SOMETHING ABOUT THE AUTHOR®

Something about
the Author *was named
an "Outstanding
Reference Source,"*
*the highest honor given
by the American
Library Association
Reference and Adult
Services Division.*

ISSN 0276-816X

something About the Author®

**Facts and Pictures about Authors
and Illustrators of Books for Young People**

volume 233

GALE
CENGAGE Learning®

Detroit • New York • San Francisco • New Haven, Conn • Waterville, Maine • London

Something about the Author, Volume 233

Project Editor: Lisa Kumar

Permissions: Leitha Etheridge-Sims

Imaging and Multimedia: Leitha Etheridge-Sims, John Watkins

Composition and Electronic Capture: Amy Darga

Manufacturing: Rhonda Dover

Product Manager: Mary Onorato

For product information and technology assistance, contact us at
Gale Customer Support, 1-800-877-4253.
For permission to use material from this text or product,
submit all requests online at **www.cengage.com/permissions.**
Further permissions questions can be emailed to
permissionrequest@cengage.com

Since this page cannot legibly accommodate all copyright notices, the acknowledgments constitute an extension of the copyright notice.

While every effort has been made to ensure the reliability of the information presented in this publication, Gale, a part of Cengage Learning, does not guarantee the accuracy of the data contained herein. Gale accepts no payment for listing; and inclusion in the publication of any organization, agency, institution, publication, service, or individual does not imply endorsement of the editors or publisher. Errors brought to the attention of the publisher and verified to the satisfaction of the publisher will be corrected in future editions.

EDITORIAL DATA PRIVACY POLICY: Does this publication contain information about you as an individual? If so, for more information about our editorial data privacy policies, please see our Privacy Statement at www.gale.cengage.com.

Gale, Cengage Learning
27500 Drake Rd.
Farmington Hills, MI, 48331-3535

LIBRARY OF CONGRESS CATALOG CARD NUMBER 62-52046

ISBN-13: 978-1-4144-6923-2
ISBN-10: 1-4144-6923-3

ISSN 0276-816X

This title is also available as an e-book.
ISBN-13: 978-1-4144-8235-4
ISBN-10: 1-4144-8235-3
Contact your Gale, Cengage Learning sales representative for ordering information.

Printed in Mexico
1 2 3 4 5 6 7 15 14 13 12 11

Contents

Authors in Forthcoming Volumes vii

Introduction ix

SATA Product Advisory Board xi

Illustrations Index 189

Author Index 225

A

al Abdullah, Rania
 See Rania, Queen of Jordan 131

Almond, David 1951- 1

Amateau, Gigi 1964- 7

Andres, Kristina 1971- 9

Arato, Rona 10

B

Bach, Bellamy
 See Windling, Terri 178

Bendinger, Jessica 1966- 13

Blake, Stephanie 1968- 14

Blau, Aljoscha 1972- 15

Blecha, Aaron 16

Bolger, Kevin 17

Bowen, Fred 1953- 18

Bracken, Alexandra 1987- 23

Braeuner, Shellie 24

Brodien-Jones, Chris
 See Brodien-Jones, Christine 25

Brodien-Jones, Christine 1950- 25

Brown, Monica 1969- 27

Browning, Diane 30

Brunelle, Lynn 31

C

Callery, Sean 33

Carman, Patrick 1966- 34

Chessa, Francesca 39

Clarkson, Karen 42

Correa, E. Shan
 See Correa, Shan 42

Correa, Shan 42

Coventry, Susan 43

Coy, John 1958- 44

Crowley, Cath 1971- 48

Croza, Laurel 49

Cummings, Gillian 1961- 50

Cypess, Leah 51

D

Dawson, Scott 53

Duane, Diane 1952- 54

Dunrea, Olivier 1953- 61

F

Flood, Bo
 See Flood, Nancy Bo 68

Flood, Nancy Bo 1945- 68

G

Grab, Daphne 1971- 70

Gruner, Jessica 71

Guarnaccia, Steven 72

H

Hamilton, Meredith 75

Harrison, Michelle 1979- 76

Hasnat, Naheed
 See Senzai, N.H. 157

Hayter, Rhonda 78

Hermes, Patricia 1936- 80

Horner, Emily 1982- 88

Authors in Forthcoming Volumes

Below are some of the authors and illustrators that will be featured in upcoming volumes of *SATA*. These include new entries on the swiftly rising stars of the field, as well as completely revised and updated entries (indicated with *) on some of the most notable and best-loved creators of books for children.

Susannah Appelbaum ▌ A former magazine editor, Appelbaum showcases her knowledge of plant lore in her "Poisons of Caux" middle-grade novel trilogy. In *The Hollow Bettle*, *The Tasters Guild*, and *The Shepherd of Weeds* readers follow a young heroine as she fights against a corrupt world where evil powers may be rooted in the soil rather than embodied in human form. In Appelbaum's unusual fantasy, the forces of nature can be harnessed through an understanding of the power of plants and used to either poison or heal, to nourish or destroy.

Lisa Brown ▌ Brown's illustrations first appeared in humor books authored by her husband, the pseudonymous Lemony Snicket: *How to Dress for Every Occasion by the Pope* and *The Latke Who Couldn't Stop Screaming: A Christmas Story*. Furthering her illustration career, she has created a series of board-book parodies collected as the "Baby Be of Use" series. In addition to creating original self-illustrated picture books such as *How to Be ....* and *Vampire Boy's Good Night*, Brown has also teamed up with writer Adele Griffin to create the acclaimed illustrated YA novel *Picture the Dead*.

*Morris Gleitzman ▌ A popular children's writer in Australia, the British-born Gleitzman has a well-deserved reputation in his adopted country for creating humorous middle-grade novels that couch highly sensitive topics and conflicts in chaotic situations peppered with amusing dialogue. In addition to teaming up with fellow writer Paul Jennings to create their entertaining "Wicked!" and "Deadly!" series, he shares his dry humor in books such as *Toad Rage*, *Bumface*, *Boy Overboard*, and *Blabber Mouth*. The versatile author has also explored a dark period in human history, the Holocaust, in his award-winning novels *Once*, *Then*, and *Now*.

*Lita Judge ▌ A former environmental geologist and paleobotanist, Judge now writes and illustrates children's books. In addition to original, self-illustrated stories *Pennies for Elephants* and *Red Sled*, her nonfiction works include *One Thousand Tracings: Healing the Wounds of World War II*, *Yellowstone Moran: Painting the American West*, *Born to Be Giants: How Baby Dinosaurs Grew to Rule the World*, and *Strange Creatures: The Story of Walter Rothschild and His Museum*. As an illustrator, Judge has also provided artwork for stories by Donna Jo Napoli, among them *Ugly*, an adaptation of Hans Christian Andersen's "The Ugly Duckling."

Winnie Mack ▌ Mack is the pen name of Canadian author Winnie French, who moved from writing humorous chick-lit novels for twenty-somethings to middle-grade novels such as *After All, You're Callie Boone*. For Lauren Peterson, star of *Full of It*, the problem is loss, first of a boyfriend and then a best friend, while in *Going Coastal* French follows Jody Rogers after she quits her waitressing job and in the wake of a disastrous romance. In *After the Rice* French tells the story of Megan, a newlywed whose future with new hubbie Matt is threatened by the intrusions and demands of various family members, including an uncle who takes up residence in the basement of the young couple's home.

*Scott Menchin ▌ An instructor at the prestigious Pratt Institute, Menchin created advertising art for companies such as Toyota, Intel, and Dr. Pepper before he began writing and illustrating children's books. His first picture-book project, Eve Bunting's *The Day the Whale Came*, was followed by toddler-pleasing collaborations with Doreen Cronin on *Wiggle* and *Bounce* as well as *Rescue Bunnies*. Menchin's colorful cartoon art is a highlight of Alison McGhee's humorous *Song of Middle C*, while *Taking a Bath with the Dog and Other Things That Make Me Happy* marked his shift to author in a self-illustrated story that was well-received by critics.

*Marjory Priceman ▌ Priceman is an author and illustrator who began her career in the late 1980s. Although her humorous and energetic artwork has appeared alongside texts by writers such as Jack Prelutsky, Amy MacDonald, Eileen Spinelli, and Nancy Van Laan, she admits that illustrating someone else's story is not nearly as fun as illustrating her own. After taking an advanced writing course, Priceman created the original self-illustrated picture books *My Nine Lives: by Clio*, *Princess Picky*, and *How to Make a Cherry Pie and See the U.S.A.*, all of which earned enthusiastic praise from critics.

*Stephanie Spinner ▌ A talented and versatile writer, Spinner is the author of *Quicksilver*, and *It's a Miracle!: A Hanukkah Storybook*. A former children's book editor, she worked with such notable writers as Robin McKinley and Garth Nix before gaining recognition for her popular "Aliens" chapter-book series, coauthored with Jonathan Etra. *Aliens for Breakfast* centers on Richard Bickerstaff, a youngster who discovers Aric, a creature from the planet Ganoob, in his cereal. The adventures of Richard and Aric continue in *Aliens for Lunch* and *Aliens for Dinner*.

Doug TenNapel ▌ TenNapel is the creator of the cartoon character "Earthworm Jim," who appeared in a video game in the mid-1990s and eventually wormed his way into the starring role in a television series. Although much of TenNapel's work has been in film, he has also produced books for children, among them the "Strange Kids Chronicles" books as well as the graphic novels *Gear*, *Earthboy Jacobus*, *Flink*, and *Ghostopolis*, which have been collected and bound as graphic-novel anthologies.

Treat Williams ▌ A respected stage, screen, and television actor who has garnered a host of Emmy and Golden Globe award nominations, Williams made his picture-book debut in 2010 with *Air Show*, a children's book featuring illustrations by noted cartoonist

Robert Neubecker. The work, which focuses on a pair of youngsters who journey aboard their father's plane to watch him perform in an air show, had its origins in an experience shared by author and illustrator: a certified flight instructor, Williams once traveled to a show with Neubecker, a friend and neighbor who shares the actor's love of airplanes.

Introduction

Something about the Author (*SATA*) is an ongoing reference series that examines the lives and works of authors and illustrators of books for children. *SATA* includes not only well-known writers and artists but also less prominent individuals whose works are just coming to be recognized. This series is often the only readily available information source on emerging authors and illustrators. You'll find *SATA* informative and entertaining, whether you are a student, a librarian, an English teacher, a parent, or simply an adult who enjoys children's literature.

What's Inside *SATA*

SATA provides detailed information about authors and illustrators who span the full time range of children's literature, from early figures like John Newbery and L. Frank Baum to contemporary figures like Judy Blume and Richard Peck. Authors in the series represent primarily English-speaking countries, particularly the United States, Canada, and the United Kingdom. Also included, however, are authors from around the world whose works are available in English translation. The writings represented in *SATA* include those created intentionally for children and young adults as well as those written for a general audience and known to interest younger readers. These writings cover the entire spectrum of children's literature, including picture books, humor, folk and fairy tales, animal stories, mystery and adventure, science fiction and fantasy, historical fiction, poetry and nonsense verse, drama, biography, and nonfiction. Obituaries are also included in *SATA* and are intended not only as death notices but also as concise overviews of people's lives and work. Additionally, each edition features newly revised and updated entries for a selection of *SATA* listees who remain of interest to today's readers and who have been active enough to require extensive revisions of their earlier biographies.

Autobiography Feature

Beginning with Volume 103, many volumes of *SATA* feature one or more specially commissioned autobiographical essays. These unique essays, averaging about ten thousand words in length and illustrated with an abundance of personal photos, present an entertaining and informative first-person perspective on the lives and careers of prominent authors and illustrators profiled in *SATA*.

Two Convenient Indexes

In response to suggestions from librarians, *SATA* indexes no longer appear in every volume but are included in alternate (odd-numbered) volumes of the series, beginning with Volume 57.

SATA continues to include two indexes that cumulate with each alternate volume: the Illustrations Index, arranged by the name of the illustrator, gives the number of the volume and page where the illustrator's work appears in the current volume as well as all preceding volumes in the series; the Author Index gives the number of the volume in which a person's biographical sketch, autobiographical essay, or obituary appears in the current volume as well as all preceding volumes in the series.

These indexes also include references to authors and illustrators who appear in *Gale's Yesterday's Authors of Books for Children, Children's Literature Review,* and *Something about the Author Autobiography Series.*

Easy-to-Use Entry Format

Whether you're already familiar with the *SATA* series or just getting acquainted, you will want to be aware of the kind of information that an entry provides. In every *SATA* entry the editors attempt to give as complete a picture of the person's life and work as possible. A typical entry in *SATA* includes the following clearly labeled information sections:

PERSONAL: date and place of birth and death, parents' names and occupations, name of spouse, date of marriage, names of children, educational institutions attended, degrees received, religious and political affiliations, hobbies and other interests.

ADDRESSES: complete home, office, electronic mail, and agent addresses, whenever available.

CAREER: name of employer, position, and dates for each career post; art exhibitions; military service; memberships and offices held in professional and civic organizations.

MEMBER: professional, civic, and other association memberships and any official posts held.

AWARDS, HONORS: literary and professional awards received.

WRITINGS: title-by-title chronological bibliography of books written and/or illustrated, listed by genre when known; lists of other notable publications, such as plays, screenplays, and periodical contributions.

ADAPTATIONS: a list of films, television programs, plays, CD-ROMs, recordings, and other media presentations that have been adapted from the author's work.

WORK IN PROGRESS: description of projects in progress.

SIDELIGHTS: a biographical portrait of the author or illustrator's development, either directly from the biographee—and often written specifically for the *SATA* entry—or gathered from diaries, letters, interviews, or other published sources.

BIOGRAPHICAL AND CRITICAL SOURCES: cites sources quoted in "Sidelights" along with references for further reading.

EXTENSIVE ILLUSTRATIONS: photographs, movie stills, book illustrations, and other interesting visual materials supplement the text.

How a *SATA* Entry Is Compiled

SATA editors examine a wide variety of published sources to gather information for an entry. Biographical and bibliographic sources are consulted, as are book reviews, feature articles, published interviews, and material sometimes obtained from the biographee's family, publishers, agent, or other associates. Whenever possible, the author or illustrator is sent a copy of the entry to check for accuracy and completeness.

Entries that have not been verified by the biographees or their representatives are marked with an asterisk (*).

Contact the Editor

We encourage our readers to examine the entire *SATA* series. Please write and tell us if we can make *SATA* even more helpful to you. Give your comments and suggestions to the editor:

Editor
Something about the Author
Gale, Cengage Learning
27500 Drake Rd.
Farmington Hills MI 48331-3535

Toll-free: 800-877-GALE
Fax: 248-699-8070

Something about the Author Product Advisory Board

The editors of *Something about the Author* are dedicated to maintaining a high standard of excellence by publishing comprehensive, accurate, and highly readable entries on a wide array of writers for children and young adults. In addition to the quality of the content, the editors take pride in the graphic design of the series, which is intended to be orderly yet inviting, allowing readers to utilize the pages of *SATA* easily and with efficiency. Despite the longevity of the *SATA* print series, and the success of its format, we are mindful that the vitality of a literary reference product is dependent on its ability to serve its users over time. As literature, and attitudes about literature, constantly evolve, so do the reference needs of students, teachers, scholars, journalists, researchers, and book club members. To be certain that we continue to keep pace with the expectations of our customers, the editors of *SATA* listen carefully to their comments regarding the value, utility, and quality of the series. Librarians, who have firsthand knowledge of the needs of library users, are a valuable resource for us. The *Something about the Author* Product Advisory Board, made up of school, public, and academic librarians, is a forum to promote focused feedback about *SATA* on a regular basis. The nine-member advisory board includes the following individuals, whom the editors wish to thank for sharing their expertise:

Eva M. Davis
Director,
Canton Public Library,
Canton, Michigan

Joan B. Eisenberg
Lower School Librarian,
Milton Academy,
Milton, Massachusetts

Francisca Goldsmith
Teen Services Librarian,
Berkeley Public Library,
Berkeley, California

Susan Dove Lempke
Children's Services Supervisor,
Niles Public Library District,
Niles, Illinois

Robyn Lupa
Head of Children's Services,
Jefferson County Public Library,
Lakewood, Colorado

Victor L. Schill
Assistant Branch Librarian/Children's Librarian,
Harris County Public Library/Fairbanks Branch,
Houston, Texas

Caryn Sipos
Community Librarian,
Three Creeks Community Library,
Vancouver, Washington

Steven Weiner
Director,
Maynard Public Library,
Maynard, Massachusetts

something ABOUT the AUTHOR

AL ABDULLAH, Rania
   See RANIA, QUEEN OF JORDAN

* * *

ALMOND, David 1951-

Personal

Born May 15, 1951, in Newcastle upon Tyne, England; son of James Arthur and Catherine Almond; married Sara Jane Palmer; children: Freya Grace Almond-Palmer. *Education:* University of East Anglia, B.A. (English and American literature; with honors), 1975. *Hobbies and other interests:* Walking, listening to music, traveling, spending time with family.

Addresses

Home—Heaton, Newcastle, England. *E-mail*—dalmond @lineone.net.

Career

Novelist. Teacher in primary, adult, and special-education schools in Gateshead, England, 1976-82; freelance writer. *Panurge* (fiction magazine), editor, 1987-93. Creative-writing tutor for Arvon Foundation, beginning 1987, and Open College of the Arts, 1995-99; Huntington School, York, England, visiting writer, 1996-98; Hartlepool Schools, writer-in-residence, spring, 1999; visiting speaker and course leader.

David Almond (Reproduced by permission of David Almond.)

1

Awards, Honors

Hawthornden fellowship, 1997; Whitbread Award, 1998, Lancashire Children's Book of the Year award, Stockton Children's Book of the Year award, *Guardian* Children's Fiction Prize shortlist, and Carnegie Medal, British Library Association, all 1999, Michael L. Printz Honor Book selection, American Library Association, 2000, and Sheffield Children's Book of the Year award shortlist, all for *Skellig;* British Arts Council Award for outstanding literature for young people, 1998, Smarties Silver Award, 1999, and Michael L. Printz Award, 2001, all for *Kit's Wilderness;* Smarties Gold Award, Carnegie Medal shortlist, and Whitbread Award shortlist, all 2003, and *Boston Globe/Horn Book* Award for fiction and poetry, 2004, all for *The Fire-Eaters;* Costa Children's Book Award shortlist, and Carnegie Medal shortlist, both 2005, both for *Clay;* Hans Christian Andersen Author Award, International Board on Books for Young People, 2010; Freedom of Town Award, City of Felling, England, 2011.

Writings

JUVENILE FICTION

Skellig (also see below), Hodder Children's Books (London, England), 1998, Delacorte Press (New York, NY), 1999.

Kit's Wilderness, Hodder Children's Books (London, England), 1999, Delacorte Press (New York, NY), 2000.

Heaven Eyes, Hodder Children's Books (London, England), 2000, Delacorte Press (New York, NY), 2001.

Counting Stars (short stories), Hodder Children's Books (London, England), 2000, Delacorte Press (New York, NY), 2002.

Secret Heart, Hodder Children's Books (London, England), 2001, Delacorte Press (New York, NY), 2002.

The Fire-Eaters, Hodder Children's Books (London, England), 2003, Delacorte Press (New York, NY), 2004.

Kate, the Cat, and the Moon, illustrated by Stephen Lambert, Hodder Children's Books (London, England), 2004, Random House (New York, NY), 2005.

Clay, Hodder Children's Books (London, England), 2005, Delacorte Press (New York, NY), 2006.

My Dad's a Birdman, illustrated by Polly Dunbar, Walker Books (London, England), 2007, Candlewick Press (Cambridge, MA), 2008.

The Savage, illustrated by Dave McKean, Candlewick Press (Cambridge, MA), 2008.

Jackdaw Summer, Hodder Children's Books (London, England), 2008, published as *Raven Summer,* Delacorte Press (New York, NY), 2009.

The Boy Who Climbed into the Moon, illustrated by Polly Dunbar, Candlewick Press (Somerville, MA), 2010.

My Name Is Mina, Delacorte Press (New York, NY), 2011.

Slog's Dad, illustration by Dave McKean, Candlewick Press (Somerville, MA), 2011.

The True Tale of the Monster Billy Dean, Puffin (London, England), 2011.

Kit's Wilderness and *Skellig* were translated and published in several other languages; short stories were broadcast on BBC Radio Four.

OTHER

Mickey and the Emperor (play for children), produced at Washington Arts Center, 1984.

Sleepless Nights (short stories), Iron Press (North Shields, Northumberland, England), 1985.

A Kind of Heaven (short stories), Iron Press (North Shields, Northumberland, England), 1997.

Skellig (play; first produced on BBC Radio 4, 2000), Hodder Children's Books (London, England), 2002, published in *Two Plays,* 2005.

Wild Girl, Wild Boy (play; produced in London, England, 2001), Hodder Children's Books (London, England), 2002, published in *Two Plays,* 2005.

Clay Boy (radio play), produced on BBC Radio 4, 2002.

Two Plays (contains *Wild Girl, Wild Boy* and *Skellig*), Delacorte Press (New York, NY), 2005.

Contributor to periodicals, including *London* and *Critical Quarterly.* Author of libretto for operatic adaptation of *Skellig,* produced in Gateshead, England, 2008.

Adaptations

Several of Almond's novels have been adapted for audiobook, including *Clay* and *Skellig. My Dad's a Birdman* was adapted for the stage and produced in London, England, 2010-11. *Clay* was adapted as a television film, produced on BBC1, 2008. *Skellig* was adapted as a feature film, 2010.

Sidelights

British author David Almond wrote for adults before achieving what amounted to overnight success with his first young-adult novel, *Skellig.* Published in 1998, Almond's tale of a young boy's discovery of a possibly supernatural creature living in his own backyard was unanimously praised by reviewers, sold out its first printing in four days, and went on to win Britain's prestigious Whitbread Children's Book of the Year award as well as a Carnegie medal. Almond has received numerous other honors for his work in the years since, including the Michael L. Printz Award for *Kit's Wilderness* and the *Boston Globe/Horn Book* Award for *The Fire-Eater.* In 2010 he was awarded an even greater honor: the International Board on Books for Young People's Hans Christian Andersen Author Award, which is the highest honor a children's writer can receive.

Like the hero in *Skellig,* Almond grew up on the fringes of a northern English city, a landscape that offered great imaginative possibilities for him as a youth. "Maybe ink was always in my blood," he once commented. "I

don't remember it, of course, but as a baby in my mother's arms I used to visit my uncle's printing works on the narrow high street of our town. I used to point and grin and gurgle as the pages of the local newspaper rolled off the machines. It was a small steep town with wild heather hills at the crest and the River Tyne flowing far below. From our windows, we looked out towards the city that packed the opposite bank, towards the distant sea, and even on clear days toward the hazy Cheviots an eternity away. It was a place that had everything necessary for the imagination."

Almond grew up as part of a large, extended Catholic family that was rich with stories. "I listened to the stories and songs at family parties," he later recalled. "I listened to the gossip that filled Dragon's coffee shop. I ran with my friends through the open spaces and the narrow lanes. We scared each other with ghost stories told in fragile tents on dark nights. We promised never-ending friendship and whispered of the amazing journeys we'd take together. I sat with my grandfather in his allotment, held tiny Easter chicks in my hands while he smoked his pipe and the factory sirens wailed and larks yelled high above. I trembled at the images presented to us in church, at the awful threats and glorious promises made by black-clad priests with Irish voices. I scribbled stories and stitched them into little books. I disliked school and loved the library, a little square building in which I dreamed that books with my name on them would stand one day on the shelves. I loved Arthurian legends, Hemingway, John Wyndham, the tales of the fake Tibetan monk, Lobsang Rampa."

After earning a degree from the University of East Anglia, Almond became a teacher. Then, in 1982, he quit his full-time job, sold his house, and moved to a commune in order to devote himself to writing. The result was a collection of stories, *Sleepless Nights,* which was published by a small press in 1985 and "appeared to a tiny amount of acclaim and a vast amount of silence," as its author remembered. "I [also] ran a fiction magazine, *Panurge,* that excited and exhausted me for six years. I wrote The Great English Novel that took five years, went to thirty-three publishers and was rejected by them all. I went on writing. More stories, more publications, a few small prizes. Another novel, never finished. Another story collection was published, *A Kind of Heaven,* twelve years after the first. Then at last I started writing about growing up in our small steep town: a whole sequence of stories, half-real, half-imaginary, that I called *Stories from the Middle of the World.* They took a year to write." It was the act of finishing these childhood stories that led Almond to the opening lines of the ten-year-old narrator of *Skellig:* "I found him in the garage on Sunday afternoon."

On the Sunday when the plot of *Skellig* begins, Michael, the narrator, and his family have just taken possession of an old, run-down house. Michael's newborn sister soon arrives home from the hospital, but she soon must return there for heart surgery. In the garage, behind a

great deal of clutter, Michael discovers Skellig, a man who is covered in dust and insects and has odd, wing-like appendages. At first the boy believes Skellig to be homeless, but the man's vague communications reveal to him that Skellig has come there to die. As Michael begins his new school, his mother is away with his sister at the hospital and his father is understandably preoccupied. Needing connection, he brings Skellig food and medicine. He also befriends his new neighbor, a girl name Mina who is an intelligent, independent thinker with interests that include ornithology and the poetry of early nineteenth-century Romantic writer William Blake. Mina shows her new friend a nest of rare owls, and Michael reciprocates by sharing the secret of Skellig. Due to the children's visits, Skellig's health improves and he eventually vanishes, leaving Michael with the revelation that love can achieve miracles science cannot.

As Perri Klass noted in reviewing *Skellig* for the *New York Times Book Review,* the book's charm lies in Almond's courage in allowing some things to remain a mystery. "In its simple but poetic language, its tender

Cover of Almond's highly acclaimed debut middle-grade novel Skellig, *which features artwork by Kamil Vojnar.* (Cover illustration copyright © 1998 by Delacorte Press. Used by permission of Delacorte Press, an imprint of Random House Children's Books, a division of Random House, Inc.)

refusal to package its mysteries neatly or offer explanations for what happens in either world, it goes beyond adventure story or family-with-a-problem story to become a story about worlds enlarging and the hope of scattering death," Klass wrote. The critic also praised Almond's talent for weaving prosaic details of daily life within larger themes involving the metaphysical world. *Skellig* "is a book about the business of everyday life proceeding on a canvas suddenly widened to include mystery and tragedy," he added, "although not everyone has eyes to see." Cathryn M. Mercier, writing in *Five Owls,* cited Almond's book as a "novel of faith and hope" as well as "a book of rare spirituality for young adults." For *Reading Time* reviewer Howard George, *Skellig* treats readers to "a haunting story" redolent with "the deep emotions evoked by the family crisis and the love given out to Skellig."

Over a decade after *Skellig* was published, Almond produced a prequel, *My Name Is Mina.* Here readers are introduced to Mina McKee independent of her future neighbor, and learn about the people and events that have shaped her quirky world view, some described using her own made-up vocabulary. Mina's sadness over her father's death, her random thoughts and ideas, her stories and her feelings, and the problems at school that led her to become a lonely home-schooled child: all these things come into focus in her notebook and crystallize at the point where she will meet her new neighbor, Michael, and be pulled into a great adventure. "Even by David Almond's standards this is a truly remarkable book," wrote Peter Hollingsdale in his *School Librarian* review of *My Name Is Mina,* the critic describing the novel as "psychologically profound, packed with ideas, [and] full of the wonder of life and of language." The novel also showcases the author's "gift of being able to grip you even when nothing much seems to be happening," noted Lisa O'Kelly in her review of the book for the London *Observer.* In *My Name Is Mina* the magic comes from "the random thoughts, dreams and wordplay" that reside in its protagonist's inner world. Calling Almond's young heroine "delightful," *Guardian* critic Marcus Sedgwick added that "everybody has met a child like Mina at least once, (metaphorically) sitting in a tree, looking down at the world, and wondering and whispering to themselves at the beauty of it all."

In Almond's second young-adult novel, *Kit's Wilderness,* he focuses on a game of pretend death that his characters play. Thirteen-year-old Kit Watson has moved with his family to the British coal-mining town of Stoneygate, where they will care for Kit's widowed grandfather. A troubled, enigmatic classmate named John Askew befriends Kit and introduces him to a bizarre game called "Death" that is played in the abandoned mines. Participants lie alone in a dark cavern and attempt to connect with the spirits of young boys who died there in a terrible accident. Although several of the players treat the game as a lark, "Kit senses something far more profound and dangerous, and the connection

Cover of Almond's haunting novel **Kit's Wilderness,** *a story about friendship and obsession that features cover art by Kamil Vojnar.* (Cover illustration copyright © 2000 by Delacorte Press, an imprint of Random House Children's Books, a division of Random House, Inc. Used by permission of Delacorte Press, an imprint of Random House Children's Books, a division of Random House, Inc.)

he forges with the ancient past also circuitously seals a deeper bond with Askew," noted a critic in *Publishers Weekly.* When John disappears, Kit determines to locate his friend and reunite him with his family. At the same time, he discovers his artistic side through his relationship with his grandfather, a storyteller who inspires Kit to write a story that mirrors his own life. According to *School Library Journal* critic Ellen Fader, Almond "brings these complicated, interwoven plots to a satisfying conclusion as he explores the power of friendship and family, the importance of memory, and the role of magic in our lives." In her review of *Kit's Wilderness,* Cooper remarked that "the story's ruminations about death and the healing power of love will strike children in unsuspected ways."

Also written for teens, *Heaven Eyes* blends everyday adventure with a dalliance in the netherworld; its characters are escapees from a juvenile home who flee on a raft to an old printing plant on the River Tyne. *Secret Heart,* which was describe as "a thought-provoking allegory" by Daniel L. Darigan in *School Library Journal,* focuses on Joe Maloney, a lonely misfit who dreams

of tigers and finds himself curiously drawn to a ragged traveling circus that arrives in his town. "Almond fans, who relish the author's skill at creating surreal landscapes and otherworldly images, will not be disappointed by this tale," remarked a critic in reviewing *Secret Heart* for *Publishers Weekly.*

Geared for middle graders, Almond's novel *The Fire-Eaters* was shortlisted for both the Carnegie Medal and the Whitbread Award and received the Smarties Gold Award. Set in 1962, during the Cuban Missile Crisis, the story concerns twelve-year-old Bobby Burns, who lives with his family in a small English seaside village. Accepted into an elite private school, Bobby must deal with a cruel teacher who practices corporal punishment while also navigating his shifting relationships with a pair of old friends and his worries when a strange illness befalls his father. Overshadowing everything is the threat of nuclear war; according to a reviewer in *Publishers Weekly,* "Bobby's reflections . . . convey the young protagonist's uncertainties and a sense of the world itself being on the cusp of change." "The apocalyptic atmosphere is personified by the tragic character McNulty, a fire-eating exhibitionist whose torturous feats raise" another significant theme in the novel, according to *Horn Book* critic Lauren Adams: "the human capacity for pain—giving it, accepting it, bearing it for another." Also praising Almond's novel, a contributor to *Kirkus Reviews* deemed *The Fire-Eaters* "breathtakingly and memorably up to Almond's best."

In *Clay* "the sinister is never far away," according to London *Guardian* contributor Philip Ardagh. This story follows the relationships that build between three boys: Davie, Geordie, and Stephen. Davie and Geordie are good friends and altar boys at their local church when Stephen moves into the village as the ward of his aunt, known as Crazy Mary. Because Stephen's father has recently died and his mother has had a mental breakdown, rumors circulate that the boy may be the cause of these family tragedies. Stephen seems to be unaffected by these problems and acts friendly toward everyone. At first Davie and Geordie befriend him, viewing the new boy as a help in the ongoing battle against town bully Mouldy. As the story plays out, however, their feelings shift to fascination. By the time Stephen has begun using these younger boys to help him construct a strange, monstrous creature out of clay, readers realize that Almond has focused them on one threat while keeping them ignorant of a threat that is far greater. The "scary monster-come-to-town story" in *Clay* "raises big issues about God, creativity, and evil," noted *Booklist* contributor Hazel Rochman, the critic adding that it "will grab readers with its gripping action and . . . important ideas." Noting that *Clay* treats readers to "a powerful and provocative tale" that contains "religious overtones," Paula Rohrlick added in her *Kliatt* review that Almond's story "will haunt readers long after they finish it."

An adventure shared by friends is also at the core of *Jackdaw Summer,* a novel for young teens that was released in the United States as *Raven Summer.* Liam and

Max live in a small village and spend much of their summer roaming in the wild areas nearby and playing war games that mimic the events reported on the nightly news. One day they spot a giant raven that cries insistently and seems to lead the boys to an abandoned and overgrown farm house. There they find an infant wrapped securely in a blanket to which is attached a note claiming the baby to be a "childe of god." This discovery ultimately affects not only the boys but also Liam's artist mom and writer dad and even the creepy town bully, Natrass, as characters transform their fears and worries into acts of violence. *Jackdaw Summer* presents what Tim Wadhams described in *School Library Journal* as "a passionate plea for peace" in an age of war, and its story will prompt readers to "think about the consequence of violence." "Nobody evokes childhood like Almond," asserted Ardagh, and in *Jackdaw Summer* he presents "a thoughtful and claustrophobic snapshot of people's lives" as they change over the

Almond shares his memories of growing up in a close-knit extended family in Counting Stars, *a book featuring artwork by Michael Morgenstern.* (Cover illustration copyright © 2002 by Delacorte Press. Used by permission of Random House Children's Books, a division of Random House, Inc.)

Polly Dunbar crafts the whimsical artwork that brings to life Almond's fanciful picture book The Boy Who Climbed into the Moon. (Illustration copyright © 2010 Polly Dunbar. Reproduced with permission of Candlewick Press, Somerville, MA.)

course of a few months. Calling the novel "a thought-provoking coming-of-age story," a *Publishers Weekly* contributor added that in *Jackdaw Summer* Almond "tackles complex questions about humanity from multiple points of view."

During his writing career, Almond has intermittently taken time away from novel writing to pen stories for younger children. His first picture book, *Kate, the Cat, and the Moon,* features illustrations by Stephen Lambert alongside a story about a little girl who is transformed into a cat and enjoys a starlit adventure that may or may not have been a dream. Both *The Boy Who Climbed into the Moon* and *My Dad's a Birdman* pair stories for elementary graders with engaging artwork by Polly Dunbar. In *The Boy Who Climbed into the Moon* nighttime is again the setting, as young Paul becomes convinced that the moon is actually a giant hole in the night sky. Encouraged by his enthusiastic new friend Molly, who lives in a world of fanciful possibilities, Paul sets out to prove his theory in a story that introduces "endearing, funny and engaging" characters and "is charming without being twee; quirky without being

whimsical; and genuinely thought-provoking without being clever-clever," according to Ardagh.

A second collaboration between Almond and Dunbar, *My Dad's a Birdman,* presents a "comic piece of magic realism" in which "birds and human flight" become "metaphors for love's transcendence over grief," according to *School Library Journal* contributor Margaret A. Chang. Set in the north of England, *My Dad's a Birdman* finds Lizzie helping her widowed father battle his depression over the death of his wife by competing in a challenge to be the first to fly over the river Tyne. Although a *Kirkus Reviews* writer described Almond's tale as "at least as emotionally complex" as his novels for older teens, the tale resolves into a "buoyant story" that is brought to life by Dunbar in colorful, sketchy images which "evoke Quentin Blake." Adapted from the author's stage play, *My Dad's a Birdman* prompted *Booklist* critic Ilene Cooper to recall the title character of *Skellig,* noting that "an undercurrent of sadness" threads through Arnold's fictional "tribute to the human spirit."

Biographical and Critical Sources

PERIODICALS

Book, May, 2001, Kathleen Odean, review of *Kit's Wilderness,* p. 80.
Booklist, January 1, 2000, Ilene Cooper, interview with Almond, p. 898, and review of *Kit's Wilderness,* p. 899; March 15, 2000, Michael Cart, "Carte Blanche," p. 1370; April 1, 2001, Ilene Cooper, interview with Almond, p. 1464; February 1, 2002, Hazel Rochman, review of *Counting Stars,* p. 934; October 1, 2002, Michael Cart, review of *Secret Heart,* p. 322; March 15, 2004, Ilene Cooper, review of *The Fire-Eaters,* pp. 1297-1298; October 1, 2005, Hazel Rochman, review of *Two Plays,* p. 51; June 1, 2006, Hazel Rochman, review of *Clay,* p. 74; September 15, 2007, Lynn Rutan, review of *Click,* p. 57; March 15, 2008, Ilene Cooper, review of *My Dad's a Birdman,* p. 54; September 15, 2008, Ian Chipman, review of *The Savage,* p. 49; January 1, 2010, Daniel Kraus, review of *The Boy Who Climbed into the Moon,* p. 79.
Bookseller, September 12, 2008, Caroline Horn, interview with Arnold, p. 21.
Carousel, summer, 1999, David Almond, "Writing for Boys," p. 29.
Guardian (London, England), January 7, 2006, Philip Ardagh, review of *Clay,* p. 17; November 1, 2008, Philip Ardagh, review of *Jackdaw Summer,* p. 10; June 26, 2010, Philip Ardagh, review of *The Boy Who Climbed into the Moon,* p. 14; August 21, 2010, Sarah Crown, "A Life in Writing," p. 10; September 4, 2010, Marcus Sedgwick, review of *My Name Is Mina,* p. 14.
Observer (London, England), October 26, 2008, Geraldine Brennan, review of *Jackdaw Summer,* p. 25; December 5, 2010, Lisa O'Kelly, review of *My Name Is Mina,* p. 40.

Five Owls, May-June, 1999, Cathryn M. Mercier, review of *Skellig,* p. 110.

Horn Book, May, 1999, review of *Skellig,* p. 326; March-April, 2002, Gregory Maguire, review of *Counting Stars,* pp. 207-208; November-December, 2002, Christine M. Heppermann, review of *Secret Heart,* pp. 745-746; May-June, 2004, review of *The Fire-Eaters,* p. 324; September-October, 2008, Jonathan Hunt, review of *The Savage,* p. 575; November-December, 2009, Christine M. Hepperman, review of *Raven Summer,* p. 662; May-June, 2010, Sarah Ellis, review of *The Boy Who Climbed into the Moon,* p. 74.

Kirkus Reviews, March 15, 2002, review of *Counting Stars,* p. 404; September 1, 2002, review of *Secret Heart,* p. 1300; April 1, 2004, review of *The Fire-Eaters,* p. 323; September 1, 2005, review of *Kate, the Cat, and the Moon,* p. 967; October 15, 2005, review of *Two Plays,* p. 1133; September 15, 2007, review of *Click*; March 15, 2008, review of *My Dad's a Birdman*; September 15, 2008, review of *Savage*; October 15, 2009, review of *Raven Summer.*

Kliatt, November, 2002, Paula Rohrlick, review of *Secret Heart,* p. 5; January, 2004, Nola Theiss, review of *Counting Stars,* p. 26; July, 2006, Paula Rohrlick, review of *Clay,* p. 7.

Los Angeles Times, April 8, 2001, "Books for Kids," p. 6.

New York Times Book Review, June 6, 1999, Perry Klass, review of *Skellig,* p. 49.

Publishers Weekly, June 28, 1999, Elizabeth Devereaux, "Flying Starts," p. 25; January 3, 2000, review of *Kit's Wilderness,* p. 77; April 1, 2002, review of *Counting Stars,* p. 85; July 1, 2002, "The British Invasion," pp. 26-29; August 19, 2002, review of *Secret Heart,* p. 90; May 3, 2004, review of *The Fire-Eaters,* p. 192; September 5, 2005, review of *Kate, the Cat, and the Moon,* p. 61; May 29, 2006, review of *Clay,* p. 60; October 15, 2007, review of *Click,* p. 62; November 9, 2009, review of *Raven Summer,* p. 47; March 29, 2010, review of *The Boy Who Climbed into the Moon,* p. 59; March 7, 2011, review of *Slog's Dad,* p. 66.

Reading Time, May, 1999, Howard George, review of *Skellig,* p. 25.

School Librarian, winter, 2010, Peter Hollindale, review of *My Name Is Mina,* p. 238.

School Library Journal, March, 2000, Ellen Fader, review of *Kit's Wilderness,* p. 233; March, 2002, William McLoughlin, review of *Counting Stars,* p. 225; May, 2004, Joel Shoemaker, review of *The Fire-Eaters,* p. 140; September, 2005, Maura Bresnahan, review of *Kate, the Cat, and the Moon,* p. 164; December, 2005, Nancy Menaldi-Scanlan, review of *Two Plays,* p. 160; May, 2008, Margaret Chang, review of *My Dad's a Birdman,* p. 92; December, 2008, Johanna Lewis, review of *The Savage,* p. 118; December, 2009, Tim Wadham, review of *Raven Summer,* p. 105; May, 2010, Susan Hepler, review of *The Boy Who Climbed into the Moon,* p. 78.

Times (London, England), September 11, 2010, Amanda Craig, review of *My Name Is Mina,* p. 12.

Voice of Youth Advocates, April, 2000, Bette Ammon, review of *Kit's Wilderness,* p. 42.

ONLINE

Achuka Web site, http://www.achuka.co.uk/ (October 19, 2001), interview with Almond.

David Almond Home Page, http://www.davidalmond.com (September 15, 2011).

Jubilee Books Web site, http://www.jubileebooks.co.uk/ (October 19, 2001), interview with Almond.

TeenReads Web site, http://www.teenreads.com (October 19, 2001), interview with Almond.

Walker Books Web site, http://www.walker.co.uk/ (September 15, 2011), "David Almond."*

*   *   *

AMATEAU, Gigi 1964-

Personal

Born October 20, 1964, in Ripley, MS; married John W. Sanderson, Jr. (an information technologist); children: Judith Ellen. *Education:* Virginia Commonwealth University, B.S. (urban studies and planning), 1988. *Hobbies and other interests:* Horses, gardening, yoga, birding.

Addresses

Home—Bon Air, VA. *Agent*—Leigh Feldman, Writer's House, 21 W. 26th St., New York, NY 10010. *E-mail*—info@gigiamateau.com.

Career

Author and nonprofit administrator. United Way of Greater Richmond and Petersburg, Richmond, VA, director of community initiatives, assistant vice president for community resources, and grant administrator, 1995-2000; Senior Navigator, Richmond, VA, director of product development and project consultant, beginning 2000; Homeward (agency), grant administrator, 2003-05. Affiliated with United Way of Greater Richmond and Petersburg, 2003-05; City of Richmond, election officer. Has also worked for nonprofit organizations.

Member

Authors Guild, Authors League of America, Society of Children's Book Writers and Illustrators.

Awards, Honors

Book Sense Children's Pick, 2005, and Editor's Pick selection, *Voice of Youth Advocates,* and New York Public Library Book for the Teen Age selection, both 2006, all for *Claiming Georgia Tate.*

Writings

Claiming Georgia Tate, Candlewick Press (Cambridge, MA), 2005.

Chancey of the Maury River, Candlewick Press (Cambridge, MA), 2008, published as *Chancey,* Walker Books (London, England), 2009.

A Certain Strain of Peculiar, Candlewick Press (Somerville, MA), 2009.

Contributor, with daughter, Judith Amateau, to anthology *Our White House: Looking in Looking Out,* introduction by David McCullough, Candlewick Press, 2010.

Sidelights

Tapping her Southern roots, Gigi Amateau has written the young-adult novels *A Certain Strain of Peculiar* and *Claiming Georgia Tate* as well as the middle-grade novel *Chancey of the Maury River.* Before becoming an author, the Mississippi-born Amateau worked in the social service sector, where her skills as a writer aided her in the grant writing needed to fund the development and administration of community-based resources.

Amateau's first book, *Claiming Georgia Tate,* deals with a difficult and controversial subject matter: incest. In the novel, twelve-year-old Georgia Tate Jamison is being raised by her maternal grandparents and has en-

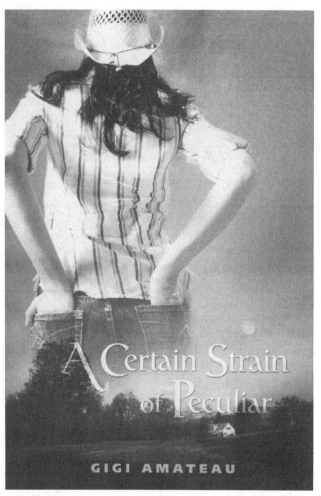

Cover of Gigi Amateau's middle-grade novel A Certain Strain of Peculiar, *which finds a young teen dealing with adult problems.* (Copyright © 2009 Gigi Amateau. Reproduced by permission of Candlewick Press, Somerville, MA.)

joyed a secure and happy childhood. That ends when Georgia's absentee father arrives and takes the preteen on a vacation with his new wife, Sissy. In addition to being subjected to the man's sexually abusive behavior, she also learns that her mother is not dead, but is instead an escapee from a mental asylum. According to *School Library Journal* writer Cindy Darling Codell, while *Claiming Georgia Tate* "encompass[es] terrible things, this is still a story of faith and differing facets of individual spirituality." *Kliatt* critic Shaunna Silva noted that Georgia's "young and naive"-sounding narrative shares a "tender and poignant story" in which Amateau's "sensitive subject matter is treated carefully" and avoids "intensely graphic scenes."

Amateau turns her attention to slightly older readers in *A Certain Strain of Peculiar,* a multigenerational story that focuses on thirteen-year-old Mary Harold. An outsider among her peers, Mary has become the target of several schoolmates, and she sees no way that the bullying can stop other than to stop being who she is. Her mother's pickup truck and a road map offer the young teen a way out of her situation, and after an all-night drive she crosses the Alabama state line and eventually reaches her grandmother's cattle ranch. Neighbor Bud accepts Mary as part of the ranch and along with chores and raising a young calf, she soon gets to know Bud's two children, Dixie and Delta, who are unusual and even eccentric. Through her grandmother's loving counsel, Mary learns that running away will not change who she is and that self-acceptance and resilience offer a more life-affirming future. In *Booklist* Frances Bradburn recommended *A Certain Strain of Peculiar* as an "unusual, sensitive story" while *School Library Journal* contributor Carol A. Edwards noted that Mary's "narrative brings an immediacy to the teen's humanity and hurt."

Amateau casts an albino horse in the central role of her children's novel *Chancey of the Maury River* (published in England as *Chancey*), and doing so provided her with fresh challenges. "Horses see color differently than people do," she explained in an interview for the *James River Writers* Web site, "so I tried to use most of the color words carefully if used by Chancey. . . . I also made up a rule that Chancey only really 'talks' within his genus, because horses do have a pretty amazing way of communicating with each other. . . . I believe animals feel; they communicate with people, and they bond with people."

An Appaloosa as well as an albino, Chancey is born under a shooting star, a sign that signals him as a horse of destiny, as he explains in *Chancey of the Maury River.* Used as a saddle horse for beginning riders for several years, he is eventually let loose by his owner after finances run dry. Chancey ultimately finds a new home at the Maury River Stables, where he becomes the companion of a young woman named Claire and competes with her in horse shows. As time passes, medical problems prevent Chancey from making his way along the trails or over jumps in the riding ring. Now almost

blind, the horse finds a new purpose in life as a therapy horse, helping to build confidence and forge trusting bonds with humans whose wounds are both physical and emotional. In *School Library Journal* Kathleen E. Gruver wrote that *Chancey of the Maury River* is "a highly enjoyable read" within which Amateau weaves "many details about equine behavior and horsemanship that lend authenticity." The horse narrator's "generous heart and deepening trust in his riders are the occasion of more than one teary moment," wrote *Horn Book* contributor Anita L. Burkam, the critic adding that the tale "winds to a stirring finish" on the strength of a "narrative [that] is immediate and fascinating."

"I try to write something every day," Amateau noted in discussing her writing career with *Teacher Librarian* interviewer Teri S. Lesesne. "I am a ritual person—rituals hold a lot of meaning for me. When I can grab a true writing day, I usually start off with a specific prayer or intention for the story that I am writing. The act of pausing to reflect and ask for guidance helps me to get my writing mind on track." "Typically," she added, "I will spend some time free writing on a legal pad, focused on one of the note cards or some aspect of the story that is still puzzling me. My dog, Poochie-Mama, is the constant companion. She snores loudly, which makes very reassuring and cozy background music."

Biographical and Critical Sources

PERIODICALS

Booklist, May 1, 2009, Frances Bradburn, review of *A Certain Strain of Peculiar,* p. 72.
Horn Book, May 1, 2008, Anita L. Burkam, review of *Chancey of the Maury River.*
Kirkus Reviews, May 15, 2005, review of *Claiming Georgia Tate,* p. 583; April 15, 2008, review of *Chancey of the Maury River;* November, 2009, Carol A. Edwards, review of *A Certain Strain of Peculiar,* p. 99.
Kliatt, July 1, 2007, Shaunna Silva, review of *Claiming Georgia Tate,* p. 22.
School Library Journal, June 1, 2005, Cindy Darling Codell, review of *Claiming Georgia Tate,* p. 147; June 1, 2008, Kathleen E. Gruver, review of *Chancey of the Maury River,* p. 134.
Teacher Librarian, April, 2006, Teri S. Lesesne, interview with Amateau, p. 58.
Voice of Youth Advocates, October, 2008, Sophie Brookover, review of *Chancey of the Maury River,* p. 329; June, 2009, Amanda McGregor, review of *A Certain Strain of Peculiar,* p. 131.

ONLINE

Authors Round the South, http://www.authorsroundthe south.com/ (April 24, 2009), interview with Amateau.
Gigi Amateau Home Page, http://www.gigiamateau.com (September 15, 2011).

James River Writers Web site, http://www.jamesriverwrit ers.org/ (August 4, 2009), interview with Amateau.*

*   *   *

ANDRES, Kristina 1971-

Personal

Born 1971, in German Democratic Republic (now Germany).

Addresses

Home—Mecklenburg, Germany *E-mail*—post@kristina andres.com.

Career

Author and illustrator. Illustrator of advent calendars. *Exhibitions:* Work exhibited at Bologna Illustrators' Exhibition, 2004-06; and at shows throughout the world.

Writings

SELF-ILLUSTRATED

Ich bin ein Wolf, NordSüd Verlag (Zürich, Switzerland), 2008, translated as *Good Little Wolf,* NorthSouth Books (New York, NY), 2008.
Die Große Seefahrt, NordSüd Verlag (Zürich, Switzerland), 2010, translated as *Elephant in the Bathtub,* NorthSouth Books (New York, NY), 2010.
Nacktkatzen—ABC, Boje Verlag (Cologne, Germany), 2010.
Wenn der Räber Beule kommt, Bajazzoverlag (Zürich, Switzerland), 2010.
Die schnurrende Kammerfrau, Little Tiger Verlag (Gifkendorf, Germany), 2011.

ILLUSTRATOR

Der bunte Hund, Beltz & Gelberg (Weinheim, Germany), 2004.
Herbert Puchta, reteller, *Lilos Lesewelt 4,* Helbling, Rum (Innsbruck, Austria), 2005.
Marjaleena Lembcke, *Bärenpolka uns Zauberflöte,* Residenz Verlag (St. Pölten, Austria), 2006.
Udo Weigelt, *Immer dieser Bär,* NordSüd Verlag (Zürich, Switzerland), 2007.
Christine Knödler, *Geschichtenkoffer für Glückskinder,* Boje Verlag (Cologne, Germany), 2007.
Christine Knödler, *Der Weinachts-Geschichten-Koffer,* Boje Verlag (Cologne, Germany), 2008.
Patacrua, *A pota que trota,* OQO Editora (Pontevedra, Spain), 2009.
Horst Bartnitzky, *Kunterbunt Lesebuch,* volumes 2-4, Ernst Klett Verlag (Leipzig, Germany), 2009–2010.

José Campanari, *Lucas y Oso,* OQO Editora (Pontevedra, Spain), 2010.

Eva Strittmatter, *Großmütterchen Gutefrau und ihre Tiere,* Aufbau Verlag (Berlin, Germany), 2011.

Books featuring Andres' illustrations have been published in Chinese, Finnish, French, Galacian, Greek, Italian, Korean, Portuguese, and Spanish editions.

Adaptations

Anders' illustrations were adapted for the film adaptation of *A pota que trota,* OQO Films.

Biographical and Critical Sources

PERIODICALS

Booklist, December 1, 2008, Janice Del Negro, review of *Good Little Wolf,* p. 54.

Kirkus Reviews, September 1, 2008, review of *Good Little Wolf;* May 1, 2010, review of *Elephant in the Bathtub.*

Publishers Weekly, October 27, 2008, review of *Good Little Wolf,* p. 53.

School Library Journal, December, 2008, Angela J. Reynolds, review of *Good Little Wolf,* p. 84; June, 2010, Tanya Boudreau, review of *Elephant in the Bathtub,* p. 64.

ONLINE

Kristina Andres Home Page, http://www.kristinaandres. com (September 15, 2011).

*   *   *

ARATO, Rona

Personal

Born in New York, NY; immigrated to Canada, 1970; married; husband's name Paul; children: Alise, Debbie, Daniel. *Education:* University of California, Los Angeles, B.A.

Addresses

Home—Toronto, Ontario, Canada. *Office*—90C Centurian Dr., Markham, Ontario L3R 8C5, Canada. *E-mail*—rona@ronaarato.com; rona@words-matter.com.

Career

Author, editor, public-relations consultant, and educator. Rona Arato Communications, Markham, Ontario, Canada, owner. Elementary school teacher in Los Angeles, CA, and Toronto, Ontario, and creative-writing instructor for Toronto District School Board; conductor of business-writing workshops. Interviewer for Survivors of the Shoah Visual History Foundation, 1994-98.

Member

Canadian Society of Children's Authors, Illustrators, and Performers, Writers' Union of Canada, Canadian Children's Book Centre, Society of Children's Book Writers and Illustrators International.

Awards, Honors

First prize, Canadian Authors' Association Short Story Contest, 1993, for "A String of Pearls"; Toronto Arts Council grant, and Canada Council grant, both 2007, and Best Books selection, Canadian Children's Book Centre (CCBC), 2010, all for *Working for Freedom;* Children's Book of the Year Award nomination, Canadian Library Association, and CCBC Best Books selection, both 2008, both for *Ice Cream Town;* Silver Birch Award nominee, Ontario Library Association, 2010, and Golden Oak Award, Ontario Library Association, 2011, both for *Courage and Compassion.*

Writings

NONFICTION

Fossils: Clues to Ancient Life, Crabtree Publishing (New York, NY), 2005.

World of Water: Essential to Life, Crabtree Publishing (New York, NY), 2005.

Courage and Compassion: Ten Canadians Who Made a Difference, Maple Tree Press (Toronto, Ontario, Canada), 2008.

Working for Freedom: The Story of Josiah Henson, Napoleon Publishing (Toronto, Ontario, Canada), 2008.

Design It!: The Ordinary Things You Use Every Day and the Unordinary Ways They Came to Be, illustrated by Claudia Newell, Tundra Books of Northern New York (Plattsburgh, NY), 2010.

Protists: Algae, Amoebas, Plankton, and Other Protists, Crabtree Publishing (New York, NY), 2010.

Contributor to magazines and newspapers, including *Toronto Star, Canadian Living, Homemakers, Trade & Commerce, Financial Times of Canada,* and *Financial Post.*

FICTION

Ice Cream Town, Fitzhenry & Whiteside (Markham, Ontario, Canada), 2007.

On a Canadian Day: Nine Story Voyages through History, illustrated by Peter Ferguson, Owlkids (Berkeley, CA), 2009.

Mrs. Kaputnik's Matzo Ball and Pool Hall Emporium, Tundra Books of Northern New York (Plattsbugh, NY), 2010.

On a Medieval Day: Story Voyages around the World, illustrated by Peter Ferguson, Owlkids (Berkley, CA), 2010.

On an American Day: Story Voyages through History 1750-1899, illustrated by Ben Shannon, Owlkids (Berkley, CA), 2011.

Sidelights

A writer, editor, and teacher, Rona Arato is the author of both fiction and nonfiction for young readers that include *Ice Cream Town* and *Working for Freedom: The Story of Josiah Henson.* Arato's books often reflect her love of history; *On a Medieval Day: Story Voyages around the World,* for example, contains nine tales that capture life in the Middle Ages. "I love telling stories and I love to learn," the author remarked in an *Open Book: Toronto* online interview. "When I research, I learn new things. I enjoy working with kids and introducing them to times and places and events. The process is fun and rewarding."

Set in New York City in the years following World War I, Arato's novel *Ice Cream Town* centers on a family of Polish immigrants. After their mother's death, Sammy Levin and his sister, Malka, endure a long and arduous journey from their hometown of Logov to be reunited

Cover of Rona Arato's humorous historical novel **Mrs. Kaputnik's Pool Hall and Matzo Ball Emporium,** *featuring artwork by Linda Hendry.* (Illustration copyright © 2010 by Linda Hendry. Reproduced with permission of Tundra Books.)

with their father, who has already settled in the United States. Their new home, a cramped tenement building, proves disappointing, however, and the pair finds it difficult to make friends. To overcome his loneliness, Sammy joins a local street gang, but he soon gets into trouble with the police after he shoplifts, an incident that forces him to make changes to his life. "Sammy is a character who will appeal to young readers," Myra Junyk observed in the *Canadian Review of Materials,* and *School Library Journal* critic Kim Dare described *Ice Cream Town* as "a richly detailed, solid piece of historical fiction that gives insight into the early-20th-century immigrant experience."

In *Mrs. Kaputnik's Matzo Ball and Pool Hall Emporium* Arato presents another tale about an immigrant family, this one containing an element of the fantastic. Escaping from Russian cossacks with the help of Snigger, a fire-breathing dragon, Mama Kaputnik and her two children make their way to America, where they encounter a host of colorful—and somewhat disreputable—characters, including the gangster Nick the Stick and the Slobbers, a group of ballplayers who use Mama's rock-hard matzo balls for batting practice. The story's "mild humor and the fantasy element introduced by the dragon . . . keep the story line fresh," a contributor concluded in *Kirkus Reviews.*

Arato, who was born in the United States but now lives in Canada, views the evolution of her adopted country through the eyes of Little Wolf, a seventeenth-century aboriginal boy, and several other fictional children in *On a Canadian Day: Nine Story Voyages through History.* According to Marilynne V. Black in the *Canadian Review of Materials,* Arato's "stories give the sense of a real child living a much different life than that of most modern children." A companion volume, *On a Medieval Day,* features tales about a child-bride in eighth-century China, a squire in twelfth-century England, and a merchant's son in fourteenth-century Mali. "What links all these unique stories together," Junyk commented in the *Canadian Review of Materials,* "is a sense of the complexity of medieval culture in the time period from 400 to 1400 A.D." *Booklist* reviewer Carolyn Phelan similarly noted that "the entries offer glimpses of different cultures within well-structured narratives."

Arato has also garnered praise for her nonfiction efforts. She offers a biography of Josiah Henson, a former slave who became a conductor on the Underground Railroad, in *Working for Freedom,* a book described as "both heartbreaking and inspiring" by Megan Moore Burns in *Quill & Quire.* In *Design It!: The Ordinary Things You Use Every Day and the Unordinary Ways They Came to Be* she presents an introduction to the field of industrial design. Mike Crisolago, writing in *Quill & Quire,* recommended Arato's work here as "a perfect introduction to the way the products we use each day, from toasters to telephones, came to be."

Biographical and Critical Sources

PERIODICALS

Booklist, April 1, 2007, Anne O'Malley, review of *Ice Cream Town,* p. 44; June 1, 2010, Hazel Rochman, review of *Mrs. Kaputnik's Matzo Ball and Pool Hall Emporium,* p. 76; January 1, 2011, Carolyn Phelan, review of *On a Medieval Day: Story Voyages around the World,* p. 105.

Canadian Review of Materials, February 16, 2007, Myra Junyk, review of *Ice Cream Town;* February 12, 2010, Marilynne V. Black, review of *On a Canadian Day: Nine Story Voyages through History;* November 12, 2010, Myra Junyk, review of *On a Medieval Day.*

Children's Bookwatch, May, 2009, review of *Working for Freedom: The Story of Josiah Henson;* January, 2010, review of *On a Canadian Day.*

Kirkus Reviews, March 1, 2010, review of *Mrs. Kaputnik's Matzo Ball and Pool Hall Emporium.*

Quill & Quire, May, 2009, Megan Moore Burns, review of *Working for Freedom;* September, 2010, Jill Bryant, review of *On a Medieval Day;* November, 2010, Mike Crisolago, review of *Design It!: The Ordinary Things We Use Every Day and the Not-So-Ordinary Ways They Came to Be.*

Resource Links, April, 2007, Myra Junyk, review of *Ice Cream Town,* p. 12; June, 2010, Lesley Little, review of *Protists,* p. 25; February, 2010, Adriane Pettit, review of *Mrs. Kaputnik's Matzo Ball and Pool Hall Emporium,* p. 7, and Moira Kirkpatrick, review of *On a Canadian Day,* p. 15.

School Library Journal, June, 2007, Kim Dare, review of *Ice Cream Town,* p. 138; July, 2010, Joanna K. Fabicon, review of *Mrs. Kaputnik's Matzo Ball and Pool Hall Emporium,* p. 81; November, 2010, Clare A. Dombrowski, review of *On a Medieval Day,* p. 134; January, 2011, Anne Chapman Callaghan, review of *Design It!,* p. 122.

ONLINE

Canadian Children's Book Centre Web site, http://www.bookcentre.ca/ (August 1, 2011), "Rona Arato."

Canadian Society of Children's Authors, Illustrators, and Performers Web site, http://www.canscaip.org/ (August 1, 2011), "Rona Arato."

Open Book: Toronto Web site, http://www.openbooktoronto.com/ (November 3, 2010), "On Writing, with Rona Arato."

Rona Arato Communications Web site, http://www.words-matter.com (August 1, 2011).

Rona Arato Home Page, http://ronaarato.com (August 1, 2011).

Writers' Union of Canada Web site, http://www.writersunion.ca/ (August 1, 2011), "Rona Arato."

B

BACH, Bellamy
See WINDLING, Terri

* * *

BENDINGER, Jessica 1966-

Personal
Born November 10, 1966, in Oak Park, IL; father a copywriter, mother a musician. *Education:* Columbia University, degree.

Addresses
Home—Los Angeles, CA.

Career
Screenwriter, director, producer, and novelist. Runway model for Elite Modeling Agency; former journalist for *Spin* magazine and MTV News, New York, NY; MTV, music-video producer and director; freelance writer. Motion picture work includes: (creative consultant) *Sex and the City,* 2001; (producer) *The Wedding Date,* 2005; and (director) *Stick It,* 2006.

Awards, Honors
Billboard Music Award nominations for Best Rap Video and Best Director, both 1991, both for Queen Latifah's "Fly Girl"; named to "Hollywood's Most Powerful Women under 40" list, *Glamour,* 2005.

Writings

NOVELS

The Seven Rays, Simon & Schuster (New York, NY), 2009.

SCREENPLAYS

Bring It On, Universal Pictures, 2000.

(With Jonathan Demme, Steve Schmidt, and Peter Joshua) *The Truth about Charlie,* Universal Pictures, 2002.
(With Kate Kondell) *First Daughter,* Twentieth Century-Fox, 2004.
(With John Quaintance) *Aquamarine,* Twentieth Century-Fox, 2006.
(And director) *Stick It,* Buena Vista Pictures, 2006.

Author of scripts for *Sous le soleil* (French television show), 1996. Uncredited contributor to films, including *Hitch,* Columbia Pictures, 2005.

Sidelights
A noted screenwriter and director, Jessica Bendinger is also the author of *The Seven Rays,* a paranormal young-adult adventure that blends elements of mystery and romance. In the film world, Bendinger is best known for her work on *Bring It On,* a hip, sassy cheerleading comedy which she wrote, and *Stick It,* her directorial debut and a story set in the world of competitive gymnastics. Although her works focus on adolescent characters, they are not targeted solely at a teen audience, as she explained to Debra Eckerling in a *Write On! Online* interview. "I call it a 'coming of consciousness' theme," Bendinger explained. "I think this is what distinguishes me a little bit. I don't think that I write movies for young people. . . . I'm just writing for people."

Bendinger developed an active imagination at a young age, fueled in part by the literary activities of her family. "My dad was very successful in advertising as a writer, [and] my grandmother wrote children's books for me as a hobby and was a volunteer at the library in her town, so books and writing and creativity were a big part of my youth," she recalled to *Austinist.com* contributor Steph Beasley. While attending Columbia University, Bendinger began writing for *Spin* magazine and MTV News, and she later produced and directed videos for MTV. After several years as a freelance writer, which included producing scripts for a French television show, she decided to try her hand at a movie screenplay. Success did not come easily, however; the

script for *Bring It On* was rejected twenty-seven times before finding a home at Universal Pictures. Starring Kirsten Dunst, the film, about an elite suburban cheer squad that learns its routines have been stolen from a predominately black team at a rival high school, proved popular with audiences and critics alike. According to Charles Taylor of *Salon.com, Bring It On* "moves along entertainingly right through to the end credit sequence, and its heart is in just the right place."

Bendinger also served as a creative consultant for the hit television show *Sex and the City* and co-wrote such films as *First Daughter* before moving behind the camera for *Stick It.* This film concerns a rebellious seventeen year old—a former gymnastics champion—who gains a shot at redemption when she returns to competition under the direction of a no-nonsense coach. *New York Times* critic Nathan Lee remarked that the film "takes the usual batch of underdogs, dirt bags, mean girls and bimbos and sends them somersaulting through happy clichés and unexpected invention," and Peter Hartlaub maintained in the *San Francisco Chronicle* that "it's a credit to Bendinger's attention to the little details that make *Stick It* feel so unique and entertaining—poking fun at elite-level child athletics while still respecting its young characters and their feelings."

Bendinger's debut novel, *The Seven Rays,* focuses on Beth Michaels, a sensitive, intelligent seventeen year old who experiences strange visions—glowing dots and colored braids—that cause her to question her sanity. After she receives a mysterious gold envelope containing the message, "You are more than you think you are," Beth's psychic powers increase, and she is soon able to sense other people's fears and secrets. With the help of her new boyfriend, Ritchie, Beth journeys to New York City, where she encounters the group responsible for the cryptic notes she has been receiving, and also learns of her amazing destiny. Reviewing *The Seven Rays* in *Booklist,* Cindy Welch observed that Bendinger takes readers on "quite a ride," and a *Publishers Weekly* critic remarked that the novel's "ambitious premise is interesting and the characters are varied."

Biographical and Critical Sources

PERIODICALS

Advocate, June 6, 2000, review of *Bring It On,* p. 50.
Booklist, February 15, 2010, Cindy Welch, review of *The Seven Rays,* p. 71.
Hollywood Reporter, April 28, 2006, Frank Scheck, review of *Stick It,* p. 13.
Kirkus Reviews, October 15, 2009, review of *The Seven Rays.*
New York Times, April 28, Nathan Lee, review of *Stick It,* p. E20.

Philadelphia Inquirer, April 27, 2006, Carrie Rickey, review of *Stick It.*
Publishers Weekly, November 23, 2009, review of *The Seven Rays,* p. 59.
San Francisco Chronicle, September 24, 2004, Carla Meyer, review of *First Daughter,* p. E5; April 28, 2006, Peter Hartlaub, review of *Bring It On,* p. E5.
School Library Journal, December, 2009, Tara Kehoe, review of *The Seven Rays,* p. 106.
Variety, August 28, 2000, Robert Koehler, review of *Bring It On,* p. 25; May 1, 2006, Robert Koehler, review of *Stick It,* p. 31.

ONLINE

Austinist.com, http://austinist.com/ (March 25, 2010), Steph Beasley, interview with Bendinger.
Jessica Bendinger Home Page, http://www.jessicabendinger.com (August 15, 2011).
Salon.com, http://www.salon.com/ (August 25, 2010), Charles Taylor, review of *Bring It On.*
Seven Rays Web site, http://www.thesevenrays.com (August 15, 2011).
Write On! Online, http://writeononline.com/ (November 13, 2009), Debra Eckerling, interview with Bendinger.*

*　　　*　　　*

BLAKE, Stephanie 1968-

Personal

Born 1968, in Northfield, MN; immigrated to France.

Addresses

Home—Paris, France.

Career

Author and illustrator.

Writings

SELF-ILLUSTRATED

Un éléphant pour se doucher, Loulou & Compagnie (Paris, France), 1994.
Ma petite soeur Lili, École de Loisirs (Paris, France), 1997.
Le noël de Lili, Loulou & Compagnie (Paris, France), 1997.
Petit-Jean, Loulou & Compagnie (Paris, France), 1997.
Les 5 Sens, Loulou & Compagnie (Paris, France), 1998.
Qui veut m'aider?, Loulou & Compagnie (Paris, France), 1998.
Violette, École de Loisirs (Paris, France), 1998.
Souk, École de Loisirs (Paris, France), 1999.

C'est l'hiver!, Loulou & Compagnie (Paris, France), 2000.

Charles, École de Loisirs (Paris, France), 2000.

Francesca, École de Loisirs (Paris, France), 2000.

La fille qui voulait être un garçon, Mouche (Paris, France), 2001.

Mic le porc-épic, École de Loisirs (Paris, France), 2001.

Caca boudin, École de Loisirs (Paris, France), 2002.

Ouf!, Loulou & Compagnie (Paris, France), 2002.

Les poissons rouges, Mouche (Paris, France), 2002.

Mon chat, mon petit chat, École de Loisirs (Paris, France), 2004.

Au loup!, École de Loisirs (Paris, France), 2005.

Superlapin, École de Loisirs (Paris, France), 2005.

Bébé Cadum, École de Loisirs (Paris, France), 2006.

Je veux pas aller a l'École, École de Loisirs (Paris, France), 2007, translated by Whitney Stahlberg as *I Don't Want to Go to School!*, Random House (New York, NY), 2009.

Donner c'est donner, École de Loisirs (Paris, France), 2007, translated by Blake as *A Deal's a Deal!*, Random House Children's Books (New York, NY), 2011.

Je veux des pâtes, École de Loisirs (Paris, France), 2008.

L'anniversaire de Scarlett, École de Loisirs (Paris, France), 2009.

Poux!, École de Loisirs (Paris, France), 2009.

Aaaah! pas le dentiste!, École de Loisirs (Paris, France), 2010.

Non pas dodo!, École de Loisirs (Paris, France), 2010.

Attends-moi!, Loulou & Compagnie (Paris, France), 2011.

Il est où mon p'tit loup?, Loulou & Compagnie (Paris, France), 2011.

Non pas le pot!, École de Loisirs (Paris, France), 2011.

Author's books have been translated into Chinese, Italian, Japanese, Korean, Norwegian, Spanish, and Swedish.

ILLUSTRATOR

Jacques Pibarot, *Touitou, le petit hibou*, École de Loisirs (Paris, France), 1999.

Audren, *Celle que j'aime*, Mouche (Paris, France), 2010.

Christophe Honoré, *J'élève ma poupée*, Neuf (France), 2010.

Biographical and Critical Sources

PERIODICALS

Booklist, July 1, 2009, Andrew Medlar, review of *I Don't Want to Go to School!*, p. 66.

Kirkus Reviews, June 15, 2009, review of *I Don't Want to Go to School!*.

Publishers Weekly, July 13, 2009, review of *I Don't Want to Go to School!*, p. 58.

School Library Journal, August, 2009, Martha Simpson, review of *I Don't Want to Go to School!*, p. 69.

ONLINE

École de Loisirs Web site, http://www.ecoledeloisirs.fr/ (September 15, 2011), "Stephanie Blake."*

*   *   *

BLAU, Aljoscha 1972-

Personal

Born 1972, in Leningrad, USSR (now Russia); immigrated to Germany, 1990; married. *Education:* Fachhochschule für Grafik (Hamburg, Germany), degree (illustration and graphic arts).

Addresses

Home—Berlin, Germany. *E-mail*—blau.ali@gmx.net.

Career

Illustrator.

Awards, Honors

Troisdorfer Bilderbuchpreis second prize, 2002, for *Hans und die Bohnenranke* by Peter Urbscheit; Deutscher Jugendliteraturpreis, 2002, for *Die Geschichte der Wirtschaft* by Nikolaus Piper, 2007, for *Schwester* by Hinrich Schmidt-Henkel; Kröte des Monats Dezember award, 2006, for *Loreley* by Heinrich Heine; Lektorix honor, Bologna Ragazzi Awards, 2006, and Empfehlungsliste Silberne Feder, 2007, both for *Rote Wangen* by Heinz Janisch; Österreichischer Staatspreis für Kinder-und Jugendliteratur, 2008, for *Der Ritt auf dem Seepferd* by Janisch.

Illustrator

Kemal Kurt, *Die fünf Finger und der Mond*, NordSüd Verlag (Gossau, Switzerland), 1997, translated by Anthea Bell as *The Five Fingers and the Moon*, North-South Books (New York, NY), 1997.

Anthea Bell, reteller, *Hans und die Bohnenranke*, NordSüd (Gossau, Switzerland), 2000, translated as *Jack and the Beanstalk: An English Fairy Tale*, North South Books (New York, NY), 2000.

Doris Schröder-Köpf and Ingke Brodersen, *Der Kanzler wohnt im Swimmingpool oder Wie Politik gemacht wird*, Droemer Knaur (Germany), 2003.

Wolfdietrich Schnurre, *Die Maus im Porzellanladen*, Aufbau (Berlin, Germany), 2003.

Reiner Engelmann and Urs M. Fiechtner, *Frei von Furcht und Not*, Sauerländer (Düsseldorf, Germany), 2004.

Henri van Daele, *Vom Grizzly, der nicht schlafen wollte*, Bajazzo Verlag (Zürich, Switzerland), 2004.

Heinz Janisch, *Rote Wangen*, Aufbau (Berlin, Germany), 2005.

Martin Baltscheit, *Die Belagerung*, Bajazzo Verlag (Zürich, Switzerland), 2005.

Martin Baltscheit, *Der Winterzirkus,* Fischer-Taschenbuch (Frankfrut am Main, Germany), 2005.

Reiner Engelmann and Urs M. Fiechtner, *Kinder ohne Kindheit,* Sauerländer (Düsseldorf, Germany), 2006.

Sylke Tempel, *Die Tagesschau erklärt die Welt,* Rohwohlt (Berlin, Germany), 2006.

Heinrich Heine, *Loreley,* Kinderman (Berlin, Germany), 2006.

Hinrich Schmidt-Henkel, *Schwester,* Bajazzo Verlag (Zürich, Switzerland), 2006.

Heinz Janisch, *Der Ritt auf dem Seepferd: Alte und durch wundersame Zufälle neu entdeckte Schriften über die unglaublichen Abenteurer des Carl Friedrich Hieronymus Freiherr von Münchhausen,* Aufbau (Berlin, Germany), 2007, translated by Belinda Cooper as *The Fantastic Adventures of Baron Munchausen: Traditional and Newly Discovered Tales of Karl Friedrich Hieronymus von Munchausen,* Enchanted Lion Books (New York, NY), 2010.

Nikolaus Piper, *Geschichte der Wirtschaft,* Beltz & Gelberg (Germany), 2007.

Hartmut von Hentig, *Paff, der Kater oder wenn wir leiben,* Sanssouci (Munich, Germany), 2007.

Freundschaften (textbook), Terzio (Munich, Germany), 2007.

Detlef Gürtler, *Die Tagesschau erklärt die Wirtschaft,* Rohwohlt (Berlin, Germany), 2008.

Heinz Janisch, *Das Kopftuch meiner Großmutter,* Bajazzo Verlag (Zürich, Switzerland), 2008.

Antonie Schneider, reteller, *Kamel bleibt Kamel* (based on the stories of Aesop), Residenz-Verlag (St. Pölten, Germany), 2009.

Die schönsten Märchen, Aufbau (Berlin, Germany), 2009.

Lemony Snicket, *Wenn die Dinge lebendig werden,* Jacoby & Stuart (Berlin, Germany), 2010.

Andrea Hensgen, *Als Häschen den Käpt'n absetzte,* Jacoby & Stuart (Berlin, Germany), 2010.

Paul Marr, *Das fliegende Kamel,* Oetinger (Hamburg, Germany), 2010.

Books featuring Blau's illustrations have been translated into several languages, including French and Spanish.

Biographical and Critical Sources

PERIODICALS

Publishers Weekly, May 10, 2010, review of *The Fantastic Adventures of Baron Munchausen: Traditional and Newly Discovered Tales of Karl Friedrich Hieronymus von Munchausen,* p. 41.

ONLINE

Aljoscha Blau Home Page, http://aljoschablau.com (September 15, 2011).

Rossipotti Literaturlexikon Web site, http://www.rossipotti. de/ (September 15, 2011), "Aljoscha Blau."*

BLECHA, Aaron

Personal

Born in Green Bay, WI; immigrated to United Kingdom, c. 2007; married.

Addresses

Home—London, England. *E-mail*—blecha@monsters quid.com.

Career

Illustrator, graphic designer, and animator. Designer of toys.

Illustrator

(With Jason Felix) *A Field Guide to Midwest Monsters,* privately published, 2005.

Lisa Trumbauer, reteller, *The Three Little Pigs: The Graphic Novel,* Stone Arch Books (Minneapolis, MN), 2009.

Martin Powell, reteller, *The Tall Tale of Paul Bunyan,* Stone Arch Books (Mankato, MN), 2010.

Martin Powell, reteller, *The Ugly Duckling: The Graphic Novel,* Stone Arch Books (Minneapolis, MN), 2010.

Kevin Bolger, *Zombiekins,* Razorbill (New York, NY), 2010.

"GEORGE BROWN, CLASS CLOWN" READER SERIES

Nancy Krulik, *Super Burp!,* Grosset & Dunlap (New York, NY), 2010.

Nancy Krulik, *Trouble Magnet,* Grosset & Dunlap (New York, NY), 2010.

Nancy Krulik, *World's Worst Wedgie,* Grosset & Dunlap (New York, NY), 2010.

Nancy Krulik, *What's Black and White and Stinks All Over?,* Grosset & Dunlap (New York, NY), 2011.

Nancy Krulik, *Wet and Wild!,* Grosset & Dunlap (New York, NY), 2011.

Nancy Krulik, *Help! I'm Stuck in a Giant Nostril!,* Grosset & Dunlap (New York, NY), 2011.

Nancy Krulik, *Attack of the Tighty Whities!,* Grosset & Dunlap (New York, NY), 2012.

"THE ROTTEN ADVENTURES OF ZACHARY RUTHLESS" READER SERIES

Allan Woodrow, *The Rotten Adventures of Zachary Ruthless,* HarperCollins (New York, NY), 2011.

Allan Woodrow, *The Stench of Goodness,* HarperCollins (New York, NY), 2011.

Sidelights

Warty green monsters, disgruntled dragons, knobby-knee'd pirates, and flesh-eating zombies are some of the many creatures Aaron Blecha has brought to life in his amusing artwork. A Wisconsin-born animator and

designer who now makes his home in England, Blecha creates art that has been paired with graphic-novel adaptations of several classical stories as well as original tales by writers Kevin Bolger, Allan Woodrow, and Nancy Kulik. "Blecha's black-and-white illustrations . . . are an added bonus" of *Zombiekins,* according to a *Kirkus Reviews* critic. Recounting a boy's adventures with a rather creepy stuffed toy, *Zombiekins* features a "cheeky humor [that] will hold interest," according to the reviewer, while *Booklist* critic Daniel Kraus wrote that the "fast and funny" story is "helped along by Blecha's art, which provides some G-rated goo and gore." The "over-the-top" cartoon illustrations he creates for Powell's *The Tall Tale of Paul Bunyan* help to "recapture the bombastic scope of the original stories," according to Benjamin Russell in *School Library Journal.*

Luring beginning readers in with such titles as *Super Burp!, World's Worst Wedgie, What's Black and White and Stinks All Over?,* and *Help! I'm Stuck in a Giant Nostril!,* Kulik's "George Brown, Class Clown" series features Blecha's interior greyscale cartoons and colorful cover art. Readers meet the titular troublemaker in *Super Burp!,* as young George is determined to win over classmates in his new school through his humor and goofball antics. Blecha's "line drawings add humor and break up the short chapters" in *Super Burp!,* according to *School Library Journal* contributor Clare A. Dombrowski, and Jackie Partch noted in the same periodical that the artist's contributions to series installment *Trouble Magnet* "expand on the child's zany behavior."

Biographical and Critical Sources

PERIODICALS

Booklist, June 1, 2010, Daniel Kraus, review of *Zombiekins,* p. 83.

Illustrator Aaron Blecha teams up with writer Kevin Bolger on the comical graphic novel **Zombiekins.** (Copyright © by Kevin Bolger. Used by permission of Razorbill, an imprint of Penguin Young Readers Group, a member of Penguin Group (USA) Inc., 375 Hudson St., New York, NY 10014. All rights reserved.)

Canadian Review of Materials, October, 29, 2010, Dave Jenkinson, review of *Zombiekins.*

Kirkus Reviews, May 1, 2010, review of *Zombiekins.*

Publishers Weekly, July 12, 2010, review of *Super Burp!,* p. 47.

Quill & Quire, July, 2010, Ian Daffer, review of *Zombiekins.*

School Library Journal, September, 2009, Carrie Rogers-Whitehead, review of *The Three Little Pigs: The Graphic Novel,* p. 190; July, 2010, Jackie Partch, review of *Trouble Magnet,* p. 62, and Benjamin Russell, review of *The Tale Tale of Paul Bunyan,* p. 107; September, 2010, Clare A. Dombrowski, review of *Super Burp!,* p. 129.

ONLINE

Aaron Blecha Home Page, http://monstersquid.com (September 15, 2011).

Aaron Blecha Web log, http://monstersquid.blogspot.com (September 15, 2011).

*　　　*　　　*

BOLGER, Kevin

Personal

Born in Ontario, Canada. *Education:* College degree.

Addresses

Home—Ottawa, Ontario, Canada.

Career

Teacher and writer. First Avenue Public School, Ottawa, Ontario, Canada, teacher.

Writings

Sir Fartsalot Hunts the Booger, illustrated by Stephen Gilpin, Razorbill (New York, NY), 2008.

Zombiekins, illustrated by Aaron Blecha, Razorbill (New York, NY), 2010.

Contributor of articles and reviews to periodicals, including *McSweeney's, Toronto Star,* and *Globe & Mail.* Collaborator, with Blecha, on internet cartoon "Sir Fartsalot versus the Dragon."

Sidelights

As a teacher, Kevin Bolger practices what he preaches. In addition to teaching writing and reading at the elementary-school level, Bolger has also crafted several entertaining stories designed to appeal to reluctant readers. His first published book, the compellingly titled *Sir*

Fartsalot Hunts the Booger, has been followed by the equally enticing *Zombiekins,* a story featuring quirky cartoon art by Aaron Blecha.

In *Sir Fartsalot Hunts the Booger,* a fanciful tale illustrated by Stephen Gilpin, a brave but flatulent knight goes on a quest to locate the source of the strange, unpleasant-smelling wind that has brought unease to his kingdom. Accompanied by young practical joker Prince Harry of Armpit, the turnip-eating Sir Fartsalot encounters a number of similarly named nobles on his journey. When Our Hero discovers that a foul monster known as the Booger is the cause of this wind, he and Prince Harry make tracking the Booger the focus of their quest, encountering a colorful galaxy of fairytale residents along the way. Calling Bolger's story "Don Quixote for nine-year-olds," John Wilson added in *Quill & Quire* that *Sir Fartsalot Hunts the Booger* keeps the jokes "coming thick and fast." "Many will cause the parents who are dragooned into reading them aloud to cringe," the critic cautioned, although adding that this will be greatly to the delight of the story's intended audience.

Zombiekins takes readers to the hum-drum town of Dementedyville, where young Stanley Nudelman's life changes after he purchases a strange stuffed toy from the witch next door. When exposed to moonlight, the toy morphs into an evil being that winds up turning all of Stanley's schoolmates into zombies. Teaming up with good friend Miranda, Stanley attempts to stop the demented cuddle toy before his whole town is transformed in a "silly zombie spoof [that] will tickle the funny bone and satisfy the gross-out quotient of any reader," according to a *Kirkus Reviews* writer. In *Booklist,* Daniel Kraus also praised the humorous story in *Zombiekins,* writing that Bolger's "fast and funny" plot is "helped along by Blecha's art, which provides some G-rated goo and gore." "Take the 'Bunnicula', 'Goosebumps' and 'Captain Underpants' series and mash them all together," asserted *Canadian Review of Materials* critic Dave Jenkinson, "and the result would be something resembling *Zombiekins.* An elementary school teacher for a decade, Bolger obviously knows what will amuse his audience."

Biographical and Critical Sources

PERIODICALS

Booklinks, May, 2009, Rebecca A. Hill, review of *Sir Fartsalot Hunts the Booger,* p. 6.
Booklist, June 1, 2010, Daniel Kraus, review of *Zombiekins,* p. 83.
Bulletin of the Center for Children's Books, July-August, 2010, Karen Coats, review of *Zombiekins,* p. 472.
Canadian Review of Materials, October 29, 2010, Dave Jenkinson, review of *Zombiekins.*
Kirkus Reviews, May 1, 2010, review of *Zombiekins.*

Quill & Quire, June, 2008, John Wilson, review of *Sir Fartsalot Hunts the Booger;* July, 2010, Ian Daffern, review of *Zombiekins.*

ONLINE

Zombiekins Web site, http://www.zombiekins.com (September 15, 2011).*

* * *

BOWEN, Fred 1953-

Personal

Born August 3, 1953, in Marblehead, MA; married Peggy Jackson; children: one son, one daughter. *Education:* University of Pennsylvania, B.A. (history and political science); George Washington University, J.D. *Hobbies and other interests:* Reading, watching sports, playing golf.

Addresses

Home—Silver Spring, MD. *E-mail*—fred@fredbowen. com.

Career

Lawyer, journalist, and children's author. Attorney for the U.S. government until 2008.

Awards, Honors

Family Channel Seal of Quality, 1966, for *T.J.'s Secret Pitch;* Best Books for the Classroom citation, Virginia Center for Children's Books, 2000, and several state awards, all for *Winners Take All* and several other books; Maryland Children's Book Award shortlist, 2002, for *Full Court Fever;* Best Children's Books of the Year selection, Bank Street College of Education, Capitol Choices Noteworthy Book selection, and Must Read selection, Massachusetts Center for the Book, all 2010, all for *No Easy Way;* Recommended title, New York State Reading Association, 2010, and South Carolina Book Award finalist, both for *Touchdown Trouble.*

Writings

No Easy Way: The Story of Ted Williams and the Last .400 Season, illustrated by Charles S. Pyle, Dutton Children's Books (New York, NY), 2010.

Contributor of weekly sports column "The Score" to *Washington Post,* beginning 2000.

"ALL-STAR SPORT STORY" SERIES

T.J.'s Secret Pitch, illustrated by Jim Thorpe, Peachtree Publishers (Atlanta, GA), 1996, revised edition, 2010.

Fred Bowen (Reproduced by permission.)

The Golden Glove, illustrated by Jim Thorpe, Peachtree Publishers (Atlanta, GA), 1996, revised edition, 2010.

The Kid Coach, illustrated by Ann Barrow, Peachtree Publishers (Atlanta, GA), 1996, revised edition, 2010.

Playoff Dreams, illustrated by Ann Barrow, Peachtree Publishers (Atlanta, GA), 1997, revised edition, 2009.

Full Court Fever, illustrated by Ann Barrow, Peachtree Publishers (Atlanta, GA), 1998, revised edition, 2009.

Off the Rim, illustrated by Ann Barrow, Peachtree Publishers (Atlanta, GA), 1998, revised edition, 2009.

The Final Cut, illustrated by Ann Barrow, Peachtree Publishers (Atlanta, GA), 1999, revised edition, 2009.

On the Line, illustrated by Ann Barrow, Peachtree Publishers (Atlanta, GA), 1999, revised edition, 2009.

Winners Take All, illustrated by Paul Casale, Peachtree Publishers (Atlanta, GA), 2000, revised edition, 2010.

"FRED BOWEN SPORTS STORY" SERIES

Soccer Team Upset, Peachtree Publishers (Atlanta, GA), 2009.

Touchdown Trouble, Peachtree Publishers (Atlanta, GA), 2009.

Dugout Rivals, Peachtree Publishers (Atlanta, GA), 2010.

Throwing Heat, Peachtree Publishers (Atlanta, GA), 2010.

Hardcourt Comeback, Peachtree Publishers (Atlanta, GA), 2010.

Quarterback Season, Peachtree Publishers (Atlanta, GA), 2011.

Real Hoops, Peachtree Publishers (Atlanta, GA), 2011.

Sidelights

Children's author Fred Bowen has earned a reputation for creating popular sports fiction, Bowen's winning mixture of sports history and action stories has attracted a devoted fan base since the appearance of his first novel, *T.J.'s Secret Pitch,* in 1996. His sports tales, geared for elementary-and middle-school readers, have managed to reach reluctant readers and sports enthusiasts alike. Additionally, each book includes a bonus history section at the back, complete with vintage photographs. The inclusion of that material is vital to his works, Bowen stated in an interview on the Reading Is Fundamental Reading Planet Web site. "One thing is that it gives the kids (readers) an idea that . . . playing in these games makes them part of an ongoing process," he commented, adding, "There's a whole historically true world that's different from mine and is fascinating."

Born in Marblehead, Massachusetts, in 1953, Bowen is one of seven siblings. "My dad loved sports," he noted on his home page. "One of my earliest memories is watching the 1957 World Series on TV with my dad and my brothers. I was four years old and the TV was black-and-white." His father coached him in Little League, and sports informed much of Bowen's early years. "My best childhood memories are taken from playing Little League in the park and basketball on the playground," he recalled on his home page. "I can remember home runs, bad calls, and great comebacks from games I played more than thirty years ago. My favorite reading back then was sports fiction and the sports section in the newspaper."

Bowen thought he was leaving all this sports craziness behind when he went off to college, first to the University of Pennsylvania, where he majored in history and political science, and then on to George Washington University Law School. After graduation, he became a lawyer for the U.S. government, but in his free time he still followed sports. He began to get the writing fever when his journalist wife suggested that he write movie reviews for the local newspaper. "The editor liked the idea and I had a lot of fun doing it," Bowen recalled on his home page. "Who wouldn't? I was getting paid to watch the movies. And it was so cool to see my name in the newspaper." As he read sports books to his young son, Bowen realized that he could write books like those himself.

During lunch hours, on his commute to work, and on weekend mornings, Bowen began to put down some of his own memories and he sculpted these into *T.J.'s Secret Pitch,* the debut title in his "All-Star Sport Story" series. Young T.J. wants to be a pitcher more than anything, but he is small of stature and lacks speed on his

pitches. However, when T.J. discovers the "eephus pitch," a crazy pitching style used by Truett "Rip" Sewell of the Pittsburgh Pirates in the 1940s, everything changes. Using this pitch, T.J. helps his team to win the championship. This first title from Bowen received critical praise, especially for its blend of play-by-play action and sports history. *School Library Journal* critic Blair Christolson wrote that "by interweaving baseball history into the plot" of *T.J.'s Secret Pitch,* Bowen "distinguishes this story from typical sports-series fare."

The second "All-Star Sport Story" book, *The Golden Glove,* deals with Jamie, a shortstop who has lost his lucky glove. He suspects that two kids in the neighborhood stole it, and his parents refuse to buy him a new one. Finally he is forced to borrow a glove, but it does not have the same magic as his old mitt. Interwoven into this story is the history of the baseball glove and the fact that early players did not use them. When players first started to use gloves, they were called sissies. It was not until the Chicago White Stocking pitcher Albert Spalding—the founder of the sporting goods company—wore the glove himself that it became acceptable.

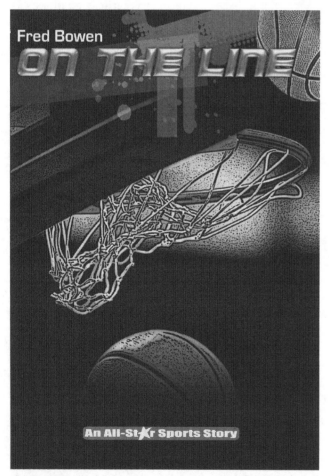

Fred Bowen

ON THE LINE

An All-St★r Sports Story

Bowen mixes basketball into the boy-friendly plot of his young-adult novel **On the Line.** (Illustration copyright © by Charles S. Pyle. Used by permission of Dutton Children's Books, a division of Penguin Young Readers Group, an imprint of Penguin Group (USA) Inc., 375 Hudson St., New York, NY 10014. All rights reserved.)

The Kid Coach, the third title in the series, features the Tigers baseball team, which has lost its coach. The kids end up coaching themselves, and in a big game they attempt to use the "Williams Shift" to stop a home run hitter. This ploy worked against the great Ted Williams in the 1940s, but the Tigers are not sure it will work in their game. Bowen blends in the history of the player-coach idea into *The Kid Coach,* particularly the story of Lou Boudreau, who was both shortstop and coach of the Cleveland Indians in the 1940s.

Reviewing the first three "All-Star Sport Story" titles, *Washington Post Book World* critic Jim Naughton commended Bowen for his restraint in not attempting too much. Noting that the author "weaves female athletes into these 'boy's books' in an admirable way, and he presents a multiracial cast of characters," Naughton further concluded that young readers "who love the game will appreciate that Bowen loves it too and that he makes no attempt to justify this love by enlisting it in the service of grander themes."

In *Playoff Dreams* skilled center fielder Brendan is a member of a team that is not winning, and his frustration turns to anger when he sees no way for his team to make it to the playoffs. Brendan's parents—a jazz-playing dad and doctor mother—are not interested in athletics, but help comes from a sports-crazy uncle who takes Brendan to a baseball game at Chicago's Wrigley Field. When this uncle tells him the story of the hard-luck Cubs and their Hall-of-Fame player Ernie Banks, Brendan begins to look at sports' ups and downs differently. Though Banks never made it to a playoff or a World Series, he always felt happy just to be playing the game. Christolson, writing in *School Library Journal,* observed that Bowen's books use "actual sports heroes to reinforce a positive attitude among young athletes." In *Booklist* Carolyn Phelan also had praise for *Playoff Dreams,* citing its combination of a "simple plot and a well-defined problem."

Bowen turns to basketball in *Full Court Fever,* in which the Falcons, a team long on skill and spirit but short in stature, try desperately to patch up a losing season. They turn to a tactic devised by the 1964 University of California—Los Angeles Bruins, a team that won a national championship without any tall players on their side. More basketball action is served up in *Off the Rim.* Here Chris, who spends too much time on the bench, gets some tips from his friend Greta, the star of the girls' team. In *Off the Rim* Bowen mixes in lore about the history of womens' basketball and how it once differed from men's, being essentially a half-court game.

In *The Final Cut* four middle-grade friends plan to try out for the eighth-grade basketball team. Although basketball is their life, the boys are not the best of athletes. They can hold their own in park games, but when it comes time for the big try-outs, will they be able to cut it and keep their friendship intact? Richard Luzer, re-

Bowen shares an exciting chapter in baseball history in* No Easy Way, *a biography of player Ted Williams that features artwork by Charles S. Pyle.
(Cover design by Thomas Gonzalez and Maureen Withee. Reproduced by permission of Peachtree Publishers.)

viewing *The Final Cut* for *School Library Journal,* wrote that Bowen hits a nerve with "the characters' obsessive interest in evaluating the competition and enhancing their own chances of making the team."

On the Line, the eighth title in the "All-Star Sport Story" series, deals with Marcus, a star forward who is tops all over the court, except at the foul line. Unsought help comes from the school custodian, who shows Marcus how to shoot an underhand foul shot. Bowen again uses a real-life example for this sports story: National Basketball Association star Rick Barry, who played in the 1970s and used the underhand foul shot to great advantage. "Bowen scores again with a satisfying blend of historical sports commentary and fiction," declared Gerry Larson in *School Library Journal* review of *On the Line.*

Focusing on baseball in *Winners Take All,* Bowen tells the story of a good kid who makes a bad decision. Kyle Holt is the Reds center fielder, and they are battling for first place against the Cubs. Kyle wants to win so much that he secretly cheats, pretending to catch a ball he actually drops, and his team wins the game. Everybody is overjoyed, but Kyle feels uneasy about the victory. Then a player from the Cubs discovers the cheating and threatens to tell. Kyle's grandmother gives the young boy a lesson in sports fairness by telling him about Hall-of-Famer Christy Mathewson, a player so honest that umpires would ask his help in making calls. After Kyle confesses to cheating, his team finally beats the Cubs fair and square. Kate Kohlbeck wrote in *School Library Journal* that *Winners Take All* is "a story with plenty of play-by-play action, a good plot, a valuable lesson, and some interesting baseball history." "Bowen pitches a winner here," Kohlbeck concluded.

Bowen's "Fred Bowen Sports Story" series focuses on the thrills and spills of athletic competition. *Touchdown Trouble* draws its plot from an actual sporting event: a 1940 football game between Dartmouth College and Cornell University in which Cornell, aided by an official's error that gave them an extra play, scored a last-second touchdown to win the game. When the players and administrators at Cornell later realized the mistake, they decided to forfeit the contest even though they were not required by any rule to do so, thus ending an eighteen-game unbeaten streak. *Touchdown Trouble* concerns Sam, a running back for the Cowboys' youth team who scores in the waning seconds to give his team the championship. Replaying the contest on video, however, Sam notices that his TD came on an illegal fifth down, and he presents the evidence to his teammates. "Bowen generates some unexpectedly potent drama" out of the ethical dilemma, Ian Chipman noted in his review of *Touchdown Trouble* for *Booklist.*

In *Dugout Rivals* shortstop Jake Daley hopes to improve on his breakthrough performance the previous season, when he was named best eleven-year-old ballplayer on his team. When a new teammate, Adam Hull,

demonstrates superior skills, however, Jake must learn to contain his jealousy while helping Adam deal with some troublesome issues at home. *Throwing Heat,* another baseball tale, centers on Jack Lerner, an eighth-grade pitcher who possesses a blazing fastball but struggles with control problems. With help from his sister's new boyfriend, a college hurler, Jack eventually learns to control his speed and develop a full arsenal of pitches. John Peters, writing in *Booklist,* noted that Jack's initial reluctance to change his approach to the game "adds a realistic touch" to *Throwing Heat.*

A star basketball player suffers a crisis of confidence in *Hardcourt Comeback,* another entry in the "Fred Bowen Sports Story" that was described by Chipman as a "quick, purposeful, and effective" novel. After Brett Carter misses an easy layup at the end of a game, his performance suffers in other areas: he freezes while climbing a rock wall at a friend's party, and he blows a simple question during his school's Brain Bowl. As an important hoops showdown approaches, Brett wonders if he can regain his swagger. According to *School Library Journal* critic H.H. Henderson, "Bowen's stories move along briskly with rapid-fire action sequences and end with surprising twists."

Bowen looks at one of the legends of baseball in his nonfiction work *No Easy Way: The Story of Ted Williams and the Last .400 Season.* Considered one of the greatest hitters in the history of the game, Williams—nicknamed the "Splendid Splinter"—played nineteen seasons for the Boston Red Sox and led the American League in batting six times. In 1941, with the chance for a rare .400 batting average on the line, Williams courageously decided to play both games of a doubleheader on the final day of the season; he collected six hits on the day, ending the season at .406, the last time any major leaguer has reached that mark. Bowen "captures all of the drama" of Williams' magical season, Marilyn Taniguchi commented in *School Library Journal.* Bill Ott, writing in *Booklist,* observed that the story of Williams's accomplishment "hasn't lost its appeal over the years, and Bowen makes the most of it in terms kids will understand."

Discussing the popularity of his books with *Smithsonian* interviewer Jordan Steffen, Bowen remarked, "I think kids really like sports. It's a big part of their lives. Sometimes I'll be in front of parents and they will say to the kids it's just a game. Well the kids are thinking, it's just school. They take the game pretty seriously. I think that the kids sense this isn't a story about a dog playing left field or something, this guy is taking it just as serious as I do."

Biographical and Critical Sources

PERIODICALS

Booklist, November 1, 1997, Carolyn Phelan, review of *Playoff Dreams,* p. 469; September 1, 2009, Ian Chip-

man, review of *Touchdown Trouble,* p. 109; December 15, 2009, Bill Ott, review of *No Easy Way: The Story of Ted Williams and the Last .400 Season,* p. 41; April 15, 2010, Ian Chipman, review of *Hardcourt Comeback,* p. 43; September 1, 2010, John Peters, review of *Throwing Heat,* p. 120.

Kirkus Reviews, February 15, 2010, review of *No Easy Way.*

Newsday, March 16, 1998, Nicole Lord and Leeza Menon, "Did You Like It?"

School Library Journal, July, 1996, Blair Christolson, review of *T.J.'s Secret Pitch,* p. 82; March, 1998, Blair Christolson, review of *Playoff Dreams,* pp. 166-167; December, 1998, Barb Lawler, review of *Full Court Fever,* p. 118; July, 1999, Richard Luzer, review of *The Final Cut,* p. 95; April, 2000, Gerry Larson, review of *On the Line,* p. 129; April, 2001, Kate Kohlbeck, review of *Winners Take All,* p. 138; May, 2006, Marilyn Taniguchi, review of *Playoff Dreams,* p. 59; January, 2010, Marilyn Taniguchi, review of *No Easy Way,* p. 85, and Blair Christolon, review of *Touchdown Trouble,* p. 96; May, 2010, H.H. Henderson, reviews of *Dugout Rivals,* and *Hardcourt Comeback,* both p. 105; October, 2010, Richard Luzer, review of *Throwing Heat,* p. 108.

Washington Post Book World, May 4, 1997, Jim Naughton, reviews of *T.J.'s Secret Pitch, The Golden Glove,* and *The Kid Coach,* all p. 16.

ONLINE

Children's Book Guild Web site, http://www.childrensbookguild.org/ (August 1, 2011), "Fred Bowen."

Fred Bowen Home Page, http://www.fredbowen.com (August 1, 2011).

Reading Is Fundamental Reading Planet Web site, http://www.rif.org/kids/readingplanet/bookzone/ (August 1, 2011), "Meet the Authors and Illustrators: Fred Bowen."

Smithsonian Magazine Online, http://www.smithsonianmag.com/ (July 15, 2009), Jordan Steffen, "Author Fred Bowen Steps up to Bat for the Nationals and the Smithsonian."

*   *   *

BRACKEN, Alexandra 1987-

Personal

Born February 27, 1987, in Phoenix, AZ. *Education:* College of William & Mary, B.A. (history and English), 2009; graduated from Columbia University publishing course.

Addresses

Home—New York, NY.

Career

Author. Works in children's book marketing in New York, NY.

Writings

Brightly Woven, Egmont USA (New York, NY), 2010.

Sidelights

During her sophomore year at the College of William & Mary, Arizona native Alexandra Bracken completed the novel-length manuscript that would eventually be published as her debut fantasy novel *Brightly Woven.* Now living in New York City, Bracken works in publishing while also continuing her work in fantasy fiction.

In *Brightly Woven* Bracken introduces the young rebel wizard Wayland North and his companion Sydelle Mirabel, a sixteen-year-old weaver who became the wizard's assistant as a reward for ending a drought in Sydelle's small mountain village. Pursued by an army of invaders that are led by another wizard, Reuel Dorwan, Wayland and Sydelle journey to the kingdom's capital city, hoping to avert the kingdom's destruction. Along the way, the young woman learns why Wayland took her from

Cover of Alexandra Bracken's young-adult fantasy **Brightly Woven,** *which finds a young artisan faced with the responsibility of protecting* **her people.** (Copyright © 2010. Jacket photo courtesy iStock.com. Reproduced with permission of Egmont USA.)

her family, a reason that is linked to her discovery of her own power and the determination of Dorwan to prevent her from reaching her goal. Elements of romance also enter the tale, contributing to what *Booklist* critic Courtney Jones described as "the pair's breathless adventure" and "ultimate triumph."

"Danger appears at every turn," noted Anthony C. Doyle in his *School Library Journal* review of *Brightly Woven,* and "Bracken weaves a compulsively readable tale" that should appeal to fans of Tamora Pierce and Kristin Cashore. Although "Sydelle's narration portrays her as the stereotypical feisty-yet-commonsensical redhead," it fuels a tale that moves at "a ripping pace, culminating in a (literally) earthshaking climax," asserted a *Kirkus Reviews* writer, and in *Publishers Weekly* a contributor predicted that the mix of "vivid prose" and compelling storytelling makes *Brightly Woven* "a delight, and Bracken . . . a debut author to watch."

Biographical and Critical Sources

PERIODICALS

Booklist, March 15, 2010, Courtney Jones, review of *Brightly Woven,* p. 38.
Kirkus Reviews, February 15, 2010, review of *Brightly Woven,*.
Publishers Weekly, February 1, 2010, review of *Brightly Woven,* p. 51.
School Library Journal, April, 2010, Anthony C. Doyle, review of *Brightly Woven,* p. 151.

ONLINE

Alexandra Bracken Home Page, http://www.alexandra bracken.com (September 15, 2011).
Alexandra Bracken Web log, http://bracken.livejournal. com (September 15, 2011).*

*   *   *

BRAEUNER, Shellie

Personal

Born in IN. *Education:* Vanderbilt University, degree (theatre, psychology).

Addresses

Home—Nashville, TN. *Agent*—Teresa Kietlinski, Prospect Agency, 551 Valley Rd., PMB 377, Upper Montclair, NJ 07043. *E-mail*—shellie@shelliebraeuner.com.

Career

Nanny and author. Worked variously as a counselor, substitute teacher, and dresser for theatre productions. Presenter at schools.

Awards, Honors

Cheerios Spoonful of Stories Children's Book Contest winner, 2007.

Writings

The Great Dog Wash, illustrated by Robert Neubecker, Simon & Schuster Books for Young Readers (New York, NY), 2009.

Sidelights

Shellie Braeuner enjoyed writing stories while growing up because they allowed her to keep in touch with good friends after her family's frequent moves. In college Braeuner's interest shifted to stage drama, and she eventually graduated with a combined major in psychology and theatre. While establishing a career that would allow her to work closely with young people, she reconnected with her love of writing, and her decision to develop this talent resulted in her first published book, *The Great Dog Wash.*

The story of how Braeuner's first children's book came to be published is almost as interesting as the tale itself. She was working as a nanny in Nashville, Tennessee, when the interest to write for children prompted her to pay attention to the stories she invented to entertain her young charges. One day, she and a young girl were washing the family dog when the girl started singing a simply worded song with the repeating refrain "Dog Wash, Dog Wash." The words inspired a story, and by the time dinner was ready that evening Braeuner had set down the first draft of her picture book on paper. She eventually submitted the tale to the 2007 Cheerios Spoonfuls of Stories New Author contest, where it was selected as the winner from among almost 1,000 entries. In addition to being published and distributed to children via over a million boxes of the popular breakfast cereal, *The Great Dog Wash* also attracted the attention of a New York City publisher and was released (without the Cheerios!) to bookstores in 2009 in both Spanish-and English-language editions.

Illustrated by Robert Neubecker and featuring Braeuner's simple, rhythmic text, *The Great Dog Wash* finds a group of children planning a neighborhood clean-up project with a twist: armed with a hose, some soap, and a sudsy tub of water, they attempt to wash all the dogs that are willing. Things get out of hand, however, when a cat saunters into view and is chased by the wet pups up and into the nearest tree. The story's "multiethnic" cast of young characters was described by a *Kirkus Reviews* writer as "a confidence-inspiring creative group whose know-how and adaptability" will inspire young readers, and a *Publishers Weekly* critic wrote that "these kids clearly have their act together." Neubecker's colorful art was praised by *Booklist* critic Abby Nolan as "vivid and lively enough to match the energy of the

Shellie Braeuner's contest-winning story was paired with Robert Neubecker's artwork in the picture book **The Great Dog Wash.** (Illustration copyright © 2009 by Robert Neubecker. Reproduced with permission of Simon & Schuster Books for Young Readers, an imprint of Simon & Schuster Children's Publishing Division.)

text" of *The Great Dog Wash,* and the *Publishers Weekly* contributor asserted that the artist exhibits his skill at "conveying the bustle and telling details of a crowd."

Biographical and Critical Sources

PERIODICALS

Booklist, May 15, 2009, Abby Nolan, review of *The Great Dog Wash,* p. 45.
Kirkus Reviews, June 15, 2009, review of *The Great Dog Wash.*
Publishers Weekly, June 29, 2009, review of *The Great Dog Wash,* p. 127.

ONLINE

Shellie Braeuner Home Page, http://www.shelliebraeuner. com (September 15, 2011).*

*   *   *

BRODIEN-JONES, Chris
See BRODIEN-JONES, Christine

*   *   *

BRODIEN-JONES, Christine 1950-
(Chris Brodien-Jones)

Personal

Born 1950; married; husband's name Peter; children: Ian, Derek. *Education:* Emerson College, degree; attended graduate school. *Hobbies and other interests:* Travel, spending time with family, hiking, kayaking and sailing, swimming, reading, watching films, listening to music.

Addresses

Home—Gloucester, MA. *Agent*—Stephen Fraser, Jennifer de Chiara Literary Agency, 31 E. 32nd St., Ste. 300, New York, NY 10016. *E-mail*—owlkeeper@verizon.net.

Career

Author and editor. Oxford University Press, London, England, former editor's assistant; Elsevier's (publisher), Amsterdam, Netherlands, former editor; Ebsco Publishing, Ipswich, MA, former member of staff. Worked variously as a freelance journalist and photographer and a teacher of special needs students. Presenter at schools.

Member

Author's League, Society of Children's Books Writers and Illustrators.

Writings

(As Chris Brodien-Jones) *The Dreamkeepers,* Bradbury Press (New York, NY), 1992.
The Owl Keeper, illustrated by Maggie Kneen, Delacorte Press (New York, NY), 2010.
The Scorpions of Zahir, Random House (New York, NY), 2012.

Contributor of stories and articles to periodicals.

Sidelights

A former editor and world traveler, Christine Brodien-Jones is the author of middle-grade fantasy novels that include *The Dreamkeepers* and *The Owl Keeper.* A visit to Wales draws two siblings into an ancient battle involving an evil sorceress and a prison of ice in the first

Cover of Christine Brodien-Jones' nature-themed fantasy **The Owl Keeper,** *featuring cover art by Fernando Juarez.* (Illustration copyright © 2010 by Delacorte Press, an imprint of Random House Children's Books, a division of Random House, Inc. Used by permission of Delacorte Press, an imprint of Random House Children's Books, a division of Random House, Inc. New York.)

story, which a *Publishers Weekly* contributor praised for its "arresting imagery." Brodien-Jones focuses on a futuristic evil in *The Owl Keeper,* and the act of writing it transported her far from her home in the quaint New England seaport town of Gloucester, Massachusetts. "I love writing for children because I remember my own excitement reading books when I was young . . . ," the author noted on her home page. "My hope is to fire the imaginations of young people so they can treasure and love the amazing power of stories."

In *The Owl Keeper* readers meet Max Unger just as the boy is about to turn twelve. Living in a near future where the government's tinkering with Earth's climate has caused a human exodus to protected domed cities, Max has difficulty tolerating the sun and only comes outside at night. His trips into the shaded forest with his late grandmother introduced him to the silver owls that dwell there; with Gran now gone, he lives in the care of the grim Mrs. Crumlin. At age twelve the boy is to be assigned a job from the ruling High Echelon, and he worries about his fate until he meets bossy Rose Eccles and she pushes him toward freedom. Gaining knowledge of the Silver Prophecy, the two preteens flee into the forest in search of the Owl Keeper, a creature that may help them destroy the government and help restore Earth's climate and humanity.

Reviewing *The Owl Keeper* in *School Library Journal,* Necia Blundy compared Brodien-Jones' novel to those of British writer Susan Cooper and noted that the author "fills her dystopic fantasy with many striking images and ideas." *Bulletin of the Center for Children's Books* contributor Kate Quealy-Gainer wrote that "the post-apocalyptic setting is nicely done" in *The Owl Keeper,* and a critic for *Publishers Weekly* cited the author's unusual mix of fantasy and science fiction, a mix in which "all science is evil and all magic is good."

Biographical and Critical Sources

PERIODICALS

Booklist, December 15, 1992, Jim Jeske, review of *The Dreamkeepers,* p. 736.
Bulletin of the Center for Children's Books, April, 2010, Kate Quealy-Gainer, review of *The Owl Keeper,* p. 327.
Publishers Weekly, October 26, 1992, review of *The Dreamkeepers,* p. 72; April 12, 2010, review of *The Owl Keeper,* p. 52.
School Library Journal, May, 2010, Necia Blundy, review of *The Owl Keeper,* p. 106.
Voice of Youth Advocates, February, 1993, review of *The Dreamkeepers,* p. 344; October, 2010, Kathleen Beck, review of *The Owl Keeper,* p. 362.

ONLINE

Christine Brodien-Jones Home Page, http://www.owl keeper.com (September 15, 2011).
Christine Brodien-Jones Web log, http://cbrodienjones. wordpress.com (September 15, 2011).*

BROWN, Monica 1969-

Personal

Born 1969; married; children: two daughters. *Education:* Earned Ph.D.

Addresses

Home—Flagstaff, AZ. *Agent*—Stefanie Von Borstel, Full Circle Literary, 7676 Hazard Ctr. Dr., Ste. 500, San Diego, CA 92108, stefanie@fullcircleliterary.com *E-mail*—monica@monicabrown.net.

Career

Author, scholar, and educator. Northern Arizona University, professor of English. Presenter at schools, libraries, and conferences.

Awards, Honors

Rockefeller fellowship on Chicano Cultural Literacies; Américas Award for Children's Literature, and Pura Belpré Honor designation, both 2004, both for *My Name Is Celia: The Life of Celia Cruz;* National Association for the Advancement of Colored People Image Award nomination, and Tejas Star Book Award finalist, both 2010, both for *Side by Side: The Story of Dolores Huerta and Cesar Chavez.*

Writings

FOR CHILDREN

My Name Is Celia: The Life of Celia Cruz/Me llamo Celia: La vida de Celia Cruz, illustrated by Rafael López, Rising Moon (Flagstaff, AZ), 2004.
My Name Is Gabriela: The Life of Gabriela Mistral/Me llamo Gabriela: La vida de Gabriela Mistral, illustrated by John Parra, Luna Rising (Flagstaff, AZ), 2005.
Butterflies on Carmen Street/Mariposas en la calle Carmen, illustrated by April Ward, Piñata Books (Houston, TX), 2007.
My Name Is Gabito: The Life of Gabriel García Márquez/Me llamo Gabito: La vida de Gabriel García Márquez, illustrated by Raúl Colón, Luna Rising (Flagstaff, AZ), 2007.
Pelé, King of Soccer/Pelé, el rey del fútbol, illustrated by Rudy Gutierrez, Rayo (New York, NY), 2009.
Chavela and the Magic Bubble, illustrated by Magaly Morales, Clarion (Boston, MA), 2010.
Side by Side: The Story of Dolores Huerta and Cesar Chavez/Lado a lado: La historia de Dolores Huerta y César Chávez, illustrated by Joe Cepeda, Rayo (New York, NY), 2010.
Pablo Neruda, Poet of the People, illustrated by Julie Paschkis, Henry Holt (New York, NY), 2011.

Waiting for the Biblioburro, illustrated by John Parra, Tricycle Press (Berkeley, CA), 2011.
Clara and the Curandera/Clara y la curandera, illustrated by Thelma Muraida, Piñata Books (Houston, TX), 2011.
Marisol McDonald Doesn't Match/Marisol McDonald no combina, illustrated by Sara Palacios, Children's Book Press (New York, NY), 2011.

OTHER

Gang Nation: Delinquent Citizens in Puerto Rican, Chicano, and Chicana Narratives, University of Minnesota Press (Minneapolis, MN), 2002.

Contributor to academic journals.

Sidelights

A woman of Peruvian, Amerindian, European, and Jewish ancestry, Monica Brown is a scholar who teaches Latino and multicultural literature in the English department of Northern Arizona University. In addition to her teaching, Brown has also crafted biographies of noted Hispanic men and women from all walks of life in books that include *My Name Is Celia: The Life of Celia Cruz/Me llamo Celia: La vida de Celia Cruz, My Name Is Gabriela: The Life of Gabriela Mistral/Me llamo Gabriela: La vida de Gabriela Mistral, My Name Is Gabito: The Life of Gabriel García Márquez/Me llamo Gabito: La vida de Gabriel García Márquez, Pelé, King of Soccer/Pelé, el rey del fútbol, Side by Side: The Story of Dolores Huerta and Cesar Chavez/Lado a lado: La historia de Dolores Huerta y César Chávez,* and *Pablo Neruda, Poet of the People.* "I write from a place of deep passion, joy, and commitment to producing the highest possible quality of literature for children," Brown noted on her home page. "In my biographies, the lives of my subjects are so interesting and transformational that I am simply giving them voice for a young audience."

Brown's first picture book, *My Name Is Celia,* is illustrated with colorful paintings by Rafael López and captures the life of the talented Cuban girl who overcame many obstacles on her way to becoming an internationally renowned salsa-singing sensation in her adopted home of Miami. In *School Library Journal* Ann Welton praised Brown's children's-book debut, calling *My Name Is Celia* "a brilliant introduction to a significant woman and her music."

Literary figures make an appearance in several books by Brown, among them *My Name Is Gabito.* Paired with Raúl Colón's pencil-and-watercolor images, Brown's text takes readers to Colombia, where noted magical realist Gabriel García Márquez was encouraged to develop the interest in writing that would eventually lead to groundbreaking novels such as *One Hundred Years of Solitude.* "Brown does a wonderful job of articulating . . . magical realism . . . in a way young-

Monica Brown's imaginative story for* Chavela and the Magic Bubble *comes to life in Magaly Morales's colorful stylized art. (Illustration copyright © 2010 by Magaly Morales. Reproduced with permission of Clarion Books, an imprint of Houghton Mifflin Harcourt Publishing Company.)

sters can grasp," asserted *School Library Journal* contributor Susan E. Murray, and in *Booklist* Carolyn Phelan praised the mix of "vivid, lyrical text" and "artwork [that] interprets the story with verve."

Hispanic poets are the focus of both *My Name Is Gabriela* and *Pablo Neruda, Poet of the People.* In the first book John Parra crafts "naive-style" folk-art paintings that "go well beyond complementing" Brown's biography of the Chilean writer who eventually received a Nobel prize for her work, according to Maria Otero-Boisvert in her *School Library Journal* review of the book. Julie Paschkis creates the artwork for *Pablo Neruda, Poet of the People,* Brown's profile of another Nobel-winning Chilean writer, a man who was actually Mistral's student. Characterizing *Pablo Neruda, Poet of the People* as "not so much a biography of the Chilean Nobel laureate as a verbal and visual paean to his art," *Horn Book* contributor Joanna Rudge Long added that the author's text "celebrates the subjects that informed his [Neruda's] poetry," including his social activism and love of travel. Brown's "simple, but impassioned telling combine[s] with Paschkis's vibrant, decorative style for a book high in child appeal," asserted *School Library Journal* contributor Wendy Lukehart, and a *Publishers Weekly* critic praised *Pablo Neruda, Poet of the People* as a paean to "a man who saw the world as a joyful, complex, and beautiful poem waiting to be unveiled."

Sports become Brown's focus in *Pelé, King of Soccer,* in which artwork by Rudy Gutierrez brings to life her bilingual biography of perhaps the best-known soccer player in the world. Born in Brazil, Pelé grew up in poverty and channeled his determination and love of the game into a career that made him world-famous. Brown's "direct prose effectively tells the soccer hero's story," wrote Mary Landrum in her *School Library Journal* review of *Pelé, King of Soccer,* while in *Kirkus Reviews* a contributor concluded that Brown and Gutierrez's "inspiring blend of art and story scores a winning goal."

Two noted twentieth-century labor activists come into focus in *Side by Side: The Story of Dolores Huerta and Cesar Chavez,* a picture book illustrated by Joe Cepeda. Here Brown describes the events leading up to a nation-wide boycott of grapes that came to fruition in the 1960s as a way to make Americans aware of the poor working and living conditions of the nation's migrant agricultural workers. Inspired by Huerta, the boycott was let by Chavez, and the two continued to advocate through the United Farm Workers Union for several decades. "The vocabulary, pictures, and length of the story lend themselves to reading aloud to younger audiences," noted *School Library Journal* contributor Shannon Dye, the critic adding that Brown's story would also be useful in sparking discussions about social-justice issues among older children.

In addition to biographies, Brown has also created several original stories that feature Hispanic children. In *Chavela and the Magic Bubble,* illustrated by Magaly

Morales, a young girl buys a package of magic gum—or chicle. When she starts to chew and then to blow, the resulting bubble is large enough to transport her from her California home all the way down to Mexico's Yucatan, where the chicle sap of the sapodilla tree is harvested. Although Brown includes information on the threatened rain-forest environment of the sapodilla tree, she separates them from her main text and "creates a charming story that celebrates the joys of gum chewing . . . without becoming didactic," according to *School Library Journal* reviewer Mary Landrum. In *Kirkus Reviews* a critic praised *Chavela and the Magic Bubble* as "a lovely, child-friendly tale that will entertain" story-hour audiences "as well as exposing them to both ecological and cultural themes."

The power of reading to inspire young imaginations is the subject of *Waiting for the Biblioburro,* a picture book illustrated by John Parra that was inspired by Soriano Bohorquez, a Colombian man who traveled to rural villages with his portable library. In the story, Ana loves to read, but her family has only a few books and she knows them all by heart. Then a librarian arrives with a wagon-load of books for loan and a knack for both teaching and storytelling. In addition to borrowing several books, Ana also writes her own story, a story about the traveling librarian that the man adds to his collection of books when she presents it to him at his next visit. Recommending *Waiting for the Biblioburro* as "perfect for read-alouds," a *Kirkus Reviews* writer added that Brown's inclusion of "onomatopoeic Spanish words . . . add[s] to the fun." Other picture-book stories by Brown include *Butterflies on Carmen Street/ Mariposas en la calle Carmen,* *Clara and the Curandera/Clara y la curandera,* and *Marisol McDonald Doesn't Match/Marisol McDonald no combina,* the last illustrated by Sara Palacios.

Biographical and Critical Sources

PERIODICALS

Booklist, February 1, 2008, Carolyn Phelan, review of *My Name Is Gabito: The Life of Gabriel García Márquez/Me llamo Gabito: La vida de Gabriel García Márquez,* p. 45; November 15, 2008, John Peters, review of *Pelé, King of Soccer/Pelé, el rey del fútbol,* p. 48; April 1, 2010, Hazel Rochman, review of *Chavela and the Magic Bubble,* p. 45; November 1, 2010, Hazel Rochman, review of *Side by Side: The Story of Dolores Huerta and Cesar Chavez/Lado a lado: La historia de Dolores Huerta y César Chávez,* p. 44; January 1, 2011, Gillian Engberg, review of *Pablo Neruda, Poet of the People,* p. 86.
Horn Book, March-April, 2010, Joanna Rudge Long, review of *Pablo Neruda, Poet of the People* p. 135.
Kirkus Reviews, November 15, 2008, review of *Pelé, King of Soccer;* April 15, 2010, review of *Chavela and the Magic Bubble;* June 15, 2011, review of *Waiting for the Biblioburro.*

Publishers Weekly, December 20, 2010, review of *Pablo Neruda, Poet of the People,* p. 52; May 2, 2011, review of *Waiting for the Biblioburro,* p. 53

School Library Journal, January, 2005, Ann Welton, review of *My Name Is Celia: The Life of Celia Cruz/Me llamo Celia: La vida de Celia Cruz,* p. 120; February, 2006, Maria Otero-Boisvert, review of *My Name Is Gabriela,* p. 126; March, 2008, Susan E. Murray, review of *My Name Is Gabito,* p. 82; April, 2009, Mary Landrum, review of *Pelé, King of Soccer,* p. 120; April, 2010, Mary Landrum, review of *Chavela and the Magic Bubble,* p. 120; November, 2010, Shannon Dye, review of *Side by Side,* p. 96; February, 2011, Wendy Lukehart, review of *Pablo Neruda, Poet of the People,* p. 94.

ONLINE

Monica Brown Home Page, http://www.monicabrown.net (September 15, 2011).*

*   *   *

BROWNING, Diane

Personal

Female. *Education:* Attended Art Center College of Design. *Hobbies and other interests:* Travel, photography, Irish music, films, cats, reading.

Addresses

Home—Blue Jay, CA. *E-mail*—dianebrowning3@gmail.com.

Career

Fine-art painter and author/illustrator. Formerly worked in advertising and graphic design; teacher of art to children. Muralist. *Exhibitions:* Work exhibited in galleries and included in permanent collection of a museum in Russia.

Member

Society of Children's Book Writers and Illustrators.

Awards, Honors

Top-Ten Historical Titles for Youth and Top-Ten Art Titles for Youth selections, both *Booklist,* both 2010, and Amelia Bloomer Recommended selection, American Library Association, and Crystal Kite Award shortlist, Society of Children's Book Writers and Illustrators, both 2011, all for *Signed, Abiah Rose.*

Writings

SELF-ILLUSTRATED

Signed, Abiah Rose, Tricycle Press (Berkeley, CA), 2009.

Contributor of activities to children's books.

Sidelights

"Almost as soon as I could sit upright I joined my sisters at a table where we each had our own stack of paper and crayons and where we could draw to our hearts' content," Diane Browning recalled on her home page. The daughter of a fashion illustrator, Browning grew up in a home that encouraged creativity. An early desire to tell stories was fueled by the children's writing club of legendary Texas librarian and author Siddie Joe Johnson. After moving to California and graduating from Hollywood High School, she enrolled at the prestigious Art Center College of Design, and studies in Europe continued to enrich her artistic vision. Browing worked as a graphic artist and illustrator in the advertising field for several years while also exhibiting her work as a painter. Her paintings have been exhibited widely and one is part of the permanent collection of a museum in Russia. During her career, Browning has also shared her enthusiasm with children as a teacher of painting and drawing.

A course in children's book creation taught by noted artist Uri Schulevitz eventually led to Browning's first published children's book, *Signed, Abiah Rose.* The first-person story was inspired by a television documentary about nineteenth-century American women artists and focuses on a young girl who loves to paint. Al-

Diane Browning captures the resolve of a creative young spirit in her self-illustrated picture book **Signed, Abiah Rose.** (Copyright © 2009 by Diane Browning. Used by permission of Tricycle Press, an imprint of the Crown Publishing Group, a division of Random House, Inc., New York.)

though Abiah exhibits a considerable talent, she is discouraged from following her dream of becoming a portrait painter, even though she sells several of her paintings to people in the surrounding countryside. Cautioned not to sign her paintings, the girl instead paints the image of a small rose into each of her works. Browning's "understated story is balanced by truly lovely art," noted Paula Willey in her *School Library Journal* review of *Signed, Abiah Rose,* and her "beautiful and inspiring" acrylic and colored-pencil images are paired with appropriately "old-fashioned, homespun language." The artist's picture-book debut "instantly evokes and sustains old-fashioned charm," asserted a *Kirkus Reviews* writer, making *Signed, Abiah Rose* an "ideal" choice for prompting discussions about "gender roles and/or folk art in pioneer America." In addition to marking "a promising debut," according to *Booklist* critic Carolyn Phelan, Browning's engaging story pairs "an idyllic view of an earlier time" with a story about a talented and creative girl confronting a society in which "women's opportunities were limited." In *Publishers Weekly* a critic dubbed *Signed, Abiah Rose* "a winning combination of historical fiction and creative resolve."

Biographical and Critical Sources

PERIODICALS

Booklist, February 15, 2010, Carolyn Phelan, review of review of *Signed, Abiah Rose,* p. 77.
Kirkus Reviews, April 15, 2010, review of *Signed, Abiah Rose.*
Publishers Weekly, April 19, 2010, review of *Signed, Abiah Rose,* p. 53.
School Library Journal, April, 2010, Paula Willey, review of *Signed, Abiah Rose,* p. 120.

ONLINE

Diane Browning Home Page, http://www.dianebrowning illustrations.com (September 15, 2011).

*   *   *

BRUNELLE, Lynn

Personal

Married; children: two sons. *Education:* B.A.; B.A., M.Ed.

Addresses

Home—Bainbridge Island, WA. *E-mail*—lynn@lynn brunelle.com.

Career

Television writer and author. Worked as a science, English, and art teacher of grades K-12; Scientific American Books for Young Readers, New York, NY, former editor. Songwriter and videographer. Consultant; contributor to National Public Radio program "Science Friday" and programming on Sirius Radio and Martha Stewart Living Radio.

Awards, Honors

Four Emmy awards for writing, for *Disney Presents: Bill Nye the Science Guy* television program; Telly Award; Gold Award, Parents' Choice Foundation, 1999, 2001, 2004, for *Pop Bottle Science,* 2007, for *Camp Out!,* 2008, for *The Zoo's Shoes.*

Writings

FOR CHILDREN

Tina L. Seelig, *Incredible Edible Science,* Scientific American Books for Young Readers (New York, NY), 1994.
(With Leslie McGuire) *Animal Singalong,* illustrated by Rhonda Voo, Weldon Owen, 1999.
(With Leslie McGuire) *Copycat!: A Book of Animal Actions,* illustrated by Jackie Snider, photography by Chris Shorten, Weldon Owen, 1999.
I Go Places: A Fun Sticker Book, illustrated by Leo Espinosa, Weldon Owen, 1999.
My Blue Zoo: A Counting Book of Blue,, photography by Chris Shorten, Weldon Owen, 1999.
(Compiler) *Nursery Rhymes Music & Dance,* illustrated by Jennifer Herbert, Weldon Owen, 1999.
Red on the Go: A Counting Book of Red, photography by Chris Shorten, Weldon Owen, 1999.
The Itsy-bitsy Spider and a Handful of Finger Rhymes, illustrated by Dona Turner, Weldon Owen, 1999.
Indiana, the Hoosier State, World Almanac Library (Milwaukee, WI), 2002.
Bite into an Apple, Blackbirch Press (San Diego, CA), 2004.
Pop Bottle Science, illustrated by Paul Meisel, Workman Publishing (New York, NY), 2004.
Turn on the Faucet, Blackbirch Press (San Diego, CA), 2004.
Yoga for Chickens: Relaxing Your Inner Chick; or, Enlightened Poses Straight from the Coop, Chronicle Books (San Francisco, CA), 2004.
Earthquake!: The 1906 San Francisco Nightmare, Bearport Pub. (New York, NY), 2005.
Camp Out!: The Ultimate Kids' Guide, from the Backyard to the Backwoods, illustrated by Brian Biggs, technical illustrated by Elara Tanguy, Workman Publishing (New York, NY), 2007.
Mama's Little Book of Tricks: Fun Games, Cool Feats, Nifty Knowledge, illustrated by Jessie Eckel, technical illustrated by Arthur Mount, Chronicle Books (San Francisco, CA), 2007.
The Zoo's Shoes: Learn to Tie Your Shoelaces!, illustrated by Emilie Chollat, Workman Publishing (New York, NY), 2008.
Why Did I Buy This Book?: Over 500 Puzzlers, Teasers, and Challenges to Boost Your Brain Power, Chronicle Books (San Francisco, CA), 2009.

(With George Shannon) *Chicken Scratches: Chicken Rhymes and Poultry Poetry,* illustrated by Scott Menchin, Chronicle Books (San Francisco, CA), 2010.

Writer for television series and documentaries, including *Bill Nye the Science Guy, All Terrain Brain, Artopia,* and *Travels to the Edge with Art Wolfe.* Contributor to periodicals, including *Explorations, Family Fun, National Geographic Extreme Explorer, Kids Contact, Metalsmith, National Geographic World, Nick, Jr., Scientific America,* and *Weekly Reader.*

Biographical and Critical Sources

PERIODICALS

Booklist, July, 1994, Mary Harris Veeder, review of *Incredible Edible Science,* p. 1942.

Publishers Weekly, September 13, 2004, review of *Pop Bottle Science,* p. 81; April 26, 2010, review of *Chicken Scratches: Poultry Poetry and Rooster Rhymes,* p. 110.

School Library Journal, November, 2005, Peg Glisson, review of *Earthquake!: The 1906 San Francisco Nightmare,* p. 112; February, 2008, Cynde Suite, review of *Camp Out!: The Ultimate Kids' Guide,* p. 132; February, 2008, Cynde Suite, review of *Camp Out!: The Ultimate Kids' Guide,* p. 13; June, 2010, Julie Roach, review of *Chicken Scratches,* p. 91.

ONLINE

Lynn Brunelle Home Page, http://www.lynnbrunelle.com (September 15, 2011).

C

CALLERY, Sean

Personal
Born in England. *Education:* Teaching degree.

Addresses
Home—Oxfordshire, England. *E-mail*—sean@caller.demon.co.uk.

Career
Writer and educator. Worked in journalism and public relations for ten years; freelance writer of adult reference and children's books. Primary-school teacher and music specialist. Presenter at schools.

Writings

Handwriting: Secrets Revealed, Sterling Pub. Co. (New York, NY), 1989.

Card Games for Two, Sterling Pub. Co. (New York, NY), 1990.

(Editor) *Basic Golfing Techniques,* Tiger Books International (London, England), 1990.

The Pictorial History of Tennis, Gallery Books (New York, NY), 1990.

Tracing Your Family Tree, Ward Lock (London, England), 1991.

First time Father, Ward Lock (London, England), 1991.

Harrods, Knightsbridge: The Story of Society's Favourite Store, Ebury Press (London, England), 1991.

Soccer: Technique, Tactics, Training, Crowood Press (Ramsbury, Marlborough, England), 1991.

Scandals: Gripping Accounts of the Exposed and Deposed, Apple (London, England), 1992.

The Bridegroom's Handbook, Ward Lock (London, England), 1992, new edition, 1994.

(Editor) *The Complete Drawing and Painting Course: The Artist's Practical Guide to Media and Techniques,* Apple (London, England), 1997.

Children's Parties, Collins (London, England), 2006.

Party Games, Collins (London, England), 2006.

Dreams, Collins (London, England), 2006.

Codes and Ciphers, Collins (London, England), 2006.

Dictators, Collins (London, England), 2007.

Five-minute Memory Workout, Collins (London, England), 2007.

(With Clive Gifford and Mike Goldsmith) *Explore,* Kingfisher (New York, NY), 2008.

I Wonder Why There's a Hole in the Sky, and Other Questions about the Environment, Kingfisher (New York, NY), 2008.

(With Tom Jackson) *Quiz Whiz,* Kingfisher (New York, NY), 2008.

The Rainforest Express ("Star Plays" series), Evans Bros. (London, England), 2009.

Rocks and Minerals, Miles Kelly (Great Bardfield, England), 2009, published as *100 Things You Should Know about Rocks and Minerals,* Mason Crest (Broomall, PA), 2010.

The Pharaoh's Toothache ("Star Plays" series), Evans Bros. (London, England), 2009.

Victor Wouk: The Father of the Hybrid Car, Crabtree (New York, NY), 2009.

Topspin ("Solo" reader series), Barrington Stoke (London, England), 2010.

Hide and Seek in the Jungle (board book), illustrated by Rebecca Robinson, Macmillan (New York, NY), 2010.

Hide and Seek Pets (board book), illustrated by Rebecca Robinson, Macmillan (New York, NY), 2010.

Money Matters, QEB Pub. (Mankato, MN), 2010.

Treasure Hunt!, Crabtree (New York, NY), 2011.

Children's History of Oxford, Hometown World (England), 2011.

(With Clive Gifford and Mike Goldsmith) *The Encyclopedia of Everything,* Kingfisher (London, England), 2012.

The Tour de France, HarperCollins (London, England), 2012.

Author's work has been translated into French, German, and Spanish.

"EXTREME SCIENCE" NONFICTION SERIES

Defying Gravity: Surviving Extreme Sports, Capstone Press (Mankato, MN), 2008.
Frozen World: Polar Meltdown, Capstone Press (Mankato, MN), 2008.
Lights Out!: Living in 24-hour Darkness, Capstone Press (Mankato, MN), 2008.

"WHAM!" NONFICTION SERIES; ILLUSTRATED BY SHONA GRANT

Wham! Undersea, Barrington Stoke (Edinburgh, Scotland), 2009.
Wham! Grasslands, Barrington Stoke (Edinburgh, Scotland), 2009.
Wham! Rainforest, Barrington Stoke (Edinburgh, Scotland), 2010.
Wham! Arctic, Barrington Stoke (Edinburgh, Scotland), 2010.

"DARK HISTORY" NONFICTION SERIES

The Dark History of America's Old West, Marshall Cavendish Benchmark (New York, NY), 2010.
The Dark History of Ancient Greece, Marshall Cavendish Benchmark (New York, NY), 2010.
The Dark History of Ancient Rome, Marshall Cavendish Benchmark (New York, NY), 2010.
The Dark History of the Aztec Empire, Marshall Cavendish Benchmark (New York, NY), 2010.

"CODEQUEST" NONFICTION SERIES

Hieroglyphs: Solve the Mystery of the Golden Cat, Kingfisher (London, England), 2010, published as *Hieroglyphs: Solve the Mystery from Ancient Egypt,* Kingfisher (New York, NY), 2010.
Inca Gold: Solve the Mystery of the Golden Corn, Kingfisher (London, England), 2011.

"TAKE 2" NONFICTION READER SERIES

Moon Walk, illustrated by Emil Dacanay, Evans Bros. (London, England), 2010.
The Ice Race, Evans Bros. (London, England), 2010.
Stowaway, illustrated by George Brunton, Evans Bros. (London, England), 2010.

"LIFECYCLES" NONFICTION SERIES

Ocean, Kingfisher (London, England), 2011.
Rainforest, Kingfisher (London, England), 2011.
Grassland, Kingfisher (London, England), 2011.
Polar Lands, Kingfisher (London, England), 2011.
Forest, Kingfisher (London, England), 2012.
River, Kingfisher (London, England), 2012.
Desert, Kingfisher (London, England), 2012.
Mountains, Kingfisher (London, England), 2012.

"SPOOKY TALES" SERIES

Ghost in the South East, Evans Bros. (London, England), 2012.
Ghost in the Midlands, Evans Bros. (London, England), 2012.
Ghost in the North West, Evans Bros. (London, England), 2012.
Ghost in the East of England, Evans Bros. (London, England), 2012.

Biographical and Critical Sources

PERIODICALS

Booklist, May 1, 2010, Courtney Jones, review of *Hide and Seek in the Jungle,* p. 90; May 15, 2010, Ilene Cooper, review of *Hieroglyphs: Solve the Mystery from Ancient Egypt,* p. 38; October 1, 2010, Daniel Kraus, review of *The Dark History of America's Old West,* p. 65.
Kirkus Reviews, May 1, 2010, review of *Hieroglyphs.*
Publishers Weekly, March 15, 2010, review of *Hide and Seek in the Jungle,* p. 54.
School Library Journal, August, 2010, Paula Willey, review of *Hieroglyphs,* p. 97.
Science and Children, February, 2010, Nancy McDonough, review of *Frozen World: Polar Meltdown,* p. 81.

ONLINE

Sean Callery Home Page, http://seancallery.co.uk (September 15, 2011).

*   *   *

CARMAN, Patrick 1966-

Personal

Born February 27, 1966; son of an entrepreneur; married; wife's name Karen; children: Reece, Sierra (daughters). *Education:* Willamette University, B.S. (economics). *Hobbies and other interests:* Fly fishing, doing crossword puzzles, basketball, tennis, reading, spending time with family.

Addresses

Home—WA. *E-mail*—fanmail@patrickcarman.com.

Career

Author, entrepreneur, and literacy advocate. Founder of four businesses, including an advertising agency. Former game designer. Volunteer on behalf of literacy campaigns. Presenter at schools.

Awards, Honors

iParenting Media Award, 2005, and Lamplighter Award, 2007, both for *The Dark Hills Divide;* Lamplighter Award, 2008, for *Beyond the Valley of Thorns;* National Literacy Explore New Worlds selection, Library of Congress, for *Land of Elyon;* E.B. White Award nomination, 2008, and Truman Award nomination, 2009, both for *Atherton;* Children's Book Council (CBC) Best Books nomination, 2010, for *The Crossbones;* CBC Best Book nomination, 2010, and YALSA Quick Picks for Reluctant Readers listee, 2011, both for *Thirteen Days to Midnight;* numerous state and child-selected awards.

Writings

The Black Circle (installment in "39 Clues" mystery series), Scholastic (New York, NY), 2009.
Thirteen Days to Midnight, Little, Brown (New York, NY), 2010.
Floors, Scholastic (New York, NY), 2011.
Dark Eden (multiplatform novel), HarperCollins (New York, NY), 2011.

Author's novels have been translated into several languages.

"LAND OF ELYON" MIDDLE-GRADE FANTASY SERIES

The Dark Hills Divide, Orchard Books (New York, NY), 2005.
Beyond the Valley of Thorns, Orchard Books (New York, NY), 2005.
The Tenth City, Orchard Books (New York, NY), 2006.
Into the Mist (prequel), Orchard Books (New York, NY), 2007.
Stargazer, Scholastic Press (New York, NY), 2008.

"ATHERTON" FANTASY SERIES

(Self-illustrated) *The House of Power,* Little, Brown (New York, NY), 2007.
Rivers of Fire, Little, Brown (New York, NY), 2008.
The Dark Planet, illustrated by Squire Broel, Little, Brown (New York, NY), 2009.

"ELLIOT'S PARK" READER SERIES

Saving Mister Nibbles, illustrated by Jim Madsen, Orchard Books (New York, NY), 2008.
Haunted Hike, illustrated by Jim Madsen, Orchard Books (New York, NY), 2008.
The Walnut Cup, illustrated by Steve James, Orchard Books (New York, NY), 2009.

"SKELETON CREEK" MULTIPLATFORM NOVEL SERIES

Skeleton Creek, illustrated by Joshua Pease, Scholastic Press (New York, NY), 2009.

Ghost in the Machine, illustrated by Joshua Pease, Scholastic Press/PC Studio (New York, NY), 2009.
The Crossbones, illustrated by Joshua Pease and Squire Broel, Scholastic Press/PC Studios (New York, NY), 2010.
The Raven, illustrated by Joshua Pease, Scholastic, PC Studios (New York, NY), 2011.

"TRACKERS" MULTIPLATFORM NOVEL SERIES

Trackers, Scholastic (New York, NY), 2010.
Shantorian, Scholastic (New York, NY), 2011.

Adaptations

The Land of Elyon was adapted for film by CGI Films. *Skeleton Creek* was optioned for film. Several of Carman's novels were adapted as audiobooks by Brilliance Audio. *The Black Circle* and *The Dark Planet* were adapted for audiobook, read by David Pittu, Scholastic Audiobooks, 2009.

Sidelights

Patrick Carman's fantasy novels for middle-grade readers have helped to encourage reading while also weaving other media into the traditional reading experience.

Cover of Patrick Carman's **The Dark Hills Divide,** *featuring artwork by Brad Weinman.* (Cover illustration copyright © 2005 by Scholastic, Inc. Reproduced by permission.)

While his "Land of Elyon" and "Atherton" books are traditional page-turners, with his "Skeleton Key" and futuristic "Trackers" books Carman mixes a written narrative with a sequence of Web-accessible videos "created" by one of the story's fictional narrator. Carman's "Elliot's Park" books, which focus on a squirrel and his friends and feature illustrations by Steve James, are geared for younger readers and include the stories *Saving Mister Nibbles, Haunted Hike,* and *The Walnut Cup.* The prolific author has also written for older readers and has contributed the novel *The Black Circle* to the popular multi-author "39 Clues" series, which focuses on sibilngs Amy and Dan Cahill and their efforts to discover the secret of their family's power.

A second-generation entrepreneur, Carman successfully launched four businesses—including an advertising agency—prior to turning to children's book writing full-time. When he began to indulge his creative side, he penned a fantasy novel for young readers that was inspired by his daughters Reece and Sierra. Completing the book in nine months, Carman decided to publish the novel himself after failing to find a publisher. *The Dark Hills Divide* became a local hit in western Washington, where Carman lives, and a representative from Scholastic publishers discovered the book while visiting a popular Seattle book store. Soon, Carman had a contract for several more novels and set about to complete his "Land of Elyon" series.

Twelve-year-old Alexa Daley, the heroine of *The Dark Hills Divide* and its sequels, has grown up in a city surrounded by high walls, and she feels increasingly claustrophobic and longs for escape. One day she finds a tunnel that allows her to leave the shelter of her protected city and venture out into the unknown, where she comes across a magical stone that enables her to communicate with animals. From these creatures Alexa learns that her home fortress has actually been penetrated by a spy who seeks to destroy the city. It is up to her to return to the city to identify this spy and eradicate the threat to her friends and loved ones.

Calling *The Dark Hills Divide* an "entertaining, accessible fantasy" that features a "highly cinematic" text, *School Library Journal* contributor Beth Wright noted that Carman's inclusion of "double identities, mysterious codes, and Alexa's magical gift of speaking with animals" creates an entertaining plot. "The most endearing parts of the story are the relationships Alexa forms with animals who help her," commented Claire Rosser in a *Kliatt* review of the novel, while a *Kirkus* reviewer praised Carman's preteen heroine as a girl who, "with her brains courage and grit, proves to be an appealingly strong female hero." "Readers of all ages will gain much from this tale," concluded a *Publishers Weekly* contributor, praising Carman for creating a "plucky, convincingly curious heroine" who "follows her passion" despite her fears.

The "Land of Elyon" series continues in *Beyond the Valley of Thorns,* the first of several sequels following Alexa's further adventures. Joined by several unusual friends, including a squirrel, a wolf, a hawk, a giant, and a midget named Yipes, the girl hopes to vanquish the evil ogre Abaddon from the land. To accomplish so she must do battle with a swarm of poisonous bats as well as with Abaddon's ogre army. In *The Tenth City* the origin of Elyon are revealed, Yipes is kidnaped by Grindall, a powerful lord beholden to Abaddon, and the battle with the supernatural ogre and his army continues. In *School Library Journal* Jessi Platt described Carman's text in *Beyond the Valley of Thorns* as "poetic, full of childlike wonder, and well written," although the critic cautioned that the vocabulary of the fantasy adventure might be too complex for reluctant readers.

In *Into the Mist* Carman begins a second sequence of "Land of Elyon" novels, as Alexa and Yipes join Captain Roland Warvold on a voyage leading to a pivotal face-off against Lord Grindall. On the way, readers as well as Alexa learn the history of their land and the reason for the kingdom's great divide. Abaddon shows his power as a shapechanger in *Stargazer,* and in his guise as a terrifying sea monster the creature follows Alexa and company to a refuge called the Five Stone Pillars. Citing the "nonstop action" of *Into the Mist,* a *Kirkus*

Carman's second fantasy series, "Atherton," includes The House of Power, *a novel featuring artwork by Phillip Straub.* (Cover artwork © 2007 by Phillip Straub. Reproduced with permission of Little, Brown and Company.)

Reviews writer added that the story propels readers "from crisis to crisis and ends on a classic Carman cliffhanger."

Comprised of *House of Power, Rivers of Fire,* and *The Dark Planet,* Carman's "Atherton" series draws readers into another fantasy world. In Atherton the richest citizens live in the Highlands while the lower flatlands, known as the Tabletop, serve as home to the peasant classes. Everything changes, however, when an earthquake causes the lands of Atherton to resolve into a level plane, and social and political chaos is the result. In *House of Power* twelve-year-old orphaned Edgar goes in search of a secret book said to contain Atherton's secrets, and the boy's quest leads him to discover the land's actual creator and learn the genesis of his world following Earth's ecological meltdown. Edgar's adventures continue in *Rivers of Fire,* as he and friends Samuel and Isabel attempt to restore water to their parched and ecologically damaged land, while in *The Dark Planet* Edgar continues to search for clues to Atherton's past and discovers away to return to his species' former home planet.

Reviewing the first "Atherton" novel, *Booklist* contributor Mattson predicted that Carman's intended middle-grade readership "will be caught up in the accessible sf premise, extended with [the author's] evocative illustrations." While admitting that *House of Power* has a typical science-fiction premise, a *Kirkus Reviews* contributor noted that Carman's technique of seeding his plot with "frequently surprises," making the dystopian novel "a humdinger of a cliff-hanger [that] will leave even reluctant readers demanding more." Equally "fast-paced and suspenseful," according to another *Kirkus Reviews* critic, *Rivers of Fire* continues to draw fans into a saga in which "danger abounds, science seems to have run amok and a neat . . . ending ties up most of the loose ends." In *The Dark Planet* "familiar and new characters . . . maintain reader interest," according to *School Library Journal* contributor Danielle Serra, the critic characterizing the "Atherton" saga as "action-driven sci-fi with unique settings populated by creative creatures."

Carman's "Skeleton Creek" series attracts reluctant readers through its adventurous, fast-moving storyline and "multi-platform" format in which readers are guided to a special Web site that fleshes out the story. "There are so many ways to tell a story," noted Carman in discussing his unique format with *Booklist* interviewer Rebecca A. Hill. "The fact that the Internet exists alongside books and games with people imagining how to put it all in a structure is so very exciting. With multiplatform books, we are reimagining what literacy can be. Kids can read the book and then do the videos or not, but they still get the story. It's just that it has this extra punch."

The saga begins in *Skeleton Creek,* as fifteen-year-old friends Ryan McRay and friend Sarah Fincher find themselves drawn into an old-fashioned mystery after a

With Skeleton Creek *Carman introduced readers to a new type of novel: a multiplatform experience that mixes text with Web videos.* (Copyright © 2009 by Patrick Carman. Reproduced with permission of Scholastic Press, an imprint of Scholastic Inc.)

night exploring a nearby creek where miners once panned for gold. Curious about how Skeleton Creek got its name, the two teens sneak out one night to investigate, but Ryan falls and breaks his leg. Although prohibited from further sleuthing by their respective parents, the friends continue their investigation, uncovering an old murder and a story of spectral haunting in the process. The teens' adventures continue in *Ghost in the Machine,* as the friends realize that someone—or something—is determined to keep them from finding the truth. A secret society figures in the plot of *The Crossbones,* while *The Raven* finds Ryan and Sarah enmeshed in an even-more-intricate mystery. In addition to Ryan's narrative, which is typeset on ruled pages to resemble an actual handwritten journal, readers can view Sarah's video of the creek and its secrets, adding a visual dimension to Carman's tale. Writing in *Booklist,* Stephanie Zvirin noted of *Skeleton Creek* that the author's "accessible, journal-type text, full of mystery and foreshadowing, pulls from the outset," and Courtney Jones concluded in the same periodical that *Ghost in the Machine* sustains an "eerie mood" that "makes this mystery a good read."

Another multimedia project, *Trackers* takes readers to near-future Seattle, where geeky teens Adam, Lewis, Finn, and Emily are channeling their technological super-savvy into jobs locating computer hackers, their hardware procured with the help of Adam's computer-repairman dad. When the Trackers' own computers are hacked by super-hacker Lasko and his accomplice and several of Adam's inventions are stolen, the Trackers go on the defensive, especially after Lasko attempts to use the stolen plans to blackmail the teens into giving him computer access to the world's banking complex. However, "nothing is as simple as it seems at first," observed Todd Morning in his *Booklist* review of Carman's high-tech mystery. *Trackers* is "an ingenious and entertaining mystery on several levels," noted *School Library Journal* contributor Jeffrey Hastings, the critic adding that Adam's narrative is supplemented by videos on the book's Web site that can be accessed using codes that are woven into the book's text. Describing the "Trackers" Web site as "darn nifty," a *Kirkus Reviews* writer recommended the series to "young technophiles," who will be attracted by the story's "gee-whiz factor." Carman's "Trackers" series continues in *Shantorian,* making converts of reluctant readers due to "its many twists and touches of humor," according to Morning.

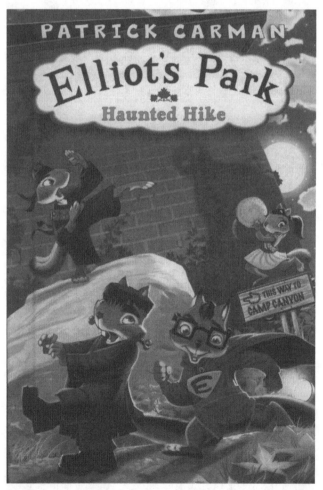

Carman turns to younger readers in his squirrel-centered "Elliot's Park" series, which includes the novel **The Haunted Hike** *and features artwork by Jim Madsen.* (Cover illustration copyright © 2008 by Jim Madsen. Reproduced by permission of Scholastic Inc.)

In *Thirteen Days to Midnight,* a standalone mystery geared for older teens, Carman returns to the traditional novel format. Teen Jacob Fielding finds himself the possessor of an extraordinary ability after his foster father dies in a car accident just after breathing his last words, "You are indestructible." In addition to gaining the ability to avoid injury and death, the teen is also able to pass his new skill along to best friends Ophelia and Milo, along with the power's unintended consequences. When Ophelia encourages the group to use their power unselfishly and only do good, things become more complex and soon the teens find themselves forced to decide who to save and who to let die. They also discover, too late, that their power comes at a very high cost. A *Kirkus Reviews* writer commended Carman for crafting a thoughtful storyline that "explores survivor's guilt and raises theological issues," then weaving it into an "action-packed and twisted tale," and Peters deemed *Thirteen Days to Midnight* "a creepy fantasy-mystery" that also serves as "a provocative take on the theme that every superpower comes with a price." "Produc[ing] . . . serous chills," the novel will attract fans "who have grown out of Carman's 'Atherton' and 'Land of Elyon' series," predicted a *Publishers Weekly* critic, while *School Library Journal* contributor Karen E. Brooks-Reese recommended *Thirteen Days to Midnight* as "a natural choice for reluctant readers and fans of both adventure stories and supernatural thrillers."

Biographical and Critical Sources

PERIODICALS

Booklist, March 1, 2005, Sally Estes, review of *The Dark Hills Divide,* p. 1193; May 15, 2007, Jennifer Mattson, review of *The House of Power,* p. 60; May 15, 2008, Jennifer Mattson, review of *Rivers of Fire,* p. 56; June 1, 2008, Kay Weisman, review of *Saving Mister Nibbles,* p. 92; December 1, 2008, Stephanie Zvirin, review of *Skeleton Creek,* p. 52; December 15, 2009, Courtney Jones, review of *Ghost in the Machine,* p. 40; March 1, 2010, Rebecca A. Hill, interview with Carman, p. S12; May 1, 2010, John Peters, review of *Thirteen Days to Midnight,* p. 50; July 1, 2010, Todd Morning, review of *Trackers,* p. 54; March 15, 2011, Todd Morning, review of *Shantorian,* p. 56.

Bulletin of the Center for Children's Books, January, 2005, Timnah Card, review of *The Dark Hills Divide,* p. 202; July-August, 2007, review of *The House of Power,* p. 455.

Kirkus Reviews, February 1, 2005, review of *The Dark Hills Divide,* p. 174; September 1, 2005, review of *Beyond the Valley of Thorns,* p. 969; May 1, 2007, review of *The House of Power;* September 1, 2007, review of *Into the Mist;* March 15, 2008, review of *Saving Mister Nibbles;* April 15, 2008, review of *Rivers of Fire;* December 1, 2008, review of *Skeleton Creek;* March 1, 2010, review of *Thirteen Days to Midnight;* April 15, 2010, review of *Trackers;* April 15, 2011, review of *Dark Eden;* August 15, 2011, review of *Floors.*

Kliatt, January, 2005, Claire Rosser, review of *The Dark Hills Divide,* p. 6.

New York Times Book Review, November 7, 2010, Sam Grobart, "Interactive Books," p. 28.

Publishers Weekly, December 13, 2004, John F. Baker, "Big Push for Self-published Kids' Author," p. 12; February 21, 2005, review of *The Dark Hills Divide,* p. 176; March 12, 2007, review of *The House of Power,* p. 58; December 15, 2008, review of *Skeleton Creek,* p. 55; March 15, 2010, review of *Thirteen Days to Midnight,* p. 5.

School Library Journal, April, 2005, Beth Wright, review of *The Dark Hills Divide,* p. 129; October, 2005, Jessi Platt, review of *Beyond the Valley of Thorns,* p. 154; August, 2006, Elizabeth Bird, review of *The Tenth City,* p. 117; June, 2007, Tasha Saecker, review of *The House of Power,* p. 140; August, 2008, Danielle Serra, review of *Rivers of Fire,* p. 116; March, 2009, Lisa Egly Lehmuller, review of *The Walnut Cup,* p. 107, and Caitlin August, review of *Skeleton Creek,* p. 142; October, 2009, Danielle Serra, review of *The Dark Planet,* p. 121; May, 2010, Karen E. Brooks-Reese, review of *Thirteen Days to Midnight,* p. 106; July, 2010, Jeffrey Hastings, review of *Trackers,* p. 83; October, 2009, Danielle Serra, review of *The Dark Planet,* p. 121.

Seattle Post-Intelligencer, March 19, 2004, Cecelia Goodnow, "For Authors with Drive and a Good Story, Self-Publishing Can Be the Ticket"; February 27, 2009, Cecelia Goodnow, "Author's Print-Video Hybrid Targets Readers for a Digital Age," p. B1.

Voice of Youth Advocates, April, 2005, Ann Welton, review of *The Dark Hills Divide,* p. 53; June, 2011, Bethany Martin, review of *Shantorian,* p. 180; August, 2011, Susan Redman-Parodi, review of *Dark Eden,* p. 264.

ONLINE

Patrick Carman Home Page, http://www.patrickcarman. com (September 15, 2011).

Scholastic Web site, http://www.scholastic.com/ (September 15, 2010), "Patrick Carman."*

*   *   *

CHESSA, Francesca

Personal

Born in Italy; married. *Education:* College degree (architecture); studied art with Aura Cesari and Stepan Zavrel. *Hobbies and other interests:* Reading, watching movies, cycling, swimming, skiing.

Addresses

Home—Turin, Italy. *Agent*—Eunice McMullen, Low Ibbotsholme Cottage, Off Bridge Ln., Troutbeck Bridge, Windermere, Cumbria LA23 1HU, England; eunicemc mullen@totalise.co.uk. *E-mail*—franchessa@tiscalinet. it.

Career

Artist, author, and illustrator. Creator of artwork for UNICEF greeting cards. Conductor of educational workshops, beginning 1999. *Exhibitions:* Works included in exhibitions staged at museums in Japan, Taiwan, Italy, and elsewhere in Europe, including U.N. Convention on the Rights of the Child, Milan, Italy, 1999; Sarmede, Italy, 2000-01; Macerata, Italy, 2002-03; and Riccione, Italy, 2004-05.

Awards, Honors

Honorable mention, Bologna Book Fair, 1998; TIBI Prize, Teheran International Biennale of Illustration, 1999, for *The Sheep Who Wanted to Fly;* several other illustration awards.

Writings

SELF-ILLUSTRATED

Balenottera mangiona, Edizioni Colors (Genoa, Italy), 1998.

A Button Muddle, Chrysalis (London, England), 2003.

Tom's Train, Gakken (Tokyo, Japan), 2004.

The Mysterious Package, Bloomsbury Children's Books (New York, NY), 2007, published as *The Mysterious Parcel,* Bloomsbury (London, England), 2007.

Holly's Red Boots, Holiday House (New York, NY), 2008.

Some Days, Gakken (Tokyo, Japan), 2008.

Ce livre est pour toi, Lirabelle (Aubais, France), 2010.

ILLUSTRATOR

Silvia Roncaglia, *Il bisonte bisunto,* Edizioni Signum Scuola (Turin, Italy), 2000.

Cristina Garelli, *Farm Friends Clean Up,* Crown Publishers (New York, NY), 2000.

Gianni Rodari, *Le Favole di esopino,* Edizioni Il Capitello (Turin, Italy), 2000.

Christina Garelli, *The Sheep Who Wanted to Fly,* Gakken (Tokyo, Japan), 2001.

Cristina Garelli, *Forest Friends' Five Senses,* Knopf (New York, NY), 2001.

Guido Quarzo, *Cecilia e il grande Gnam,* Fabbri Editori (Milan, Italy), 2001.

Loredana Frescura, *L'avventura straordinaria,* Edizioni il Capitello (Turin, Italy), 2001.

Juliane Hartmann Stuckelberger, *Stella und der Weihnachtsstern,* Friedrich Reinhardt Verlag (Basel, Switzerland), 2001.

Fulvia Degl'Innocenti, *Celluloso gigante goloso,* Edizioni i Colori del Mondo (Naples, Italy), 2002.

Marcello Bernardi, *Educazione e libertà,* Fabbri Editori (Milan, Italy), 2002.

Cristina Garelli, *Jungle Friends and Their Teeth,* Gakken (Tokyo, Japan), 2002.

Pino Pace, *L'odore di pepenero,* Edizioni Signum Scuola (Turin, Italy), 2002.

Francesca Chessa's colorful art brings to life the family-centered story in Alan James Brown's story for **Love-a-Duck.** (Illustration copyright © 2010 by Francesca Chessa. Reproduced with permission of Holiday House, Inc.)

Mario Lodi, *Il drago del vulcano e altre storie,* Giunti (Florence, Italy), 2002.

Silvia Rocaglia, *Animali pronti in favola,* Editrice Piccoli (Turin, Italy), 2004.

Donatella Ziliotto, *Anelli di drago,* Giunti Editore (Florence, Italy), 2004.

Lo Vorrei . . . (anthology), Edizioni Condè Nast (Italy), 2004.

Helen Bannerman, *The Story of Little Black Sambo,* Kyowon Co (Seoul, Korea), 2005.

Anna Vivarelli, *Il labirinto sotto il letto,* Fabbri Editori (Milan, Italy), 2005.

Fulvia Degli'Innocenti, *Martina ed il coccodrillo,* Paoline Editori (Milan, Italy), 2005.

Hans Christian Andersen, *Il brutto anatroccolo,* Corriere della sera (Milan, Italy), 2005.

Brothers Grimm, *Il lupo ed i sette capretti,* Corriere della sera (Milan, Italy), 2005.

Cristina Garelli, *Dog and I,* Gakken (Tokyo, Japan), 2006.

Carrie Weston, *When Brian Was a Lion,* Gullane Children's Books (London, England), 2006.

Roberto Piumini, *Il gatto con gli Stivali,* Edizioni EL (Trieste, Italy), 2006.

Silvio d'Arzo, *Il Pinuino senza frac,* Editrice Signum (Turin, Italy), 2007.

Giovanna Ferri, *Girotondi, conte e indovinelli,* Giunti Junior (Florence, Italy), 2008.

Jonathan Shipton, *Baby Baby Blah Blah Blah!*, Gullane (London, England), 2008, Holiday House (New York, NY), 2009.

The Mitten, Gakken (Tokyo, Japan), 2009.

Alan James Brown, *Love-a-Duck,* Holiday House (New York, NY), 2010.

Roberto Piumini, reteller, *Puss in Boots,* Picture Window Books (Mankato, MN), 2010.

Ramón Aragüés, *El ombligo de Juanito,* Oqo Editora (Pontevedra, Spain), 2010.

Lucia Panzieri, *Un leone e due bici,* Lapis Edizioni (Rome, Italy), 2010.

Gillian Shields, *Library Lily,* Eerdmans (Grand Rapids MI), 2011.

Also contributor to periodicals.

Sidelights

An Italian illustrator, Francesca Chessa has provided the artwork for more than thirty children's books, among them *Farm Friends Clean Up* by Cristina Garelli and *Baby Baby Blah Blah Blah!* by Jonathan Shipton. In the former, a collection of three short tales, Wolf learns the importance of dental care, Sheep gets a much-needed haircut, and odiferous Pig takes a bath to avoid offending his friends. According to a critic in *Publishers Weekly,* "Chessa's textured brushwork and sophisticated palette . . . provide a fitting stage for the merry antics," and Susan Marie Pitard noted in *School Library Journal* that the illustrations "combine bright colors and rich textures with sharp black outlines defining most objects."

Chessa and Garelli also collaborate on *Forest Friends' Five Senses,* in which a group of forest dwellers gathers around a campfire one night to share their experiences with sight, sound, touch, taste, and smell. Although *Booklist* contributor Gillian Engberg observed that "the friendly animal pals are appealing," a *Publishers Weekly* critic maintained that "Chessa's earth-toned, dense brushwork . . . supplies the book's real pleasure." Karen Scott similarly noted in *School Library Journal* that Chessa's "brightly colored paintings with heavy black outlines match the story to a tee"

In Shipton's *Baby Baby Blah Blah Blah!,* young Emily approaches the birth of her new sister with trepidation. After she prepares a list of the pros and cons of having a baby in the house, her parents attempt to ease her mind, assuring Emily that she will always be loved. "Chessa's colorfully messy, childlike illustrations perfectly match the breezy tone of the story," Kathleen Kelly MacMillan reported in *School Library Journal,* and a *Kirkus Reviews* contributor noted that the protagonist's "shifting moods are enhanced through varied perspectives and disproportionate characters." *Love-a-Duck,* a picture book by Alan James Brown, centers on the escapades of a rubber ducky that inadvertently ends up outside the safety of its owner's house. A critic in *Kirkus Reviews* stated that Chessa's "cheery, inviting paintings are the just-right complement to this quirky tale."

In addition to her work for other authors, Chessa has produced several original self-illustrated stories. *The Mysterious Package* concerns a pair of curious siblings, Charlie and Frances, whose imaginations run wild when a large box arrives on their doorstep. Informed that they must wait until their father arrives home before the package can be opened, Charlie and Frances convince themselves that the box must contain something exotic and dangerous, like a pet lion. Chessa's bold pictures, "done in a flat and childlike style, capture the story's innocence and exuberance," remarked Suzanne Myers Harold in *School Library Journal,* and a *Kirkus Reviews* contributor stated that the illustrations "imbue the world of Charlie and Frances with an endearing simplicity."

A young girl plans an exciting adventure in the snow in *Holly's Red Boots,* another self-illustrated title. As Holly prepares to head out the door to build a snowman, her mother insists that she wear her red boots, which prove nearly impossible to find among all the other red items that belong to the youngster. When Holly finally discovers her boots under the stairs, the snow has already melted; fortunately, her mother shows her how to enjoy the puddles that remain. "The seamless combination of art and text will be rollicking fun for young readers," observed a writer in *Kirkus Reviews.*

Biographical and Critical Sources

PERIODICALS

Booklist, December 1, 2001, Gillian Engberg, review of *Forest Friends' Five Senses,* p. 649; July 1, 2007, Hazel Rochman, review of *The Mysterious Package,* p. 66.

Children's Bookwatch, May, 2010, review of *Love-a-Duck.*

Kirkus Reviews, April 15, 2007, review of *The Mysterious Package;* August 1, 2008, review of *Holly's Red Boots;* January 15, 2009, review of *Baby Baby Blah Blah Blah;* March 1, 2010, review of *Love-a-Duck.*

Publishers Weekly, November 13, 2000, review of *Farm Friends Clean Up,* p. 103; November 12, 2001, review of *Forest Friends' Five Senses,* p. 58.

School Library Journal, October, 2000, Susan Marie Pitard, review of *Farm Friends Clean Up,* p. 125; November, 2001, Karen Scott, review of *Forest Friends' Five Senses,* p. 122; July, 2007, Suzanne Myers Harold, review of *The Mysterious Package,* p. 73; September, 2008, Marge Loch-Wouters, review of *Holly's Red Boots,* p. 142; March, 2009, Kathleen Kelly MacMillan, review of *Baby Baby Blah Blah Blah!,* p. 128; July, 2010, Maryann H. Owen, review of *Love-a-Duck,* p. 56.

ONLINE

Eunice McMullen Web site, http://www.eunicemcmullen.co.uk/ (August 1, 2011), "Francesca Chessa."

Francesca Chessa Home Page, http://www.francesca chessa.it (August 1, 2011).*

* * *

CLARKSON, Karen

Personal

Married; husband's name Bill. *Ethnicity:* "Choctaw."

Addresses

Home—Prescott, AZ. *E-mail*—clarksonart@gmail.com.

Career

Fine artist and illustrator. Member, Indian Arts and Crafts Board, U.S. Department of the interior.

Member

National Registry of Native American Artists, Indian Arts and Crafts Board, Choctaw Nation Artist Registry, Artist against Drunk Driving.

Awards, Honors

Awards from Choctaw Nation Art Show, Santa Fe Indian Art Show, and other competitions; Patterson Prize for Books for Young People, *Storytelling World* Resource Award, and ALSC Notable Children's Book designation, all 2011, all for *Saltypie* by Tim Tingle.

Illustrator

Tim Tingle, *Saltypie: A Choctaw Journey from Darkness into Light,* Cinco Puntos Press (El Paso, TX), 2010.

Biographical and Critical Sources

PERIODICALS

Booklist, May 1, 2010, John Peters, review of *Saltypie: A Choctaw Journey from Darkness into Light,* p. 83.
Kirkus Reviews, April 15, 2010, review of *Saltypie.*
Publishers Weekly, April 26, 2010, review of *Saltypie,* p. 108.
School Library Journal, May, 2010, Sharon Morrison, review of *Saltypie,* p. 101.
Tribune Books (Chicago, IL), July 10, 2010, Mary Harris Russell, review of *Saltypie,* p.12.

ONLINE

Cinco Puntos Press Web site, http://www.cincopuntos.com/ (September 15, 2011), "Karen Clarkson."
Karen Clarkson Home Page, http://www.clarksonart.com (September 15, 2011).

CORREA, E. Shan
See CORREA, Shan

* * *

CORREA, Shan
(E. Shan Correa)

Personal

Married Leslie Correa (a university administrator); children: Evan, Brandon. *Education:* Attended graduate school.

Addresses

Home—Honolulu, HI.

Career

Author and educator. Former banker in Seattle, WA; teacher of English and journalism for fourteen years at Honolulu Community College and Hawai'i Pacific University; freelance writer.

Member

National League of American Pen Women, Society of Children's Book Writers and Illustrators.

Writings

(And editor, under name E. Shan Correa) *Learning from Each Other: The Official Proceedings of the 1995 International Symposium of Japan-America Societies: June 18-21, 1995,* Japan-America Society of Hawai'i (Honolulu, HI), 1996.
Gaff, Peachtree Press (Atlanta, GA), 2009.

Contributor to periodicals, including *Cricket, Jack and Jill,* and *Ranger Rick.*

Sidelights

Although Shan Correa hails from the Pacific Northwest, she now makes her home on the island of Hawai'i, where she attended graduate school and where her first novel, *Gaff,* is set. A former banker, Correa taught English and journalism for over a dozen years before focusing full-time on fiction writing. While much of her time as a professional writer is spent on client-related projects, she has also produced articles for children's magazines as well as book-length fiction.

Geared for middle-grade readers, *Gaff* finds seventh-grader Paulie Silva living in a hilly part of the large island, where his father has the space to raise his flock of roosters. The birds are hatched as chicks and begin to show their natural aggression within a few months;

Paulie's father then trains them to fight in the cockfighting competitions that are so popular in the region. Although Paulie knows that the sport is violent—and illegal—he still views the colorfully plumaged roosters as pets, until friend Sal's older brother shows him the reality of cockfighting by taking both boys to a competition. When he expresses to his father his view that it is not right for the family to support itself through the pain of other creatures, Paulie's father understands, and the challenge for both father and son now becomes finding a new way to keep their beloved island homestead.

"Paulie's narrative voice is spot-on for his 12 years," wrote John Peters, the critic adding in his *Booklist* review that *Gaff* "is strongly colored by its distinctive regional setting and culture." Correa's use of Hawaiian dialect "add[s] local flavor to this interesting tale on an unusual topic," asserted Joel Shoemaker in his *School Library Journal* review of the story, while in *Kirkus Reviews* a contributor wrote of *Gaff* that, in addition to capturing the island's "lush mélage of sights, sounds and smells," Paulie's story will give readers "a reason to cheer."

***Shan Correa introduces readers to life in rural Hawai'i in her coming-of-age novel* Gaff.** (Cover design by Maureen Withee. Reproduced with permission of Peachtree Publishers.)

Biographical and Critical Sources

PERIODICALS

Booklist, April 1, 2010, John Peters, review of *Gaff,* p. 38.
Kirkus Reviews, March 1, 2010, review of *Gaff.*
Publishers Weekly, April 12, 2010, review of *Gaff,* p. 49.
School Library Journal, May, 2010, Joel Shoemaker, review of *Gaff,* p. 108.

ONLINE

Society of Children's Book Writers and Illustrators Web site, http://www.scbwi.org/ (September 15, 2011), "Shan Correa."*

*   *   *

COVENTRY, Susan

Personal

Born in NJ; married; has children. *Education:* New Jersey Medical School, M.D., 1989.

Addresses

Home—Louisville, KY. *Agent*—Irene Kraas, Kraas Literary Agency, irenekraas@sbcglobal.net. *E-mail*—susan@susancoventry.com.

Career

Medical doctor and author. Pediatric pathologist in Louisville, KY, beginning c. 1994.

Member

Historical Novel Society, Society of Pediatric Pathology.

Awards, Honors

Best Children's Book selection, Bank Street College of Education, 2011, for *The Queen's Daughter.*

Writings

The Queen's Daughter, Henry Holt (New York, NY), 2010.

Sidelights

A board-certified physician as well as a wife and mother, Susan Coventry has always relied on conveniently placed historical novels to whisk her away from the pressures of daily life: in addition to drawing her into an eventful story peopled with interesting characters, historical novels also include facts about the past

Susan Coventry (Photograph by Yono. Reproduced by permission.)

Queen's Daughter follows her as she grows into womanhood, marries a Sicilian king ten years her senior, and eventually falls in love with Raymond VI, count of Toulouse and a man she has loved since childhood.

Combining romance and drama in a coming-of-age story that *Voice of Youth Advocates* critic Laura Woodruff deemed "an intricate picture of a distant life and time," *The Queen's Daughter* brings to life a character about what little is known and captures two decades in the life of a young woman who is "lonely and without a sense of identity apart from her royal role." A *Kirkus Reviews* writer noted that Coventry's "impressive" narrative reveals both the richness of the Middle Ages and the "virtual imprisonment" endured by "wealthy women in an era that many romanticize." Few novels for young adults are set against the complex backdrop of the Middle Ages, noted *Booklist* contributor Melissa Moore, and in *The Queen's Daughter* Coventry serves up a "solid choice" that mixes dynamic and realistic characters with "settings [that] are vividly imagined." "Readers will champion Joan in her search for love," concluded Moore, while in *School Library Journal* Wendy Scalfaro predicted that "fans of historical fiction, and especially historical romance, will devour this volume."

Biographical and Critical Sources

PERIODICALS

Booklist, April 15, 2010, Melissa Moore, review of *The Queen's Daughter,* p. 57.
Kirkus Reviews, May 1, 2010, review of *The Queen's Daughter.*
School Library Journal, July, 2010, Wendy Scalfaro, review of *The Queen's Daughter,* p. 84.
Voice of Youth Advocates, October, 2010, Laura Woodruff, review of *The Queen's Daughter,* p. 344.

ONLINE

Susan Coventry Home Page, http://www.susancoventry. com (September 15, 2011).

*   *   *

that help to diminish any guilt over wasted time on the part of the reader. For Coventry, the fictional setting of choice has always been medieval Europe, the time of Robin Hood, the Second and Third Crusade, and continuous friction between the British Isles and France. After years of reading, she realized that she knew enough about this historical epoch to imagine what life was like for the men and women living in the shadows of such stories' central protagonists. With the help of an online writers' group and her commitment to thorough background research, Coventry eventually contributed to her favorite literary genre with her own historical novel, *The Queen's Daughter.*

In *The Queen's Daughter* readers are transported back to twelfth-century Britain and the reign of Henry II. Henry's queen is the beautiful Eleanor of Aquitaine, born in France and queen consort to French king Louis VI before ending that marriage and becoming engaged to Norman duke Henry. In addition to bearing her husband eight children, Eleanor became involved in political intrigue following Henry's coronation in 1154; her support of her son Henry in his efforts to unseat the English crown from his father's head even landed Eleanor in prison for a time. She eventually became queen dowager after her son, Richard ascended the throne as Richard the Lionhearted. Coventry's novel focuses on Eleanor's youngest daughter Joan, a girl who must navigate the politics of her parents' fractious relationship as she also receives counsel from her worldly-wise mother. Beginning during Joan's seventh year, *The*

COY, John 1958-

Personal

Born August 9, 1958, in Minneapolis, MN; son of Richard (a professor) and Luanne (a teacher) Coy; married Fiona McCrae (a publisher), June 18, 1999; children: Sophia. *Education:* St. John's University, B.A. (summa cum laude), 1980; St. Mary's University, M.A., 1993. *Hobbies and other interests:* Basketball, yoga, travel, reading, politics, history.

John Coy (Reproduced by permission.)

Addresses

Home—Minneapolis, MN. *E-mail*—comments@ johncoy.com.

Career

Writer. Visiting author and writing teacher, 1994—, workshop presenter for groups, including Children's Theater Company, Minneapolis, MN, 1999; participant in literature-based theatre productions. Anderson Center for Interdisciplinary Studies resident, 2000, 2002, 2004. Participant in National Basketball Association's Read to Achieve program.

Member

Society of Children's Book Writers and Illustrators, PEN American Center, Children's Literature Network, Minnesota Literature, Kerlan Collection of Children's Literature.

Awards, Honors

Choice selection, Cooperative Children's Book Center (CCBC), 1996, Marion Vannett Ridgway Memorial Award for excellence in an author's or illustrator's first picture book, 1997, Best Children's Book of the Year selection, Children's Book Committee of Bank Street College of Education, 1998, and Seal of Quality, Family Channel Entertainment Guide, all for *Night Driving;* grant from The Loft, 1999; Notable Book designation, American Library Association (ALA), CCBC Choice

designation, Bank Street College Best Children's Book of the Year designation, Notable Book for a Global Society designation, International Reading Association (IRA), and Notable Social Studies Trade Book for Young People designation, all 2000, all for *Strong to the Hoop;* Children's Literature Choice Book of Excellence designation, and Bank Street College Children's Book of the Year selection, both 2001, both for *Vroomaloom Zoom;* Ohio Farm Bureau Federation Honor Book designation, CCBC Choice designation, Bank Street College Best Children's Book designation, and Charlotte Zolotow Award Honor Book designation, all 2003, all for *Two Old Potatoes and Me;* Chicago Public Library Best of the Best designation, 2005, and ALA Quick Pick for Reluctant Young-Adult Readers selection, IRA Young Adult Choices selection, and CBCC Choice designation, all for *Crackback;* CCBC Choice designation, and Best Children's Book selection, Bank Street College of Education, both 2011, both for *Top of the Order;* CCBC Choice designation, 2011, for *Eyes on the Goal.*

Writings

FOR CHILDREN

Night Driving, illustrated by Peter McCarty, Holt (New York, NY), 1996.

(Editor) *A Special Stretch of Sky* (anthology of student writing), COMPAS, 1997.

Strong to the Hoop, illustrated by Leslie Jean-Bart, Lee & Low (New York, NY), 1999.

Vroomaloom Zoom, illustrated by Joe Cepeda, Knopf/ Crown (New York, NY), 2000.

Two Old Potatoes and Me, illustrated by Carolyn Fisher, Knopf (New York, NY), 2003.

Around the World, illustrated by Antonio Reonegro and Tom Lynch, Lee & Low (New York, NY), 2005.

Author's work has been translated into Chinese and Spanish.

"FOUR FOR FOUR" NOVEL SERIES

Top of the Order, Feiwel & Friends (New York, NY), 2009.

Eyes on the Goal, Feiwel & Friends (New York, NY), 2010.

Love of the Game, Feiwel & Friends (New York, NY), 2011.

Take Your Best Shot, Feiwel & Friends (New York, NY), 2012.

OTHER

Crackback (young-adult novel), Scholastic Press (New York, NY), 2005.

Box Out (young-adult novel), Scholastic Press (New York, NY), 2008.

Librettist for *All around Sound,* composed by Libby Larsen, 1999; writer and narrator of *Copland Portrait* (orchestral piece based on the work of Aaron Copland), produced by Minnesota Orchestra, 2000. Contributor to anthology *Libraries of Minnesota,* Minnesota Historical Society Press (St. Paul, MN), 2011; contributor to periodicals, including *Hungry Mind Review, Riverbank Review, Five Owls Review, Organica,* and *Five Owls for Parents.* Science Museum of Minnesota, collaborator on Thinking Fountain Web site, 1996—.

Sidelights

An award-winning author, John Coy often focuses on the world of sports in his picture books for children and his novels for older readers. His picture book *Strong to the Hoop* and the comic-book-styled *Around the World* both focus on basketball, while the works in his "Four for Four" series concern four boys who learn life lessons while competing in a different sport each season. In addition, Coy teaches in schools throughout the country and around the world.

As Coy once told *SATA:* "Each summer when I was a boy, we took long car trips as a family. Because I was the oldest child, I sat up front with my dad as everybody else fell asleep. He would tell me stories, and we'd watch for animals and have the road to ourselves. These memories formed the basis for my first picture book, *Night Driving,* which was beautifully illustrated by Peter McCarty." A family road trip is also the focus of another picture book by Coy. *Vroomaloom Zoom,* featuring illustrations by Joe Cepeda, follows the automobile adventures of Carmela, a young girl who hopes that a car ride with her dad will help her fall asleep. Praised as a "delightful" story featuring a "rhythmic, repetitive text" according to *School Library Journal* contributor Sheilah Kosco, the book finds the pair motoring through the city, forest, swamp, and seaside. Although the hum of the motor makes Carmela sleepy, Coy's energetic story in *Vroomaloom Zoom* was dubbed "a giggly, wiggly winner, but not for bedtime!," by Ilene Cooper in *Booklist.*

Another story featuring a father and daughter, Coy's award-winning picture book *Two Old Potatoes and Me* is narrated by a young girl who describes how two wrinkled, sprouted potatoes are transformed into a garden of purple flowers and then a bowl of tasty mashed potatoes through the pair's careful gardening. Noting the subtext in the story—the multiracial father and daughter do not live together all the time due to a divorce—a *Kirkus Reviews* contributor praised Coy's alliterative narrative as "colloquial and casual and just right." In *Publishers Weekly* a reviewer wrote of *Two Old Potatoes and Me* that the author's "well-realized" tale "brims with affection" and concludes with sixty-seven new potatoes and a recipe.

Coy's efforts with the National Basketball Association's Read to Achieve program were the driving force behind *Around the World,* a tribute to the international reach of the sport that takes readers from New York City to Perth, Australia, Shanghai, China, and Istanbul, Turkey, among other locales. "I love to travel, so to combine two passions—basketball and travel—was wonderful," Coy stated on the Lee & Low Books Web site. "I picked the countries to highlight the geographical reach of basketball. I also tried to represent some of the countries that have sent many international players to the NBA (National Basketball Association)." Featuring bold, vibrant illustrations by Antonio Reonegro and Tom Lynch, *Around the World* "helps reaffirm the commonalities of the sport, regardless of the setting," as Steven Engelfried noted in his *School Library Journal* review.

In *Crackback* readers meet Miles Manning, a high-school sophomore who lives and breathes football. Pushed by his dad to excel at the sport, he is thwarted in his dreams of a starring career when his coach benches him. While tensions at home rise, Miles learns from his fellow second-stringers—as well as from new friend Lucia—that there is more to life than winning the game. When steroids begin to circulate among his teammates, Miles realizes that he must make his own decisions in life and accept the outcome. "When I was

Cover of Coy's sports-themed young-adult novel Crackback, *which finds a young athlete dealing with challenges both on the field and off.* (Copyright © 2005 by Scholastic Press. Jacket photo © Art Becker/Potonica. Reproduced by permission of Scholastic, Inc.)

a teen, I loved football," Coy explained on his home page in discussing the novel. "I loved smashing into people. Football was the one place that hitting somebody was not only okay, it was prized. In *Crackback*, I wanted to convey that physical love of the game. I wanted to convey how much of Miles's identity comes from football and what happens when that is taken away." Praising the book as a "welcome" addition to the sports-fiction genre, a *Kirkus Reviews* writer noted that Coy's text combines "girlfriends, serious social history and family dynamics seamlessly," while in *School Library Journal* Julie Webb wrote that "great football action" combines with "well-rounded characters" in *Crackback*.

Box Out, another work for young adults, focuses on Liam Bergstrom, a high-school basketball player who finds himself at the center of a controversy involving the separation of church and state. After earning an unexpected promotion to the varsity team, Liam quickly becomes disenchanted with his new coach, who insists that players join him in a pregame prayer and runs off the team's star, the only African American on the squad. After Liam voices his complaints about the coach's behavior to a watchdog organization, he feels pressure from his friends and family and quits the team, finding consolation in a new relationship with the coach of the girls' varsity squad, who recruits Liam as a practice player. "The message that one must choose one's own road is certainly worthy," Joel Shoemaker observed in his *School Library Journal* review of *Box Out,* and a critic in *Kirkus Reviews* stated that "the moral tenor of the novel make this a solid choice for sports fans." Writing in *Booklist,* John Peters complimented the serious tone of the book, adding that Coy "weaves in plenty of breathlessly compelling game action, too."

Coy's "Four for Four" series of sports novels, aimed at middle-grade readers, centers on one year in the life of four friends making the transition from elementary school to middle school. In *Top of the Order,* Jackson, Isaac, Gig, and Diego realize they have the makings of a championship baseball team as long as they can fill their opening at second base. When Gig's sister, Sydney, arrives at practice, pink glove in tow, the boys reluctantly allow her to try out for the squad despite Gig's protests. After Sydney displays considerable talents in the field, however, Jackson, Isaac, and Diego must convince an outraged Gig to change his mind. "Coy . . . brings his successful combination of relatable characters and sports action" to the work, a critic in *Publishers Weekly* noted, and Peters commented that the author "underscores the importance of teamwork, bonding, and being open to change both on and off the field." The four pals head to soccer camp in *Eyes on the Goal,* a "solid, simply told sports story," according to a *Kirkus Reviews* contributor. While Diego and Gig try to convince the counselors to allow the less-skilled Jackson and Isaac to join their team, the foursome investigates rumors of ghosts that may haunt the campus. The novel

garnered praise from Blair Christolon in *School Library Journal,* who stated of *Eyes on the Goal* that "Coy has created a story of just the right length to keep his fans engaged."

An outspoken literacy advocate, Coy remarked in a *Children's Literature Network* online interview: "We need to find books that speak to the genuine interests of young people. For many of them that is sports. Teachers and parents also need to be careful that they don't convey the attitude that books about sports aren't 'real books.' That's a sure way to turn a sports-interested youngster away from books."

Coy often speaks to students who identify themselves and nonreaders or reluctant readers. He challenges them to think about all the reading they do in a day: texting, online, Facebook, Twitter. "Students today read much more than they realize," the author noted. "We have to tap into their desire to read what interests them in order for them to develop a life-long love of reading."

Biographical and Critical Sources

PERIODICALS

Booklist, September 1, 1996, Bill Ott, review of *Night Driving,* p. 141; December 15, 1999, Bill Ott, review of *Strong to the Hoop,* p. 784; December 1, 2000, Ilene Cooper, review of *Vroomaloom Zoom,* p. 717; September 1, 2005, Gillian Engberg, review of *Crackback,* p. 115; September 1, 2008, John Peters, review of *Box Out,* p. 110; March 1, 2009, John Peters, review of *Top of the Order,* p. 46.

Bulletin of the Center for Children's Books, December, 1996, review of *Night Driving,* p. 131; October, 2003, Deborah Stevenson, review of *Two Old Potatoes and Me,* p. 54.

Children's Book Review Service, October, 1996, review of *Night Driving,* p. 14.

Horn Book, September-October, 1996, Roger Sutton, review of *Night Driving,* p. 574.

Hungry Mind Review, winter, 1996, review of *Night Driving,* p. 40.

Kirkus Reviews, September 1, 1996, review of *Night Driving,* p. 1320; June 1, 2003, review of *Two Old Potatoes and Me,* p. 801; November 1, 2005, reviews of *Crackback* and *Around the World,* p. 1182; June 15, 2008, review of *Box Out.*

Kliatt, November, 2005, Claire Rosser, review of *Crackback,* p. 5; July, 2008, Paula Rohrlick, review of *Box Out,* p. 10; January 15, 2009, review of *Top of the Order;* March 1, 2010, review of *Eyes on the Goal.*

Los Angeles Times Book Review, December 8, 1996, review of *Night Driving,* p. 18.

New York Times, December 9, 1996, Christopher Lehmann-Haupt, review of *Night Driving,* p. B3.

New York Times Book Review, December 22, 1996, Sam Swope, review of *Night Driving,* p. 16.

Publishers Weekly, August 26, 1996, review of *Night Driving,* p. 97; September 27, 1999, review of *Strong to the Hoop,* p. 105; November 6, 2000, review of *Vroomaloom Zoom,* p. 90; May 19, 2003, review of *Two Old Potatoes and Me,* p. 74; March 16, 2009, review of *Top of the Order,* p. 61.

Resource Links, October, 2003, Linda Berezowski, review of *Two Old Potatoes and Me,* p. 3.

School Library Journal, October, 1996, Lauralyn Persson, review of *Night Driving,* p. 91; October, 2000, Sheilah Kosco, review of *Strong to the Hoop,* p. 119; December, 2005, Julie Webb, review of *Crackback,* p. 143; January, 2006, Steven Engelfried, review of *Around the World,* p. 94; September, 2008, Joel Shoemaker, review of *Box Out,* p. 177; March, 2009, Kim Dare, review of *Top of the Order,* p. 142; April, 2010, Blair Christolon, review of *Eyes on the Goal,* p. 152.

Star Tribune, (Minneapolis, MN), June 3, 2010, Kim Ode, "Is This Author Smarter than These Fifth-Graders?," p. P1E.

ONLINE

Children's Literature Network, http://www.childrenslitera turenetwork.org/ (May 10, 2010), "Eyes on the Goal: An Interview with John Coy."

John Coy Home Page, http://johncoy.com (August 1, 2011).

John Coy Web log, http://onepotatoten.blogspot.com (August 1, 2011).

Lee & Low Books Web site, http://www.leeandlow.com/ (August 1, 2011), "John Coy."

Macmillan Web site, http://us.macmillan.com/ (August 1, 2011), "John Coy: Q&A."

Scholastic Web site, http://www2.scholastic.com/ (August 1, 2011), "John Coy."

* * *

CROWLEY, Cath 1971-

Personal

Born 1971, in Melbourne, Victoria, Australia. *Education:* Swinburne University, B.A. (Medieval studies and literature); Royal Melbourne Institute of Technology, Diploma of Professional Writing and Editing, 2001. *Hobbies and other interests:* Reading, politics, education, art.

Addresses

Home—Yarraville, Victoria, Australia. *Agent*—Catherine Drayton, InkWell Management, 521 5th Ave., 26th Fl., New York, NY 10175; info@inkwellmanagement.com. *E-mail*—cathcrowley@iprimus.com.au.

Career

Writer and educator. Has taught English and creative writing in Australia.

Cath Crowley (Photograph by Darren James. Reproduced by permission.)

Awards, Honors

Notable Book for Older Readers selection, Children's Book Council of Australia (CBCA), 2005, for *The Life and Times of Gracie Faltrain;* CBCA Book of the Year Award for Older Readers shortlist, 2006, for *Chasing Charlie Duskin;* CBCA Notable Book for Older Readers, 2009, for *Gracie Faltrain Gets It Right (Finally);* Best Books for Young Adults designation, America Library Association, 2010, for *A Little Wanting Song;* Ethel Turner Prize for Young People's Literature, Prime Minister's Literary Award for Young-Adult Fiction, Victorian Premier's Award shortlist, and Queensland Premier's Award shortlist, all 2011, and CBCA Book of the Year for Older Readers shortlist, all for *Graffiti Moon.*

Writings

The Life and Times of Gracie Faltrain, Pan Macmillan Australia (Sydney, New South Wales, Australia), 2004.

Chasing Charlie Duskin, Pan Macmillan Australia (Sydney, New South Wales, Australia), 2005, published as *A Little Wanting Song,* Knopf (New York, NY), 2010.

Gracie Faltrain Takes Control, Pan Macmillan Australia (Sydney, New South Wales, Australia), 2006.

Gracie Faltrain Gets It Right (Finally), Pan Macmillan Australia (Sydney, New South Wales, Australia), 2008.

Rosie Staples' Minor Magical Misunderstanding, Pan Macmillan Australia (Sydney, New South Wales, Australia), 2010.

Graffiti Moon, Pan Macmillan Australia (Sydney, New South Wales, Australia), 2010, Knopf (New York, NY), 2012.

Contributor to anthologies, including *Picture This 2,* Pearson, and to periodicals, including the *Age.*

Sidelights

In her young-adult novel *Chasing Charlie Duskin*—published in the United States as *A Little Wanting Song*—Australian author Cath Crowley depicts the unlikely relationship between a pair of teenaged girls from

vastly different backgrounds. The work focuses on Charlie, a talented but shy singer/songwriter from Melbourne who spends the summer in the countryside visiting her widowed grandfather. When Rose Butler, an aloof neighbor who feels stifled by small-town life, wins a scholarship to a prestigious high school, she attempts to befriend Charlie, hoping the sensitive teen will help convince Rose's parents to let their daughter move to the city. As the summer progresses, brash Rose learns to appreciate Charlie's sense of compassion while Charlie gains confidence in her abilities. "Crowley captures quiet moments with aching beauty and tenderness," Debbie Carton noted in her *School Library Journal* review, and a critic in *Kirkus Reviews* observed of *A Little Wanting Song* that "Charlie's quirky song lyrics add a pleasing poetic element to the narrative."

Using alternating narrators, Crowley's story for *Graffiti Moon* concerns a group of friends on the cusp of adulthood and their search for an elusive graffiti artist. "*Graffiti Moon* is a story about a group of teenagers who are outsiders," Crowley explained in a *Good Reading* online interview. "They spend one night together, out in the city, and it changes things for them. They don't work out who they are—that would be hard in one night—but they work out that it's okay to be different."

Crowley's works for young adults often focus on issues of love, family, and friendship. "I know I have the same reactions to these things now that I did when I was younger; it's just that when I was a teenager the emotion was raw because it was happening for the first time," she remarked in her *Good Reading* interview. "I like writing about those 'firsts': first love, first love disaster, first loss, first friendship."

Biographical and Critical Sources

PERIODICALS

Booklist, May 1, 2010, Debbie Carton, review of *A Little Wanting Song,* p. 77.
Kirkus Reviews, May 1, 2010, review of *A Little Wanting Song.*
School Library Journal, June, 2010, Rhona Campbell, review of *A Little Wanting Song,* p. 98.

ONLINE

Booked Out Web site, http://bookedout.com.au/ (August 1, 2011), "Cath Crowley."
Cath Crowley Home Page, http://cathcrowley.com.au (August 1, 2011).
Good Reading Online, http://www.goodreadingmagazine.com.au/ (August 1, 2011), "Meet the Author: Cath Crowley."
New South Wales Association for Gifted and Talented Children Web site, http://nswagtc.org.au/ (August 1, 2011), review of *Graffiti Moon.*

* * *

CROZA, Laurel

Personal

Born in Canada; married; husband's name Mike; children: Shannon, Caitie, Allie, Jake. *Education:* Attended Ryerson University, 2003. *Hobbies and other interests:* Biking.

Addresses

Home—Markham, Ontario, Canada. *E-mail*—contact@laurelcroza.com.

Career

Writer.

Member

Canadian Society of Children's Authors, Illustrators, and Performers.

Cover of Crowley's novel A Little Wanting Song, *which focuses on an unlikely friendship between two Australian teens.* (Cover copyright © 2005 by Alfred A. Knopf. Used by permission of Alfred A. Knopf, an imprint of Random House Children's Books, a division of Random House, Inc.)

Awards, Honors

Boston Globe/Horn Book Award, 2010, and Outstanding International Books Honor selection, U.S. Board on Books for Young People, and New Writer Award, New York Public Library/Ezra Jack Keats Foundation, both 2011, all for *I Know Here.*

Writings

I Know Here, illustrated by Matt James, Groundwood Books (Toronto, Ontario, Canada), 2010.

Contributor to periodicals, including *Toronto Star.*

Sidelights

Canadian author Laurel Croza won both the prestigious *Boston Globe/Horn Book* Award and the Ezra Jack Keats New Writer Award for her debut work, *I Know Here,* a "regional look at a universal slice of childhood," according to *School Library Journal* critic Luann Toth. Croza's picture book, which concerns a young girl's reaction to her family's impending move from rural Saskatchewan to cosmopolitan Toronto, was inspired by its author's reminiscences of growing up in remote areas of Canada. After reading *I Know Here,* Myra Junyk predicted in the *Canadian Review of Materials* that the book's "readers will be inspired to ask questions such as: How does our environment impact us? What would we remember about our homes if we had to leave them tomorrow? How can we preserve our memories?"

Croza was an avid reader from an early age. "It all began with fairy tales," the author recalled on her home page. "There's a special place in my heart and on my bookshelf for Hilda Boswell's *Treasury of Fairy Tales*—scribbled on, tattered, binding completely come undone. To this day, I feel wonder and awe when I open it (carefully, it has fallen apart after all) and turn its pages." Though she often considered a career as a writer while growing up, Croza did not seriously pursue her literary interests until she was diagnosed with cancer as an adult. Recalling a fateful meeting with her oncologist in her acceptance speech for the Ezra Jack Keats award, she explained: "He said that successful surgery, like mine, was about as hopeful as hopeful gets with lung cancer. As we were leaving he did hand me one option: He said, 'Don't wait for five years to live your dreams.'"

In 2003 Croza enrolled in a creative-writing class titled "True to Life: Writing Your Own Story" at Ryerson University in Toronto. "I am a steadfast believer in serendipity—a gift from my illness—and, as it happens, the very first class assignment was this: draw a map of your earliest remembered neighborhood," she noted in her *Boston Globe/Horn Book* Award acceptance speech. "Bring this neighborhood to life and then tell a story from the map." The assignment resonated with Croza, the daughter of a construction engineer who built roads, bridges, and dams throughout Canada. "By the time I was fourteen, I'd moved nine times," she explained. "That writing assignment transported me back to living beside a dam site in Saskatchewan just before leaving for Toronto. I was four when I arrived and barely turned seven when I left. And the memories of that time became the nucleus, the heart, of *I Know Here.*"

Featuring illustrations by Matt James, *I Know Here* depicts a young girl's efforts to recall the familiar sights and sounds of northern Saskatchewan before her family relocates to the big city. At the suggestion of her caring teacher, the youngster begins drawing pictures of the things that are most important to her, creating a keepsake she can take to her new home. Roger Sutton, reviewing the tale in *Horn Book,* described Croza's narrative as "deliberate and declarative," and *Booklist* critic Hazel Rochman observed that *I Know Here* "captures a child's fear of moving with a touch of magic realism." According to *New York Times Book Review* contributor David Barringer, the story "could have been treated as a weepy leave-taking shaded with sepia sentiment. Heroically, Croza balances her story on something far more hopeful and true: a child realizing that the act of making art is a way to preserve memories of home."

Biographical and Critical Sources

PERIODICALS

Booklist, May 15, 2010, Hazel Rochman, review of *I Know Here,* p. 43.
Canadian Review of Materials, June 11, 2010, Myra Junyk, review of *I Know Here.*
Horn Book, May-June, 2010, Roger Sutton, review of *I Know Here,* p. 65; January-February, 2011, review of *I Know Here,* and Laurel Croza, transcript of *Boston Globe/Horn Book* Award acceptance speech, both p. 25.
Kirkus Reviews, May 1, 2010, review of *I Know Here.*
New York Times Book Review, May 16, 2010, David Barringer, review of *I Know Here,* p. 17.
Quill & Quire, June, 2010, Chelsea Donaldson, review of *I Know Here.*
School Library Journal, October, 2010, Luann Toth, review of *I Know Here,* p. 82.

ONLINE

Ezra Jack Keats Foundation Web site, http://www.ezra-jack-keats.org/ (June 6, 2011), transcript of New Writer Award acceptance speech.
Laurel Croza Home Page, http://www.laurelcroza.com (August 1, 2011).*

*   *   *

CUMMINGS, Gillian 1961-

Personal

Born 1961, in Perth, Scotland; immigrated to Canada, 1966; married; children: two daughters. *Education:* University of Toronto, B.A. (music history); University of Western Ontario, M.A. (journalism).

Addresses

Home—Toronto, Ontario, Canada.

Career

Journalist and author. London Free Press, London, Ontario, Canada, former music critic; freelance writer. Researcher and production assistant for Canadian television programs. Presenter at schools.

Awards, Honors

Young Adults Best Bets selection, Ontario Library Association, 2010, and Best Books for Kids and Teens selection, Canadian Children's Book Centre, 2011, both for *Somewhere in Blue.*

Writings

Somewhere in Blue, Lobster Press (Montreal, Quebec, Canada), 2010.

Contributor to periodicals, including *Canadian Living* and *Style at Home.*

Biographical and Critical Sources

PERIODICALS

Booklist, April 15, 2010, Heather Booth, review of *Somewhere in Blue,* p. 43.
Kirkus Reviews, April 15, 2010, review of *Somewhere in Blue.*

ONLINE

Gillian Cummings Home Page, http://www.gillian cummings.com (September 15, 2011).
Lobster Press Web site, http://www.lobsterpress.com/ (July 12, 2011), "Gillian Cummings."*

*   *   *

CYPESS, Leah

Personal

Married Aaron M. Cypess (a physician and researcher); children: two daughters, one son. *Education:* Brooklyn College, B.S. (biology); Columbia University, J.D. *Hobbies and other interests:* Hiking, travel, spending time with family.

Addresses

Home—Brookline, MA. *E-mail*—lcypess@gmail.com.

Leah Cypess (Reproduced by permission.)

Career

Attorney and author. Debevois & Plimpton (law firm), New York, NY, attorney for two years; freelance writer. Presenter at schools.

Awards, Honors

YALSA Best Fiction for Young Adults nomination, 2012, for *Nightspell.*

Writings

Mistwood, Greenwillow (New York, NY), 2010.
Nightspell, Greenwillow (New York, NY), 2011.

Contributor of short fiction to periodicals, including *Asimov's Science Fiction, HelixSF, Odyssey, Marion Zimmer Bradley's Fantasy Magazine, Strange Horizons,* and *Sword & Sorceress.* Contributor of articles to *Writer.*

Sidelights

Although Leah Cypess began her writing career in the first grade, she took a giant sidestep into a biology degree and a career as a lawyer. She started work on the manuscript that would grow into her first novel, *Mistwood,* as an antidote to the stress of law school, and alternated her job at a New York City law firm with writing and publishing short fantasy fiction. During the

seven years it took to complete her debut novel, Cypess traded her job as an attorney for the more-challenging job of parenting her two young children. This juggling act proved to be successful; a companion novel, *Nightspell,* was produced a year after *Mistwood* appeared in bookstores.

Cypess grounds *Mistwood* in the kingdom of Samorna, a land in which an immortal creature called a Shifter is charged with protecting Samorna's anointed leaders. Isabel is one such shifter, and while peace reins in Samorna the ancient one lives a quiet life in the Mistwood, unaware of her special gifts. Then Crown Prince Rokan arrives in the forest. He captures Isabel by encircling her wrist with the powerful Shifter's Seal, then brings her to the palace to act in his defense. Rokan knows that the shifter can change from human to animal and even into a grey mist, and that Isabel possesses great strength and speed. As Isabel tries to understand these inner powers, she must also navigate the politics of the Samornan court and try to understand why Rokan's requests leave her uneasy and feeling threatened. Recommending *Mistwood* to fans of Megan Whalen Turner, *School Library Journal* contributor Jessica Miller noted that Cypess's novel "unfolds gracefully, mirroring the slow path Isabel must travel to begin understanding herself and her place in the world." "The greatest magic is the power of choice in this lush, romantic debut fantasy," proclaimed a *Kirkus Reviews* writer, and in *Booklist* Lynn Rutan recommended *Mistwood* as "an unusual, suspenseful fantasy that is propelled by well-placed clues."

Set in a similar fantasy kingdom, Ghostland, *Nightspell* introduces threats of a ghostly nature. Callie, a princess of the nomadic Raellian people, was betrothed to a Ghostland prince as a child and she has lived in that kingdom since girlhood. Like others of his kind, the prince is long dead but continues to move among the living, drawing his energy from the intrigue and excesses of the palace court. When Callie's older siblings Darri and her brother Varis enter Ghostland in the hope of rescuing her, they find their sister strangely reluctant. Soon Darri recognizes that the decision is hers: in order to save her sister she must sacrifice her future to marriage with this strangely compelling prince. Praising *Nightspell* for its "elegant, allusive prose," a *Kirkus Reviews* critic went on to note of Cypess's second novel that it effectively evokes "both the claustrophobic horror and overripe allure of the decadent [Ghostland] court." In *Booklist* Lynn Rutan listed plot elements that would appeal to fans of sword-and-sorcery novels, writing that "swordfights, blood, and double-dealing" help to fuel the author's "action-filled story . . . to a surprising conclusion."

Biographical and Critical Sources

PERIODICALS

Booklist, April 1, 2010, Lynn Rutan, review of *Mistwood,* p. 34; April 1, 2011, Lynn Rutan, review of *Nightspell,* p. 70.

Kirkus Reviews, April 15, 2010, review of *Mistwood;* May 1, 2011, review of *Nightspell.*

Publishers Weekly, May 17, 2010, review of *Mistwood,* p. 51.

School Library Journal, May, 2010, Jessica Miller, review of *Mistwood,* p. 108.

Voice of Youth Advocates, June, 2010, Marlyn Beebe, review of *Mistwood,* p. 162.

ONLINE

HarperCollins Web site, http://www.harpercollins.com/ (September 15, 2011), "Leah Cypess."

Leah Cypess Home Page, http://www.leahcypess.com (September 15, 2011).

D

DAWSON, Scott

Personal

Three children. *Education:* Wichita State University, B.F.A.; studied at Rhode Island School of Design and Art Center School of Design. *Hobbies and other interests:* Tennis, music, golf.

Addresses

Home—Wichita, KS. *Agent*—Suzanne Craig, Suzanne Craig Represents, 4015 E. 53rd St., Tulsa, OK 74135. *E-mail*—scott@scottdawsonillustration.com.

Career

Illustrator and graphic artist.

Illustrator

Barbara Rosenstock, *Fearless: The Story of Racing Legend Louise Smith,* Dutton (New York, NY), 2010.
Adam Blade, *Beast Quest: Vipero the Snake Man,* Scholastic (New York, NY), 2011.

Contributor to periodicals, including *Texas Co-op Power* and *Wall Street Journal.*

"WORLD OF INVENTORS" NONFICTION SERIES; FOR CHILDREN

Nancy Honovich, *Alexander Graham Bell,* Silver Dolphin Books (Charlotte, NC), 2009.
Dennis Schnatz, *Thomas Edison,* Silver Dolphin Books (Charlotte, NC), 2009.

"I SURVIVED" NONFICTION SERIES BY LAUREN TARSHIS; FOR CHILDREN

The Sinking of the Titanic, 1912, Scholastic (New York, NY), 2010.
The Shark Attacks of 1916, Scholastic (New York, NY), 2010.

Hurricane Katrina, 2005, Scholastic (New York, NY), 2011.
The Bombing of Pearl Harbor, 1941, Scholastic (New York, NY), 2011.
The San Francisco Earthquake, 1906, Scholastic (New York, NY), 2011.

"MYSTERY AND THE MINISTER'S WIFE" NOVEL SERIES

Diane Noble, *Through the Fire,* Guideposts (New York, NY), 2011.
Traci Depree, *A State of Grace,* Guideposts (New York, NY), 2011.
Beth Pattillo, *Beauty Shop Tales,* Guideposts (New York, NY), 2011.
Carol Cox, *A Test of Faith,* Guideposts (New York, NY), 2011.
Eve Fisher, *The Best Is Yet to Be,* Guideposts (New York, NY), 2011.
Diane Noble, *Angels Undercover,* Guideposts (New York, NY), 2011.

Sidelights

Artist Scott Dawson began working as a freelance illustrator in the mid-1980s, and his projects include images for advertising, graphic design projects, and art for corporations. His strong grasp of design and color made Dawson a good fit as a children's book illustrator, and his artwork has appeared in both nonfiction and fiction books since the late 2000s. In addition to capturing the high points of the biographical profiles included in the "World of Inventors" series, Dawson's acrylic paintings also bring to life the real-world drama of Lauren Tarshis's "I Survived" books, which include *The Sinking of the Titanic, 1912, The Shark Attacks of 1916,* and *Hurricane Katrina, 2005.* Reviewing the last-named book, *Booklist* contributor Erin Anderson noted that Dawson's "expressive illustrations capture the drama of the storm and its aftermath." The artist's "black-and-white illustrations that resemble old photographs enhance the events" in *The Shark Attacks of 1916,* according to *School Library Journal* contributor Delia Carruthers.

Scott Dawson's paintings capture the excitement and energy in Barb Rosenstock's picture-book biography **Fearless: The Story of Racing Legend Louise Smith.** (Illustration copyright © 2010 by Scott Dawson. Reproduced with permission of Dutton Children's Books, a division of Penguin Young Readers Group, an imprint of Penguin Group (USA) Inc., 375 Hudson St., New York, NY 10014. All rights reserved.)

Dawson's illustration projects also include creating the artwork for Barbara Rosenstock's picture-book biography *Fearless: The Story of Racing Legend Louise Smith.* Rosenstock's text profiles the long career of a woman who, born in 1906, built her first racing car at age seven and became a professional stock-car racer in the early days of auto racing. In capturing Smith's eventful life, which included both excitement and danger, Dawson creates "realistic, action-filled, mixed-media images" that capture the life story of "a person once called 'the craziest woman we know,'" according to *Booklist* critic Andrew Medlar. "Gorgeous, light-infused acrylics convey Louise's self-assured nature," noted a *Publishers Weekly* reviewer in appraising *Fearless,* and in *School Library Journal* Patricia Manning praised "Dawson's color-saturated paintings" for capturing the energy of "a determined woman" who went on to become the first female to be elected to the International Motorsports Hall of Fame.

Biographical and Critical Sources

PERIODICALS

Booklist, December 1, 2010, Andrew Medlar, review of *Fearless: The Story of Racing Legend Louise Smith,* p. 43; February 1, 2011, Erin Anderson, review of *Hurricane Katrina, 2005,* p. 78.
Bulletin of the Center for Children's Books, November, 2010, Elizabeth Bush, review of *Fearless,* p. 145.

Publishers Weekly, October 11, 2011, review of *Fearless,* p. 42.
School Library Journal, December, 2010, Patricia Manning, review of *Fearless,* p. 97, and Delia Carruthers, review of *The Shark Attacks of 1916,* p. 129.

ONLINE

Scott Dawson Home Page, http://www.scottdawsonillustration.com (September 15, 2011).

*   *   *

DUANE, Diane 1952-

Personal

Born May 18, 1952, in New York, NY; daughter of Edward David (an aircraft engineer) and Elizabeth Kathryn Duane; married Robert Peter Smyth (a writer under pseudonym Peter Morwood), February 15, 1987. *Education:* Attended Dowling College, 1970-71; Pilgrim State Hospital School of Nursing, degree, 1974. *Hobbies and other interests:* Collecting recipes and cookbooks, traveling, gardening, astronomy, computer graphics and modeling, iaido, cartography, desktop publishing, fractals.

Addresses

Home—County Wicklow, Ireland. *Agent*—Donald Maass Literary Agency, Ste. 801, 121 W. 27th St., New York, NY 10001; info@maassagency.com.

Career

Novelist and television writer. Pilgrim State Hospital, Brentwood, NY, registered nurse, 1974; Payne Whitney Clinic, Cornell/New York Hospital Medical Center, New York, NY, psychiatric nurse, 1974-76; writer's assistant, 1976-78; freelance writer, beginning 1978; Filmation Studios, Reseda, CA, staff writer, 1983-84; story editor and consultant for television programs.

Awards, Honors

Best Books selection, *School Library Journal,* 1985, and Best Science Fiction and Fantasy Titles for Young Adults selection, *Voice of Youth Advocates,* 1986, both for *Deep Wizardry;* Best Science Fiction and Fantasy Titles for Young Adults selection, *Voice of Youth Advocates,* 1986, for *The Door into Shadow;* Books for the Teen Age citation, New York Public Library, 1994, for *Dark Mirror,* and 2003, for *A Wizard Alone;* special commendation, Anne Spencer Lindbergh Prize in Children's Literature, Charles A. and Anne Morrow Lindbergh Foundation, for "Young Wizards" series.

Writings

"YOUNG WIZARDS" NOVEL SERIES

So You Want to Be a Wizard (also see below), Delacorte (New York, NY), 1983, reprinted, Harcourt (Orlando, FL), 2003.
Deep Wizardry (also see below), Delacorte (New York, NY), 1985.
High Wizardry (also see below), Delacorte (New York, NY), 1990.
Support Your Local Wizard (contains *So You Want to Be a Wizard, Deep Wizardry,* and *High Wizardry*), Guild American (New York, NY), 1990.
A Wizard Abroad, Corgi (London, England), 1993, Harcourt (San Diego, CA), 1997.
The Wizard's Dilemma, Harcourt (San Diego, CA), 2001.
A Wizard Alone, Harcourt (San Diego, CA), 2003.
Wizard's Holiday, Harcourt (Orlando, FL), 2003.
Wizards at War, Harcourt (Orlando, FL), 2005.
A Wizard of Mars, Harcourt (Boston, MA), 2010.

"MIDDLE KINGDOM" NOVEL SERIES

The Door into Fire (also see below), Dell (New York, NY), 1979.
The Door into Shadow (also see below), Bluejay Books (New York, NY), 1984.
The Door into Sunset, Tor Books (New York, NY), 1993.
The Tale of the Five: The Sword and the Dragon (includes *The Door into Fire* and *The Door into Shadow*), Meisha Merlin Books (Decatur, GA), 2002.

SCIENCE-FICTION NOVELS; BASED ON "STAR TREK" TELEVISION SERIES

The Wounded Sky, Pocket Books (New York, NY), 1983.
Spock's World, Pocket Books (New York, NY), 1988.
Doctor's Orders, Pocket Books (New York, NY), 1990.

Diane Duane (Photo by Gary Jordan. Reproduced by permission.)

The Next Generation: Dark Mirror, Pocket Books (New York, NY), 1993.
The Next Generation: Intellivore, Pocket Books (New York, NY), 1997.
(With A.C. Crispin) *Star Trek: Sand and Stars* (contains *Star Trek: Spock's World*), Pocket Books (New York, NY), 2004.

"RIHANNSU" SERIES; BASED ON "STAR TREK" TELEVISION SERIES

My Enemy, My Ally, Pocket Books (New York, NY), 1984.
(With husband, Peter Morwood) *The Romulan Way,* Pocket Books (New York, NY), 1987.
Swordhunt, Pocket Books (New York, NY), 2000.
Honor Blade, Pocket Books (New York, NY), 2000.
(With Peter Morwood) *The Bloodwing Voyages,* Pocket Books (New York, NY), 2006.
The Empty Chair, Pocket Books (New York, NY), 2006.

"SPACE COPS" NOVEL SERIES; WITH PETER MORWOOD

Mindblast, Avon (New York, NY), 1991.
Kill Station, Avon (New York, NY), 1992.
High Moon, Avon (New York, NY), 1992.

"MARVEL COMICS NOVELS" SERIES

Spider-Man: The Venom Factor, illustrated by Ron Lim, Byron Preiss Multimedia/Putnam (New York, NY), 1994.
Spider-Man: The Lizard Sanction, illustrated by Darick Robertson and Scott Koblish, Byron Preiss Multimedia/Putnam (New York, NY), 1995.

Spider-Man: The Octopus Agenda, illustrated by Darick Robertson, Byron Preiss Multimedia/Putnam (New York, NY), 1996.

X-Men: Empire's End, Byron Preiss Multimedia/Putnam (New York, NY), 1997.

"STARDRIVE: THE HARBINGER" NOVEL TRILOGY

Starrise at Corrivale, TSR (Lake Geneva, WI), 1998.
Storm at Eldala, TSR (Renton, WA), 1999.
Nightfall at Algemron, TSR (Renton, WA), 2000.

"TOM CLANCY'S NET FORCE" NOVEL SERIES; BASED ON A CONCEPT BY TOM CLANCY AND STEVE PIECZENIK

Deathworld, Berkley (New York, NY), 2000.
Safe House, Berkley (New York, NY), 2000.
Runaways, Berkley (New York, NY), 2001.
Death Match, Berkley (New York, NY), 2003.

OTHER

(With Peter Morwood) *Keeper of the City* (fantasy), Bantam (New York, NY), 1989.

(Adapter, with Peter Morwood) *SeaQuest DSV* (based on the Steven Spielberg television program), Ace (New York, NY), 1993.

X-COM UFO Defense (science-fiction novel; based on the computer game), Prima (New York, NY), 1995.

Raetian Tales: A Wind from the South, Badfort Press (Dublin, Ireland), 1995.

The Cats of Grand Central, Warner (New York, NY), 1997.

The Book of Night with Moon ("Cat Wizards" series), Warner (New York, NY), 1997.

On Her Majesty's Wizardly Service ("Cat Wizards" series), Hodder & Stoughton (London, England), 1998, published as *To Visit the Queen,* Aspect/Warner Books (New York, NY), 1999.

Stealing the Elf-King's Roses, Warner Books (New York, NY), 2002.

Uptown Local and Other Interventions (e-book anthology), Badfort Press, 2010.

Omnitopia Dawn, DAW Books (New York, NY), 2010.

Writer for television, including (as coauthor, with Michael Reaves) for *Star Trek: The Next Generation.* Contributor to *Star Trek: The Kobayashi Alternative* (computer game), Simon & Schuster Interactive (New York, NY), 1985.

Work represented in anthologies, including *Flashing Swords! 5,* edited by Lin Carter, Dell (New York, NY), 1981; *Sixteen: Short Stories by Outstanding Young-Adult Writers,* edited by Donald R. Gallo, Delacorte (New York, NY), 1984; *Dragons and Dreams: A Collection of New Fantasy and Science-Fiction Stories,* edited by Jane Yolen and others, Harper (New York, NY), 1986; *Xanadu Two,* edited by Yolen, Tor (New York, NY), 1994; *On Crusade: More Tales of the Knights Templar,* edited by Katherine Kurtz, Warner (New York, NY), 2003; *Through the Wardrobe: Your Favorite Au-*

thors on C.S. Lewis's Chronicles of Narnia, edited by Herbie Brennan, BenBella Books, 2008; and *Mystery Date,* edited by Denise Little, DAW Books (New York, NY), 2008. Contributor to periodicals, including *Fantasy Book* and *Amazing.*

Adaptations

Several titles in the "Wizardry" series were adapted for audiocassette by Recorded Books. *Spock's World* was released on audiocassette, 1989. *So You Want to Be a Wizard, Deep Wizardry,* and *High Wizardry* were adapted into books for younger readers, Harcourt (San Diego, CA), 2003.

Sidelights

Best known for her "Young Wizards" science-fiction and fantasy series, which has drawn comparisons to J.K. Rowling's "Harry Potter" books, prolific novelist Diane Duane is the author of dozens of novels for adults, teens, and children. A versatile writer, Duane produces both series and stand-alone titles, creates screenplays, and writes as a stable author for established series. She plans each of her books far in ad-

Cover of Duane's young-adult novel **The Book of Night with Moon,** *featuring artwork for Robert Goldstrom.* (Copyright © 1997 by Diane Duane. Reproduced by permission of Grand Central Publishing.)

vance and dedicates a great deal of time to researching her science-based plots. Called "not only highly talented but highly unpredictable," by Jessica Yates in *Twentieth-Century Young-Adult Writers,* Duane's diverse output is characterized by imaginative plots, strong, well-rounded male and female characters, and a firm grounding in such time-honored virtues as beauty, heroism, and loyalty.

Raised in Roosevelt, Long Island, in the suburbs of New York City, Duane experienced a childhood that was "essentially quite boring and sometimes rather unhappy," as the author once told *SATA.* Fortunately, "the unhappiness was tempered with a great love of books and writing in general." When she had read all the books she desired at her local library, Duane "began to write my own," as she later recalled, "occasionally illustrating them (usually in crayon). When I left high school, I went on to study astronomy (something else I had loved greatly from a young age), didn't do too well at that, and then on a friend's recommendation went on to study nursing, which I did much better at. But the writing, for my own enjoyment, went on all the time." Duane's health-care career led her to a staff position as a psychiatric nurse, but by 1976 she had decided to give serious attention to becoming a writer. She moved to California for a time, where she made her first sale: *The Door into Fire,* the initial volume of her "Middle Kingdom" series. She also began writing for the screen while in California, then moved to Pennsylvania for a time. In 1987, Duane married Northern Irish writer Peter Morwood and now makes her home in County Wicklow, Ireland.

The Door into Fire introduces five characters, some human, some not, whose adventures span several volumes in the "Middle Kingdom" series. These adult fantasies, which include *The Door into Shadow* and *The Door into Sunset,* encompass an epic battle between good and evil that hinges on the paranormal abilities and growth of each character. In *The Door into Shadow,* for instance, a young woman named Segnbora vows to support the fugitive Prince Frelorn's Ferrant in his attempt to regain the throne of the kingdom of Arlen against the usurpation of his greedy half-brother, Cillmod, whose rule is guided by the ancient Shadow. In opposition to the Shadow's evil powers stands the Goddess, the creator of life in Duane's mythical world. In *The Door into Sunset,* the prince is still supported by Segnbora, who has focused her magic powers and now rallies dragons to Frelorn's cause, as well as by Queen Eftgan d'Arienn and her troops from the neighboring kingdom of Darthan. Thus strengthened, the Prince now engages in a war of absolutes in a novel that a *Publishers Weekly* reviewer deemed an "intelligent and exhilarating Swords and Sorcery adventure."

While many of her books are suitable for a teen audience, Duane never consciously decided to write with that age group in mind. "I always wrote what pleased me," she once admitted to *SATA,* "and was rather shocked when it began to sell (though the shock was very pleasant). Occasionally I find I'm writing a story which younger readers would probably appreciate more thoroughly than older ones, or rather, it would take older readers of taste and discernment to have fun with a story that younger readers would have no problem with at all. I let my publishers label or target the markets for my books, and I myself sit home and get on with the storytelling."

Duane began her popular series of teen novels about the fantastic exploits of two modern adolescents in an alternate Earth in *So You Want to Be a Wizard.* From reading a book in the local library, twelve-year-old Kit Rodriguez and thirteen-year-old Nita Callahan learn how to harness the powers of magic as a defense against several neighborhood bullies. However, instead of simplifying their lives, the magic complicates things, as the friends suddenly find themselves in an alternate New York City which is inhabited by machines that attack living creatures. They enter this realm through Worldgates that are hidden in locations such as Rockefeller Center. Given the task of rescuing a magical book from a dragon's lair, the middle schoolers incur the wrath of the evil Starsnuffer, who follows them back into their own world and snuffs out the light of Earth's Sun. Using their powers along with magical incantations from the book to vanquish their foe, Kit and Nita are also aided by Fred, a "white hole" from the edge of the galaxy. Praising *So You Want to Be a Wizard* as "outstanding" and "original," *Horn Book* reviewer Ann A. Flowers added that the novel "stands between the works of Diane Wynne Jones, in its wizardry and spells, and those of Madeleine L'Engle, in its scientific concepts and titanic battles between good and evil." Writing in *Five Owls,* Judy Rosenbaum noted that "Duane makes brilliant use of the Manhattan setting to give her fantasy real individuality" and praised the "Young Wizards" books as "one of the most gripping, exhilarating, and inventive fantasy series for young people."

Further novels in the "Young Wizards" series include *Deep Wizardry, High Wizardry,* and *A Wizard Abroad.* In *Deep Wizardry* Nita and Kit must come to the rescue again, this time to help an injured Whale wizard named S'reee prevent the evil Lone Power from coaxing a dormant volcano beneath Manhattan into unleashing its power and destroying the city. Nita's eleven-year-old sister, Dairine, a budding computer hacker, finds a way to incorporate the ancient laws of wizardry with modern technology in *High Wizardry.* Programming the family's laptop computer to transport her across the Universe, Dairine is followed by caretakers Nita and Kit as she is initiated into wizardom by confronting the malevolent Lone One. Reviewing the third title in the series, a *Publishers Weekly* critic called it a "rollicking yarn" that illustrates why "Duane is tops in the high adventure business." Margaret A. Chang, writing in *School Library Journal,* dubbed *High Wizardry* "audacious in theme" and an obvious "homage to the science fiction of the 1950s, particularly [Robert] Heinlein."

A Wizard Abroad finds the teens in Ireland where they rally the country's wizards to help battle the ghostly Fomori, an army of ancient invaders that are the pawns of the Lone One. *Booklist* critic Chris Sherman noted that Duane "weaves the heroes and demons of Irish legends" in this fourth installment into a tale as "equally satisfying" as the first three. According to *Science Fiction Chronicle* contributor Don D'Ammassa, *A Wizard Abroad* is an "exceptional work of children's fantasy." Appraising the "Young Wizards" series to date, Jessica Yates commented in *School Librarian* that Duane "has succeeded in writing an exciting and moral fantasy which doesn't preach, and her style . . . lives up to the challenge of her cosmic theme."

The "Young Wizards" series continues with *The Wizard's Dilemma.* Here Nita taking a break after the adventures she had in Ireland, but there will be little rest for her. It becomes apparent that Kit is growing away from her, and then Nita's mother develops brain cancer.

Cliff Nielsen creates the cover art for Duane's fantasy novel **The Wizard's Dilemma**, *another installment in her "Young Wizards" series.*
(Cover illustration copyright © 2001 by Cliff Nielsen. Reprinted by permission of Houghton Mifflin Harcourt Publishing Company. All rights reserved.)

The only way Nita can save her mom is to go to the alternate universe to search for a cure. There the Lone One offers her a Faustian bargain: her mother's life for the power that she, Nita, possesses. Meanwhile, Kit faces his own inner demons as he must decide whether or not he will retreat within himself or continue to battle evil. In *School Library Journal,* Beth Wright praised the "well-crafted plot, occasional dry humor, and appealing main characters" in *The Wizard's Dilemma,* while a critic for *Kirkus Reviews* dubbed Duane's book "powerful and satisfying on many levels." Writing for the *Green Man Review* online, Michael M. Jones commented that with *The Wizard's Dilemma* Nita and Kit's "adventures take on both macro levels, as they explore a panoply of strange new universes, and micro levels, as they discover that we are each our own universe."

Book six of "Young Wizards," *A Wizard Alone,* finds Nita mourning the death of her mother and closing herself off from friend Kit. At the same time, Kit is involved in a life-and-death struggle to save a young wizard in training, Darryl, an autistic boy. When Kit and his dog become trapped in Darryl's world, Nita finally comes out of herself in order to save her friend. Lisa Prolman, reviewing *A Wizard Alone* for *School Library Journal,* wrote that "the incorporation of Darryl's autism is seamless and drives the plot forward," while *Booklist* contributor GraceAnne A. DeCandido, recommended Duane's novel as "a fine fantasy." DeCandido also noted that the author "expertly weaves" the manner in which Nita and Kit explain their wizardry to their respective families into her story while also showing how the teens have "integrated wizard training into urban teen life."

Duane continues the adventures of Kit and Nita in *Wizard's Holiday.* After Dairine applies to a wizard exchange program without asking permission, she is placed on confinement, with Kit and Nita taking her place on the planet Alaalu, a veritable utopia. Soon the duo, along with Kit's dog, Ponch, discovers a startling truth about the planet's inhabitants. More ominously, they detect the presence of the Lone Power on Alaalu. Meanwhile, back home, Dairine and her father host three most unusual wizards—Sker'ret, a giant centipede; Filif, a shrub-like being; and Roshaun, an egotistical prince—who claim to have detected a problem with Earth's sun. Farida S. Dowler, writing in *School Library Journal,* applauded the compelling narrative in *Wizard's Holiday,* writing that "the presentation of imaginative scenarios and challenges that are anything but clear-cut provide enough interest for fans of the series."

The Lone Power unleashes a diabolical scheme to destroy the universe in *Wizards at War,* which reintroduces a number of characters from earlier "Young Wizards" novels. Arriving home from their vacation, Kit and Nita learn that their nemesis has tampered with the very fabric of the universe, filling it with a rapidly expanding dark matter that also causes adult wizards to

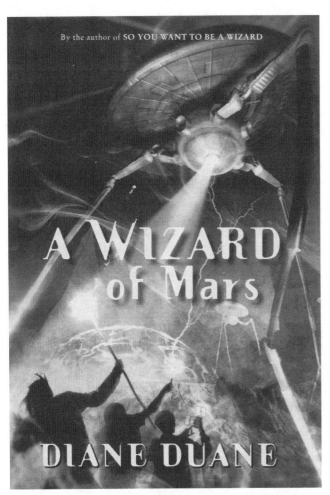

Cover of A Wizard of Mars, *a novel in Duane's "Young Wizards" series that features cover art by Cliff Nielsen.* (Cover illustration copyright © 2010 by Cliff Nielsen. Reprinted by permission of Houghton Mifflin Harcourt Publishing Company. All rights reserved.)

lose their powers. Joining forces with Dairine and her trio of magical houseguests, Kit and Nita embark on an intergalactic search for a weapon powerful enough to prevent annihilation. Though some critics cautioned that Duane's references to previous titles might confuse those new to the "Young Wizards" novels, a contributor in *Kirkus Reviews* described *Wizards at War* as "a solid pleasure for fans of the series." Walter Minkel commented in *School Library Journal* that readers "who are familiar with the series will thoroughly enjoy this story, especially its grand and wistful conclusion."

Kit's fascination with the Red Planet reignites an ancient conflict in *A Wizard of Mars.* As part of an investigative team exploring Mars, the teen examines a mysterious artifact that appears to hold clues to the disappearance of that world's ancient inhabitants, and in unlocking its secrets he unleashes powers he cannot control. As the fate of Earth hangs in the balance, Nita begins searching for Kit, who has vanished into the Red Planet's past. "Duane's worldbuilding gleams with crystalline precision, a-glitter with lapidary characterization," remarked a critic in an appraisal of *A Wizard of Mars* for *Kirkus Reviews.*

In her "Cat Wizards" series Duane employs concepts and characters that first appeared in her "Young Wizards" novels, this time setting them in tales that feature magical felines. In *The Book of Night with Moon,* for example, she describes the fight of a band of sorcerers against the Lone Power. Four cats—Rhiow, Saash, Urruah, and Arhu—guard the gates between worlds at Grand Central Station. They are forced to enter the world of Lone Power to avoid an invasion by the creatures of Downside. In the course of the telling, Duane also supplies minutiae of the cat civilization she has created, including their language and customs. A *Publishers Weekly* reviewer concluded that Duane's story "purrs with charms that even ailurophobes will find irresistible." Similarly, *Kliatt* critic Rita M. Fontinha predicted that "cat lovers who also enjoy fantasy will delight in this well-constructed tale." Likewise, Susan Allen noted in her *Voice of Youth Advocates* review that "the reader need only be a cat lover or fantasy reader to delve into the surreal worlds that are described."

Duane's "Cat Wizards" series continues in *To Visit the Queen,* which was originally published as *On Her Majesty's Wizardly Service.* Here the cats are in action again, traveling back in time to Victorian London to stop the assassination of Queen Victoria. Their mission is complicated when the felines of London resent the assistance of cats from the United States. Allen, writing again in *Voice of Youth Advocates,* maintained that "there is something for most readers in this delightful fantasy," and a *Publishers Weekly* critic anticipated that "even those who don't fancy felines should enjoy this purr of a tale." Jackie Cassada, reviewing *To Visit the Queen* for *Library Journal,* called it a "whimsical adventure," while for *Booklist* critic Sally Estes the book serves up "fun fare for fantasy and cat lovers."

While best known for her "Young Wizards" series, Duane has also written several other series and in numerous other genres, from fantasy to horror to science fiction. In 1983, she published the first of her "Star Trek" novels. Based on the characters from the original television series, *The Wounded Sky* has been followed by several other books; *Dark Mirror* is actually based on the cast of characters familiar to viewers of television's *Star Trek: The Next Generation.* In *My Enemy, My Ally* Captain Kirk and the crew of the starship *Enterprise* join a Romulan commander in a brief peace, during which time the two commanders team up to stop Romulan scientists from channeling Vulcan mind powers into weaponry. A political debate on whether the planet Vulcan should secede from the Federation is the subject of *Spock's World,* while "Bones" McCoy becomes the central character in *Doctor's Orders.* With Kirk gone on a routine mission to a newly discovered planet, Dr. McCoy is left as acting captain and must confront an aggressive attack by a Klingon spaceship with designs on the yet-unclaimed planet. Praising Duane for staying close to the facts set out in the original series, a *School Library Journal* reviewer dubbed *Doctor's Orders* "a fast-paced, well-written adventure."

In addition to her popular "Wizards" and "Star Trek" books, Duane has contributed several stories to the "Marvel Comic Novels" series, which mixes modern-day reality with super-hero fantasy in an entertaining and believable fashion. Reviewing *Spider-Man: The Venom Factor* in *Booklist,* Dennis Winters concluded: "Great Literature it ain't, but it's fun, which, after all, is what it's supposed to be." Along with her husband, who writes under the name Peter Morwood, Duane has also written several books featuring the pair's "Space Cop" heroes.

Featuring a story inspired by Duane's love of multi-player online role-playing games, *Omnitopia Dawn* centers on Dev Logan, the billionaire creator of Omnitopia, a virtual world that allows its millions of devotees to create their own universes and even profit from their designs, which can lure swindlers and speculators as well as gamers. As Logan's company gears up for an expansion of its product, a group of hackers plans an attack on the game's servers, and it turns out that Logan's former friend and business partner hopes to reap the financial windfall from Omnitopia's failure. In an *io9* online interview, Duane recalled that her experiences working on a computer game for Electronic Arts (EA) proved helpful when writing *Omnitopia Dawn.* "It was their first foray into interactive entertainment. They were almost trying to do choose-your-own-movie, with game modules to help you determine your path. And that left me with a very clear sense of how to structure a game. The EA people taught me an incredible amount about the structure of building computer games in general and this kind of interactive, flow-dictated game in particular." According to *Booklist* reviewer Kristine Huntley, readers familiar with role-playing games (RPG's) "will appreciate Duane's rich description of Omnitopia's many universes."

Despite the fact that their settings are products of the author's vivid imagination, Duane's fantasy books require extensive background research—"a great deal of reading in myths and legends of all countries, comparative religions, folklore, fairy tales, and (every now and then) other people's fantasy novels," as she once explained to *SATA.* "But I find the oldest material the most useful for my purposes. Fraser's *Golden Bough* and the *Larousse Encyclopedia of Mythology* have been two major helps to my fantasy work: the old themes, the Jungian 'archetypes,' are what makes fantasy work best in any time and place it's set—ancient Greece or modern Manhattan."

Although Duane's books range from space operas to magical escapades, they share similar themes. "They're [also] subject to change without notice," she once admitted, "and in any case I don't care to spell them out. I prefer to let the reader find them, if he or she cares to. If the themes aren't obvious, so much the better—a book made primarily for entertainment purposes is not the place for a writer to shout. People who are listening hard enough will hear even the whispers, the rest shouldn't be distracted from being entertained, which in itself is a noble thing, in this busy, crazy world."

Cover of Duane's middle-grade sci-fi adventure **Starrise at Corrivale,** *featuring artwork by R.K. Post.* (Illustration by R.K. Post. Wizards of the Coast and Dungeons & Dragons are trademarks of Wizards of the Coast LLC. Cover used with permission.)

Biographical and Critical Sources

BOOKS

St. James Guide to Science Fiction Writers, 4th edition, St. James Press (Detroit, MI), 1996.
Twentieth-Century Young-Adult Writers, St. James Press (Detroit, MI), 1994.

PERIODICALS

Booklist, February 15, 1993, Roland Green, review of *The Door into Sunset,* p. 10; October 15, 1993, John Mort, review of *The Dark Mirror,* p. 195; October 15, 1994,

Dennis Winters, review of *Spider-Man: The Venom Factor,* p. 405; October 1, 1997, Chris Sherman, review of *A Wizard Abroad,* p. 319; March 1, 1999, Sally Estes, review of *To Visit the Queen,* p. 1160; June 1, 2001, Sally Estes, review of *The Wizard's Dilemma,* p. 1862; November 15, 2002, GraceAnne A. DeCandido, review of *A Wizard Alone,* p. 588; January 1, 2004, John Peters, review of *Wizard's Holiday,* p. 854; October 15, 2005, Jennifer Mattson, review of *Wizards at War,* p. 50; August 1, 2010, Kristine Huntley, review of *Omnitopia Dawn,* p. 36.

Five Owls, January-February, 2001, Judy Rosenbaum, review of *So You Want to Be a Wizard,* p. 63.

Horn Book, December, 1983, Ann A. Flowers, review of *So You Want to Be a Wizard,* p. 716.

Kirkus Reviews, June 1, 2001, review of *The Wizard's Dilemma,* p. 800; September 15, 2005, review of *Wizards at War,* p. 1024; March 1, 2010, review of *A Wizard of Mars.*

Kliatt, March, 1998, Rita M. Fontinha, review of *The Book of Night with Moon,* p. 18; March, 2003, Donna L. Scanlon, review of *The Wizard's Dilemma,* p. 32; September, 2005, Deirdre Root, review of *Wizard's Holiday,* p. 26.

Library Journal, February 15, 1999, Jackie Cassada, review of *To Visit the Queen,* p. 188.

Magazine of Fantasy and Science Fiction, June, 1998, Charles de Lint, review of *The Book of Night with Moon,* pp. 37-38; March, 2002, Michelle West, review of *The Wizard's Dilemma,* pp. 34-39.

Publishers Weekly, March 9, 1984, review of *The Door into Shadow,* p. 111; April 13, 1990, review of *High Wizardry,* p. 67; January 4, 1993, review of *The Door into Sunset,* p. 62; October 3, 1994, review of *Spider-Man: The Venom Factor,* p. 54; September 22, 1997, p. 74; November 10, 1997, review of *The Book of Night with Moon,* pp. 59-60; January 25, 1999, review of *To Visit the Queen,* p. 77; November 24, 2003, review of *Wizard's Holiday,* p. 66.

School Librarian, August, 1992, Jessica Yates, reviews of *So You Want to Be a Wizard, Deep Wizardry,* and *High Wizardry,* all p. 113.

School Library Journal, March, 1985, Holly Sanhuber, review of *Deep Wizardry,* p. 176; March, 1990, Margaret A. Chang, review of *High Wizardry,* pp. 216-217; December, 1990, review of *Doctor's Orders,* p. 140; August, 2001, Beth Wright, review of *The Wizard's Dilemma,* p. 178; February, 2003, Lisa Prolman, review of *A Wizard Alone,* p. 140; December, 2003, Farida S. Dowler, review of *Wizard's Holiday,* p. 149; November, 2005, Walter Minkel, review of *Wizards at War,* p. 132.

Science Fiction Chronicle, June, 1998, Don D'Ammassa, review of *A Wizard Abroad,* pp. 42-43; February, 2003, Lisa Prolman, review of *A Wizard Alone,* p. 140.

Voice of Youth Advocates, April, 1998, Susan Allen, review of *The Book of Night with Moon,* p. 54; August, 1999, Susan Allen, review of *To Visit the Queen,* p. 190.

ONLINE

Diane Duane Home Page, http://www.dianeduane.com (August 15, 2011).

Green Man Review Online, http://www.greenmanreview.com/ (September 1, 2003), Michael M. Jones, review of *The Wizard's Dilemma.*

Harcourt Books Web site, http://www.harcourtbooks.com/ (August 15, 2011), interview with Duane.

io9.com, http://io9.com/ (November 28, 2010), "Diane Duane Says All Fiction—Even Science Fiction—Is a Subset of Fantasy."

January Online, http://www.januarymagazine.com/ (September, 2001), Monica Stark, review of *The Wizard's Dilemma.*

SFF.net, http://www.sff.net/ (September 1, 2003), Victoria Strauss, review of *The Wizard's Dilemma.*

Young Wizards Web site, http://www.youngwizards.com/ (August 15, 2011).*

*   *   *

DUNREA, Olivier 1953-

Personal

Surname is pronounced "DUN-ray"; born Clarence Miller, Jr., September 22, 1953, in Virginia Beach, VA; son of Clarence (a baker) and Marian (a homemaker) Miller; partner's name John. *Education:* Attended University of Delaware, 1971-73; West Chester State College (now University), B.A., 1975; Washington State University, M.A. (theater and music), 1976. *Hobbies and other interests:* Reading, mapmaking, running, gardening, camping, canoeing and kayaking.

Addresses

Home and office—Moel Eyris Studio at Henwoodie, 23 4th Ave., Narrowsburg, NY 12764. *E-mail*—odunrea@ henwoodie.com.

Career

Illustrator and author. Worked variously as a waiter, secretary, and management consultant; freelance artist and actor in Philadelphia, PA, San Francisco, CA, and New York, NY, 1976-79; writer and illustrator, beginning 1976. Teacher of art and theater to children; leader of workshops in makeup design, watercolor illustration, mask making, movement and nonverbal communication, and model building. *Exhibitions:* Work has been exhibited in Philadelphia, PA, and New York, NY.

Awards, Honors

Cooper/Woods Award (travel grant), English-speaking Union, 1980; residency grant, National Endowment for the Arts/Delaware State Arts Council, 1981-83; named Outstanding Pennsylvania Children's Author, 1985; Celebrating Literacy Award, International Reading Association, 1987; *Skara Brae* selected one of Child Study Association of America's Children's Books of the Year, 1987; One Hundred Titles for Reading and Sharing selection, New York Public Library, 2009, for *It's Snowing.*

Writings

PICTURE BOOKS; SELF-ILLUSTRATED

Eddy B, Pigboy, Atheneum (New York, NY), 1983.

Ravena, Holiday House (New York, NY), 1984.

Fergus and Bridey, Holiday House (New York, NY), 1985.

Mogwogs on the March!, Holiday House (New York, NY), 1985.

Skara Brae: The Story of a Prehistoric Village, Holiday House (New York, NY), 1986.

Deep down Underground, Macmillan (New York, NY), 1989.

Eppie M. Says . . . , Macmillan (New York, NY), 1990.

The Broody Hen, Doubleday (New York, NY), 1992.

The Painter Who Loved Chickens, Farrar, Straus (New York, NY), 1995.

Noggin and Bobbin by the Sea, Celebration Press (Glenview, IL), 1996.

The Tale of Hilda Louise, Farrar, Straus (New York, NY), 1996.

The Trow-Wife's Treasure, Farrar, Straus (New York, NY), 1998.

Appearing Tonight! Mary Heather Elizabeth Livingstone, Farrar, Straus (New York, NY), 1999.

Bear Noel, Farrar, Straus (New York, NY), 2000.

It's Snowing, Farrar, Straus (New York, NY), 2002.

Essie and Myles, Farrar, Straus (New York, NY), 2003.

Hanne's Quest, Philomel (New York, NY), 2005.

Old Bear and His Cub, Philomel Books (New York, NY), 2010.

A Christmas Tree for Pyn, Philomel Books (New York, NY), 2011.

Gideon, Houghton Mifflin Books for Children (Boston, MA), 2012.

Gideon and Otto, Houghton Mifflin Harcourt (Boston, MA), 2012.

"GOSSIE AND FRIENDS" BOARD-BOOK SERIES; SELF-ILLUSTRATED

Gossie, Houghton Mifflin (Boston, MA), 2002.

Gossie and Gertie, Houghton Mifflin (Boston, MA), 2002.

Ollie, Houghton Mifflin (Boston, MA), 2003.

Ollie the Stomper, Houghton Mifflin (Boston, MA), 2003.

Peedie, Houghton Mifflin (Boston, MA), 2004.

BooBoo, Houghton Mifflin (Boston, MA), 2004.

Merry Christmas, Ollie!, Houghton Mifflin (Boston, MA), 2005.

Gosling on the Prowl, Houghton Mifflin (Boston, MA), 2005.

Gossie and Friends: A First Flap Book, Houghton Mifflin (New York, NY), 2006.

Gossie's Busy Day: A First Tab Book, Houghton Mifflin (Boston, MA), 2007.

Gossie Plays Hide and Seek: A Flap, Tab, Sniff, and Squeak Hide-and-Seek!, Houghton Mifflin Harcourt (New York, NY), 2009.

Ollie's Easter Eggs, Houghton Mifflin (Boston, MA), 2009.

Ollie's Halloween, Houghton Mifflin (Boston, MA), 2010.

ILLUSTRATOR

Nathan Zimelman, *The Star of Melvin,* Macmillan (New York, NY), 1987.

Barbara Brenner, *The Boy Who Loved to Draw: Benjamin West,* Houghton Mifflin (Boston, MA), 1998.

Joy Cowley, *The Rusty, Trusty Tractor,* Boyds Mills Press (Mankato, MN), 1999.

Alice Schertle, *A Very Hairy Bear,* Harcourt (San Diego, CA), 2004.

Corey Rosen Schwartz and Tali Klein, *Hop! Plop!,* Walker (New York, NY), 2006.

OTHER

The Writing Process, Stronetrow Studio, 1990.

Sidelights

Since his debut in 1983, author and illustrator Olivier Dunrea has created a steady stream of picture books, including concept books, stories of family life—modern and ancient—and stories about artists. Many of Dunrea's picture books testify to his love of animals and his interest in the archaeology and folklore of the British Isles, and several—including *Ravena, The Trow-Wife's Treasure,* and *Bear Noel*—take place in a similar land of Dunrea's own creation: the mythic island of Moel Eyris. "I don't write books or make pictures for children," Dunrea once told *SATA*. "I make them for myself. It just so happens that children like what I do as much as I do!"

Dunrea was born in Virginia Beach, Virginia, in 1953, and grew up in a busy household full of siblings and pets, where storytelling was an important entertainment. "As a child my major fascination was with farm animals and rocks," the author/illustrator once explained. "Most of my time was spent either taking care of livestock on our homestead or drawing them and making up stories about them. Chickens, geese, and pigs are my favorites." In addition to drawing, Dunrea also learned to sculpt animals out of clay, a hobby he has continued into adulthood, with increasing sophistication. Several of his books for children, including the chapter book *Hanne's Quest,* reflect the author/illustrator's love of farmyard creatures.

Encouraged by adults who recognized his talent and creativity, Dunrea became the first member of his family to attend college, and he earned a master of arts degree in theater arts and music. For five years, he worked as a professional actor, singer, and dancer, and also designed stage sets and costumes. He was inspired to begin his career in children's books during the late 1970s, when he made several trips to Scotland, the Orkney Islands, and the Outer Hebrides islands. There he researched—including sketching, painting, and photographing—ancient monuments. As Dunrea later recalled, "the world seems so very complicated—to both chil-

Olivier Dunrea treats readers to a visit within his mythical kingdom of Moel Eyris in his original picture book **The Trow-Wife's Treasure.** (Copyright ©
1998 by Olivier Dunrea. Used by permission of the author.)

dren and adults alike. My fascination is with the ancient past, when things were more mysterious, more magical, and more permanent. Therefore, my favorite kind of stories to write and illustrate usually center around my own characters that I've created from my imagination. They live in a prehistoric, stony setting."

In early books such as *Ravena, Mogwogs on the March!, Deep down Underground,* and *The Trow-Wife's Treasure* Dunrea demonstrates his interest in archaeology and folklore, setting these stories in an unique world of his own creation called Moel Eyris. *Ravena* tells the story of a nonconformist banshee, a female spirit common to Scottish folklore, that searches for a new home, while a group of gnomes going on a hike are the focus of *Mogwogs on the March!* Noting Dunrea's pastel illustrations for *Ravena,* which are contained with frames of stones, a *Publishers Weekly* contributor wrote that they "convey the atmosphere of the locale," while

School Library Journal critic Hayden E. Atwood deemed the story's artwork "superior." In *Publishers Weekly* Jean F. Mercier found the brightly attired gnomes in *Mogwogs on the March!* to be "beguiling."

A concept book, *Deep down Underground* teaches counting by following the trail of a mole through its underground passageways. Critics praised the work for its art as well as for Dunrea's rhyming, alliterative, and onomatopoetic text. A *Publishers Weekly* reviewer pointed out the book's "unusual theme and lovely art," while *Horn Book* critic Ellen Fader described the work as "out of the ordinary and intriguing." *Deep down Underground* is a "celebration of nature, a delightful puzzle, and an invitation to look sharply at the small wonders around us," concluded Anna Biagioni Hart in her review of Dunrea's story for *School Library Journal.*

In *The Trow-Wife's Treasure* Dunrea uses Scots dialect to recount how a farmer named Bracken van Eyck helps a troll-like woman find her missing child after the infant is blown away by a gust of wind. Although *Horn Book* reviewer Nancy Vasilakis noted that the plot appears to tell a "simple story of kindness rewarded," she added that the illustrations in Dunrea's "arresting book suggest something deeper and more mystical." *Booklist* critic Helen Rosenberg remarked on the "detailed and striking" artwork in the book and called *The Trow-Wife's Treasure* a "satisfying tale, with true Scottish flavor."

In the nonfiction picture book *Skara Brae: The Story of a Prehistoric Village* Dunrea reveals to young readers a glimpse of prehistoric life in Skara Brae, an ancient community whose vestiges have been discovered in the Orkney Islands, north of Scotland. Among Dunrea's many pen-and-ink drawings are seascapes, architectural diagrams and site plans, and imagined scenes of village life. Writing in the *Bulletin of the Center for Children's Books,* Zena Sutherland praised the text as "well written and organized," adding that "graceful illustrations elaborate significantly on an inherently interesting subject." *Horn Book* critic Ann A. Flowers wrote that Dunrea's text "gives a clear description of the settlers' primitive way of life" and that his "illustrations are fascinating." "Children and adults are sure to be intrigued," Marguerite F. Raybould asserted in a *School Library Journal* review of *Skara Brae.*

Readers have continued to return with Dunrea to Moel Eyris in several other books. In *Bear Noel* a polar bear takes on the role of Santa Claus to the creatures of the north woods. As a gentle snow falls, the bear presents a gift to the many animals of the area: a tree decorated with seeds, nuts, and berries. Praising the book as a "quiet" tale, *Booklist* contributor GraceAnne A. DeCandido added that in his lush opaque watercolor artwork Dunrea "beautifully creates the effect of falling snow." By using a restrained palette of earth tones highlighted by a warm red, he imbues the book with "a celebratory feel," the critic continued. A *Publishers Weekly* reviewer wrote that the book's "gorgeous, lifelike landscapes . . . exude a quiet, satisfying beauty," while in *School Library Journey* a contributor announced that "the paintings area the best part" of *Bear Noel.* In addition to praising the art in her *New York Times Book Review* article, Karen Leggett called *Bear Noel* "as simple, complex and elegant a story as each single snowflake."

Another winter-themed tale, *It's Snowing!,* also showcases Dunrea's gouache paintings to good effect. In the story, a sleeping bear cub is awakened by Mama Bear's song honoring the first snowflakes of the winter season. In *Old Bear and His Cub* a bear cub's relationship with his father is Dunrea's focus, producing "a winter story to be savored by all," according to *School Library Journal* reviewer Sara Lissa Paulson. Both Little Cub and Old Bear are spending a winter day together, and while the younger bear refuses to finish his porridge or snug up his woolen scarf or take his nap unless his father in-

sists, the caring is shown to extend both ways when Old Bear's sneezing and coughing draw his son's parent-like concern later in the day. "A beautifully crafted story for beginning readers," according to *Booklist* contributor Carolyn Phelan, *Old Bear and His Cub* pairs a text containing "simple sentences and repeated phrases" with "beguiling pencil-and-gouache" art that captures the bears and their world with "simplicity, sensitivity, and restraint." Paulson also praised *Old Bear and His Cub* as "elegant" and "innovative," while in *Horn Book* Roger Sutton wrote that Dunrea's "bedtime-friendly text" engages young imaginations in its depiction of a "loving battle of wills."

Dunrea focuses on the very young reader in many of his picture-book tales. Small in size and designed for toddler reading, his "Gossie and Friends" board books first appeared in 2001 with *Gossie.* The series was inspired by a flock of Canada geese that flew over Dunrea's studio one day while he was working. "A pair of red rubber toy boots sat on my bookshelf for some strange reason," he added on his home page. "As I sketched goslings I started drawing them wearing red rubber boots. And that is how the idea for Gossie and her 'bright red boots' came to life."

In *Gossie* Dunrea's foolish but loveable goosling decides to share her love of fashionable shoes with her friend Gertie, and the two ducklings return in *Gossie and Gertie.* A *Publishers Weekly* contributor wrote of this second story that the author/illustrator "imbues both goslings with distinctive, endearing personalities and chronicles experiences every preschooler can recognize." Noting that Dunrea's tales are "as unassuming

Dunrea tells a poignant multigenerational story in his self-illustrated picture book **Old Bear and His Cub.** (Copyright © 2010 by Olivier Dunrea. Used by permission of Philomel Books, a division of Penguin Young Readers Group, a member of Penguin Group (USA) Inc., 375 Hudson St., New York, NY 10014. All rights reserved.)

yet satisfying as the art that illustrates them," Carolyn Phelan predicted in *Booklist* that, with their use of primary colors, repetitive texts, simple stories, and a dash of rhyme, both *Gossie* and *Gossie and Gertie* will be equally entertaining to toddlers and older preschool children.

Other characters are introduced in *Peedie*, *BooBoo*, and *Ollie*. In *Ollie* readers meet a stubborn little gosling who takes his time hatching from his egg. Ollie continues forge his own path in *Ollie the Stomper*, which finds the gosling enjoying some colorful new boots. In *BooBoo* a blue gosling eats anything that crosses her path, while *Peedie* introduces a yellow gosling who forgets everything. *School Library Journal* contributor Gay Lynn Van Vleck wrote that Dunrea's small-sized picture books are a "perfect match of simple sentence and spare but precious" pen-and-ink and watercolor art, while other critics praised the use of a large font and uncluttered artwork. A *Publishers Weekly* reviewer dubbed several of the volumes "winsome," while in *School Library Journal* Marge Louch-Wouters wrote that "Dunrea's feathered characters have the look and feel of preschoolers rapt in their own discovery of the world."

Ollie returns in several other adventures, among them *Merry Christmas, Ollie*, *Ollie's Halloween*, and *Ollie's Easter Eggs*. In *Merry Christmas, Ollie* the gosling joins Gossie, Gertie, BooBoo, and Peedie as they wait up to see Father Christmas Goose. While the other youngsters eventually become distracted by other activities, Ollie remains steadfast and is rewarded with a special responsibility. The little gosling turns the tables during a hunt for colored eggs on the farm in *Ollie's Easter Eggs*, and the colorfully costumed goslings search the farm for candy and fun in *Ollie's Halloween*. "Remaining true to his uncomplicated watercolor style, Dunrea maintains and element of charm to Ollie's waiting," noted Joanna K. Fabicon in her *School Library Journal* review of *Merry Christmas, Ollie*, while Catherine Calegari predicted in the same periodical that Dunrea's "low-key story" in *Ollie's Halloween* "is a great addition to the 'Gossie and Friends' books and will work well in storytime."

In addition to his large-format picture books and his smaller "gosling" books for tiny hands, Dunrea has illustrated several texts by other authors, among them Barbara Brenner's picture-book biography of colonial American artist Benjamin West, titled *The Boy Who Loved to Draw*, and Joy Cowley's *The Rusty, Trusty Tractor*. For Brenner's book Dunrea created period paintings that "pay their respects to the art of the period but retain . . . a childlike puckishness," to quote a *Publishers Weekly* reviewer. According to Carolyn Phelan in *Booklist*, Dunrea's illustrations for *The Boy Who Loved to Draw* "present clear visual expressions of the activities and emotions related in the story." *Horn Book* critic Mary M. Burns declared the work a "handsome interpretation, faithful to its subject, lively to read, distinctively colonial in pictorial content, and cast in a well-designed format."

In *The Painter Who Loved Chickens* Dunrea opens a window into his own life. In the story, a painter loves fowl of all sorts. After halfheartedly painting other subjects, he finally gains acclaim by painting the animal he loves the most. The "unassuming text straightforwardly conveys his emotion-filled, clearly delineated story," praised a *Publishers Weekly* reviewer. Mary M. Burns wrote in *Horn Book* that the book is a "tribute to individual talent and dogged determination," while in *Booklist* Hazel Rochman dubbed *The Painter Who Loved Chickens* "a zany story" and "a joyful celebration of following your dreams."

Dunrea makes his home in the Catskill Mountains of New York State. His house, called Henwoodie, houses his studio and living quarters, as well as a gallery space. Dunrea shares his home with his partner, John, as well as with number of dogs, some of which the couple has rescued. On the *Henwoodie* Web site Dunrea offers advice for beginning wordsmiths: "As a writer it is important to write about the things and people you care about. Write from the heart. Pay close attention to the details—both in your writing and your illustrating. . . . Listen to your words. Let your ear tell you when something doesn't sound right."

Biographical and Critical Sources

PERIODICALS

Booklist, March 1, 1995, Hazel Rochman, review of *The Painter Who Loved Chickens*, p. 1247; April 15, 1998, Helen Rosenberg, review of *The Trow-Wife's Treasure*, pp. 1450-1451; September 15, 1999, Carolyn Phelan, review of *The Boy Who Loved to Draw: Benjamin West*, p. 262; September 1, 2000, GraceAnne A. De Candido, review of *Bear Noel*, p. 131; August, 2002, Carolyn Phelan, review of *Gossie*, p. 1970; November 15, 2002, Gillian Engberg, review of *It's Snowing!*, p. 609; October 1, 2003, Jennifer Locke, reviews of *Ollie* and *Ollie the Stomper*, both p. 326; August, 2004, Carolyn Phelan, reviews of *Boo Boo* and *Peedie*, both p. 1941; April 15, 2006, Jennifer Mattson, review of *Hop! Plop!*, p. 55; October 15, 2008, Carolyn Phelan, review of *Merry Christmas, Ollie!*, p. 46; January 1, 2010, Carolyn Phelan, review of *Ollie's Easter Eggs*, p. 96; November 1, 2010, Carolyn Phelan, review of *Old Bear and His Cub*, p. 53.

Bulletin of the Center for Children's Books, May, 1986, Zena Sutherland, review of *Skara Brae: The Story of a Prehistoric Village*, p. 164.

Horn Book, September-October, 1986, Ann A. Flowers, review of *Skara Brae*, p. 607; November-December, 1989, Ellen Fader, review of *Deep down Underground*, p. 757; July-August, 1995, Mary M. Burns, review of *The Painter Who Loved Chickens*, pp. 448-449; July-August, 1998, Nancy Vasilakis, review of *The Trow-Wife's Treasure*, pp. 471-472; September, 1999, Mary M. Burns, review of *The Boy Who Loved to Draw*, p. 622; September-October, 2002, Joanna Rudge Long,

Dunrea recalls his rural childhood in his self-illustrated picture book The Painter Who Loved Chickens. (Copyright © 1995 by Olivier Dunrea. Reprinted by permission of Farrar, Straus & Giroux, LLC.)

review of *It's Snowing!,* p. 550; January-February, 2003, Martha V. Parravano, review of *Gossie,* p. 55; March-April, 2006, Joanna Rudge Long, review of *Hanne's Quest,* p. 185; May-June, 2006, Kitty Flynn, review of *Hop! Plop!,* p. 303; November-December, 2008, Jennifer M. Brabander, review of *Merry Christmas, Ollie!,* p. 648; January-February, 2011, Roger Sutton, review of *Old Bear and His Cub,* p. 78.

Kirkus Reviews, June 15, 2002, review of *Gossie,* p. 879; July 1, 2003, review of *Ollie,* p. 909; July 15, 2004, review of *Boo Boo* and *Peedie,* p. 684; January 1, 2006, review of *Hanne's Quest,* p. 39; February 15, 2006, review of *Gossie and Friends,* p. 181; March 15, 2006, review of *Hop! Plop!,* p. 300.

New York Times Book Review, December 3, 2000, Karen Leggett, review of *Bear Noel.*

Publishers Weekly, November 9, 1984, review of *Ravena,* p. 65; March 22, 1985, review of *Fergus and Bridey,* p. 59; December 6, 1985, Jean F. Mercier, review of *Mogwogs on the March!,* p. 75; September 29, 1989, review of *Deep down Underground,* p. 67; March 13, 1995, review of *The Painter Who Loved Chickens,* p.

69; July 5, 1999, review of *The Boy Who Loved to Draw,* p. 70; September, 25, 2000, review of *Bear Noel,* p. 69; July 15, 2002, reviews of *Gossie* and *Gossie and Gertie,* both p. 72; October 21, 2002, review of *It's Snowing!,* p. 73; July 14, 2003, reviews of *Ollie,* and *Ollie the Stomper,* both p. 75; January 2, 2006, review of *Hanne's Quest,* p. 62; October 11, 2010, review of *Old Bear and His Cub,* p. 40.

School Library Journal, November, 1984, Hayden E. Atwood, review of *Ravena,* p. 106; May, 1986, Marguerite F. Raybould, review of *Skara Brae,* p. 90; September, 1989, Anna Biagioni Hart, review of *Deep down Underground,* p. 224; October, 1990, John Peters, review of *Eppie M. Says . . . ,* p. 90; October, 2000, review of *Bear Noel,* p. 59; September, 2002, Laurie von Mehren, review of *Gossie,* p. 189; October, 2002, Susan Pine, review of *It's Snowing!,* p. 103; July, 2003, Gay Lynn Van Vleck, review of *Ollie,* p. 95; October, 2004, Marge Loch-Wouters, reviews of *Boo Boo* and *Peedie,* both p. 112; February, 2006, Wendy Lukehart, review of *Hanne's Quest,* p. 96; May, 2006, Catherine Callegari, review of *Hop!*

Plop!, p. 103; October, 2008, Joanna K. Fabicon, review of *Merry Christmas, Ollie!,* p. 93; March, 2010, Laura Butler, review of *Ollie's Easter Eggs,* p. 117; November, 2010, Sara Lissa Paulson, review of *Old Bear and His Cub,* p. 68; December, 2010, Catherine Calegari, review of *Ollie's Halloween,* p. 82.

ONLINE

Macmillan Web site, http://us.macmillan.com/ (September 15, 2011), "Olivier Dunrea."

Olivier Dunrea Home Page, http://www.olivierdunrea.com (September 15, 2011).*

F-G

FLOOD, Bo
    See FLOOD, Nancy Bo

   *   *   *

FLOOD, Nancy Bo 1945-
   (Bo Flood)

Personal

Born September 24, 1945, in IL; daughter of Frank John (a teacher and coach) and Shirley (a homemaker) Bohac; married William L. Flood (a pediatrician), August, 1967; children: Megan, Michael, Elizabeth, Macey. *Education:* Beloit College, B.A. (cum laude), 1967; University of Minnesota—Twin Cities, Ph.D., 1970; University of London, postdoctoral study, 1971; Vermont College, M.F.A., 2007. *Hobbies and other interests:* Baking cookies, writing letters, walking.

Addresses

Home—Chinle, AZ. *E-mail*—wflood@hotmail.com.

Career

Writer, psychologist, and educator. Center for Retarded Children, Rolling Meadows, IL, teacher and therapist, 1968; University of Hawai'i—Manoa, Honolulu, assistant professor of psychology, 1971-72; University of Minnesota—Twin Cities, Minneapolis, assistant professor of psychology, 1972-74; Colorado Mountain College, Glenwood Springs, instructor in psychology, 1974-95; Northern Marianas College, Saipan, instructor in psychology, 1989-91, instructor and counselor in education, arts, and humanities, 1995-2001, director of programs for persons with disabilities, 1995-97; Community College of Samoa, Pago Pago, instructor, 1995; University of Guam, UOG Station, Mangilao, instructor, 1995-2001; Navajo Diné Community College, Tuba City, AZ, instructor, beginning 2001; Northern Arizona University, Flagstaff, distant education instructor, begin-

Nancy Bo Flood (Reproduced by permission.)

ning 2002; Kaplan University, instructor for online courses, beginning 2007. Sopris Mental Health Center, staff psychologist, 1974-81; private practitioner of child and family counseling, 1981-90. Presenter of writing and psychology workshops and lectures.

Member

International Reading Association (founding member of Saipan chapter), Society of Children's Book Writers and Illustrators, American Psychological Association, Colorado Authors League, Phi Beta Kappa.

Awards, Honors

Outstanding Teacher award, Northern Marianas College, 1990; HarperCollins Multicultural Children's Mentoring Program award, 1992; Outstanding Service Award, Colorado Mountain College, 1995; named Outstanding Literary Artist, Saipan Annual Governor's Art Awards, 1997; Colorado Authors' League Award, 2002, for "The Coconut Palm, the Tree of Life," 2006, for *One Hundred Coconuts and a Top Hat,* 2006, for "Puppets without Strings," 2011, for *Warriors in the Crossfire;* Society of Children's Book Writers and Illustrators Merit Award, 2006, for *One Hundred Coconuts and a Top Hat,* 2007, for "Girls Scouts Break out of Prison"; Harcourt scholarship, 2007; Notable Social Studies Trade Books for Young People, National Council for the Social Studies/Children's Book Council, 2007, for *The Navajo Year, Walk through Many Seasons;* Best Fiction for Young Adults designation, American Library Association, 2011, for *Warriors in the Crossfire.*

Writings

The Navajo Year, Walk through Many Seasons, illustrated by Billy Whitethorne, Salina Bookshelf (Flagstaff, AZ), 2006.

Sand to Stone and Back Again, illustrated with photographs by Tony Kuyper, Fulcrum Publishing (Golden, CO), 2009.

Warriors in the Crossfire, Front Street (Honesdale, PA), 2010.

UNDER NAME BO FLOOD

Working Together against World Hunger, Rosen Publishing (New York, NY), 1995.

(With Lida Lafferty) *Born Early: A Children's Story about Premature Birth,* Songbird Publishing (CO), 1995.

(Compiler) *From the Mouth of the Monster Eel: Stories from Micronesia,* Fulcrum Publishing (Golden, CO), 1996.

I'll Go to School, If . . ., Fairview Press (Minneapolis, MN), 1996.

(With Maureen Nuckols) *The Counseling Handbook: Practical Strategies to Help Children with Common Problems,* Center for Applied Psychology (Philadelphia, PA), 1998.

(Compiler, with Beret E. Strong and husband, William Flood) *Pacific Island Legends: Tales from Micronesia, Melanesia, Polynesia, and Australia* (with teacher's resource guide), Bess Press (Honolulu, HI), 1999.

(Compiler) *Marianas Island Legends: Myth and Magic* (includes teacher's resource guide and children's writing curriculum), Bess Press (Honolulu, HI), 2001.

(Compiler, with Beret E. Strong and husband, William Flood) *Micronesian Legends: History and Culture,* Bess Press (Honolulu, HI), 2001.

Also author of *My Homes and Places* (therapeutic game for counselors, teachers, and children), Kidsrights. Member of editorial board, *Northern Marianas College Electronic Journal of the Humanities;* Member of editorial board and contributor, *Proa* newsletter, Northern Marianas College. Contributor to scientific books, including *Brain Mechanisms of Behavior in Lower Vertebrates,* edited by P. Taming, Cambridge University Press (London, England), 1981. Contributor of articles and short stories to children's magazines, including *Boy's Life, Cricket, Falcon, Hopscotch, New Moon, Pockets, Quest, Storytelling,* and *Teaching Tolerance;* contributor to professional journals, including *Physiology and Behavior* and *Psychological Reports.*

Sidelights

A respected psychologist and educator, Nancy Bo Flood is also the author of *Warriors in the Crossfire,* a critically acclaimed work of historical fiction that is set on the island of Saipan during World War II. Flood, a child and family counselor who has lived and worked in Malawi, Japan, and Haiti, among other places, became interested in writing fiction after watching her patients work through trauma using play therapy. "I observed the power of story and realized that is what we do, as children and as adults," she told *Cynsations* online interviewer Cynthia Leitich Smith. "In every culture, in many different ways—through dance, sand painting, song, chants, movies, plays, paintings—and books. Story is a powerful way to build compassion and bridge understanding between cultures and between generations. Story has the power to entertain but more profoundly, to teach and to heal."

In *Warriors in the Crossfire* Flood focuses on two boys whose friendship is tested under dire circumstances. Narrated by Joseph, the son of a village chief on Saipan, the novel depicts his relationship with Kento, whose father serves as an administrator for the occupying Japanese forces. When U.S. troops arrive in the summer of 1944, fierce fighting ensues and Joseph must lead his family to safety using the survival secrets he shared with Kento. "Conflicted yet determined, Joseph is an ideal mix for a story of heroism," observed *Booklist* critic Ian Chipman, while Riva Pollard described Joseph in *School Library Journal* as "an engaging and three-dimensional character." According to a critic in *Publishers Weekly,* "Flood's concise and passionate fictionalized account raises myriad complicated questions about friendship, family, and honor." A number of reviewers cited Flood's depiction of the tragedy of war as a strength of *Warriors in the Crossfire,* a *Kirkus Reviews* writer noting that her account of Japanese civilians committing suicide by leaping off of cliffs into the sea is "so horrifying that this small tale will long linger."

In her work as a writer, Flood has also compiled several collections of folklore from the Pacific Islands, among them *From the Mouth of the Monster Eel: Stories from Micronesia* and *Marianas Island Legends: Myth and Magic,* the latter a collaboration with Beret E. Strong and her own husband, pediatrician William

Cover of Flood's young-adult novel Warriors in the Crossfire, *which focuses on a young teen's heroism while living on the island of Saipan during World War II.* (Jacket photograph © 2010 by JupiterImages Corporation. Copyright © 2010 by Nancy Bo Flood. Reproduced with permission of Front St., an imprint of Boyds Mills Press.)

Flood. "People living in other places as part of other cultures fascinate me. I continue to discover that we are different in how we do daily life, but we are the same in how we feel inside," she remarked in an interview on the *Salina Bookshelf* Web log.

Biographical and Critical Sources

PERIODICALS

Booklist, April 15, 2010, Ian Chipman, review of *Warriors in the Crossfire,* p. 57.
Bulletin of the Center for Children's Books, April, 2010, Elizabeth Bush, review of *Warriors in the Crossfire,* p. 335.
Independent Publisher, August 3, 1999, Hallie Lowe, review of *Pacific Island Legends: Tales from Micronesia, Melanesia, Polynesia, and Australia.*
Kirkus Reviews, March 1, 2010, review of *Warriors in the Crossfire.*

Publishers Weekly, April 12, 2010, review of *Warriors in the Crossfire,* p. 52.
School Library Journal, October, 2006, S.K. Joiner, review of *The Navajo Year, Walk through Many Seasons,* p. 134; May, 2010, Riva Pollard, review of *Warriors in the Crossfire,* p. 112.

ONLINE

Cynsations Web log, http://cynleitichsmith.livejournal.com/ (August 31, 2009), Cynthia Leitich Smith, interview with Flood.
Nancy Bo Flood Home Page, http://www.nancyboflood. com (August 1, 2011).
Salina Bookshelf Web log, http://www.salinabookshelf. com/ (August 1, 2011), "Nancy Bo Flood."*

*   *   *

GRAB, Daphne 1971-

Personal

Born 1971, in Rhinebeck, NY; mother an English teacher; married; children: two. *Education:* Bard College, degree (history), 1993; New School University, M.F.A. (writing for children), 2006.

Addresses

Home—New York, NY. *E-mail*—daphnegrab@yahoo. com.

Career

Author. Worked variously as a social worker and waitress. Teacher of English as a second language in China for two years; teacher of high-school history in Los Angeles, CA.

Writings

Alive and Well in Prague, NY, Laura Geringer Books (New York, NY), 2008.

Sidelights

In her first novel, *Alive and Well in Prague, NY,* Daphne Grab describes the experiences of an urban teen whose family relocates from upscale Manhattan to a small upstate community after her artist father is diagnosed with a serious illness. Grab began the work while pursuing an advanced degree in writing at New York City's New School University. Several aspects of the novel are drawn from the author's own life, including the small-town setting and family worries over a disabling medical condition. Grab's own father suffered from ALS, and her fictional heroine deals with similar symptoms while caring for a father with Parkinson's disease.

Matisse Osgood is the central character in *Alive and Well in Prague, NY*, and the story revolves around her unwillingness to accept the situation in which she finds herself following her family's move north. While attempting to navigate the alien terrain of her new rural home town, the sixteen year old is also forced to create certain fictions to dispel the rumors that are passing among her former classmates back in the city. Ultimately, the change of setting forces Matisse to come to terms with both her father's illness and her attitudes toward the people whose friendship she once valued so highly. Reviewing *Alive and Well in Prague, NY* in *Kirkus Reviews*, a critic cited Grab's ability to craft an "excellent narrative voice" while also recommending the "touching emotional connection and playful rural activities" that enrich Matisse's story. "The heroine's strong, clear voice and heartbreaking vulnerability" will attract fans of "character-driven fiction," predicted *Booklist* contributor Anne O'Malley, while in *Publishers Weekly* a critic recommended *Alive and Well in Prague, NY* as a "sympathetic portrayal [that] may comfort those affected by sickness and loss."

Biographical and Critical Sources

PERIODICALS

Booklist, May 15, 2008, Anne O'Malley, review of *Alive and Well in Prague, NY*, p. 38.
Kirkus Reviews, May 1, 2008, review of *Alive and Well in Prague, NY*.
Kliatt, May 1, 2008, Claire Rosser, review of *Alive and Well in Prague, NY*, p. 10.
Publishers Weekly, May 26, 2008, review of *Alive and Well in Prague, NY*, p. 67.
School Library Journal, June 1, 2008, Debra Banna, review of *Alive and Well in Prague, NY*, p. 142.
Voice of Youth Advocates, August 1, 2008, Kathleen Beck, review of *Alive and Well in Prague, NY*, p. 242.

ONLINE

Daphne Grab Home Page, http://www.daphnegrab.com (September 15, 2011).
HarperCollins Web site, http://www.harpercollins.com/ (March 11, 2009), "Daphne Grab."*

                    *   *   *

GRUNER, Jessica

Personal

Female. *Education:* College degree.

Addresses

Home—San Francisco, CA.

Career

Writer. Taught high-school English for four years in San Francisco, CA; owner of a clothing boutique.

Writings

"EMILY THE STRANGE" NOVEL SERIES; WITH ROB REGER

The Lost Days, illustrated by Reger and Buzz Parker, Harper (New York, NY), 2009.
Stranger and Stranger, illustrated by Reger and Buzz Parker, Harper (New York, NY), 2010.
Dark Times, illustrated by Reger and Buzz Parker, Harper (New York, NY), 2010.
Piece of Mind, illustrated by Reger and Buzz Parker, Harper (New York, NY), 2011.

Coauthor, with Reger, of "Emily the Strange" comic books, Dark Horse Comics, 2007-08.

Sidelights

A former high-school English teacher, San Francisco-based writer Jessica Gruner now teams up with author/illustrator Rob Reger to promote Reger's character creation Emily the Strange. Resembling television character Morticia Adams with her long, straight, black hair, dour outlook, and penchant for black, thirteen-year-old Emily the Strange first appeared on stickers and T-shirts in the early 1990s. Her growing popularity as a counterculture Goth icon eventually inspired Reger to craft Emily's back story. From her adoption as a symbol of skater culture, in 2007 Emily migrated to comic books published by Oregon-based Dark Horse Comics. With Gruner's talent as a writer, Emily the Strange made the jump to full-fledged fictional heroine when she was cast in the illustrated middle-grade novel *The Lost Days* and its sequels. Lists are Emily's forte, and each "Emily the Strange" book functions as a diary in which thirteen-item lists punctuate her wry narrative, along with black, white, and red cartoon art by Reger and Buzz Parker.

Gruner started working with Reger to develop the "Emily the Strange" character in at the suggestion of a mutual friend who knew that Gruner had developed a similar Goth character. She began by helping to develop content for the Emily the Strange Web site, which content included Emily's characteristic lists. Gruner was enthusiastic about joining the Emily the Strange project because she views Emily as an inspiration for girls breaking out on their own as individuals. The iconic teen's intelligence and interest in science (Emily is an inventor), her creativity, and her self-reliance (she prefers the company of her four cats and excels at the slingshot) allow her to break from the "typical teen" category while Emily's interests in rock music, skateboarding, and playing the guitar allow a broad base of teen and preteen readers to identify with her.

When readers first meet Emily in *The Lost Days,* they know more about her than she knows about herself; a bout of amnesia has left her wandering, alone and confused, in a small town named Blackrock, with only her slingshot and her diary to help her sort out her past. While noting that the story's "plot perambulations" make readers as confused as amnesiac Emily, Ian Chipman added in his *Booklist* review that in *The Lost Days* the girl's "lighthearted but darkly hued creativity [is] on display." Emily's "sarcastic, nerdy individualism . . . will make readers want to spend more time with her," predicted a *Publishers Weekly* contributor, while *School Library Journal* critic Suanne Roush asserted that Gruner's "highly enjoyable read . . . will appeal to readers new to the series and Emily fans alike."

Stranger and Stranger chronicles Emily's encounter with an identical twin, courtesy of a copy machine run amok. While sorting out the confusion caused by this twin, the teen also finds time to perfect several scientific inventions, craft some new golems, and commune with her beloved cats. In *Dark Times* Emily shares her home-school curricula, a range of classes that encompasses everything from spy photography and time travel to germ theory and a study of cats throughout history. *Stranger and Stranger* "dresses up teen identity issues in midnight-black humor," wrote Chipman, while in *School Library Journal* Mara Alpert characterized Reger and Gruner's Goth iconoclast as an "evil genius and skateboarder extraordinaire" whose second novel-length outing is narrated, diary style, "with demented wit and great relish."

Biographical and Critical Sources

PERIODICALS

Booklist, May 1, 2009, Ian Chipman, review of *The Lost Days,* p. 38; January 1, 2010, Ian Chipman, review of *Stranger and Stranger,* p. 86.
Publishers Weekly, June 1, 2009, review of *The Lost Days,* p. 47.
School Library Journal, June, 2009, Suanne Roush, review of *The Lost Days,* p. 136; January, 2010, Mara Alpert, review of *Stranger and Stranger,* p. 112.
Voice of Youth Advocates, August, 2010, Shari Fesko, review of *Stranger and Stranger,* p. 272.

ONLINE

Emily the Strange Home Page, http://www.emilystrange.com/ (September 15, 2011).
Fanpop Web site, http://www.fanpop.com/ (May 29, 2008), video interview with Gruner.
HarperCollins Web site, http://www.harpercollins.com/ (July 12, 2011), "Jessica Gruner."*

GUARNACCIA, Steven

Personal

Married Susan Hochbaum (a graphic designer). *Education:* Brown University, degree, 1974; attended Rhode Island School of Design.

Addresses

Home—Montclair, NJ. *Office*—Parsons the New School for Design, 66 5th Ave., Office 806A, New York, NY 10011. *Agent*—Bernstein & Andriulli, 58 W. 40th St., 6th Fl., New York, NY 10018; info@ba-reps.com. *E-mail*—sguarnaccia@hotmail.com; guarnacs@new school.edu.

Career

Illustrator, designer, and educator. Studio Guarnaccia, owner, beginning 1977; *New York Times,* New York, NY, art director of op-ed page, 2001-04; Parsons the New School for Design, New York, NY, director of illustration program and associate professor of illustration, beginning 2005. School of Visual Arts, New York, NY, founding faculty of M.F.A. design program; illustrator of greeting cards for Museum of Modern Art, of watches for Swatch, and of murals for Disney Cruise Lines. Member of illustration juries for American Illustration, Society of Illustrators, and American Institute of Graphic Arts; chair of Objects of Design jury, American Institute of Graphic Artists. *Exhibitions:* Work included in solo shows in New York, NY; Milan, Italy; and Toronto, Ontario, Canada. Work included in group show at Museum of Modern Art, New York, NY.

Member

Alliance Graphique Internationale, American Institute of Graphic Arts.

Awards, Honors

Numerous honors from American Institute of Graphic Artists, New York Art Directors Club, Society of Publication Designers, and other professional organizations; Hallmark fellow, Aspen Design Conference.

Writings

(With Steven Heller) *School Days,* Abbeville Press (New York, NY), 1992.
(With Steven Heller) *Designing for Children,* Watson-Guptill (New York, NY), 1994.
(With Susan Hochbaum) *Black and White,* Chronicle Books (San Francisco, CA), 2002.

SELF-ILLUSTRATED

Skeleton Closet: A Spooky Pop-up Book, Hyperion Books for Children (New York, NY), 1995.

(Reteller) *Goldilocks and the Three Bears: A Tale Moderne,* Abrams Books (New York, NY), 2000.

(Reteller) *The Three Little Pigs: An Architectural Tale,* Abrams Books (New York, NY), 2010.

ILLUSTRATOR

Alfa-Betty Olsen and Marshall Efron, *Sin City Fables,* A & W Publishers (New York, NY), 1981.

Gardner McFall, *Jonathan's Cloud,* Harper & Row (New York, NY), 1986.

William Irvine, *Madam I'm Adam and Other Palindromes,* Scribner's (New York, NY), 1987.

Brian Gleeson, *Anansi,* Picture Book Studio (Saxonville, MA), 1991, Rabbit Ears Books (South Norwalk, CT), 2006.

William Irvine, *If I Had a Hi-fi and Other Palindromes,* Laurel (New York, NY), 1992.

Gardner McFall, *Naming the Animals,* Viking (New York, NY), 1994.

Bob Sloan, *A Stiff Drink and a Close Shave,* Chronicle Books (San Francisco, CA), 1995.

Bob Sloan, *Hi-fi's and Hi-balls: The Golden Age of the American Bachelor,* Chronicle Books (San Francisco, CA), 1997.

Brothers, Running Press (Philadelphia, PA), 1998.

Paola Antonelli, *Achille Castiglioni,* Corraini (Mantova, Italy), 2000.

Carl Meister, *Busy, Busy City Street,* Viking (New York, NY), 2000.

Beverly Mills and Alicia Ross, *Cheap, Fast, Good!: A Cookbook,* Workman Publishing (New York, NY), 2005.

Atony Shugaar, *I Lie for a Living: Greatest Spies of All Time,* National Geographic (Washington, DC), 2006.

Contributor to periodicals.

Sidelights

Steven Guarnaccia, an artist and world-renowned director of the illustration program at Parsons the New School for Design, has provided the artwork for a number of children's books, among them *The Three Little Pigs: An Architectural Tale,* his own contemporary retelling of a familiar folktale. Guarnaccia's illustrations have also appeared in magazines as well as several books for adult readers, and he has designed murals for Disney Cruise Lines, greeting cards for New York City's Museum of Modern Art, and watches for Swatch. A former art director for the *New York Times,* Guarnaccia has received honors for his work from such esteemed institutions as the American Institute of Graphic Arts and the New York Art Directors Club.

Guarnaccia's *Goldilocks and the Three Bears: A Tale Moderne* presents a stylish take on an old favorite. After the bears return to their split-level house, which is tastefully decorated with furnishings by celebrated designers Arne Jacobsen, George Nelson, Eva Zeisel, and Charles and Ray Eames, they discover a certain blonde intruder attempting a swift escape out a window.

Steven Guarnaccia pairs a unique retelling of a beloved story in his picture book The Three Little Pigs: An Architectural Tale. (Illustration copyright © 2010 by Steven Guarnaccia. Reproduced with permission of Abrams Books for Young Readers, an imprint of ABRAMS. All rights reserved.)

Booklist reviewer Gillian Engberg noted that "the story is illustrated in a spare, angled style derivative of modern art," and a *Publishers Weekly* critic wrote that Guarnaccia's "generous, fluid line and 1930s cartoon aesthetic pump up the nostalgic feel."

In *The Three Little Pigs* Guarnaccia pays homage to famed architects Frank Gehry, Phillip Johnson, and Frank Lloyd Wright at the same time that his porcine protagonists attempt to thwart a tough, leather-jacketed wolf. Guarnaccia's illustrations are quirky and stylish, incorporating notable 20th-and 21st-century architecture and interior design elements," a contributor stated in *Kirkus Reviews*. Introducing young readers to the fields of design and architecture is "a sophisticated idea," Angela Redfern commented in *School Librarian*, "but it works brilliantly" in *The Three Little Pigs*.

In addition to his self-illustrated titles, Guarnaccia has created art for stories by other authors. *Naming the Animals*, a creation tale by Gardner McFall, finds the biblical Adam choosing names for the world's creatures by studying their unique characteristics. A *Publishers Weekly* critic applauded Guarnaccia's contributions to this work, writing that his "buoyant style [is] recognizable by its vivid colors and zigzaggy, contemporary lines." In Carl Meister's *Busy, Busy City Street*, a work told in verse, young readers are introduced to the sights and sounds of an urban environment. Here the illustrator's "palette of olive, rust and gold contrasts with tight angles and solid black details," according to a contributor in *Publishers Weekly*, "and the atmosphere is charged."

Biographical and Critical Sources

PERIODICALS

Booklist, May 15, 2000, Gillian Engberg, review of *Goldilocks and the Three Bears: A Tale Moderne*, p. 1755.

Kirkus Reviews, May 1, 2010, review of *The Three Little Pigs: An Architectural Tale.*

Library Journal, June 15, 2006, Daniel K. Blewett, review of *Lie for a Living: Greatest Spies of All Time*, p. 85.

New York Times, March 12, 2000, Elaine Louie, review of *Goldilocks and the Three Bears*, p. 3.

Print, November-December, 1994, Jane Clark Chermayeff, review of *Designing for Children*, p. 141; May, 2000, Joyce Rutter Kaye, review of *Goldilocks and the Three Bears*, p. 15; May-June, 2002, Andrea Moed, review of *Black and White*, p. 16.

Publishers Weekly, December 6, 1993, review of *Naming the Animals*, p. 72; April 17, 2000, review of *Goldilocks and the Three Bears*, p. 79; August 21, 2000, review of *Busy, Busy City Street*, p. 72; June 14, 2010, review of *The Three Little Pigs*, p. 50.

School Librarian, autumn, 2010, Angela Redfern, review of *The Three Little Pigs*, p. 164.

School Library Journal, April, 2000, Julie Cummins, review of *Goldilocks and the Three Bears*, p. 149; February, 2001, Marianne Saccardi, review of *Busy, Busy City Street*, p. 104.

ONLINE

Parsons the New School for Design Web site, http://www.newschool.edu/ (August 1, 2011), "Steven Guarnaccia."

Steven Guarnaccia Home Page, http://stevenguarnaccia.com (August 1, 2011).*

H

HAMILTON, Meredith

Personal

Daughter of university professors. *Education:* Brown University, A.B. (comparative literature); attended Parson's School of Design; School of Visual Arts, M.F.A.

Addresses

Home—Brooklyn, NY. *E-mail*—meredith@meredith hamilton.com.

Career

Illustrator and art director. Universal Press Syndicate, assistant art director, 1983-86; *Discover* magazine, assistant art director, 1985-87; *Newsweek* magazine, art director of information graphics and associate editor, 1987-93; freelance illustrator, beginning 1998.

Member

Graphic Artists Guild.

Awards, Honors

Parent's Choice Award, 2003, for *A Child's Introduction to Poetry* by Michael Driscoll; Parent's Choice Award, and Teachers' Choice Award, both 2004, both for *A Child's Introduction to the Night Sky* by Driscoll; Gold Moonbeam Award, c. 2008, for *A Child's Introduction to the Environment* by Driscoll.

Illustrator

FOR CHILDREN

Robert Levine, *The Story of the Orchestra: Listen While You Learn about the Instruments, the Music, and the Composers Who Wrote the Music* (includes audio CD), Black Dog & Leventhal (New York, NY), 2001.

Michael Driscoll, *A Child's Introduction to Poetry: Listen While You Learn about the Magic Words That Have Moved Mountains, Won Battles, and Made Us Laugh and Cry* (includes audio CD), Black Dog & Leventhal (New York, NY), 2003.

Michael Driscoll, *A Child's Introduction to the Night Sky: The Story of the Stars, Planets, and Constellations and How You Can Find Them in the Sky,* Black Dog & Leventhal (New York, NY), 2004.

Laura Lee, *A Child's Introduction to Ballet: The Stories, Music, and Magic of Classical Dance* (includes audio CD), Black Dog & Leventhal (New York, NY), 2007.

They're Poets and They Know It!: A Collection of Thirty Timeless Poems, Scholastic (New York, NY), 2007.

Michael Driscoll and Dennis Driscoll, *A Child's Introduction to the Environment: The Air, Earth, and Sea around Us—Plus Experiments, Projects, and Activities You Can Do to Help Our Planet!,* Black Dog & Leventhal (New York, NY), 2008.

Heather Alexander, *A Child's Introduction to the World: Geography, Cultures, and People: From the Grand Canyon to the Great Wall of China,* Black Dog & Leventhal (New York, NY), 2010.

Heather Alexander, *A Child's Introduction to Greek Mythology: The Stories of the Gods, Goddesses, Heroes, Monsters, and Other Mythical Creatures,* Black Dog & Leventhal (New York, NY), 2011.

OTHER

Helen Gustafson, *The Green Tea User's Manual,* Clarkson Potter (New York, NY), 2001.

Carole Walter, *Great Coffee Cakes, Sticky Buns, Muffins, and More: 200 Anytime Treats and Special Sweets for Morning to Midnight,* Clarkson Potter (New York, NY), 2007.

Contributor to books, including *The Pilates Body* and *Your Ultimate Pilates Body,* both Broadway Books; *In Italiano,* McGraw Hill; *En Français,* McGraw Hill; *Stylish One-Dish Dinners,* Doubleday; *The Menopause Cookbook,* Norton; *The Olive and the Caper,* Workman;

and *Development Girl,* Broadway Books. Contributor to periodicals, including the *New York Times* and *Town & Country.*

Sidelights

Meredith Hamilton, a former art director for *Newsweek* magazine, has served as the illustrator for a number of nonfiction works for children. Hamilton's works range from narrative drawings that illustrate myths and fairy tales to humorous illustrations that communicate sophisticated scientific concepts such as the rotation of the planets and deforestation. She often inserts wry portraits of her children in her loose ink-and-watercolor drawings, as well as sprinkling her images with obscure animals and historical details. In the pages of one of Hamilton's illustration projects, Robert Levine's *The Story of the Orchestra: Listen While You Learn about the Instruments, the Music, and the Composers Who Wrote the Music,* readers are introduced to such musical giants as Johann Sebastian Bach, Maurice Ravel, and Antonio Vivaldi as well as to the wide variety of instruments that are played during an orchestral performance. "Text and images are extremely lively: the drawings are whimsical and often amusing," remarked GraceAnne A. DeCandido in her *Booklist* review of the book.

Hamilton's illustration projects also include Michael Driscoll's *A Child's Introduction to Poetry: Listen While You Learn about the Magic Words That Have Moved Mountains, Won Battles, and Made Us Laugh and Cry,* which provides an overview of poetic forms and offers brief profiles of William Shakespeare, Maya Angelou, and other versifying luminaries. Here her "warm cartoon watercolors" garnered praise from *School Library Journal* reviewer Donna Cardon. Driscoll explores the mysteries of the universe in *A Child's Introduction to the Night Sky: The Story of the Stars, Planets, and Constellations and How You Can Find Them in the Sky,* which features "a mix of cartoon vignettes [and] elaborately detailed illustrations of constellations," according to John Peters in *Booklist.*

A Child's Introduction to Ballet: The Stories, Music, and Magic of Classical Dance, a work by Laura Lee, contains Hamilton's "colorful illustrations of scenes" drawn from *Swan Lake, The Rite of Spring,* and other famous ballets, as Carol Schene noted in *School Library Journal.* The father-and-son team of Michael Driscoll and Dennis Driscoll explores humankind's relationship to the natural world in the award-winning *A Child's Introduction to the Environment: The Air, Earth, and Sea around Us—Plus Experiments, Projects, and Activities You Can Do to Help Our Planet!* Here "the conversational writing style, [Hamilton's] plentiful watercolor illustrations, and varied page layouts add reader appeal," observed Kathy Piehl in her review of this book for *School Library Journal.*

Biographical and Critical Sources

PERIODICALS

Booklist, December 15, 2001, GraceAnne A. DeCandido, review of *The Story of the Orchestra: Listen While You Learn about the Instruments, the Music, and the Composers Who Wrote the Music,* p. 726; November 15, 2003, Hazel Rochman, review of *A Child's Introduction to Poetry: Listen While You Learn about the Magic Words That Have Moved Mountains, Won Battles, and Made Us Laugh and Cry,* p. 595.

Children's Bookwatch, July, 2010, review of *A Child's Introduction to the World: Geography, Cultures, and People: From the Grand Canyon to the Great Wall of China.*

Kirkus Reviews, April 15, 2010, review of *A Child's Introduction to the World.*

Publishers Weekly, March 10, 2008, review of *A Child's Introduction to the Environment: The Air, Earth, and Sea around Us—Plus Experiments, Projects, and Activities You Can Do to Help Our Planet!,* p. 83.

School Library Journal, September, 2001, Susan Shaver, review of *The Story of the Orchestra,* p. 249; January, 2004, Donna Cardon, review of *A Child's Introduction to Poetry,* p. 146; September, 2004, John Peters, review of *A Child's Introduction to the Night Sky: The Story of the Stars, Planets, and Constellations and How You Can Find Them in the Sky,* p. 226; August, 2007, Carol Schene, review of *A Child's Introduction to Ballet: The Stories, Music, and Magic of Classical Dance,* p. 135; June, 2008, Kathy Piehl, review of *A Child's Introduction to the Environment,* p. 158.

ONLINE

Ispot Web site, http://www.theispot.com/ (August 1, 2011), "Meredith Hamilton."

Meredith Hamilton Home Page, http://www.meredithhamilton.com (August 1, 2011).

*   *   *

HARRISON, Michelle 1979-

Personal

Born 1979, in Essex, England. *Education:* College degree (illustration).

Addresses

Home—Oxfordshire, England. *E-mail*—info@michelleharrisonbooks.com.

Career

Writer. Worked variously as a barmaid, art gallery attendant, and children's bookseller; assistant editor at a children's publisher in London, England, for over three years.

Awards, Honors

Waterstone's Children's Book Prize, 2009, for *The 13 Treasures.*

Writings

"THIRTEEN TREASURES" FANTASY TRILOGY

The 13 Treasures, Simon & Schuster Children's (London, England), 2009, Little, Brown (New York, NY), 2010.
The 13 Curses, Simon & Schuster Children's (London, England), 2010, Little, Brown (New York, NY), 2011.
The 13 Secrets, Simon & Schuster Children's (London, England), 2011, Little, Brown (New York, NY), 2012.

Author's work has been translated into several languages, including German.

Sidelights

British writer Michelle Harrison was inspired to begin her "Thirteen Treasures" fantasy trilogy by her own love of myths and her research into the way different cultures have described and attempted to deal with the faery world. Geared for middle-grade readers, the series unfolds in the novels *The 13 Treasures, The 13 Curses,* and *The 13 Secrets,* all which *School Library Journal* contributor Kathy Kirchoefer praised as "an intriguing, exciting blend of fantasy and mystery."

Harrison knew that she wanted to become a writer and illustrator by the time she was fourteen, and while focusing on an art curriculum during college, she spent her off hours writing what would become the first part of *The 13 Treasures.* In her story, she wove elements from her own life together with information about fairies and legends that she learned through her substantial research: Her story's heroine is based on a family relative and its woodland setting was inspired by the area where Harrison grew up. "The Thirteen Treasures is a legend I came across," she noted on her home page, adding that this ancient tale "sparked my imagination and led me to my own interpretation." Harrison continued to develop her manuscript after graduation, where jobs such as barmaid, art gallery staffer, and children's bookstore clerk helped her pay the bills. She also learned the ins and outs of publishing while employed as an assistant editor, a job that proved useful when it came time to market her work. Her art training also cam in handy when she created the interior art for the U.K. edition of the book.

Thirteen-year-old Tanya is the central character in *The 13 Treasures,* which a *Publishers Weekly* critic dubbed a "sprightly contemporary fantasy." When readers first meet her, Tanya is staying with her elderly grandmother at Elvesden Manor, a vast pile of a house complete with tunnels and hidden rooms. Through an old photograph, the teen learns about the disappearance of Morwenna, a girl who was last seen entering the dark and cavern-riddled local forest half a century before. Although her grandmother will not speak of the girl, Morwenna's disappearance has been linked by rumors to the family of the manor's caretaker. Tanya also has a secret: she is able to see the fairies that inhabit this nearby forest and also overrun the manor, and she senses that some fairies may be more evil than good. With the help of the caretaker's son, Fabian, she now sets out into the dangerous forest to discover the truth behind Morwenna's disappearance, but with her supernatural insight she soon realizes that the children of the nearby town have been besieged by the same evil at the root of the fifty-year-old tragedy.

"Harrison is an excellent storyteller," exclaimed *Booklist* contributor Francisca Goldsmith, and in *The 13 Treasures* her "command of language wonderfully matches the scenarios and characters she creates." Also recommending the novel, Kirchoefer added in her *School Library Journal* review that Harrison's fiction debut "is fresh and clever" and will keep fantasy fans tantalized.

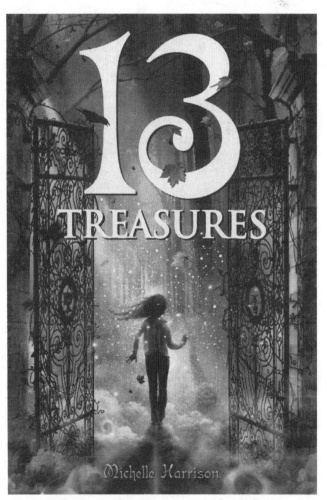

Michelle Harrison introduces her engaging "Thirteen Treasures" fantasy trilogy with this colorful mix of myth and magic. (Copyright © 2010 by Hachette Book Group, Inc. Reproduced with permission of Little Brown & Company, a division of Hachette Book Group, Inc.)

A sequel to *The 13 Treasures* that can also be read independently, *The 13 Curses* finds orphaned teenager Rowan turning to Tanya for help when her little brother James is kidnapped by fairies. Rowan also is able to sense the presence of the fairy folk, and she soon finds that she is threatened in two worlds. First trapped by a witch and then held captive in the faery realm, Rowan is subsequently suspected of kidnapping children in the world of humans. "Informed by the strangest poems of Yeats and Keats," *The 13 Secrets* also evokes "the inspired irrationality of Celtic myth," noted London *Times* contributor Amanda Craig, the critic going on to praise Harrison's novel as "edgier" than many stories in its genre. While that "genre is fairy fantasy," the creatures that inhabit its supernatural realm are "definitely non-pink," according to *School Librarian* contributor Chris Brown: these are "self-centred, cruel and vindictive fairy-folk," according to the reviewer. In *Kirkus Reviews* a critic commended Harrison for crafting "a fully realized world" and added of *The 13 Curses* that her "sure-handed storytelling" shapes that world into one that is "by turns violent and tender, sinister and poignant" and one that "afford[s] opportunities for heroism for the young protagonists."

On her home page, Harrison offered concrete advice for beginning writers. In addition to encouraging reading and writing, she also advises budding authors to get their work out to the reading public. "Enter writing competitions, or put your work forward for your school/college/local newspaper or creative writing magazine—or even start one of your own," she suggested. "It's great practice and will give you a sense of achievement if your work wins a prize or is selected for publication." "Don't expect immediate success," Harrison added; "It can take time. Enjoy writing and have fun with it."

Biographical and Critical Sources

PERIODICALS

Booklist, April 1, 2010, Francisca Goldsmith, review of *The 13 Treasures*, p. 37; May 15, 2011, Francisca Goldsmith, review of *The 13 Curses*, p. 57.
Bulletin of the Center for Children's Books, September, 2010, April Spisak, review of *The 13 Treasures*, p. 22.
Kirkus Reviews, March 1, 2010, review of *The 13 Treasures;* May 15, 2011, review of *The Thirteen Curses.*
Publishers Weekly, March 8, 2010, review of *The 13 Treasures*, p. 56.
School Librarian, summer, 2010, Chris Brown, review of *The 13 Curses*, p. 112.
School Library Journal, April, 2010, Kathy Kirchoefer, review of *The 13 Treasures*, p. 158.
Times (London, England), January 10, 2009, Amanda Craig, review of *The 13 Treasures*, p. 15; January 9, 2010, Amanda Craig, review of *The 13 Curses*, p. 8.

ONLINE

Michelle Harrison Home Page, http://www.michelleharrisonbooks.com (September 15, 2011).
Thirteen Treasures Trilogy Web site, http://13treasurestrilogy.com/ (September 13, 2011).

* * *

HASNAT, Naheed
See SENZAI, N.H.

* * *

HAYTER, Rhonda

Personal

Born in St. Jean, Quebec, Canada; immigrated to United States; married; children: two sons. *Education:* Attended college.

Addresses

Home—Los Angeles, CA. *E-mail*—rhondahayter1@sbcglobal.net.

Career

Author and story analyst. Former stage actress in New York, NY, and Los Angeles, CA; currently works as a story analyst for a film production company.

Writings

The Witchy Worries of Abbie Adams, Dial Books for Young Readers (New York, NY), 2010.

Sidelights

Canadian-born writer Rhonda Hayter began her career as a stage actress before a move to Los Angeles allowed her to expand her career to a different branch of the entertainment industry. Now working as a story analyst for a film producer, where she helps to determine which screenplays merit consideration as feature films, she also works raising her two sons. While watching, dispassionately, as her then six year old engaged in a prolonged tantrum, Hayter was inspired with the "What if . . . ?" scenario that eventually became her first book for children.

In *The Witchy Worries of Abbie Adams* readers meet eleven-year-old Abbie Adams, a girl who is far too old to engage in temper tantrums. For Abbie, school is her main difficulty, although friendship issues and difficulties memorizing her lines for an upcoming Drama Club

Rhonda Hayter (Photograph by Jody Frank. Reproduced by permission.)

lies who followed them were young. They were uniformly white, English-speaking, physically able, and primarily Anglican or Catholic. I never tasted any sort of ethnic food, never met a person of color, or a disabled person, or someone of another faith. I seldom even saw anyone over the age of forty, unless grandparents happened to visit.

"Except in books.

"In my tiny town there was no bus or subway, so when the Bobbsey Twins took a jitney excursion to the beach, it was an outsized adventure for me. The first pig and sheep I ever encountered were the ones in *Charlotte's Web*. And don't even mention the South Seas Island trip I took with Pippi Longstocking. It was only through books that I learned there was a larger world out there. My boys are growing up in Los Angeles. Their circle of friends is fantastically diverse: Six different languages are spoken on my older guy's soccer team. They love Japanese, Mexican, Chinese, and Italian food. Computer games vie with TV, Facebook, and Wii for their attention. But I'm thrilled to say that even so, they of-

play also rank in life's "Problem" category. The fact that Abbie is also a witch should make thing easier, but she is not the only one in her family with supernatural abilities. Her parents are both witches and her little brother is a budding werewolf. Even their new kitten seems unusual. When it turns out that the family feline is actually noted inventor Thomas Edison, who has been cursed and transported into the future before he could invent the light bulb, Abbie joins her witch parents in their efforts to return the thirteen-year-old future inventor to human form and his own time. Reviewing *The Witchy Worries of Abbie Adams*, Kelly Roth noted in *School Library Journal* that "Abbie is a likable character" and a preteen that elementary graders can relate to. The girl's "breezy, personable narrative incorporates droll asides," according to *Booklist* contributor Shelle Rosenfeld, and in *Kirkus Reviews* a reviewer concluded of Hayter's "frothy debut novel" that its mix of comedy, suspense, and time-travel elements results in a story as "light as cotton candy and just as tasty."

"I spent most of my childhood in a place in northern Canada called Labrador City," Hayter told *SATA*. "It was a tiny mining town, cut out of the wilderness with no way to reach it aside from infrequent trains or planes. There was no TV because the location was too remote. All of the men who went up there to work and the fami-

Cover of Hayter's humorous chapter book **The Witchy Worries of Abbie Adams**, *featuring cover art by Luisa Montalto.* (Illustration © 2010 by Luisa Montalto. Used by permission of Dial Books for Young Readers, a division of Penguin Young Readers Group, 345 Hudson St., New York, NY 10014.)

ten find a book that propels them right into the kind of misty, magical worlds I visited as a child, to visit with a Harry Potter, or a Percy Jackson, or a Katniss Everdeen."

Biographical and Critical Sources

PERIODICALS

Booklist, February 15, 2010, Shelle Rosenfeld, review of *The Witchy Worries of Abbie Adams,* p. 78.

Bulletin of the Center for Children's Books, May, 2010, Kate Quealy-Gainer, review of *The Witchy Worries of Abbie Adams,* p. 380.

Kirkus Reviews, March 1, 2010, review of *The Witchy Worries of Abbie Adams.*

Publishers Weekly, April 5, 2010, review of *The Witchy Worries of Abbie Adams,* p. 60.

School Library Journal, April, 2010, Kelly Roth, review of *The Witchy Worries of Abbie Adams,* p. 158.

ONLINE

Authors Now! Web site, http://www.authorsnow.com/ (September 15, 2011), "Rhonda Hayter."

Rhonda Hayter Home Page, http://rhondahayter.com (September 15, 2011).

*   *   *

HERMES, Patricia 1936-

Personal

Born February 21, 1936, in Brooklyn, NY; daughter of Fred Joseph (a bank vice president) and Jessie Martin; married Matthew E. Hermes (a research and development director for a chemical company), August 24, 1957 (divorced 1984); children: Paul, Mark, Timothy, Matthew, Jr., Jennifer. *Education:* St. John's University, B.A., 1957.

Addresses

Home—Fairfield, CT. *Agent*—Dorothy Markinko, McIntosh & Otis, Inc., 310 Madison Ave., New York, NY 10017. *E-mail*—patriciahermes@snet.net.

Career

Writer and educator. Rollingcrest Junior High School, Takoma Park, MD, teacher of English and social studies, 1957-58; Delcastle Technical High School, Delcastle, DE, teacher of home-bound children, 1972-73; writer, beginning 1977. Teacher of gifted middle-grade children, Norfolk, VA, 1981-82; adult education instructor. Speaker at schools.

Patricia Hermes (Photograph by David Bravo. Reproduced by permission.)

Member

Authors Guild, Authors League, Society of Children's Book Writers and Illustrators.

Awards, Honors

CRABbery Award, International Reading Association/Children's Book Council (CBC), 1980, for *What If They Knew?;* Pine Tree Book Award, Iowa Young Reader Medal, Hawai'i Nene Award, California Young Reader Medal, and Notable Children's Trade Book in the Field of Social Studies citation, NCSS/CBC, all 1983, all for *You Shouldn't Have to Say Goodbye;* Notable Children's Trade Book in the Field of Social Studies citation, NCSS/CBC, 1983, for *Who Will Take Care of Me?;* Best Book for Young Adults citation, American Library Association, 1985, and Notable Children's Trade Book in the Field of Social Studies citation, National Council for Social Studies (NCSS)/CBC, both 1985, both for *A Solitary Secret;* Best Book of the Year citation, *School Library Journal,* 1991, for *Mama, Let's Dance;* C.S. Lewis Honor Book designation; New York Library Best Book for the Teen Age designation; numerous child-selected awards.

Writings

FOR CHILDREN

What If They Knew?, Harcourt (San Diego, CA), 1980.

Nobody's Fault?, Harcourt (San Diego, CA), 1981.

You Shouldn't Have to Say Goodbye, Harcourt (San Diego, CA), 1982, published as *You Shouldn't Have to Say Goodbye: It's Hard Losing the Person You Love the Most,* Sourcebooks Jabberwocky (Naperville, IL), 2008.

Who Will Take Care of Me?, Harcourt (San Diego, CA), 1983.

Friends Are like That, Harcourt (San Diego, CA), 1984.

A Solitary Secret, Harcourt (San Diego, CA), 1985.

Kevin Corbett Eats Flies, illustrated by Carol Newsom, Harcourt (San Diego, CA), 1986.

A Place for Jeremy (sequel to *What If They Knew?*), Harcourt (San Diego, CA), 1987.

Heads, I Win (sequel to *Kevin Corbett Eats Flies*), illustrated by Carol Newsom, Harcourt (San Diego, CA), 1988.

Be Still My Heart, Putnam's (New York, NY), 1989.

I Hate Being Gifted, Putnam's (New York, NY), 1990.

(With Laurice Elehwany) *My Girl* (novelization), Pocket Books (New York, NY), 1991.

Mama, Let's Dance, Little, Brown (Boston, MA), 1991.

Take Care of My Girl, Little, Brown (Boston, MA), 1992.

Someone to Count On, Little, Brown (Boston, MA), 1993.

Nothing but Trouble, Trouble, Trouble, Scholastic (New York, NY), 1994.

(With Janet Kovalcik) *My Girl II,* Pocket Books (New York, NY), 1994.

On Winter's Wind, Little, Brown (Boston, MA), 1995.

When Snow Lay Soft on the Mountain (picture book), illustrated by Leslie A. Baker, Little, Brown (Boston, MA), 1996.

My Secret Valentine, Scholastic (New York, NY), 1996.

Something Scary, illustrated by John Gurney, Scholastic (New York, NY), 1996.

Turkey Trouble, illustrated by John Gurney, Scholastic (New York, NY), 1996.

Christmas Magic, illustrated by John Gurney, Scholastic (New York, NY), 1996.

Fly away Home (novelization; based on the screenplay by Robert Rodat and Vince McKewin), Newmarket (New York, NY), 1996.

Zeus and Roxanne (novelization; based on the screenplay by Tom Benedek), Pocket Books (New York, NY), 1997.

Hoppy Easter, illustrated by Amy Wummer, Scholastic (New York, NY), 1998.

Calling Me Home, Avon (New York, NY), 1998.

Cheat the Moon, Little, Brown (Boston, MA), 1998.

In God's Novel, Marshall Cavendish (New York, NY), 2000.

Sweet By and By, HarperCollins (New York, NY), 2002.

Summer Secrets, Marshall Cavendish (New York, NY), 2004.

The Brothers' War ("My Side of the Story" series; includes *Melody's Story* and *Marshall's Story*), Kingfisher (Boston, MA), 2005.

Salem Witch ("My Side of the Story" series; includes *Elizabeth's Story* and *George's Story*), Kingfisher (Boston, MA), 2006.

Koda, illustrated by Ruth Sanderson, Random House (New York, NY), 2009.

"COUSINS' CLUB" CHAPTER-BOOK SERIES

I'll Pulverize You, William, Pocket Books (New York, NY), 1994.

Everything Stinks, Minstrel Books (New York, NY), 1995.

Thirteen Things Not to Tell a Parent, Pocket Books (New York, NY), 1995.

Boys Are Even Worse than I Thought, Pocket Books (New York, NY), 1995.

"MY AMERICA" SERIES

Our Strange New Land: Elizabeth's Jamestown Colony Diary, Scholastic (New York, NY), 2000.

Westward to Home: Joshua's Oregon Trail Diary, Scholastic (New York, NY), 2001.

The Starving Time: Elizabeth's Jamestown Colony Diary, Book Two, Scholastic (New York, NY), 2001.

Season of Promise; Elizabeth's Jamestown Colony Diary, Book Three, Scholastic (New York, NY), 2002.

A Perfect Place: Joshua's Oregon Trail Diary, Book Two, Scholastic (New York, NY), 2002.

The Wild Year: Joshua's Oregon Trail Diary, Book Three, Scholastic (New York, NY), 2003.

"EMILY DILEMMA" CHAPTER-BOOK SERIES

Emma Dilemma and the New Nanny, Marshall Cavendish (Tarrytown, NY), 2006.

Emma Dilemma and the Two Nannies, Marshall Cavendish (Tarrytown, NY), 2007.

Emma Dilemma and the Soccer Nanny, Marshall Cavendish (Tarrytown, NY), 2008.

Emma Dilemma and the Camping Nanny, Marshall Cavendish (Tarrytown, NY), 2009.

Emma Dilemma, the Nanny, and the Secret Ferret, Marshall Cavendish (Tarrytown, NY), 2010.

Emma Dilemma, the Nanny, and the Best Horse Ever, Marshall Cavendish (New York, NY), 2011.

OTHER

A Time to Listen: Preventing Youth Suicide, Harcourt (New York, NY), 1987.

(With Stanley Rosner) *The Self-Sabotage Cycle: Why We Repeat Behaviors That Create Hardships and Ruin Relationships,* Praeger (Westport, CT), 2006.

Contributor to textbooks, including *On Reading and Writing for Kids.* Contributor to periodicals, including *Woman's Day, Life and Health, Connecticut, American Baby, Mother's Day,* and *New York Times.*

Author's work has been translated into Danish, French, Italian, Portuguese, and Japanese.

Sidelights

In her novels for middle-grade readers and young adults, Patricia Hermes creates fictional characters who confront and transcend difficult and trying times—life in foster care, uncaring parents, intolerant classmates—while also finding joy and even engaging in a bit of mischief. A young girl attempting to come to terms with her mother's terminal illness is the subject of Hermes' poignant novel *You Shouldn't Have to Say Goodbye,* while abandoned children find their way in life in *Mama, Let's Dance. Cheat the Moon,* another popular novel by Hermes, finds a girl dealing with both her mother's death and her father's alcoholic neglect. The versatile author also shows her lighter side in her picture books, the humorous stories in her "Cousins' Club" and "Emily Dilemma" series, while her contributions to Scholastic's "My America" series feature young people enduring the challenges of different epochs in their nation's history. In her unusual "My Side of the Story" flip-book novels *Salem Witch* and *The Brothers' War,* Hermes weaves two distinct and contemporary points of view regarding an historic controversy into compelling contrasting narratives. "As adults, we often try to deceive ourselves that childhood is a safe, pleasant place to be," the author once told *SATA.* "It isn't—at least, some of the time. For me, it is important to say this to young people so children know they are not alone."

While growing up in Brooklyn, New York, Hermes enjoyed being active as a child, but she was also a bookworm. She got a lot of practice reading and writing after she contracted rheumatic fever and was required to spend several months in bed. In college Hermes majored in speech and English, then married and taught school for a short time before leaving to raise her children. Although she returned to teaching after her children were older, Hermes became interested in writing professionally after taking a class taught by biographer Russell Freedman at New York City's New School for Social Research (now New School University). "I took some things I wrote in the course and sent them out to publishers and to my utter amazement, people started buying them," Hermes once recalled to *SATA.* "You get hooked pretty quickly that way." She continued to write nonfiction articles for several years, including many pieces on sudden infant death syndrome (SIDS), a condition that she had dealt with first hand.

From nonfiction, Hermes eventually shifted her focus to children's fiction, and her first novel, *What If They Knew?,* was published in 1980. *What If They Knew?* introduces a girl named Jeremy who has epilepsy and is starting at a new school. While *What If They Knew?* deals with a serious subject, it also features Hermes' refreshingly light approach. In *A Place for Jeremy,* a sequel, Jeremy spends part of her fifth-grade year with her grandparents in Brooklyn while her parents are abroad, adopting a baby. Jeremy calls the unknown child "Stupid Baby," fearing that the infant will steal her parents' affections. A *Publishers Weekly* contributor remarked of *A Place for Jeremy* that "scenes between Jeremy and her grandfather are heartwarming."

Hermes deals with the difficult subject of death in several books for children. In *You Shouldn't Have to Say Goodbye* welve-year-old Sarah is losing her mother to cancer. While confronting this crisis, the girl moves between fear for her mother and her own typically preteen concerns. Sarah deals with her worries and fears by joining both her parents in planning a party to celebrate what may be her mom's last Christmas. In the end, she is left with a journal her mother has written, a book that offers guidance in dealing with life's various trials. *You Shouldn't Have to Say Goodbye* was described as "moving, but . . . not maudlin" by a *Bulletin of the Center for Children's Books* contributor, and in *Voice of Youth Advocates* Vicki Hardesty deemed the novel "an excellent portrayal of a teenager adjusting to the terminal illness of a parent." Hermes' novel has proved so popular with preteen readers that it has been more-recently released in a new edition as *You Shouldn't Have to Say Goodbye: It's Hard Losing the Person You Love the Most.*

Geared for younger children, *Who Will Take Care of Me?* focuses on Mark and his developmentally disabled younger brother Pete. Both boys live with their grandmother, and when the elderly woman dies the boys hide in the woods so that Pete will not be sent away to a special school. Reviewing Hermes' story, *School Library Journal* critic Nancy Berkowitz described Mark as "sympathetic" and Pete's characterization "honest and unsentimental."

Mama, Let's Dance "tugs at the heart without manipulating its audience," according to *Horn Book* contributor Mary M. Burns. The story involves three children—aged sixteen, eleven, and seven—who are left to fend for themselves when their mother leaves home and abandons them. The children pretend nothing has changed until the youngest becomes seriously ill and the siblings must reach out to their neighbors for help. Carolyn Noah, reviewing the novel for *School Library Journal,* described *Mama, Let's Dance* as a "tightly woven tale" in which "rhythmic, homey text and genuine characters resonate with authenticity."

Young girls are forced to make difficult decisions after the death of a parent in Hermes' novels *Someone to Count On* and *Cheat the Moon.* In the former book, Sam and her mother have been traveling around the country since the death of her father, and now they move to Colorado to live on her grandfather's ranch. Just as Sam is settling in, her mother informs her that they are moving again, and the girl is faced with a difficult choice in what *Horn Book* critic Maeve Visser Knoth described as a "powerful" and "engaging" story with "richly drawn" characters. In *Cheat the Moon* Gabrielle takes responsibility for her younger brother Will and herself after their mother dies and their father dis-

appears on an alcoholic binge. A budding writer, Gabrielle records her feelings in a journal, and Susan P. Bloom described the girl's reflections as "bittersweet" in her *Horn Book* review of the novel. Debbie Carton, reviewing *Cheat the Moon* for *Booklist,* praised Hermes for offering readers a "poignant, compassionate story."

Along with tackling difficult topics, Hermes also indulges her lighthearted side in stories such as *Kevin Corbett Eats Flies* and *Heads, I Win.* In *Kevin Corbett Eats Flies* the titular hero regularly gains his classmates' attention by tackling bizarre stunts, like eating flies or swallowing the class goldfish. Kevin meets his match, however, in tough but likeable Bailey, who eventually becomes his friend. *Heads, I Win* focuses on Bailey's life both in school and with foster mother Ms. Henderson and her four-year-old son. Bailey is afraid that her social worker will decide to transfer her to yet another foster home; to help combat this fear, she decides to run for class president to show everyone how well she is doing in school. Kevin volunteers to be Bailey's campaign manager, "and their analysis of how best to 'buy' individual students makes up much of the

Hermes captures the attention of young readers in* Kevin Corbett Eats Flies, *a story featuring art by Carol Newsom. (Illustration copyright © 1986 by Carol Newsom. Reproduced by permission of Houghton Mifflin Harcourt Publishing Company. This material may not be reproduced in any form or by any means without the prior permission of the publisher.)

humor of the book," wrote Candy Colborn in *School Library Journal.* Hermes' "characters are well drawn, and the fifth-grade in-fighting is very realistic," the critic added.

Hermes' lighthearted "Cousins' Club" series kicks off with *I'll Pulverize You, William,* in which best friends and cousins Marcie and Meghann are introduced. The two eleven year olds are looking forward to summer until they learn that another, less-enjoyable cousin—William—is scheduled to arrive for a visit. The cousins quickly develop a plan to keep William at a distance: Knowing that he is allergic to animals, they start a pet-sitting service. Of course, things do not go according to plan in this "chipper start" to the series, according to a reviewer for *Publishers Weekly.*

The "Cousins' Club" series continues in *Everything Stinks,* as Meghann and Marcie visit twin cousins Jennifer and Amy. Jennifer is of the opinion that everything stinks because she is always treated like a little kid, and she dreams of the time when she will be in charge of her life. When her parents go on vacation, Jennifer decides that this time has come, with near disastrous and rather humorous results. Mary Harris Veeder, writing in *Booklist,* asserted that Hermes gives some "good descriptions of fifth-grade embarrassments" in her book. The humorous adventures of the "Cousins' Club" protagonists continue in *Thirteen Things Not to Tell a Parent* and *Boys Are Even Worse than I Thought.*

Readers are introduced to spunky young Emma O'Fallon and her four siblings in *Emma Dilemma and the New Nanny,* the first installment in Hermes' "Emily Dilemma" chapter-book series. When her pet ferret, Marmaduke, escapes from his cage and winds up inside her mother's mattress, Emma finds her role as pet owner somewhat tenuous. Fortunately, a new nanny named Annie O'Reilly enters the household and soon sets things to rights, managing to keep the children's good-natured mishaps under wraps. Comparing Emma to literary heroines such as Beverly Cleary's Ramona and Barbara Park's Junie B. Jones, Terrie Dorio wrote in *School Library Journal* that Hermes' "lively" character "goes about living in her own way and in her own style." *Emma Dilemma and the New Nanny* "will leave thoughtful young readers mulling issues of trust and responsibility," noted John Peters in *Booklist,* the critic adding of the story that Hermes "lightly but effectively" shows the value in admitting mistakes.

Emma returns in *Emma Dilemma and the Two Nannies,* as Annie is scheduled to depart on a three-week holiday in Ireland. While Emma and her siblings will miss Annie, her absence descends into tragedy when the replacement nanny turns out to be grouchy, ferret-hating Mrs. Potts. The O'Fallon children team up and go on strike in *Emma Dilemma and the Soccer Nanny,* hopeful that Annie be allowed to chaperone Emma's upcoming soccer team away game to Washington, DC. The efforts of the younger siblings to expand their pet

Cover of Hermes' chapter book Emma Dilemma and the Two Nannies, *featuring cover art by Abby Carter.* (Illustration copyright © Marshall Cavendish Corporation. Reproduced by permission of Marshall Cavendish.)

menagerie to include a kitten and a second ferret also figure in Hermes' lighthearted story. The "headstrong but sympathetic heroine" in *Emma Dilemma and the Two Nannies* "learns from her mistakes," explained *Booklist* critic Abby Nolan, and with the help of well-meaning adults "recognizes her missteps and makes amends." In addition to a humorous story, *Emma Dilemma and the Soccer Nanny* shares "messages about the importance of honest" and "the challenges and unexpected rewards of compromise," according to *Booklist* contributor Shelle Rosenfeld.

Emma Dilemma and the Camping Nanny and *Emma Dilemma, the Nanny, and the Secret Ferret* continue the humorous saga of the O'Fallon children. Jealousy sets in in the former, as Annie's decision to study Irish dancing with boyfriend Bo keeps her away from home more than Emily would like. The sixth grader's feelings are further hurt when best friend Luisa also seems to be keeping her distance. Marmaduke the ferret is smuggled aboard the family car on a vacation trip to Maine in *Emma Dilemma, the Nanny, and the Secret Ferret*, leaving Emma with a multitude of challenges while trying to juggle ferret care with her attempt to keep the stowaway hidden from her parents. "Many children will re-

late to Emma's feelings of being left out and jealous," asserted *School Library Journal* contributor Maryilyn Teicher, and in *Booklist* Engberg noted that *Emma Dilemma and the Camping Nanny* shows Hermes' young and sometimes misguided heroine at her finest, and the "reassuring read makes another strong entry in the series." Citing the "surprising sweet ending" in *Emma Dilemma, the Nanny, and the Secret Ferret*, Elizabeth Swistock added in her *School Library Journal* review of Hermes' lighthearted chapter book that "the nice thing . . . is that it sends the message that sometimes we judge people too harshly."

Several of Hermes' books feature a mix of history and storytelling. Set in the early 1800s, *On Winter's Wind* takes readers back to the time of slavery as eleven-year-old Genevieve and her family deal with hardship now that her father has been presumed lost at sea. When she learns that there is a bounty on a slave who is being hidden in her little town, Genevieve is sorely tempted to turn the fugitive in, but she is convinced to do otherwise by the Quakers who are sheltering the young runaway. "Hermes does a fine job of depicting the situa-

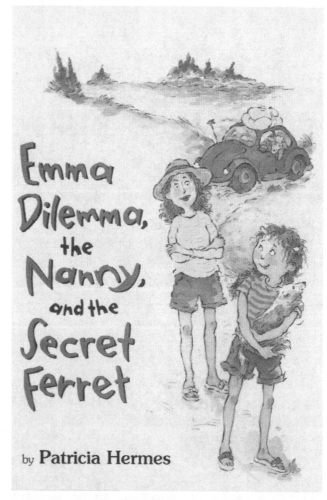

Emma's humorous adventures continue in Emma Dilemma, the Nanny, and the Secret Ferret, *which pairs Hermes' text with Abby Carter's humorous art.* (Illustration copyright © Marshall Cavendish Corporation. Reproduced by permission of Marshall Cavendish.)

tion," wrote *Booklist* contributor Chris Sherman, while Knoth praised *On Winter's Wind* as "poignant" in her *Horn Book* review.

Calling Me Home is set on the Nebraska prairie in the 1850s. For Abbie her twelfth year is marked by her family's journey from St. Joseph, Missouri, to their Nebraska homestead. The girl goes from living in a proper house with a piano to a sod house on the prairie; there is no school and no other children live nearby. Although Abbie enjoys the freedom of the prairie, she also misses the ease of the city, especially when her brother dies during a cholera outbreak. In *Calling Me Home* Hermes "takes a fresh path with a feminist angle" on this familiar territory, according to a *Publishers Weekly* critic, the reviewer also deeming the story "solid . . . [and] neatly told." Janet Gillen noted in *School Library Journal* that the novel's "strengths lie in Hermes' ability to convey sensitive issues of death and the loss of faith through succinct, well-written scenes."

Drawing readers closer to their own era, Hermes' *Sweet By and By* is set during World War II and deals with the effects of the death of an elderly family member. Blessing is eleven years old and has lived with her grandmother in the Tennessee mountains since she was a toddler. She is secure in the woman's love and is bonded partly by the gift for music that they share. Now Blessing must acknowledge that her beloved grandmother is dying, a fact that means that the preteen will soon have to adapt to life in a new home. A reviewer for *Publishers Weekly* commended *Sweet By and By* as a "gracefully composed story of love, loss and courage," while Kay Weisman wrote in *Booklist* that the "loving relationship between grandmother and grandchild" that is captured in the novel "will touch the heart." Barbara Auerbach, writing in *School Library Journal,* lauded the "poetic prose" that enriches Hermes' "heartfelt story."

Also featuring a World War II setting, *In God's Novel* takes readers to rural Mississippi and introduces an eleven year old named Missy. When her mother suddenly goes "sick crazy," Missy wonders why God allows such bad things to happen. Fortunately, the family maid, Geneva, is there during the girl's search for security and answers. In a sequel, *Summer Secrets,* Missy is a year older and wiser as she continues to come to terms with her mother's condition. In addition to confiding her concerns to her new diary, the twelve year old and her two boy-crazy best friends also share personal secrets during the long, hot summer, amid welcome news from overseas that the war in Europe is winding down. In a *Kirkus Reviews* appraisal of *Summer Secrets* a contributor commended Hermes for introducing Missie as a "delightful, multifaceted" protagonist "who is at once innocent, strong-willed, compassionate, insightful, and curious." "An evocative and satisfying coming-of-age story," according to *School Library Journal* contributor Cindy Darling Codell, *Summer Secrets* features a "child's-eye view of a small southern town [that] is on target."

Part of the "Cousins Club" series, Hermes' novel **Thirteen Things Not to Tell a Parent,** *featuring artwork by Chuck Pyle.* (Reproduced with permission of Chuck Pyle, conveyed through Lindgren & Smith.)

Scholastic's "My America" series presents fictionalized diary accounts that bring to life historical times for young readers. In her contribution to this series, Hermes details life in Virginia's Jamestown Colony in a sequence of books about nine-year-old Elizabeth, and she also follows a pioneer family along the Oregon Trail via the journals of a boy named Joshua. *Our Strange New Land: Elizabeth's Jamestown Colony Diary* introduces Elizabeth as she records her experiences with Native Americans, helps her family build a new home, and deals with hunger and death in the first years of the seventeenth century. Shawn Brommer, writing in *School Library Journal,* deemed *Our Strange New Land* a "quick, easy read."

The Starving Time: Elizabeth's Jamestown Colony Diary, Book Two furthers the girl's saga, the "historical details . . . woven so intricately into the plot that they become an integral part of the story," according to Kristen Oravec in *School Library Journal. Season of Promise; Elizabeth's Jamestown Colony Diary, Book Three* continues the story as Elizabeth, now aged ten, learns of her newly widowed father's plan to remarry. "Beautifully written," according to *School Library Journal* contributor Leslie Barban, *Season of Promise* "gives

children a glimpse of colonial life through the eyes of a warm, spunky, and heroic young girl."

Westward to Home: Joshua's Oregon Trail Diary presents the first diary entries of nine-year-old Joshua McCullough as he and his family follow the Oregon Trail from their home in St. Joseph, Missouri. John McAndrew, writing in *Childhood Education,* praised the way that Joshua "vividly records his dreams, hopes, frustrations, and fears" in the book's journal-like format. Ellen Mandel, writing in *Booklist,* also had praise for the novel, noting that *Westward to Home* "will stick in the readers' minds and enrich their studies of the era" of U.S. westward expansion.

Joshua records further adventures in *A Perfect Place: Joshua's Oregon Trail Diary, Book Two* in which the boy and his family settle down to life in Oregon's Willamette Valley, and *The Wild Year: Joshua's Oregon Trail Diary, Book Three,* the nine year old finds frontier life normalizing as the territory establishes a new government and he begins to attend school. A contributor for *Kirkus Reviews* called *A Perfect Place* "fascinating history," and Sally Bates Goodroe wrote in *School Li-*

Cover of Hermes' middle-grade novel Summer Secrets, *featuring artwork by Steve McAfee.* (Copyright © 2004 by Marshall Cavendish. Jacket illustration copyright © 2004 by Steve McAfee. Reproduced by permission of Marshall Cavendish.)

brary Journal that "details of the life in Oregon Country . . . are vividly integrated" into Hermes' historical narrative. "Despite the diary format, Hermes creates a smooth, economical narrative" in *The Wild Year,* concluded Sue Sherif in *School Library Journal.*

Hermes focuses on older teens in her novel *A Solitary Secret,* "a spellbinding book that drops the reader deep into the soul" of a girl who has endured incest, according to *Voice of Youth Advocates* contributor Marijo Duncan. The unnamed protagonist, who ages from fourteen to eighteen during the story, chronicles her experiences via a journal and eventually shares her secret with a friend's parent. *Be Still My Heart,* another young-adult novel, finds Allison infatuated with David, who loves Leslie, Allison's best friend. David and Allison are ultimately brought together when a teacher's husband develops AIDS and becomes a victim of discrimination. *Be Still My Heart* "shows through its female characters that looks aren't everything to all boys, and that intelligence, enthusiasm, and conviction are just as appealing," declared *School Library Journal* contributor Kathryn Havris of the novel.

One of two nonfiction books authored by Hermes, *A Time to Listen: Preventing Youth Suicide* is intended to help young adults understand issues related to suicide. The book consists of interviews with teens who have tried suicide, parents and friends of victims, and a therapist specializing in the problems confronting contemporary young people. "The interviews are probing, but sensitive to the privacy of subjects," commented Libby K. White in a review of *A Time to Listen* for *School Library Journal,* the critic adding that "the great myths of teen suicide . . . are refuted" in Hermes' account. Of special use to teens, *A Time to Listen* also includes suggestions for helping depressed friends. Overall, it serves as "a sensible, approachable book for those who need it," concluded Rosemary Moran in a review for *Voice of Youth Advocates.*

In a further change of pace, Hermes' first picture book, *When Snow Lay Soft on the Mountain,* introduces prereaders to Hallie as she copes with life during a difficult winter on Hairy Bear Mountain while also caring for her ill father. A contributor to *Kirkus Reviews* called *When Snow Lay Soft on the Mountain* a "sweet and sentimental tale," and a *Publishers Weekly* critic wrote that Hermes' picture book "should satisfy readers in the mood for an old-fashioned moral tale."

Commenting on her work as a children's writer, Hermes once told *SATA* that there is a childlike part of us "we never lose, if we're lucky. Every good teacher has that. I think that child is a part of me, and she needs to speak—and does—through my books. I don't write for some child out there, I write for the child in me."

When asked if she had any advice for young writers, Hermes said: "If I could preach for a minute, I'd say 'If you're going to be a writer, you must be a reader.' It

doesn't matter what you read. Forget what those teachers tell you. You don't have to read 'good' literature. Read anything, because eventually, if you become a reader you will someday find good literature. No, there's nothing wrong with trivial reading.

"Also don't throw away anything you've ever written. I tell kids that if their mothers get in cleaning fits, tell them they can throw away their school books, or their baby brother, but do not throw away anything they've written."

Biographical and Critical Sources

BOOKS

Encyclopedia of Children's Literature, edited by Bernice E. Cullinan and Diane G. Person, Continuum (New York, NY), 2001.

St. James Guide to Young-Adult Writers, 2nd edition, edited by Tom Pendergast and Sara Pendergast, St James Press (Detroit, MI), 1999.

PERIODICALS

Booklist, November 15, 1992, Janice Del Negro, review of *Take Care of My Girl;* January 15, 1995, Mary Harris Veeder, review of *Everything Stinks*, p. 928; October 1, 1995, Chris Sherman, review of *On Winter's Wind*, p. 314; June 1, 1998, Debbie Carton, review of *Cheat the Moon*, p. 1766; January 1, 1999, Kay Weisman, review of *Calling Me Home*, p. 876; February 1, 2001, Ellen Mandel, review of *Westward to Home: Joshua's Oregon Trail Diary*, p. 1053; October 1, 2002, Kay Weisman, review of *Sweet By and By*, pp. 341-342; January 1, 2003, Todd Morning, review of *A Perfect Place: Joshua's Oregon Trail Diary, Book Two*, p. 890; April 15, 2006, John Peters, review of *Emma Dilemma and the New Nanny*, p. 47; May 15, 2007, Abby Nolan, review of *Emma Dilemma and the Two Nannies*, p. 50; July 1, 2008, Shelle Rosenfeld, review of *Emma Dilemma and the Soccer Nanny*, p. 62; March 15, 2009, Gillian Engberg, review of *Emma Dilemma and the Camping Nanny*, p. 55.

Bulletin of the Center for Children's Books, March, 1983, review of *You Shouldn't Have to Say Goodbye*, p. 127; November, 1995, review of *On Winter's Wind*, p. 92; June, 2004, Karen Coats, review of *Summer Secrets*, p. 421.

Childhood Education, fall, 2001, John McAndrew, review of *Westward to Home*, p. 50.

Horn Book, January-February, 1992, Mary M. Burns, review of *Mama, Let's Dance*, p. 70; January-February, 1994, Maeve Visser Knoth, review of *Someone to Count On*, pp. 69-70; November-December, 1995, Maeve Visser Knoth, review of *On Winter's Wind*, pp. 742-743; September-October, 1998, Susan P. Bloom, review of *Cheat the Moon*, pp. 608-609.

Kirkus Reviews, December, 15, 1994, review of *I'll Pulverize You, William*, p. 1564; September 15, 1996, review of *When Snow Lay Soft on the Mountain*, p. 1401; November 15, 1998, review of *Calling Me Home*, p. 1669; October 15, 2002, reviews of *A Perfect Place*, p. 1530, and *Sweet By and By*, p. 1531; March 15, 2004, review of *Summer Secrets*, p. 270; March 15, 2007, review of *Emma Dilemma and the Two Nannies*; July 1, 2008, review of *Emma Dilemma and the Soccer Nanny*.

New York Times Book Review, May 20, 1984, review of *You Shouldn't Have to Say Goodbye*, p. 29; January 10, 1988, review of *A Time to Listen: Preventing Youth Suicide*, p. 36.

Publishers Weekly, April 24, 1987, review of *A Place for Jeremy*, p. 70; November 23, 1990, review of *I Hate Being Gifted*, p. 66; November 21, 1994, review of *I'll Pulverize You, William*, pp. 76-77; October 30, 1995, review of *On Winter's Wind*, p. 62; October 21, 1996, review of *When Snow Lay Soft on the Mountain*, p. 82; December 14, 1998, review of *Calling Me Home*, p. 76; May 27, 2002, review of *Our Strange New Land: Elizabeth's Jamestown Colony Diary*, p. 62; November 11, 2002, review of *Sweet By and By*, p. 64.

School Library Journal, October, 1983, Nancy Berkowitz, review of *Who Will Take Care of Me?*, p. 158; March, 1988, Libby K. White, review of *A Time to Listen*, p. 220; August, 1988, Candy Colborn, review of *Heads, I Win*, p. 95; December, 1989, Kathryn Havris, review of *Be Still My Heart*, p. 118; September, 1991, Carolyn Noah, review of *Mama, Let's Dance*, p. 253; December, 1992, Cindy Darling Codell, review of *Take Care of My Girl*, p. 112; March, 1995, Elaine Lesh Morgan, review of *Everything Stinks*, p. 204; September, 1995, Nancy P. Veeder, review of *On Winter's Wind*, p. 200; January, 1997, Mollie Bynum, review of *When Snow Lay Soft on the Mountain*, p. 83; June, 1998, Connie Tyrrell Burns, review of *Cheat the Moon*, p. 146; December, 1998, Janet Gillen, review of *Calling Me Home*, p. 1998; August, 2000, Shawn Brommer, review of *Our Strange New Land*, p. 156; June, 2001, Kristen Oravec, review of *The Starving Time: Elizabeth's Jamestown Colony Diary, Book Two*, p. 118; October, 2002, Barbara Auerbach, review of *Sweet By and By*, p. 164; November, 2002, Sally Bates Goodroe, review of *A Perfect Place*, p. 124; February, 2003, Leslie Barban, review of *Season of Promise*, p. 112; May, 2004, Sue Sherif, review of *The Wild Year: Joshua's Oregon Trail Diary, Book Three*, p. 114, and Cindy Darling Codell, review of *Summer Secrets*, p. 148; November, 2005, S.K. Joiner, review of *The Brother's War*, p. 137; May, 2006, Terrie Dorio, review of *Emma Dilemma and the New Nanny*, p. 89; February, 2007, Kristen Oravec, review of *Salem Witch*, p. 118; April, 2007, Kelly Roth, review of *Emma Dilemma and the Two Nannies*, p. 108; June, 2008, Jane Barrer, review of *Emma Dilemma and the Soccer Nanny*, p. 104; May, 2009, Marilyn Teicher, review of *Emma Dilemma and the Camping Nanny*, p. 80; April, 2010, Elizabeth Swistock, review of *Emma Dilemma, the Nanny, and the Secret Ferret*, p. 128.

Voice of Youth Advocates, December, 1985, Marijo Duncan, review of *A Solitary Secret*, p. 320; June, 1988, Rosemary Moran, review of *A Time to Listen*, p. 101; October, 1993, Vicki Hardesty, review of *You Shouldn't*

Have to Say Goodbye, p. 203; December, 1995, review of *On Winter's Wind,* p. 302; February, 1997, Susan Dunn, review of *Fly away Home,* pp. 327-328; August, 1998, review of *Cheat the Moon,* p. 201; August, 2004, Pam Carlson, review of *Summer Secrets,* p. 216.

ONLINE

Balkin Buddies Web site, http://www.balkinbuddies.com/ (May 25, 2008), "Patricia Hermes."
Patricia Hermes Home Page, http://www.patriciahermes. com (September 11, 2011).*

* * *

HORNER, Emily 1982-

Personal

Born 1982, in Ottawa, Ontario, Canada. *Education:* College degree; University of North Carolina—Chapel Hill, M.L.S., 2006. *Hobbies and other interests:* Musicals, bicycles, knitting, baking, Japanese music films.

Addresses

Home—Brooklyn, NY. *E-mail*—emily@emilyhorner. com.

Career

Librarian and author. Librarian in Brooklyn, NY.

Writings

A Love Story Starring My Dead Best Friend, Dial Books (New York, NY), 2010.

Sidelights

Describing herself on her home page as "a geeky person with a lot of momentary obsessions and strange hobbies," librarian Emily Horner weaves everything from ninjas to stage musicals into the plot of her first novel, *A Love Story Starring My Dead Best Friend.* Horner's eclectic education has contributed to her unusual approach: although she earned her master's degree in library science, her undergraduate years were spent studying linguistics and the Japanese language; she even supplemented her language studies with a trip to Nagasaki, Japan, during in her early twenties. It was after she discovered the colorful underground fan comic publications that proliferate in Japan that Horner decided to take her own talent seriously and write her first novel.

Sixteen-year-old Cass Meyer, the main character in *A Love Story Starring My Dead Best Friend,* is devastated when her best friend and secret crush, Julia, is killed in

a car accident just as she was on the verge of making her big break toward her dream of becoming a stage composer. To honor their late friend, Julia's boyfriend Oliver and her fellow thespians decide to produce her work in progress, *Totally Sweet Ninja Death Squad.* Cass feels left out because she has never been a theatre geek, and when her middle-school nemesis is cast in the play's lead, the broken-hearted eteen decides that it is time for a road trip. Even though her favored form of transportation is a single-saddle bicycle, Cass will not be traveling alone from her Mid-West home to California: she has her late friend's ashes securely packed on board in a plastic pop-top container. From Cass's trip across the western United States, Horner flashes forward to senior year, when the young woman's relationships resolve themselves in a surprising way in a novel that *School Library Journal* contributor Misti Tidman characterized as a "funny, touching, and sweet coming-of-age story."

"Cass is a fascinating and believable character, a Quaker and committed cyclist incredibly competent in matters mechanical and awkwardly inept in matters of the

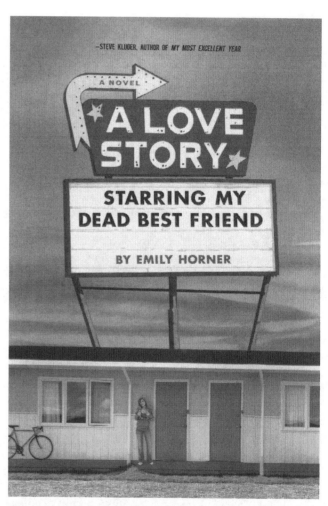

Cover of **A Love Story Starring My Dead Best Friend,** *Emily Horner's story of a teen who gains self-understanding during a road trip inspired by grief and loss.* (Cover images courtesy of iStockphoto. Reproduce with permission of Dial Books, an imprint of Penguin Group (USA) Inc., 375 Hudson St., New York, NY 10014. All rights reserved.)

heart," noted Debbie Carton in her *Booklist* review of *A Love Story Starring My Dead Best Friend.* Horner "treat[s] the grieving process with respect while maintaining a positive tone, a balance that allows the triumphant conclusions of both story lines to feel unforced," asserted *Horn Book* critic Claire E. Gross. Also praising Horner's novel, a *Kirkus Reviews* writer recommended the work as "bittersweet but never mawkish and punctuated with just the right amount of teen hipster humor," while Regina Marler wrote in the *New York Times Book Review* that "the strength of this promising novel is its emotional reach, from mourning through identity crisis through new love."

Biographical and Critical Sources

PERIODICALS

Booklist, June 1, 2010, Debbie Carton, review of *A Love Story Starring My Dead Best Friend,* p. 56.

Horn Book, July-August, 2010, Claire E. Gross, review of *A Love Story Starring My Dead Best Friend,* p. 112.

Kirkus Reviews, May 1, 2010, review of *A Love Story Starring My Dead Best Friend.*

New York Times Book Review, June 20, 2010, Regina Marler, review of *A Love Story Starring My Dead Best Friend,* p. 12.

School Library Journal, July, 2010, Misti Tidman, review of *A Love Story Starring My Dead Best Friend,* p. 91.

Voice of Youth Advocates, October, 2010, Jennifer Ingram, review of *A Love Story Starring My Dead Best Friend,* p. 350.

ONLINE

Emily Horner Home Page, http://emilyhorner.com (September 15, 2011).*

I-K

IGNATOW, Amy 1977-

Personal

Born 1977, in Huntington, NY; married; husband's name Mark. *Education:* Moore College of Art and Design, degree, 2002.

Addresses

Home—Philadelphia, PA. *Agent*—Dan Lazar, Writer's House, 21 W. 26th St., New York, NY 10010; dlazar@writershouse.com.

Career

Writer and illustrator. Worked variously as a teacher, farmer, florist, short-order vegan cook, wedding singer, and ghostwriter for Internet personal ads.

Member

Society of Children's Book Writers and Illustrators.

Awards, Honors

Gold Award, National Parenting Publications Awards, 2010, and Best of the Best listee, Chicago Public Library, and Rainbow Project selection, both 2011, all for *Research for the Social Improvement and General Betterment of Lydia Goldblatt and Julie Graham-Chang.*

Writings

"POPULARITY PAPERS" YOUNG-ADULT NOVEL SERIES; SELF-ILLUSTRATED

Research for the Social Improvement and General Betterment of Lydia Goldblatt and Julie Graham-Chang, Amulet Books (New York, NY), 2010.
A Record of the Continued Transatlantic Discoveries of Lydia Goldblatt and Julie Graham-Chang, Amulet Books (New York, NY), 2011.

OTHER

Creator of *Ig City* Web comic.

Sidelights

Cartoonist Amy Ignatow is the author and illustrator of the "Popularity Papers" novels, which includes *Research for the Social Improvement and General Betterment of Lydia Goldblatt and Julie Graham-Chang* and chronicles the efforts of two fifth graders to uncover the secret to enduring popularity before they enter junior high. To achieve their goal, the friends concoct a plan to observe the habits of the most popular students in their school, then attempt to mimic those behaviors with Lydia, the more courageous of the two, serving as the guinea pig for their experiments. Julie, blessed with better penmanship and artistic skills than her comrade, will record the results in a special journal, which Ignatow illustrates with ink, colored pencil, colored marker, yarn, and digital art. Describing *Research for the Social Improvement and General Betterment of Lydia Goldblatt and Julie Graham-Chang* in a *Society of Children's Book Writers and Illustrators* interview with Alice Pope, Ignatow commented: "Instead of writing it as a straight graphic novel (panels, word-bubbles) I wanted readers to feel like they were really holding a journal that these two girls made—Lydia writes in cursive, Julie prints, and they both draw (as the better artist, Julie takes the lead, but Lydia makes due with her stick figure illustrations when Julie isn't around). They paste notes that they've passed back and forth into the book, as well as photos they've printed off the Internet, plants, and yarn samples."

The "Popularity Papers" books have earned praise for their humorous narrative and endearing characters. *School Library Journal* critic Laurie Slagenwhite described *Research for the Social Improvement and General Betterment of Lydia Goldblatt and Julie Graham-Chang* as an "entertaining look at the social hierarchy of preteens," and Andrew Medlar remarked in *Booklist* that "Ignatow offers a quick, fun, well-developed story

Amy Ignatow creates both art and story in her quirky middle-grade novel **Research for the Social Improvement and General Betterment of Lydia Goldblatt and Julie Graham-Chang,** *part of her "Popularity Papers" series.* (Illustration copyright © 2010 by Amy Ignatow. Reproduced with permission of Amulet Books, an imprint of Harry Abrams.)

that invites repeated readings." "It is testimony to Ignatow's skill that the two friends emerge as individual personalities," stated *New York Times Book Review* contributor Barbara Feinberg, the critic adding that "this is done largely through the characters' very distinct prose and drawing styles, and also their different handwriting . . . . This graphological dimension contributes, somehow, to how we know them. The girls feel very real."

Biographical and Critical Sources

PERIODICALS

Booklist, March 1, 2010, Andrew Medlar, review of *Research for the Social Improvement and General Betterment of Lydia Goldblatt and Julie Graham-Chang,* p. 74.

Bulletin of the Center for Children's Books, May, 2010, review of *Research for the Social Improvement and General Betterment of Lydia Goldblatt and Julie Graham-Chang,* p. 382.

New York Times Book Review, June 6, 2010, Barbara Feinberg, review of *Research for the Social Improvement and General Betterment of Lydia Goldblatt and Julie Graham-Chang,* p. 24.

Publishers Weekly, March 8, 2011, review of *Research for the Social Improvement and General Betterment of Lydia Goldblatt and Julie Graham-Chang,* p. 56.

School Librarian, autumn, 2010, Rosemary Woodman, review of *Research for the Social Improvement and General Betterment of Lydia Goldblatt and Julie Graham-Chang,* p. 165.

School Library Journal, April, 2010, Laurie Slagenwhite, review of *Research for the Social Improvement and General Betterment of Lydia Goldblatt and Julie Graham-Chang,* p. 160.

Voice of Youth Advocates, August, 2010, Robbie Flowers, review of *Research for the Social Improvement and General Betterment of Lydia Goldblatt and Julie Graham-Chang,* p. 247.

ONLINE

Fuse #8 Production Web log, http://blog.schoollibrary journal.com/afuse8production/ (September 2, 2010), Elizabeth Bird, review of *Research for the Social Improvement and General Betterment of Lydia Goldblatt and Julie Graham-Chang.*

GraphicNovelReporter.com, http://www.graphicnovelreport er.com/ (August 15, 2011), Snow Wildsmith, review of *Research for the Social Improvement and General Betterment of Lydia Goldblatt and Julie Graham-Chang.*

Harry Abrams Web site, http://www.abramsbooks.com/ (August 15, 2011), "Amy Ignatow."

Society of Children's Book Writers and Illustrators Web log, http://scbwi.blogspot.com/ (May 13, 2010), Alice Pope, interview with Ignatow.*

*   *   *

JACOBSON, Jennifer
See JACOBSON, Jennifer Richard

*   *   *

JACOBSON, Jennifer Richard 1958-
(Jennifer Jacobson)

Personal

Born 1958, in Peterborough, NH; married; children: two. *Education:* Harvard University, M.A. (education). *Hobbies and other interests:* Hiking, swimming, skiing, reading.

Addresses

Home—Cumberland, ME. *E-mail*—jennifer@jennifer jacobson.com.

Career

Teacher, educational consultant, editor, and author. Writer, beginning 1995. Sixth-grade teacher, curriculum coordinator, and language-arts specialist at various schools in New England; educational consultant. Presenter at schools.

Awards, Honors

Bank Street College of Education Best Children's Book selection, and Top Ten First Novels listee, *Booklist*, both 2001, both for *Winnie Dancing on Her Own;* Children's Curriculum Choice selection, *School Library Journal*, and Rhode Island Children's Book Award nominee, 2004, both for *Truly Winnie;* Best Children's Book selection, Chicago Public Library, and Texas 2X2 listee, both 2005, both for *Andy Shane and the Very Bossy Dolores Starbuckle;* New York Public Library Books for the Teen Age selection, Lupine Award for Juvenile Title (ME), and American Library Association Best Books for Young Adults selection, all 2006, all for *Stained;* Bank Street College of Education 100 Best Books selection, 2008, for *Andy Shane and the Queen of Egypt;* Parents' Choice Gold Fiction Award, 2011, for *Small as an Elephant.*

Writings

FOR CHILDREN

(As Jennifer Jacobson) *Mr. Lee* (picture book), illustrated by John Agee, Open Court Pub. (Chicago, IL), 1995.

(As Jennifer Jacobson) *Getting to Know Sharks* (nonfiction), Sadlier-Oxford (New York, NY), 1997.

(As Jennifer Jacobson) *A Net of Stars* (picture book), illustrated by Greg Shed, Dial Books for Young Readers (New York, NY), 1998.

Moon Sandwich Mom (picture book), illustrated by Benrei Huang, Albert Whitman (Morton Grove, IL), 1999.

Winnie Dancing on Her Own (chapter book), illustrated by Alissa Imre Geis, Houghton Mifflin (Boston, MA), 2001.

Truly Winnie (chapter book), illustrated by Alissa Imre Geis, Houghton Mifflin (Boston, MA), 2003.

Winnie at Her Best (chapter book), illustrated by Alissa Imre Geis, Houghton Mifflin (Boston, MA), 2005.

Small as an Elephant, Candlewick Press (Somerville, MA), 2011.

"ANDY SHANE" BEGINNING READER SERIES; ILLUSTRATED BY ABBY CARTER

Andy Shane and the Very Bossy Dolores Starbuckle, Candlewick Press (Cambridge, MA), 2005.

Andy Shane and the Pumpkin Trick Candlewick Press (Cambridge, MA), 2006.

Andy Shane Is NOT in Love, Candlewick Press (Cambridge, MA), 2008.

Andy Shane and the Queen of Egypt, Candlewick Press (Cambridge, MA), 2008.

Andy Shane and the Barn Sale Mystery, Candlewick Press (Somerville, MA), 2009.

Andy Shane, Hero at Last, Candlewick Press (Cambridge, MA), 2010.

YOUNG-ADULT NOVELS

Stained, Atheneum Books for Young Readers (New York, NY), 2005.

The Complete History of Why I Hate Her, Atheneum Books for Young Readers (New York, NY), 2010.

FOR ADULTS

How Is My First Grader Doing in School?: What to Expect and How to Help, Simon & Schuster (New York, NY), 1998.

(With Dottie Raymer) *How Is My Second Grader Doing in School?: What to Expect and How to Help,* Simon & Schuster (New York, NY), 1998.

How Is My Third Grader Doing in School?: What to Expect and How to Help, Simon & Schuster (New York, NY), 1999.

The Big Book of Reproducible Graphic Organizers, Scholastic (New York, NY), 1999.

(With Dottie Raymer) *How Is My Fourth Grader Doing in School?: What to Expect and How to Help,* Simon & Schuster (New York, NY), 2000.

(With Dottie Raymer) *How Is My Fifth Grader Doing in School?: What to Expect and How to Help,* Simon & Schuster (New York, NY), 2000.

(With Dottie Raymer) *How Is My Sixth Grader Doing in School?: What to Expect and How to Help,* Simon & Schuster (New York, NY), 2000.

(As Jennifer Jacobson; with Dottie Raymer) *Reading Renaissance Power Lessons: Literature-based Lessons to Teach Reading Skills,* School Renaissance Institute (Madison, WI), 2001.

(As Jennifer Jacobsen) *No More "I'm Done!": Fostering Independent Writing in the Primary Grades,* Stenhouse Publishers (Portland, ME), 2010.

Adaptations

Truly Winnie was adapted for audiobook, narrated by Laura Hamilton, Live Oak Media, 2009. The "Andy Shane" chapter books were also adapted as audiobooks.

Sidelights

Jennifer Richard Jacobson is a teacher-turned-writer who has produced guides for parents and educators that include *How Is My First Grader Doing in School?: What to Expect and How to Help* and its sequels. Also writing for both teens and children in the elementary grades, Jacobson has produced the "Winnie" and "Andy Shane" chapter books as well as picture books and the young-adult novels *Stained* and *The Complete History of Why I Hate Her.*

Reviewing Jacobson's picture book *A Net of Stars,* about how a little girl manages to overcome her fear of heights by riding a Ferris wheel during a starlit night, *Booklist* reviewer Hazel Rochman praised the author for relating her tale "quietly in the first person." A writer for *Publishers Weekly* was also positive about this "nostalgic" work, predicting that "young readers conquering anxieties of their own will want to linger over this comforting drama." In *Moon Sandwich Mom* Jacobson provides another learning experience, this time introducing a young fox who discovers that life is not really any better at his friends' houses. Kathy Broderick, writing in *Booklist,* observed that in *Moon Sandwich Mom* Jacobson "does a good job getting this 'grass-is-greener' story to a level little ones can understand."

Middle graders are Jacobson's chosen audience in *Small as an Elephant,* which finds a preteen trying to make sense of the unpredictability of his busy mom. Although he has always had to look out for himself where the little things in life are concerned, Jack Martel also enjoyed pursuing his interest in elephants, an animal he loves for its reliability. On a camping trip along the Maine coast, Jack wakes up to find his mother gone.

Jennifer Richard Jacobson's story in* Winnie Dancing on Her Own *comes to life in Alissa Imre Geis's charming pen-and-ink art. (Illustration copyright © 2001 by Alissa Imre Geis. Reprinted by permission of Houghton Mifflin Harcourt Publishing Company. All rights reserved.)

With barely enough food or money to get by, the eleven year old decides to make the journey back to Boston on his own, trusting that modelling his decisions on the instincts of elephants will keep him safe and out of foster care. By keeping her focus on Jack rather than on the adults who are dedicated to tracking him down, Jacobson shows that the boy's perception of the world is "nicely tied together by the elephant theme" and helps his adventure resolve in a "happy yet realistic ending," according to *Horn Book* contributor Dean Schneider.

With *Winnie Dancing on Her Own* Jacobson introduces third-grader Winnie and her friends Zoe and Vanessa. Ballet class threatens the friendship of these three, since Winnie would much rather go to the library than to dance class. Gradually finding herself an outsider to her other friends' growing intimacy, Winnie learns important lessons about herself and her relationship to her widowed father as a result. A critic for *Kirkus Reviews* noted that in *Winnie Dancing on Her Own* the author "does a skillful job of showing the heart-wrenching emotions felt by a child left behind by unfeeling friends," and a reviewer for *Publishers Weekly* called Jacobson's chapter book an "uplifting tale."

Jacobson reprises her youthful protagonist in *Truly Winnie* and *Winnie at Her Best,* both of which feature Alissa Imre Geis's whimsical line drawings. A "winning second episode," according to a *Kirkus Reviews* critic, *Truly Winnie* finds the three girls at summer camp, but when Winnie is separated from Zoe and Vanessa she must make new friends. When Winnie tells one white lie to deflect sympathy over the death of her mother, she discovers that the lies suddenly multiply and she ends up in trouble. The girls are in fourth grade in *Winnie at Her Best,* as Winnie's feelings of being bested by her friends' varied accomplishments are resolved during a project helping kindergarten readers. *Booklist* contributor Rochman noted of *Truly Winnie* that "young readers will find a lot to talk about; they'll recognize that Winnie's lie is also a wish." Jean Gaffney, reviewing the same title in *School Library Journal,* praised Jacobson's "satisfying, quick-moving story" as one that "portrays the fun and challenge of camp life and making new friends," while in *Booklist* Phelan dubbed *Winnie at Her Best* a "rewarding choice" due to its "fine-tuned, realistic dialogue." "Winnie Fletcher is the kind of friend we all wish we could be," concluded a *Kirkus Reviews* writer in reviewing the third book in the series.

While Jacobson's "Winnie" stories focus on a likeable young girl, boys find a friend in her "Andy Shane" beginning readers, which feature pencil-and-wash illustrations by Abby Carter. Praised by *School Library Journal* contributor Rachael Vilmar for presenting "a refreshing perspective on a common childhood issue," *Andy Shane and the Very Bossy Dolores Starbuckle* introduces Andy and his arch enemy, class know-it-all Dolores Starbuckle. The boy's adventures continue in *Andy Shane and the Pumpkin Trick* as an invitation to Dolores's birthday party falls on the same day as Hal-

Jacobson teams up with illustrator Abby Carter in her humorous picture book **Andy Shane and the Queen of Egypt.** (Illustration copyright © 2008 by Abby Carter. Reproduced with permission of Candlewick Press, Somverville, MA.)

loween, and romantic jealousy comes to the fore when he becomes a special helper to the new girl in school in *Andy Shane Is NOT in Love.* Dolores makes continued attempts to upstage Andy in both *Andy Shane and the Queen of Egypt* and *Andy Shane, Hero at Last,* but she proves to be a loyal friend and helps him buy a special gift for his beloved Granny Webb in *Andy Shane and the Barn Sale Mystery.* In *Booklist,* Phelan praised *Andy Shane and the Queen of Egypt* as "sensitively written and expressively illustrated," while *School Library Journal* critic Linda Staskus called *Andy Shane and the Pumpkin Trick* "an entertaining, easy chapter book." "Jacobson's light touch and respect for her audience make the ordinary happenings of a little boy in a small town universal," concluded Robin L. Smith in her *Horn Book* review of *Andy Shane, Hero at Last.*

Jacobson's young-adult novel *Stained* focuses on teenage relationships and the harm caused by the sexual predations of a priest. This "carefully written novel tells how adolescents are vulnerable to sexual abuse," according to *Kliatt* reviewer Claire Rosser. Set in 1975, *Stained* is told from the point of view of teenager Jocelyn, who has found real affection with Benny, a boy who is new to her neighborhood. Meanwhile Gabe, whom Jocelyn has known since childhood, is acting odder than usual. Soon Benny, feeling guilty about his relationship with Jocelyn, begins visiting the local priest and avoids her. When Gabe suddenly disappears, things come to a head in what a *Publishers Weekly* reviewer described as a "quietly powerful, expertly told tale." Similarly, a contributor for *Kirkus Reviews* called Jacobson's first young-adult offering a "well-written and

suspenseful story." Writing in *Horn Book,* Lauren Adams praised Jocelyn's narrative voice as "honest and compelling," and Rosser asserted that Jocelyn's narration "grips the reader with her honesty, her confusion, and her growing wisdom."

High schooler Nola Werth plans a summer alternating her time between friends and her job waitressing at a coastal vacation resort when readers meet her in *The Complete History of Why I Hate Her,* a YA novel that "has undeniable appeal," according to a *Publishers Weekly* critic. When Nola first meets her, Carly seems to be the perfect summer best friend, and the girls share fashion tips and stories and adventures while also working at the same Maine hotel. However, Carly soon begins to show flashes of a darker, jealous side. As their relationship develops a competitive edge, the competition soon extends to Nola's beloved younger sister, thirteen-year-old Song, who is suffering with cancer. *The Complete History of Why I Hate Her* was praised by *School Library Journal* critic Robyn Zaneski as a "well-written" coming-of-age story, and *Booklist* critic Francesca Goldsmith recommended Jacobson's novel as "a compelling story of self-discovery with plenty of insights into the motivations that drive relationships."

Biographical and Critical Sources

PERIODICALS

Booklist, June 1, 1998, Hazel Rochman, review of *A Net of Stars,* p. 1779; July, 1999, Kathy Broderick, review of *Moon Sandwich Mom,* p. 1951; September 15, 2001, Hazel Rochman, review of *Winnie Dancing on Her Own,* p. 232; September 1, 2003, Hazel Rochman, review of *Truly Winnie,* p. 119; July, 2005, John Peters, review of *Andy Shane and the Very Bossy Dolores Starbuckle,* p. 1929; August 1, 2006, Carolyn Phelan, review of *Winnie at Her Best,* p. 88; September 1, 2006, Julie Cummins, review of *Andy Shane and the Pumpkin Trick,* p. 137; April 1, 2008, Carolyn Phelan, review of *Andy Shane and the Queen of Egypt,* p. 50; February 15, 2010, Francisca Goldsmith, review of *The Complete History of Why I Hate Her,* p. 47.

Horn Book, March-April, 2005, Lauren Adams, review of *Stained,* p. 202; September-October, 2006, Betty Carter, review of *Andy Shane and the Pumpkin Trick,* and Christine M. Heppermann, review of *Winnie at Her Best,* both p. 586; March-April, 2010, Robin L. Smith, review of *Andy Shane, Hero at Last,* p. 58; March-April, 2011, Dean Schneider, review of *Small as an Elephant,* p. 119.

Kirkus Reviews, August 1, 2001, review of *Winnie Dancing on Her Own,* p. 1125; August 1, 2003, review of *Truly Winnie,* p. 1018; March 1, 2005, review of *Stained,* p. 288; June 15, 2005, review of *Andy Shane and the Very Bossy Dolores Starbuckle,* p. 684; July 15, 2006, reviews of *Winnie at Her Best* and *Andy Shane and the Pumpkin Trick,* both p. 724.

Kliatt, January, 2005, Claire Rosser, review of *Stained,* p. 8.

Publishers Weekly, June 22, 1998, review of *A Net of Stars,* p. 90; August 6, 2001, review of *Winnie Dancing on Her Own,* p. 90; August 25, 2003, review of *Truly Winnie,* p. 66; February 1, 2005, review of *Stained,* p. 176; April 19, 2010, review of *The Complete History of Why I Hate Her,* p. 55.

School Library Journal, December, 2001, Elaine Lesh Morgan, review of *Winnie Dancing on Her Own,* p. 104; November, 2003, Jean Gaffney, review of *Truly Winnie,* p. 96; March, 2005, Francisca Goldsmith, review of *Stained,* p. 212; August, 2005, Rachael Vilmar, review of *Andy Shane and the Very Bossy Dolores Starbuckle,* p. 97; September, 2006, Tina Zubak, review of *Winnie at Her Best,* p. 174; October, 2006, Linda Staskus, review of *Andy Shane and the Pumpkin Trick,* p. 113; July, 2008, Laura Scott, review of *Andy Shane and the Queen of Egypt,* p. 75; December, 2009, Beth Cuddy, review of *And Shane and the Barn Sale Mystery,* p. 85; August, 2010, Robyn Zaneski, review of *The Complete History of Why I Hate Her,* p. 104.

ONLINE

Jennifer Richard Jacobson Home Page, http://www.jenniferjacobson.com (September 15, 2011).*

*   *   *

KLING, Heidi R.

Personal

Born in CA; married; has children. *Education:* University of California—Santa Cruz, B.A. (literature), 1994; New School University, M.F.A. (creative writing), 2001.

Addresses

Home—Palo Alto, CA. *Agent*—Sara Crowe, Harvey Klinger, Inc., sara@harveyklinger.com. *E-mail*—heidi writesstuff@gmail.com.

Career

Writer.

Awards, Honors

Best Pick selection, International Teachers Association, 2010, and Northern California Independent Booksellers Book of the Year finalist, both for *Sea.*

Writings

Sea, G.P. Putnam's Sons (New York, NY), 2010.

Contributor to anthologies, including *A Visitor's Guide to Mystic Falls,* 2010, *Truth and Dare,* 2011, and *Firsts,* 2011.

Sidelights

In *Sea* California-based author Heidi R. Kling weaves together a story of varied threads. Sienna "Sea" Jones is a fifteen-year-old Californian who is still haunted by her mother's disappearance several years ago during a flight for a relief misson that took her over the Indian Ocean. When her psychologist father learns of the devastation in the wake of an Indonesian tsunami, he now volunteers to go and asks a reluctant Sienna to accompany him. As she attempts to navigate the Muslim culture of Indonesia, the teen stands out due to her blonde hair and Western ways. Surprisingly, in this alien country she finds a kindred spirit in newly orphaned seventeen-year-old Deni. At night Deni sneaks Sienna out onto the back streets and shows her the many sides of Islamic life while also helping her to reassess her own possibilities.

Reviewing *Sea* in *Kirkus Reviews,* a contributor dubbed Kling's novel "well-meaning" but added that the romantic aspects are diminished by the story's tragic setting. *School Library Journal* contributor Suanne Roush recommended *Sea* to "teens who like relationship novels," while a *Publishers Weekly* reviewer predicted that "fans of . . . teen romance" will discover an "exotic" twist to the genre in *Sea.*

Biographical and Critical Sources

PERIODICALS

Kirkus Reviews, May 1, 2010, review of *Sea.*
Publishers Weekly, June 21, 2010, review of *Sea,* p. 50.
School Library Journal, June, 2010, Suanne Roush, review of *Sea,* p. 108.

ONLINE

Heidi R. Kling Web log, http://heidirkling.tumblr.com (September 15, 2011).*

L

LAIRAMORE, Dawn

Personal

Female. *Education:* University of California, Davis, B.A. (English); paralegal degree.

Addresses

Home—Sacramento, CA. *Agent*—Nancy Gallt Literary Agency, 273 Charlton Ave., South Orange, NJ, 07079. *E-mail*—dawn.lairamore@yahoo.com.

Career

Writer. Worked as an editorial assistant for a small publisher; former technical writer for software company. Presenter at schools.

Awards, Honors

Bank Street College Best Children's Books selection, 2011, for *Ivy's Ever After.*

Writings

"IVY" NOVEL SERIES

Ivy's Ever After, Holiday House (New York, NY), 2010.
Ivy and the Meanstalk, Holiday House (New York, NY), 2011.

Sidelights

In her "Ivy" novels for middle-grade readers, Dawn Lairamore taps her long-held love of fairy stories while also introducing a surprising twist. A "military brat" who spent her childhood moving from one group of friends to another, Lairamore found retained longtime friends in the small collection of books she carried with her to each new home. By high school, her family was permanently settled in California, and she went on to earn her English degree at the University of California, Davis. A job as an editorial assistant for a publisher and work as a technical writer allowed Lairamore to use her talent for writing but not her creativity. This changed when she came up with the idea for the story that would become her first novel, *Ivy's Ever After.*

In *Ivy's Ever After* readers are transported to Ardendale, where the reigning princess is locked in a tall tower and a fearsome dragon stands guard. While it sounds like a traditional fairy tale will unfold from such a premise, complete with a love-besotted prince and a royal wedding, such is not the case in Lairamore's story. Fourteen-year-old Ivy, the princess in question, would rather not be rescued by a brave and handsome prince, and the dragon on guard is a timid beast named Elridge. Unfortunately, when Prince Romil arrives from a cold northern land, he seems determined to win Ivy's hand in marriage—and thereby become king of a much more temperate clime—despite the presence of the fearsome-looking Elridge. Romil's persistence forces Ivy and Elridge into an unusual partnership, and they set off to find Ivy's fairy godmother and discover how to avoid a fairytale ending to their story. Calling Ivy "an engaging alternative to the standard damsel-in-distress figure," Melissa Moore added in *Booklist* that *Ivy's Ever After* also benefits from a "lushly vivid setting" and "witty dialogue." Eva Mitnick also enjoyed Lairamore's story, calling the novel an "entertaining" story "with a nice balance of character development and action" in her *School Library Journal* review, while a *Kirkus Reviews* writer dubbed *Ivy's Ever After* a "fractured fairy tale [that] will delight tween readers."

Ivy and Elridge locate Ivy's fairy godmother in *Ivy's ever After,* but another adventure awaits them in *Ivy and the Meanstalk.* This time Lairamore's likeable characters stumble sideways into the plot of "Jack and the Beanstalk," as a giant who misses her magic harp decides to hold the kingdom hostage until her prized instrument is returned. The author's "lighthearted quest

tale" is buoyed by a "heroine with engaging stubbornness," noted a *Kirkus Reviews* contributor, making *Ivy and the Meanstalk* "breezy and entertaining."

Biographical and Critical Sources

PERIODICALS

Booklist, May 15, 2010, Melissa Moore, review of *Ivy's Ever After,* p. 53.

Kirkus Reviews, April 1, 2010, review of *Ivy's Ever After;* April 15, 2011, review of *Ivy and the Meanstalk.*

School Library Journal, August, 2010, Eva Mitnick, review of *Ivy's Ever After,* p. 106.

ONLINE

Dawn Lairamore Home Page, http://www.dawnbooks.com (September 15, 2011).*

*   *   *

LANGDO, Bryan 1973-

Personal

Born January 7, 1973, in Denville, NJ; son of Steven (an engineer) and Barbara (a homemaker) Langdo; married; wife's name Nikki; children: Oliver. *Education:* Attended Art Student's League of New York, 1992-95; Rutgers University, B.A. (cum laude), 1998. *Hobbies and other interests:* Hiking, cooking, playing in the yard.

Addresses

Home and office—NY. *E-mail*—bryanlangdo@gmail.com.

Career

Illustrator. Mount Olive Child Care and Learning Center, Flanders, NJ, head teacher, 1998-99, 2000-01; Children's Institute, Verona, NJ, teacher's assistant, beginning 2001; Tusk Entertainment, Califon, NJ, production assistant, 2001. *Exhibitions:* Work included in Original Art show, Society of Illustrators, New York, NY, 2002.

Awards, Honors

Best Children's Books of the Year selection, Bank Street College of Education, 2002, for *Joe Cinders* by Marianne Mitchell.

Writings

SELF-ILLUSTRATED

The Dog Who Loved the Good Life, Henry Holt (New York, NY), 2001.

Tornado Slim and the Magic Cowboy Hat, Marshall Cavendish (Tarrytown, NY), 2011.

ILLUSTRATOR

Marianne Mitchell, *Joe Cinders,* Henry Holt (New York, NY), 2002.

Brian James, *Spooky Hayride,* Scholastic (New York, NY), 2003.

Eileen Spinelli, *The Best Time of Day,* Harcourt (Orlando, FL), 2005.

Cindy Neuschwander, *Mummy Math: An Adventure in Geometry,* Henry Holt (New York, NY), 2005.

Sandra Levins, *Was It the Chocolate Pudding?: A Story for Little Kids about Divorce,* Magination Press (Washington, DC), 2005.

Else Holmelund Minarik, *Cat and Dog,* HarperCollins (New York, NY), 2005.

Alison Inches, *The Stuffed Animals Get Ready for Bed,* Harcourt (Orlando, FL), 2006.

Cindy Neuschwander, *Patterns in Peru: An Adventure in Patterning,* Henry Holt (New York, NY), 2007.

Jean M. Malone, *No Room at the Inn: The Nativity Story,* Grosset & Dunlap (New York, NY), 2009.

Cindy Neuschwander, *Pastry School in Paris: An Adventure in Capacity,* Henry Holt (New York, NY), 2009.

Jane Annunziata and Marc Nemiroff, *Sometimes I'm Scared,* Magination Press (Washington, DC), 2009.

Trish Trinco, *The Leaf That Wouldn't Leave,* Tristan Publishing (Minneapolis, MN), 2009.

Sarah Burell, *Diamond Jim Dandy and the Sheriff,* Sterling (New York, NY), 2010.

Sandra Levins, *Do You Sing Twinkle?: A Story about Remarriage and New Family,* Magination Press (Washington, DC), 2010.

Melinda Hardin, *Hero Dad,* Marshall Cavendish (New York, NY), 2010.

Jean M. Malone, *The Miracle of Easter,* Grosset & Dunlap (New York, NY), 2010.

Malachy Doyle, *Jack and the Jungle,* A & C Black (London, England), 2010.

Sidelights

Bryan Langdo is the author and illustrator of *The Dog Who Loved the Good Life,* his debut picture book, as well as *Tornado Slim and the Magic Cowboy Hat,* a tall tale. Langdo has also provided the artwork for more than a dozen books by other writers, including Eileen Spinelli's *The Best Time of Day* Sarah Burell's *Diamond Jim Dandy and the Sheriff,* and Melinda Hardin's *Hero Dad.* "I think working on children's books inspires me to think about my childhood more than I would otherwise," Langdo admitted in an interview on the Macmillan Web site. "It keeps me young at heart, I think. This may or may not help with my work, but it certainly helps to keep me a happy person."

The Dog Who Loved the Good Life introduces readers to a canine named Jake who expects to be treated just like a pampered human being. Jake wants to eat at the

dinner table, sit on the furniture, and use the television remote control. The pup's owner, Mr. Hibble, is not pleased with the situation, but he is unsure about the best way to control his pet. Instead, Mr. Hibble tries to rid himself of the demanding dog, first by putting Jake on a bus and then sending him into outer space. Jake keeps coming back, however, until Mr. Hibble finally comes up with a better solution: giving the dog to his niece. Although some critics were disturbed by Mr. Hibble's efforts to rid himself of the dog, others noted that Langdo's illustrations clearly convey the fact that his story is intended to be taken tongue in cheek. A *Kirkus Reviews* contributor wrote that while *The Dog Who Loved the Good Life* "ought to give lawless kiddos

a pause . . . [it] is softened considerably by Langdo's meltingly affectionate artwork." Writing in *Booklist,* Michael Cart remarked that the artist's "cartoon illustrations add nice comic touches" to an "appealing" tale.

Tornado Slim and the Magic Cowboy Hat, set in the Old West, centers on a cowboy whose new hat, a gift from a wily coyote, spells trouble wherever he goes. He returns to the Old West in illustrating *Joe Cinder,* a collaboration with Marianne Mitchell that was described as "a knee-slapping, rootin'-tootin' Wild West version of the classic Cinderella tale" by a *Kirkus Reviews* critic. A lowly ranch hand, Joe Cinders does the bidding of his three lazy stepbrothers, including toting the

***Bryan Langdo's illustration assignments include Cindy Neuschwander's math concept book* Patterns in Peru.** (Copyright © 2007 Cindy Neuschwander. Illustrations copyright © 2007 by Bryan Langdo. All rights reserved. Reprinted by permission of Henry Holt and Company, LLC.)

water for their annual baths. When the Bronco boys receive an invitation to a fiesta at the ranch of the lovely Rosalinda, Joe harbors no illusions of attending the event. A mysterious, sombrero-clad stranger provides Joe with new jeans and a shiny pick-up, however, and the ranch hand makes a positive impression on his beautiful host, although he leaves a cowboy boot behind in his rush to meet the stranger's midnight deadline. "Langdo's watercolor cartoons are light and cheerful," noted Ruth Semrau in *School Library Journal,* and the *Kirkus Reviews* contributor added that "Langdo's illustrations hit the mark and add to the appeal of the storyline."

Spinelli's *The Best Time of Day,* a work told in verse, depicts the special moments within a farming community. As the day progresses, readers learn that the rooster looks forward to crowing at sunrise, the farmer's son enjoys recess at school, and the little boy's grandmother waits patiently for a visit from a special guest. According to a contributor in *Kirkus Reviews,* "Langdo's earth-toned watercolors are just right for the country and farm setting" in *The Best Time of Day.* Shelle Rosenfeld, writing in *Booklist,* observed that his "illustrations portray [Spinelli's] characters and an idyllic rural setting with cartoonlike simplicity," and *School Library Journal* reviewer Lisa S. Schindler remarked that Langdo's pictures "are colorful and laugh-out-loud funny."

Langdo has also contributed artwork to a trio of arithmetic books by Cindy Neuschwander. In *Mummy Math: An Adventure in Geometry,* Matt and Bibi Zill journey to Egypt with their parents to locate the burial chamber of a pharaoh. "The book is reminiscent of those old-fashioned easy puzzle books; the illustrations . . . are bright and clever, and there's a straightforward lesson in geometry built into the promise of Egypt," Meg Wolitzer wrote in the *New York Times Book Review.* A companion volume, *Patterns in Peru: An Adventure in Patterning,* finds the Zills searching for the Lost City of Quwi. Here "Langdo's vibrantly colored watercolors support the text," as a contributor in *Kirkus Reviews* observed, and his "cartoonlike illustrations adequately depict patterns to decipher," according to *School Library Journal* critic Kathy Piehl. Matt and Bibi return in Neuschwander's *Pastry School in Paris: An Adventure in Capacity,* which finds the twins using the knowledge gleaned from their cooking class to prepare a special meal for an influential visitor. "Appealing watercolor illustrations suggest the Parisian setting with views of a few famous sites," Carolyn Phelan maintained in *Booklist,* while Langdo's "bold, bright, and amusing watercolor illustrations" for *Pastry School in Paris:* garnered praise from *School Library Journal* contributor Kathleen Finn.

First published in 1960, Else Holmelund Minarik's *Cat and Dog* was reissued in 2005 with new illustrations by Langdo. The work concerns the unlikely friendship between a frisky canine and a cautious feline. Laura Scott, writing in *School Library Journal,* applauded the book's "colorful, cheerful" artwork. In another illustration project, *The Stuffed Animals Get Ready for Bed* by Alison Inches, a little girl attempts to get her menagerie of toys ready for a night of slumber. As the youngster brushes her teeth, however, her spotted cow begins singing, her red hen dines on a bowl of soup, and her kitten finds a hiding place. Here Langdo's "pictures artistically convey the energy of the text," noted *Booklist* contributor Ilene Cooper, while Catherine Callegari wrote in *School Library Journal* that his "watercolor spreads enliven the text with fun depictions of the toys' antics."

Hardin pays tribute to military families in *Hero Dad,* another picture book featuring Langdo's pencil-and-watercolor illustrations. In the work, a youngster compares his father, a U.S. soldier now serving in the Middle East, to a comic-book superhero, citing his ability to fly (parachute from a plane), his X-ray vision (using night-vision goggles), and his bravery (patrolling the desert). "The bright, cartoon artwork makes the book child-friendly," Mary Landrum maintained in *School Library Journal,* and *Booklist* reviewer Ray Enos applauded "the solemn, uncluttered illustrations clearly portraying the father's actions." A *Publishers Weekly* critic praised the combination of story and art in *Hero Dad,* remarking that Hardin's "minimal, confident text is in perfect sync with the khaki and fatigue-hued combat scenes."

A sleepy Western town gets a jolt of excitement from an unexpected source in *Diamond Jim Dandy and the Sheriff,* a work by Burell. Little of consequence happens in Dustpan, Texas, a town so deadly dull that its sheriff takes babysitting jobs just to pass the time. When a rattlesnake arrives for a visit, however, the lawman jumps into action, telling the snake to leave town. In contrast, the townspeople welcome the kindhearted reptile with open arms, finding it to be a most pleasant and entertaining companion. When young Idie Mae Tumbleweed goes missing the rattler comes to the rescue, thereby proving its worth to the sheriff. "Langdo's watercolors have an appropriately dusty feel to them," a contributor in *Kirkus Reviews* observed in a review of *Diamond Jim Dandy and the Sheriff,* while other reviewers complimented the artist's use of humor in his pictures. "The Old West-infused comic illustrations are a good match for this tale," Julie Cummins stated in her *Booklist* appraisal of *Diamond Jim Dandy and the Sheriff,* and a *Publishers Weekly* critic reported that Langdo's "chipper, homespun cartoons bring additional comedic dimension" to Burell's narrative.

Langdo once told *SATA:* "I have been drawing for as long as I can remember. It has always been the one area of my life where I have total focus. Growing up, I most often would draw from comic books and fantasy art. I also loved Dr. Seuss as a young kid, just like everyone else. My favorite book was *The Sailor Dog,* though, by Margaret Wise Brown. I've always loved big adventures, and I think that book does a great job capturing the feel of a big adventure in a small book.

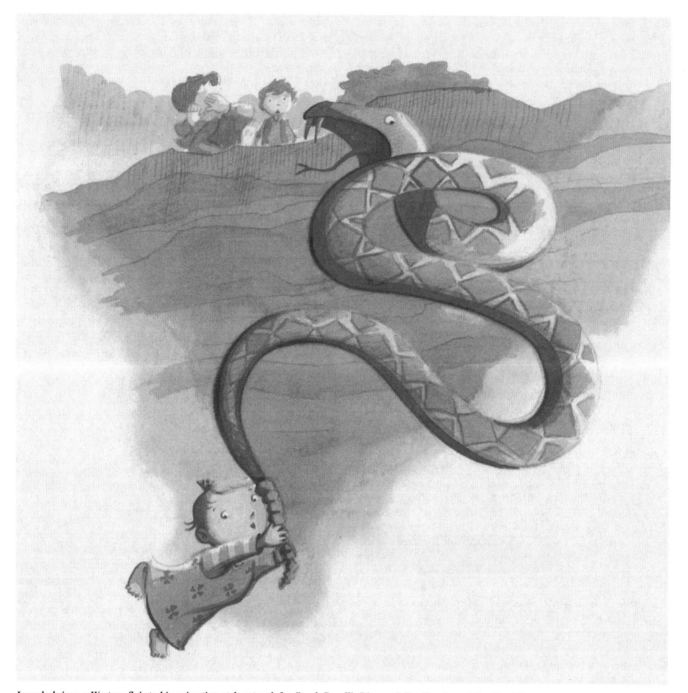

Langdo brings a Western flair to his animation-style artwork for Sarah Burell's Diamond Jim Dandy and the Sheriff. (Illustration copyright © 2010 by Bryan Langdo. Reproduced with permission of Sterling Publishing Co., Inc.)

"I never considered doing picture books until I met Robert J. Blake, from whom I took lessons all through middle and high school. Watching his books develop and come to completion week by week firsthand was an invaluable experience alone, not to mention all he taught me about composition, drawing, and painting. After high school, I studied at the Art Student's League of New York, doing life drawing and life painting—very academic.

"How I got into writing was just the next logical step. In order to practice illustrating and to develop a personal style, I began making up scenarios and/or stories to make pictures about. I sent out stories and illustrations constantly for a year, hoping to get published. A big part of me assumed it would never happen, but I stuck with it anyway. The day I found out *The Dog Who Loved the Good Life* was going to be published was possibly the best day of my life. I remember it like it was yesterday, and I'm still having trouble believing it.

"I write sporadically at best. If and when an idea comes, I try to develop it and work when inspired. I draw every day and usually am working on an illustration, even if it's not for something being published. I just can't

stop myself from working on art. My main goal in making a book is to entertain kids, make them laugh out loud if possible. Hopefully, their parents will laugh, too."

Biographical and Critical Sources

PERIODICALS

Booklist, December 1, 2001, Michael Cart, review of *The Dog Who Loved the Good Life,* p. 649; October 15, 2002, Connie Fletcher, review of *Joe Cinders,* p. 408; October 15, 2005, Shelle Rosenfeld, review of *The Best Time of Day,* p. 60; August 1, 2006, Ilene Cooper, review of *The Stuffed Animals Get Ready for Bed,* p. 88; June 1, 2009, Carolyn Phelan, review of *Pastry School in Paris: An Adventure in Capacity,* p. 76; November 15, 2009, Gillian Engberg, review of *Do You Sing Twinkle?: A Story about Remarriage and New Family,* p. 42; February 15, 2010, Julie Cummins, review of *Diamond Jim Dandy and the Sheriff,* p. 80; December 15, 2010, Randall Enos, review of *Hero Dad,* p. 57.

Children's Bookwatch, June, 2005, review of *Mummy Math: An Adventure in Geometry;* June, 2007, review of *Patterns in Peru: An Adventure in Patterning;* January, 2010, review of *The Leaf That Wouldn't Leave.*

Kirkus Reviews, October 1, 2001, review of *The Dog Who Loved the Good Life,* p. 1426; September 1, 2002, review of *Joe Cinders,* p. 1315; March 15, 2005, review of *Mummy Math,* p. 355; September 15, 2005, review of *The Best Time of Day,* p. 1034; March 15, 2007, review of *Patterns in Peru;* May 15, 2009, review of *Pastry School in Paris;* March 1, 2010, review of *Diamond Jim Dandy and the Sheriff.*

New York Times Book Review, March 15, 2005, Meg Wolitzer, review of *Mummy Math.*

Publishers Weekly, November 19, 2001, review of *The Dog Who Loved the Good Life,* p. 66; March 15, 2010, review of *Diamond Jim Dandy and the Sheriff,* p. 50; October 25, 2010, review of *Hero Dad,* p. 45.

School Library Journal, December, 2001, Lucinda Snyder Whitehurst, review of *The Dog Who Loved the Good Life,* p. 105; May, 2002, Lynda Ritterman, review of *Mummy Math,* p. 114; December, 2002, Ruth Semrau, review of *Joe Cinders,* p. 102; August, 2005, Laura Scott, review of *Cat and Dog,* p. 103; January, 2006, Lisa S. Schindler, review of *The Best Time of Day,* p. 114; September, 2006, Catherine Callegari, review of *The Stuffed Animals Get Ready for Bed,* p. 174; March, 2007, Kathy Piehl, review of *Patterns in Peru,* p. 200; August, 2009, Kathleen Finn, review of *Pastry School in Paris,* p. 81; March, 2010, Madeline J. Bryant, review of *Diamond Jim Dandy and the Sheriff,* p. 116; October, 2010, Mary Landrum, review of *Hero Dad,* p. 86.

ONLINE

Bryan Langdo Home Page, http://www.bryanlangdo.com (August 1, 2011).

Macmillan Web site, http://us.macmillan.com/ (August 1, 2011), "Bryan Langdo."*

*   *   *

LOPSHIRE, Robert 1927-2002

Personal

Born April 14, 1927, in Sarasota, FL; died of emphysema and congestive heart failure, May 4, 2002, in Gainesville, FL; son of Conrad A. and Jessie Davidson; adopted by Roy Howard and Dorothy Lopshire; married Jane Haller Ingalls, October 21, 1946 (divorced); married Selma Dorothy Stefel, February 21, 1974; children: (first marriage) Robert Martin, Jr., Howard Christian, Terri Jane, Victoria Anne; (stepchildren) Sandee, Debbie, Wendy. *Education:* Attended Vesper George School of Art and School of Practical Art (Boston, MA), 1946-48. *Hobbies and other interests:* Model aircraft, painting, "stimulating young minds to think and go further than the immediate limits of their own small world."

Career

Author and artist. Freelance artist and illustrator, Philadelphia, PA, 1948-54, Boston, MA, 1954-56, and New York, NY, 1956-59; Random House, New York, NY, creative art director, 1959-61; owner of advertising agency in Sergeantsville, NJ, 1961-64; writer. Consulting art director for companies in New York; public relations director for Academy of Model Aeronautics. *Exhibitions:* Paintings included in private collections. *Military service:* U.S. Coast Guard, 1944-45, served in Pacific theatre; Air Sea Rescues, 1945-46, combat photographer; received invasion awards.

Awards, Honors

Numerous painting awards for realistic still life and landscapes.

Writings

SELF-ILLUSTRATED

Put Me in the Zoo, Beginner Books (New York, NY), 1960, puzzle book edition, 1999, board-book edition, Random House (New York, NY), 2002.

How to Make Flibbers, Etc.: A Book of Things to Make and Do, Beginner Books (New York, NY), 1964, published as *The Beginner's Book of Things to Make: Fun Stuff You Can Make Yourself,* 1977.

A Beginner's Guide to Building and Flying Model Airplanes, Harper & Row (New York, NY), 1967.

I Am Better than You!, Harper & Row (New York, NY), 1968.

It's Magic?, Macmillan (New York, NY), 1969.

Radio Control Miniature Aircraft, Macmillan (New York, NY), 1974.

How to Make Snop Snappers and Other Fine Things, Greenwillow Books (New York, NY), 1977.

The Biggest, Smallest, Fastest, Tallest Things You've Ever Heard Of, Crowell (New York, NY), 1980.

ABC Games, Crowell (New York, NY), 1986.

I Want to Be Somebody New!, Beginner Books (New York, NY), 1986.

I Can Draw, Scholastic (New York, NY), 1988.

Shut the Door!, Western Publishing (Racine, WI), 1993.

New Tricks I Can Do!, Beginner Books (New York, NY), 1996.

Put Me in the Alphabet!: A Beginner Workbook about ABC's, Beginner Books (New York, NY), 1997.

ILLUSTRATOR

Frederick Phleger, *Ann Can Fly,* Random House (New York, NY), 1959.

Kin Platt, *Big Max,* HarperCollins (New York, NY), 1965, with new illustrations, HarperTrophy (New York, NY), 1992.

Betty Baker, *The Pig War,* Harper & Row (New York, NY), 1969.

Richard J. Margolis, *Wish Again, Big Bear,* Macmillan (New York, NY), 1972.

Bernard Wiseman, *Little New Kangaroo,* Macmillan (New York, NY), 1973.

Richard J. Margolis, *Big Bear to the Rescue,* Greenwillow Books (New York, NY), 1975.

Kin Platt, *Big Max in The Mystery of the Missing Moose,* Harper & Row (New York, NY), 1977.

OTHER

Contributor to *World Book Encyclopedia* and to magazines, including *Model Airplane News* and *R/C Modeler.*

Sidelights

An accomplished author and illustrator, Robert Lopshire earned recognition for his whimsical and brightly colored picture books, which include *Put Me in the Zoo, How to Make Snop Snappers and Other Fine Things,* and *New Tricks I Can Do!* Born in Florida in 1927, Lopshire earned his pilot's license at the age of fifteen, and after graduating from high school he served on invasion forces in the Pacific Theatre during World War II. He later found work as an illustrator in studios in Boston, Massachusetts, and Philadelphia, Pennsylvania, before moving to New York City, where he served as an art director at Random House. Lopshire's illustrations for Frederick Phleger's *Ann Can Fly* caught the

attention of Theodor Geisel, better known as Dr. Seuss. "Geisel felt Bob's illustrations really captured the stories well and strongly urged him to try his hand at writing and illustrating his own book," Lopshire's wife, Selma, recalled to Lou Kennedy in the *Sarasota Herald Tribune.* "That launched it all."

Lopshire is probably best known for his debut self-illustrated title, 1960's *Put Me in the Zoo.* As the author/illustrator later explained, "I came to write my first book because, at the time, I was employed as creative art director on the 'Beginner Book' project at Random House, the first of the truly planned assaults on young minds." Later, he explained, "Geisel . . . said that the old 'Dick, Jane and Spot' concept was horrible, and that no one could ever do anything more with the three—he bet me on this. . . . *Put Me in the Zoo* uses Dick, Jane and Spot and I won the bet."

Put Me in the Zoo introduces Spot, a multi-talented leopard (he can even juggle his own spots!) who wants to join the zoo. It was followed by two sequels: *I Want to Be Somebody New!* and *New Tricks I Can Do!* In *I Want to Be Somebody New!* Spot tries on the forms of an elephant, a giraffe, and a mouse. However, he discovers that as an elephant he is too big for his favorite chair, as a giraffe he is too tall for his friends, and as a mouse he cannot even open the door of his house. Finally, his friends convince him that he is fine just as he is. "This intelligent, cheerful sequel, with its simple rhyming text, lives up to the reputation of its predecessor," a *Publishers Weekly* contributor commented. "The theme of self-acceptance is quite admirable," Tom S. Hurlburt noted in his review of *I Want to Be Somebody New!* for *School Library Journal.*

A determined Spot must demonstrate his versatility in *New Tricks I Can Do!,* which was released by Lopshire more than three decades after *Put Me in the Zoo.* Dismissed as a one-trick pony by zoo officials, who begin seeking a new attraction, the leopard shows two youngsters that he has the ability to transform himself into a host of different colors and patterns. The work "ably employ[s] Seussian repetitions and cadences," according to a critic in a *Publishers Weekly* appraisal of *New Tricks I Can Do!*

Lopshire is also the author of "how-to" books for kids. In *The Beginner Book of Things to Make, How to Make Snop Snappers and Other Fine Things* and *How to Make Flibbers, Etc.: A Book of Things to Make and Do* he explains how to craft a variety of child-friendly toys, including homemade Frisbees, bird feeders, dancing dolls, and even a balloon rocket. A *Booklist* contributor appreciated the "ultra-simple design" of the projects in the "usable, readable" *How to Make Snop Snappers and Other Fine Things,* while a *Junior Bookshelf* reviewer dubbed *The Beginner Book of Things to Make* "a zany Seuss-like account of ingenious tricks and gadgets." In *Publishers Weekly* a critic also cited the latter book,

Robert Lopshire is the author/illustrator of the classic children's book **Put Me in the Zoo,** *a beginning readers starring a sociable leopard with disappearing spots.* (Copyright © 1960, renewed 1988 by Random House Children's Books. Used by permission of Random House Children's Books, a division of Random House, Inc.)

praising the way Lopshire "excites imagination by leaving up to his audience to discover what happens when they" put some of his gadgets to use.

"Personally, the best award I've ever received was the news that one of my books was the most often stolen from a large metropolitan library system," noted Lopshire prior to his death in 2002. "I put a tremendous amount of effort into trying to give kids what *they* want . . . what better tribute could any writer ask for than a theft record?"

Biographical and Critical Sources

BOOKS

Shaw, John Mackay, *Childhood in Poetry,* Gale (Detroit, MI), 1967.
Ward, Martha E., and others, *Authors of Books for Young People,* 3rd edition, Scarecrow Press (Metuchen, NJ), 1990.

PERIODICALS

Booklist, September 1, 1974, review of *Radio Control Miniature Aircraft,* p. 9; March 15, 1977, review of *How to Make Snop Snappers and Other Fine Things,* p. 1098; October 15, 1980, review of *The Biggest, Smallest, Fastest, Tallest Things You've Ever Heard Of,* p. 328.
Hobbies, October, 1974, review of *Radio Control Miniature Aircraft,* p. 159.
Horn Book, December, 1980, review of *The Biggest, Smallest, Fastest, Tallest Things You've Ever Heard Of,* pp. 654-655.
Junior Bookshelf, June, 1978, review of *The Beginner Book of Things to Make,* p. 143.
Kirkus Reviews, December 15, 1980, review of *The Biggest, Smallest, Fastest, Tallest Things You've Ever Heard Of,* p. 1569.
New York Times Book Review, May 1, 1977, Nancy Larrick, review of *How to Make Snop Snappers and Other Fine Things,* p. 43.
Publishers Weekly, May 9, 1977, review of *How to Make Snop Snappers and Other Fine Things,* p. 92; October 28, 1983, review of *Big Max in The Mystery of the Missing Moose,* p. 70; June 27, 1986, review of *I Want to Be Somebody New!,* p. 89; October 31, 1986, review of *ABC Games,* p. 64; April 15, 1996, review of *New Tricks I Can Do!,* p. 68.
Reading Teacher, October, 1987, review of *I Want to Be Somebody New!,* p. 36.
School Library Journal, May, 1977, review of *How to Make Snop Snappers and Other Fine Things,* p. 76; October, 1978, review of *It's Magic?,* p. 120; December, 1980, Nancy Palmer, review of *The Biggest, Smallest, Fastest, Tallest Things You've Ever Heard Of,* p. 65; December, 1981, review of *How to Make Flibbers, Etc.: A Book of Things to Make and Do,* p. 79; November, 1986, Tom S. Hurlburt, review of *I Want to Be Somebody New!,* p. 79; December, 1986, Leda Schubert, review of *ABC Games,* p. 92; September, 1996, Marilyn Taniguchi, review of *New Tricks I Can Do!,* p. 184.
Tribune Books (Chicago, IL), September 21, 1986, review of *ABC Games,* p. 9.

Obituaries

PERIODICALS

Sarasota Herald Tribune, May 11, 2002.*

M

MANNING, Jane
(Jane K. Manning)

Personal

Female.

Addresses

Home—Deep River, CT.

Career

Author and illustrator. Presenter at schools.

Writings

SELF-ILLUSTRATED

This Little Piggy, HarperFestival (New York, NY), 1997.
My First Songs, HarperFestival (New York, NY), 1998.
Who Stole the Cookies from the Cookie Jar?, HarperFestival (New York, NY), 2001.
My First Baby Games, HarperFestival (New York, NY), 2001.
Cat Nights, Greenwillow Books (New York, NY), 2008.

ILLUSTRATOR

Susan Saunders, *The Ghost Who Ate Chocolate,* HarperCollins (New York, NY), 1996.
Susan Saunders, *The Haunted Skateboard,* HarperTrophy (New York, NY), 1996.
Alvin Granowsky, *Help Yourself, Little Red Hen!,* Steck-Vaughn (Austin, TX), 1996.
Susan Saunders, *The Revenge of the Pirate Ghost,* HarperCollins (New York, NY), 1997.
Susan Saunders, *The Phantom Pen Pal,* HarperCollins (New York, NY), 1997.
Susan Saunders, *The Ghost of Spirit Lake,* HarperTrophy (New York, NY), 1997.

Susan Saunders, *The Curse of the Cat Mummy,* HarperTrophy (New York, NY), 1997.
Susan Saunders, *The Chilling Tale of Crescent Pond,* HarperCollins (New York, NY), 1998.
Susan Saunders, *The Case of the Eyeball Surprise,* HarperTrophy (New York, NY), 1998.
Susan Saunders, *The Creature Double Feature,* HarperTrophy (New York, NY), 1998.
Susan Saunders, *The Creepy Camp-Out,* HarperTrophy (New York, NY), 1998.
Alice Low, *The Witch Who Was Afraid of Witches,* HarperCollins (New York, NY), 1999.
Sarah Weeks, *Drip, Drop,* HarperCollins (New York, NY), 2000.
Susan Lowell, *Cindy Ellen: A Wild Western Cinderella,* HarperCollins (New York, NY), 2000.
Shirley Climo, *Cobweb Christmas,* HarperCollins (New York, NY), 2001.
Melinda Luke, *The Green Dog,* Kane Press (New York, NY), 2002.
Linda Smith, *There Was an Old Woman Who Lived in a Boot,* HarperCollins (New York, NY), 2003.
Lee Bennett Hopkins, selector, *A Pet for Me,* HarperCollins (New York, NY), 2004.
Sarah Weeks, *Baa-choo!,* HarperCollins (New York, NY), 2004.
Pattie L. Schnetzler, *Fast 'n' Snappy,* Carolrhoda Books (Minneapolis, MN), 2004.
Megan McDonald, *Beetle McGrady Eats Bugs!,* Greenwillow Books (New York, NY), 2005.
Jane Kurtz, *Do Kangaroos Wear Seat Belts?,* Dutton Children's Books (New York, NY), 2005.
Gary L. Blackwood, *The Just-So Woman,* HarperCollins (New York, NY), 2006.
Sarah Weeks, *Pip Squeak,* Laura Geringer Books (New York, NY), 2007.
Lola M. Schaefer and Heather Miller, *Look Behind!: Tales of Animal Ends,* Greenwillow Books (New York, NY), 2008.
Sarah Weeks, *Mac and Cheese,* Laura Geringer Books (New York, NY), 2010.
Sarah Weeks, *Mac and Cheese and the Perfect Plan,* Harper (New York, NY), 2010.

Bobbi Katz, *Nothing but a Dog,* Dutton Children's Books (New York, NY), 2010.

Jack Prelutsky, selector, *There's No Place like School: Classroom Poems,* Greenwillow Books (New York, NY), 2010.

Pamela Jane, *Little Goblins Ten,* Harper (New York, NY), 2011.

Sidelights

A children's author and illustrator who makes her home in a small New England town, Jane Manning is the author of the original self-illustrated picture books *This Little Piggy, My First Songs, Who Stole the Cookies from the Cookie Jar?, My First Baby Games,* and *Cat Nights.* Manning brings something unique to each of her works: in *My First Songs* she shares her own childhood favorites while the traditional toe-counting rhyme that she illustrates in *This Little Piggy* is printed on pages shaped like a foot. *Cat Nights,* which is based on an Irish legend, features a rhyming text that introduces a 263-year-old witch who is close to perfecting a transformative spell that will allow her to prowl like a cat at night. Paired with Manning's "easy-to-read text," the large and colorful illustrations in *Cat Nights* make the book "a great read-aloud choice for storytimes," according to *School Library Journal* contributor Lee Bock.

As an illustrator, Manning crafts art that captures the fun of stories by a wide range of writers, among them Shirley Climo, Alice Low, Lola M. Shaefer, Garry L. Blackwood, Jack Prelutsky, Lee Bennett Hopkins, Bobbi Katz, and Sarah Weeks. In Hopkins' poetry collection *A Pet for Me* verses come to life in full-sized illustrations featuring "appealing animals and cute [multiethnic] children with stylized, elongated eyes," according to a *Kirkus Reviews* writer, while in *School Library Journal* Jane Marino asserted that Manning's "cheerful watercolor illustrations" "suit both the format and the poetry perfectly." Katz's *Nothing but a Dog* captures a child's dream of owning a pet in a simple story that Manning enhances in what *School Library Journal* contributor C.J. Connor described as "delightful watercolor illustrations" that add to the story's "feel-good" spirit. Something scary mixes with something funny in Megan McDonald's *Beetle McGrady Eats Bugs!,* a story about an adventurous second grader that includes appropriately quirky illustrations. Citing Manning's "amiably disgusting" water-color representation of McGrady's wriggling cuisine, a *Kirkus Reviews* judged *Beetle McGrady Eats Bugs!* to be "agreeably icky fun."

In illustrating Susan Lowell's amusing picture book *Cindy Ellen: A Wild Western Cinderella,* Manning was inspired by her memories of Killarny, a horse she rode years before, and his image found its way into her artwork. According to *Book* contributor Kathleen Odean, the "colorful, exaggerated" images in *Cindy Ellen* "add to the tall-tale tone" of Lowell's fairy-tale adaptation, and Manning has continued to exhibit this talent in her artwork for Linda Smith's *There Was an Old Woman Who Lived in a Boot.* Also based on a folk tale and featuring what a *Kirkus Reviews* writer described as an "irascible senior citizen" who cohabits her unusual home with an equally cantankerous kitty, Smith's story benefits from a "bucolic, shoe-dotted landscape" and humorous "children-turned-geezer scenes," according to a *Publishers Weekly* writer.

One of Manning's most frequent collaborators has been author Weeks, for whom she has illustrated the beginning readers *Baa-Choo!, Drip Drop, Pip Squeak,* and *Mac and Cheese.* Pip Squeak the mouse finds a way to cope with a leaky roof in *Drip Drop,* and here Manning's "animated illustrations make the story's action clear and fun to follow," according to *Booklist* contributor Gillian Engberg. In a return engagement, Weeks's resourceful rodent must deal with a terribly untidy houseguest in *Pip Squeak,* while a sneezy sheep sets in motion a series of farmyard antics in *Baa-Choo!* A back alley inhabited by a frisky but rotund cat named Macaroni and a slim but lazy cat named Cheese is the setting for *Mac and Cheese,* and here Weeks's "rhyming text" is well matched by Manning's "appealing, stylized illustrations," according to Carolyn Phelan in *Booklist.* Also recommending the story as a "solid selection for all libraries," Mary Elam noted in her *School Library Journal* review of *Mac and Cheese* that the "action" captured in the book's art "lead[s] readers in turning the page." Reviewing the illustrations for *Pip Squeak,* *School Library Journal* contributor Melinda Piehler noted that Manning's images are "filled with amusing details" and "provide good picture cues" for budding readers.

Biographical and Critical Sources

PERIODICALS

Book, September, 2000, Kathleen Odeon, review of *Cindy Ellen: A Wild Western Cinderella,* p. 86.

Booklist, December 15, 1996, Denia Hester, review of *The Ghost Who Ate Chocolate,* p. 727; November 15, 1998, Kay Weisman, review of *That Toad Is Mine!,* p. 596; September 1, 1999, Kathy Broderick, review of *The Witch Who Was Afraid of Witches,* p. 146; September 15, 1999, Shelley Townsend-Hudson, review of *Lost Little Angel,* p. 269; May 15, 2000, GraceAnne A. DeCandido, review of *Cindy Ellen,* p. 1757; July, 2000, Gillian Engberg, review of *Drip, Drop,* p. 2046; August, 2004, Hazel Rochman, review of *Baa-Choo!,* p. 1946; December 1, 2006, Hazel Rochman, review of *The Just-So Woman,* p. 51; October 1, 2007, Shelle Rosenfeld, review of *My Mom Is a Firefighter,* p. 65; December 15, 2010, Carolyn Phelan, review of *Mac and Cheese,* p. 58.

Horn Book, January-February, 2005, Martha V. Parravano, review of *Baa-Choo!,* p. 99; July-August, 2007, Betty Carter, review of *Pip Squeak,* p. 406.

Jane Manning's illustration projects include Bobbi Katz's entertaining girl-wants-a-pet picture book **Nothing but a Dog.** (Illustration copyright © 2010 by Jane Manning. Used by permission of Dutton Children's Books, a division of Penguin Young Readers Group, a member of Penguin Group (USA) Inc., 375 Hudson St., New York, NY 10014. All rights reserved.)

Kirkus Reviews, February 15, 2003, review of *A Pet for Me,* p. 307; April 15, 2003, review of *There Was an Old Woman Who Lived in a Boot,* p. 1079; November 1, 2004, review of *Baa-Choo!,* p. 1047; January 1, 2005, review of *Do Kangaroos Wear Seat Belts?,* p. 53; April, 2005, review of *Beetle McGrady Eats Bugs!,* p. 421; October 15, 2006, review of *The Just-So Woman,* p. 1066; June 15, 2007, review of *Pip Squeak;* March 1, 2010, review of *Nothing but a Dog.*

Publishers Weekly, December 3, 2001, review of *Cindy Ellen,* p. 63; August 4, 2003, review of *There Was an Old Woman Who Lived in a Boot,* p. 79; February 28, 2005, reviews of *Do Kangaroos Wear Seat Belts?,* p. 65, and *Beetle McGrady Eats Bugs!,* p. 66.

School Library Journal, June, 2000, Starr LaTronica, review of *Cindy Ellen,* p. 134; September, 2000, Martha Topol, review of *Drip, Drop,* p. 211; March, 2003, Jane Marino, review of *A Pet for Me,* p. 219; December, 2003, Blair Christolon, review of *There Was an Old Woman Who Lived in a Boot,* p. 128; April, 2004,

Donna Cardon, review of *Fast 'n' Snappy,* p. 124; January, 2005, Susan Lissim, review of *Baa-Choo!,* p. 98; April, 2005, Piper L. Nyman, review of *Do Kangaroos Wear Seat Belts?,* p. 105; May, 2005, Suzanne Meyers Harold, review of *Beetle McGrady Eats Bugs!,* p. 90; November, 2006, Melinda Piehler, review of *The Just-So Woman,* p. 84; October, 2007, Linda M. Kenton, review of *My Mom Is a Firefighter,* p. 116; February, 2008, Melinda Piehler, review of *Pip Squeak,* p. 98; January, 2009, Lee Bock, review of *Cat Nights,* p. 80; February, 2010, C.J. Connor, review of *Nothing but a Dog,* p. 88; September, 2010, Mary Elam, review of *Mac and Cheese,* p. 135.

ONLINE

Houghton Mifflin Reading Web site, http://www.eduplace. com/ (September 15, 2011), "Jane Manning."*

MANNING, Jane K.
See MANNING, Jane

* * *

MILFORD, Kate 1976-

Personal

Born 1976, in MD; married; husband's name Nathan. *Education:* Ithaca College, B.A. (English, theatre), 1998. *Hobbies and other interests:* Photography.

Addresses

Home—Brooklyn, NY. *Agent*—Ann Behar, Scovil Galen Ghoush, annbehar@sgglit.com. *E-mail*—kate@clock workfoundry.com.

Career

Novelist and columnist. Worked in retail management for Williams-Sonoma, New York, NY, 2003-06, Restoration Hardware, 2006-07, and Estee Lauder Companies, 2007-10; freelance writer, beginning 2001. McNally Jackson Books, New York, NY, children's specialist, beginning 2010.

Member

Science Fiction Writers of America, Society of Children's Book Writers and Illustrators.

Awards, Honors

YALSA Best Fiction for Young Adults selection, 2010, for *The Boneshaker.*

Writings

The Boneshaker, illustrated by Andrea Offermann, Clarion Books (Boston, MA), 2010.
The Broken Lands, illustrated by Andrea Offermann, Clarion Books (Boston, MA), 2012.

Author of plays; contributor of articles to periodicals.

Sidelights

Maryland native Kate Milford's love of mechanical wonders as well as the arcane, and the aberrant inspired her to write "steampunk" fiction before she even knew that there was such a genre. Milford's first novel, *The Boneshaker,* was lauded by numerous fans of steampunk, a branch of science fiction that mixes a speculative scenario with alternate history and usually features a late-nineteenth-century industrialized setting. In addition to her novel, Milford also writes for a Web site promoting the town of Nagspeake. A fictional place of her own creation, Nagspeake exists only online at www.Nagspeake.com, but many fans of *The Boneshaker* anticipate a time when it will become the setting for another of Milford's imaginative tales.

Illustrated by German artist Andrea Offermann, *The Boneshaker* transports readers back to 1913 and a small, shuttered town in Missouri called Arcane. Thirteen-year-old Arcane resident Natalie Minks has always been fascinated by the gear-driven, clicking, and whirring machines she has seen come and go due to her father's work as a mechanic. A carnival has now come to town—Dr. Jake Limberleg's Nostrum Fair and Technological Magic Show—and Natalie is excited until she sees the performances and realizes that each of the acts is strangely syncronized and shadowed by some sort of malevolence. With Dr. Jake's promises that he can cure all manner of disease, the population of Arcane quickly seems to fall under his spell, and not even her father will heed Natalie's warnings. When she bravely ventures behind the curtain concealing the magic show's inner workings, the logic-minded teen realizes that her fears are well founded, and she may be the only one able to save her community.

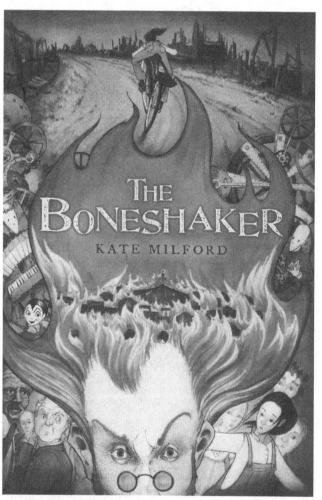

Cover of Kate Milford's intriguing middle-grade novel The Boneshaker, *featuring cover art by Andrea Offermann.* (Illustration copyright © 2010 by Andrea Offerman. Reprinted by permission of Harcourt Children's Books, an imprint of Houghton Mifflin Harcourt Publishing Company. All rights reserved.)

While inspired by Milford's interest in society's more unsettling side, *The Boneshaker* required a great deal of research on the part of the author, including an in-depth study of nineteenth-century patent medicines, which were popular tonics due to their high alcohol content. During her research, she unearthed a bit of history that became her novel's key ingredient: a neurological condition known as Jake Leg, which surfaced during the Prohibition era of the 1930s. Patent medicines were self-administered with abandon as a replacement for alcoholic beverages, and one of the cheapest was called Jamaica Ginger or Jake. To mask the alcohol, the manufacturer added a substance that proved toxic, leaving tens of thousands of users with neurological damage that exhibited itself as trembling of the legs. Hence the title of the carnival in *The Boneshaker*—Dr. Jake Limberleg's Nostrum Fair—and the doctor's easy seduction of the populace or Arcane to the promise of miraculous cures.

In *School Library Journal* Heather M. Campbell compared Milford's debut novel to the work of acclaimed science-fiction writer Ray Bradbury. *The Boneshaker* "unfolds with the almost audible click of puzzle pieces coming together," she noted, revealing an "intricate story" that is captured in Offermann's surreal drawings. A *Kirkus Reviews* critic cited the mix of "folklore, tall tales, and steampunk" in the novel and called its heroine "a well drawn protagonist with sturdy supporting characters around her." In spinning her story of good versus evil, Milford molds her "eerie and atmospheric vision of early-twentieth-century Americana" into what *Booklist* contributor Ian Chipman described as an "impressive and ambitious" first novel, and a *Publishers Weekly* critic observed that "Milford's detail-rich prose makes it all the more haunting." *The Boneshaker* is without a doubt Steampunk's best bet at making headway into the juvenile reader genre," asserted *School Library Journal* blogger Elizabeth Bird. "However, above and beyond this rote category, the book's just a damn good bit of writing." "Once you pick it up you'll be hard pressed to set it down again," Bird predicted.

Biographical and Critical Sources

PERIODICALS

Booklist, May 15, 2010, Ian Chipman, review of *The Boneshaker,* p. 52.
Kirkus Reviews, April 15, 2010, review of *The Boneshaker.*
Publishers Weekly, May 10, 2010, review of *The Boneshaker,* p. 45.
School Library Journal, June, 2010, Heather M. Campbell, review of *The Boneshaker,* p. 113.

ONLINE

Kate Mildford Home Page, http://clockworkfoundry.com (September 15, 2011).

Nagspeake Web site, http://www.nagspeake.com/ (September 15, 2011).
School Library Journal Web site, http://blog.schoollibrary journal.com/afuse8production/ (April 29, 2010), Elizabeth Bird, review of *The Boneshaker.**

*   *   *

MOORE, Cyd 1957-

Personal

Born July 4, 1957, in GA; daughter of Henry and Joy (an art teacher) Shealy; children: Branden, Lindsay. *Education:* University of Georgia, B.F.A., 1979. *Hobbies and other interests:* Painting, yoga, running, cooking, gardening, mosaics.

Addresses

Home—Sylvan Lake, MI. *E-mail*—mail@cydmoore. com.

Career

Illustrator. WMAZ-TV/Radio, Macon, GA, art director, 1978-80; *Macon Telegraph & News,* Macon, staff artist, 1980-83; freelance illustrator/designer, 1983—; founder of *Picturebook* (artist directory and Web site), 1997—. *Exhibitions:* Works have been exhibited at solo shows in galleries in Birmingham and Montgomery, AL, and Birmingham, MI; work exhibited at group show of children's book art in New York, NY.

Awards, Honors

National Parenting Publications Honors Award, for *I Love You, Stinky Face* by Lisa McCourt; National Parenting Publications Award Honors selection, 2008, Children's Choice listee, International Reading Association/Children's Book Council, Eric Hoffer Book Award honorable mention, and *Storytelling World* Award, all 2009, Oprah Book Club selection, 2010, Creative Child Award, 2011, and several state awards, all for *Willow* by Denise Brennan-Nelson and Rosemarie Brennan; Parent's Choice Approved Award, 2010, for *Arbor Day Square* by Kathryn O. Galbraith.

Writings

ILLUSTRATOR

Jane Yolen, *Jane Yolen's Songs of Summer,* Boyds Mills Press (Honesdale, PA), 1993.
Fay Robinson, compiler, *A Frog inside My Hat,* Troll Publications (Mahwah, NJ), 1993.
Judy Barron, *I Want to Learn to Fly* (with audiocassette), Scholastic (New York, NY), 1994.

Cyd Moore (Photograph by Rachel Holland. Reproduced by permission.)

Shulamith Levey Oppenheim, *I Love You Bunny Rabbit,* Boyds Mills Press (Honesdale, PA), 1994.

Charles Ghigna, *Tickle Day: Poems from Father Goose,* Hyperion (New York, NY), 1994.

Rozanne L. Williams, *Scaredy Cat,* Creative Teaching Press (Huntington Beach, CA), 1995.

Marlene Beierel, *What Comes in Threes?,* Creative Teaching Press (Huntington Beach, CA), 1995.

Rozanne L. Williams, *The Time Song,* Creative Teaching Press (Huntington Beach, CA), 1995.

Rozanne L. Williams, *Scaredy Cat Runs Away,* Creative Teaching Press (Huntington Beach, CA), 1995.

Eileen Spinelli, *Where's the Night Train Going?,* Boyds Mills Press (Honesdale, PA), 1996.

Shulamith Levey Oppenheim, *What Is the Full Moon Full Of?,* Boyds Mills Press (Honesdale, PA), 1997.

Steven J. Simmons, *Alice and Greta: A Tale of Two Witches,* Charlesbridge Publishers (Watertown, MA), 1997.

Lisa McCourt, *I Love You, Stinky Face,* Troll Publications (Mahwah, NJ), 1997.

Lisa McCourt, *It's Time for School, Stinky Face,* Bridgewater Books (Mahwah, NJ), 1997.

Rozanne L. Williams, *Can You Read a Map?,* Creative Teaching Press (Huntington Beach, CA), 1997.

Big Book: Goldilocks and the Three Bears, William Sadlier (New York, NY), 1997.

Lisa McCourt, *I Miss You, Stinky Face,* Bridgewater Books (Mahwah, NJ), 1999.

Steven J. Simmons, *Greta's Revenge: More Alice and Greta,* Crown Publishers (New York, NY), 1999.

Lisa McCourt, *Good Night, Princess Pruney-Toes,* Bridgewater Books (Mahwah, NJ), 2001.

Steven J. Simmons, *Alice and Greta's Color Magic,* Knopf (New York, NY), 2001.

Roni Schotter, *Missing Rabbit,* Clarion Books (New York, NY), 2001.

Lisa McCourt, *Merry Christmas, Stinky Face,* Bridgewater Books (Mahwah, NJ), 2002.

Roni Schotter, *Room for Rabbit,* Clarion Books (New York, NY), 2003.

Lisa McCourt, *The Most Thankful Thing,* Bridgewater (Mahwah, NJ), 2003.

Lesléa Newman, *A Fire Engine for Ruthie,* Clarion Books (New York, NY), 2004.

Raffi, adaptor, *If You're Happy and You Know It,* Knopf (New York, NY), 2005.

Tony Johnston, *Sticky People,* HarperCollins (New York, NY), 2006.

Jeanie Franz Ransom, *What Do Parents Do (When You're Not Home)?,* Peachtree (Atlanta, GA), 2007.

Lisa McCourt, *Happy Halloween, Stinky Face,* Scholastic (New York, NY), 2007.

Marjorie Blain Parker, *Your Kind of Mommy,* Dutton (New York, NY), 2007.

Lisa McCourt, *Granny's Dragon,* Dutton (New York, NY), 2008.

Denise Brennan-Nelson and Rosemarie Brennan, *Willow,* Sleeping Bear Press (Chelsea, MI), 2008.

Marcia Thornton Jones, *Leprechaun on the Loose,* Scholastic (New York, NY), 2008.

Kathryn O. Galbraith, *Arbor Day Square,* Peachtree Publishers (Atlanta, GA), 2010.

Lisa McCourt, *It's the 100th Day, Stinky Face!,* Scholastic (New York, NY), 2010.

Lisa McCourt, *Ready for Kindergarten, Stinky Face?,* Cartwheel Books (New York, NY), 2010.

Denise Brennan-Nelson, *Willow and the Snow Day Dance,* Sleeping Bear Press (Ann Arbor, MI), 2011.

EDITOR; WITH AMY GARY

Picturebook '98: The Directory of Children's Illustration, Menasha Ridge Press, 1999.

Picturebook '99: The Directory of Children's Illustration, WaterMark, 1999.

Picturebook 2K: The Directory of Children's Illustration, WaterMark, 2000.

Picturebook 2001: The Directory of Children's Illustration, WaterMark, 2001.

Sidelights

An accomplished and respected children's book illustrator, Cyd Moore chooses from among a variety of styles and palettes when accentuating the unique qualities of each story she brings to life. Her work has been paired with tales by Lisa McCourt, Steven J. Simmons, Kathryn O. Galbraith, and Denise Brennan-Nelson, among others, often to critical acclaim. Reviewing Moore's work for Lesléa Newman's *A Fire Engine for Ruthie,* which finds a little girl more interested in playing with toy trains and trucks than dolls, a *Publishers Weekly* contributor concluded that the book's "vibrant watercolors pack in plenty of detail and the cheery hues of the busy spreads echo Ruthie's sunny optimism." Turning to another example from the illustrator's long list of successes, a *Kirkus Reviews* writer noted that Moore's detailed illustrations "will prove engrossing for young readers" of Marjorie Blain Parker's *Your Kind of Mommy.*

Growing up in Georgia, Moore was encouraged in her creative endeavors by her mother, also an artist. In school, her artistic talent earned her the job of design-

ing posters as well as a position on the yearbook committee. After high school, Moore attended the University of Georgia, where she earned her B.F.A. and then started on a career as a graphic illustrator, creating art for newspapers, television, and product advertisements. In the mid-1980s she decided to make the shift to book illustration, where children's picture books were the perfect fit for her humorous, whimsical approach. Since that time, she has provided the artwork for dozens of picture books. Additionally, Moore has served as the driving force behind Picturebook, a directory of children's illustrators. "Picturebook has helped hundreds of children's book artists showcase their work in a very effective way," she remarked in an essay on the *Embracing the Child* Web site.

In her art for McCourt's picture-book series that includes *I Love You, Stinky Face, I Miss You, Stinky Face,* and *Ready for Kindergarten, Stinky Face?*, Moore contributes neon-colored monsters and brightly colored scenes to emphasize the unlikely nature of the child's fears and the consequent humor of imagining that they could really happen. Reviewing *I Love You, Stinky Face,*

in which a little boy being tucked into bed tests his mother's love with frightful scenarios, Hazel Rochman wrote in *Booklist* that "Moore's paintings, in neon colors with lots of purple and green, contrast the gentle bedtime caresses with the wild scenarios." A similar scene is enacted in *I Miss You, Stinky Face,* in which Mom, phoning her son at home while she is away on business, is questioned closely about her ability to overcome a series of unlikely obstacles that might delay her return. *Merry Christmas, Stinky Face* continues the amusing interchange between mother and son. Reviewing *It's Time for School, Stinky Face,* Tim Wadham wrote in *School Library Journal* that Moore's "lively cartoon style is perfect for the over-the-top scenarios" presented in McCourt's text, while Rochman praised the illustrator's ability to "express the rambunctious party fun as well as the tender family bond" in *Merry Christmas, Stinky Face.*

In *Happy Halloween, Stinky Face* the inquisitive youngster poses a series of endless questions about the holiday to his mother, who acts as a reassuring presence. According to *Booklist* contributor Ilene Cooper, Moore's

Moore's collaborations with writer Lisa McCourt include the humorous picture book It's Time for School, Stinky Face. (Illustration copyright © 2000 by Cyd Moore. Reproduced by permission of Scholastic, Inc.)

Moore crafts a nostalgic vision in her artwork for Kathryn O. Galbraith's family-themed picture book **Arbor Day Square.** (Illustration copyright © 2010 by Cyd Moore. Reproduced with permission of Peachtree Publishers.)

fall-colored, ink-and-watercolor paintings are full of detailed fun as they pair imagination with reality." A familiar childhood scenario—preparing for the first day of school—is the subject of *Ready for Kindergarten, Stinky Face?* As always, the ever-curious protagonist cannot help but wonder what awaits him in the classroom, and he peppers his mother with queries about everything from hungry armadillos to grape-juice-spouting faucets. "Cheery illustrations and amusing facial expressions add humor to the exaggerated fears," remarked Mary Hazelton in her *School Library Journal* review of *Ready for Kindergarten, Stinky Face?*

Other collaborations with McCourt center on the love between a caregiver and a child. In *Good Night, Princess Pruney Toes* the two tell the story of a father bathing and putting his daughter to bed, creating "a delightful romp," according to Susan Marie Pitard in *School Library Journal.* Moore's "exuberant watercolors include warm domestic details" that readers will easily identify with, according to a contributor to *Publishers Weekly. The Most Thankful Thing,* another team effort, pairs McCourt's "breezy" text about a mother and daughter's perusal of a family photo album with Moore's "effective" pastel-hued cartoon art, according to *Booklist* critic Carolyn Phelan. In *School Library Journal* Deborah Rothaug dubbed *The Most Thankful Thing* "a wonderful, reassuring read-aloud for storytime and for individual sharing," and a *Publishers Weekly*

critic concluded that the illustrator's "heartfelt, cartoonish illustrations manage to keeps things lively."

In *Granny's Dragon,* another Moore-McCourt collaboration, a youngster spending the night at her grandparent's house worries about a scary monster appearing in the bedroom, until Granny soothes her nerves by placing a special stuffed toy near the child's bed. Amy Lilien-Harper, writing in *School Library Journal,* called Moore's artwork the "real star" of *Granny's Dragon,* noting that the imaginary creature "is distinctly monstrous without being overly scary."

Moore contributes cheerful watercolors to Fay Robinson's poetry collection *A Frog inside My Hat* as well as to Charles Ghigna's *Tickle Day: Poems from Father Goose.* Her watercolor-and-pencil compositions for the latter reflect the poet's optimism through "vaguely Chagall-like touches" and the use of "rich and vibrant" colors, according to a contributor to *Publishers Weekly.* For Spinelli's collection of poems titled *Where Is the Night Train Going?,* Moore creates a crew of shaggy cartoon characters in a style that recalls the reassuring art of beloved picture-book illustrator Mercer Mayer.

A range of emotions is reflected in Moore's paintings for Shulamith Levey Oppenheim's *I Love You, Bunny Rabbit,* in which a little boy's favorite rabbit becomes so dirty that he (briefly) contemplates giving it up in favor of a new toy. A *Publishers Weekly* contributor

Popular children's entertainer Raffi crafts the text that comes to life in Moore's art for **If You're Happy and You Know It.** (Illustration copyright © 2005 by Cyd Moore. Used by permission of Alfred A. Knopf, an imprint of Random House Children's Books, a division of Random House, Inc.)

dubbed *I Love You, Bunny Rabbit* "a winsome tale of love remaining love in spite of dirt and grime." Another rabbit stars in both *Missing Rabbit* and *Room for Rabbit*, "reassuring" picture books by Roni Schotter that feature "Moore's warm, cartoonlike watercolors," according to *School Library Journal* contributor Kathleen Kelly MacMillan. "Gentle humor is also reflected in Moore's illustrations for Oppenheim's *What Is the Full Moon Full Of?* Here, a little boy asks the title question of a cow, a firefly, a squirrel, and his grandmother, and finally comes up with his own hypothesis. "Moore's pictures are lighthearted and goofy," remarked Stephanie Zvirin in her *Booklist* review of the story.

Moore fittingly gives way to flights of illustrative fancy in *I Want to Learn to Fly!* The book's text is composed of lyrics written by Judy Barron and recorded on an accompanying CD by Maureen McGovern that focuses on a child's wish for adventure. "Fanciful, full-page illustrations . . . playfully depict the girl's exotic destinations," remarked a *Publishers Weekly* reviewer of the work. Other lyrics brought to life through Moore's art include popular singer/storyteller Raffi's version of *If You're Happy and You Know It*.

Two toddlers spend a day fiddling around with one sticky object after another in Tony Johnston's *Sticky People,* a picture book that is injected with even more humor via Moore's watercolor art. The story's illustrations depict the two toddlers as they move from breakfast with sugary jam to playing in the mud to pasting together craft projects, ultimately winding up in the bathtub after a playful dinner with their parents. Moore's art sets the story within a loving family in which the "feeling of familiarity" show "characters . . . having so much fun readers will want to join right in," according to a *Kirkus Reviews* writer. In a turn of the tables, adults cause the mess in the pages of Jenanie Franz Ransom's *What Do Parents Do (When You're Not Home?)*. In watercolor-and-pencil illustrations, Moore contributes what *School Library Journal* critic Linda L. Walkins described as "humorous details" to Ransom's revelations regarding parents who get into all sorts of trouble while their children are spending the night at Grandma's. In Marjorie Blain Parker's *Your Kind of Mommy,* a mother describes the ways elephants, wolves, and other animals care for their young as she tends to her own child's needs. "Moore's . . . illustrations work equally well at depicting both the animal mothers and their human counterpart," a contributor in *Kirkus Reviews* noted, and Martha Topol, writing in *School Library Journal,* called the artwork "vibrant and expressive, with the mother and child making a friendly and secure duo."

Moore has teamed up with author Steven J. Simmons in a number of picture-book projects. Among these are the "Alice and Greta" stories about two little witches, one always good and the other always bad. In her art, Moore plays with the meanings associated with color: In *Alice and Greta: A Tale of Two Witches* she dresses sweet Alice in pink while poisonous Greta wears a nasty shade of green. The tables are turned in *Greta's Revenge: More Alice and Greta,* as nasty Greta casts a spell on Alice to make her mean, and formerly pink Alice turns green. In *Alice and Greta's Color Magic* Greta succeeds in casting a spell that drains the entire world of color, even the vile shade of green that she adores. Sharon McNeil, writing in *School Library Journal,* praised Moore's humorous, pastel-colored cartoons in *Alice and Greta's Color Magic,* noting that "the facial expressions of all of the characters are very telling."

In *Willow,* a picture book co-written by Denise Brennan-Nelson and Rosemarie Brennan, a vibrant youngster with her own unique take on the world enters the classroom of a strict, neat-as-a-pin teacher. Although Mrs. Hawthorne fails to appreciate Willow's inventiveness at first, the new student's Christmas gift softens the dour teacher's heart, prompting her to renovate the classroom. "Expressive faces show wonderment and joy as teacher and students discover—as Willow has—the intense power of imagination," Mary Jean Smith remarked in *School Library Journal*. In Brennan-Nelson's sequel, *Willow and the Snow Day Dance,* the sprightly youngster attempts to win the heart of a grouchy new neighbor. "Brimming with details, Moore's cheerful pictures capture Willow's outsize personality," commented a reviewer in *Publishers Weekly.*

Set in the nineteenth century, Galbraith's *Arbor Day Square* follows the efforts of a pioneer girl and her father to beautify their treeless village by ordering and planting fifteen saplings from back east, an event that is subsequently celebrated annually by appreciative neighbors. "Moore's gentle pencil and watercolors lend a classic 'storybook' feel to the story," a *Kirkus Reviews* contributor stated, and Phelan wrote that Moore's "charming, naive illustrations . . . give this large-scale picture book great visual appeal."

"Illustration does not have to be just a picture of the words written on a page," Moore once told *SATA*. "It can be—and, in my opinion, *must* be—more than that. Illustration, approached with a larger purpose, is art of the highest form . . . just as important and inspiring as an oil painting in the finest museum. My single purpose in illustrating each book is to make that book more than the words . . . to go beyond the words . . . to lift readers young and old to places within themselves that make their lives more than they were a moment before. One beautifully painted picture, filled with imagination and love, does that to those who are able to see.

"Great art must flow from higher spaces through the artist's hands and onto a smooth white page. It is always spontaneous and never contrived. It is like a living thing that must have a vehicle by which to travel in order to arrive where it needs to be. Great art can arrive anywhere: in a gallery, in a subway, in a children's book. It only depends upon the spirit of the artist and whether he can or *will* allow that art to come. The goal is to be that open every time for every page in every book that is illustrated. The goal is hard and frustrating

at times. Deadlines and time schedules must be factored in to all of this wonderful *flow*. But when the goal is grasped even once, the feeling of getting it right forces you to try again and again for that perfection.

The love between a parent and child is captured in Moore's pencil-and-watercolor artwork for McCourt's **The Most Thankful Thing.** (Illustration copyright © 2004 by Cyd Moore. Reproduced by permission of Scholastic, Inc.)

"These may seem like lofty statements for the illustration of children's books. But I remember some of the pictures in some of my books from childhood to this day. I remember how they made me feel. Children and their parents don't go to museums much. Museums can be boring and hard to understand. Video games are a lot more fun, and so is golf on Saturday. But most kids get to open a book and look at the pictures, and sometimes the parents share those moments. And if those pictures happen to have some substance behind them . . . some magic . . . then the artist's show has been viewed, hopefully a spark has been lit, and the artist's job has been well done."

Biographical and Critical Sources

PERIODICALS

Booklist, June 1, 1993, Deborah Abbott, review of *Jane Yolen's Songs of Summer*, p. 1846; January 1, 1995, April Judge, review of *I Love You, Bunny Rabbit*, p. 826; January 1, 1996, Hazel Rochman, review of *Where's the Night Train Going?*, p. 841; October 15, 1997, Hazel Rochman, review of *I Love You, Stinky Face*, p. 403; December 1, 1997, Stephanie Zvirin, review of *What Is the Full Moon Full Of?*, p. 643; May 1, 2002, Gillian Engberg, review of *Missing Rabbit*, p. 1536; September 15, 2002, Hazel Rochman, review of *Merry Christmas, Stinky Face*, p. 246; March 1, 2003, Gillian Engberg, review of *Room for Rabbit*, p. 1204; November 1, 2003, Carolyn Phelan, review of *The Most Thankful Thing*, p. 502; August, 2004, Ilene Cooper, review of *A Fire Engine for Ruthie*, p. 1944; April 1, 2007, Abby Nolan, review of *What Do Parents Do (When You're Not Home)?*, p. 60; September 1, 2007, Ilene Cooper, review of *Happy Halloween, Stinky Face*, p. 126; April 15, 2010, Carolyn Phelan, review of *Arbor Day Square*, p. 48.
Bulletin of the Center for Children's Books, February, 1995, review of *I Love You, Bunny Rabbit*, p. 211; September, 2004, Hope Morrison, review of *A Fire Engine for Ruthie*, p. 33; April, 2007, Deborah Stevenson, review of *What Do Parents Do (When You're Not Home)?*, p. 342.
Kirkus Reviews, February 15, 2002, review of *Missing Rabbit*, p. 265; November 1, 2002, review of *Merry Christmas, Stinky Face*, p. 1622; July 1, 2004, review of *A Fire Engine for Ruthie*, p. 625; May 1, 2006, review of *Sticky People*, p. 461; February 1, 2007, review of *Your Kind of Mommy*, p. 128; February 15, 2007, review of *What Do Parents Do (When You're Not Home)?*; July 15, 2007, review of *Happy Halloween, Stinky Face*; April 15, 2008, review of *Willow*; July 1, 2008, review of *Granny's Dragon*; March 1, 2010, review of *Arbor Day Square*.
Oakland Press (Oakland, MI), October 12, 2004, Garry Graff, "Moore, Moore, Moore," pp. D1-D2.
Publishers Weekly, July 26, 1993, review of *A Frog inside My Hat*, p. 70; September 12, 1994, review of *Tickle Day: Poems from Father Goose*, p. 91; December 12,

1994, review of *I Love You, Bunny Rabbit*, p. 61; March 20, 1995, review of *I Want to Learn to Fly!*, p. 31; February 5, 1996, review of *Where's the Night Train Going?*, p. 90; August 18, 1997, review of *Alice and Greta: A Tale of Two Witches*, p. 91; August 25, 1997, review of *I Love You, Stinky Face*, p. 70; July 19, 1999, review of *Alice and Greta*, p. 197; September 6, 1999, review of *Greta's Revenge: More Alice and Greta*, p. 103; February 5, 2001, review of *Good Night, Princess Pruney Toes*, p. 88; January 21, 2002, review of *Missing Rabbit*, p. 88; August 25, 2003, review of *Alice and Greta's Color Magic*, p. 67; November 3, 2003, review of *The Most Thankful Thing*, p. 73; September 6, 2004, review of *A Fire Engine for Ruthie*, p. 61; December 6, 2004, review of *The Most Thankful Thing*, p. 58; January 10, 2011, review of *Willow and the Snow Day Dance*, p. 50.
School Library Journal, August, 1993, Jane Marino, review of *Jane Yolen's Songs of Summer*, p. 162; October, 1993, Barbara Chatton, review of *A Frog inside My Hat*, p. 121; September, 1994, Kathleen Whalin, review of *Tickle Day*, p. 208; February, 1995, Lynn Cockett, review of *I Love You, Bunny Rabbit*, p. 78; April, 1996, Liza Bliss, review of *Where's the Night Train Going?*, p. 130; October, 1997, Elizabeth Trotter, review of *I Love You, Stinky Face*, p. 104; December, 1997, Peggy Morgan, review of *What Is the Full Moon Full Of?*, p. 99; January, 1998, Tana Elias, review of *Alice and Greta*, p. 93; May, 1999, Linda Ludke, review of *I Miss You, Stinky Face*, p. 92; December, 1999, Maryann H. Owen, review of *Greta's Revenge*, p. 112; October, 2000, Tim Wadham, review of *It's Time for School, Stinky Face*, p. 130; May, 2001, Susan Marie Pitard, review of *Good Night, Princess Pruney Toes*, p. 129; October, 2001, Sharon McNeil, review of *Alice and Greta's Color Magic*, p. 132; April, 2002, Susan Weitz, review of *Missing Rabbit*, p. 122; April, 2003, Kathleen Kelly MacMillan, review of *Room for Rabbit*, p. 138; August, 2003, Deborah Rothaug, review of *The Most Thankful Thing*, p. 138; September, 2004, Roxanne Burg, review of *A Fire Engine for Ruthie*, p. 176; July, 2006, Julie Roach, review of *Sticky People*, p. 79; March, 2007, Martha Topol, review of *Your Kind of Mommy*, p. 184; June, 2007, Linda L. Walkins, review of *What Do Parents Do (When You're Not Home)?*, p. 120; August, 2008, Mary Jean Smith, review of *Willow*, p. 84, and Amy Lilien-Harper, review of *Granny's Dragon*, p. 98; April, 2010, Mary Jean Smith, review of *Arbor Day Square*, p. 124; September, 2010, Mary Hazelton, review of *Ready for Kindergarten, Stinky Face?*, p. 123.

ONLINE

Cyd Moore Home Page, http://www.cydmoore.com (August 1, 2011).
Embracing the Child Web site, http://www.embracingthechild.org/ (January 10, 2007), "Cyd Moore, Illustrator."
Picturebook Web site, http://picture-book.com/ (August 1, 2011), "Cyd Moore."

N-Q

NEWSOME, Richard 1964-

Personal

Born October 13, 1964, in Wanganui, New Zealand; married; children: three. *Education:* B.Econ. (economics; with first-class honours).

Addresses

Home—Brisbane, Queensland, Australia. *E-mail*—richard@richardnewsome.com.

Career

Writer Worked as a print, radio, and television journalist; Bain & Co., Boston, MA, corporate business strategist; communications director for a media company in Sydney, New South Wales, Australia.

Writings

"BILLIONAIRE"/"ARCHER LEGACY" MIDDLE-GRADE NOVEL TRILOGY

The Billionaire's Curse, Text Publishing (Melbourne, Victoria, Australia), 2009, illustrated by Jonny Duddle, Walden Pond Press (New York, NY), 2010.
The Emerald Casket, Text Publishing (Melbourne, Victoria, Australia), 2010, illustrated by Jonny Duddle, Walden Pond Press (New York, NY), 2011.
The Mask of Destiny, Text Publishing (Melbourne, Victoria, Australia), 2011 illustrated by Jonny Duddle, Walden Pond Press (New York, NY), 2012.

Author's work has been translated into German, Italian, Polish, Spanish, and Turkish.

Sidelights

Winner of New Zealand's prestigious Esther Glen Medal in 2010, Richard Newsome's debut novel *The Billionaire's Curse* is the first volume in his "Billion-

Richard Newsome (Reproduced by permission.)

aire" series, a middle-grade mix of mystery and adventure that has been introduced to U.S. readers as the "Archer Legacy" novel collection. Illustrated with spot art by Jonny Duddle, *The Billionaire's Curse* has been followed by *The Emerald Casket* and *The Mask of Destiny.*

Newsome was born in rural New Zealand but migrated with his family to Queensland, Australia, as a toddler. After high school he worked as a newspaper and television journalist for seven years, then earned an econom-

ics degree. Work as a business strategist while supporting his family kept Newsome busy, but then his interest in storytelling was sparked—"in an attempt to bore [my] . . . children to sleep at night," as Newsome quipped on his home page. One of the most popular of these bedtime stories eventually developed into *The Billionaire's Curse,* but it was a decade between the time Newsome started transcribing the tale in an old notebook and its publication and appearance on bookshop shelves.

Newsome's fictional hero, thirteen-year-old Aussie Gerald Archer Wilkins, is introduce to readers in *The Billionaire's Curse,* just after his life has changed drastically. Great-Aunt Geraldine has died and left Gerald her fortune, which includes a Caribbean island and a London estate. Unfortunately, her death was the result of murder, and in a letter Geraldine wrote to the teen just before she died, she revealed her suspicions that evildoers were after her and hinted that her demise would involve a recent theft of a valuable diamond from the British Museum. As Gerald investigates, with the help of twin friends Ruby and Sam, he learns that the mys-

tery reaches back further than Geraldine's death; perhaps all the way to ancient times. In part due to the inclusion of "dramatic escape scenes [that] create a delicious urgency," *The Billionaire's Curse* will appeal to middle-grade adventure fans, according to *School Library Journal* contributor Caitlin Augusta, and in *Booklist* Karen Cruze noted that Newsome's story is "rife with killings, suspects, ancient clues, and booby-trapped caverns straight out of an Indiana Jones movie." "There's no letup in the pacing," wrote a *Kirkus Reviews,* "and all the tried-and-true mystery elements add up to an Anthony Horowitz-style romp."

Gerald, Ruby, and Sam return for more adventures in *The Emerald Casket,* and this time India becomes the scene of their adventure. Drawn there through their discovery of a cache of papers which show that the fate of the world may be at stake, the teens make some startling discoveries, including a lost city and a den of thieves who are intent on stealing a casket of valuable gemstones. Newsome's "Billionaire" trilogy concludes in *The Mask of Destiny,* which will serve as yet another "fun romp for action-loving readers," according to *Booklist* critic Cruze. Describing *The Emerald Casket* as a "lighter-than-air caper," a *Kirkus Reviews* writer predicted that "fans of [Scholastic's popular] *39 Clues*-style adventures will be swept along" with Newsome's tale.

Biographical and Critical Sources

PERIODICALS

Booklist, May 1, 2010, Karen Cruze, review of *The Billionaire's Curse,* p. 50; April 1, 2011, Karen Cruze, review of *The Emerald Casket,* p. 70.

Bulletin of the Center for Children's Books, September, 2010, Elizabeth Bush, review of *The Billionaire's Curse,* p. 34.

Kirkus Reviews, May 1, 2010, review of *The Billionaire's Curse;* April 1, 2011, review of *The Emerald Casket.*

School Library Journal, July, 2010, Caitlin Augusta, review of *The Billionaire's Curse,* p. 94.

ONLINE

Richard Newsome Home Page, http://www.richardnewsome.com (September 15, 2011).

* * *

OLSON, Julie 1976-

Personal

Born 1976. *Education:* Brigham Young University, B.F.A., 1998.

Cover of Newsome's middle-grade adventure The Billionaire's Curse, *featuring cover art by Jonny Duddle.* (Illustration copyright © 2010 by Jonny Duddle. Reproduced with permission of Walden Pond Press, an imprint of HarperCollins Publishers.)

Julie Olson (Photograph by Rhett Olson. Reproduced by permission.)

Addresses

Home—UT. *Agent*—Tammy Shannon, Shannon Associates, 333 W. 57th St., Ste. 809, New York, NY 10036. *E-mail*—julie@jujubeeillustrations.com.

Career

Illustrator.

Member

Utah Children's Writers and Illustrators.

Awards, Honors

Best Children's Book of the Year selection, Bank Street College of Education, 2010, for *The Chihuahua Chase* by A.E. Cannon.

Writings

SELF-ILLUSTRATED

Tickle, Tickle! Itch, Twitch!, Marshall Cavendish (New York, NY), 2010.

ILLUSTRATOR

Brad Wilcox, *Hip, Hip, Hooray for Annie McRae!,* Gibbs Smith (Layton, UT), 2001.

Rick Walton, *Herd of Cows! Flock of Sheep!,* Gibbs Smith (Layton, UT), 2002, revised edition published as *Herd of Cows, Flock of Sheep: An Adventure in Collective Nouns,* 2011.

L.N. Dion, *The Opposites of My Jewish Year,* Kar-Ben Publishing (Minneapolis, MN), 2005.

A.D. Tarbox, *Already Asleep,* Moo Press (Warwick, NY), 2006.

Dena Fox Luchsinger, *Playing by the Rules: A Story about Autism,* Woodbine House (Bethesda, MD), 2007.

Candy Chand, *Christmas Love,* Gibbs Smith (Layton, UT), 2008.

Cari Meister, *The Kickball Kids,* Stone Arch Books (Mankato, MN), 2009.

A.E. Cannon, *The Chihuahua Chase,* Farrar, Straus & Giroux (New York, NY), 2010.

Jonathan London, *Little Penguin: The Emperor of Antarctica,* Marshall Cavendish (New York, NY), 2011.

Marian Moore and Mary Jane Kensington, *Dear Cinderella,* Orchard Books (New York, NY), 2012.

Sidelights

A freelance illustrator based in Utah, Julie Olson has contributed artwork to a host of children's books, among them Rick Walton's *Herd of Cows! Flock of Sheep!* Couching a grammar lesson in its humorous story, *Herd of Cows! Flock of Sheep!* centers on a group of farm animals racing to save their exhausted owner as he sleeps through a downpour so intense that rising floodwaters threaten to sweep him away mid-snooze. "Olson's illustrations flow right along with the story's action," Carolyn Janssen remarked in her *School Library Journal* review of the entertaining picture book.

Olson has also provided black-and-white drawings for *The Chihuahua Chase,* a chapter book by A.E. Cannon. After Teddy's speedy dog, Phantom, vanishes just before a big Chihuahua race, the fourth grader must join forces with his classmate (and rival) Addie May to solve the mystery of the canine's disappearance. Olson's illustrations "draw attention to some pivotal scenes" in *The Chihuahua Case,* according to *School Library Journal* reviewer Tanya Boudreau.

In her first self-illustrated title, *Tickle, Tickle! Itch, Twitch!,* Olson follows the exploits of a mischievous mouse and a gullible groundhog. While Gus the groundhog enjoys a lazy day by basking in the sun, a mouse sneaks up behind him and begins tickling Gus's back with a feather. Hoping to relieve the itch, the groundhog searches for a stick to use as a backscratcherm but mistakenly picks up a snake instead. Having found a suitable target for his practical joke, the mouse continues to irritate Gus, whose efforts to find a solution to each successive irritant only lead to more surprising encounters. *Tickle, Tickle! Itch, Twitch!* garnered praise from *School Library Journal* critic Lora Van Marel, who predicted that readers will appreciate "the simple and silly humor and the bright, colorful illustrations that fill the pages."

Olson's humorous approach to her subject matter can be seen in her illustration "Dog Walking Job." (Reproduced by permission.)

"I love illustrating for children," Olson told *SATA*. "There's an honesty, a sweetness, and a nostalgia that comes along with it. My own children have provided so much inspiration, knowledge, and reference when it comes to my writing and illustrating. I hope everyone can find joy in picture books."

Biographical and Critical Sources

PERIODICALS

Booklist, May 1, 2010, Kathleen Isaacs, review of *The Chihuahua Chase,* p. 52.

Children's Bookwatch, January, 2008, review of *Playing by the Rules: A Story about Autism.*

School Library Journal, September, 2002, Carolyn Janssen, review of *Herd of Cows! Flock of Sheep!,* p. 208; November, 2005, Rachel Kamin, review of *The Opposites of My Jewish Year,* p. 113; December, 2007, Mary

Hazelton, review of *Playing by the Rules,* p. 94; June, 2010, Tanya Boudreau, review of *The Chihuahua Chase,* p. 65; December, 2010, Lora Van Marel, review of *Tickle, Tickle! Itch, Twitch!,* p. 87.

ONLINE

Julie Olson Home Page, http://www.jujubeeillustrations. com (August 1, 2011).

Julie Olson Web log, http://jujubeeillustrations.blogspot. com (August 1, 2011).

Utah Children's Writers and Illustrators Web site, http:// ucwi.org/ (July 7, 2003), interview with Olson.

*   *   *

PATNEAUDE, David 1944-

Personal

Born January 2, 1944, in St. Paul, MN; son of Mervin and Florence Patneaude; married Judy Voeller (a

teacher/librarian), September 21, 1985; children: Matt, Jaime, Jeff. *Education:* University of Washington, B.A., 1971. *Politics:* "Progressive." *Religion:* Lutheran. *Hobbies and other interests:* Reading, running, outdoor activities, travel, watching movies and plays.

Addresses

Home—Woodinville, WA. *E-mail*—david@patneaude. com.

Career

Novelist. Speaker and presenter at schools and libraries. *Military service:* U.S. Navy, 1966-70; received Vietnam Service Medal.

Member

Society of Children's Book Writers and Illustrators.

Awards, Honors

Prairie Pasque Children's Book Award, South Dakota, Children's Book Award, Utah, and Best of the Texas Lone Star Reading Lists citation, all c. 1993, all for *Someone Was Watching;* Books for the Teen Age citation, New York Public Library, 1996, for *The Last Man's Reward;* Honor Book citation, Society of School Librarians International, 1999, for *Framed in Fire;* Tennessee Volunteer State Book Award nomination, 2010, for *A Piece of the Sky;* books named to dozens of state young-readers' lists.

David Patneaude (Reproduced by permission.)

Writings

Someone Was Watching, Albert Whitman (Morton Grove, IL), 1993.

Dark Starry Morning: Stories of This World and Beyond, Albert Whitman (Morton Grove, IL), 1995.

The Last Man's Reward, Albert Whitman (Morton Grove, IL), 1996.

Framed in Fire, Albert Whitman (Morton Grove, IL), 1999.

Haunting at Home Plate, Albert Whitman (Morton Grove, IL), 2000.

Colder than Ice, Albert Whitman (Morton Grove, IL), 2003.

Thin Wood Walls, Houghton Mifflin (Boston, MA), 2004.

Deadly Drive, Albert Whitman (Morton Grove, IL), 2005.

A Piece of the Sky, Albert Whitman (Morton Grove, IL), 2007.

Epitaph Road, Egmont USA (New York, NY), 2010.

Sidelights

David Patneaude has made his name as a children's book author by crafting creepy, suspenseful tales, sometimes featuring supernatural forces and sometimes purely human wrongdoers. *Someone Was Watching, The Last Man's Reward, Deadly Drive,* and *Epitaph Road;* The titles of Patneaude's books hint to readers that they will enjoy spine-tingling stories between the covers.

Patneaude's first published book, *Someone Was Watching,* introduces thirteen-year-old Chris Barton, whose little sister Molly is missing and presumed to have drowned in a river near their summer home in Florida. After watching a home video of Molly's last day with the family, Chris thinks that there may be another explanation for her disappearance. Along with his friend Pat, Chris withdraws all of his money from his savings account and heads off to Florida in search of her. "Middle schoolers will love it," John Sigwald declared in *School Library Journal.* Sigwald and a *Kirkus Reviews* critic both pointed out that the fact that no one questions two thirteen-year-old boys traveling cross-country alone is slightly unrealistic, but, as the *Kirkus Reviews* contributor concluded, the characters' "grief and reactions to various dilemmas are so pure and credible that readers will willingly put doubts aside to join in the search."

The Last Man's Reward centers on four friends, all of whom are living in the same temporary apartment complex. When they pool their resources and buy a boxful of baseball cards at a yard sale, they end up with a serious dilemma: among the run-of-the-mill cards, they also find a rare Willie Mays rookie card that is worth thousands of dollars. Which of them should get the card? They finally decide that it should be the reward of the last of them to move out of their current apartments. Then one of the boys, Albert, discovers that their unfriendly gym teacher desperately needs money

Patneaude takes on the subject of bullying in his middle-grade novel **Colder than Ice,** *featuring cover art by Doron Ben-Ami.* (Cover illustration © 2003 by Doron Ben-Ami. Reproduced with permission of Albert Whitman & Company.)

to pay for his wife's cancer treatment. Albert decides that the teacher should have the money from the sale of the card, but when he attempts to retrieve the card from the cave where the boys have hidden it, he becomes trapped. In *The Last Man's Reward* Patneaude "shows that suspense is possible without outright villainy," wrote a *Kirkus Reviews* critic, and *Booklist* reviewer Francis Bradburn predicted that "most early adolescents will be able to identify . . . totally" with this "truly exciting adventure."

Colder than Ice is another chilling tale, in more ways than one. In the midst of a north Idaho winter, Josh becomes the new kid in school. If just being new is not enough to make Josh a target for the school's bullies, his excess weight also attracts unwanted attention. However, one bully, Corey, soon becomes very friendly with Josh—suspiciously friendly in the opinion of Josh's other friends, Mark and Skye. The two turn out to be right, although Corey's true motive is much worse than they suspected. The novel's climax is a "dramatic, heart-pounding scene that will stay with readers long after they put down the novel," according to *Booklist* reviewer Lauren Peterson. "Anyone who has ever been

new to a school, dealt with bullies, or just not known whom to trust will relate to Josh and his dilemmas," Karen T. Bilton concluded in her *School Library Journal.*

With *Thin Wood Walls* Patneaude branches out into a new genre: historical fiction. The book follows Japanese-American boy named Joe Hanada as he and his family cope with prejudice against people of Japanese ancestry during World War II. The Hanadas are relocated from their home near Seattle, Washington, to an internment camp in California, all except Joe's father, who was taken away by the FBI shortly after the Japanese attack on Pearl Harbor. The novel's title refers to the walls of the miserable one-room shack in which the Hanada family is now forced to live, but this is just one of the many indignities they face in the camp. Even after Joe's older brother, Mike, volunteers to join the U.S. army, white Americans still question the Hanadas' patriotism. "Joe's first-person narrative is moving and clear in its depiction of this life, so cruel and unfair," wrote a *Kirkus Reviews* contributor. *Thin Wood Walls* is also notable for depicting the divisions among the Japa-

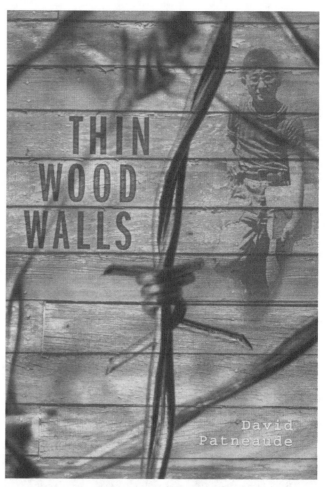

Focusing on the internment of a Japanese-American family during World War II, Patneaude's young-adult novel **Thin Wood Walls** *follows its teen protagonist from Seattle to a California camp.* (Copyright © 2004. Reprinted by permission of Houghton Mifflin Harcourt Publishing Company. All rights reserved.)

nese Americans who are subjected to this ordeal; while some, like Mike, remain patriotic, others renounce their American identity, even going so far as to prohibit their children from speaking English. Patneaude "does a fine job of bringing the daily experience [of Japanese-Americans during World War II] up close through the story of an American kid torn from home," Hazel Rochman concluded in *Booklist.*

Patneaude interweaves stories from two different eras in *A Piece of the Sky.* Russell, a fourteen-year-old Californian, has joined his mom on a trip to Port Orford, Oregon, to help move his grandfather to a retirement community. While sorting through the man's possessions, Russell comes upon a piece of meteorite, a heirloom that was originally given to Russell's great-great-great grandfather Matthew by a scientist named Dr. John Evans. Curious, Russell decides to search for the rest of the meteorite, which supposedly is located somewhere in Port Orford, aided by friend Phoebe and her older brother. Flash back to 1856, and the third-person story of thirteen-year-old Matthew as he joins Dr. Evans on his meteorite hunt. Unfortunately for the three modern-day teens, a relentless man known as Full Moon also desires the meteorite, and his efforts to secretly track Russell and his progress are recounted in what *Booklist* contributor Carolyn Phelan described as "a suspenseful quest tale" with "contemporary appeal." Fans of Gordon Korman's 'On the Run' series . . . will enjoy the sense of danger and the self-sufficiency of the main characters," concluded Kristin Anderson in her *School Library Journal* review of *A Piece of the Sky.*

The year is 2097 when readers tap into the adventure in *Epitaph Road,* and it has been thirty years since a plague-like supervirus killed almost all the males on Earth. Now women are forced to assume the reins of world governments, and their feminist oversight has resulted in a planet without violence or hunger or poverty. However, as fourteen-year-old Kellen Dent knows, life is not rosy for those males that have remained: they have been kept cloistered and treated as virtual untouchables, their numbers maintained at five percent and culled by suspicious mini-plagues. Some men, including Kellen's father, have established a new community far away from the woman-focused cities. When Kellen overhears talk of an outbreak about to start in this community, he realizes that other strange occurrences may have had some evil intent behind them. His efforts to warn his father in time to save the man's life lead to a terrible discovery in a novel that mixes a "fast-paced" plot in an "intriguing" way: "a specific current-events issue is incorporated into a science-fiction context," according to *School Library Journal* critic Kristin Anderson. In *Booklist* Daniel Kraus wrote that *Epitaph Road* features an "intelligent and reasonable" teen cast and a plot in which "a moving sense of loss blankets everything" despite the many high-energy "action sequences." Patneaude's "first-person" narration and

Cover of Patneaude's young-adult novel **Framed in Fire,** *featuring cover art by Layne Johnson.* (Cover illustration copyright © 2001 by Layne Johnson. Reproduced by permission of Albert Whitman & Company.)

"page-turning plot of this post-apocalyptic thriller will hook readers," predicted a *Kirkus Reviews* writer.

Patneaude once told *SATA:* "Like a lot of other writers, I loved to read as a young person, and I often thought about what it would be like to be a real writer—an author of real books. After several decades of thinking about it, reading books, reading about writers, and taking writing courses, I decided it was time for me to try it, to write something intended for someone else to read. And I decided that I wanted to write for young people.

"My motivation? First, to entertain—to give them the kind of enjoyment I used to get when I dove into a really good story. Beyond that, I'd like to prompt readers to think about a bigger picture without writing some kind of heavy-handed 'message' story. *Someone Was Watching,* for instance, is a mystery/adventure, but it's also about love and responsibility and commitment and the importance of believing in yourself, in your ideas when others tell you you're wrong, when they say it's impossible, when they try to take away your dreams."

Biographical and Critical Sources

PERIODICALS

Booklist, July, 1993, Susan DeRonne, review of *Someone Was Watching,* p. 1958; September 1, 1995, review of *Dark Starry Morning: Stories of This World and Beyond,* p. 78; June 1, 1996, Frances Bradburn, review of *The Last Man's Reward,* p. 1720; September 1, 2000, Denia Hester, review of *Haunting at Home Plate,* p. 118; November 1, 2003, Lauren Peterson, review of *Colder than Ice,* p. 497; September 15, 2004, Hazel Rochman, review of *Thin Wood Walls,* p. 234; May 1, 2005, John Peters, review of *Deadly Drive,* p. 1544; September 1, 2007, Carolyn Phelan, review of *A Piece of the Sky,* p. 118; January 1, 2010, Daniel Kraus, review of *Epitaph Road,* p. 60.

Bulletin of the Center for Children's Books, November, 1993, review of *Someone Was Watching,* p. 94.

Kirkus Reviews, July 1, 1993, review of *Someone Was Watching;* August 15, 1995, review of *Dark Starry Morning;* March 15, 1996, review of *Last Man's Reward;* March 15, 1999, review of *Framed in Fire;* September 1, 2004, review of *Thin Wood Walls,* p. 872; February 15, 2010, review of *Epitaph Road.*

Publishers Weekly, March 1, 1999, review of *Framed in Fire,* p. 70; February 8, 2010, review of *Epitaph Road,* p. 51.

School Library Journal, July, 1993, John Sigwald, review of *Someone Was Watching,* p. 86; September, 1995, John Sigwald, review of *Dark Starry Morning,* p. 220; July, 1996, Elaine Lesh Morgan, review of *The Last Man's Reward,* p. 1720; September, 2000, Barb Lawler, review of *Haunting at Home Plate,* p. 235; October, 2003, Karen T. Bilton, review of *Colder than Ice,* p. 175; October, 2004, Ginny Gustin, review of *Thin Wood Walls,* p. 175; May, 2005, Amy Patrick, review of *Deadly Drive,* p. 135; May, 2006, Marilyn Taniguchi, review of *Haunting at Home Plate,* p. 60; May, 2007, Kristin Anderson, review of *A Piece of the Sky,* p. 140; April, 2010, Kristin Anderson, review of *Epitaph Road,* p. 165.

ONLINE

David Patneaude Home Page, http://www.patneaude.com (September 15, 2011).

Cover of Patneaude's futuristic novel Epitaph Road, *which draws readers into a world where males have been relegated to the level of* livestock. (Copyright © 2010. Jacket art and design by JDrift Design. Reproduced with permission of Egmont USA.)

* * *

PETERSON, John 1924-2002

Personal

Born 1924, in Bradford, PA; died November, 2002, in NY; married Holly Simmonds; children: John Christopher, Matthew James, Joel David Barnes, Elizabeth Hollly. *Education:* Pratt Institute, degree, 1948.

Career

Illustrator and author/illustrator of books for children. Volunteer for Boy Scouts of America. Speaker at schools. *Military service:* U.S. Military, 11th Airborne Division, paratrooper during World War II.

Writings

SELF-ILLUSTRATED

Tulips; a Science Story without Words, Holt, Rinehart & Winston (New York, NY), 1963.

The Secret Hide-out, Four Winds Press (New York, NY), 1965.

Enemies of the Secret Hide-out, Four Winds Press (New York, NY), 1966.

How to Write Codes and Send Secret Messages, illustrated by Bernice Myers, Four Winds Press (New York, NY), 1970.

"LITTLES" SERIES

(Self-illustrated) *The Littles to the Rescue,* Platt & Munk (New York, NY), 1981.

(Self-illustrated) *The Littles and Their Friends,* Platt & Munk (New York, NY), 1981.

(Self-illustrated) *The Littles' Scrapbook: A Facsimile Reproduction of Pages from a Tiny Person's Book, Enlarged Six Times,* Scholastic (New York, NY), 1984.

The Littles and the Terrible Tiny Kid, illustrated by Roberta Carter Clark, Scholastic (New York, NY), 1993.

The Littles and Their Amazing New Friend, illustrated by Roberta Carter Clark, Scholastic (New York, NY), 1999.

ILLUSTRATOR

Gladys Rhiner, *Jimmy Goes Camping,* Broadman Press (Nashville, TN), 1978.

(With Jack Storholm) Gary Paulsen and John Morris, *Canoeing, Kayaking, and Rafting,* Messner (New York, NY), 1979.

Adaptations

The "Littles" books were adapted as an animate cartoon series by DiC Entertainment and were adapted into storybooks by Teddy Slater and illustrated by Jacqueline Rogers, Scholastic, 2000-03.

Biographical and Critical Sources

PERIODICALS

Publishers Weekly, June 26, 1981, Jean F. Mercier, review of *The Littles and Their Friends,* p. 61.*

*   *   *

PETRONE, Valeria

Personal

Female. *Education:* Attended St. Martin School of Art (London, England); studied in Milan, Italy.

Addresses

Home—Italy. *Agent*—Morgan Gaynin, 194 3rd Ave., New York, NY 10003. *E-mail*—valeria@valeriapetrone.com.

Career

Illustrator. *Exhibitions:* Work exhibited in Italy and elsewhere around the world, including at Society of Illustrators' Original Art Show, New York, NY.

Member

Italian Association of Illustrators (former vice president), Society of Illustrators New York.

Illustrator

Carol Watson, *If You Were a Puppy,* Dinosaur (London, England), 1989.

Wes Magee, *Morning Break, and Other Poems,* Cambridge University Press (New York, NY), 1990.

Dennis Bond, *The Granny Who Wasn't like Other Grannies,* 1993, new edition, Coach House Press (London, England), 2003.

Incy Wincy Spider, and Other Nursery Rhymes, Ladybird (London, England), 1994.

Linda Jennings, *This Little Piggy,* Levinson Books (London, England), 1997.

Kate Burns, *Round and Round the Garden,* Levinson Books (London, England), 1997.

Denis Bond, *The Shark Who Bit Things He Shouldn't,* Little Hippo (London, England), 1998.

Lori Haskins, *Ducks in Muck,* Random House (New York, NY), 2000.

Nancy Smiler Levinson, *Say Cheese!,* Golden Books (New York, NY), 2000.

Mary Serfozo, *Plumply, Dumply Pumpkin,* Margaret K. McElderry Books (New York, NY), 2001.

Marion Dane Bauer, *Uh-oh!: A Lift-the-Flap Story,* Little Simon (New York, NY), 2002.

Leslie Parrott, *God Made You Nose to Toes,* Zonderkidz (Grand Rapids, MI), 2002.

Teresa Imperato, *Colors All Around,* Piggy Toes Press (Los Angeles, CA), 2003.

Joan N. Keener, *God Thought of It First,* Standard Publishing, 2003.

Anna Jane Hays, *The Pup Speaks Up: A Phonics Reader,* Random House (New York, NY), 2003.

Teresa Imperato, *How Many Ducks in a Row?,* Piggy Toes Press (Los Angeles, CA), 2003.

Stuart J. Murphy, *Double the Ducks,* HarperCollins (New York, NY), 2003.

Jan Peck, *Way down Deep in the Deep Blue Sea,* Simon & Schuster Books for Young Readers (New York, NY), 2004.

Cari Meister, *Luther's Halloween,* Viking (New York, NY), 2004.

Helen Bannerman, *The Boy and the Tigers,* Golden Books (New York, NY), 2004.

Jan Peck, *Way up High in a Tall Green Tree,* Simon & Schuster Books for Young Readers (New York, NY), 2005.

Patricia Ryan, *My Blankie: A Book to Touch and Feel,* Little Simon (New York, NY), 2005.

Michelle Knudsen, *Fish and Frog,* Candlewick Press (Cambridge, MA), 2005.

Jan Peck, *Way Far away on a Wild Safari,* Simon & Schuster Books for Young Readers (New York, NY), 2006.

Shari Becker, *Horris Grows Down,* G.P. Putnam's Sons (New York, NY), 2007.

Gianni Rodari, *Il pittore,* Edizioni EL (Trieste, Italy), 2007.

Gianni Rodari, *I viaggi di Giovannino Perdigiorno,* Edizioni EL (Trieste, Italy), 2008.

Kersten Hamilton, *Red Truck,* Viking Children's Books (New York, NY), 2008.

Gianni Rodari, *Gelsomino nel Paese dei Bugiardi,* Edizioni EL (Trieste, Italy), 2009.

Hope Vestergaard, *Potty Animals: What to Know When You've Gotta Go!,* Sterling Pub. (New York, NY), 2009.

Danna Smith, *Two at the Zoo,* Clarion Books (New York, NY), 2009.

Agnès De Lestrade, *L'abécédaire de la famille,* Milan Edition (Toulouse, France), 2010.

Gianni Rodari, *Le favolette di Alice,* Edizioni EL (Trieste, Italy), 2011.

Danna Smith, *Pirate Nap: A Book of Colors,* Clarion Books (Boston, MA), 2011.

Contributor of illustrations to periodicals, including *Elle, Express, Flair Living, Guardian, Los Angeles Times, Red,* and *Time Asia.*

Sidelights

Italian artist Valeria Petrone is internationally known for her work as a children's book illustrator. Although her images appear primarily in stories by English-language authors, books featuring Petrone's art have also reached young readers in Japan, France, and her native Italy through translation. Her work is inspired by British book illustration—she trained at London's St. Martin School of Art as well as in Italy—and it brings to life texts written by such well-known children's authors as Jan Peck, Stuart J. Murphy, Cari Meister, Hope Vestergaard, and Marion Dane Bauer. In her *School Library Journal* appraisal of Peck's *Way up High in a Tall Green Tree,* Suzanne Meyers-Harold cited Petrone for contributing "bold, colorful, digitally rendered" images that are distinguished by a "creative use of perspective." Susan E. Murray wrote in the same periodi-

Petrone heaps on the humor in her illustrations for Hope Vestergaard's entertaining picture book Potty Animals: What to Know When You've Gotta Go! *(Illustration © 2010 by Valeria Petrone. Reproduced with permission of Sterling Publishing Co., Inc.)*

cal that the cast of Petrone-rendered critters that stars in Vestergaard's *Potty Animals: What to Know When You've Gotta Go!* "are endearing and friendly." This lighthearted book will "make for uproarious reading," predicted Susan E. Murray in another *School Library Journal* review.

Petrone's signature mix of bold colors and digital images are on display in the pages of Shari Becker's *Horris Grows Down,* the story of an overgrown four year old who towers over his mother and dad. Told by his parents to find a job, the oversized preschooler is hampered by the fact that he can neither read nor count. In creating art for Becker's quirky tale, Petrone uses vivid colors in her "smooth digital illustrations, which mimic acrylic painting in retro oranges and turquoise," as noted by a *Publishers Weekly* reviewer. Julie Cummins, in her review of *Horris Grows Down* for *Booklist,* compared Petrone's unique images to those of other unique artists, writing that her "wacky illustrations . . . call up the work of J. Otto Seibold and Dan Yaccarino."

Kersten Hamilton's *Red Truck* is another book featuring Petrone's art. The author's simply worded, rhyming text spins out the story of a rainy school day and the yellow school bus that becomes stuck on slushy roads while making its way to school. Images featuring "bold primary colors . . . sparkle against the gray winter back-

Valeria Petrone's naive-styled artwork adds an air of whimsy to Jan Peck's rhyming story in Way Down Deep in the Deep Blue Sea. *(Illustrations copyright ©2004 by Valeria Petrone. Reprinted with the permission of Simon & Schuster Books for Young Readers, an imprint of Simon & Schuster Children's Publishing Division.)*

drops," according to *School Library Journal* contributor Julie R. Ranelli, and these "bright illustrations" make *Red Truck* a good choice for story hours featuring young boys. Petrone's "vibrant" artwork "will draw listeners in and make them right at home," predicted a *Kirkus Reviews* writer, and *Booklist* critic Carolyn Phelan noted that the artist's "strong, flowing lines and . . . simplified forms create a certain retro look" in the "appealing" children's book.

Biographical and Critical Sources

PERIODICALS

Booklist, April 15, 2000, Hazel Rochman, review of *Ducks in Muck,* p. 1555; September 1, 2001, Shelle Rosenfeld, review of *Plumply, Dumply Pumpkin,* p. 122; March 15, 2003, Hazel Rochman, review of *Double the Ducks,* p. 1328; July, 2003, Ilene Cooper, review of *The Pup Speaks Up: A Phonics Reader,* p. 1899; February 15, 2007, Julie Cummins, review of *Horris Grows Down,* p. 82; January 1, 2008, Carolyn Phelan, review of *Red Truck,* p. 79; March 15, 2010, Hazel Rochman, review of *Potty Animals: What to Know When You've Gotta Go!,* p. 47.

Books, February 11, 2007, Mary Harris Russell, review of *Horris Grows Down,* p. 7.

Bulletin of the Center for Children's Books, September, 2004, Gay Lynn Van Vleck, review of *Luther's Halloween,* p. 174; September, 2005, Hope Morrison, review of *Way up High in a Tall Green Tree,* p. 34; February, 2007, Deborah Stevenson, review of *Horris Grows Down,* p. 244.

Kirkus Reviews, July 1, 2001, review of *Plumply, Dumply Pumpkin,* p. 947; December 1, 2002, review of *Double the Ducks,* p. 1770; April 1, 2004, review of *Way Down Deep in the Deep Blue Sea,* p. 335; July 1, 2004, review of *Luther's Halloween,* p. 633; June 15, 2005, review of *Way up High in a Tall Green Tree,* p. 688; May 1, 2006, review of *Way Far away on a Wild Safari,* p. 465; December 15, 2006, review of *Horris Grows Down,* p. 1264; January 15, 2008, review of *Red Truck;* January 15, 2009, review of *Two at the Zoo;* February 15, 2010, review of *Potty Animals.*

Publishers Weekly, January 4, 1999, review of *Round and Round the Garden,* p. 92; September 24, 2001, review of *Plumply, Dumply Pumpkin,* p. 42; May 10, 2004, review of *Way down Deep in the Deep Blue Sea,* p. 57; August 9, 2004, review of *Luther's Halloween,* p. 31; January 22, 2007, review of *Horris Grows Down,* p. 184.

School Librarian, November, 1989, review of *If You Were a Puppy,* p. 146; August, 1993, review of *The Granny Who Wasn't like Other Grannies,* p. 101.

School Library Journal, August, 2000, Susan Hepler, review of *Give a Little Love: Stories of Love and Friendship,* p. 164; February, 2001, Barb Lawler, review of *Ducks in Muck,* p. 100; September, 2001, Piper L. Myman, review of *Plumply, Dumply Pumpkin,* p. 206; July, 2004, Julie Roach, review of *Way down Deep in the Deep Blue Sea,* p. 84; August, 2005, Melinda Piehler, review of *Fish and Frog,* p. 98; September, 2005, Suzanne Myers Harold, review of *Way up High in a Tall Green Tree,* p. 184; June, 2006, Marge Loch-Wouters, review of *Way Far away on a Wild Safari,* p. 124; February, 2007, Maryann H. Owen, review of *Horris Grows Down,* p. 84; April, 2008, Julie R. Ranelli, review of *Red Truck,* p. 110; February, 2009, Linda M. Kenton, review of *Two at the Zoo: A Counting Book,* p. 86; May, 2010, Susan E. Murray, review of *Potty Animals: What to Know When You've Gotta Go,* p. 93.

ONLINE

Valeria Petrone Home Page, http://www.valeriapetrone. com (September 15, 2011).

*   *   *

QUALLS, Sean

Personal

Married Selina Alko (an illustrator); children: Isaiah, Ginger.

Addresses

Home and office—Brooklyn, NY. *E-mail*—seanqualls@ hotmail.com.

Career

Artist and children's book illustrator. *Exhibitions:* Work exhibited in galleries in New York, NY, and elsewhere in the United States.

Member

Society of Children's Book Writers and Illustrators.

Awards, Honors

Honors from Society of Illustrators New York and Society of Illustrators Los Angeles; Silver Award, Parents' Choice, 2004, for *Powerful Words;* Blue Ribbon Award, *Bulletin of the Center for Children's Books,* 2006, for both *Dizzy* by Jonah Winter and *The Poet Slave of Cuba* by Margarita Engle; *Horn Book* Fanfare designation, 2006, and American Library Association (ALA) Notable Children's Book designation, 2007, both for *Dizzy;* Best Book for Young Adults, ALA, 2007, for *The Poet Slave of Cuba;* Christopher Award, for *How We Are Smart* by W. Nikola Lisa; Coretta Scott King Illustration Honor Book designation, 2008, for *Before John Was a Jazz Giant* by Carole Boston Weatherford.

Illustrator

Wade Hudson, *Powerful Words: More than 200 Years of Extraordinary Writing by African Americans,* Scholastic (New York, NY), 2004.

Karen English, *The Baby on the Way,* Farrar, Straus & Giroux (New York, NY), 2005.

Margarita Engle, *The Poet Slave of Cuba: A Biography of Juan Francisco Manzano,* Henry Holt (New York, NY), 2006.

W. Nikola-Lisa, *How We Are Smart,* Lee & Low (New York, NY), 2006.

Jonah Winter, *Dizzy,* Arthur A. Levine Books (New York, NY), 2006.

Carole Boston Weatherford, *Before John Was a Jazz Giant,* Henry Holt (New York, NY), 2008.

Catherine Clinton, *Phillis's Big Test,* Houghton Mifflin (Boston, MA), 2008.

Vaunda Micheaux Nelson, *Who Will I Be, Lord?,* Random House (New York, NY), 2009.

Toni Morrison and Slade Morrison, *Little Cloud and Lady Wind,* Simon & Schuster Books for Young Readers (New York, NY), 2010.

Roxane Orgill, *Skit-scat Raggedy Cat: Ella Fitzgerald,* Candlewick Press (Somerville, MA), 2010.

Sally M. Walker, *Freedom Song: The Story of Henry "Box" Brown,* Harper (New York, NY), 2011.

Spike and Tonya Lewis Lee, *Giant Steps to Change the World,* Simon & Schuster Books for Young Readers (New York, NY), 2011.

Andrea Davis Pinkney, *Bird in a Box,* Little, Brown (New York, NY), 2011.

Cover of Margarita Engle's The Poet Slave of Cuba, *an award-winning picture book featuring Sean Qualls' illustrations.* (Illustration © 2006 by Sean Qualls. Reprinted by permission of Henry Holt & Company, LLC.)

Contributor to periodicals, including *Function Design, Great Life, Hartford Courant, Harvard Business Review, Ladies' Home Journal, Las Vegas Life, Pennsylvania Gazette, READ,* and the *Wall Street Journal.*

Sidelights

Sean Qualls had an auspicious start to his career in children's-book illustration, earning several significant awards with only a few publications to his credit. At the beginning of his career his mixed-media art garnered two Blue Ribbon citations from the *Bulletin of the Center for Children's Books,* an accomplishment that was cited as "a little unusual" by the periodical's editor, Deborah Stevenson. Stevenson was quick to add, however, that Qualls' double honor was a result of his "serious craftsmanship" and an "original style" that combines acrylic paints with other artistic media. Not surprisingly, the influences cited by the artist on his home page are diverse: "movies, television, childhood memories, aging and decaying surfaces, old buildings, architecture, nature, folk art, fairy tales, Americana, Black memorabilia, outsider art, cave paintings, collectibles, African art, Little Golden Books, vintage advertisements, psychology, mythology, science fiction, music, and literature."

Referencing Qualls' work for such books as *Powerful Words: More than 200 Years of Extraordinary Writing by African Americans* by Wade Hudson and *The Baby on the Way* by Karen English, Stevenson summarized the artist's unique collage artwork as "sometimes crisp and close-cropped . . . and sometimes adding subtle tracery to backgrounds." In a joint online interview with wife and fellow illustrator Selina Alko for *AltPick.com,* Qualls commented that his art work is predominantly "about emotion and atmosphere. . . . I try to capture a feeling and perhaps not tangible things like music and a character's history." In the same interview, the artist/illustrator noted that his inspiration comes from "memories of my childhood and a sense of nostalgia," as well as from the works of well-known artists such as Jacob Lawrence and Romare Bearden.

Among Qualls' award-winning illustration projects is *The Poet Slave of Cuba: A Biography of Juan Francisco Manzano.* Featuring a rhyming text by Margarita Engle and based on the childhood of the noted Cuban poet, *The Poet Slave of Cuba* contains high-contrast black-and-white illustrations. Hazel Rochman, writing in *Booklist,* asserted that Qualls' charcoal drawings "express Juan's suffering and strength," while Carol Jones Collins wrote in her *School Library Journal* review that the book's highly visual aspect provides readers with a "suitably stark and compelling" counterpoint to Manzano's life story.

Phillis's Big Test, a vignette retold by writer Catherine Clinton, focuses on eighteenth-century African-American poet Phillis Wheatley and her need to prove authorship of her verses before the governor of the

Qualls captures the up beat of Roxane Orgill's picture-book biography Skit-Scat Raggedy Cat: Ella Fitzgerald. (Illustration copyright © 2010 by Sean Qualls. Reproduced with permission of Candlewick Press, Somerville, MA.)

Massachusetts Bay Colony. Here the artist "employ[s] strong diagonal lines, swirling ribbons of thought, and a combination of opaque images and outlined, transparent figures over washes of color to create visual interest," according to *School Library Journal* contributor Wendy Lukehart.

Dizzy, another picture-book portrait of a creative black American that features Qualls' art, pairs a text by Jonah Winter with what a *Publishers Weekly* critic described as "expressionistic" acrylic paintings that "bloom with the blaring hot red and pink streams of sound emanating from [the] . . . horn" blown by the noted jazz trumpeter. "Qualls is able to translate the story . . . into shapes and colors that undulate and stream across the pages with a beat and bounce of their own," asserted Ilene Cooper in her *Booklist* appraisal of *Dizzy.*

Also focusing on music, Carole Boston Weatherford teams up with Qualls to create *Before John Was a Jazz Giant: A Song of John Coltrane,* and here the artist's "muted palette of rich hues suggests the smoky jazz moods he [Coltrane] would [later] create," according to *School Library Journal* contributor Joyce Adams Burner. Yet another jazz great is profiled in Roxane Orgill's *Skit-Scat Raggedy Cat: Ella Fitzgerald,* and here Qualls "firmly establishes himself as a leading illustrator of jazz biographies for children," according to Mary Landrum in her *School Library Journal* review of the book.

Biographical and Critical Sources

PERIODICALS

Black Issues Book Review, Suzanne Rust, "Learning as We Climb: Stories about the Civil Rights Movement for Young Readers," p. 58.

Booklist, February 15, 2004, Carolyn Phelan, review of *Powerful Words: More than 200 Years of Extraordinary Writing by African Americans,* p. 1068; October 1, 2005, Hazel Rochman, review of *The Baby on the Way,* p. 62; February 15, 2006, Hazel Rochman, review of *The Poet Slave of Cuba: A Biography of Juan Francisco Manzano,* p. 95; April 1, 2006, Hazel Rochman, review of *How We Are Smart,* p. 38; November 1, 2006, Ilene Cooper, review of *Dizzy,* p. 63; February 1, 2008, Ilene Cooper, review of *Phillis's Big Test,* p. 61; June 1, 2010, Ian Chipman, review of *Skit-Scat Raggedy Cat: Ella Fitzgerald,* p. 99; February 1, 2011, Hazel Rochman, review of *Giant Steps to Change the World,* p. 75.

Horn Book, July-August, 2006, Lelac Almagor, review of *The Poet Slave of Cuba,* p. 459; November-December, 2009, Susan Dove Lempke, review of *Who Will I Be, Lord?,* p. 657.

Kirkus Reviews, October 1, 2005, review of *The Baby on the Way,* p. 1079; March 15, 2006, review of *The Poet Slave of Cuba,* p. 289; April 15, 2006, review of *How We Are Smart;* September 15, 2006, review of *Dizzy,* p. 970; March 15, 2008, review of *Before John Was a Jazz Giant;* September 1, 2009, review of *Who Will I Be, Lord?;* February 15, 2010, review of *Little Cloud and Lady Wind.*

New York Times Book Review, November 13, 2005, review of *The Baby on the Way,* p. L30.

Publishers Weekly, October 31, 2005, review of *The Baby on the Way,* p. 55; April 17, 2006, review of *The Poet Slave of Cuba,* p. 190; October 30, 2006, review of *Dizzy,* p. 61; January 4, 2010, review of *Little Cloud and Lady Wind,* p. 45; July 26, 2010, review of *Skit-Scat Raggedy Cat,* p. 73.

School Library Journal, February, 2004, Mary N. Oluonye, review of *Powerful Words,* p. 164; November, 2005, Mary N. Oluonye, review of *The Baby on the Way,* p. 89; April, 2006, Carol Jones Collins, review of *The Poet Slave of Cuba,* p. 154; Joy Fleishhacker, June, 2006, review of *How We Are Smart,* p. 182; October, 2006, Lee Bock, review of *Dizzy,* p. 143; March, 2008, Wendy Lukehart, review of *Phillis's Big Test,* p. 183; October, 2009, Lisa Egly Lehmuller, review of *Who Will I Be, Lord,* p. 100; July, 2010, Mary Landrum, review of *Skit-Scat Raggedy Cat,* p. 75; February, 2011, Sara Lissa Paulson, review of *Giant Steps to Change the World,* p. 85.

ONLINE

AltPick.com, http://altpick.com/ (February 20, 2007), interview with Qualls and Selina Alko.

Bulletin of the Center for Children's Books Online, http://bccb.lis.uiuc.edu/ (February 20, 2007), Maggie Hommel, review of *The Poet Slave of Cuba;* Deborah Stevenson, "Rising Star: Sean Qualls."

Sean Qualls Home Page, http://www.seanqualls.com (September 15, 2011).

ZoomInfo.com, http://www.zoominfo.com/ (September 15, 2011), "Sean Qualls."

R

RANIA, QUEEN of JORDAN 1970-
(Rania al Abdullah)

Personal

Born August 31, 1970, in Kuwait; immigrated to Jordan, 1990; daughter of a pediatrician; married King Abdullah II ibn Al Hussein, June 10, 1993; children: Crown Prince Hussein, Princess Iman, Princess Salma, Prince Hashem. *Education:* American University in Cairo, B.A. (business administration), 1991. *Religion:* Muslim. *Hobbies and other interests:* Running.

Addresses

Home—Amman, Jordan.

Career

Philanthropist and author. Citibank, Amman, Jordan, former investment banker; Apple Computer, Amman, former member of marketing staff; proclaimed queen of Jordan, March 22, 1999. Participant in international gatherings, including Clinton Global Initiative. Member of board, International Youth Foundation, United Nations Foundation, World Economic Forum, Foundation for International Community Assistance, and Forum of Young Global Leaders; Royal Health Awareness Society, chairperson; established Queen Rania scholarship program.

Awards, Honors

Life Achievement Award, American Osteoporosis Foundation, 2001; James C. Morgan Global Humanitarian Award, 2010; named Dama di Gran Croce, Republic of Italy Order of Merit; named to Royal Norwegian Order of St. Olav; named honorary member of international advisory council, International Center for Research on Women; honorary chairperson of philanthropic organizations, including U.N. Girls' Education Initiative and Operation Smile.

Rania, Queen of Jordan (Uli Deck/DPA/Landov. Reproduced by permission.)

Writings

The King's Gift: A Tribute to His Majesty the Late King Hussein of Jordan (in Arabic), illustrated by Angel Dominguez, Michael O'Mara Books (London, England), 2000.

Eternal Beauty, [Jordan], 2008.

Maha of the Mountains, Global Campaign for Education (Amman, Jordan), 2009.

(With Kelly DiPucchio) *The Sandwich Swap,* illustrated by Tricia Tusa, Disney-Hyperion Books (New York, NY), 2010.

Sidelights

Rania, Queen of Jordan is wife to Jordan's King Abdullah II ibn al Hussein. Beloved by many around the world for both the example she sets as a mother to her four children and the grace she brings to her office, Queen Rania is also active in the education of future generations of Jordanians through her work promoting computer literacy, consistent teaching standards, and the increased involvement of families, businesses, and communities in the educational process. Her position as queen also allows her to work on the international level, advocating for all children's right to a quality education and also serving as a spokesperson for UNICEF. On an individual level, Queen Rania shares a lesson in tolerating differences in *The Sandwich Swap,* a picture book coauthored by Kelly DiPucchio and illustrated by Tricia Tusa.

Queen Rania was born in Kuwait to Palestinian parents, and her father supported the family's upper-middle-class lifestyle through his work as a pediatrician. She was educated in a private school where she learned to master English and also gained exposure to non-Muslim culture. Queen Rania was earning a degree in business administration at the American University in Cairo in 1990 when Saddam Hussein invaded Kuwait and her family was forced to flee to nearby Jordan. She rejoined her parents after graduation and took a job with Citibank. Rania was twenty-two years old and working in the marketing department of Apple Computer's Amman branch when she met Prince Abdullah at a dinner party, and the couple was married eighteen months later. Prince Abdullah expected to continue his career in the Jordanian Army. However, when his father, King Hussein, died five years later he had altered the succession, passing the crown from his brother, the Prince Regent, to his son and making Rania queen.

One of Queen Rania's first published books, a tribute to the late King Hussein, was the children's book *The King's Gift: A Tribute to His Majesty the Late King Hussein of Jordan,* and the proceeds from its sales were donated to a Jordanian children's charity. *Eternal Beauty,* her next book, honors Mother's Day, while *Maha of the Mountains* was written for Jordan's 2009 Big Read event and focuses on a child's determination to gain an education.

Queen Rania's story for her fourth book, *The Sandwich Swap,* is based on a childhood memory. Coauthored by

Queen Rania teams up with Kelly DiPucchio on the friendship story The Sandwich Swap, *featuring artwork by Tricia Tusa.*

veteran children's-book author DiPucchio, it focuses on the relationship between best friends Lily and Salma when each decides that the other's favorite sandwich is distasteful. Lily loves peanut butter and jelly, just like most everyone else she knows. Therefore, Salma's hummus-on-pita bread sandwich does not seem normal to her, and even more not-normal is the fact that Salma finds peanut butter and jelly less than appealing. Fortunately, although their disagreement escalates into a lunchroom brawl, the two friends make up while waiting in the principal's office, and they even trade sandwiches! Writing in *Booklist,* Hazel Rochman called *The Sandwich Swap* a "lively picture book" and praised Tusa for crafting "harmonious" illustrations for the collaborative text. A *Publishers Weekly* critic noted the story's "readily apparent themes of acceptance and sharing," while Marjorie Kehe concluded in her *Christian Science Monitor* review that *The Sandwich Swap* contains "a lesson to remember."

Biographical and Critical Sources

PERIODICALS

Booklist, February 15, 2010, Hazel Rochman, review of *The Sandwich Swap,* p. 81.
Children's Bookwatch, June, 2010, review of *The Sandwich Swap.*
Christian Science Monitor, April 2, 1010, Marjorie Kehe, review of *The Sandwich Swap.*
Harper's Bazaar, March, 2003, Lisa DePaulo, "Up Close with Queen Rania," p. 276.
Middle East, March, 1999, Adel Darwish, "Spotlight on a Queen," p. 7.
People, November 21, 2005, Michelle Tauber, "A Very Modern Queen," p. 110.
Publishers Weekly, March 15, 2010, review of *The Sandwich Swap,* p. 50.
Sunday Times (London, England), May 28, 2006, "Her Majesty Won't Be Wearing a Burqa," p. 5.
Time for Kids, January 11, 2008, Ritu Upadhyay, "A Royal Quest for Peace," p. 7.
Time International, November 13, 2006, Scott MacLeod, "Queen Rania," p. 102.

ONLINE

Campaign for Education Web site, http://www.campaign foreducation.org/ (May 15, 2011), "Maha of the Mountains."
Rania al Abdullah Home Page, http://www.queenrania.jo (May 27, 2011).*

*   *   *

ROCKWELL, Lizzy 1961-

Personal

Born 1961; daughter of Harlow (a painter and illustrator) and Anne F. (an author and artist) Rockwell; mar-

Lizzy Rockwell (Photograph by Kenneth Alcorn. Reproduced by permission.)

ried Kenneth Alcorn; children: Nicholas, Nigel. *Education:* Attended Connecticut College and School of Visual Arts. *Hobbies and other interests:* Gardening, baking, watching movies, camping, skiing, traveling, playing piano, spending time with family.

Addresses

Home and office—401 Grovers Ave., Bridgeport, CT 06605. *E-mail*—lizzyrockwell@mac.com.

Career

Writer and illustrator. Illustrator, beginning 1984. Presenter at schools.

Awards, Honors

Best Children's Science Books selection, 1995, for *A Nest Full of Eggs* by Patricia Belz Jenkins; Top-Ten Science and Technology Books for Youth inclusion, *Booklist,* and Best Books for Youth selection, American Library Association, both 2004, both for *The Busy Body Book.*

Writings

SELF-ILLUSTRATED

Hello Baby!, Crown (New York, NY), 1999.

Good Enough to Eat: A Kid's Guide to Food and Nutrition, HarperCollins (New York, NY), 1999.

The Busy Body Book: A Kid's Guide to Fitness, Crown (New York, NY), 2004.

ILLUSTRATOR

Anne Rockwell, *Apples and Pumpkins,* Macmillan (New York, NY), 1989, reprinted, Aladdin (New York, NY), 2011.

(With father, Harlow Rockwell) Anne Rockwell, *My Spring Robin,* Macmillan (New York, NY), 1989.

Amy Hest, *A Sort-of Sailor,* Four Winds (New York, NY), 1990.

(With Pam Braun and Rina Horiuchi) Pyke Johnson, *Pyke's Poems: Verse for Kids,* Shorelands (Old Greenwich, CT), 1992.

Anne Rockwell, *Our Yard Is Full of Birds,* Collier (New York, NY), 1992.

Anne Rockwell, *Pots and Pans,* Macmillan (New York, NY), 1993.

Anne Rockwell, *Ducklings and Pollywogs,* Macmillan (New York, NY), 1994.

Priscilla Belz Jenkins, *A Nest Full of Eggs,* HarperCollins (New York, NY), 1995.

Deborah Heiligman, *On the Move,* HarperCollins (New York, NY), 1996.

Anne Rockwell, *Halloween Day,* HarperCollins (New York, NY), 1997.

Anne Rockwell, *Show and Tell Day,* HarperCollins (New York, NY), 1997.

I.K. Swobud, *Don't Go up Haunted Hill—or Else!,* Golden Books (New York, NY), 1999.

Anne Rockwell, *Thanksgiving Day,* HarperCollins (New York, NY), 1999.

Anne Rockwell, *Career Day,* HarperCollins (New York, NY), 2000.

Anne Rockwell, *Valentine's Day,* HarperCollins (New York, NY), 2001.

Anne Rockwell, *One Hundred School Days,* HarperCollins (New York, NY), 2002.

Gloria Rothstein, *Sheep Asleep,* HarperCollins (New York, NY), 2003.

Maya Angelou, *Izak of Lapland,* Random House (New York, NY), 2004.

Maya Angelou, *Renée Marie of France,* Random House (New York, NY), 2004.

Maya Angelou, *Mikale of Hawai'i,* Random House (New York, NY), 2004.

Maya Angelou, *Angelina of Italy,* Random House (New York, NY), 2004.

Anne Rockwell, *Mother's Day,* HarperCollins (New York, NY), 2004.

Anne Rockwell, *Father's Day,* HarperCollins (New York, NY), 2005.

Anne Rockwell, *Who Lives in an Alligator Hole?,* Collier (New York, NY), 2006.

Joy Hulme, *Mary Clare Likes to Share: A Math Reader,* Random House (New York, NY), 2006.

Anne Rockwell, *Presidents' Day,* HarperCollins (New York, NY), 2007.

Anne Rockwell, *First Day of School,* Harper (New York, NY), 2010.

Anne Rockwell, *St. Patrick's Day,* by Harper (New York, NY), 2010.

Sidelights

Lizzy Rockwell is an illustrator whose work has appeared in picture books and magazines, as well as in games and other products for children. A prolific artist, she has illustrated more than thirty books, many of them written by her mother, children's author Anne Rockwell. In addition to her work as an artist, Rockwell has also created art for her original texts, which include *Hello Baby!, Good Enough to Eat: A Kid's Guide to Food and Nutrition*, and *The Busy Body Book: A Kid's Guide to Fitness.*

As the daughter of two creative parents—her father, the late Harlow Rockwell, was an illustrator and art director—Rockwell grew up around art and storytelling and watched her parents collaborate on books together. "There were plenty of art materials around the house and my brother, sister, and I were always encouraged to be creative and to express our ideas," she recalled on her home page. After attending college and art school, Rockwell started her career in 1984, illustrating magazines and book jackets. Her first picture-book project, illustrating her mother's text for *Apples and Pumpkins,* was published in 1989 and has remained perennially in print.

As an illustrator, Rockwell is noted for her use of color. Her "realistically rendered illustrations are drenched in color," wrote Lisa Gangemi in a *School Library Jour-*

Rockwell and mother Anne Rockwell take a walk through the holidays in a series of picture books that include **President's Day.** (Illustration copyright © 2008 by Lizzy Rockwell. Reproduced with permission of HarperCollins Children's Books, a division of HarperCollins Publishers.)

Rockwell's illustration projects include the original holiday illustration "Let There Be Peace." (Reproduced by permission of Lizzy Rockwell.)

nal review of the artist's contribution to *One Hundred School Days,* a mother-daughter project. In appraising another Rockwell-and-Rockwell collaboration, *Pots and Pans,* a *Publishers Weekly* wrote that the "bright watercolors capture an impressive variety of textures." Another *Publishers Weekly* critic, reviewing *Halloween Day,* noted that author and artist collaborate to "create believable multiethnic characters," while *School Library Journal* contributor Wendy S. Carroll complimented the easy-to-read text in *Career Day* and asserted that Lizzy Rockwell's "colorful pictures are [as] . . . appealing" as her mother's text.

Of her work on *Who Lives in an Alligator Hole?,* a *Kirkus Reviews* contributor wrote that "a non-reading child would be able to get much of the text's information from Lizzy Rockwell's pictures alone." *Father's Day,* part of a series by Anne Rockwell that focuses on Mrs. Madoff's class of spunky second graders, contains artwork that features "rounded shapes and smooth colors," giving it "a simple, friendly look that puts the focus on the characters," according to *Booklist* critic Ilene Cooper. The series also includes *President's Day,* and here the "clean, uncluttered illustrations" Lizzy Rock-

well contributes "are bright and bold" and contribute to making the book "an excellent introduction to the holiday for younger grades," according to Grace Oliff in *School Library Journal.*

Rockwell's illustration projects have extended beyond books authored by her mother and include bringing to life stories by Deborah Heiligman, Patricia Belz Jenkins, Maya Angelou, and Joy Hulme. In a review of *Angelina of Italy,* a story by noted author Angelou, Hazel Rochman wrote in *Booklist* that the illustrator's "clear, cheerful pictures will appeal to kids," while Hulme's story in *Mary Clare Likes to Share: A Math Reader* benefits from Rockwell's "cheerful illustrations of children of many different ethnicities," according to a *Kirkus Reviews* critic.

In her self-illustrated work, Rockwell explains the laws of balanced nutrition to a young audience in *Good Enough to Eat.* Designed for the preschool set, the book addresses such topics as fighting germs, vitamins, and how good foods help improve movement, respiration, warmth, and growing. "This could be a valuable classroom tool for teaching about health and nutrition,"

Rochman concluded in a *Booklist* review. Regarding the illustrations, a *Publishers Weekly* critic wrote that Rockwell's "compositions are cheerful and sometimes playful."

Another original self-illustrated picture book, *Hello Baby!*, is also geared for very young readers and was created by Rockwell to help soon-to-be-older-siblings prepare for an infant's arrival. The picture book shows parents including their child in the entire process of pregnancy, even doctor visits, and describes the biology behind a growing baby. Noting that some of the concepts might be beyond the scope of the youngest readers, Rochman nonetheless wrote that parents may "welcome the chance to include the fascinating biology as well as the usual reassuring message." The narrator's voice and explanations "accurately reflect a happy child's point of view," wrote a *Publishers Weekly* contributor.

The Busy Body Book uses some of the same techniques as *Good Enough to Eat*, presenting factual material in a way that makes it easy for preschoolers to understand. "The design is clear and inviting," wrote Rochman of the title in her *Booklist* review. Shauna Yusko, writing in *School Library Journal*, concluded of *The Busy Body Book* that Rockwell's "text is purposely motivating, yet easy to understand and informative."

On her home page, Rockwell explained that she enjoys both writing and illustrating. "It is such a great challenge to tell a story or explain something complicated using as few words as possible," she explained. "It's fun to write picture books, because you know that the pictures will do a lot of the work for you. Even when I am writing nonfiction, I want the words to sound as beautiful as a poem, flow from the mouth as easily as a song, and have meaning as compelling as a novel." "In my pictures, I want all children to recognize themselves, and feel proud and included," Rockwell once told *SATA*. "I strive to model good citizenship, high self-esteem, and positive interpersonal relationships in ways that are realistic and natural, but never sentimental or preachy." Of being an author and illustrator as a career, she wrote:

***Rockwell teams up with mother Anne Rockwell on the fall-themed picture book* Apples and Pumpkins.** (Illustration copyright © 1989 Lizzy Rockwell. Reprinted with the permission of Simon & Schuster Books for Young Readers, an imprint of Simon & Schuster Children's Publishing Division.)

"My job is one of the most creative and expressive things I can imagine doing. I love carrying on my parents' tradition in children's books."

Biographical and Critical Sources

BOOKS

Marcus, Leonard S., *Pass It Down: Five Picture-Book Families Make Their Mark,* Walker (New York, NY), 2006.

PERIODICALS

Booklist, December 15, 1994, Mary Harris Veeder, review of *Ducklings and Pollywogs,* p. 760; June 1, 1995, Hazel Rochman, review of *A Nest Full of Eggs,* p. 1778; May 1, 1996, Hazel Rochman, review of *On the Move,* p. 1510; April 1, 1997, Hazel Rochman, review of *Show and Tell Day,* p. 1339; January 1, 1999, Hazel Rochman, review of *Good Enough to Eat: A Kid's Guide to Food and Nutrition,* p. 883; March 15, 1999, review of *Hello Baby!,* p. 1334; September 1, 1999, Shelley Townsend-Hudson, review of *Thanksgiving Day,* p. 150; May 1, 2000, review of *Career Day,* p. 1679; December 1, 2003, review of *The Busy Body Book: A Kid's Guide to Fitness,* p. 681; November 15, 2004, Hazel Rochman, review of *Angelina of Italy,* p. 589; January 1, 2005, review of *The Busy Body Book,* p. 776; May 15, 2005, Ilene Cooper, review of *Father's Day,* p. 1666; December 1, 2006, Carolyn Phelan, review of *Who Lives in an Alligator Hole?,* p. 62; February 15, 2008, Ilene Cooper, review of *President's Day,* p. 87.

Horn Book, May-June, 1993, Martha V. Parravano, review of *Pots and Pans,* p. 350; March, 2001, Martha V. Parravano, review of *Valentine's Day,* p. 202.

Kirkus Reviews, January 15, 2004, review of *The Busy Body Book,* p. 88; October 15, 2006, review of *Mary Clare Likes to Share,* p. 1073; November 1, 2006, review of *Who Lives in an Alligator Hole?,* p. 1124.

Publishers Weekly, April 5, 1993, review of *Pots and Pans,* p. 75; October 6, 1997, review of *Halloween Day,* p. 48; January 18, 1999, review of *Good Enough to Eat,* p. 338; May 10, 1999, review of *Hello Baby!,* p. 67.

School Library Journal, July, 2000, Wendy S. Carroll, review of *Career Day,* p. 86; September, 2002, Lisa Gangemi, review of *One Hundred School Days,* p. 205; January, 2004, Shauna Yusko, review of *The Busy Body Book,* p. 121; July, 2004, Lisa Gangemi Kropp, review of *One Hundred School Days,* p. 44; May, 2005, Mary Hazelton, review of *Father's Day,* p. 95; November, 2006, Christine Markley, review of *Who Lives in an Alligator Hole?,* p. 123; January, 2008, Grace Oliff, review of *Presidents' Day,* p. 97; January, 2010, Lisa Egly Lehmuller, review of *St. Patrick's Day,* p. 81.

ONLINE

Kids at Random Web site, http://www.randomhouse.com/kids/ (November 21, 2007), profile of Rockwell.

Lizzy Rockwell Home Page, http://www.lizzyrockwell.com (September 15, 2011).

*   *   *

ROGÉ 1972-

Personal

Born 1972, in Quebec, Canada. *Education:* Attended Laval University.

Addresses

Home—Montreal, Quebec, Canada. *Agent*—Lori Nowicki; lori@painted-words.com. *E-mail*—roge@bellnet.ca.

Career

Painter and children's-book author and illustrator. Former artistic director for Cossette and LG2 (advertising agencies). *Exhibitions:* Work included in exhibitions at Salon international du Livre de Taipei, Taiwan, 2010; Galerie IQ, Montreal, Quebec, Canada, 2010; Galerie du Café de la Grave, Îles-de-la-Madeleine, Quebec, 2010; and Librairie Monet, Montreal, 2011.

Awards, Honors

Named among Top Fifty Canadian Children's Picture Books (2000-2003), International Board on Books for Young People, Blue Spruce Award, Ontario Library Association, Governor General's Award for Illustration shortlist, Canada Council for the Arts, and Our Choice selection, Canadian Children's Book Centre (CCBC), all 2003, and Outstanding Canadian Book selection, Association for the Export of Canadian Books, 2004, all for *When Pigs Fly* by Valerie Coulman; Best Children's Picture Book finalist, Independent Publisher Book Awards, Blue Spruce Award shortlist, CCBC Our Choice selection, Shining Willow Award shortlist, and Saskatchewan Young Readers' Choice selection, all 2004, all for *Sink or Swim* by Coulman; Governor General's Award for Illustration, 2006, for *Le gros monstre qui aimait trop lire* by Lili Chartrand; Prix TD finalist, CCBC, Governor General's Award for Illustration shortlist, and honorable mention, Salon du livre de Trois-Rivières, all 2009, and Prix Cécile-Gagnon finalist, 2010, all for *La vraie histoire de Léo Pointu;* numerous honors for editorial illustrations.

Writings

SELF-ILLUSTRATED

La vraie histoire de Léo Pointu, Dominique et Compagnie (Saint-Lambert, Quebec, Canada), 2008.

Le roi de la patate, Dominique et Compagnie (Saint-Lambert, Quebec, Canada), 2010.

Haïti, mon pays: Poèmes d''coliers haïtiens, Éditions de la Bagnole (Montreal, Quebec, Canada), 2010.

ILLUSTRATOR

Lisa Mallen, *Elton the Elf,* Lobster Press (Montreal, Quebec, Canada), 2000.

Louise Tondreau-Levert, *Parents Do the Weirdest Things!,* Dominique et Compagnie (Saint-Lambert, Quebec, Canada), 2001.

Valerie Coulman, *When Pigs Fly,* Lobster Press (Montreal, Quebec, Canada), 2001.

Louise Tondreau-Levert, *Les bêtises des parents,* Dominique et Compagnie (Saint-Lambert, Quebec, Canada), 2001.

Marie-Danielle Croteau, *Un gnome à la mer,* Dominique et Compagnie (Saint-Lambert, Quebec, Canada), 2002.

Valerie Coulman, *Sink or Swim,* Lobster Press (Montreal, Quebec, Canada), 2003.

Barbara Todd, *The Rainmaker,* Annick Press (Toronto, Ontario, Canada, 2003.

Louise Tondreau Levert, *Les bêtises des parents,* Dominique et Compagnie (Saint-Lambert, Quebec, Canada), 2004.

Johanne Gagné, *Les vacances du Petit Chaperon rouge,* Les 400 coups (Montreal, Quebec, Canada, 2004.

Dennis Lee, *Ragoût de crocodile: Délicieux poèmes,* Key Porter Kids (Toronto, Ontario, Canada), 2005.

Barbara Todd, *Roger Gets Carried Away,* Annick Press (Toronto, Ontario, Canada), 2005.

Lili Chartrand, *Le gros monstre qui aimait trop lire,* Dominique et Compagnie (Saint-Lambert, Quebec, Canada), 2005.

Dennis Lee, *Alligator Stew: Favourite Poems,* Key Porter Kids (Toronto, Ontario, Canada), 2005.

Lili Chartrand, *Taming Horrible Harry,* Tundra Books (Toronto, Ontario, Canada), 2006.

Gilles Chouinard, *Le tyranno nez rouge: Une préhistoire de Noël,* DesJardins (Montreal, Quebec, Canada), 2007, published as *Dinah Red Nose: A Christmas Tale,* 2007.

Gilles Chouinard, *Tyrano de Bergerac: Une préhistoire d'amour,* DesJardins (Montreal, Quebec, Canada), 2008.

Susan Collins, *Cesar Takes a Break,* Sterling (New York, NY), 2008.

Johanne Gagné, *Les vacances du petit chaperon rouge,* Les 400 coups (Montreal, Quebec, Canada), 2009.

***Rogé's illustrations add spark to picture-book stories such as Stephen Krensky's* Noah's Bark.** (Illustration copyright © 2010 by Rogé. Reproduced with permission of Carolrhoda Books, a division of Lerner Publishing Group. All rights reserved.)

Stephen Krensky, *Noah's Bark,* Carolrhoda Books (Minneapolis, MN), 2010.

Louise Tondreau-Levert, *Les bêtises des parents,* Dominique et Compagnie (Saint-Lambert, Quebec, Canada), 2010.

Sidelights

A respected Canadian artist, Rogé has provided the artwork for more than twenty children's books, including *When Pigs Fly,* an award-winning title by Valerie Coulman, and *Noah's Bark,* a critically acclaimed work by Stephen Krensky. Rogé made his picture-book debut in 2000 with Lisa Mallen's *Elton the Elf,* which describes an arduous journey undertaken by one of Santa's helpers. The illustrator's characteristic "bright-as-a-button acrylics" for this work garnered praise from a critic in *Publishers Weekly.*

When Pigs Fly centers on Ralph, a young cow that has his heart set on learning to ride a bicycle. When his disapproving father tells Ralph that he will purchase a bike "when pigs fly," the youngster takes the statement literally, signing up for helicopter lessons so he can take his piglet pals for a ride. According to Ian Stewart in the *Canadian Review of Materials,* "Rogé's comic style illustrations add to the whimsical charm" of the story, and Linda Berezowski noted in *Resource Links* that the book's "bright, bold, eye-catching illustrations" in *When Pigs Fly* "capture" the protagonist's persistent nature.

Ralph makes a return appearance in *Sink or Swim,* a work by Coulman that focuses on the bovine's efforts to learn how to swim with help from a duck, a turtle, and a frog. "The artwork conveys a chipper mood and lots of energy," remarked a contributor in *Publishers Weekly,* and *Resource Links* reviewer Isobel Lang described Rogé's illustrations for *Sink or Swim* as "energetic and vibrant." In the words of *Canadian Review of Materials* critic Sandi Harrison, "The underwater illustrations are especially fun, with colourful, friendly fish darting in and out of the pages, sometimes eating dinner, playing cards, or reading a book."

Rogé has also enjoyed a successful collaboration with author Barbara Todd. In *The Rainmaker,* a young boy creates a torrential downpour by opening a special faucet, after which he meets an unusual fellow known as the Rainmaker who dispenses magical umbrellas. "Rogé peoples this nonlinear world with button-eyed characters and funky, distorted perspectives," commented a reviewer in *Publishers Weekly.* An imaginative youngster learns to appreciate his new eyeglasses after an unanticipated encounter with an alien in Todd's *Roger Gets Carried Away.* "The illustrations are bold and colourful," Berezowski stated of the work in *Resource Links,* "adding action to the text and interest to the story," and Christina Neigel concluded in *Canadian Review of Materials* that the pictures in *Roger Gets Carried Away* "convey fun and lightheartedness."

In Lili Chartrand's *Taming Horrible Harry* a frightening creature discovers the joys of reading. "Rogé's splashy artwork includes plenty of grinning monsters," remarked a contributor in reviewing *Taming Horrible Harry* for *Publishers Weekly,* and *School Library Journal* critic Corrina Austin maintained that the "pictures have that ghastly but humorous quality so enjoyed by children." *Cesar Takes a Break,* a tale by Susan Collins, follows the exploits of Cesar the iguana, a classroom pet that explores his school while the students are on spring vacation. In *School Library Journal,* Gay Lynn Van Vleck observed that "Rogé's acrylic cartoons emphasize the comedy with bright colors and creative poses."

Krensky offers a humorous retelling of a Biblical tale in *Noah's Bark.* Here, according to *Booklist* contributor Julie Cummins, Rogé's "stylized, brushstroked paintings are embellished with highlighted sound effects and subtle comic expressions."

Biographical and Critical Sources

PERIODICALS

Booklist, December 1, 2003, Jennifer Mattson, review of *Sink or Swim,* p. 684; May 1, 2008, John Peters, review of *Cesar Takes a Break,* p. 92; March 1, 2010, Julie Cummins, review of *Noah's Bark,* p. 78.

Canadian Review of Materials, May 24, 2002, Ian Stewart, review of *When Pigs Fly;* September 30, 2005, Christina Neigel, review of *Roger Gets Carried Away;* January 20, 2006, Sandi Harrison, review of *Sink or Swim;* June 9, 2006, Rosemary Hollett, review of *Taming Terrible Harry.*

Children's Bookwatch, August, 2010, review of *Noah's Bark.*

Kirkus Reviews, November 1, 2003, review of *Sink or Swim,* p. 1310; June 15, 2005, review of *Roger Gets Carried Away,* p. 692.

Publishers Weekly, September 24, 2001, review of *Elton the Elf,* p. 50; April 7, 2003, review of *The Rainmaker,* p. 65; November 17, 2003, review of *Sink or Swim,* p. 62; May 22, 2006, review of *Taming Horrible Harry,* p. 51; March 22, 2010, review of *Noah's Bark,* p. 67.

Resource Links, April, 2002, Linda Berezowski, review of *When Pigs Fly,* p. 3; October, 2005, Linda Berezowski, review of *Roger Gets Carried Away,* p. 10; April, 2006, Rachel Steen, review of *Taming Horrible Harry,* p. 3.

School Library Journal, August, 2003, Susan Lissim, review of *The Rainmaker,* p. 144; February, 2004, Isobel Lang, review of *Sink or Swim,* p. 1; May, 2004, Jane Barrer, review of *Sink or Swim,* p. 108; July, 2006, Corrina Austin, review of *Taming Horrible Harry,* p. 70; June, 2008, Gay Lynn Van Vleck, review of *Cesar Takes a Break,* p. 115.

ONLINE

Lobster Press Web site, http://www.lobsterpress.com/ (August 1, 2011), "Rogé."
Painted-Words.com, http://www.painted-words.com/ (August 1, 2011), "Rogé."
Rogé Home Page, http://roge-ca.squarespace.com (August 1, 2011).*

*   *   *

RUE, Nancy 1951-
(Nancy N. Rue)

Personal

Born July 27, 1951, in Riverside, NJ; daughter of William Theodore (a civil servant) and Jean Naylor; married James Rue (in theatre management), June 2, 1973; children: Marijean Suzanne. *Education:* John B. Stetson University, B.A. (English), 1973; College of William and Mary, M.A. (education), 1978; University of Nevada, Reno, B.A. (theatre). *Religion:* Episcopalian.

Addresses

Office—P.O. Box 217, Lebanon, TN 37088. *E-mail*—nancy@nancyrue.com.

Career

Writer and educator. High-school language and fine-arts teacher in Norfolk, VA, 1973-78, and Carson City, NV, 1978-80; Dayton High School, Dayton, NV, teacher of language and fine arts and chairman of department, 1982-84; freelance writer and speaker, beginning 1984. Founder, Nevada Children's Theatre. Motivational speaker; presenter at schools, libraries, and churches.

Awards, Honors

Women of Faith Novel of the Year award, 2009, for *Healing Waters;* Christian Book Award finalist, Evangelical Christian Publishing Association, 2010; Christy awards, for both *The Reluctant Prophet* and *Motorcycles, Sushi, and One Strange Book..*

Writings

YOUNG-ADULT NOVELS

Row This Boat Ashore, Crossway Books (Westchester, IL), 1986.
The Janis Project, Crossway Books (Westchester, IL), 1988.
Stop in the Name of Love, Rosen Publishing (New York, NY), 1988.
Home by Another Way, Crossway Books (Wheaton, IL), 1991.

"B" Is for Bad at Getting into Harvard ("Raise the Flag" series), Waterbrook Press (Colorado Springs, CO), 1998.
Do I Have to Paint You a Picture? ("Raise the Flag" series), Waterbrook Press (Colorado Springs, CO), 1998.
Don't Count on Homecoming Queen ("Raise the Flag" series), Waterbrook Press (Colorado Springs, CO), 1998.
I Only Binge on Holy Hungers ("Raise the Flag" series), Waterbrook Press (Colorado Springs, CO), 1998.
Friends Don't Let Friends Date Jason ("Raise the Flag" series), Waterbrook Press (Colorado Springs, CO), 1999.
When Is Perfect, Perfect Enough? ("Raise the Flag" series), Waterbrook Press (Colorado Springs, CO), 1999.
New Girl in Town ("Nama Beach High" series), Zondervan/Youth Specialties (El Cajon, CA), 2003.
False Friends and True Strangers ("Nama Beach High" series), Zondervan/Youth Specialties (El Cajon, CA), 2004.
Fault Lines ("Nama Beach High" series), Zondervan/Youth Specialties (El Cajon, CA), 2004.
Totally Unfair ("Nama Beach High" series), Zondervan/Youth Specialties (El Cajon, CA), 2005.

"CHRISTIAN HERITAGE" HISTORICAL NOVEL SERIES

The Accused, Focus on the Family Publishing (Colorado Springs, CO), 1995.
The Guardian, Focus on the Family Publishing (Colorado Springs, CO), 1995.
The Stowaway, Focus on the Family Publishing (Colorado Springs, CO), 1995.
The Secret, Focus on the Family Publishing (Colorado Springs, CO), 1996.
The Thief, Focus on the Family Publishing (Colorado Springs, CO), 1996.
The Ally, Focus on the Family Publishing (Colorado Springs, CO), 1997.
The Battle, Focus on the Family Publishing (Colorado Springs, CO), 1997.
The Burden, Focus on the Family Publishing (Colorado Springs, CO), 1997.
The Prisoner, Focus on the Family Publications (Colorado Springs, CO), 1997.
The Invasion, Focus on the Family Publications (Colorado Springs, CO), 1997.
The Misfit, Focus on the Family Publications (Colorado Springs, CO), 1997.
The Rescue, Bethany House Publishers (Minneapolis, MN), 1998.
The Threat, Bethany House Publishers (Minneapolis, MN), 1998.
The Trap, Bethany House Publishers (Minneapolis, MN), 1998.
The Escape, Bethany House Publishers (Minneapolis, MN), 1998.
The Hostage, Bethany House Publishers (Minneapolis, MN), 1998.
The Chase, Bethany House Publishers (Minneapolis, MN), 1999.
The Capture, Bethany House Publishers (Minneapolis, MN), 1999.

The Stunt, Bethany House Publishers (Minneapolis, MN), 1999.

The Trick, Bethany House Publishers (Minneapolis, MN), 1999.

The Caper, Bethany House Publishers (Minneapolis, MN), 2000.

The Pursuit, Bethany House Publishers (Minneapolis, MN), 2000.

The Discovery, Focus on the Family Publishing (Colorado Springs, CO), 2001.

The Mission, Focus on the Family Publishing (Colorado Springs, CO), 2001.

The Mirage, Focus on the Family Publishing (Minneapolis, MN), 2001.

The Stand, Focus on the Family Publishing (Minneapolis, MN), 2001.

The Choice, Focus on the Family Publishing (Minneapolis, MN), 2002.

The Struggle, Bethany House Publishers (Minneapolis, MN), 2002.

"LILY" NOVEL SERIES

Here's Lily!, Zonderkidz (Grand Rapids, MI), 2000.

Lily Robbins, M.D. (Medical Dabbler), Zonderkidz (Grand Rapids, MI), 2000.

Lily the Rebel, Zonderkidz (Grand Rapids, MI), 2001.

Lily and the Creep, Zonderkidz (Grand Rapids, MI), 2001.

Lily's Ultimate Party, Zonderkidz (Grand Rapids, MI), 2001.

Lights, Action, Lily!, Zonderkidz (Grand Rapids, MI), 2002.

Lily Rules, Zonderkidz (Grand Rapids, MI), 2002.

Lily Speaks!, Zonderkidz (Grand Rapids, MI), 2002.

Rough and Rugged Lily, Zonderkidz (Grand Rapids, MI), 2002.

Horse Crazy Lily, Zonderkidz (Grand Rapids, MI), 2003.

Lily's Church Camp Adventure, Zonderkidz (Grand Rapids, MI), 2003.

Lily's in London?!, Zonderkidz (Grand Rapids, MI), 2003.

Lily's Passport to Paris, Zonderkidz (Grand Rapids, MI), 2003.

"SOPHIE'S WORLD" MIDDLE-GRADE NOVEL SERIES

Sophie's World, Zonderkidz (Grand Rapids, MI), 2004.

Sophie's Secret, Zonderkidz (Grand Rapids, MI), 2004.

Sophie and the Scoundrels, Zonderkidz (Grand Rapids, MI), 2005, published as *Sophie under Pressure*, 2009.

Sophie Breaks the Code, Zonderkidz (Grand Rapids, MI), 2005, published as *Sophie's Friendship Fiasco*, 2009.

Sophie Tracks a Thief, Zonderkidz (Grand Rapids, MI), 2005, published as *Sophie and the New Girl*, 2009.

Sophie's First Dance?, Zonderkidz (Grand Rapids, MI), 2005.

Sophie's Irish Showdown, Zonderkidz (Grand Rapids, MI), 2005, published as *Sophie Steps Up*, 2009.

Sophie's Stormy Summer, Zonderkidz (Grand Rapids, MI), 2005.

Sophie Flakes Out, Zonderkidz (Grand Rapids, MI), 2006.

Sophie Loses the Lead, Zonderkidz (Grand Rapids, MI), 2006, published as *Sophie's Drama*, 2009.

Sophie Loves Jimmy, Zonderkidz (Grand Rapids, MI), 2006.

Sophie's Encore, Zonderkidz (Grand Rapids, MI), 2006, published as *Sophie Gets Real*, 2009.

"LUCY" MIDDLE-GRADE NOVEL SERIES

Lucy Doesn't Wear Pink, Zonderkidz (Grand Rapids, MI), 2008.

Lucy out of Bounds, Zonderkidz (Grand Rapids, MI), 2008.

Lucy Finds Her Way, Zonderkidz (Grand Rapids, MI), 2009.

Lucy's "Perfect" Summer, Zonderkidz (Grand Rapids, MI), 2009.

"REAL LIFE" YOUNG-ADULT NOVEL SERIES

Boyfriends, Burritos, and an Ocean of Trouble, Zondervan (Grand Rapids, MI), 2010.

Motorcycles, Sushi, and One Strange Book, Zonderkidz (Grand Rapids, MI), 2010.

Tournaments, Cocoa, and One Wrong Move, Zondervan (Grand Rapids, MI), 2010.

Limos. Lattes, and My Life on the Fringe, Zondervan (Grand Rapids, MI), 2011.

ADULT NOVELS

Pascal's Wager, Multnomah Publishers (Sisters, OR), 2001.

Antonia's Choice, Multnomah Publishers (Sisters, OR), 2003.

Tristan's Gap, Waterbrook Press (Colorado Springs, CO), 2006.

(With Stephen Arterburn) *Healing Stones* ("Sullivan Crisp" series), Thomas Nelson Publishers (Nashville, TN), 2007.

(With Stephen Arterburn) *Healing Waters* ("Sullivan Crisp" series), Thomas Nelson Publishers (Nashville, TN), 2008.

(With Stephen Arterburn) *Healing Sands* ("Sullivan Crisp" series), Thomas Nelson (Nashville, TN), 2009.

The Reluctant Prophet, David C. Cook, 2010.

Unexpected Dismounts (sequel to *The Reluctant Prophet*), David C. Cook, 2011.

TEEN NONFICTION

Coping with Dating Violence, Rosen Publishing (New York, NY), 1989.

Coping with an Illiterate Parent, Rosen Publishing (New York, NY), 1990.

Everything You Need to Know about Getting Your Period, Rosen Publishing (New York, NY), 1995.

Everything You Need to Know about Abusive Relationships, Rosen Publishing (New York, NY), 1996, revised edition, 1998.

Choosing a Career in Hotels, Motels, and Resorts, Rosen Publishing (New York, NY), 1997.

Everything You Need to Know about Peer Mediation, Rosen Publishing (New York, NY), 1997, revised edition, 2001.

The Whole Guy Thing, Zondervan (Grand Rapids, MI), 2012.

"YOUNG WOMEN OF FAITH LIBRARY" TEEN NONFICTION SERIES

The Beauty Book, illustrated by Steven Mach, Zonderkidz (Grand Rapids, MI), 2000.

The Body Book, illustrated by Steven Mach, Zonderkidz (Grand Rapids, MI), 2000.

The Best Bash Book, illustrated by Lyn Boyer, Zonderkidz (Grand Rapids, MI), 2001.

The Blurry Rules Book, illustrated by Lyn Boyer, Zonderkidz (Grand Rapids, MI), 2001.

The Buddy Book, illustrated by Lyn Boyer, Zonderkidz (Grand Rapids, MI), 2001.

The It's My Life Book, illustrated by Lyn Boyer, Zonderkidz (Grand Rapids, MI), 2001.

The Creativity Book, illustrated by Lyn Boyer, Zonderkidz (Grand Rapids, MI), 2002.

Year 'Round Holiday Book, illustrated by Lyn Boyer, Zonderkidz (Grand Rapids, MI), 2002.

The Uniquely Me Book, illustrated by Lyn Boyer, Zonderkidz (Grand Rapids, MI), 2002.

The Values and Virtue Book, illustrated by Lyn Boyer, Zonderkidz (Grand Rapids, MI), 2002.

The Fun-Finder Book, illustrated by Lyn Boyer, Zonderkidz (Grand Rapids, MI), 2003.

The Walk-the-Walk Book, illustrated by Lyn Boyer, Zonderkidz (Grand Rapids, MI), 2003.

"FAITHGIRLZ" NONFICTION SERIES

The Faithgirlz! Bible, Zonderkidz (Grand Rapids, MI), 2006.

(With daughter Marijean Rue) *Beauty Lab,* Zonderkidz (Grand Rapids, MI), 2007.

The Skin You're in: Discovering True Beauty, Zonderkidz (Grand Rapids, MI), 2007.

Girl Politics: Friends, Cliques, and Really Mean Chicks, Zonderkidz (Grand Rapids, MI), 2007.

Body Talk, Zonderkidz (Grand Rapids, MI), 2007.

Everybody Tells Me to Be Myself, but I Don't Know Who I Am!, Zonderkidz (Grand Rapids, MI), 2007.

Dear Nancy: Answers to Letters from Girls like You, compiled by Marijean S. Rue, Zonderkidz (Grand Rapids, MI), 2008.

Moms' Ultimate Guide to the Tween Girl World, Zondervan (Grand Rapids, MI), 2010.

That Is SO Me: 365 Days of Devotions, Zonderkidz (Grand Rapids, MI), 2010.

(With Jim Rue) *What Happened to My Little Girl?: The Dad's Ultimate Guide to His Tween Daughter,* Zondervan (Grand Rapids, MI), 2010.

OTHER

(With David Wayne) *Home: Love It and Leave It,* Baker Books (Grand Rapids, MI), 1983.

The Christmas Closet (one-act play; produced in Carson City, NV, 1986), United Methodist Publishing House, 1984.

Cradled in God's Loving Arms, Here's Life (San Bernadino, CA), 1987.

Handling the Heartbreak of Miscarriage, Here's Life (San Bernadino, CA), 1987.

Give It Up (one-act play; produced in Carson City, NV, 1987), United Methodist Publishing House, 1985.

The Christian Heritage Teaching Guide, five volumes, Bethany House (Minneapolis, MN), 1998–2002.

(Editor) *Guys and Other Things That Fry Your Brains: Eighteen Awesome Short Reads,* Vine Books (Ann Arbor, MI), 1999.

(Editor) *Bringing up Good Parents and Other Jobs for Teenage Girls: A Collection of Short Stories,* Vine Books/Servant Publications (Ann Arbor, MI), 2001.

Contributor to magazines, including *Breakaway, Brio, Campus Life, Christian Adventurer, Christian Writer, Clubhouse, Focus on the Family, Straight, Teacher in Focus, Teen Quest,* and *Youth Teacher.*

Sidelights

A prolific author whose novels and self-help books for young teens are inspired by her optimistic personality and strong Christian faith, Nancy Rue can count over a hundred books among her works. Reviewing Rue's "Faithgirlz" books, which span nonfiction and fiction, "*Library Journal* contributor Graham Christian asserted that the author "writes in an accessible, from-the-hip style" that is designed to appeal to "the important but elusive 'tween' female market."

Born in New Jersey, Rue moved to Florida and earned an English degree from John B. Stetson University with the goal of becoming a high-school English teacher. Four years later, in 1978, she completed a master's degree in education at the College of William and Mary; she would pursue yet another degree—one in theatre—several years later. In the meantime, Rue taught English in her adopted state of Nevada, and expanded her teaching to include theatre.

All this while, Rue had been writing, a hobby she has enjoyed since childhood. By now her teaching experience had coupled with her faith walk and transformed this hobby into a calling with the goal of writing full time. At first Rue got up extra early to steal some writing time before leaving for the classroom, producing articles and occasional works of nonfiction. In 1980, she finally took time off from her teaching assignment and devoted forty hours per week to writing. Her perseverance paid off when her first published teen novel, *Row This Boat Ashore,* was released by a Christian publishing house in 1986. Other novels soon followed, and by 1995 Rue was a full-time writer.

Cover of Nancy Rue's young-adult novel Motorcycles, Sushi, and One Strange Book, *part of her "Real Life" series.* (Copyright © 2010 by Nancy Rue. Reproduced with permission of Zondervan.)

Most of Rue's books are included in series that follow the lives of a central character. Her first series for middle-graders, the "Christian Heritage" novels, spans the years 1690 to 1945 and focuses on middle graders whose lives intersect with pivotal epochs in U.S. history. Reviewing *The Rescue*, which is set in the late 1600s and focuses on Salem resident Josiah Hutchinson and his sister Hope, the author tells a "well-paced" story about characters who "live according to their religious convictions in spite of the intolerance of others," according to *Booklist* contributor Lois Schultz.

Moving into contemporary times, Rue's "Lucy" series introduces eleven-year-old Lucy Rooney, an independent preteen who has been raised by a blind and widowed father and who is now in need of strong female role models. The first novel in Rue's "Lily" series, *Here's Lily*, follows the antics of another likeable girl, sixth-grader Lily, as she embarks on the first of many "Things" that she thinks might define her—in this case a modeling career. The "Sophie" books capture the imaginative perspective of Christian preteen Sophie La-Croix as she fights to stay true to herself following a

family move that brings the challenge of gaining acceptance from students at a new school. Predicting that series opener *Sophie's World* would be welcomed by tween fans of faith-based fiction, Stephanie Zvirin added in *Booklist* that the author "smoothly works the idea of prayer in daily life" into a story that has "the ring of truth."

Slightly older teens are Rue's chosen audience for her "Real Life" novels, which include *Motorcycles, Sushi, and One Strange Book*, *Boyfriends, Burritos, and an Ocean of Trouble*, and *Tournaments, Cocoa, and One Wrong Move*. In the series opener, fifteen-year-old Jessie has a double shock: not only is her father alive, but she is going to be his new roommate now that her mom has been hospitalized due to an emotional disorder. Stepping into a new family in another state, the teen is aided by her father's faith-based approach to life as introduced in a modern version of the New Testament. Another fifteen year old, Bryn, is attempting to detach from an abusive relationship with the help of both her with-it surfer grandmother and a fellow teen who shares her deepening Christian perspective. With its contemporary approach, *Motorcycles, Sushi, and One Strange Book* "make[s] a strong statement for reading and understanding the Bible and its teachings," observed *School Library Journal* contributor Karen Alexander, while a *Kirkus Reviews* writer commended the novel for its "hugely sympathetic protagonist-narrator, . . . genuine supporting characters and a well-realized setting." In *Booklist*, Hazel Rochman concluded that while "Rue folds . . . quite a lot" into the plot of *Boyfriends, Burritos, and an Ocean of Trouble*, the plot twists "will grab readers, and the dialogue is right on target."

"My major target audience is young people, aged thirteen to nineteen," Rue once commented. "These folks are on that marvelous edge between the world of the child and the realm of the adult. They have the uncanny ability to dip back into childhood and be spontaneous, creative, and alive, yet at the same time they can reach in like adults and reason, and reach out like adults to communicate. I enjoy catching them on that edge and appealing to both facets."

Biographical and Critical Sources

PERIODICALS

Booklist, September 1, 1995, Lois Schultz, review of *The Rescue*, p. 58; September 1, 1995, Lois Schultz, review of *The Stowaway*, p. 58; November 1, 1995, Stephanie Zvirin, review of *Everything You Need to Know about Getting Your Period*, p. 462; October 1, 2004, Stephanie Zvirin, review of *Sophie's World*, p. 345; June 1, 2010, Frances Bradburn, review of *Motorcycles, Sushi, and One Strange Book*, p. 56; September 15, 2010, Hazel Rochman, review of *Boyfriends, Burritos, and an Ocean of Trouble*, p. 72.
Kirkus Reviews, May 1, 2010, review of *Motorcycles, Sushi, and One Strange Book*.

Library Journal, October 1, 2007, Graham Christian, review of "Faithgirlz" series, p. 52.

Publishers Weekly, August 28, 2000, reviews of *Here's Lily* and *The Beauty Book: It's a God Thing!,* both p. 79; October 13, 2008, review of *Healing Waters,* p. 38.

School Library Journal, February, 2005, Heather Ulesoo, review of *Sophie's World,* p. 140; August, 2010, Karen Alexander, review of *Motorcycles, Sushi, and One Strange Book,* p. 110.

ONLINE

Nancy Rue Home Page, http://www.nancyrue.com (September 15, 2011).

*   *   *

RUE, Nancy N.
 See RUE, Nancy

S

SALTZBERG, Barney 1955-

Personal
Born April 30, 1955, in Los Angeles, CA; son of Irving and Ruth Saltzberg; married 1985; wife's name Susan; children: two children. *Education:* Sonoma State College, degree, 1977.

Addresses
Home—Los Angeles, CA. *E-mail*—info@barney saltzberg.com.

Career
Artist, illustrator, author, and singer-songwriter. Performer at concerts for children; songwriter and producer of recordings adapted from Public Broadcasting System (PBS) children's television series *Arthur.* Teacher of annual class in writing and illustrating at University of California—Los Angeles. Founder, Crazy Hair Day Literacy Campaign (reading initiative).

Member
Society of Children's Book Writers and Illustrators.

Awards, Honors
Oppenheim Toy Portfolio award, 1998, for *The Flying Garbanzos;* California Young Reader Medal finalist, 1999, for *Mrs. Morgan's Lawns;* Parents' Choice Award, 2000, and California Young Reader Medal nomination, 2003, both for *The Soccer Mom from Outer Space.*

Writings

SELF-ILLUSTRATED

Utter Nonsense, McGraw-Hill (New York, NY), 1980.

Barney Saltzberg (Photograph by Linda Vanoff. Reproduced by permission of Barney Saltzberg.)

It Must Have Been the Wind, Harper & Row (New York, NY), 1982.

What to Say to Clara, Atheneum (New York, NY), 1984.

The Yawn, Atheneum (New York, NY), 1985.

Cromwell, Atheneum (New York, NY), 1986.

Hi Bird, Bye Bird, Barron's (New York, NY), 1990.

What Would You Do with a Bone?, Barron's (New York, NY), 1990.

Mrs. Morgan's Lawn, Hyperion (New York, NY), 1993.

This Is a Great Place for a Hot Dog Stand, Hyperion (New York, NY), 1994.

Where, Oh, Where's My Underwear?, Hyperion (New York, NY), 1994.

Show and Tell, Hyperion (New York, NY), 1994.

Phoebe and the Spelling Bee, Hyperion (New York, NY), 1996.

Backyard Cowboy, paper engineering by Renée Jablow, Hyperion (New York, NY), 1996.

The Flying Garbanzos, Crown (New York, NY), 1998.

Animal Kisses, Harcourt (San Diego, CA), 2000.

The Soccer Mom from Outer Space, Crown (New York, NY), 2000.

Baby Animal Kisses, Harcourt (New York, NY), 2000.

The Problem with Pumpkins: A Hip and Hop Story, Harcourt (San Diego, CA), 2001.

Hip, Hip, Hooray Day!: A Hip and Hop Story, Harcourt (San Diego, CA), 2002.

Peekaboo Kisses, Harcourt (San Diego, CA), 2002.

Crazy Hair Day, Candlewick Press (Cambridge, MA), 2003.

Noisy Kisses: A Touch and Feel Book, Harcourt (San Diego, CA), 2004.

I Love Cats, Candlewick Press (Cambridge, MA), 2005.

I Love Dogs, Candlewick Press (Cambridge, MA), 2005.

Cornelius P. Mud, Are You Ready for Bed?, Candlewick Press (Cambridge, MA), 2005.

Star of the Week, Candlewick Press (Cambridge, MA), 2006.

Goodnight Kisses, Harcourt (New York, NY), 2006.

Hi, Bunny. Bye, Bunny, Harcourt (New York, NY), 2007.

Hi, Blueberry!, Harcourt (San Diego, CA), 2007.

Cornelius P. Mud, Are You Ready for School?, Candlewick Press (Cambridge, MA), 2007.

Stanley and the Class Pet, Candlewick Press (Cambridge, MA), 2008.

Peekaboo, Blueberry!, Harcourt (Orlando, FL), 2008.

Cornelius P. Mud, Are You Ready for Baby?, Candlewick Press (Somerville, MA), 2009.

Good Egg, Workman Publishing (New York, NY), 2009.

All around the Seasons, Candlewick Press (Somerville, MA), 2010.

Beautiful Oops!, Workman Pub. (New York, NY), 2010.

Kisses: A Pull, Touch, Lift, Squeak, and Smooch Book!, Houghton Mifflin Harcourt (Boston, MA), 2010.

Would You Rather Be a Princess or a Dragon?, Tricycle Press (Berkeley, CA), 2011.

FOR CHILDREN

(With Laura Numeroff) *Two for Stew,* illustrated by Salvatore Murdocca, Simon & Schuster (New York, NY), 1996.

ILLUSTRATOR

Lisa Rojany, *Jake and Jenny on the Farm* (interactive book), Price Stern Sloan (Los Angeles, CA), 1990.

Wendy Boyd-Smith, *There's No Barking at the Table Cookbook,* Lip Smackers, Inc., 1991.

Lisa Rojany, *Jake and Jenny on the Town* (interactive book), Price Stern Sloan (Los Angeles, CA), 1993.

Lisa A. Marsoli and Stacie Strong, *Bow, Wow, and You on the Farm,* Child's Play of England, 1996.

Judy Sierra, *There's a Zoo in Room 22,* Harcourt (San Diego, CA), 2000.

Amy Ehrlich, *Kazam's Magic,* Candlewick Press (Cambridge, MA), 2001.

Amy Ehrlich, *Bravo, Kazam!,* Candlewick Press (Cambridge, MA), 2002.

Stuart J. Murphy, *Slugger's Carwash,* HarperCollins (New York, NY), 2002.

How Many Elephants? (lift-the-flap book), Candlewick Press (Cambridge, MA), 2004.

Adaptations

Many of Saltzberg's books have been adapted as audiobooks, including *Crazy Hair Day,* produced by Inkless Music as a benefit for Concern Foundation for Cancer Research, 2007.

Sidelights

Barney Saltzberg is an author and illustrator of children's books whose work includes *The Flying Garbanzos, The Soccer Mom from Outer Space, Crazy Hair Day,* and several books featuring an unlikely porcine hero named Cornelius P. Mud. In addition to writing, Saltzberg also composes songs, often performing concerts for children in schools, libraries, and hospitals across the United States. Discussing the beginning of his writing career on his home page, the versatile author/artist explained that although he dreamt of being a musician early on in his life, a career in children's books did not become a possibility until he took a printmaking class while studying art at Sonoma State College in California. The assignment Saltzberg completed for this class resulted in one of his first children's books, *It Must Have Been the Wind.*

Like *It Must Have Been the Wind,* most of Saltzberg's books for children feature original stories and art. In *What to Say to Clara,* for example, he pairs his text with black-and-white cartoons that bring to life the simple story of a shy boy named Otis and his attempt to gather enough courage to speak to a classmate. "Droll" and "firmly etched" drawings accompany the text of this "larky" story, noted a reviewer in *Publishers Weekly.* Saltzberg features another simple narrative in *The Yawn,* a wordless book in which a young boy begins his day with a huge yawn, passing it on to a dog that passes it on again, fueling a chain reaction that even affects the Man in the Moon. In a review for *School Library Journal,* Deb Andrews praised the simple illustrations in *The Yawn,* predicting that Saltzberg's work will "spark discussion among young children."

Several of Saltzberg's stories weave basic concepts into an engaging, toddler-friendly text. In *All around the Seasons* readers first experience the sights of early

spring, as snowpiles melt away and tiny birds and animals emerge to start a new year—and sometimes a new life. Summer, fall, and winter follow in succession, each month captured in artwork that *School Library Journal* critic Kara Schaff Dean cited for possessing a "childlike simplicity that should appeal to young children. Saltzberg's "simple verse" also makes *All around the Seasons* an enjoyable challenge for budding readers, Dean added, and a *Kirkus Reviews* writer asserted that this "rhyming salute to the four seasons" features a text "made for reading aloud."

A classic picture-book villain, the crabby and unpleasant neighbor, is the star of *Mrs. Morgan's Lawn*. In Saltzberg's story, a boy dreads asking Mrs. Morgan to return his ball after it lands in her yard, he imagines various other alternative methods he can use to retrieve the toy. "The boy's forthright narration rings true," reflected by the author's humorous and "naïve . . . illustrations," observed Elizabeth Bush in her *Booklist* review of *Mrs. Morgan's Lawn*. Saltzberg also focuses on everyday activities and realistic actions in books such as *Where, Oh Where Is My Underwear?*, *Show and Tell*, and *Backyard Cowboy*.

The author/illustrator shares a more-involved story in *This Is a Great Place for a Hot Dog Stand*, a tale highlighting "individual enterprise and ingenuity" according to Jane Marino in *School Library Journal*. The book tells of hopes and dreams as Izzy, a factory worker, quits his job to begin a business selling hot dogs. In *Phoebe and the Spelling Bee*, Saltzberg returns to a familiar theme: dealing with fear and unpleasant tasks. Writing in *Booklist*, Stephanie Zvirin remarked that although the spelling list Phoebe is confronted with in *Phoebe and the Spelling Bee* might seem a bit complicated to the book's intended audience, readers "will readily recognize themselves in Phoebe's . . . attempts to avoid . . . something new and scary." A reviewer for *Publishers Weekly* praised Saltzberg's story for providing children with a new tactic to learning words.

A family of circus acrobats takes center-stage in *The Flying Garbanzos*, in which the five-member Garbanzo family—including a two-year-old baby named Beanie—fly and perform acrobatic tricks even when they are not on stage. Saltzberg's whimsical picture book is "sure to be a hit," predicted *School Library Journal* critic Virginia Golodetz, while in *Publishers Weekly* a reviewer remarked that the story's "fast action and shouted dialogue ensure that the pages turn in a hurry."

Outrageous behavior of another sort is the focus of *The Soccer Mom from Outer Space*, Saltzberg's exaggerated look at an overly enthusiastic mother. Lena's mom's excitement in the days leading up to her daughter's first soccer game prompts Dad to recount the story of his own mother and her antics during his own childhood sports career. Reviewing the picture book for *School Library Journal*, Blair Christolon noted that while chil-

dren will certainly relate to the story, *The Soccer Mom from Outer Space* is also a "particularly good choice for coaches to use for a meeting with new soccer parents."

A less-involved set of parents provides the humor in Saltzberg's picture books featuring a rambunctious young pig. In *Cornelius P. Mud, Are You Ready for Bed?* the young pig is queried regarding his daily nighttime ritual: putting away toys, using the bathroom, etcetera. Although Saltzberg's story shows the piglet answering in the affirmative, his illustrations tell a quite different story. In *Horn Book* Kitty Flynn noted that the "simple text" in the book features a "twist on a familiar storyline and the bold dynamic pictures are . . . attention grabbers." A similar story plays out in *Cornelius P. Mud, Are You Ready for School?* as Cornelius answers his mother's questions while getting ready to leave for school. Another perennial toddler experience, making introductions to a new baby-big brother, sparks little enthusiasm from the toddler stand-in in *Cornelius P. Mud, Are You Ready for Baby?* "The cheerful colors and Cornelius's lively antics make his world the happy-go-lucky kind of place that children enjoy visiting," wrote *Booklist* critic Randall Enos in reviewing *Cornelius P. Mud, Are You Ready for School?*, and Kay Weisman asserted in the same periodical that because "Saltzberg keeps the discussion concrete, never muddying the waters with more complex issues," *Cornelius P. Mud, Are You Ready for Baby?* would be a "perfect" choice for toddler storytimes.

Saltzberg introduces a humorous porcine hero in his book series that includes **Cornelius P. Mud, Are You Ready for School?** (Copyright © 2007 by Barney Saltzberg. Reproduced with permission of Candlewick Press, Somerville, MA.)

A young boy's creative zeal backfires in Saltzberg's humorous self-illustrated picture book Crazy Hair Day. (Copyright © 2003 by Barney Saltzberg. Reproduced by permission of Candlewick Press, Inc., Somerville, MA.)

Inspired by a young cancer patient's worries about returning to school following chemotherapy, *Crazy Hair Day* introduces a young hamster named Stanley Birdbaum as he prepares for school. This is no ordinary day, however; as Stanley tells his mom, it is Crazy Hair Day, and the two have fun fluffing, spiking, and coloring the hamster's fur. When Stanley arrives at school, however, he is mortified to learn that it is actually school picture day. After hiding in the bathroom for a while, the hamster emerges and finds that all his classmates have followed his lead, transforming the day into Crazy Hair Picture Day. "Saltzberg conveys the pleasing goofiness of special days at school," noted a *Kirkus Reviews* contributor in a review of *Crazy Hair Day*, while in *Booklist* Jennifer Mattson concluded that "the authenticity of Stanley's situation is likely to put readers in the mood to share their most embarrassing moments." In *School Library Journal*, Jody McCoy dubbed *Crazy Hair Day* a "delightful tale of confusion and compassion."

Stanley returns in *Star of the Week* as the young hamster is selected to share his favorite things with the class. When Stanley's favorite foods and favorite toy do not elicit enthusiasm, he feels a tad rejected. However, on the third day his chalkboard art wins raves. Another adventure captures toddler attention in *Stanley and the Class Pet*, as Stanley is selected to care for the class bird for the weekend. Problems arise when he takes a friend's advice and opens the bird's cage. In his ink-and-acrylic art, Saltzberg "creates Stanley's world with warmth and keen attention to detail," wrote *Booklist*

critic Carolyn Phelan in a review of *Star of the Week*, and *School Library Journal* critic Kathy Piehl remarked that the same book "perfectly captures the stage fright that almost everyone has experienced." Noting that the acrylic illustrations of *Stanley and the Class Pet* "perfectly capture" a boy's "delight at finally acting as caregiver," a *Kirkus Reviews* contributor recommended Saltzberg's story as "an excellent choice for discussions about both peer pressure and friendship."

Biographical and Critical Sources

BOOKS

Ward, Martha E., and others, *Authors of Books for Young People,* Scarecrow Press (Metuchen, NJ), 1990.

PERIODICALS

Booklist, December 1, 1993, Elizabeth Bush, review of *Mrs. Morgan's Lawn,* p. 701; October 1, 1997, Stephanie Zvirin, review of *Phoebe and the Spelling Bee,* p. 339; September 15, 2001, Ilene Cooper, review of *The Problem with Pumpkins: A Hip and Hop Story,* p. 236; November 1, 2003, Jennifer Mattson, review of *Crazy Hair Day,* p. 506; May 1, 2005, Ilene Cooper, review of *Cornelius P. Mud, Are You Ready for Bed?,* p. 1593; February 1, 2006, Carolyn Phelan, review of *Star of the Week,* p. 57; June 1, 2007, Randall Enos, review of *Cornelius P. Mud, Are You Ready for School?,* p. 80; March 1, 2009, Kay Weisman, review of *Cornelius P. Mud, Are You Ready for Baby?,* p. 50.

Bulletin of the Center for Children's Books, December, 2003, Karen Coats, review of *Crazy Hair Day,* p. 164; September, 2005, Timnah Card, review of *Cornelius P. Mud, Are You Ready for Bed?,* p. 41.

Horn Book, May-June, 2005, Kitty Flynn, review of *Cornelius P. Mud, Are You Ready for Bed?,* p. 314.

Kirkus Reviews, February 15, 2002, review of *Hip, Hip, Hooray Day!,* p. 264; July 15, 2003, review of *Crazy Hair Day,* p. 967; April 1, 2005, review of *Cornelius P. Mud, Are You Ready for Bed?,* p. 424; January 15, 2006, review of *Star of the Week,* p. 89; June 15, 2007, review of *Cornelius P. Mud, Are You Ready for School?;* May 15, 2008, review of *Stanley and the Class Pet.*

Publishers Weekly, December 21, 1984, review of *What to Say to Clara,* p. 88; November 8, 1993, review of *Mrs. Morgan's Lawn,* p. 75; October 13, 1997, review of *Phoebe and the Spelling Bee,* p. 74; September 7, 1998, review of *The Flying Garbanzos,* p. 93; September 24, 2001, review of *The Problem with Pumpkins,* p. 43; July 1, 2002, review of *Peekaboo Kisses,* p. 81; August 18, 2003, review of *Crazy Hair Day,* p. 78.

School Library Journal, August, 1982, review of *It Must Have Been the Wind,* p. 105; December, 1984, review of *What to Say to Clara,* p. 76; December, 1985, Deb

Andrews, review of *The Yawn,* p. 82; April, 1986, Ronald Van de Voorde, review of *Cromwell,* p. 79; May, 1995, Jane Marino, review of *This Is a Great Place for a Hot Dog Stand,* p. 94; September, 1998, Virginia Golodetz, review of *The Flying Garbanzos,* p. 181; August, 2000, Blair Christolon, review of *The Soccer Mom from Outer Space,* p. 164; April, 2002, Roxanne Burg, review of *Hip, Hip, Hooray Day!,* p. 122; December, 2003, Jody McCoy, review of *Crazy Hair Day,* p. 125; March, 2005, Kelley Rae Unger, review of *Cornelius P. Mud, Are You Ready for Bed?,* p. 186; August, 2004, Andrea Tarr, reviews of *I Love Cats* and *I Love Dogs,* both p. 105; February, 2006, Kathy Piehl, review of *Star of the Week,* p. 109; October, 2007, Martha Simpson, review of *Cornelius P. Mud, Are You Ready for School?,* p. 127; July, 2008, Grace Oliff, review of *Stanley and the Class Pet,* p. 80; February, 2009, Kathleen Kelly MacMillian, review of *Cornelius P. Mud, Are You Ready for Baby?,* p. 85; February, 2010, Kara Schaff Dean, review of *All around the Seasons,* p. 94; June, 2010, Linda Ludke, review of *Kisses: A Pull, Touch, Lift, Squeak, and Smooch Book!,* p. 83.

Tribune Books (Chicago, IL), September 7, 2003, review of *Crazy Hair Day,* p. 51; February 26, 2006, Mary Harris Russell, review of *Star of the Week,* p. 7.

ONLINE

Barney Saltzberg Home Page, http://www.barneysaltzberg. com (September 15, 2011).

Barney Saltzberg Web Log, http://barneysaltzberg.blogspot. com (September 15, 2011).*

*   *   *

SAWYER, Kim Vogel

Personal

Married; husband's name Don; children: three daughters. *Religion:* Christian. *Hobbies and other interests:* Drama, quilting, calligraphy.

Addresses

Home—Hutchinson, KS.

Career

Writer, novelist, evangelist, and educator. Elementary-school teacher, 2005. Motivational speaker.

Member

American Christian Fiction Writers.

Awards, Honors

Historical Book of the Year selection, American Christian Fiction Writers (ACFW), 2008, for *Where Willows Grow,* ACFW award, Gayle Wilson Award of Excellence, and Romance Writers Award of Excellence, all 2009, all for *My Heart Remembers.*

Writings

A Seeking Heart, ACW Press, 2002.

Dear John, Heartsong Presents (Uhrichsville, OH), 2006.

That Wilder Boy, Heartsong Presents (Uhrichsville, OH), 2006.

Waiting for Summer's Return, Bethany House (Minneapolis, MN), 2006.

Where Willows Grow, Bethany House (Minneapolis, MN), 2007.

Promising Angela, Heartsong Presents (Uhrichsville, OH), 2007.

Montana Mistletoe, Barbour Publishing (Uhrichsville, OH), 2007.

Kansas Weddings, Barbour Publishing (Uhrichsville, OH), 2007.

My Heart Remembers, Bethany House (Minneapolis, MN), 2008.

Where the Heart Leads (sequel to *Waiting for Summer's Return*), Bethany House (Minneapolis, MN), 2008.

A Promise for Spring, Bethany House (Minneapolis, MN), 2009.

Fields of Grace, Bethany House (Minneapolis, MN), 2009.

A Hopeful Heart, Bethany House (Minneapolis, MN), 2010.

In Every Heartbeat (sequel to *My Heart Remembers*), Bethany House (Minneapolis, MN), 2010.

Courting Miss Amsel, Bethany House (Minneapolis, MN), 2011.

A Whisper of Peace, Bethany House (Minneapolis, MN), 2011.

Song of My Heart, Bethany House (Minneapolis, MN), 2012.

Work included in anthologies.

"SOMMERFELD" NOVEL TRILOGY

Bygones, Barbour Publishing (Uhrichsville, OH), 2007.

Beginnings, Barbour Publishing (Uhrichsville, OH), 2007.

Blessings, Barbour Publishing (Uhrichsville, OH), 2007.

Sommerfeld Trilogy (includes *Bygones, Beginnings,* and *Blessings*), Barbour Publishing (Uhrichsville, OH), 2008.

"KATY LAMBRIGHT" NOVEL SERIES

Katy's Debate, Zondervan (Grand Rapids, MI), 2010.

Katy's New World, Zondervan (Grand Rapids, MI), 2010.

Katy's Decision, Zondervan (Grand Rapids, MI), 2011.

Katy's Homecoming, Zondervan (Grand Rapids, MI), 2011.

Adaptations

Several of author's novels have been adapted for audiobook.

Sidelights

Kim Vogel Sawyer introduces characters whose determination and perseverance are inspired by their Christian faith in novels such as *My Heart Remembers, Fields*

of Grace, *Waiting for Summer's Return, A Hopeful Heart,* and *Courting Miss Amsel,* as well as in the books comprising her "Sommerfeld" and "Katy Lambright" series. Sawyer's fiction transports readers to America's heartland and often take place generations in the past, as men, women, and young people confront often-conflicting concerns involving their hopes and dreams, their love for others, and their responsibility to do what is right or what is necessary. On her home page, Sawyer explained her goal as "writing gentle stories of hope" that illustrate the "hope we can all possess when we place our hearts and souls in God's very capable hands."

Sawyer worked as an elementary-school teacher until 2005, when she discovered a new calling through the success of her first novel, *A Seeking Heart.* She is no stranger to the difficulties that many of her fictional characters face: her life's ups and downs have included periods of poverty, chronic pain, and serving as the parent of a special-needs child. Supplementing writing as part of her evangelical mission, Sawyer speaks to groups around the Midwest and has contributed inspiring essays to several faith-based self-help anthologies.

When readers first meet her, Summer Steadman, the title character of one of Sawyer's early novels, *Waiting for Summer's Return,* is reeling from losing her entire family to typhoid fever during their migration west. Devastated by this loss, the woman withdraws into depression and hopes that God will soon take her as well. In her grief, Summer blames the Lord for ignoring her prayers in her time of greatest need. With no other options, she decides to remain where she is, in the Midwestern town of Gaeddert, where her children are buried. To support herself, Summer accepts a job offered by local resident Peter Ollenburger, who asks her to teach his son, Thomas, now that a serious injury has prevented the boy from attending the local school. Exposed to the close-knit Ollenburger family and their sincere devotion to their Mennonite faith, the young woman emerges from her personal pain and begins to heal. Sawyer focuses on Thomas Ollenburger's story in *Where the Heart Leads,* as the young man attempts to reconcile his faith with his life in the wider world. In reviewing *Waiting for Summer's Return* in *Armchair Interviews* online, Marty Medley recommended Sawyer's tale as "wonderful light reading for summer vacation."

Also set in the late 1800s, *My Heart Remembers* follows the lives of three young sisters after their Irish-born parents die during a fire after bringing the family to America. Taken to Missouri aboard an orphan train, the siblings are separated and oldest sister Maelle determines to one day reunite them. Almost two decades later, her hope of doing so has almost faded despite her efforts to seek out her sisters in a novel that a *Library Journal* critic recommended as a "sweet, simple story of family bonds and faith." Taking place in 1888 Kansas and joining a gawky but well-heeled young Easterner on her journey west to make some struggling

rancher a wife, *A Hopeful Heart* introduces readers to the "bride-train experiences on the American frontier," according to *Booklist* contributor Lynne Welch. The author's "plainspoken historical and inspirational coming-of-age romance" will find enthusiastic readers among teenage Western fans, Welch added, while a *Publishers Weekly* contributor predicted that *A Hopeful Heart* will be "appreciat[ed] . . . for its heart."

Rural Nebraska of 1882 is the setting for *Courting Miss Amsel,* which finds Omaha-born Edythe Amsel moving to a rural farming community to serve as a teacher. Although Edythe has the knowledge and enthusiasm to inspire her students, her provocative views on women's rights raise more than a few eyebrows among parents. Fortunately, the young woman finds faith-based support from her landlady, Luthenia, as well as discovering an ally in Joel Townsend, a local farmer who is acting as father to his two young nephews. Reviewing *Courting Miss Amsel* in *Booklist,* Welch praised Sawyer's novel as a "first-rate . . . Christian historical prairie romance."

Bygones, the first book of Sawyer's "Sommerfeld" trilogy, tells the story of Marie Koeppler Quinn, a wid-

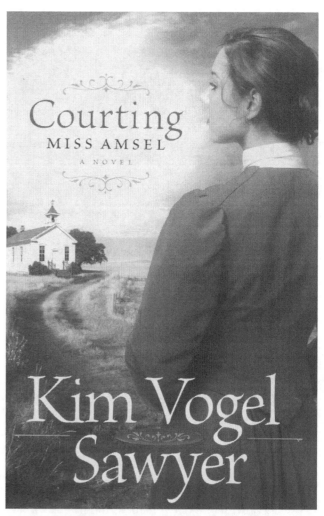

Cover of Kim Vogel Sawyer's Christian-themed historical novel Courting Miss Amsel, *featuring cover art by Steve Gardner.* (Cover photography by Steve Gardner, PixelWorks Studio, Inc. Reproduced with permission of Bethany House Publishers, a division of Baker Publishing Group.)

owed mother who has been drawn back to the Mennonite community she abandoned almost two dozen years ago when she fell in love with a young truck driver. After she left Sommerfeld, Marie's family disowned her and will not welcome her back. Now, her Aunt Lisabeth has died and willed the estranged young woman her house on the condition that Marie return and live in it for at least six months. Together with her daughter, the woman returns to Sommerfeld to fulfill the conditions of her aunt's will, only to find the primitive living conditions troubling and old memories resurfacing. In addition to being haunted by thoughts of a former love named Henry Braun, Marie must deal with the fallout when she is suspected in a rash of thefts of antiques from residents' houses. Sawyer's contemporary-themed "Sommerfeld" saga continues in *Beginnings* and *Blessings.*

In addition to her novels for adult readers, Sawyer has also written for teens in her "Katy Lambright" books. In the first installment, *Katy's New World,* a Mennonite girl has the opportunity to attend a secular high school near her close-knit Old Order community of Schellberg during her sophomore year. Things change for the teen as new friends and new ideas begin to challenge her traditional views of life. *Katy's Debate* finds the teen attempting to derail her widowed father's efforts to court a new wife while also experiencing twinges of first love herself.

Sawyer's "Katy Lambright" saga continues in *Katy's Homecoming,* as the girl's election to the court of her new school's homecoming dance may give her the chance to get to know a young man she is smitten with, while an injured friend from high school causes problems with hometown best friend Annika when the girl stays with Katy and her family in *Katy's Decision.* In *Library Journal* Nanci Milone Hill wrote that Sawyer's "Katy Lambright" novels "bring . . . a new dimension to the ever-popular Amish subgenre" of faith-based teen novels, and a *Kirkus Reviews* writer asserted that in *Katy's New World* the author "stays focused on what many teens will find they have in common with Katy." *Katy's Homecoming* serves up more of the same, noted another *Kirkus Reviews* contributor, the critic predicting that Sawyer's story should appeal to teens "intrigued by the moral dilemma between personal choice and adhering to a religious code."

Biographical and Critical Sources

PERIODICALS

Booklist, June 1, 2010, Lynne Welch, review of *A Hopeful Heart,* p. 45; August 1, 2010, Lynne Welch, review of *In Every Heartbeat,* p. 24; December 1, 2010, Lynne Welch, review of *Courting Miss Amsel,* p. 34.

Kirkus Reviews, January 15, 2010, review of *Katy's New World;* February 1, 2011, review of *Katy's Homecoming.*

Library Journal, February 1, 2008, review of *My Heart Remembers,* p. 54; February 15, 2010, Nanci Milone Hill, review of *Katy's New World,* p. 81.

Publishers Weekly, July 6, 2009, review of *Fields of Grace,* p. 35; April 12, 2010, review of *A Hopeful Heart,* p. 35.

ONLINE

Armchair Interviews Web site, http://www.armchair interviews.com/ (July 30, 2007), Jamie Driggers, review of *Bygones;* Marty Medley, review of *Waiting for Summer's Return.*

Barbour Publishing Web site, http://www.barbourbooks. com/ (July 30, 2007), "Kim Vogel Sawyer."

Kim Vogel Sawyer Home Page, http://www.kimvogelsaw yer.com (September 15, 2011).*

* * *

SAYRE, April Pulley 1966-

Personal

Born April 11, 1966, in Greenville, SC; daughter of David Clarence (a university professor) and Elizabeth Richardson (a science educator and businesswoman) Pulley; married Jeffrey Peter Sayre (an author and ecologist), 1989. *Education:* Duke University, B.A. (biology), 1987; Vermont College, M.F.A. (creative writing). *Hobbies and other interests:* Travel, birdwatching, herb gardening, SCUBA diving.

Addresses

Home and office—South Bend, IN. *E-mail*—asayre@me.com.

Career

Author; National Wildlife Federation, associate editor for school programs, 1988-91; author and video producer, beginning 1991. Presenter at schools.

Member

Society of Children's Book Writers and Illustrators, National Audubon Society, Nature Conservancy, American Birding Association.

Awards, Honors

John Burroughs Award, Best Books citation, *School Library Journal,* and Notable Books for Children citation, *Smithsonian* magazine, all 1995, all for *If You Should Hear a Honeyguide;* Best Books for the Teen Age selection, New York Public Library, 1996, for *Endangered Birds of North America;* Outstanding Science Trade Book for Children selection, National Science Teachers Association/Children's Book Council, 1999, for *Home at Last* and 2001, for *Dig, Wait, Listen;* John

April Pulley Sayre (Photograph by Jeff Sayre. Reproduced by permission.)

Burroughs Award, 2001, for *The Hungry Hummingbird;* *Riverbank Review* Children's Book of Distinction designation, 2002, for *Dig, Wait, Listen;* Bank Street College of Education Best Books designation, 2003, and Notable Book designation, American Library Association (ALA), 2004, both for *One Is a Snail;* John Burroughs Award, 2005, for *The Bumblebee Queen;* Subaru Prize for Excellence in Science Books, American Association for the Advancement of Science/*Science Books & Films,* and Notable Book designation, ALA, both 2005, both for *Stars beneath Your Bed;* Theodor Geisel Honor Book Award, ALA, and Subaru Prize for Excellence in Science Books finalist, both 2008, both for *Vulture View;* Best Book selection, Bank Street College of Education, 2010, for *Turtle, Turtle, Watch Out!*

Writings

If You Should Hear a Honeyguide, illustrated by S.D. Schindler, Houghton Mifflin (Boston, MA), 1995.

Endangered Birds of North America, Holt (New York, NY), 1996.

Hummingbirds: The Sun Catchers, NorthWord Press (Minocqua, WI), 1996.

Put on Some Antlers and Walk like a Moose: How Scientists Find, Follow, and Study Wild Animals, Twenty-first Century Books (Brookfield, CT), 1997.

Home at Last: A Song of Migration, illustrated by Alix Berenzy, Holt (New York, NY), 1998.

El Niño and La Niña: Weather in the Headlines, Twenty-first Century Books (Brookfield, CT), 2000.

Turtle, Turtle, Watch Out!, illustrated by Lee Christiansen, Orchard Books (New York, NY), 2000, revised edition, illustrated by Annie Patterson, Charlesbridge (New York, NY), 2010.

Splish! Splash! Animal Baths, Millbrook Press (Brookfield, CT), 2000.

Crocodile Listens, illustrated by JoEllen McAllister Stammen, Greenwillow Books (New York, NY), 2001.

It's My City!: A Singing Map, illustrated by Denis Roche, Greenwillow Books (New York, NY), 2001.

Dig, Wait, Listen: A Desert Toad's Tale, illustrated by Barbara Bash, Greenwillow Books (New York, NY), 2001.

The Hungry Hummingbird, illustrated by Gay W. Holland, Millbrook Press (Brookfield, CT), 2001.

Noodle Man: The Pasta Superhero, illustrated by Stephen Costanza, Orchard Books (New York, NY), 2002.

Army Ant Parade, illustrated by Rick Chrustowski, Holt (New York, NY), 2002.

Shadows, illustrated by Harvey Stevenson, Holt (New York, NY), 2002.

Secrets of Sound: Studying the Calls and Songs of Whales, Elephants, and Birds, Houghton Mifflin (Boston, MA), 2002.

Rain Forest, Scholastic Reference, 2002.

One Is a Snail, Ten Is a Crab: A Counting by Feet Book, illustrated by Randy Cecil, Candlewick Press (Cambridge, MA), 2003.

Trout, Trout, Trout!: A Fish Chant, illustrated by Trip Park, NorthWord Press (Chanhassen, MN), 2004.

Stars beneath Your Bed: The Surprising Story of Dust, illustrated by Ann Jonas, Greenwillow Books (New York, NY), 2005.

The Bumblebee Queen, illustrated by Patricia J. Wynne, Charlesbridge (Watertown, MA), 2005.

Ant, Ant, Ant!: An Insect Chant, illustrated by Trip Park, NorthWord Books for Young Readers (Minnetonka, MN), 2005.

Vulture View, illustrated by Steve Jenkins, Henry Holt (New York, NY), 2007.

Hush, Little Puppy, illustrated by Susan Winter, Henry Holt (New York, NY), 2007.

Bird, Bird, Bird!: A Chirping Chant, illustrated by Gary Locke, NorthWord Books for Young Readers (Minnetonka, MN), 2007.

Trout Are Made of Trees, illustrated by Kate Endle, Charlesbridge (Watertown, MA), 2008.

Honk, Honk, Goose!: Canada Geese Start a Family, illustrated by Huy Voun Lee, Henry Holt (New York, NY), 2009.

Meet the Howlers!, illustrated by Woody Miller, Charlesbridge (Watertown, MA), 2010.

If You're Hoppy, illustrated by Jackie Urbanovic, Greenwillow Books (New York, NY), 2011.

Rah, Rah, Radishes!: A Vegetable Chant, Beach Lane Books (New York, NY), 2011.

Contributor to *World, Ranger Rick, Earth Explorer Encyclopedia* (CD-ROM), and various educator's guides and scientific curricula.

Author's books have been translated into several languages, among them Dutch, French, Japanese, and Korean.

"EXPLORING EARTH'S BIOMES" SERIES

Tropical Rain Forest, Twenty-first Century Books (Brookfield, CT), 1994.
Desert, Twenty-first Century Books (Brookfield, CT), 1994.
Grassland, Twenty-first Century Books (Brookfield, CT), 1994.
Temperate Deciduous Forest, Twenty-first Century Books (Brookfield, CT), 1994.
Tundra, Twenty-first Century Books (Brookfield, CT), 1994.
Taiga, Twenty-first Century Books (Brookfield, CT), 1994.
River and Stream, Twenty-first Century Books (Brookfield, CT), 1996.
Lake and Pond, Twenty-first Century Books (Brookfield, CT), 1996.
Wetland, Twenty-first Century Books (Brookfield, CT), 1996.
Seashore, Twenty-first Century Books (Brookfield, CT), 1996.
Coral Reef, Twenty-first Century Books (Brookfield, CT), 1996.
Ocean, Twenty-first Century Books (Brookfield, CT), 1996.

"SEVEN CONTINENTS" SERIES

North America, Twenty-first Century Books (Brookfield, CT), 1998.
Europe, Twenty-first Century Books (Brookfield, CT), 1998.
Antarctica, Twenty-first Century Books (Brookfield, CT), 1998.
Australia, Twenty-first Century Books (Brookfield, CT), 1998.
South America, Twenty-first Century Books (Brookfield, CT), 1999.
Africa, Twenty-first Century Books (Brookfield, CT), 1999.
Asia, Twenty-first Century Books (Brookfield, CT), 1999.

"OUR AMAZING CONTINENTS" SERIES

G'Day, Australia!, Millbrook Press (Brookfield, CT), 2003.
Welcome to North America!, Millbrook Press (Brookfield, CT), 2003.
South America, Surprise!, Millbrook Press (Brookfield, CT), 2003.

Sidelights

April Pulley Sayre is the author of dozens of science books for children, among them award-winning books in multi-volume series and stand-alone titles. An adventurous person, "Sayre has followed lemurs in Madagascar, pursued army ants in Panama, and eaten piranha in the Peruvian Amazon," as she revealed on her home page. Each of these experiences has inspired and influenced her work, from story books such as *Hush, Little Puppy* and *If You're Hoppy* to nonfiction picture books that include *Trout Are Made of Trees* to well-illustrated, fact-based references such as *Endangered Birds of North America* and her "Our Amazing Continents" series.

In her "Exploring Earth's Biomes" series Sayre presents elementary-grade readers with information about the various habitats found on earth, and her "Seven Continents" series provides overviews on the geography, wildlife, and weather to be found on each of earth's continent. Several critics singled out the author's "lively and precise" writing style, to quote *Booklist* contributor Carolyn Phelan in a review of both *Wetland* and *Lake and Pond.* In a joint review of *Coral Reef* and *Ocean* for *Voice of Youth Advocates,* Mary Ojibway praised the "conversational style" in which Sayre presents both "clear, accurate information."

Sayre is an avid bird watcher, as books such as *If You Should Hear a Honeyguide, Hummingbirds: The Sun Catchers, The Hungry Hummingbird, Endangered Birds of North America, Bird, Bird, Bird!: A Chirping Chant,* and *Vulture View* each attest. In her picture books *If You Should Hear a Honeyguide* and *Hummingbirds* she allows glimpses into the life of the birds mentioned, fol-

Woody Miller crafts the stylized illustrations that keep the pages turning in Sayre's humorous nature-themed story in **Meet the Howlers!** *(Illustration copyright © 2010 by Woody Miller. Used with permission of Charlesbridge Publishing, Inc. All rights reserved.)*

Shadows, *Sayre's imaginative picture-book story, is brought to life in evocative paintings by Harvey Stevenson.* (Illustration copyright © 2002 by Harvey Stevenson. Reprinted by permission of Henry Holt & Company, LLC.)

lowing them up with an author's note to give more detailed information. According to Maryann H. Owen in *School Library Journal,* the artwork and easily accessible facts combine to make *The Hungry Hummingbird* "a winner" and a "pleasant, versatile book." Written for somewhat older juvenile readers, *Endangered Birds of North America* presents information on the snail kite, Kirtland's warbler, red-cockaded woodpecker, piping plover, and whooping crane, all in what *Booklist* critic Stephanie Zvirin called "a stimulating fashion." In *School Library Journal,* Patricia Manning praised Sayre's text for *Endangered Birds of North America* as "clear" and "readable," and also remarked favorably on the photographs and maps.

Winner of the Theodor Geisel Honor Book award, *Vulture View* pairs Sayre's text with collage art by award-winning illustrator Steve Jenkins to explore the life of a much-maligned bird. In addition, she discusses the way birds travel through the air on rising warm air and cooling sinking air. In what *School Library Journal* contributor Robin L. Gibson described as a "spare, rhyming text," the author provides basic information about these much-maligned carrion eaters while Jenkins' "dynamic" images "are often quite dramatic." "Sayre's text is positively gleeful" in depicting the lowly vulture "not as cartoon villains but as a necessary part of nature," according to a *Kirkus Reviews* writer. As Cooper noted, author and illustrator "buoyantly approach" their un-

usual subject, "celebrating the majesty of an underappreciated creature" in a book combining "fascinating content and sprightly execution." "Rarely has a book about these scavengers gotten such a gorgeous treatment," Cooper added in a nod to Jenkins' collage art.

Turtle, Turtle, Watch Out!, *Crocodile Listens*, *Dig, Wait, Listen: A Desert Toad's Tale*, and *The Bumblebee Queen* number among Sayre's picture-book treatments of individual animal species. In the popular *Turtle, Turtle, Watch Out!*—which was published in two editions with different illustrations—she shows the life cycle of the sea turtle, "drawing readers into the turtle's story without anthropomorphism," wrote Phelan. Similarly, in *Crocodile Listens* she provides readers with a glimpse into the habitat of this dangerous African reptile, producing a work that a *Kirkus Reviews* contributor called "playful without being precious." The only book for children that presents the life cycle of the desert-dwelling spadefoot toad, *Dig, Wait, Listen* features a text that Phelan described as "clear, precise, and poetic."

Younger readers are introduced to selected species in the companion volumes *Trout, Trout, Trout!: A Fish Chant*, *Ant, Ant, Ant!: An Insect Chant*, *Bird, Bird, Bird!*, and *Rah, Rah, Radishes!: A Vegetable Chant*. Sayre includes common names as well as assorted facts about each creature that are echoed in the books' amusing art. Reviewing *Ant, Ant, Ant!* for *School Library Journal*, Carolyn Janssen wrote that Sayre's "text and illustrations [by Trip Park] are a natural pairing for exploring the insect world."

Illustrated by Huy Voun Lee with colorful cut-paper collage art, *Honk Honk Goose!: Canada Geese Start a Family* serves up "a fun read-aloud grounded by great informational back matter," according to *Booklist* critic Abby Nolan. Here Sayre's expressive and animated rhymes chronicle the life cycle of one of North America's best-known birds, and her text "conveys personality without slipping into anthropomorphism," according to *School Library Journal* contributor Farida S. Dowler. Lee's multidimensional "geese seem . . . ready to fly off the page and honk at the reader," observed a *Kirkus Reviews* writer, the critic concluding that the combination of art and Sayre's child-friendly text make *Honk Honk Goose!* a "terrific introduction."

Sayre has also treated various topics from a wider point of view. In *Put on Some Antlers and Walk like a Moose: How Scientists Find, Follow, and Study Wild Animals* she introduces methods that biologists use in the field to track and study a variety of species and presents the pros and cons of such work. Reviewing the work for *School Library Journal*, Arwen Marshall declared it a "lively and informative book" as well as an "excellent resource." Both *Splish! Splash! Animal Baths* and *Home at Last: A Song of Migration* are picture-book treatments focusing respectively on how animals bathe and

find their way "home." In the former title, which *Booklist* critic Ellen Mandel called "wonderfully entertaining," readers learn about how elephants, birds, horses, and even fish groom themselves. Birds, sea turtles, and Monarch butterflies number among the animals discussed in *Home at Last,* which with its combination of text and pastel art, may "strike a chord in young readers," according to a *Kirkus Reviews* writer.

Sayre focuses on a tantalizing topic in *Stars beneath Your Bed: The Surprising Story of Dust.* The narrative here prompted Cooper to cite the author's "poetic treatment" of her "lowly" subject, while in *Kirkus Reviews* a contributor noted that Sayre's book "will leave readers with a greater appreciation" for the ubiquitous and timeless substance.

Sayre's picture-book texts are accompanied by child-friendly artwork by several talented illustrators. In *Trout Are Made of Trees* she draws readers into an introduction to the life cycle while Kate Endle brings the circular story to life in "attractive collage illustrations in natural colors," according to *School Library Journal* critic Christine Markley. *Hush, Little Puppy,* in which a boy and his pup recall their daytime play as they fall asleep, features what *Booklist* contributor Hazel Rochman described as "soft-toned illustrations" by Susan Winter. Woody Miller crafts what Rochman described as the "eye-catching artwork" that brings to life *Meet the Howlers!,* an entertaining mix of rhyme and science fact that describes the life of the howler monkeys that live in Panama's rain-forest environment. Alongside Miller's creative mix of acrylics, crayon, colored pencil, and water color, Sayre's "bouncing rhymes" will

Sayre's picture book **Trout Are Made of Trees** *features artwork by Kate Endle.* (Illustration copyright © 2008 by Kate Endle. Used with permission of Charlesbridge Publishing, Inc. All rights reserved.)

Randy Cecil's cartoon art adds a humorous element to Sayre's ocean-themed concept book **One Is a Snail, Ten Is a Crab.** (Illustration copyright © 2003 by Randy Cecil. Reprinted by permission of Candlewick Press, Inc., Somerville, MA.)

animate young storyhour crowds, Rochman added, and in *School Library Journal* Nancy Call dubbed *Meet the Howlers!* "a whimsical introduction" that shows "active animals against backdrops of lush green." Reviewing the same book, a *Kirkus Reviews* writer announced that Sayre "delivers yet another entertaining and accessible guide to the natural world."

Sayre once told *SATA:* "As a child, I spent hours picking flowers, watching insects and birds, reading books, and writing. Now I do the same thing, only as a career. My favorite part of the work is researching—reading books and magazines, calling people on the phone, and visiting museums, parks, and aquariums. The writing itself is difficult. But I write and rewrite until I'm satisfied with every paragraph. I try to communicate the excitement I feel about nature and my fascination with the way scientists discover how nature works. I also feel it's important to write about the environmental problems our planet faces and what's being done to solve those problems.

"My favorite activity is traveling. I have been fortunate to visit many of the grasslands, forests, seashores, rain forests, deserts, and other biomes I describe in my books. I SCUBA dive and snorkel over coral reefs. My husband and I spent a month in the rain forest of Madagascar, studying lemurs. But most of the time we tromp through wetlands, forests, and grasslands nearby, in order to watch birds.

"My advice to young writers/naturalists is to read a lot, write a lot, and grab a hand lens, go outdoors, and check out all the bizarre and beautiful insects and spiders that live on the plants in your neighborhood. Like me, you'll probably be amazed by what you find living close to home."

Biographical and Critical Sources

PERIODICALS

Booklist, January 1, 1995, Mary Harris Veeder, reviews of *Temperate Deciduous Forest, Tropical Rain Forest,* and *Desert,* all p. 821; September 1, 1995, Julie Corsaro, review of *If You Should Hear a Honeyguide,* p. 80; June 1, 1996, Carolyn Phelan, reviews of *Wetland* and *Lake and Pond,* both pp. 1712-1713; December 1, 1997, Susan Dove Lempke, review of *Put on Some Antlers and Walk like a Moose: How Scientists Find, Follow, and Study Wild Animals,* and Stephanie Zvirin, review of *Endangered Birds of North America,* both p. 632; December 1, 1998, Hazel Rochman, review of *Home at Last: A Song of Migration,* p. 682; February 1, 1999, Carolyn Phelan, review of *Antarctica,* p. 972; August, 1999, Hazel Rochman, review of *Asia,* p. 2055; April 1, 2000, Ellen Mandel, review of *Splish! Splash! Animal Baths,* p. 1466; August, 2000, Carolyn Phelan, review of *Turtle, Turtle, Watch Out!,* p. 2150; September 15, 2000, Catherine Andronik, review of *El Niño and La Niña: Weather in the Headlines,* p. 238; December 1, 2000, Stephanie Zvirin, *Splish! Splash! Animal Baths,* p. 73; June 1, 2001, Carolyn Phelan, review of *Dig, Wait, Listen: A Desert Toad's Tale,* p. 1881; November 15, 2001, Gillian Engberg, review of *The Hungry Hummingbird,* p. 579; December 1, 2001, Stephanie Zvirin, review of *Dig, Wait, Listen,* p. 658; February 15, 2002, Kay Weisman, review of *Noodle Man: The Pasta Superhero,* p. 1021; March 1, 2002, Lauren Peterson, review of *Army Ant Parade,* p. 1138; April 1, 2005, Ilene Cooper, review of *Stars beneath Your Bed: The Surprising Story of Dust,* p. 1362; June 1, 2007, Hazel Rochman, review of *Hush, Little Puppy,* p. 76; November 1, 2007, Ilene Cooper, review of *Vulture View,* p. 44; February 15, 2008, Stephanie Zvirin, review of *Trout Are Made of Trees,* p. 94; March 1, 2009, Abby Nolan, review of *Honk, Honk, Goose!: Canada Geese Start a Family,* p. 45; March 15, 2010, Hazel Rochman, review of *Meet the Howlers!,* p. 44.

Horn Book, November-December, 2001, Lolly Robinson, review of *It's My City!: A Singing Map,* p. 738; July-August, 2008, Danielle J. Ford, review of *Trout Are Made of Trees,* p. 472; May-June, 2009, Danielle J. Ford, review of *Honk, Honk, Goose!,* p. 327; May-June, 2010, Danielle J. Ford, review of *Turtle, Turtle, Watch Out!,* p. 113.

Kirkus Reviews, October 1, 1998, review of *Home at Last,* p. 1464; August 15, 2001, review of *Crocodile Listens,* p. 1221; April 1, 2005, review of *Stars beneath Your Bed,* p. 424; March 15, 2007, review of *Hush, Little Puppy;* September 1, 2007, review of *Vulture View;* September 15, 2007, review of *Bird, Bird, Bird!: A Chirping Chant;* January 15, 2008, review of *Trout Are Made of Trees;* April 1, 2009, review of *Honk, Honk, Goose!;* February 15, 2010, review of *Meet the Howlers!*

Publishers Weekly, July 9, 2001, review of *It's My City,* p. 67; February 11, 2002, review of *Shadows,* p. 184; April 8, 2002, review of *Noodle Man,* p. 226; November 5, 2007, review of *Vulture View,* p. 63; February 18, 2008, review of *Trout Are Made of Trees,* p. 153.

School Library Journal, January, 1995, Eva Elisabeth Von Ancken, reviews of *Tropical Rain Forest, Desert,* and *Temperate Deciduous Forest,* all p. 131; February, 1995, Eva Elisabeth Von Ancken, reviews of *Tundra, Taiga,* and *Grassland,* all p. 110; October, 1995, Susan Scheps, review of *If You Should Hear a Honeyguide,* p. 129; June, 1996, Lisa Wu Stowe, reviews of *Wetland, River and Stream,* and *Lake and Pond,* all p. 148; January, 1997, Frances E. Millhouser, reviews of *Seashore, Ocean,* and *Coral Reef,* all pp. 134-135; January, 1998, Patricia Manning, review of *Endangered Birds of North America,* pp. 130-131; February, 1998, Arwen Marshall, review of *Put on Some Antlers and Walk like a Moose,* pp. 124-123; December, 1998, Patricia Manning, review of *Home at Last,* pp. 113-114; February, 1999, Jeanette Larson, reviews of *Australia* and *Europe,* both p. 125; April, 1999, Mollie Bynum, review of *Antarctica,* p. 156; May, 2000, Blair Christolon, review of *Splish! Splash! Animal Baths,* p. 164; October, 2000, Susan Scheps, review of *Turtle, Turtle, Watch Out!,* p. 136; June, 2001, Ellen Heath, review of *Dig, Wait, Listen,* p. 129; October, 2001, Anne Knickerbocker, review of *It's My City,* and Kathleen Kelly MacMillan, review of *Crocodile Listens,* both p. 130; November, 2001, Maryann H. Owen, review of *The Hungry Hummingbird,* p. 150; April, 2005, Patricia Manning, review of *The Bumblebee Queen,* p. 126; December, 2005, Carolyn Janssen, review of *Ant, Ant, Ant!: An Insect Chant,* p. 134; August, 2007, Alyssa G. Parkinson, review of *Hush, Little Puppy,* p. 105; December, 2007, Robin L. Gibson, review of *Vulture View,* p. 115; January, 2008, Martha Simpson, review of *Bird, Bird, Bird!,* p. 111; April, 2008, Christine Markley, review of *Trout Are Made of Trees,* p. 13; April, 2009, Farida S. Dowler, review of *Honk, Honk, Goose!,* p. 126; March, 2010, Frances E. Millhouser, review of *Turtle, Turtle, Watch Out!,* p. 130, and Nancy Call, review of *Meet the Howlers!,* p. 143; January, 2011, Linda Ludke, review of *If You're Hoppy,* p. 82.

Teacher Librarian, March, 1999, Shirley Lewis, review of *Home at Last,* p. 44.

Voice of Youth Advocates, April, 1997, Mary Ojibway, reviews of *Coral Reef* and *Ocean,* both p. 60; February, 1998, Marilyn Brien, review of *Put on Some Antlers and Walk like a Moose,* p. 404.

ONLINE

April Pulley Sayre Home Page, http://www.aprilsayre.com (September 15, 2011).

Kirkus Reviews Online, http://www.kirkusreviews.com/ (August 12, 2011), Jessie Grearson, interview with Sayre.

*   *   *

SENZAI, N.H.
(Naheed Hasnat)

Personal

Born in Chicago, IL; daughter of a civil engineer father; married; husband a professor of political science;

children: one son. *Education:* University of California, Berkeley, B.S., 1997; Columbia University, M.I.B., 2001.

Addresses

Home—San Francisco Bay Area, CA. *Agent*—Michael Bourret, Dystel & Goderich Literary Management, One Union Square W., Ste. 904, New York, NY 10003; mbourret@dystel.com *E-mail*—nhsenzai@yahoo.com.

Career

Writer and intellectual property consultant. AcrossWorld Communications, Santa Clara, CA, director of market development, 1998-2000; Intellectual Capital Management Group, Sonoma, CA, consultant, 2000-05; LECG Corporation, senior consultant, 2005-07; EnnovationZ (environmental services company), Mountain View, CA, cofounder, 2007-08; Foresight Valuation Group, Palo Alto, CA, director, 2009—.

Member

Society of Children's Book Writers and Illustrators.

Awards, Honors

Notable Social Studies Trade Books for Young People, National Council for the Social Studies/Children's Book Council, Asian/Pacific American Award for Young Adult Literature, and Middle East Book Award for Youth Literature, all 2010, and Bank Street Best Children's Book of the Year, Bank Street College of Education, and Teachers Choice Award, International Reading Association, both 2011, all for *Shooting Kabul.*

Writings

Shooting Kabul (novel), Simon & Schuster Books for Young Readers (New York, NY), 2010.

Sidelights

In *Shooting Kabul,* her debut novel for young-adult readers, N.H. Senzai follows the efforts of an Afghani immigrant to locate his younger sister, who was left behind when his family fled their homeland. The work is based in part on the experiences of Senzai's husband, whose own family escaped from war-torn Afghanistan in 1979. "They had an amazing journey that had them fleeing Soviet forces which were after my husband's father because he was an intellectual and a professor at Kabul University," the author noted on her home page. "Some of the elements of the story are similar to my husband's, but overall [*Shooting Kabul*] . . . is a work of fiction."

Shooting Kabul centers on Fadi, a middle-school student who is adjusting to his new life in San Francisco, California, where he resides with his father, mother, and older sister. Fadi is haunted by memories of the fateful night in the summer of 2001, when his family was pursued by Taliban forces and hastily left Afghanistan. In the confusion, Fadi's six-year-old sister, Mariam, let go of his hand and disappeared into the darkness. Still searching for ways to rescue his sister, Fadi enters a photography contest, hoping to win a trip to India and reenter his homeland.

Shooting Kabul earned solid reviews. "This is a sweet story of family unity," observed Kristin Anderson in *School Library Journal,* and Steven Kral similarly noted in *Voice of Youth Advocates* that "Fadi's world is one of strong familial ties, Islam, and a vibrant, strong immigrant community." A contributor in *Kirkus Reviews* also recommended the book, commenting that Senzai's debut offers "an original and engaging plot and a lens through which readers will learn much about the . . . conflict" in Afghanistan.

Biographical and Critical Sources

PERIODICALS

Booklist, June 1, 2010, Gillian Engberg, review of *Shooting Kabul,* p. 78.
Bulletin of the Center for Children's Books, July-August, 2010, Maggie Hommel, review of *Shooting Kabul.*
Kirkus Reviews, May 1, 2010, review of *Shooting Kabul.*
School Library Journal, June, 2010, Kristin Anderson, review of *Shooting Kabul,* p. 120.
Voice of Youth Advocates, August, 2010, Steven Kral, review of *Shooting Kabul,* p. 256.

ONLINE

Cynsations Web log, http://cynthialeitichsmith.blogspot.com/ (July 26, 2010), Cynthia Leitich Smith, interview with Senzai.
N.H. Senzai Home Page, http://www.nhsenzai.com (August 1, 2011).*

* * *

SHEINMEL, Alyssa B.

Personal

Born in Stanford, CA; married. *Education:* Columbia University, degree. *Hobbies and other interests:* Reading, cooking, entertaining friends.

Addresses

Home—New York, NY. *Agent*—Sarah Burnes, The Gernert Company, 136 E. 57th St., New York, NY 10022.

Career

Novelist and editor. Random House Children's Books, New York, NY, member of editorial staff.

Writings

The Beautiful Between, Alfred A. Knopf (New York, NY), 2010.

The Lucky Kind, Alfred A. Knopf (New York, NY), 2011.

The Stone Girl, Alfred A. Knopf (New York, NY), 2012.

Sidelights

A habitual journal-writer who also enjoyed crafting stories from childhood through college, Alyssa B. Sheinmel stopped writing, when she got a job in an emotionally draining office setting. She resumed the writing habit that would lead to her debut young-adult novel, *The Beautiful Between,* after moving to a position on the editorial staff of a major New York City publishing house. The company of book-lovers and published writers inspired Sheinmel to write again, and two years later she had completed her book-length manuscript. "The great thing about writing, at least in my experience, is that it comes out best when you're doing it for the very, very fun of it," Sheinmel noted on her home page.

Sheinmel has continued to focus on teen readers, authoring *The Lucky Kind* and *The Stone Girl.* Interestingly, she is not the only published writer in her family. Older sister Courtney Sheinmel led the way, both in her choice of alma mater (Barnard College) and her decision to become an author of YA fiction (Courtney's first novel, *My So-Called Family,* was published in the fall of 2009).

In *The Beautiful Between* readers meet high-schooler Connelly Sternin. With college looming in her future, the sixteen year old is juggling a lot of balls right now: maintaining her grades at her exclusive private school, studying for her SAT's, rating potential colleges, and trying to keep her friends from discovering her secret regarding her father's mysterious death years ago. Imagining her life as a modern-day princess trapped in a tower, Connelly soon finds a kindred soul in Jeremy Cole, a potential Prince Charming and the son of an affluent Manhattan family. When Jeremy confides a secret about his own family—his sister is dying—and reveals his knowledge regarding Courtney's dad's death from leukemia, the teens quickly form a bond. Along with homework, they share intimate details as best friends, although Connelly soon realizes that current truths are more of a threat to their friendship than the secrets from their pasts.

"Sheinmel makes an impressive debut with an absorbing tale of unlikely friendship, loss, and family secrets," asserted a *Publishers Weekly* critic in a laudatory review of *The Beautiful Between.* Recommending the novel to teens dealing with death in their own families, *Voice of Youth Advocates* contributor Laura Woodruff praised the author's characterization of Connelly as a girl who is "genuinely scarred by her family's secrecy, [and] matures with Jeremy's help." The teen's relationship is "realistically portrayed" with a "steady pace," noted Geri Diorio, the *School Library Journal* critic recommending *The Beautiful Between* as "a terrific alternative to the clique-y high school novels that are al sex, drugs, and rock 'n' roll."

Another close-knit relationship among sixteen year olds is the focus of *The Lucky Kind.* Nick Brandt is lucky by anyone's standards: he has a stable family with understanding parents, a loyal friend in buddy Stevie, and his grades foretell a successful future. The only thing missing as far as Nick is concerned is Eden Reiss, a girl he has crushed since his freshman year. Just as he breaks the ice with Eden, his parents drop a bombshell that threatens to topple Nick's world: he actually has a much-older half brother, Sam, who was given up for adoption decades before. Angry and resentful, Nick

Cover of Alyssa B. Sheinmel's evocative young-adult novel **The Beautiful Between.** (Copyright © 2010 by Alfred A. Knopf. Reproduced with permission of Alfred A. Knopf, an imprint of Random House Children's Books, a division of Random House, Inc.)

loses his self-assured confidence when relating to Eden and their relationship becomes sexualized too soon. As the teen attempts to sort out his family's shifting emotional landscape, his reactions will either help or hurt his budding romance in a novel showcases the dilemma of what *Voice of Youth Advocates* contributor Pam Carlson described as a "frequently unsympathetic main character." Nick's emotional confusion is "effectively" captured by Sheinmel in "a breezy, often humorous first-person voice that's deceptively slight in its handling of deep issues," noted a *Kirkus Reviews* critic, also praising *The Lucky Kind.*

Biographical and Critical Sources

PERIODICALS

Bulletin of the Center for Children's Books, May, 2010, Kate Quealy-Gainer, review of *The Beautiful Between,* p. 399.

Kirkus Reviews, April 15, 2010, review of *The Beautiful Between;* April 15, 2011, review of *The Lucky Kind.*

Publishers Weekly, May 10, 2010, review of *The Beautiful Between,* p. 47.

School Library Journal, May, 2010, Geri Diorio, review of *The Beautiful Between,* p. 123.

Voice of Youth Advocates, August, 2010, Laura Woodruff, review of *The Beautiful Between,* p. 256; June, 2011, Pam Carlson, review of *The Lucky Kind,* p. 173.

ONLINE

Alyssa Sheinmel Home Page, http://www.alyssasheinmel. com (September 15, 2011).

Alyssa Sheinmel Web Log, http://www.alyssasheinmel. blogspot.com (September 15, 2011).

TeenReads Web site, http://www.teenreads.com/ (May, 2010), interview with Sheinmel.*

*   *   *

SOLHEIM, James 1959-

Personal

Born 1959, in Kensal, ND; married; wife's name Joyce; children: Jenny, Justin. *Education:* Northwest Missouri State University, B.A. (English), 1981; University of Iowa, M.F.A. (creative writing), 1983.

Addresses

Home—Omaha, NE. *E-mail*—jim@jamessolheim.com.

Career

Writer and educator. Southern Illinois University, Carbondale, creative writing instructor, 1985-93. Presenter at schools.

Writings

It's Disgusting—and We Ate It!: True Food Facts from around the World and throughout History, illustrated by Eric Brace, Simon & Schuster Books for Young Readers (New York, NY), 1998.

Santa's Secrets Revealed: All Your Questions Answered about Santa's Super Sleigh, His Flying Reindeer, and Other Wonders, illustrated by Barry Gott, Carolrhoda Books (Minneapolis, MN), 2004.

In It's Disgusting—-and We Ate It! *James Solheim and illustrator Eric Brace team up to reveal the odd things people consume in different parts of the world.* (Illustration copyright © 1998 by Eric Brace. Reprinted with permission of Simon & Schuster Books for Young Readers, an imprint of Simon & Schuster Children's Publishing Division.)

Solheim captures an unusual perspective on babyhood in his quirky picture book **Born Yesterday: The Diary of a Young Journalist.** (Illustration copyright © 2010 by Simon James. Reproduced with permission of Philomel Books, a division of Penguin Young Readers Group, a division of Penguin Group (USA), Inc. 375 Hudson St., New York, NY 10014. All rights reserved.)

Born Yesterday: The Diary of a Young Journalist, illustrated by Simon James, Philomel Books (New York, NY), 2010.

Contributor of poems to literary magazines, including *Kenyon Review* and *Poetry.*

Sidelights

The title of James Solheim's first book for children, *It's Disgusting—and We Ate It!: True Food Facts from around the World and throughout History,* served as flypaper to young readers, as did the second, the intriguing holiday exposé *Santa's Secrets Revealed: All Your Questions Answered about Santa's Super Sleigh, His Flying Reindeer, and Other Wonders.* "'I knew the idea of [disgusting foods] . . . would capture kids' imaginations," Solheim admitted to *St. Louis Post-Dispatch* writer Renee Stovsky. "But the main purpose of my book *It's Disgusting—and We Ate It!* was to write something fascinating that would use every grade school subject—science, math, social studies, language arts— and prove that learning from books can be fun."

Solheim knew by age eight that he wanted to be a writer; his childhood works included stories of a housefly who saved the day and a boy who fell into his trumpet and found a lost universe. In addition to writing, he now performs as a Norwegian folk dancer and includes folk-dance performances or teaches energetic dance steps in his school presentations on writing. Solheim also shares his own childhood writings with students

and emphasizes the fun of creativity and revising through imagination. His overarching goal is to inspire children to write.

In his first book for children, Solheim reveals some of the unusual foods eaten by individuals around the world. *It's Disgusting—and We Ate It!* offers readers poems, recipes, and interesting food facts about things people eat, both past and present. Divided into three chapters, Solheim's text reveals strange delicacies like flowers, snakes, and frog legs; unusual foods consumed in the past, such as squirrels, rats, and swans; and products likely found in the refrigerator of the average American, including the seaweed that thickens many brands of ice cream. "With enough information for several sittings," remarked a *Publishers Weekly* critic, "this compendium lives up to its title's rich promise." Describing the book as "fact-packed with fun from beginning to end," *School Library Journal* contributor Joyce Adams Burner added that Solheim's work "appeals to the gross-out side of kids." In *Booklist,* Stephanie Zvirin described the food facts in *It's Disgusting—and We Ate It!* "fascinating and fun" and given added spunk from Eric Brace's "zany illustrations."

Santa's Secrets Revealed, illustrated by Barry Gott, finds a skeptical eight year old named Stevie going on national television to proclaim his contention that Santa Claus is a fiction, a deception, and a lie that has been perpetrated on children everywhere. Tuned in to the show, Santa decides to take the young doubter on a tour

of his Christmas-making operations, from his naughtiness-tracking system housed in Cleveland, Ohio, to the high-tech toymaking operation at his North Pole headquarters. Barry Gott's quirky digital art for *Santa's Secrets Revealed* adds suitable humor to a text rife with "tongue-in-cheek flair," according to a *Publishers Weekly* reviewer.

Solheim's third book for children, *Born Yesterday: The Diary of a Young Journalist,* is illustrated by Simon James and purports to be the diary of a newly born infant. The book's chubby-knee'd journalist discovers her ability to use her fingers to grab and hold things, questions why her older sister can do things she cannot, attempts to mentally deconstruct the colorful mobile hanging above her crib, and strategizes ways to keep her tummy full. In *Booklist* Ilene Cooper predicted that *Born Yesterday* will generate "giggles" among the kindergarten crowd, and a *Publishers Weekly* critic quipped: "As fake memoirs go, this one is a hoot." The illustrator's "reportorial watercolor-and-ink cartoons make terrific visual punctuation,"the same critic added, while in *School Library Journal* Judith Constantinides dubbed Solheim's mock-chronicle "a fresh and amusing slant on sibling adjustment."

Biographical and Critical Sources

PERIODICALS

Booklist, April, 1998, Stephanie Zvirin, review of *It's Disgusting—and We Ate It!: True Food Facts from around the World and throughout History,* p. 1318; March 1, 2010, Ilene Cooper, review of *Born Yesterday: The Diary of a Young Journalist,* p. 76.
Bulletin of the Center for Children's Books, April, 1998, Deborah Stevenson, review of *It's Disgusting—and We Ate It!,* pp. 296-297.
Kirkus Reviews, January 15, 2010, review of *Born Yesterday.*
New York Times Book Review, December 5, 2004, Emily Jenkins, review of *Santa's Secrets Revealed:: All Your Questions Answered about Santa's Super Sleigh, His Flying Reindeer, and Other Wonders,* p. 54.
Publishers Weekly, May 18, 1998, review of *It's Disgusting—and We Ate It!,* p. 79; September 27, 2004, review of *Santa's Secrets Revealed,* p. 63; February 22, 2010, review of *Born Yesterday,* p. 63.
St. Louis Post-Dispatch, March 11, 1999, Renee Stovsky, profile of Solheim, p. G1.
School Library Journal, June, 1998, Joyce Adams Burner, review of *It's Disgusting—and We Ate It!,* p. 136; March, 2010, Judith Constantinides, review of *Born Yesterday,* p. 132.

ONLINE

James Solheim Home Page, http://www.jamessolheim.com (September 1, 2011).

STAIB, Walter

Personal

Born in Pforzheim, Germany; children: Patrick, Elizabeth.

Addresses

Home—Bryn Mawr, PA.

Career

Chef, restaurateur, and author. Sommerberg Hotel, Bad Wildbad, Germany, chef, 1963-65; Chessery, Gstaad, Switzerland, chef, 1965-69; Casa Berno (resort), Ascona, Switzerland, executive sous chef, 1967-69; Mid America Club, Chicago, IL, chef, 1969-72; Hyatt Regency, executive chef, 1972-75; Hotel Quatro Rodas, São Paulo, Brazil, corporate director of food and beverage and director of concept development; Dunfy Hotels, corporate director, beginning 1977, then senior vice president of food and beverage operations, 1982-89; Concepts by Staib, Ltd. (restaurant consulting firm), founder, 1989. Cofounder, Caribbean Culinary Federation. Guest instructor, Culinary Institute of America, Hyde Park, 2011. Appeared on cooking programs, including *Talk Philly* and *A Taste of History;* host of *World Cuisine of the Black Forest.*

Member

German Society of Pennsylvania.

Awards, Honors

Named chevalier, Ordre du Mérite Agricole, Republic of France; named Commandeur, Association Internationale des Maîtres Conseils en Gastronomie Française, 1986; Silver Plate award, 1987; inducted into Caribbean Culinary Hall of Fame, 1995; ambassador to Culinary Institute of America; appointed Culinary Ambassador to the City of Philadelphia, 1996; named Restaurateur of the Year, Philadelphia Delaware Valley Restaurant Association, 1999; March of Dimes Star Chef Award, 2002; Federal Republic of Germany, German-American Friendship Award, 2003, Knight's Cross of the Order of Merit, 2007; Distinguished Visiting Author Award, Johnson & Wales University, 2003, Founder's Trophy and induction into World Gourmet Club, 2004; Keystone Humanitarian Award, Pennsylvania, National Restaurant Association, 2007; Leadership and Service award, German-American Chamber of Commerce, 2008; Emmy Award, Academy of Television Arts and Sciences, nomination, 2008, and award for Best Host, 2010; Contemporary Pioneer Award, Colonial Society of Pennsylvania, 2011; Silver Medal Award, American Culinary Federation, 2011; numerous other industry and culinary honors.

Writings

(With Beth D'Addono) *City Tavern Cookbook: 200 Years of Classic Recipes from America's First Gourmet Restaurant,* Running Press (Philadelphia, PA), 1999.

(With Jennifer Lindner) *City Tavern Baking and Dessert Cookbook: 200 Years of Authentic American Recipes,* Running Press (Philadelphia, PA), 2003.

(With Jennifer Lindner McGlinn) *Black Forest Cuisine: The Classic Blending of European Flavors,* Running Press (Philadelphia, PA), 2006.

City Tavern: Recipes from the Birthplace of American Cuisine, Running Press (Philadelphia, PA), 2008.

(With Jennifer Fox) *A Feast of Freedom: Tasty Tidbits from the City Tavern,* illustrated by Fernando Juarez, Running Press Kids (Philadelphia, PA), 2010.

Newspaper columnist.

Sidelights

Award-winning chef and restaurateur Walter Staib operates City Tavern, a Philadelphia eatery that specializes in recreating the food and ambiance of eighteenth-century America. Built in 1773 as a gathering spot and designed in the manner of an English tavern, City Tavern hosted meetings of the men who would eventually sign their names to the Declaration of Independence, as well as providing a venue for the First Continental Congress. In his book *A Feast of Freedom: Tasty Tidbits from the City Tavern* Staib teams up with coauthor Jennifer Fox and illustrator Fernando Juarez to mix his love of historic cuisine and the tavern's lush setting with an interesting story designed to capture the imagination of budding history buffs.

For the German-born Staib, his role as a children's book author is a definite sidestep from his career, which was sparked during a childhood spent working in his grandfather's restaurant. As a young man Staib apprenticed at the Hotel Post, and working at this historic five-star hotel located in Germany's Black Forest inspired his interest in time-honored recipes and traditional food-preparation techniques. In 1963 he accepted the first of a series of appointments that eventually led him to the United States, among them positions at Switzerland's Chessery and five-star restaurant Casa Berno in Ascona, Switzerland. His first position in the United States was at Chicago's Mid America Club; other positions include serving as executive chef at the Hyatt Regency, as a director at Brazil's Hotel Quatro Rodas resorts, and as a senior vice president of food and beverage operation at OMNI Hotels. In addition to starting his own restaurant at City Tavern, Staib also operates a successful consulting service, Concepts by Staib, Ltd.

In City Tavern, Staib's guests are treated to open-hearth cookery and beers crafted using recipes from the Founding Fathers. In *A Feast of Freedom* readers also get to experience what dining out was like during the late 1700s, their journey guided by a scrappy mouse wearing a tricornered hat. Featured in Juarez's large, full-color illustrations, the bewhiskered narrator describes the whirl of history that surrounded the tavern, from the decision to break the American colonies loose from

British control to Paul Revere's historic ride to the meeting of the Constitutional Convention and the signing of the Declaration of Independence. The tavern served its Philadelphia neighborhood as the place where political plots were hatched, business conducted, and entertainments performed, all enriched by a mug of ale and popular meals prepared from foods grown or raised nearby. Readers also learn about the history of the tavern building, from its construction through a fire and ultimate destruction in 1954 to its eventual restoration and status as a National Park Service property and an award-winning restaurant.

Reviewing *A Feast of Freedom,* Carol S. Surges recommended the book in *School Library Journal,* noting Staib's inclusion of the tavern's prize-winning cornbread recipe and praising the coauthors for taking "a fresh look at a requisite time in U.S. history." The book serves up "a great slice of illustrated American history for students aged 4-8," asserted a *Children's Bookwatch* reviewer, and in *Publishers Weekly* a contributor praised Juarez's acrylic paintings for contributing "a distinctly modern sculptural element" that "heightens the drama and intimacy of the action" in *A Feast of Freedom.*

Biographical and Critical Sources

PERIODICALS

Booklist, November 16, 1999, Mark Knoblauch, review of *City Tavern Cookbook: 200 Years of Classic Recipes from America's First Gourmet Restaurant,* p. 1999.

Children's Bookwatch, July, 2010, review of *A Feast of Freedom: Tasty Tidbits from the City Tavern.*

Kirkus Reviews, April 15, 2010, review of *A Feast of Freedom.*

Publishers Weekly, August 21, 2006, review of *Black Forest Cuisine: The Classic Blending of European Flavors,* p. 65; April 26, 2010, review of *A Feast of Freedom,* p. 107.

School Library Journal, August, 2010, Carol S. Surges, review of *A Feast of Freedom,* p. 122.

ONLINE

Reluctant Gourmet Web site, http://www.reluctantgourmet.com/ (September 15, 2011), "Walter Staib."

Walter Staib Home Page, http://staib.com (December 15, 2011).*

* * *

STRINGAM, Jean 1945-

Personal

Born 1945, in Alberta, Canada; children: five. *Education:* University of Alberta, Ph.D., 1998. *Hobbies and other interests:* Writing music, travel, theater, Nordic skiing.

Jean Stringam (Reproduced by permission.)

Addresses

Office—English Department, Siceluff Hall 342, Missouri State University, 901 S. National Ave., Springfield, MO 65897. *E-mail*—JeanStringam@Missouri State.edu.

Career

Educator and writer. Missouri State University, Springfield, member of faculty, 2001-04, associate professor, beginning 2004, exchange professor to Qingdao University, People's Republic of China, 2004-06, and professor of English.

Member

Society of Children's Book Writers and Illustrators, Children's Literature Association, Ozark Romance Authors.

Awards, Honors

Summer faculty fellowship, Missouri State University, 2002; University Award for Teaching, Missouri State University, 2006.

Writings

"COUSINS" NOVEL CYCLE

The Hoarders, Bonneville Books (Springville, UT), 2010.
Balance, Bonneville Books (Springville, UT), 2011.

OTHER

Contributor to *Canadian Children's Literature, Dominant Expressions, Voices of the Other,* and *Language and Writing 11.*

Sidelights

Jean Stringam, a native of Canada who lives and works in the United States, is the author of *The Hoarders* and *Balance,* the first two novels in her four-part "Cousins" cycle for young adults. On her Web log, Stringam noted that her stories, which chronicle one year in the lives of a large, extended family, "investigate ways the current generation of teens respond to being raised by their Gen-Me parents and Boomer grandparents."

The Hoarders centers on ten-year-old Cheyenne and his younger brother, Joaquin, who live with their irresponsible, spendthrift mother. Often neglected, the boys begin hoarding food to survive, stockpiling supplies in their backpacks and closet. When their mother abandons them entirely, Cheyenne and Joaquin are placed in the care of their aunt Amy, a sympathetic adult who offers stability and security. Unfortunately, Amy soon encounters problems of her own, suffering an accident that leaves her hospitalized. The brothers are once again forced to fend for themselves, taking shelter in a van and foraging through dumpsters while their aunt recovers. Michael Cart, writing in *Booklist,* applauded Stringam's portrayal of Cheyenne and Joaquin, commenting that "their compelling, dramatic story will captivate most readers." A contributor in *Kirkus Reviews* stated of *The Hoarders* that "Cheyenne's authentic voice is lovable enough to make this a worthy . . . read."

Biographical and Critical Sources

PERIODICALS

Booklist, June 1, 2010, Michael Cart, review of *The Hoarders,* p. 73.
Kirkus Reviews, May 1, 2010, review of *The Hoarders.*

ONLINE

Jean Stringam Web log, http://jeanstringamauthor.word press.com (August 15, 2011).*

T-V

TERRY, Michael 1947-

Personal

Born 1947, in Folkestone, Kent, England; married (divorced); in a second relationship; children: (first marriage) David, Timothy, Mark; (second relationship) Jamie (son). *Education:* College degree (graphic design and illustration), 1967.

Addresses

Home—Folkestone, Kent, England. *Agent*—Folio Illustration Agency, 10 Gate St., Lincoln's Inn Fields, London WC2A 3HP, England. *E-mail*—mike@thepaint brush.co.uk.

Career

Illustrator and author of children's books. Typographer and graphic designer in London, England, 1967-72; freelance illustrator beginning c. 1972.

Awards, Honors

D&AD award for illustration; Mecanorma award for best poster illustration; Bishop's Stortford Picture Book Award shortlist, 2009, for *The Wide-mouthed Frog* by Iain Smyth; Red House Children's Book Award shortlist, 2009, for *Crunch Munch Dinosaur Lunch!* by Paul Bright.

Writings

SELF-ILLUSTRATED

Banana Skins (cartoon collection), Banana Books (Folkestone, England), 1990.
Rhino's Horns, Bloomsbury Children's Books (London, England), 2001.
Captain Wag the Pirate Dog, Bloomsbury Children's Books (London, England), 2007.

Captain Wag and the Big Blue Whale, Bloomsbury Children's Books (London, England), 2008.
Captain Wag and the Polar Bears, Bloomsbury Children's Books (London, England), 2009.
How to Draw Leprechauns in Simple Steps, Search Press (Tunbridge Wells, England), 2009.
Who Lives Here?, Bloomsbury Children's Books (London, England), 2012.

ILLUSTRATOR

Ann Jungman, *Vlad the Drac Goes Travelling,* Lions (London, England), 1994.
Dick King-Smith, *Smasher,* Viking (London, England), 1996.
Dick King-Smith, *Clever Duck,* Viking (London, England), 1996.
Elizabeth Hawkins, *A Monster of a Hamster,* Puffin (London, England), 1997.
Dick King-Smith, *Hogsel and Gruntel and Other Animal Stories,* Puffin (London, England), 1997, Orchard Books (New York, NY), 1998, selection published as *Fat Lawrence,* Puffin, 2001.
Faustin Charles, *The Selfish Crocodile* (also see below), Bloomsbury Children's Books (London, England), 1998.
Patricia Borlenghi, compiler, *Animal Joke Book,* Bloomsbury Children's Books (London, England), 1998.
Dick King-Smith, *Martin's Mice,* new edition, Puffin (London, England), 1998.
Dick King-Smith, *Poppet,* Puffin (London, England), 1999.
Dick King-Smith, *More Animal Stories,* Puffin (London, England), 1999.
Dick King-Smith, *Magnus Powermouse,* new edition, Puffin (London, England), 1999.
Dick King-Smith, *The Fox Busters,* new edition, Puffin (London, England), 1999.
Dick King-Smith, *Ace,* new edition, Puffin (London, England), 1999.
Brian Patten, *Little Hotchpotch,* Bloomsbury Children's Books (London, England), 2000.
Ian Whybrow, *Three Little Rascals,* Gullane Children's (London, England), 2002.

Marsha Diane Arnold, *The Tail of Little Skunk,* Golden Books (New York, NY), 2002.

Sally Grindley, *The Sulky Vulture,* Bloomsbury Children's Books (London, England), 2002, Bloomsbury Children's Books (New York, NY), 2003.

Shen Roddie, *The Gossipy Parrot* (also see below), Bloomsbury Children's Books (London, England), 2003.

Nicola Grant, *Chameleon's Crazy Colours,* Little Tiger (London, England), 2004.

Peter Blight, *The Lonely Giraffe* (also see below), Bloomsbury Children's Books (London, England), 2004.

Faustin Charles, Shen Roddie, and Peter Blight, *The Selfish Crocodile, and Other Animals* (includes CD; includes *The Gossipy Parrot* and *The Lonely Giraffe*), Bloomsbury Children's Books (London, England), 2006.

Ragnhild Scamell, *Ouch!,* Good Books (Intercourse, PA), 2006.

Vivian French, *Ellie and Elvis,* Bloomsbury Children's Books (London, England), 2006.

Faustin Charles, *The Selfish Crocodile Book of Nursery Rhymes,* Bloomsbury Children's Books (London, England), 2008.

Paul Bright, *Crunch Munch Dinosaur Lunch!,* Little Tiger Press (London, England), 2009.

Iain Smyth, *The Wide-mouthed Frog,* Bloomsbury Children's Books (London, England), 2009.

Paul Bright, *What's More Scary than a Shark?,* Little Tiger Press (London, England), 2010.

Anna Claybourne, *Silly Barney,* Little Tiger Press (London, England), 2011.

Faustin Charles, *The Selfish Crocodile Book of Words* (board book), Bloomsbury Children's Books (London, England), 2012.

Faustin Charles, *The Selfish Crocodile Book of Numbers* (board book), Bloomsbury Children's Books (London, England), 2012.

Contributor to periodicals, including *Observer, Penthouse, TV Times, Telegraph, Time Out,* and London *Times.*

Books featuring Terry's art have been translated into several languages, including Arabic and French.

Sidelights

Michael Terry worked in advertising and illustration art for several years before expanding his focus to include children's book illustration. His first illustration project,

Michael Terry's art brings to life such engaging animal characters as the prickly young hedgehog star of Ragnhild Scammell's **Ouch!** (Illustration copyright © Michael Terry 2006. Reproduced with permission of Little Tiger Press, an imprint of Magi Publications.)

creating art for Ann Jungman's 1994 picture book *Vlad the Drac Goes Travelling,* was followed soon after by a book that has become something of a picture-book classic. With a text by Faustin Charles, *The Selfish Crocodile* focuses on a crocodile that discovers that it is much more fun to share the river with friends than keep it all to himself. In addition to remaining in print for over a decade, *The Selfish Crocodile* has also been published as part of a story anthology as well as expanded as *The Selfish Crocodile Book of Nursery Rhymes* and several concept board books, each featuring what a *Publishers Weekly* contributor characterized as "broadly portrayed animals [that] sport bug eyes and cartoonish grins." Terry's "bright, amusing illustrations add plenty of energy" to *The Selfish Crocodile Book of Nursery Rhymes,* wrote *School Library Journal* contributor Kathy Peihl, while in *Booklist* Helen Rosenberg asserted that the "hilarious, large, bright illustrations" in *The Selfish Crocodile* make the picture book "perfect" for group story-hour sharing.

In his artwork, Terry uses a variety of media, working on stretched water color paper or water color board. Beginning with a pencil sketch, he adds color with gouache, pastels, or colored pencil as he sees fit. When gathering visual material to help him capture what a particular animal looks like, he studies reference books and images on the Internet.

Terry's more-recent illustration projects include stories by such noted children's writers as Vivian French, Ragnhild Scammel, Paul Bright, Dick King-Smith, and Sally Grindley, the last whose picture book *The Sulkey Vulture* inspired a *Kirkus Reviews* critic to predict that "recalcitrant youngsters will recognize themselves" in the author's "hard-to-please hero." "Terry strikes a smooth balance between cartooning and realism" in depicting the animal cast of Grindley's story, asserted a *Publishers Weekly* critic in discussing the same picture book. Bright's *The Lonely Giraffe* is awash with what Andrea Tarr described in *School Library Journal* as "vivid, splashy colors" that radiate toddler appeal, while in Shen Roddie's "arch" retelling of a traditional tale in *The Gossipy Parrot* the artist's focus assures that "even very young viewers will have no trouble" picking up on Roddie's humor, according to a *Kirkus Reviews* writer. "Terry's illustrations are delightful, full of expression and movement, and perfectly suited to" Scamell's hedgehog-themed story in *Ouch!*, according to another *Kirkus Reviews* critic.

In addition to his work with other children's authors, Terry has also created a series of original self-illustrated stories featuring Captain Wag the Pirate Dog. In *Captain Wag the Pirate Dog,* the floppy-eared pirate discovers a treasure map and sails off with best friends Old Scratch and One-Eye Jack to see what they can find. Feline pirate Ginger Tom and his catty crew are determined to capture the treasure first, but ultimately it becomes clear that not everyone views the same things as precious. *Captain Wag and the Big Blue Whale* and *Captain Wag and the Polar Bears* continue the canine pirate's adventures as the sharp-clawed Ginger Tom continues to play the role of arch enemy until adversity prompts cats and dogs to band together. In addition to stories, Terry inspires budding artists with his whimsically titled primer *How to Draw Leprechauns in Simple Steps,* which includes directions for drawing twenty-eight different leprechaun figures, some complete with pots of gold.

Biographical and Critical Sources

PERIODICALS

Booklist, June 1, 1999, Helen Rosenberg, review of *The Selfish Crocodile,* p. 1838.
Kirkus Reviews, November 15, 2002, review of *The Sulky Vulture,* p. 1693; December 15, 2003, review of *The Gossipy Parrot,* p. 1454; May 1, 2006, review of *Ouch!,* p. 466.
Publishers Weekly, March 8, 1999, review of *The Selfish Crocodile,* p. 66; August 23, 1999, review of *Hogsel and Gruntel and Other Animal Stories,* p. 61; November 18, 2002, review of *The Sulky Vulture,* p. 59.
School Library Journal, October, 1999, Sally Bates Goodroe, review of *Hogsel and Gruntel and Other Animal Stories,* p. 117; July, 2005, Andrea Tarr, review of *The Lonely Giraffe,* p. 65; July, 2005, Maryann H. Owen, review of *Ouch!,* p. 87; October, 2009, Kathy Piehl, review of *The Selfish Crocodile Book of Nursery Rhymes,* p. 110.

ONLINE

Great British Life Online, http://kent.greatbritishlife.co.uk/ (September 15, 2011), Sarah Sturt, "Kent Life Meets Michael Terry, Author and Illustrator."
Michael Terry Home Page, http://www.thepaintbrush.co.uk (September 15, 2011).

*   *   *

TOFT, Di 1958-

Personal

Born 1958, in Watford, Hertfordshire, England; married; children: one son, one daughter.

Addresses

Home—Somerset, England. *Agent*—Rogers, Coleridge & White Literary Agents, 20 Powis Mews, London W11 1JN, England.

Career

Writer and librarian. Worked variously in advertising, sales, and editing; Gordano School, Portishead, Somerset, England, school librarian.

Writings

"WOLVEN" MIDDLE-GRADE NOVEL SERIES

Wolven, Chicken House (Frome, England), 2009, Chicken House/Scholastic (New York, NY), 2010.

The Twilight Circus, Chicken House (Frome, England), 2010, Chicken House (New York, NY), 2011.

Bad Wolf Rising, Chicken House (New York, NY), 2011.

Author's books have been translated into several languages, including Chinese, French, German, and Portuguese.

Sidelights

British librarian and author Di Toft channels her love of fantasy in her lighthearted "Wolven" novel series for middle graders. In crafting the series, which includes *Wolven, The Twilight Circus,* and *Bad Wolf Rising,* Toft invented an entire mythology around the creature after which the series is named, even weaving in historical elements from the middle ages to link them to actual

Cover of Di Toft's humorous supernatural-themed picture book **Wolven,** *featuring kid-magnet cover art by Martin Simpson.* (Jacket art © 2009 by Martin Simpson. Reproduced with permission of The Chicken House, an imprint of Scholastic, Inc.)

human history. Traditional werewolves take their human form most of the time and only revert to a wolf during the full moon. For Toft's wolfen, things are reversed: once bitten, they are destined to spend most of their time as a wolf and can only return to their human form when the moon is full.

Although Toft has always enjoyed reading fantasy stories, she did not begin writing until later in life, while working as a school librarian in her native Somerset. When writing for adults proved to be a challenge, she shifted her focus to preteens and based the central canine character of *Wolfen* on her loveable but oversized family dog, an Alsatian named Dave.

Twelve-year-old Nate Carver is the hero of *Wolven,* and he lives with his grandparents in Temple Gurney, a small town that borders a forest where secret government experiments are rumored to occur. Seeking companionship, Nate asks for a dog and is given Woody, a scruffy pup with such a knowing gaze that he seems almost human. When Woody morphs into a human boy one night Nate is not as shocked as he otherwise would be, and he listens with fascination to Woody's story: a member of a werewolf clan whose members were active as far back as the thirteenth century, Woody now needs Nate's help to fight a government scientist named Dr. Gabriel Gruber. Gruber's Proteus Project is headquartered in the nearby forest and is designed to capture and train werewolves such as Woody for military purposes.

When readers catch up with Nate and Woody in *The Twilight Circus,* the friends are traveling with a troupe known as the Twilight Circus of Illusion, all the while being shadowed by Gruber's agents. Although they hope to locate Nate's dad as well as any scattered members of Woody's Wolven clan, boy and wolven discover something far different . . . and far worse: a vampiric black widow spider that is intent on capturing them in her web. Nate has discovered that he also has wolven blood in *Bad Wolf Rising,* and now he shares Woody's fears of being captured by the evil Gruber. As the scientist marshals a band of vicious werewolves, the friends know that they are running out of time and options. Soon they discover that the past may hold the key to helping them stop the building threat to both the Wolven and human populations.

Reviewing the first "Wolven" novel in *School Library Journal,* Donna Rosenblum wrote that Toft's "hair-raising adventure" features a "fresh perspective on werewolf lore" and serves up "a satisfying read with a fly-off-the-shelves cover." *Wolven* mixes "magic and slapstick into a madcap scramble" that should entertain preteen fantasy fans, according to a *Kirkus Reviews* writer, and a *Publishers Weekly* critic cited the story's entertaining mix of "fun action sequences, over-the-top villains, . . . and some intriguing magic."

Biographical and Critical Sources

PERIODICALS

Bristol Evening Post (Bristol, England), June 9, 2010, David Clensy, "Librarian Starts New Chapter as Author."

Kirkus Reviews, May 1, 2010, review of *Wolven.*

Publishers Weekly, May 31, 2010, review of *Wolven,* p. 48.

School Library Journal, August, 2010, Donna Rosenblum, review of *Wolven,* p. 114.

ONLINE

Kidsread Web site, http://www.kidsread.com/ (June, 2010), interview with Toft.*

*   *   *

VENABLE, Colleen A.F. 1980-

Personal

Born 1980, in NY. *Education:* Wagner College, B.A. (English and studio art).

Addresses

Home—New York, NY.

Career

Graphic designer, playwright, photographer, and author. First Second Books, New York, NY, art and design editor. Children's Book Council, former programs associate. Presenter at schools and festivals.

Awards, Honors

CYBILS Award finalist, and 100 Titles for Reading and Sharing selection, New York Public Library, both 2010, both for *Hamster and Cheese.*

Writings

"GUINEA PIG, PET SHOP PRIVATE EYE" GRAPHIC-CHAPTER-BOOK SERIES

Hamster and Cheese, illustrated by Stephanie Yue, Graphic Universe (Minneapolis, MN), 2010.

And Then There Were Gnomes, illustrated by Stephanie Yue, Graphic Universe (Minneapolis, MN), 2010.

The Ferret's a Foot, illustrated by Stephanie Yue, Graphic Universe (Minneapolis, MN), 2011.

Fish You Were Here, illustrated by Stephanie Yue, Graphic Universe (Minneapolis, MN), 2011.

Creator of Web comic "Fluff in Brooklyn," 2004-07. Contributor of book reviews to *Hybridmagazine.com.*

Sidelights

Colleen A.F. Venable teams up with sequential artist Stephanie Yue to create the engaging "Guinea Pig, Pet Shop Private Eye" stories. Modeled on the popular graphic-novel format, Venable's stories are designed to attract beginning readers with their cuddly rodent characters, word play, and simple-reading texts. The series begins with *Hamster and Cheese* and the lighthearted humor continues in *And Then There Were Gnomes, The Ferret's a Foot,* and *Fish You Were Here.*

Venable was raised in upstate New York, and at Staten Island's Wagner College she earned a double major in English and studio art while also seeing several of her plays produced. A fan of comic strips such as "Calvin and Hobbes" and "The Far Side," Venable began channeling her creativity in a similar direction, merging photos of friends with drawings of stuffed animals in the quirky Web comic "Fluff in Brooklyn" between 2004 and 2007. In her day job, she now works at New York City-based comic-book publisher First Second Books, where her title of art and design editor encompasses responsibility for everything from book covers and logos to catalogue copy and design, copy proofing, and the hiring of freelance artists and writers. "And my night job is writing graphic novels about a . . . hyperactive hamster named Hamisher," Venable quipped on her home page. "The world is a very lovely place."

The aforementioned hyperactive Hamisher is the energy behind Venable's "Guinea Pig, Pet Shop Private Eye" books, and he and costar, Sasspants the Guinea Pig, are introduced in *Hamster and Cheese.* The story takes place in Mr. Venezi's pet shop, where the absentminded store owner has attached incorrect names to several animal cages. Persnickety and reclusive Sasspants is fortunate: her sign reads "GUINEA PIG," . . . until the final letter falls off. When Mr. Venezi's sandwiches start to disappear, Hamisher becomes excited about the prospect of discovering the culprit. When he sees the sign "GUINEA PI", Hamisher begs Sasspants to put down her book and help him in his sleuthing. Other volumes in the "Guinea Pig, Pet Shop Private Eye" series include *And Then There Were Gnomes,* in which caged mice begin to disappear without a trace; *The Ferret's a Foot,* in which a crazy new resident throws the pet shop into chaos; and *Fish You Were Here,* in which an efficient new assistant prompts the beloved Mr. Venezi to take an extended vacation.

Reviewing Venable's first "Guinea Pig, Pet Shop Private Eye" book, Kat Kan predicted in *Booklist* that fans "will appreciate the zaniness of the pet shop and the fun mystery." "Children will love Sasspants," exclaimed *School Library Journal* critic Marilyn Ackerman, the critic adding of *Hamster and Cheese* that Yue's "full-

color cartoons enhance the comic appeal." Appraising *And Then There Were Gnomes,* a *Publishers Weekly* contributor concluded of the book that "everything about it could be described as cute, from the art to the characters' personalities."

Biographical and Critical Sources

PERIODICALS

Booklist, March 15, 2010, Kat Kan, review of *Hamster and Cheese,* p. 62.

Publishers Weekly, April 5, 2010, review of *Hamster and Cheese,* p. 64; September 6, 2010, review of *And Then There Were Gnomes,* p. 43.

School Library Journal, May, 2010, Marilyn Ackerman, review of *Hamster and Cheese,* p. 143.

ONLINE

Colleen A.F. Venable Home Page, http://www.colleenaf. com (September 15, 2011).

Colleen A.F. Venable Web log, http://colleenaf.livejournal. com (September 15, 2011).

Daily Crosshatch Online, http://thedailycrosshatch.com/ (April 20, 2010), interview with Venable.*

W-Z

WALLACE, Rich 1957-

Personal

Born January 29, 1957, in Hackensack, NJ; married (divorced, 1996); married Sandra Neil Wallace (a writer), 2000; children: two sons. *Education:* Montclair State College (now University), B.A., 1980. *Hobbies and other interests:* Track and field.

Addresses

Home—NH. *E-mail*—richxw@aol.com.

Career

Writer. *Herald News,* Passaic, NJ, editorial assistant, 1978-79; sports reporter, 1979-82; *Daily Advance,* Dover, NJ, sports editor, 1982-84, news editor, 1984-85; *Trenton Times,* Trenton, NJ, copy editor, 1985-86, assistant city editor, 1986-87; *Highlights for Children* magazine, copy editor, 1988-90, assistant editor, 1990-92, coordinating editor, 1992-98, senior editor, beginning 1998. Highlights Foundation, Boyds Mills, PA, writing instructor.

Awards, Honors

Best Books for Young Adults selection, American Library Association (ALA), and ALA Quick Pick for Reluctant Young-Adult Readers selection, both 1997, both for *Wrestling Sturbridge;* ALA Best Books for Young Adults selection, ALA Quick Pick for Reluctant Young-Adult Readers selection, and Books for the Teen Age selection, New York Public Library, all 2001, all for *Playing without the Ball;* Books for the Teen Age selection, New York Public Library, 2004, for *Restless;* ALA Best Books for Young Adults selection, 2008, for *One Good Punch.*

Writings

Wrestling Sturbridge, Knopf (New York, NY), 1996.
Shots on Goal, Knopf (New York, NY), 1997.

Rich Wallace (Reproduced by permission.)

Playing without the Ball: A Novel in Four Quarters, Knopf (New York, NY), 2000.
Losing Is Not an Option (short stories), Knopf (New York, NY), 2003.
Restless: A Ghost's Story, Viking (New York, NY), 2003.
One Good Punch, Knopf (New York, NY), 2007.
Dishes, Viking (New York, NY), 2008.
Perpetual Check, Knopf (New York, NY), 2009.
Sports Camp, Knopf (New York, NY), 2010.
War and Watermelon, Viking (New York, NY), 2011.

Contributor to anthologies, including *Lost and Found: Award-winning Authors Sharing Real-life Experiences through Fiction,* edited by M. Jerry Weiss and Helen S. Weiss, 2000; *On the Edge: Stories at the Brink,* edited by Lois Duncan, 2000; *One Hot Second: Stories about Desire,* edited by Cathy Young, 2002; *Guys Write for Guys Read,* edited by Jon Scieszka, 2005; and *Dreams and Visions: Fourteen Flights of Fantasy,* edited by Weiss and Weiss, 2006. Contributor to periodicals, including *ALAN Review, Highlights for Children, Runner's World,* and *Track and Field News.*

"WINNING SEASON" NOVEL SERIES

The Roar of the Crowd, Viking (New York, NY), 2004.

Technical Foul, Viking (New York, NY), 2004.

Fast Company, Viking (New York, NY), 2004.

Double Fake, Viking (New York, NY), 2005.

Emergency Quarterback, Viking (New York, NY), 2005.

Southpaw, Viking (New York, NY), 2006.

Dunk under Pressure, Viking (New York, NY), 2006.

Takedown, Viking (New York, NY), 2006.

Curveball, Viking (New York, NY), 2007.

Second-string Center, Viking (New York, NY), 2007.

"KICKERS" CHAPTER-BOOK SERIES

The Ball Hogs, illustrated by Jimmy Holder, Knopf (New York, NY), 2010.

Fake Out, illustrated by Jimmy Holder, Knopf (New York, NY), 2010.

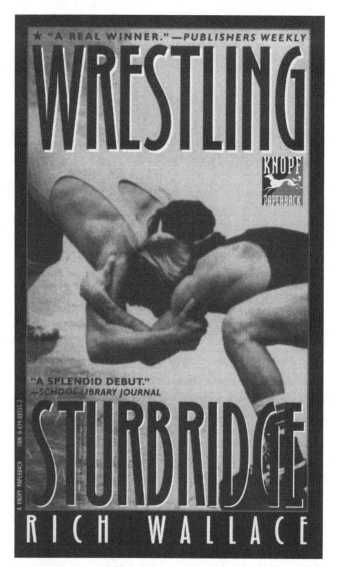

Cover of Wallace's sports-themed novel Wrestling Sturbridge, *featuring artwork by Scott Hunt.* (Illustration copyright © 1996 by Alfred A. Knopf. Reproduced by permission of Alfred A. Knopf, an imprint of Random House, Inc.)

Benched, illustrated by Jimmy Holder, Knopf (New York, NY), 2010.

Game-day Jitters, illustrated by Jimmy Holder, Knopf (New York, NY), 2011.

Adaptations

Wrestling Sturbridge was adapted as an audiobook, Recorded Books, 1996. *Shots on Goal* was adapted as an audiobook, Recorded Books, 1998.

Sidelights

In his young-adult novels *Wrestling Sturbridge, Southpaw,* and *Perpetual Check* Rich Wallace uses "the metaphors of sports to explore universal themes of emerging adulthood and self-definition," according to *Horn Book* reviewer Maeve Visser Knoth. "I look for the universal in the very specific," Wallace explained in an essay for the *St. James Guide to Young-Adult Writers.* "The moment of self-examination in the seconds before an athletic event, the painful truth in being rejected by a love interest, the sobering idea that a kid might be more mature than one of his parents." Wallace also deals with sports themes in his books for a younger audience, such as his "Kickers" chapter-book series about a coed youth soccer team.

Raised in Hackensack, New Jersey, as one of six children born to college-educated parents, Wallace began writing as a first grader. Academics were not his strong suit, however; he found school to be dull and he did not read much beyond what was required for classes from sixth grade until after college. As a teenager, Wallace was primarily interested in sports, especially track and cross country.

During high school Wallace began writing extensively, keeping a diary in which he poured out his emotions. He also gained valuable experience by working on his school newspaper. His evolution as a writer continued at New Jersey's Montclair State College, where he took creative-writing classes, including one that required him to pen an entire novel, one chapter per week. He also interned at the *Passaic Herald-News,* where he was eventually offered a paid writing and reporting position. Although Wallace left college just two credits short of a degree, he returned a couple of years later and completed the two physical education courses he needed to earn his B.A.

In 1980 Wallace reworked the novel that he had started in his creative-writing class and sent it to publishers, where it was consistently rejected. Meanwhile, he continued his eight-year newspaper career, working variously as a sports reporter, news editor, and assistant city editor at a variety of New Jersey newspapers. He also married and became a father to two boys. In 1988, he began working for *Highlights for Children* as a copy editor and eventually moved on to senior editor, where publishing well-written stories became his passion. When he completed a story that he knew had promise,

Wallace sent the manuscript to a Philomel editor who had offered him constructive comments while rejecting his first manuscript years before. The editor suggested several changes and in 1996 *Wrestling Sturbridge* was published to critical acclaim.

Wrestling Sturbridge is the story of Ben, a high-school senior and varsity wrestler who tires of being practice fodder for Al, his teammate and close friend. Faced with a bleak future in a dead-end town, Ben decides to challenge for Al's spot on the squad despite the fact that Al is a top contender for the state title. Ben also begins a romance with the intelligent, tough-minded Kim, who believes in Ben more than he believes in himself. "Wallace isn't writing a sports fairy story," a *Publishers Weekly* contributor declared in a review of *Wrestling Sturbridge,* and in *Horn Book* Maeve Visser Knoth wrote that the book "strong portrait of a smothering small town and the hopelessness that it engenders in an adolescent." "Anyone even remotely curious about small-town America need look no further than this exemplary first novel," stated a *Publishers Weekly* critic in praise of Wallace's book. Ben "tells the story in a spare way appropriate to his undemonstrative, nonverbal nature," a *Kirkus Reviews* critic wrote, "recording fast and furious wrestling action, the steady burn of his own anger and frustration, and brief but telling glimpses of the people around him." *Wrestling Sturbridge* "is about young people who care about life and about keeping promises they've made to themselves and others," Ken Donelson concluded in the *St. James Guide to Young-Adult Writers.* "It is a rare sports story because there is no super-hero and no villain."

Wallace also sets *Shots on Goal* in Sturbridge, but her he moves the action to the soccer field. A critic in *Kirkus Reviews* declared that the author "flattens the sophomore jinx in this taut, present-tense tale of an underdog high-school soccer team battling internal dissension." The instigators of this internal dissension are Barry "Bones" Austin and his best friend, Joey. Bones realizes that he is stuck in second place, not only on the soccer field, where he is the team's second-best player after Joey, but also at home, where his older brother, Tommy, is the favored son of their parents. Tension arises when Bones' object of desire, Shannon, begins dating Joey. Bones also grows resentful of Joey's increasingly selfish behavior on the field. As the soccer season rolls on, "a face-off between the two teens" occurs, as *Booklist* critic Frances Bradburn stated, the critic adding that each boy is "striving to find his own identity without the other, in spite of the other." The face-off finally comes to an end in *Shots on Goal* after "the two friends square off in a fight that makes both aware how important their soccer team and their friendship are," according to Donelson.

Like *Wrestling Sturbridge, Shots on Goal* earned praise for its fully developed characters and exciting action. Dina Sherman, writing in *School Library Journal,* maintained that the "situations and emotions that Bones ex-

Soccer is the focus of Wallace's high-energy novel Shots on Goal, *featuring artwork by Jim Erickson.* (Copyright © 1997 by Alfred A. Knopf. Used by permission of Alfred A. Knopf Children's Books, a division of Random House, Inc.)

periences are all very real, and young people will relate to them." A critic for the *Bulletin of the Center for Children's Books* added that "the soccer matches are fast, the interaction with girls unromantically realistic, and the voice is engaging, as Bones tells his story as a rueful eyewitness account."

In *Playing without the Ball: A Novel in Four Quarters* Wallace again invites readers to enter the world of high-school sports in Sturbridge. Jay is a seventeen-year-old basketball player who supports himself by working part-time in a bar while also living upstairs from his job. After Jay is cut from the high-school team he joins a YMCA squad that offers him the competitive outlet he needs. He also develops a relationship with Spit, the female lead singer in a punk band that often performs at the bar. According to *School Library Journal* contributor Jack Forman, *Playing without the Ball* "has a lot to say about friendship, independence, and self-realization." A *Publishers Weekly* reviewer praised Wallace's well-written game sequences, adding that, "with equal

skill, the author limns the resilient Jay and his realistically awkward and tentative forays into romance."

A seventeen-year-old athlete encounters a supernatural being in *Restless: A Ghost's Story.* While running through a graveyard late one night, Herbie senses that an unusual presence is following him. Intrigued, he returns again and again to the cemetery and eventually meets the spirit of a young man named Eamon. Herbie eventually comes to believe that he has also contacted the ghost of his older brother, Frank, who died ten years earlier and serves as the book's narrator. According to Donna M. Knott in *School Library Journal,* Herbie, Eamon, and Frank "are intertwined in a search for an understanding of one another's experiences in life and in death and how to move on from them." In *Restless,* as *Kliatt* reviewer Paula Rohrlick observed, Wallace "raises interesting questions about an afterlife."

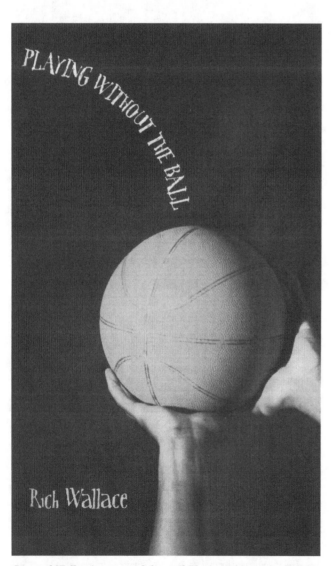

Cover of Wallace's young-adult novel **Playing without the Ball,** *in which a teen gains a new understanding of teamwork after moving from a high-profile school team to playing with members of the local* **YMCA.** (Cover illustration copyright © 2000 by Laurel-Leaf, an imprint of Random House Children's Books, a division of Random House, Inc. Used by permission of Laurel-Leaf, an imprint of Random House Children's Books, a division of Random House, Inc.)

In his short novel *One Good Punch* Wallace introduces Michael Kerrigan, a high-school senior who is gunning for a track scholarship. A straight arrow, Michael takes on a part-time job as an editorial assistant, writing obituaries for the local newspaper. When police discover marijuana stashed in Michael's school locker, the senior is faced with expulsion and must decide whether to reveal the identity of the friend who hid these drugs in his locker or accept a punishment that may end his dream of attending college. "Wallace's sobering novel is as quick and tight as a taut jab and packs about as much heft," Ian Chipman wrote in *Booklist,* and Rohrlick praised the author's skill in "conveying the experience and importance of sports in a teenage boy's life."

A restless nineteen year old tries to connect with his absentee father in *Dishes,* a departure of sorts for Wallace. Living in Ogunquit, Maine, an oceanfront resort town that caters to gay tourists, college dropout Danny takes a job at Dishes, a gay bar that also employs his father, Jack, as a bartender. Jack was only seventeen when Danny was born, and he still lives recklessly and aimlessly, as Danny finds out when the two decide to share an apartment. Although he is straight, Danny begins to make friends with the patrons and staff at Dishes, among them a cute waitress named Mercy, and this social network offers him opportunities for growth that his father cannot provide. A contributor in *Publishers Weekly* remarked that in *Dishes* Wallace "looks beneath stereotypes about gays and teen fatherhood as he shares Danny's induction into a new subculture." Rohrlick predicted that mature readers "will appreciate the accurate portrait of a young man trying to sort out his emotional life, seeking love and finally finding it."

The game of chess is at the heart of *Perpetual Check,* a slim novel that is told from the alternating points of view of two dissimilar brothers. High-school senior Zeke Mansfield, whose aggressive nature mirrors that of his father, shares little in common with his younger, laid-back brother Randy save for their love of chess. During an intense weekend of competition at a regional chess tournament, the siblings meet meet in a semifinal match that helps them gain a greater appreciation of each other's strengths and weaknesses. "Wallace cleverly positions Randy and Zeke for a win-win conclusion in this satisfying, engaging, and deceptively simple story," Joel Shoemaker commented in a *School Library Journal* review of the novel, and *Booklist* critic Todd Morning described *Perpetual Check* as "a fascinating study of two fully formed characters."

Inspired by Wallace's childhood experiences, *Sports Camp* introduces Riley Liston, a sensitive eleven year old from Jersey City who spends two weeks in the backwoods of Pennsylvania, engaged in heated summer-camp contests at Camp Olympia. Smaller and less skilled than most of the other campers, the optimistic and determined Riley earns the admiration of his cabinmates as they pursue the Big Joe Trophy, named after a legendary snapping turtle that purportedly haunts the

Wallace focuses his sports-themed story in **The Ball Hogs** ***on younger readers with the help of Jimmy Holder's art.*** (Illustration copyright © 2010 by Jimmy Holder. Used by permission of Alfred A. Knopf, an imprint of Random House Children's Books, a division of Random House, Inc.)

camp's lake. "The tale sticks fairly close to realism, allowing Riley to win and lose," remarked a contributor in *Kirkus Reviews*. Morning also offered praise for *Sports Camp*, noting that "the exciting, tightly written sports passages will keep kids turning the pages." "Wallace has a talent for capturing adolescent boys' behavior," reported *School Library Journal* critic Kim Dare, the reviewer adding that *Sports Camp* "has appeal."

The Roar of the Crowd, the first of Wallace's "Winning Season" series for middle-grade readers, is set in Hudson City, New Jersey, and concerns sixth-grader Manny Ramos. A short, scrawny football player, Manny's mistakes cost his team a win and land him on the bench. The speedy Manny never loses heart, however, and when he gets another chance to prove himself, he makes the most of his opportunity. Reviewing *The Roar of the Crowd* in *School Library Journal*, Kate Kohlbeck remarked that "this story conveys an all-important message about perseverance and making the most of one's strengths."

The "Winning Season" series continues in *Technical Foul*, as a talented but hot-headed basketball player named Jared learns to rely on his teammates when his squad falls into a slump. Ilene Cooper, reviewing the novel in *Booklist*, noted that "most of the text is play-by-play action, which will engage young sports fans." *Dunk under Pressure*, a sequel to *Technical Foul*, centers on Jared's teammate, Cornell "Dunk" Duncan. When the team advances to the state finals, Cornell, a sharp-shooting reserve, must come off the bench to hit a clutch free throw. According to *School Library Journal* contributor Sharon R. Pearce, in *Dunk under Pressure* "Wallace offers a good portrayal of sixth-grade boys and team dynamics." In *Second-string Center*, another book in the series, Wallace focuses on the relationship between Jared, the starter on his seventh-grade team, and Cornell, his backup. When Jared's play starts to suffer because of his parents' divorce, Cornell offers his sympathy and support and the team gets back to its winning ways. A contributor in *Kirkus Reviews* described *Second-string Center* as "a strong choice" for readers interested in sports.

In *Takedown*, another title in the "Winning Season" series, seventh-grader Donald Jenkins must learn to harness his anger and aggression before he can earn a win on the wrestling mat. *Southpaw* concerns Jimmy Fleming, who moves from rural Pennsylvania to Hudson City after his parents' divorce. Pressured by his father to succeed but faced with a mounting series of losses, Jimmy must turn to his new teammates for encouragement. Comparing Wallace's novel to the sports stories of Matt Christopher, *Booklist* contributor John Peters called *Southpaw* an "uplifting entry" in the series.

Wallace's "Kickers" series of soccer tales features illustrations by Jimmy Holder and also targets young readers. In *The Ball Hogs* nine-year-old Ben joins his first soccer team, the Bobcats, which also includes good friend Erin as well as Ben's nemesis, Mark, a brash, boastful fourth grader who refuses to share the ball. Convinced that Mark's showboating is costing him a chance to showcase his own talents, Ben gradually realizes that the Bobcats' best chance for a victory depends on his ability to share the spotlight. According to *Booklist* reviewer Carolyn Phelan, *The Ball Hogs* presents "realistic scenes on the field, at home, and at school."

The Bobcats' march to the playoffs continues in *Fake Out*, the second chapter book in the "Kickers" series. As he becomes more comfortable on the field, Ben decides to add an especially difficult move to his soccer repertoire. Unfortunately, he loses control of the ball during an important game, and after suffering the resultant crisis of confidence learns to refocus his energies. "Readers who look for play-by-play action will relish" these titles, observed Blair Christolon in *School Library Journal*.

In *Benched* Ben's troubles at home affect his behavior at the schoolyard as well as his play on the soccer field,

leading to a suspension from the team. Phelan complimented Wallace's ability to make the sports scenes in this "Kickers" installment "as readable as those set at home and at school."

Wallace turns to the short-story form in *Losing Is Not an Option,* a collection of nine interconnected tales that focus on Ron, a student athlete growing up in a small, working-class Pennsylvania town. Many of the stories "are filled with subtlety and ambiguity, offering snapshots of the protagonist at various points of his teenage life," wrote Todd Morning in *School Library Journal.* In "Night Game," for example, an adolescent Ron realizes that his best friend has left him behind, while "I Voted for Mary Ann" finds Ron coping with the death of his beloved grandfather. In the title story, the boy, now a high-school senior, competes for the state track championship. Although a *Publishers Weekly* critic noted that not all of the tales are equally successful, "together they powerfully render an athlete's coming of age." According to *Booklist* contributor Michael Cart, the best stories in *Losing Is Not an Option* "have a wonderful emotional integrity and remind readers that Wallace is a writer to watch."

In his fiction, Wallace hopes to offer an honest representation of how adolescent boys struggle to find their identity. Critics agree that his novels resonate with his fans; as Donelson stated in the *St. James Guide to Young-Adult Writers,* "It's safe to say that many readers . . . await whatever Wallace has to offer." For his part, Wallace intends to continue writing for young adults. As he remarked in an essay on the Random House Web site, "I wonder sometimes if I'll ever move away from my teenage years, in either direction, and write about little kids or adults. There's this fiery orb of matter centered on the years from fifteen to eighteen, and I don't think it will expire in my lifetime."

Biographical and Critical Sources

BOOKS

St. James Guide to Young-Adult Writers, St. James Press (Detroit, MI), 1999.

PERIODICALS

Booklist, September 1, 1996, Debbie Carton, review of *Wrestling Sturbridge,* p. 128; September 15, 1997, Frances Bradburn, review of *Shots on Goal,* p. 224; September 1, 1998, Sally Estes, review of *Shots on Goal,* p. p. 119; September 1, 2000, Frances Bradburn, review of *Playing without the Ball: A Novel in Four Quarters,* p. 116; September 1, 2001, Gillian Engberg, review of *Playing without the Ball,* p. 101; August, 2003, Michael Cart, review of *Losing Is Not an Option,* p. 1973; September 1, 2004, Ilene Cooper,

reviews of *Roar of the Crowd* and *Technical Foul,* both p. 111; February 15, 2006, John Peters, review of *Southpaw,* p. 92; September 1 2007, Ian Chipman, review of *One Good Punch,* p. 131; January 1, 2009, Todd Morning, review of *Perpetual Check,* p. 71; March 1, 2010, Todd Morning, review of *Sports Camp,* p. 74; May 15, 2010, Carolyn Phelan, review of *The Ball Hogs,* p. 38; January 1, 2011, Carolyn Phelan, review of *Benched,* p. 106.

Bulletin of the Center for Children's Books, December, 1997, review of *Shots on Goal,* pp. 143-144.

Horn Book, November-December, 1996, Mave Visser Knoth, review of *Wrestling Sturbridge,* p. 747; November, 1997, Susan P. Bloom, review of *Shots on Goal,* p. 687; November, 2000, Susan P. Bloom, review of *Playing without the Ball,* p. 763.

Kirkus Reviews, May 15, 1996, review of *Wrestling Sturbridge,* p. 752; July 15, 1997, review of *Shots on Goal,* p. 1118; July 1, 2003, review of *Losing Is Not an Option,* p. 916; August 1, 2003, review of *Restless: A Ghost's Story,* p. 1025; September 15, 2007, review of *One Good Punch;* September 15, 2008, review of *Dishes;* January 1, 2009, review of *Perpetual Check;* March 1, 2010, review of *Sports Camp;* May 15, 2010, review of *The Ball Hogs.*

Kliatt, November, 2002, Claire Rosser, review of *Playing without the Ball,* p. 22; September, 2003, Paula Rohrlick, review of *Restless,* p. 14; March, 2006, Annette Wells, review of *Losing Is Not an Option,* p. 33; September, 2007, Paula Rohrlick, review of *One Good Punch,* p. 19; November, 2008, Paula Rohrlick, review of *Dishes,* p. 19.

Publishers Weekly, June 3, 1996, review of *Wrestling Sturbridge,* p. 84; July 1, 1996, Heather Vogel Frederick, "Flying Starts: Six Children's Book Newcomers Share Thoughts on Their Debut Projects," pp. 34-37; August 21, 2000, review of *Playing without the Ball,* p. 74; August 18, 2003, review of *Losing Is Not an Option,* p. 80; October 6, 2008, review of *Dishes,* p. 55.

Quill & Quire, June 14, 2010, review of *The Ball Hogs,* p. 52.

School Library Journal, November, 1997, Dina Sherman, review of *Shots on Goal,* pp. 124-125; October, 2000, Jack Forman, review of *Playing without the Ball,* p. 173; September, 2003, Todd Morning, review of *Losing Is Not an Option,* p. 222; November, 2003, Donna M. Knott, review of *Restless,* p. 150; March, 2004, Andrew Medlar, review of *Losing Is Not an Option,* p. 69; September, 2004, Kate Kohlbeck, review of *The Roar of the Crowd,* p. 219; October, 2004, Michael Giller, review of *Technical Foul,* p. 181; March, 2006, Kara Schaff Dean, review of *Southpaw,* p. 232; June, 2006, Sharon R. Pearce, review of *Dunk under Pressure,* p. 167; December, 2006, Michael Giller, review of *Takedown,* p. 158; January, 2009, Natasha Forrester, review of *Dishes,* p. 121; February, 2009, Joel Shoemaker, review of *Perpetual Check,* p. 112; April, 2010, Kim Dare, review of *Sports Camp,* p. 170; September, 2010, Blair Christolon, reviews of *The Ball Hogs* and *Fake Out,* both p. 135.

ONLINE

Random House Web site, http://www.randomhouse.com/ (January 1, 2009), "Rich Wallace."

Rich Wallace Home Page, http://www.richwallacebooks. com (August 1, 2011).*

*   *   *.

WATSON, Renée 1978-

Personal

Born July 29, 1978, in Paterson, NJ. *Education:* The New School, B.A. (creative writing) and drama therapy certificate.

Addresses

Home—New York, NY. *E-mail*—renee@reneewatson. net.

Career

Author, poet, educator, and performer.

Awards, Honors

Named New Voice for 2010, Independent Children's Booksellers Association, for *What Momma Left Me.*

Writings

A Place Where Hurricanes Happen, illustrated by Shadra Strickland, Random House (New York, NY), 2010.
What Momma Left Me (novel), Bloomsbury (New York, NY), 2010.

Harlem's Little Blackbird: The Story of Florence Mills (novel), illustrated by Christian Robinson, Bloomsbury (New York, NY), 2012.

Author of one-woman show *Roses Are Red, Women Are Blue,* produced at Lincoln Center, New York, NY. Contributor of poetry and articles to periodicals, including *Rethinking Schools.*

Sidelights

A writer, educator, and performer who teaches poetry and theater to middle school and high school students, Renée Watson is the author of *A Place Where Hurricanes Happen,* a critically acclaimed picture book set in New Orleans, Louisiana, and *What Momma Left Me,* an award-winning young-adult novel. "My stories naturally center around children and teenagers," she remarked in a *Brown Bookshelf* online interview, adding: "The pains and joys of adolescents are moments I witness on a daily basis, so their stories are always with me as I write. Also, for me, the lives of children and teens are interesting—they are always changing. There's just so much to sort through. All of this makes for good plots and complex characters."

Illustrated by Shadra Strickland, *A Place Where Hurricanes Happen* concerns the aftermath of Hurricane Katrina, a devastating storm that hit the U.S. Gulf Coast on August 29, 2005, toppling levees in New Orleans and leaving catastrophic damage in its wake. Watson's narrative centers on four neighbors—Adrienne, Michael, Keesha, and Tommy—whose lives are dramatically altered by Katrina. Michael witnesses the power of the storm while hiding in his attic; Keesha, after spending

Renee Watson tells a dramatic story with the help of Shadra Strickland's evocative art in her picture book **A Place Where Hurricanes Happen.** (Illustration copyright © 2010 by Shadra Strickland. Reproduced with permission of Random House Children's Books, a division of Random House, Inc.)

five days in the Superdome awaiting rescue, now lives in a trailer; and Adrienne and Tommy ultimately relocate to new cities with their families. "Both the words and pictures personalize the events," Hazel Rochman noted in *Booklist,* and a critic in *Kirkus Reviews* observed that the author realistically portrays "the impact of the hurricane on people's lives." Writing in *School Library Journal,* Judith Constantinides remarked that *A Place Where Hurricanes Happen* "beautifully encapsulates the story of the tragedy in words and pictures that children can understand, without dwelling on the horror," and a *Publishers Weekly* contributor cited a reunion scene at the book's end while noting that, "although Watson's story delivers some difficult emotional blows, it has plenty of sweetness, too."

In *What Momma Left Me* thirteen-year-old Serenity and younger brother Danny are taken in by their grandparents after their mother is killed and their father skips town. As she copes with her loss, Serenity must also adjust to a new neighborhood, school, and church, where she joins the youth ministry and makes friends with a trustworthy, supportive girl. She also worries about her brother's future after Danny begins to associate with some unsavory characters. "Serenity's struggles and insights . . . are inspiring, authentic, and told in a straightforward yet poetic style," according to a reviewer in *Publishers Weekly,* and Stephanie Malosh reported in *School Library Journal* that the novel's "overall message of staying true to one's self is strong and reassuring." According to *Voice of Youth Advocates* contributor Lynne Farrell Stover, Watson "is a natural storyteller, weaving the details of the daily life of an extended African American family into a complex and often unjust society" in *What Momma Left Me.*

Biographical and Critical Sources

PERIODICALS

Booklist, May 1, 2010, Carolyn Phelan, review of *What Momma Left Me,* p. 87; May 15, 2010, Hazel Rochman, review of *A Place Where Hurricanes Happen,* p. 38.

Kirkus Reviews, May 1, 2010, review of *A Place Where Hurricanes Happen.*

Oregonian, June 16, 2010, Jeff Baker, "Jefferson High Alum Renee Watson Finds Literary Success in New York."

Publishers Weekly, May 31, 2010, review of *A Place Where Hurricanes Happen,* p. 47; June 28, 2010, review of *What Momma Left Me,* p. 129.

School Library Journal, June, 2010, Judith Constantinides, review of *A Place Where Hurricanes Happen,* p. 86; August, 2010, Stephanie Malosh, review of *What Momma Left Me,* p. 115.

Voice of Youth Advocates, August, 2010, Lynne Farrell Stover, review of *What Momma Left Me,* p. 258.

ONLINE

Brown Bookshelf Web site, http://thebrownbookshelf.com/ (February 5, 2011), Tameka Fryar Brown, interview with Watson.

Cynsations Web log, http://cynthialeitichsmith.blogspot. com/ (January 27, 2011), Renée Watson, "Writing about Serious Topics in Children's Books."

Reading Local Portland Online, http://portland.reading local.com/ (June 21, 2010), Amy Baskin, interview with Watson.

Reneé Watson Home Page, http://www.reneewatson.net (August 1, 2011).

*   *   *

WINDLING, Terri 1958-
(Bellamy Bach, a joint pseudonym)

Personal

Born 1958, in Fort Dix, NJ; married Howard Gayton (a dramatist), 2008; children: (stepdaughter) Victoria Gayton. *Education:* Attended Antioch University; studied in London, England, and Dublin, Ireland.

Addresses

Home—Devon, England. *E-mail*—TheEndicottStudio@ gmail.com.

Career

Editor, author, artist, and illustrator. Ace Books/Grosset & Dunlap, New York, NY, editorial assistant, beginning 1979, became associate editor, then fantasy editor, then senior editor, executive editor, 1984-86; affiliated with Armadillo Press, New York, NY, 1985-86; Tor Books, New York, NY, consulting editor, 1986—. Endicott Studio, founder, Boston, MA, 1987-91, then Devon, England, and Tucson, AZ, beginning 1991. Endicott West, cofounder, 2001. Founder and coeditor, with Midori Snyder, of *Journal of Mythic Arts,* 1997-2008. Mythic Imagination Institute, advisory board member; judge, World Fantasy Awards, 1985. *Exhibitions;* Paintings exhibited in museums and galleries, both nationally and internationally, including at Boston Museum of Fine Arts, West Virginia Museum of Art, Words and Pictures Museum, Book Arts Gallery, Mythic Garden (England), Abbaye Daoulas (France), and University of Arizona.

Member

Interstitial Arts Foundation.

Awards, Honors

World Fantasy Award for Best Anthology (with Mark Alan Arnold), 1982, for *Elsewhere;* World Fantasy Award for Best Anthology (with Ellen Datlow), 1989,

for *The Year's Best Fantasy: First Annual Collection;* World Fantasy Special Award for Editing, 1989; World Fantasy Award for Best Anthology (with Datlow), 1990, for *The Year's Best Fantasy: Second Annual Collection;* World Fantasy Award for Best Anthology (with Datlow), 1992, for *The Year's Best Fantasy and Horror: Fourth Annual Collection;* Tiptree Award shortlist, 1995, for *The Armless Maiden, and Other Tales for Childhood's Survivors;* Mythopoeic Award for Best Novel of the Year, 1997, for *The Wood Wife;* World Fantasy Award for Best Anthology (with Datlow), 2000, for *Silver Birch, Blood Moon;* Bram Stoker Award for Best Anthology (with Datlow), Horror Writers Association, 2000, for *The Year's Best Fantasy and Horror: Thirteenth Annual Collection;* World Fantasy Award for Best Anthology (with Datlow), 2003, for *The Green Man;* World Fantasy Award for Best Anthology (with Datlow), 2007, for *Salon Fantastique;* World Fantasy Special Award (with Midori Snyder), 2008, for Endicott Studios Web site; Soltice Award, Science Fiction and Fantasy Writers of America, 2010, for outstanding contributions to the speculative fiction field.

Writings

NOVELS

The Changeling (for children), Random House (New York, NY), 1995.

The Wood Wife, Tor Books (New York, NY), 1996.

A Midsummer Night's Faery Tale, illustrated with dolls created by Wendy Froud, photographs by John Lawrence Jones with sets and photographic art direction by Brian Froud, Simon & Schuster (New York, NY), 1999.

(With Ellen Steiber) *The Raven Queen,* Random House (New York, NY), 1999.

The Winter Child, illustrated with dolls created by Wendy Froud, photographs by John Lawrence Jones with sets and photographic art direction by Brian Froud, Simon & Schuster (New York, NY), 2001.

The Faeries of Spring Cottage, illustrated with dolls created by Wendy Froud, photographs by John Lawrence Jones with sets and photographic art direction by Brian Froud, Simon & Schuster (New York, NY), 2003.

EDITOR

(With Mark Alan Arnold; and illustrator) *Elsewhere* (anthology), Ace (New York, NY), Volume 1, 1981, Volume 2, 1982, Volume 3, 1984.

Faery!, Berkley/Ace (New York, NY), 1985.

(With Mark Alan Arnold) *Borderland,* NAL/Signet (New York, NY), 1986.

(With Mark Alan Arnold) *Bordertown: A Chronicle of the Borderlands,* Signet (New York, NY), 1986.

(With Ellen Datlow) *The Year's Best Fantasy* (annual), St. Martin's Press (New York, NY), 1988–1989, published as *The Year's Best Fantasy and Horror,* St. Martin's Press (New York, NY), 1990–2004.

Life on the Border (third volume of "Bordertown" series), Tor Books (New York, NY), 1991.

(With Ellen Datlow) *Snow White, Blood Red,* Morrow/AvoNova (New York, NY), 1993.

(With Ellen Datlow) *Black Thorn, White Rose,* Morrow/AvoNova (New York, NY), 1994.

The Armless Maiden, and Other Tales for Childhood's Survivors, Tor Books (New York, NY), 1995.

(With Ellen Datlow) *Ruby Slippers, Golden Tears,* Morrow/AvoNova (New York, NY), 1995.

(With Ellen Datlow) *Black Swan, White Raven,* Avon (New York, NY), 1997.

(With Ellen Datlow) *Sirens and Other Daemon Lovers,* HarperPrism (New York, NY), 1998.

(With Delia Sherman) *The Essential Bordertown: A Traveller's Guide to the Edge of Faerie,* Tor Books (New York, NY), 1998.

(With Ellen Datlow) *Silver Birch, Blood Moon,* Avon (New York, NY), 1999.

(With Ellen Datlow) *A Wolf at the Door and Other Retold Fairy Tales,* Simon & Schuster (New York, NY), 2000.

(With Ellen Datlow) *Black Heart, Ivory Bones,* Avon (New York, NY), 2000.

(With Ellen Datlow) *The Green Man: Tales from the Mythic Forest,* illustrated by Charles Vess, Viking (New York, NY), 2001.

(With Ellen Datlow; and author of introduction) *Swan Sister: Fairy Tales Retold,* Simon & Schuster Books for Young Readers (New York, NY), 2003.

(With Ellen Datlow; and author of introduction) *The Faery Reel: Tales from the Twilight Realm,* illustrated by Charles Vess, Firebird (New York, NY), 2004.

(With Ellen Datlow; and author of introduction) *Salon Fantastique: Fifteen Original Tales of Fantasy,* Thunder's Mouth Press (New York, NY), 2006.

(With Ellen Datlow; and author of introduction) *The Coyote Road: Trickster Tales,* illustrated by Charles Vess, Viking (New York, NY), 2007.

(With Ellen Datlow; and author of introduction) *Troll's-eye View: A Book of Villainous Tales,* illustrated by Charles Vess, Viking (New York, NY), 2009.

(With Ellen Datlow; and author of introduction) *The Beastly Bride: Tales of the Animal People,* illustrated by Charles Vess, Viking (New York, NY), 2010.

(With Ellen Datlow; and author of introduction) *Teeth: Vampire Tales,* HarperTeen (New York, NY), 2011.

OTHER

(Author of introduction) Patti Perret, *The Faces of Fantasy,* Tor Books (New York, NY), 1996.

Author of stories under the group pseudonym Bellamy Bach. Work anthologized in *Horns of Elfland,* edited by Ellen Kushner, Donald G. Keller, and Delia Sherman, Roc (New York, NY), 1997. Columnist, *Realms of Fantasy* magazine, beginning 1995.

Sidelights

Terri Windling has made an enormous impact on the world of fantasy literature through her work as an editor and artist as well as a writer. Best known for editing

Dollmaker Wendy Froud joins Brian Froud and photographer John Lawrence Jones to create the fanciful illustrations that bring to life Windling's engaging fantasy **The Winter Child.** (Photographs copyright © 2001 Wendy Froud. Reprinted with the permission of Simon & Schuster, Inc.)

numerous anthologies of fantasy fiction for adults, including the annual *The Year's Best Fantasy and Horror* compendiums with Ellen Datlow, Windling has also written several original adult novels in addition to authoring and editing works for younger readers. She has received a host of honors for her work, including numerous World Fantasy Awards as well as the 2010 Solstice Award from the Science Fiction and Fantasy Writers of America. "I'm particularly drawn to art that crosses the borders critics have erected between 'high art' and 'popular culture,' between 'mainstream' and 'genre,' or between one genre and another," Windling stated in a *Locus* interview. "I love that moment of passage between the two; that place on the border where two worlds meet and energize each other."

Windling stumbled into her first publishing job almost accidentally, as she explained to Michael Jones of the *Green Man Review.* After graduating from college, she moved to New York City hoping to get a job working on *The Dark Crystal,* a fantasy film by Jim Henson. She was not hired, so "I looked around to see what else I could do with my passion for folklore and folkloric art," she recalled. She applied for several different jobs in publishing, both artistic and editorial positions, and was finally offered a job as an editorial assistant. This job proved to be the starting point that would begin Windling's career as a highly regarded editor of fantasy.

During the next decade Windling worked as an editor for some of the premiere publishers in the fantasy genre. She joined fellow editor Mark Alan Arnold to create the popular "Borderland" series, which is set in a city on the border between everyday Earth and the land of the elves. Normally, humans and elves are separated by a magical border, but sometimes the barrier is lifted and the two groups can interact. The four long stories in the opening volume of the series were called "unusually well written in terms of character development, plot tension, and innovation" by *Kliatt* contributor Eugene E. LaFaille, Jr. The third volume, *Life on the Border,* which Windling edited on her own, was also praised by reviewers. In *Locus* Tom Whitmore wrote that the book shows that there are "people writing in this vein who write very well indeed." *Voice of Youth Advocate* contributor Joyce Davidson also concluded that *Life on the Border* contains "great stories," concluding that "the world of Bordertown has become a very real place, a place that would be great to visit."

"As I worked with writers and artists, it became clear that I was too envious of them," Windling continued to Jones. "I wanted to be writing and doing art myself." Gradually, she shifted her focus to that side of the field, founding Endicott Studio in 1987 and publishing a children's fantasy novella, *The Changeling,* in 1995. At the same time, Windling remained a consulting editor and in that role has helped to edit numerous anthologies, a job she enjoys much more than editing novels. "Editing an anthology, even though the stories in them are the work and creative children of the authors involved, you

have more of an influence on the whole shape of the book," she told Jones. "Your name is on it, you're providing the theme for it, whereas it's a whole different skill being a novel editor. A good novel editor is invisible."

In *A Wolf at the Door and Other Retold Fairy Tales,* Windling and her *The Year's Best Fantasy and Horror* coeditor Ellen Datlow take a theme common to their adult anthologies—retelling classic fairy tales in contemporary settings—and collect several youth-friendly stories in this vein. As in their compendiums for adults, the stories are darker and more complex than the sanitized versions of fairy tales that most Americans are familiar with. Windling and Datlow explain in their introduction that these retellings are actually closer to the original European folktales than today's familiar happily-ever-after versions, which were popularized during the Victorian era. Garth Nix's "Hansel's Eyes," in which the witch lures children in order to sell their organs on the black market, is perhaps the darkest of the lot. It "may be too lurid, even for teens," predicted

Terri Windling collaborates with Ellen Datlow on editing several popular anthologies, among them **A Wolf at the Door and Other Retold Fairy Tales,** *featuring cover art by Tristan Ellwell.* (Cover illustration copyright © 2000 by Tristan Elwell. Reproduced by permission of Shannon Associates, illustrator's agent.)

Booklist critic Hazel Rochman, although *Rocky Mountain News* reviewer Natalie Soto asserted that there was nothing in the volume "so shocking that a middle-grader wouldn't love [it]." Other entries are more poetic. In Gregory Maguire's "The Seven Stage a Comeback," the Seven Dwarves lament the loss of Snow White in long soliloquies and plot to win her back from the prince, while Neil Gaiman contributes a poem of "Instructions" for what to do if you find yourself in a fairy tale. "The diversity of content, style, and tone makes this an excellent collection for sampling," asserted *School Library Journal* contributor Ellen A. Greever.

A companion volume, *Swan Sister: Fairy Tales Retold*, features Will Shetterly's take on Red Riding Hood, a Neil Gaiman poem about Scheherazade, and Lois Metzger's version of Rapunzel, among other writings. A critic in *Kirkus Reviews* described *Swan Sister* as "an above-average gathering."

In *Troll's-eye View: A Book of Villainous Tales,* another collection of fairytale retellings, Windling and Datlow asked contributors to turn their attentions to the most

Cover of Windling and Datlow's unusual anthology The Beastly Bride, *featuring cover art by Charles Vess.* (Cover illustration copyright © Charles Vess, 2010. Used by permission of Viking Children's Books, a division of Penguin Young Reader's Group (USA) Inc., 345 Hudston St., New York, NY 10014. All rights reserved.)

unpopular of fairy-tale characters. "Witches, wizards, giants, trolls, ogres: what's the truth behind their stories?," the editors ask in their introduction. "And are the fairy-tale heroes and heroines pitted against them quite as noble as they first appear?" In Peter S. Beagle's "Up the Down Beanstalk: A Wife Remembers," for example, the spouse of the infamous giant gives a scathing newspaper interview regarding Jack, her husband's nemesis. Daniel Kraus, reviewing the work in *Booklist,* concluded that *Troll's-eye View* offers "a mixed bag of funny, quirky, and downright creepy entries."

Windling and Datlow have also released a collection of fairy tales for young adults, *The Green Man: Tales from the Mythic Forest.* The fifteen stories and three poems included all feature young adults interacting with nature in some way. As with *A Wolf at the Door,* the tones of the pieces vary widely. A humorous story by Gregory Maguire, "Fee, Fie, Foe, et Cetera," tells the other side of the story of Jack and the Beanstalk, while other works feature "mature themes and an often sophisticated view of the world and how one survives in it," according to Amy Kellman in *School Library Journal.* "All in all, this is a tasty treat for fantasy fans," Sally Estes concluded in her *Booklist* review of *The Green Man.*

Windling and Datlow's *The Faery Reel: Tales from the Twilight Realm* contains stories and poems from twenty writers, including Delia Sherman, whose "CATNYP," an urban fantasy set in New York City, concerns the changeling myth. Another contributor, Bruce Glassco, presents "Never Never," which offers a grim, unusual look at the relationship between Captain Hook and Peter Pan. Windling's "fine introductory essay on the origins, varieties, and attitudes toward fairies in different cultures" earned praise from *Booklist* contributor Carolyn Phelan, and a *Kirkus Reviews* critic deemed *The Faery Reel* "a treasure chest." *The Coyote Road: Trickster Tales,* a third volume of mythic fiction, contains more than two dozen stories about the rascally fictional character, an archetype that also appears as a fox maiden in Japanese legends, a spider in African and Native-American stories, and a hare in Indian and Tibetan tales. "This excellent collection is bound to find an audience," Susan Hepler commented in her *School Library Journal* review of *The Coyote Road.*

The Beastly Bride: Tales of the Animal People, the fourth anthology in Windling and Datlow's mythic fiction series, focuses on therianthropic figures, shapeshifters that can transform from animal to human. The volume includes Midori Snyder's "The Monkey Bride," a story based on a Kordofan folktale; Carol Emshwiller's "The Abominable Child's Tale," which concerns the relationship between a bigfoot and a human female; and Hiromi Goto's "The Hikikomori," about an outcast who is transformed into a rat. According to Misti Tidman, writing in *School Library Journal,* "Windling's

fascinating introduction details the history of shape-shifters in legends from around the globe."

In *Salon Fantastique: Fifteen Original Tales of Fantasy* Windling and Datlow eschew a central theme, hoping "to evoke the liberating, creative spirit of a literary salon," as they note in their introduction to the volume. According to *Booklist* reviewer Ray Olson, contributions by Beagle, Maguire, Lucius Shepard, and Paul Di Filippo "all pleasingly blend stylization and substance."

A Midsummer Night's Faery Tale, The Winter Child, and *The Faeries of Spring Cottage* are picture books that pair a story by Windling with artwork by Wendy Froud, a fiber artist best known for her puppet-making work on *The Dark Crystal* and the *Star Wars* films. These three books follow a young tree-root faery named Sneezle and his sidekick Twig (a marsh thistle faery) as they save the day for the better-known faery king and queen Oberon and Titania. In the first volume, Sneezle saves Queen Titiana from a magical enchantment; in *The Winter Child,* he recovers Oberon's lost cup and breaks a spell that prevents winter from coming to the faery kingdom.

These creative collaborations feature an uncommon form of illustration: Froud and her husband Brian created dolls of the characters and arranged them into tableaux representing various scenes that were then photographed by John Lawrence Jones. *Booklist* reviewer Michael Cart offered a mixed reaction to the illustrations in *A Midsummer Night's Faery Tale,* writing that "some readers will love the elaborately staged, brightly lit pictures," while others may find them "inherently static, and even a bit creepy." A *Publishers Weekly* reviewer was more positive, noting that the photographs in *The Winter Child* mesh "seamlessly with [Windling's] sensitive text" to produce a finished product that is "flawlessly conceived and exquisitely produced."

Fantasy, mythic fiction, and fairy tales have long held a fascination for Windling, who views such stories as universal. As she wrote on her home page, "the symbols to be found in folklore and myth (the collective dreams of entire cultures) provide useful metaphors for the journeys, struggles and transformations we experience throughout our lives."

Biographical and Critical Sources

BOOKS

St. James Guide to Young-Adult Writers, second edition, St. James Press (Detroit, MI), 1999.

Windling, Terry, and Ellen Datlow, editors, *Salon Fantastique: Fifteen Original Tales of Fantasy,* Thunder's Mouth Press (New York, NY), 2006.

PERIODICALS

Booklist, July, 1992, Candace Smith, review of *The Year's Best Fantasy and Horror,* p. 1925; August, 1994, Ray Olson, review of *Black Thorn, White Rose,* p. 2030; August, 1995, Roland Green, review of *The Year's Best Fantasy and Horror: Eighth Annual Collection,* p. 1933; December 15, 1995, Roland Green, review of *Ruby Slippers, Golden Tears,* p. 692; July, 1996, Ray Olson, review of *The Year's Best Fantasy and Horror: Ninth Annual Collection,* p. 1812; April 15, 1997, Roland Green, review of *Black Swan, White Raven,* p. 1387; September 15, 1998, Roland Green, review of *The Essential Bordertown: A Traveller's Guide to the Edge of Faerie,* p. 205; March 15, 1999, Roland Green, review of *Silver Birch, Blood Moon,* p. 1293; July, 1999, Ray Olson, review of *The Year's Best Fantasy and Horror: Twelfth Annual Edition,* p. 1930; February 1, 2000, Michael Cart, review of *A Midsummer Night's Fairy Tale,* p. 1022; September 1, 2000, Roland Green, review of *The Year's Best Fantasy and Horror: Thirteenth Annual Collection,* p. 71, and Hazel Rochman, review of *A Wolf at the Door and Other Retold Fairy Tales,* p. 73; July, 2001, Roland Green, review of *The Year's Best Fantasy and Horror: Fourteenth Annual Collection,* p. 1993; April 15, 2002, Sally Estes, review of *The Green Man: Tales from the Mythic Forest,* p. 1412; August, 2002, Kristine Huntley, review of *The Year's Best Fantasy and Horror: Fifteenth Annual Collection,* p. 1939; September 15, 2003, Hazel Rochman, review of *Swan Sister: Fairy Tales Retold,* p. 232; April 15, 2004, Carolyn Phelan, review of *The Faery Reel: Tales from the Twilight Realm,* p. 1450; December 15, 2006, Ray Olson, review of *Salon Fantastique: Fifteen Original Tales of Fantasy,* p. 31; September 15, 2007, Carolyn Phelan, review of *The Coyote Road: Trickster Tales,* p. 61; March 1, 2009, Daniel Kraus, review of *Troll's-eye View: A Book of Villainous Tales,* p. 46.

Kirkus Reviews, May 1, 2002, review of *The Green Man,* p. 651; June 15, 2002, review of *The Year's Best Fantasy and Horror: Fifteenth Annual Collection,* p. 847; September 1, 2003, review of *Swan Sister,* p. 1121; May 15, 2004, review of *The Faery Reel,* p. 489.

Kliatt, fall, 1986, Eugene E. LaFaille, Jr., review of *Borderland,* p. 30.

Library Journal, December, 1988, C. Robert Nixon, review of *The Year's Best Fantasy: First Annual Collection,* p. 113; August, 1992, Jackie Cassada, review of *The Year's Best Fantasy and Horror: Fifth Annual Collection,* p. 155; November 15, 1995, Jackie Cassada, review of *Ruby Slippers, Golden Tears,* p. 103; June 15, 1997, Susan Hamburger, review of *Black Swan, White Raven,* p. 100; October 15, 1997, Susan Hamburger, review of *The Year's Best Fantasy and Horror: Tenth Annual Collection,* p. 98; August, 2000, Ann Kim, review of *The Year's Best Fantasy and Horror: Thirteenth Annual Collection,* p. 168.

Locus, August, 1991, Tom Whitmore, review of *Life on the Border,* pp. 29, 52; October, 2003, "Terri Windling: Border Coyote," p. 76.

Los Angeles Times Book Review, February 6, 1983, Don Strachan, review of *Elsewhere,* Volume II, p. 8.

Magazine of Fantasy and Science Fiction, June, 1995, Charles de Lint, review of *The Armless Maiden, and Other Tales for Childhood's Survivors,* p. 33; October-November, 1996, Charles de Lint, review of *The Year's Best Fantasy and Horror: Ninth Annual Collection,* pp. 59-60; December, 1996, Charles de Lint, review of *The Wood Wife,* p. 42; September, 1997, Charles de Lint, review of *Black Swan, White Raven,* pp. 34-36; September, 2003, Charles de Lint, review of *The Faeries of Spring Cottage,* pp. 40-41; February, 2004, Charles de Lint, review of *The Year's Best Fantasy and Horror: Seventeenth Annual Collection,* p. 34.

New York Times Book Review, January 31, 1993, Meg Wolitzer, review of *Snow White, Blood Red,* p. 29.

Publishers Weekly, July 29, 1988, Peggy Kaganoff, review of *The Year's Best Fantasy: First Annual Collection,* p. 227; June 22, 1990, Penny Kaganoff, review of *The Year's Best Fantasy and Horror: Third Annual Collection,* p. 49; July 12, 1991, review of *The Year's Best Fantasy and Horror: Fourth Annual Collection,* p. 61; July 6, 1992, review of *The Year's Best Fantasy and Horror: Fifth Annual Collection,* p. 50; November 23, 1992, review of *Snow White, Blood Red,* p. 57; July 5, 1993, review of *The Year's Best Fantasy and Horror: Sixth Annual Collection,* p. 68; August 8, 1994, review of *Black Thorn, White Rose,* p. 392; April 10, 1995, review of *The Armless Maiden, and Other Tales for Childhood's Survivors,* p. 58; July 17, 1995, review of *The Year's Best Fantasy and Horror: Eighth Annual Collection,* p. 227; November 6, 1995, review of *Ruby Slippers, Golden Tears,* p. 86; July 8, 1996, review of *The Year's Best Fantasy and Horror: Ninth Annual Collection,* p. 80; September 16, 1996, review of *The Wood Wife,* p. 74; May 26, 1997, review of *Black Swan, White Raven,* p. 71; August 11, 1997, review of *The Year's Best Fantasy and Horror: Tenth Annual Collection,* p. 390; September 4, 2000, review of *The Year's Best Fantasy and Horror: Thirteenth Annual Collection,* p. 90; July 9, 2001, review of *The Year's Best Fantasy and Horror: Fourteenth Annual Collection,* p. 52; September 10, 2001, review of *The Winter Child,* p. 66; May 27, 2002, review of *The Green Man,* p. 62; July 29, 2002, review of *The Year's Best Fantasy and Horror: Fifteenth Annual Collection,* p. 59; July 28, 2003, review of *The Year's Best Fantasy and Horror: Sixteenth Annual Collection,* pp. 83-84; October 6, 2003, review of *Swan Sister,* p. 86; October 9, 2006, review of *Salon Fantastique,* p. 41.

Rocky Mountain News (Denver, CO), August 6, 2000, Natalie Soto, review of *A Wolf at the Door,* p. 4E.

School Library Journal, April 15, 1982, review of *Elsewhere,* p. 88; July, 1997, Dottie Kraft, review of *The Wood Wife,* p. 117; August, 2000, Ellen A. Greever, review of *A Wolf at the Door,* p. 180; November, 2000, Francisca Goldsmith, review of *Black Heart, Ivory Bones,* p. 182; June, 2002, Margaret A. Chang, review of *The Winter Child,* p. 116; July, 2002, Amy Kellman, review of *The Green Man,* pp. 118-119; July, 2004, Sharon Rawlins, review of *The Faery Reel,* p. 104; September, 2007, Susan Hepler, review of *The Coyote Road,* p. 215; April, 2009, Eva Mitnick, review of *Troll's-eye View,* p. 130; May, 2010, Misti Tidman, review of *The Beastly Bride: Tales of the Animal People,* p. 108.

Voice of Youth Advocates, Joyce Davidson, review of *Life on the Border,* p. 324.

ONLINE

Endicott Studio Web Site, http://www.endicott-studio.com/ (August 1, 2011).

Green Man Review Online, http://www.greenmanreview/ (January 14, 2004), Michael Jones, interview with Windling.

Terri Windling Home Page, http://www.terriwindling.com (August 1, 2011).*

*   *   *

WRIGHT, Maureen 1961-

Personal

Born 1961; married; husband's name Don; children: three sons.

Addresses

Home—Athens, PA. *E-mail*—wright@booksbymaureenwright.com

Career

Writer. Presenter at schools.

Awards, Honors

Best Bedtime Book selection, *Nick Jr.* magazine, and Ladybug Picture Book Award shortlist inclusion, both 2009, and Wanda Gág Book Award Honor Book selection, Minnesota State University, 2010, all for *Sleep, Big Bear, Sleep!*

Writings

To Mom, Keeper of the Zoo, 1995.

Sleep, Big Bear, Sleep!, illustrated by Will Hillenbrand, Marshall Cavendish Children (Tarrytown, NY), 2009.

Sneezy the Snowman, illustrated by Stephen Gilpin, Marshall Cavendish (New York, NY), 2010.

Sneeze, Big Bear, Sneeze!, illustrated by Will Hillenbrand, Marshall Cavendish Children (Tarrytown, NY), 2011.

Earth Day, Birthday, illustrated by Violet Kim, Marshall Cavendish Children (Tarrytown, NY), 2012.

Barnyard Fun on April One!, illustrated by Paul Ratz de Tagyos, Marshall Cavendish Children (Tarrytown, NY), 2013.

Contributor to *Cicada* magazine.

Maureen Wright (Smith Photography. Reproduced by permission.)

Sidelights

The writing talent of Maureen Wright is teamed up with the artistic skill of noted artist/illustrator Will Hillenbrand in several entertaining picture books featuring a drowsy brown bear. In *Sleep, Big Bear, Sleep!* a lumbering brown bear is too tired to clearly hear Old Man Winter explain that it is time to go into hibernation. Instead of "sleep," the befuddled Big Bear hears "leap," "sweep," and several other rhyming words, all which signify some sort of humor-inducing action. Another collaborative work, *Sneeze, Big Bear, Sneeze!*, finds the seasonal clock set to autumn as Big Bear watches the leaves fall from the trees and foolishly believes that his gusty sneezes must be the cause. Reviewing *Sleep, Big Bear, Sleep!*, Amy Lilien-Harper noted in *School Library Journal* that the story "moves at a steady clip, and the refrain will encourage child participation," while a *Kirkus Reviews* writer recommended Wright's picture book as "a terrific read-aloud." "The bounce of Wright's verse is welcome," asserted a *Kirkus Reviews* writer in discussing *Sneeze, Big Bear, Sneeze!*, and Hillenbrand's mixed-media illustrations "use a bright and appealing palette" to capture the story's fall setting.

Sleep, Big Bear, Sleep! was voted best bedtime book by *Nick Jr.* magazine as well as earning several other honors, but its publication only occurred as a result of Wright's dogged determination to become a children's author: after twenty years of submitting manuscripts,

Sleep, Big Bear, Sleep! was her first story to attract the attention of a publisher, and she now shares her lesson of persistence with the children she visits in schools and libraries.

In addition to Hillenbrand, Wright's stories have also been brought to life by several other artists. *Sneezy the Snowman,* the story of a snowman with little tolerance for cold weather, features illustrations by Stephen Gilpin that capture the silliness in three children's efforts to help Sneezy warm up (and melt!) with a cup of hot cocoa, a woolen coat, and even a campfire. Wright's "rhyming text keeps the snow show moving along at a brisk, bouncing pace," noted *Booklist* contributor Andrew Medlar. Citing the story's "new take on a popular seasonal theme," Laura Butler predicted in *School Library Journal* that *Sneezy the Snowman* "should find a warm audience during cold months."

"It took me a long time to get published—twenty years of trying and being rejected!," Wright told *SATA*. "There were times when I wanted to give up, but I'm so glad that I didn't. I hope that whatever your dream or goal is that you will always keep on trying! Following your dream isn't easy, getting good grades isn't easy, not giving up isn't easy, but it is worth it!

"I live out in the country with my husband, Don, and our youngest son, Mark. We have a cat named Lyle and I dog-sit for my middle son, Jeff. His two-year-old black lab, Gus, stays with me while Jeff works. I write in my recliner and Lyle is usually on my lap, although sometimes Gus sneaks up on my lap one leg at a time. He is an eighty-pound dog who thinks he's a lap dog.

"When I'm not writing or doing things around the house, I am volunteering at our local nursing home. I love helping out in the activity department and being with the elderly residents. Some of my best friends live there. I also enjoy baking cookies and pies!

"Check out my Web site, www.booksbymaureenwright. com, and remember to keep following your dream!"

Biographical and Critical Sources

PERIODICALS

Booklist, November 1, 2010, Andrew Medlar, review of *Sneezy the Snowman,* p. 78.
Horn Book, January-February, 2010, Joanna Rudge Long, review of *Sleep, Big Bear, Sleep!,* p. 79.
Kirkus Reviews, October 15, 2009, review of *Sleep, Big Bear, Sleep!;* August 15, 2011, review of *Sneeze, Big Bear, Sneeze!*
School Library Journal, September, 2009, Amy Lilien-Harper, review of *Sleep, Big Bear, Sleep!,* p. 137; September, 2010, Laura Butler, review of *Sneezy the Snowman,* p. 136.

ONLINE

Maureen Wright Home Page, http://www.booksbymaureen wright.com (September 15, 2011).

*   *   *

WYSHYNSKI, Sue

Personal

Born in Canada. *Hobbies and other interests:* Surfing, BMX riding, travel.

Addresses

Home—Honolulu, HI. *E-mail*—poserthebook@gmail. com.

Career

Author and surfer. Works in film and television as body double/stand-in. Visitor to schools and libraries.

Writings

Poser, Walker & Co. (New York, NY), 2010.

Biographical and Critical Sources

PERIODICALS

Kirkus Reviews, May 1, 2010, review of *Poser.*
School Library Journal, August, 2010, Kimberly Garnick Giarratano, review of *Poser,* p. 117.

ONLINE

Sue Wyshynski Home Page, http://www.suewyshynski.com (September 15, 2011).
Sue Wyshynski Web log, http://triksyfun.blogspot.com (September 15, 2011).*

*   *   *

YOUNG, Ned

Personal

Born in UT; married; wife's name Melanie; children: three.

Addresses

Home—Brigham City, UT.

Career

Artist and author/illustrator of children's books. *Exhibitions:* Paintings included in private and corporate collections.

Writings

SELF-ILLUSTRATED

Zoomer, Harper (New York, NY), 2010.
Zoomer's Summer Snowstorm, HarperCollins (New York, NY), 2011.

Sidelights

Self-taught artist Ned Young shares his humorous vision through illustration projects that include posters and calendars, cards, puzzles, and various small housewares. The Utah-based Young has also earned a host of young fans through his companion picture books *Zoomer* and *Zoomer's Summer Snowstorm.*

In *Zoomer* readers meet the members of a three-pup litter: Hooper, Cooper, and Zoomer. It is morning and all three puppies are busy getting ready for school, . . . all except for Zoomer. Despite Father Dog's coaxing, Zoomer would rather chase soap bubbles, make sand sculptures, and otherwise play. Finally, even Dad becomes convinced that Zoomer has the right idea. Young continues the fun in *Zoomer's Summer Snowstorm,* as a scheme to manufacture a refreshing snow cone results in a journey into the puppy's overactive imagination. Reviewing *Zoomer,* a *Publishers Weekly* critic wrote that Young's "fanciful visual illustrations" alert readers that "Zoomer's world is one in which just about anything can happen," and *School Library Journal* contributor Amanda Moss Struckmeyer enjoyed the "bright, fun illustrations detailing Zoomer's ambitious undertakings." In capturing his canine hero's over-the-top "silly" antics, author/illustrator Young "show[s] that he can illustrate wildly improbably animal antics in a humorous and . . . believable way," asserted a *Kirkus Reviews* writer, and *Booklist* contributor Abby Nolan dubbed *Zoomer* a "lively picture-book debut" that has "an appealing retro feel."

Biographical and Critical Sources

PERIODICALS

Booklist, May 1, 2010, Abby Nolan, review of *Zoomer,* p. 94; April 15, 2011, Shelle Rosenfeld, review of *Zoomer's Summer Snowstorm,* p. 60.
Kirkus Reviews, May 1, 2010, review of *Zoomer;* April 1, 2011, review of *Zoomer's Summer Snowstorm.*
Publishers Weekly, April 5, 2010, review of *Zoomer,* p. 59.

Ned Young introduces an exuberant young canine character in his self-illustrated picture book **Zoomer.** (Copyright © 2010 by Ned Young. Reproduced with permission of Harper, an imprint of HarperCollins Publishers.)

School Library Journal, May, 2010, Amanda Moss Struckmeyer, review of *Zoomer,* p. 95.

ONLINE

Ned Young Studio Web Log, http://www.nedyoung. blogspot.com (September 15, 2011).*

* * *

ZAHEDI, Morteza 1978-
(Murtiza Zahidi)

Personal

Born March 31, 1978, in Rasht, Iran. *Education:* Azad University of Islamic Art and Architecture, B.A. (painting). *Religion:* Muslim.

Addresses

Home—Tehran, Iran. *E-mail*—mortezahedi@yahoo.com.

Career

Educator and writer. Teacher of art at Shahrood University of Technology, Semnan Province, Iran. *Exhibitions:* Work exhibited at Bologna Book Fair and at galleries in Tehran, Iran, and in Tokyo, Osaka, Fukuoka, and Nagano, Japan.

Awards, Honors

Second prize, Tehran Illustrator's Biennial for Children's Book, 2003; second prize, Belgrade Biennal for Children's Book Illustration, 2003; Outstanding Books for Young People with Disabilities selection, IBBY, 2010, for *Good Night, Commander* by Ahmad Akbarpour.

Illustrator

Ahmad Akbarpour, *Shab Bekheyr Farmandeh!,* 2003, translated from the Iranian by Shadi Eskandani and Helen Mixter as *Good Night, Commander,* Groundwood Books (Toronto, Ontario, Canada), 2010.

Illustrator of books published in Iran, including *Butterfly's Travels, Look, Look, This Way, Multiplication Table, Aunt Cockroach, Where Are You Going To?, Two Turtles, Two Human,* and *Sneeze.*

Works featuring Zahedi's art have been translated into French and Japanese.

Biographical and Critical Sources

PERIODICALS

Booklist, May 1, 2010, John Peters, review of *Good Night, Commander,* p. 86.
Kirkus Reviews, April 15, 2010, review of *Good Night, Commander.*
Publishers Weekly, April 12, 2010, review of *Good Night, Commander,* p. 49.
School Library Journal, May, 2010, Maryann H. Owen, review of *Good Night, Commander,* p. 78.

ONLINE

Morteza Zahedi Home Page, http://www.mortezahedi.com (September 15, 2011).*

* * *

ZAHIDI, Murtiza
See ZAHEDI, Morteza

Illustrations Index

(In the following index, the number of the *volume* in which an illustrator's work appears is given *before* the colon, and the *page number* on which it appears is given *after* the colon. For example, a drawing by Adams, Adrienne appears in Volume 2 on page 6, another drawing by her appears in Volume 3 on page 80, another drawing in Volume 8 on page 1, and so on and so on. . . .)

YABC

Index references to *YABC* refer to listings appearing in the two-volume *Yesterday's Authors of Books for Children,* also published by Gale, Cengage Learning. *YABC* covers prominent authors and illustrators who died prior to 1960.

A

Aas, Ulf *5:* 174
Abbe, S. van
 See van Abbe, S.
Abel, Raymond *6:* 122; *7:* 195; *12:* 3; *21:* 86; *25:* 119
Abelliera, Aldo *71:* 120
Abolafia, Yossi *60:* 2; *93:* 163; *152:* 202
Abrahams, Hilary *26:* 205; *29:* 24, 25; *53:* 61
Abrams, Kathie *36:* 170
Abrams, Lester *49:* 26
Abulafia, Yossi *154:* 67; *177:* 3
Accardo, Anthony *191:* 3, 8
Accornero, Franco *184:* 8
Accorsi, William *11:* 198
Acs, Laszlo *14:* 156; *42:* 22
Acuna, Ed *198:* 79
Adams, Adrienne *2:* 6; *3:* 80; *8:* 1; *15:* 107; *16:* 180; *20:* 65; *22:* 134, 135; *33:* 75; *36:* 103, 112; *39:* 74; *86:* 54; *90:* 2, 3
Adams, Connie J. *129:* 68
Adams, John Wolcott *17:* 162
Adams, Kathryn *224:* 1
Adams, Lynn *96:* 44
Adams, Norman *55:* 82
Adams, Pam *112:* 1, 2
Adams, Sarah *98:* 126; *164:* 180
Adams, Steve *209:* 64
Adamson, George *30:* 23, 24; *69:* 64
Addams, Charles *55:* 5
Addison, Kenneth *192:* 173; *231:* 166
Addy, Sean *180:* 8; *222:* 31
Ade, Rene *76:* 198; *195:* 162
Adinolfi, JoAnn *115:* 42; *176:* 2; *217:* 79
Adkins, Alta *22:* 250
Adkins, Jan *8:* 3; *69:* 4; *144:* 2, 3, 4; *210:* 11, 17, 18, 19
Adl, Shirin *225:* 2
Adler, Kelynn *195:* 47
Adler, Peggy *22:* 6; *29:* 31
Adler, Ruth *29:* 29
Adlerman, Daniel *163:* 2
Adragna, Robert *47:* 145
Agard, Nadema *18:* 1
Agee, Jon *116:* 8, 9, 10; *157:* 4; *196:* 3, 4, 5, 6, 7, 8
Agre, Patricia *47:* 195
Aguirre, Alfredo *152:* 218
Ahl, Anna Maria *32:* 24

Ahlberg, Allan *68:* 6, 7, 9; *165:* 5; *214:* 9
Ahlberg, Janet *68:* 6, 7, 9; *214:* 9
Ahlberg, Jessica *229:* 2, 191
Aicher-Scholl, Inge *63:* 127
Aichinger, Helga *4:* 5, 45
Aitken, Amy *31:* 34
Ajhar, Brian *207:* 126; *220:* 2
Akaba, Suekichi *46:* 23; *53:* 127
Akasaka, Miyoshi *YABC 2:* 261
Akib, Jamel *181:* 13; *182:* 99; *220:* 74
Akino, Fuku *6:* 144
Alain *40:* 41
Alajalov *2:* 226
Albert, Chris *200:* 64
Alborough, Jez *86:* 1, 2, 3; *149:* 3
Albrecht, Jan *37:* 176
Albright, Donn *1:* 91
Alcala, Alfredo *91:* 128
Alcantará, Felipe Ugalde *171:* 186
Alcorn, John *3:* 159; *7:* 165; *31:* 22; *44:* 127; *46:* 23, 170
Alcorn, Stephen *110:* 4; *125:* 106; *128:* 172; *150:* 97; *160:* 188; *165:* 48; *201:* 113; *203:* 39; *207:* 3; *226:* 25
Alcott, May *100:* 3
Alda, Arlene *44:* 24; *158:* 2
Alden, Albert *11:* 103
Aldridge, Andy *27:* 131
Aldridge, George *105:* 125
Aldridge, Sheila *192:* 4
Alejandro, Cliff *176:* 75
Alex, Ben *45:* 25, 26
Alexander, Claire *228:* 2
Alexander, Ellen *91:* 3
Alexander, Lloyd *49:* 34
Alexander, Martha *3:* 206; *11:* 103; *13:* 109; *25:* 100; *36:* 131; *70:* 6, 7; *136:* 3, 4, 5; *169:* 120; *230:* 78
Alexander, Paul *85:* 57; *90:* 9
Alexeieff, Alexander *14:* 6; *26:* 199
Alfano, Wayne *80:* 69
Aliki
 See Brandenberg, Aliki
Alko, Selina *218:* 2
Allamand, Pascale *12:* 9
Allan, Judith *38:* 166
Alland, Alexandra *16:* 255
Allen, Gertrude *9:* 6
Allen, Graham *31:* 145
Allen, Jonathan *131:* 3, 4; *177:* 8, 9, 10
Allen, Joy *168:* 185; *217:* 6, 7

Allen, Pamela *50:* 25, 26, 27, 28; *81:* 9, 10; *123:* 4, 5
Allen, Raul *207:* 94
Allen, Rowena *47:* 75
Allen, Thomas B. *81:* 101; *82:* 248; *89:* 37; *104:* 9
Allen, Tom *85:* 176
Allender, David *73:* 223
Alley, R.W. *80:* 183; *95:* 187; *156:* 100, 153; *169:* 4, 5; *179:* 17
Allison, Linda *43:* 27
Allon, Jeffrey *119:* 174
Allport, Mike *71:* 55
Almquist, Don *11:* 8; *12:* 128; *17:* 46; *22:* 110
Aloise, Frank *5:* 38; *10:* 133; *30:* 92
Alsenas, Linas *186:* 2
Alter, Ann *206:* 4, 5
Althea
 See Braithwaite, Althea
Altschuler, Franz *11:* 185; *23:* 141; *40:* 48; *45:* 29; *57:* 181
Alvin, John *117:* 5
Ambrus, Victor G. *1:* 6, 7, 194; *3:* 69; *5:* 15; *6:* 44; *7:* 36; *8:* 210; *12:* 227; *14:* 213; *15:* 213; *22:* 209; *24:* 36; *28:* 179; *30:* 178; *32:* 44, 46; *38:* 143; *41:* 25, 26, 27, 28, 29, 30, 31, 32; *42:* 87; *44:* 190; *55:* 172; *62:* 30, 144, 145, 148; *86:* 99, 100, 101; *87:* 66, 137; *89:* 162; *134:* 160
Ames, Lee J. *3:* 12; *9:* 130; *10:* 69; *17:* 214; *22:* 124; *151:* 13; *223:* 69
Amini, Mehrdokht *211:* 119
Amon, Aline *9:* 9
Amoss, Berthe *5:* 5
Amstutz, André *152:* 102; *214:* 11, 16; *223:* 99
Amundsen, Dick *7:* 77
Amundsen, Richard E. *5:* 10; *24:* 122
Ancona, George *12:* 11; *55:* 144; *145:* 7; *208:* 13
Anderson, Alasdair *18:* 122
Andersen, Bethanne *116:* 167; *162:* 189; *175:* 17; *191:* 4, 5; *218:* 20
Anderson, Bob *139:* 16
Anderson, Brad *33:* 28
Anderson, Brian *211:* 8
Anderson, C.W. *11:* 10
Anderson, Carl *7:* 4
Anderson, Catherine Corley *72:* 2
Anderson, Cecil *127:* 152
Anderson, David Lee *118:* 176

Anderson, Derek *169:* 9; *174:* 180
Anderson, Doug *40:* 111
Anderson, Erica *23:* 65
Anderson, G.E. *223:* 181
Anderson, Laurie *12:* 153, 155
Anderson, Lena *99:* 26
Anderson, Peggy Perry *179:* 2
Anderson, Sara *173:* 3
Anderson, Scoular *138:* 13; *201:* 6
Anderson, Stephanie *225:* 3
Anderson, Susan *90:* 12
Anderson, Tara *188:* 132; *211:* 115
Anderson, Wayne *23:* 119; *41:* 239; *56:* 7; *62:* 26; *147:* 6; *202:* 4, 5
Andreasen, Daniel *86:* 157; *87:* 104; *103:* 201, 202; *159:* 75; *167:* 106, 107; *168:* 184; *180:* 247; *186:* 9; *212:* 101; *220:* 110, 111; *221:* 56; *227:* 3, 4, 5, 6
Andrew, Ian *111:* 37; *116:* 12; *166:* 2
Andrew, John *22:* 4
Andrews, Benny *14:* 251; *31:* 24; *57:* 6, 7; *183:* 8
Andrews, Vaughn *166:* 28
Anelay, Henry *57:* 173
Angel, Marie *47:* 22
Angelo, Valenti *14:* 8; *18:* 100; *20:* 232; *32:* 70
Anglund, Joan Walsh *2:* 7, 250, 251; *37:* 198, 199, 200
Anholt, Catherine *74:* 8; *131:* 7; *141:* 5
Anholt, Laurence *141:* 4
Anno, Mitsumasa *5:* 7; *38:* 25, 26, 27, 28, 29, 30, 31, 32; *77:* 3, 4; *157:* 10, 11
Antal, Andrew *1:* 124; *30:* 145
Antram, David *152:* 133
Apostolou, Christy Hale
    See Hale, Christy
Apple, Margot *33:* 25; *35:* 206; *46:* 81; *53:* 8; *61:* 109; *64:* 21, 22, 24, 25, 27; *71:* 176; *77:* 53; *82:* 245; *92:* 39; *94:* 180; *96:* 107; *152:* 4, 5; *162:* 192, 194; *173:* 44; *214:* 21, 22, 23, 24
Appleyard, Dev *2:* 192
Aragones, Sergio *48:* 23, 24, 25, 26, 27
Araneus *40:* 29
Arbo, Cris *103:* 4; *220:* 4, 5
Archambault, Matt *85:* 173; *138:* 19, 20; *143:* 33; *145:* 144; *179:* 103; *187:* 7; *219:* 2
Archer, Janet *16:* 69; *178:* 156
Ardizzone, Edward *1:* 11, 12; *2:* 105; *3:* 258; *4:* 78; *7:* 79; *10:* 100; *15:* 232; *20:* 69,178; *23:* 223; *24:* 125; *28:* 25, 26, 27, 28, 29, 30, 31,33, 34, 35, 36, 37; *31:* 192, 193; *34:* 215, 217; *60:* 173; *64:* 145; *87:* 176; *YABC 2:* 25
Arena, Jill *176:* 49
Arenella, Roy *14:* 9
Argemi, David *197:* 2
Argent, Kerry *103:* 56; *138:* 17; *158:* 134
Arihara, Shino *201:* 98
Arisman, Marshall *162:* 50
Armer, Austin *13:* 3
Armer, Laura Adams *13:* 3
Armer, Sidney *13:* 3
Armitage, David *47:* 23; *99:* 5; *155:* 4
Armitage, Eileen *4:* 16
Armstrong, George *10:* 6; *21:* 72
Armstrong, Shelagh *102:* 114; *224:* 4
Armstrong-Ellis, Carey *185:* 196
Arno, Enrico *1:* 217; *2:* 22, 210; *4:* 9; *5:* 43; *6:* 52; *29:* 217, 219; *33:* 152; *35:* 99; *43:* 31, 32, 33; *45:* 212, 213, 214; *72:* 72; *74:* 166; *100:* 169
Arnold, Alli *187:* 40, 41
Arnold, Andrew *219:* 155; *221:* 155
Arnold, Caroline *174:* 5
Arnold, Emily *76:* 7, 9, 10
Arnold, Katya *115:* 11; *168:* 2, 3
Arnold, Tedd *116:* 14; *133:* 152; *160:* 5; *208:* 24, 25, 26, 176

Arnosky, Jim *22:* 20; *70:* 9, 10, 11; *118:* 3, 5; *160:* 8, 10; *189:* 5, 7, 8, 9, 10; *217:* 11, 12, 13, 14
Arnsteen, Katy Keck *105:* 97; *116:* 145
Arsenault, Isabelle *207:* 7; *226:* 109
Arrowood, Clinton *12:* 193; *19:* 11; *65:* 210
Artell, Mike *89:* 8
Arting, Fred J. *41:* 63
Artzybasheff, Boris *13:* 143; *14:* 15; *40:* 152, 155
Aruego, Ariane *6:* 4
Aruego, José *4:* 140; *6:* 4; *7:* 64; *33:* 195; *35:* 208; *68:* 16, 17; *75:* 46; *93:* 91, 92; *94:* 197; *109:* 65, 67; *125:* 2, 3, 4, 5; *127:* 188; *143:* 25; *178:* 17, 19, 74; *188:* 166; *202:* 164; *231:* 176
Arzoumanian, Alik *177:* 12; *194:* 115
Asare, Meshack *86:* 9; *139:* 19
Ascensios, Natalie *105:* 139
Asch, Frank *5:* 9; *66:* 2, 4, 6, 7, 9, 10; *102:* 18, 19,21; *154:* 12
Ashby, Gail *11:* 135
Ashby, Gil *146:* 4
Ashby, Gwynneth *44:* 26
Ashley, C.W. *19:* 197
Ashmead, Hal *8:* 70
Ashton, Tim *211:* 204
Aska, Warabe *56:* 10
Assel, Steven *44:* 153; *77:* 22, 97
Astrop, John *32:* 56
Atene, Ann *12:* 18
Atherton, Lisa *38:* 198
Atkinson, Allen *60:* 5
Atkinson, J. Priestman *17:* 275
Atkinson, Janet *86:* 147; *103:* 138
Atkinson, Mike *127:* 74
Atkinson, Wayne *40:* 46
Attard, Karl *196:* 22, 23
Attebery, Charles *38:* 170
Atwell, Debby *150:* 6
Atwood, Ann *7:* 9
Aubrey, Meg Kelleher *77:* 159
Auch, Herm *173:* 7, 8
Auch, Mary Jane *173:* 7
Augarde, Steve *25:* 22; *159:* 7; *210:* 43, 44
Austerman, Miriam *23:* 107
Austin, Margot *11:* 16
Austin, Robert *3:* 44
Austin, Virginia *81:* 205; *127:* 221; *232:* 190
Auth, Tony *51:* 5; *192:* 18
Avendano, Dolores *158:* 74
Avedon, Richard *57:* 140
Averill, Esther *1:* 17; *28:* 39, 40, 41
Avilés, Martha *218:* 6
Axeman, Lois *2:* 32; *11:* 84; *13:* 165; *22:* 8; *23:* 49; *61:* 116; *101:* 124
Axtel, David *155:* 110
Ayer, Jacqueline *13:* 7
Ayer, Margaret *15:* 12; *50:* 120
Ayers, Alan *91:* 58; *107:* 169
Ayliffe, Alex *95:* 164
Ayto, Russell *111:* 5; *112:* 54; *206:* 7, 8; *213:* 56
Azarian, Mary *112:* 9, 10; *114:* 129; *117:* 171; *137:* 163; *171:* 4, 5; *181:* 161; *188:* 128; *232:* 174

B

B.T.B.
    See Blackwell, Basil T.
Baasansuren, Bolormaa *216:* 40
Babbitt, Bradford *33:* 158
Babbitt, Natalie *6:* 6; *8:* 220; *68:* 20; *70:* 242, 243; *194:* 8, 9
Baca, Maria *104:* 5
Bacchus, Andy *94:* 87
Bacha, Andy *109:* 169
Bachelet, Gilles *196:* 18

Bachem, Paul *48:* 180; *67:* 65; *144:* 206
Back, Adam *63:* 125
Back, George *31:* 161
Backes, Nick *190:* 72
Backhouse, Colin *78:* 142
Bacon, Bruce *4:* 74
Bacon, Paul *7:* 155; *8:* 121; *31:* 55; *50:* 42; *56:* 175; *62:* 82, 84
Bacon, Peggy *2:* 11, 228; *46:* 44
Baek, Matthew J. *169:* 95; *202:* 8
Baer, Julie *161:* 2
Baicker-McKee, Carol *177:* 15; *180:* 215
Bailey, Peter *58:* 174; *87:* 221; *194:* 12
Bailey, Sheila *155:* 11
Baker, Alan *22:* 22; *61:* 134; *93:* 11, 12; *146:* 6, 7, 10
Baker, Charlotte *2:* 12
Baker, Garin *89:* 65
Baker, Jeannie *23:* 4; *88:* 18, 19, 20
Baker, Jim *22:* 24
Baker, Joe *82:* 188; *111:* 55; *124:* 70; *197:* 73
Baker, Keith *179:* 6, 7; *222:* 36
Baker, Leslie *112:* 214; *132:* 103, 246; *180:* 74, 246
Baker-Smith, Grahame *223:* 10; *225:* 132
Baldacci, Rudy *184:* 9
Baldridge, Cyrus LeRoy *19:* 69; *44:* 50
Baldus, Jackie *216:* 81
Baldus, Zachary *152:* 231; *187:* 60
Balet, Jan *11:* 22
Balian, Lorna *9:* 16; *91:* 16
Balit, Christina *102:* 24; *159:* 9; *162:* 118, 119; *212:* 2, 3
Ballantyne, R.M. *24:* 34
Ballis, George *14:* 199
Balouch, Kristen *176:* 11
Baltzer, Hans *40:* 30
Banbery, Fred *58:* 15
Bancroft, Bronwyn *216:* 42
Banfill, A. Scott *98:* 7; *112:* 59
Bang, Molly *24:* 37, 38; *69:* 8, 9, 10; *111:* 7,9, 10, 11; *140:* 11; *158:* 37, 38, 39; *195:* 3; *215:* 11, 12, 13, 14
Banik, Yvette Santiago *21:* 136
Banks, Erin Bennett *211:* 12
Banner, Angela
    See Maddison, Angela Mary
Bannerman, Helen *19:* 13, 14
Banning, Greg *202:* 98
Bannon, Laura *6:* 10; *23:* 8
Bantock, Nick *74:* 229; *95:* 6
Banyai, Istvan *185:* 209; *193:* 14, 16; *209:* 155; *223:* 166, 167
Baptist, Michael *37:* 208
Baracca, Sal *135:* 206
Baranaski, Marcin *182:* 113
Barasch, Lynne *126:* 16; *186:* 15
Barbarin, Lucien C., Jr. *89:* 88
Barbour, Karen *96:* 5; *74:* 209; *170:* 16
Bare, Arnold Edwin *16:* 31
Bare, Colleen Stanley *32:* 33
Barger, Jan *147:* 11
Bargery, Geoffrey *14:* 258
Barkat, Jonathan *149:* 177; *164:* 254; *181:* 106; *184:* 186; *196:* 11; *198:* 148
Barker, Carol *31:* 27
Barker, Cicely Mary *49:* 50, 51
Barkley, James *4:* 13; *6:* 11; *13:* 112
Barks, Carl *37:* 27, 28, 29, 30, 31, 32, 33, 34
Barling, Joy *62:* 148
Barling, Tom *9:* 23
Barlow, Gillian *62:* 20
Barlow, Perry *35:* 28
Barlowe, Dot *30:* 223
Barlowe, Wayne *37:* 72; *84:* 43; *105:* 5
Barnard, Bryn *88:* 53; *13:* 55; *169:* 13; *193:* 194
Barneda, David *206:* 11
Barner, Bob *29:* 37; *128:* 33; *136:* 19, 20; *177:* 27
Barnes, Hiram P. *20:* 28

Barnes, Tim *137:* 28
Barnes-Murphy, Rowan *88:* 22
Barnett, Charles II *175:* 150
Barnett, Ivan *70:* 14
Barnett, Moneta *16:* 89; *19:* 142; *31:* 102; *33:* 30, 31, 32; *41:* 153; *61:* 94, 97
Barney, Maginel Wright *39:* 32, 33, 34; *YABC 2:* 306
Barnum, Jay Hyde *11:* 224; *20:* 5; *37:* 189, 190
Baron, Alan *80:* 3; *89:* 123
Barr, George *60:* 74; *69:* 64
Barragán, Paula S. *134:* 116; *186:* 158; *216:* 43, 44, 197; *232:* 133
Barrall, Tim *115:* 152
Barraud, Martin *189:* 38
Barrauds *33:* 114
Barrer-Russell, Gertrude *9:* 65; *27:* 31
Barret, Robert *85:* 134
Barrett, Angela *40:* 136, 137; *62:* 74; *75:* 10; *76:* 142; *144:* 137; *145:* 14; *223:* 14
Barrett, Jennifer *58:* 149
Barrett, John E. *43:* 119
Barrett, Moneta *74:* 10
Barrett, Peter *55:* 169; *86:* 111
Barrett, Robert *62:* 145; *77:* 146; *82:* 35
Barrett, Ron *14:* 24; *26:* 35
Barron, John N. *3:* 261; *5:* 101; *14:* 220
Barrow, Ann *136:* 27
Barrows, Walter *14:* 268
Barry, Ethelred B. *37:* 79; *YABC 1:* 229
Barry, James *14:* 25
Barry, Katharina *2:* 159; *4:* 22
Barry, Robert E. *6:* 12
Barry, Scott *32:* 35
Barshaw, Ruth McNally *203:* 9
Bartenbach, Jean *40:* 31
Barth, Ernest Kurt *2:* 172; *3:* 160; *8:* 26; *10:* 31
Bartholomew, Caty *208:* 153
Bartholomew, Marie *200:* 66
Bartlett, Alison *101:* 88; *165:* 93; *209:* 51
Barton, Byron *8:* 207; *9:* 18; *23:* 66; *80:* 181; *90:* 18, 19, 20, 21; *126:* 29, 30
Barton, Harriett *30:* 71
Barton, Jill *129:* 108; *135:* 120; *145:* 185, 189; *184:* 177; *224:* 142, 143
Barton, Patrice *226:* 14
Bartram, Robert *10:* 42
Bartram, Simon *218:* 8
Bartsch, Jochen *8:* 105; *39:* 38
Bascove, Barbara *45:* 73
Base, Graeme *101:* 15, 16, 17, 18; *162:* 8, 10, 12
Baseman, Gary *174:* 12
Bash, Barbara *132:* 9
Baskin, Leonard *30:* 42, 43, 46, 47; *49:* 125, 126, 128, 129,133; *173:* 120
Bass, Saul *49:* 192
Bassett, Jeni *40:* 99; *64:* 30
Basso, Bill *99:* 139; *189:* 134
Batchelor, Joy *29:* 41, 47, 48
Bate, Norman *5:* 16
Bates, Amy June *188:* 170; *189:* 27, 28
Bates, Leo *24:* 35
Batet, Carmen *39:* 134
Batherman, Muriel *31:* 79; *45:* 185
Battaglia, Aurelius *50:* 44
Batten, John D. *25:* 161, 162
Batten, Mary *162:* 14, 15
Battles, Asa *32:* 94, 95
Bauer, Carla *193:* 6
Bauer, Jutta *150:* 32
Bauernschmidt, Marjorie *15:* 15
Baum, Allyn *20:* 10
Baum, Willi *4:* 24, 25; *7:* 173
Bauman, Leslie *61:* 121
Baumann, Jill *34:* 170
Baumhauer, Hans *11:* 218; *15:* 163, 165, 167
Baxter, Glen *57:* 100
Baxter, Leon *59:* 102

Baxter, Robert *87:* 129
Bayer, Herbert *181:* 16
Bayley, Dorothy *37:* 195
Bayley, Nicola *40:* 104; *41:* 34, 35; *69:* 15; *129:* 33, 34, 35
Baylin, Mark *158:* 233
Baynes, Pauline *2:* 244; *3:* 149; *13:* 133, 135,137, 141; *19:* 18, 19, 20; *32:* 208, 213, 214; *36:* 105, 108; *59:* 12, 13, 14, 16, 17, 18, 20; *100:* 158, 159, 243; *133:* 3, 4
Beach, Lou *150:* 150; *207:* 117, 118
Beaky, Suzanne *232:* 11
Beame, Rona *12:* 40
Bean, Jonathan *196:* 102
Bear's Heart *73:* 215
Beard, Alex *222:* 40
Beard, Dan *22:* 31, 32
Beard, J.H. *YABC 1:* 158
Bearden, Romare *9:* 7; *22:* 35
Beardshaw, Rosalind *169:* 22; *190:* 22; *224:* 12; *225:* 6, 7, 8; *226:* 71
Beardsley, Aubrey *17:* 14; *23:* 181; *59:* 130, 131
Bearman, Jane *29:* 38
Beaton, Cecil *24:* 208
Beaton, Clare *125:* 28; *208:* 67; *220:* 10, 11, 12
Beauce, J.A. *18:* 103
Beaujard, Sophie *81:* 54
Beavers, Ethen *225:* 9
Beccia, Carlyn *189:* 29
Bechtold, Lisze *208:* 29
Beck, Andrea *226:* 16
Beck, Charles *11:* 169; *51:* 173
Beck, Ian *138:* 27; *182:* 150; *190:* 25; *225:* 130
Beck, Melinda *203:* 112
Beck, Ruth *13:* 11
Becker, Harriet *12:* 211
Beckerman, Jonathan *208:* 194
Beckett, Sheilah *25:* 5; *33:* 37, 38
Beckhoff, Harry *1:* 78; *5:* 163
Beckhorn, Susan Williams *189:* 32
Beckman, Kaj *45:* 38, 39, 40, 41
Beckman, Per *45:* 42, 43
Beddows, Eric *72:* 70
Bedford, F.D. *20:* 118, 122; *33:* 170; *41:* 220, 221,230, 233
Bee, Joyce *19:* 62
Bee, William *188:* 6
Beeby, Betty *25:* 36
Beech, Carol *9:* 149
Beech, Mark *192:* 122
Beek *25:* 51, 55, 59
Beeke, Tiphanie *177:* 127; *204:* 140; *212:* 178; *218:* 102
Beekman, Doug *125:* 146, 148
Beerbohm, Max *24:* 208
Beeson, Bob *108:* 57
Begin, Mary Jane *82:* 13; *206:* 13
Beha, Philippe *172:* 85
Behr, Joyce *15:* 15; *21:* 132; *23:* 161
Behrens, Hans *5:* 97
Beier, Ellen *135:* 170; *139:* 47; *183:* 164; *221:* 177; *222:* 151
Beingessner, Laura *220:* 14
Beinicke, Steve *69:* 18
Beisner, Monika *46:* 128, 131; *112:* 127
Belden, Charles J. *12:* 182
Belina, Renate *39:* 132
Bell, Corydon *3:* 20
Bell, Graham *54:* 48
Bell, Julia *151:* 214
Bell, Julie *159:* 172; *165:* 18
Bell, Thomas P. *76:* 182
Bellamy, Glen *127:* 15
Beltran, Alberto *43:* 37
Bemelmans, Ludwig *15:* 19, 21; *100:* 27
Ben-Ami, Doron *75:* 96; *84:* 107; *108:* 132; *110:* 63; *159:* 157; *197:* 142; *233:* 122

Bendall-Brunello, John *150:* 4; *157:* 163; *185:* 3, 4; *203:* 5
Benda, Wladyslaw T. *15:* 256; *30:* 76, 77; *44:* 182
Bender, Robert *77:* 162; *79:* 13; *160:* 23
Bendick, Jeanne *2:* 24; *68:* 27, 28
Benioff, Carol *121:* 42; *175:* 23; *232:* 12
Benner, Cheryl *80:* 11
Bennett, Charles H. *64:* 6
Bennett, Erin Susanne *165:* 216
Bennett, F.I. *YABC 1:* 134
Bennett, James *146:* 240
Bennett, Jill *26:* 61; *41:* 38, 39; *45:* 54
Bennett, Rainey *15:* 26; *23:* 53
Bennett, Richard *15:* 45; *21:* 11, 12, 13; *25:* 175
Bennett, Susan *5:* 55
Benny, Mike *142:* 78; *203:* 13, 14; *207:* 85
Benoit, Elise *77:* 74
Benson, Linda *60:* 130; *62:* 91; *75:* 101; *79:* 156; *134:* 129
Benson, Patrick *68:* 162; *147:* 17, 18, 19, 20
Bentley, Carolyn *46:* 153
Bentley, James *149:* 30
Bentley, Roy *30:* 162
Benton, Jim *172:* 22
Benton, Thomas Hart *2:* 99
Bereal, JaeMe *228:* 16
Berelson, Howard *5:* 20; *16:* 58; *31:* 50
Berenstain, Jan *12:* 47; *64:* 33, 34, 36, 37, 38, 40, 42, 44; *135:* 25, 28, 31, 35
Berenstain, Stan *12:* 47; *64:* 33, 34, 36, 37, 38, 40, 42, 44; *135:* 25, 28, 31, 35
Berenzy, Alix *65:* 13; *73:* 6; *78:* 115
Berg, Joan *1:* 115; *3:* 156; *6:* 26, 58
Berg, Ron *36:* 48, 49; *48:* 37, 38; *67:* 72
Bergen, David *115:* 44; *207:* 34
Berger, Barbara *77:* 14
Berger, Carin *185:* 6; *232:* 14
Berger, Joe *221:* 9
Berger, William M. *14:* 143; *YABC 1:* 204
Bergherr, Mary *74:* 170; *151:* 123
Bergin, Mark *114:* 8, 9; *143:* 95; *160:* 26, 27
Bergstreser, Douglas *69:* 76
Bergum, Constance R. *121:* 14, 15; *208:* 31, 32, 33; *209:* 176
Bering, Claus *13:* 14
Berkeley, Jon *139:* 218
Berkowitz, Jeanette *3:* 249
Berman, Paul *66:* 14
Berman, Rachel *217:* 26
Bernadette
See Watts, Bernadette
Bernard, Gary *216:* 71
Bernardin, James *112:* 24; *167:* 94; *227:* 14, 15
Bernasconi, Pablo *183:* 10, 11
Bernath, Stefen *32:* 76
Berner, Rotraut Susanne *214:* 32
Bernhard, Durga *80:* 13
Bernstein, Michel J. *51:* 71
Bernstein, Ted *38:* 183; *50:* 131
Bernstein, Zena *23:* 46
Berridge, Celia *86:* 63
Berrill, Jacquelyn *12:* 50
Berry, Erick
See Best, Allena
Berry, Holly *205:* 116; *210:* 49, 50
Berry, William D. *14:* 29; *19:* 48
Berry, William A. *6:* 219
Berson, Harold *2:* 17, 18; *4:* 28, 29, 220; *9:* 10; *12:* 19; *17:* 45; *18:* 193; *22:* 85; *34:* 172; *44:* 120; *46:* 42; *80:* 240
Bertholf, Bret *187:* 9; *189:* 32, 33
Berton, Patsy *99:* 16
Bertschmann, Harry *16:* 1
Besco, Don *70:* 99
Beskow, Elsa *20:* 13, 14, 15
Bess, Clayton *63:* 94
Best, Allena *2:* 26; *34:* 76

Betera, Carol *74:* 68
Bethell, Thomas N. *61:* 169
Bethers, Ray *6:* 22
Betteridge, Deirdre *214:* 34
Bettina
   See Ehrlich, Bettina
Betts, Ethel Franklin *17:* 161, 164, 165; *YABC 2:* 47
Betz, Rudolf *59:* 161
Bewick, Thomas *16:* 40, 41, 43, 44, 45, 47; *54:* 150; *YABC 1:* 107
Beyer, Paul J. III *74:* 24
Bezencon, Jacqueline *48:* 40
Biamonte, Daniel *40:* 90
Bianchi, John *91:* 19
Bianco, Pamela *15:* 31; *28:* 44, 45, 46
Bible, Charles *13:* 15
Bice, Clare *22:* 40
Biedrzycki, David *186:* 170; *219:* 7
Bierman, Don *57:* 184
Biggers, John *2:* 123
Biggs, Brian *192:* 38; *196:* 15; *207:* 170
Bikadoroff, Roxanna *201:* 74
Bileck, Marvin *3:* 102; *40:* 36, 37
Bilibin, Ivan *61:* 8, 9, 12, 13, 14, 15, 151, 152, 154, 162
Billington, Patrick *98:* 71
Billout, Guy *144:* 38, 39
Bimen, Levent *5:* 179
Binch, Caroline *81:* 18; *140:* 15, 16; *144:* 115; *211:* 82
Binder, Hannes *169:* 163
Bing, Christopher *126:* 34
Binger, Bill *121:* 46
Binks, Robert *25:* 150
Binzen, Bill *24:* 47
Birch, Reginald *15:* 150; *19:* 33, 34, 35, 36; *37:* 196,197; *44:* 182; *46:* 176; *YABC 1:* 84; *2:* 34, 39
Birch, Wendy *223:* 70
Birchall, Mark *123:* 188
Bird, Esther Brock *1:* 36; *25:* 66
Birdsong, Keith *167:* 85; *219:* 105
Birkett, Georgie *204:* 121
Birkett, Rachel *78:* 206
Birling, Paul *109:* 30
Birmingham, Christian *132:* 243; *143:* 114; *209:* 58; *220:* 20
Birmingham, Lloyd P. *12:* 51; *83:* 13
Biro, Val *1:* 26; *41:* 42; *60:* 178; *67:* 23, 24; *84:* 242, 243
Bischoff, Ilse *44:* 51
Bishop, Don *199:* 133
Bishop, Gavin *97:* 17, 18; *144:* 42, 44; *216:* 52, 55, 56, 57
Bishop, Kathleen Wong *115:* 67
Bishop, Rich *56:* 43
Bite, I. *60:* 14
Bittinger, Ned *93:* 117; *205:* 115
Bjorklund, Lorence *3:* 188, 252; *7:* 100; *9:* 113; *10:* 66; *19:* 178; *33:* 122, 123; *35:* 36, 37, 38, 39,41, 42, 43; *36:* 185; *38:* 93; *47:* 106; *66:* 194; *YABC 1:* 242
Björkman, Steve *91:* 199; *160:* 110; *198:* 18; *218:* 188; *223:* 20, 21
Blabey, Aaron *214:* 35
Black Sheep *164:* 100
Blackburn, Loren H. *63:* 10
Blackall, Sophie *194:* 140; *209:* 157; *231:* 31, 115
Blackford, John *137:* 105; *180:* 36
Blackwell, Basil T. *YABC 1:* 68, 69
Blackwood, Freya *199:* 9
Blackwood, Gary L. *118:* 17
Blades, Ann *16:* 52; *37:* 213; *50:* 41; *69:* 21; *99:* 215
Blair, Jay *45:* 46; *46:* 155
Blaisdell, Elinore *1:* 121; *3:* 134; *35:* 63
Blake, Anne Catharine *189:* 71
Blake, Francis *198:* 4

Blake, Quentin *3:* 170; *10:* 48; *13:* 38; *21:* 180; *26:* 60; *28:* 228; *30:* 29, 31; *40:* 108; *45:* 219; *46:* 165, 168; *48:* 196; *52:* 10, 11, 12,13, 14, 15, 16, 17; *73:* 41, 43; *78:* 84, 86; *80:* 250, 251; *84:* 210, 211, 212; *87:* 177; *96:* 24, 26, 28; *124:* 79; *125:* 32, 34; *181:* 139; *211:* 26, 27; *227:* 176; *229:* 167
Blake, Robert J. *37:* 90; *53:* 67; *54:* 23; *160:* 28, 29
Blake, William *30:* 54, 56, 57, 58, 59, 60
Blakeslee, Lys *218:* 11, 105
Blanchard, N. Taylor *82:* 140
Blass, Jacqueline *8:* 215
Blazek, Scott R. *91:* 71
Blecha, Aaron *233:* 17
Bleck, Cathie *118:* 116
Bleck, Linda *204:* 124
Blegvad, Erik *2:* 59; *3:* 98; *5:* 117; *7:* 131; *11:* 149; *14:* 34, 35; *18:* 237; *32:* 219; *60:* 106; *66:* 16, 17, 18, 19; *70:* 233; *76:* 18; *82:* 106; *87:* 45; *100:* 188; *129:* 125; *132:* 17, 18, 19, 20; *176:* 14; *200:* 100; *YABC 1:* 201
Blessen, Karen *93:* 126
Bliss, Corinne Demas *37:* 38
Bliss, Harry *196:* 27, 28, 29
Blitt, Barry *179:* 199; *187:* 13; *225:* 198
Bloch, Lucienne *10:* 12
Blondon, Herve *129:* 48; *183:* 22
Bloom, Lloyd *35:* 180; *36:* 149; *47:* 99; *62:* 117; *68:* 231; *72:* 136; *75:* 185; *83:* 99; *108:* 19; *229:* 114
Bloom, Suzanne *172:* 23, 24; *232:* 17
Blossom, Dave *34:* 29
Blumenschein, E.L. *YABC 1:* 113, 115
Blumer, Patt *29:* 214
Blundell, Kim *29:* 36
Bluthenthal, Diana Cain *93:* 32; *104:* 106; *177:* 26; *232:* 21
Blythe, Benjamin *128:* 7
Blythe, Gary *112:* 52; *181:* 166; *182:* 64; *185:* 7; *186:* 116, 117
Boake, Kathy *176:* 185
Board, Perry *171:* 99
Boardman, Gwenn *12:* 60
Boase, Susan *224:* 53
Boatwright, Phil *211:* 195
Bober, Richard *125:* 145; *132:* 40
Bobri, *30:* 138; *47:* 27
Bock, Vera *1:* 187; *21:* 41
Bock, William Sauts *8:* 7; *14:* 37; *16:* 120; *21:* 141; *36:* 177; *62:* 203
Bodecker, N(iels) M(ogens) *8:* 13; *14:* 2; *17:* 55, 56, 57; *73:* 22, 23, 24
Boehm, Linda *40:* 31
Bogacki, Tomek *138:* 31, 32; *144:* 123; *202:* 13
Bogan, Paulette *197:* 152; *201:* 17
Bogdan, Florentina *107:* 43
Bohdal, Susi *22:* 44; *101:* 20
Bohlen, Nina *58:* 13
Boies, Alex *96:* 53
Bok, Chip *205:* 16
Bolam, Emily *101:* 216; *159:* 12; *205:* 59
Bolian, Polly *3:* 270; *4:* 30; *13:* 77; *29:* 197
Bolle, Frank *87:* 100; *208:* 101
Bollen, Roger *79:* 186; *83:* 16
Bolling, Vickey *114:* 44
Bollinger, Peter *101:* 7; *128:* 198; *172:* 26
Bolognese, Don *2:* 147, 231; *4:* 176; *7:* 146; *17:* 43; *23:* 192; *24:* 50; *34:* 108; *36:* 133; *71:* 24, 25; *103:* 131; *129:* 39, 40
Bolster, Rob *186:* 169
Bolton, A.T. *57:* 158
Bond, Arnold *18:* 116
Bond, Barbara Higgins *21:* 102
Bond, Bruce *52:* 97
Bond, Felicia *38:* 197; *49:* 55, 56; *89:* 170; *90:* 171; *126:* 37
Bond, Higgins *177:* 22, 23; *209:* 175; *220:* 22, 23, 24
Bone, J. *230:* 11, 181

Bonn, Pat *43:* 40
Bonner, Hannah *197:* 13, 14
Bonners, Susan *41:* 40; *85:* 36; *94:* 99, 100; *151:* 105, 106
Bonnet, Rosalinde *230:* 79
Bono, Mary *184:* 73
Bonsall, Crosby *23:* 6
Booker, Philip *225:* 16
Boon, Debbie *103:* 6; *144:* 188
Boon, Emilie *86:* 23, 24
Boone, Debbie *165:* 77
Boore, Sara *60:* 73
Bootman, Colin *155:* 13; *159:* 35; *174:* 192; *222:* 128
Booth, Franklin *YABC 2:* 76
Booth, George *191:* 13
Booth, Graham *32:* 193; *37:* 41, 42
Borda, Juliette *102:* 188
Bordier, Georgette *16:* 54
Boren, Tinka *27:* 128
Borges, Jose Francisco *119:* 62
Borja, Robert *22:* 48
Born, Adolf *49:* 63
Bornstein, Ruth *14:* 44; *88:* 45, 46; *107:* 30
Borten, Helen *3:* 54; *5:* 24
Bosin, Blackbear *69:* 104
Bossom, Naomi *35:* 48
Bostock, Mike *83:* 221; *114:* 14; *188:* 205
Boston, Peter *19:* 42
Bosustow, Stephen *34:* 202
Boszko, Ron *75:* 47
Bottner, Barbara *14:* 46
Boucher, Joelle *41:* 138
Boulat, Pierre *44:* 40
Boulet, Susan Seddon *50:* 47
Bouma, Paddy *118:* 25; *128:* 16
Bour, Daniele *66:* 145
Bourke-White, Margaret *15:* 286, 287; *57:* 102
Boutavant, Marc *200:* 136
Boutet de Monvel, M. *30:* 61, 62, 63, 65
Bowen, Betsy *105:* 222
Bowen, Richard *42:* 134
Bowen, Ruth *31:* 188
Bower, Ron *29:* 33
Bowers, David *95:* 38; *115:* 20; *127:* 169, 170; *165:* 57; *207:* 11
Bowers, Tim *185:* 35; *201:* 41; *218:* 13
Bowman, Claire *174:* 177
Bowman, Eric *151:* 23
Bowman, Leslie *85:* 203; *105:* 108; *116:* 76; *128:* 234; *182:* 24, 25
Bowman, Peter *146:* 214, 215; *150:* 115
Bowser, Carolyn Ewing *22:* 253
Boxall, Ed *178:* 28
Boyd, Aaron *158:* 242
Boyd, Patti *45:* 31
Boyle, Eleanor Vere *28:* 50, 51
Boynton, Sandra *57:* 13, 14, 15; *107:* 36, 37; *152:* 12, 13, 14
Bozzo, Frank *4:* 154
Brabbs, Derry *55:* 170
Brace, Eric *132:* 193, 194; *152:* 71; *184:* 195; *197:* 6; *201:* 54; *233:* 160
Brackers de Hugo, Pierre *115:* 21
Bradford, June *158:* 138
Bradford, Ron *7:* 157
Bradley, David P. *69:* 105
Bradley, Richard D. *26:* 182
Bradley, William *5:* 164
Brady, Irene *4:* 31; *42:* 37; *68:* 191
Bragg, Michael *32:* 78; *46:* 31
Bragg, Ruth Gembicki *77:* 18
Brainerd, John W. *65:* 19
Braithwaite, Althea *23:* 12, 13; *119:* 16
Brak, Syd *146:* 187
Bralds, Braldt *90:* 28; *91:* 151
Bram, Elizabeth *30:* 67
Bramley, Peter *4:* 3
Brandenberg, Aliki *2:* 36, 37; *24:* 222; *35:* 49, 50, 51,52, 53, 54, 56, 57; *75:* 15, 17; *92:* 205; *113:* 18, 19, 20; *157:* 28; *156:* 111

Brandenburg, Alexa *75:* 19
Brandenburg, Jim *47:* 58; *150:* 212
Brandi, Lillian *31:* 158
Brandon, Brumsic, Jr. *9:* 25
Brannen, Sarah S. *202:* 15; *216:* 199
Bransom, Paul *17:* 121; *43:* 44
Braren, Loretta Trezzo *87:* 193
Brassard, France *186:* 22
Braun, Wendy *80:* 17, 18; *213:* 14
Brautigam, Don *115:* 175, 176; *225:* 109
Brazell, Derek *75:* 105; *79:* 9
Breathed, Berkeley *86:* 27, 28, 29; *161:* 13,
   14; *229:* 10, 11, 12
Breckenreid, Julia *192:* 209
Breen, Steve *186:* 23
Brennan, Steve *83:* 230; *101:* 184
Brenner, Fred *22:* 85; *36:* 34; *42:* 34
Brett, Bernard *22:* 54
Brett, Harold M. *26:* 98, 99, 100
Brett, Jan *30:* 135; *42:* 39; *71:* 31, 32; *130:*
   23, 24, 25, 26, 27; *171:* 15, 16
Brewer, Paul *106:* 115; *145:* 202; *230:* 13
Brewer, Sally King *33:* 44
Brewster, Patience *40:* 68; *45:* 22, 183; *51:* 20;
   66: 144; *89:* 4; *97:* 30, 31; *212:* 99
Brick, John *10:* 15
Brickman, Robin D. *131:* 88; *142:* 150; *155:*
   18; *178:* 109; *184:* 32
Bridge, David R. *45:* 28
Bridgman, L.J. *37:* 77
Bridwell, Norman *4:* 37; *138:* 36, 37, 40
Brierley, Louise *91:* 22; *96:* 165; *183:* 51
Briggs, Harry *172:* 187
Briggs, Raymond *10:* 168; *23:* 20, 21; *66:* 29,
   31, 32; *131:* 28, 29; *184:* 15, 16
Brigham, Grace A. *37:* 148
Bright, Robert *24:* 55
Brighton, Catherine *107:* 39; *206:* 23
Brinckloe, Julie *13:* 18; *24:* 79, 115; *29:* 35;
   63: 140; *81:* 131
Brion *47:* 116
Brisley, Joyce L. *22:* 57
Brisson, James F. *110:* 60
Brittingham, Geoffrey *88:* 37
Brix-Henker, Silke *81:* 194
Broadway, Hannah *208:* 104
Brock, Charles E. *15:* 97; *19:* 247, 249; *23:*
   224, 225; *36:* 88; *42:* 41, 42, 43, 44, 45;
   100: 189; *YABC 1:* 194, 196, 203
Brock, Emma *7:* 21
Brock, Henry Matthew *15:* 81; *16:* 141; *19:*
   71; *34:* 115; *40:* 164; *42:* 47, 48, 49; *49:* 66
Brocksopp, Arthur *57:* 157
Broda, Ron *136:* 180; *174:* 123
Brodkin, Gwen *34:* 135
Brodovitch, Alexi *52:* 22
Bromhall, Winifred *5:* 11; *26:* 38
Bromley, Lizzy *159:* 179
Bronson, Linda *150:* 210; *174:* 133; *203:* 16,
   17; *225:* 178
Brooke, L. Leslie *16:* 181, 182, 183, 186; *17:*
   15, 16, 17; *18:* 194
Brooker, Christopher *15:* 251
Brooker, Kyrsten *111:* 94; *140:* 28; *162:* 111;
   175: 108; *186:* 42, 225; *199:* 12; *201:* 30;
   219: 98
Brooks, Erik *166:* 52; *182:* 30; *232:* 139
Brooks, Karen Stormer *110:* 186; *220:* 65
Brooks, Maya Itzna *92:* 153
Brooks, Ron *94:* 15; *197:* 188; *212:* 6, 7, 8, 9
Brooks, S.G. *178:* 127
Broomfield, Maurice *40:* 141
Brotman, Adolph E. *5:* 21
Brown, Buck *45:* 48
Brown, Calef *179:* 18; *210:* 206; *217:* 30, 31;
   225: 201
Brown, Christopher *62:* 124, 125, 127, 128
Brown, Craig *73:* 28; *84:* 65; *224:* 18
Brown, Dan *61:* 167; *115:* 183, 184; *116:* 28,
   29; *193:* 190; *200:* 21, 23
Brown, David *7:* 47; *48:* 52

Brown, Denise *11:* 213
Brown, Don *172:* 29
Brown, Elbrite *195:* 39; *198:* 5
Brown, Ford Madox *48:* 74
Brown, Gayle *224:* 184
Brown, Hunter *191:* 111, 112
Brown, Judith Gwyn *1:* 45; *7:* 5; *8:* 167; *9:*
   182, 190; *20:* 16, 17, 18; *23:* 142; *29:* 117;
   33: 97; *36:* 23, 26; *43:* 184; *48:* 201, 223;
   49: 69; *86:* 227; *110:* 188; *153:* 7
Brown, Kathryn *98:* 26
Brown, Lisa *187:* 175
Brown, Laurie Krasny *99:* 30
Brown, Leo *225:* 18
Brown, Marc (Tolon) *10:* 17, 197; *14:* 263;
   51: 18; *53:* 11, 12, 13, 15, 16, 17; *75:* 58;
   80: 24, 25, 26; *82:* 261; *99:* 29; *145:* 22, 23,
   25, 27; *162:* 198; *224:* 136
Brown, Marcia *7:* 30; *25:* 203; *47:* 31, 32, 33,
   34, 35,36, 37, 38, 39, 40, 42, 43, 44; *YABC*
   1: 27
Brown, Margery W. *5:* 32, 33; *10:* 3
Brown, Martin *101:* 43
Brown, Mary Barrett *97:* 74
Brown, Palmer *36:* 40
Brown, Paul *25:* 26; *26:* 107
Brown, Richard *61:* 18; *67:* 30
Brown, Rick *78:* 71; *150:* 154; *224:* 16
Brown, Robert S. *85:* 33
Brown, Rod *157:* 142; *232:* 32, 33
Brown, Ruth *55:* 165; *86:* 112, 113; *105:* 16,
   17, 18; *171:* 178
Brown, Trevor *99:* 160; *139:* 247; *189:* 206
Browne, Anthony *45:* 50, 51, 52; *61:* 21, 22,
   23, 24, 25; *105:* 21, 22, 23, 25
Browne, Dik *8:* 212; *67:* 32, 33, 35, 37, 39
Browne, Gordon *16:* 97; *64:* 114, 116, 117,
   119, 121
Browne, Hablot K. *15:* 65, 80; *21:* 14, 15, 16,
   17, 18, 19,20; *24:* 25
Browne, Jane *165:* 222
Browning, Coleen *4:* 132
Browning, Diane *233:* 30
Browning, Mary Eleanor *24:* 84
Bruce, Robert *23:* 23
Brude, Dick *48:* 215
Bruel, Nick *166:* 41; *205:* 17, 18
Brule, Al *3:* 135
Brumbeau, Jeff *157:* 29
Bruna, Dick *43:* 48, 49, 50; *76:* 27, 28
Brundage, Frances *19:* 244
Brunhoff, Jean de *24:* 57, 58
Brunhoff, Laurent de *24:* 60; *71:* 35, 36, 37
Brunkus, Denise *84:* 50; *123:* 117; *178:* 209;
   193: 99; *204:* 10, 11, 12; *209:* 202
Brunson, Bob *43:* 135
Bryan, Ashley *31:* 44; *72:* 27, 28, 29; *107:* 92;
   116: 192; *132:* 24; *178:* 33, 34, 35; *208:* 83
Bryant, Laura J. *176:* 36; *183:* 168; *214:* 141;
   222: 49, 152
Bryant, Michael *93:* 74
Brychta, Alex *21:* 21
Bryer, Diana *107:* 121
Bryson, Bernarda *3:* 88, 146; *39:* 26; *44:* 185;
   131: 40
Buba, Joy *12:* 83; *30:* 226; *44:* 56
Buchanan, George *166:* 198
Buchanan, Lilian *13:* 16
Buchanan, Rachel *171:* 71
Bucholtz-Ross, Linda *44:* 137
Buchs, Thomas *40:* 38
Buck, Margaret Waring *3:* 30
Buckhardt, Marc *172:* 59
Buckley, Mike *166:* 180
Budwine, Greg *175:* 172
Buehner, Mark *104:* 12, 15; *105:* 160; *119:* 98;
   157: 188; *159:* 39, 40, 43; *192:* 111; *219:*
   13, 14, 15, 16; *221:* 17, 18, 19
Buehr, Walter *3:* 31
Buell, Carl *222:* 68
Buff, Conrad *19:* 52, 53, 54

Buff, Mary *19:* 52, 53
Bull, Charles Livingston *18:* 207; *88:* 175, 176
Bullen, Anne *3:* 166, 167
Buller, Jon *205:* 21
Bullock, Kathleen *77:* 24
Bumgarner-Kirby, Claudia *77:* 194
Burbank, Addison *37:* 43
Burchard, Peter Duncan *3:* 197; *5:* 35; *6:* 158,
   218; *143:* 17
Burckhardt, Marc *94:* 48; *110:* 89; *196:* 41;
   199: 116
Burden, Andrea *227:* 26
Burger, Carl *3:* 33; *45:* 160, 162
Burgeson, Marjorie *19:* 31
Burgess, Anne *76:* 252
Burgess, Gelett *32:* 39, 42
Burgess, Mark *157:* 31
Burke, Jim *179:* 19; *185:* 63
Burke, Phillip *95:* 117
Burkert, Nancy Ekholm *18:* 186; *22:* 140; *24:*
   62, 63,64, 65; *26:* 53; *29:* 60, 61; *46:* 171;
   YABC 1: 46
Burkhardt, Bruce *142:* 86
Burkhardt, Melissa A. *142:* 86
Burleson, Joe *104:* 35; *172:* 139; *227:* 124
Burn, Doris *6:* 172
Burn, Jeffrey *89:* 125; *152:* 132
Burn, Ted
   See Burn, Thomas E.
Burn, Thomas E. *151:* 41; *232:* 40
Burnard, Damon *115:* 23
Burnett, Lindy *210:* 59
Burnett, Virgil *44:* 42
Burningham, John *9:* 68; *16:* 60, 61; *59:* 28,
   29, 30,31, 32, 33, 35; *111:* 18, 19, 21; *160:*
   37; *225:* 21, 24
Burns, Howard M. *12:* 173
Burns, Jim *47:* 70; *86:* 32; *91:* 197; *123:* 16
Burns, M.F. *26:* 69
Burns, Raymond *9:* 29
Burns, Robert *24:* 106
Burr, Dan *65:* 28; *108:* 134; *164:* 203; *182:* 68
Burr, Dane *12:* 2
Burra, Edward *YABC 2:* 68
Burrell, Galen *56:* 76
Burri, Rene *41:* 143; *54:* 166
Burridge, Marge Opitz *14:* 42
Burris, Burmah *4:* 81
Burroughs, John Coleman *41:* 64
Burroughs, Studley O. *41:* 65
Burton, Marilee Robin *46:* 33
Burton, Virginia Lee *2:* 43; *44:* 49, 51; *100:*
   46, 47; *YABC 1:* 24; *147:* 56
Buscema, Stephanie *232:* 34
Bush, Timothy *228:* 138
Busoni, Rafaello *1:* 186; *3:* 224; *6:* 126; *14:* 5;
   16: 62, 63
Butchkes, Sidney *50:* 58
Butler, Geoff *94:* 20
Butler, Ralph *116:* 212
Butterfield, Ned *1:* 153; *27:* 128; *79:* 63
Butterworth, Ian *184:* 48, 49
Butterworth, Nick *106:* 43, 44; *149:* 34
Buxton, John *123:* 12
Buzelli, Christopher *105:* 149
Buzonas, Gail *29:* 88
Buzzell, Russ W. *12:* 177
Byard, Carole *39:* 44; *57:* 18, 19, 20; *60:* 60;
   61: 93, 96; *69:* 210; *78:* 246; *79:* 227
Byars, Betsy *46:* 35
Byfield, Barbara Ninde *8:* 18
Byfield, Graham *32:* 29
Bynum, Janie *176:* 50
Byrd, Robert *13:* 218; *33:* 46; *158:* 70; *212:*
   100; *226:* 39, 40; *229:* 102; *232:* 167
Byrd, Samuel *123:* 104

C

Cabat, Erni 74: 38
Cabban, Vanessa 138: 73; 176: 39; 185: 65; 227: 70
Cabrera, Jane 103: 24; 152: 27; 182: 33, 34
Caceres, Ana Palmero 198: 106
Caddy, Alice 6: 41
Cady, Harrison 17: 21, 23; 19: 57, 58
Caffrey, Aileen 72: 223; 141: 154
Cairns, Julia 177: 37
Caldecott, Randolph 16: 98, 103; 17: 32, 33, 36, 38, 39; 26: 90; 100: 49, 50; YABC 2: 172
Calder, Alexander 18: 168
Calderón, Gloria 179: 5
Calderon, W. Frank 25: 160
Caldwell, Ben 105: 75; 149: 60; 195: 61
Caldwell, Clyde 98: 100; 116: 39; 208: 145
Caldwell, Doreen 23: 77; 71: 41
Caldwell, John 46: 225
Call, Greg 126: 135; 165: 49; 182: 105, 163; 197: 18, 19; 200: 159; 209: 166; 212: 161; 229: 122
Callahan, Kevin 22: 42
Callahan, Philip S. 25: 77
Callan, Jamie 59: 37
Callen, Liz 231: 37
Calvert, Rosemary 218: 96
Calvin, James 61: 92
Camburn-Bracalente, Carol A. 118: 22
Cameron, Chad 190: 144
Cameron, Julia Margaret 19: 203
Cameron, Scott 99: 18
Camm, Martin 140: 208, 209, 210
Campbell, Ann 11: 43; 123: 182; 183: 68
Campbell, Bill 89: 39
Campbell, Ken 126: 143; 205: 162
Campbell, Robert 55: 120
Campbell, Rod 51: 27; 98: 34
Campbell, Walter M. YABC 2: 158
Camps, Luis 28: 120, 121; 66: 35
Canga, C.B. 187: 165
Caniglia, Jeremy 201: 89
Cann, Helen 124: 50; 141: 78; 170: 138; 179: 22, 23
Cannell, Jon 196: 43
Cannon, Janell 78: 25; 128: 40
Canright, David 36: 162
Cantone, AnnaLaura 182: 146; 196: 80
Canty, Thomas 85: 161; 92: 47; 113: 192; 134: 60; 185: 117
Canyon, Christopher 150: 44; 151: 112
Cáparo, Antonio Javier 204: 128; 218: 88; 220: 114; 221: 167; 227: 125; 231: 154
Caple, Laurie 228: 9
Caporale, Wende 70: 42
Capp, Al 61: 28, 30, 31, 40, 41, 43, 44
Cappon, Manuela 154: 64; 218: 149
Caras, Peter 36: 64
Caraway, Caren 57: 22
Caraway, James 3: 200, 201
Carbe, Nino 29: 183
Cardinale, Christopher 231: 38
Cares, Linda 67: 176
Carigiet, Alois 24: 67
Carle, Eric 4: 42; 11: 121; 12: 29; 65: 32,33, 34, 36; 73: 63, 65; 163: 55, 56
Carling, Amelia Lau 164: 46
Carlino, Angela 168: 43; 188: 20
Carlson, Nancy L. 41: 116; 56: 25; 90: 45; 144: 48, 50; 213: 24, 25, 26
Carluccio, Maria 175: 129; 221: 119
Carmi, Giora 79: 35; 149: 40; 208: 126
Carpenter, Nancy 76: 128; 86: 173; 89: 171; 131: 186; 134: 8; 138: 215; 153: 204; 159: 93; 165: 232; 211: 134; 216: 113
Carr, Archie 37: 225

Carrick, Donald 5: 194; 39: 97; 49: 70; 53: 156; 63: 15, 16, 17, 18, 19, 21; 80: 131; 86: 151; 118: 24
Carrick, Malcolm 28: 59, 60
Carrick, Paul 118: 26; 194: 28
Carrick, Valery 21: 47
Carrier, Lark 71: 43
Carroll, Jim 88: 211; 140: 177; 153: 99; 195: 75
Carroll, Lewis
    See Dodgson, Charles L.
Carroll, Michael 72: 5
Carroll, Pamela 84: 68; 128: 214; 199: 130
Carroll, Ruth 7: 41; 10: 68
Carter, Abby 81: 32; 97: 121; 102: 61; 163: 139; 164: 125; 184: 22, 23; 191: 85; 222: 51; 233: 84, 94
Carter, Barbara 47: 167, 169
Carter, David A. 114: 24, 25; 170: 42, 43; 228: 29
Carter, Don 124: 54; 184: 100; 192: 43, 44, 45
Carter, Harry 22: 179
Carter, Helene 15: 38; 22: 202, 203; YABC 2: 220, 221
Carter, Penny 173: 91
Cartlidge, Michelle 49: 65; 96: 50, 51
Cartwright, Reg 63: 61, 62; 78: 26; 143: 4
Cartwright, Shannon 176: 81
Carty, Leo 4: 196; 7: 163; 58: 131
Cary 4: 133; 9: 32; 20: 2; 21: 143
Cary, Page 12: 41
Casale, Paul 71: 63; 109: 122; 136: 28
Case, Chris 209: 23
Case, Sandra E. 16: 2
Caseley, Judith 87: 36; 159: 47, 48, 49
Casilla, Robert 78: 7; 167: 124; 211: 41; 212: 165
Casino, Steve 85: 193
Cassel, Lili
    See Wronker, Lili Cassel
Cassel-Wronker, Lili
    See Wronker, Lili Cassel
Cassels, Jean 8: 50; 150: 119; 173: 37; 186: 182
Cassen, Melody 140: 51
Cassity, Don 104: 24
Cassler, Carl 75: 137, 138; 82: 162
Casson, Hugh 65: 38, 40, 42, 43
Castellon, Federico 48: 45, 46, 47, 48
Castle, Jane 4: 80
Castro L., Antonio 84: 71; 226: 43
Casu, Danny "casroc" 201: 10
Catalano, Dominic 94: 79; 163: 60, 61; 162: 54
Catalanotto, Peter 63: 170; 70: 23; 71: 182; 72: 96; 74: 114; 76: 194, 195; 77: 7; 79: 157; 80: 28, 67; 83: 157; 85: 27; 108: 11; 113: 30, 31, 33, 34, 36; 114: 27, 28, 29; 117: 53; 124: 168; 159: 54, 55; 195: 19, 20, 21, 22, 24, 174; 200: 156; 207: 103; 209: 184; 226: 4
Catania, Tom 68: 82
Cather, Carolyn 3: 83; 15: 203; 34: 216
Catlin, George 214: 172
Catrow, David 117: 179; 152: 31, 33; 173: 24; 206: 29; 231: 107
Catusanu, Mircea 222: 53
Cauley, Lorinda Bryan 44: 135; 46: 49
Cayard, Bruce 38: 67
Cazet, Denys 52: 27; 99: 39, 40; 163: 65, 66; 191: 25, 27, 28
Ceccoli, Nicoletta 181: 39; 188: 99; 199: 118; 209: 6
Cecil, Randy 127: 132, 133; 187: 16, 17; 191: 168; 209: 5; 223: 37, 38; 224: 83; 233: 156
Cellini, Joseph 2: 73; 3: 35; 16: 116; 47: 103
Cepeda, Joe 90: 62; 109: 91; 134: 172; 159: 57, 58, 164; 197: 157; 203: 69, 95; 215: 38, 39, 40
Chabrian, Debbi 45: 55

Chabrian, Deborah 51: 182; 53: 124; 63: 107; 75: 84; 79: 85; 82: 247; 89: 93; 101: 197; 212: 13
Chagnon, Mary 37: 158
Chalmers, Mary 3: 145; 13: 148; 33: 125; 66: 214
Chamberlain, Christopher 45: 57
Chamberlain, Margaret 46: 51; 106: 89; 188: 193; 212: 16, 17; 224: 181
Chamberlain, Nigel 78: 140
Chambers, C.E. 17: 230
Chambers, Dave 12: 151
Chambers, Jill 134: 110
Chambers, Mary 4: 188
Chambliss, Maxie 42: 186; 56: 159; 93: 163, 164; 103: 178; 186: 33, 34; 196: 39; 223: 182
Champlin, Dale 136: 124
Chan, Harvey 96: 236; 99: 153; 143: 218; 179: 144; 211: 219
Chan, Peter 207: 21; 221: 39
Chandler, David P. 28: 62
Chaney, Howard 139: 27
Chang, Warren 101: 209
Chapel, Jody 68: 20
Chapman, C.H. 13: 83, 85, 87
Chapman, Frederick T. 6: 27; 44: 28
Chapman, Gaye 203: 133
Chapman, Gaynor 32: 52, 53
Chapman, Jane 145: 186; 150: 56; 166: 220; 174: 202; 176: 43, 44; 179: 131; 202: 189; 212: 20, 21, 22; 216: 123, 225; 221: 181, 182
Chapman, Lynne 175: 31; 197: 25; 208: 44
Chapman-Crane, Jeff 220: 101
Chappell, Warren 3: 172; 21: 56; 27: 125
Charles, Donald 30: 154, 155
Charlip, Remy 4: 48; 34: 138; 68: 53, 54; 119: 29, 30; 210: 63, 64
Charlot, Jean 1: 137, 138; 8: 23; 14: 31; 48: 151; 56: 21
Charlot, Martin 64: 72
Charlton, Michael 34: 50; 37: 39
Charmatz, Bill 7: 45
Chartier, Normand 9: 36; 52: 49; 66: 40; 74: 220; 145: 169; 168: 91; 177: 108
Chase, Lynwood M. 14: 4
Chast, Roz 97: 39, 40; 212: 25
Chastain, Madye Lee 4: 50
Chateron, Ann 152: 19
Chatterton, Martin 68: 102; 152: 19; 225: 42
Chau, Tungwai 140: 35
Chauncy, Francis 24: 158
Chayka, Doug 145: 97; 177: 150; 196: 46; 212: 58
Chee, Cheng-Khee 79: 42; 81: 224; 180: 245
Chen, Chih-sien 90: 226
Chen, Tony 6: 45; 19: 131; 29: 126; 34: 160
Chen, Wendy 221: 76
Chen, Yong 183: 34
Cheney, T.A. 11: 47
Cheng, Andrea 205: 28
Cheng, Judith 36: 45; 51: 16
Chermayeff, Ivan 47: 53
Cherry, David 93: 40
Cherry, Lynne 34: 52; 65: 184; 87: 111; 99: 46, 47
Chesak, Lina 135: 118
Chess, Victoria 12: 6; 33: 42, 48, 49; 40: 194; 41: 145; 69: 80; 72: 100; 92: 33, 34; 104: 167
Chessa, Francesca 233: 40
Chessare, Michele 41: 50; 56: 48; 69: 145
Chesterton, G.K. 27: 43, 44, 45, 47
Chestnutt, David 47: 217
Chesworth, Michael 75: 24, 152: 88: 136; 94: 25; 98: 155; 160: 42; 207: 23, 24, 25; 214: 145
Chetham, Celia 134: 34
Chetwin, Grace 86: 40
Cheung, Irving 158: 96

Chevalier, Christa *35:* 66
Chew, Ruth *7:* 46; *132:* 147
Chewning, Randy *92:* 206
Chichester Clark, Emma *72:* 121; *77:* 212; *78:* 209; *87:* 143; *117:* 37, 39, 40; *144:* 138; *156:* 24, 25; *209:* 26
Chifflart *47:* 113, 127
Child, Lauren *119:* 32; *183:* 30, 31
Chin, Alex *28:* 54
Chitwood, Susan Tanner *163:* 16
Cho, Shinta *8:* 126
Chodos-Irvine, Margaret *52:* 102, 103, 107; *152:* 44
Choi, Yangsook *171:* 134; *173:* 135; *178:* 38, 39, 40
Choksi, Nishant *222:* 54
Chollat, Emilie *170:* 203
Chollick, Jay *25:* 175
Choma, Christina *99:* 169
Chomey, Steve *188:* 53
Chorao, Kay *7:* 200, 201; *8:* 25; *11:* 234; *33:* 187; *35:* 239; *69:* 35; *70:* 235; *123:* 174; *193:* 179; *215:* 43, 44, 45, 46; *229:* 174
Chorney, Steve *221:* 63
Chow, Frances J. Soo Ping *206:* 36
Chowdhury, Subrata *62:* 130; *162:* 22, 23
Christelow, Eileen *38:* 44; *83:* 198, 199; *90:* 57, 58; *184:* 26
Christensen, Bonnie *93:* 100; *153:* 67; *213:* 29, 30
Christensen, Gardell Dano *1:* 57
Christensen, James C. *140:* 226
Christiana, David *90:* 64; *135:* 13; *171:* 7; *195:* 26, 27
Christiansen, Per *40:* 24
Christie, R. Gregory *116:* 107; *127:* 20, 21; *162:* 179; *164:* 114; *165:* 137; *174:* 157; *179:* 172; *185:* 17, 18, 19; *200:* 2; *204:* 85; *215:* 207; *218:* 57; *220:* 80, 130; *225:* 45, 46, 47; *226:* 211; *231:* 113
Christy, Howard Chandler *17:* 163, 164, 165, 168, 169; *19:* 186, 187; *21:* 22, 23, 24, 25
Christy, Jana *194:* 21
Chronister, Robert *23:* 138; *63:* 27; *69:* 167
Church, Caroline Jayne *179:* 27; *219:* 28, 29
Church, Frederick *YABC 1:* 155
Chute, Marchette *1:* 59
Chwast, Jacqueline *1:* 63; *2:* 275; *6:* 46, 47; *11:* 125; *12:* 202; *14:* 235
Chwast, Seymour *3:* 128, 129; *18:* 43; *27:* 152; *92:* 79; *96:* 56, 57, 58; *146:* 32, 33; *197:* 99
Cieslawski, Steve *101:* 142; *127:* 116; *158:* 169, 171; *190:* 174; *212:* 85; *228:* 123
Cinelli, Lisa *146:* 253
Cirlin, Edgard *2:* 168
Clairin, Georges *53:* 109
Clapp, John *105:* 66; *109:* 58; *126:* 7; *129:* 148; *130:* 165; *195:* 48; *220:* 102
Clark, Brenda *119:* 85; *153:* 55
Clark, David *77:* 164; *134:* 144, 145, *216:* 66, 67
Clark, Emma Chichester
  See Chichester Clark, Emma
Clark, Robert *227:* 170
Clark, Victoria *35:* 159
Clarke, Greg *169:* 134; *215:* 47, 115
Clarke, Gus *72:* 226; *134:* 31
Clarke, Harry *23:* 172, 173
Clarke, Peter *75:* 102
Claverie, Jean *38:* 46; *88:* 29
Clavis, Philippe Goossens *182:* 167
Clay, Wil *203:* 29
Clayton, Elaine *159:* 60; *209:* 32
Clayton, Robert *9:* 181
Cleary, Brian P. *186:* 37
Cleaver, Elizabeth *8:* 204; *23:* 36
Cleland, Janet *225:* 111; *226:* 48
Cleland, T.M. *26:* 92
Clemens, Peter *61:* 125
Clement, Charles *20:* 38

Clement, Gary *186:* 79; *191:* 32
Clement, Janet *182:* 50
Clement, Nathan *200:* 30
Clement, Rod *97:* 42
Clement, Stephen *88:* 3
Clementson, John *84:* 213
Clemesha, David *192:* 49, 50
Cleminson, Kate *221:* 26
Clevin, Jorgen *7:* 50
Clifford, Judy *34:* 163; *45:* 198
Clokey, Art *59:* 44
Clouse, Dennis *187:* 158
Clouse, James *84:* 15
Clouse, Nancy L. *78:* 31; *114:* 90; *225:* 117
Clover, Peter *152:* 45
Cneut, Carll *156:* 166; *165:* 67; *197:* 26
Coalson, Glo *9:* 72, 85; *25:* 155; *26:* 42; *35:* 212; *53:* 31; *56:* 154; *94:* 37, 38, 193
Cober, Alan E. *17:* 158; *32:* 77; *49:* 127
Cober-Gentry, Leslie *92:* 111
Cocca-Leffler, Maryann *80:* 46; *136:* 60; *139:* 193; *194:* 31, 33, 34
Cochran, Bobbye *11:* 52
Cochran, Josh *221:* 27
CoConis, Ted *4:* 41; *46:* 41; *51:* 104
Cocozza, Chris *87:* 18; *110:* 173; *111:* 149
Cockroft, Jason *152:* 20
Coerr, Eleanor *1:* 64; *67:* 52
Coes, Peter *35:* 172
Cogancherry, Helen *52:* 143; *69:* 131; *77:* 93; *78:* 220; *109:* 204; *110:* 129; *203:* 92
Coggins, Jack *2:* 69
Cohen, Alix *7:* 53
Cohen, Lisa *225:* 49
Cohen, Miriam *155:* 23, 24
Cohen, Nancy R. *165:* 35
Cohen, Santiago *164:* 26; *215:* 52, 199
Cohen, Sheldon *105:* 33, 34; *166:* 46, 47
Cohen, Vincent O. *19:* 243
Cohen, Vivien *11:* 112
Coker, Paul *51:* 172
Colbert, Anthony *15:* 41; *20:* 193
Colby, C.B. *3:* 47
Cole, Babette *58:* 172; *96:* 63, 64; *155:* 29
Cole, Brock *68:* 223; *72:* 36, 37, 38, 192; *127:* 23; *136:* 64, 65; *197:*
Cole, Gwen *87:* 185
Cole, Henry *178:* 120; *181:* 42, 43; *189:* 60; *213:* 35, 36; *222:* 139
Cole, Herbert *28:* 104
Cole, Michael *59:* 46
Cole, Olivia H.H. *1:* 134; *3:* 223; *9:* 111; *38:* 104
Cole, Rachael *209:* 39
Colin, Paul *102:* 59; *123:* 118; *126:* 152; *192:* 129
Colley, Jacqui *202:* 20
Collicott, Sharleen *98:* 39; *143:* 29, 30
Collier, Bryan *126:* 54; *151:* 166; *174:* 16, 17, 18; *204:* 18, 19; *208:* 84; *211:* 143; *228:* 128
Collier, David *13:* 127
Collier, John *27:* 179; *208:* 154
Collier, Steven *50:* 52
Collier-Morales, Roberta *168:* 61
Collins, Heather *66:* 84; *67:* 68; *81:* 40; *98:* 192, 193; *129:* 95, 96, 98
Collins, Matt *167:* 90; *231:* 9
Collins, Ross *140:* 23, 24; *200:* 36, 37; *209:* 54
Colman, Audrey *146:* 161
Colón, Raul *108:* 112; *113:* 5; *117:* 167; *134:* 112; *146:* 23; *159:* 92; *166:* 73; *180:* 107; *186:* 156; *190:* 6; *193:* 24, 205; *202:* 21, 22, 23; *217:* 68; *220:* 126, 157; *226:* 118; *227:* 165; *232:* 122
Colonna, Bernard *21:* 50; *28:* 103; *34:* 140; *43:* 180; *78:* 150
Comport, Sally Wern *117:* 169; *169:* 104; *190:* 42; *207:* 50
Conahan, Carolyn *215:* 17
Conde, J.M. *100:* 120

Condon, Grattan *54:* 85 Condon, Ken *161:* 44; *195:* 28, 29
Cone, Ferne Geller *39:* 49
Cone, J. Morton *39:* 49
Conklin, Paul *43:* 62
Connelly, Gwen *212:* 30
Connelly, James *198:* 12
Connolly, Howard *67:* 88
Connolly, Jerome P. *4:* 128; *28:* 52
Connolly, Peter *47:* 60
Conoly, Walle *110:* 224
Conover, Chris *31:* 52; *40:* 184; *41:* 51; *44:* 79; *213:* 39
Conroy, Melissa *226:* 54
Constantin, Pascale *207:* 159
Contreras, Gerry *72:* 9
Converse, James *38:* 70
Conway *62:* 62
Conway, Michael *69:* 12; *81:* 3; *92:* 108
Cook, Ande *188:* 135
Cook, G.R. *29:* 165
Cook, Joel *108:* 160
Cook, Lynette *228:* 211
Cookburn, W.V. *29:* 204
Cooke, Donald E. *2:* 77
Cooke, Tom *52:* 118
Coomaraswamy, A.K. *50:* 100
Coombs, Charles *43:* 65
Coombs, Deborah *139:* 175
Coombs, Patricia *2:* 82; *3:* 52; *22:* 119; *51:* 32, 33, 34, 35, 36, 37, 38, 39, 40, 42, 43
Cooney, Barbara *6:* 16, 17, 50; *12:* 42; *13:* 92; *15:* 145; *16:* 74, 111; *18:* 189; *23:* 38, 89, 93; *32:* 138; *38:* 105; *59:* 48, 49, 51, 52, 53; *74:* 222; *81:* 100; *91:* 25; *96:* 71, 72, 74; *100:* 149; *YABC2:* 10
Cooper, Elisha *157:* 38, 39
Cooper, Floyd *79:* 95; *81:* 45; *84:* 82; *85:* 74; *91:* 118; *96:* 77, 78; *103:* 149; *144:* 54; *145:* 151; *159:* 198; *176:* 133, 134; *187:* 26, 27, 28, 29; *188:* 22; *199:* 175; *219:* 66; *227:* 38, 39, 40, 42
Cooper, Heather *50:* 39
Cooper, Helen *102:* 42, 43, 44
Cooper, Mario *24:* 107
Cooper, Marjorie *7:* 112
Cope, Jane *61:* 201; *108* 52
Copeland, Mark *180:* 12
Copelman, Evelyn *8:* 61; *18:* 25
Copley, Heather *30:* 86; *45:* 57
Corace, Jen *208:* 48
Corbett, Grahame *30:* 114; *43:* 67
Corbino, John *19:* 248
Corcos, Lucille *2:* 223; *10:* 27; *34:* 66
Cordell, Matthew *197:* 93; *199:* 20, 21
Córdova, Amy *220:* 194
Corey, Robert *9:* 34
Corlass, Heather *10:* 7
Cornell, James *27:* 60
Cornell, Jeff *11:* 58
Cornell, Laura *94:* 179; *95:* 25
Corr, Christopher *204:* 98
Corral, Ridrigs *212:* 87
Corrigan, Barbara *8:* 37
Corrigan, Patrick *145:* 149
Corwin, Judith Hoffman *10:* 28
Corwin, Oliver *191:* 119
Cory, Fanny Y. *20:* 113; *48:* 29
Cosentino, Ralph *169:* 32
Cosgrove, Margaret *3:* 100; *47:* 63; *82:* 133
Costabel, Eva Deutsch *45:* 66, 67
Costanza, John *58:* 7, 8, 9
Costello, Chris *86:* 78
Costello, David F. *23:* 55
Côté, Geneviéve *184:* 37, 39; *210:* 256; *211:* 151
Cote, Nancy *126:* 139; *156:* 101; *174:* 101; *182:* 53, 54, 55; *222:* 49
Cottenden, Jeff *190:* 45
Couch, Greg *94:* 124; *110:* 13; *162:* 31; *168:* 149; *199:* 22; *216:* 144; *229:* 103

Councell, Ruth Tietjen 79: 29
Courtney, Cathy 58: 69, 144; 59: 15; 61: 20, 87
Courtney, R. 35: 110
Counihan, Claire 133: 106
Cousineau, Normand 89: 180; 112: 76; 227: 75
Cousins, Lucy 172: 53, 54; 205: 34, 35
Couture, Christin 41: 209
Covarrubias, Miguel 35: 118, 119, 123, 124, 125
Coville, Katherine 32: 57; 36: 167; 92: 38
Covington, Neverne 113: 87
Cowdrey, Richard 169: 170; 178: 205; 204: 22, 23; 215: 31
Cowell, Cressida 140: 39
Cowell, Lucinda 77: 54
Cowles, Rose 203: 164, 167
Cox 43: 93
Cox, Charles 8: 20
Cox, David 56: 37; 90: 63; 119: 38
Cox, Palmer 24: 76, 77
Cox, Paul 226: 57, 58
Cox, Steve 140: 96
Coxe, Molly 69: 44
Coxon, Michele 158: 80
Crabb, Gordon 70: 39
Crabtree, Judith 98: 42
Craft, Kinuko 22: 182; 36: 220; 53: 122, 123, 148,149; 74: 12; 81: 129; 86: 31; 89: 139; 127: 27, 28, 29; 132: 142; 139: 38
Craig, Daniel 177: 67; 180: 11; 185: 203; 211: 212; 224: 27; 229: 59
Craig, David 136: 198; 205: 37
Craig, Helen 49: 76; 62: 70, 71, 72; 69: 141; 94: 42, 43, 44; 112: 53; 135: 101, 102; 213: 45, 46, 47, 55, 81, 82
Crane, Alan H. 1: 217
Crane, H.M. 13: 111
Crane, Jack 43: 183
Crane, Jordan 174: 21
Crane, Walter 18: 46, 47, 48, 49, 53, 54, 56, 57, 59, 60, 61; 22: 128; 24: 210, 217; 100: 70, 71
Cravath, Lynne Avril 98: 45; 182: 58, 59; 216: 48; 219: 61; 220: 124; 224: 183; 228: 74; 229: 89
Crawford, Allen 212: 181
Crawford, Denise 137: 213
Crawford, Will 43: 77
Credle, Ellis 1: 69
Czekaj, Jef 217: 44; 218: 77
Czernecki, Stefan 154: 104; 178: 68, 69
Cresci, Anne 232: 148
Crespi, Francesca 87: 90
Cressy, Michael 124: 55; 203: 132
Crews, Donald 32: 59, 60; 76: 42, 43, 44
Crews, Nina 97: 49
Crichlow, Ernest 74: 88; 83: 203
Crilley, Mark 210: 71
Croft, James 150: 57
Crofut, Bob 80: 87; 81: 47
Crofut, Susan 23: 61
Croll, Carolyn 80: 137; 102: 52
Cross, Peter 56: 78; 63: 60, 65
Crossman, David A. 219: 38
Crowe, Elizabeth 88: 144
Crowell, Pers 3: 125
Cruikshank, George 15: 76, 83; 22: 74, 75, 76, 77, 78, 79,80, 81, 82, 84, 137; 24: 22, 23
Crump, Fred H. 11: 62
Cruz, Ray 6: 55; 70: 234; 123: 173; 172: 192
Csatari, Joe 44: 82; 55: 152; 63: 25, 28; 102: 58
Cuetara, Mittie 158: 85
Cuffari, Richard 4: 75; 5: 98; 6: 56; 7: 13,84, 153; 8: 148, 155; 9: 89; 11: 19; 12: 55, 96,114; 15: 51, 202; 18: 5; 20: 139; 21: 197; 22: 14, 192; 23: 15, 106; 25: 97; 27: 133; 28: 196; 29: 54; 30: 85; 31: 35; 36: 101; 38: 171; 42: 97; 44: 92, 192; 45: 212, 213; 46:

36, 198; 50: 164; 54: 80, 136, 137, 145; 56: 17; 60: 63; 66: 49, 50; 70: 41; 71: 132; 77: 157; 78: 58, 149; 79: 120; 85: 2, 152
Cugat, Xavier 19: 120
Cumings, Art 35: 160
Cummings, Chris 29: 167
Cummings, Michael 159: 142
Cummings, Pat 42: 61; 61: 99; 69: 205; 71: 57,58; 78: 24, 25; 93: 75; 107: 49, 50; 164: 259; 203: 45, 46
Cummings, Richard 24: 119
Cummings, Terrance 227: 49, 172
Cunette, Lou 20: 93; 22: 125
Cunningham, Aline 25: 180
Cunningham, David 11: 13
Cunningham, Imogene 16: 122, 127
Cunningham, Kelley 176: 159
Cupples, Pat 107: 12; 126: 109; 182: 13; 198: 68; 217: 21, 22
Curlee, Lynn 98: 48; 141: 39; 190: 48
Currey, Anna 190: 145; 202: 130, 132
Curry, John Steuart 2: 5; 19: 84; 34: 36; 144: 126
Curry, Tom 127: 131; 185: 25, 26
Curtis, Bruce 23: 96; 30: 88; 36: 22
Curtis, Neil 167: 30
Curtis, Stacy 205: 38
Cusack, Margaret 58: 49, 50, 51
Cushman, Doug 65: 57; 101: 39, 40; 133: 179; 157: 45; 186: 157; 210: 76, 77; 232: 132
Cutting, Ann 196: 194
Cyrus, Kurt 132: 39; 179: 36, 37
Czechowski, Alicia 95: 21; 171: 37
Czernecki, Stefan 117: 173

D

Dabcovich, Lydia 25: 105; 40: 114; 99: 75, 76
Dacey, Bob 82: 175; 152: 65
d'Achille, Gino 127: 175, 176
Daily, Don 78: 197; 220: 154
Dain, Martin J. 35: 75
Dale, Penny 127: 224; 151: 57; 160: 89; 197: 75; 232: 188
Dale, Rae 72: 197
Daley, Joann 50: 22
Dalton, Anne 40: 62; 63: 119
Daly, Deborah M. 74: 213
Daly, Jim 103: 60; 150: 48
Daly, Jude 138: 118, 119; 213: 41; 222: 56, 57
Daly, Nicholas 37: 53; 76: 48, 49
Daly, Niki 107: 15; 114: 38, 39, 40; 164: 86; 192: 53; 198: 26, 27
Daly, Paul 97: 205
Dalziel, Brothers 33: 113
D'Amato, Alex 9: 48; 20: 25
D'Amato, Janet 9: 48; 20: 25; 26: 118
D'Amico, Steve 170: 52
Danalis, Johnny 167: 27
D'Andrea, Domenick 183: 108
Daniel, Alan 23: 59; 29: 110; 76: 50, 53, 55, 56; 153: 76 115: 74; 134: 70
Daniel, Lea 76: 53, 55; 153: 76
Daniel, Lewis C. 20: 216
Daniels, Beau 73: 4
Daniels, Steve 22: 16
Daniels, Stewart 56: 12
Dann, Bonnie 31: 83
Dann, Penny 82: 128
Danska, Herbert 24: 219
Danyell, Alice 20: 27
Darbyshire, Kristen 218: 41
Dardik, Helen 208: 200
Darley, F.O.C. 16: 145; 19: 79, 86, 88, 185; 21: 28,36; 35: 76, 77, 78, 79, 80, 81; YABC 2: 175
Darling, Lois 3: 59; 23: 30, 31
Darling, Louis 1: 40, 41; 2: 63; 3: 59; 23: 30,31; 43: 54, 57, 59; 121: 53

Darnell, K.L. 210: 247
Darrow, David R. 84: 101
Darrow, Whitney, Jr. 13: 25; 38: 220, 221
Darwin, Beatrice 43: 54
Darwin, Len 24: 82
Dastolfo, Frank 33: 179
Dauber, Liz 1: 22; 3: 266; 30: 49
Daugherty, James 3: 66; 8: 178; 13: 27, 28, 161; 18: 101; 19: 72; 29: 108; 32: 156; 42: 84; YABC 1: 256; 2: 174
d'Aulaire, Edgar Parin 5: 51; 66: 53
d'Aulaire, Ingri Parin 5: 51; 66: 53
Davalos, Felipe 99: 197; 159: 66; 174: 163
Davenier, Christine 125: 88; 127: 32; 128: 152; 179: 39, 40; 216: 84, 85, 86, 87; 218: 62, 63; 224: 73
Davick, Linda 151: 124; 208: 187
David, Jacques-Louis 193: 22
David, Jonathan 19: 37
Davidson, Kevin 28: 154
Davidson, Raymond 32: 61
Davie, Helen K. 77: 48, 49
Davies, Andy Robert 205: 169
Davies, Lottie 214: 69
Davis, Allen 20: 11; 22: 45; 27: 222; 29: 157; 41: 99; 47: 99; 50: 84; 52: 105
Davis, Bette J. 15: 53; 23: 95
Davis, Dimitris 45: 95
Davis, Eleanor 209: 33
Davis, Hendon 151: 122
Davis, Jack E. 145: 139; 175: 84, 85; 208: 102; 210: 81, 82; 213: 151
Davis, Jim 32: 63, 64
Davis, Katie 152: 52, 53, 54; 208: 52
Davis, Lambert 110: 23, 24; 176: 58
Davis, Marguerite 31: 38; 34: 69, 70; 100: 34; YABC 1: 126, 230
Davis, Nelle 69: 191
Davis, Paul 78: 214
Davis, Rich 206: 38
Davis, Stuart 211: 69
Davis, Yvonne LeBrun 94: 144
Davisson, Virginia H. 44: 178
DaVolls, Andy 85: 53
Dawson, Diane 24: 127; 42: 126; 52: 130; 68: 104
Dawson, Janine 215: 198
Dawson, Willow 208: 54; 216: 119
Day, Alexandra 67: 59; 97: 54; 166: 65; 169: 40; 197: 50, 51, 52, 54
Day, Larry 169: 88; 185: 59; 227: 55
Day, Rob 94: 110; 127: 24; 197: 32
Dean, Bob 19: 211
Dean, David 192: 55
de Angeli, Marguerite 1: 77; 27: 62, 65, 66, 67, 69, 70, 72; 100: 75, 76; YABC 1: 166
DeArmond, Dale 70: 47
Deas, Michael 27: 219, 221; 30: 156; 67: 134; 72: 24; 75: 155; 84: 206; 88: 124
Deas, Rich 191: 87; 193: 10; 212: 79
deBarros, Jim 196: 60
Debon, Nicolas 151: 60; 177: 46
de Bosschere, Jean 19: 252; 21: 4; 186: 44, 45
De Bruyn, M(onica) G. 13: 30, 31
Decker, C.B. 172: 120; 215: 94
De Cuir, John F. 1: 28, 29
Deeter, Catherine 74: 110; 103: 150; 137: 50
Degen, Bruce 40: 227, 229; 57: 28, 29; 56: 156; 75: 229; 76: 19; 81: 36, 37; 92: 26; 93: 199; 97: 56, 58, 59; 124: 40; 147: 39, 40, 41; 168: 23; 205: 45, 46; 231: 46, 47, 48, 49
De Grazia 14: 59; 39: 56, 57
DeGrazio, George 88: 40
deGroat, Diane 9: 39; 18: 7; 23: 123; 28: 200, 201; 31: 58, 59; 34: 151; 41: 152; 43: 88; 46: 40, 200; 49: 163; 50: 89; 52: 30, 34; 54: 43; 63: 5; 70: 136; 71: 99; 73: 117,156; 77: 34; 85: 48; 86: 201; 87: 142; 90: 72, 73, 143; 95: 182; 111: 123; 118: 160; 126: 8; 130: 130; 138: 93, 94; 169: 46, 47
de Groot, Lee 6: 21

Deines, Brian *110:* 139; *220:* 36, 37
DeJohn, Marie *89:* 78
Dekhteryov, B. *61:* 158
de Kiefte, Kees *94:* 107
Delacre, Lulu *36:* 66; *156:* 35; *202:* 10, 53; *209:* 36
Delaney, A. *21:* 78
Delaney, Michael *180:* 16
Delaney, Molly *80:* 43
Delaney, Ned *28:* 68; *56:* 80; *102:* 11
DeLapine, Jim *79:* 21
De La Roche Saint Andre, Anne *75:* 37
de Larrea, Victoria *6:* 119, 204; *29:* 103; *72:* 203; *87:* 199
Delehanty, Joan W. *223:* 165
DeLeon, Melanie *210:* 43
Delessert, Étienne *7:* 140; *46:* 61, 62, 63, 65, 67, 68; *130:* 38, 39, 40, 41, 42; *179:* 46, 47, 48, 49; *YABC 2:* 209
Delezenne, Christine *186:* 126
Delinois, Alix *228:* 40
Del Negro, Janice *196:* 161
Delon, Melanie *216:* 30
DeLorenzo, Christopher *154:* 149
Delulio, John *15:* 54
DeLuna, Tony *88:* 95
Demarest, Chris L. *45:* 68, 69, 70; *73:* 172, 173, 176; *78:* 106; *82:* 48, 49; *89:* 212; *92:* 86; *128:* 57, 58; *175:* 46, 48
De Mejo, Oscar *40:* 67
De Muth, Roger *205:* 184; *221:* 35
Demi *11:* 135; *15:* 245; *66:* 129, 130; *89:* 216; *102:* 66, 67, 68; *210:* 86, 87, 89
Denetsosie, Hoke *13:* 126; *82:* 34
Denise, Christopher *147:* 43, 44; *176:* 101; *193:* 35, 36, 37; *201:* 37
Dennis, Morgan *18:* 68, 69; *64:* 89
Dennis, Wesley *2:* 87; *3:* 111; *11:* 132; *18:* 71, 72, 73, 74; *22:* 9; *24:* 196, 200; *46:* 178; *69:* 94, 96; *129:* 62
Denos, Julia *202:* 26
Denslow, W.W. *16:* 84, 85, 86, 87; *18:* 19, 20, 24; *29:* 211; *100:* 21
Denton, Kady MacDonald *110:* 82; *130:* 70; *181:* 54, 55, 56; *192:* 75
Denton, Phil *220:* 6
Denton, Terry *72:* 163; *174:* 26; *186:* 52; *196:* 83, 84
DePalma, Mary Newell *132:* 114; *139:* 75; *185:* 30, 31; *186:* 121; *213:* 62
dePaola, Tomie *8:* 95; *9:* 93; *11:* 69; 25; 103; *28:* 157; *29:* 80; *39:* 52, 53; *40:* 226; *46:* 187; *59:* 61, 62, 63, 64, 65, 66, 67, 68, 69, 71, 72, 74; *62:* 19; *108:* 63, 67, 68, 70; *155:* 62, 64, 66; *180:* 105; *200:* 47, 48, 49, 50; *226:* 116
Deraney, Michael J. *77:* 35; *78:* 148
deRosa, Dee *70:* 48; *71:* 210; *91:* 78
Dervaux, Isabelle *111:* 117
DeSaix, Deborah Durland *180:* 15; *188:* 24
De Saulles, Tony *119:* 39
de Sève, Peter *146:* 261; *207:* 78; *219:* 42
Deshaprabhu, Meera Dayal *86:* 192
Desimini, Lisa *86:* 68; *94:* 47; *96:* 7; *104:* 107; *125:* 194; *131:* 180; *172:* 56; *216:* 89, 90
de St. Menin, Charles *70:* 17
Detmold, Edward J. *22:* 104, 105, 106, 107; *35:* 120; *64:* 5; *YABC 2:* 203
Detrich, Susan *20:* 133
Deutermann, Diana *77:* 175
DeVelasco, Joseph E. *21:* 51
de Veyrac, Robert *YABC 2:* 19
DeVille, Edward A. *4:* 235
de Visser, John *55:* 119
Devito, Bert *12:* 164
Devlin, Harry *11:* 74; *74:* 63, 65; *136:* 77, 78
Dewan, Ted *108:* 73; *157:* 55; *165:* 129; *226:* 67, 68, 69
Dewar, Nick *133:* 122
Dewdney, Anna *184:* 43, 44; *232:* 46, 47, 48

Dewey, Ariane *7:* 64; *33:* 195; *35:* 208; *68:* 16,17; *75:* 46; *93:* 91; *94:* 197; *109:* 65, 66, 67; *125:* 2, 3, 4, 5; *127:* 188; *143:* 25; *178:* 17, 19, 74; *188:* 166; *202:* 164; *231:* 176
Dewey, Jennifer (Owings) *58:* 54; *64:* 214; *65:* 207; *88:* 169; *103:* 45
Dewey, Kenneth *39:* 62; *51:* 23; *56:* 163
de Zanger, Arie *30:* 40
Diakité, Baba Wagué *174:* 28
Diamond, Donna *21:* 200; *23:* 63; *26:* 142; *35:* 83, 84, 85, 86, 87, 88, 89; *38:* 78; *40:* 147; *44:* 152; *50:* 144; *53:* 126; *69:* 46, 47, 48, 201; *71:* 133; *123:* 19
Dias, Ron *71:* 67
Diaz, David *80:* 213; *96:* 83, 84; *108:* 228; *110:* 29; *149:* 106; *150:* 63; *179:* 160; *184:* 95, 97; *189:* 51, 52, 53; *221:* 86; *229:* 37, 38, 39, 40
di Bartolo, Jim *225:* 53
Dibley, Glin *138:* 83; *141:* 128; *211:* 162; *221:* 61
DiCesare, Joe *70:* 38; *71:* 63, 106; *79:* 214; *93:* 147; *116:* 217; *143:* 111; *166:* 57
Dick, John Henry *8:* 181
Dickens, Frank *34:* 131
Dickey, Robert L. *15:* 279
Dickson, Mora *84:* 21
Didier, Sam *166:* 114
Dietz, James *128:* 223; *193:* 136
di Fate, Vincent *37:* 70; *90:* 11; *93:* 60; *109:* 219, 220
Di Fiori, Lawrence *10:* 51; *12:* 190; *27:* 97; *40:* 219; *93:* 57; *130:* 45
Digby, Desmond *97:* 180
Dignan, James *196:* 143
Di Grazia, Thomas *32:* 66; *35:* 241
Dillard, Annie *10:* 32
Dillard, Sarah *136:* 186; *217:* 53
Dillon, Corinne B. *1:* 139
Dillon, Diane *4:* 104, 167; *6:* 23; *13:* 29; *15:* 99; *26:* 148; *27:* 136, 201; *51:* 29, 48, 51, 52, 53, 54,55, 56, 57, 58, 59, 60, 61, 62; *54:* 155; *56:* 69; *58:* 127,128; *61:* 95; *62:* 27; *64:* 46; *68:* 3; *69:* 209; *74:* 89; *79:* 92; *86:* 89; *92:* 28, 177; *93:* 7, 210; *94:* 239, 240; *97:* 167; *106:* 58, 59,61, 64; *107:* 3; *139:* 246; *167:* 77; *189:* 202; *191:* 191; *194:* 45, 46, 48, 49
Dillon, Leo *4:* 104, 167; *6:* 23; *13:* 29; *15:* 99; *26:* 148; *27:* 136, 201; *51:* 29, 48, 51, 52, 53, 54,55, 56, 57, 58, 59, 60, 61, 62; *54:* 155; *56:* 69; *58:* 127,128; *61:* 95; *62:* 27; *64:* 46; *68:* 3; *69:* 209; *74:* 89; *79:* 92; *86:* 89; *92:* 28, 177; *93:* 7, 210; *94:* 239, 240; *97:* 167; *106:* 58, 59,61, 64; *107:* 3; *139:* 246; *167:* 77; *189:* 202; *191:* 191; *194:* 45, 46, 48, 49
Dillon, Sharon Saseen *59:* 179, 188
DiMaccio, Gerald *121:* 80
DiMaggio, Joe *36:* 22
DiMassi, Gina *169:* 17
Dinan, Carol *25:* 124; *59:* 75
Dines, Glen *7:* 66, 67
Dinesen, Thomas *44:* 37
Dinh, Pham Viet *167:* 184
Dinnerstein, Harvey *42:* 63, 64, 65, 66, 67, 68; *50:* 146
Dinsdale, Mary *10:* 65; *11:* 171
Dinyer, Eric *86:* 148; *109:* 163; *110:* 239; *124:* 11; *150:* 69; *170:* 4; *171:* 30
Dion, Nathalie *170:* 124; *213:* 52
DiPucchio, Kelly *230:* 3
DiRocco, Carl *181:* 23
DiSalvo-Ryan, DyAnne *59:* 77; *62:* 185; *117:* 46; *144:* 64; *150:* 153; *186:* 162
Disney, Walt *28:* 71, 72, 73, 76, 77, 78, 79, 80, 81, 87, 88, 89,90, 91, 94
DiTerlizzi, Tony *105:* 7; *147:* 22; *154:* 31, 32, 33; *214:* 74
Divito, Anna *83:* 159
Dixon, Don *74:* 17; *109:* 196

Dixon, Larry *127:* 125
Dixon, Maynard *20:* 165
Dizin, Pascal *230:* 25, 26
Doares, Robert G. *20:* 39
Dob, Bob *205:* 14
Dobias, Frank *22:* 162
Dobrin, Arnold *4:* 68
Dobson, Steven Gaston *102:* 103
Docherty, Thomas *218:* 45, 46
Dockray, Tracy *139:* 77
Docktor, Irv *43:* 70
Dodd, Ed *4:* 69
Dodd, Emma *203:* 57
Dodd, Julie *74:* 73
Dodd, Lynley *35:* 92; *86:* 71; *132:* 45, 46, 47
Dodge, Bill *96:* 36; *118:* 7, 8, 9; *133:* 135
Dodgson, Charles L. *20:* 148; *33:* 146; *YABC 2:* 98
Dodson, Bert *9:* 138; *14:* 195; *42:* 55; *54:* 8; *60:* 49; *101:* 125
Dodson, Liz Brenner *105:* 117; *111:* 15
Dohanos, Stevan *16:* 10
Dolce, J. Ellen *74:* 147; *75:* 41
Dolch, Marguerite P. *50:* 64
Dolesch, Susanne *34:* 49
Dollar, Diane *57:* 32
Dolobowsky, Mena *81:* 54
Dolson, Hildegarde *5:* 57
Domanska, Janina *6:* 66, 67; *YABC 1:* 166
Domi *134:* 113
Dominguez, El *53:* 94
Domjan, Joseph *25:* 93
Domm, Jeffrey C. *84:* 69; *135:* 70
Donahey, William *68:* 209
Donahue, Dorothy *76:* 170
Donahue, Vic *2:* 93; *3:* 190; *9:* 44
Donald, Elizabeth *4:* 18
Donalty, Alison *149:* 195, 196, 197
Donato *85:* 59; *149:* 204; *191:* 19
Donato, Michael A. *200:* 143
Doner, Kim *208:* 57
Doney, Todd L.W. *87:* 12; *93:* 112; *98:* 135; *101:* 57; *104:* 40; *118:* 163; *135:* 162, 163; *151:* 18; *227:* 79
Donna, Natalie *9:* 52
Donohue, Dorothy *95:* 2; *132:* 30; *176:* 54, 55; *178:* 77, 78, 79
Dooling, Michael *82:* 19; *105:* 55; *106:* 224; *125:* 135; *171:* 46; *172:* 12; *176:* 120; *197:* 89; *220:* 39, 40
Doran, Ben-Ami *128:* 189
Doran, Colleen *211:* 48
Dore, Gustave *18:* 169, 172, 175; *19:* 93, 94, 95, 96, 97, 98,99, 100, 101, 102, 103, 104, 105; *23:* 188; *25:* 197, 199
Doremus, Robert *6:* 62; *13:* 90; *30:* 95, 96, 97; *38:* 70
Dorfman, Ronald *11:* 128
Doriau *86:* 59; *91:* 152
Dorman, Brandon *197:* 35; *204:* 6; *210:* 104; *212:* 95; *216:* 156; *222:* 133
Dormer, Frank W. *200:* 55; *222:* 48
Dorros, Arthur *78:* 42, 43; *91:* 28
Doruyter, Karel *165:* 105
dos Santos, Joyce Audy *57:* 187, 189
Doty, Roy *28:* 98; *31:* 32; *32:* 224; *46:* 157; *82:* 71; *142:* 7
Doucet, Bob *132:* 238; *169:* 159
Dougherty, Charles *16:* 204; *18:* 74
Doughty, Rebecca *177:* 174; *222:* 159
Doughty, Thomas *118:* 31; *140:* 60
Douglas, Aaron *31:* 103
Douglas, Allen *223:* 53; *230:* 148
Douglas, Carole Nelson *73:* 48
Douglas, Goray *13:* 151
Dow, Brian *150:* 92
Dowd, Jason *132:* 51, 52; *164:* 244
Dowd, Vic *3:* 244; *10:* 97
Dowden, Anne Ophelia *7:* 70, 71; *13:* 120
Dowdy, Mrs. Regera *29:* 100
Downard, Barry *202:* 32

Downes, Belinda *180:* 29
Downing, Julie *60:* 140; *81:* 50; *86:* 200; *99:* 129
Doyle, Janet *56:* 31
Doyle, Richard *21:* 31, 32, 33; *23:* 231; *24:* 177; *31:* 87
Draper, Angie *43:* 84
Drath, Bill *26:* 34
Drawson, Blair *17:* 53; *126:* 65
Dray, Matt *177:* 47
Drescher, Henrik *105:* 60, 62, 63; *172:* 72
Drescher, Joan *30:* 100, 101; *35:* 245; *52:* 168; *137:* 52
Dressell, Peggy *186:* 41
Drew, Janet *201:* 177
Drew, Patricia *15:* 100
Dronzek, Laura *199:* 28, 29; *207:* 69
Drummond, Allan *209:* 41
Drummond, V.H. *6:* 70
Drury, Christian Potter *105:* 97; *186:* 224
Dubanevich, Arlene *56:* 44
Dubin, Jill *205:* 56; *217:* 25
Dubois, Claude K. *196:* 2
Dubois, Gerard *182:* 9
DuBurke, Randy *187:* 89; *222:* 136; *224:* 35
Ducak, Danilo *99:* 130; *108:* 214
Duchesne, Janet *6:* 162; *79:* 8
Duda, Jana *102:* 155; *209:* 134
Dudash, C. Michael *32:* 122; *77:* 134; *82:* 149; *212:* 93, 94
Duddle, Jonny *233:* 118
Duer, Douglas *34:* 177
Duewell, Kristina *195:* 76
Duffy, Daniel Mark *76:* 37; *101:* 196; *108:* 147, 148
Duffy, Joseph *38:* 203
Duffy, Pat *28:* 153
Dugan, Karen *181:* 26; *202:* 35
Dugin, Andrej *77:* 60
Dugina, Olga *77:* 60
Duke, Chris *8:* 195; *139:* 164
Duke, Kate *87:* 186; *90:* 78, 79, 80, 81; *192:* 21, 59, 60, 61, 63
Duke, Marion *165:* 87
Dulac, Edmund *19:* 108, 109, 110, 111, 112, 113, 114, 115, 117; *23:* 187; *25:* 152; *YABC 1:* 37; *2:* 147
Dulac, Jean *13:* 64
Dumas, Philippe *52:* 36, 37, 38, 39, 40, 41, 42, 43, 45; *119:* 40, 41, 42
Dunaway, Nancy *108:* 161
Dunbar, James *76:* 63
Dunbar, Polly *181:* 60, 61; *211:* 51, 52, 53; *212:* 42; *233:* 6
Duncan, Beverly *72:* 92
Duncan, John *116:* 94
Dunn, H.T. *62:* 196
Dunn, Harvey *34:* 78, 79, 80, 81
Dunn, Iris *5:* 175
Dunn, Phoebe *5:* 175
Dunne, Jeanette *72:* 57, 173, 222
Dunnick, Regan *176:* 51; *178:* 83, 84; *219:* 36; *224:* 144; *229:* 83
Dunnington, Tom *3:* 36; *18:* 281; *25:* 61; *31:* 159; *35:* 168; *48:* 195; *79:* 144; *82:* 230
Dunn-Ramsey, Marcy *117:* 131
Dunrea, Olivier *59:* 81; *118:* 53, 54; *124:* 43; *233:* 63, 64, 66
Duntze, Dorothee *88:* 28; *160:* 76
Dupasquier, Philippe *86:* 75; *104:* 76; *151:* 63
duPont, Lindsay Harper *207:* 39
DuQuette, Keith *90:* 83; *155:* 73, 74
Durand, Delphine *200:* 56
Durham, Sarah *192:* 248
Durney, Ryan *208:* 122
Duroussy, Nathalie *146:* 150
Durrell, Julie *82:* 62; *94:* 62
Dusíková, Maja *223:* 49
Dutz *6:* 59

Duvoisin, Roger *2:* 95; *6:* 76, 77; *7:* 197; *28:* 125; *30:* 101, 102, 103, 104, 105, 107; *47:* 205; *84:* 254
Dyer, Dale *141:* 71
Dyer, Jane *75:* 219; *129:* 28; *147:* 49, 50, 51; *168:* 121; *190:* 4; *191:* 57, 59, 60; *203:* 4
Dyer, Sarah *212:* 40
Dypold, Pat *15:* 37

E

E.V.B.
See Boyle, Eleanor Vere (Gordon)
Eachus, Jennifer *29:* 74; *82:* 201; *164:* 153
Eadie, Bob *63:* 36
Eagle, Bruce *95:* 119
Eagle, Ellen *82:* 121; *89:* 3
Eagle, Jeremy *141:* 71
Eagle, Michael *11:* 86; *20:* 9; *23:* 18; *27:* 122; *28:* 57; *34:* 201; *44:* 189; *73:* 9; *78:* 235; *85:* 43
Earl-Bridges, Michele *159:* 128
Earle, Edwin *56:* 27
Earle, Olive L. *7:* 75
Earle, Vana *27:* 99
Earley, Lori *132:* 2; *186:* 4; *195:* 8
Early, Margaret *72:* 59
East, Jacqueline *218:* 198; *224:* 38
East, Stella *131:* 223
Eastman, P.D. *33:* 57
Easton, Reginald *29:* 181
Eaton, Tom *4:* 62; *6:* 64; *22:* 99; *24:* 124
Eaves, Edward *224:* 13
Ebbeler, Jeffrey *193:* 62; *206:* 45
Ebel, Alex *11:* 89
Eberbach, Andrea *192:* 115
Ebert, Len *9:* 191; *44:* 47
Echevarria, Abe *37:* 69
Echo Hawk, Bunky *187:* 192
Eckersley, Maureen *48:* 62
Eckert, Horst *72:* 62
Ede, Janina *33:* 59
Edens, Cooper *49:* 81, 82, 83, 84, 85; *112:* 58
Edens, John *109:* 115
Edgar, Sarah E. *41:* 97
Edgerton, Perky *195:* 144
Edliq, Emily S. *131:* 107
Edrien *11:* 53
Edwards, Freya *45:* 102
Edwards, George Wharton *31:* 155
Edwards, Gunvor *2:* 71; *25:* 47; *32:* 71; *54:* 106
Edwards, Jeanne *29:* 257
Edwards, Linda Strauss *21:* 134; *39:* 123; *49:* 88, 89
Edwards, Michelle *152:* 62, 63
Edwards, Wallace *170:* 55
Egan, Tim *155:* 76, 77, 78
Egge, David *102:* 71
Eggenhofer, Nicholas *2:* 81
Eggleton, Bob *74:* 40; *81:* 190, 191; *105:* 6; *121:* 183; *149:* 203; *166:* 215
Egielski, Richard *11:* 90; *16:* 208; *33:* 236; *38:* 35; *49:* 91, 92, 93, 95, 212, 213, 214, 216; *79:* 122; *106:* 67, 68, 69; *134:* 135; *144:* 244; *163:* 82, 84; *207:* 125; *225:* 200
Ehlert, Lois *35:* 97; *69:* 51; *112:* 7; *113:* 208; *128:* 63, 64, 65; *172:* 77, 79, 80; *220:* 43, 44, 45, 46, 47, 48
Ehrlich, Bettina *1:* 83
Eitan, Ora *160:* 165
Eichenberg, Fritz *1:* 79; *9:* 54; *19:* 248; *23:* 170; *24:* 200; *26:* 208; *50:* 67, 68, 69, 70, 71, 72, 73,74, 75, 77, 79, 80, 81; *60:* 165; *100:* 137; *YABC 1:* 104, 105; *2:* 213
Einsel, Naiad *10:* 35; *29:* 136
Einsel, Walter *10:* 37
Einzig, Susan *3:* 77; *43:* 78; *67:* 155; *129:* 154
Eisner, Will *165:* 82, 83

Eitzen, Allan *9:* 56; *12:* 212; *14:* 226; *21:* 194; *38:* 162; *76:* 218
Eldridge, H. *54:* 109
Eldridge, Harold *43:* 83
Elgaard, Greta *19:* 241
Elgin, Kathleen *9:* 188; *39:* 69
Ellacott, S.E. *19:* 118
Elliot, David *192:* 26; *208:* 62, 63
Elliott, Mark *93:* 69; *105:* 108; *107:* 123; *140:* 53; *165:* 189; *173:* 67; *195:* 95; *203:* 67; *210:* 99; *221:* 57, 70; *230:* 147
Elliott, Sarah M. *14:* 58
Ellis, Carson *216:* 210
Ellis, Dianne *130:* 208
Ellis, Jan Davey *88:* 50; *115:* 80
Ellis, Richard *130:* 47, 48
Ellison, Chris *196:* 66; *199:* 131; *207:* 193
Ellison, Pauline *55:* 21
Ellwand, David *213:* 60
Elmer, Richard *78:* 5
Elmore, Larry *90:* 8
Elschner, Géraldine *183:* 38
Elwell, Peter *195:* 150
Elwell, Tristan *110:* 39; *121:* 182; *127:* 46; *137:* 144; *141:* 173; *151:* 236; *158:* 264; *167:* 119, 120, 121; *169:* 20; *190:* 12; *202:* 16; *226:* 6; *233:* 181
Elzbieta *88:* 80, 81
Ember, Kathi *214:* 147
Emberley, Ed *8:* 53; *70:* 53, 54; *146:* 65, 69, 70; *218:* 50
Emberley, Rebecca *218:* 50
Emberley, Michael *34:* 83; *80:* 72; *119:* 47, 48; *147:* 100; *158:* 115; *189:* 62, 64; *203:* 87, 89; *232:* 51, 52, 54
Emerling, Dorothy *104:* 27
Emery, Leslie *49:* 187
Emmett, Bruce *49:* 147; *80:* 175; *101:* 206; *220:* 200
Emond, Stephen *231:* 59
Emry-Perrott, Jennifer *61:* 57
Emshwiller, Ed *174:* 45
Endle, Kate *191:* 167; *207:* 41; *233:* 155
Engel, Christiane *231:* 61
Engel, Diana *70:* 57
Engle, Mort *38:* 64
Englebert, Victor *8:* 54
English, Mark *101:* 207; *220:* 201
Enik, Ted *142:* 39
Enos, Randall *20:* 183
Enright, Maginel Wright *19:* 240, 243; *39:* 31, 35, 36
Enrique, Romeo *34:* 135
Ensor, Barbara *180:* 30
Epstein, Stephen *50:* 142, 148
Erdogan, Buket *174:* 179
Erdrich, Louise *141:* 62
Erhard, Walter *1:* 152
Erickson, Jim *196:* 190; *233:* 173
Erickson, Phoebe *11:* 83; *59:* 85
Erikson, Mel *31:* 69
Eriksson, Eva *63:* 88, 90, 92, 93; *203:* 99; *207:* 44
Ering, Timothy Basil *131:* 100; *176:* 63, 64; *202:* 29; *204:* 8
Erlbruch, Wolf *181:* 66
Ernst, Lisa Campbell *47:* 147; *95:* 47; *154:* 46, 47, 48; *164:* 88; *212:* 45
Esco, Jo *61:* 103
Escourido, Joseph *4:* 81
Escrivá, Viví *119:* 51; *181:* 36
Essakalli, Julie Klear *200:* 58
Este, Kirk *33:* 111
Estep, David *73:* 57
Estes, Eleanor *91:* 66
Estoril, Jean *32:* 27
Estrada, Pau *74:* 76
Estrada, Ric *5:* 52, 146; *13:* 174
Etchemendy, Teje *38:* 68
Etheredges, the *73:* 12
Etienne, Kirk-Albert *145:* 184

Ets, Marie Hall 2: 102
Ettlinger, Doris 171: 98; 186: 106; 197: 126; 214: 125
Eulalie YABC 2: 315
Eustace, David 224: 24
Evangelista, Theresa M. 213: 67
Evans, Greg 73: 54, 55, 56; 143: 40, 41
Evans, Katherine 5: 64
Evans, Leslie 144: 227; 207: 57; 214: 88; 221: 28
Evans, Shane W. 159: 142; 160: 190; 168: 39; 188: 88; 189: 66, 67, 68; 229: 150
Everitt, Betsy 151: 110
Ewart, Claire 76: 69; 145: 59, 60
Ewing, Carolyn 66: 143; 79: 52
Ewing, Juliana Horatia 16: 92
Eyolfson, Norman 98: 154

F

Fabian, Limbert 136: 114
Facklam, Paul 132: 62
Falconer, Ian 125: 66; 179: 59
Falconer, Pearl 34: 23
Falkenstern, Lisa 70: 34; 76: 133; 78: 171; 127: 16; 191: 151
Fallone, Gianluca 231: 23
Falls, C.B. 1: 19; 38: 71, 72, 73, 74
Falter, John 40: 169, 170
Falwell, Cathryn 118: 77; 137: 185; 196: 71, 72
Fancher, Lou 138: 219; 141: 64; 144: 199; 177: 51; 214: 95; 221: 63; 228: 42, 43, 44; 230: 44, 45, 46
Fanelli, Sara 89: 63; 126: 69
Faria, Rosana 150: 143
Faricy, Patrick 185: 182; 212: 61
Farooqi, Musharraf Ali 207: 46
Farmer, Andrew 49: 102
Farmer, Peter 24: 108; 38: 75
Farnsworth, Bill 93: 189; 116: 147; 124: 8; 135: 52; 146: 242, 243, 244; 182: 176; 186: 31, 83, 84, 85; 191: 197; 222: 2
Farquharson, Alexander 46: 75
Farrell, Darren 228: 45
Farrell, David 40: 135
Farrell, Russell 196: 38
Farris, David 74: 42
Fasolino, Teresa 118: 145
Fatigati, Evelyn 24: 112
Fatus, Sophie 182: 74; 190: 218; 225: 131
Faul-Jansen, Regina 22: 117
Faulkner, Jack 6: 169
Faulkner, Matt 161: 174; 167: 75
Faust, Anke 230: 166
Fava, Rita 2: 29
Fax, Elton C. 1: 101; 4: 2; 12: 77; 25: 107
Fay 43: 93
Fearing, Mark 223: 142; 224: 39, 40
Fearnley, Jan 153: 82, 83; 205: 63, 64, 65
Fearrington, Ann 146: 80
Federspiel, Marian 33: 51
Fedorov, Nickolai Ivanovich 110: 102
Feelings, Tom 5: 22; 8: 56; 12: 153; 16: 105; 30: 196; 49: 37; 61: 101; 69: 56, 57; 93: 74; 105: 88
Fehr, Terrence 21: 87
Feiffer, Jules 3: 91; 8: 58; 61: 66, 67, 70, 74, 76,77, 78; 111: 47, 48, 49, 50; 132: 122; 157: 62; 201: 48, 49, 50; 230: 66
Feigeles, Neil 41: 242
Feldman, Elyse 86: 7
Feller, Gene 33: 130
Fellows, Muriel H. 10: 42
Felstead, Cathie 116: 85
Felts, Shirley 33: 71; 48: 59
Fennell, Tracy 171: 69
Fennelli, Maureen 38: 181
Fenton, Carroll Lane 5: 66; 21: 39

Fenton, Mildred Adams 5: 66; 21: 39
Ferguson, Peter 177: 30, 31; 181: 154; 197: 4; 199: 40; 215: 104; 221: 66; 229: 15, 16
Ferguson, Walter W. 34: 86
Fernandes, Eugenie 77: 67; 205: 68
Fernandes, Stanislaw 70: 28
Fernandez, Fernando 77: 57
Fernandez, Laura 77: 153; 101: 117; 131: 222; 170: 119; 175: 182
Ferrari, Alex 188: 121
Ferrington, Susan 172: 22
Fetz, Ingrid 11: 67; 12: 52; 16: 205; 17: 59; 29: 105; 30: 108, 109; 32: 149; 43: 142; 56: 29; 60: 34; 85: 48; 87: 146
Fiammenghi, Gioia 9: 66; 11: 44; 12: 206; 13: 57, 59; 52: 126, 129; 66: 64; 85: 83; 91: 161; 166: 169
Fiedler, Joseph Daniel 96: 42; 113: 173; 129: 164; 146: 17; 159: 68; 162: 104
Field, Rachel 15: 113
Fielding, David 70: 124
Fieser, Stephen 152: 36
Fine, Howard 145: 159; 159: 64; 165: 134; 174: 129; 181: 68
Fine, Peter K. 43: 210
Finger, Helen 42: 81
Fink, Sam 18: 119
Finlay, Winifred 23: 72
Finney, Pat 79: 215
Fiore, Peter 99: 196; 125: 139; 144: 225; 160: 169; 180: 72; 212: 103
Fiorentino, Al 3: 240
Firehammer, Karla 174: 202; 221: 183; 228: 84
Firmin, Charlotte 29: 75; 48: 70
Firmin, Peter 58: 63, 64, 65, 67, 68, 70, 71
Firth, Barbara 81: 208; 127: 218; 179: 62; 232: 189
Fischel, Lillian 40: 204
Fischer, Hans 25: 202
Fischer, Scott M. 207: 37; 217: 29
Fischer-Nagel, Andreas 56: 50
Fischer-Nagel, Heiderose 56: 50
Fisher, Carolyn 154: 50
Fisher, Chris 79: 62; 158: 248; 188: 195
Fisher, Cynthia 117: 45; 137: 118; 195: 40
Fisher, Jeffrey 142: 80
Fisher, Leonard Everett 3: 6; 4: 72, 86; 6: 197; 9: 59; 16: 151, 153; 23: 44; 27: 134; 29: 26; 34: 87, 89, 90, 91, 93, 94, 95, 96; 40: 206; 50: 150; 60: 158; 73: 68, 70, 71, 72, 73; 176: 71, 72, 73; 208: 131; YABC 2: 169
Fisher, Lois 20: 62; 21: 7
Fisher, Valorie 177: 55; 214: 92
Fisk, Nicholas 25: 112
Fitschen, Marilyn 2: 20, 21; 20: 48
Fitz-Maurice, Jeff 175: 2
Fitzgerald, F.A. 15: 116; 25: 86, 87
Fitzgerald, Joanne 157: 153, 154; 198: 34, 35
Fitzgerald, Royce 205: 5
Fitzhugh, Louise 1: 94; 9: 163; 45: 75, 78
Fitzhugh, Susie 11: 117
Fitzpatrick, Jim 109: 130
Fitzpatrick, Marie-Louise 125: 69, 70; 189: 72, 73
Fitzsimmons, Arthur 14: 128
Fix, Philippe 26: 102
Flack, Marjorie 21: 67; 100: 93; YABC 2: 122
Flagg, James Montgomery 17: 227
Flavin, Teresa 132: 115; 186: 119
Flax, Zeona 2: 245
Fleetwood, Tony 171: 51
Fleishman, Seymour 14: 232; 24: 87
Fleming, Denise 71: 179; 81: 58; 126: 71, 72, 73; 173: 52, 53
Fleming, Guy 18: 41
Flesher, Vivienne 85: 55
Fletcher, Claire 80: 106; 157: 159
Flint, Russ 74: 80
Floate, Helen 111: 163

Floca, Brian 155: 88, 89; 190: 10, 66, 67
Floethe, Richard 3: 131; 4: 90
Floherty, John J., Jr. 5: 68
Flook, Helen 160: 81
Flora, James 1: 96; 30: 111, 112
Florczak, Robert 166: 51
Florian, Douglas 19: 122; 83: 64, 65; 125: 71, 72, 74, 76; 128: 130; 177: 58, 60; 226: 119
Flory, Jane 22: 111
Flower, Renee 125: 109
Floyd, Gareth 1: 74; 17: 245; 48: 63; 62: 35,36, 37, 39, 40, 41; 74: 245; 79: 56
Fluchere, Henri A. 40: 79
Flynn, Alice 183: 2
Flynn, Barbara 7: 31; 9: 70
Fogarty, Thomas 15: 89
Foley, Greg 190: 69
Folger, Joseph 9: 100
Folkard, Charles 22: 132; 29: 128, 257, 258
Foott, Jeff 42: 202
Forberg, Ati 12: 71, 205; 14: 1; 22: 113; 26: 22; 48: 64, 65
Ford, A.G. 230: 40; 231: 69
Ford, George 24: 120; 31: 70, 177; 58: 126; 81: 103; 107: 91; 136: 100; 194: 47; 208: 81; 218: 56
Ford, Gilbert 199: 10
Ford, H.J. 16: 185, 186
Ford, Jason 174: 119
Ford, Pamela Baldwin 27: 104
Fordham, John 168: 160, 161
Foreman, Michael 2: 110, 111; 67: 99; 73: 78, 79, 80,81, 82; 93: 146; 135: 55, 56, 57; 184: 58, 59; 216: 100, 101, 102, 103; 225: 144
Forrester, Victoria 40: 83
Forsey, Chris 140: 210
Fortnum, Peggy 6: 29; 20: 179; 24: 211; 26: 76, 77, 78; 39: 78; 58: 19, 21, 23, 27; YABC 1: 148
Fortune, Eric 191: 52
Foster, Brad W. 34: 99
Foster, Genevieve 2: 112
Foster, Gerald L. 7: 78; 198: 40
Foster, Jon 146: 18; 198: 7
Foster, Laura Louise 6: 79
Foster, Marian Curtis 23: 74; 40: 42
Foster, Sally 58: 73, 74
Fotheringham, Edwin 219: 32
Foucher, Adele 47: 118
Foust, Mitch 168: 50
Fowler, Jim 184: 190
Fowler, Mel 36: 127
Fowler, Richard 87: 219
Fowles, Shelley 165: 127; 205: 72
Fox, Charles Phillip 12: 84
Fox, Christyan 188: 36
Fox, Jim 6: 187
Fox, Nathan 208: 64
Fox-Davies, Sarah 76: 150; 182: 63; 199: 42, 43
Frace, Charles 15: 118
Frailey, Joy 72: 108
Frame, Paul 2: 45, 145; 9: 153; 10: 124; 21: 71; 23: 62; 24: 123; 27: 106; 31: 48; 32: 159; 34: 195; 38: 136; 42: 55; 44: 139; 60: 39, 40, 41, 42, 43, 44, 46; 73: 183
Frampton, David 85: 72; 102: 33; 139: 182; 152: 37; 189: 171
Francis, Guy 198: 164; 224: 91; 225: 65
Francois, Andre 25: 117
Francoise
    See Seignobosc, Francoise
Frank, Lola Edick 2: 199
Frank, Mary 4: 54; 34: 100
Franke, Phil 45: 91
Frankel, Alona 66: 70
Frankel, Julie 40: 84, 85, 202
Frankenberg, Robert 22: 116; 30: 50; 38: 92, 94, 95; 68: 111
Frankfeldt, Gwen 84: 223; 110: 92

Frankland, David *169:* 137; *182:* 164; *201:* 159; *224:* 7; *231:* 27

Franklin, Ashton *165:* 144; *225:* 107

Franklin, John *24:* 22

Franson, Leanne R. *111:* 57, 58; *151:* 7; *223:* 63, 64, 158

Frascino, Edward *9:* 133; *29:* 229; *33:* 190; *48:* 80, 81, 82, 83, 84, 85, 86

Frasconi, Antonio *6:* 80; *27:* 208; *53:* 41, 43, 45, 47,48; *68:* 145; *73:* 226; *131:* 68

Fraser, Betty *2:* 212; *6:* 185; *8:* 103; *31:* 72,73; *43:* 136; *111:* 76

Fraser, Eric *38:* 78; *41:* 149, 151

Fraser, F.A. *22:* 234

Fraser, James *171:* 68

Fraser, Mary Ann *137:* 63; *214:* 98

Frasier, Debra *69:* 60; *112:* 67; *182:* 81, 82, 83

Fraustino, Lisa Rowe *146:* 87

Frazee, Marla *72:* 98; *105:* 79, 80; *151:* 67, 68; *164:* 165; *171:* 190, 191; *187:* 53, 54, 55, 56, 143; *222:* 173; *225:* 68, 69, 70; *226:* 180

Frazetta, Frank *41:* 72; *58:* 77, 78, 79, 80, 81, 82, 83

Frazier, Craig *177:* 63; *221:* 47

Freas, John *25:* 207

Fredrickson, Mark *103:* 33

Freeland, Michael J. *118:* 115

Freeman, Don *2:* 15; *13:* 249; *17:* 62, 63, 65, 67, 68; *18:* 243; *20:* 195; *23:* 213, 217; *32:* 155; *55:* 129

Freeman, Irving *67:* 150

Freeman, Laura *144:* 111; *200:* 62, 63

Freeman, Pietri *140:* 223

Freeman, Tom *167:* 118

Freeman, Tor *164:* 93

Fregosi, Claudia *24:* 117

Fremaux, Charlotte Murray *138:* 29; *141:* 95

French, Fiona *6:* 82, 83; *75:* 61; *109:* 170; *132:* 79, 80, 81, 82

French, Martin *163:* 4

French, S. Terrell *216:* 106

Frendak, Rodney *126:* 97, 98

Freschet, Gina *175:* 73

Freynet, Gilbert *72:* 221

Fried, Janice *202:* 121

Frieden, Sarajo *213:* 119

Friedman, Judith *43:* 197; *131:* 221

Friedman, Marvin *19:* 59; *42:* 86

Frinta, Dagmar *36:* 42

Frith, Michael K. *15:* 138; *18:* 120

Fritz, Ronald *46:* 73; *82:* 124

Fromm, Lilo *29:* 85; *40:* 197

Frost, A.B. *17:* 6, 7; *19:* 123, 124, 125, 126, 127, 128, 129,130; *100:* 119; *YABC 1:* 156, 157, 160; *2:* 107

Frost, Helen *183:* 51

Frost, Kristi *118:* 113; *231:* 114

Frost, Michael *151:* 209; *209:* 44; *212:* 70

Froud, Brian *150:* 82, 83

Froud, Wendy *151:* 237

Fry, Guy *2:* 224

Fry, Rosalie *3:* 72; *YABC 2:* 180, 181

Fry, Rosalind *21:* 153, 168

Fryer, Elmer *34:* 115

Fuchs, Bernie *110:* 10; *162:* 46

Fuchs, Erich *6:* 84

Fuchshuber, Annegert *43:* 96

Fucile, Tony *221:* 48

Fufuka, Mahiri *32:* 146

Fuge, Charles *144:* 91, 93

Fujikawa, Gyo *39:* 75, 76; *76:* 72, 73, 74

Fulford, Deborah *23:* 159

Fuller, Margaret *25:* 189

Fulweiler, John *93:* 99

Funai, Mamoru *38:* 105

Funfhausen, Christian *196:* 30

Funk, Tom *7:* 17, 99

Furchgott, Terry *29:* 86

Furness, William Henry, Jr. *94:* 18

Furukawa, Mel *25:* 42

Fusari, Erika *164:* 227

G

Gaadt, David *78:* 212; *121:* 166; *201:* 171

Gaadt, George *71:* 9

Gaber, Susan *99:* 33; *115:* 57, 58; *164:* 195; *169:* 61, 62, 63; *185:* 50, 51; *188:* 124

Gaberell, J. *19:* 236

Gable, Brian *195:* 68, 69

Gabler, Mirko *99:* 71; *195:* 32

Gabor, Tim *216:* 61

Gackenbach, Dick *19:* 168; *41:* 81; *48:* 89, 90, 91, 92,93, 94; *54:* 105; *79:* 75, 76, 77

Gad, Victor *87:* 161

Gaetano, Nicholas *23:* 209

Gaffney-Kessell, Walter *94:* 219; *174:* 188

Gag, Flavia *17:* 49, 52

Gag, Wanda *100:* 101, 102; *YABC 1:* 135, 137, 138, 141, 143

Gagnon, Cecile *11:* 77; *58:* 87

Gaillard, Jason *200:* 69; *204:* 74

Gal, Laszlo *14:* 127; *52:* 54, 55, 56; *65:* 142; *68:* 150; *81:* 185; *96:* 104, 105

Gal, Susan *228:* 58

Galazinski, Tom *55:* 13

Galbraith, Ben *200:* 70

Galdone, Paul *1:* 156, 181, 206; *2:* 40, 241; *3:* 42,144; *4:* 141; *10:* 109, 158; *11:* 21; *12:* 118, 210; *14:* 12; *16:* 36, 37; *17:* 70, 71, 72, 73, 74; *18:* 111, 230; *19:* 183; *21:* 154; *22:* 150, 245; *33:* 126; *39:* 136, 137; *42:* 57; *51:* 169; *55:* 110; *66:* 80, 82, 139; *72:* 73; *100:* 84

Gale, Cathy *140:* 22; *143:* 52; *213:* 166

Gall, Chris *176:* 79, 80

Gallagher, Jack *187:* 100

Gallagher, S. Saelig *105:* 154; *198:* 91

Gallagher, Sears *20:* 112Gallagher-Cole, Mernie *206:* 56

Galloway, Ewing *51:* 154

Galouchka, Annouchka Gravel *95:* 55; *182:* 40

Galster, Robert *1:* 66

Galsworthy, Gay John *35:* 232

Galvez, Daniel *125:* 182

Gamble, Kim *112:* 64, 65; *124:* 77; *183:* 40, 42, 43, 56, 57; *187:* 170

Gammell, Stephen *7:* 48; *13:* 149; *29:* 82; *33:* 209; *41:* 88; *50:* 185, 186, 187; *53:* 51, 52, 53, 54, 55, 56,57, 58; *54:* 24, 25; *56:* 147, 148, 150; *57:* 27, 66; *81:* 62, 63; *87:* 88; *89:* 10; *106:* 223; *126:* 2; *128:* 71, 73, 74, 77; *154:* 34; *211:* 210; *226:* 80, 81, 82

Gamper, Ruth *84:* 198

Gampert, John *58:* 94

Ganly, Helen *56:* 56

Gannett, Ruth Chrisman *3:* 74; *18:* 254; *33:* 77, 78

Gannon, Ned *205:* 6

Gantschev, Ivan *45:* 32

Garafano, Marie *73:* 33

Garbot, Dave *131:* 106

Garbutt, Bernard *23:* 68

Garcia *37:* 71

Garcia, Geronimo *222:* 73

Garcia, Manuel *74:* 145

Garcia-Franco, Rebecca *173:* 46

Gardiner, Lindsey *178:* 128; *186:* 137

Gardner, Earle *45:* 167

Gardner, Joan *40:* 87

Gardner, Joel *40:* 87, 92

Gardner, John *40:* 87

Gardner, Lucy *40:* 87

Gardner, Richard
    See Cummings, Richard

Gardner, Sally *171:* 177; *177:* 66, 68; *229:* 58

Gargiulo, Frank *84:* 158

Garland, Michael *36:* 29; *38:* 83; *44:* 168; *48:* 78, 221, 222; *49:* 161; *60:* 139; *71:* 6, 11; *72:* 229; *74:* 142; *89:* 187; *93:* 183; *104:* 110; *131:* 55; *139:* 209; *168:* 56; *208:* 72, 73, 75

Garland, Peggy *60:* 139

Garland, Sarah *62:* 45; *135:* 67, 68; *171:* 118

Garn, Aimee *75:* 47

Garner, Joan *128:* 170

Garneray, Ambroise Louis *59:* 140

Garnett, Eve *3:* 75

Garnett, Gary *39:* 184

Garns, Allen *80:* 125; *84:* 39; *165:* 231; *209:* 44

Garófoli, Viviana *186:* 123

Garraty, Gail *4:* 142; *52:* 106

Garrett, Agnes *46:* 110; *47:* 157

Garrett, Edmund H. *20:* 29

Garrett, Tom *107:* 194; *215:* 179

Garrick, Jacqueline *67:* 42, 43; *77:* 94

Garrison, Barbara *19:* 133; *104:* 146; *109:* 87

Garro, Mark *108:* 131; *128:* 210

Garvey, Robert *98:* 222

Garza, Carmen Lomas *80:* 211; *182:* 86

Garza, Xavier *184:* 64

Gates, Frieda *26:* 80

Gaughan, Jack *26:* 79; *43:* 185

Gaver, Becky *20:* 61

Gavril, David *211:* 196

Gawing, Toby *72:* 52

Gay, Marie-Louise *68:* 76, 77, 78; *102:* 136; *126:* 76, 78, 81, 83; *127:* 55, 56; *179:* 70, 72, 73, 74; *224:* 81

Gay, Zhenya *19:* 135, 136

Gaydos, Tim *62:* 201

Gazsi, Ed *80:* 48

Gazso, Gabriel *73:* 85

Geary, Clifford N. *1:* 122; *9:* 104; *51:* 74

Geary, Rick *142:* 44, 46

Gee, Frank *33:* 26

Geehan, Wayne *157:* 181

Geer, Charles *1:* 91; *3:* 179; *4:* 201; *6:* 168; *7:* 96; *9:* 58; *10:* 72; *12:* 127; *39:* 156,157, 158, 159, 160; *42:* 88, 89, 90, 91; *55:* 111, 116

Geerinck, Manuel *173:* 128

Gehm, Charlie *36:* 65; *57:* 117; *62:* 60, 138

Geis, Alissa Imre *189:* 77; *233:* 93

Geisel, Theodor Seuss *1:* 104, 105, 106; *28:* 108, 109, 110,111, 112, 113; *75:* 67, 68, 69, 70, 71; *89:* 127, 128; *100:* 106, 107, 108

Geisert, Arthur *92:* 67, 68; *133:* 72, 73, 74; *165:* 97, 98; *171:* 64, 65

Geldart, William *15:* 121; *21:* 202

Genia *4:* 84

Gentry, Cyrille R. *12:* 66

Genzo, John Paul *136:* 74

George, Jean *2:* 113

George, Lindsay Barrett *95:* 57; *155:* 97, 98

Geraghty, Paul *130:* 60, 61

Gerard, Jean Ignace *45:* 80

Gerard, Rolf *27:* 147, 150

Gerber, Mark *61:* 105

Gerber, Mary Jane *112:* 124; *171:* 56

Gerber, Stephanie *71:* 195

Gerdstein, Mordecai *169:* 105

Gergely, Tibor *54:* 15, 16

Geritz, Franz *17:* 135

Gerlach, Geff *42:* 58

Gerrard, Roy *47:* 78; *90:* 96, 97, 98, 99

Gerritsen, Paula *177:* 69; *217:* 166

Gershinowitz, George *36:* 27

Gerstein, Mordicai *31:* 117; *47:* 80, 81, 82, 83, 84, 85, 86; *51:* 173; *69:* 134; *107:* 122; *142:* 49, 52; *165:* 209; *176:* 119; *178:* 95, 97, 99; *215:* 173; *222:* 76

Gervase *12:* 27

Geter, Tyrone *146:* 249; *150:* 86

Getz, Arthur *32:* 148

Gévry, Claudine *188:* 47

Gewirtz, Bina *61:* 81

Giancola, Donato *95:* 146; *164:* 226; *229:* 181
Gibala-Broxholm, Scott *205:* 76; *219:* 186
Gibbons, Gail *23:* 78; *72:* 77, 78, 79; *82:* 182; *104:* 65; *160:* 99, 100; *201:* 59, 60, 62
Gibbs, Tony *40:* 95
Gibran, Kahlil *32:* 116
Gibson, Barbara Leonard *205:* 77; *212:* 151
Gider, Iskender *81:* 193
Giebfried, Rosemary *170:* 135
Giesen, Rosemary *34:* 192, 193
Giffard, Hannah *83:* 70
Giguere, George *20:* 111
Gilbert, John *19:* 184; *54:* 115; *YABC 2:* 287
Gilbert, W.S. *36:* 83, 85, 96
Gilbert, Yvonne *116:* 70; *128:* 84; *149:* 119; *185:* 69; *192:* 25; *195:* 81
Gilchrist, Jan Spivey *72:* 82, 83, 84, 85, 87; *77:* 90; *105:* 89, 91; *130:* 63, 64; *155:* 105, 107; *182:* 67
Giles, Will *41:* 218
Gili, Phillida *70:* 73
Gill, Margery *4:* 57; *7:* 7; *22:* 122; *25:* 166; *26:* 146, 147
Gillen, Denver *28:* 216
Gillette, Henry J. *23:* 237
Gilliam, Stan *39:* 64, 81
Gillies, Chuck *62:* 31
Gilliland, Jillian *87:* 58
Gillman, Alec *98:* 105
Gilman, Esther *15:* 124
Gilman, Phoebe *104:* 70, 71
Gilpin, Stephen *213:* 68
Ginsberg, Sari *111:* 184
Ginsburg, Max *62:* 59; *68:* 194 *Girard, Roge 161:* 30
Girouard, Patrick *155:* 100; *218:* 165
Giovanopoulos, Paul *7:* 104; *60:* 36
Giovine, Sergio *79:* 12; *93:* 118; *139:* 118; *205:* 114
Gist, E.M. *206:* 60
Githens, Elizabeth M. *5:* 47
Gladden, Scott *99:* 108; *103:* 160; *193:* 46, 47
Gladstone, Gary *12:* 89; *13:* 190
Gladstone, Lise *15:* 273
Glanzman, Louis S. *2:* 177; *3:* 182; *36:* 97, 98; *38:* 120, 122; *52:* 141, 144; *71:* 191; *91:* 54, 56
Glaser, Byron *154:* 59, 60
Glaser, Milton *3:* 5; *5:* 156; *11:* 107; *30:* 26; *36:* 112; *54:* 141; *151:* 70
Glass, Andrew *36:* 38; *44:* 133; *48:* 205; *65:* 3; *68:* 43, 45; *90:* 104, 105; *150:* 89; *223:* 73, 74
Glass, Marvin *9:* 174
Glasser, Judy *41:* 156; *56:* 140; *69:* 79; *72:* 101
Glattauer, Ned *5:* 84; *13:* 224; *14:* 26
Glauber, Uta *17:* 76
Gleeson, J.M. *YABC 2:* 207
Glegg, Creina *36:* 100
Glienke, Amelie *63:* 150
Gliewe, Unada *3:* 78, 79; *21:* 73; *30:* 220
Gliori, Debi *72:* 91; *138:* 82; *162:* 37; *189:* 79, 81, 82
Glovach, Linda *7:* 105
Gobbato, Imero *3:* 180, 181; *6:* 213; *7:* 58; *9:* 150; *18:* 39; *21:* 167; *39:* 82, 83; *41:* 137, 251; *59:* 177
Goble, Paul *25:* 121; *26:* 86; *33:* 65; *69:* 68, 69; *131:* 79, 80
Goble, Warwick *46:* 78, 79; *194:* 143
Godal, Eric *36:* 93
Godbey, Cory *221:* 154
Godkin, Celia *145:* 84, 86
Godfrey, Michael *17:* 279
Godon, Ingrid *166:* 163; *186:* 99
Goede, Irene *208:* 87
Goembel, Ponder *42:* 124
Goffe, Toni *61:* 83, 84, 85; *89:* 11; *90:* 124; *178:* 118
Goffstein, M.B. *8:* 71; *70:* 75, 76, 77

Golbin, Andre *15:* 125
Gold, Robert *166:* 151, 152
Goldfeder, Cheryl *11:* 191
Goldfinger, Jennifer P. *185:* 71
Goldman, Todd H. *221:* 50, 51
Goldsborough, June *5:* 154, 155; *8:* 92, *14:* 226; *19:* 139; *54:* 165
Goldsmith, Robert *110:* 77
Goldstein, Barry *198:* 147
Goldstein, Leslie *5:* 8; *6:* 60; *10:* 106
Goldstein, Nathan *1:* 175; *2:* 79; *11:* 41, 232; *16:* 55
Goldstrom, Robert *98:* 36; *145:* 51, 52; *233:* 56
Golembe, Carla *79:* 80, 81; *136:* 91; *144:* 113; *193:* 53
Golin, Carlo *74:* 112
Gomez, Elena *188:* 122; *191:* 72
Gomez, Elizabeth *127:* 70; *133:* 76
Gomi, Taro *64:* 102; *103:* 74, 76
Gon, Adriano *101:* 112
Gonsalves, Ron *178:* 213; *212:* 196
Gonzalez, Maya Christina *104:* 3; *136:* 92; *215:* 4, 5
Gonzalez, Thomas *226:* 157
Gonzalez, Yolanda *212:* 65
Good, Karen Hillard *212:* 143; *214:* 103
Goodall, John S. *4:* 92, 93; *10:* 132; *66:* 92, 93; *YABC 1:* 198
Goode, Diane *15:* 126; *50:* 183; *52:* 114, 115; *76:* 195; *84:* 94; *99:* 141; *114:* 76, 77, 78; *170:* 99, 101; *225:* 80, 81, 82, 83, 84
Goodelman, Aaron *40:* 203
Goodenow, Earle *40:* 97
Goodfellow, Peter *62:* 95; *94:* 202
Goodman, Joan Elizabeth *50:* 86
Goodman, Vivienne *82:* 251; *146:* 181, 182
Goodnow, Patti *117:* 33
Goodrich, Carter *221:* 52, 53
Goodwin, Harold *13:* 74
Goodwin, Philip R. *18:* 206
Goor, Nancy *39:* 85, 86
Goor, Ron *39:* 85, 86
Goossens, Philippe *195:* 71
Gorbachev, Valeri *89:* 96; *112:* 97; *143:* 63, 64; *184:* 66, 67, 68, 101; *222:* 84, 85, 86, 87
Gordon, David *216:* 159
Gordon, Gwen *12:* 151
Gordon, Margaret *4:* 147; *5:* 48, 49; *9:* 79
Gordon, Mike *101:* 62, 63, 64
Gordon, Russell *136:* 204; *137:* 214; *228:* 34
Gordon, Walter *138:* 9
Gore, Leonid *89:* 51; *94:* 74; *136:* 8; *158:* 117; *166:* 136; *168:* 36; *170:* 107; *181:* 94; *185:* 73; *222:* 89, 90, 91, 92
Gorecka-Egan, Erica *18:* 35
Gorey, Edward *1:* 60, 61; *13:* 169; *18:* 192; *20:* 201; *29:* 90, 91, 92, 93, 94, 95, 96, 97, 98, 99, 100; *30:* 129; *32:* 90; *34:* 200, *65:* 48; *68:* 24, 25; *69:* 79; *70:* 80, 82, 83, 84; *85:* 136; *127:* 62
Gorman, Mike *222:* 167
Gorsline, Douglas *1:* 98; *6:* 13; *11:* 113; *13:* 104; *15:* 14; *28:* 117, 118; *YABC 1:* 15
Gorton, Julia *108:* 94; *178:* 81, 82
Gosfield, Josh *118:* 165, 166; *149:* 67
Gosner, Kenneth *5:* 135
Gosney, Joy *167:* 142
Gotlieb, Jules *6:* 127
Goto, Scott *115:* 86; *136:* 69; *203:* 77, 78
Gott, Barry *197:* 95; *212:* 102
Gottlieb, Dale *67:* 162; *107:* 16; *149:* 6
Goudey, Ray *97:* 86
Gough, Alan *91:* 57
Gough, Philip *23:* 47; *45:* 90
Gould, Chester *49:* 112, 113, 114, 116, 117, 118
Gould, Jason *151:* 232
Gourbault, Martine *177:* 159
Govern, Elaine R. *26:* 94
Gower, Teri *102:* 184

Gowing, Toby *60:* 25; *63:* 33; *78:* 70, 252; *83:* 228; *86:* 187; *93:* 145; *108:* 133; *110:* 217; *184:* 125; *225:* 142
Grabianski *20:* 144
Grabianski, Janusz *39:* 92, 93, 94, 95
Graboff, Abner *35:* 103, 104
Graef, Renée *61:* 188; *72:* 207; *204:* 45; *210:* 249
Grafe, Max *156:* 173; *178:* 237; *192:* 240; *198:* 51
Graham, A.B. *11:* 61
Graham, Bob *101:* 66, 67, 68; *151:* 74, 75; *187:* 65, 67, 68, 70
Graham, Georgia *188:* 3; *190:* 75
Graham, L. *7:* 108
Graham, Margaret Bloy *11:* 120; *18:* 305, 307
Graham, Mark *88:* 208; *159:* 153; *182:* 3
Grahame-Johnstone, Janet *13:* 61
Grahame-Johnstone, Anne *13:* 61
Grainger, Sam *42:* 95
Gralley, Jean *166:* 86
Gramatky, Hardie *1:* 107; *30:* 116, 119, 120, 122, 123
Gran, Julie *168:* 118
Granahan, Julie *84:* 84
GrandPré, Mary *84:* 131; *109:* 199; *118:* 76; *180:* 65; *184:* 70, 71, 180; *192:* 87; *215:* 24; *229:* 68, 69, 70
Grandström, Brita *176:* 139
Grandville, J.J. *45:* 81, 82, 83, 84, 85, 86, 87, 88; *47:* 125; *64:* 10
Granger, Paul *39:* 153
Granström, Brita *162:* 35; *167:* 46; *224:* 56, 57
Grant, (Alice) Leigh *10:* 52; *15:* 131; *20:* 20; *26:* 119; *48:* 202
Grant, Gordon *17:* 230, 234; *25:* 123, 124, 125, 126; *52:* 69; *YABC 1:* 164
Grant, Melvyn *159:* 186, 187; *170:* 48, 49; *213:* 168, 169; *226:* 163
Grant, Michelle *210:* 95
Grant, Renee *77:* 40
Grant, Shirley *109:* 45
Graves, Elizabeth *45:* 101
Graves, Keith *167:* 89; *191:* 74; *216:* 34; *223:* 103
Gray, Harold *33:* 87, 88
Gray, Les *82:* 76; *83:* 232
Gray, Reginald *6:* 69
Gray, Steve *226:* 206; *231:* 77, 78
Greco, Tony *184:* 6
Greder, Armin *76:* 235
Green, Ann Canevari *62:* 48
Green, Eileen *6:* 97
Green, Elizabeth Shippen *139:* 109
Green, Jonathan *86:* 135; *105:* 109; *221:* 73
Green, Ken *111:* 68
Green, Michael *32:* 216
Green, Robina *87:* 138
Green, Jonathan *157:* 105
Greene, Jeffrey *117:* 93
Greenaway, Kate *17:* 275; *24:* 180; *26:* 107; *41:* 222, 232; *100:* 115, 116; *YABC 1:* 88, 89; *2:* 131, 133, 136,138, 139, 141
Greenberg, Melanie Hope *72:* 93; *80:* 125; *101:* 174; *133:* 180; *186:* 189; *214:* 105
Greenseid, Diane *178:* 106, 107
Greenstein, Elaine *150:* 100
Greenwald, Sheila *1:* 34; *3:* 99; *8:* 72
Greger, Carol *76:* 86
Gregorian, Joyce Ballou *30:* 125
Gregory, Emilian *177:* 146; *187:* 10
Gregory, Fran *130:* 4; *140:* 93
Gregory, Frank M. *29:* 107
Greiffenhagen, Maurice *16:* 137; *27:* 57; *YABC 2:* 288
Greiner, Robert *6:* 86
Gretter, J. Clemens *31:* 134
Gretz, Susanna *7:* 114
Gretzer, John *1:* 54; *3:* 26; *4:* 162; *7:* 125; *16:* 247; *18:* 117; *28:* 66; *30:* 85, 211; *33:* 235; *56:* 16

Grey, Mini *166:* 90; *192:* 71
Grey Owl *24:* 41
Gri *25:* 90
Grieder, Walter *9:* 84
Griesbach/Martucci *59:* 3
Grifalconi, Ann *2:* 126; *3:* 248; *11:* 18; *13:* 182; *46:* 38; *50:* 145; *66:* 99, 100, 101, 104, 106; *69:* 38; *70:* 64; *87:* 128; *90:* 53; *93:* 49; *128:* 48; *133:* 79, 81; *210:* 111
Griffin, Gillett Good *26:* 96
Griffin, James *30:* 166
Griffin, John Howard *59:* 186
Griffin, Rachel *131:* 23
Griffith, Gershom *94:* 214
Griffiths, Dave *29:* 76
Griffiths, Dean *168:* 180; *169:* 182
Grimly, Gris *186:* 102; *192:* 112; *197:* 86; *219:* 34
Grimsdell, Jeremy *83:* 75
Grimwood, Brian *82:* 89
Gringhuis, Dirk *6:* 98; *9:* 196
Gripe, Harald *2:* 127; *74:* 98
Grisha *3:* 71
Grobler, Piet *201:* 100
Grohmann, Susan *84:* 97
Gropper, William *27:* 93; *37:* 193
Gros *60:* 199
Grose, Helen Mason *YABC 1:* 260; *2:* 150
Grossman, Nancy *24:* 130; *29:* 101
Grossman, Robert *11:* 124; *46:* 39
Groth, John *15:* 79; *21:* 53, 54; *83:* 230
Grover, Lorie Ann *168:* 59
Grubb, Lisa *160:* 116
Grue, Lisa *187:* 193
Gruelle, Johnny *35:* 107
Gschwind, William *11:* 72
Guarnaccia, Steven *201:* 170, 173; *233:* 73
Guay-Mitchell, Rebecca *110:* 95, 96; *135:* 240; *180:* 76; *181:* 71, 73; *216:* 77
Guback, Georgia *88:* 102
Gudeon, Karla *212:* 67
Guerguerion, Claudine *105:* 73
Guevara, Susan *97:* 87; *167:* 49; *194:* 54
Guggenheim, Hans *2:* 10; *3:* 37; *8:* 136
Guhathaakurta, Ajanta *183:* 199
Guida, Lisa Chauncy *172:* 188
Guilbeau, Honore *22:* 69
Guillette, Joseph *137:* 37
Guisewite, Cathy *57:* 52, 53, 54, 56, 57
Gukova, Julia *95:* 104; *154:* 103; *168:* 195
Gundersheimer, Karen *35:* 240; *82:* 100
Gunderson, Nick *57:* 120
Gunnella *192:* 144
Gurney, James *76:* 97; *86:* 32
Gurney, John Steven *75:* 39, 82; *110:* 175; *143:* 67, 68; *169:* 172; *217:* 50, 88; *227:* 86, 87, 88; *228:* 139, 140, 141
Gusman, Annie *38:* 62
Gustafson, Scott *34:* 111; *43:* 40
Gustavson, Adam *104:* 10; *171:* 183; *176:* 87; *197:* 94; *204:* 35; *219:* 187
Guthridge, Bettina *108:* 79; *186:* 92
Guthrie, R. Dale *64:* 143
Guthrie, Robin *20:* 122
Gutierrez, Akemi *172:* 87; *205:* 135
Gutierrez, Alan *136:* 31, 32
Gutierrez, Rudy *97:* 162; *203:* 79; *216:* 158
Gutmann, Bessie Pease *73:* 93, 94
Gwynne, Fred *41:* 94, 95
Gyberg, Bo-Erik *38:* 131

H

Haas, Irene *17:* 77; *87:* 46; *96:* 117
Hack, Konrad *51:* 127
Hader, Berta H. *16:* 126
Hader, Elmer S. *16:* 126
Haeffele, Deborah *76:* 99
Haemer, Alan *62:* 109

Hafner, Marylin *22:* 196, 216; *24:* 44; *30:* 51; *35:* 95; *51:* 25, 160, 164; *86:* 16; *105:* 196; *121:* 93, 94; *149:* 208, 209; *179:* 82, 83, 84, 115; *190:* 200; *201:* 29; *217:* 91
Hagerty, Sean *62:* 181
Hague, Michael *32:* 128; *48:* 98, 99, 100, 101, 103, 105,106, 107, 108, 109, 110; *49:* 121; *51:* 105; *64:* 14, 15; *79:* 134; *80:* 91, 92; *83:* 135; *100:* 241; *102:* 29; *129:* 101, 103, 104; *185:* 80, 81, 82; *215:* 89
Hair, Jonathan *115:* 135
Halas, John *29:* 41, 47, 48
Haldane, Roger *13:* 76; *14:* 202
Hale, Bruce *203:* 83
Hale, Christy *79:* 124; *84:* 200; *114:* 201; *128:* 2, 3; *146:* 203; *158:* 243; *167:* 99; *179:* 87
Hale, Irina *26:* 97
Hale, James Graham *88:* 207
Hale, Kathleen *17:* 79; *66:* 114, 116, 118
Hale, Nathan *210:* 115, 116; *214:* 179
Haley, Amanda *205:* 82, 83
Haley, Gail E. *43:* 102, 103, 104, 105; *78:* 65, 67; *136:* 106, 107
Hall, Amanda *96:* 110
Hall, Angus *224:* 192
Hall, August N. *217:* 74
Hall, Chuck *30:* 189
Hall, Douglas *15:* 184; *43:* 106, 107; *86:* 100; *87:* 82; *129:* 72
Hall, H. Tom *1:* 227; *30:* 210
Hall, Melanie *116:* 48, 49; *169:* 77, 78; *219:* 170; *228:* 65, 66, 67
Hall, Michael *228:* 69
Hall, Sydney P. *31:* 89
Hall, Tim *164:* 196; *202:* 41
Hall, Vicki *20:* 24
Hallinan, P.K. *39:* 98
Hallman, Tom *98:* 166
Hally, Greg *101:* 200; *151:* 224
Halperin, Wendy Anderson *96:* 151; *125:* 96, 97, 98, 99; *139:* 22; *140:* 84; *200:* 77, 78; *210:* 157; *215:* 65; *228:* 24, 76
Halpern, Joan *10:* 25
Halpern, Shari *174:* 172
Halsey, Megan *96:* 172; *114:* 185; *180:* 8; *185:* 85
Halstead, Virginia *125:* 105
Halverson, Janet *49:* 38, 42, 44
Hallensleben, Georg *134:* 5, 6; *172:* 17
Hallett, Mark *220:* 63
Hamanaka, Sheila *71:* 100
Hamann, Brad *78:* 151
Hamann, Sigune *104:* 115
Hamberger, John *6:* 8; *8:* 32; *14:* 79; *34:* 136; *88:* 78
Hamil, Tom *14:* 80; *43:* 163
Hamilton, Bill and Associates *26:* 215
Hamilton, Helen S. *2:* 238
Hamilton, J. *19:* 83, 85, 87
Hamilton, Laurie *116:* 210
Hamilton, Todd Cameron *84:* 15
Hamlin, Janet *97:* 136; *124:* 90; *137:* 157; *182:* 117
Hamlin, Louise *71:* 135
Hammill, Matt *206:* 65
Hammond, Chris *21:* 37
Hammond, Elizabeth *5:* 36, 203
Hampshire, Michael *5:* 187; *7:* 110, 111; *48:* 150; *51:* 129
Hampson, Denman *10:* 155; *15:* 130
Hampton, Blake *41:* 244
Handford, Martin *64:* 105, 106, 107, 109
Handforth, Thomas *42:* 100, 101, 102, 103, 104, 105, 107
Handville, Robert *1:* 89; *38:* 76; *45:* 108, 109
Hane, Roger *17:* 239; *44:* 54
Haney, Elizabeth Mathieu *34:* 84
Hanke, Ted *71:* 10
Hankinson, Phil *181:* 164
Hanley, Catherine *8:* 161
Hann, Jacquie *19:* 144

Hanna, Cheryl *91:* 133
Hanna, Wayne A. *67:* 145
Hanrahan, Kelly-Anne *203:* 142
Hansen, Gaby *159:* 11; *186:* 25; *224:* 11
Hansen, Mia *149:* 76
Hanson, Glen *229:* 84
Hanson, Joan *8:* 76; *11:* 139
Hanson, Peter E. *52:* 47; *54:* 99, 100; *73:* 21; *84:* 79; *116:* 144
Hansson, Gunilla *64:* 111, 112
Harbour, Elizabeth *221:* 68
Hardcastle, Nick *121:* 82; *175:* 185; *222:* 135
Hardy, David A. *9:* 96; *119:* 74
Hardy, Paul *YABC 2:* 245
Hargis, Wes *219:* 70 *Haring, Keith 145:* 65
Harlan, Jerry *3:* 96
Harlin, Greg *89:* 194; *103:* 82; *118:* 161; *121:* 167; *182:* 76; *201:* 172; *215:* 76
Harman, Dominic *206:* 48
Harness, Cheryl *106:* 80; *131:* 87; *178:* 111; *200:* 39
Harnischfeger *18:* 121
Harper, Arthur *YABC 2:* 121
Harper, Betty *126:* 90
Harper, Jamie *174:* 71; *214:* 212
Harper, Piers *79:* 27; *105:* 102; *161:* 67
Harrington, Glenn *82:* 18; *94:* 66, 68; *185:* 118
Harrington, Jack *83:* 162
Harrington, Richard *5:* 81
Harris, Andrew N. *191:* 78
Harris, Jim *127:* 130; *183:* 4
Harris, John *83:* 25
Harris, Nick *86:* 177
Harris, Susan Yard *42:* 121
Harrison, Florence *20:* 150, 152
Harrison, Harry *4:* 103
Harrison, Jack *28:* 149
Harrison, Mark *105:* 157; *165:* 190
Harrison, Ted *56:* 73
Harsh, Fred *72:* 107
Harston, Jerry *105:* 143
Hart, Lewis *98:* 115
Hart, Thomas *181:* 165
Hart, William *13:* 72
Hartland, Jessie *171:* 80, 81; *186:* 165; *223:* 58
Hartung, Susan Kathleen *150:* 107, 108; *173:* 106; *175:* 106; *192:* 78; *211:* 19
Hartelius, Margaret *10:* 24
Hartshorn, Ruth *5:* 115; *11:* 129
Harvey, Amanda *145:* 44
Harvey, Bob *48:* 219
Harvey, Gerry *7:* 180
Harvey, Lisa *97:* 21
Harvey, Paul *88:* 74
Harvey, Roland *71:* 88; *123:* 63; *179:* 94; *218:* 94; *219:* 74
Haskamp, Steve *195:* 36; *229:* 29
Hassall, Joan *43:* 108, 109
Hassell, Hilton *YABC 1:* 187
Hassett, John *162:* 59
Hasselriis, Else *18:* 87; *YABC 1:* 96
Hastings, Glenn *89:* 183
Hastings, Ian *62:* 67
Hauman, Doris *2:* 184; *29:* 58, 59; *32:* 85, 86, 87
Hauman, George *2:* 184; *29:* 58, 59; *32:* 85, 86, 87
Hausherr, Rosmarie *15:* 29
Haverfield, Mary *225:* 87
Hawkes, Kevin *78:* 72; *104:* 198; *105:* 197; *112:* 109; *126:* 87; *144:* 88; *149:* 210; *150:* 110, 135; *156:* 94; *164:* 35; *186:* 18; *190:* 197; *198:* 152; *201:* 70, 71, 72; *220:* 99; *221:* 90, 92, 93
Hawkins, Jacqui *112:* 86; *162:* 64
Hawkinson, John *4:* 109; *7:* 83; *21:* 64
Hawkinson, Lucy *21:* 64
Hawthorne, Mike *140:* 228

Haxton, Elaine *28:* 131
Haydock, Robert *4:* 95
Hayes, Geoffrey *26:* 111; *44:* 133; *91:* 85; *207:* 63
Hayes, Karel *207:* 65
Haynes, Max *72:* 107
Hays, Michael *73:* 207; *83:* 93; *139:* 197; *146:* 202, 250; *202:* 47
Haywood, Carolyn *1:* 112; *29:* 104
Heale, Jonathan *104:* 117
Healy, Daty *12:* 143
Healy, Deborah *58:* 181, 182; *101:* 111
Heap, Sue *102:* 207; *150:* 113, 114; *187:* 84, 85, 87
Hearn, Diane Dawson *79:* 99; *113:* 13; *209:* 71, 72; *211:* 106
Hearon, Dorothy *34:* 69
Heaslip, William *57:* 24, 25
Hechtkopf, H. *11:* 110
Heck, Ed *173:* 81
Hector, Julian *205:* 85
Hedderwick, Mairi *30:* 127; *32:* 47; *36:* 104; *77:* 86; *145:* 91, 93, 95
Heffernan, Phil *146:* 197; *195:* 172; *218:* 123
Hefter, Richard *28:* 170; *31:* 81, 82; *33:* 183
Hehenberger, Shelly *126:* 91
Heigh, James *22:* 98
Heighway, Richard *25:* 160; *64:* 4
Heighway-Bury, Robin *159:* 89
Heine, Helme *67:* 86; *135:* 91, 92
Heinly, John *45:* 113
Hellard, Susan *81:* 21; *204:* 82; *209:* 92
Hellebrand, Nancy *26:* 57
Heller, Linda *46:* 86
Heller, Ruth M. *66:* 125; *77:* 30, 32
Hellmuth, Jim *38:* 164
Helms, Georgeann *33:* 62
Helquist, Brett *142:* 203; *146:* 133, 134; *156:* 10; *173:* 25; *180:* 106; *187:* 90, 91; *193:* 12; *224:* 186; *226:* 117; *229:* 76, 77, 78
Helweg, Hans *41:* 118; *50:* 93; *58:* 22, 26
Hemingway, Edward *212:* 71
Hemphill, Helen *179:* 95
Henba, Bobbie *90:* 195
Henderling, Lisa *214:* 65
Henderson, Dave *73:* 76; *75:* 191, 192, 193, 194; *82:* 4
Henderson, D.F. *216:* 77
Henderson, Douglas *103:* 68
Henderson, Kathy *55:* 32; *155:* 118
Henderson, Keith *35:* 122
Henderson, Meryl *127:* 58, 60; *169:* 81; *228:*
Hendrix, John *187:* 133; *208:* 106, 107, 108; *216:* 115
Hendry, Linda *80:* 104; *83:* 83; *164:* 216; *233:* 11
Hengeveld, Dennis *142:* 86
Henkes, Kevin *43:* 111; *108:* 106, 107, 108
Henneberger, Robert *1:* 42; *2:* 237; *25:* 83
Henriksen, Harold *35:* 26; *48:* 68
Henriquez, Celeste *103:* 137
Henriquez, Elsa *82:* 260
Henriquez, Emile F. *89:* 88; *211:* 56
Henry, Everett *29:* 191
Henry, Matthew *117:* 58
Henry, Paul *93:* 121; *194:* 125
Henry, Rohan *217:* 77
Henry, Thomas *5:* 102
Hensel *27:* 119
Henshaw, Jacqui *141:* 127
Henstra, Friso *8:* 80; *36:* 70; *40:* 222; *41:* 250; *73:* 100, 101
Henterly, Jamichael *93:* 4
Heo, Yumi *89:* 85, 86; *94:* 89, 90; *146:* 40, 137, 138; *163:* 227; *201:* 192
Hepple, Norman *28:* 198
Herbert, Helen *57:* 70
Herbert, Jennifer *189:* 47
Herbert, Wally *23:* 101
Herbster, Mary Lee *9:* 33
Herder, Edwin *182:* 104

Herge
  See Remi, Georges
Hermansen, Pal *133:* 113
Hermanson, Dennis *10:* 55
Hermes, Gertrude *54:* 161
Herr, Margo *57:* 191
Herr, Susan *83:* 163
Herriman, George *140:* 74, 75, 76, 77, 78
Herriman, Lisa *87:* 190
Herring, Michael *121:* 76; *182:* 103
Herrington, Roger *3:* 161
Herscovici, C. *165:* 240
Hescox, Richard *85:* 86; *90:* 30; *139:* 35
Heslop, Mike *38:* 60; *40:* 130
Hess, Lydia J. *85:* 17
Hess, Mark *111:* 146; *113:* 207
Hess, Paul *134:* 47; *166:* 133; *193:* 13
Hess, Richard *42:* 31
Hester, Ronnie *37:* 85
Heuser, Olga J. *121:* 116
Heusser, Sibylle *168:* 195
Heustis, Louise L. *20:* 28
Hewgill, Jody *201:* 90
Hewitson, Jennifer *74:* 119; *124:* 167
Hewitt, Kathryn *80:* 126; *149:* 105; *184:* 93; *196:* 36; *229:* 99
Hewitt, Margaret *84:* 112
Heyduck-Huth, Hilde *8:* 82
Heyer, Carol *74:* 122; *130:* 72, 73; *192:* 35; *203:* 78
Heyer, Hermann *20:* 114, 115
Heyer, Marilee *102:* 108
Heyman, Ken *8:* 33; *34:* 113
Heyne, Ulrike *146:* 151
Heywood, Karen *48:* 114
Hickling, P.B. *40:* 165
Hickman, Stephen *85:* 58; *136:* 33; *171:* 128
Hierstein, Judith *56:* 40; *162:* 168; *212:* 72; *227:* 46
Higashi, Sandra *154:* 59, 60
Higginbottom, J. Winslow *8:* 170; *29:* 105, 106
Higgins, Chester *101:* 79
Higham, David *50:* 104
Hilb, Nora *176:* 8
Hild, Anja *215:* 194
Hildebrandt, Greg *8:* 191; *55:* 35, 36, 38, 39, 40, 42, 46; *172:* 110
Hildebrandt, Tim *8:* 191; *55:* 44, 45, 46
Hilder, Rowland *19:* 207
Hill, Eric *66:* 127, 128; *133:* 91
Hill, Gregory *35:* 190
Hill, Pat *49:* 120
Hillenbrand, Will *84:* 115; *92:* 76, 80; *93:* 131; *104:* 168; *128:* 137; *145:* 187; *146:* 184; *147:* 105, 106, 107; *152:* 59; *184:* 179; *195:* 34, 180; *196:* 125; *210:* 122, 123, 124; *217:* 62; *224:* 145
Hilliard, Richard *183:* 74
Hillier, Matthew *45:* 205
Hillman, Priscilla *48:* 115
Hills, Tad *113:* 4; *137:* 147; *173:* 83; *208:* 199
Himler, Ronald *6:* 114; *7:* 162; *8:* 17, 84, 125; *14:* 76; *19:* 145; *26:* 160; *31:* 43; *38:* 116; *41:* 44, 79; *43:* 52; *45:* 120; *46:* 43; *54:* 44, 83; *58:* 180; *59:* 38; *68:* 146; *69:* 231; *70:* 98; *71:* 177, 178; *77:* 219; *79:* 212; *83:* 62; *89:* 5; *91:* 160; *92:* 91, 92, 93; *94:* 93; *95:* 69, 174, 194; *99:* 99, 111, 112; *113:* 92; *118:* 114; *137:* 73, 74, 77, 167; *163:* 99; *165:* 138; *178:* 9, 220; *183:* 77, 79, 80, 81; *184:* 80, 83; *215:* 151; *231:* 11, 112
Himmelman, John *47:* 109; *65:* 87; *94:* 96, 97; *159:* 85; *221:* 79, 80, 81, 82
Hinds, Bill *37:* 127, 130
Hines, Anna Grossnickle *51:* 90; *74:* 124; *95:* 78, 79,80, 81
Hines, Bob *135:* 149, 150
Hirao, Amiko *203:* 98
Hiroko *99:* 61
Hiroshige *25:* 71

Hirsh, Marilyn *7:* 126
Hiscock, Bruce *137:* 80, 81; *204:* 51, 53
Hissey, Jane *103:* 90; *130:* 81
Hitch, Jeff *99:* 206; *128:* 86
Hitz, Demi *11:* 135; *15:* 245; *66:* 129, 130; *152:* 94, 95
Hnizdovsky, Jacques *32:* 96; *76:* 187
Ho, David *227:* 32
Ho, Kwoncjan *15:* 132
Hoban, Lillian *1:* 114; *22:* 157; *26:* 72; *29:* 53; *40:* 105, 107, 195; *41:* 80; *69:* 107, 108; *71:* 98; *77:* 168; *106:* 50; *113:* 36; *136:* 118
Hoban, Tana *22:* 159; *104:* 82, 83, 85
Hobbie, Holly *225:* 90, 91
Hobbie, Jocelyn *190:* 78; *196:* 92
Hobbie, Nathaniel *196:* 92
Hobbs, Leigh *166:* 95
Hoberman, Norman *5:* 82
Hobson, Sally *77:* 185
Hockerman, Dennis *39:* 22; *56:* 23
Hodgell, P.C. *42:* 114
Hodges, C. Walter *2:* 139; *11:* 15; *12:* 25; *23:* 34; *25:* 96; *38:* 165; *44:* 197; *45:* 95; *100:* 57; *YABC 2:* 62, 63
Hodges, David *9:* 98
Hodgetts, Victoria *43:* 132
Hofbauer, Imre *2:* 162
Hoff, Syd *9:* 107; *10:* 128; *33:* 94; *72:* 115,116, 117, 118; *138:* 114, 115
Hoffman, Rosekrans *15:* 133; *50:* 219; *63:* 97
Hoffman, Sanford *38:* 208; *76:* 174; *88:* 160, 161; *151:* 156
Hoffmann, Felix *9:* 109
Hoffnung, Gerard *66:* 76, 77
Hofsinde, Robert *21:* 70
Hogan, Inez *2:* 141
Hogan, Jamie *192:* 94; *198:* 177
Hogarth, Burne *41:* 58; *63:* 46, 48, 49, 50, 52, 53, 54, 55,56
Hogarth, Paul *41:* 102, 103, 104; *YABC 1:* 16
Hogarth, William *42:* 33
Hogenbyl, Jan *1:* 35
Hogner, Nils *4:* 122; *25:* 144
Hogrogian, Nonny *3:* 221; *4:* 106, 107; *5:* 166; *7:* 129; *15:* 2; *16:* 176; *20:* 154; *22:* 146; *25:* 217; *27:* 206; *74:* 127, 128, 129, 149, 152; *127:* 99; *YABC 2:* 84, 94
Hokanson, Lars *93:* 111; *172:* 137; *212:* 88
Hokusai *25:* 71
Hol, Colby *126:* 96
Holberg, Richard *2:* 51
Holbrook, Kathy *107:* 114
Holdcroft, Tina *38:* 109; *227:* 99, 100, 160
Holden, Caroline *55:* 159
Holder, Heidi *36:* 99; *64:* 9
Holder, Jim *204:* 163
Holder, Jimmy *151:* 224; *233:* 175
Holderness, Grizelda *215:* 107
Hole, Stian *204:* 55
Holiday, Henry *YABC 2:* 107
Holl, F. *36:* 91
Holland, Brad *45:* 59, 159
Holland, Gay W. *128:* 105; *225:* 76
Holland, Janice *18:* 118
Holland, Marion *6:* 116
Holland, Richard *216:* 109, 124
Holldobler, Turid *26:* 120
Holliday, Keaf *144:* 236
Holling, Holling C. *15:* 136, 137
Hollinger, Deanne *12:* 116
Holm, Sharon Lane *114:* 84; *115:* 52
Holmes, B. *3:* 82
Holmes, Bea *7:* 74; *24:* 156; *31:* 93
Holmes, Dave *54:* 22
Holmes, Lesley *135:* 96
Holmgren, George Ellen *45:* 112
Holmlund, Heather D. *150:* 140
Holt, Norma *44:* 106
Holt, Pater *151:* 188
Holtan, Gene *32:* 192
Holub, Joan *149:* 72; *229:* 82

Holyfield, John *149:* 231; *227:* 101; *230:* 9
Holz, Loretta *17:* 81
Hom, Nancy *79:* 195
Homar, Lorenzo *6:* 2
Homer, Winslow *128:* 8; *YABC 2:* 87
Honey, Elizabeth *112:* 95, 96; *137:* 93, 94
Honeywood, Varnette P. *110:* 68, 70
Hong, Lily Toy *76:* 104
Honigman, Marian *3:* 2
Honore, Paul *42:* 77, 79, 81, 82
Hood, Alun *69:* 145, 218; *72:* 41; *80:* 226; *87:* 4; *95:* 139
Hood, Susan *12:* 43
Hook, Christian *104:* 103
Hook, Frances *26:* 188; *27:* 127
Hook, Jeff *14:* 137; *103:* 105
Hook, Richard *26:* 188
Hooks *63:* 30
Hooper, Hadley *177:* 145
Hoover, Carol A. *21:* 77
Hoover, Russell *12:* 95; *17:* 2; *34:* 156
Hope, James *141:* 116
Hopkins, Chris *99:* 127
Hopkinson, Leigh *202:* 70
Hopman, Philip *178:* 184
Hoppe, Paul *209:* 85
Hoppin, Augustus *34:* 66
Horacek, Judy *211:* 86
Horacek, Petr *163:* 117; *214:* 113
Horder, Margaret *2:* 108; *73:* 75
Horen, Michael *45:* 121
Horne, Daniel *73:* 106; *91:* 153; *109:* 127; *110:* 232; *164:* 176
Horne, Richard *111:* 80
Horowitz, Dave *204:* 58
Horse, Harry *128:* 195; *169:* 86
Horstman, Lisa *219:* 79
Horton, Anthony *211:* 98
Horvat, Laurel *12:* 201
Horvath, David *192:* 95
Horvath, Ferdinand Kusati *24:* 176
Horvath, Maria *57:* 171
Horwitz, Richard *57:* 174
Hotchkiss, De Wolfe *20:* 49
Hough, Charlotte *9:* 112; *13:* 98; *17:* 83; *24:* 195
Houlihan, Ray *11:* 214
House, Caroline *183:* 121
Housman, Laurence *25:* 146, 147
Houston, James *13:* 107; *74:* 132, 134, 135
Hovland, Gary *88:* 172; *171:* 148
Hoyt, Eleanor *158:* 231
How, W.E. *20:* 47
Howard, Alan *16:* 80; *34:* 58; *45:* 114
Howard, Arthur *165:* 111, 112; *190:* 5; *229:* 30
Howard, J.N. *15:* 234
Howard, John *33:* 179
Howard, Kim *116:* 71
Howard, Paul *142:* 126, 129; *144:* 187
Howard, Rob *40:* 161
Howarth, Daniel *170:* 34; *222:* 97, 98; *224:* 20; *225:* 77
Howe, John *79:* 101; *80:* 150; *115:* 47; *176:* 106; *207:* 32, 35
Howe, Phillip *79:* 117; *175:* 115
Howe, Stephen *1:* 232
Howell, Karen *119:* 123
Howell, Pat *15:* 139
Howell, Troy *23:* 24; *31:* 61; *36:* 158; *37:* 184; *41:* 76, 235; *48:* 112; *56:* 13; *57:* 3; *59:* 174; *63:* 5; *74:* 46; *89:* 188; *90:* 231; *95:* 97; *98:* 130; *99:* 189; *153:* 156, 157, 158; *176:* 104; *199:* 96, 98; *222:* 65
Howells, Tania *229:* 87
Howes, Charles *22:* 17
Hoyt, Ard *145:* 141; *190:* 82; *207:* 148
Hranilovich, Barbara *127:* 51
Hu, Ying-Hwa *116:* 107; *152:* 236; *173:* 171
Huang, Benrei *137:* 55
Huang, Zhong-Yang *117:* 30, 32; *213:* 18

Hubbard, Woodleigh Marx *98:* 67; *115:* 79; *160:* 138; *214:* 120
Hubbell, Patricia *222:* 31
Hubley, Faith *48:* 120, 121, 125, 130, 131, 132, 134
Hubley, John *48:* 125, 130, 131, 132, 134
Hudak, Michal *143:* 74
Hudnut, Robin *14:* 62
Huerta, Catherine *76:* 178; *77:* 44, 45; *90:* 182; *210:* 202
Huffaker, Sandy *10:* 56
Huffman, Joan *13:* 33
Huffman, Tom *13:* 180; *17:* 212; *21:* 116; *24:* 132; *33:* 154; *38:* 59; *42:* 147
Hughes, Arthur *20:* 148, 149, 150; *33:* 114, 148, 149
Hughes, Darren *95:* 44
Hughes, David *36:* 197
Hughes, Shirley *1:* 20, 21; *7:* 3; *12:* 217; *16:* 163; *29:* 154; *63:* 118; *70:* 102, 103, 104; *73:* 169; *88:* 70; *110:* 118, 119; *159:* 103
Hugo, Victor *47:* 112
Huliska-Beith, Laura *204:* 108; *220:* 137; *232:* 97, 98
Hull, Cathy *78:* 29
Hull, Richard *95:* 120; *123:* 175; *172:* 195
Hulsmann, Eva *16:* 166
Hume, Lachie *189:* 93
Hummel, Berta *43:* 137, 138, 139
Hummel, Lisl *29:* 109; *YABC 2:* 333, 334
Humphrey, Henry *16:* 167
Humphreys, Graham *25:* 168
Humphries, Tudor *76:* 66; *80:* 4; *124:* 4, 5; *226:* 112
Huneck, Stephen *183:* 88, 89
Hunt, James *2:* 143
Hunt, Jonathan *84:* 120
Hunt, Paul *119:* 104; *129:* 135; *139:* 160; *173:* 112
Hunt, Robert *110:* 206, 235; *147:* 136, 137; *170:* 3; *211:* 76; *226:* 189
Hunt, Scott *190:* 143; *233:* 172
Hunter, Anne *133:* 190; *178:* 150
Huntington, Amy *180:* 99
Hurd, Clement *2:* 148, 149; *64:* 127, 128, 129, 131, 133, 134,135, 136; *100:* 37, 38
Hurd, Peter *24:* 30, 31,; *YABC 2:* 56
Hurd, Thacher *46:* 88, 89; *94:* 114, 115, 116; *123:* 81, 82, 84; *219:* 82
Hurlimann, Ruth *32:* 99
Hurst, Carol Otis *185:* 92
Hurst, Elise *221:* 98
Hurst, Philip *196:* 79
Hurst, Tracey *192:* 238
Hussar, Michael *114:* 113; *117:* 159
Hustler, Tom *6:* 105
Hutchins, Laurence *55:* 22
Hutchins, Pat *15:* 142; *70:* 106, 107, 108; *178:* 131, 132
Hutchinson, Sascha *95:* 211
Hutchinson, William M. *6:* 3, 138; *46:* 70
Hutchison, Paula *23:* 10
Hutton, Clarke *YABC 2:* 335
Hutton, Kathryn *35:* 155; *89:* 91
Hutton, Warwick *20:* 91
Huyette, Marcia *29:* 188
Hyatt, John *54:* 7
Hyatt, Mitch *178:* 162
Hyde, Maureen *82:* 17; *121:* 145, 146
Hyman, David *117:* 64
Hyman, Miles *210:* 132
Hyman, Trina Schart *1:* 204; *2:* 194; *5:* 153; *6:* 106; *7:* 138, 145; *8:* 22; *10:* 196; *13:* 96; *14:* 114; *15:* 204; *16:* 234; *20:* 82; *22:* 133; *24:* 151; *25:* 79, 82; *26:* 82; *29:* 83; *31:* 37, 39; *34:* 104; *38:* 84, 100, 128; *41:* 49; *43:* 146; *46:* 91, 92, 93, 95, 96, 97, 98, 99, 100, 101, 102, 103, 104, 105,108, 109, 111, 197; *48:* 60, 61; *52:* 32; *60:* 168; *66:* 38; *67:* 214;

72: 74; *75:* 92; *79:* 57; *82:* 95, 238; *89:* 46; *95:* 91, 92, 93; *100:* 33, 199; *132:* 12; *147:* 33, 35, 36; *167:* 58, 60; *177:* 189, 190; *211:* 188

I

Ibarra, Rosa *147:* 91
Ibatoulline, Bagram *156:* 48; *174:* 33, 82; *202:* 30; *211:* 213; *224:* 84; *225:* 98, 99; *232:* 60
Ichikawa, Satomi *29:* 152; *41:* 52; *47:* 133, 134,135, 136; *78:* 93, 94; *80:* 81; *146:* 143, 145, 146; *208:* 117, 118, 119
Ide, Jacqueline *YABC 1:* 39
Idle, Molly Schaar *223:* 95
Ignatow, Amy *233:* 91
Ilsley, Velma *3:* 1; *7:* 55; *12:* 109; *37:* 62; *38:* 184
Imai, Ayano *190:* 85, 86
in den Bosch, Nicole *150:* 204
Inga *1:* 142
Ingman, Bruce *134:* 50; *182:* 91, 92; *214:* 10
Ingpen, Robert *109:* 103, 104; *132:* 138; *137:* 177; *166:* 103; *181:* 140; *229:* 169
Ingraham, Erick *21:* 177; *84:* 256; *103:* 66
Inkpen, Mick *99:* 104, 105; *106:* 44
Innerst, Stacy *149:* 104; *232:* 101, 102
Innocenti, Roberto *21:* 123; *96:* 122; *159:* 111, 197; *199:* 176
Inoue, Yosuke *24:* 118
Iofin, Michael *97:* 157
Iosa, Ann *63:* 189
Ipcar, Dahlov *1:* 124, 125; *49:* 137, 138, 139, 140, 141, 142,143, 144, 145; *147:* 122, 124, 126
Irvin, Fred *13:* 166; *15:* 143, 144; *27:* 175
Irving, Jay *45:* 72
Irving, Laurence *27:* 50
Isaac, Joanne *21:* 76
Isaacs, Gary *170:* 188
Isadora, Rachel *43:* 159, 160; *54:* 31; *79:* 106, 107,108; *121:* 100, 102; *165:* 116, 117; *204:* 61, 63, 64
Ishmael, Woodi *24:* 111; *31:* 99
Isol *220:* 73
Ives, Ruth *15:* 257
Iwai, Melissa *149:* 233; *183:* 92; *199:* 115
Iwamura, Kazuo *213:* 87

J

Jabar, Cynthia *101:* 201; *210:* 134, 135
Jackness, Andrew *94:* 237
Jackson, Julian *91:* 104, 106
Jackson, Michael *43:* 42
Jackson, Shelley *79:* 71; *99:* 109; *187:* 82
Jacob, Murv *89:* 30
Jacobi, Kathy *62:* 118
Jacobs, Barbara *9:* 136
Jacobs, Lou, Jr. *9:* 136; *15:* 128
Jacobsen, Laura *176:* 98; *177:* 85, 86
Jacobson, Rick *131:* 222; *170:* 119; *222:* 52
Jacobus, Tim *79:* 140; *109:* 126; *129:* 180
Jacques, Robin *1:* 70; *2:* 1; *8:* 46; *9:* 20; *15:* 187; *19:* 253; *32:* 102, 103, 104; *43:* 184; *73:* 135; *YABC 1:* 42
Jaeggi, Yoshiko *186:* 184
Jaffee, Al *66:* 131, 132
Jago *216:* 122
Jagr, Miloslav *13:* 197
Jahn-Clough, Lisa *88:* 114; *152:* 104; *193:* 70, 71
Jahnke, Robert *84:* 24
Jainschigg, Nicholas *80:* 64; *91:* 138; *95:* 63; *99:* 25; *108:* 50; *171:* 41
Jakesevic, Nenad *85:* 102; *226:* 215

Jakobsen, Kathy *116:* 83
Jakubowski, Charles *14:* 192
Jambor, Louis *YABC 1:* 11
James, Ann *73:* 50; *82:* 113; *158:* 61; *183:* 44
James, Brian *140:* 91
James, Curtis E. *182:* 93
James, Derek *35:* 187; *44:* 91; *61:* 133; *74:* 2; *80:* 57; *86:* 88; *130:* 30; *179:* 29; *218:* 31
James, Gilbert *YABC 1:* 43
James, Gordon C. *195:* 89
James, Harold *2:* 151; *3:* 62; *8:* 79; *29:* 113; *51:* 195; *74:* 90
James, Kennon *126:* 211
James, Robin *50:* 106; *53:* 32, 34, 35
James, Simon *202:* 73, 74, *233:* 161
James, Will *19:* 150, 152, 153, 155, 163
Janosch
  See Eckert, Horst
Janovitch, Marilyn *68:* 168
Janovitz, Marilyn *87:* 187; *130:* 198; *194:* 91
Jansons, Inese *48:* 117
Jansson, Alexander *216:* 59
Jansson, Tove *3:* 90; *41:* 106, 108, 109, 110, 111, 113, 114
Jaques, Faith *7:* 11, 132, 133; *21:* 83, 84; *69:* 114, 116; *73:* 170
Jaques, Frances Lee *29:* 224
Jarka, Jeff *221:* 94
Jarrett, Clare *201:* 77
Jarrie, Martin *219:* 86
Jauss, Anne Marie *1:* 139; *3:* 34; *10:* 57, 119; *11:* 205; *23:* 194
Jay, Alison *158:* 97, 98; *183:* 126, 127; *196:* 95, 96, 97, 98; *200:* 72, 73, 74; *212:* 39
Jeffers, Oliver *175:* 111; *213:* 89
Jeffers, Susan *17:* 86, 87; *25:* 164, 165; *26:* 112; *50:* 132, 134, 135; *70:* 111, 112, 113; *137:* 107, 108, 109, 110, 111; *202:* 77, 78
Jefferson, Louise E. *4:* 160
Jenkin-Pearce, Susie *78:* 16
Jenkins, Debra Reid *85:* 202; *114:* 89; *173:* 134; *225:* 116
Jenkins, Jean *98:* 79, 102
Jenkins, Leonard *157:* 169; *167:* 128; *189:* 96, 97; *190:* 89
Jenkins, Patrick *72:* 126
Jenkins, Steve *124:* 177; *154:* 90, 91, 92, 93; *185:* 194; *188:* 81, 82, 83, 84, 85, 86; *218:* 67, 69, 70, 71, 72
Jenks, Aleta *73:* 117; *124:* 225
Jenkyns, Chris *51:* 97
Jensen, Bruce *95:* 39
Jensinius, Kirsten *56:* 58
Jeram, Anita *89:* 135; *102:* 122, 123; *129:* 112; *154:* 96, 97, 98; *164:* 154; *203:* 123, 124; *219:* 88, 89, 90, 91
Jernigan, E. Wesley *85:* 92
Jerome, Elaine *227:* 45
Jerome, Karen A. *72:* 194
Jeruchim, Simon *6:* 173; *15:* 250
Jeschke, Susan *20:* 89; *39:* 161; *41:* 84; *42:* 120
Jessel, Camilla *29:* 115
Jessell, Tim *159:* 3; *177:* 87; *181:* 95; *205:* 4; *213:* 74; *223:* 187; *225:* 102; *226:* 190
Jeyaveeran, Ruth *182:* 100
Jiang, Cheng An *109:* 108
Jiang, Wei *109:* 108
Jimenez, Maria *77:* 158; *93:* 127
Jobling, Curtis *138:* 74
Jocelyn, Marthe *118:* 83; *137:* 219; *163:* 119, 120; *198:* 62
Joerns, Consuelo *38:* 36; *44:* 94
John, Diana *12:* 209
John, Helen *1:* 215; *28:* 204
Johns, Elizabeth *127:* 33
Johns, Jasper *61:* 172
Johns, Jeanne *24:* 114
Johnson, Adrian *143:* 50
Johnson, Bruce *9:* 47
Johnson, Cathy *92:* 136; *218:* 112

Johnson, Crockett
  See Leisk, David
Johnson, D. William *23:* 104
Johnson, D.B. *183:* 98, 139
Johnson, David A. *175:* 18; *191:* 91; *218:* 19
Johnson, Gillian *119:* 175; *164:* 217; *215:* 99
Johnson, Harper *1:* 27; *2:* 33; *18:* 302; *19:* 61; *31:* 181; *44:* 46, 50, 95
Johnson, Ingrid *37:* 118
Johnson, James Ralph *1:* 23, 127
Johnson, James David *12:* 195
Johnson, Jane *48:* 136
Johnson, Joel Peter *98:* 18; *128:* 111; *201:* 13; *213:* 189
Johnson, John E. *34:* 133
Johnson, Kevin *72:* 44
Johnson, Kevin Eugene *109:* 215
Johnson, Larry *47:* 56; *123:* 107; *159:* 203
Johnson, Layne *187:* 94; *209:* 63; *222:* 100, 101; *233:* 123
Johnson, Margaret S. *35:* 131
Johnson, Meredith Merrell *71:* 181; *83:* 158; *89:* 103; *104:* 88
Johnson, Milton *1:* 67; *2:* 71; *26:* 45; *31:* 107; *60:* 112; *68:* 96
Johnson, Pamela *16:* 174; *52:* 145; *62:* 140; *73:* 116; *85:* 64
Johnson, Paul Brett *83:* 95; *132:* 119
Johnson, Stephen T. *80:* 15; *131:* 35; *141:* 96; *145:* 40; *164:* 187; *175:* 32; *189:* 99, 100; *208:* 43
Johnson, Steve *138:* 219; *141:* 64; *144:* 199; *177:* 51; *214:* 95; *221:* 63; *228:* 42, 43, 44; *230:* 44, 45, 46
Johnson, William R. *38:* 91
Johnson-Petrov, Arden *115:* 206
Johnston, David McCall *50:* 131, 133
Johnston, Lynne *118:* 85, 87, 89; *216:* 127, 128, 131
Johnstone, Anne *8:* 120; *36:* 89
Johnstone, Janet Grahame *8:* 120; *36:* 89
Jolivet, Joëlle *231:* 71
Jonas, Ann *50:* 107, 108, 109; *135:* 113
Jones, Bob *71:* 5; *77:* 199
Jones, Carol *5:* 131; *72:* 185, 186; *153:* 111, 112
Jones, Chuck *53:* 70, 71
Jones, Curtis *211:* 144
Jones, Davy *89:* 176
Jones, Douglas B. *185:* 192; *202:* 82
Jones, Elizabeth Orton *18:* 124, 126, 128, 129
Jones, Harold *14:* 88; *52:* 50
Jones, Holly *127:* 3
Jones, Jeff *41:* 64
Jones, Laurian *25:* 24, 27
Jones, Margaret *74:* 57
Jones, Noah Z. *182:* 37; *203:* 159
Jones, Randy *131:* 104
Jones, Richard *127:* 222
Jones, Robert *25:* 67
Jones, Wilfred *35:* 115; *YABC 1:* 163
Jordan, Charles *89:* 58
Jordan, Jess *158:* 136; *203:* 111
Jordan, Martin George *84:* 127
Jordan, Richard *84:* 36
Jorgenson, Andrea *91:* 111
Jorisch, Stéphane *153:* 56, 193; *177:* 29; *178:* 138, 139; *187:* 23; *211:* 182
Joseph, James *53:* 88
Joudrey, Ken *64:* 145; *78:* 6
Joyce, William *72:* 131, 132, 133, 134; *73:* 227; *145:* 37
Joyner, Jerry *34:* 138
Joyner, Loraine M. *209:* 17
Joysmith, Brenda *210:* 237
Juan, Ana *175:* 38; *179:* 111, 112; *213:* 9
Juarez, Fernando *233:* 26
Jucker, Sita *5:* 93
Judge, Lita *192:* 99
Judkis, Jim *37:* 38
Juhasz, Victor *31:* 67

Jullian, Philippe *24:* 206; *25:* 203
Jung, Tom *91:* 217
Junge, Alexandra *183:* 37
Junge, Walter *67:* 150
Jupo, Frank *7:* 148, 149
Jurisch, Stephane *154:* 105
Justice, Martin *34:* 72

K

Kabatova-Taborska, Zdenka *107:* 153
Kachik, John *165:* 230
Kaczman, James *156:* 98
Kadair, Deborah Ousley *184:* 45, 89
Kahl, David *74:* 95; *97:* 35; *109:* 174; *110:* 213; *198:* 15
Kahl, M.P. *37:* 83
Kahl, Virginia *48:* 138
Kahn, Katherine Janus *90:* 135; *211:* 155; *218:* 75, 76; *220:* 89,90
Kakimoo, Kozo *11:* 148
Kalett, Jim *48:* 159, 160, 161
Kalin, Victor *39:* 186
Kalis, Jennifer *207:* 82; *219:* 62
Kalman, Maira *96:* 131, 132; *137:* 115
Kalmenoff, Matthew *22:* 191
Kalow, Gisela *32:* 105
Kamen, Gloria *1:* 41; *9:* 119; *10:* 178; *35:* 157; *78:* 236; *98:* 82
Kaminsky, Jef *102:* 153
Kandell, Alice *35:* 133
Kane, Henry B. *14:* 90; *18:* 219, 220
Kane, Robert *18:* 131
Kanfer, Larry *66:* 141
Kangas, Juli *200:* 88
Kappes, Alfred *28:* 104
Karalus, Bob *41:* 157
Karas, G. Brian *80:* 60; *99:* 179; *115:* 41; *118:* 50; *136:* 168; *145:* 166; *149:* 245; *159:* 65; *171:* 192; *178:* 142, 143; *202:* 38; *209:* 142; *222:* 106, 107, 108, 109; *225:* 62
Karasz, Ilonka *128:* 163
Karlin, Eugene *10:* 63; *20:* 131
Karlin, Nurit *63:* 78; *103:* 110
Karpinski, Tony *134:* 160
Kasamatsu, Shiro *139:* 155
Kasparavicius, Kestutis *139:* 210
Kassian, Olena *64:* 94
Kastner, Jill *79:* 135; *117:* 84, 85
Kasuya, Masahiro *41:* 206, 207; *51:* 100
Kasza, Keiko *191:* 99, 100, 101, 102, 103
Katona, Robert *21:* 85; *24:* 126
Katz, Avi *199:* 55
Katz, Karen *158:* 123; *232:* 108, 109, 110
Kauffer, E. McKnight *33:* 103; *35:* 127; *63:* 67
Kaufman, Angelika *15:* 156
Kaufman, Joe *33:* 119
Kaufman, John *13:* 158
Kaufman, Stuart *62:* 64; *68:* 226; *137:* 44
Kaufmann, John *1:* 174; *4:* 159; *8:* 43, 1; *10:* 102; *18:* 133, 134; *22:* 251
Kaye, Graham *1:* 9; *67:* 7, 8
Kaye, M.M. *62:* 95
Kazalovski, Nata *40:* 205
Keane, Bil *4:* 135
Kearney, David *72:* 47; *121:* 83
Keating, Pamel T. *77:* 37
Keats, Ezra Jack *3:* 18, 105, 257; *14:* 101, 102; *33:* 129; *57:* 79, 80, 82, 83, 84, 87
Keegan, Charles *166:* 211
Keegan, Marcia *9:* 122; *32:* 93
Keeler, Patricia A. *81:* 56; *183:* 102, 103
Keely, Jack *119:* 95
Keely, John *26:* 104; *48:* 214
Keen, Eliot *25:* 213
Keep, Richard C. *170:* 122
Keeping, Charles *9:* 124, 185; *15:* 28, 134; *18:* 115; *44:* 194, 196; *47:* 25; *52:* 3; *54:* 156; *69:* 123, 124; *74:* 56; *155:* 9

Keeter, Susan *168:* 46; *183:* 192

Keith, Eros *4:* 98; *5:* 138; *31:* 29; *43:* 220; *52:* 91, 92, 93, 94; *56:* 64, 66; *60:* 37; *79:* 93

Keleinikov, Andrei *65:* 101, 102

Kelen, Emery *13:* 115

Keller, A.J. *62:* 198

Keller, Arthur I. *26:* 106

Keller, Dick *36:* 123, 125

Keller, Holly *45:* 79; *76:* 118, 119, 120, 121; *108:* 137, 138, 140; *157:* 117, 118, 119; *216:* 136

Keller, Katie *79:* 222; *93:* 108

Keller, Laurie *196:* 105, 106

Keller, Ronald *45:* 208

Kelley, Gary *183:* 105; *216:* 78; *217:* 95, 96, 97

Kelley, Marty *211:* 91

Kelley, True *41:* 114, 115; *42:* 137; *75:* 35; *92:* 104, 105; *124:* 62; *130:* 100, 101; *179:* 120, 121, 122; *192:* 251

Kellogg, Steven *8:* 96; *11:* 207; *14:* 130; *20:* ; *201:* 38 58; *29:* 140, 141; *30:* 35; *41:* 141; *57:* 89, 90, 92,93, 94, 96; *59:* 182; *73:* 141; *77:* 129; *130:* 105, 106; *177:* 94, 95, 96, 97; *199:* 57; *217:* 61; *YABC 1:* 65, 73

Kelly, Billy *158:* 143

Kelly, Geoff *97:* 196; *112:* 25

Kelly, Irene *147:* 134; *210:* 144, 145

Kelly, Jennifer *230:* 137

Kelly, John *194:* 186

Kelly, Joseph *174:* 94

Kelly, Kathleen M. *71:* 109

Kelly, Laura *89:* 217

Kelly, True *163:* 87

Kelly, Walt *18:* 136, 137, 138, 139, 140, 141, 144, 145, 146, 148, 149

Kemble, E.W. *34:* 75; *44:* 178; *YABC 2:* 54, 59

Kemly, Kathleen *209:* 165

Kemp-Welsh, Lucy *24:* 197; *100:* 214

Kendall, Jane *150:* 105; *186:* 109

Kendall, Peter *152:* 85

Kendrick, Dennis *79:* 213

Kennaway, Adrienne *60:* 55, 56; *171:* 88, 89

Kennedy, Anne *212:* 34

Kennedy, Doug *189:* 104

Kennedy, Paul Edward *6:* 190; *8:* 132; *33:* 120

Kennedy, Richard *3:* 93; *12:* 179; *44:* 193; *100:* 15; *YABC 1:* 57

Kent, Jack *24:* 136; *37:* 37; *40:* 81; *84:* 89; *86:* 150; *88:* 77

Kent, Rockwell *5:* 166; *6:* 129; *20:* 225, 226, 227,229; *59:* 144

Kenyon, Tony *81:* 201; *127:* 74; *231:* 86

Kepes, Juliet *13:* 119

Kerins, Anthony *76:* 84

Kerr, Judity *24:* 137

Kerr, Phyllis Forbes *72:* 141

Kessler, Leonard *1:* 108; *7:* 139; *14:* 107, 227; *22:* 101; *44:* 96; *67:* 79; *82:* 123

Kest, Kristin *168:* 99; *173:* 23

Kesteven, Peter *35:* 189

Ketcham, Hank *28:* 140, 141, 142

Kettelkamp, Larry *2:* 164

Key, Alexander *8:* 99

Khalsa, Dayal Kaur *62:* 99

Kiakshuk *8:* 59

Kid, Tom *207:* 54

Kidd, Chip *94:* 23

Kidd, Richard *152:* 110

Kidd, Tom *64:* 199; *81:* 189; *185:* 173

Kiddell-Monroe, Joan *19:* 201; *55:* 59, 60; *87:* 174; *121:* 112

Kidder, Harvey *9:* 105; *80:* 41

Kidwell, Carl *43:* 145

Kieffer, Christa *41:* 89

Kiesler, Kate *110:* 105; *136:* 142

Kiff, Ken *40:* 45

Kilaka, John *223:* 107

Kilbride, Robert *37:* 100

Kilby, Don *141:* 144

Kim, David *201:* 79; *202:* 97

Kim, Glenn *99:* 82

Kimball, Anton *78:* 114; *119:* 105

Kimball, Yeffe *23:* 116; *37:* 88

Kimber, Murray *171:* 91

Kimmel, Warren *176:* 112

Kincade, Orin *34:* 116

Kindersley, Barnabas *96:* 110

Kindred, Wendy *7:* 151

King, Colin *53:* 3

King, Robin *10:* 164, 165

King, Stephen Michael *141:* 31; *197:* 191; *218:* 81, 82

King, Tara Calahan *139:* 172

King, Tony *39:* 121

Kingman, Dong *16:* 287; *44:* 100, 102, 104

Kingsley, Charles *YABC 2:* 182

Kingston, Julie *147:* 14

Kingston, Maxine Hong *53:* 92

Kinney, Jeff *187:* 97

Kipling, John Lockwood *YABC 2:* 198

Kipling, Rudyard *YABC 2:* 196

Kipniss, Robert *29:* 59

Kirchherr, Astrid *55:* 23

Kirchhoff, Art *28:* 136

Kirk, Daniel *153:* 115, 116, 117; *173:* 101; *196:* 113, 114, 115, 116

Kirk, David *117:* 88, 89; *161:* 97, 98

Kirk, Ruth *5:* 96

Kirk, Steve *170:* 37

Kirk, Tim *32:* 209, 211; *72:* 89; *83:* 49

Kirmse, Marguerite *15:* 283; *18:* 153

Kirsch, Vincent X. *124:* 207

Kirschner, Ruth *22:* 154

Kirwan, Wednesday *198:* 73

Kish, Ely *73:* 119; *79:* 2

Kitamura, Satoshi *62:* 102; *98:* 91; *101:* 147; *138:* 2; *143:* 83, 85, 86; *201:* 83; *223:* 3, 4

Kiss, Andrew *168:* 115

Kitchel, JoAnn E. *133:* 32

Kitchen, Bert *70:* 126; *193:* 49

Kittelsen, Theodor *62:* 14

Kiuchi, Tatsuro *114:* 71

Kiwak, Barbara *172:* 135

Klahr, Susan *176:* 196

Klapholz, Mel *13:* 35

Klee, Jutte *209:* 136

Klein, Bill *89:* 105

Klein, Robert *55:* 77

Klein, Suzanna *63:* 104

Kleinman, Zalman *28:* 143

Kleven, Elisa *173:* 96, 97; *217:* 100, 102

Kliban, B. *35:* 137, 138

Kline, Michael *127:* 66

Klinger, Shula *230:* 55

Klise, M. Sarah *180:* 117, 118; *181:* 97; *221:* 100, 102

Knabel, Lonnie *73:* 103; *75:* 187, 228; *194:* 216

Kneen, Maggie *140:* 139; *221:* 104, 105

Knight, Ann *34:* 143

Knight, Christopher *13:* 125

Knight, Hilary *1:* 233; *3:* 21; *15:* 92, 158, 159; *16:* 258, 259, 260; *18:* 235; *19:* 169; *35:* 242; *46:* 167; *52:* 116; *69:* 126, 127; *132:* 129; *YABC 1:* 168, 169, 172

Knorr, Laura *200:* 91

Knorr, Peter *126:* 92, 93

Knotts, Howard *20:* 4; *25:* 170; *36:* 163

Knutson, Barbara *112:* 134; *202:* 108

Knutson, Kimberley *115:* 90

Kobayashi, Ann *39:* 58

Kochalka, James *196:* 120, 121, 122

Kocsis, J.C.
  See Paul, James

Kodman, Stanislawa *201:* 85; *224:* 72

Koehler, Hanne Lore *176:* 203

Koehn, Ilse *34:* 198; *79:* 123

Koelsch, Michael *99:* 182; *107:* 164; *109:* 239; *138:* 142; *150:* 94; *176:* 105; *187:* 63; *198:* 63; *230:* 204

Koering, Ursula *3:* 28; *4:* 14; *44:* 5; *64:* 140,141; *85:* 46

Koerner, Henry
  See Koerner, W.H.D.

Koerner, W.H.D. *14:* 216; *21:* 88, 89, 90, 91; *23:* 211

Koetsch, Mike *166:* 68

Koffler, Camilla *36:* 113

Kogan, Deborah Ray *161:* 101, 102

Koide, Yasuko *50:* 114

Kolado, Karen *102:* 228

Kolesova, Juliana *217:* 81; *222:* 185; *229:* 183

Komarck, Michael *227:* 48

Komoda, Kiyo *9:* 128; *13:* 214

Kompaneyets, Marc *169:* 92

Konashevich, Vladimir *61:* 160

Konashevicha, V. *YABC 1:* 26

Konigsburg, E.L. *4:* 138; *48:* 141, 142, 144, 145; *94:* 129, 130; *126:* 129, 130, 131; *194:* 95, 98

Kono, Erin Eitter *177:* 99

Kooiker, Leonie *48:* 148

Koonook, Simon *65:* 157

Koontz, Robin Michal *136:* 155

Koopmans, Loek *101:* 121

Kopelke, Lisa *154:* 107

Kopper, Lisa *72:* 152, 153; *105:* 135, 136

Korach, Mimi *1:* 128, 129; *2:* 52; *4:* 39; *5:* 159; *9:* 129; *10:* 21; *24:* 69

Koren, Edward *5:* 100; *65:* 65, 67

Kosaka, Fumi *164:* 130

Koscielniak, Bruce *99:* 122; *153:* 120, 121, 122

Koshkin, Alexander *92:* 180

Kossin, Sandy *10:* 71; *23:* 105

Kostin, Andrej *26:* 204

Kosturko, Bob *164:* 56

Kotzky, Brian *68:* 184

Kovacevic, Zivojin *13:* 247

Kovalski, Maryann *58:* 120; *84:* 88; *97:* 124, 125, 126; *158:* 3; *186:* 80

Kozjan, Drazen *209:* 99; *231:* 130

Krahn, Fernando *2:* 257; *34:* 206; *49:* 152

Krall, Dan *218:* 84, 85

Kramek, Oren *231:* 119

Kramer, Anthony *33:* 81

Kramer, David *96:* 162; *109:* 132; *150:* 220

Kramer, Frank *6:* 121

Krantz, Kathy *35:* 83

Kratter, Paul *139:* 65

Kraus, Robert *13:* 217; *65:* 113; *93:* 93, 94

Krause, Jon *176:* 62

Krauss, Trisha *174:* 10

Kredel, Fritz *6:* 35; *17:* 93, 94, 95, 96; *22:* 147; *24:* 175; *29:* 130; *35:* 77; *YABC 2:* 166, 300

Kreloff, Eliot *189:* 107, 108; *205:* 182

Krementz, Jill *17:* 98; *49:* 41

Krenina, Katya *117:* 106; *125:* 133; *176:* 117; *221:* 107

Kresin, Robert *23:* 19

Kretschmar, Sonia *226:* 97

Krieger, Salem *54:* 164

Kriegler, Lyn *73:* 29

Krinitz, Esther Nisenthal *193:* 196

Krommes, Beth *128:* 141; *149:* 136; *181:* 100, 101; *184:* 105; *188:* 125; *208:* 135; *209:* 185

Krone, Mike *101:* 71

Kronheimer, Ann *135:* 119

Krosoczka, Jarrett J. *155:* 142; *200:* 93, 94

Kruck, Gerald *88:* 181

Krudop, Walter Lyon *199:* 19

Krupinski, Loretta *67:* 104; *102:* 131; *161:* 105, 106

Krupp, Robin Rector *53:* 96, 98

Krush, Beth *1:* 51, 85; *2:* 233; *4:* 115; *9:* 61; *10:* 191; *11:* 196; *18:* 164, 165; *32:* 72; *37:* 203; *43:* 57; *60:* 102, 103, 107, 108, 109

Krush, Joe *2:* 233; *4:* 115; *9:* 61; *10:* 191; *11:* 196; *18:* 164, 165; *32:* 72, 91; *37:* 203; *43:* 57; *60:* 102, 103, 107, 108, 109

Krych, Duane 91: 43
Krykorka, Vladyana 96: 147; 143: 90, 91; 168: 14
Kubick, Dana 165: 91; 212: 104, 105, 212
Kubinyi, Laszlo 4: 116; 6: 113; 16: 118; 17: 100; 28: 227; 30: 172; 49: 24, 28; 54: 23; 167: 149
Kubricht, Mary 73: 118
Kucharik, Elena 139: 31
Kuchera, Kathleen 84: 5
Kuhn, Bob 17: 91; 35: 235
Kulikov, Boris 163: 185; 185: 23; 205: 99, 100; 217: 160
Kulka, Joe 188: 110
Kukalis, Romas 90: 27; 139: 37
Kuklin, Susan 63: 82, 83, 84
Kunhardt, Dorothy 53: 101
Kunhardt, Edith 67: 105, 106
Kunstler, Mort 10: 73; 32: 143
Kurchevsky, V. 34: 61
Kurczok, Belinda 121: 118
Kurelek, William 8: 107
Kuriloff, Ron 13: 19
Kurisu, Jane 160: 120
Kurilla, Renée 231: 117
Kuskin, Karla 2: 170; 68: 115, 116; 111: 116
Kutzer, Ernst 19: 249
Kuzma, Steve 57: 8; 62: 93
Kuznetsova, Berta 74: 45
Kvasnosky, Laura McGee 93: 103; 142: 83; 182: 108
Kwas, Susan Estelle 179: 116; 217: 90
Kyong, Yunmee 165: 139

L

LaBlanc, Andre 24: 146
Laboccetta, Mario 27: 120
LaBrose, Darcie 157: 134
Labrosse, Darcia 58: 88; 108: 77; 178: 89
LaCava, Vince 95: 118
Laceky, Adam 32: 121
Lacis, Astra 85: 117
Lacome, Julie 174: 96, 97
La Croix YABC 2: 4
Ladd, London 206: 50
Ladwig, Tim 98: 212; 117: 76; 215: 32; 223: 111, 112
La Farge, Margaret 47: 141
LaFave, Kim 64: 177; 72: 39; 97: 146; 99: 172; 106: 123; 149: 126; 196: 128, 129
Lafontaine, Roger 167: 158
Lafrance, Marie 197: 109
Lagarrigue, Jerome 136: 102; 187: 81
Laimgruber, Monika 11: 153
Laínez, René Colato 226: 50
Laio, Jimmy 213: 57
Laite, Gordon 1: 130, 131; 8: 209; 31: 113; 40: 63; 46: 117
Laliberté, Louise-Andrée 169: 98
LaMarche, Jim 46: 204; 61: 56; 94: 69; 114: 22; 129: 163; 162: 78, 80
Lamb, Jim 10: 117
Lambase, Barbara 101: 185; 150: 221; 166: 234
Lambert, J.K. 38: 129; 39: 24
Lambert, Sally Anne 133: 191
Lambert, Saul 23: 112; 33: 107; 54: 136
Lambert, Stephen 109: 33; 174: 59
Lambo, Don 6: 156; 35: 115; 36: 146
Lamontagne, Jacques 166: 227
Lamut, Sonja 57: 193
Lamut, Sonya 85: 102
Landa, Peter 11: 95; 13: 177; 53: 119
Landau, Jacob 38: 111
Landis, Joan 104: 23; 203: 32
Landon, Lucinda 79: 31
Landshoff, Ursula 13: 124
Landström, Lena 146: 165, 166

Landström, Olof 146: 166, 168; 170: 22; 232: 22
Lane, Daniel 112: 60
Lane, John R. 8: 145
Lane, John 15: 176, 177; 30: 146
Lane, Nancy 166: 74
Lang, G.D. 48: 56
Lang, Gary 73: 75
Lang, Glenna 221: 113
Lang, Jerry 18: 295
Langdo, Bryan 186: 187; 191: 113, 114, 115; 233: 98, 100
Lange, Dorothea 50: 141
Langley, Jonathan 162: 128
Langner, Nola 8: 110; 42: 36
Lanino, Deborah 105: 148
Lantz, Paul 1: 82, 102; 27: 88; 34: 102; 45: 123
Larkin, Bob 84: 225
Laroche, Giles 126: 140; 146: 81; 221: 116, 117
LaRochelle, David 171: 97
Larrañaga, Ana Martín 229: 106
Larrecq, John 44: 108; 68: 56
Larsen, Suzanne 1: 13
Larson, Gary 57: 121, 122, 123, 124, 125, 126, 127
Larsson, Carl 35: 144, 145, 146, 147, 148, 149, 150, 152, 153, 154
Larsson, Karl 19: 177
Lartitegui, Ana G. 105: 167
LaRue, Jenna 167: 20
La Rue, Michael D. 13: 215
Lasker, Joe 7: 186, 187; 14: 55; 38: 115; 39: 47; 83: 113, 114, 115
Latham, Barbara 16: 188, 189; 43: 71
Lathrop, Dorothy 14: 117, 118, 119; 15: 109; 16: 78, 79, 81; 32: 201, 203; 33: 112; YABC 2: 301
Lattimore, Eleanor Frances 7: 156
Lauden, Claire 16: 173
Lauden, George, Jr. 16: 173
Laune, Paul 2: 235; 34: 31
Laure, Jason 49: 53; 50: 122
Lauter, Richard 63: 29; 67: 111; 77: 198
Lavallee, Barbara 74: 157; 92: 154; 96: 126; 145: 193; 166: 125, 126; 186: 155; 192: 172; 231: 165; 232: 131
Lave, Fitz Hugh 59: 139
Lavis, Steve 43: 143; 87: 137, 164, 165; 222: 161; 225: 121
Layton, Neal 152: 120, 121; 182: 65; 187: 103, 105, 106
Law, Jenny 201: 31
Lawrason, June 168: 30
Lawrence, John 25: 131; 30: 141; 44: 198, 200; 214: 7
Lawrence, Stephen 20: 195
Lawson, Carol 6: 38; 42: 93, 131; 174: 56; 189: 89; 209: 59
Lawson, George 17: 280
Lawson, Robert 5: 26; 6: 94; 13: 39; 16: 11; 20: 100, 102, 103; 54: 3; 66: 12; 100: 144, 145; YABC 2: 222, 224, 225, 227, 228, 229, 230, 231, 232, 233, 234, 235, 237, 238, 239, 240, 241
Layfield, Kathie 60: 194
Lazare, Jerry 44: 109; 74: 28
Lazarevich, Mila 17: 118
Lazarus, Claire 103: 30
Lazarus, Keo Felker 21: 94
Lazzaro, Victor 11: 126
Lea, Bob 166: 208; 203: 108
Lea, Tom 43: 72, 74
Leacroft, Richard 6: 140
Leaf, Munro 20: 99
Leake, Donald 70: 41
Leander, Patricia 23: 27
Lear, Edward 18: 183, 184, 185
Lear, Rebecca 149: 46

Lebenson, Richard 6: 209; 7: 76; 23: 145; 44: 191; 87: 153
Le Cain, Errol 6: 141; 9: 3; 22: 142; 25: 198; 28: 173; 68: 128, 129; 86: 49
Lechon, Daniel 113: 211
Leder, Dora 129: 172
Ledger, Bill 181: 58
Leduc, Bernard 102: 36
Lee, Alan 62: 25, 28
Lee, Bryce 99: 60; 101: 195; 196: 53
Lee, Chinlun 181: 138; 182: 112
Lee, Declan 191: 20
Lee, Dom 83: 118, 120; 93: 123; 121: 121, 126; 146: 174, 175, 206, 207; 174: 204
Lee, Doris 13: 246; 32: 183; 44: 111
Lee, Hector Viveros 115: 96
Lee, Ho Baek 200: 160
Lee, Huy Voun 217: 106
Lee, Jeanne M. 158: 56
Lee, Jared 93: 200; 157: 229; 215: 113, 191, 192, 193; 228: 177
Lee, Jody 81: 121; 82: 225; 91: 155; 100: 182
Lee, Jody A. 127: 124, 126, 127
   See also Lee, Jody
Lee, Manning de V. 2: 200; 17: 12; 27: 87; 37: 102, 103, 104; YABC 2: 304
Lee, Margaret 213: 179
Lee, Marie G. 138: 157
Lee, Paul 97: 100; 105: 72, 209; 109: 177; 128: 113; 202: 45
Lee, Robert J. 3: 97; 67: 124
Lee, Victor 96: 228; 105: 182; 140: 196; 208: 191
Lee, Virginia 208: 139, 140; 218: 28
Leech, Dorothy 98: 76
Leech, John 15: 59
Leedy, Loreen 84: 142; 128: 144, 145, 146; 175: 125, 126, 127
Leeman, Michael 44: 157
Leeming, Catherine 87: 39
Lees, Harry 6: 112
LeFever, Bill 88: 220, 221
Legenisel 47: 111
Legrand, Edy 18: 89, 93
Lehman, Barbara 73: 123; 170: 130
Lehrman, Rosalie 2: 180
Leichman, Seymour 5: 107
Leick, Bonnie 205: 104
Leighton, Clare 25: 130; 33: 168; 37: 105, 106, 108,109
Leisk, David 1: 140, 141; 11: 54; 30: 137, 142, 143,144
Leister, Bryan 89: 45; 106: 37; 114: 67; 149: 236; 222: 181
Leloir, Maurice 18: 77, 80, 83, 99
Lemaître, Pascal 144: 175; 176: 130; 189: 135; 225: 124, 125
Lemieux, Michele 100: 148; 139: 153
Lemke, Horst 14: 98; 38: 117, 118, 119
Lemke, R.W. 42: 162
Lemon, David Gwynne 9: 1
LeMoult, Adolph 82: 116
Lenn, Michael 136: 89
Lennon, John 114: 100
Lennox, Elsie 95: 163; 143: 160
Lenski, Lois 1: 144; 26: 135, 137, 139, 141; 100: 153, 154
Lent, Blair 1: 116, 117; 2: 174; 3: 206, 207; 7: 168, 169; 34: 62; 68: 217; 133: 101; 183: 60
Leon, Jana 226: 214
Leonard, David 212: 149
Leonard, Richard 91: 128
Leonard, Tom 207: 95; 219: 55
Leone, Leonard 49: 190
Lerner, Carol 86: 140, 141, 142
Lerner, Judith 116: 138
Lerner, Sharon 11: 157; 22: 56
Leroux-Hugon, Helene 132: 139
Leslie, Cecil 19: 244

Lessac, Frané *80:* 182, 207; *96:* 182; *202:* 58;
    209: 104
Lessing, Erich *167:* 52; *173:* 60
Lester, Alison *50:* 124; *90:* 147, 148; *129:*
    130; *218:* 91, 93
Lester, Mike *208:* 50
Lethcoe, Jason *191:* 116, 117
Le Tord, Bijou *49:* 156; *95:* 112
Leutz, Emanuel *165:* 27
Levai, Blaise *39:* 130
Levert, Mireille *211:* 101
Levin, Ted *12:* 148
Levine, David *43:* 147, 149, 150, 151, 152;
    64: 11
Levine, Joe *71:* 88; *219:* 74
Levine, Marge *81:* 127
Levinson, David *178:* 232
Levit, Herschel *24:* 223
Levstek, Ljuba *131:* 192; *134:* 216; *149:* 65;
    168: 180
Levy, Jessica Ann *19:* 225; *39:* 191
Levy, Lina *117:* 126
Lewin, Betsy *32:* 114; *48:* 177; *90:* 151; *91:*
    125; *92:* 85; *115:* 105; *169:* 110, 111; *178:*
    47; *186:* 188; *194:* 201; *222:* 120; *226:* 139
Lewin, Ted *4:* 77; *8:* 168; *20:* 110; *21:* 99,100;
    27: 110; *28:* 96, 97; *31:* 49; *45:* 55; *48:* 223;
    60: 20, 119, 120; *62:* 139; *66:* 108; *71:* 12;
    72: 21; *74:* 226; *76:* 139, 140; *77:* 82; *79:*
    87; *85:* 49, 177; *86:* 55; *88:* 182; *93:* 28, 29;
    94: 34, 182, 194; *99:* 156; *104:* 8; *115:* 123;
    118: 74; *119:* 114, 116; *131:* 54; *145:* 99;
    165: 151; *177:* 75; *178:* 42; *190:* 30; *192:*
    86; *195:* 101, 102; *203:* 52; *222:* 119; *226:*
    136, 137, 138, 139
Lewis, Allen *15:* 112
Lewis, Anthony *227:* 114
Lewis, E.B. *88:* 143; *93:* 109; *119:* 79; *124:*
    113; *128:* 49; *151:* 167; *168:* 110; *173:* 121;
    174: 66; *176:* 7; *184:* 150; *185:* 191; *211:*
    108, 109, 110, 111; *223:* 17
Lewis, H.B. *170:* 124
Lewis, J. Patrick *162:* 83
Lewis, Jan *81:* 22
Lewis, Kim *136:* 165; *217:* 109, 111
Lewis, Richard W. *52:* 25
Lewis, Robin Baird *98:* 193
Lew-Vriethoff, Joanne *225:* 181
Leydon, Rita Floden *21:* 101
Li, Xiojun *187:* 172
Liao, Jimmy *202:* 100
Lichtenheld, Tom *152:* 125, 126; *222:* 160;
    224: 9
Lieblich, Irene *22:* 173; *27:* 209, 214
Lieder, Rick *108:* 197; *199:* 58, 59, 60
Lies, Brian *92:* 40; *141:* 101; *150:* 138; *190:*
    97, 98, 99
Liese, Charles *4:* 222
Liew, Sonny *219:* 108
Life, Kay *79:* 49
Lifton, Robert Jay *66:* 154
Lightburn, Ron *86:* 153; *91:* 122
Lightfoot, Norman R. *45:* 47
Lignell, Lois *37:* 114
Lill, Debra *121:* 70
Lilly, Charles *8:* 73; *20:* 127; *48:* 53; *72:* 9,16;
    77: 98; *102:* 94
Lilly, Ken *37:* 224
Lim, John *43:* 153
Limona, Mercedes *51:* 183
Lin, Grace *143:* 217; *162:* 86, 87; *174:* 185
Lincoln, Patricia Henderson *27:* 27; *78:* 127
Lindahn, Ron *84:* 17
Lindahn, Val *84:* 17
Lindberg, Howard *10:* 123; *16:* 190
Lindberg, Jeffrey *64:* 77; *77:* 71; *79:* 54; *80:*
    149; *174:* 109; *179:* 52
Linden, Seymour *18:* 200, 201; *43:* 140
Lindenbaum, Pija *144:* 143; *183:* 113
Linder, Richard *27:* 119
Lindman, Maj *43:* 154

Lindsay, Norman *67:* 114
Lindsay, Vachel *40:* 118
Lindstrom, Jack *145:* 118
Line, Les *27:* 143
Linell
    See Smith, Linell
Lintern, Tom *228:* 101
Lionni, Leo *8:* 115; *72:* 159, 160, 161
Lipinsky, Lino *2:* 156; *22:* 175
Lippincott, Gary A. *70:* 35; *119:* 118; *220:*
    105, 106, 107
Lippman, Peter *8:* 31; *31:* 119, 120, 160
Lisi, Victoria *89:* 145
Lisker, Emily *169:* 114
Lisker, Sonia O. *16:* 274; *31:* 31; *44:* 113, 114
Lisowski, Gabriel *47:* 144; *49:* 157
Lissim, Simon *17:* 138
Little, Ed *89:* 145; *151:* 53
Little, Harold *16:* 72
Little, Mary E. *28:* 146
Littlewood, Karen *165:* 126; *211:* 112
Litty, Julie *111:* 63
Litzinger, Rosanne *151:* 101; *176:* 118; *196:*
    133, 134, 135; *208:* 129; *209:* 147
Liu, Lesley *143:* 72
Lively, Lorna *19:* 216
Livingston, Susan *95:* 22
Liwska, Renata *164:* 113; *199:* 25, 69; *220:* 79
Ljungkvist, Laura *180:* 120
Llerena, Carlos Antonio *19:* 181
Lloyd, Errol *11:* 39; *22:* 178
Lloyd, Megan *77:* 118; *80:* 113; *97:* 75; *117:*
    94, 95; *189:* 121, 122; *208:* 128; *211:* 72
Lloyd, Sam *183:* 116, 117
Lo, Beth *165:* 154
Lo, Koon-chiu *7:* 134
Loates, Glen *63:* 76
Lobel, Anita *6:* 87; *9:* 141; *18:* 248; *55:* 85,86,
    87, 88, 93, 104; *60:* 67; *78:* 263; *82:* 110;
    96: 157, 159; *101:* 84; *132:* 35; *162:* 93, 94
Lobel, Arnold *1:* 188, 189; *5:* 12; *6:* 147; *7:*
    167, 209; *18:* 190, 191; *25:* 39, 43; *27:* 40;
    29: 174; *52:* 127; *55:* 89, 91, 94, 95, 97, 98,
    99, 100, 101, 102,103, 105, 106; *60:* 18, 31;
    66: 181, 183; *75:* 57; *82:* 246; *136:* 146
Lobel, Gillian *190:* 21
Lobo, Jen *229:* 53
Locker, Thomas *109:* 134
Lodge, Bernard *107:* 125, 126; *153:* 93
Loeb, Jeph *153:* 177
Lodge, Jo *112:* 119
Loefgren, Ulf *3:* 108
Loescher, Ann *20:* 108
Loescher, Gil *20:* 108
Loew, David *93:* 184; *171:* 120; *211:* 187
Lofting, Hugh *15:* 182, 183; *100:* 161, 162
Lofts, Pamela *60:* 188
Loh, George *38:* 88
Lomberg, Jon *58:* 160
Lonette, Reisie *11:* 211; *12:* 168; *13:* 56; *36:*
    122; *43:* 155
Long, Ethan *168:* 146; *178:* 12; *182:* 120, 121;
    196: 124; *223:* 116, 117
Long, Laurel *162:* 135; *190:* 11; *203:* 113,
    114; *228:* 212
Long, Loren *99:* 176; *172:* 65; *182:* 78; *188:*
    114, 115
Long, Melinda *152:* 128
Long, Miles *115:* 174
Long, Sally *42:* 184
Long, Sylvia *74:* 168; *132:* 63; *179:* 134
Longoni, Eduardo *73:* 85
Longtemps, Ken *17:* 123; *29:* 221; *69:* 82
Looser, Heinz *YABC 2:* 208
Lopez, Loretta *190:* 100
López, Rafael *197:* 160; *198:* 85
Lopshire, Robert *6:* 149; *21:* 117; *34:* 166; *73:*
    13; *233:* 103
Lord, John Vernon *21:* 104; *23:* 25; *51:* 22
Lorenz, Albert *40:* 146; *115:* 127
Lorenzen, Geoffrey *229:* 24

Loretta, Sister Mary *33:* 73
Lorraine, Walter H. *3:* 110; *4:* 123; *16:* 192;
    103: 119
Los, Marek *146:* 22; *193:* 23
Loss, Joan *11:* 163
Louderback, Walt *YABC 1:* 164
Loughridge, Stuart *214:* 131
Louis, Catherine *212:* 186
Lousada, Sandra *40:* 138
Louth, Jack *149:* 252; *151:* 191, 192
Love, Judy *173:* 43; *196:* 40
Lovelock, Brian *214:* 132, 197
Low, Joseph *14:* 124, 125; *18:* 68; *19:* 194;
    31: 166; *80:* 239
Low, William *62:* 175; *80:* 147; *112:* 194; *150:*
    202; *169:* 175; *177:* 110; *192:* 27
Lowe, Vicky *177:* 130
Lowenheim, Alfred *13:* 65, 66
Lowenstein, Sallie *116:* 90, 91
Lowery, Mike *227:* 115
Lowitz, Anson *17:* 124; *18:* 215
Lowrey, Jo *8:* 133
Loxton, Daniel *229:* 109
Lubach, Vanessa *142:* 152
Lubell, Winifred *1:* 207; *3:* 15; *6:* 151
Lubin, Leonard B. *19:* 224; *36:* 79, 80; *45:*
    128, 129,131, 132, 133, 134, 135, 136, 137,
    139, 140, 141; *70:* 95; *YABC2:* 96
Lucas, David *208:* 148
Lucht, Irmgard *82:* 145
Ludwig, Helen *33:* 144, 145
Luebs, Robin *212:* 109
Lufkin, Raymond *38:* 138; *44:* 48
Luhrs, Henry *7:* 123; *11:* 120
Lujan, Tonita *82:* 33
Lum, Bernice *230:* 70
Lupo, Dom *4:* 204
Lustig, Loretta *30:* 186; *46:* 134, 135, 136,
    137
Lutes, Jason *210:* 163
Luthardt, Kevin *172:* 125, 126; *217:* 2
Luxbacher, Irene *153:* 145; *219:* 112, 113
Luzak, Dennis *52:* 121; *99:* 142
Lydbury, Jane *82:* 98
Lydecker, Laura *21:* 113; *42:* 53
Lynch, Charles *16:* 33
Lynch, Marietta *29:* 137; *30:* 171
Lynch, P.J. *126:* 228; *129:* 110; *132:* 247; *183:*
    64; *207:* 184; *213:* 100, 101, 102
Lyne, Alison Davis *188:* 118, 198
Lyon, Carol *102:* 26
Lyon, Elinor *6:* 154
Lyon, Fred *14:* 16
Lyon, Lea *212:* 110
Lyon, Tammie *175:* 170
Lyons, Oren *8:* 193
Lyster, Michael *26:* 41

M

Maas, Dorothy *6:* 175
Maas, Julie *47:* 61
Macaulay, David *46:* 139, 140, 141, 142, 143,
    144, 145, 147, 149, 150; *72:* 167, 168, 169;
    137: 129, 130, 131, 132
MacCarthy, Patricia *69:* 141
Macdonald, Alister *21:* 55
Macdonald, Roberta *19:* 237; *52:* 164
MacDonald, Norman *13:* 99
MacDonald, Ross *201:* 103
MacDonald, Suse *54:* 41; *109* 138; *130:* 156;
    193: 106, 107, 109, 110
Mace, Varian *49:* 159
MacEachern, Stephen *206:* 2
Macguire, Robert Reid *18:* 67
Machetanz, Fredrick *34:* 147, 148
MacInnes, Ian *35:* 59
MacIntyre, Elisabeth *17:* 127, 128

Mack, Jeff *161:* 128; *194:* 119, 120; *219:* 67; *225:* 135
Mack, Stan *17:* 129; *96:* 33
Mackay, Donald *17:* 60
MacKaye, Arvia *32:* 119
Mackenzie, Robert *204:* 78
Mackenzie, Stuart *73:* 213
MacKenzie, Garry *33:* 159
Mackie, Clare *87:* 134
Mackinlay, Miguel *27:* 22
MacKinstry, Elizabeth *15:* 110; *42:* 139, 140, 141, 142, 143,144, 145
MacLeod, Lee *91:* 167
Maclise, Daniel *YABC 2:* 257
Macnaughton, Tina *182:* 145; *218:* 106, 107
MacRae, Tom *181:* 112
Madden, Don *3:* 112, 113; *4:* 33, 108, 155; *7:* 193; *78:* 12; *YABC 2:* 211
Maddison, Angela Mary *10:* 83
Madrid, Erwin *229:* 117
Madsen, Jim *146:* 259; *152:* 237; *184:* 106; *197:* 21; *202:* 103, 104; *233:* 38
Maestro, Giulio *8:* 124; *12:* 17; *13:* 108; *25:* 182; *54:* 147; *59:* 114, 115, 116, 117, 118, 121, 123, 124, 125,126, 127; *68:* 37, 38; *106:* 129, 130, 131, 136, 137, 138
Maffia, Daniel *60:* 200
Maggio, Viqui *58:* 136, 181; *74:* 150; *75:* 90; *85:* 159; *90:* 158; *109:* 184; *193:* 113
Magnus, Erica *77:* 123
Magnuson, Diana *28:* 102; *34:* 190; *41:* 175
Magoon, Scott *181:* 104; *217:* 165; *222:* 126
Magovern, Peg *103:* 123; *218:* 164
Maguire, Sheila *41:* 100
Magurn, Susan *91:* 30
Mahony, Will *37:* 120
Mahony, Will *85:* 116
Mahood, Kenneth *24:* 141
Mahurin, Matt *164:* 225; *175:* 95; *189:* 37; *196:* 14; *209:* 163; *229:* 179
Maik, Henri *9:* 102
Maione, Heather *106:* 5; *178:* 8; *189:* 126, 127; *193:* 58
Maisto, Carol *29:* 87
Maitland, Antony *1:* 100, 176; *8:* 41; *17:* 246; *24:* 46; *25:* 177, 178; *32:* 74; *60:* 65, 195; *67:* 156; *87:* 131; *101:* 110
Majewski, Dawn W. *169:* 95
Mak, Kam *72:* 25; *75:* 43; *87:* 186; *97:* 24; *102:* 154; *149:* 195; *186:* 28; *209:* 132
Makie, Pam *37:* 117
Maktima, Joe *116:* 191
Maland, Nick *99:* 77
Male, Alan *132:* 64
Malone, James Hiram *84:* 161
Malone, Nola Langner *82:* 239
Malone, Peter *191:* 121, 122, 123
Malsberg, Edward *51:* 175
Malvern, Corinne *2:* 13; *34:* 148, 149
Manchess, Gregory *165:* 241; *203:* 119
Mancusi, Stephen *63:* 198, 199
Mandelbaum, Ira *31:* 115
Manders, John *138:* 152, 155; *188:* 171; *190:* 92; *199:* 5; *217:* 52; *219:* 35; *219:* 115, 116, 117
Mandine, Selma *228:* 103
Manet, Edouard *23:* 170
Mangiat, Jeff *173:* 127
Mangurian, David *14:* 133
Manham, Allan *42:* 109; *77:* 180; *80:* 227
Manley, Matt *103:* 167; *117:* 98; *172:* 49; *212:* 207
Manna, Giovanni *178:* 44
Manniche, Lise *31:* 121
Manning, Jane *96:* 203; *233:* 107
Manning, Jo *63:* 154
Manning, Lawrence *191:* 153
Manning, Maurie J. *211:* 116
Manning, Mick *176:* 139; *224:* 57
Manning, Samuel F. *5:* 75
Mantel, Richard *57:* 73; *63:* 106; *82:* 255

Mantha, John *205:* 164; *217:* 117
Maraja *15:* 86; *YABC 1:* 28; *2:* 115
Marcellino, Fred *20:* 125; *34:* 222; *53:* 125; *58:* 205; *61:* 64, 121, 122; *68:* 154, 156, 157, 158, 159; *72:* 25; *86:* 184; *98:* 181; *118:* 129, 130, 131; *149:* 218; *194:* 7
Marchesi, Stephen *34:* 140; *46:* 72; *50:* 147; *66:* 239; *70:* 33; *73:* 18, 114, 163; *77:* 47, 76,147; *78:* 79; *80:* 30; *81:* 6; *89:* 66; *93:* 21,130; *94:* 94; *97:* 66; *98:* 96; *114:* 115, 116
Marchiori, Carlos *14:* 60
Marciano, John Bemelmans *118:* 133; *167:* 110, 111, 112
Marconi, Guilherme *220:* 143
Marcus, Barry David *139:* 248; *145:* 18
Maren, Julie *199:* 73
Margules, Gabriele *21:* 120
Mariana
See Foster, Marian Curtis
Mariano, Michael *52:* 108
Marino, Dorothy *6:* 37; *14:* 135
Mario, Heide Stetson *101:* 202
Maris, Ron *71:* 123
Maritz, Nicolaas *85:* 123
Mark, Mona *65:* 105; *68:* 205; *116:* 213
Markham, R.L. *17:* 240
Marklew, Gilly *211:* 118
Marks, Alan *104:* 104; *109:* 182; *164:* 92; *185:* 134; *187:* 120, 121, 122; *218:* 114, 115; *230:* 165
Marks, Cara *54:* 9
Marks, Colin *203:* 129
Marokvia, Artur *31:* 122
Marquez, Susan *108:* 121; *219:* 95
Marrella, Maria Pia *62:* 116
Marriott, Pat *30:* 30; *34:* 39; *35:* 164, 165, 166; *44:* 170; *48:* 186, 187, 188, 189, 191, 192, 193; *91:* 92
Mars, W.T. *1:* 161; *3:* 115; *4:* 208, 225; *5:* 92, 105, 186; *8:* 214; *9:* 12; *13:* 121; *27:* 151; *31:* 180; *38:* 102; *48:* 66; *62:* 164, 165; *64:* 62; *68:* 229; *79:* 55
Marschall, Ken *85:* 29
Marsh, Christine *3:* 164
Marsh, James *73:* 137
Marsh, Reginald *17:* 5; *19:* 89; *22:* 90, 96
Marshall, Anthony D. *18:* 216
Marshall, Felicia *170:* 190
Marshall, James *6:* 160; *40:* 221; *42:* 24, 25, 29; *51:* 111, 112, 113, 114, 115, 116, 117, 118, 119, 120, 121; *64:* 13; *75:* 126, 127, 128, 129; *102:* 10, 12; *216:* 26, 28
Marshall, Janet *97:* 154
Marstall, Bob *55:* 145; *84:* 153, 170; *104:* 145; *154:* 166, 167, 168
Martchenko, Michael *50:* 129, 153, 155, 156, 157; *83:* 144,145; *154:* 137, 138, 139
Marten, Ruth *129:* 52
Martin, Brad *199:* 186
Martin, Charles E. *70:* 144
Martin, Courtney A. *214:* 28
Martin, David Stone *24:* 232; *62:* 4
Martin, Fletcher *18:* 213; *23:* 151
Martin, Rene *7:* 144; *42:* 148, 149, 150
Martin, Richard E. *51:* 157; *131:* 203
Martin, Ron *32:* 81
Martin, Stefan *8:* 68; *32:* 124, 126; *56:* 33
Martin, Whitney *166:* 137
Martinez, Ed *58:* 192; *72:* 231; *77:* 33; *80:* 214; *167:* 123
Martinez, John *6:* 113; *118:* 13; *139:* 143
Martinez, Sergio *158:* 190; *220:* 156
Martini, Angela *183:* 161; *226:* 195
Martiniere, Stephan *171:* 130
Marton, Jirina *95:* 127, 128; *144:* 145; *230:* 73, 74, 75
Martorell, Antonio *84:* 6; *97:* 161
Martucci, Griesbach *52:* 106
Marvin, Frederic *83:* 86
Marx, Robert F. *24:* 143

Marzollo, Jean *190:* 127
Masefield, Judith *19:* 208, 209
Masheris, Robert *78:* 51
Masiello, Ralph *186:* 171; *214:* 134
Mason, George F. *14:* 139
Mason, Robert *84:* 96
Masse, Josée *208:* 45; *217:* 19; *221:* 134
Massey, Barbara *68:* 142
Massie, Diane Redfield *16:* 194
Massie, Kim *31:* 43
Massini, Sarah *213:* 79
Mataya, David *121:* 66
Mathers, Petra *119:* 135; *163:* 104; *176:* 143, 144; *187:* 142; *196:* 101
Mathewuse, James *51:* 143
Mathieu, Joseph *14:* 33; *39:* 206; *43:* 167; *56:* 180; *79:* 126; *94:* 147; *185:* 140
Matje, Martin *169:* 177, 178; *172:* 180
Matsubara, Naoko *12:* 121
Matsuda, Shizu *13:* 167
Matsuoka, Mei *192:* 135; *214:* 84
Matte, L'Enc *22:* 183
Mattelson, Marvin *36:* 50, 51
Matheson, Jenny *180:* 132; *222:* 153
Matthews, Elizabeth *194:* 128; *223:* 35
Matthews, F. Leslie *4:* 216
Matthews, Tina *190:* 130
Mattingly, David *71:* 76, 77; *82:* 64; *91:* 216, 217; *109:* 25
Matulay, Laszlo *5:* 18; *43:* 168
Matus, Greta *12:* 142
Maughan, Bill *181:* 31; *211:* 211
Mauldin, Bill *27:* 23
Mauterer, Erin Marie *119:* 5
Mawicke, Tran *9:* 137; *15:* 191; *47:* 100
Mawson, Matt *74:* 115
Max, Peter *45:* 146, 147, 148, 149, 150
Maxie, Betty *40:* 135
Maxwell, John Alan *1:* 148
May, Katie *225:* 128
May, Steve *204:* 30
Mayan, Earl *7:* 193
Maydak, Michael S. *220:* 117
Mayer, Bill *200:* 138
Mayer, Danuta *117:* 103
Mayer, Marianna *32:* 132
Mayer, Mercer *11:* 192; *16:* 195, 196; *20:* 55, 57; *32:* 129, 130, 132, 133, 134; *41:* 144, 248, 252; *58:* 186; *73:* 140, 142, 143; *137:* 137, 138
Mayforth, Hal *166:* 77
Mayhew, James *85:* 121; *138:* 187; *149:* 140; *204:* 81
Mayhew, Richard *3:* 106
Mayo, Gretchen Will *38:* 81; *84:* 166
Mays, Victor *5:* 127; *8:* 45, 153; *14:* 245; *23:* 50; *34:* 155; *40:* 79; *45:* 158; *54:* 91; *66:* 240
Mazal, Chanan *49:* 104
Maze, Deborah *71:* 83
Mazellan, Ron *75:* 97, 98; *210:* 169
Mazetti, Alan *112:* 72
Mazille, Capucine *96:* 168
Mazza, Adriana Saviozzi *19:* 215
Mazzella, Mary Jo *82:* 165
Mazzetti, Alan *45:* 210
McAfee, Steve *135:* 146; *167:* 176; *191:* 84; *210:* 117; *218:* 34; *233:* 86
McAlinden, Paul *112:* 128
McBride, Angus *28:* 49; *103:* 40
McBride, Will *30:* 110
McCaffery, Janet *38:* 145
McCall, Bruce *209:* 119
McCallum, Graham *78:* 78
McCallum, Stephen *141:* 143; *156:* 5; *166:* 228
McCann, Gerald *3:* 50; *4:* 94; *7:* 54; *41:* 121
McCarthy, Dan *174:* 74
McCarthy, Linda *177:* 128; *218:* 104
McCarthy, Meghan *168:* 134; *199:* 74

McCauley, Adam *157:* 36; *184:* 199; *193:* 100; *209:* 122

McCay, Winsor *41:* 124, 126, 128, 129, 130, 131; *134:* 77, 79

McClary, Nelson *1:* 111

McClements, George *196:* 146

McClennan, Connie *210:* 181

McClintock, Barbara *57:* 135; *95:* 130; *146:* 190; *213:* 3, 5, 107, 108

McClintock, Theodore *14:* 141

McCloskey, Robert *1:* 184, 185; *2:* 186, 187; *17:* 209; *39:* 139, 140, 141, 142, 143, 146, 147, 148; *85:* 150, 151; *100:* 172, 173, 174

McClung, Robert *2:* 189; *68:* 166, 167

McClure, Gillian *31:* 132; *150:* 53

McClure, Nikki *218:* 120

McConnel, Jerry *31:* 75, 187

McConnell, Mary *102:* 49

McCord, Kathleen Garry *78:* 236

McCormack, John *66:* 193

McCormick, A.D. *35:* 119

McCormick, Dell J. *19:* 216

McCoy, Glenn *212:* 132

McCrady, Lady *16:* 198; *39:* 127

McCrea, James *3:* 122; *33:* 216

McCrea, Ruth *3:* 122; *27:* 102; *33:* 216

McCue, Lisa *65:* 148, 149; *77:* 54; *80:* 132; *175:* 33; *177:* 133, 135; *212:* 136, 137, 138

McCully, Emily Arnold *2:* 89; *4:* 120, 121, 146, 197; *5:* 2, 129; *7:* 191; *11:* 122; *15:* 210; *33:* 23; *35:* 244; *37:* 122; *39:* 88; *40:* 103; *50:* 30,31, 32, 33, 34, 35, 36, 37; *52:* 89, 90; *57:* 6; *62:* 3; *70:* 195; *86:* 82; *96:* 192; *97:* 93; *110:* 143,144; *117:* 47; *167:* 96; *210:* 175, 176; *225:* 179; *231:* 157

McCurdy, Michael *13:* 153; *24:* 85; *81:* 160; *82:* 157, 158; *86:* 125; *97:* 92; *117:* 178; *132:* 6; *147:* 159, 160

McCusker, Paul *99:* 19

McDaniel, Jerry *132:* 135

McDaniel, Preston *160:* 206; *170:* 139

McDermott, Beverly Brodsky *11:* 180

McDermott, Gerald *16:* 201; *74:* 174, 175; *163:* 150, 151

McDermott, Mike *96:* 187

McDonald, Jill *13:* 155; *26:* 128

McDonald, Mercedes *169:* 118

McDonald, Ralph J. *5:* 123, 195

McDonnell, Flora *146:* 199, 200

McDonnell, Patrick *179:* 153, 154; *221:* 136, 137, 138

McDonough, Don *10:* 163

McElligott, Matt *196:* 147

McElmurry, Jill *137:* 148; *163:* 141; *202:* 186

McElrath-Eslick, Lori *129:* 145; *142:* 21; *173:* 123; *202:* 194; *204:* 88, 89

McEntee, Dorothy *37:* 124

McEwan, Keith *88:* 116; *165:* 122, 123

McEwen, Katharine *169:* 34

McFall, Christie *12:* 144

McFeely, Daniel *160:* 213

McGaw, Laurie *109:* 243; *143:* 216; *211:* 218

McGee, Barbara *6:* 165

McGee, Marni *163:* 153

McGillvray, Kim *158:* 171; *165:* 213; *186:* 183; *190:* 175

McGinley-Nally, Sharon *131:* 19

McGinnis, Robert *110:* 113; *177:* 80

McGovern, Tara *98:* 171

McGraw, Sheila *83:* 146

McGregor, Barbara *200:* 155

McGregor, Malcolm *23:* 27

McGrory, Anik *193:* 120

McGuire, Robert *204:* 57; *209:* 86

McGuirk, Leslie *152:* 159

McHale, John *138:* 190

McHenry, E.B. *193:* 122

McHugh, Tom *23:* 64

McIntosh, Jon *42:* 56

McKay, Donald *2:* 118; *32:* 157; *45:* 151, 152

McKean, Dave *150:* 71; *174:* 156; *197:* 83, 118; *229:* 45, 46

McKeating, Eileen *44:* 58

McKee, David *10:* 48; *21:* 9; *70:* 154, 155; *107:* 139, 140, 141; *134:* 218; *158:* 148, 149, 150, 151; *228:* 171

McKee, Diana *109:* 185

McKelvey, Patrick *164:* 141

McKendry, Joe *170:* 136

McKeveny, Tom *164:* 60; *173:* 79

McKie, Roy *7:* 44

McKie, Todd *205:* 181

McKillip, Kathy *30:* 153

McKinney, Ena *26:* 39

McKinnon, James *136:* 75

McKowen, Scott *172:* 63; *202:* 49

McLachlan, Edward *5:* 89

McLaren, Chesley *133:* 53; *213:* 112; *219:* 31

McLaren, Kirsty *123:* 99; *124:* 226

Mclean, Andrew *113:* 117, 118, 120, 121; *172:* 130, 131

Mclean, Janet *172:* 130

McLean, Meg *94:* 196

McLean, Sammis *32:* 197

McLean, Wilson *90:* 29; *113:* 195

McLoughlin, John C. *47:* 149

McLoughlin, Wayne *102:* 230; *134:* 178; *216:* 196

McMahon, Robert *36:* 155; *69:* 169

McManus, Shawn *85:* 71

McMenemy, Sarah *156:* 139; *211:* 93; *224:* 139; *226:* 152

McMillan, Bruce *22:* 184

McMullan, James *40:* 33; *67:* 172; *87:* 142; *99:* 63, 64; *189:* 133; *196:* 51

McMullen, Nigel *146:* 177

McNeely, Tom *162:* 55

McNaught, Harry *12:* 80; *32:* 136

McNaughton, Colin *39:* 149; *40:* 108; *92:* 144, 145, 146; *134:* 104, 106; *211:* 122, 123, 124

McNicholas, Maureen *38:* 148

McNicholas, Shelagh *173:* 61; *191:* 125, 126

McPhail, David *14:* 105; *23:* 135; *37:* 217, 218, 220,221; *47:* 151, 152, 153, 154, 155, 156, 158, 159, 160, 162, 163, 164; *71:* 211; *81:* 139, 140, 142; *86:* 123; *132:* 150; *140:* 129, 131, 132; *183:* 134, 135, 137; *189:* 132; *219:* 121, 122, 123, 125; *231:* 158

McPhee, Richard B. *41:* 133

McPheeters, Neal *78:* 132; *86:* 90; *99:* 162; *111:* 141; *142:* 162; *231:* 146

McQuade, Jacqueline *124:* 223

McQueen, Lucinda *28:* 149; *41:* 249; *46:* 206; *53:* 103

McQuillan, Mary *153:* 97; *200:* 140

McVay, Tracy *11:* 68

McVicker, Charles *39:* 150

McWilliam, Howard *219:* 135

Mead, Ben Carlton *43:* 75

Meade, Holly *90:* 102; *94:* 101; *149:* 8; *151:* 107

Mecray, John *33:* 62

Meddaugh, Susan *20:* 42; *29:* 143; *41:* 241; *77:* 50; *84:* 173, 174, 175, 176, 177, 178; *125:* 160, 161, 162; *176:* 148, 149, 150, 151

Meehan, Dennis B. *56:* 144

Meents, Len W. *73:* 147, 150

Meers, Tony *99:* 113

Meisel, Paul *98:* 137; *124:* 18; *162:* 180; *179:* 16; *181:* 62; *194:* 154; *221:* 5; *224:* 100, 101, 102, 133; *231:* 25

Melanson, Luc *149:* 229; *198:* 97, 98; *221:* 166

Melendez, Francisco *72:* 180

Melling, David *202:* 199

Melnychuk, Monika *153:* 65

Melo, Esperança *196:* 90

Melo, John *16:* 285; *58:* 203

Meloni, Maria Teresa *98:* 62

Meltzer, Ericka
See O'Rourke, Ericka

Menasco, Milton *43:* 85

Menchin, Scott *188:* 129

Mendelson, Steven T. *86:* 154

Mendelssohn, Felix *19:* 170

Mendola, Christopher *88:* 223

Meng, Heinz *13:* 158

Merian, Maria Sibylla *140:* 88

Mero, Lee *34:* 68

Merrell, David *205:* 3

Merrill, Frank T. *16:* 147; *19:* 71; *YABC 1:* 226, 229,273

Merriman, Rachel *98:* 108; *114:* 122; *149:* 142

Merveille, David *200:* 142

Meryman, Hope *27:* 41

Meryweather, Jack *10:* 179

Meseldzija, Petar *168:* 97

Meserve, Jessica *184:* 137; *211:* 127

Messick, Dale *64:* 150, 151, 152

Meth, Harold *24:* 203

Meyer, Alex Eben *226:* 60

Meyer, Herbert *19:* 189

Meyer, Renate *6:* 170

Meyers, Bob *11:* 136

Meyers, Nancy *172:* 124

Meynell, Louis *37:* 76

Micale, Albert *2:* 65; *22:* 185

Miccuci, Charles *82:* 163; *144:* 150

Micich, Paul *164:* 163

Middleton, Charlotte *230:* 81

Middleton, Jeffrey *177:* 173; *222:* 157

Middleton, Joshua *208:* 146; *219:* 24

Middleton-Sandford, Betty *2:* 125

Mieke, Anne *45:* 74

Mighell, Patricia *43:* 134

Miglio, Paige *101:* 203; *151:* 223; *201:* 118, 119; *204:* 162

Mikec, Larry *204:* 125

Mikolaycak, Charles *9:* 144; *12:* 101; *13:* 212; *21:* 121; *22:* 168; *30:* 187; *34:* 103, 150; *37:* 183; *43:* 179; *44:* 90; *46:* 115, 118, 119; *49:* 25; *78:* 121, 122, 205, 207; *81:* 4

Milelli, Pascal *129:* 66; *135:* 153; *187:* 45

Miles, Elizabeth *117:* 77

Miles, Jennifer *17:* 278

Milgrim, David *158:* 157; *187:* 125, 126, 128; *223:* 124, 125, 126, 127

Milhous, Katherine *15:* 193; *17:* 51

Millais, John E. *22:* 230, 231

Millar, H.R. *YABC 1:* 194, 195, 203

Millard, C.E. *28:* 186

Millard, Kerry *105:* 124; *204:* 93, 94

Miller, Don *15:* 195; *16:* 71; *20:* 106; *31:* 178

Miller, Edna *29:* 148

Miller, Edward *115:* 64; *183:* 140, 141; *218:* 129, 130, 131

Miller, Frank J. *25:* 94

Miller, Grambs *18:* 38; *23:* 16

Miller, Ian *99:* 128

Miller, Jane *5:* 196

Miller, Marcia *13:* 233

Miller, Marilyn *1:* 87; *31:* 69; *33:* 157

Miller, Mitchell *28:* 183; *34:* 207

Miller, Phil *175:* 150

Miller, Shane *5:* 140

Miller, Virginia *81:* 206

Miller, Woody *233:* 153

Millman, Isaac *172:* 18

Mills, Elaine *72:* 181

Mills, Judith Christine *130:* 168, 169

Mills, Lauren *92:* 170

Mills, Yaroslava Surmach *35:* 169, 170; *46:* 114

Millsap, Darrel *51:* 102

Milone, Karen *89:* 169; *222:* 149

Milord, Susan *147:* 163, 164; *200:* 144

Milot, René *226:* 127

Milton, Debbie *162:* 161

Mims, Ashley *170:* 51

Min, Willemien *222:* 62

Miner, Julia *98:* 69

Minor, Wendell *39:* 188; *52:* 87; *56:* 171; *58:* 116; *62:* 56; *66:* 109; *74:* 93; *78:* 129; *94:* 67; *117:* 12, 13; *124:* 84, 86; *136:* 121; *164:* 168, 169; *170:* 71; *199:* 79, 80, 81, 82; *217:* 63; *223:* 149; *226:* 90, 91, 92
Minter, Daniel *176:* 154; *179:* 177
Mirocha, Paul *81:* 133; *192:* 148; *194:* 36
Misako Rocks! *192:* 149, 150
Mitchell, Judith *109:* 117
Mitchell, Mark *91:* 208
Mitchell, Tracy *190:* 15
Mitgutsch, Ali *76:* 161
Mitsuhashi, Yoko *45:* 153
Miyake, Yoshi *38:* 141
Mizumura, Kazue *10:* 143; *18:* 223; *36:* 159
Mochi, Ugo *8:* 122; *38:* 150
Mock, Paul *55:* 83; *123:* 32
Modarressi, Mitra *90:* 236; *126:* 168; *173:* 165, 166; *200:* 147, 148
Modell, Frank *39:* 152
Mogenson, Jan *74:* 183
Mohn, Susan *89:* 224
Mohr, Mark *133:* 201
Mohr, Nicholasa *8:* 139; *113:* 127
Molan, Christine *60:* 177; *84:* 183
Moldon, Peter L. *49:* 168
Molk, Laurel *92:* 150; *230:* 217, 219
Mollica, Gene *197:* 11
Momaday, N. Scott *48:* 159
Mombourquette, Paul *112:* 91; *126:* 142
Monk, Julie *165:* 231; *191:* 96
Monks, Lydia *189:* 136, 137
Monroe, Chris *219:* 133
Monroy, Manuel *199:* 192
Montalto, Luisa *233:* 79
Montgomery, Lucy *150:* 126
Montgomery, Michael G. *208:* 159
Montgomery-Higham, Amanda *169:* 131
Monteiel, David *201:* 95
Montiel, David *69:* 106; *84:* 145
Montijo, Rhode *193:* 164
Montresor, Beni *2:* 91; *3:* 138; *38:* 152, 153, 154,155, 156, 157, 158, 159, 160; *68:* 63
Montserrat, Pep *128:* 135; *181:* 119; *184:* 53
Moon, Carl *25:* 183, 184, 185
Moon, Eliza *14:* 40
Moon, Ivan *22:* 39; *38:* 140
Moore, Adrienne *67:* 147
Moore, Agnes Kay Randall *43:* 187
Moore, Cyd *117:* 107, 108; *159:* 137, 138; *186:* 148, 149, 151; *203:* 15; *214:* 138, 139; *233:* 111, 112, 113, 115
Moore, Gustav *127:* 181, 182; *170:* 162, 163
Moore, Jackie *128:* 79
Moore, Janet *63:* 153
Moore, Margie *176:* 156; *221:* 125; *224:* 106, 107
Moore, Mary *29:* 160
Moore, Patrick *184:* 121
Moore, Yvette *101:* 11, 12; *154:* 141
Mora, Giovanni *179:* 127; *184:* 11
Mora, Raul Mina *20:* 41
Moraes, Odilon *102:* 144
Morales, Magaly *225:* 137; *233:* 28
Morales, Yuyi *154:* 144; *226:* 120
Moran, Rosslyn *111:* 26
Moran, Tom *60:* 100
Mordan, C.B. *193:* 115
Mordvinoff, Nicolas *15:* 179
Moreno, René King *169:* 59; *190:* 133, 209; *212:* 52
Morgan, Barbara *169:* 116
Morgan, Jacqui *58:* 57
Morgan, Mary *114:* 133, 134, 135; *123:* 11; *213:* 115, 116, 117
Morgan, Tom *42:* 157
Morgan, Pierr *173:* 148
Morgenstern, Michael *158:* 7, 57; *171:* 103; *174:* 60; *226:* 12; *233:* 5
Morice, Dave *93:* 142

Morin, Paul *73:* 132; *79:* 130; *88:* 140; *137:* 143
Moriuchi, Mique *177:* 203
Morozumi, Atsuko *110:* 155; *217:* 126, 127
Morrill, Leslie *18:* 218; *29:* 177; *33:* 84; *38:* 147; *42:* 127; *44:* 93; *48:* 164, 165, 167, 168, 169, 170,171; *49:* 162; *63:* 136, 180; *70:* 72; *71:* 70, 91,92; *72:* 228; *80:* 163, 164, 165; *90:* 121; *121:* 88; *178:* 117
Morrill, Rowena A. *84:* 16; *98:* 163
Morris *47:* 91
Morris, Frank *55:* 133; *60:* 28; *76:* 2
Morris, Harry O. *119:* 138
Morris, Jackie *128:* 194; *144:* 119; *151:* 146; *202:* 126, 127; *204:* 83; *211:* 80; *214:* 163
Morris, Jennifer E. *179:* 157
Morris, Oradel Nolen *128:* 180
Morris, Tony *62:* 146; *70:* 97
Morrison, Bill *42:* 116; *66:* 170; *69:* 40
Morrison, Gordon *87:* 150; *113:* 93; *128:* 181, 182; *183:* 144, 145, 146
Morrison, Frank *169:* 162; *205:* 156; *224:* 121; *226:* 154
Morrison, Taylor *159:* 144, 145; *187:* 131
Morrow, Gray *2:* 64; *5:* 200; *10:* 103, 114; *14:* 175
Morse, Scott *200:* 149, 150
Morstad, Julie *232:* 137
Morton, Lee Jack *32:* 140
Morton, Marian *3:* 185
Mosberg, Hilary *117:* 195; *118:* 164; *149:* 55
Moser, Barry *56:* 68, 117, 118, 119, 120, 121, 122, 123, 124; *59:* 141; *60:* 160; *79:* 91, 147, 149, 151, 152; *82:* 81; *90:* 118; *91:* 35; *95:* 210; *97:* 91, 93; *102:* 152; *126:* 4; *128:* 175; *133:* 141; *138:* 167, 171, 174; *153:* 205; *174:* 130; *185:* 152, 154; *195:* 163; *204:* 115; *209:* 201
Moser, Cara *90:* 118; *138:* 167
Moses, Grandma *18:* 228
Moses, Will *178:* 170, 171
Moskof, Martin Stephen *27:* 152
Mosley, Francis *57:* 144
Moss, Donald *11:* 184
Moss, Geoffrey *32:* 198
Moss, Marissa *71:* 130; *104:* 127; *163:* 156; *216:* 164, 165, 166
Most, Bernard *48:* 173; *91:* 142, 143; *134:* 120
Mourning, Tuesday *205:* 25; *220:* 68; *221:* 42
Mowll, Joshua *188:* 133
Mowry, Carmen *50:* 62
Moxley, Sheila *96:* 174; *169:* 26; *206:* 16
Moyers, William *21:* 65
Moyler, Alan *36:* 142
Mozley, Charles *9:* 87; *20:* 176, 192, 193; *22:* 228; *25:* 205; *33:* 150; *43:* 170, 171, 172, 173, 174; *YABC2:* 89
Mueller, Hans Alexander *26:* 64; *27:* 52, 53
Mugnaini, Joseph *11:* 35; *27:* 52, 53; *35:* 62
Mujica, Rick *72:* 67; *88:* 95; *111:* 53; *180:* 185; *197:* 70
Mullen, Douglas *180:* 178
Muller, Robin *86:* 161
Muller, Steven *32:* 167
Muller, Jorg *35:* 215; *67:* 138, 139
Mulock, Julie *163:* 112
Mullins, Edward S. *10:* 101
Mullins, Patricia *51:* 68
Multer, Scott *80:* 108
Munari, Bruno *15:* 200
Munch, Edvard *140:* 143
Munowitz, Ken *14:* 148; *72:* 178, 179
Muñoz, Claudio *208:* 161
Munoz, William *42:* 160
Munro, Roxie *58:* 134; *136:* 177; *137:* 218; *184:* 133, 134; *223:* 130, 132, 133

Munsinger, Lynn *33:* 161; *46:* 126; *71:* 92; *82:* 80; *89:* 218; *92:* 125; *94:* 157, 158, 159, 160; *98:* 196; *103:* 198; *142:* 143; *145:* 133, 134, 136; *153:* 203; *176:* 162; *177:* 140, 141, 142; *189:* 113, 114, 116, 117; *201:* 42; *221:* 148, 149,150
Munson, Russell *13:* 9
Munster, Sebastian *166:* 107
Munzar, Barbara *149:* 75
Murdocca, Salvatore *73:* 212; *98:* 132; *111:* 157; *157:* 228; *164:* 257
Murphy, Bill *5:* 138; *130:* 170
Murphy, Jill *37:* 142; *70:* 166; *142:* 132, 134
Murphy, Kelly *130:* 212; *143:* 119; *176:* 158; *190:* 135
Murphy, Liz *210:* 183; *212:* 157
Murphy, Mary *196:* 158
Murphy, Tom *192:* 40
Murr, Karl *20:* 62
Murray, Joe *175:* 37
Murray, Ossie *43:* 176
Mussino, Attilio *29:* 131; *100:* 164
Mutchler, Dwight *1:* 25
Myers, Bernice *9:* 147; *36:* 75; *81:* 146, 147, 148
Muth, Jon J. *165:* 169; *167:* 109; *190:* 227; *193:* 59; *228:* 206
Myers, Christopher *183:* 150; *193:* 139
Myers, Duane O. *99:* 145
Myers, Tim *147:* 168
Myers, V.G. *142:* 41
Myers, Lou *11:* 2

N

Na, Il Sung *231:* 136
Nachreiner, Tom *29:* 182
Nacht, Merle *65:* 49
Nadler, Ellis *88:* 91
Nagle, Shane *180:* 223
Nagy, Ian *195:* 64
Najaka, Marlies *62:* 101
Nakai, Michael *30:* 217; *54:* 29
Nakata, Hiroe *157:* 156; *162:* 30; *205:* 124, 125
Nakatani, Chiyoko *12:* 124
Narahashi, Keiko *77:* 188; *82:* 213; *115:* 142, 143, 144
Nascimbene, Yan *133:* 128; *173:* 132, 133
Nash, Lesa *87:* 135
Nash, Linell *46:* 175
Nash, Scott *130:* 36; *188:* 196; *224:* 180
Naso, John *33:* 183
Nason, Thomas W. *14:* 68
Nasser, Muriel *48:* 74
Nast, Thomas *21:* 29; *28:* 23; *51:* 132, 133, 134, 135,136, 137, 138, 139, 141
Nasta, Vincent *78:* 185
Natale, Vincent *76:* 3; *78:* 125; *112:* 47; *166:* 81; *174:* 189; *185:* 212; *197:* 59; *218:* 35
Natchev, Alexi *96:* 177
Nathan, Charlott *125:* 151
Nathan, Cheryl *150:* 104; *186:* 112
Natti, Susanna *20:* 146; *32:* 141, 142, *35:* 178; *37:* 143; *71:* 49; *93:* 98; *125:* 166, 168; *126:* 228; *151:* 6; *178:* 8; *188:* 106; *231:* 10
Navarra, Celeste Scala *8:* 142
Naylor, Penelope *10:* 104
Nazz, James *72:* 8
Nebel, M. *45:* 154
Neebe, William *7:* 93
Needham, Dave *196:* 85
Needler, Jerry *12:* 93
Neel, Alice *31:* 23
Neely, Beth *119:* 184
Neely, Keith R. *46:* 124
Neff, Leland *78:* 74
Negri, Rocco *3:* 213; *5:* 67; *6:* 91, 108; *12:* 159

Negrin, Fabian *174:* 125; *175:* 15; *223:* 91
Neidigh, Sherry *128:* 53; *204:* 101, 102, 103; *222:* 95
Neilan, Eujin Kim *180:* 241; *200:* 151, 152
Neill, John R. *18:* 8, 10, 11, 21, 30; *100:* 22
Neilsen, Cliff *158:* 131; *177:* 112, 121; *209:* 8; *215:* 150; *230:* 62
Neilsen, Terese *116:* 74
Nelson, Craig *62:* 151; 153; *183:* 86
Nelson, Gail White *68:* 140
Nelson, Jennifer *129:* 152; *199:* 132
Nelson, Kadir *151:* 185; *154:* 146, 147; *157:* 189, 222; *181:* 122, 124; *197:* 155; *213:* 122, 123, 124
Nelson, Melissa *224:* 87
Nelson, S.D. *131:* 34; *181:* 126, 127; *228:* 23
Ness, Evaline *1:* 164, 165; *2:* 39; *3:* 8; *10:* 147; *12:* 53; *26:* 150, 151, 152, 153; *49:* 30, 31, 32; *56:* 30; *60:* 113
Neubecker, Robert *170:* 143; *214:* 157; *233:* 25
Neville, Vera *2:* 182
Nevins, Daniel *191:* 173
Nevwirth, Allan *79:* 168
Newberry, Clare Turlay *1:* 170
Newbold, Greg *108:* 125; *145:* 199; *151:* 23; *193:* 178; *197:* 10; *199:* 92, 93
Newfeld, Frank *14:* 121; *26:* 154
Newhouse, Maxwell *232:* 144
Newland, Gillian *220:* 132
Newman, Andy *149:* 61; *195:* 63
Newman, Ann *43:* 90
Newman, Barbara Johansen *191:* 137, 138; *231:* 13
Newsham, Ian *143:* 162
Newsom, Carol *40:* 159; *44:* 60; *47:* 189; *65:* 29; *70:* 192; *80:* 36; *85:* 137, 138; *92:* 167; *191:* 82; *233:* 83
Newsom, Tom *49:* 149; *71:* 13, 62; *75:* 156; *91:* 113
Newton, Jill *83:* 105; *200:* 154
Nez, John *218:* 136
Ng, Michael *29:* 171
Ng, Simon *167:* 7
Ngui, Marc *229:* 50
Nguyen, Vincent *189:* 49; *226:* 160; *229:* 172
Nichols, Sandy *219:* 103
Nicholson, William *15:* 33, 34; *16:* 48
Nickens, Bessie *104:* 153
Nicklaus, Carol *45:* 194; *62:* 132, 133
Nickle, John *181:* 128
Nickless, Will *16:* 139
Nicholas, Corasue *154:* 20
Nicolas *17:* 130, 132, 133; *YABC 2:* 215
Niebrugge, Jane *6:* 118
Nielsen, Cliff *95:* 207, 208; *105:* 58; *114:* 112; *124:* 12; *125:* 91, 92; *132:* 224; *135:* 187; *136:* 40; *137:* 168; *145:* 54; *149:* 28; *158:* 129; *165:* 64, 158; *168:* 169; *170:* 6; *175:* 114, 116; *187:* 75, 76; *194:* 107; *197:* 172; *201:* 14; *208:* 192; *211:* 186; *216:* 215; *217:* 67; *224:* 61, 62; *230:* 21; *233:* 58, 59
Nielsen, Jon *6:* 100; *24:* 202
Nielsen, Kay *15:* 7; *16:* 211, 212, 213, 215, 217; *22:* 143; *YABC 1:* 32, 33
Niemann, Christoph *191:* 141
Nikola-Lisa, W. *180:* 180
Niland, Deborah *25:* 191; *27:* 156; *135:* 50; *172:* 143
Niland, Kilmeny *25:* 191; *75:* 143
Nino, Alex *59:* 145
Ninon *1:* 5; *38:* 101, 103, 108
Nissen, Rie *44:* 35
Nithael, Mark *158:* 237
Nivola, Claire A. *78:* 126; *140:* 147; *208:* 164
Nixon, K. *14:* 152
Nobati, Eugenia *194:* 118
Noble, Louise *61:* 170
Noble, Marty *97:* 168; *125:* 171
Noble, Trinka Hakes *39:* 162; *84:* 157
Nobles, Scott *226:* 159

Noda, Takayo *168:* 143
Noguchi, Yoshie *30:* 99
Nolan, Dennis *42:* 163; *67:* 163; *78:* 189; *82:* 225; *83:* 26; *92:* 169, 170; *103:* 166; *111:* 35; *112:* 213; *127:* 171; *166:* 161; *194:* 218
Noll, Sally *82:* 171
Nolte, Larry *121:* 63, 65
Nones, Eric Jon *61:* 111; *76:* 38; *77:* 177
Noonan, Daniel *100:* 224
Noonan, Julia *4:* 163; *7:* 207; *25:* 151; *91:* 29; *95:* 149; *231:* 163
Norcia, Ernie *108:* 155; *140:* 47
Nordenskjold, Birgitta *2:* 208
Noreika, Robert *173:* 20; *217:* 24
Norling, Beth *149:* 153, 154; *209:* 77
Norman, Elaine *77:* 72, 176; *94:* 35; *136:* 63; *178:* 42
Norman, Mary *36:* 138, 147
Norman, Michael *12:* 117; *27:* 168
Normandin, Luc *227:* 180
Northway, Jennifer *85:* 96
Nostlinger, Christiana *162:* 131
Novak, Linda *166:* 205
Novak, Matt *104:* 132, 133; *165:* 173, 174; *204:* 104, 106
Novelli, Luca *61:* 137
Novgorodoff, Danica *215:* 133
Nugent, Cynthia *106:* 189; *205:* 126, 127; *209:* 180
Numberman, Neil *220:* 133
Numeroff, Laura Joffe *28:* 161; *30:* 177
Nurse, Chris *164:* 91
Nussbaumer, Paul *16:* 219; *39:* 117
Nutt, Ken *72:* 69; *97:* 170
Nyce, Helene *19:* 219
Nygren, Tord *30:* 148; *127:* 164

O

Oakley, Graham *8:* 112; *30:* 164, 165; *84:* 188,189, 190, 191, 192
Oakley, Thornton *YABC 2:* 189
Oberheide, Heide *118:* 37
Obligado, Lilian *2:* 28, 66, 67; *6:* 30; *14:* 179; *15:* 103; *25:* 84; *61:* 138, 139, 140, 141, 143
Oblinski, Rafael *190:* 139
Obrant, Susan *11:* 186
O'Brien, Anne Sibley *53:* 116, 117; *155:* 115; *213:* 127; *224:* 71; *227:* 9
O'Brien, John *41:* 253; *72:* 12; *89:* 59, 60; *98:* 16; *161:* 185; *169:* 16; *180:* 196; *228:* 38
O'Brien, Patrick *193:* 142, 143, 144
O'Brien, Teresa *87:* 89
O'Brien, Tim *93:* 25; *136:* 94; *164:* 57; *169:* 57; *173:* 55; *175:* 86; *184:* 192; *191:* 134; *193:* 137; *210:* 159; *224:* 28, 29; *229:* 140; *232:* 166
O'Clair, Dennis *127:* 25
O'Connor, George *183:* 153; *228:* 113, 114
Odell, Carole *35:* 47
Odem, Mel *99:* 164; *167:* 84, 87
O'Donohue, Thomas *40:* 89
Oechsli, Kelly *5:* 144, 145; *7:* 115; *8:* 83, 183; *13:* 117; *20:* 94; *81:* 199
Ofer, Avi *208:* 143
Offen, Hilda *42:* 207
Offermann, Andrea *233:* 108
Ogden, Bill *42:* 59; *47:* 55
Ogg, Oscar *33:* 34
Ogle, Nancy Gray *163:* 144
Ohi, Ruth *90:* 175, 177; *131:* 63; *135:* 106; *175:* 107; *179:* 55
Ohlsson, Ib *4:* 152; *7:* 57; *10:* 20; *11:* 90; *19:* 217; *41:* 246; *82:* 106; *92:* 213
Ohtomo, Yasuo *37:* 146; *39:* 212, 213
O'Keefe, Jennifer *184:* 184
O'Kelley, Mattie Lou *36:* 150
Olbinski, Rafal *149:* 27; *158:* 77; *203:* 36
Oldland, Nicholas *223:* 136

O'Leary, Chris *208:* 166
Olander, Johan *231:* 138
Oleynikov, Igor *202:* 134
Oliver, Isaac *171:* 182
Oliver, Jenni *23:* 121; *35:* 112
Oliver, Narelle *152:* 192; *197:* 129, 130
Oller, Erika *128:* 186; *134:* 126
Olschewski, Alfred *7:* 172
Olsen, Ib Spang *6:* 178, 179; *81:* 164
Olson, Alan *77:* 229
Olson, Julie *233:* 120
Olson-Brown, Ellen *183:* 154
Olugebefola, Ademola *15:* 205
O'Malley, Kevin *94:* 180; *106:* 8; *113:* 108; *136:* 70; *157:* 193; *191:* 146; *203:* 78; *217:* 84; *230:* 115, 117, 118
O'Neil, Dan IV *7:* 176
O'Neill, Catharine *72:* 113; *84:* 78; *134:* 153
O'Neill, Jean *22:* 146
O'Neill, Martin *187:* 39; *203:* 118
O'Neill, Michael J. *54:* 172
O'Neill, Rose *48:* 30, 31
O'Neill, Steve *21:* 118
Ono, Chiyo *7:* 97
Orbaan, Albert *2:* 31; *5:* 65, 171; *9:* 8; *14:* 241; *20:* 109
Orbach, Ruth *21:* 112
Orback, Craig *197:* 132
Orfe, Joan *20:* 81
Org, Ed *119:* 93
Ormai, Stella *72:* 129
Ormerod, Jan *55:* 124; *70:* 170, 171; *90:* 39; *132:* 172, 173, 174; *147:* 98
Ormsby, Virginia H. *11:* 187
O'Rourke, Ericka *108:* 216; *117:* 194; *111:* 142; *119:* 194; *137:* 152; *150:* 134; *167:* 64; *172:* 164; *188:* 163; *191:* 172; *201:* 15; *203:* 75; *209:* 130; *219:* 99
O'Rourke, Ericka Meltzer
   See O'Rourke, Ericka
Orozco, Jose Clemente *9:* 177
Orr, Forrest W. *23:* 9
Orr, N. *19:* 70
Ortiz, Vilma *88:* 158
Osborn, Kathy *152:* 232; *199:* 101, 102; *206:* 67
Osborn, Robert *65:* 49
Osborne, Billie Jean *35:* 209
Osmond, Edward *10:* 111
Ostow, David *223:* 138
O'Sullivan, Tom *3:* 176; *4:* 55; *78:* 195
Otani, June *124:* 42; *156:* 53
Otis, Rebecca *185:* 92
Ottley, Matt *147:* 221; *171:* 133
Otto, Svend *22:* 130, 141; *67:* 188, 189
Oudry, J.B. *18:* 167
Oughton, Taylor *5:* 23; *104:* 136
Overeng, Johannes *44:* 36
Overlie, George *11:* 156
Owens, Carl *2:* 35; *23:* 521
Owens, Gail *10:* 170; *12:* 157; *19:* 16; *22:* 70; *25:* 81; *28:* 203, 205; *32:* 221, 222; *36:* 132; *46:* 40; *47:* 57; *54:* 66, 67, 68, 69, 70, 71, 72, 73; *71:* 100; *73:* 64; *77:* 157; *80:* 32; *82:* 3; *99:* 226; *224:* 198
Owens, Mary Beth *113:* 202, 203; *191:* 148, 149
Owens, Nubia *84:* 74
Oxenbury, Helen *3:* 150, 151; *24:* 81; *68:* 174, 175,176; *81:* 209; *84:* 213, 245; *129:* 56; *149:* 159; *184:* 181; *224:* 147
Oz, Robin *88:* 167; *185:* 181

P

Padgett, Jim *12:* 165
Page, Gail *205:* 128
Page, Homer *14:* 145
Page, Mark *162:* 70

Paget, Sidney *24:* 90, 91, 93, 95, 97
Paget, Walter *64:* 122
Paillot, Jim *173:* 89
Pajouhesh, Noushin *160:* 121
Pak *12:* 76
Pak, Yu Cha *86:* 174
Paladino, Lance *134:* 30
Palazzo, Tony *3:* 152, 153
Palecek, Josef *56:* 136; *89:* 158
Palen, Debbie *135:* 88; *195:* 148, 149
Palencar, John Jude *84:* 12, 45; *85:* 87; *92:* 187; *99:* 128; *110:* 204; *150:* 122; *171:* 86; *207:* 36
Palin, Nicki *81:* 201; *89:* 161
Palisi, Heather *231:* 109
Palladini, David *4:* 113; *40:* 176, 177, 178, 179, 181,224, 225; *50:* 138; *78:* 186
Pallarito, Don *43:* 36
Palmer, Carol *158:* 230; *195:* 187
Palmer, Gary *232:* 39
Palmer, Heidi *15:* 207; *29:* 102
Palmer, Jan *42:* 153; *82:* 161
Palmer, Judd *153:* 160, 161
Palmer, Juliette *6:* 89; *15:* 208
Palmer, Kate Salley *104:* 143; *154:* 169
Palmer, Lemuel *17:* 25, 29
Palmisciano, Diane *110:* 62; *162:* 26; *202:* 138, 139
Palmquist, Eric *38:* 133
Pamintuan, Macky *214:* 160
Panesis, Nicholas *3:* 127
Panter, Gary *182:* 191
Panton, Doug *52:* 99
Paparone, Pamela *129:* 174
Papas, William *11:* 223; *50:* 160
Papin, Joseph *26:* 113
Papish, Robin Lloyd *10:* 80
Papp, Robert *198:* 41; *205:* 130; *219:* 53
Paradis, Susan *40:* 216
Paraquin, Charles H. *18:* 166
Pardo DeLange, Alex *179:* 128; *211:* 135, 136
Paris, Peter *31:* 127
Parisi, Elizabeth B. *141:* 82; *164:* 57
Park, Nick *113:* 143
Park, Seho *39:* 110
Park, W.B. *22:* 189
Parker, Ant *82:* 87, 88; *104:* 121
Parker, Buzz *227:* 154
Parker, Jake *227:* 134
Parker, Lewis *2:* 179
Parker, Nancy Winslow *10:* 113; *22:* 164; *28:* 47, 144; *52:* 7; *69:* 153; *91:* 171, 174; *132:* 175
Parker, Robert *4:* 161; *5:* 74; *9:* 136; *29:* 39
Parker, Robert Andrew *11:* 81; *29:* 186; *39:* 165; *40:* 25; *41:* 78; *42:* 123; *43:* 144; *48:* 182; *54:* 140; *74:* 141; *91:* 24; *111:* 115; *151:* 201; *154:* 156; *200:* 163, 164; *211:* 67
Parker-Rees, Guy *149:* 145; *193:* 149, 150
Parkin, Trevor *140:* 151
Parkins, David *114:* 123; *146:* 176; *176:* 168; *192:* 107; *218:* 139, 140, 141, 148; *224:* 92
Parkinson, Kathy *71:* 143; *144:* 234
Parkinson, Keith *70:* 66
Parks, Gordon, Jr. *33:* 228
Parlato, Stephen *222:* 137
Parnall, Peter *5:* 137; *16:* 221; *24:* 70; *40:* 78; *51:* 130; *69:* 17, 155; *136:* 22, 23, 24
Parnall, Virginia *40:* 78
Paros, Jennifer *210:* 197
Parow, Lorraine *158:* 127
Parr, Todd *134:* 139, 140; *179:* 163, 164, 165
Parra, John *225:* 150; *232:* 134
Parrish, Anne *27:* 159, 160
Parrish, Dillwyn *27:* 159
Parrish, Maxfield *14:* 160, 161, 164, 165; *16:* 109; *18:* 12, 13; *YABC 1:* 149, 152, 267; *2:* 146, 149
Parry, David *26:* 156
Parry, Marian *13:* 176; *19:* 179
Parsons, Garry *197:* 135

Partch, Virgil *45:* 163, 165
Pascal, David *14:* 174
Paschkis, Julie *177:* 153, 154; *220:* 140, 141; *231:* 64
Pasquier, J.A. *16:* 91
Pastel, Elyse *201:* 123
Pasternak, Robert *119:* 53
Paterson, Diane *13:* 116; *39:* 163; *59:* 164, 165, 166,167; *72:* 51, 53; *129:* 175; *177:* 156, 157
Paterson, Helen *16:* 93
Patkau, Karen *112:* 123
Paton, Jane *15:* 271; *35:* 176
Patricelli, Leslie *207:* 129
Patrick, John *139:* 190
Patrick, Pamela *90:* 160; *93:* 211; *105:* 12
Patrick, Tom *190:* 103
Patterson, Geoffrey *54:* 75
Patterson, Robert *25:* 118
Patti, Joyce *187:* 145, 146
Patz, Nancy *111:* 40; *154:* 161; *214:* 80
Paul, James *4:* 130; *23:* 161
Paul, Korky *102:* 85
Paull, Grace *24:* 157; *87:* 127
Paulsen, Ruth Wright *79:* 160, 164; *189:* 146; *231:* 150
Pavlov, Elena *80:* 49
Payne, Adam S. *135:* 166
Payne, C.F. *145:* 138, 140; *179:* 168
Payne, Joan Balfour *1:* 118
Payne, Tom *170:* 27
Payson, Dale *7:* 34; *9:* 151; *20:* 140; *37:* 22
Payzant, Charles *21:* 147
Peacock, Phyllis Hornung *230:* 124
Peacock, Ralph *64:* 118
Peake, Mervyn *22:* 136, 149; *23:* 162, 163, 164; *YABC2:* 307
Pearce, Carl *228:* 107; *229:* 148
Pearson, Larry *38:* 225
Pearson, Tracey Campbell *64:* 163, 164, 167, 168, 169; *118:* 51; *156:* 169, 171, 172; *163:* 140; *219:* 140, 141, 142, 143
Peat, Fern B. *16:* 115
Peck, Anne Merriman *18:* 241; *24:* 155
Peck, Beth *66:* 242; *79:* 166; *80:* 136; *91:* 34; *95:* 9; *101:* 77; *164:* 197; *190:* 170
Peddicord, Jane Ann *199:* 106
Pedersen, Janet *193:* 152; *217:* 57; *218:* 15; *228:* 85
Pedersen, Judy *66:* 217; *121:* 36; *172:* 67
Pedersen, Vilhelm *YABC 1:* 40
Pederson, Sharleen *12:* 92
Pedlar, Elaine *161:* 45
Peek, Merle *39:* 168
Peet, Bill *2:* 203; *41:* 159, 160, 161, 162, 163; *78:* 158, 159, 160, 161
Peguero, Adrian *116:* 133
Peguero, Gerard *116:* 133
Peirce, Lincoln *232:* 150
Pels, Winslow Pinney *55:* 126
Peltier, Leslie C. *13:* 178
Peltzer, Marc *202:* 92
Penberthy, Mark *171:* 78
Pendle, Alexy *7:* 159; *13:* 34; *29:* 161; *33:* 215; *86:* 62
Pendola, Joanne *76:* 203; *81:* 125; *105:* 181; *178:* 152, 153
Pene du Bois, William *4:* 70; *10:* 122; *26:* 61; *27:* 145, 211; *35:* 243; *41:* 216; *68:* 180, 181; *73:* 45
Penfound, David *102:* 185
Pennington, Eunice *27:* 162
Peppe, Mark *28:* 142
Peppe, Rodney *4:* 164, 165; *74:* 187, 188, 189
Pepper, Hubert *64:* 143
Percy, Graham *63:* 2
Pericoli, Matteo *178:* 177
Perini, Ben *173:* 77
Perkins, David *60:* 68
Perkins, Lucy Fitch *72:* 199
Perkins, Lynne Rae *172:* 146; *212:* 153

Perl, Susan *2:* 98; *4:* 231; *5:* 44, 45, 118; *6:* 199; *8:* 137; *12:* 88; *22:* 193; *34:* 54, 55; *52:* 128; *YABC 1:* 176
Perlman, Janet *222:* 141
Perrone, Donna *78:* 166
Perry, Marie Fritz *165:* 180
Perry, Patricia *29:* 137; *30:* 171
Perry, Roger *27:* 163
Perske, Martha *46:* 83; *51:* 108, 147
Persson, Stina *175:* 166
Pesek, Ludek *15:* 237
Petach, Heidi *149:* 166; *200:* 207
Peters, David *72:* 205; *182:* 116
Petersen, Jeff *181:* 95
Petersham, Maud *17:* 108, 147, 148, 149, 150, 151, 152, 153
Petersham, Miska *17:* 108, 147, 148, 149, 150, 151, 152, 153
Peterson, Eric *109:* 125
Peterson, Nisse *99:* 27
Peterson, R.F. *7:* 101
Peterson, Russell *7:* 130
Petie, Haris *2:* 3; *10:* 41, 118; *11:* 227; *12:* 70
Petit-Roulet, Philippe *227:* 12
Petricic, Dusan *153:* 75, 76, 77; *170:* 12; *172:* 13; *176:* 170; *179:* 56
Petrides, Heidrun *19:* 223
Petrone, Valeria *159:* 160; *171:* 92; *186:* 173, 204: 49; *216:* 208; *220:* 98; *233:* 126
Petrosino, Tamara *177:* 40; *193:* 154, 155
Petruccio, Steven James *67:* 159; *127:* 5
Pettingill, Ondre *64:* 181; *70:* 64; *222:* 167, 168
Peyo *40:* 56, 57
Peyton, K.M. *15:* 212
Pfeifer, Herman *15:* 262
Pfister, Marcus *83:* 165, 166, 167; *146:* 152; *150:* 160; *207:* 132, 134, 135, 136
Pfloog, Jan *124:* 60
Pham, LeUyen *160:* 48; *175:* 154, 156; *179:* 149; *201:* 124, 125, 126, 127; *204:* 28; *208:* 206; *217:* 92
Phelan, Matt *182:* 160; *184:* 222; *215:* 140, 141; *221:* 157; *231:* 28
Phillipps, J.C. *218:* 142
Phillips, Craig *70:* 151; *207:* 74; *221:* 159; *229:* 22
Phillips, Douglas *1:* 19
Phillips, F.D. *6:* 202
Phillips, Gary R. *223:* 23
Phillips, Louise *133:* 67
Phillips, Matt *184:* 173
Phillips, Thomas *30:* 55
Philpot, Glyn *54:* 46
Phiz
See Browne, Hablot K.
Piatti, Celestino *16:* 223
Pica, Steve *115:* 181
Picarella, Joseph *13:* 147
Picart, Gabriel *121:* 165; *201:* 169
Picasso, Pablo *228:* 131
Pichon, Liz *174:* 139
Pickard, Charles *12:* 38; *18:* 203; *36:* 152
Picken, George A. *23:* 150
Pickens, David *22:* 156
Pickering, Jimmy *195:* 152; *197:* 163
Pien, Lark *222:* 143, 144
Pienkowski, Jan *6:* 183; *30:* 32; *58:* 140, 141, 142,143, 146, 147; *73:* 3; *87:* 156, 157; *131:* 189
Pieper, Christiane *200:* 168
Pignataro, Anna *163:* 220; *223:* 143 *Pile, Emma 218:* 156 *Pileggi, Steve 145:* 122
Pilkey, Dav *68:* 186; *115:* 164, 166; *166:* 173, 174, 175
Pimlott, John *10:* 205
Pincus, Harriet *4:* 186; *8:* 179; *22:* 148; *27:* 164, 165; *66:* 202
Pini, Wendy *89:* 166
Pinkett, Neil *60:* 8

Pinkney, Brian *81:* 184, 185; *94:* 107; *113:* 146, 147; *117:* 121, 166; *132:* 145; *158:* 108, 191; *160:* 189; *200:* 8
Pinkney, Jerry *8:* 218; *10:* 40; *15:* 276; *20:* 66; *24:* 121; *33:* 109; *36:* 222; *38:* 200; *41:* 165, 166, 167, 168, 169, 170, 171, 173, 174; *44:* 198; *48:* 51; *53:* 20; *56:* 61, 68; *58:* 184; *60:* 59; *61:* 91; *71:* 146, 148, 149; *72:* 17; *73:* 149; *74:* 159,192; *75:* 45; *80:* 206; *81:* 44; *85:* 144; *95:* 50; *107:* 158, 159, 160; *108:* 164; *112:* 114, 115; *133:* 58; *195:* 140; *227:* 131
Pinkwater, Daniel Manus *8:* 156; *46:* 180, 181, 182, 185, 188, 189, 190; *151:* 161 *76:* 178, 179, 180; *210:* 203
Pinkwater, Manus
See Pinkwater, Daniel Manus
Pinkwater, Jill *114:* 160, 161; *158:* 179; *188:* 143, 145, 146
Pinto, Ralph *10:* 131; *45:* 93
Pinto, Sara *200:* 165
Pinon, Mark *74:* 22
Piven, Hanoch *173:* 142
Pistolesi *73:* 211
Pitcairn, Ansel *188:* 10; *227:* 20
Pittman, Helena Clare *71:* 151
Pitz, Henry C. *4:* 168; *19:* 165; *35:* 128; *42:* 80; *YABC 2:* 95, 176
Pitzenberger, Lawrence J. *26:* 94
Pitzer, Susanna *181:* 131
Place, François *218:* 42
Plant, Andrew *214:* 166
Player, Stephen *82:* 190
Plecas, Jennifer *84:* 201; *106:* 124; *149:* 168; *205:* 180; *220:* 81; *229:* 152, 153, 154
Ploog, Mike *180:* 19
Plowden, David *52:* 135, 136
Plume, Ilse *170:* 149
Plummer, William *32:* 31
Podevin, Jean François *184:* 185
Podwal, Mark *56:* 170, 173; *101:* 154, 155, 157; *149:* 176; *160:* 194; *224:* 127, 128, 129
Pogany, Willy *15:* 46, 49; *19:* 222, 256; *25:* 214; *44:* 142, 143, 144, 145, 146, 147, 148
Pohrt, Tom *67:* 116; *104:* 80; *152:* 199; *195:* 154; *199:* 85
Poirson, V.A. *26:* 89
Polacco, Patricia *74:* 195, 196, 197, 198; *123:* 121, 122, 123; *180:* 189, 190, 191, 193, 194; *212:* 168, 170, 171
Polgreen, John *21:* 44
Polhemus, Coleman *210:* 209
Polhumus, Rien *6:* 212; *65:* 165, 166, 167
Politi, Leo *1:* 178; *4:* 53; *21:* 48; *47:* 173,174, 176, 178, 179, 180, 181
Pollack, Barbara *219:* 60
Pollema-Cahill, Phyllis *123:* 126
Pollen, Samson *64:* 80
Polonsky, Arthur *34:* 168
Polseno, Jo *1:* 53; *3:* 117; *5:* 114; *17:* 154; *20:* 87; *32:* 49; *41:* 245
Pomaska, Anna *117:* 148
Pons, Bernadette *184:* 100
Ponter, James *5:* 204
Poole, Colin *111:* 27
Poortvliet, Rien *6:* 212; *65:* 165, 166, 167
Pope, Kevin *183:* 158
Popp, Wendy *72:* 122; *158:* 68
Poppel, Hans *71:* 154, 155
Porfirio, Guy *76:* 134
Portal, Colette *6:* 186; *11:* 203
Porter, George *7:* 181
Porter, Janice Lee *136:* 175; *164:* 37
Porter, John *113:* 47
Porter, Pat Grant *84:* 112; *125:* 101
Porter, Sue *146:* 246, 247; *213:* 139, 140, 141; *221:* 91
Porter, Walter *124:* 175
Porto, James *221:* 14
Posada, Mia *187:* 151
Posen, Michael *175:* 82
Post, R.K. *233:* 60

Posthuma, Sieb *150:* 163
Postier, Jim *202:* 140; *204:* 25
Postma, Lidia *79:* 17
Potter, Beatrix *100:* 194, 195; *132:* 179, 180, 181, 182; *YABC 1:* 208, 209, 210, 212, 213
Potter, Giselle *117:* 123; *143:* 44; *144:* 170, 197; *149:* 7; *150:* 165; *187:* 152, 153; *190:* 198; *196:* 152; *200:* 12; *225:* 60; *227:* 105
Potter, Katherine *104:* 147; *171:* 135; *173:* 136; *217:* 130, 131
Potter, Miriam Clark *3:* 162
Poulin, Stephane *98:* 140, 141
Poullis, Nick *146:* 210
Powell, Constance Buffington *174:* 141
Powell, Gary *151:* 208
Powell, Ivan *67:* 219
Power, Margaret *105:* 122
Powers, Daniel *161:* 173
Powers, Richard M. *1:* 230; *3:* 218; *7:* 194; *26:* 186
Powledge, Fred *37:* 154
Powzyk, Joyce *74:* 214
Poydar, Nancy *96:* 149; *190:* 180, 181, 182
Pracher, Richard *91:* 166
Prachaticka, Marketa *126:* 126
Prange, Beckie *181:* 169
Prap, Lila *177:* 165
Prater, John *103:* 142, 143, 144; *149:* 172
Pratt, Charles *23:* 29
Pratt, Christine Joy *214:* 167
Pratt, George *116:* 208; *212:* 37
Pratt, Pierre *150:* 73; *166:* 183; *168:* 172; *201:* 27; *208:* 171, 172, 173
Prebenna, David *73:* 174
Preiss-Glasser, Robin *123:* 176; *152* 40; *172:* 194
Press, Jenny *116:* 95
Preston, Mark *152:* 162
Pretro, Korinna *91:* 126
Prevost, Mikela *209:* 111
Price, Christine *2:* 247; *3:* 163, 253; *8:* 166
Price, Cynthia *118:* 156
Price, Edward *33:* 34
Price, Garrett *1:* 76; *2:* 42
Price, Hattie Longstreet *17:* 13
Price, Nick *216:* 173; *220:* 7
Price, Norman *YABC 1:* 129
Price, Willard *48:* 184
Priceman, Marjorie *81:* 171; *136:* 169; *156:* 200; *168:* 153, 154; *188:* 45; *226:* 7
Priestley, Alice *168:* 33; *227:* 142
Priestley, Chris *198:* 144
Primavera, Elise *26:* 95; *58:* 151; *73:* 37; *80:* 79; *86:* 156; *105:* 161; *213:* 157; *230:* 132, 133, 134
Primrose, Jean *36:* 109
Prince, Alison *86:* 188, 189
Prince, Leonora E. *7:* 170
Pritchett, Shelley *116:* 148
Prittie, Edwin J. *YABC 1:* 120
Proimos, James *176:* 4; *217:* 132, 133, 134
Proimos, John *173:* 144
Prosmitsky, Jenya *132:* 33
Provensen, Alice *37:* 204, 215, 222; *70:* 176, 177, 178, 180; *71:* 213; *147:* 184; *191:* 190
Provensen, Martin *37:* 204, 215, 222; *70:* 176, 177, 178, 180; *71:* 213; *191:* 190
Pucci, Albert John *44:* 154
Pudlo *8:* 59
Puggaard, Ulla *196:* 25
Pullen, Zachary *211:* 161
Pulver, Harry, Jr. *129:* 159
Pulver, Robin *160:* 4
Punchatz, Don *99:* 57
Purdy, Susan *8:* 162
Pursell, Weimer *55:* 18
Purston, Oliver *229:* 156
Purtscher, Alfons *97:* 6
Purvis, Leland *232:* 156
Puskas, James *5:* 141
Pyk, Jan *7:* 26; *38:* 123

Pyle, Charles S. *99:* 149; *191:* 83; *233:* 20, 21; *233:* 85
Pyle, Howard *16:* 225, 226, 227, 228, 230, 231, 232, 235; *24:* 27; *34:* 124, 125, 127, 128; *59:* 132; *100:* 198

Q

Quackenbush, Robert *4:* 190; *6:* 166; *7:* 175, 178; *9:* 86; *11:* 65, 221; *41:* 154; *43:* 157; *70:* 185, 186; *71:* 137; *85:* 47; *92:* 148; *133:* 154, 164, 169
Qualls, Sean *177:* 167, 168; *193:* 43; *228:* 108; *233:* 128, 129
Quennell, Marjorie (Courtney) *29:* 163, 164
Quidor, John *19:* 82
Quirk, John *62:* 170
Quirk, Thomas *12:* 81

R

Rackham, Arthur *15:* 32, 78, 214-227; *17:* 105, 115; *18:* 233; *19:* 254; *20:* 151; *22:* 129, 131, 132, 133; *23:* 175; *24:* 161, 181; *26:* 91; *32:* 118; *64:* 18; *100:* 9, 16, 203, 204; *YABC 1:* 25, 45, 55, 147; *2:* 103, 142, 173, 210
Racz, Michael *56:* 134
Raczka, Bob *191:* 155, 156
Radcliffe, Andrew *82:* 215
Rader, Laura *101:* 219; *197:* 147; *203:* 53
Radunsky, Vladimir *177:* 170; *192:* 30
Radzinski, Kandy *212:* 174
Rafilson, Sidney *11:* 172
Raglin, Tim *125:* 24
Raible, Alton *1:* 202, 203; *28:* 193; *35:* 181; *110:* 207
Raine, Patricia *82:* 74; *88:* 154
Ramá, Sue *173:* 45; *185:* 186; *190:* 184
Ramhorst, John *117:* 11
Ramirez, Gladys *177:* 19
Ramirez, Jose *207:* 27
Ramsey, James *16:* 41
Ramsey, Marcy Dunn *82:* 11; *180:* 186
Ramus, Michael *51:* 171
Rand, Paul *6:* 188
Rand, Ted *67:* 9, 10, 121, 123; *74:* 190; *84:* 170; *103:* 170; *112:* 6; *114:* 73; *139:* 168; *143:* 194; *156:* 154; *161:* 9, 10; *200:* 38; *204:* 7
Randazzo, Tony *81:* 98
Randell, William *55:* 54
Rane, Walter *93:* 144; *143:* 109; *184:* 126
Rankin, Joan *163:* 40; *212:* 176
Rankin, Laura *176:* 173, 174; *179:* 150
Ransome, Arthur *22:* 201
Ransome, James E. *74:* 137; *75:* 80; *84:* 181; *94:* 108; *117:* 115; *123:* 128, 129, 130; *158:* 101, 102; *159:* 205; *178:* 188, 189, 190; *216:* 114; *227:* 146, 148, 149, 150
Rantz, Don *119:* 184
Rao, Anthony *28:* 126
Raphael, Elaine *23:* 192; *71:* 24, 25
Rappaport, Eva *6:* 190
Raschka, Chris *80:* 187, 189, 190; *97:* 211; *115:* 210; *117:* 151, 152, 153, 154; *143:* 195; *145:* 153; *166:* 190, 191; *170:* 114; *207:* 140, 143, 144, 145; *208:* 82; *220:* 85
Rash, Andy *158:* 178; *162:* 172; *210:* 204; *219:* 145; *226:* 194
Raskin, Ellen *2:* 208, 209; *4:* 142; *13:* 183; *22:* 68; *29:* 139; *36:* 134; *38:* 173, 174, 175, 176, 177, 178,179, 180, 181; *60:* 163; *86:* 81
Rathmann, Peggy *93:* 32; *94:* 168; *157:* 212, 214
Ratkus, Tony *77:* 133

Rattray, Gail 227: 96
Ratzkin, Lawrence 40: 143
Rau, Margaret 9: 157
Raverat, Gwen YABC 1: 152
Ravid, Joyce 61: 73
Ravielli, Anthony 1: 198; 3: 168; 11: 143
Ravilious, Robin 77: 169
Rawlins, Donna 72: 198; 73: 15, 129
Rawlins, Janet 76: 79
Rawlings, Steve 143: 139; 151: 54; 208: 150
Rawlinson, Debbie 75: 132
Ray, Deborah Kogan 8: 164; 29: 238; 50: 112, 113; 62: 119; 78: 191; 203: 149, 150, 151
Ray, Jane 96: 166; 97: 104; 152: 208; 190: 221; 196: 165
Ray, Ralph 2: 239; 5: 73
Rayann, Omar 162: 205; 186: 29, 30
Rayevsky, Robert 64: 17; 70: 173; 80: 204; 117: 79; 190: 187, 188
Raymond, Larry 31: 108; 97: 109
Rayner, Hugh 151: 170
Rayner, Mary 22: 207; 47: 140; 72: 191; 87: 171, 172; 192: 104
Rayner, Shoo
   See Rayner, Hugh
Raynes, John 71: 19
Raynor, Dorka 28: 168
Raynor, Paul 24: 73
Rayyan, Omar 110: 222; 112: 17; 125: 131
Razzi, James 10: 127
Read, Alexander D. 20: 45
Reader, Dennis 71: 157
Reasoner, Charles 53: 33, 36, 37
Rebenschied, Shane 203: 76; 215: 124
Reczuch, Karen 115: 132; 145: 131
Redlich, Ben 163: 221; 198: 193
Reddy, Mike 203: 67
Reed, Joseph 116: 139
Reed, Lynn Rowe 115: 173; 171: 146; 208: 177; 215: 144, 145
Reed, Mike 211: 147; 215: 131
Reed, Tom 34: 171
Reeder, Colin 74: 202; 77: 113
Rees, Mary 134: 219
Reese, Bob 60: 135
Reeve, Philip 171: 50
Reeves, Eira B. 130: 173, 174; 141: 151
Reeves, Rick 181: 179
Reeves, Rosie 202: 200
Regan, Dana 117: 116
Regan, Laura 103: 198; 153: 206
Reichert, Renée 169: 127
Reid, Barbara 82: 178; 92: 17; 93: 169, 170; 222: 45
Reid, Stephen 19: 213; 22: 89
Reim, Melanie 104: 151; 150: 98
Reinert, Kirk 89: 138; 195: 129
Reinertson, Barbara 44: 150; 62: 103
Reiniger, Lotte 40: 185
Reisberg, Mira 119: 2
Reisch, Jesse 158: 130
Reiser, Lynn 81: 175; 138: 184; 180: 200
Reiss, John J. 23: 193
Relf, Douglas 3: 63
Relyea, C.M. 16: 29; 31: 153
Remi, Georges 13: 184
Remington, Frederic 19: 188; 41: 178, 179, 180, 181, 183,184, 185, 186, 187, 188; 62: 197
Remkiewicz, Frank 67: 102; 77: 171; 80: 130; 113: 107; 152: 116; 152: 211, 212; 157: 148; 217: 120, 138, 139, 140, 141
Rendon, Maria 116: 141; 192: 134; 134: 152
Renfro, Ed 79: 176
Renier, Aaron 202: 141; 207: 119
Renlie, Frank 11: 200
Reschofsky, Jean 7: 118
Rethi 60: 181
Rethi, Lili 2: 153; 36: 156
Reusswig, William 3: 267
Revell, Cindy 195: 93

Rex, Adam 156: 172; 169: 91; 186: 178, 179; 215: 103; 223: 11; 225: 154
Rex, Michael 157: 147; 191: 159, 160; 221: 124
Rey, H.A. 1: 182; 26: 163, 164, 166, 167, 169; 69: 172, 173, 174, 175; 86: 195, 196, 197; 100: 211; YABC 2: 17
Rey, Luis V. 201: 162
Reynish, Jenny 222: 155
Reynolds, Adrian 192: 159, 160
Reynolds, Doris 5: 71; 31: 77
Reynolds, Peter H. 142: 12; 179: 175, 176; 202: 113, 114; 226: 30, 166, 167; 228: 132
Rhead, Louis 31: 91; 100: 228
Rhodes, Andrew 38: 204; 50: 163; 54: 76; 61: 123, 124; 87: 200
Ribbons, Ian 3: 10; 37: 161; 40: 76
Ricci, Regolo 93: 22; 164: 148
Rice, Elizabeth 2: 53, 214
Rice, Eve 34: 174, 175; 91: 172
Rice, James 22: 210; 93: 173
Rich, Anna 212: 180
Rich, Martha 195: 16
Richards, Chuck 170: 154
Richards, George 40: 116, 119, 121; 44: 179
Richards, Henry YABC 1: 228, 231
Richardson, Ernest 2: 144
Richardson, Frederick 18: 27, 31
Richardson, John 110: 88
Richman, Hilda 26: 132
Richmond, George 24: 179
Riddell, Chris 114: 170, 195; 166: 179; 199: 164, 166, 167; 218: 146, 148; 219: 149, 150, 152, 153; 228: 125
Riddle, Tohby 74: 204; 151: 179; 223: 154, 156
Riding, Peter 63: 195
Rieniets, Judy King 14: 28
Riger, Bob 2: 166
Riggio, Anita 73: 191; 85: 63; 137: 184; 172: 165
Rigano, Giovanni 219: 45
Riley, Jon 74: 70
Riley, Kenneth 22: 230
Riley, Terry 203: 100
Riley-Webb, Charlotte 153: 143
Rim, Sujean 225: 157
Rinaldi, Angelo 165: 60, 69; 227: 53
Ringgold, Faith 71: 162; 114: 173, 174, 176; 187: 160, 161, 163
Ringi, Kjell 12: 171
Rios, Tere
   See Versace, Marie
Rioux, Jo 215: 110; 226: 170
Ripper, Charles L. 3: 175
Ripplinger, Henry 117: 31
Ritchie, Scot 217: 145
Ritchie, William 74: 183
Ritter, John 175: 14
Ritz, Karen 41: 117; 72: 239; 87: 125; 102: 7; 106: 6
Rivas, Victor 209: 193; 226: 144
Rivers, Ruth 178: 193
Rivkin, Jay 15: 230
Rivoche, Paul 45: 125
Roach, Marilynne 9: 158
Robbin, Jodi 44: 156, 159
Robbins, Frank 42: 167
Robbins, Ken 147: 191, 192
Robbins, Ruth 52: 102
Roberton, Fiona 230: 142
Roberts, Cliff 4: 126
Roberts, David 154: 4, 6; 191: 162; 196: 184; 197: 105; 210: 257
Roberts, Doreen 4: 230; 28: 105
Roberts, Jim 22: 166; 23: 69; 31: 110
Roberts, Tony 109: 195, 214
Roberts, W. 22: 2, 3
Robertson, M.P. 197: 153
Robins, Arthur 137: 172; 151: 225; 204: 161

Robinson, Aminah Brenda Lynn 86: 205; 103: 55; 159: 175
Robinson, Charles [1870-1937] 17: 157, 171, 172, 173, 175, 176; 24: 207; 25: 204; YABC 2: 308, 309, 310, 331
Robinson, Charles 3: 53; 5: 14; 6: 193; 7: 150; 7: 183; 8: 38; 9: 81; 13: 188; 14: 248, 249; 23: 149; 26: 115; 27: 48; 28: 191; 32: 28; 35: 210; 36: 37; 48: 96; 52: 33; 53: 157; 56: 15; 62: 142; 77: 41; 111: 148
Robinson, Fiona 225: 158
Robinson, Jerry 3: 262
Robinson, Joan G. 7: 184
Robinson, Lolly 90: 227
Robinson, T.H. 17: 179, 181, 182, 183; 29: 254
Robinson, W. Heath 17: 185, 187, 189, 191, 193, 195, 197, 199, 202; 23: 167; 25: 194; 29: 150; YABC 1: 44; 2: 183
Rocco, John 187: 4; 188: 151; 208: 180, 181, 182; 213: 94; 222: 34
Roche, Christine 41: 98
Roche, Denis 99: 184; 180: 32; 196: 168
Roche, P.K. 57: 151, 152
Rocker, Fermin 7: 34; 13: 21; 31: 40; 40: 190,191
Rocklen, Margot 101: 181
Rockwell, Anne 5: 147; 33: 171, 173; 71: 166, 167,168; 114: 183, 184; 194: 152, 155
Rockwell, Gail 7: 186
Rockwell, Harlow 33: 171, 173, 175
Rockwell, Lizzy 114: 182; 162: 182; 185: 189; 233: 134, 135, 136
Rockwell, Norman 23: 39, 196, 197, 199, 200, 203, 204, 207; 41: 140, 143; 123: 47; YABC 2: 60
Rockwood, Richard 119: 75
Rodanas, Kristina 156: 183, 184; 221: 127
Rodegast, Roland 43: 100
Rodgers, Frank 69: 177
Rodriguez, Albert G. 182: 50
Rodriguez, Christina 184: 12; 225: 94
Rodriguez, Edel 204: 86
Rodriguez, Joel 16: 65
Rodriguez, Robert 145: 145; 212: 33
Rodriguez-Howard, Pauline 177: 18
Roe, Monika 210: 94
Roeckelein, Katrina 134: 223
Roennfeldt, Robert 66: 243
Roever, J.M. 4: 119; 26: 170
Roffey, Maureen 33: 142, 176, 177
Rogasky, Barbara 46: 90
Rogé 173: 160; 233: 138
Rogers, Carol 2: 262; 6: 164; 26: 129
Rogers, Chris M. 150: 59; 196: 61
Rogers, Forest 87: 160; 101: 76
Rogers, Frances 10: 130
Rogers, Gregory 104: 76; 126: 57; 171: 26
Rogers, Jacqueline 78: 249; 80: 34; 86: 54; 103: 70; 115: 72; 129: 173; 131: 57, 225; 143: 211; 153: 100; 193: 186; 203: 51; 213: 144, 145, 146; 214: 142
Rogers, Sherry 191: 66
Rogers, Walter S. 31: 135, 138; 67: 65, 168; 100: 81
Rogers, William A. 15: 151, 153, 154; 33: 35
Rogoff, Barbara 95: 20
Rohmann, Eric 103: 152; 198: 151
Rojankovsky, Feodor 6: 134, 136; 10: 183; 21: 128,129, 130; 25: 110; 28: 42; 68: 120
Rolfsen, Alf 62: 15
Rolston, Steve 209: 154; 223: 113
Romain, Trevor 134: 157
Roman, Barbara J. 103: 171
Romas 114: 111; 165: 63
Romano, Robert 64: 68
Romero, Alejandro 187: 185
Roos, Maryn 168: 198; 225: 160; 226: 143
Root, Barry 80: 212; 90: 196; 146: 78; 156: 165; 159: 161; 182: 18, 172; 232: 160, 161, 162

Root, Kimberly Bulcken *86:* 72; *98:* 21; *108:* 111; *127:* 114; *159:* 162; *176:* 134; *192:* 163
Roper, Bob *65:* 153
Roraback, Robin *111:* 156
Rorer, Abigail *43:* 222; *85:* 155
Rosales, Melodye *80:* 35
Rosamilia, Patricia *36:* 120
Rose, Carl *5:* 62
Rose, David S. *29:* 109; *70:* 120
Rose, Gerald *68:* 200, 201; *86:* 48
Rose, Naomi C. *228:* 136
Rose, Ted *93:* 178
Rosen, Elizabeth *205:* 137
Rosenbaum, Jonathan *50:* 46
Rosenberg, Amye *74:* 207, 208
Rosenberry, Vera *87:* 22, 26; *144:* 212, 213; *158:* 120; *219:* 163, 164
Rosenblum, Richard *11:* 202; *18:* 18
Rosenstiehl, Agnès *203:* 153
Rosier, Lydia *16:* 236; *20:* 104; *21:* 109; *22:* 125; *30:* 151, 158; *42:* 128; *45:* 214; *77:* 227, 228
Rosing, Jens *85:* 142
Ross
See Thomson, Ross
Ross, Christine *83:* 172, 173
Ross, Clare Romano *3:* 123; *21:* 45; *48:* 199
Ross, Dave *32:* 152; *57:* 108
Ross, Graham *199:* 4
Ross, Herbert *37:* 78
Ross, John *3:* 123; *21:* 45
Ross, Johnny *32:* 190
Ross, Larry *47:* 168; *60:* 62
Ross, Ruth *109:* 233
Ross, Tony *17:* 204; *56:* 132; *65:* 176, 177, 179; *90:* 123; *123:* 186, 187, 190; *130:* 188, 190, 191, 192; *132:* 242; *174:* 159; *176:* 181, 182, 183; *202:* 198; *225:* 168, 170
Rossetti, Dante Gabriel *20:* 151, 153
Rostant, Larry *180:* 221; *194:* 108; *195:* 96; *197:* 12; *207:* 53; *210:* 189; *226:* 22
Roth, Arnold *4:* 238; *21:* 133
Roth, Julie Jersild *180:* 206
Roth, Marci *135:* 223
Roth, R.G. *184:* 50
Roth, Rob *105:* 98; *146:* 41
Roth, Robert *176:* 159
Roth, Roger *61:* 128; *190:* 192
Roth, Ruby *216:* 185
Roth, Stephanie *136:* 171, 172
Roth, Susan L. *80:* 38; *93:* 78; *134:* 165, 166; *181:* 145, 146
Rothenberg, Joani Keller *162:* 190, 191
Rothman, Michael *139:* 62; *184:* 34 *Rotman, Jeffrey L. 145:* 30
Rotondo, Pat *32:* 158
Roughsey, Dick *35:* 186
Rouille, M. *11:* 96
Rounds, Glen *8:* 173; *9:* 171; *12:* 56; *32:* 194; *40:* 230; *51:* 161, 162, 166; *56:* 149; *70:* 198, 199; *YABC 1:* 1, 2, 3; *112:* 163
Roundtree, Katherine *114:* 88; *168:* 102
Rovetch, Lissa *201:* 164
Rowan, Evadne *52:* 51
Rowe, Eric *111:* 161
Rowe, Gavin *27:* 144; *72:* 47; *88:* 201
Rowe, John *132:* 70, 71; *180:* 126
Rowell, Kenneth *40:* 72
Rowen, Amy *52:* 143
Rowena *116:* 101
Rowland, Andrew *164:* 136
Rowland, Jada *83:* 73
Rowles, Daphne *58:* 24
Roy, Jeroo *27:* 229; *36:* 110
Royo *118:* 32; *144:* 105, 106, 108; *165:* 19; *166:* 166
Rubbino, Salvatore *220:* 147
Rubel, Nicole *18:* 255; *20:* 59; *81:* 66, 67; *95:* 169, 170; *119:* 60; *135:* 177, 179, 180; *169:* 68; *181:* 150
Rubel, Reina *33:* 217

Rud, Borghild *6:* 15
Ruddell, Gary *110:* 238; *116:* 207
Rudolph, Norman Guthrie *17:* 13
Rue, Leonard Lee III *37:* 164
Rueda, Claudia *183:* 170, 171
Ruelle, Karen Gray *126:* 193
Ruff, Donna *50:* 173; *72:* 203; *78:* 49; *80:* 120,121; *93:* 162; *164:* 121
Ruffins, Reynold *10:* 134, 135; *41:* 191, 192, 193, 194, 195, 196; *125:* 187, 188, 189; *162:* 197
Ruhlin, Roger *34:* 44
Rui, Paolo *217:* 115
Ruiz, Art *95:* 154; *110:* 91
Rumford, James *193:* 167
Runnerstroem, Bengt Arne *75:* 161
Ruse, Margaret *24:* 155
Rush, Ken *98:* 74
Rush, Peter *42:* 75
Russell, Charles M. *167:* 171
Russell, E.B. *18:* 177, 182
Russell, Jim *53:* 134
Russell, Natalie *218:* 170, 171
Russell, P. Craig *80:* 196; *146:* 102; *162:* 186
Russo, Marisabina *84:* 51; *106:* 164; *151:* 183; *188:* 153, 154, 155, 156
Russo, Susan *30:* 182; *36:* 144
Russon, Mary *87:* 145
Ruth, Greg *183:* 125
Ruth, Rod *9:* 161
Rutherford, Alexa *110:* 108
Rutherford, Jenny *78:* 5
Rutherford, Meg *25:* 174; *34:* 178, 179; *69:* 73; *72:* 31
Rutland, Jonathan *31:* 126
Ruurs, Margriet *147:* 195
Ruzzier, Sergio *159:* 176, 177; *163:* 184; *210:* 214, 216
Ryan, Amy *188:* 50
Ryan, Will *86:* 134
Rycroft, Nina *228:* 143
Ryden, Hope *8:* 176
Rylant, Cynthia *112:* 170, 172
Rymer, Alta M. *34:* 181
Ryniak, Christopher *178:* 11
Rystedt, Rex *49:* 80

S

Saaf, Chuck *49:* 179
Saaf, Donald *101:* 220; *124:* 180
Sabaka, Donna R. *21:* 172
Sabin, Robert *45:* 35; *60:* 30; *99:* 161; *223:* 29
Sabuda, Robert *170:* 166, 167, 168
Sacker, Amy *16:* 100
Sadler, Sonia Lynn *230:* 42, 163
Saelig, S.M. *129:* 73; *173:* 59
Saffioti, Lino *36:* 176; *48:* 60; *223:* 26
Saflund, Birgitta *94:* 2
Sagsoorian, Paul *12:* 183; *22:* 154; *33:* 106; *87:* 152
Sahara, Tony *168:* 106; *177:* 181; *178:* 228; *186:* 132; *207:* 89; *231:* 54
Sahlberg, Myron *57:* 165
Saidens, Amy *145:* 162; *191:* 131; *210:* 129
Saint Exupery, Antoine de *20:* 157
Saint James, Synthia *152:* 220; *188:* 90; *200:* 7
Sakai, Komako *213:* 148
Saldutti, Denise *39:* 186; *57:* 178
Sale, Morton *YABC 2:* 31
Sale, Tim *153:* 177
Salerno, Steven *150:* 79; *176:* 188; *202:* 39; *216:* 190
Salter, George *72:* 128, 130
Saltzberg, Barney *135:* 184, 185; *194:* 160; *233:* 147, 148
Saltzman, David *86:* 209
Salwowski, Mark *71:* 54

Salzman, Yuri *86:* 12
Sambourne, Linley *YABC 2:* 181
Sampson, Katherine *9:* 197
Samson, Anne S. *2:* 216
San Souci, Daniel *40:* 200; *96:* 199, 200; *113:* 171; *157:* 149; *170:* 69; *192:* 167, 168; *220:* 152; *221:* 126
Sancha, Sheila *38:* 185
Sanchez, Enrique O. *155:* 84
Sand, George X. *45:* 182
Sandberg, Lasse *15:* 239, 241
Sanders, Beryl *39:* 173
Sanderson, Ruth *21:* 126; *24:* 53; *28:* 63; *33:* 67; *41:* 48, 198, 199, 200, 201, 202, 203; *43:* 79; *46:* 36,44; *47:* 102; *49:* 58; *62:* 121, 122; *85:* 3; *109:* 207, 208, 209, 210; *172:* 157, 158; *223:* 85; *224:* 152, 153, 154
Sandia *119:* 74
Sandin, Joan *4:* 36; *6:* 194; *7:* 177; *12:* 145,185; *20:* 43; *21:* 74; *26:* 144; *27:* 142; *28:* 224, 225; *38:* 86; *41:* 46; *42:* 35; *59:* 6; *80:* 136; *94:* 188; *140:* 116; *153:* 179, 180; *197:* 168; *232:* 6
Sandland, Reg *39:* 215
Sandoz, Edouard *26:* 45, 47
Sanford, John *66:* 96, 97
Sanger, Amy Wilson *205:* 140
Sankey, Tom *72:* 103
Sano, Kazuhiko *153:* 208; *195:* 171; *203:* 21; *221:* 71
Santat, Dan *188:* 160; *221:* 62; *223:* 163; *224:* 157, 158, 159
Santiago, Wilfred *210:* 48
Santore, Charles *54:* 139; *200:* 171, 172
Santoro, Christopher *74:* 215
Santos, Jesse J. *99:* 24
Sapieha, Christine *1:* 180
Saport, Linda *123:* 137, 138; *215:* 29
Sara
See De La Roche Saint Andre, Anne
Sarcone-Roach, Julia *215:* 158
Sardinha, Rick *175:* 151
Sarg, Tony *YABC 2:* 236
Sargent, Claudia *64:* 181
Sargent, Robert *2:* 217
Saris *1:* 33
Sarony *YABC 2:* 170
Saroff, Phyllis V. *202:* 160
Sasaki, Goro *170:* 46
Sasaki, Ellen Joy *216:* 49
Sasek, Miroslav *16:* 239, 240, 241, 242
Sassman, David *9:* 79
Sattler, Jennifer Gordon *218:* 175
Satty *29:* 203, 205
Sauber, Robert *40:* 183; *76:* 256; *78:* 154; *87:* 92
Saunders, Dave *85:* 163, 164, 165
Savadier, Elivia *84:* 50; *145:* 45; *164:* 206; *228:* 146
Savage, Naomi *56:* 172
Savage, Steele *10:* 203; *20:* 77; *35:* 28
Savage, Stephen *174:* 182
Savio *76:* 4
Savitt, Sam *8:* 66, 182; *15:* 278; *20:* 96; *24:* 192; *28:* 98
Sawyer, Kem Knapp *84:* 228, 229
Say, Allen *28:* 178; *69:* 182, 183, 232; *110:* 194, 195,196; *161:* 154, 155
Sayles, Elizabeth *82:* 93; *105:* 155; *109:* 116; *180:* 64; *220:* 160, 161; *232:* 177
Scabrini, Janet *13:* 191; *44:* 128
Scalora, Suza *224:* 160
Scanlan, Peter *83:* 27; *153:* 165; *187:* 149
Scanlon, Paul *83:* 87
Scannell, Reece *105:* 105
Scarry, Huck *35:* 204, 205
Scarry, Richard *2:* 220, 221; *18:* 20; *35:* 193, 194, 195,196, 197, 198, 199, 200, 201, 202; *75:* 165, 167, 168

Schachner, Judith Byron *88:* 180; *92:* 163; *93:* 102; *142:* 82; *178:* 199, 200; *190:* 140; *228:* 83

Schade, Susan *205:* 21

Schaeffer, Mead *18:* 81, 94; *21:* 137, 138, 139; *47:* 128

Schaffer, Amanda *90:* 206

Schallau, Daniel *222:* 164

Schanzer, Rosalyn *138:* 192, 193

Scharl, Josef *20:* 132; *22:* 128

Scheel, Lita *11:* 230

Scheffler, Axel *180:* 23, 24; *230:* 169, 170

Scheib, Ida *29:* 28

Schermer, Judith *30:* 184

Schick, Eleanor *82:* 210, 211; *144:* 222

Schick, Joel *16:* 160; *17:* 167; *22:* 12; *27:* 176; *31:* 147, 148; *36:* 23; *38:* 64; *45:* 116, 117; *52:* 5, 85; *104:* 159

Schields, Gretchen *75:* 171, 203

Schindelman, Joseph *1:* 74; *4:* 101; *12:* 49; *26:* 51; *40:* 146; *56:* 158; *73:* 40

Schindler, Edith *7:* 22

Schindler, S.D. *38:* 107; *46:* 196; *74:* 162; *75:* 172, 173; *99:* 133; *112:* 177; *118:* 185, 186; *121:* 71; *136:* 159; *143:* 45; *149:* 120; *156:* 30; *169:* 135; *171:* 161, 162, 163; *172:* 9; *186:* 163; *194:* 109; *195:* 35; *198:* 170, 171, 172

Schlesinger, Bret *7:* 77

Schlossberg, Elisabeth *221:* 161

Schmid, Eleanore *12:* 188; *126:* 196, 197

Schmid, Paul *231:* 169

Schmiderer, Dorothy *19:* 224

Schmidt, Bill *73:* 34; *76:* 220, 222, 224

Schmidt, Elizabeth *15:* 242

Schmidt, George Paul *132:* 122

Schmidt, Karen Lee *54:* 12; *71:* 174; *92:* 56; *94:* 190, 191; *127:* 103

Schmidt, Lynette *76:* 205

Schmitz, Tamara *207:* 147

Schneider, Christine M. *171:* 165

Schneider, Howie *181:* 159

Schneider, Rex *29:* 64; *44:* 171

Schnurr, Edward *170:* 62

Schoberle, Cecile *80:* 200; *92:* 134; *218:* 113

Schoenherr, Ian *32:* 83; *173:* 41

Schoenherr, John *1:* 146, 147, 173; *3:* 39, 139; *17:* 75; *29:* 72; *32:* 83; *37:* 168, 169, 170; *43:* 164, 165; *45:* 160, 162; *51:* 127; *66:* 196, 197, 198; *68:* 83; *72:* 240; *75:* 225; *88:* 176

Scholder, Fritz *69:* 103

Schomburg, Alex *13:* 23

Schongut, Emanuel *4:* 102; *15:* 186; *47:* 218, 219; *52:* 147, 148, 149, 150; *185:* 27

Schoonover, Frank *17:* 107; *19:* 81, 190, 233; *22:* 88,129; *24:* 189; *31:* 88; *41:* 69; *YABC 2:* 282, 316

Schories, Pat *164:* 210; *232:* 170, 171, 172

Schottland, Miriam *22:* 172

Schramm, Ulrik *2:* 16; *14:* 112

Schreiber, Elizabeth Anne *13:* 193

Schreiber, Ralph W. *13:* 193

Schreiter, Rick *14:* 97; *23:* 171; *41:* 247; *49:* 131

Schroades, John *214:* 129

Schroeder, Binette *56:* 128, 129

Schroeder, E. Peter *12:* 112

Schroeder, Ted *11:* 160; *15:* 189; *30:* 91; *34:* 43

Schrotter, Gustav *22:* 212; *30:* 225

Schubert, Dieter *101:* 167, 168; *217:* 151, 152, 153, 155

Schubert, Ingrid *217:* 151, 152, 153, 155

Schubert-Gabrys, Ingrid *101:* 167, 168

Schucker, James *31:* 163

Schuett, Stacey *72:* 137; *208:* 204

Schulder, Lili *146:* 29

Schulke, Debra *57:* 167

Schulke, Flip *57:* 167

Schulz, Barbara *167:* 24

Schulz, Charles M. *10:* 137, 138, 139, 140, 141, 142; *118:* 192, 193, 194, 196, 199

Schutzer, Dena *109:* 32

Schwark, Mary Beth *51:* 155; *72:* 175

Schwartz, Amy *47:* 191; *82:* 100; *83:* 178, 179, 180,181; *129:* 107; *131:* 197, 198; *189:* 166, 168; *226:* 174

Schwartz, Carol *124:* 41; *130:* 199

Schwartz, Charles *8:* 184

Schwartz, Daniel *46:* 37

Schwartz, Joanie *124:* 170

Schwartzberg, Joan *3:* 208

Schwarz, Viviane *204:* 132

Schweitzer, Iris *2:* 137; *6:* 207

Schweninger, Ann *29:* 172; *82:* 246; *159:* 202; *168:* 166; *211:* 193

Schwinger, Laurence *84:* 44; *91:* 61

Scofield, Penrod *61:* 107; *62:* 160

Scott, Anita Walker *7:* 38

Scott, Art *39:* 41

Scott, Frances Gruse *38:* 43

Scott, Jane Wooster *226:* 181

Scott, Julian *34:* 126

Scott, Roszel *33:* 238

Scott, Sally *87:* 27

Scott, Steve *166:* 230, 231; *171:* 93

Scott, Trudy *27:* 172

Scotton, Rob *214:* 183

Scrace, Carolyn *143:* 95, 96

Scrambly, Crab *198:* 196

Scribner, Joanne *14:* 236; *29:* 78; *33:* 185; *34:* 208; *78:* 75; *164:* 237; *203:* 73

Scrofani, Joseph *31:* 65; *74:* 225

Scroggs, Kirk *187:* 169

Seaman, Mary Lott *34:* 64

Searle, Ronald *24:* 98; *42:* 172, 173, 174, 176, 177, 179; *66:* 73, 74; *70:* 205, 206, 207

Searle, Townley *36:* 85

Sebree, Charles *18:* 65

Sedacca, Joseph M. *11:* 25; *22:* 36

Seder, Jason *108:* 102

Seeger, Laura Vaccaro *172:* 162

Seegmiller, Don *57:* 57

Seely, David *164:* 173

Seeley, Laura L. *97:* 105

Segal, John *178:* 202

Segar, E.C. *61:* 179, 181

Segur, Adrienne *27:* 121

Seibold, J. Otto *83:* 188, 190, 191; *149:* 212, 214, 215, 216; *196:* 177, 179; *215:* 204

Seignobosc, Francoise *21:* 145, 146

Sejima, Yoshimasa *8:* 187

Selig, Sylvie *13:* 199

Seltzer, Isadore *6:* 18; *133:* 59

Seltzer, Meyer *17:* 214

Selven, Maniam *144:* 133

Selway, Martina *169:* 157

Selznick, Brian *79:* 192; *104:* 25; *117:* 175; *126:* 156; *134:* 171; *158:* 76, 78; *169:* 70; *171:* 172, 173; *191:* 106; *192:* 130; *197:* 158; *203:* 35; *205:* 92; *210:* 219, 220, 221, 222

Sempe, Jean-Jacques *47:* 92; *YABC 2:* 109

Sendak, Maurice *1:* 135, 190; *3:* 204; *7:* 142; *15:* 199; *17:* 210; *27:* 181, 182, 183, 185, 186, 187, 189,190, 191, 192, 193, 194, 195, 197, 198, 199, 203; *28:* 181, 182; *32:* 108; *33:* 148, 149; *35:* 238; *44:* 180, 181; *45:* 97, 99; *46:* 174; *73:* 225; *91:* 10, 11 *YABC1:* 167; *113:* 163, 165, 167, 168; *118:* 153; *127:* 161

Senders, Marci *180:* 79

Sengler, Johanna *18:* 256

Senn, Steve *60:* 145

Seredy, Kate *1:* 192; *14:* 20, 21; *17:* 210

Sergeant, John *6:* 74

Serra, Sebastià *212:* 215

Servello, Joe *10:* 144; *24:* 139; *40:* 91; *70:* 130, 131; *146:* 159

Seton, Ernest Thompson *18:* 260-269, 271

Seuss, Dr.
See Geisel, Theodor

Severin, John Powers *7:* 62

Sewall, Marcia *15:* 8; *22:* 170; *37:* 171, 172, 173; *39:* 73; *45:* 209; *62:* 117; *69:* 185, 186; *71:* 212; *90:* 232; *96:* 127; *102:* 101; *107:* 129; *119:* 176, 177, 178, 180

Seward, James *70:* 35

Seward, Prudence *16:* 243

Sewell, Helen *3:* 186; *15:* 308; *33:* 102; *38:* 189, 190, 191, 192

Seymour, Stephen *54:* 21

Sfar, Joann *182:* 183

Shachat, Andrew *82:* 179

Shadbolt, Robert *203:* 68

Shahn, Ben *39:* 178; *46:* 193

Shalansky, Len *38:* 167

Shanks, Anne Zane *10:* 149

Shannon, David *57:* 137; *107:* 184; *112:* 216; *135:* 12; *152:* 223, 224, 225; *158:* 192; *212:* 159, 160, 163; *228:* 162, 163, 164, 165

Sharkey, Niamh *213:* 152

Sharp, Paul *52:* 60

Sharp, William *6:* 131; *19:* 241; *20:* 112; *25:* 141

Sharratt, Nick *102:* 207, 208; *104:* 163; *153:* 198; *175:* 176; *192:* 208; *199:* 141, 142, 143, 184, 187, 188

Shaw, Barclay *74:* 14, 16; *118:* 138

Shaw, Charles *21:* 135; *38:* 187; *47:* 124; *126:* 219

Shaw, Charles G. *13:* 200

Shaw, Hannah *227:* 163, 164

Shaw-Smith, Emma *144:* 117

Shea, Bob *231:* 170, 171

Shea, Edmund *56:* 19

Shearer, Ted *43:* 193, 194, 195, 196

Sheban, Chris *182:* 185; *190:* 102, 104; *202:* 28; *204:* 112, 114; *209:* 150; *210:* 107; *220:* 103; *224:* 185

Shecter, Ben *16:* 244; *25:* 109; *33:* 188, 191; *41:* 77

Shed, Greg *74:* 94; *84:* 204; *129:* 149, 167; *91:* 179: 192; *223:* 104

Sheeban, Chris *144:* 190; *158:* 163

Shefcik, James *48:* 221, 222; *60:* 141

Shefelman, Karl *58:* 168

Shefelman, Tom *204:* 137

Shefts, Joelle *48:* 210

Shein, Bob *139:* 189

Sheinkin, Stephen *204:* 139

Shekerjian, Haig *16:* 245

Shekerjian, Regina *16:* 245; *25:* 73

Sheldon, David *184:* 174; *185:* 204; *211:* 189

Shelley, John *186:* 223

Shemie, Bonnie *96:* 207

Shenton, Edward *45:* 187, 188, 189; *YABC 1:* 218, 219, 221

Shepard, Ernest H. *3:* 193; *4:* 74; *16:* 101; *17:* 109; *25:* 148; *33:* 152, 199, 200, 201, 202, 203, 204, 205, 206,207; *46:* 194; *98:* 114; *100:* 111, 178, 179, 217, 219, 220,221; *YABC 1:* 148, 153, 174, 176, 180, 181

Shepard, Mary *4:* 210; *22:* 205; *30:* 132, 133; *54:* 150, 152, 153, 157, 158; *59:* 108, 109, 111; *100:* 246

Shepherd, Amanda *198:* 14

Shepherd, Irana *171:* 112

Sheppard, Kate *195:* 176

Shepperson, Rob *96:* 153; *177:* 163; *178:* 204; *197:* 34; *205:* 108

Sheridan, Brian *196:* 193

Sherman, Theresa *27:* 167

Sherwan, Earl *3:* 196

Shields, Charles *10:* 150; *36:* 63

Shields, Leonard *13:* 83, 85, 87

Shiffman, Lena *139:* 167; *168:* 136

Shiga, Jason *228:* 168

Shigley, Neil K. *66:* 219

Shillabeer, Mary *35:* 74

Shilston, Arthur *49:* 61; *62:* 58

Shimin, Symeon *1:* 93; *2:* 128, 129; *3:* 202; *7:* 85; *11:* 177; *12:* 139; *13:* 202, 203; *27:* 138; *28:* 65; *35:* 129; *36:* 130; *48:* 151; *49:* 59; *56:* 63, 65, 153
Shimizu, Yuko *215:* 197
Shine, Andrea *104:* 165; *128:* 34
Shinn, Everett *16:* 148; *18:* 229; *21:* 149, 150, 151; *24:* 218
Shinn, Florence Scovel *63:* 133, 135
Shore, Robert *27:* 54; *39:* 192, 193; *YABC 2:* 200
Shortall, Leonard *4:* 144; *8:* 196; *10:* 166; *19:* 227, 228, 229, 230; *25:* 78; *28:* 66, 167; *33:* 127; *52:* 125; *73:* 12, 212
Shortt, T.M. *27:* 36
Shpitalnik, Vladimir *83:* 194
Shroades, John *230:* 24
Shropshire, Sandy *170:* 191
Shtainments, Leon *32:* 161
Shulevitz, Uri *3:* 198, 199; *17:* 85; *22:* 204; *27:* 212; *28:* 184; *50:* 190, 191, 192, 193, 194, 195, 196,197, 198, 199, 201; *106:* 181, 182, 183; *165:* 203, 205; *166:* 138
Shulman, Dee *180:* 140
Shupe, Bobbi *139:* 80, 81
Shute, A.B. *67:* 196
Shute, Linda *46:* 59; *74:* 118
Siberell, Anne *29:* 193
Sibley, Don *1:* 39; *12:* 196; *31:* 47
Sibthorp, Fletcher *94:* 111, 112
Sidjakov, Nicolas *18:* 274
Siebel, Fritz *3:* 120; *17:* 145
Siebold, J. Otto *158:* 227
Siegel, Hal *74:* 246
Sieger, Ted *189:* 172
Siegl, Helen *12:* 166; *23:* 216; *34:* 185, 186
Silin-Palmer, Pamela *184:* 102
Sill, John *140:* 194; *141:* 157; *221:* 163; *222:* 171
Sills, Joyce *5:* 199
Silva, Simon *108:* 122
Silver, Maggie *85:* 210
Silveria, Gordon *96:* 44
Silverstein, Alvin *8:* 189
Silverstein, Shel *33:* 211; *92:* 209, 210
Silverstein, Virginia *8:* 189
Silvey, Joe *135:* 203
Simard, Rémy *95:* 156; *221:* 144
Siminovich, Laura *219:* 172
Simmons, Elly *110:* 2; *127:* 69; *134:* 181
Simon, Eric M. *7:* 82
Simon, Hilda *28:* 189
Simon, Howard *2:* 175; *5:* 132; *19:* 199; *32:* 163, 164, 165
Simont, Marc *2:* 119; *4:* 213; *9:* 168; *13:* 238,240; *14:* 262; *16:* 179; *18:* 221; *26:* 210; *33:* 189, 194; *44:* 132; *58:* 122; *68:* 117; *73:* 204, 205, 206; *74:* 221; *126:* 199, 200; *133:* 195; *163:* 40; *164:* 128; *223:* 28
Simpson, Martin *233:* 168
Sims, Agnes *54:* 152
Sims, Blanche *44:* 116; *57:* 129; *75:* 179, 180; *77:* 92; *104:* 192; *152:* 117; *156:* 160; *160:* 70; *168:* 174, 175; *198:* 17
Singer, Edith G. *2:* 30
Singer, Gloria *34:* 56; *36:* 43
Singer, Julia *28:* 190
Singh, Jen *178:* 146
Sinquette, Jaclyn *215:* 83
Siomades, Lorianne *134:* 45; *204:* 48; *217:* 157
Siracusa, Catherine *68:* 135; *82:* 218
Sís, Peter *67:* 179, 181, 183, 184, 185; *96:* 96, 98; *106:* 193, 194, 195; *149:* 224, 226; *180:* 177; *192:* 180, 182; *222:* 64
Sivard, Robert *26:* 124
Sivertson, Liz *116:* 84
Skardinski, Stanley *23:* 144; *32:* 84; *66:* 122; *84:* 108
Slack, Michael *185:* 108; *189:* 173, 174
Slackman, Charles B. *12:* 201

Slade, Christian *193:* 187; *204:* 134
Slade, Paul *61:* 170
Slark, Albert *99:* 212; *205:* 161
Slater, Rod *25:* 167
Slavin, Bill *182:* 14, 15; *196:* 90; *199:* 148, 149, 150; *217:* 20
Sloan, Joseph *16:* 68
Sloane, Eric *21:* 3; *52:* 153, 154, 155, 156, 157, 158, 160
Sloat, Teri *164:* 231
Slobodkin, Louis *1:* 200; *3:* 232; *5:* 168; *13:* 251; *15:* 13, 88; *26:* 173, 174, 175, 176, 178, 179; *60:* 180
Slobodkina, Esphyr *1:* 201
Slonim, David *166:* 167, 168
Small, David *50:* 204, 205; *79:* 44; *95:* 189, 190, 191; *126:* 203, 204; *136:* 119; *143:* 201, 202, 203; *144:* 246; *150:* 5; *161:* 176; *183:* 181, 182, 183, 184; *200:* 211; *212:* 86; *216:* 202, 203, 204; *230:* 222; *232:* 95
Small, W. *33:* 113
Smalley, Janet *1:* 154
Smath, Jerry *198:* 179, 180
Smedley, William T. *34:* 129
Smee, David *14:* 78; *62:* 30
Smee, Nicola *167:* 156
Smith, A.G., Jr. *35:* 182
Smith, Ali *204:* 68
Smith, Alvin *1:* 31, 229; *13:* 187; *27:* 216; *28:* 226; *48:* 149; *49:* 60
Smith, Andy *188:* 20; *207:* 151
Smith, Anne *194:* 35
Smith, Anne Warren *41:* 212
Smith, Barry *75:* 183
Smith, Brian *200:* 183
Smith, Carl *36:* 41
Smith, Cat Bowman *146:* 39; *164:* 219; *201:* 55, 184
Smith, Craig *97:* 197; *172:* 175; *206:* 40; *215:* 19; *217:* 129; *220:* 145
Smith, Donald A. *178:* 7
Smith, Doris Susan *41:* 139
Smith, Douglas *189:* 159; *213:* 170
Smith, Duane *171:* 152; *208:* 97
Smith, E. Boyd *19:* 70; *22:* 89; *26:* 63; *YABC 1:* 4, 5, 240, 248, 249
Smith, Edward J. *4:* 224
Smith, Elwood H. *157:* 231; *181:* 79; *203:* 160, 161, 162; *231:* 108
Smith, Eunice Young *5:* 170
Smith, Gary *113:* 216
Smith, George *102:* 169
Smith, Howard *19:* 196
Smith, J. Gerard *95:* 42
Smith, Jacqueline Bardner *27:* 108; *39:* 197
Smith, Jay J. *61:* 119
Smith, Jeff *93:* 191
Smith, Jessie Willcox *15:* 91; *16:* 95; *18:* 231; *19:* 57, 242; *21:* 29, 156, 157, 158, 159, 160, 161; *34:* 65; *100:* 223; *YABC 1:* 6; *2:* 180, 185, 191, 311, 325
Smith, Jos. A. *52:* 131; *72:* 120; *74:* 151; *84:* 147, 148; *85:* 146; *87:* 96; *94:* 219; *96:* 97; *104:* 33; *108:* 126, 127, 128; *111:* 140; *136:* 145; *181:* 173; *200:* 213; *201:* 94; *231:* 148
Smith, Kenneth R. *47:* 182
Smith, Keri *216:* 60
Smith, Kevin Warren *89:* 112
Smith, Kristin *209:* 197
Smith, L.H. *35:* 174
Smith, Lane *76:* 211, 213; *88:* 115; *105:* 202, 203,204, 205; *131:* 207; *160:* 217, 221; *179:* 183, 184, 185, 186; *199:* 122, 123, 124, 126; *224:* 164
Smith, Lee *29:* 32
Smith, Linell Nash *2:* 195
Smith, Maggie Kaufman *13:* 205; *35:* 191; *110:* 158; *178:* 226; *190:* 204; *209:* 145
Smith, Mavis *101:* 219
Smith, Moishe *33:* 155
Smith, Philip *44:* 134; *46:* 203

Smith, Ralph Crosby *2:* 267; *49:* 203
Smith, Robert D. *5:* 63
Smith, Sally J. *84:* 55
Smith, Susan Carlton *12:* 208
Smith, Terry *12:* 106; *33:* 158
Smith, Virginia *3:* 157; *33:* 72
Smith, William A. *1:* 36; *10:* 154; *25:* 65
Smith-Moore, J.J. *98:* 147
Smolinski, Dick *84:* 217
Smoljan, Joe *112:* 201
Smollin, Mike *39:* 203
Smyth, Iain *105:* 207
Smyth, M. Jane *12:* 15
Smythe, Fiona *151:* 213
Smythe, Theresa *141:* 37
Snair, Andy *176:* 4
Sneed, Brad *125:* 25; *191:* 175, 176; *211:* 194; *232:* 152
Snow, Sarah *228:* 47
Snyder, Andrew A. *30:* 212
Snyder, Betsy *230:* 173
Snyder, Jerome *13:* 207; *30:* 173
Snyder, Joel *28:* 163
So, Meilo *162:* 201; *208:* 188
Soentpiet, Chris K. *97:* 208; *110:* 33; *159:* 184; *161:* 10; *163:* 130
Sofia *1:* 62; *5:* 90; *32:* 166; *86:* 43
Sofilas, Mark *93:* 157
Sogabe, Aki *207:* 153; *221:* 110
Sohn, Jiho *182:* 78
Sokol, Bill *37:* 178; *49:* 23
Sokolov, Kirill *34:* 188
Solbert, Ronni *1:* 159; *2:* 232; *5:* 121; *6:* 34; *17:* 249
Solomon, Michael *174:* 115
Solonevich, George *15:* 246; *17:* 47
Soloviov, Michael *223:* 122
Soma, Liana *81:* 118
Soman, David *90:* 122; *102:* 126; *140:* 120; *93:* 188; *188:* 43, 89; *200:* 180, 181
Sommer, Robert *12:* 211
Song, Jae *203:* 27
Soo, Kean *201:* 185
Sorel, Edward *4:* 61; *36:* 82; *65:* 191, 193; *126:* 214
Sorensen, Henri *196:* 58
Sorensen, Henrik *62:* 16
Sorensen, Svend Otto *22:* 130, 141; *67:* 188, 189
Sorra, Kristin *155:* 80; *229:* 85
Sosa, Hernan *198:* 66
Sostre, Maria *187:* 36
Sotomayor, Antonio *11:* 215
Souhami, Jessica *112:* 128; *176:* 193
Sousa, Natalie C. *209:* 89
Souza, Diana *71:* 139
Sovak, Jan *115:* 190
Sowards, Ben *215:* 62
Soyer, Moses *20:* 177
Spaenkuch, August *16:* 28
Spafford, Suzy *160:* 228
Spain, Valerie *105:* 76
Spain, Sunday Sahara *133:* 204
Spalenka, Greg *149:* 69; *151:* 228; *184:* 195; *191:* 21; *196:* 12; *198:* 181, 182, 201; *208:* 92
Spanfeller, James *1:* 72, 149; *2:* 183; *19:* 230, 231,232; *22:* 66; *36:* 160, 161; *40:* 75; *52:* 166; *76:* 37
Spangler, Brie *212:* 188
Sparks, Mary Walker *15:* 247
Spearing, Craig J. *228:* 172
Spears, Rick *182:* 187; *220:* 67
Speidel, Sandra *78:* 233; *94:* 178; *134:* 180; *210:* 67
Speirs, John *67:* 178
Spence, Geraldine *21:* 163; *47:* 196
Spence, Jim *38:* 89; *50:* 102
Spencer, Laurie *113:* 12
Spencer, Mark *57:* 170
Spengler, Kenneth J. *146:* 256

Sperling, Andrea *133:* 182
Spiegel, Beth *184:* 203
Spiegel, Doris *29:* 111
Spiegelman, Art *109:* 227
Spier, Jo *10:* 30
Spier, Peter *3:* 155; *4:* 200; *7:* 61; *11:* 78; *38:* 106; *54:* 120, 121, 122, 123, 124, 125, 126, 127, 128, 129, 130,131, 132, 133, 134
Spilka, Arnold *5:* 120; *6:* 204; *8:* 131
Spires, Ashley *231:* 96
Spirin, Gennady *95:* 196, 197; *113:* 172; *128:* 9; *129:* 49; *134:* 210; *153:* 9; *204:* 143, 144, 145; *220:* 153
Spiro, Ruth *208:* 197
Spivak, I. Howard *8:* 10; *13:* 172
Spohn, David *72:* 233
Spohn, Kate *87:* 195; *147:* 201, 202
Spollen, Christopher J. *12:* 214
Spooner, Malcolm *40:* 142
Spoor, Mike *220:* 92
Spowart, Robin *82:* 228; *92:* 149; *133:* 131; *176:* 163; *177:* 183, 184; *217:* 123, 124
Sprague, Kevin *150:* 60; *196:* 62
Spranger, Nina *201:* 199
Sprattler, Rob *12:* 176
Spring, Bob *5:* 60
Spring, Ira *5:* 60
Springer, Harriet *31:* 92
Spudvilas, Anne *110:* 74; *197:* 192; *199:* 154
Spurll, Barbara *78:* 199; *88:* 141, 142; *99:* 215
Spurrier, Steven *28:* 198
Spuvilas, Anne *85:* 114
Spy
    See Ward, Leslie
Squires, Stuart *127:* 74
St. Aubin, Bruno *179:* 54
St. John, J. Allen *41:* 62
Staake, Bob *209:* 168, 169; *229:* 132
Stabin, Victor *101:* 131; *164:* 158
Stadler, John *62:* 33; *204:* 149
Stadnyk, Greg *212:* 55
Staffan, Alvin E. *11:* 56; *12:* 187
Stahl, Ben *5:* 181; *12:* 91; *49:* 122; *71:* 128; *87:* 206; *112:* 107
Stair, Gobin *35:* 214
Stallwood, Karen *73:* 126
Stamaty, Mark Alan *12:* 215; *230:* 175
Stammen, JoEllen McAllister *113:* 14
Stamp, Jørgen *225:* 184
Stampnick, Ken *51:* 142
Stanbridge, Joanne *150:* 91
Stanley, Diane *3:* 45; *37:* 180; *80:* 217, 219
Stanley, Sanna *145:* 228
Star, Lindsay *219:* 39
Starcke, Helmut *86:* 217
Stark, Ken *197:* 102
Starr, Branka *73:* 25
Stasiak, Krystyna *49:* 181; *64:* 194
Staub, Leslie *103:* 54
Stauffer, Brian *220:* 123
Staunton, Ted *112:* 192
Stawicki, Matt *164:* 250
Stead, Erin E. *232:* 179
Stead, L. *55:* 51, 56
Steadman, Broeck *97:* 185, 186; *99:* 56; *121:* 48; *208:* 190
Steadman, Henry *211:* 130
Steadman, Ralph *32:* 180; *123:* 143, 145
Stearn, Nick *183:* 26
Stearn, Todd *218:* 179
Steckler, June *90:* 178
Steele, Robert Gantt *169:* 174
Steichen, Edward *30:* 79
Steig, William *18:* 275, 276; *70:* 215, 216, 217, 218; *111:* 173, 174, 175, 176, 177
Stein, David Ezra *211:* 168
Stein, Harve *1:* 109
Steinberg, Saul *47:* 193
Steinel, William *23:* 146
Steiner, Charlotte *45:* 196
Steiner, Joan *110:* 219; *199:* 160, 161

Steirnagel, Michael *80:* 56
Stemp, Eric *60:* 184
Stengel, Christopher *229:* 200; *232:* 57
Stephens, Alice Barber *66:* 208, 209
Stephens, Charles H. *YABC 2:* 279
Stephens, Pam *198:* 69
Stephens, Pat *126:* 110; *128:* 101
Stephens, William M. *21:* 165
Stephenson, Kristina *224:* 169
Steptoe, Javaka *151:* 203, 204; *190:* 169; *213:* 163, 164
Steptoe, John *8:* 197; *57:* 9; *63:* 158, 159, 160, 161,163, 164, 165, 166, 167; *96:* 4; *105:* 87
Stern, Simon *15:* 249, 250; *17:* 58; *34:* 192, 193
Sterret, Jane *53:* 27
Stetsios, Debbie *165:* 108, 109
Steven, Kat *158:* 237
Stevens, David *62:* 44
Stevens, Helen *189:* 31; *207:* 83
Stevens, Janet *40:* 126; *57:* 10, 11; *80:* 112; *90:* 221, 222; *109:* 156; *130:* 34; *166:* 202; *176:* 53, 116; *193:* 199, 200, 202; *208:* 127; *212:* 182
Stevens, Mary *11:* 193; *13:* 129; *43:* 95
Stevenson, Harvey *66:* 143; *80:* 201, 221; *153:* 60; *191:* 166; *233:* 154
Stevenson, James *42:* 182, 183; *51:* 163; *66:* 184; *71:* 185, 187, 188; *78:* 262; *87:* 97; *113:* 182, 183,184, 185; *161:* 182, 183
Stevenson, Sucie *92:* 27; *104:* 194, 195; *112:* 168; *160:* 202; *194:* 172, 173; *195:* 166
Stewart, April Blair *75:* 210
Stewart, Arvis *33:* 98; *36:* 69; *60:* 118; *75:* 91; *127:* 4
Stewart, Charles *2:* 205
Stewart, Joel *151:* 205; *211:* 170, 171; *229:* 168
Stieg, William *172:* 58
Stiles, Fran *26:* 85; *78:* 56; *82:* 150
Stillman, Susan *44:* 130; *76:* 83
Stimpson, Tom *49:* 171
Stimson, James *208:* 46
Stinemetz, Morgan *40:* 151
Stinson, Paul *110:* 86
Stirnweis, Shannon *10:* 164
Stites, Joe *86:* 96
Stobbs, William *1:* 48, 49; *3:* 68; *6:* 20; *17:* 117, 217; *24:* 150; *29:* 250; *60:* 179; *87:* 204, 205,206
Stock, Catherine *37:* 55; *65:* 198; *72:* 7; *99:* 225; *114:* 197, 198, 199; *126:* 3; *145:* 161; *161:* 82; *173:* 149; *208:* 210; *214:* 192, 194; *224:* 196, 197
Stockman, Jack *113:* 24
Stoeke, Janet Morgan *90:* 225; *136:* 196; *202:* 182, 183
Stoerrle, Tom *55:* 147
Stolp, Jaap *49:* 98
Stolp, Todd *89:* 195
Stone, David L. *87:* 154
Stone, David *9:* 173
Stone, David K. *4:* 38; *6:* 124; *9:* 180; *43:* 182; *60:* 70
Stone, Helen V. *6:* 209
Stone, Helen *44:* 121, 122, 126
Stone, Kazuko G. *134:* 43
Stone, Kyle M. *202:* 185
Stone, Phoebe *86:* 212; *134:* 213; *162:* 188; *205:* 145
Stone, Steve *166:* 213; *208:* 185; *220:* 57,58; *224:* 124
Stone, Tony *150:* 34, 35
Storms, Patricia *217:* 163
Storrings, Michael *191:* 108; *216:* 217
Stoud, Virginia A. *89:* 31
Stover, Jill *82:* 234
Stower, Adam *217:* 89; *227:* 53
Strachan, Bruce *205:* 146
Stratton, Helen *33:* 151

Stratton-Porter, Gene *15:* 254, 259, 263, 264, 268, 269
Straub, Matt *192:* 176; *229:* 176
Straub, Phillip *197:* 22; *233:* 36
Streano, Vince *20:* 173
Street, Janet Travell *84:* 235
Streeter, Clive *121:* 2
Strickland, Shadra *209:* 179; *233:* 177
Stringer, Lauren *129:* 187; *154:* 172, 173; *161:* 127; *183:* 187, 188; *232:* 153
Strodl, Daniel *47:* 95
Strogart, Alexander *63:* 139
Stromoski, Rick *111:* 179; *124:* 161, 190
Strong, Joseph D., Jr. *YABC 2:* 330
Stroyer, Poul *13:* 221
Strugnell, Ann *27:* 38
Stubbs, William *73:* 196
Stubis, Talivaldis *5:* 182, 183; *10:* 45; *11:* 9; *18:* 304; *20:* 127
Stubley, Trevor *14:* 43; *22:* 219; *23:* 37; *28:* 61; *87:* 26
Stuck, Marion *104:* 44
Stuecklen, Karl W. *8:* 34, 65; *23:* 103
Stull, Betty *11:* 46
Stutzman, Mark *119:* 99
Stutzmann, Laura *73:* 185
Suarez, Maribel *162:* 208; *200:* 202
Suave, Gordon *209:* 66
Suba, Susanne *4:* 202, 203; *14:* 261; *23:* 134; *29:* 222; *32:* 30
Sue, Majella Lue *209:* 182; *212:* 146
Sueling, Barbara *98:* 185
Sueling, Gwenn *98:* 186
Sugarman, Tracy *3:* 76; *8:* 199; *37:* 181, 182
Sugimoto, Yugo *170:* 144; *223:* 137
Sugita, Yutaka *36:* 180, 181
Suh, John *80:* 157
Sullivan, Dorothy *89:* 113
Sullivan, Edmund J. *31:* 86
Sullivan, James F. *19:* 280; *20:* 192
Sully, Tom *104:* 199, 200; *182:* 77
Sumichrast, Jozef *14:* 253; *29:* 168, 213
Sumiko *46:* 57
Summers, Leo *1:* 177; *2:* 273; *13:* 22
Summers, Mark *118:* 144
Summers, Mike *190:* 176
Sutton, Judith *94:* 164
Svarez, Juan *56:* 113
Svendsen, Mark *181:* 176
Svolinsky, Karel *17:* 104
Swain, Carol *172:* 182
Swain, Su Zan Noguchi *21:* 170
Swan, Susan *22:* 220, 221; *37:* 66; *60:* 146; *145:* 205; *181:* 168
Swann, Susan *86:* 55
Swanson, Karl *79:* 65; *89:* 186
Swarner, Kristina *203:* 62; *215:* 184
Swayne, Sam *53:* 143, 145
Swayne, Zoa *53:* 143, 145
Swearingen, Greg *152:* 56; *165:* 135; *173:* 2; *224:* 32; *225:* 188
Sweat, Lynn *25:* 206; *57:* 176; *73:* 184; *168:* 178
Sweet, Darrell K. *60:* 9; *69:* 86; *74:* 15; *75:* 215; *76:* 130, 131; *81:* 96, 122; *82:* 253; *83:* 11; *84:* 14; *85:* 37; *89:* 140; *90:* 6; *91:* 137,139; *95:* 160, 161; *126:* 25; *185:* 175; *195:* 132
Sweet, Darrell K. *1:* 163; *4:* 136; *164:* 175
Sweet, Melissa *71:* 94; *72:* 172; *111:* 82; *139:* 53, 58; *141:* 88; *142:* 231; *155:* 121; *159:* 121, 122; *172:* 185; *188:* 127; *209:* 81; *211:* 174, 175; *218:* 21
Sweet, Ozzie *31:* 149, 151, 152
Sweetland, Robert *12:* 194
Swiatkowska, Gabi *132:* 43; *175:* 139; *180:* 218; *183:* 176
Swope, Martha *43:* 160; *56:* 86, 87, 89
Sylvada, Peter *154:* 174
Sylvester, Natalie G. *22:* 222

Syme, Hugh *232:* 8
Szafran, Gene *24:* 144
Szasz, Susanne *13:* 55, 226; *14:* 48
Szekeres, Cyndy *2:* 218; *5:* 185; *8:* 85; *11:*
    166; *14:* 19; *16:* 57, 159; *26:* 49, 214; *34:*
    205; *60:* 150, 151, 152, 153, 154; *73:* 224;
    74: 218; *131:* 213, 215
Szpura, Beata *81:* 68; *119:* 65; *168:* 201
Szuc, Jeff *220:* 188

T

Taback, Simms *40:* 207; *52:* 120; *57:* 34; *80:*
    241; *104:* 202, 203; *170:* 176, 177; *205:* 183
Taber, Patricia *75:* 124
Tabor, Nancy Maria Grande *89:* 210; *161:* 188
Taddei, Richard *112:* 13, 14
Tadgell, Nicole *150:* 77; *161:* 20; *177:* 186;
    209: 16; *220:* 190, 191
Tadiello, Ed *133:* 200
Tafuri, Nancy *39:* 210; *75:* 199, 200; *92:* 75;
    130: 215, 216, 217
Tailfeathers, Gerald *86:* 85
Tait, Douglas *12:* 220; *74:* 105, 106
Takabayashi, Mari *113:* 112; *130:* 22; *156:* 169
Takahashi, Hideko *136:* 160; *187:* 6; *209:* 152,
    187
Takakjian, Portia *15:* 274
Takashima, Shizuye *13:* 228
Talarczyk, June *4:* 173
Talbott, Hudson *84:* 240; *163:* 100; *212:* 191,
    192, 193
Tallarico, Tony *116:* 197
Tallec, Olivier *218:* 4
Tallon, Robert *2:* 228; *43:* 200, 201, 202, 203,
    204, 205,206, 207, 209
Tamaki, Jillian *201:* 188
Tamas, Szecsko *29:* 135
Tamburine, Jean *12:* 222
Tanaka, Yoko *215:* 187
Tancredi, Sharon *215:* 127
Tandy, H.R. *13:* 69
Tandy, Russell H. *65:* 9; *100:* 30, 131
Tang, Charles *81:* 202; *90:* 192
Tang, Susan *80:* 174; *108:* 158
Tang, You-shan *63:* 100
Tankersley, Paul *69:* 206; *133:* 219
Tannenbaum, Robert *48:* 181
Tanner, Jane *87:* 13; *97:* 37
Tanner, Tim *72:* 192; *84:* 35
Tanobe, Miyuki *23:* 221
Tarabay, Sharif *110:* 149; *113:* 123; *169:* 83
Tarkington, Booth *17:* 224, 225
Tarlow, Phyllis *61:* 198
Tate, Don *159:* 141, 191; *183:* 69; *186:* 120
Tauss, Herbert *95:* 179
Tauss, Marc *117:* 160; *126:* 155; *178:* 221;
    197: 7; *223:* 168
Tavares, Matt *159:* 192, 193; *198:* 188, 189,
    190; *199:* 86
Taylor, Ann *41:* 226
Taylor, Dahl *129:* 157
Taylor, Geoff *93:* 156; *197:* 173, 175; *204:*
    151, 152
Taylor, Isaac *41:* 228
Taylor, Jennifer *226:* 128; *232:* 154
Taylor, Mike *143:* 99, 100
Teague, Mark *83:* 6; *139:* 241; *170:* 180, 181;
    205: 150, 151
Teale, Edwin Way *7:* 196
Teason, James *1:* 14
Teckentrup, Britta *200:* 191, 192
Teeple, Lyn *33:* 147
Tee-Van, Helen Damrosch *10:* 176; *11:* 182
Teevee, Ningeokuluk *223:* 173
Teicher, Dick *50:* 211
Teichman, Mary *77:* 220; *124:* 208; *127:* 22;
    197: 33
Telgemeier, Raina *228:* 180, 181, 182

Temertey, Ludmilla *96:* 232; *104:* 43, 45; *109:*
    244
Tempest, Margaret *3:* 237, 238; *88:* 200
Temple, Frances *85:* 185, 186, 187
Temple, Herbert *45:* 201
Templeton, Owen *11:* 77
ten Cate, Marijke *183:* 193
Tenggren, Gustaf *18:* 277, 278, 279; *19:* 15;
    28: 86; *YABC2:* 145
Tennent, Julie *81:* 105
Tenneson, Joyce *153:* 166
Tenney, Gordon *24:* 204
Tenniel, John *74:* 234, 235; *100:* 89; *YABC 2:*
    99; *153:* 63
Teplin, Scott *231:* 180
Tepper, Matt *116:* 80
Terkel, Ari *103:* 162
Terry, Michael *180:* 209; *233:* 166
Terry, Will *131:* 73; *205:* 155; *223:* 105
Teskey, Donald *71:* 51
Tessler, Manya *200:* 193
Thacher, Mary M. *30:* 72
Thackeray, William Makepeace *23:* 224, 228
Thamer, Katie *42:* 187
Tharlet, Eve *146:* 149
Thelwell, Norman *14:* 201
Theobalds, Prue *40:* 23
Theurer, Marilyn Churchill *39:* 195
Thiesing, Lisa *89:* 134; *95:* 202; *156:* 190;
    159: 195
Thiewes, Sam *133:* 114
Thisdale, François *223:* 55
Thistlethwaite, Miles *12:* 224
Thollander, Earl *11:* 47; *18:* 112; *22:* 224
Thomas, Allan *22:* 13
Thomas, Art *48:* 217
Thomas, Eric *28:* 49
Thomas, Harold *20:* 98
Thomas, Jacqui *125:* 95
Thomas, Jan *197:* 180; *226:* 198
Thomas, Mark *42:* 136
Thomas, Martin *14:* 255
Thomas, Middy *177:* 114; *230:* 63
Thompson, Arthur *34:* 107
Thompson, Carol *85:* 189; *95:* 75; *102:* 86;
    147: 166; *189:* 179, 180, 181; *190:* 84; *207:*
    18
Thompson, Colin *95:* 204
Thompson, Ellen *51:* 88, 151; *60:* 33; *67:* 42;
    77: 148; *78:* 75, 219; *79:* 122, 170; *84:* 219;
    85: 97; *87:* 37; *88:* 192, 194; *89:* 80; *93:* 37;
    98: 59; *132:* 14
Thompson, George W. *22:* 18; *28:* 150; *33:*
    135
Thompson, John *58:* 201; *102:* 226; *124:* 154;
    128: 228; *129:* 157; *150:* 49; *185:* 160; *191:*
    192; *224:* 110
Thompson, Julie *44:* 158
Thompson, Katherine *132:* 146
Thompson, K. Dyble *84:* 6
Thompson, Miles *152:* 77
Thompson, Sharon *74:* 113; *158:* 60; *165:* 87
Thomson, Arline K. *3:* 264
Thomson, Bill *186:* 160
Thomson, Hugh *26:* 88
Thomson, Ross *36:* 179
Thorkelson, Gregg *95:* 183, 184; *98:* 58; *165:*
    30, 31; *225:* 31, 32
Thorn, Lori *189:* 119
Thornberg, Dan *104:* 125
Thornburgh, Rebecca McKillip *143:* 37
Thorne, Diana *25:* 212
Thornhill, Jan *77:* 213
Thorpe, Peter *58:* 109
Thorvall, Kerstin *13:* 235
Threadgall, Colin *77:* 215
Thurber, James *13:* 239, 242, 243, 245, 248,
    249
Thurman, Mark *63:* 173; *168:* 116
Tibbles, Jean-Paul *115:* 200
Tibbles, Paul *45:* 23

Tibo, Gilles *67:* 207; *107:* 199, 201
Tichenor, Tom *14:* 207
Tichnor, Richard *90:* 218
Tiegreen, Alan *36:* 143; *43:* 55, 56, 58; *77:*
    200; *94:* 216, 217; *121:* 54, 59
Tierney, Tom *113:* 198, 200, 201
Tildes, Phyllis Limbacher *210:* 240
Tilley, Debbie *102:* 134; *133:* 226; *137:* 101;
    159: 96; *190:* 211, 212; *213:* 51
Tillman, Nancy *211:* 129, 178
Tillotson, Katherine *224:* 175
Tilney, F.C. *22:* 231
Timbs, Gloria *36:* 90
Timmins, Harry *2:* 171
Timmons, Bonnie *194:* 189
Tinkelman, Murray *12:* 225; *35:* 44
Titherington, Jeanne *39:* 90; *58:* 138; *75:* 79;
    135: 161
Tjader, Ella *209:* 14
Tobin, Nancy *145:* 197
Toddy, Irving *172:* 144
Tokunbo, Dimitrea *181:* 183; *187:* 182, 183;
    226: 209
Tolbert, Jeff *128:* 69
Toledo, Francisco *197:* 182; *198:* 199
Toledo, Natalia *197:* 182
Tolford, Joshua *1:* 221
Tolkien, J.R.R. *2:* 243; *32:* 215
Tolman, Marije *195:* 43
Tolmie, Ken *15:* 292
Tomei, Lorna *47:* 168, 171
Tomes, Jacqueline *2:* 117; *12:* 139
Tomes, Margot *1:* 224; *2:* 120, 121; *16:* 207;
    18: 250; *20:* 7; *25:* 62; *27:* 78, 79; *29:* 81,
    199; *33:* 82; *36:* 186, 187, 188, 189, 190;
    46: 129; *56:* 71; *58:* 183; *70:* 228; *75:* 73,
    75; *80:* 80; *83:* 97; *90:* 205
Tommaso, Rich *200:* 198
Tommorow, Tom *223:* 176
Toner, Raymond John *10:* 179
Tong, Gary *66:* 215
Tongier, Stephen *82:* 32
Tooke, Susan *173:* 162
Toothill, Harry *6:* 54; *7:* 49; *25:* 219; *42:* 192
Toothill, Ilse *6:* 54
Topaz, Ksenia *224:* 94
Topolski, Feliks *44:* 48
Torbert, Floyd James *22:* 226
Torgersen, Don *55:* 157
Torline, Kevin *169:* 171
Tormey, Bertram M. *75:* 3, 4
Torrecilla, Pablo *176:* 207
Torres, Leyla *156:* 199, 201
Torrey, Helen *87:* 41
Torrey, Marjorie *34:* 105
Torrey, Richard *189:* 182; *205:* 24
Toschik, Larry *6:* 102
Totten, Bob *13:* 93
Townsend, Michael *231:* 183
Toy, Julie *128:* 112
Trachok, Cathy *131:* 16; *228:* 10
Tracy, Libba *82:* 24
Trago, Keith *158:* 253
Trail, Lee *55:* 157
Trang, To Ngoc *167:* 180
Trang, Winson *89:* 151
Trapani, Iza *116:* 202; *214:* 203
Travers, Bob *90:* 100; *63:* 145
Treatner, Meryl *95:* 180
Tremain, Ruthven *17:* 238
Tresilian, Stuart *25:* 53; *40:* 212
Trez, Alain *17:* 236
Trezzo, Loretta *86:* 45
Trier, Walter *14:* 96
Trimby, Elisa *47:* 199
Trinkle, Sally *53:* 27
Triplett, Gina *182:* 193; *188:* 100; *198:* 38
Tripp, F.J. *24:* 167
Tripp, Wallace *2:* 48; *7:* 28; *8:* 94; *10:* 54,76;
    11: 92; *31:* 170, 171; *34:* 203; *42:* 57; *60:*
    157; *73:* 182

Trivas, Irene *53:* 4; *54:* 168; *82:* 46, 101
Trnka, Jiri *22:* 151; *43:* 212, 213, 214, 215; *YABC 1:* 30, 31
Trondheim, Lewis *182:* 183
Troughton, Joanna *37:* 186; *48:* 72
Troyer, Johannes *3:* 16; *7:* 18
Trudeau, G.B. *35:* 220, 221, 222; *48:* 119, 123, 126, 127,128, 129, 133; *168:* 189
Trueman, Matthew *165:* 208; *183:* 191; *220:* 61; *222:* 174
Truesdell, Sue *55:* 142; *108:* 219, 220; *212:* 202; *220:* 78
Tryon, Leslie *84:* 7; *139:* 214; *143:* 10; *181:* 10
Tseng, Jean *72:* 195; *94:* 102; *119:* 126; *151:* 106; *173:* 138, 139; *200:* 158
Tseng, Mou-sien *72:* 195; *94:* 102; *119:* 126; *151:* 106; *173:* 138, 139; *200:* 158
Tsinajinie, Andy *2:* 62
Tsinganos, Jim *180:* 142
Tsugami, Kyuzo *18:* 198, 199
Tucker, Ezra *156:* 31
Tuckwell, Jennifer *17:* 205
Tudor, Bethany *7:* 103
Tudor, Tasha *18:* 227; *20:* 185, 186, 187; *36:* 111; *69:* 196, 198; *100:* 44; *YABC 2:* 46, 314; *160:* 234
Tuerk, Hanne *71:* 201
Tugeau, Jeremy *199:* 170; *203:* 96
Tulloch, Maurice *24:* 79
Tunis, Edwin *1:* 218, 219; *28:* 209, 210, 211, 212
Tunnicliffe, C.F. *62:* 176; *177:* 178, 179; 181
Turkle, Brinton *1:* 211, 213; *2:* 249; *3:* 226; *11:* 3; *16:* 209; *20:* 22; *50:* 23; *67:* 50; *68:* 65; *79:* 205, 206, 207; *128:* 47; *YABC 1:* 79
Turnbull, Christopher J. *143:* 99, 100
Turner, Gwenda *59:* 195
Turner, Helen *203:* 154
Turska, Krystyna *12:* 103; *31:* 173, 174, 175; *56:* 32,34; *100:* 66
Tusa, Tricia *72:* 242; *111:* 180, 181; *157:* 165; *164:* 186; *189:* 40; *201:* 9; *207:* 163, 164; *233:* 132
Tusan, Stan *6:* 58; *22:* 236, 237
Tuschman, Richard *219:* 100; *224:* 188; *225:* 175; *231:* 149
Tworkov, Jack *47:* 207
Tyers, Jenny *89:* 220
Tylden-Wright, Jenny *114:* 119
Tyrol, Adelaide Murphy *103:* 27
Tyrrell, Frances *107:* 204
Tzimoulis, Paul *12:* 104

U

Uchida, Yoshiko *1:* 220
Uderzo *47:* 88
Udovic, David *189:* 185; *195:* 201
Ueno, Noriko *59:* 155
Ugliano, Natascia *196:* 186
Ulm, Robert *17:* 238
Ulrich, George *73:* 15; *75:* 136, 139; *99:* 150
Ulriksen, Mark *101:* 58; *182:* 43; *210:* 243
Unada *84:* 67; *227:* 80
See Gliewe, Unada
Underhill, Liz *53:* 159
Underwood, Beck *192:* 36
Underwood, Clarence *40:* 166
Unger, Jim *67:* 208
Ungerer, Tomi *5:* 188; *9:* 40; *18:* 188; *29:* 175; *33:* 221, 222, 223, 225; *71:* 48; *106:* 209, 210, 211, 212
Unwin, Nora S. *3:* 65, 234, 235; *4:* 237; *44:* 173, 174; *YABC 1:* 59; *2:* 301
Unzner, Christa *230:* 186
Upitis, Alvis *145:* 179
Urban, Helle *149:* 243
Urbanovic, Jackie *86:* 86; *189:* 186, 187

Urberuaga, Emilio *219:* 110, 175
U'ren, Andrea *213:* 177; *232:* 175
Uris, Jill *49:* 188, 197
Ursell, Martin *50:* 51
Utpatel, Frank *18:* 114
Utz, Lois *5:* 190

V

Vagin, Vladimir *66:* 10; *142:* 215
Vaillancourt, Francois *107:* 199
Vainio, Pirkko *123:* 157, 158
Valério, Geraldo *180:* 225; *194:* 116
Vallejo, Boris *62:* 130; *72:* 212; *91:* 38; *93:* 61
Van Abbe, S. *16:* 142; *18:* 282; *31:* 90; *YABC 2:* 157, 161
Van Allsburg, Chris *37:* 205, 206; *53:* 161, 162, 163, 165,166, 167, 168, 169, 170, 171; *105:* 215, 216, 217, 218; *156:* 176, 177, 178
Vance, James *65:* 28
Van Der Linde, Henry *99:* 17
van der Meer, Ron *98:* 204, 205
van der Meer, Atie *98:* 204, 205
Vandivert, William *21:* 175
Van Dongen, H.R. *81:* 97
Van Dusen, Chris W. *173:* 169; *228:* 192
Vane, Mitch *210:* 160; *218:* 152
Van Everen, Jay *13:* 160; *YABC 1:* 121
Van Fleet, John *165:* 12, 13
Van Frankenhuyzen, Gijsbert *145:* 230; *149:* 164; *184:* 151; *210:* 248
van Genechten, Guido *165:* 226
van Haeringen, Annemarie *193:* 206
Van Horn, William *43:* 218
van Hout, Mies *195:* 191; *207:* 58
van Kampen, Vlasta *194:* 217
van Lawick, Hugo *62:* 76, 79
Van Lieshout, Maria *201:* 196; *223:* 119
Van Loon, Hendrik Willem *18:* 285, 289, 291
Van Munching, Paul *83:* 85
van Ommen, Sylvia *186:* 192
Van Patter, Bruce *183:* 195
Van Rynbach, Iris *102:* 192
Van Sciver, Ruth *37:* 162
VanSeveren, Joe *63:* 182
Van Stockum, Hilda *5:* 193
Van Vleet, John *213:* 180
Van Wassenhove, Sue *202:* 193
Van Wely, Babs *16:* 50; *79:* 16
Van Wright, Cornelius *72:* 18; *102:* 208; *116:* 107; *152:* 236; *173:* 170, 171; *199:* 185
Van Zyle, Jon *103:* 125; *160:* 181, 182; *176:* 199, 200; *221:* 128; *232:* 125
Vardzigulyants, Ruben *90:* 54
Varga, Judy *29:* 196
Vargo, Kurt *79:* 224
Varley, Susan *61:* 199; *63:* 176, 177; *101:* 148; *134:* 220
Varon, Sara *195:* 208
Vasconcellos, Daniel *80:* 42
Vasiliu, Mircea *2:* 166, 253; *9:* 166; *13:* 58; *68:* 42
Vaughn, Frank *34:* 157
Vavra, Robert *8:* 206
Vawter, Will *17:* 163
Vayas, Diana *71:* 61
Vazquez, Carlos *125:* 184
Veeder, Larry *18:* 4
Velasquez, Eric *45:* 217; *61:* 45; *63:* 110, 111; *88:* 162; *90:* 34, 144; *94:* 213; *107:* 147; *132:* 192; *138:* 213; *159:* 126; *181:* 184; *184:* 96; *191:* 16; *192:* 234; *208:* 37; *214:* 81; *226:* 201, 203, 212
Velasquez, Jose A. *63:* 73
Velez, Walter *71:* 75; *91:* 154; *121:* 181; *168:* 49; *207:* 52
Velthuijs, Max *110:* 228, 229
Vendrell, Carme Sole *42:* 205
Venezia, Mike *54:* 17

Venti, Anthony Bacon *124:* 103; *126:* 26
Venturo, Piero *61:* 194, 195
Ver Beck, Frank *18:* 16, 17
Verkaaik, Ben *110:* 209
Verling, John *71:* 27
Verney, John *14:* 225; *75:* 8
Vernon, Ursula *204:* 157
Verrier, Suzanne *5:* 20; *23:* 212
Verroken, Sarah *223:* 178
Versace, Marie *2:* 255
Verstraete, Randy *108:* 193
Vess, Charles *215:* 201; *233:* 182
Vestal, H.B. *9:* 134; *11:* 101; *27:* 25; *34:* 158
Vestergaard, Hope *190:* 203
Vicatan *59:* 146
Vickrey, Robert *45:* 59, 64
Victor, Joan Berg *30:* 193
Vieceli, Emma *210:* 245
Viereck, Ellen *3:* 242; *14:* 229
Vigna, Judith *15:* 293; *102:* 194, 195, 196, 197
Vila, Laura *207:* 172
Vilato, Gaspar E. *5:* 41
Villeneuve, Anne *230:* 189
Villiard, Paul *51:* 178
Vimnera, A. *23:* 154
Vincent, Eric *34:* 98
Vincent, Felix *41:* 237
Vincent, Gabrielle *121:* 175
Vip *45:* 164
Viskupic, Gary *83:* 48
Vitale, Stefano *109:* 71, 107; *114:* 219, 220; *123:* 106; *138:* 232; *180:* 228, 229; *212:* 38; *225:* 191, 192, 193
Vivas, Julie *51:* 67, 69; *96:* 225; *197:* 190; *199:* 71
Voake, Charlotte *114:* 221, 222; *180:* 232
Vo-Dinh, Mai *16:* 272; *60:* 191
Vogel, Ilse-Margret *14:* 230
Vojnar, Kamil *95:* 31; *114:* 4; *115:* 62; *121:* 90; *124:* 72; *130:* 31; *141:* 81; *146:* 196; *150:* 123; *158:* 5, 6; *158:* 154; *171:* 119, 188; *179:* 15; *180:* 112; *203:* 74; *223:* 30; *229:* 43; *230:* 199; *231:* 53, 121, 122; *233:* 3, 4
Vojtech, Anna *42:* 190; *108:* 222, 223; *150:* 203; *174:* 173; *228:* 21
von Buhler, Cynthia *149:* 237; *162:* 177; *177:* 205; *180:* 77; *185:* 214, 215, 216
von Roehl, Angela *126:* 191
von Schmidt, Eric *8:* 62; *50:* 209, 210
von Schmidt, Harold *30:* 80
Vosburgh, Leonard *1:* 161; *7:* 32; *15:* 295, 296; *23:* 110; *30:* 214; *43:* 181
Voss, Tom *127:* 104
Voter, Thomas W. *19:* 3, 9
Vroman, Tom *10:* 29
Vulliamy, Clara *72:* 65
Vyner, Tim *228:* 198

W

Waber, Bernard *47:* 209, 210, 211, 212, 213, 214; *95:* 215, 216, 217; *156:* 203, 205, 206, 207
Waber, Paulis *231:* 189
Wachenje, Benjamin *194:* 170
Wack, Jeff *95:* 140; *110:* 90
Wagner, John *8:* 200; *52:* 104
Wagner, Ken *2:* 59
Wagner, Michael *211:* 159
Wahman, Wendy *218:* 186
Waide, Jan *29:* 225; *36:* 139
Wainwright, Jerry *14:* 85
Waites, Joan *171:* 2; *226:* 184
Wakeen, Sandra *47:* 97
Wakiyama, Hanako *171:* 96; *192:* 236; *200:* 16
Waldherr, Kris *81:* 186
Waldman, Bruce *15:* 297; *43:* 178

Waldman, Neil *35:* 141; *50:* 163; *51:* 180; *54:* 78; *77:* 112; *79:* 162; *82:* 174; *84:* 5, 56, 106; *94:* 232, 233, 234; *96:* 41; *111:* 139; *113:* 9; *118:* 30; *142:* 220, 223; *203:* 173, 174
Waldrep, Richard *111:* 147; *198:* 202
Waldron, Kevin *230:* 191
Walker, Brian *144:* 128
Walker, Charles *1:* 46; *4:* 59; *5:* 177; *11:* 115; *19:* 45; *34:* 74; *62:* 168; *72:* 218
Walker, Dugald Stewart *15:* 47; *32:* 202; *33:* 112
Walker, Gil *8:* 49; *23:* 132; *34:* 42
Walker, Jeff *55:* 154; *123:* 116
Walker, Jim *10:* 94
Walker, Mort *8:* 213
Walker, Norman *41:* 37; *45:* 58
Walker, Stephen *12:* 229; *21:* 174
Walker, Steve *231:* 119
Wallace, Beverly Dobrin *19:* 259
Wallace, Chad *229:* 198
Wallace, Cly *87:* 93
Wallace, Ian *53:* 176, 177; *56:* 165, 166; *58:* 4; *98:* 4; *101:* 191; *112:* 124; *141:* 197, 198, 199, 200; *151:* 212; *219:* 180, 182
Wallace, John *105:* 228
Wallace, Nancy Elizabeth *141:* 204; *186:* 195, 197, 199; *222:* 191, 192, 193, 194
Wallenta, Adam *123:* 180
Waller, S.E. *24:* 36
Wallner, Alexandra *15:* 120; *156:* 183
Wallner, John C. *9:* 77; *10:* 188; *11:* 28; *14:* 209; *31:* 56, 118; *37:* 64; *51:* 186, 187, 188, 189, 190, 191,192, 193, 194, 195; *52:* 96; *53:* 23, 26; *71:* 99; *73:* 158; *89:* 215; *141:* 9
Wallner, John *162:* 17
Wallower, Lucille *11:* 226
Walotsky, Ron *93:* 87
Walsh, Ellen Stoll *99:* 209; *147:* 219; *194:* 194, 195, 196
Walsh, Rebecca *158:* 193; *217:* 169, 170
Walsh, Vivian *149:* 215; *158:* 227
Walters, Anita *205:* 163
Walters, Audrey *18:* 294
Walther, Tom *31:* 179
Walton, Garry *69:* 149
Walton, Tony *11:* 164; *24:* 209; *153:* 8; *177:* 73
Waltrip, Lela *9:* 195
Waltrip, Mildred *3:* 209; *37:* 211
Waltrip, Rufus *9:* 195
Wan *12:* 76
Wan, Shelly *212:* 131
Wang, Lin *221:* 179
Wang, Shaoli *216:* 220
Wang, Suling *191:* 183; *213:* 194
Warburton, Sarah *154:* 187
Wappers, G. *121:* 40
Ward, Chad Michael *217:* 121
Ward, Fred *52:* 19
Ward, Helen *72:* 244; *144:* 240, 242
Ward, John *42:* 191; *96:* 54; *97:* 110; *123:* 105; *124:* 71; *173:* 66; *221:* 55
Ward, Keith *2:* 107; *132:* 69
Ward, Leslie *34:* 126; *36:* 87
Ward, Lynd *1:* 99, 132, 133, 150; *2:* 108, 158, 196, 259; *18:* 86; *27:* 56; *29:* 79, 187, 253, 255; *36:* 199,200, 201, 202, 203, 204, 205, 206, 207, 209; *43:* 34; *56:* 28; *60:* 116; *100:* 65
Ward, Peter *37:* 116
Waring, Geoff *172:* 84
Warhola, James *92:* 5; *115:* 85, 87; *118:* 174, 175, 177; *176:* 84; *187:* 189, 190; *223:* 102
Warner, Bob *230:* 5
Warner, Ben *159:* 171
Warner, Peter *14:* 87
Warner, Sally *214:* 210
Warnes, Tim *175:* 159; *202:* 188; *216:* 224
Warnick, Elsa *113:* 223
Warren, Betsy *2:* 101

Warren, Jim *85:* 81
Warren, Marion Cray *14:* 215
Warshaw, Jerry *30:* 197, 198; *42:* 165
Wasden, Kevin *102:* 162
Washington, Nevin *20:* 123
Washington, Phyllis *20:* 123
Wasserman, Amy L. *92:* 110; *209:* 95
Waterman, Stan *11:* 76
Watkins-Pitchford, D.J. *6:* 215, 217
Watling, James *67:* 210; *78:* 112; *101:* 81; *117:* 189, 190; *127:* 119, 120
Watson, Aldren A. *2:* 267; *5:* 94; *13:* 71; *19:* 253; *32:* 220; *42:* 193, 194, 195, 196, 197, 198, 199, 200, 201; *YABC 2:* 202
Watson, G. *83:* 162
Watson, Gary *19:* 147; *36:* 68; *41:* 122; *47:* 139
Watson, J.D. *22:* 86
Watson, Jesse Joshua *197:* 124; *199:* 181; *202:* 136
Watson, Karen *11:* 26
Watson, Mary *117:* 193
Watson, Richard Jesse *62:* 188, 189; *211:* 201
Watson, Wendy *5:* 197; *13:* 101; *33:* 116; *46:* 163; *64:* 12; *74:* 242, 243; *91:* 21; *142:* 228; *215:* 79
Watt, Mélanie *136:* 206; *193:* 211
Wattenberg, Jane *174:* 200; *185:* 46; *187:* 108
Watterson, Bill *66:* 223, 225, 226
Watts, Bernadette *4:* 227; *103:* 182, 183; *230:* 193, 194, 195
Watts, James *59:* 197; *74:* 145; *86:* 124
Watts, John *37:* 149
Watts, Leslie Elizabeth *150:* 207; *165:* 106; *209:* 67
Watts, Stan *116:* 205
Weatherby, Mark Alan *77:* 141
Web, Hannah *228:* 215
Webb, Jennifer *110:* 79
Webb, Lanny *142:* 175
Webb, Sophie *135:* 214
Webber, Helen *3:* 141
Webber, Irma E. *14:* 238
Weber, Erik *56:* 19, 20
Weber, Florence *40:* 153
Weber, Jill *127:* 227, 228; *189:* 163; *208:* 157; *209:* 190, 191; *216:* 46
Weber, Roland *61:* 204
Weber, Sam *190:* 227
Weber, William J. *14:* 239
Webster, Jean *17:* 241
Weeks, Sarah *162:* 39
Wegman, William *78:* 243
Wegner, Fritz *14:* 250; *20:* 189; *44:* 165; *86:* 62
Weidenear, Reynold H. *21:* 122
Weigel, Jeff *170:* 193
Weihs, Erika *4:* 21; *15:* 299; *72:* 201; *107:* 207, 208
Weil, Lisl *7:* 203; *10:* 58; *21:* 95; *22:* 188,217; *33:* 193
Weiman, Jon *50:* 162, 165; *52:* 103; *54:* 78, 79, 81; *78:* 80; *82:* 107; *93:* 82; *97:* 69; *105:* 179; *193:* 65
Weiner, Greg *215:* 21
Weiner, Sandra *14:* 240
Weiner, Scott *55:* 27
Weinhaus, Karen Ann *53:* 90; *71:* 50; *86:* 124
Weinman, Brad *197:* 20; *233:* 35
Weinstock, Robert *204:* 165, 166
Weisgard, Leonard *1:* 65; *2:* 191, 197, 204, 264, 265; *5:* 108; *21:* 42; *30:* 200, 201, 203, 204; *41:* 47; *44:* 125; *53:* 25; *85:* 196, 198, 200, 201; *100:* 139,207; *YABC 2:* 13
Weisman, David *173:* 47
Weiss, Ellen *44:* 202
Weiss, Emil *1:* 168; *7:* 60
Weiss, Harvey *1:* 145, 223; *27:* 224, 227; *68:* 214; *76:* 245, 246, 247
Weiss, Nicki *33:* 229
Weissman, Bari *49:* 72; *90:* 125; *139:* 142

Weitzman, David L. *172:* 199
Welch, Sheila Kelly *130:* 221
Welkes, Allen *68:* 218
Wellington, Monica *99:* 223; *157:* 259, 260, 261; *222:* 197, 198, 199, 200
Welliver, Norma *76:* 94
Wellner, Fred *127:* 53
Wells, Frances *1:* 183
Wells, H.G. *20:* 194, 200
Wells, Haru *53:* 120, 121
Wells, Robert E. *184:* 208
Wells, Rosemary *6:* 49; *18:* 297; *60:* 32; *66:* 203; *69:* 215, 216; *114:* 227; *118:* 149, 150; *156:* 188, 189, 190, 191; *207:* 180, 181, 182, 183
Wells, Rufus III *56:* 111, 113
Wells, Susan *22:* 43
Wendelin, Rudolph *23:* 234
Wengenroth, Stow *37:* 47
Weninger, Brigitte *189:* 192, 194
Werenskiold, Erik *15:* 6; *62:* 17
Werner, Honi *24:* 110; *33:* 41; *88:* 122
Werth, Kurt *7:* 122; *14:* 157; *20:* 214; *39:* 128
Wesson,
West, Harry A. *124:* 38; *227:* 16
Westcott, Nadine Bernard *68:* 46; *84:* 49; *86:* 133; *106:* 199; *111:* 78; *113:* 111; *130:* 224; *139:* 54; *158:* 256; *194:* 199
Westerberg, Christine *29:* 226
Westerduin, Anne *105:* 229
Westerman, Johanna *162:* 206
Weston, Martha *29:* 116; *30:* 213; *33:* 85, 100; *53:* 181, 182, 183, 184; *77:* 95; *80:* 152; *119:* 196,197, 198, 199; *127:* 189; *133:* 196; *209:* 199
Wetherbee, Margaret *5:* 3
Wexler, Jerome *49:* 73; *150:* 129
Whalley, Peter *50:* 49
Whamond, Dave *222:* 203
Whatley, Bruce *186:* 93, 95; *207:* 127; *213:* 183, 184
Wheatley, Arabelle *11:* 231; *16:* 276
Wheeler, Cindy *49:* 205
Wheeler, Dora *44:* 179
Wheelright, Rowland *15:* 81; *YABC 2:* 286
Whelan, Michael *56:* 108; *70:* 27, 29, 67, 68, 148; *74:* 18; *84:* 14; *91:* 195, 196; *95:* 147; *98:* 150, 151; *106:* 157; *113:* 218, 220; *116:* 99, 100
Whelan, Patrick *135:* 145
Whistler, Rex *16:* 75; *30:* 207, 208
White, Beth *216:* 139
White, Craig *110:* 130; *119:* 193; *130:* 33; *179:* 31
White, David Omar *5:* 56; *18:* 6
White, Joan *83:* 225
White, Lee *221:* 176; *223:* 188, 189, 190
White, Martin *51:* 197; *85:* 127
Whitear *32:* 26
Whitehead, Beck *86:* 171
Whitehead, Jenny *221:* 16
Whitehead, S.B. *154:* 132
Whithorne, H.S. *7:* 49
Whitman, Candace *208:* 208
Whitney, George Gillett *3:* 24
Whitney, Jean *99:* 53
Whitson, Paul *102:* 161
Whittam, Geoffrey *30:* 191
Whyte, Mary *96:* 127; *232:* 39
Wiberg, Harald *38:* 127; *93:* 215
Wick, Walter *77:* 128
Wickstrom, Sylvie *106:* 87; *169:* 180; *214:* 110
Wickstrom, Thor *200:* 205
Widener, Terry *105:* 230; *106:* 7; *163:* 23; *200:* 17; *209:* 195; *231:* 12
Wiese, Kurt *3:* 255; *4:* 206; *14:* 17; *17:* 18, 19; *19:* 47; *24:* 152; *25:* 212; *32:* 184; *36:* 211,213, 214, 215, 216, 217, 218; *45:* 161; *100:* 92

Wiesner, David *33:* 47; *51:* 106; *57:* 67; *58:* 55; *64:* 78, 79, 81; *69:* 233; *72:* 247, 248, 249, 251,252, 253, 254; *83:* 134; *104:* 31; *117:* 197, 199, 200, 202; *139:* 223, 224; *151:* 51; *181:* 189, 190
Wiesner, William *4:* 100; *5:* 200, 201; *14:* 262
Wight, Eric *218:* 190; *232:* 195
Wiggins, George *6:* 133
Wijngaard, Juan *111:* 36; *114:* 124; *227:* 136; *230:* 202
Wikkelsoe, Otto *45:* 25, 26
Wikland, Ilon *5:* 113; *8:* 150; *38:* 124, 125, 130; *127:* 162
Wikler, Madeline *114:* 233
Wilbur, C. Keith, M.D. *27:* 228
Wilburn, Kathy *53:* 102; *68:* 234
Wilcox, Cathy *105:* 123
Wilcox, J.A.J. *34:* 122
Wilcox, Lydia *207:* 187
Wilcox, R. Turner *36:* 219
Wild, Jocelyn *46:* 220, 221, 222; *80:* 117
Wilde, George *7:* 139
Wildish, Lee *231:* 34, 193
Wildsmith, Brian *16:* 281, 282; *18:* 170, 171; *66:* 25; *69:* 224, 225, 227; *77:* 103; *83:* 218; *124:* 214,217, 219
Wildsmith, Mike *140:* 229
Wilhelm, Hans *58:* 189, 191; *73:* 157; *77:* 127; *135:* 229, 230, 233, 234; *196:* 209
Wilkin, Eloise *36:* 173; *49:* 208, 209, 210
Wilkinson, Barry *50:* 213
Wilkinson, Gerald *3:* 40
Wilkon, Jozef *31:* 183, 184; *71:* 206, 207, 209; *133:* 222
Wilks, Mike *34:* 24; *44:* 203; *224:* 193
Willems, Mo *154:* 245, 246, 247; *180:* 236, 237, 239; *228:* 204, 208
Willey, Bee *103:* 129; *139:* 159; *173:* 115
Willhoite, Michael A. *71:* 214
William, Maria *168:* 51
Williams, Berkeley, Jr. *64:* 75
Williams, Ferelith Eccles *22:* 238
Williams, Garth *1:* 197; *2:* 49, 270; *4:* 205; *15:* 198, 302, 304, 307; *16:* 34; *18:* 283, 298, 299, 300, 301; *29:* 177, 178, 179, 232, 233, 241, 242, 243, 244, 245, 248; *40:* 106; *66:* 229, 230, 231, 233, 234; *71:* 192; *73:* 218, 219, 220; *78:* 261; *100:* 251, 252, 255; *136:* 117; *YABC 2:* 15, 16, 19
Williams, J. Scott *48:* 28
Williams, Jennifer *102:* 201
Williams, Jenny *60:* 202; *81:* 21; *88:* 71
Williams, Kent *180:* 18
Williams, Kit *44:* 206, 207, 208, 209, 211, 212
Williams, Marcia *97:* 214; *159:* 208, 209
Williams, Maureen *12:* 238
Williams, Patrick *14:* 218
Williams, Richard *44:* 93; *72:* 229; *74:* 133; *78:* 155, 237; *91:* 178; *110:* 212; *136:* 201, 202, 203; *152:* 115
Williams, Sam *124:* 222; *153:* 11; *177:* 201, 202; *180:* 34; *212:* 49; *232:* 155
Williams, Sophy *135:* 236
Williams, Vera B. *53:* 186, 187, 188, 189; *102:* 201, 202, 203; *210:* 65
Williamson, Alex *177:* 180; *205:* 50
Williamson, Mel *60:* 9
Willingham, Fred *104:* 206; *154:* 157
Willis, Adam *181:* 75; *209:* 11
Willmore, J.T. *54:* 113, 114
Wilsdorf, Anne *180:* 122; *189:* 124; *191:* 195
Wilson, Anne *160:* 114; *224:* 199, 200
Wilson, Charles Banks *17:* 92; *43:* 73
Wilson, Connie *113:* 179
Wilson, Dagmar *10:* 47
Wilson, Dawn *67:* 161; *81:* 120; *113:* 158
Wilson, Edward A. *6:* 24; *16:* 149; *20:* 220, 221; *22:* 87; *26:* 67; *38:* 212, 214, 215, 216, 217
Wilson, Forrest *27:* 231
Wilson, Gahan *35:* 234; *41:* 136

Wilson, George *76:* 87
Wilson, Helen Miranda *140:* 61
Wilson, Jack *17:* 139
Wilson, Janet *77:* 154; *96:* 114; *99:* 219, 220; *153:* 64 *106:* 122; *130:* 210; *145:* 178; *173:* 64
Wilson, John *22:* 240
Wilson, Maurice *46:* 224
Wilson, Patten *35:* 61
Wilson, Peggy *15:* 4; *84:* 20
Wilson, Phil *181:* 29
Wilson, Rowland B. *30:* 170
Wilson, Sarah *50:* 215
Wilson, Tom *33:* 232
Wilson, W.N. *22:* 26
Wilson-Max, Ken *170:* 196; *180:* 181
Wilton, Nicholas *103:* 52; *183:* 111
Wilwerding, Walter J. *9:* 202
Wimmer, Mike *63:* 6; *70:* 121; *75:* 186; *76:* 21,22, 23; *91:* 114; *97:* 45, 68; *98:* 28; *107:* 130; *146:* 21; *149:* 47; *173:* 126; *193:* 21, 25; *194:* 204, 205
Winborn, Marsha *78:* 34; *99:* 70; *192:* 20
Winch, John *165:* 233
Winchester, Linda *13:* 231
Wind, Betty *28:* 158
Windham, Kathryn Tucker *14:* 260
Windham, Sophie *212:* 212
Winfield, Alison *115:* 78; *214:* 121
Winfield, Wayne *72:* 23
Wing, Gary *64:* 147
Wing, Ron *50:* 85
Wingerter, Linda S. *132:* 199; *174:* 181; *200:* 196
Winick, Judd *124:* 227, 228, 229
Winn-Lederer, Ilene *202:* 91
Winnick, Karen B. *211:* 207
Winslow, Will *21:* 124
Winstead, Rosie *180:* 243
Winsten, Melanie Willa *41:* 41
Winter, Jeanette *151:* 240, 241, 242; *184:* 215, 217, 218, 219
Winter, Milo *15:* 97; *19:* 221; *21:* 181, 203, 204, 205; *64:* 19; *YABC 2:* 144
Winter, Paula *48:* 227
Winter, Susan *163:* 177; *182:* 201; *226:* 173
Winters, Greg *70:* 117
Winters, Nina *62:* 194
Wise, Louis *13:* 68
Wiseman, Ann *31:* 187
Wiseman, B. *4:* 233
Wishnefsky, Phillip *3:* 14
Wiskur, Darrell *5:* 72; *10:* 50; *18:* 246
Wisniewski, David *95:* 220, 221
Wisniewski, Robert *95:* 10; *119:* 192
Withee, Maureen *225:* 42
Witschonke, Alan *153:* 149, 150
Witt, Dick *80:* 244
Wittmann, Patrick *162:* 204
Wittman, Sally *30:* 219
Wittner, Dale *99:* 43
Wittwer, Hala *158:* 267; *195:* 80
Woehr, Lois *12:* 5
Wohlberg, Meg *12:* 100; *14:* 197; *41:* 255
Wohnoutka, Mike *137:* 68; *190:* 199; *195:* 218; *205:* 132; *221:* 6; *230:* 206, 207
Wojtowycz, David *167:* 168
Woldin, Beth Weiner *34:* 211
Wolf, Elizabeth *133:* 151; *208:* 175
Wolf, J. *16:* 91
Wolf, Janet *78:* 254
Wolf, Linda *33:* 163
Wolfe, Corey *72:* 213
Wolfe, Frances *216:* 227
Wolfe, Gillian *199:* 193
Wolff, Ashley *50:* 217; *81:* 216; *156:* 216, 217; *170:* 57; *174:* 174; *184:* 72; *203:* 181, 182, 183, 184
Wolff, Glenn *178:* 230
Wolff, Jason *213:* 186
Wolfsgruber, Linda *166:* 61

Wondriska, William *6:* 220
Wong, Janet S. *98:* 225; *152:* 43
Wong, Ken *224:* 23
Wong, Nicole *174:* 13; *214:* 216; *215:* 25
Wonsetler, John C. *5:* 168
Wood, Audrey *50:* 221, 222, 223; *81:* 219, 221; *198:* 206
Wood, Don *50:* 220, 225, 226, 228, 229; *81:* 218, 220; *139:* 239, 240
Wood, Grant *19:* 198
Wood, Heather *133:* 108
Wood, Ivor *58:* 17
Wood, Jakki *211:* 209
Wood, Muriel *36:* 119; *77:* 167; *171:* 55; *187:* 46
Wood, Myron *6:* 220
Wood, Owen *18:* 187; *64:* 202, 204, 205, 206, 208, 210
Wood, Rob *193:* 48
Wood, Ruth *8:* 11
Woodbridge, Curtis *133:* 138; *204:* 113
Wooding, Sharon L. *66:* 237
Woodruff, Liza *132:* 239; *182:* 46, 204
Woodruff, Thomas *171:* 73
Woods, John, Jr. *109:* 142
Woods, Maria *227:* 69
Woodson, Jack *10:* 201
Woodson, Jacqueline *94:* 242
Woodward, Alice *26:* 89; *36:* 81
Wool, David *26:* 27
Wooley, Janet *112:* 75; *227:* 74
Woolman, Steven *106:* 47; *163:* 73
Wooten, Vernon *23:* 70; *51:* 170
Worboys, Evelyn *1:* 166, 167
Word, Reagan *103:* 204
Wormell, Christopher *154:* 251; *202:* 206
Worth, Jo *34:* 143
Worth, Wendy *4:* 133
Wosmek, Frances *29:* 251
Wrenn, Charles L. *38:* 96; *YABC 1:* 20, 21
Wright, Barbara Mullarney *98:* 161
Wright, Cliff *168:* 203
Wright, Dare *21:* 206
Wright-Frierson, Virginia *58:* 194; *110:* 246
Wright, George *YABC 1:* 268
Wright, Joseph *30:* 160
Wronker, Lili Cassel *3:* 247; *10:* 204; *21:* 10
Wu, Donald *200:* 18
Wummer, Amy *154:* 181; *168:* 150; *176:* 85; *201:* 202, 203; *218:* 154
Wyant, Alexander Helwig *110:* 19
Wyatt, David *97:* 9; *101:* 44; *114:* 194; *140:* 20; *167:* 13; *188:* 48; *227:* 60
Wyatt, Stanley *46:* 210
Wyeth, Andrew *13:* 40; *YABC 1:* 133, 134
Wyeth, Jamie *41:* 257
Wyeth, N.C. *13:* 41; *17:* 252, 253, 254, 255, 256, 257, 258, 259, 264, 265, 266, 267, 268; *18:* 181; *19:* 80, 191, 200; *21:* 57, 183; *22:* 91; *23:* 152; *24:* 28, 99; *35:* 61; *41:* 65; *100:* 206; *YABC1:* 133, 223; *2:* 53, 75, 171, 187, 317
Wyman, Cherie R. *91:* 42
Wynne, Patricia J. *210:* 260; *223:* 184

X

Xuan, YongSheng *119:* 202, 207, 208; *140:* 36; *187:* 21; *226:* 221, 227, 230, 232, 233

Y

Yaccarino, Dan *141:* 208, 209; *147:* 171; *192:* 244, 245; *207:* 168
Yakovetic, Joe *59:* 202; *75:* 85
Yalowitz, Paul *93:* 33; *211:* 92

Yamaguchi, Marianne *85:* 118
Yamasaki, James *167:* 93
Yang, Belle *170:* 198
Yang, Jay *1:* 8; *12:* 239
Yap, Weda *6:* 176
Yaroslava
  See Mills, Yaroslava Surmach
Yashima, Taro *14:* 84
Yates, John *74:* 249, 250
Yates, Kelly *208:* 214
Yayo *178:* 88; *226:* 235
Yeatts, Tabatha *215:* 210
Yee, Cora *166:* 233
Yee, Wong Herbert *115:* 216, 217; *172:* 204, 205; *194:* 59
Yelchin, Eugene *204:* 4; *232:* 198
Yeo, Brad *135:* 121; *192:* 106
Yerxa, Leo *181:* 195
Yezerski, Thomas F. *162:* 29
Ylla
  See Koffler, Camilla
Yohn, F.C. *23:* 128; *YABC 1:* 269
Yoo, Taeeun *191:* 198
Yorinks, Adrienne *144:* 248; *200:* 214
Yorke, David *80:* 178
Yoshida, Toshi *77:* 231
Yoshikawa, Sachiko *168:* 104; *177:* 28; *181:* 196, 197; *225:* 115
Youll, Paul *91:* 218
Youll, Stephen *92:* 227; *118:* 136, 137; *164:* 248; *202:* 92
Young, Amy L. *185:* 218; *190:* 46
Young, Cybéle *167:* 9
Young, Ed *7:* 205; *10:* 206; *40:* 124; *63:* 142; *74:* 250, 251, 252, 253; *75:* 227; *81:* 159; *83:* 98; *94:* 154; *115:* 160; *137:* 162; *YABC 2:* 242; *173:* 174, 175, 176; *205:* 29; *212:* 82; *221:* 72
Young, Mary O'Keefe *77:* 95; *80:* 247; *134:* 214; *140:* 213; *211:* 223, 225
Young, Ned *233:* 187
Young, Noela *8:* 221; *89:* 231; *97:* 195; *230:* 145, 146

Young, Paul *190:* 222; *225:* 38
Young, Selina *153:* 12; *201:* 204, 205
Yuen, Sammy *223:* 46
Yum, Hyewon *211:* 228
Yun, Cheng Mung *60:* 143
Yung, Jennifer *220:* 136

Z

Zacharow, Christopher *88:* 98
Zacks, Lewis *10:* 161
Zadig *50:* 58
Zaffo, George *42:* 208
Zagwyn, Deborah Turney *138:* 227
Zahares, Wade *193:* 219
Zaid, Barry *50:* 127; *51:* 201
Zaidenberg, Arthur *34:* 218, 219, 220
Zahedi, Morteza *232:* 2
Zalben, Jane Breskin *7:* 211; *79:* 230, 231, 233; *170:* 202
Zallinger, Jean *4:* 192; *8:* 8, 129; *14:* 273; *68:* 36; *80:* 254; *115:* 219, 220, 222
Zallinger, Rudolph F. *3:* 245
Zakanitch, Robert Rahway *231:* 195
Zakrajsek, Molly *177:* 146
Zappa, Ahmet *180:* 250
Zebot, George *83:* 214
Zecca, Katherine *207:* 195
Zeck, Gerry *40:* 232
Zeff, Joe *181:* 98; *221:* 101
Zeifert, Harriet *154:* 265, 267
Zeiring, Bob *42:* 130
Zeldich, Arieh *49:* 124; *62:* 120
Zeldis, Malcah *86:* 239; *94:* 198; *146:* 265, 266
Zelinsky, Paul O. *14:* 269; *43:* 56; *49:* 218-223; *53:* 111; *68:* 195; *102:* 219, 222, 221, 222; *154:* 255, 256, 257; *171:* 141; *185:* 96
Zelvin, Diana *72:* 190; *76:* 101; *93:* 207
Zemach, Kaethe *149:* 250

Zemach, Margot *3:* 270; *8:* 201; *21:* 210, 211; *27:* 204, 205, 210; *28:* 185; *49:* 22, 183, 224; *53:* 151; *56:* 146; *70:* 245, 246; *92:* 74
Zeman, Ludmila *153* 212
Zemsky, Jessica *10:* 62
Zepelinsky, Paul *35:* 93
Zerbetz, Evon *127:* 34; *158:* 109
Zezejl, Daniel *197:* 74
Zhang, Ange *101:* 190; *172:* 41
Zhang, Son Nang *163:* 113; *170:* 206
Ziegler, Jack *84:* 134
Zimdars, Berta *129:* 155
Zimet, Jay *147:* 94; *152:* 74; *196:* 75
Zimic, Tricia *72:* 95
Zimmer, Dirk *38:* 195; *49:* 71; *56:* 151; *65:* 214; *84:* 159; *89:* 26; *147:* 224
Zimmer, Tracie Vaughn *169:* 183
Zimmerman, Andrea *192:* 49, 50
Zimmermann, H. Werner *101:* 223; *112:* 197
Zimnik, Reiner *36:* 224
Zingone, Robin *180:* 134
Zinkeisen, Anna *13:* 106
Zinn, David *97:* 97
Zoellick, Scott *33:* 231
Zollars, Jaime *190:* 190
Zonia, Dhimitri *20:* 234, 235
Zorn, Peter A., Jr. *142:* 157
Zudeck, Darryl *58:* 129; *63:* 98; *80:* 52
Zug, Mark *88:* 131; *204:* 169
Zulewski, Tim *164:* 95; *232:* 59
Zuma *99:* 36
Zvorykin, Boris *61:* 155
Zweifel, Francis *14:* 274; *28:* 187
Zwerger, Lisbeth *54:* 176, 178; *66:* 246, 247, 248; *130:* 230, 231, 232, 233; *181:* 92; *194:* 224, 225, 226
Zwinger, Herman H. *46:* 227
Zwolak, Paul *67:* 69, 71, 73, 74

Author Index

The following index gives the number of the volume in which an author's biographical sketch, Autobiography Feature, Brief Entry, or Obituary appears.

This index includes references to all entries in the following series, which are also published by The Gale Group.

YABC—*Yesterday's Authors of Books for Children: Facts and Pictures about Authors and Illustrators of Books for Young People from Early Times to 1960*
CLR—*Children's Literature Review: Excerpts from Reviews, Criticism, and Commentary on Books for Children*
SAAS—*Something about the Author Autobiography Series*

A

Aardema, Verna 1911-2000 .... *107*
  Obituary *119*
  Earlier sketches in SATA *4, 68*
  See also CLR *17*
  See also SAAS *8*
Aaron, Chester 1923- *216*
  Autobiography Feature *216*
  Earlier sketches in SATA *9, 74*
  See also SAAS *12*
Aaseng, Nate
  See Aaseng, Nathan
Aaseng, Nathan 1953- *172*
  Brief entry *38*
  Earlier sketches in SATA *51, 88*
  See also CLR *54*
  See also SAAS *12*
Abadzis, Nick 1965- *193*
Abalos, Rafael 1956-
  See Abalos, Rafael
Abalos, Rafael 1956- *197*
Abbas, Jailan 1952- *91*
Abbey, Lynn
  See Abbey, Marilyn Lorraine
Abbey, Marilyn Lorraine 1948- *156*
Abbott, Alice
  See Borland, Kathryn Kilby
  and Speicher, Helen Ross S(mith)
Abbott, Jacob 1803-1879 .... *22*
Abbott, Manager Henry
  See Stratemeyer, Edward L.
Abbott, R(obert) Tucker 1919-1995 .... *61*
  Obituary *87*
Abbott, Sarah
  See Zolotow, Charlotte
Abbott, Tony 1952- *205*
  Earlier sketch in SATA *159*
Abdelsayed, Cindy 1962- *123*
Abdul, Raoul 1929- *12*
Abeele, Veronique van den *196*
Abel, Raymond 1911- *12*
Abell, Kathleen 1938- *9*
Abelove, Joan *110*
Abels, Harriette S(heffer) 1926- *50*
Abercrombie, Barbara 1939- *182*
  Earlier sketch in SATA *16*
Abercrombie, Barbara Mattes
  See Abercrombie, Barbara

Abercrombie, Lynn
  See Sorrells, Walter
Abernethy, Robert G(ordon) 1927- *5*
Abisch, Roslyn Kroop 1927- *9*
Abisch, Roz
  See Abisch, Roslyn Kroop
Ablow, Gail 1962- *198*
Abodaher, David J. (Naiph) 1919- *17*
Abolafia, Yossi 1944-
  See Abulafia, Yossi
Abolivier, Aurelie *219*
Abouzeid, Chris *175*
Abrahall, Clare Hoskyns
  See Hoskyns-Abrahall, Clare (Constance Drury)
Abrahams, Hilary (Ruth) 1938- *29*
Abrahams, Peter 1947- *194*
Abrahams, Robert David 1905-1998 .... *4*
Abramovitz, Anita (Zeltner Brooks) 1914- *5*
Abrams, Joy 1941- *16*
Abrams, Lawrence F. *58*
  Brief entry *47*
Abrashkin, Raymond 1911-1960 .... *50*
Abulafia, Yossi 1944- *177*
  Brief entry *46*
  Earlier sketch in SATA *60*
Acampora, Paul *175*
Accardo, Anthony *191*
Acer, David *206*
Achebe, Albert Chinualumogu
  See Achebe, Chinua
Achebe, Chinua 1930- *40*
  Brief entry *38*
  Earlier sketch in SATA *38*
  See also CLR *156*
Acheson, Alison 1964- *222*
Ackerman, Diane 1948- *102*
Ackerman, Eugene (Francis) 1888-1974 ...... *10*
Ackerman, Karen 1951- *126*
Ackerman, Susan Yoder 1945- *92*
Ackison, Wendy Wassink 1956- *103*
Ackley, Peggy Jo 1955- *58*
Ackroyd, Peter 1949- *153*
Acorn, John (Harrison) 1958- *79*
Acredolo, Linda (Potter) 1947- *159*
Acs, Laszlo (Bela) 1931- *42*
  Brief entry *32*
Acuff, Selma Boyd 1924- *45*

Ada, Alma Flor 1938- *222*
  Autobiography Feature *222*
  Earlier sketches in SATA *43, 84, 143, 181*
  See also CLR *62*
Adair, Gilbert 1944- *98*
Adair, Ian 1942- *53*
Adair, Margaret Weeks (?)-1971 .... *10*
Adam, Cornel
  See Lengyel, Cornel Adam
Adam, Mark
  See Alexander, Marc
Adam, Paul 1958- *231*
Adam, Robert 1948- *93*
Adams, Adrienne 1906- *90*
  Earlier sketch in SATA *8*
  See also CLR *73*
Adams, Andy 1859-1935
  See YABC *1*
Adams, Barbara Johnston 1943- *60*
Adams, Bruin
  See Ellis, Edward S.
Adams, Captain Bruin
  See Ellis, Edward S.
Adams, Captain J. F. C.
  See Ellis, Edward S.
Adams, Dale
  See Quinn, Elisabeth
Adams, Daniel
  See Nicole, Christopher
Adams, Debra
  See Speregen, Devra Newberger
Adams, Diane 1960- *217*
Adams, Douglas 1952-2001 .... *116*
  Obituary *128*
Adams, Douglas Noel
  See Adams, Douglas
Adams, Edith
  See Shine, Deborah
Adams, Florence 1932- *61*
Adams, Georgie 1945- *216*
Adams, Harriet S(tratemeyer) 1892(?)-1982 .. *1*
  Obituary *29*
Adams, Harrison
  See Rathborne, St. George (Henry)
  and Stratemeyer, Edward L.
Adams, Hazard 1926- *6*
Adams, Hazard Simeon
  See Adams, Hazard
Adams, John Anthony 1944- *67*

Adams, Kathryn 224
Adams, Laurie 1941- 33
Adams, Lowell
　See Joseph, James (Herz)
Adams, Nicholas
　See Pine, Nicholas
Adams, Nicholas
　See Smith, Sherwood
Adams, Nicholas
　See Doyle, Debra
　and Macdonald, James D.
Adams, Pam 1919- 112
Adams, Pamela
　See Adams, Pam
Adams, Richard 1920- 69
　Earlier sketch in SATA 7
　See also CLR 121
Adams, Richard George
　See Adams, Richard
Adams, Ruth Joyce 14
Adams, S.J.
　See Selzer, Adam
Adams, Tricia
　See Kite, Pat
Adams, William Taylor 1822-1897 28
Adam Smith, Janet (Buchanan) 1905-1999 .. 63
Adamson, Gareth 1925-1982(?) 46
　Obituary 30
Adamson, George 1906-1989
　Obituary 63
Adamson, George (Worsley) 1913-2005 30
Adamson, Graham
　See Groom, Arthur William
Adamson, Joy(-Friederike Victoria)
　1910-1980 11
　Obituary 22
Adamson, Wendy Writson 1942- 22
Addasi, Maha 1968- 205
Addison, Kenneth 1949(?)-2005 187
Addison, Kenneth L.
　See Addison, Kenneth
Addona, Angelo F. 1925- 14
Addy, Sean 1976- 222
Addy, Sharon Hart 1943- 192
　Earlier sketch in SATA 108
Addy, Ted
　See Winterbotham, R(ussell) R(obert)
Adelberg, Doris
　See Orgel, Doris
Adelson, Leone 1908- 11
Adinolfi, JoAnn 176
Adkins, Jan 1944- 210
　Autobiography Feature 210
　Earlier sketches in SATA 8, 69, 144
　See also CLR 77
　See also SAAS 19
Adl, Shirin 1975- 225
Adler, C. S. 1932- 126
　Earlier sketches in SATA 26, 63, 102
　See also CLR 78
　See also SAAS 15
Adler, Carole Schwerdtfeger
　See Adler, C. S.
Adler, David A. 1947- 231
　Earlier sketches in SATA 14, 70, 106, 151,
　178
　See also CLR 108
Adler, Emily 230
Adler, Irene
　See Penzler, Otto
　and Storr, Catherine (Cole)
Adler, Irving 1913- 29
　Autobiography Feature 164
　Earlier sketch in SATA 1
　See also CLR 27
　See also SAAS 15
Adler, Larry 1939- 36
Adler, Peggy 22
Adler, Ruth 1915-1968 1
Adlerman, Daniel (Ezra) 1963- 163
　Earlier sketch in SATA 96

Adlerman, Kim
　See Adlerman, Kimberly M(arie)
Adlerman, Kimberly M(arie) 1964- 163
　Earlier sketch in SATA 96
Adoff, Arnold 1935- 96
　Earlier sketches in SATA 5, 57
　See also CLR 7
　See also SAAS 15
Adoff, Jaime 163
Adoff, Jaime Levi
　See Adoff, Jaime
Adorjan, Carol (Madden) 1934- 71
　Earlier sketch in SATA 10
Adrian, Frances
　See Polland, Madeleine A(ngela Cahill)
Adrian, Mary
　See Jorgensen, Mary Venn
Adshead, Gladys L(ucy) 1896-1985 3
Aesop 620(?)B.C.-560(?)B.C. 64
　See also CLR 14
Aesop, Abraham
　See Newbery, John
Affabee, Eric
　See Stine, R.L.
Agapida, Fray Antonio
　See Irving, Washington
Agard, John 1949- 223
　Earlier sketch in SATA 138
Agard, Nadema 1948- 18
Agarwal, Deepa 1947- 141
Agee, Jon 1960- 196
　Earlier sketches in SATA 116, 157
Agell, Charlotte 1959- 214
　Earlier sketches in SATA 99, 150
Agent Orange
　See Moseley, James W(illett)
Aghill, Gordon
　See Garrett, Randall
　and Silverberg, Robert
Agle, Nan Hayden 1905- 3
　See also SAAS 10
Agnew, Edith J(osephine) 1897-1988 11
Agnew, Lincoln 222
Agonito, Joseph 177
Agonito, Rosemary 1937- 177
Aguilar, David 214
Aguilar, David A.
　See Aguilar, David
Ahern, Margaret McCrohan 1921- 10
Ahl, Anna Maria 1926- 32
Ahlberg, Allan 1938- 214
　Brief entry 35
　Earlier sketches in SATA 68, 120, 165
　See also CLR 18
Ahlberg, Janet 1944-1994 120
　Brief entry 32
　Obituary 83
　Earlier sketch in SATA 68
　See also CLR 18
Ahlberg, Jessica 1980- 229
Aho, Julia Kay
　See Kay, Julia
Aichinger, Helga 1937- 4
Aiken, Clarissa (M.) Lorenz 1899-1992 12
　Obituary 109
Aiken, Conrad 1889-1973 30
　Earlier sketch in SATA 3
Aiken, Conrad Potter
　See Aiken, Conrad
Aiken, Joan (Delano) 1924-2004 73
　Autobiography Feature 109
　Obituary 152
　Earlier sketches in SATA 2, 30
　See also CLR 90
　See also SAAS 1
Aillaud, Cindy Lou 1955- 184
Ainsley, Alix
　See Steiner, Barbara A(nnette)
Ainsworth, Catherine Harris 1910- 56
Ainsworth, Norma 1911-1987 9

Ainsworth, Ruth (Gallard) 1908- 73
　Earlier sketch in SATA 7
Ainsworth, William Harrison 1805-1882 24
Aistrop, Jack 1916- 14
Aitken, Amy 1952- 54
　Brief entry 40
Aitken, Dorothy 1916- 10
Aitmatov, Chingiz 1928-2008 56
Aitmatov, Chingiz Torekulovich
　See Aitmatov, Chingiz
Ajhar, Brian 1957- 220
Akaba, Suekichi 1910- 46
Akbarpour, Ahmad 1970- 232
Akers, Floyd
　See Baum, L. Frank
Akib, Jamel 181
Aks, Patricia 1926-1994 68
al Abdullah, Rania
　See Rania, Queen of Jordan
Alagoa, Ebiegberi Joe 1933- 108
Alain
　See Brustlein, Daniel
Alajalov, Constantin 1900-1987
　Obituary 53
Alalou, Ali 203
Alalou, Elizabeth 203
Alan, David
　See Horsfield, Alan
Alan, Robert
　See Silverstein, Robert Alan
Alarcon, Francisco X. 1954- 215
　Earlier sketch in SATA 104
Alarcon, Francisco Xavier
　See Alarcon, Francisco X.
Alarcon, Karen Beaumont
　See Beaumont, Karen
Albee, Sarah 1962- 231
Albert, Burton 1936- 22
Albert, Louise 1928- 157
Albert, Michael 1966- 202
Albert, Richard E. 1909-1999 82
Albert, Susan Wittig 1940- 107
Alberts, Frances Jacobs 1907-1989 14
Albertson, Susan
　See Wojciechowski, Susan
Albion, Lee Smith 29
Alborough, Jez 1959- 149
　Earlier sketch in SATA 86
Albrecht, Lillie (Vanderveer H.)
　1894-1985 12
Albyn, Carole Lisa 1955- 83
Alchemy, Jack
　See Gershator, David
Alcock, Gudrun 1908- 56
　Brief entry 33
Alcock, Vivien (Dolores) 1924-2003 76
　Brief entry 38
　Obituary 148
　Earlier sketch in SATA 45
　See also CLR 26
Alcorn, John 1935- 31
　Brief entry 30
Alcorn, Stephen 1958- 207
　Earlier sketch in SATA 110
Alcott, Louisa May 1832-1888 100
　See also YABC 1
　See also CLR 109
Alda, Arlene 1933- 205
　Brief entry 36
　Earlier sketches in SATA 44, 106, 158
　See also CLR 93
Alden, Isabella (Macdonald) 1841-1930 115
　See also YABC 2
Alden, Sue
　See Francis, Dorothy
Alderman, Clifford Lindsey 1902-1988 3
Alderson, Sue Ann 1940- 59
　Brief entry 48
Alding, Peter
　See Jeffries, Roderic
Aldis, Dorothy (Keeley) 1896-1966 2

Aldiss, Brian W. 1925- 34
Aldiss, Brian Wilson
  See Aldiss, Brian W.
Aldon, Adair
  See Meigs, Cornelia Lynde
Aldous, Allan (Charles) 1911- 27
Aldrich, Ann
  See Meaker, Marijane
Aldrich, Bess Streeter 1881-1954
  See CLR 70
Aldrich, Thomas (Bailey) 1836-1907 114
  Earlier sketch in SATA 17
Aldridge, (Harold Edward) James 1918- 87
Aldridge, Josephine Haskell 14
Aldridge, Sheila 1974- 192
Aleas, Richard
  See Ardai, Charles
Alegria, Malin 1974(?)- 190
Alegria, Ricardo E(nrique) 1921- 6
Aleksin, Anatolii Georgievich 1924- 36
Alenov, Lydia 1948- 61
Alex, Ben (a pseudonym) 1946- 45
Alex, Marlee (a pseudonym) 1948- 45
Alexander, Alma 1963- 217
Alexander, Anna B(arbara Cooke) 1913- 1
Alexander, Anne
  See Alexander, Anna B(arbara Cooke)
Alexander, Claire 228
Alexander, Ellen 1938- 91
Alexander, Frances (Laura) 1888-1979 4
Alexander, Heather 1967- 232
Alexander, Janet 1907-1994 97
  Earlier sketch in SATA 1
Alexander, Jill S. 1964- 223
Alexander, Jill Shurbet
  See Alexander, Jill S.
Alexander, Jocelyn Anne Arundel 1930- 22
Alexander, Linda 1935- 2
Alexander, Lloyd 1924-2007 135
  Obituary 182
  Earlier sketches in SATA 3, 49, 81, 129
  See also CLR 48
  See also SAAS 19
Alexander, Lloyd Chudley
  See Alexander, Lloyd
Alexander, Marc 1929- 117
Alexander, Martha 1920- 136
  Earlier sketches in SATA 11, 70
Alexander, Rae Pace
  See Alexander, Raymond Pace
Alexander, Raymond Pace 1898-1974 22
Alexander, R.C. 232
Alexander, Robert 200
Alexander, Robert C.
  See Alexander, R.C.
Alexander, Rod
  See Pellowski, Michael (Joseph)
Alexander, Sally Hobart 1943- 84
Alexander, Sue 1933-2008 136
  Obituary 195
  Earlier sketches in SATA 12, 89
  See also SAAS 15
Alexander, Vincent Arthur 1925-1980
  Obituary 23
Alexeieff, Alexandre A. 1901-1979 14
Alger, Horatio, Jr.
  See Stratemeyer, Edward L.
Alger, Horatio, Jr. 1832-1899 16
  See also CLR 170
Alger, Leclaire (Gowans) 1898-1969 15
Aliki
  See Brandenberg, Aliki
Alkema, Chester Jay 1932- 12
Al-Khalili, Jim 1962- 124
Alkiviades, Alkis 1953- 105
Alko, Selina 1968- 218
Alkouatli, Claire 186
Allaby, John Michael
  See Allaby, Michael
Allaby, Michael 1933- 167
Allamand, Pascale 1942- 12

Allan, Mabel Esther 1915-1998 75
  Earlier sketches in SATA 5, 32
  See also CLR 43
  See also SAAS 11
Allan, Nicholas 1956- 123
  Earlier sketch in SATA 79
Allan-Meyer, Kathleen 1918- 51
  Brief entry 46
Allard, Harry, Jr. 1928- 216
  Earlier sketches in SATA 42, 102
  See also CLR 85
Allard, Harry G.
  See Allard, Harry, Jr.
Allee, Marjorie Hill 1890-1945 17
Allen, Adam
  See Epstein, Beryl
  and Epstein, Samuel
Allen, Alex B.
  See Heide, Florence Parry
Allen, Allyn
  See Eberle, Irmengarde
Allen, Betsy
  See Harrison, Elizabeth (Allen) Cavanna
Allen, Bob 1961- 76
Allen, Constance
  See Albee, Sarah
Allen, Gertrude E(lizabeth) 1888-1984 9
Allen, Grace
  See Hogarth, Grace (Weston Allen)
Allen, Jeffrey (Yale) 1948- 42
Allen, John
  See Perry, Ritchie (John Allen)
Allen, Jonathan 1957- 177
  Earlier sketch in SATA 131
Allen, Jonathan Dean
  See Allen, Jonathan
Allen, Joy 1948- 217
Allen, Judy (Christina) 1941- 124
  Earlier sketch in SATA 80
Allen, Kenneth S. 1913-1981 56
Allen, Leroy 1912- 11
Allen, Linda 1925- 33
Allen, Marjorie 1931- 22
Allen, Maury 1932-2010 26
Allen, Merritt Parmelee 1892-1954 22
Allen, Nancy Kelly 1949- 171
  Earlier sketch in SATA 127
Allen, Nina (Stroemgren) 1935- 22
Allen, Pamela (Kay) 1934- 123
  Earlier sketches in SATA 50, 81
  See also CLR 44
Allen, Raul 205
Allen, Rodney F. 1938-1999 27
Allen, Roger MacBride 1957- 105
Allen, Ruth
  See Peterson, Esther (Allen)
Allen, Samuel W(ashington) 1917- 9
Allen, T. D.
  See Allen, Terril Diener
Allen, Terril Diener 1908- 35
Allen, Terry D.
  See Allen, Terril Diener
Allen, Thomas B. 1929- 193
  Earlier sketches in SATA 45, 140
Allen, Thomas Benton
  See Allen, Thomas B.
Allen, Tom
  See Allen, Thomas B.
Allende, Isabel 1942- 163
  See also CLR 99
Allerton, Mary
  See Govan, (Mary) Christine Noble
Alley, Robert W.
  See Alley, R.W.
Alley, R.W. 211
  Earlier sketch in SATA 169
Alley, Zoe B. 214
Alleyn, Ellen
  See Rossetti, Christina
Allington, Richard L(loyd) 1947- 39
  Brief entry 35

Allison, Amy 1956- 138
Allison, Bob 14
Allison, Diane Worfolk 78
Allison, Jennifer 173
Allison, Linda 1948- 43
Allison, Margaret
  See Klam, Cheryl
Allman, Barbara 1950- 137
Allmendinger, David F(rederick), Jr. 1938- . 35
Allred, Alexandra Powe 1965- 144
Allred, Gordon T(hatcher) 1930- 10
Allsop, Kenneth 1920-1973 17
Allsopp, Sophie 188
Alma, Ann 1946- 201
Almedingen, E. M.
  See Almedingen, Martha Edith von
Almedingen, Martha Edith von 1898-1971 3
Almon, Russell
  See Clevenger, William R.
  and Downing, David A(lmon)
Almond, David 1951- 233
  Earlier sketches in SATA 114, 158
  See also CLR 168
Almond, Linda Stevens 1881(?)-1987
  Obituary 50
Almquist, Don 1929- 11
Alonzo, Sandra 199
Alphin, Elaine Marie 1955- 232
  Autobiography Feature 139
  Earlier sketches in SATA 80, 130, 139
Alsenas, Linas 1979- 186
Alsop, Mary O'Hara 1885-1980 34
  Obituary 24
  Earlier sketch in SATA 2
Alter, Anna 1974- 206
  Earlier sketch in SATA 135
Alter, Judith 1938- 101
  Earlier sketch in SATA 52
Alter, Judith MacBain
  See Alter, Judith
Alter, Judy
  See Alter, Judith
Alter, Robert Edmond 1925-1965 9
Alter, Stephen 1956- 187
Althea
  See Braithwaite, Althea
Altman, Linda Jacobs 1943- 21
Altman, Suzanne
  See Orgel, Doris
  and Schecter, Ellen
Alton, Steve 169
Altschuler, Franz 1923- 45
Altsheler, Joseph A(lexander) 1862-1919
  See YABC 1
Alvarez, John
  See del Rey, Lester
Alvarez, Joseph A. 1930- 18
Alvarez, Julia 1950- 129
al-Windawi, Thura
  See Windawi, Thura al-
Alyer, Philip A.
  See Stratemeyer, Edward L.
Amado, Elisa 193
Amann, Janet 1951- 79
Amateau, Gigi 1964- 233
Amato, Carol A. 1942- 92
Amato, Mary 1961- 178
  Earlier sketch in SATA 140
Ambrose, Stephen E. 1936-2002 138
  Earlier sketch in SATA 40
Ambrose, Stephen Edward
  See Ambrose, Stephen E.
Ambrus, Gyozo Laszlo 1935- 1
  See also SAAS 4
Ambrus, Victor G.
  See Ambrus, Gyozo Laszlo
Amend, Bill 1962- 147
Amerman, Lockhart 1911-1969 3
Ames, Evelyn 1908-1990 13
  Obituary 64

Ames, Gerald 1906-1993 .... *11*
  Obituary *74*
Ames, Lee J. 1921-2011 .... *151*
  Earlier sketch in SATA *3*
Ames, Lee Judah
  See Ames, Lee J.
Ames, Mildred 1919-1994 .... *85*
  Earlier sketches in SATA *22, 81*
Amico, Tom 1960(?)- *176*
Amit, Ofra 1966- *205*
Ammon, Richard 1942- *124*
Amon, Aline 1928- *9*
Amory, Jay
  See Lovegrove, James
Amoss, Berthe 1925- *112*
  Earlier sketch in SATA *5*
Amstutz, Andre 1925- *214*
Anastasio, Dina 1941- *94*
  Brief entry *30*
  Earlier sketch in SATA *37*
Anaya, Rudolfo 1937-
  See CLR *129*
Anaya, Rudolfo A.
  See Anaya, Rudolfo
Anaya, Rudolpho Alfonso
  See Anaya, Rudolfo
Anckarsvard, Karin Inez Maria 1915-1969 .... *6*
Ancona, George 1929- *208*
  Autobiography Feature *208*
  Earlier sketches in SATA *12, 85, 145, 192*
  See also SAAS *18*
Anders, C. J.
  See Bennett, Cherie
Anders, Isabel 1946- *101*
Anders, Lou *176*
Andersdatter, Karla M. 1938- *34*
Andersen, Bethanne 1954- *191*
Andersen, Hans Christian 1805-1875 .... *100*
  See also YABC *1*
  See also CLR *113*
Andersen, Ted
  See Boyd, Waldo T.
Andersen, Yvonne 1932- *27*
Anderson, Bernice G(oudy) 1894-1997 .... *33*
Anderson, Bob 1944- *139*
  Earlier sketch in SATA *136*
Anderson, Brad 1924- *33*
  Brief entry *31*
Anderson, Bradley Jay
  See Anderson, Brad
Anderson, Brian 1974- *211*
Anderson, C. C.
  See Anderson, Catherine Corley
Anderson, C(larence) W(illiam) 1891-1971 . *11*
Anderson, Carolyn Dunn
  See Dunn, Carolyn
Anderson, Catherine C.
  See Anderson, Catherine Corley
Anderson, Catherine Corley 1909-2001 .... *72*
  See Lee, Cora
Anderson, Clifford
  See Gardner, Richard (M.)
Anderson, Daryl Shon 1963- *93*
Anderson, Dave
  See Anderson, David
Anderson, David 1929- *60*
Anderson, Derek 1969- *169*
Anderson, Eloise Adell 1927- *9*
Anderson, George
  See Groom, Arthur William
Anderson, Grace Fox 1932- *43*
Anderson, J(ohn) R(ichard) L(ane)
  1911-1981 .... *15*
  Obituary *27*
Anderson, Jessica Lee 1980- *224*
Anderson, Jodi Lynn *182*
Anderson, John David *197*
Anderson, John L. 1905- *2*
Anderson, Joy 1928- *1*
Anderson, Kevin J. 1962- *117*
  Earlier sketch in SATA *74*

Anderson, Kevin James
  See Anderson, Kevin J.
Anderson, Kirsty 1978- *108*
Anderson, K.J.
  See Moesta, Rebecca
Anderson, Laurie Halse 1961- *186*
  Earlier sketches in SATA *95, 132*
  See also CLR *138*
Anderson, LaVere Francis Shoenfelt
  1907-1998 .... *27*
Anderson, Leone Castell 1923- *53*
  Brief entry *49*
Anderson, Lisa G. 1963- *108*
Anderson, Lonzo
  See Anderson, John L.
Anderson, Lucia (Lewis) 1922- *10*
Anderson, Madelyn Klein 1926-2005 .... *28*
Anderson, Margaret J(ean) 1931- *27*
  See also SAAS *8*
Anderson, Marilyn D. 1943- *144*
Anderson, Mary 1939- *82*
  Earlier sketch in SATA *7*
  See also SAAS *23*
Anderson, Matthew Tobin
  See Anderson, M.T.
Anderson, Mona 1910-2004 .... *40*
Anderson, Mrs. Melvin
  See Anderson, Catherine Corley
Anderson, M.T. 1968- *182*
  Earlier sketches in SATA *97, 146*
Anderson, Norman Dean 1928- *22*
Anderson, Peggy Perry 1953- *179*
  Earlier sketch in SATA *84*
Anderson, Poul 1926-2001 .... *90*
  Autobiography Feature *106*
  Brief entry *39*
  See also CLR *58*
Anderson, Poul William
  See Anderson, Poul
Anderson, Rachel 1943- *86*
  Earlier sketch in SATA *34*
  See also SAAS *18*
Anderson, Rebecca J.
  See Anderson, R.J.
Anderson, Rebecca M.
  See Moesta, Rebecca
Anderson, Rebecca Moesta
  See Moesta, Rebecca
Anderson, Richard
  See Anderson, J(ohn) R(ichard) L(ane)
Anderson, R.J. 1970(?)- *216*
Anderson, Sara *173*
Anderson, Scoular *201*
Anderson, (Tom) Scoular *138*
Anderson, Stephanie 1976- *225*
Anderson, Susan 1952- *90*
Anderson, Thomas Scoular
  See Anderson, Scoular
Anderson, W. B.
  See Schultz, James Willard
Anderson, Wayne 1946- *202*
  Earlier sketches in SATA *56, 147*
Andersson, Kenneth 1970- *200*
Andre, Evelyn M. 1924- *27*
Andre, Evelyn Marie
  See Andre, Evelyn M.
Andreasen, Dan *227*
  Earlier sketch in SATA *186*
Andreassen, Karl
  See Boyd, Waldo T.
Andreassi, K. Robert
  See DeCandido, Keith R.A.
Andree, Louise
  See Coury, Louise Andree
Andres, Kristina 1971- *233*
Andrew, Ian 1962- *166*
  Earlier sketch in SATA *116*
Andrew, Ian Peter
  See Andrew, Ian
Andrew, Prudence (Hastings) 1924- *87*

Andrews, Benny 1930-2006 .... *31*
  Obituary *178*
Andrews, Eleanor Lattimore
  See Lattimore, Eleanor Frances
Andrews, Elton V.
  See Pohl, Frederik
Andrews, F(rank) Emerson 1902-1978 .... *22*
Andrews, J(ames) S(ydney) 1934- *4*
Andrews, Jan 1942- *167*
  Brief entry *49*
  Earlier sketches in SATA *58, 98*
Andrews, Julie 1935- *153*
  Earlier sketch in SATA *7*
  See also CLR *85*
Andrews, Laura
  See Coury, Louise Andree
Andrews, Roy Chapman 1884-1960 .... *19*
Andrews, Tamra 1959- *129*
Andrews, V(irginia) C(leo) 1924(?)-1986
  Obituary *50*
Andrews, Wendy
  See Sharmat, Marjorie Weinman
Andrews, William G. 1930- *74*
Andrews, William George
  See Andrews, William G.
Andrezel, Pierre
  See Blixen, Karen
Andriani, Renee
  See Williams-Andriani, Renee
Andriola, Alfred J. 1912-1983
  Obituary *34*
Andrist, Ralph K. 1914-2004 .... *45*
Andronik, Catherine M. *189*
Andryszewski, Tricia 1956- *148*
  Earlier sketch in SATA *88*
Anelli, Melissa 1979- *215*
Angaramo, Roberta 1974- *229*
Angel, Ann 1952- *192*
Angel, Carl *178*
Angel, Marie 1923- *47*
Angeles, Peter A. 1931- *40*
Angeletti, Roberta 1964- *124*
Angeli, Marguerite (Lofft) de
  See de Angeli, Marguerite (Lofft)
Angell, Judie 1937- *78*
  Earlier sketch in SATA *22*
  See also CLR *33*
Angell, Madeline 1919- *18*
Angelo, Valenti 1897- *14*
Angelou, Maya 1928- *136*
  Earlier sketch in SATA *49*
  See also CLR *53*
Angier, Bradford -1997 .... *12*
Angle, Kimberly Greene *203*
Angle, Paul M(cClelland) 1900-1975
  Obituary *20*
Anglund, Joan Walsh 1926- *2*
  See also CLR *94*
Ango, Fan D.
  See Longyear, Barry B(rookes)
Angrist, Stanley W(olff) 1933- *4*
Anhalt, Ariela 1990(?)- *227*
Anholt, Catherine 1958- *131*
  Earlier sketch in SATA *74*
Anholt, Laurence 1959- *141*
  Earlier sketch in SATA *74*
Aninno, J.G.
  See Annino, Jan Godown
Anita
  See Daniel, Anita
Anmar, Frank
  See Nolan, William F.
Annett, Cora
  See Scott, Cora Annett (Pipitone)
Annie-Jo
  See Blanchard, Patricia
  and Suhr, Joanne
Annino, Jan Godown 1952- *228*
Annixter, Jane
  See Sturtzel, Jane Levington

Annixter, Paul
    See Sturtzel, Howard A(llison)
Anno, Mitsumasa 1926- 157
    Earlier sketches in SATA *5, 38, 77*
    See also CLR *122*
Anrooy, Francine Van
    See Van Anrooy, Francine
Ansary, Mir Tamim 1948- 140
Anstey, Caroline 1958- 81
Antell, Will D. 1935- 31
Anthony, Barbara
    See Barber, Antonia
Anthony, C. L.
    See Smith, Dorothy Gladys
Anthony, Edward 1895-1971 21
Anthony, Joelle 232
Anthony, John
    See Beckett, Ronald Brymer
    and Ciardi, John (Anthony)
    and Sabini, John Anthony
Anthony, Joseph Patrick 1964- 103
Anthony, Patricia 1947- 109
Anthony, Piers 1934- 129
    Autobiography Feature 129
    Earlier sketch in SATA *84*
    See also CLR *118*
    See also SAAS *22*
Anthony, Susan C(arol) 1953- 87
Anticaglia, Elizabeth 1939- 12
Antieau, Kim 214
Antilles, Kem
    See Moesta, Rebecca
Antle, Nancy 1955- 102
Antolini, Margaret Fishback 1904-1985
    Obituary 45
Anton, Michael J(ames) 1940- 12
Antonacci, Robert J(oseph) 1916- 45
    Brief entry 37
Anvil, Christopher 1925-2009 102
Anzaldua, Gloria (Evanjelina) 1942-2004
    Obituary 154
Aoki, Hisako 1942- 45
Aoyagi, Nora 229
Apfel, Necia H(alpern) 1930- 51
    Brief entry 41
Aphrodite, J.
    See Livingston, Carole
Apikuni
    See Schultz, James Willard
Apostolina, M. 184
Apostolina, Michael
    See Apostolina, M.
Apostolou, Christine Hale 1955- 179
    Earlier sketches in SATA *82, 128*
Appel, Allen (R.) 1945- 115
Appel, Benjamin 1907-1977 39
    Obituary 21
Appel, Martin 1948- 45
Appel, Martin Eliot
    See Appel, Martin
Appel, Marty
    See Appel, Martin
Appelbaum, Diana Muir Karter 1953- 132
Appelt, Kathi 1954- 190
    Earlier sketches in SATA *83, 129*
Apperley, Dawn 1969- 135
Appiah, Peggy 1921-2006 84
    Earlier sketch in SATA *15*
    See also SAAS *19*
Apple, Margot 214
    Brief entry 42
    Earlier sketches in SATA *64, 152*
Applebaum, Stan 1922- 45
Applegate, K.A.
    See Applegate, Katherine
Applegate, Katherine 1956- 196
    Earlier sketches in SATA *109, 162*
    See also CLR *90*
Applegate, Katherine Alice
    See Applegate, Katherine

Appleton, Victor
    See Barrett, Neal, Jr.
    and Doyle, Debra
    and Stratemeyer, Edward L.
    and Vardeman, Robert E.
Appollo 1969- 214
Appollodorus, Olivier
    See Appollo
Apsler, Alfred 1907-1982 10
Aragones, Sergio 1937- 48
    Brief entry 39
Arato, Rona 233
Araujo, Frank P. 1937- 86
Arbo, Cris 1950- 220
    Earlier sketch in SATA *103*
Arbuckle, Dorothy Fry 1910-1982
    Obituary 33
Arbuthnot, May Hill 1884-1969 2
Archambault, John 163
    Earlier sketches in SATA *67, 112*
Archambault, Matthew 1968- 219
Archbold, Rick 1950- 97
Archer, Colleen Rutherford 1949- 164
Archer, Frank
    See O'Connor, Richard
Archer, Jules 1915- 85
    Earlier sketch in SATA *4*
    See also SAAS *5*
Archer, Lily 1981- 193
Archer, Marion Fuller 1917- 11
Archer, Nathan
    See Watt-Evans, Lawrence
Archer, Peggy 1947- 199
Archibald, Joe
    See Archibald, Joseph S(topford)
Archibald, Joseph S(topford) 1898-1986 3
    Obituary 47
Ard, William
    See Jakes, John
Ardagh, Philip 1961- 154
Ardai, Charles 1969- 85
Arden, Barbi
    See Stoutenburg, Adrien (Pearl)
Arden, William
    See Lynds, Dennis
Ardizzone, Edward (Jeffrey Irving)
    1900-1979 28
    Obituary 21
    Earlier sketch in SATA *1*
    See also CLR *3*
Ardley, Neil 1937- 121
    Earlier sketch in SATA *43*
Ardley, Neil Richard
    See Ardley, Neil
Arehart-Treichel, Joan 1942- 22
Arena, Felice 1968- 151
Arenella, Roy 1939- 14
Arevamirp, Esile
    See Primavera, Elise
Argent, Kerry 1960- 138
Arguelles, Francisco Xavier
    See Stork, Francisco X.
Argueta, Jorge 179
Arihara, Shino 1973- 201
Arkin, Alan 1934- 59
    Brief entry 32
Arkin, Alan Wolf
    See Arkin, Alan
Arksey, Neil 158
Arlen, Leslie
    See Nicole, Christopher
Arley, Robert
    See Jackson, Mike
Armer, Alberta (Roller) 1904-1986 9
Armer, Laura Adams 1874-1963 13
Armistead, John 1941- 130
Armitage, David 1943- 155
    Brief entry 38
    Earlier sketch in SATA *99*
Armitage, Frank
    See Carpenter, John

Armitage, Ronda (Jacqueline) 1943- 155
    Brief entry 38
    Earlier sketches in SATA *47, 99*
Armour, Richard (Willard) 1906-1989 14
    Obituary 61
Armstrong, Alan 1939- 172
Armstrong, Alan W.
    See Armstrong, Alan
Armstrong, George D. 1927- 10
Armstrong, Gerry (Breen) 1929- 10
Armstrong, Jeannette (C.) 1948- 102
Armstrong, Jennifer 1961- 165
    Autobiography Feature 120
    Earlier sketches in SATA *77, 111*
    See also CLR *66*
    See also SAAS *24*
Armstrong, Louise 43
    Brief entry 33
Armstrong, Martin Donisthorpe
    1882-1974 115
Armstrong, Matthew 1975- 188
Armstrong, Matthew S.
    See Armstrong, Matthew
Armstrong, Ralph Richard
    See Armstrong, Richard
Armstrong, Richard 1903-1986 11
Armstrong, Shelagh 1961- 224
Armstrong, William H(oward) 1914-1999 4
    Obituary 111
    See also CLR *117*
    See also SAAS *7*
Armstrong-Ellis, Carey (Fraser) 1956- 145
Armstrong-Hodgson, Shelagh
    See Armstrong, Shelagh
Arndt, Ursula (Martha H.) 56
    Brief entry 39
Arneson, D(on) J(on) 1935- 37
Arnett, Caroline
    See Cole, Lois Dwight
Arnett, Jack
    See Goulart, Ron
Arnette, Robert
    See Silverberg, Robert
Arno, Enrico 1913-1981 43
    Obituary 28
Arnold, Ann 1953(?)- 207
Arnold, Caroline 1944- 228
    Brief entry 34
    Earlier sketches in SATA *36, 85, 131, 174*
    See also CLR *61*
    See also SAAS *23*
Arnold, Elizabeth 1944- 164
Arnold, Elliott 1912-1980 5
    Obituary 22
Arnold, Emily 1939- 210
    Autobiography Feature 134
    Earlier sketches in SATA *5, 50, 76, 110, 134*
    See also CLR *46*
    See also SAAS *7*
Arnold, Gillian Clare
    See Cross, Gillian
Arnold, Katya 1947- 168
    Earlier sketches in SATA *82, 115*
Arnold, Louise 175
Arnold, Louise Claire
    See Arnold, Louise
Arnold, Marsha Diane 1948- 147
    Earlier sketch in SATA *93*
Arnold, Nick 1961- 113
Arnold, Oren 1900-1980 4
Arnold, Susan (Riser) 1951- 58
Arnold, Tedd 1949- 208
    Earlier sketches in SATA *69, 116, 160*
Arnoldy, Julie
    See Bischoff, Julia Bristol
Arnosky, James Edward 1946- 189
    Earlier sketches in SATA *70, 118*
    See also CLR *93*
Arnosky, Jim
    See Arnosky, James Edward
Arnott, Kathleen 1914- 20

Arnov, Boris, Jr. 1926- 12
Arnow, Harriette (Louisa) Simpson
  1908-1986 42
  Obituary 47
Arnsteen, Katy Keck 1934- 68
Arnstein, Helene S(olomon) 1915- 12
Arntson, Herbert E(dward) 1911-1982 12
Aroner, Miriam 82
Aronin, Ben 1904-1980
  Obituary 25
Aronson, Marc 1950- 189
  Autobiography Feature 189
  Earlier sketches in SATA *126, 175*
Aronson, Marc Henry
  See Aronson, Marc
Aronson, Sarah 196
Aronson, Virginia 1954- 122
Arora, Shirley (Lease) 1930- 2
Arrasmith, Patrick 176
Arrick, Fran
  See Angell, Judie
Arrigan, Mary 1943- 142
Arrington, Aileen 183
Arrington, Stephen L. 1948- 97
Arrington, Stephen Lee
  See Arrington, Stephen L.
Arrley, Richmond
  See Delany, Samuel R., Jr.
Arrou-Vignod, Jean-Philippe 1958- 218
Arrowood, (McKendrick Lee) Clinton
  1939- 19
Arrowsmith, Pat 1930- 59
Arsenault, Isabelle 1978- 207
Artell, Mike 1948- 183
  Earlier sketches in SATA *89, 134*
Arthur, Robert (Andrew) 1909-1969
  See Arthur, Robert, (Jr.)
Arthur, Robert, (Jr.) 1909-1969 118
Arthur, Ruth M(abel) 1905-1979 26
  Earlier sketch in SATA *7*
Artis, Vicki Kimmel 1945- 12
Artzybasheff, Boris (Miklailovich)
  1899-1965 14
Aruego, Ariane
  See Dewey, Ariane
Aruego, Jose 1932- 178
  Earlier sketches in SATA *6, 68, 125*
  See also CLR *5*
Aruego, Jose Espiritu
  See Aruego, Jose
Arundel, Honor (Morfydd) 1919-1973 4
  Obituary 24
  See also CLR *35*
Arundel, Jocelyn
  See Alexander, Jocelyn Anne Arundel
Arvey, Michael 1948- 79
Arzoumanian, Alik 177
Asare, Meshack (Yaw) 1945- 139
  Earlier sketch in SATA *86*
Asaro, Catherine 1955- 165
  Earlier sketch in SATA *101*
Asaro, Catherine Ann 1955-
  See Asaro, Catherine
Asay, Donna Day 1945- 127
Asbjornsen, Peter Christen 1812-1885 15
  See also CLR *104*
Asch, Frank 1946- 154
  Earlier sketches in SATA *5, 66, 102*
Ash, Jutta 1942- 38
Ashabranner, Brent 1921- 166
  Earlier sketches in SATA *1, 67, 130*
  See also CLR *28*
  See also SAAS *14*
Ashabranner, Brent Kenneth
  See Ashabranner, Brent
Ashbless, William
  See Blaylock, James P.
  and Powers, Tim
Ashby, Gil 1958- 146
Ashby, Gwynneth 1922- 44
Ashby, Ruth 170

Ashby, Yvonne 1955- 121
Ashe, Arthur (Robert, Jr.) 1943-1993 65
  Obituary 87
Ashe, Geoffrey (Thomas) 1923- 17
  Autobiography Feature 125
Ashe, Mary Ann
  See Lewis, Mary
Asher, Bridget
  See Baggott, Julianna
Asher, Sandra Fenichel
  See Asher, Sandy
Asher, Sandy 1942- 71
  Autobiography Feature 158
  Brief entry 34
  Earlier sketch in SATA *36*
  See also SAAS *13*
Asheron, Sara
  See Moore, Lilian
Ashey, Bella
  See Breinburg, Petronella
Ashford, Daisy
  See Ashford, Margaret Mary
Ashford, Jeffrey
  See Jeffries, Roderic
Ashford, Margaret Mary 1881-1972 10
Ashland, Monk 1972- 207
Ashley, Bernard (John) 1935- 155
  Brief entry 39
  Earlier sketches in SATA *47, 79*
  See also CLR *4*
Ashley, Elizabeth
  See Salmon, Annie Elizabeth
Ashley, Ray
  See Abrashkin, Raymond
Ashman, Linda 1960- 203
  Earlier sketch in SATA *150*
Ashton, Lorayne
  See Gottfried, Theodore Mark
Ashton, Warren T.
  See Adams, William Taylor
Asimov, Isaac 1920-1992 74
  Earlier sketches in SATA *1, 26*
  See also CLR *79*
Asinof, Eliot 1919-2008 6
Asinof, Eliot Tager
  See Asinof, Eliot
Aska, Warabe
  See Masuda, Takeshi
Askani, Tanja 1962- 227
Asprin, Robert 1946-2008 92
Asprin, Robert L.
  See Asprin, Robert
Asprin, Robert Lynn
  See Asprin, Robert
Asquith, Cynthia Mary Evelyn (Charteris)
  1887-1960 107
Asquith, Ros 153
Astley, Juliet
  See Lofts, Norah (Robinson)
Aston, Dianna Hutts 1964- 176
Aston, James
  See White, T(erence) H(anbury)
Ata, Te 1895-1995 119
Atene, Ann
  See Atene, (Rita) Anna
Atene, (Rita) Anna 1922- 12
Atheling, William, Jr.
  See Blish, James
Atkins, Catherine 160
Atkins, Jeannine 1953- 172
  Earlier sketch in SATA *113*
Atkinson, Allen G. 1953(?)-1987 60
  Brief entry 46
  Obituary 55
Atkinson, Elizabeth 215
Atkinson, Elizabeth Jane
  See Atkinson, Elizabeth
Atkinson, M. E.
  See Frankau, Mary Evelyn Atkinson
Atkinson, Margaret Fleming 14
Atteberry, Kevan J. 186

Attema, Martha 1949- 156
  Earlier sketch in SATA *94*
Atticus
  See Davies, Hunter
  and Fleming, Ian
  and Pawle, Gerald Strachan
  and Wilson, (Thomas) Woodrow
Atwater, Florence 1896-1979 66
  Earlier sketch in SATA *16*
  See also CLR *19*
Atwater, Florence Hasseltine Carroll
  See Atwater, Florence
Atwater, Montgomery Meigs 1904-1976 15
Atwater, Richard 1892-1948 66
  Brief entry 27
  Earlier sketch in SATA *54*
  See also CLR *19*
Atwater, Richard Tupper
  See Atwater, Richard
Atwater-Rhodes, Amelia 1984- 170
  Earlier sketch in SATA *124*
Atwell, Debby 1953- 150
  Earlier sketch in SATA *87*
Atwood, Ann (Margaret) 1913-1992 7
Atwood, Margaret 1939- 170
  Earlier sketch in SATA *50*
Atwood, Margaret Eleanor
  See Atwood, Margaret
Aubrey, Meg Kelleher 1963- 83
Aubry, Claude B. 1914-1984 29
  Obituary 40
Auch, Herm 173
Auch, Mary Jane 173
  Earlier sketch in SATA *138*
Auch, M.J.
  See Auch, Mary Jane
Auclair, Joan 1960- 68
Auel, Jean 1936- 91
Auel, Jean M.
  See Auel, Jean
Auel, Jean Marie
  See Auel, Jean
Auer, Martin 1951- 77
Augarde, Steve 1950- 210
  Earlier sketches in SATA *25, 159*
Augarde, Steven Andre
  See Augarde, Steve
Augelli, John P(at) 1921- 46
Augustine, Mildred
  See Benson, Mildred
Ault, Phil
  See Ault, Phillip H(alliday)
Ault, Phillip H(alliday) 1914- 23
Ault, Rosalie Sain 1942- 38
Ault, Roz
  See Ault, Rosalie Sain
Aung, (Maung) Htin 1909- 21
Auntie Deb
  See Coury, Louise Andree
Auntie Louise
  See Coury, Louise Andree
Aunt Weedy
  See Alcott, Louisa May
Auseon, Andrew 1976- 217
  Earlier sketch in SATA *166*
Austen, Carrie
  See Bennett, Cherie
Austen, Catherine 1965- 223
Austin, Carrie
  See Seuling, Barbara
Austin, Elizabeth S. 1907-1977 5
Austin, Harry
  See McInerny, Ralph
Austin, Margot 1909(?)-1990 11
  Obituary 66
Austin, Michael 178
Austin, Oliver L(uther), Jr. 1903-1988 7
  Obituary 59
Austin, Patricia 1950- 137

Austin, R. G.
　See Gelman, Rita Golden
　and Lamb, Nancy
Austin, Virginia 1951- *152*
　Earlier sketch in SATA *80*
Auteur, Hillary
　See Gottfried, Theodore Mark
Auth, Tony
　See Auth, William Anthony, Jr.
Auth, William Anthony, Jr. 1942- *192*
Autry, Gloria Diener
　See Allen, Terril Diener
Auvil, Peggy A 1954- *122*
Auvil, Peggy Appleby
　See Auvil, Peggy A
Avasthi, Swati 1971- *231*
Aveni, Anthony F. 1938- *181*
Aveni, Anthony Francis
　See Aveni, Anthony F.
Averbeck, Jim 1963- *201*
Averill, Esther (Holden) 1902-1992 .... *28*
　Obituary *72*
　Earlier sketch in SATA *1*
Avery, A. A.
　See Montgomery, Rutherford George
Avery, Al
　See Montgomery, Rutherford George
Avery, Gillian 1926- *137*
　Autobiography Feature *137*
　Earlier sketches in SATA *7, 75*
　See also SAAS *6*
Avery, Gillian Elise
　See Avery, Gillian
Avery, Kay 1908- *5*
Avery, Lorraine
　See Older, Effin
　and Older, Jules
Avery, Lynn
　See Cole, Lois Dwight
Avi 1937- *226*
　Earlier sketches in SATA *14, 71, 108, 156,
　190*
　See also CLR *68*
Aviles, Martha *218*
Avishai, Susan 1949- *82*
Avraham, Kate Aver *227*
Avril, Francois 1961- *191*
Avril, Lynne
　See Cravath, Lynne W.
Awdry, Christopher Vere 1940- *67*
Awdry, Wilbert Vere 1911-1997 .... *94*
　See also CLR *23*
Axelrod, Amy *131*
Axelsen, Stephen 1953- *165*
Axton, David
　See Koontz, Dean
Ayars, James S(terling) 1898-1986 .... *4*
Aye, A. K.
　See Edwards, Hazel (Eileen)
Ayer, Eleanor H. 1947-1998 .... *121*
　Earlier sketch in SATA *78*
Ayer, Jacqueline 1930- *13*
Ayer, Margaret (?)-1981 .... *15*
Aylesworth, Jim 1943- *213*
　Earlier sketches in SATA *38, 89, 139*
　See also CLR *89*
Aylesworth, Thomas G(ibbons) 1927-1995 .. *88*
　Earlier sketch in SATA *4*
　See also CLR *6*
　See also SAAS *17*
Ayliffe, Alex *190*
Aylward, Marcus
　See Alexander, Marc
Aymar, Brandt 1911- *22*
Ayme, Marcel (Andre) 1902-1967 .... *91*
　See also CLR *25*
Ayres, Becky
　See Hickox, Rebecca (Ayres)
Ayres, Katherine 1947- *187*
Ayres, Pam 1947- *90*

Ayres, Patricia Miller 1923-1985
　Obituary *46*
Aytmatov, Chingiz
　See Aitmatov, Chingiz
Ayto, Russell 1960- *206*
　Earlier sketches in SATA *111, 166*
Azaid
　See Zaidenberg, Arthur
Azar, Penny 1952- *121*
Azarian, Mary 1940- *171*
　Earlier sketch in SATA *112*
Azore, Barbara 1934- *188*

B

Baasansuren, Bolormaa 1982- *216*
Baastad, Babbis Friis
　See Friis-Baastad, Babbis Ellinor
Bab
　See Gilbert, W(illiam) S(chwenck)
Babbis, Eleanor
　See Friis-Baastad, Babbis Ellinor
Babbitt, Lucy Cullyford 1960- *85*
Babbitt, Natalie 1932- *194*
　Earlier sketches in SATA *6, 68, 106*
　See also CLR *141*
　See also SAAS *5*
Babbitt, Natalie Zane Moore
　See Babbitt, Natalie
Babcock, Chris 1963- *83*
Babcock, Dennis 1948- *22*
Babcock, Dennis Arthur
　See Babcock, Dennis
Baber, Carolyn Stonnell 1936- *96*
Baboni, Elena *198*
Baca, Ana 1967- *191*
Baca, Maria 1951- *104*
Baccalario, Pierdomenico 1974- *222*
Bach, Alice (Hendricks) 1942- *93*
　Brief entry *27*
　Earlier sketch in SATA *30*
Bach, Bellamy
　See Windling, Terri
Bach, Mary 1960- *125*
Bach, Richard 1936- *13*
Bach, Richard David
　See Bach, Richard
Bache, Ellyn 1942- *124*
Bachel, Beverly K. 1957- *142*
Bachelet, Gilles 1952- *196*
Bachem, Paul *231*
Bachman, Fred 1949- *12*
Bachman, Richard
　See King, Stephen
Bachorz, Pam 1973- *226*
Bachrach, Deborah 1943- *80*
Bacigalupi, Paolo 1973- *230*
Backus, James Gilmore 1913-1989
　Obituary *63*
Backus, Jim
　See Backus, James Gilmore
Bacmeister, Rhoda W(arner) 1893-1991 .... *11*
Bacon, Betty
　See Bacon, Elizabeth
Bacon, Elizabeth 1914-2001 .... *3*
　Obituary *131*
Bacon, Joan Chase
　See Bowden, Joan Chase
Bacon, Josephine Dodge (Daskam)
　1876-1961 .... *48*
Bacon, Margaret Frances
　See Bacon, Peggy
Bacon, Margaret Hope 1921- *6*
Bacon, Martha Sherman 1917-1981 .... *18*
　Obituary *27*
　See also CLR *3*
Bacon, Melvin 1950- *93*
Bacon, Melvin L.
　See Bacon, Melvin

Bacon, Peggy 1895-1987 .... *50*
Bacon, R(onald) L(eonard) 1924- *84*
　Earlier sketch in SATA *26*
Baddiel, Ivor 1963- *210*
Baden, Robert 1936- *70*
Baden-Powell, Robert (Stephenson Smyth)
　1857-1941 .... *16*
Badt, Karin L(uisa) 1963- *91*
Bae, Hyun-Joo *186*
Baehr, Kingsley M. 1937- *89*
Baehr, Patricia 1952- *65*
Baehr, Patricia Goehner
　See Baehr, Patricia
Baek, Matthew J. 1971- *202*
Baer, Jill
　See Gilbert, (Agnes) Joan (Sewell)
Baer, Judy 1951- *71*
Baer, Julie 1960- *161*
Baer-Block, Roxanna *172*
Baerg, Harry J(ohn) 1909-1996 .... *12*
Baeten, Lieve 1954- *83*
Bagert, Brod 1947- *191*
　Earlier sketch in SATA *80*
Baggette, Susan K. 1942- *126*
Baggott, Julianna 1969- *197*
Bagnold, Enid 1889-1981 .... *25*
　Earlier sketch in SATA *1*
Baguley, Elizabeth 1959- *199*
Bahlke, Valerie Worth -1994
　See Worth, Valerie
Bahous, Sally 1939- *86*
Bahr, Mary (Madelyn) 1946- *95*
Bahr, Robert 1940- *38*
Bahti, Tom 1926-1972 .... *57*
　Brief entry *31*
Bai, Durga *211*
Baicker-McKee, Carol 1958- *177*
Bailey, Alice Cooper 1890-1978 .... *12*
Bailey, Anne 1958- *71*
Bailey, Bernadine (Freeman) 1901-1995 ...... *14*
Bailey, Carolyn Sherwin 1875-1961 .... *14*
Bailey, Debbie 1954- *123*
Bailey, Donna (Veronica Anne) 1938- *68*
Bailey, Jane H(orton) 1916- *12*
Bailey, John (Robert) 1940- *52*
Bailey, Len *193*
Bailey, Linda 1948- *217*
　Earlier sketches in SATA *107, 182*
Bailey, Maralyn Collins (Harrison) 1941- *12*
Bailey, Matilda
　See Radford, Ruby L(orraine)
Bailey, Maurice Charles 1932- *12*
Bailey, Pearl (Mae) 1918-1990 .... *81*
Bailey, Peter 1946- *194*
Bailey, Ralph Edgar 1893-1982 .... *11*
Bailey, Sheila (Lucas) 1960- *155*
Baillie, Allan 1943- *151*
　Earlier sketch in SATA *87*
　See also CLR *49*
　See also SAAS *21*
Baillie, Allan Stuart
　See Baillie, Allan
Baines, John (David) 1943- *71*
Bains, Larry
　See Sabin, Louis
Baird, Alison 1963- *138*
Baird, Bil 1904-1987 .... *30*
　Obituary *52*
Baird, Thomas (P.) 1923-1990 .... *45*
　Brief entry *39*
　Obituary *64*
Baird, William Britton
　See Baird, Bil
Baity, Elizabeth Chesley 1907-1989 .... *1*
Baiul, Oksana 1977- *108*
Bajoria, Paul 1964- *187*
Bakeless, John (Edwin) 1894-1978 .... *9*
Bakeless, Katherine Little 1895-1992 .... *9*
Baker, Alan 1951- *146*
　Earlier sketches in SATA *22, 93*
Baker, Augusta 1911-1998 .... *3*

Baker, Barbara 1947- *192*
Baker, Betty Lou 1928-1987 .... *73*
   Obituary *54*
   Earlier sketch in SATA 5
Baker, Carin Greenberg 1959- *79*
Baker, Charlotte 1910- *2*
Baker, Christina
   See Kline, Christina Baker
Baker, Christopher W. 1952- *144*
Baker, Deirdre 1955- *195*
Baker, E.D. *190*
Baker, (Mary) Elizabeth (Gillette) 1923- *7*
Baker, Gayle Cunningham 1950- *39*
Baker, James W. 1924- *65*
   Earlier sketch in SATA 22
Baker, James W. 1926- *122*
Baker, Janice E(dla) 1941- *22*
Baker, Jeanette *178*
Baker, Jeannie 1950- *156*
   Earlier sketches in SATA 23, 88
   See also CLR 28
Baker, Jeffrey J(ohn) W(heeler) 1931- *5*
Baker, Jim
   See Baker, James W.
Baker, Keith 1953- *222*
   Earlier sketch in SATA 179
Baker, Ken 1962- *133*
Baker, Laura Nelson 1911- *3*
Baker, Margaret 1890-1965 .... *4*
Baker, Margaret J(oyce) 1918- *12*
   See also SAAS 8
Baker, Mary Gladys Steel 1892-1974 .... *12*
Baker, (Robert) Michael (Graham) 1938- *4*
Baker, Nina (Brown) 1888-1957 .... *15*
Baker, Pamela J. 1947- *66*
Baker, Rachel 1904-1978 .... *2*
   Obituary *26*
Baker, Roberta *206*
Baker, Rosalie F. 1945- *166*
Baker, Samm Sinclair 1909-1997 .... *12*
   Obituary *96*
Baker, Sharon Reiss 1962- *207*
Baker, Susan (Catherine) 1942-1991 .... *29*
Baker-Smith, Grahame *223*
Balaam
   See Lamb, G(eoffrey) F(rederick)
Balan, Bruce 1959- *113*
Balcavage, Dynise 1965- *137*
Balch, Glenn 1902-1989 .... *3*
   Obituary *83*
   See also SAAS 11
Baldacci, David 1960- *184*
Baldacci, David G.
   See Baldacci, David
   and Baldacci, David
Balderose, Nancy Ward 1952- *93*
Balderson, Margaret 1935- *151*
Baldini, Michelle *205*
Baldry, Cherith 1947- *167*
   Earlier sketch in SATA 72
Balducci, Carolyn 1946- *5*
Balducci, Carolyn Feleppa
   See Balducci, Carolyn
Baldwin, Alex
   See Griffin, W. E. B.
Baldwin, Anne Norris 1938- *5*
Baldwin, Clara *11*
Baldwin, Gordo
   See Baldwin, Gordon C(ortis)
Baldwin, Gordon C(ortis) 1908-1983 .... *12*
Baldwin, James 1841-1925 .... *24*
Baldwin, James 1924-1987 .... *9*
   Obituary *54*
Baldwin, Louis 1919- *110*
Baldwin, Margaret
   See Weis, Margaret
Baldwin, Stan(ley C.) 1929- *62*
   Brief entry *28*
Bales, Carol Ann 1940- *57*
   Brief entry *29*
Balet, Jan (Bernard) 1913- *11*

Balgassi, Haemi 1971- *131*
Balian, Lorna 1929- *91*
   Earlier sketch in SATA 9
Balit, Christina 1961- *212*
   Earlier sketches in SATA 102, 159
Ball, Duncan 1941- *73*
Ball, Zachary
   See Janas, Frankie-Lee
   and Masters, Kelly R(ay)
Ballantine, Lesley Frost
   See Frost, Lesley
Ballantyne, R(obert) M(ichael) 1825-1894 ... *24*
   See also CLR 137
Ballard, James G.
   See Ballard, J.G.
Ballard, James Graham
   See Ballard, J.G.
Ballard, Jane
   See Gorman, Carol
Ballard, J.G. 1930-2009 .... *93*
   Obituary *203*
Ballard, Jim G.
   See Ballard, J.G.
Ballard, John 1945- *110*
Ballard, Lowell C(lyne) 1904-1986 .... *12*
   Obituary *49*
Ballard, (Charles) Martin 1929- *1*
Ballard, Mignon F. 1934- *64*
   Brief entry *49*
Ballard, Mignon Franklin
   See Ballard, Mignon F.
Ballard, Robert D(uane) 1942- *85*
   See also CLR 60
Ballard, Robin 1965- *126*
Balliett, Blue 1955- *156*
Ballinger, Bryan 1968- *161*
Ballouhey, Pierre 1944- *90*
Balog, Cyn *221*
Balogh, Penelope 1916-1975 .... *1*
   Obituary *34*
Balouch, Kristen *176*
Balow, Tom 1931- *12*
Baltazzi, Evan S(erge) 1921- *90*
Balterman, Marcia Ridlon 1942- *22*
Baltimore, J.
   See Catherall, Arthur
Baltzer, Hans (Adolf) 1900- *40*
Balzano, Jeanne (Koppel) 1912- *7*
Bambara, Toni Cade 1939-1995 .... *112*
Bamfylde, Walter
   See Bevan, Tom
Bamman, Henry A. 1918- *12*
Banat, D. R.
   See Bradbury, Ray
Bancks, Tristan 1974- *231*
Bancroft, Bronwyn 1958- *216*
Bancroft, Griffing 1907-1999 .... *6*
Bancroft, Laura
   See Baum, L. Frank
Bandel, Betty 1912- *47*
Baner, Skulda Vanadis 1897-1964 .... *10*
Banerjee, Anjali *174*
Banfill, A. Scott 1956- *98*
Bang, Betsy 1912- *48*
   Brief entry *37*
Bang, Garrett
   See Bang, Molly
Bang, Molly 1943- *215*
   Earlier sketches in SATA 24, 69, 111, 158
   See also CLR 8
Bang, Molly Garrett
   See Bang, Molly
Bang-Campbell, Monika 1975(?)- *195*
   Earlier sketch in SATA 140
Banjo, The
   See Paterson, A(ndrew) B(arton)
Banke, Cecile de
   See de Banke, Cecile
Banks, Erin Bennett 1978- *211*
Banks, Kate 1960- *200*
   Earlier sketches in SATA 134, 172

Banks, Laura Stockton Voorhees 1908(?)-1980
   Obituary *23*
Banks, Lynne Reid
   See Reid Banks, Lynne
Banks, Merry *197*
Banks, Michael A. 1951- *101*
Banks, Paul 1952- *174*
Banks, Sara
   See Harrell, Sara Gordon
Banks, Sara Jeanne Gordon Harrell
   See Harrell, Sara Gordon
Bannatyne-Cugnet, Elizabeth Jo-Anne
   See Bannatyne-Cugnet, Jo
Bannatyne-Cugnet, Jo 1951- *101*
Banner, Angela
   See Maddison, Angela Mary
Bannerman, Helen (Brodie Cowan Watson)
   1862(?)-1946 .... *19*
   See also CLR 144
Banning, Evelyn I. 1903-1993 .... *36*
Bannon, Laura (?)-1963 .... *6*
Bannor, Brett 1959- *143*
Bansch, Helga 1957- *224*
Banta, Susan *181*
Bantock, Nick 1950(?)- *95*
Banyai, Istvan *193*
Barakat, Ibtisam 1963- *186*
Barasch, Lynne 1939- *186*
   Earlier sketches in SATA 74, 126
Barbalet, Margaret 1949- *77*
Barbary, James
   See Baumann, Amy Beeching
   and Beeching, Jack
Barbash, Shepard 1957- *84*
Barbauld, Anna Laetitia 1743-1825
   See CLR 160
Barbe, Walter Burke 1926- *45*
Barber, Alison *222*
Barber, Antonia 1932- *163*
   Earlier sketch in SATA 29
Barber, Atiim Kiambu
   See Barber, Tiki
Barber, Lynda
   See Graham-Barber, Lynda
Barber, Lynda Graham
   See Graham-Barber, Lynda
Barber, Richard (William) 1941- *35*
Barber, Ronde 1975- *182*
Barber, Tiki 1975- *182*
Barbera, Joe 1911-2006 .... *51*
   Obituary *179*
Barbera, Joseph
   See Barbera, Joe
Barbera, Joseph Roland
   See Barbera, Joe
Barberis, Juan C(arlos) 1920- *61*
Barbour, Karen 1956- *170*
   Earlier sketches in SATA 63, 121
Barbour, Ralph Henry 1870-1944 .... *16*
Barclay, Bill
   See Moorcock, Michael
Barclay, Isabel
   See Dobell, I(sabel) M(arian) B(arclay)
Barclay, William Ewert
   See Moorcock, Michael
Barclay, William Ewert
   See Moorcock, Michael
Bardhan-Quallen, Sudipta 1977- *214*
   Earlier sketch in SATA 168
Bardoe, Cheryl *181*
Bare, Arnold Edwin 1920- *16*
Bare, Colleen Stanley *32*
Bar-el, Dan *199*
Barenholtz, Bernard 1914-1989
   Obituary *64*
Bargar, Gary W. 1947-1985 .... *63*
Barger, Jan 1948- *147*
Barish, Matthew 1907-2000 .... *12*
Barkan, Joanne *127*
   Earlier sketch in SATA 77
Barker, Albert W. 1900- *8*

Barker, Carol (Minturn) 1938- 31
Barker, Cicely Mary 1895-1973 49
  Brief entry 39
  See also CLR 88
Barker, Melvern 1907-1989 11
Barker, S. Omar 1894-1985 10
Barker, Squire Omar
  See Barker, S. Omar
Barker, Will 1913-1983 8
Barkin, Carol 1944- 52
  Earlier sketch in SATA 42
Barklem, Jill 1951- 96
  See also CLR 31
Barkley, Brad 178
Barkley, James Edward 1941- 6
Barks, Carl 1901-2000 37
Barley, Janet Crane 1934- 95
Barlow, Steve 1952- 211
Barnaby, Ralph S(tanton) 1893-1986 9
Barnard, A. M.
  See Alcott, Louisa May
Barnard, Bryn 1956- 169
  Earlier sketch in SATA 115
Barne, Kitty
  See Barne, Marion Catherine
Barne, Marion Catherine 1883-1957 97
Barneda, David 206
Barner, Bob 1947- 136
  Earlier sketch in SATA 29
Barnes, Dawn 1957- 175
Barnes, Derrick 191
Barnes, Derrick D.
  See Barnes, Derrick
Barnes, (Frank) Eric Wollencott 1907-1962 . 22
Barnes, Joyce Annette 1958- 85
Barnes, Laura T. 1958- 119
Barnes, Loutricia
  See Barnes-Svarney, Patricia L(ou)
Barnes, Malcolm 1909(?)-1984
  Obituary 41
Barnes, Michael 1934- 55
Barnes-Murphy, Frances 1951- 88
Barnes-Murphy, Rowan 1952- 88
Barnes-Svarney, Patricia L(ou) 1953- 67
Barnet, Nancy 1954- 84
Barnett, Ivan 1947- 70
Barnett, Lincoln (Kinnear) 1909-1979 36
Barnett, Mac 223
Barnett, Moneta 1922-1976 33
Barnett, Naomi 1927- 40
Barney, Maginel Wright 1881(?)-1966 39
  Brief entry 32
Barnhart, Clarence L(ewis) 1900-1993 48
  Obituary 78
Barnholdt, Lauren 1980(?)- 232
Barnhouse, Rebecca 1961- 225
Barnouw, Adriaan Jacob 1877-1968
  Obituary 27
Barnouw, Victor 1915-1989 43
  Brief entry 28
Barnstone, Willis 1927- 20
Barnum, Jay Hyde 1888(?)-1962 20
Barnum, P. T., Jr.
  See Stratemeyer, Edward L.
Barnum, Richard 67
  Earlier sketch in SATA 1
Barnum, Theodore
  See Stratemeyer, Edward L.
Barnwell, Ysaye M. 1946- 200
Baron, Kathi 1956- 226
Baron, Kathy 1954- 90
Baron, Virginia Olsen 1931- 46
  Brief entry 28
Barr, Donald 1921-2004 20
  Obituary 152
Barr, George 1907-1992 2
Barr, Jene 1922-1985 16
  Obituary 42
Barr, Nevada 1952- 126
  Earlier sketch in SATA 115
Barragan, Paula 1963- 216

Barratt, Mark 1954- 224
Barrer, Gertrude
  See Barrer-Russell, Gertrude
Barrer-Russell, Gertrude 1921- 27
Barrett, Angela 1955- 223
Barrett, Angela (Jane) 1955- 145
  Earlier sketch in SATA 75
Barrett, Ethel 87
  Brief entry 44
Barrett, Joyce Durham 1943- 138
Barrett, Judi
  See Barrett, Judith
Barrett, Judith 1941- 204
  Earlier sketch in SATA 26
  See also CLR 98
Barrett, Robert T(heodore) 1949- 92
Barrett, Ron 1937- 14
Barrett, Susan (Mary) 1938- 113
Barrett, Tracy 1955- 207
  Earlier sketches in SATA 84, 115, 156
Barrett, William E(dmund) 1900-1986
  Obituary 49
Barretta, Gene 214
  Earlier sketch in SATA 176
Barretton, Grandall
  See Garrett, Randall
Barrie, Baronet
  See Barrie, J. M.
Barrie, J. M. 1860-1937 100
  See also YABC 1
  See also CLR 124
Barrie, James Matthew
  See Barrie, J. M.
Barringer, William 1940-1996 153
Barrington, Michael
  See Moorcock, Michael
Barris, George 1925- 47
Barrol, Grady
  See Bograd, Larry
Barron, Rex 1951- 84
Barron, T.A. 1952- 192
  Earlier sketches in SATA 83, 126
  See also CLR 86
Barron, Thomas Archibald
  See Barron, T.A.
Barron, Tom
  See Barron, T.A.
Barrow, Lloyd H. 1942- 73
Barrows, Annie 1962- 180
Barry, Dan 1958- 177
Barry, Dana (Marie Malloy) 1949- 139
Barry, James P(otvin) 1918- 14
Barry, Katharina Watjen 1936- 4
Barry, Robert 1931- 6
Barry, Robert Everett
  See Barry, Robert
Barry, Scott 1952- 32
Barry, Sheila Anne -2003 91
Barshaw, Ruth McNally 203
Bartell, Susan S. 175
Bartenbach, Jean 1918- 40
Barth, Edna 1914-1980 7
  Obituary 24
Barth, Kelly L. 1964- 152
Barthelme, Donald 1931-1989 7
  Obituary 62
Barth-Grozinger, Inge 1950- 185
Bartholomew, Barbara 1941- 86
  Brief entry 42
Bartholomew, Jean
  See Beatty, Patricia (Robbins)
Bartlett, Alison 153
Bartlett, Philip A. 1
Bartlett, Robert Merrill 1899-1995 12
Bartoletti, Susan Campbell 1958- 173
  Earlier sketches in SATA 88, 129, 135
Barton, Byron 1930- 126
  Earlier sketches in SATA 9, 90
Barton, Chris 224
Barton, Jill(ian) 1940- 75

Barton, May Hollis 67
  Earlier sketch in SATA 1
Barton, Pat
  See Arrowsmith, Pat
Barton, Patrice 1955- 226
Bartos-Hoeppner, Barbara 1923- 5
Bartram, Simon 218
  Earlier sketch in SATA 156
Bartsch, Jochen 1906- 39
Baruch, Dorothy W(alter) 1899-1962 21
Barunga, Albert 1912(?)-1977 120
Baryshnikov, Mikhail 1948- 192
Bas, Rutger
  See Rutgers van der Loeff-Basenau, An(na)
  Maria Margaretha
Base, Graeme 1958- 162
  Earlier sketches in SATA 67, 101
  See also CLR 22
Base, Graeme Rowland
  See Base, Graeme
Baseman, Gary 1960- 174
Bash, Barbara 1948- 132
Bashevis, Isaac
  See Singer, Isaac Bashevis
Bashevis, Yitskhok
  See Singer, Isaac Bashevis
Bashista, Adrienne Ehlert 203
Basile, Gloria Vitanza 1929- 180
Baskin, Leonard 1922-2000 120
  Brief entry 27
  Earlier sketch in SATA 30
Baskin, Nora Raleigh 1961- 189
  Earlier sketch in SATA 129
Bason, Lillian 1913- 20
Bass, Hester 1956- 223
Bass, L.G.
  See Geringer, Laura
Bassett, Jeni 1959- 64
  Brief entry 43
Bassett, John Keith
  See Keating, Lawrence A.
Bassett, Lisa 1958- 61
Bassil, Andrea
  See Nilsen, Anna
Bastyra, Judy 108
Basye, Dale E. 205
Bataille, Marion 1963- 209
Bat-Ami, Miriam 1950- 150
  Autobiography Feature 150
  Earlier sketches in SATA 82, 122
Bate, Lucy 1939-1993 18
Bate, Norman (Arthur) 1916- 5
Bateman, Colin 1962- 172
Bateman, Donna M. 190
Bateman, Teresa 1957- 216
  Earlier sketches in SATA 112, 168
Bates, Amy June 189
Bates, Barbara S(nedeker) 1919- 12
Bates, Betty
  See Bates, Elizabeth
Bates, Dianne 1948- 147
Bates, Elizabeth 1921- 19
Bates, Ivan 175
Bates, Katharine Lee 1859-1929 113
Bates, Martine
  See Leavitt, Martine
Bateson, Catherine 1960- 197
  Earlier sketch in SATA 157
Batey, Tom 1946- 52
  Brief entry 41
Bath, Kevin P.
  See Bath, K.P.
Bath, K.P. 1959- 171
Batherman, Muriel
  See Sheldon, Muriel
Batson, Larry 1930- 35
Batt, Tanya Robyn 1970- 131
Battaglia, Aurelius 1910- 50
  Brief entry 33
Batten, H(arry) Mortimer 1888-1958 25

Batten, Mary 1937- 162
Earlier sketches in SATA 5, 102
Batterberry, Ariane Ruskin 1935- 13
Batterberry, Michael Carver 1932-2010 32
Battle-Lavert, Gwendolyn 1951- 155
Earlier sketches in SATA 85, 131
Battles, (Roxy) Edith 1921- 7
Baudouy, Michel-Aime 1909- 7
Bauer, A.C.E. 201
Bauer, Caroline Feller 1935- 98
Brief entry 46
Earlier sketch in SATA 52
See also SAAS 24
Bauer, Fred 1934- 36
Bauer, Helen 1900-1988 2
Bauer, Joan 1951- 160
Earlier sketch in SATA 117
Bauer, Jutta 1955- 150
Bauer, Marion Dane 1938- 192
Autobiography Feature 144
Earlier sketches in SATA 20, 69, 113, 144
See also SAAS 9
Bauer, Michael Gerard 1955(?)- 167
Bauer, Steven 1948- 125
Bauerschmidt, Marjorie 1926- 15
Baughman, Dorothy 1940- 61
Baum, Allyn Z(elton) 1924-1997 98
Earlier sketch in SATA 20
Baum, L. Frank
See Thompson, Ruth Plumly
Baum, L. Frank 1856-1919 100
Earlier sketch in SATA 18
See also CLR 107
Baum, Louis 1948- 182
Brief entry 52
Earlier sketch in SATA 64
Baum, Louis F.
See Baum, L. Frank
Baum, Lyman Frank
See Baum, L. Frank
Baum, Maxie 188
Baum, Willi 1931- 4
Bauman, Beth Ann 1964- 220
Baumann, Amy Beeching 1922- 10
Baumann, Amy Brown Beeching
See Baumann, Amy Beeching
Baumann, Hans 1914- 2
See also CLR 35
Baumann, Kurt 1935- 21
Baumgartner, Barbara 1939- 86
Baurys, Flo 1938- 122
Baurys, Florence
See Baurys, Flo
Bausum, Ann 173
Bawden, Nina 1925- 132
Earlier sketches in SATA 4, 72
See also CLR 51
See also SAAS 16
Bawden, Nina Mary Mabey
See Bawden, Nina
Baxter, Andy
See Dakin, Glenn
Baxter, Roberta 1952- 219
Baxter, Valerie
See Meynell, Laurence Walter
Bay, Jeanette Graham 1928- 88
Bayer, Harold
See Gregg, Andrew K.
Bayer, Jane E. (?)-1985
Obituary 44
Bayley, Nicola 1949- 129
Earlier sketches in SATA 41, 69
Baylor, Byrd 1924- 136
Earlier sketches in SATA 16, 69
See also CLR 3
Baynes, Pauline 1922-2008 133
Obituary 196
Earlier sketches in SATA 19, 59
Baynes, Pauline Diana
See Baynes, Pauline
Bayoc, Cbabi 186

Bayrock, Fiona 215
BB
See Watkins-Pitchford, Denys James
Beach, Charles
See Reid, (Thomas) Mayne
Beach, Charles Amory 1
Beach, Edward L. 1918-2002 12
Obituary 140
Beach, Edward Latimer
See Beach, Edward L.
Beach, Lisa 1957- 111
Beach, Lynn
See Lance, Kathryn
Beach, Stewart T(aft) 1899-1979 23
Beachcroft, Nina 1931- 18
Beagle, Peter S. 1939- 130
Earlier sketch in SATA 60
Beagle, Peter Soyer
See Beagle, Peter S.
Beaglehole, Helen 1946- 117
Beake, Lesley 1949- 209
Beaky, Suzanne 1971- 230
Beale, Fleur 107
Bealer, Alex W(inkler III) 1921-1980 8
Obituary 22
Beales, Valerie 1915- 74
Beals, Carleton 1893-1979 12
Beals, Frank Lee 1881-1972
Obituary 26
Beam, Matt 1970- 187
Beame, Rona 1934- 12
Beamer, Charles 1942- 43
Beamer, George Charles, Jr.
See Beamer, Charles
Bean, Jonathan 1979- 194
Bean, Normal
See Burroughs, Edgar Rice
Beaney, Jan
See Udall, Jan Beaney
Beaney, Jane
See Udall, Jan Beaney
Bear, Carolyn
See Rayban, Chloe
Bear, Greg 1951- 105
Earlier sketch in SATA 65
Bear, Gregory Dale
See Bear, Greg
Bearanger, Marie
See Messier, Claire
Beard, Alex 1970- 222
Beard, Charles A(ustin) 1874-1948 18
Beard, Dan(iel Carter) 1850-1941 22
Beard, Darleen Bailey 1961- 96
Bearden, Romare (Howard) 1914(?)-1988 ... 22
Obituary 56
Beardmore, Cedric
See Beardmore, George
Beardmore, George 1908-1979 20
Beardshaw, Rosalind 1969- 225
Earlier sketch in SATA 190
Beardsley, Martyn R. 1957- 150
Bearman, Jane (Ruth) 1917- 29
Bearn, Emily 220
Beaton, Clare 1947- 220
Earlier sketch in SATA 125
Beatty, Elizabeth
See Holloway, Teresa (Bragunier)
Beatty, Hetty Burlingame 1907-1971 5
Beatty, Jerome, Jr. 1918- 5
Beatty, John (Louis) 1922-1975 6
Obituary 25
Beatty, Patricia (Robbins) 1922-1991 73
Obituary 68
Earlier sketches in SATA 1, 30
See also SAAS 4
Beaty, Andrea 186
Beaty, Mary (T.) 1947- 146
Beaudoin, Sean 210
Beauford, Jhenne Tyler
See Beauford, Tyler
Beauford, Tyler 1990- 225

Beaumont, Karen 1954- 204
Beavers, Ethen 1971- 225
Beccia, Carlyn 189
Bechard, Margaret 1953- 164
Earlier sketch in SATA 85
Bechtel, Louise Seaman 1894-1985 4
Obituary 43
Bechtold, Lisze 208
Beck, Andrea 1956- 226
Beck, Barbara L. 1927- 12
Beck, Ian 1947- 190
Earlier sketch in SATA 138
See Beck, Ian Archibald
Beck, Peggy 1949- 171
Beck, Scott 197
Becker, Beril 1901-1999 11
Becker, Bonny 184
Becker, Deborah Zimmett 1955- 138
Becker, Helaine 1961- 142
Becker, John (Leonard) 1901- 12
Becker, John E(mil) 1942- 148
Becker, Joyce 1936- 39
Becker, May Lamberton 1873-1958 33
Becker, Neesa 1951- 123
Becker, Shari 174
Beckerman, Chad W. 198
Beckett, Sheilah 1913- 33
Beckhorn, Susan Williams 1953- 189
Beckles Willson, Robina 1930- 27
Beckman, Delores 1914-1994 51
Beckman, Gunnel 1910- 6
See also CLR 25
See also SAAS 9
Beckman, Kaj
See Beckman, Karin
Beckman, Karin 1913- 45
Beckman, Per (Frithiof) 1913- 45
Bedard, Michael 1949- 154
Earlier sketch in SATA 93
See also CLR 35
Beddor, Frank 194
Beddows, Eric
See Nutt, Ken
Bedford, A. N.
See Watson, Jane Werner
Bedford, Annie North
See Watson, Jane Werner
Bedford, David 224
Earlier sketch in SATA 159
Bedford, David J.
See Bedford, David
Bedoukian, Kerop 1907-1981 53
Bee, Jay
See Brainerd, John W(hiting)
Bee, William 188
Beebe, B. F.
See Johnson, B. F.
Beebe, (Charles) William 1877-1962 19
Beeby, Betty 1923- 25
Beech, Mark 1971- 191
Beech, Webb
See Griffin, W. E. B.
Beecham, Jahnna 161
Beechcroft, William
See Hallstead, William F(inn III)
Beeching, Jack 1922- 14
Beeke, Tiphanie 219
Earlier sketch in SATA 163
Beeler, Janet
See Shaw, Janet
Beeler, Nelson F(rederick) 1910-1978 13
Beere, Peter 1951- 97
Beers, Dorothy Sands 1917- 9
Beers, Lorna 1897-1989 14
Beers, V(ictor) Gilbert 1928- 130
Earlier sketch in SATA 9
Beeton, Max
See Redding, Robert Hull
Begay, Shonto 1954- 137
Begaye, Lisa Shook
See Beach, Lisa

Begin, Mary Jane 1963- 82
Begin-Callanan, Mary Jane
    See Begin, Mary Jane
Begley, Kathleen A. 1948- 21
Begley, Kathleen Anne
    See Begley, Kathleen A.
Beguine, Anna
    See Saintcrow, Lilith
Beha, Eileen 221
Beha, Philippe 211
Behan, Leslie
    See Gottfried, Theodore Mark
Behler, Deborah A. 1947- 145
Behler, John L. 1943-2006 145
    Obituary 173
Behler, John Luther
    See Behler, John L.
Behn, Harry 1898-1973 2
    Obituary 34
Behnke, Frances L. 8
Behr, Joyce 1929- 15
Behrens, Andy 228
Behrens, June York 1925- 19
Behrman, Carol H(elen) 1925- 144
    Earlier sketch in SATA 14
Beifuss, John, (Jr.) 1959- 92
Beil, Karen Magnuson 1950- 221
    Earlier sketch in SATA 124
Beil, Michael D. 226
Beiler, Edna 1923- 61
Beingessner, Laura 1965- 220
Beinicke, Steve 1956- 69
Beirne, Barbara 1933- 71
Beiser, Arthur 1931- 22
Beiser, Germaine 1931- 11
Belair, Richard L. 1934- 45
Belaney, Archibald Stansfeld 1888-1938 24
    See also CLR 32
Belasen, Amy 1983- 213
Belbin, David 1958- 164
    Earlier sketch in SATA 106
Belden, Wilanne Schneider 1925- 56
Belfrage, Sally 1936-1994 65
    Obituary 79
Belknap, B. H.
    See Ellis, Edward S.
Belknap, Boynton
    See Ellis, Edward S.
Belknap, Boynton M.D.
    See Ellis, Edward S.
Bell, Anthea 1936- 148
    Earlier sketch in SATA 88
Bell, Cathleen Davitt 1971- 203
Bell, Cece 202
Bell, Clare (Louise) 1952- 99
Bell, Corydon Whitten 1894-1980 3
Bell, David Owen 1949- 99
Bell, Emerson
    See Stratemeyer, Edward L.
Bell, Emily Mary
    See Cason, Mabel Earp
Bell, Frank
    See Benson, Mildred
Bell, Gertrude (Wood) 1911-1987 12
Bell, Gina
    See Balzano, Jeanne (Koppel)
Bell, Hilari 1958- 226
    Earlier sketches in SATA *151, 197*
Bell, Jadrien
    See Golden, Christie
Bell, Janet
    See Clymer, Eleanor
Bell, Janet Cheatham 1937- 127
Bell, Krista 1950- 215
    Earlier sketch in SATA 126
Bell, Krista Anne Blakeney
    See Bell, Krista
Bell, Margaret E(lizabeth) 1898-1990 *........ 2*
Bell, Mary Reeves 1946- 88
Bell, Norman (Edward) 1899- 11
Bell, Raymond Martin 1907-1999 13

Bell, Siobhan 177
Bell, Thelma Harrington 1896-1985 3
Bell, William 1945- 90
    See also CLR 91
Bellairs, John (Anthony) 1938-1991 160
    Obituary 66
    Earlier sketches in SATA 2, 68
    See also CLR 37
Beller, Susan Provost 1949- 128
    Earlier sketch in SATA 84
    See also CLR 106
Bellingham, Brenda 1931- 99
    Brief entry 51
Bello, Rosario de
    See De Bello, Rosario
Belloc, Hilaire 1870-1953 112
    See also YABC 1
    See also CLR 102
Belloc, Joseph Hilaire Pierre Sebastien Rene
    Swanton
    See Belloc, Hilaire
Belloc, Joseph Peter Rene Hilaire
    See Belloc, Hilaire
Belloc, Joseph Pierre Hilaire
    See Belloc, Hilaire
Belloli, Andrea P. A. 1947- 86
Bell-Rehwoldt, Sheri 1962- 199
Bellville, Cheryl Walsh 1944- 54
    Brief entry 49
Bell-Zano, Gina
    See Balzano, Jeanne (Koppel)
Belpre, Pura 1899-1982 16
    Obituary 30
Belting, Natalia Maree 1915-1997 6
Belton, John Raynor 1931- 22
Belton, Sandra 1939- 186
    Earlier sketches in SATA 85, 134
Belton, Sandra Yvonne
    See Belton, Sandra
Beltran, Alberto 1923- 43
Beltran-Hernandez, Irene 1945- 74
Belvedere, Lee
    See Grayland, Valerie (Merle Spanner)
Bemelmans, Ludwig 1898-1962 100
    Earlier sketch in SATA 15
    See also CLR 93
Benander, Carl D. 1941- 74
Benary, Margot
    See Benary-Isbert, Margot
Benary-Isbert, Margot 1889-1979 2
    Obituary 21
    See also CLR 12
Benasutti, Marion 1908-1992 6
Benatar, Raquel 1955- 167
Benchley, Nathaniel (Goddard) 1915-1981 .. 25
    Obituary 28
    Earlier sketch in SATA 3
Benchley, Peter 1940-2006 164
    Earlier sketches in SATA 3, 89
Benchley, Peter Bradford
    See Benchley, Peter
Bendall-Brunello, John 185
Bender, Edna 1941- 92
Bender, Esther 1942- 88
Bender, Lucy Ellen 1942- 22
Bender, Robert 1962- 160
    Earlier sketch in SATA 79
Bendick, Jeanne 1919- 135
    Earlier sketches in SATA 2, 68
    See also CLR 5
    See also SAAS 4
Bendick, Robert L(ouis) 1917- 11
Bendinger, Jessica 1966- 233
Benedetto, William R. 1928- 180
Benedetto, William Ralph
    See Benedetto, William R.
Benedict, Andrew
    See Arthur, Robert, (Jr.)
Benedict, Dorothy Potter 1889-1979 11
    Obituary 23
Benedict, Lois Trimble 1902-1967 12

Benedict, Rex 1920-1995 8
Benedict, Stewart H(urd) 1924- 26
Beneduce, Ann Keay 128
Benet, Laura 1884-1979 3
    Obituary 23
Benet, Stephen Vincent 1898-1943
    See YABC 1
Benet, Sula 1906-1982 21
    Obituary 33
Ben-Ezer, Ehud 1936- 122
Benezra, Barbara (Beardsley) 1921- 10
Benham, Leslie 1922- 48
Benham, Lois (Dakin) 1924- 48
Benham, Mary Lile 1914-1991 55
Benioff, Carol 232
Benjamin, E. M. J.
    See Bache, Ellyn
Benjamin, Floella 1949- 206
Benjamin, Nora
    See Kubie, Nora Gottheil Benjamin
Benjamin, Saragail Katzman 1953- 86
Benner, Cheryl 1962- 80
Benner, Judith Ann 1942- 94
Bennett, Alice
    See Ziner, Florence
Bennett, Artie 227
Bennett, Cherie 1960- 158
    Earlier sketch in SATA 97
Bennett, Dorothea
    See Young, Dorothea Bennett
Bennett, Erin Susanne
    See Banks, Erin Bennett
Bennett, Holly 1957- 181
Bennett, James (W.) 1942- 153
    Autobiography Feature 153
    Earlier sketches in SATA 93, 148
Bennett, Jay 1912- 87
    Brief entry 27
    Earlier sketch in SATA 41
    See also SAAS 4
Bennett, Jill (Crawford) 1934- 41
Bennett, John 1865-1956
    See YABC 1
Bennett, Kelly 1958- 231
Bennett, Kelly Goldman
    See Bennett, Kelly
Bennett, Penelope (Agnes) 1938- 94
Bennett, Rachel
    See Hill, Margaret (Ohler)
Bennett, Rainey 1907-1998 15
    Obituary 111
Bennett, Richard 1899- 21
Bennett, Russell H(oradley) 1896- 25
Bennett, Veronica 1953- 178
Bennett, William (John) 1943- 102
Benning, Elizabeth
    See Rice, Bebe Faas
Benny, Mike 1964- 203
Benson, Elizabeth P(olk) 1924- 65
Benson, Kathleen 1947- 183
    Earlier sketches in SATA 62, 111
Benson, Linda M(aria) 1959- 84
Benson, Mildred 1905-2002 100
    Obituary 135
    Earlier sketches in SATA 1, 65, 67
Benson, Mildred Augustine Wirt
    See Benson, Mildred
Benson, Mildred Wirt
    See Benson, Mildred
Benson, Millie
    See Benson, Mildred
Benson, Patrick 1956- 147
Benson, Sally 1900-1972 35
    Obituary 27
    Earlier sketch in SATA 1
Bentley, Judith (McBride) 1945- 89
    Earlier sketch in SATA 40
Bentley, Karen
    See Taschek, Karen
Bentley, Nancy (L.) 1946- 78

Bentley, Nicolas Clerihew 1907-1978
    Obituary 24
Bentley, Phyllis Eleanor 1894-1977 6
    Obituary 25
Bentley, Roy 1947- 46
Bentley, William (George) 1916- 84
Bently, Peter 1960- 221
Benton, Jim 1963- 172
ben Uzair, Salem
    See Horne, Richard Henry Hengist
Ben-Zvi, Rebeccca Tova
    See O'Connell, Rebecca
Bercaw, Edna Coe 1961- 124
Berck, Judith 1960- 75
Bereal, JaeMe 1959(?)- 228
Berelson, Howard 1940- 5
Berends, Polly Berrien 1939- 50
    Brief entry 38
Berenstain, Jan 1923- 135
    Earlier sketches in SATA *12, 64, 129*
    See also CLR *150*
    See also SAAS *20*
Berenstain, Janice
    See Berenstain, Jan
Berenstain, Michael 1951- 220
    Earlier sketch in SATA *45*
Berenstain, Mike
    See Berenstain, Michael
Berenstain, Stan 1923-2005 135
    Obituary 169
    Earlier sketches in SATA *12, 64, 129*
    See also CLR *150*
    See also SAAS *20*
Berenstain, Stanley
    See Berenstain, Stan
Berenzy, Alix 1957- 168
    Earlier sketch in SATA *65*
Beresford, Elisabeth 1928-2010 141
    Earlier sketches in SATA *25, 86*
    See also SAAS *20*
Berg, Adriane G(ilda) 1948- 152
Berg, Dave
    See Berg, David
Berg, David 1920-2002 27
    Obituary 137
Berg, Elizabeth 1948- 104
Berg, Jean Horton 1913-1995 6
Berg, Joan
    See Victor, Joan Berg
Berg, Ron 1952- 48
Bergaust, Erik 1925-1978 20
Bergel, Colin J. 1963- 137
Bergen, Joyce 1949- 95
Berger, Barbara (Helen) 1945- 77
Berger, Carin 232
    Earlier sketch in SATA *185*
Berger, Gilda 1935- 88
    Brief entry 42
Berger, Joe 1970- 221
Berger, Josef 1903-1971 36
Berger, Lou 1950- 213
Berger, Melvin H. 1927- 158
    Autobiography Feature 124
    Earlier sketches in SATA *5, 88*
    See also CLR *32*
    See also SAAS *2*
Berger, Phil 1942-2001 62
Berger, Samantha 1969- 140
Berger, Samantha Allison
    See Berger, Samantha
Berger, Terry 1933- 8
Bergey, Alyce 1934- 45
Bergey, Alyce Mae
    See Bergey, Alyce
Bergin, Mark 1961- 160
    Earlier sketch in SATA *114*
Berglin, Ruth Marie 1970- 181
Bergman, Donna 1934- 73
Bergman, Mara 1956- 196
Bergman, Tamar 1939- 95

Bergren, Lisa T.
    See Bergren, Lisa Tawn
Bergren, Lisa Tawn 200
Bergsma, Jody Lynn 163
Bergstein, Rita M. 211
Bergum, Constance R. 1952- 208
    Earlier sketch in SATA *121*
Berk, Ari 208
Berk, Josh 1976- 227
Berkebile, Fred D(onovan) 1900-1978
    Obituary 26
Berkeley, Jon 1962- 204
Berkes, Marianne 217
    Earlier sketch in SATA *173*
Berkey, Barry Robert 1935- 24
Berkowitz, Freda Pastor 1908-1994 12
Berkus, Clara Widess 1909- 78
Berlan, Kathryn Hook 1946- 78
Berlfein, Judy Reiss 1958- 79
Berlin, Eric 1968- 195
Berliner, Don 1930- 33
Berliner, Franz 1930- 13
Berlitz, Charles (L. Frambach) 1914-2003 ... 32
    Obituary 151
Berman, Len 1947- 229
Berman, Linda 1948- 38
Berman, Paul (Lawrence) 1949- 66
Berman, Rachel 1946- 217
Berna, Paul 1910-1994 15
    Obituary 78
    See also CLR *19*
Bernadette
    See Watts, Bernadette
Bernard, Bruce 1928-2000 78
    Obituary 124
Bernard, George I. 1949- 39
Bernard, Jacqueline (de Sieyes) 1921-1983 ... 8
    Obituary 45
Bernard, Patricia 1942- 181
    Earlier sketch in SATA *106*
Bernard, Trish
    See Bernard, Patricia
Bernardin, James 1966- 227
    Earlier sketch in SATA *112*
Bernardo, Anilu 184
Bernards, Neal 1963- 71
Bernasconi, Pablo 1973- 183
Bernays, Anne 1930- 32
Berner, Rotraut Susanne 1948- 214
Bernhard, Durga T. 1961- 80
Bernhard, Emery 1950- 80
Bernheimer, Kate 201
Bernier-Grand, Carmen T. 1947- 202
Bernstein, Daryl (Evan) 1976- 81
Bernstein, Joanne E(ckstein) 1943- 15
Bernstein, Jonathan 217
Bernstein, Margery 1933- 114
Bernstein, Nina 1949- 180
Bernstein, Theodore M(enline) 1904-1979 ... 12
    Obituary 27
Berrien, Edith Heal
    See Heal, Edith
Berrill, Jacquelyn (Batsel) 1905- 12
Berrington, John
    See Brownjohn, Alan
Berry, B. J.
    See Berry, Barbara J.
Berry, Barbara J. 1937- 7
Berry, Erick
    See Best, (Evangel) Allena Champlin
Berry, Holly 1957- 210
Berry, James 1924- 110
    Earlier sketch in SATA *67*
    See also CLR *143*
Berry, Jane Cobb 1915(?)-1979
    Obituary 22
Berry, Joy 1944- 58
    Brief entry 46
Berry, Joy Wilt
    See Berry, Joy
Berry, Julie 1974- 218

Berry, Lynne 190
Berry, William D(avid) 1926- 14
Bersani, Shennen 1961- 164
Berson, Harold 1926- 4
Bertagna, Julie 1962- 151
Bertholf, Bret 189
Bertin, Charles-Francois
    See Berlitz, Charles (L. Frambach)
Bertolet, Paul
    See McLaughlin, Frank
Berton, Pierre (Francis de Marigny)
    1920-2004 99
    Obituary 158
Bertrand, Cecile 1953- 76
Bertrand, Diane Gonzales 1956- 177
    Earlier sketch in SATA *106*
Bertrand, Lynne 1963- 164
    Earlier sketch in SATA *81*
Beskow, Elsa (Maartman) 1874-1953 20
    See also CLR *17*
Bess, Clayton
    See Locke, Robert
Besson, Luc 1959- 199
Best, (Evangel) Allena Champlin 1892-1974 . 2
    Obituary 25
Best, Cari 1951- 200
    Earlier sketches in SATA *107, 149*
Best, (Oswald) Herbert 1894-1980 2
Bestall, A(lfred) E(dmeades) 1892-1986 97
    Obituary 48
Betancourt, Jeanne 1941- 148
    Brief entry 43
    Earlier sketches in SATA *55, 96*
Beth, Mary
    See Miller, Mary Beth
Bethancourt, T. Ernesto
    See Paisley, Tom
Bethel, Dell 1929- 52
Bethell, Jean (Frankenberry) 1922- 8
Bethers, Ray 1902-1973 6
Bethke, Bruce Raymond 1955- 114
Bethlen, T.D.
    See Silverberg, Robert
Bethune, J. G.
    See Ellis, Edward S.
Bethune, J. H.
    See Ellis, Edward S.
Betteridge, Anne
    See Potter, Margaret
Betteridge, Deirdre 214
Bettina
    See Ehrlich, Bettina Bauer
Bettmann, Otto Ludwig 1903-1998 46
Bettoli, Delana 187
Betts, James
    See Haynes, Betsy
Betz, Eva Kelly 1897-1968 10
Bevan, Tom 1868-1930(?)
    See YABC *2*
Bevis, Mary 1939- 202
Bewick, Thomas 1753-1828 16
Beyer, Audrey White 1916- 9
Beyer, Paul J. III 1950- 74
Beynon, John
    See Harris, John (Wyndham Parkes Lucas)
    Beynon
Bezencon, Jacqueline (Buxcel) 1924- 48
Bhatia, Jamunadevi 1919- 48
Bhatia, June
    See Bhatia, Jamunadevi
Bial, Morrison David 1917- 62
Bial, Raymond 1948- 225
    Earlier sketches in SATA *76, 116, 165*
Biala
    See Brustlein, Janice Tworkov
Biale, Rachel 1952- 99
Bialk, Elisa
    See Krautter, Elisa (Bialk)
Bianchi, John 1947- 91
Bianchi, Robert S(teven) 1943- 92

Bianco, Margery
  See Bianco, Margery Williams
Bianco, Margery Williams 1881-1944 .... *15*
  See also CLR *146*
Bianco, Pamela 1906- *28*
Bibby, Violet 1908-1996 .... *24*
Bible, Charles 1937- *13*
Bibo, Bobette
  See Gugliotta, Bobette
Bice, Clare 1909-1976 .... *22*
Bickerstaff, Isaac
  See Swift, Jonathan
Bidner, Jenni 1963- *193*
Biedrzycki, David 1955- *219*
Biegel, Paul 1925- *79*
  Earlier sketch in SATA *16*
  See also CLR *27*
  See also SAAS *18*
Biemiller, Carl L(udwig), Jr.) 1912-1979 ..... *40*
  Obituary *21*
Bienenfeld, Florence L(ucille) 1929- *39*
Bierhorst, John (William) 1936- *149*
  Autobiography Feature *149*
  Earlier sketches in SATA *6, 91*
  See also SAAS *10*
Biggar, Joan R. 1936- *120*
Biggar, Joan Rawlins
  See Biggar, Joan R.
Biggle, Lloyd, Jr. 1923-2002 .... *65*
Biggs, Brian 1968- *192*
Bilal, Abdel W(ahab) 1970- *92*
Bilbrough, Norman 1941- *111*
Bildner, Phil *230*
  Earlier sketch in SATA *173*
Bileck, Marvin 1920- *40*
Bilibin, Ivan (Iakolevich) 1876-1942 .... *61*
Bill, Alfred Hoyt 1879-1964 .... *44*
Bill, Tannis *228*
Billam, Rosemary 1952- *61*
Billings, Charlene W(interer) 1941- *41*
Billingsley, Franny 1954- *132*
Billington, Elizabeth T(hain) *50*
  Brief entry *43*
Billout, Guy (Rene) 1941- *144*
  Earlier sketch in SATA *10*
  See also CLR *33*
Bilson, Geoffrey 1938-1987 .... *99*
Binch, Caroline (Lesley) 1947- *140*
  Earlier sketch in SATA *81*
Bing, Christopher (H.) *126*
Bingham, Caroline 1962- *158*
Bingham, Jane M. 1941- *163*
Bingham, Jane Marie
  See Bingham, Jane M.
Bingham, Janet 1959- *200*
Bingham, Kelly 1967- *207*
Bingham, Sam 1944- *96*
Bingham, Samuel A.
  See Bingham, Sam
Bingley, Margaret (Jane Kirby) 1947- *72*
Binkley, Anne
  See Rand, Ann (Binkley)
Binzen, Bill
  See Binzen, William
Binzen, William *24*
Birch, David (W.) 1913-1996 .... *89*
Birch, Reginald B(athurst) 1856-1943 .... *19*
Birchman, David 1949- *72*
Birchmore, Daniel A. 1951- *92*
Bird, Carmel 1940- *124*
Bird, E(lzy) J(ay) 1911- *58*
Birdsall, Jeanne 1951- *231*
Birdsall, Jeanne 1952(?)- *170*
Birdseye, Tom 1951- *148*
  Earlier sketches in SATA *66, 98*
Birenbaum, Barbara 1941- *65*
Birmingham, Christian 1970- *220*
Birmingham, Lloyd P(aul) 1924- *83*
  Earlier sketch in SATA *12*
Birmingham, Ruth
  See Sorrells, Walter

Birney, Betty G. 1947- *169*
  Earlier sketch in SATA *98*
Biro, B.
  See Biro, B. S.
Biro, B. S. 1921- *1*
  See also CLR *28*
  See also SAAS *13*
Biro, Val
  See Biro, B. S.
Birtha, Becky 1948- *229*
Bischoff, Julia Bristol 1899-1970 .... *12*
Bishop, Bonnie 1943- *37*
Bishop, Claire Huchet 1899(?)-1993 .... *14*
  Obituary *74*
  See also CLR *80*
Bishop, Courtney
  See Ruemmler, John D(avid)
Bishop, Curtis (Kent) 1912-1967 .... *6*
Bishop, Elizabeth 1911-1979
  Obituary *24*
Bishop, Gavin 1946- *216*
  Earlier sketches in SATA *97, 144*
Bishop, Kathleen Wong 1954- *120*
Bishop, Kathy
  See Bishop, Kathleen Wong
Bishop, Nic 1955- *161*
  Earlier sketch in SATA *107*
Bishop, Rudine Sims *224*
Bisset, Donald 1910-1995 .... *86*
  Earlier sketch in SATA *7*
Bisson, Terry 1942- *99*
Bisson, Terry Ballantine
  See Bisson, Terry
Bitter, Gary G(len) 1940- *22*
Bixby, William (Courtney) 1920-1986 .... *6*
  Obituary *47*
Bjoerk, Christina 1938- *99*
  Earlier sketch in SATA *67*
  See also CLR *22*
Bjork, Christina
  See Bjoerk, Christina
Bjorklund, Lorence F. 1913-1978 .... *35*
  Brief entry *32*
Bjorkman, Lauren *222*
Bjorkman, Steve *223*
  Earlier sketch in SATA *163*
Blabey, Aaron 1975(?)- *214*
Black, Algernon David 1900-1993 .... *12*
  Obituary *76*
Black, Holly 1971- *210*
  Earlier sketch in SATA *147*
Black, Irma Simonton 1906-1972 .... *2*
  Obituary *25*
Black, Joe 1959- *224*
Black, Rabbi Joe
  See Black, Joe
Black, Kat *217*
Black, Katherine
  See Black, Kat
Black, Mansell
  See Trevor, Elleston
Black, MaryAnn
  See Easley, MaryAnn
Black, Susan Adams 1953- *40*
Blackall, Bernie 1956- *126*
Blackall, Sophie *231*
  Earlier sketch in SATA *182*
Blackburn, Claire
  See Altman, Linda Jacobs
Blackburn, John(ny) Brewton 1952- *15*
Blackburn, Joyce Knight 1920- *29*
Blacker, Terence 1948- *194*
Blacker, Tina
  See Louise, Tina
Blackett, Veronica Heath 1927- *12*
Blackie, Jean Cutler 1943- *79*
Blacklin, Malcolm
  See Chambers, Aidan
Blacklock, Dyan 1951- *112*
Blackman, Malorie 1962- *196*
  Earlier sketches in SATA *83, 128*

Blackton, Peter
  See Wilson, Lionel
Blackwood, Alan 1932- *70*
Blackwood, Freya *199*
Blackwood, Gary
  See Blackwood, Gary L.
Blackwood, Gary L. 1945- *226*
  Earlier sketches in SATA *72, 118, 169*
Blade, Alexander
  See Garrett, Randall
  and Hamilton, Edmond
  and Silverberg, Robert
Blades, Ann (Sager) 1947- *69*
  Earlier sketch in SATA *16*
  See also CLR *15*
Bladow, Suzanne Wilson 1937- *14*
Blaine, Chris
  See Gardner, Craig Shaw
Blaine, John
  See Goodwin, Harold L(eland)
Blaine, Marge
  See Blaine, Margery Kay
Blaine, Margery Kay 1937- *11*
Blair, Alison
  See Lerangis, Peter
Blair, Anne Denton 1914-1993 .... *46*
Blair, David Nelson 1954- *80*
Blair, Eric
  See Orwell, George
Blair, Jay 1953- *45*
Blair, Lucile
  See Yeakley, Marjory Hall
Blair, Margaret Whitman 1951- *227*
  Earlier sketch in SATA *124*
Blair, Mary 1911-1978 .... *195*
Blair, Pauline Hunter
  See Clarke, Pauline
Blair, Ruth Van Ness 1912-1999 .... *12*
Blair, Shannon
  See Kaye, Marilyn
Blair, Walter 1900-1992 .... *12*
  Obituary *72*
Blaisdell, Bob
  See Blaisdell, Robert
Blaisdell, Robert 1959- *105*
Blake, Bronwyn 1940- *149*
Blake, Francis *198*
Blake, Jon 1954- *171*
  Earlier sketch in SATA *78*
Blake, Olive
  See Supraner, Robyn
Blake, Quentin 1932- *211*
  Earlier sketches in SATA *9, 52, 96, 125*
  See also CLR *31*
Blake, Robert 1949- *42*
Blake, Robert J. *160*
Blake, Stephanie *233*
  See Pearl, Jacques Bain
Blake, Walker E.
  See Griffin, W. E. B.
Blake, William 1757-1827 .... *30*
  See also CLR *52*
Blakely, Gloria 1950- *139*
Blakely, Roger K. 1922- *82*
Blakeney, Jay D.
  See Chester, Deborah
Blakeslee, Lys 1985- *218*
Blakey, Nancy 1955- *94*
Blanc, Esther S. 1913-1997 .... *66*
Blanc, Mel 1908-1989
  Obituary *64*
Blanchard, Patricia *125*
Blanchet, M(uriel) Wylie 1891-1961 .... *106*
Blanco, Richard L(idio) 1926- *63*
Bland, E.
  See Nesbit, E.
Bland, Edith Nesbit
  See Nesbit, E.
Bland, Fabian
  See Nesbit, E.

Blane, Gertrude
  See Blumenthal, Gertrude
Blank, Clarissa Mabel 1915-1965 62
Blankenship, LeeAnn 1944- 181
Blassingame, Wyatt Rainey 1909-1985 34
  Obituary 41
  Earlier sketch in SATA *1*
Blatchford, Claire H. 1944- 94
Blau, Aljoscha 1972- 233
Blauer, Ettagale 1940- 49
Blecha, Aaron 233
Bleck, Linda 207
Bledsoe, Glen L. 1951- 108
Bledsoe, Glen Leonard
  See Bledsoe, Glen L.
Bledsoe, Karen E. 1962- 167
  Earlier sketch in SATA *108*
Bledsoe, Karen Elizabeth
  See Bledsoe, Karen E.
Bledsoe, Lucy Jane 1957- 162
  Earlier sketch in SATA *97*
Bleeker, Sonia
  See Zim, Sonia Bleeker
Blegen, Daniel M. 1950- 92
Blegvad, Erik 1923- 132
  Earlier sketches in SATA *14, 66*
Blegvad, Lenore 1926- 176
  Earlier sketches in SATA *14, 66*
Blessing, Charlotte 223
Bley, Anette 1967- 188
Blish, James 1921-1975 66
Blish, James Benjamin
  See Blish, James
Blishen, Edward (William) 1920-1996 66
  Obituary 93
  Earlier sketch in SATA *8*
Bliss, Corinne Demas
  See Demas, Corinne
Bliss, Frederick
  See Card, Orson Scott
Bliss, Gillian
  See Paton Walsh, Jill
Bliss, Harry 1964- 196
  Earlier sketch in SATA *156*
Bliss, Reginald
  See Wells, H. G.
Bliss, Ronald G(ene) 1942- 12
Blitt, Barry 187
Bliven, Bruce, Jr. 1916-2002 2
Blixen, Karen 1885-1962 44
Blizzard, Gladys S. (?)-1992 79
Blobaum, Cindy 1966- 123
Bloch, Lucienne 1909-1999 10
Bloch, Marie Halun 1910-1998 6
  See also SAAS *9*
Bloch, Robert (Albert) 1917-1994 12
  Obituary 82
Bloch, Serge 1956- 213
Blochman, Lawrence G(oldtree)
  1900-1975 22
Block, Francesca Lia 1962- 213
  Earlier sketches in SATA *80, 116, 158*
  See also CLR *116*
  See also SAAS *21*
Block, Irvin 1917- 12
Blomgren, Jennifer (Alice) 1954- 136
Blonder, Terry Joyce
  See Golson, Terry
Blood, Charles Lewis 1929- 28
Bloom, Barbara Lee 1943- 146
Bloom, Freddy 1914-2000 37
  Obituary 121
Bloom, Lloyd 1947- 108
  Brief entry 43
Bloom, Suzanne 1950- 232
  Earlier sketch in SATA *172*
Bloomfield, Michaela 1966- 70
Bloor, Edward 1950- 201
  Earlier sketches in SATA *98, 155*
Bloor, Edward William
  See Bloor, Edward

Blos, Joan W. 1928- 153
  Autobiography Feature 153
  Brief entry 27
  Earlier sketches in SATA *33, 69, 109*
  See also CLR *18*
  See also SAAS *11*
Blos, Joan Winsor
  See Blos, Joan W.
Bloss, Josie 1981- 232
Blough, Glenn O(rlando) 1907-1995 1
Blue, Rose 1931- 166
  Autobiography Feature 117
  Earlier sketches in SATA *5, 91, 93*
  See also SAAS *24*
Blue, Zachary
  See Stine, R.L.
Bluemle, Elizabeth 209
Bluggage, Oranthy
  See Alcott, Louisa May
Blumberg, Leda 1956- 59
Blumberg, Rhoda 1917- 123
  Earlier sketches in SATA *35, 70*
  See also CLR *21*
Blume, Judy 1938- 195
  Earlier sketches in SATA *2, 31, 79, 142*
  See also CLR *69*
Blume, Judy Sussman
  See Blume, Judy
Blume, Lesley M.M. 1975- 180
Blumenthal, Deborah 204
  Earlier sketch in SATA *161*
Blumenthal, Gertrude 1907-1971
  Obituary 27
Blumenthal, Shirley 1943- 46
Blutig, Eduard
  See Gorey, Edward (St. John)
Bly, Janet 1945- 43
Bly, Janet Chester
  See Bly, Janet
Bly, Stephen A(rthur) 1944- 116
  Earlier sketch in SATA *43*
Blyler, Allison Lee 1966- 74
Blythe, Gary 1959- 185
Blyton, Carey 1932-2002 9
  Obituary 138
Blyton, Enid 1897-1968 25
  See also CLR *31*
Blyton, Enid Mary
  See Blyton, Enid
Bo, Ben
  See Richardson, V.A.
Boardman, Fon Wyman, Jr. 1911-2000 6
Boardman, Gwenn R.
  See Petersen, Gwenn Boardman
Boase, Susan 226
Boase, Wendy 1944-1999 28
  Obituary 110
Boatner, Mark Mayo III 1921- 29
Bobbe, Dorothie de Bear 1905-1975 1
  Obituary 25
Bober, Natalie S. 1930- 134
  Earlier sketch in SATA *87*
  See also SAAS *23*
Bobette, Bibo
  See Gugliotta, Bobette
Bobri, Vladimir V. 1898-1986 47
  Brief entry 32
Bobritsky, Vladimir
  See Bobri, Vladimir V.
Bochak, Grayce 1956- 76
Bock, Hal
  See Bock, Harold I.
Bock, Harold I. 1939- 10
Bock, William Sauts Netamux'we 1939- 14
Bodanis, David 179
Bode, Janet 1943-1999 96
  Obituary 118
  Earlier sketch in SATA *60*
Bode, N.E.
  See Baggott, Julianna

Bodecker, N(iels) M(ogens) 1922-1988 73
  Obituary 54
  Earlier sketch in SATA *8*
Bodeen, S. A. 1965- 158
  Earlier sketch in SATA *114*
Boden, Hilda
  See Bodenham, Hilda Morris
Bodenham, Hilda Morris 1901- 13
Bodett, Thomas Edward 1955- 70
Bodett, Tom
  See Bodett, Thomas Edward
Bodie, Idella F(allaw) 1925- 89
  Earlier sketch in SATA *12*
Bodker, Cecil
  See Bodker, Cecil
Bodker, Cecil 1927- 133
  Earlier sketch in SATA *14*
  See also CLR *23*
Bodsworth, (Charles) Fred(erick) 1918- 27
Boeckman, Charles 1920- 12
Boegehold, Betty (Doyle) 1913-1985
  Obituary 42
Boelts, Maribeth 1964- 200
  Earlier sketches in SATA *78, 163*
Boerst, William J. 1939- 170
  Earlier sketch in SATA *121*
Boesch, Mark J(oseph) 1917- 12
Boesen, Victor 1908- 16
Bogacki, Tomek 1950- 214
  Earlier sketch in SATA *138*
Bogaerts, Gert 1965- 80
Bogan, Paulette 1960- 201
  Earlier sketch in SATA *129*
Bogart, Jo Ellen 1945- 222
  Earlier sketch in SATA *92*
  See also CLR *59*
Boggs, Ralph Steele 1901-1994 7
Bograd, Larry 1953- 89
  Earlier sketch in SATA *33*
  See also SAAS *21*
Bogue, Gary 1938- 195
Bogue, Gary L.
  See Bogue, Gary
Bohdal, Susi 1951- 101
  Earlier sketch in SATA *22*
Bohlen, Nina 1931- 58
Bohlmeijer, Arno 1956- 94
Bohner, Charles (Henry) 1927- 62
Bohnhoff, Maya Kaathryn 1954- 88
Boie, Kirsten 1950- 221
Boiger, Alexandra 178
Boissard, Janine 1932- 59
Bojunga, Lygia
  See Nunes, Lygia Bojunga
Bojunga-Nunes, Lygia
  See Nunes, Lygia Bojunga
Bok, Arthur
  See Bok, Chip
Bok, Chip 1952- 205
Bolam, Emily 1969- 206
Boland, Janice 98
Bolden, Tonya 1959- 227
  Earlier sketches in SATA *79, 138, 188*
Bolden, Tonya Wilyce
  See Bolden, Tonya
Boles, Paul Darcy 1916-1984 9
  Obituary 38
Bolger, Kevin 233
Bolian, Polly 1925- 4
Bollen, Roger 1941(?)- 83
  Brief entry 29
Bolliger, Max 1929- 7
Bollinger, Max 1929- 167
Bollinger, Peter 172
Bolognese, Don(ald Alan) 1934- 129
  Earlier sketches in SATA *24, 71*
Bolognese, Elaine 1933- 23
Bolotin, Norman (Phillip) 1951- 93
Bolton, Carole 1926- 6
Bolton, Elizabeth
  See St. John, Nicole

Bolton, Evelyn
  See Bunting, Eve
Bonar, Veronica
  See Bailey, Donna (Veronica Anne)
Bond, B. J.
  See Heneghan, James
Bond, Bruce 1939- 61
Bond, Felicia 1954- 219
  Earlier sketches in SATA *49, 126*
Bond, Gladys Baker 1912- 14
Bond, Higgins 1951- 220
  Earlier sketches in SATA *83, 177*
Bond, J. Harvey
  See Winterbotham, R(ussell) R(obert)
Bond, (Thomas) Michael 1926- 157
  Earlier sketches in SATA *6, 58*
  See also CLR 95
  See also SAAS 3
Bond, Nancy 1945- 159
  Autobiography Feature 159
  Earlier sketches in SATA *22, 82*
  See also CLR *11*
  See also SAAS *13*
Bond, Nancy Barbara
  See Bond, Nancy
Bond, Rebecca 1972- 214
  Earlier sketch in SATA *130*
Bond, Ruskin 1934- 87
  Earlier sketch in SATA *14*
Bondie, J. D.
  See Cunningham, Chet
Bondoux, Anne-Laure 1971- 175
Bone, Ian 1956- 158
  Earlier sketch in SATA *117*
Bone, J. 230
Bone, Jason
  See Bone, J.
Bonehill, Captain Ralph
  See Stratemeyer, Edward L.
Bonestell, Chesley 1888-1986
  Obituary 48
Bonham, Barbara Thomas 1926- 7
Bonham, Frank 1914-1989 49
  Obituary 62
  Earlier sketch in SATA *1*
  See also SAAS 3
Boniface, William 1963- 182
  Earlier sketch in SATA *102*
Bonino, Louise
  See Williams, Louise Bonino
Bonk, John J. 189
Bonn, Pat
  See Bonn, Patricia Carolyn
Bonn, Patricia Carolyn 1948- 43
Bonner, Hannah 197
Bonner, Mary Graham 1890-1974 19
Bonner, Mike 1951- 121
Bonners, Susan 1947- 85
  Brief entry 48
Bonnet, Rosalinde 1978- 226
Bonnett-Rampersaud, Louise 173
Bonning, Tony 1948- 169
Bonsall, Crosby Barbara (Newell)
  1921-1995 23
  Obituary 84
Bonsall, Joseph S. 1948- 119
Bonsignore, Joan 1959- 140
Bontemps, Arna 1902-1973 44
  Obituary 24
  Earlier sketch in SATA *2*
  See also CLR 6
Bontemps, Arnaud Wendell
  See Bontemps, Arna
Bonzon, Paul-Jacques 1908-1978 22
Boock, Paula 1964- 134
Booher, Dianna Daniels 1948- 33
Book, Rick 1949- 119
Book, Rita
  See Holub, Joan
Bookman, Charlotte
  See Zolotow, Charlotte

Boon, Debbie 1960- 103
Boon, Emilie (Laetitia) 1958- 86
Boone, Charles Eugene
  See Boone, Pat
Boone, Pat 1934- 7
Booraem, Ellen 211
Boorman, Linda 1940- 46
Boorman, Linda Kay
  See Boorman, Linda
Boorstin, Daniel J(oseph) 1914-2004 52
Boos, Ben 1971- 206
Booth, Coe 187
Booth, Ernest Sheldon 1915-1984 43
Booth, George 1926- 191
Booth, Graham (Charles) 1935- 37
Bootman, Colin 159
Borden, Louise 1949- 190
  Autobiography Feature 141
  Earlier sketches in SATA *68, 104, 141*
Bordier, Georgette 1924- 16
Borgman, James
  See Borgman, Jim
Borgman, James Mark
  See Borgman, Jim
Borgman, Jim 1954- 122
Borgo, Lacy Finn 1972- 194
Boring, Mel 1939- 168
  Earlier sketch in SATA *35*
Borja, Corinne 1929- 22
Borja, Robert 1923- 22
Borland, Hal
  See Borland, Harold Glen
Borland, Harold Glen 1900-1978 5
  Obituary 24
Borland, Kathryn Kilby 1916- 16
Borlenghi, Patricia 1951- 79
Born, Adolf 1930- 49
Bornstein, Ruth Lercher
  See Bornstein-Lercher, Ruth
Bornstein-Lercher, Ruth 1927- 88
  Autobiography Feature 107
  Earlier sketch in SATA *14*
Borris, Albert 221
Borski, Lucia Merecka 18
Borten, Helen Jacobson 1930- 5
Bortolotti, Dan 1969- 157
Borton, Elizabeth
  See Trevino, Elizabeth B(orton) de
Borton, Lady 1942- 98
Borton de Trevino, Elizabeth
  See Trevino, Elizabeth B(orton) de
Bortstein, Larry 1942-2010 16
Bortz, Alfred B(enjamin) 1944- 139
  Earlier sketch in SATA *74*
Bortz, Fred
  See Bortz, Alfred B(enjamin)
Bosch, Pseudonymous 199
Bosco, Jack
  See Holliday, Joseph
Bose, Mitali
  See Perkins, Mitali
Boshell, Gordon 1908-1991 15
Boshinski, Blanche 1922- 10
Bosman, Paul 1929- 107
Bosse, Malcolm (Joseph, Jr.) 1926-2002 136
  Earlier sketch in SATA *35*
Bosserman, Charles Phillip
  See Bosserman, Phillip
Bosserman, Phillip 1931- 84
Bossley, Michele Martin 1969- 219
Bossom, Naomi 1933- 35
Bostock, Mike 1962- 114
Boston, L(ucy) M(aria Wood) 1892-1990 19
  Obituary 64
  See also CLR 3
Bostrom, Kathleen (Susan) Long 1954- 139
Bostrom, Kathy
  See Bostrom, Kathleen (Susan) Long
Boswell, Addie 208
Boswell, Addie Kay
  See Boswell, Addie

Bosworth, J. Allan 1925- 19
Bothwell, Jean (?)-1977 2
Botkin, B(enjamin) A(lbert) 1901-1975 40
Botsford, Ward 1927-2004 66
Botting, Douglas (Scott) 1934- 43
Bottner, Barbara 1943- 232
  Autobiography Feature 121
  Earlier sketches in SATA *14, 93, 170*
  See also SAAS 26
Bottone, Frank G., Jr. 1969- 141
Bouchard, David 1952- 213
  Earlier sketch in SATA *117*
Boucher, (Clarence) Carter 1954- 129
Boudelang, Bob
  See Pell, Ed(ward)
Boughton, Richard 1954- 75
Boulet, Susan Seddon 1941- 50
Boulle, Pierre 1912-1994 22
  Obituary 78
Boulle, Pierre Francois Marie-Louis
  See Boulle, Pierre
Boulton, Jane 1921- 91
Bouma, Paddy 1947- 128
Bour, Daniele 1939- 62
Bourbonniere, Sylvie 1966- 182
Bourdon, David 1934-1998 46
Bourgeois, Paulette 1951- 153
Bourne, Lesley
  See Marshall, Evelyn
Bourne, Miriam Anne 1931-1989 16
  Obituary 63
Boutavant, Marc 1970- 200
Boutet de Monvel, (Louis) M(aurice)
  1850(?)-1913 30
  See also CLR 32
Bouwman, Heather M.
  See Bouwman, H.M.
Bouwman, H.M. 209
Bova, Ben 1932- 133
  Earlier sketches in SATA *6, 68*
  See also CLR 96
Bova, Benjamin William
  See Bova, Ben
Bovaird, Anne E(lizabeth) 1960- 90
Bow, Patricia 1946- 168
Bowden, Joan Chase 1925- 51
  Brief entry 38
Bowe, Julie 1962- 194
Bowen, Alexandria Russell 97
Bowen, Andy Russell
  See Bowen, Alexandria Russell
Bowen, Anne 1952- 202
  Earlier sketch in SATA *170*
Bowen, Betty Morgan
  See West, Betty
Bowen, Catherine (Shober) Drinker
  1897-1973 7
Bowen, David
  See Bowen, Joshua David
Bowen, Fred 1953- 233
  Earlier sketch in SATA *136*
Bowen, Joshua David 1930- 22
Bowen, Rhys
  See Quin-Harkin, Janet
Bowen, Robert Sydney 1900-1977 52
  Obituary 21
Bowermaster, Jon 1954- 135
  Earlier sketch in SATA *77*
Bowers, Richard J.
  See Bowers, Rick
Bowers, Rick 1952- 227
Bowers, Terrell L. 1945- 101
Bowers, Terry
  See Bowers, Terrell L.
Bowers, Tim 218
  Earlier sketch in SATA *185*
Bowie, C. W.
  See Old, Wendie C(orbin)
  and Wirths, Claudine (Turner) G(ibson)

Bowie, Jim
  See Norwood, Victor G(eorge) C(harles)
  and Stratemeyer, Edward L.
Bowkett, Stephen 1953- 67
Bowler, Jan Brett
  See Brett, Jan
Bowler, Tim 1953- 209
  Earlier sketch in SATA *149*
Bowman, Catherine
  See Smith, Cat Bowman
Bowman, Crystal 1951- 105
Bowman, James Cloyd 1880-1961 23
Bowman, John S(tewart) 1931- 16
Bowman, Kathleen (Gill) 1942- 52
  Brief entry 40
Bowman, Leslie
  See Bowman, Leslie W.
Bowman, Leslie W. 182
Bowsher, Melodie 195
Boxall, Ed 178
Boyce, Frank Cottrell 182
Boyce, George A(rthur) 1898- 19
Boyd, Candy Dawson 1946- 72
  See also CLR *50*
Boyd, Pauline
  See Schock, Pauline
Boyd, Selma
  See Acuff, Selma Boyd
Boyd, Waldo T. 1918- 18
Boyden, Linda 1948- 143
Boyer, Allen B. 1963- 153
Boyer, Robert E(rnst) 1929- 22
Boyes, Vivien 1952- 106
Boyes, Vivien Elizabeth
  See Boyes, Vivien
Boyle, Ann (Peters) 1916- 10
Boyle, Bob 232
Boyle, Eleanor Vere (Gordon) 1825-1916 28
Boyle, Robert II
  See Boyle, Bob
Boyle, Robert H. 1928- 65
Boylston, Helen Dore 1895-1984 23
  Obituary 39
Boyne, John 1971- 181
Boynton, Sandra (Keith) 1953- 152
  Brief entry 38
  Earlier sketches in SATA *57, 107*
  See also CLR *105*
Boz
  See Dickens, Charles
Bozarth, Jan 227
Braasch, Gary 201
Bracken, Alexandra 1987- 233
Bracken, Charles
  See Pellowski, Michael (Joseph)
Brackers de Hugo, Pierre 1960- 115
Brackett, Dolli Tingle 1911-1993 137
Brackett, Virginia 1950- 166
  Earlier sketch in SATA *121*
Brackett, Virginia Roberts Meredith
  See Brackett, Virginia
Bradbury, Bianca (Ryley) 1908-1982 56
  Earlier sketch in SATA *3*
Bradbury, Edward P.
  See Moorcock, Michael
Bradbury, Ray 1920- 123
  Earlier sketches in SATA *11, 64*
Bradbury, Ray Douglas
  See Bradbury, Ray
Bradby, Marie 161
Bradfield, Carl 1942- 91
Bradford, Ann (Liddell) 1917- 56
  Brief entry 38
Bradford, Barbara Taylor 1933- 66
Bradford, Chris 1974- 215
Bradford, Emma
  See Perrin, Pat
Bradford, Karleen 1936- 96
  Earlier sketch in SATA *48*
Bradford, Lois J(ean) 1936- 36

Bradford, Richard (Roark) 1932-2002 59
  Obituary 135
Bradford, Sally
  See Bradford, Barbara Taylor
Bradley, Duane
  See Sanborn, Duane
Bradley, Kimberly Brubaker 1967- 179
Bradley, Marion Zimmer 1930-1999 139
  Obituary 116
  Earlier sketch in SATA *90*
  See also CLR *158*
Bradley, Timothy J. 193
Bradley, Virginia 1912- 23
Bradley, Will
  See Strickland, Brad
Bradman, Tony 1954- 152
  Earlier sketch in SATA *81*
Bradshaw, Gillian (Joan) 1949- 118
Bradshaw, Gillian 1956- 127
Bradshaw, Gillian Marucha
  See Bradshaw, Gillian
Bradstreet, T. J.
  See Thesman, Jean
Brady, Esther Wood 1905-1987 31
  Obituary 53
Brady, Irene 1943- 4
Brady, Kimberley S. 1953- 101
Brady, Kimberley Smith
  See Brady, Kimberley S.
Brady, Lillian 1902- 28
Braeuner, Shellie 1966(?)- 233
Bragdon, Elspeth MacDuffie 1897-1980 6
Bragdon, Lillian Jacot 24
Brager, Bruce L. 1949- 146
Bragg, Georgia 225
Bragg, Mabel Caroline 1870-1945 24
Bragg, Michael 1948- 46
Bragg, Ruth Gembicki 1943- 77
Brahm, Sumishta 1954- 58
Brailsford, Frances
  See Wosmek, Frances
Brainerd, John W(hiting) 1918- 65
Braithwaite, Althea 1940- 23
  Autobiography Feature 119
  See also SAAS *24*
Brallier, Jess M. 1953- 226
Bram, Elizabeth 1948- 30
Bramsen, Carin 227
Bramsen, Kirsten 228
Brancato, Robin F. 1936- 97
  See also CLR *32*
  See also SAAS *9*
Brancato, Robin Fidler
  See Brancato, Robin F.
Branch, Muriel Miller 1943- 152
  Earlier sketch in SATA *94*
Brand, Christianna
  See Lewis, Mary
Brand, Rebecca
  See Charnas, Suzy McKee
Brande, Robin 194
Brandel, Marc 1919- 71
Brandenberg, Alexa (Demetria) 1966- 97
Brandenberg, Aliki 1929- 157
  Earlier sketches in SATA *2, 35, 75, 113*
  See also CLR *71*
Brandenberg, Franz 1932- 75
  Earlier sketches in SATA *8, 35*
Brandenburg, Jim 1945- 87
Brandhorst, Carl T(heodore) 1898-1988 23
Brandis, Marianne 1938- 149
  Earlier sketches in SATA *59, 96*
Brandon, Brumsic, Jr. 1927- 9
Brandon, Curt
  See Bishop, Curtis (Kent)
Brandreth, Gyles 1948- 28
Brandreth, Gyles Daubeney
  See Brandreth, Gyles
Brandt, Catharine 1905-1997 40
Brandt, Keith
  See Sabin, Louis

Brandt, Sue R(eading) 1916- 59
Branfield, John (Charles) 1931- 11
Branford, Henrietta 1946-1999 106
Branley, Franklyn M(ansfield) 1915-2002 .. 136
  Earlier sketches in SATA *4, 68*
  See also CLR *13*
  See also SAAS *16*
Brannen, Sarah S. 202
Branscum, Robbie (Tilley) 1937-1997 72
  Obituary 96
  Earlier sketch in SATA *23*
  See also SAAS *17*
Bransom, (John) Paul 1885-1979 43
Brashares, Ann 1967- 188
  Earlier sketch in SATA *145*
  See also CLR *113*
Brassard, France 1963- 186
Braswell, E.J.
  See Lynn, Tracy
Braswell, Elizabeth J.
  See Lynn, Tracy
Braswell, Liz
  See Lynn, Tracy
Bratton, Helen 1899-1986 4
Bratun, Katy 1950- 160
  Earlier sketch in SATA *83*
Braude, Michael 1936- 23
Braun, Lilian Jackson 1916(?)-2011 109
Brautigan, Richard 1935-1984 56
Brautigan, Richard Gary
  See Brautigan, Richard
Bray, Libba 1964- 203
  Earlier sketch in SATA *159*
Bray, Martha E.
  See Bray, Libba
Braymer, Marjorie Elizabeth 1911-1988 6
Brazil, Angela 1869(?)-1947
  See CLR *157*
Breathed, Berke 1957- 161
  Earlier sketch in SATA *86*
  See Breathed, Berkeley
Breathed, Berkeley 229
  See Breathed, Berke
Breathed, Guy Berkeley
  See Breathed, Berke
Brecht, Edith 1895-1975 6
  Obituary 25
Breck, Vivian
  See Breckenfeld, Vivian Gurney
Breckenfeld, Vivian Gurney 1895-1992 1
Breda, Tjalmar
  See DeJong, David C(ornel)
Bredeson, Carmen 1944- 163
  Earlier sketch in SATA *98*
Breen, M.E. 216
Breen, Molly
  See Breen, M.E.
Breen, Steve 1970- 186
Breinburg, Petronella 1927- 11
  See also CLR *31*
Breisky, William J(ohn) 1928- 22
Brenaman, Miriam 172
Brenna, Beverley 1962- 226
Brennan, Caitlin
  See Tarr, Judith
Brennan, Gale (Patrick) 1927- 64
  Brief entry 53
Brennan, Herbie 1940- 214
  Autobiography Feature 214
  Earlier sketches in SATA *140, 183*
Brennan, J. H.
  See Brennan, Herbie
Brennan, James Herbert
  See Brennan, Herbie
Brennan, Jan
  See Brennan, Herbie
Brennan, Joseph Lomas 1903-2000 6
Brennan, Linda Crotta 1952- 130
Brennan, Sarah Rees 1983- 221
Brennan, Tim
  See Conroy, John Wesley

Brennan-Nelson, Denise 203
Brenner, Anita 1905-1974 56
Brenner, Barbara (Johnes) 1925- 124
  Earlier sketches in SATA 4, 42, 76
  See also SAAS 14
Brenner, Fred 1920- 36
  Brief entry 34
Brent, Hope 1935(?)-1984
  Obituary 39
Brent, Stuart 1912-2010 14
Breskin, Jane
  See Zalben, Jane Breskin
Breslin, Theresa 128
  Autobiography Feature 128
  Earlier sketch in SATA 70
Breslow, Maurice 1935- 72
Breslow, Maurice A
  See Breslow, Maurice
Breslow, Susan 1951- 69
Brett, Bernard 1925- 22
Brett, Grace N(eff) 1900-1975 23
Brett, Jan 1949- 171
  Earlier sketches in SATA 42, 71, 130
  See also CLR 27
Brett, Jan Churchill
  See Brett, Jan
Brett Bowler, Jan
  See Brett, Jan
Brewer, Heather 1973- 196
Brewer, James D. 1951- 108
Brewer, Paul 1950- 230
Brewer, Sally King 1947- 33
Brewster, Benjamin
  See Folsom, Franklin (Brewster)
Brewster, Hugh 1950- 191
  Earlier sketch in SATA 95
Brewster, Patience 1952- 97
Brewton, John E(dmund) 1898-1982 5
Breznak, Irene 218
Brian, Dennis 1971- 229
Brian, Janeen (Paulette) 1948- 141
Briant, Ed 218
  Earlier sketch in SATA 180
Brick, John 1922-1973 10
Brickman, Robin D. 1954- 155
Bride, Nadja
  See Nobisso, Josephine
Bridgers, Sue Ellen 1942- 90
  Autobiography Feature 109
  Earlier sketch in SATA 22
  See also CLR 18
  See also SAAS 1
Bridges, Laurie
  See Bruck, Lorraine
Bridges, Ruby (Nell) 1954- 131
Bridges, William (Andrew) 1901-1984 5
Bridwell, Norman (Ray) 1928- 138
  Earlier sketches in SATA 4, 68
  See also CLR 96
Brier, Howard M(axwell) 1903-1969 8
Brierley, (Louise) 1958- 59
Briggs, Katharine Mary 1898-1980 101
  Obituary 25
Briggs, Peter 1921-1975 39
  Obituary 31
Briggs, Raymond 1934- 184
  Earlier sketches in SATA 23, 66, 131
  See also CLR 168
Briggs, Raymond Redvers
  See Briggs, Raymond
Bright, Paul 1949- 231
  Earlier sketch in SATA 182
Bright, Robert Sr.) 1902-1988 63
  Obituary 60
  Earlier sketch in SATA 24
Bright, Robert Douglas
  See Bright, Robert Sr.)
Bright, Sarah
  See Shine, Deborah
Brightfield, Richard 1927- 65
  Brief entry 53

Brightfield, Rick
  See Brightfield, Richard
Brighton, Catherine 1943- 206
  Earlier sketches in SATA 65, 107
Brill, Marlene Targ 1945- 124
  Earlier sketch in SATA 77
Brimberg, Stanlee 1947- 9
Brimner, Larry Dane 1949- 232
  Autobiography Feature 112
  Earlier sketches in SATA 79, 170
Brin, David 1950- 65
Brin, Ruth Firestone 1921- 22
Brinckloe, Julie 1950- 13
Brinckloe, Julie Lorraine
  See Brinckloe, Julie
Brindel, June (Rachuy) 1919- 7
Brindle, Max
  See Fleischman, Sid
Brindze, Ruth 1903-1984 23
Brink, Carol Ryrie 1895-1981 100
  Obituary 27
  Earlier sketches in SATA 1, 31
  See also CLR 149
Brinsmead, H. F.
  See Brinsmead, H(esba) F(ay)
Brinsmead, H. F(ay)
  See Brinsmead, H(esba) F(ay)
Brinsmead, H(esba) F(ay) 1922- 78
  Earlier sketch in SATA 18
  See also CLR 47
  See also SAAS 5
Briquebec, John
  See Rowland-Entwistle, (Arthur) Theodore
  (Henry)
Brisbane, Henry R.
  See Ellis, Edward S.
Brisco, P. A.
  See Matthews, Patricia
Brisco, Patty
  See Matthews, Patricia
  and Matthews, Clayton (Hartley)
Briscoe, Jill (Pauline) 1935- 56
  Brief entry 47
Brisley, Joyce Lankester 1896-1978 22
  Obituary 84
Brissenden, Connie
  See Brissenden, Constance
Brissenden, Constance 1947- 150
Brisson, Pat 1951- 177
  Autobiography Feature 133
  Earlier sketches in SATA 67, 128, 133
Britt, Albert 1874-1969
  Obituary 28
Britt, Dell 1934- 1
Brittain, Bill
  See Brittain, William
Brittain, C. Dale 1948- 82
Brittain, William 1930- 76
  Earlier sketch in SATA 36
  See also SAAS 7
Brittingham, Geoffrey (Hugh) 1959- 76
Brittney, L. 209
Britton, Kate
  See Stegeman, Janet Allais
Britton, Louisa
  See McGuire, Leslie (Sarah)
Britton, Rick 1952- 82
Bro, Margueritte (Harmon) 1894-1977 19
  Obituary 27
Broach, Elise 1963- 173
Broadhead, Helen Cross 1913- 25
Broadway, Hannah 208
Brochmann, Elizabeth 1938- 41
Brock, Betty (Carter) 1923-2003 4
  Obituary 150
Brock, C(harles) E(dmund) 1870-1938 42
  Brief entry 32
Brock, Delia
  See Ephron, Delia
Brock, Emma L(illian) 1886-1974 8
Brock, H(enry) M(atthew) 1875-1960 42

Brockett, Eleanor Hall 1913-1967 10
Brockman, C(hristian) Frank 1902-1985 26
Brockmeier, Kevin 1972- 176
Broda, Ron 1954- 209
Broderick, Dorothy M. 1929- 5
Brodeur, Ruth Wallace
  See Wallace-Brodeur, Ruth
Brodie, Sally
  See Cavin, Ruth
Brodien-Jones, Chris
  See Brodien-Jones, Christine
Brodien-Jones, Christine 1950- 233
Brodsky, Beverly
  See McDermott, Beverly Brodsky
Brody, Wendy
  See Staub, Wendy Corsi
Broekel, Rainer Lothar
  See Broekel, Ray
Broekel, Ray 1923- 38
Broekstra, Lorette 1964- 189
  Earlier sketch in SATA 124
Brogden, Sherryl
  See Jordan, Sherryl
Broger, Achim
  See Broger, Achim
Broger, Achim 1944- 31
Broida, Marian 154
Brokamp, Marilyn 1920- 10
Broman, Fred
  See Moseley, James W(illett)
Bromhall, Winifred 26
Brommer, Gerald F(rederick) 1927- 28
Brondfield, Jerome 1913-1998 22
Brondfield, Jerry
  See Brondfield, Jerome
Bronner, Stephen Eric 1949- 101
Bronowski, Jacob 1908-1974 55
Bronson, Alice
  See Watkins, Dawn L.
Bronson, Linda 203
Bronson, Lynn
  See Lampman, Evelyn Sibley
Bronson, Wilfrid Swancourt 1894-1985
  Obituary 43
Brook, Judith (Penelope) 1926- 59
  Brief entry 51
Brook, Judy
  See Brook, Judith (Penelope)
Brooke, L(eonard) Leslie 1862-1940 17
  See also CLR 20
Brooke, William J. 1946- 139
Brooke-Haven, P.
  See Wodehouse, P. G.
Brooker, Kyrsten 199
Brookins, Dana 1931- 28
Brooks, Anita
  See Abramovitz, Anita (Zeltner Brooks)
Brooks, Bill 1939- 59
Brooks, Bruce 1950- 112
  Brief entry 53
  Earlier sketch in SATA 72
  See also CLR 25
Brooks, Caryl 1924- 84
Brooks, Charlotte K(endrick) 1918-1998 24
  Obituary 112
Brooks, Erik 1972- 182
  Earlier sketch in SATA 152
Brooks, George
  See Baum, L. Frank
Brooks, Gwendolyn 1917-2000 6
  Obituary 123
  See also CLR 27
Brooks, Gwendolyn Elizabeth
  See Brooks, Gwendolyn
Brooks, Jerome 1931- 23
Brooks, Kevin 1959- 197
  Earlier sketch in SATA 150
Brooks, Kevin M.
  See Brooks, Kevin
Brooks, Laurie 209
Brooks, Lester 1924- 7

Brooks, Martha 1944- *134*
  Autobiography Feature *134*
  Earlier sketches in SATA *68, 121*
Brooks, Maurice (Graham) 1900- *45*
Brooks, Polly Schoyer 1912- *12*
Brooks, Ron 1948- *212*
  Brief entry *33*
  Earlier sketch in SATA *94*
Brooks, Ronald George
  See Brooks, Ron
Brooks, Terry 1944- *60*
Brooks, Walter R(ollin) 1886-1958 .... *17*
Brooks-Hill, Helen (Mason) 1908-1994 ...... *59*
Broome, Errol 1937- *158*
  Earlier sketch in SATA *105*
Brophy, Nannette 1963- *73*
Brosnan, James Patrick 1929- *14*
Brosnan, Jim
  See Brosnan, James Patrick
Brostoff, Anita 1931- *132*
Brothers Grimm
  See Grimm, Jacob Ludwig Karl
  and Grimm, Wilhelm Karl
Brothers Hildebrandt, The
  See Hildebrandt, Greg
  and Hildebrandt, Tim
Broun, Emily
  See Sterne, Emma Gelders
Brouwer, S. W.
  See Brouwer, Sigmund (W.)
Brouwer, Sigmund (W.) 1959- *109*
Brow, Thea 1934- *60*
Brower, Millicent *8*
Brower, Pauline 1929- *22*
Browin, Frances Williams 1898-1986 .... *5*
Brown, Alan
  See Brown, Alan James
Brown, Alan James 1947- *232*
Brown, Alexis
  See Baumann, Amy Beeching
Brown, Anne Ensign 1937- *61*
Brown, Beverly Swerdlow *97*
Brown, Bill
  See Brown, William L(ouis)
Brown, Billye Walker
  See Cutchen, Billye Walker
Brown, Bob
  See Brown, Robert Joseph
Brown, Buck 1936- *45*
Brown, Calef *217*
  Earlier sketch in SATA *179*
Brown, Cassie 1919-1986 .... *55*
Brown, Charlotte Lewis *181*
Brown, Conrad 1922- *31*
Brown, Craig 1947- *224*
Brown, Craig 1947- *224*
  Earlier sketch in SATA *73*
Brown, Craig McFarland
  See Brown, Craig
Brown, David
  See Brown, David A(lan)
  and Myller, Rolf
Brown, Dee 1908-2002 .... *110*
  Obituary *141*
  Earlier sketch in SATA *5*
Brown, Dee Alexander
  See Brown, Dee
Brown, Don 1949- *200*
  Earlier sketch in SATA *172*
Brown, Drew T. III 1955- *83*
Brown, Drollene P. 1939- *53*
Brown, Elbrite *198*
Brown, Eleanor Frances 1908-1987 .... *3*
Brown, Elizabeth Ferguson 1937- *153*
Brown, Elizabeth M(yers) 1915- *43*
Brown, Fern G. 1918- *34*
Brown, (Robert) Fletch 1923- *42*
Brown, Fornan 1901-1996 .... *71*
  Obituary *88*
Brown, George Earl 1883-1964 .... *11*
Brown, George Mackay 1921-1996 .... *35*

Brown, Irene Bennett 1932- *3*
Brown, Irving
  See Adams, William Taylor
Brown, Ivor (John Carnegie) 1891-1974 .... *5*
  Obituary *26*
Brown, Jane Clark 1930- *81*
Brown, Janet Mitsui *87*
Brown, Jennifer 1972- *227*
Brown, Jo 1964- *170*
Brown, Joanne 1933- *147*
Brown, Joe David 1915-1976 .... *44*
Brown, Joseph E(dward) 1929- *59*
  Brief entry *51*
Brown, Judith Gwyn 1933- *20*
Brown, Kathryn 1955- *168*
  Earlier sketch in SATA *98*
Brown, Kathy
  See Brown, Kathryn
Brown, Ken (James) *129*
Brown, Kevin 1960- *101*
Brown, Laurene Krasny 1945- *99*
  Earlier sketch in SATA *54*
Brown, Laurie Krasny
  See Brown, Laurene Krasny
Brown, Leo *225*
Brown, Lloyd Arnold 1907-1966 .... *36*
Brown, Mahlon A.
  See Ellis, Edward S.
Brown, Marc (Tolon) 1946- *145*
  Earlier sketches in SATA *10, 53, 80*
  See also CLR *29*
Brown, Marcia (Joan) 1918- *47*
  Earlier sketch in SATA *7*
  See also CLR *12*
Brown, Margaret Wise 1910-1952 .... *100*
  See also YABC *2*
  See also CLR *107*
Brown, Margery (Wheeler) *78*
  Earlier sketch in SATA *5*
Brown, Marion Marsh 1908-2001 .... *6*
Brown, Monica 1969- *233*
Brown, Myra Berry 1918- *6*
Brown, Palmer 1919- *36*
Brown, Pamela (Beatrice) 1924-1989 .... *5*
  Obituary *61*
Brown, Paul 1942- *221*
Brown, Peter 1979- *178*
Brown, Rachel W.N. 1947- *203*
Brown, Reeve Lindbergh
  See Lindbergh, Reeve
Brown, Richard
  See Brown, Rick
Brown, Richard E.
  See Brown, Rick
Brown, Rick 1946- *226*
  Earlier sketch in SATA *61*
Brown, Robert Joseph 1907-1989 .... *14*
Brown, Rod 1961- *232*
Brown, Roderick (Langmere) Haig-
  See Haig-Brown, Roderick (Langmere)
Brown, Rosalie
  See Moore, Rosalie (Gertrude)
Brown, Roswell
  See Webb, Jean Francis (III)
Brown, Roy (Frederick) 1921-1982 .... *51*
  Obituary *39*
Brown, Ruth 1941- *170*
  Earlier sketch in SATA *105*
Brown, Scott 1971- *134*
Brown, Sue Ellen 1954- *81*
Brown, Tricia 1954- *114*
Brown, Vinson 1912-1991 .... *19*
Brown, Walter R(eed) 1929- *19*
Brown, Will
  See Ainsworth, William Harrison
Brown, William L(ouis) 1910-1964 .... *5*
Browne, Anthony 1946- *163*
  Brief entry *44*
  Earlier sketches in SATA *45, 61, 105*
  See also CLR *156*

Browne, Anthony Edward Tudor
  See Browne, Anthony
Browne, Dik
  See Browne, Richard Arthur Allen
Browne, Hablot Knight 1815-1882 .... *21*
Browne, Matthew
  See Rands, William Brighty
Browne, Nicki M.
  See Browne, N.M.
Browne, Nicky Matthews
  See Browne, N.M.
Browne, N.M. 1960- *167*
Browne, Richard Arthur Allen 1917-1989 ... *67*
  Brief entry *38*
Browne, Vee F. 1956- *214*
  Earlier sketch in SATA *90*
Browning, Diane *233*
Browning, Robert 1812-1889
  See YABC *1*
  See also CLR *97*
Browning, Tom 1949- *226*
Brownjohn, Alan 1931- *6*
Brownlee, Walter 1930- *62*
Brownlie, Betty 1946- *159*
Brownlow, Kevin 1938- *65*
Brownlow, Mike *183*
Brownridge, William R(oy) 1932- *94*
Broyles, Anne 1953- *201*
Bruce, Dorita Fairlie 1885-1970
  Obituary *27*
Bruce, Harry 1934- *77*
Bruce, Mary 1927- *1*
Bruchac, Joseph III
  See Bruchac, Joseph
Bruchac, Joseph 1942- *228*
  Autobiography Feature *176*
  Earlier sketches in SATA *42, 89, 131, 176*
  See also CLR *46*
Bruchac, Margaret M.
  See Bruchac, Marge
Bruchac, Marge *181*
Bruck, Lorraine 1921- *55*
  Brief entry *46*
Bruel, Nick *205*
  Earlier sketch in SATA *166*
Bruel, Robert O. 1929-2002 .... *189*
Bruemmer, Fred 1929- *47*
Brugman, Alyssa (F.) 1974- *152*
Brumbeau, Jeff 1955- *157*
Bruna, Dick 1927- *76*
  Brief entry *30*
  Earlier sketch in SATA *43*
  See also CLR *7*
Brunelle, Lynn *233*
Brunhoff, Jean de 1899-1937 .... *24*
  See also CLR *116*
Brunhoff, Laurent de 1925- *150*
  Earlier sketches in SATA *24, 71*
  See also CLR *116*
Brunkus, Denise *204*
Bruno, Elsa Knight 1935-2009 .... *221*
Brunskill, Elizabeth Ann Flatt
  See Flatt, Lizann
Brush, Karen A(lexandra) 1960- *85*
Brussel-Smith, Bernard 1914- *58*
Brust, Steven 1955- *121*
  Earlier sketch in SATA *86*
Brust, Steven Karl Zoltan
  See Brust, Steven
Brustlein, Daniel 1904- *40*
Brustlein, Janice Tworkov -2000 .... *40*
  Obituary *126*
Brutschy, Jennifer 1960- *84*
Bryan, Ashley 1923- *178*
  Earlier sketches in SATA *31, 72, 132*
  See also CLR *66*
Bryan, Ashley F.
  See Bryan, Ashley
Bryan, Dorothy M. 1896(?)-1984
  Obituary *39*
Bryan, Jennifer *190*

Bryan, Sean *192*
Bryant, Bernice (Morgan) 1908-1976 .... *11*
Bryant, Jen 1960- *218*
 Earlier sketches in SATA *94, 175*
Bryant, Jennifer
 See Bryant, Jen
Bryant, Jennifer Fisher
 See Bryant, Jen
Bryant, Laura J. *176*
Brychta, Alex 1956- *21*
Brynie, Faith H. 1946- *113*
Brynie, Faith Hickman
 See Brynie, Faith H.
Bryson, Bernarda 1903-2004 .... *9*
Buba, Joy Flinsch 1904- *44*
Buchan, Bryan 1945- *36*
Buchan, John 1875-1940
 See YABC *2*
Buchan, Stuart 1942-1987
 Obituary *54*
Buchanan, Debby 1952- *82*
Buchanan, Deborah Leevonne
 See Buchanan, Debby
Buchanan, Jane 1956- *160*
Buchanan, Paul 1959- *116*
Buchanan, Sue 1939- *139*
Buchheimer, Naomi Barnett
 See Barnett, Naomi
Buchignani, Walter 1965- *84*
Buchmann, Stephen L. *194*
Buchwald, Art 1925-2007 .... *10*
Buchwald, Arthur
 See Buchwald, Art
Buchwald, Emilie 1935- *7*
Buck, Gisela 1941- *101*
Buck, Lewis 1925- *18*
Buck, Margaret Waring 1905-1997 .... *3*
Buck, Nola
 See Godwin, Laura
Buck, Pearl S. 1892-1973 .... *25*
 Earlier sketch in SATA *1*
Buck, Pearl Sydenstricker
 See Buck, Pearl S.
Buck, Siegfried 1941- *101*
Buckalew, Clare B.
 See Dunkle, Clare B.
Buckeridge, Anthony (Malcolm)
 1912-2004 .... *85*
 Earlier sketch in SATA *6*
Buckholtz, Eileen (Garber) 1949- *54*
 Brief entry *47*
Buckingham, Royce 1966- *210*
Buckingham, Royce Scott
 See Buckingham, Royce
Buckler, Ernest 1908-1984 .... *47*
Buckless, Andrea K. 1968- *117*
Buckley, Helen E(lizabeth) 1918- *90*
 Earlier sketch in SATA *2*
Buckley, James, Jr. 1963- *166*
 Earlier sketch in SATA *114*
Buckley, Michael *229*
 Earlier sketch in SATA *177*
Buckley, Susan *184*
Buckley, Susan Washburn
 See Buckley, Susan
Buckley-Archer, Linda *185*
Buckmaster, Henrietta
 See Stephens, Henrietta Henkle
Bucks, Brad
 See Holub, Joan
Budd, E. S.
 See Sirimarco, Elizabeth
Budd, Lillian (Peterson) 1897-1989 .... *7*
Budhos, Marina *173*
Buehler, Stephanie Jona 1956- *83*
Buehner, Caralyn 1963- *219*
 Earlier sketches in SATA *104, 159*
Buehner, Mark 1959- *221*
 Earlier sketches in SATA *104, 159*
Buehr, Walter Franklin 1897-1971 .... *3*

Buell, Ellen Lewis
 See Cash, Ellen Lewis Buell
Buell, Janet 1952- *185*
 Earlier sketch in SATA *106*
Buergel, Paul-Hermann H. 1949- *83*
Buettner, Dan 1960- *95*
Buff, Conrad 1886-1975 .... *19*
Buff, Mary (E. Marsh) 1890-1970 .... *19*
Buffett, Jimmy 1946- *110*
 Earlier sketch in SATA *76*
Buffie, Margaret 1945- *161*
 Earlier sketches in SATA *71, 107*
 See also CLR *39*
Bugbee, Emma 1888(?)-1981
 Obituary *29*
Bugni, Alice 1951- *122*
Buhhos, Marina Tamar
 See Budhos, Marina
Bujold, Lois McMaster 1949- *136*
Bulfinch, Thomas 1796-1867 .... *35*
Bulion, Leslie 1958- *209*
 Earlier sketch in SATA *161*
Bull, Angela (Mary) 1936- *45*
Bull, Emma 1954- *190*
 Autobiography Feature *103*
 Earlier sketch in SATA *99*
Bull, Norman John 1916- *41*
Bull, Peter (Cecil) 1912-1984
 Obituary *39*
Bull, Schuyler M. 1974- *138*
Bulla, Clyde R. 1914-2007 .... *139*
 Obituary *182*
 Earlier sketches in SATA *2, 41, 91*
 See also SAAS *6*
Bullard, Lisa 1961- *142*
Bullen, Alexandra *227*
Buller, Jon *205*
Bullock, Kathleen (Mary) 1946- *77*
Bullock, Robert (D.) 1947- *92*
Bulpin, (Barbara) Vicki *92*
Bulwer-Lytton, Edward 1803-1873 .... *23*
Bulwer-Lytton, Edward George Earle Lytton
 See Bulwer-Lytton, Edward
Bumstead, Kathleen Mary 1918-1987 .... *53*
Bundles, A'Lelia Perry 1952- *76*
Bunge, Daniela 1973- *207*
Bunin, Catherine 1967- *30*
Bunin, Sherry 1925- *30*
Bunkers, Suzanne L. 1950- *136*
Bunting, A.E.
 See Bunting, Eve
Bunting, Anne Evelyn
 See Bunting, Eve
Bunting, Eve 1928- *196*
 Earlier sketches in SATA *18, 64, 110, 158*
 See also CLR *82*
Bunting, Glenn (Davison) 1957- *22*
Bunyan, John 1628-1688
 See CLR *124*
Bupp, Walter
 See Garrett, Randall
Burack, Sylvia K. 1916-2003 .... *35*
 Obituary *143*
Burbank, Addison (Buswell) 1895-1961 .... *37*
Burch, Joann J(ohansen) *75*
Burch, Robert J(oseph) 1925- *74*
 Earlier sketch in SATA *1*
 See also CLR *63*
Burchard, Peter Duncan 1921- *143*
 Earlier sketches in SATA *5, 74*
 See also SAAS *13*
Burchard, S. H.
 See Burchard, Sue
Burchard, Sue 1937- *22*
Burchardt, Nellie 1921- *7*
Burckhardt, Marc 1962- *196*
Burden, Andrea 1969-2009 .... *227*
Burdett, Lois *117*
Burdick, Eugene (Leonard) 1918-1965 .... *22*
Burford, Eleanor
 See Hibbert, Eleanor Alice Burford

Burg, Ann E. 1954- *217*
Burg, Shana 1968- *204*
Burgan, Michael 1960- *167*
 Earlier sketch in SATA *118*
Burger, Carl 1888-1967 .... *9*
Burgess, Ann Marie
 See Gerson, Noel Bertram
Burgess, Barbara Hood 1926- *69*
Burgess, Em
 See Burgess, Mary Wyche
Burgess, (Frank) Gelett 1866-1951 .... *32*
 Brief entry *30*
Burgess, Mark *157*
Burgess, Mary Wyche 1916- *18*
Burgess, Melvin 1954- *198*
 Earlier sketches in SATA *96, 146*
Burgess, Michael
 See Gerson, Noel Bertram
Burgess, Robert F(orrest) 1927- *4*
Burgess, Starling
 See Tudor, Tasha
Burgess, Thornton Waldo 1874-1965 .... *17*
Burgess, Trevor
 See Trevor, Elleston
Burgwyn, Mebane Holoman 1914-1992 .... *7*
Burke, David 1927- *46*
Burke, Diana G.
 See Gallagher, Diana G.
Burke, Diana Gallagher
 See Gallagher, Diana G.
Burke, Dianne O'Quinn 1940- *89*
Burke, Janine 1952- *139*
Burke, Jim 1973- *179*
Burke, John
 See O'Connor, Richard
Burke, Katie 1953- *168*
Burke, Patrick 1958- *114*
Burke, Ralph
 See Garrett, Randall
 and Silverberg, Robert
Burkert, Nancy Ekholm 1933- *24*
 See also SAAS *14*
Burkett, D. Brent *194*
Burke-Weiner, Kimberly 1962- *95*
Burks, Brian 1955- *95*
Burland, Brian (Berkeley) 1931- *34*
Burland, C. A.
 See Burland, Cottie (Arthur)
Burland, Cottie (Arthur) 1905-1983 .... *5*
Burleigh, Robert 1936- *193*
 Earlier sketches in SATA *55, 98, 146*
Burlingame, (William) Roger 1889-1967 .... *2*
Burman, Alice Caddy 1896(?)-1977
 Obituary *24*
Burman, Ben Lucien 1896-1984 .... *6*
 Obituary *40*
Burn, Doris 1923- *1*
Burn, Ted
 See Burn, Thomas E.
Burn, Thomas E. 1940- *150*
Burnard, Damon 1963- *115*
Burnett, Constance Buel 1893-1975 .... *36*
Burnett, Frances Eliza Hodgson
 See Burnett, Frances Hodgson
Burnett, Frances Hodgson 1849-1924 .... *100*
 See also YABC *2*
 See also CLR *122*
Burnett, Lindy *210*
Burnett Bossi, Lisa *193*
Burney, Anton
 See Hopkins, (Hector) Kenneth
Burnford, Sheila (Philip Cochrane Every)
 1918-1984 .... *3*
 Obituary *38*
 See also CLR *2*
Burnham, Gretchen
 See Sprague, Gretchen
Burnham, Nicole 1970- *161*
Burnham, Niki
 See Burnham, Nicole
Burnham, Sophy 1936- *65*

Burningham, John 1936- *225*
  Earlier sketches in SATA *16, 59, 111, 160*
  See also CLR *9*
Burningham, Robin Yoko
  See Racoma, Robin Yoko
Burningham, Sarah O'Leary *216*
Burns, Diane L. 1950- *81*
  See also SAAS *24*
Burns, Eloise Wilkin
  See Wilkin, Eloise
Burns, Florence M. 1905-1988 .... *61*
Burns, Khephra 1950- *92*
Burns, Loree Griffin *193*
Burns, Marilyn 1941- *96*
  Brief entry *33*
Burns, Olive Ann 1924-1990 .... *65*
Burns, Patrick 1968- *227*
Burns, Paul C. *5*
Burns, Ray
  See Burns, Raymond (Howard)
Burns, Raymond (Howard) 1924- *9*
Burns, Theresa 1961- *84*
Burns, William A. 1909-1999 .... *5*
Burr, Dan 1951- *65*
Burr, Dan 1960- *219*
Burr, Lonnie 1943- *47*
Burrell, Roy E(ric) C(harles) 1923- *72*
Burroughs, Edgar Rice 1875-1950 .... *41*
  See also CLR *157*
Burroughs, Jean Mitchell 1908- *28*
Burroughs, Polly 1925- *2*
Burroway, Janet 1936- *23*
Burroway, Janet Gay
  See Burroway, Janet
Burstein, Chaya M(alamud) 1923- *64*
Burstein, Fred 1950- *83*
Burstein, John 1949- *54*
  Brief entry *40*
Burstein, Stanley M.
  See Burstein, Stanley Mayer
Burstein, Stanley Mayer 1941- *175*
Bursztynski, Sue 1953- *114*
Burt, Jesse Clifton 1921-1976 .... *46*
  Obituary *20*
Burt, Olive Woolley 1894-1981 .... *4*
Burtinshaw, Julie *185*
Burton, Gennett 1945- *95*
Burton, Hester (Wood-Hill) 1913-2000 .... *74*
  Earlier sketch in SATA *7*
  See also CLR *1*
  See also SAAS *8*
Burton, Leslie
  See McGuire, Leslie (Sarah)
Burton, Marilee Robin 1950- *82*
  Earlier sketch in SATA *46*
Burton, Maurice 1898-1992 .... *23*
Burton, Rebecca 1970- *183*
Burton, Robert (Wellesley) 1941- *22*
Burton, Virginia Lee 1909-1968 .... *100*
  Earlier sketch in SATA *2*
  See also CLR *11*
Burton, William H(enry) 1890-1964 .... *11*
Busby, Ailie *192*
Busby, Cylin 1970- *118*
Busby, Edith (A. Lake) (?)-1964
  Obituary *29*
Busby, John 1942- *209*
Buscaglia, (Felice) Leo(nardo) 1924-1998 ... *65*
Buscaglia, Leo F.
  See Buscaglia, (Felice) Leo(nardo)
Buscema, Stephanie *232*
Busch, Phyllis S. 1909- *30*
Bush, Anne Kelleher
  See Kelleher, Anne
Bush, Catherine 1961- *128*
Bush, Jenna 1981- *208*
Bush, Laura 1946- *208*
Bushmiller, Ernest Paul 1905-1982 .... *31*
Bushmiller, Ernie
  See Bushmiller, Ernest Paul
Bushnell, Jack 1952- *86*

Busoni, Rafaello 1900-1962 .... *16*
Buss, Helen M.
  See Clarke, Margaret
Busse, Sarah Martin *194*
Busselle, Rebecca 1941- *80*
Bustard, Anne 1951- *173*
Butcher, Kristin 1951- *140*
Butenko, Bohdan 1931- *90*
Butler, Beverly Kathleen 1932- *7*
Butler, Bill
  See Butler, William Vivian
  and Butler, Ernest Alton
  and Butler, William Huxford
Butler, Charles 1963- *175*
  Earlier sketch in SATA *121*
Butler, Charles Cadman
  See Butler, Charles
Butler, Dori Hillestad 1965- *207*
  Earlier sketch in SATA *164*
Butler, Dorothy 1925- *73*
Butler, Geoff 1945- *94*
Butler, John 1952- *225*
Butler, M. Christina 1934- *224*
  Earlier sketches in SATA *72, 170*
Butler, Octavia 1947-2006 .... *84*
  See also CLR *65*
Butler, Octavia E.
  See Butler, Octavia
Butler, Octavia Estelle
  See Butler, Octavia
Butler, Vivian
  See Butler, William Vivian
Butler, William
  See Butler, William Vivian
Butler, William Vivian 1927-1987 .... *79*
Butterfield, Moira 1960- *219*
Butters, Dorothy Gilman
  See Gilman, Dorothy
Butterworth, Emma Macalik 1928- *43*
Butterworth, Nick 1946- *149*
  Earlier sketch in SATA *106*
Butterworth, Oliver 1915-1990 .... *1*
  Obituary *66*
Butterworth, W. E.
  See Griffin, W. E. B.
Butterworth, William E.
  See Griffin, W. E. B.
Butterworth, William Edmund III
  See Griffin, W. E. B.
Button, Lana 1968- *229*
Butts, Ed 1951- *177*
Butts, Edward P.
  See Butts, Ed
Butts, Ellen R. 1942- *93*
Butts, Ellen Rubinstein
  See Butts, Ellen R.
Butzer, C. M. 1974- *212*
Buxton, Ralph
  See Silverstein, Alvin
  and Silverstein, Virginia B.
Buzzeo, Toni 1951- *215*
  Earlier sketch in SATA *135*
Byalick, Marcia 1947- *141*
  Earlier sketch in SATA *97*
Byard, Carole (Marie) 1941- *57*
Byars, Betsy 1928- *223*
  Autobiography Feature *108*
  Earlier sketches in SATA *4, 46, 80, 163*
  See also CLR *72*
  See also SAAS *1*
Byars, Betsy Cromer
  See Byars, Betsy
Byfield, Barbara Ninde 1930-1988 .... *8*
Byman, Jeremy 1944- *129*
Bynum, Janie *133*
Byrd, Elizabeth 1912-1989 .... *34*
Byrd, Nicole
  See Zach, Cheryl (Byrd)
Byrd, Robert 1942- *226*
  Earlier sketches in SATA *33, 112, 158*

Byrd, Robert John
  See Byrd, Robert
Byrd, Tim 1964- *216*
Byrne, Gayle *218*
Byrne, Mary Gregg 1951- *162*

C

C. 3. 3.
  See Wilde, Oscar
C. E. M.
  See Mastrangelo, Charles E(lmer)
Cabaniss, J(ames) Allen 1911-1997 .... *5*
Cabat, Erni 1914- *74*
Cabban, Vanessa 1971- *176*
Cable, Mary 1920- *9*
Cabot, Meg 1967- *217*
  Earlier sketches in SATA *127, 175*
  See also CLR *85*
Cabot, Meggin
  See Cabot, Meg
Cabot, Meggin Patricia
  See Cabot, Meg
Cabot, Patricia
  See Cabot, Meg
Cabral, O. M.
  See Cabral, Olga
Cabral, Olga 1909- *46*
Cabrera, Cozbi A. 1963- *177*
Cabrera, Jane 1968- *182*
  Earlier sketches in SATA *103, 152*
Cabrera, Marcela 1966- *90*
Caddy, Alice
  See Burman, Alice Caddy
Cade, Toni
  See Bambara, Toni Cade
Cadena, Beth *222*
Cadmus and Harmonia
  See Buchan, John
Cadnum, Michael 1949- *225*
  Earlier sketches in SATA *87, 121, 165*
  See also CLR *78*
Caduto, Michael J. 1955- *103*
Cadwallader, Sharon 1936- *7*
Cady, (Walter) Harrison 1877(?)-1970 .... *19*
Caffey, Donna (J.) 1954- *110*
Cagle, Malcolm W(infield) 1918- *32*
Cahn, Rhoda 1922- *37*
Cahn, William 1912-1976 .... *37*
Cain, Arthur H(omer) 1913-1981 .... *3*
Cain, Christopher
  See Fleming, Thomas
Cain, Sheridan 1952- *186*
Caine, Geoffrey
  See Walker, Robert W.
Caines, Jeannette (Franklin) 1938- *78*
  Brief entry *43*
  See also CLR *24*
Cairns, Trevor 1922- *14*
Calabro, Marian 1954- *79*
Caldecott, Moyra 1927- *22*
Caldecott, Randolph (J.) 1846-1886 .... *100*
  Earlier sketch in SATA *17*
  See also CLR *110*
Calder, Charlotte 1952- *125*
Calder, David 1932-1997 .... *105*
Calder, Lyn
  See Calmenson, Stephanie
Calder, Marie D(onais) 1948- *96*
Calderone-Stewart, Lisa
  See Calderone-Stewart, Lisa-Marie
Calderone-Stewart, Lisa-Marie 1958- *123*
Caldwell, Ben 1973- *230*
Caldwell, Doreen (Mary) 1942- *71*
Caldwell, John C(ope) 1913-1984 .... *7*
Caletti, Deb 1963- *221*
  Earlier sketch in SATA *171*
Calhoun, B. B. 1961- *98*

Calhoun, Chad
　See Barrett, Neal, Jr.
　and Cunningham, Chet
　and Goulart, Ron
Calhoun, Dia 1959- *183*
　Earlier sketch in SATA *129*
Calhoun, Mary
　See Wilkins, Mary Huiskamp
Calhoun, T.B.
　See Bisson, Terry
Cali, Davide 1972- *190*
Calif, Ruth 1922- *67*
Calkhoven, Laurie 1959- *229*
Calkins, Franklin
　See Stratemeyer, Edward L.
Call, Greg *197*
Call, Hughie Florence 1890-1969 .... *1*
Callahan, Dorothy M. 1934- *39*
　Brief entry *35*
Callahan, Dorothy Monahan
　See Callahan, Dorothy M.
Callahan, Philip Serna 1923- *25*
Callahan, Sean 1965- *222*
Callan, Jamie 1954- *59*
Callan, Jim 1951- *181*
Callaway, Bernice (Anne) 1923- *48*
Callaway, Kathy 1943- *36*
Callen, Larry
　See Callen, Lawrence Willard, Jr.
Callen, Lawrence Willard, Jr. 1927- *19*
Callen, Liz 1951- *231*
Callery, Sean *233*
Calley, Karin 1965- *92*
Calmenson, Stephanie 1952- *211*
　Brief entry *37*
　Earlier sketches in SATA *51, 84, 139*
Calonita, Jen *216*
Calvert, Elinor H.
　See Lasell, Elinor H.
Calvert, John
　See Leaf, (Wilbur) Munro
Calvert, Pam 1966- *205*
Calvert, Patricia 1931- *132*
　Earlier sketches in SATA *45, 69*
　See also SAAS *17*
Camburn, Carol A.
　See Camburn-Bracalente, Carol A.
Camburn-Bracalente, Carol A. 1962- *118*
Cameron, Ann 1943- *129*
　Earlier sketches in SATA *27, 89*
　See also SAAS *20*
Cameron, Edna M. 1905-1999 .... *3*
Cameron, Eleanor (Frances) 1912-1996 ... *25*
　Obituary *93*
　Earlier sketch in SATA *1*
　See also CLR *72*
　See also SAAS *10*
Cameron, Elizabeth
　See Nowell, Elizabeth Cameron
Cameron, Elizabeth Jane 1910-1976 .... *32*
　Obituary *30*
Cameron, Ian
　See Payne, Donald Gordon
Cameron, M(alcolm) G(ordon) Graham
　See Graham-Cameron, M(alcolm) G(ordon)
Cameron, M. Graham
　See Graham-Cameron, M(alcolm) G(ordon)
Cameron, Mike Graham
　See Graham-Cameron, M(alcolm) G(ordon)
Cameron, Natalie Russell
　See Russell, Natalie
Cameron, Polly 1928- *2*
Cameron, Scott 1962- *84*
Camp, Charles L. 1893-1975
　Obituary *31*
Camp, Lindsay 1957- *133*
Camp, Madeleine L'Engle
　See L'Engle, Madeleine
Camp, Walter (Chauncey) 1859-1925
　See YABC *1*
Campbell, (Elizabeth) Andrea 1963- *50*

Campbell, Ann R. 1925- *11*
Campbell, Bill 1960- *89*
Campbell, Bruce
　See Epstein, Samuel
Campbell, Camilla 1905-1992 .... *26*
Campbell, Carole R. 1939- *125*
Campbell, Hope 1925- *20*
Campbell, Hugh 1930- *90*
Campbell, Jane
　See Edwards, Jane Campbell
Campbell, Julie
　See Tatham, Julie Campbell
Campbell, Patricia J(ean) 1930- *45*
Campbell, Patty
　See Campbell, Patricia J(ean)
Campbell, Peter A. 1948- *99*
Campbell, R. W.
　See Campbell, Rosemae Wells
Campbell, Robin
　See Strachan, Ian
Campbell, Rod 1945- *98*
　Brief entry *44*
　Earlier sketch in SATA *51*
Campbell, Rosemae Wells 1909- *1*
Campbell, Sarah C. 1966- *207*
Camper, Cathy 1956- *170*
Campion, Nardi Reeder 1917-2007 .... *22*
Campling, Elizabeth 1948- *53*
Campos, Maria de Fatima *229*
Campoy, F. Isabel 1946- *181*
　Earlier sketch in SATA *143*
Camps, Luis 1928- *66*
Canales, Viola 1957- *141*
Candell, Victor 1903-1977
　Obituary *24*
Canfield, Dorothea F.
　See Fisher, Dorothy (Frances) Canfield
Canfield, Dorothea Frances
　See Fisher, Dorothy (Frances) Canfield
Canfield, Dorothy
　See Fisher, Dorothy (Frances) Canfield
Canfield, Jack 1944- *164*
Canfield, Jane White 1897-1984 .... *32*
　Obituary *38*
Canfield, Muriel 1935- *94*
Canga, C.B. 1976- *216*
Canga, Chris
　See Canga, C.B.
Caniff, Milton 1907-1988
　Obituary *58*
Caniff, Milton Arthur Paul
　See Caniff, Milton
Cann, Helen 1969- *179*
　Earlier sketch in SATA *124*
Cann, Kate 1954- *152*
　Earlier sketch in SATA *103*
Cannan, Joanna
　See Pullein-Thompson, Joanna Maxwell
Cannell, Jon *196*
Cannell, Jonathan C.
　See Cannell, Jon
Cannon, A.E. *202*
　Earlier sketches in SATA *93, 163*
Cannon, Ann Edwards
　See Cannon, A.E.
Cannon, Bettie (Waddell) 1922- *59*
Cannon, Curt
　See Hunter, Evan
Cannon, Eileen E(mily) 1948- *119*
Cannon, Frank
　See Mayhar, Ardath
Cannon, Janell 1957- *128*
　Earlier sketch in SATA *78*
　See also CLR *120*
Cannon, Marian G. 1923- *85*
Cannon, Taffy
　See Cannon, Eileen E(mily)
Cantone, AnnaLaura *182*
Cantrell, Julie 1973- *217*
Canusi, Jose
　See Barker, S. Omar

Canyon, Christopher 1966- *150*
　Earlier sketch in SATA *104*
Caparo, Antonio
　See Caparo, Antonio Javier
Caparo, Antonio Javier *205*
Capek, Michael 1947- *142*
　Earlier sketch in SATA *96*
Capes, Bernard (Edward Joseph)
　1854-1918 .... *116*
Caple, Kathy *193*
Caple, Laurie 1958- *201*
Caplin, Alfred Gerald 1909-1979 .... *61*
　Obituary *21*
Caponigro, John Paul 1965- *84*
Capote, Truman 1924-1984 .... *91*
Capp, Al
　See Caplin, Alfred Gerald
Cappel, Constance 1936- *22*
Cappetta, Cynthia 1949- *125*
Cappo, Nan Willard 1955- *143*
Capps, Benjamin (Franklin) 1922- *9*
Cappy Dick
　See Cleveland, George
Captain Kangaroo
　See Keeshan, Robert J.
Captain Wheeler
　See Ellis, Edward S.
Captain Young of Yale
　See Stratemeyer, Edward L.
Capucilli, Alyssa Satin 1957- *203*
　Earlier sketches in SATA *115, 163*
Capucine
　See Mazille, Capucine
Carafoli, Marci
　See Balterman, Marcia Ridlon
Caraher, Kim(berley Elizabeth) 1961- *105*
Caraker, Mary 1929- *74*
Caras, Roger A(ndrew) 1928-2001 .... *12*
　Obituary *127*
Caravantes, Peggy 1935- *140*
Caraway, Caren 1939- *57*
Carbone, Elisa 1954- *173*
　Earlier sketches in SATA *81, 137*
Carbone, Elisa Lynn
　See Carbone, Elisa
Carbonnier, Jeanne 1894-1974 .... *3*
　Obituary *34*
Card, Orson Scott 1951- *127*
　Earlier sketch in SATA *83*
　See also CLR *116*
Cardinale, Christopher *231*
Cardon, Laurent 1962- *230*
Care, Felicity
　See Coury, Louise Andree
Carew, Jan 1925- *51*
　Brief entry *40*
Carew, Jan Rynveld
　See Carew, Jan
Carey, Benedict 1960- *219*
Carey, Bonnie
　See Marshall, Bonnie C.
Carey, Charles W., Jr. 1951- *170*
Carey, Ernestine Gilbreth 1908-2006 ...... *2*
　Obituary *177*
Carey, Janet Lee 1954(?)- *225*
　Earlier sketch in SATA *185*
Carey, Lisa *110*
Carey, M. V.
　See Carey, Mary V(irginia)
Carey, Mary V(irginia) 1925-1994 .... *44*
　Brief entry *39*
Carey, Peter 1943- *94*
Carey, Peter Philip
　See Carey, Peter
Carey, Valerie Scho 1949- *60*
Carheden, Goorel Kristina
　See Naaslund, Goorel Kristina
Carigiet, Alois 1902-1985 .... *24*
　Obituary *47*
　See also CLR *38*
Carini, Edward 1923- *9*

Carkeet, David 1946- 75
Carle, Eric 1929- 163
  Earlier sketches in SATA *4, 65, 120*
  See also CLR *72*
  See also SAAS *6*
Carleton, Captain L. C.
  See Ellis, Edward S.
Carleton, Captain Latham C.
  See Ellis, Edward S.
Carleton, Latham C.
  See Ellis, Edward S.
Carley, V(an Ness) Royal 1906-1976
  Obituary 20
Carling, Amelia Lau 1949- 164
  Earlier sketch in SATA *119*
Carlisle, Carolyn
  See Hawes, Louise
Carlisle, Clark
  See Holding, James (Clark Carlisle, Jr.)
Carlisle, Olga Andreyev 1930- 35
Carlock, Miriam
  See Eyerly, Jeannette
Carls, Claudia 1978- 198
Carlsen, G(eorge) Robert 1917- 30
Carlsen, Ruth C(hristoffer) 1918- 2
Carlson, Bernice Wells 1910- 8
Carlson, Christopher C. 202
Carlson, Dale (Bick) 1935- 1
Carlson, Daniel (Bick) 1960- 27
Carlson, Kirsten 1968- 192
Carlson, Kirsten M.
  See Carlson, Kirsten
Carlson, Laurie 1952- 173
  Earlier sketch in SATA *101*
Carlson, Laurie Winn
  See Carlson, Laurie
Carlson, Melody 1956- 171
  Earlier sketch in SATA *113*
Carlson, Nancy 1953- 213
  Brief entry 45
  Earlier sketches in SATA *56, 90, 144*
Carlson, Nancy L.
  See Carlson, Nancy
Carlson, Natalie Savage 1906-1997 68
  Earlier sketch in SATA *2*
  See also SAAS *4*
Carlson, Susan Johnston 1953- 88
Carlson, Vada F. 1897- 16
Carlstrom, Nancy White 1948- 215
  Brief entry 48
  Earlier sketches in SATA *53, 92, 156*
Carlton, Keith
  See Robertson, Keith (Carlton)
Carlton, Susan 1960- 195
Carlyon, Richard 55
Carman, Bill
  See Carman, William
Carman, Patrick 1966- 233
  Earlier sketches in SATA *161, 197*
Carman, William 223
Carmer, Carl (Lamson) 1893-1976 37
  Obituary 30
Carmer, Elizabeth Black 1904- 24
Carmi, Giora 1944- 149
  Earlier sketch in SATA *79*
Carmichael, Carrie
  See Carmichael, Harriet
Carmichael, Clay 218
Carmichael, Harriet 40
Carmody, Isobelle 1958- 191
  Earlier sketch in SATA *161*
Carmody, Isobelle Jane
  See Carmody, Isobelle
Carney, Elizabeth 1981- 199
Carney, Jeff 1962- 196
Carney, Mary Lou 1949- 170
Carol, Bill J.
  See Knott, William C(ecil, Jr.)
Caron, Romi
  See Caron-Kyselkova', Romana
Caron-Kyselkova', Romana 1967- 94

Caroselli, Remus F(rancis) 1916- 36
Carpelan, Bo 1926- 8
Carpelan, Bo Gustaf Bertelsson
  See Carpelan, Bo
Carpenter, (John) Allan 1917- 81
  Earlier sketch in SATA *3*
Carpenter, Angelica Shirley 1945- 153
  Earlier sketch in SATA *71*
Carpenter, Frances 1890-1972 3
  Obituary 27
Carpenter, John 1948- 58
Carpenter, John Howard
  See Carpenter, John
Carpenter, Johnny
  See Carpenter, John
Carpenter, Nancy 215
Carpenter, Nancy Sippel
  See Carpenter, Nancy
Carpenter, Patricia (Healy Evans) 1920- 11
Carr, Glyn
  See Styles, (Frank) Showell
Carr, Harriett H(elen) 1899-1977 3
Carr, Jan 1953- 132
  Earlier sketch in SATA *89*
Carr, M. J.
  See Carr, Jan
Carr, Mary Jane 1899-1988 2
  Obituary 55
Carr, Philippa
  See Hibbert, Eleanor Alice Burford
Carr, Roger Vaughan 1937- 95
Carrel, Annette Felder 1929- 90
Carrick, Carol (Hatfield) 1935- 118
  Earlier sketches in SATA *7, 63*
  See also SAAS *18*
Carrick, Donald (F.) 1929-1989 63
  Earlier sketch in SATA *7*
Carrick, Malcolm 1945- 28
Carrick, Paul 1972- 194
Carrier, Lark 1947- 71
  Brief entry 50
Carrier, Roch 1937- 166
  Earlier sketch in SATA *105*
Carrighar, Sally 1898-1985 24
Carrillo, Patricia S.
  See Carrillo, P.S.
Carrillo, P.S. 209
Carrington, G. A.
  See Cunningham, Chet
Carrington, Marsha Gray 1954- 168
  Earlier sketch in SATA *111*
Carris, Joan 1938- 182
  Brief entry 42
  Earlier sketch in SATA *44*
Carris, Joan Davenport
  See Carris, Joan
Carroll, Curt
  See Bishop, Curtis (Kent)
Carroll, Elizabeth
  See Barkin, Carol
  and James, Elizabeth
Carroll, Jaye
  See Carroll, Michael
Carroll, Jenny
  See Cabot, Meg
Carroll, (Archer) Latrobe 1894-1996 7
Carroll, Laura
  See Parr, Lucy
Carroll, Lewis 1832-1898 100
  See also YABC *2*
  See also CLR *108*
Carroll, Michael 1966- 203
Carroll, Raymond 1924- 86
  Brief entry 47
Carruth, Hayden 1921-2008 47
  Obituary 197
Carryl, Charles E. 1841-1920 114
Carryl, Charles Edward
  See Carryl, Charles E.
Carse, Robert 1902-1971 5

Carson, J(ohn) Franklin 1920-1981 1
  Obituary 107
Carson, Mary Kay 1964- 200
  Earlier sketch in SATA *150*
Carson, Rachel 1907-1964 23
Carson, Rachel Louise
  See Carson, Rachel
Carson, Rosalind
  See Chittenden, Margaret
Carson, S. M.
  See Gorsline, (Sally) Marie
Carson, William C. 1928- 154
Carter, Abby 222
  Earlier sketch in SATA *184*
Carter, Alden R 1947- 137
  Earlier sketch in SATA *67*
  See also CLR *22*
  See also SAAS *18*
Carter, Alden Richardson
  See Carter, Alden R
Carter, Andy 1948- 134
Carter, Angela 1940-1992 66
  Obituary 70
Carter, Angela Olive
  See Carter, Angela
Carter, Anne Laurel 1953- 209
  Earlier sketch in SATA *135*
Carter, Asa Earl
  See Carter, Forrest
Carter, Avis Murton
  See Allen, Kenneth S.
Carter, Bruce
  See Hough, Richard (Alexander)
Carter, Carol S(hadis) 1948- 124
Carter, David A. 1957- 228
  Earlier sketches in SATA *114, 170*
Carter, Don 1958- 192
  Earlier sketch in SATA *124*
Carter, Dorothy Sharp 1921- 8
Carter, Forrest 1927(?)-1979 32
Carter, Helene 1887-1960 15
Carter, (William) Hodding, Jr. 1907-1972 2
  Obituary 27
Carter, James Earl, Jr.
  See Carter, Jimmy
Carter, Jimmy 1924- 79
Carter, Katharine J(ones) 1905-1984 2
Carter, Lin(wood Vrooman) 1930-1988 91
Carter, Mike 1936- 138
Carter, Nick
  See Avallone, Michael (Angelo, Jr.)
  and Ballard, (Willis) Todhunter
  and Crider, Bill
  and Cassiday, Bruce (Bingham)
  and Chastain, Thomas
  and Dey, Frederic (Merrill) Van Rensselaer
  and Garside, Jack
  and Hayes, Ralph E(ugene)
  and Henderson, M(arilyn) R(uth)
  and Lynds, Dennis
  and Lynds, Gayle (Hallenbeck)
  and Randisi, Robert J.
  and Rasof, Henry
  and Stratemeyer, Edward L.
  and Smith, Martin Cruz
  and Swain, Dwight V(reeland)
  and Vardeman, Robert E.
  and Wallmann, Jeffrey M(iner)
  and White, Lionel
Carter, Peter 1929- 57
Carter, Phyllis Ann
  See Eberle, Irmengarde
Carter, Samuel (Thomson) III 1904-1988 37
  Obituary 60
Carter, Scott William 231
Carter, Timothy 1972- 224
Carter, William E. 1926-1983 1
  Obituary 35
Cartlidge, Michelle 1950- 96
  Brief entry 37
  Earlier sketch in SATA *49*

Cartner, William Carruthers 1910- *11*
Cartwright, Ann 1940- *78*
Cartwright, Reg(inald Ainsley) 1938- *64*
Cartwright, Sally 1923- *9*
Carusone, Al 1949- *89*
Carvell, Marlene *172*
Carver, John
  See Gardner, Richard (M.)
Carwell, L'Ann
  See McKissack, Patricia C.
Cary
  See Cary, Louis F(avreau)
Cary, Barbara Knapp 1912(?)-1975
  Obituary *31*
Cary, Kate 1967(?)- *174*
Cary, Louis F(avreau) 1915- *9*
Caryl, Jean
  See Kaplan, Jean Caryl Korn
Casanova, Mary 1957- *186*
  Earlier sketches in SATA *94, 136*
Cascone, A.G.
  See Cascone, Annette
  and Cascone, Gina
Cascone, Annette 1960- *103*
Cascone, Gina 1955- *103*
Case, Chris 1976- *209*
Case, Marshal T(aylor) 1941- *9*
Case, Michael
  See Howard, Robert West
Caseley, Judith 1951- *159*
  Brief entry *53*
  Earlier sketch in SATA *87*
Casewit, Curtis W(erner) 1922-2002 .... *4*
Casey, Barbara (Louise) 1944- *147*
  Earlier sketch in SATA *79*
Casey, Brigid 1950- *9*
Casey, Tina 1959- *141*
Cash, Ellen Lewis Buell 1905-1989
  Obituary *64*
Cash, John Carter 1970- *218*
Cash, Megan Montague *160*
Cashore, Kristin 1976(?)- *206*
Casilla, Robert 1959- *211*
  Earlier sketches in SATA *75, 146*
Cason, Mabel Earp 1892-1965 .... *10*
Cass, Joan E(velyn) *1*
Cass-Beggs, Barbara 1904- *62*
Cassedy, Patrice (Rinaldo) 1953- *149*
Cassedy, Sylvia 1930-1989 .... *77*
  Obituary *61*
  Earlier sketch in SATA *27*
  See also CLR *26*
Cassel, Lili
  See Wronker, Lili Cassel
Cassels, Jean *173*
Cassidy, Anne 1952- *166*
Cassidy, Anne Josephine
  See Cassidy, Anne
Cassidy, Cathy 1962- *183*
Cassidy, Kay *232*
Cassino, Mark *228*
Casson, Hugh Maxwell 1910-1999 .... *65*
  Obituary *115*
Cassutt, Michael 1954- *78*
Cassutt, Michael Joseph
  See Cassutt, Michael
Castaldi, Elicia *194*
Castaldo, Nancy Fusco 1962- *151*
  Earlier sketch in SATA *93*
Castaneda, Omar S. 1954- *71*
Castell, Megan
  See Williams, Jeanne
Castellanos, Jane Mollie Robinson
  1913-2001 .... *9*
Castellon, Federico 1914-1971 .... *48*
Castellucci, Cecil 1969- *176*
Castillo, Edmund L. 1924-2005 .... *1*
  Obituary *167*
Castillo, Lauren *195*

Castle, Lee
  See Ogan, George F.
  and Ogan, Margaret E. (Nettles)
Castle, Paul
  See Howard, Vernon (Linwood)
Castle, Robert
  See Hamilton, Edmond
Castro L., Antonio 1941- *226*
Castrovilla, Selene 1966- *186*
Caswell, Brian 1954- *171*
  Earlier sketch in SATA *97*
Caswell, Deanna *223*
Caswell, Helen (Rayburn) 1923- *12*
Catalano, Dominic 1956- *163*
  Earlier sketch in SATA *76*
Catalano, Grace (A.) 1961- *99*
Catalanotto, Peter 1959- *195*
  Autobiography Feature *113*
  Earlier sketches in SATA *70, 114, 159*
  See also CLR *68*
  See also SAAS *25*
Catanese, P.W. 1961- *227*
  Earlier sketch in SATA *179*
Cate, Annette LeBlanc *196*
Cate, Dick
  See Cate, Richard Edward Nelson
Cate, Richard Edward Nelson 1932- *28*
Cather, Willa 1873-1947 .... *30*
  See also CLR *98*
Catherall, Arthur 1906-1980 .... *74*
  Earlier sketches in SATA *3, 4*
Cathon, Laura E(lizabeth) 1908-1991 .... *27*
Catlett, Elizabeth 1919(?)- *82*
Catlin, Wynelle 1930- *13*
Catlow, Nikalas
  See Catlow, Niki
Catlow, Niki 1975- *193*
Cato, Heather *105*
Cato, Sheila *114*
Catran, Ken 1944- *190*
Catrow, David
  See Catrow, David J. III
Catrow, David J. III *206*
  Earlier sketch in SATA *152*
Catt, Louis
  See French, Vivian
Cattell, James 1954- *123*
Catton, (Charles) Bruce 1899-1978 .... *2*
  Obituary *24*
Catusanu, Mircea *222*
Catz, Max
  See Glaser, Milton
Caudell, Marian 1930- *52*
Caudill, Rebecca 1899-1985 .... *1*
  Obituary *44*
Cauley, Lorinda Bryan 1951- *46*
  Brief entry *43*
Caulfield, Peggy F. 1926-1987
  Obituary *53*
Cauman, Samuel 1910-1971 .... *48*
Causley, Charles (Stanley) 1917-2003 .... *66*
  Obituary *149*
  Earlier sketch in SATA *3*
  See also CLR *30*
Cavallaro, Ann (Abelson) 1918- *62*
Cavallo, Diana 1931- *7*
Cavanagh, Helen (Carol) 1939- *98*
  Brief entry *37*
  Earlier sketch in SATA *48*
Cavanah, Frances 1899-1982 .... *31*
  Earlier sketch in SATA *1*
Cavanna, Betty
  See Harrison, Elizabeth (Allen) Cavanna
Cavanna, Elizabeth
  See Harrison, Elizabeth (Allen) Cavanna
Cave, Kathryn 1948- *123*
  Earlier sketch in SATA *76*
Cavendish, Peter
  See Horler, Sydney
Caveney, Philip 1951- *219*

Caveney, Philip Richard
  See Caveney, Philip
Cavin, Ruth 1918-2011 .... *38*
Cavin, Ruth Brodie
  See Cavin, Ruth
Cavoukian, Raffi 1948- *68*
Cawley, Winifred 1915- *13*
Cazeau, Charles J(ay) 1931- *65*
Cazet, Denys 1938- *191*
  Brief entry *41*
  Earlier sketches in SATA *52, 99, 163*
Cazzola, Gus 1934- *73*
Cebulash, Mel 1937- *91*
  Earlier sketch in SATA *10*
Ceccoli, Nicoletta *181*
Cecil, Randy 1968- *223*
  Earlier sketch in SATA *187*
Cecka, Melanie *199*
Ceder, Georgiana Dorcas -1985 .... *10*
Celenza, Anna Harwell *133*
Celestino, Martha Laing
  See Laing, Martha
Cepeda, Joe *215*
  Earlier sketch in SATA *159*
Cerf, Bennett (Alfred) 1898-1971 .... *7*
Cerf, Christopher (Bennett) 1941- *2*
Cermak, Martin
  See Duchacek, Ivo D(uka)
Cerullo, Mary M. 1949- *145*
  Earlier sketch in SATA *86*
Cervon, Jacqueline
  See Moussard, Jacqueline
Cetin, Frank Stanley 1921- *2*
Chabon, Michael 1963- *145*
Chabrian, Deborah
  See Chabrian, Deborah L.
Chabrian, Deborah L. *212*
Chaconas, D.J.
  See Chaconas, Dori
Chaconas, Dori 1938- *208*
  Earlier sketches in SATA *145, 175*
Chaconas, Doris J.
  See Chaconas, Dori
Chadda, Sarwat *224*
Chadwick, Lester *67*
  Earlier sketch in SATA *1*
Chaffee, Allen *3*
Chaffin, Lillie D(orton) 1925- *4*
Chaikin, Miriam 1924- *152*
  Earlier sketches in SATA *24, 102*
Chall, Marsha Wilson *150*
Challand, Helen J(ean) 1921- *64*
Challans, Mary
  See Renault, Mary
Chalmers, Mary (Eileen) 1927- *6*
  See also SAAS *14*
Chamberlain, Barbara A.
  See Azore, Barbara
Chamberlain, Margaret 1954- *212*
  Earlier sketch in SATA *46*
Chamberlin, Kate 1945- *105*
Chamberlin, Mary 1960- *177*
Chamberlin, Rich *177*
Chamberlin, Richard
  See Chamberlin, Rich
Chambers, Aidan 1934- *171*
  Earlier sketches in SATA *1, 69, 108*
  See also CLR *151*
  See also SAAS *12*
Chambers, Bradford 1922-1984
  Obituary *39*
Chambers, Catherine E.
  See St. John, Nicole
Chambers, John W. 1933- *57*
  Brief entry *46*
Chambers, Kate
  See St. John, Nicole
Chambers, Margaret Ada Eastwood 1911- *2*
Chambers, Peggy
  See Chambers, Margaret Ada Eastwood
Chambers, Robert W(illiam) 1865-1933 .... *107*

Chambliss, Maxie *186*
Champlin, Susan 1961- *225*
Chan, Gillian 1954- *147*
    Earlier sketch in SATA *102*
Chan, Peter 1980(?)- *207*
Chance, James T.
    See Carpenter, John
Chance, John T.
    See Carpenter, John
Chance, Stephen
    See Turner, Philip (William)
Chandler, Caroline A(ugusta) 1906-1979 ..... *22*
    Obituary *24*
Chandler, David P. 1933- *28*
Chandler, David Porter
    See Chandler, David P.
Chandler, Edna Walker 1908-1982 .... *11*
    Obituary *31*
Chandler, Jennifer
    See Westwood, Jennifer
Chandler, Karen 1959- *122*
Chandler, Kristen *230*
Chandler, Linda S(mith) 1929- *39*
Chandler, Pauline *175*
Chandler, Robert 1953- *40*
Chandler, Ruth Forbes 1894-1978 .... *2*
    Obituary *26*
Chandonnet, Ann F. 1943- *92*
Chaney, Jill 1932- *87*
Chang, Chih-Wei 1966- *111*
Chang, Cindy 1968- *90*
Chang, Grace 1961- *226*
Chang, Margaret 1941- *71*
Chang, Margaret Scrogin
    See Chang, Margaret
Chang, Raymond 1939- *142*
    Earlier sketches in SATA *71, 142 PEN*
Chanin, Michael 1952- *84*
Channel, A. R.
    See Catherall, Arthur
Chapian, Marie 1938- *29*
Chapin, Alene Olsen Dalton 1915(?)-1986
    Obituary *47*
Chapin, Tom 1945- *83*
Chapman, Allen *67*
    Earlier sketch in SATA *1*
Chapman, Cheryl O(rth) 1948- *80*
Chapman, (Constance) Elizabeth (Mann)
    1919- *10*
Chapman, Gaye 1970- *200*
Chapman, Gaye Coralie
    See Chapman, Gaye
Chapman, Gaynor 1935- *32*
Chapman, Gillian 1955- *120*
Chapman, Jane 1970- *212*
    Earlier sketches in SATA *122, 176*
Chapman, Jean *104*
    Earlier sketch in SATA *34*
    See also CLR *65*
Chapman, John Stanton Higham 1891-1972
    Obituary *27*
Chapman, Lee
    See Bradley, Marion Zimmer
Chapman, Linda 1969- *223*
Chapman, Lynne 1960- *197*
Chapman, Lynne F(erguson) 1963- *150*
    Earlier sketch in SATA *94*
Chapman, Maristan
    See Chapman, John Stanton Higham
Chapman, Vera (Ivy May) 1898-1996 .... *33*
Chapman, Walker
    See Silverberg, Robert
Chappell, Audrey 1954- *72*
Chappell, Crissa-Jean *198*
Chappell, Warren 1904-1991 .... *68*
    Obituary *67*
    Earlier sketch in SATA *6*
    See also SAAS *10*
Chapra, Mimi *182*
Charbonneau, Eileen 1951- *118*
    Earlier sketch in SATA *84*

Charbonnet, Gabrielle 1961- *227*
    Earlier sketch in SATA *81*
Chardiet, Bernice 1927(?)- *27*
Chardiet, Bernice Kroll
    See Chardiet, Bernice
Charest, Emily MacLachlan *198*
Charles, Donald
    See Meighan, Donald Charles
Charles, Louis
    See Stratemeyer, Edward L.
Charles, Nicholas
    See Kuskin, Karla
Charles, Nicholas J.
    See Kuskin, Karla
Charles, Norma *153*
Charles, Veronika Martenova *182*
Charlip, Remy 1929- *119*
    Earlier sketches in SATA *4, 68*
    See also CLR *8*
Charlot, Jean 1898-1979 .... *8*
    Obituary *31*
Charlot, Martin 1944- *64*
Charlot, Martin Day
    See Charlot, Martin
Charlton, Michael (Alan) 1923- *34*
Charlton-Trujillo, e.E. *189*
Charmatz, Bill 1925-2005 .... *7*
Charnas, Suzy McKee 1939- *110*
    Earlier sketch in SATA *61*
Charosh, Mannis 1906- *5*
Chartier, Normand L. 1945- *66*
Chase, Alice
    See McHargue, Georgess
Chase, Alyssa 1965- *92*
Chase, Andra 1942- *91*
Chase, Emily
    See Aks, Patricia
    and Garwood, Julie
    and Sachs, Judith
    and White, Carol
Chase, Mary (Coyle) 1907-1981 .... *17*
    Obituary *29*
Chase, Mary Ellen 1887-1973 .... *10*
Chase, Paula *214*
Chase, Richard 1904-1988 .... *64*
    Obituary *56*
Chase, Samantha
    See Glick, Ruth
Chast, Roz 1954- *212*
    Earlier sketch in SATA *97*
Chastain, Madye Lee 1908-1989 .... *4*
Chataway, Carol 1955- *140*
Chatterjee, Debjani 1952- *83*
Chatterton, Martin 1961- *225*
Chauncy, Nan(cen Beryl Masterman)
    1900-1970 .... *6*
    See also CLR *6*
Chaundler, Christine 1887-1972 .... *1*
    Obituary *25*
Chayka, Doug *196*
Chbosky, Stephen 1972- *164*
Cheaney, Janie B.
    See Cheaney, J.B.
Cheaney, J.B. 1950- *188*
Chee, Cheng-Khee 1934- *79*
Cheese, Chloe 1952- *118*
Chekhonte, Antosha
    See Chekhov, Anton
Chekhov, Anton 1860-1904 .... *90*
Chekhov, Anton Pavlovich
    See Chekhov, Anton
Chelushkin, Kirill 1968- *186*
Chen, Anthony 1929- *6*
Chen, Chih-Yuan 1975- *216*
    Earlier sketch in SATA *155*
Chen, Ju-Hong 1941- *78*
Chen, Pauline 1966- *202*
Chen, Sara
    See Odgers, Sally Farrell
Chen, Tony
    See Chen, Anthony

Chen, Yong 1963- *183*
Chen, Yuan-tsung 1932- *65*
Chen, Zhiyuan
    See Chen, Chih-Yuan
Chenault, Nell
    See Smith, Linell Nash
Chen Chih-Yuan
    See Chen, Chih-Yuan
Chenery, Janet (Dai) 1923- *25*
Cheney, Cora 1916-1999 .... *3*
    Obituary *110*
Cheney, Glenn (Alan) 1951- *99*
Cheney, Lynne V. 1941- *152*
Cheney, Lynne Vincent
    See Cheney, Lynne V.
Cheney, Ted
    See Cheney, Theodore Albert
Cheney, Theodore A. Rees
    See Cheney, Theodore Albert
Cheney, Theodore Albert 1928- *11*
Cheng, Andrea 1957- *205*
    Earlier sketches in SATA *128, 172*
Cheng, Christopher 1959- *173*
    Earlier sketch in SATA *106*
Cheng, Judith 1955- *36*
Cheng, Shan
    See Jiang, Cheng An
Cheripko, Jan 1951- *155*
    Earlier sketch in SATA *83*
Chermayeff, Ivan 1932- *47*
Chernenko, Dan
    See Turtledove, Harry
Chernett, Dan *224*
Chernoff, Dorothy A.
    See Ernst, (Lyman) John
Chernoff, Goldie Taub 1909- *10*
Cherry, Carolyn Janice
    See Cherryh, C.J.
Cherry, Lynne 1952- *99*
    Earlier sketch in SATA *34*
Cherryh, C.J. 1942- *172*
    Earlier sketch in SATA *93*
Cherryholmes, Anne
    See Price, Olive
Cheshire, Simon *172*
Chesler, Bernice 1932-2002 .... *59*
Chess, Victoria (Dickerson) 1939- *92*
    Earlier sketch in SATA *33*
Chessa, Francesca *233*
    Earlier sketch in SATA *191*
Chester, Deborah 1957- *85*
Chester, Kate
    See Guccione, Leslie Davis
Chesterton, G. K. 1874-1936 .... *27*
Chesterton, Gilbert Keith
    See Chesterton, G. K.
Chesworth, Michael *207*
    Earlier sketch in SATA *160*
Chetin, Helen 1922- *6*
Chetwin, Grace *86*
    Brief entry *50*
Chevalier, Christa 1937- *35*
Chevalier, Tracy 1962- *128*
Chew, Ruth 1920-2010 .... *7*
Chichester Clark, Emma 1955- *209*
    Earlier sketches in SATA *117, 156, 69*
Chidsey, Donald Barr 1902-1981 .... *3*
    Obituary *27*
Chiefari, Janet D. 1942- *58*
Chien, Catia *193*
Chien-min, Lin
    See Rumford, James
Child, L. Maria
    See Child, Lydia Maria
Child, Lauren 1965- *183*
    Earlier sketches in SATA *119, 160*
Child, Lincoln 1957- *113*
Child, Lincoln B.
    See Child, Lincoln
Child, Lydia Maria 1802-1880 .... *67*

Child, Mrs.
  See Child, Lydia Maria
Child, Philip 1898-1978 47
Children's Shepherd, The
  See Westphal, Arnold Carl
Childress, Alice 1920-1994 81
  Earlier sketches in SATA 7, 48
  See also CLR 14
Childs, H(alla) Fay (Cochrane) 1890-1971 1
  Obituary 25
Chilton, Charles (Frederick William)
  1917- 102
Chima, Cinda Williams 226
  Earlier sketch in SATA 192
Chimaera
  See Farjeon, Eleanor
Chin, Jason 1978- 218
Chin, Richard (M.) 1946- 52
Chinery, Michael 1938- 26
Chin-Lee, Cynthia 1958- 102
Chin-Lee D., Cynthia
  See Chin-Lee, Cynthia
Chippendale, Lisa A. 158
Chipperfield, Joseph Eugene 1912-1980(?) .. 87
  Earlier sketch in SATA 2
Chisholm, P. F.
  See Finney, Patricia
Chislett, Gail (Elaine) 1948- 58
Chittenden, Elizabeth F. 1903-1999 9
Chittenden, Margaret 1935- 28
Chittum, Ida 1918- 7
Chitwood, Suzanne Tanner 1958- 160
Chmielarz, Sharon Lee 1940- 72
Choate, Judith (Newkirk) 1940- 30
Chocolate, Debbi 1954- 223
  Earlier sketch in SATA 96
Chocolate, Deborah H. Newton
  See Chocolate, Debbi
Chodos-Irvine, Margaret 211
  Earlier sketch in SATA 152
Choi, Sook Nyul 1937- 73
  Autobiography Feature 126
  See also CLR 53
Choi, Yangsook 178
Choksi, Nishant 1975- 222
Choldenko, Gennifer 1957- 182
  Earlier sketch in SATA 135
Chorao, Kay 1936- 215
Chorao, (Ann Mc)Kay (Sproat) 1936- 162
  Earlier sketches in SATA 8, 69
Choron, Sandra (Zena Samelson) 1950- 146
Choung, Eun-hee 199
Chown, Marcus 1959- 137
Choyce, Lesley 1951- 165
  Earlier sketch in SATA 94
Choyce, Lesley Willis
  See Choyce, Lesley
Chrisman, Arthur Bowie 1889-1953 124
  See also YABC 1
Christelow, Eileen 1943- 184
  Autobiography Feature 120
  Brief entry 35
  Earlier sketches in SATA 38, 90
Christensen, Bonnie 1951- 213
  Earlier sketches in SATA 110, 157
Christensen, Gardell Dano 1907-1991 1
Christensen, Laurie
  See Steding, Laurie
Christesen, Barbara 1940- 40
Christgau, Alice Erickson 1902-1977 13
Christian, Mary Blount 1933- 9
Christiana, David 195
Christie, Agatha 1890-1976 36
Christie, Agatha Mary Clarissa
  See Christie, Agatha
Christie, Ann Philippa
  See Pearce, Philippa
Christie, Gregory
  See Christie, R. Gregory
Christie, Philippa
  See Pearce, Philippa

Christie, R. Gregory 1971- 225
  Earlier sketches in SATA 127, 185
Christopher, John
  See Youd, Samuel
Christopher, Louise
  See Hale, Arlene
Christopher, Matt(hew Frederick)
  1917-1997 80
  Obituary 99
  Earlier sketches in SATA 2, 47
  See also CLR 119
  See also SAAS 9
Christopher, Milbourne 1914(?)-1984 46
Christy, Howard Chandler 1873-1952 21
Chrustowski, Rick 176
Chrystie, Frances N(icholson) 1904-1986 60
Chu, Daniel 1933- 11
Chukovsky, Kornei (Ivanovich) 1882-1969 . 34
  Earlier sketch in SATA 5
Church, Caroline Jayne 219
  Earlier sketch in SATA 179
Church, Richard 1893-1972 3
Churchill, E(lmer) Richard 1937- 11
Churchill, Elizabeth
  See Hough, Richard (Alexander)
Chute, B(eatrice) J(oy) 1913-1987 2
  Obituary 53
Chute, Marchette (Gaylord) 1909-1994 1
Chwast, Jacqueline 1932- 6
Chwast, Seymour 1931- 146
  Earlier sketches in SATA 18, 96
Ciardi, John (Anthony) 1916-1986 65
  Obituary 46
  Earlier sketch in SATA 1
  See also CLR 19
  See also SAAS 26
Ciccone, Madonna Louise Veronica
  See Madonna
Ciddor, Anna 1957- 213
Ciment, James D. 1958- 140
Cirrone, Dorian 182
Cisneros, Sandra 1954-
  See CLR 123
Citra, Becky 1954- 137
Citrin, Michael 1965(?)- 183
Claflin, Willy 1944- 208
Clair, Andree 19
Clampett, Bob 1914(?)-1985 44
  Obituary 38
Clampett, Robert
  See Clampett, Bob
Clapp, John 1968- 109
Clapp, Patricia 1912- 74
  Earlier sketch in SATA 4
  See also SAAS 4
Clare, Ellen
  See Sinclair, Olga
Clare, Helen
  See Clarke, Pauline
Claremont, Chris 1950- 87
Claremont, Christopher Simon
  See Claremont, Chris
Clark, Ann Nolan 1896-1995 82
  Obituary 87
  Earlier sketch in SATA 4
  See also CLR 16
  See also SAAS 16
Clark, Champ 1923-2002 47
Clark, Christopher (Anthony) Stuart
  See Stuart-Clark, Christopher (Anthony)
Clark, Clara Gillow 1951- 154
  Earlier sketch in SATA 84
Clark, David
  See Hardcastle, Michael
Clark, David Allen
  See Ernst, (Lyman) John
Clark, Emma Chichester
  See Chichester Clark, Emma
Clark, Frank J(ames) 1922- 18
Clark, Garel
  See Garelick, May

Clark, Halsey
  See Deming, Richard
Clark, Joan
  See Benson, Mildred
Clark, Joan 1934- 182
  Earlier sketches in SATA 59, 96
Clark, Leonard 1905-1981 30
  Obituary 29
Clark, M. R.
  See Clark, Mavis Thorpe
Clark, Margaret (D.) 1943- 126
Clark, Margaret Goff 1913- 82
  Earlier sketch in SATA 8
Clark, Mary Higgins 1929- 46
Clark, Mavis Thorpe 1909-1999 74
  Earlier sketch in SATA 8
  See also CLR 30
  See also SAAS 5
Clark, Merle
  See Gessner, Lynne
Clark, Patricia Denise
  See Robins, Patricia
Clark, Patricia Finrow 1929- 11
Clark, Ronald Harry 1904-1999 193
Clark, Ronald William 1916-1987 2
  Obituary 52
Clark, Sherryl 1956- 149
Clark, Van D(eusen) 1909-1974 2
Clark, Virginia
  See Gray, Patricia (Clark)
Clark, Walter Van Tilburg 1909-1971 8
Clarke, Arthur
  See Clarke, Arthur C.
Clarke, Arthur C. 1917-2008 115
  Obituary 191
  Earlier sketches in SATA 13, 70
  See also CLR 119
Clarke, Arthur Charles
  See Clarke, Arthur C.
Clarke, Clorinda 1917- 7
Clarke, Elizabeth L. 1934- 103
Clarke, Greg 1959- 215
Clarke, Gus 1948- 134
Clarke, J.
  See Clarke, Judith
Clarke, James Hall
  See Rowland-Entwistle, (Arthur) Theodore
  (Henry)
Clarke, Joan B. 1921- 42
  Brief entry 27
Clarke, John
  See Laklan, Carli
  and Sontup, Dan(iel)
Clarke, Judith 1943- 164
  Earlier sketches in SATA 75, 110
  See also CLR 61
Clarke, Julia 1950- 138
Clarke, Kenneth 1957- 107
Clarke, Lea
  See Rowland-Entwistle, (Arthur) Theodore
  (Henry)
Clarke, Margaret 1941-
  See CLR 99
Clarke, Mary Stetson 1911-1994 5
Clarke, Michael
  See Newlon, (Frank) Clarke
Clarke, Pauline 1921- 131
  Earlier sketch in SATA 3
  See also CLR 28
Clarkson, E(dith) Margaret 1915- 37
Clarkson, Ewan 1929- 9
Clarkson, Karen 233
Claudia, Susan
  See Goulart, Ron
  and Johnston, William
Claverie, Jean 1946- 38
Clay, Patrice 1947- 47
Clay, Wil 203
Clayman, Deborah Paula
  See Da Costa, Deborah

Claypool, Jane
  See Miner, Jane Claypool
Clayton, Elaine 1961- 209
  Earlier sketches in SATA *94, 159*
Clayton, Lawrence (Otto, Jr.) 1945- 75
Clayton, Sally Pomme 218
Clayton, Sandra 1951- 110
Cle, Troy 202
Clea, Super
  See Hantman, Clea
Cleary, Beverly 1916- 121
  Earlier sketches in SATA *2, 43, 79*
  See also CLR *72*
  See also SAAS *20*
Cleary, Beverly Atlee Bunn
  See Cleary, Beverly
Cleary, Brian P. 1959- 186
  Earlier sketches in SATA *93, 132*
Cleaver, Bill
  See Cleaver, William J.
Cleaver, Carole 1934- 6
Cleaver, Elizabeth (Ann Mrazik)
  1939-1985 23
  Obituary 43
  See also CLR *13*
Cleaver, Hylton Reginald 1891-1961 49
Cleaver, Vera 1919-1993 76
  Earlier sketch in SATA *22*
  See also CLR *6*
Cleaver, Vera Allen
  See Cleaver, Vera
Cleaver, William J. 1920-1981 22
  Obituary 27
  See also CLR *6*
Cleishbotham, Jebediah
  See Scott, Sir Walter
Cleland, Janet 226
Cleland, Mabel
  See Widdemer, Mabel Cleland
Clem, Margaret H(ollingsworth) 1923- 90
Clemens, James
  See Rollins, James
Clemens, Samuel
  See Twain, Mark
Clemens, Samuel Langhorne
  See Twain, Mark
Clemens, Virginia Phelps 1941- 35
Clement, Gary 191
Clement, Janet 182
Clement, Nathan 1966- 200
Clement, Priscilla Ferguson 1942- 171
Clement, Rod 97
Clement-Moore, Rosemary 229
  Earlier sketch in SATA *188*
Clements, Andrew 1949- 203
  Earlier sketches in SATA *104, 158*
Clements, Bruce 1931- 178
  Earlier sketches in SATA *27, 94*
Clemesha, David 192
Cleminson, Katie 221
Clemons, Elizabeth
  See Nowell, Elizabeth Cameron
Clerk, N. W.
  See Lewis, C. S.
Cleveland, Bob
  See Cleveland, George
Cleveland, George 1903(?)-1985
  Obituary 43
Cleveland-Peck, Patricia 80
Cleven, Cathrine
  See Cleven, Kathryn Seward
Cleven, Kathryn Seward 2
Clevenger, William R. 1954- 84
Clevenger, William Russell
  See Clevenger, William R.
Clevin, Joergen 1920- 7
Clevin, Jorgen
  See Clevin, Joergen
Clewes, Dorothy (Mary) 1907-2003 86
  Obituary 138
  Earlier sketch in SATA *1*

Clifford, David
  See Rosenberg, Eth Clifford
Clifford, Eth
  See Rosenberg, Eth Clifford
Clifford, Harold B(urton) 1893-1988 10
Clifford, Margaret Cort 1929- 1
Clifford, Martin
  See Hamilton, Charles (Harold St. John)
Clifford, Mary Louise Beneway 1926- 23
Clifford, Peggy
  See Clifford, Margaret Cort
Clifford, Rachel Mark
  See Lewis, Brenda Ralph
Clifton, Lucille 1936-2010 128
  Earlier sketches in SATA *20, 69*
  See also CLR *5*
Clifton, Thelma Lucille
  See Clifton, Lucille
Climo, Shirley 1928- 166
  Autobiography Feature 110
  Brief entry 35
  Earlier sketches in SATA *39, 77*
  See also CLR *69*
Cline-Ransome, Lesa 201
Clinton, Catherine 1952- 203
Clinton, Cathryn 1957- 136
Clinton, Dirk
  See Silverberg, Robert
Clinton, Jon
  See Prince, J(ack) H(arvey)
Clippinger, Carol 193
Clish, (Lee) Marian 1946- 43
Clive, Clifford
  See Hamilton, Charles (Harold St. John)
Clokey, Art 1921- 59
Cloudsley-Thompson, J(ohn) L(eonard)
  1921- 19
Clouse, Nancy L. 1938- 78
Clover, Peter 1952- 215
  Earlier sketch in SATA *152*
Clutha, Janet
  See Frame, Janet
Clutha, Janet Paterson Frame
  See Frame, Janet
Clymer, Eleanor 1906-2001 85
  Obituary 126
  Earlier sketch in SATA *9*
  See also SAAS *17*
Clyne, Patricia (Edwards) 31
Cneut, Carll 1969- 197
Coalson, Glo 1946- 94
  Earlier sketch in SATA *26*
Coates, Anna 1958- 73
Coates, Belle 1896-1986 2
Coates, Ruth Allison 1915- 11
Coats, Alice M(argaret) 1905-1976 11
Coatsworth, Elizabeth (Jane) 1893-1986 100
  Obituary 49
  Earlier sketches in SATA *2, 56*
  See also CLR *2*
Cobalt, Martin
  See Mayne, William
Cobb, Jane
  See Berry, Jane Cobb
Cobb, Mary 1931- 88
Cobb, Vicki 1938- 136
  Autobiography Feature 136
  Earlier sketches in SATA *8, 69, 131*
  See also CLR *2*
  See also SAAS *6*
Cobbett, Richard
  See Pluckrose, Henry
Cober, Alan E(dwin) 1935-1998 7
  Obituary 101
Cobham, Sir Alan
  See Hamilton, Charles (Harold St. John)
Coburn, Jake 1978- 155
Cocagnac, Augustin Maurice(-Jean) 1924- 7
Cocca-Leffler, Maryann 1958- 194
  Earlier sketches in SATA *80, 136*
Cochran, Bill 187

Cochran, Bobbye A. 1949- 11
Cochran, Josh 221
Cochran, Thomas 1955- 198
Cochrane, Hamilton E.
  See Cochrane, Mick
Cochrane, Mick 1956- 215
Cockcroft, Jason 217
Cockett, Mary 3
Cocks, Peter 204
Cocovini, Abby 202
Coddell, Esme Raji
  See Codell, Esme Raji
Codell, Esme Raji 1968- 160
Cody, C. S.
  See Waller, Leslie
Cody, Jess
  See Cunningham, Chet
Cody, Matthew 229
Coe, Anne (E.) 1949- 95
Coe, Douglas
  See Epstein, Beryl
  and Epstein, Samuel
Coe, Lloyd 1899(?)-1976
  Obituary 30
Coen, Rena Neumann 1925- 20
Coerr, Eleanor (Beatrice) 1922- 67
  Earlier sketch in SATA *1*
Cofer, Judith Ortiz 1952- 164
  Earlier sketch in SATA *110*
Coffelt, Nancy 1961- 189
Coffey, Brian
  See Koontz, Dean
Coffin, Geoffrey
  See Mason, F(rancis) van Wyck
Coffin, M. T.
  See Stanley, George Edward
Coffin, M.T.
  See Stanley, George Edward
Coffman, Ramon Peyton 1896-1989 4
Cogan, Karen 1954- 125
Coggins, Jack (Banham) 1911-2006 2
Cohagan, Carolyn 1972- 228
Cohen, Barbara 1932-1992 77
  Obituary 74
  Earlier sketch in SATA *10*
  See also SAAS *7*
Cohen, Daniel (E.) 1936- 70
  Earlier sketch in SATA *8*
  See also CLR *43*
  See also SAAS *4*
Cohen, Deborah Bodin 1968- 180
Cohen, Jan Barger
  See Barger, Jan
Cohen, Jene Barr
  See Barr, Jene
Cohen, Joan Lebold 1932- 4
Cohen, Judith Love 1933- 78
Cohen, Lisa 1963- 225
Cohen, Miriam 1926-1955 155
  Earlier sketches in SATA *29, 106*
  See also SAAS *11*
Cohen, Nora 75
Cohen, Paul 1945- 58
Cohen, Paul S.
  See Cohen, Paul
Cohen, Peter Zachary 1931- 150
  Earlier sketch in SATA *4*
Cohen, Robert Carl 1930- 8
Cohen, Santiago 1954- 215
Cohen, Sholom 1951- 94
Cohn, Angelo 1914-1997 19
Cohn, Diana 194
Cohn, Rachel 1968- 228
  Earlier sketch in SATA *161*
Coit, Margaret Louise 1922-2003 2
  Obituary 142
Colasanti, Susane 1973- 214
Colato Lainez, Rene 1970- 226
  Earlier sketch in SATA *176*
Colbert, Anthony 1934-2007 15
Colbert, Nancy A. 1936- 139

Author Index

Colby, C(arroll) B(urleigh) 1904-1977 35
    Earlier sketch in SATA 3
Colby, Jean Poindexter 1909-1993 23
Cole, Annette
    See Steiner, Barbara A(nnette)
Cole, Babette 1949- 155
    Earlier sketches in SATA 61, 96
Cole, Betsy 1940- 83
Cole, Brock 1938- 200
    Earlier sketches in SATA 72, 136
    See also CLR 18
Cole, Davis
    See Elting, Mary
Cole, Hannah 1954- 74
Cole, Henry 1955- 213
    Earlier sketch in SATA 181
Cole, Jack -1974
    See Stewart, John
Cole, Jackson
    See Curry, Thomas Albert
    and Germano, Peter B.
    and Heckelmann, Charles N(ewman)
    and Newton, D(wight) B(ennett)
    and Schisgall, Oscar
Cole, Jennifer
    See Zach, Cheryl (Byrd)
Cole, Joanna 1944- 231
    Brief entry 37
    Earlier sketches in SATA 49, 81, 120, 168
    See also CLR 40
Cole, Lois Dwight 1903-1979 10
    Obituary 26
Cole, Michael 1947- 59
Cole, Samantha
    See Cole, Stephen
Cole, Sheila 1939- 171
    Earlier sketches in SATA 24, 95
Cole, Sheila R.
    See Cole, Sheila
Cole, Sheila Rotenberg
    See Cole, Sheila
Cole, Stephen 1971- 230
    Earlier sketch in SATA 161
Cole, Steve
    See Cole, Stephen
Cole, William (Rossa) 1919-2000 71
    Earlier sketch in SATA 9
    See also SAAS 9
Coleman, Andrew
    See Pine, Nicholas
Coleman, Clare
    See Bell, Clare (Louise)
    and Easton, M(alcolm) Coleman
Coleman, Janet Wyman 184
Coleman, Loren 1947- 164
Coleman, Loren Elwood, Jr.
    See Coleman, Loren
Coleman, Mary Ann 1928- 83
Coleman, Michael
    See Jones, Allan Frewin
Coleman, Michael 1946- 199
    Autobiography Feature 133
    Earlier sketches in SATA 108, 133
Coleman, Rowan 187
Coleman, William L(eRoy) 1938- 49
    Brief entry 34
Coleman, Wim 1926- 212
Coles, Robert 1929- 23
Coles, Robert Martin
    See Coles, Robert
Colfer, Eoin 1965- 197
    Earlier sketch in SATA 148
    See also CLR 112
Colin, Ann
    See Ure, Jean
Collard, Sneed B. III 1959- 184
    Earlier sketches in SATA 84, 139
Colledge, Anne 1939- 142
Colley, Jacqui 1965- 202
Collicott, Sharleen 1937- 143
    Earlier sketch in SATA 98

Collicutt, Paul 229
Collier, Bryan 204
    Earlier sketches in SATA 126, 174
Collier, Christopher 1930- 70
    Earlier sketch in SATA 16
    See also CLR 126
Collier, Ethel 1903-1999 22
Collier, James Lincoln 1928- 166
    Earlier sketches in SATA 8, 70
    See also CLR 126
    See also SAAS 21
Collier, Jane
    See Collier, Zena
Collier, Kristi 182
Collier, Steven 1942- 61
Collier, Zena 1926- 23
Collings, Gillian 1939- 102
Collington, Peter 1948- 99
    Earlier sketch in SATA 59
Collins, Ace 1953- 82
Collins, Andrew J.
    See Collins, Ace
Collins, B. R. 1981- 214
Collins, David R(aymond) 1940-2001 121
    Earlier sketch in SATA 7
Collins, Heather 1946- 81
Collins, Hunt
    See Hunter, Evan
Collins, Michael
    See Lynds, Dennis
Collins, Michael 1930- 58
Collins, Pat Lowery 1932- 217
    Earlier sketches in SATA 31, 151
Collins, Paul 1954- 126
Collins, Ross 1972- 200
Collins, Ruth Philpott 1890-1975
    Obituary 30
Collins, Suzanne 1963(?)- 224
    Earlier sketch in SATA 180
Collins, Yvonne 194
Collinson, A. S.
    See Collinson, Alan S.
Collinson, Alan S. 1934- 80
Collinson, Roger (Alfred) 1936- 133
Collison, Linda 1953- 185
Collodi, Carlo 1826-1890 100
    Earlier sketch in SATA 29
    See also CLR 120
Colloms, Brenda 1919- 40
Colman, Hila 1909-2008 53
    Earlier sketch in SATA 1
    See also SAAS 14
Colman, Morris 1899(?)-1981
    Obituary 25
Colman, Penny (Morgan) 1944- 160
    Autobiography Feature 160
    Earlier sketches in SATA 77, 114
Colman, Warren (David) 1944- 67
Coloma, Cindy
    See Martinusen-Coloma, Cindy
Colombo, John Robert 1936- 50
Colon, Raul 156
Colon, Raul 1952- 202
Colonius, Lillian 1911-1992 3
Colorado, Antonio J.
    See Colorado (Capella), Antonio J(ulio)
Colorado (Capella), Antonio J(ulio)
    1903-1994 23
    Obituary 79
Colquhoun, Glenn 1964- 165
Colston, Fifi E. 1960- 150
Colt, Martin
    See Epstein, Beryl
    and Epstein, Samuel
Colum, Padraic 1881-1972 15
    See also CLR 36
Columbus, Chris 1959- 97
Columbus, Christopher
    See Columbus, Chris
Columella
    See Moore, Clement Clarke

Colver, Anne 1908- 7
Colvin, James
    See Moorcock, Michael
Colwell, Eileen (Hilda) 1904-2002 2
Colwyn, Stewart
    See Pepper, Frank S.
Coman, Carolyn 1951- 197
    Earlier sketch in SATA 127
Combres, Elisabeth 1967- 226
Combs, Lisa M.
    See McCourt, Lisa
Combs, Robert
    See Murray, John
Comfort, Jane Levington
    See Sturtzel, Jane Levington
Comfort, Mildred Houghton 1886-1976 3
Comins, Ethel M(ae) 11
Comins, Jeremy 1933- 28
Commager, Henry Steele 1902-1998 23
    Obituary 102
Comora, Madeleine 190
Compere, Mickie
    See Davidson, Margaret
Compestine, Ying Chang 1963- 187
    Earlier sketch in SATA 140
Comport, Sally Wern 190
Compton, Patricia A. 1936- 75
Comte, The Great
    See Hawkesworth, Eric
Comus
    See Ballantyne, R(obert) M(ichael)
Comyns, Nance
    See Comyns-Toohey, Nantz
Comyns-Toohey, Nantz 1956- 86
Conahan, Carolyn
    See Conahan, Carolyn Digby
Conahan, Carolyn Digby 1961- 216
Conan Doyle, Arthur
    See Doyle, Sir Arthur Conan
Condie, Ally 204
Condie, Allyson B.
    See Condie, Ally
Condit, Martha Olson 1913- 28
Condon, Bill 1949- 142
Condon, Judith 83
Condon, Ken 195
Condy, Roy 1942- 96
Cone, Ferne Geller 1921- 39
Cone, Molly (Lamken) 1918- 151
    Autobiography Feature 151
    Earlier sketches in SATA 1, 28, 115
    See also SAAS 11
Cone, Patrick 1954- 89
Coney, Michael G. 1932-2005 61
    Obituary 170
Coney, Michael Greatrex
    See Coney, Michael G.
Coney, Mike
    See Coney, Michael G.
Conford, Ellen 1942- 162
    Earlier sketches in SATA 6, 68, 110
    See also CLR 71
Conger, Lesley
    See Suttles, Shirley (Smith)
Conklin, Gladys Plemon 1903- 2
Conklin, Paul S. 1929(?)-2003 43
    Brief entry 33
    Obituary 147
Conkling, Hilda 1910-1986 23
Conlan, Kathleen Elizabeth 1950- 145
Conlan, Kathy
    See Conlan, Kathleen Elizabeth
Conley, Robyn 1963- 125
Conley-Weaver, Robyn
    See Conley, Robyn
Conlon-McKenna, Marita 1956- 71
Conly, Jane Leslie 1948- 164
    Earlier sketches in SATA 80, 112
Conly, Robert Leslie
    See O'Brien, Robert C.

Connell, Kirk
   See Chapman, John Stanton Higham
Connell, Tom 206
Connelly, Gwen 1952- 212
Connelly, Marc(us Cook) 1890-1980
   Obituary 25
Connolly, Jerome P(atrick) 1931- 8
Connolly, Pat 1943- 74
Connolly, Peter 1935- 105
   Earlier sketch in SATA 47
Conover, Chris 1950- 213
   Earlier sketch in SATA 31
Conquest, Owen
   See Hamilton, Charles (Harold St. John)
Conrad, Joseph 1857-1924 27
Conrad, Pam 1947-1996 133
   Brief entry 49
   Obituary 90
   Earlier sketches in SATA 52, 80
   See also CLR 18
   See also SAAS 19
Conroy, Jack
   See Conroy, John Wesley
Conroy, John Wesley 1899-1990 19
   Obituary 65
Conroy, Melissa 1969- 226
Conroy, Robert
   See Goldston, Robert (Conroy)
Constable, Kate 1966- 172
Constant, Alberta Wilson 1908-1981 22
   Obituary 28
Constantin, Pascale 185
Conway, Celeste 210
Conway, David 1970- 213
Conway, Diana C. 1943- 91
Conway, Diana Cohen
   See Conway, Diana C.
Conway, Gordon
   See Hamilton, Charles (Harold St. John)
Cook, Ande 192
Cook, Bernadine 1924- 11
Cook, Fred J(ames) 1911-2003 2
   Obituary 145
Cook, Glen 1944- 171
   Earlier sketch in SATA 108
Cook, Glen Charles
   See Cook, Glen
Cook, Hugh 1956- 85
Cook, Hugh, Walter Gilbert
   See Cook, Hugh
Cook, Jean Thor 1930- 94
Cook, Joel 1934- 79
Cook, Joseph Jay 1924- 8
Cook, Lisa Broadie 157
Cook, Lyn
   See Waddell, Evelyn Margaret
Cook, Roy
   See Silverberg, Robert
Cook, Sally 207
Cook, Trish 175
Cooke, Ann
   See Cole, Joanna
Cooke, Arthur
   See Lowndes, Robert A(ugustine) W(ard)
Cooke, Barbara
   See Alexander, Anna B(arbara Cooke)
Cooke, David Coxe 1917- 2
Cooke, Donald Ewin 1916-1985 2
   Obituary 45
Cooke, Frank E. 1920- 87
Cooke, Jean (Isobel Esther) 1929- 74
Cooke, John Estes
   See Baum, L. Frank
Cooke, Trish 1962- 129
Cookson, Catherine (McMullen) 1906-1998 .. 9
   Obituary 116
Cooley, Beth 210
Cooley, Elizabeth
   See Cooley, Beth
Cooley, Regina Francoise 1940- 177

Coolidge, Olivia E(nsor) 1908- 26
   Earlier sketch in SATA 1
Cooling, Wendy 169
   Earlier sketch in SATA 111
Coombs, Charles I(ra) 1914-1994 43
   Earlier sketch in SATA 3
   See also SAAS 15
Coombs, Chick
   See Coombs, Charles I(ra)
Coombs, Jonathan 204
Coombs, Kate 190
Coombs, Patricia 1926- 51
   Earlier sketch in SATA 3
   See also SAAS 22
Cooney, Barbara 1917-2000 96
   Obituary 123
   Earlier sketches in SATA 6, 59
   See also CLR 23
Cooney, Caroline B. 1947- 218
   Brief entry 41
   Earlier sketches in SATA 48, 80, 113, 130,
   179
Cooney, Doug 181
Cooney, Nancy Evans 1932- 42
Coontz, Otto 1946- 33
Cooper, Ann (Catharine) 1939- 104
Cooper, Dutch
   See Kuyper, Sjoerd
Cooper, Elisha 1971- 157
   Earlier sketch in SATA 99
Cooper, Elizabeth Keyser -1992 47
Cooper, Floyd 227
   Earlier sketches in SATA 96, 144, 187
   See also CLR 60
Cooper, Gordon 1932- 23
Cooper, Helen 1963- 169
   Earlier sketch in SATA 102
Cooper, Henry S. F., Jr. 1933- 65
Cooper, Henry Spotswood Fenimore, Jr.
   See Cooper, Henry S. F., Jr.
Cooper, Ilene 1948- 145
   Earlier sketches in SATA 66, 97
Cooper, James Fenimore 1789-1851 19
   See also CLR 105
Cooper, John R. 1
Cooper, Kay 1941- 11
Cooper, Lee Pelham 1926- 5
Cooper, Lester (Irving) 1919-1985 32
   Obituary 43
Cooper, Lettice (Ulpha) 1897-1994 35
   Obituary 82
Cooper, Louise 1952-2009 152
Cooper, M.E.
   See Davis, Maggie S.
Cooper, M.E.
   See Lerangis, Peter
Cooper, Melrose
   See Kroll, Virginia L.
Cooper, Michael L. 1950- 181
   Earlier sketches in SATA 79, 117
Cooper, Michelle 1969- 226
Cooper, Patrick 1949- 134
Cooper, Susan 1935- 151
   Earlier sketches in SATA 4, 64, 104
   See also CLR 161
   See also SAAS 6
Cooper, Susan Mary
   See Cooper, Susan
Cope, Jane U(rsula) 1949- 108
Copeland, Helen 1920- 4
Copeland, Mark 1956- 180
Copeland, Paul W. 23
Coplans, Peta 1951- 84
Copley (Diana) Heather Pickering 1918- 45
Coppard, A(lfred) E(dgar) 1878-1957
   See YABC 1
Copper, Melinda 1952- 172
Copper, Melinda McConnaughey
   See Copper, Melinda
Corace, Jen 208

Coralie
   See Anderson, Catherine Corley
Corbett, Grahame 43
   Brief entry 36
Corbett, Scott 1913- 42
   Earlier sketch in SATA 2
   See also CLR 1
   See also SAAS 2
Corbett, Sue 174
Corbett, W(illiam) J(esse) 1938- 102
   Brief entry 44
   Earlier sketch in SATA 50
   See also CLR 19
Corbin, Sabra Lee
   See Malvern, Gladys
Corbin, William
   See McGraw, William Corbin
Corbman, Marjorie 1987- 179
Corby, Dan
   See Catherall, Arthur
Corcoran, Barbara (Asenath) 1911-2003 77
   Autobiography Feature 125
   Earlier sketch in SATA 3
   See also CLR 50
   See also SAAS 20
Corcos, Lucille 1908-1973 10
Cordell, Alexander
   See Graber, Alexander
Cordell, Matthew 1975- 199
Corder, Zizou
   See Young, Louisa
Cordova, Amy 232
Corella, Joseph
   See Odgers, Sally Farrell
Coren, Alan 1938-2007 32
   Obituary 187
Corey, Dorothy 23
Corey, Shana 1974- 219
   Earlier sketch in SATA 133
Corfe, Thomas Howell 1928- 27
Corfe, Tom
   See Corfe, Thomas Howell
Corfield, Robin Bell 1952- 74
Corke, Estelle 1969- 220
Corlett, William 1938-2005 46
   Brief entry 39
Cormack, M(argaret) Grant 1913- 11
Cormack, Maribelle B. 1902-1984 39
Cormier, Robert 1925-2000 83
   Obituary 122
   Earlier sketches in SATA 10, 45
   See also CLR 167
Cormier, Robert Edmund
   See Cormier, Robert
Cornelius, Carol 1942- 40
Cornelius, Kay 1933- 157
Cornell, J.
   See Cornell, Jeffrey
Cornell, James (Clayton, Jr.) 1938- 27
Cornell, Jean Gay 1920- 23
Cornell, Jeffrey 1945- 11
Cornell, Laura 189
Cornish, D.M. 1972- 185
Cornish, Sam(uel James) 1935- 23
Cornwall, Nellie
   See Sloggett, Nellie
Cornwell, Autumn 195
Corr, Christopher 1955- 189
Correa, E. Shan
   See Correa, Shan
Correa, Shan 233
Correy, Lee
   See Stine, G(eorge) Harry
Corrick, James A. 1945- 76
Corrigan, (Helen) Adeline 1909- 23
Corrigan, Barbara 1922- 8
Corrigan, Eireann 1977- 163
Corrin, Sara 1918- 86
   Brief entry 48
Corrin, Stephen 86
   Brief entry 48

Corriveau, Art *231*
Corsi, Wendy
  See Staub, Wendy Corsi
Cort, M. C.
  See Clifford, Margaret Cort
Cort, Margaret
  See Clifford, Margaret Cort
Corwin, Judith H(offman) 1946- *10*
Corwin, Oliver
  See Corwin, Oliver J.
Corwin, Oliver J. *206*
Cory, Rowena
  See Lindquist, Rowena Cory
Cosby, Bill 1937- *110*
  Earlier sketch in SATA *66*
Cosby, William Henry, Jr.
  See Cosby, Bill
  and Cosby, Bill
Cosentino, Ralph *169*
Cosgrave, John O'Hara II 1908-1968
  Obituary *21*
Cosgrove, Margaret (Leota) 1926- *47*
Cosgrove, Stephen E(dward) 1945- *53*
  Brief entry *40*
Coskey, Evelyn 1932- *7*
Cosner, Shaaron 1940- *43*
Cossi, Olga 1921- *216*
  Earlier sketches in SATA *67, 102*
Costabel, Eva Deutsch 1924- *45*
Costabel-Deutsch, Eva
  See Costabel, Eva Deutsch
Costales, Amy 1974- *227*
Coste, Marion 1938- *183*
Costello, David *174*
Costello, David F(rancis) 1904-1990 .... *23*
Cte, Genevieve 1964- *184*
Cote, Nancy 1952- *182*
Cott, Jonathan 1942- *23*
Cottam, Clarence 1899-1974 .... *25*
Cotten, Cynthia *188*
Cottin, Menena 1950- *213*
Cottle, Joan 1960- *135*
Cottler, Joseph 1899-1996 .... *22*
Cottonwood, Joe 1947- *92*
Cottrell, Leonard 1913-1974 .... *24*
Cottringer, Anne 1952- *150*
  Earlier sketch in SATA *97*
Couch, Greg *199*
Coulman, Valerie 1969- *161*
Couloumbis, Akila 1932-2009 .... *225*
Couloumbis, Audrey *173*
Counsel, June 1926- *70*
Countryman, The
  See Whitlock, Ralph
Courlander, Harold 1908-1996 .... *6*
  Obituary *88*
Coursen, Valerie 1965(?)- *102*
Courtis, Stuart Appleton 1874-1969
  Obituary *29*
Courtland, Tyler
  See Stevens, Serita
Courtney, Dayle
  See Goldsmith, Howard
Coury, Louise Andree 1895(?)-1983
  Obituary *34*
Cousins, Linda 1946- *90*
Cousins, Lucy 1964- *205*
  Earlier sketch in SATA *172*
Cousins, Margaret 1905-1996 .... *2*
  Obituary *92*
Cousteau, Jacques 1910-1997 .... *98*
  Earlier sketch in SATA *38*
Cousteau, Jacques-Yves
  See Cousteau, Jacques
Couture, Christin 1951- *73*
Couvillon, Jacques *195*
Coventry, Susan *233*
Coverly, Dave 1964- *223*
Covert, Ralph 1968- *197*

Coville, Bruce 1950- *216*
  Autobiography Feature *155*
  Earlier sketches in SATA *32, 77, 118, 155*
Covington, Dennis *109*
Covington, Linda
  See Windsor, Linda
Cowan, Catherine *121*
Cowan, Rebecca M.
  See Moesta, Rebecca
Cowan, Rebecca Moesta
  See Moesta, Rebecca
Coward, Fiona 1963- *178*
Cowdrey, Richard 1959- *204*
Cowell, Cressida 1966- *140*
Cowen, Eve
  See Werner, Herma
Cowen, Ida 1898-1993 .... *64*
Cowie, Leonard W(allace) 1919- *4*
Cowles, Kathleen
  See Krull, Kathleen
Cowley, Cassia Joy
  See Cowley, Joy
Cowley, Joy 1936- *164*
  Autobiography Feature *118*
  Earlier sketches in SATA *4, 90*
  See also CLR *55*
  See also SAAS *26*
Cowley, Marjorie 1925- *111*
Cox, (Christopher) Barry 1931- *62*
Cox, Clinton 1934- *108*
  Earlier sketch in SATA *74*
Cox, David 1933- *56*
Cox, David Dundas
  See Cox, David
Cox, Donald William 1921- *23*
Cox, Jack
  See Cox, John Roberts
Cox, John Roberts 1915-1981 .... *9*
Cox, Judy 1954- *198*
  Earlier sketches in SATA *117, 160*
Cox, Marion Monroe 1898-1983
  Obituary *34*
Cox, Palmer 1840-1924 .... *24*
  See also CLR *24*
Cox, Paul 1957- *226*
Cox, Vic 1942- *88*
Cox, Vicki 1945- *158*
Cox, Victoria 1945- *44*
Cox, Wallace 1924-1973 .... *25*
Cox, Wally
  See Cox, Wallace
Cox, William R(obert) 1901-1988 .... *46*
  Brief entry *31*
  Obituary *57*
Coxe, Molly 1959- *101*
  Earlier sketch in SATA *69*
Coxon, Michele 1950- *158*
  Earlier sketch in SATA *76*
Coy, Harold 1902-1986 .... *3*
Coy, John 1958- *233*
  Earlier sketches in SATA *120, 171*
Craats, Rennay 1973- *131*
Crabtree, Judith 1928- *98*
  Earlier sketch in SATA *63*
Crabtree, Julie 1970- *214*
Cracker, Edward E.B.
  See Odgers, Sally Farrell
Craft, Elizabeth 1971(?)- *204*
Craft, K. Y.
  See Craft, Kinuko Y.
Craft, Kinuko Y. 1940- *127*
  Earlier sketch in SATA *65*
Craft, Kinuko Yamabe
  See Craft, Kinuko Y.
Craft, Ruth 1935- *87*
  Brief entry *31*
Craig, A. A.
  See Anderson, Poul
Craig, Alisa
  See MacLeod, Charlotte (Matilda)

Craig, David
  See James, Bill
Craig, Helen 1934- *213*
  Earlier sketches in SATA *46, 49, 94*
Craig, Joe 1979- *198*
Craig, Joe Alexander
  See Craig, Joe
Craig, John Eland
  See Chipperfield, Joseph Eugene
Craig, John Ernest 1921- *23*
Craig, Kit
  See Reed, Kit
Craig, M. F.
  See Craig, Mary (Francis) Shura
Craig, M. Jean *17*
Craig, M. S.
  See Craig, Mary (Francis) Shura
Craig, Margaret (Maze) 1911-1964 .... *9*
Craig, Mary
  See Craig, Mary (Francis) Shura
Craig, Mary Shura
  See Craig, Mary (Francis) Shura
Craig, Mary (Francis) Shura 1923-1991 .... *86*
  Obituary *65*
  Earlier sketch in SATA *6*
  See also SAAS *7*
Craig, Ruth 1922- *95*
Craik, Mrs.
  See Craik, Dinah Maria (Mulock)
Craik, Dinah Maria (Mulock) 1826-1887 ..... *34*
Crandall, Court 1965- *175*
Crandell, Rachel 1943- *152*
Crane, Barbara (Joyce) 1934- *31*
Crane, Carol 1933- *232*
Crane, Caroline 1930- *11*
Crane, Jordan 1973- *174*
Crane, M. A.
  See Wartski, Maureen (Ann Crane)
Crane, Royston Campbell 1901-1977
  Obituary *22*
Crane, Stephen 1871-1900
  See YABC *2*
  See also CLR *132*
Crane, Stephen Townley
  See Crane, Stephen
Crane, Walter 1845-1915 .... *100*
  Earlier sketch in SATA *18*
  See also CLR *56*
Crane, William D(wight) 1892-1976 .... *1*
Cranfield, Ingrid 1945- *74*
Cranshaw, Stanley
  See Fisher, Dorothy (Frances) Canfield
Crary, Elizabeth (Ann) 1942- *99*
  Brief entry *43*
Crary, Margaret (Coleman) 1906-1986 .... *9*
Craste, Marc *201*
Cravath, Lynne Avril
  See Cravath, Lynne W.
Cravath, Lynne W. 1951- *182*
  Earlier sketches in SATA *98, 148*
Craven, Thomas 1889-1969 .... *22*
Crawford, Brent 1975- *220*
Crawford, Charles P. 1945- *28*
Crawford, Deborah 1922- *6*
Crawford, John E(dmund) 1904-1971 .... *3*
Crawford, K(aren) Michael 1959- *155*
Crawford, Laura 1977(?)- *227*
Crawford, Mel 1925- *44*
  Brief entry *33*
Crawford, Phyllis 1899- *3*
Crawley, Dave *177*
Cray, Roberta
  See Emerson, Ru
Crayder, Dorothy *7*
Crayder, Teresa
  See Colman, Hila
Crayon, Geoffrey
  See Irving, Washington
Craz, Albert G. 1926- *24*
Crebbin, June 1938- *169*
  Earlier sketch in SATA *80*

Crecy, Jeanne
See Williams, Jeanne
Credle, Ellis 1902-1998 1
Creech, Sharon 1945- 226
Earlier sketches in SATA 94, 139, 172
See also CLR 164
Creeden, Sharon 1938- 91
Creel, Ann Howard 1953- 187
Creighton, (Mary) Helen 1899-1989
Obituary 64
Creighton, Jill 1949- 96
Crelin, Bob 1959(?)- 221
Crenson, Victoria 1952- 159
Earlier sketch in SATA 88
Cresp, Gael 1954- 119
Crespo, George 1962- 82
Cresswell, Helen 1934-2005 79
Obituary 168
Earlier sketches in SATA 1, 48
See also CLR 18
See also SAAS 20
Cressy, Michael 1955- 124
Cressy, Mike
See Cressy, Michael
Cretan, Gladys (Yessayan) 1921- 2
Cretzmeyer, Stacy (Megan) 1959- 124
Crew, Gary 1947- 163
Earlier sketches in SATA 75, 110
See also CLR 42
Crew, Helen (Cecilia) Coale 1866-1941
See YABC 2
Crew, Linda (Jean) 1951- 137
Earlier sketch in SATA 71
Crewe, Megan 1980- 225
Crews, Donald 1938- 76
Brief entry 30
Earlier sketch in SATA 32
See also CLR 7
Crews, Nina 1963- 158
Earlier sketch in SATA 97
Crichton, John Michael
See Crichton, Michael
Crichton, Michael 1942-2008 88
Obituary 199
Earlier sketch in SATA 9
Crider, Allen Billy
See Crider, Bill
Crider, Bill 1941- 99
Crilley, Mark 1966- 210
Autobiography Feature 148
Earlier sketches in SATA 120, 148
Crilley, Paul 1975- 227
Crimi, Carolyn 1959- 219
Earlier sketch in SATA 176
Cripps, Enid Margaret
See Appiah, Peggy
Crisler, Curtis L. 188
Crisman, Ruth 1914- 73
Crisp, Marta Marie
See Crisp, Marty
Crisp, Marty 1947- 128
Crispin, A(nn) C(arol) 1950- 86
Crist, James J. 1961- 168
Cristall, Barbara 79
Crist-Evans, Craig 1954- 153
Crocker, Carter 193
Crocker, Nancy 1956- 185
Crofford, Emily (Ardell) 1927- 61
Crofut, William E. III 1934- 23
Croggon, Alison 1962- 194
Croll, Carolyn 1945- 102
Brief entry 52
Earlier sketch in SATA 56
Croman, Dorothy Young
See Rosenberg, Dorothy
Cromie, Alice Hamilton 1914-2000 24
Cromie, William J(oseph) 1930- 4
Crompton, Anne Eliot 1930- 73
Earlier sketch in SATA 23
Crompton, Richmal
See Lamburn, Richmal Crompton

Cronbach, Abraham 1882-1965 11
Crone, Ruth 1919-2003 4
Cronin, A(rchibald) J(oseph) 1896-1981 47
Obituary 25
Cronin, Doreen (A.) 125
Cronin, Doreen 1966(?)- 178
See also CLR 136
Cronin, Doreen A.
See Cronin, Doreen
Cronn-Mills, Kirstin 1968- 224
Crook, Beverly Courtney 38
Brief entry 35
Crook, Connie Brummel 1930- 168
Earlier sketch in SATA 98
Crook, Constance
See Crook, Connie Brummel
Crosby, Alexander L. 1906-1980 2
Obituary 23
Crosby, Harry C.
See Anvil, Christopher
Crosby, Margaret
See Rathmann, Peggy
Crosher, G. R. 14
Cross, Gilbert B. 1939- 60
Brief entry 51
Cross, Gillian 1945- 178
Autobiography Feature 178
Earlier sketches in SATA 38, 71, 110, 165
See also CLR 28
Cross, Gillian Clare
See Cross, Gillian
Cross, Helen Reeder
See Broadhead, Helen Cross
Cross, Peter 1951- 95
Cross, Sarah 216
Cross, Shauna 1976(?)- 196
Cross, Tom 1954- 146
Cross, Verda 1914- 75
Cross, Wilbur Lucius III 1918- 2
Crossingham, John 1974- 226
Crossland, Caroline 1964- 83
Crossley-Holland, Kevin 1941- 165
Earlier sketches in SATA 5, 74, 120
See also CLR 84
See also SAAS 20
Crossley-Holland, Kevin John William
See Crossley-Holland, Kevin
Crossman, David A. 1951- 219
Crouch, Karen Hillard
See Good, Karen Hillard
Crouch, Marcus 1913-1996 4
Crout, George C(lement) 1917- 11
Crow, Donna Fletcher 1941- 40
Crow, Francis Luther
See Luther, Frank
Crow, Kristyn 208
Crowe, Andrew 111
Crowe, Carole 1943- 204
Crowe, Chris 206
Crowe, Ellie 203
Crowe, John
See Lynds, Dennis
Crowe, (Bettina) Peter Lum 1911- 6
Crowell, Grace Noll 1877-1969 34
Crowell, Pers 1910-1990 2
Crowell, Robert Leland 1909-2001 63
Crowfield, Christopher
See Stowe, Harriet Beecher
Crowley, Arthur 1945- 38
Crowley, Arthur McBlair
See Crowley, Arthur
Crowley, Cath 1971- 233
Crowley, John 1942- 140
Earlier sketch in SATA 65
Crowley, Suzanne 1963- 196
Crowley, Suzanne Carlisle
See Crowley, Suzanne
Crownfield, Gertrude 1867-1945
See YABC 1
Crowther, James Gerald 1899-1983 14
Crowther, Kitty 1970- 220

Crowther, Robert 1948- 163
Croza, Laurel 233
Cruikshank, George 1792-1878 22
See also CLR 63
Cruise, Robin 1951- 179
Crum, Shutta 192
Earlier sketch in SATA 134
Crummel, Susan Stevens 1949- 176
Earlier sketch in SATA 130
Crump, Fred H., Jr. 1931- 76
Earlier sketch in SATA 11
Crump, J(ames) Irving 1887-1979 57
Obituary 21
Crump, William D(rake) 1949- 138
Crunden, Reginald
See Cleaver, Hylton Reginald
Crunk, T.
See Crunk, Tony
Crunk, Tony 1956- 130
Crutcher, Chris 1946- 196
Earlier sketches in SATA 52, 99, 153
See also CLR 159
Crutcher, Christopher C.
See Crutcher, Chris
Cruz, Ray(mond) 1933- 6
Cruz Martinez, Alejandro (?)-1987 74
Crystal, Billy 1947- 154
Crystal, William
See Crystal, Billy
Ctvrtek, Vaclav 1911-1976
Obituary 27
Cuate, Melodie A. 219
Cuetara, Mittie 1957- 158
Earlier sketch in SATA 106
Cuffari, Richard 1925-1978 66
Obituary 25
Earlier sketch in SATA 6
Cuffe-Perez, Mary 1946- 199
Cullen, Countee 1903-1946 18
Cullen, Lynn 1955- 190
Culliford, Pierre 1928-1992 40
Obituary 74
Cullinan, Bernice E(llinger) 1926- 135
Culp, Louanna McNary 1901-1965 2
Culper, Felix
See McCaughrean, Geraldine
Cumbaa, Stephen 1947- 72
Cumming, Peter 1951- 168
Cumming, Primrose Amy 1915- 24
Cumming, Robert 1945- 65
Cummings, Betty Sue 1918- 15
See also SAAS 9
Cummings, Gillian 1961- 233
Cummings, John Michael 1963(?)- 216
Cummings, Mary 1951- 185
Cummings, Parke 1902-1987 2
Obituary 53
Cummings, Pat 1950- 203
Earlier sketches in SATA 42, 71, 107
See also CLR 48
See also SAAS 13
Cummings, Phil 1957- 232
Earlier sketches in SATA 74, 123
Cummings, Priscilla 1951- 170
Earlier sketch in SATA 129
Cummings, Richard
See Gardner, Richard (M.)
Cummings, Terrance 227
Cummings, Troy 232
Cummins, Julie 200
Cummins, Maria Susanna 1827-1866
See YABC 1
Cumpliano, Ina 207
Cuneo, Mary Louise -2001 85
Cunliffe, John Arthur 1933- 86
Earlier sketch in SATA 11
Cunliffe, Marcus (Falkner) 1922-1990 37
Obituary 66
Cunnane, Kelly 175
Cunningham, Bob
See May, Julian

Cunningham, Captain Frank
  See Glick, Carl (Cannon)
Cunningham, Cathy
  See Cunningham, Chet
Cunningham, Chet 1928- 23
Cunningham, Dale S(peers) 1932- 11
Cunningham, Dru 91
Cunningham, E. V.
  See Fast, Howard
Cunningham, Julia (Woolfolk) 1916- 132
  Earlier sketches in SATA 1, 26
  See also SAAS 2
Cunningham, Lawrence J. 1943- 125
Cunningham, Virginia
  See Holmgren, Virginia C(unningham)
Cunxin, Li 1961- 220
Curiae, Amicus
  See Fuller, Edmund (Maybank)
Curie, Eve 1904-2007 1
  Obituary 188
Curlee, Lynn 1947- 190
  Earlier sketches in SATA 98, 141
Curley, Daniel 1918-1988 23
  Obituary 61
Curley, Marianne 1959- 175
  Earlier sketch in SATA 131
Currey, Anna 194
Currie, Robin 1948- 120
Currie, Stephen 1960- 132
  Earlier sketch in SATA 82
Curry, Ann (Gabrielle) 1934- 72
Curry, Jane L(ouise) 1932- 138
  Autobiography Feature 138
  Earlier sketches in SATA 1, 52, 90
  See also CLR 31
  See also SAAS 6
Curry, Peggy Simson 1911-1987 8
  Obituary 50
Curry, Tom 185
Curtis, Bruce (Richard) 1944- 30
Curtis, Chara M(ahar) 1950- 78
Curtis, Christopher Paul 1953- 187
  Earlier sketches in SATA 93, 140
  See also CLR 68
Curtis, Gavin 1965- 107
Curtis, Jamie Lee 1958- 144
  Earlier sketch in SATA 95
  See also CLR 88
Curtis, Jennifer Keats 185
Curtis, Marci 160
Curtis, Munzee
  See Caseley, Judith
Curtis, Neil 1950-2006 202
Curtis, Patricia 1921- 101
  Earlier sketch in SATA 23
Curtis, Peter
  See Lofts, Norah (Robinson)
Curtis, Philip (Delacourt) 1920- 62
Curtis, Richard 1937- 29
Curtis, Richard Alan
  See Curtis, Richard
Curtis, Richard Hale
  See Deming, Richard
  and Levinson, Leonard
  and Rothweiler, Paul Roger
Curtis, Stacy 205
Curtis, Wade
  See Pournelle, Jerry
Curtiss, A(rlene) B. 1934- 90
Cusack, Margaret 1945- 58
Cushman, Doug 1953- 210
  Earlier sketches in SATA 65, 101, 157
Cushman, Jerome 2
Cushman, Karen 1941- 147
  Earlier sketch in SATA 89
  See also CLR 55
Cusick, Richie Tankersley 1952- 231
  Earlier sketches in SATA 67, 140
Cusimano, Maryann K.
  See Love, Maryann Cusimano
Cutbill, Andy 1972- 201

Cutchen, Billye Walker 1930- 15
Cutchins, Judy 1947- 59
Cutler, Daniel S. 1951- 78
Cutler, Daniel Solomon
  See Cutler, Daniel S.
Cutler, Ebbitt 1923- 9
Cutler, Ivor 1923-2006 24
  Obituary 174
Cutler, Jane 1936- 162
  Earlier sketches in SATA 75, 118
Cutler, May Ebbitt
  See Cutler, Ebbitt
Cutler, Samuel
  See Folsom, Franklin (Brewster)
Cutlip, Kimbra L(eigh-Ann) 1964- 128
Cutrate, Joe
  See Spiegelman, Art
Cutt, W(illiam) Towrie 1898-1981 16
  Obituary 85
Cuyler, Margery 1948- 229
  Earlier sketches in SATA 39, 99, 156, 195
Cuyler, Margery Stuyvesant
  See Cuyler, Margery
Cuyler, Stephen
  See Bates, Barbara S(nedeker)
Cypess, Leah 233
Cyrus, Kurt 1954- 179
  Earlier sketch in SATA 132
Czajkowski, James
  See Rollins, James
Czekaj, Jef 1969- 217
Czernecki, Stefan 1946- 178

                        D

Daagnese, Joseph 228
Dabba Smith, Frank 174
Dabcovich, Lydia 99
  Brief entry 47
  Earlier sketch in SATA 58
Dace, Dolores B(oelens) 1929- 89
Da Costa, Deborah 193
Daddo, Andrew 1967- 198
Dadey, Debbie 1959- 217
  Earlier sketches in SATA 73, 136
Dahl, Borghild (Margarethe) 1890-1984 7
  Obituary 37
Dahl, Roald 1916-1990 73
  Obituary 65
  Earlier sketches in SATA 1, 26
  See also CLR 111
Dahlberg, Maurine F. 1951- 171
Dahlstedt, Marden (Stewart) 1921-1983 8
  Obituary 110
Dahme, Joanne 206
Dain, Martin J. 1924-2000 35
Dakin, Glenn 1960- 224
Dakos, Kalli 1950- 115
  Earlier sketch in SATA 80
Dale, Anna 1971- 170
Dale, Gary
  See Reece, Colleen L.
Dale, George E.
  See Asimov, Isaac
Dale, Jack
  See Holliday, Joseph
Dale, Kim 1957- 123
Dale, Margaret J(essy) Miller 1911- 39
Dale, Mitzi
  See Hemstock, Gillian
Dale, Norman
  See Denny, Norman (George)
Dale, Penny 1954- 151
  Earlier sketch in SATA 70
Daley, Michael J. 170
Dalgliesh, Alice 1893-1979 17
  Obituary 21
  See also CLR 62
Dalkey, Kara 1953- 132

Dalkey, Kara Mia
  See Dalkey, Kara
Dallas, Ruth 1919- 86
Dalmas, John
  See Jones, John R(obert)
Dalton, Alene
  See Chapin, Alene Olsen Dalton
Dalton, Annie 1948- 140
  Earlier sketch in SATA 40
Dalton, Kit
  See Cunningham, Chet
Dalton, Pamela
  See Johnson, Pamela
Dalton, Sean
  See Chester, Deborah
Dalton, Sheila 1949- 108
D'Aluisio, Faith 1957- 205
Daly, James 217
Daly, Jim
  See Stratemeyer, Edward L.
Daly, Jude 1951- 222
  Earlier sketch in SATA 177
Daly, Kathleen N(orah) 124
  Brief entry 37
Daly, Maureen 1921-2006 129
  Obituary 176
  Earlier sketch in SATA 2
  See also CLR 96
  See also SAAS 1
Daly, Nicholas
  See Daly, Niki
Daly, Niki 1946- 198
  Earlier sketches in SATA 37, 76, 114, 164
  See also CLR 41
  See also SAAS 21
D'Amato, Alex 1919- 20
D'Amato, Janet (Potter) 1925- 9
Damerow, Gail 1944- 83
Damerow, Gail Jane
  See Damerow, Gail
D'Amico, Carmela 170
D'Amico, Steve 170
Damrell, Liz 1956- 77
Damrosch, Helen
  See Tee-Van, Helen Damrosch
Dana, Barbara 1940- 218
  Earlier sketch in SATA 22
Dana, Richard Henry, Jr. 1815-1882 26
Danachair, Caoimhin O
  See Danaher, Kevin
Danaher, Kevin 1913-2002 22
Danakas, John 1963- 94
Dandi
  See Mackall, Dandi Daley
D'Andrea, Kate
  See Steiner, Barbara A(nnette)
Dangerfield, Balfour
  See McCloskey, (John) Robert
Daniel, Alan 1939- 76
  Brief entry 53
Daniel, Anita 1893(?)-1978 23
  Obituary 24
Daniel, Anne
  See Steiner, Barbara A(nnette)
Daniel, Becky 1947- 56
Daniel, Claire 1949- 164
Daniel, Colin
  See Windsor, Patricia
Daniel, Hawthorne 1890- 8
Daniel, (Donna) Lee 1944- 76
Daniel, Rebecca
  See Daniel, Becky
Daniels, Guy 1919-1989 11
  Obituary 62
Daniels, Kit
  See Diver, Lucienne
Daniels, Lucy
  See Oldfield, Jenny
Daniels, Max
  See Gellis, Roberta

Daniels, Olga
    See Sinclair, Olga
Daniels, Patricia 1955- 93
Daniels, Zoe
    See Laux, Constance
Dank, Gloria Rand 1955- 56
    Brief entry 46
Dank, Leonard D(ewey) 1929- 44
Dank, Milton 1920- 31
Dann, Max 1955- 62
Danneberg, Julie 1958- 173
Dantz, William R.
    See Philbrick, Rodman
Danzig, Dianne 213
Danziger, Paula 1944-2004 149
    Brief entry 30
    Obituary 155
    Earlier sketches in SATA *36, 63, 102*
    See also CLR *20*
Darby, Gene Kegley
    See Darby, Jean (Kegley)
Darby, J. N.
    See Govan, (Mary) Christine Noble
Darby, Jean (Kegley) 1921- 68
Darby, Patricia (Paulsen) 14
Darby, Ray(mond) 1912-1982 7
Darbyshire, Kristen 218
d'Arcy, Willard
    See Cox, William R(obert)
Dare, Geena
    See McNicoll, Sylvia (Marilyn)
D'arge, Mackie 218
Darian, Shea 1959- 97
Daringer, Helen Fern 1892-1986 1
Darke, Marjorie 1929- 87
    Earlier sketch in SATA *16*
Darley, F(elix) O(ctavius) C(arr)
    1822-1888 35
Darling, David J. 1953- 60
    Brief entry 44
Darling, Kathy
    See Darling, Mary Kathleen
Darling, Lois (MacIntyre) 1917-1989 3
    Obituary 64
Darling, Louis, (Jr.) 1916-1970 3
    Obituary 23
Darling, Mary Kathleen 1943- 124
    Earlier sketches in SATA *9, 79*
Darling, Sandra Louise Woodward
    See Day, Alexandra
Darnell, K(athryn) L(ynne) 1955- 150
Darroll, Sally
    See Odgers, Sally Farrell
Darrow, Sharon 181
Darrow, Whitney, (Jr.) 1909-1999 13
    Obituary 115
Darwin, Len
    See Darwin, Leonard
Darwin, Leonard 1916- 24
Dasent, Sir George Webbe 1817-1896 62
    Brief entry 29
Dash, Joan 1925- 142
Daskam, Josephine Dodge
    See Bacon, Josephine Dodge (Daskam)
D'ath, Justin 1953- 174
    Earlier sketch in SATA *106*
Dauer, Rosamond 1934- 23
Daugherty, Charles Michael 1914- 16
Daugherty, James (Henry) 1889-1974 13
    See also CLR *78*
Daugherty, Richard D(eo) 1922- 35
Daugherty, Sonia Medwedeff (?)-1971
    Obituary 27
d'Aulaire, Edgar Parin 1898-1986 66
    Obituary 47
    Earlier sketch in SATA *5*
    See also CLR *21*
d'Aulaire, Ingri 1904-1980 66
    Obituary 24
    Earlier sketch in SATA *5*
    See also CLR *21*

d'Aulaire, Ingri Mortenson Parin
    See d'Aulaire, Ingri
Dave, Dave
    See Berg, David
Daveluy, Paule Cloutier 1919- 11
Davenier, Christine 1961- 216
    Earlier sketches in SATA *127, 179*
Davenport, John 1960- 156
Daves, Michael 1938- 40
David, A. R.
    See David, A(nn) Rosalie
David, A(nn) Rosalie 1946- 103
David, Jonathan
    See Ames, Lee J.
David, Lawrence 1963- 165
    Earlier sketch in SATA *111*
David, Peter 1956- 72
David, Peter Allen
    See David, Peter
David, Rosalie
    See David, A(nn) Rosalie
Davidson, Alice Joyce 1932- 54
    Brief entry 45
Davidson, Basil 1914-2010 13
Davidson, (Marie) Diane 1924- 91
Davidson, Hugh
    See Hamilton, Edmond
Davidson, Jessica 1915-1986 5
Davidson, Judith 1953- 40
Davidson, Lionel 1922-2009 87
Davidson, Margaret 1936- 5
Davidson, Marion
    See Garis, Howard R.
Davidson, Mary R. 1885-1973 9
Davidson, Mary S. 1940- 61
Davidson, Mickie
    See Davidson, Margaret
Davidson, Nicole
    See Jensen, Kathryn
Davidson, R.
    See Davidson, Raymond
Davidson, Raymond 1926- 32
Davidson, Rosalie 1921- 23
Davie, Helen K(ay) 1952- 148
    Earlier sketch in SATA *77*
Davies, Andrew (Wynford) 1936- 27
Davies, Andy Robert 200
Davies, Bettilu D(onna) 1942- 33
Davies, Hunter 1936- 55
    Brief entry 45
Davies, Jacqueline 1962- 186
    Earlier sketch in SATA *155*
Davies, Joan 1934- 50
    Brief entry 47
Davies, Nicola 1958- 182
    Earlier sketches in SATA *99, 150*
Davies, Peter J(oseph) 1937- 52
Davies, Sumiko 1942- 46
Davis, (A.) Aubrey 1949- 153
Davis, Barbara Steincrohn
    See Davis, Maggie S.
Davis, Bette J. 1923- 15
Davis, Burke 1913- 4
Davis, Christopher 1928- 6
Davis, D(elbert) Dwight 1908-1965 33
Davis, Daniel S(heldon) 1936- 12
Davis, David R. 1948- 106
Davis, Donald 1944- 169
    Earlier sketch in SATA *93*
Davis, Donald D.
    See Davis, Donald
Davis, Eleanor 1983(?)- 209
Davis, Emma
    See Davis, Maggie S.
Davis, Gibbs 1953- 102
    Brief entry 41
    Earlier sketch in SATA *46*
Davis, Grania 1943- 88
    Brief entry 50
Davis, H(arold) L(enoir) 1896-1960 114
Davis, Heather 1970- 221

Davis, Hubert J(ackson) 1904-1997 31
Davis, Jack E. 210
Davis, Jacky 204
Davis, James Robert 1945- 32
Davis, Jenny 1953- 74
Davis, Jim
    See Davis, James Robert
Davis, Julia 1900(?)-1993 6
    Obituary 75
Davis, Karen (Elizabeth) 1944- 109
Davis, Katie 1959(?)- 208
    Earlier sketch in SATA *152*
Davis, Lambert 176
Davis, Leslie
    See Guccione, Leslie Davis
Davis, Louise Littleton 1921- 25
Davis, Maggie S. 1943- 57
Davis, Marguerite 1889- 34
Davis, Mary L(ee) 1935- 9
Davis, Mary Octavia 1901-1976 6
Davis, Nancy 1958(?)- 229
Davis, Nelle 1958- 73
Davis, Ossie 1917-2005 81
    See also CLR *56*
Davis, Paxton 1925-1994 16
Davis, Rich 1958- 206
Davis, Robert 1881-1949
    See YABC *1*
Davis, Robin W(orks) 1962- 87
Davis, Russell Gerard 1922- 3
Davis, Tanita S. 212
Davis, Tim(othy N.) 1957- 94
Davis, Tony 1961- 222
Davis, Verne Theodore 1889-1973 6
Davis, Yvonne 1927- 115
Davol, Marguerite W. 1928- 146
    Earlier sketch in SATA *82*
DaVolls, Andy (P.) 1967- 85
DaVolls, Linda 1966- 85
Davys, Sarah
    See Manning, Rosemary
Dawes, Claiborne 1935- 111
Dawson, Arthur L. 207
Dawson, Elmer A. 67
    Earlier sketch in SATA *1*
Dawson, Imogen (Zoe) 1948- 126
    Earlier sketch in SATA *90*
Dawson, Janine 1957- 196
Dawson, Mary 1919- 11
Dawson, Scott 233
Dawson, Willow 1975- 208
Day, A(rthur) Grove 1904-1994 59
Day, Alexandra 1941- 197
    Autobiography Feature 197
    Earlier sketches in SATA *67, 97, 169*
    See also CLR *22*
    See also SAAS *19*
Day, Beth (Feagles) 1924- 33
Day, Donna
    See Asay, Donna Day
Day, Edward C. 1932- 72
Day, Jon 1936(?)- 79
Day, Karen 187
Day, Larry 1956- 227
    Earlier sketch in SATA *181*
Day, Nancy 1953- 140
Day, Nancy Raines 1951- 148
    Earlier sketch in SATA *93*
Day, Shirley 1962- 94
Day, Susie 1975- 231
Day, Thomas 1748-1789
    See YABC *1*
Day, Trevor 1955- 124
Dazey, Agnes J(ohnston) 2
Dazey, Frank M. 2
Deacon, Alexis 1978- 139
Deacon, Eileen
    See Geipel, Eileen
Deacon, Richard
    See McCormick, (George) Donald (King)

Deadman, Ronald 1919-1988(?)
Obituary 56
Deak, Erzsi 1959- 152
Dean, Anabel 1915- 12
Dean, Carolee 1962- 148
Dean, Claire 215
Dean, David 1976- 192
Dean, Karen Strickler 1923- 49
Dean, Ruth (Brigham) 1947- 145
Dean, Zoey
See Bennett, Cherie
de Angeli, Marguerite (Lofft) 1889-1987 ... 100
Obituary 51
Earlier sketches in SATA *1, 27*
See also CLR *1*
Deans, Karen 195
Deans, Sis Boulos 1955- 136
Earlier sketch in SATA *78*
DeArmand, Frances Ullmann 1904(?)-1984 . 10
Obituary 38
DeArmond, Dale 1914- 70
DeArmond, Dale Burlison
See DeArmond, Dale
Deary, Terry 1946- 171
Brief entry 41
Earlier sketches in SATA *51, 101*
Deaver, Julie Reece 1953- 68
de Banke, Cecile 1889-1965 11
De Bello, Rosario 1923- 89
Debon, Nicolas 186
Earlier sketch in SATA *151*
de Bono, Edward 1933- 66
de Brissac, Malcolm
See Dickinson, Peter
de Brunhoff, Jean
See Brunhoff, Jean de
De Brunhoff, Laurent
See Brunhoff, Laurent de
De Bruyn, Monica G. 1952- 13
De Bruyn, Monica Jean Grembowicz
See De Bruyn, Monica G.
DeBry, Roger K. 1942- 91
de Camp, Catherine Crook 1907-2000 83
Earlier sketch in SATA *12*
de Camp, L. Sprague 1907-2000 83
Earlier sketch in SATA *9*
de Camp, Lyon Sprague
See de Camp, L. Sprague
DeCandido, Keith R.A. 112
Dechausay, Sonia E. 94
Decker, C.B. 172
Decker, Cynthia B.
See Decker, C.B.
Decker, Duane 1910-1964 5
Decker, Timothy 1974- 197
DeClements, Barthe 1920- 131
Earlier sketches in SATA *35, 71*
See also CLR *23*
DeClements, Barthe Faith
See DeClements, Barthe
de Clercq Zubli, Rita la Fontaine 1929- 199
de Conte, Sieur Louis
See Twain, Mark
Dedman, Stephen 108
Dee, Barbara 1958- 220
Dee, Catherine 1964- 138
Dee, Ruby
See Wallace, Ruby Ann
Deeble, Jason 1979- 221
Deedy, Carmen Agra 1960- 196
Deedy, John 1923- 24
Deegan, Paul Joseph 1937- 48
Brief entry 38
Deem, James M. 1950- 191
Autobiography Feature 191
Earlier sketches in SATA *75, 134*
Deem, James Morgan
See Deem, James M.
Deeter, Catherine 1947- 137
DeFelice, Cynthia 1951- 165
Earlier sketches in SATA *79, 121*

DeFelice, Cynthia C.
See DeFelice, Cynthia
Defoe, Daniel 1660(?)-1731 22
See also CLR *164*
de Fombelle, Timothee
See Fombelle, Timothee de
DeFord, Deborah H. 123
deFrance, Anthony
See DiFranco, Anthony (Mario)
Degen, Bruce 1945- 205
Brief entry 47
Earlier sketches in SATA *57, 97, 147*
DeGering, Etta (Belle) Fowler 1898-1996 7
De Goldi, Kate 1959- 123
De Goldi, Kathleen Domenica
See De Goldi, Kate
de Goursac, Olivier 1959- 184
De Grazia, Ettore 1909-1982 39
De Grazia, Ted
See De Grazia, Ettore
deGroat, Diane 1947- 169
Earlier sketches in SATA *31, 90*
deGros, J. H.
See Villiard, Paul
de Grummond, Lena Young 62
Earlier sketch in SATA *6*
de Hamel, Joan Littledale 1924- 86
De Haven, Tom 1949- 72
de Hugo, Pierre
See Brackers de Hugo, Pierre
Deines, Brian 1955- 220
Deiss, Joseph Jay 1912-1999 12
de Jenkins, Lyll Becerra 1925-1997 102
DeJong, David C(ornel) 1905-1967 10
de Jong, Dola
See de Jong, Dorothea Rosalie
de Jong, Dorothea Rosalie 1911-2003 7
Obituary 149
DeJong, Meindert 1906-1991 2
Obituary 68
See also CLR *73*
DeJonge, Joanne E. 1943- 56
Deka, Connie
See Laux, Constance
de Kay, Ormonde (Jr.) 1923-1998 7
Obituary 106
DeKeyser, Stacy 1959- 214
de Kiriline, Louise
See Lawrence, Louise de Kiriline
Dekker, Carl
See Laffin, John (Alfred Charles)
and Lynds, Dennis
deKruif, Paul (Henry) 1890-1971 50
Earlier sketch in SATA *5*
Delacre, Lulu 1957- 209
Earlier sketches in SATA *36, 156*
DeLaCroix, Alice 1940- 195
Earlier sketch in SATA *75*
de la Cruz, Melissa 1971- 179
De la Garza, Phyllis 1942- 169
De Lage, Ida 1918- 11
de la Mare, Walter (John) 1873-1956 16
See also CLR *148*
Delaney, Harry 1932- 3
Delaney, Joseph 1945- 172
Delaney, M.C.
See Delaney, Michael
Delaney, Michael 1955- 180
Earlier sketch in SATA *96*
Delaney, Michael Clark
See Delaney, Michael
Delaney, Ned 1951- 28
Delaney, Thomas Nicholas III
See Delaney, Ned
DeLange, Alex Pardo
See Pardo DeLange, Alex
Delano, Hugh 1933- 20
Delano, Marfe Ferguson 215
Delany, Samuel R., Jr. 1942- 92
Delany, Samuel Ray
See Delany, Samuel R., Jr.

de la Pena, Matt 205
De La Ramee, Marie Louise 1839-1908 20
de la Roche, Mazo 1879-1961 64
De La Roche Saint Andre, Anne 1950- 75
de Las Casas, Dianne 1970- 221
Delaune, (Jewel) Lynn (de Grummond) 7
DeLaurentis, Louise Budde 1920- 12
del Barco, Lucy Salamanca 1900(?)-1989
Obituary 64
Delderfield, Eric R(aymond) 1909-1995 14
Delderfield, Ronald Frederick 1912-1972 ... 20
DeLeeuw, Adele (Louise) 1899-1988 30
Obituary 56
Earlier sketch in SATA *1*
De Leon, Nephtali 1945- 97
Delessert, Etienne 1941- 179
Brief entry 27
Earlier sketches in SATA *46, 130*
See also CLR *81*
Delgado, James P. 1958- 122
Delinois, Alix 228
de Lint, Charles 1951- 207
Earlier sketches in SATA *115, 157*
de Lint, Charles Henri Diederick Hofsmit
See de Lint, Charles
Delmar, Roy
See Wexler, Jerome (LeRoy)
Del Negro, Janice M. 197
Deloria, Vine, Jr. 1933-2005 21
Obituary 171
Deloria, Vine Victor, Jr.
See Deloria, Vine, Jr.
del Rey, Lester 1915-1993 22
Obituary 76
Delrio, Martin
See Doyle, Debra
and Macdonald, James D.
Delton, Judy 1931-2001 77
Obituary 130
Earlier sketch in SATA *14*
See also SAAS *9*
Delulio, John 1938- 15
Delving, Michael
See Williams, Jay
de Marcken, Gail 186
Demarest, Chris L. 1951- 175
Brief entry 44
Earlier sketches in SATA *45, 82, 128*
Demarest, Christopher Lynn
See Demarest, Chris L.
Demarest, Doug
See Barker, Will
De Mari, Silvana 1953- 193
Demas, Corinne 1947- 203
Earlier sketches in SATA *37, 131*
Demas, Vida 1927- 9
Dematons, Charlotte 1957- 203
DeMatteis, J.M. 1953- 180
DeMatteis, John Marc
See DeMatteis, J.M.
De Mejo, Oscar 1911-1992 40
Demers, Dominique 1956- 177
de Messieres, Nicole 1930- 39
DeMeulemeester, Linda 1956- 230
Demi 1942- 210
Earlier sketches in SATA *11, 66, 102, 152*
See also CLR *58*
Demijohn, Thom
See Disch, Thomas M.
and Sladek, John
Deming, Richard 1915-1983 24
Deming, Sarah 191
de Monfreid, Dorothee 1973- 189
Demuth, Patricia Brennan 1948- 84
Brief entry 51
De Muth, Roger 1948- 221
Dendinger, Roger E. 1952- 158
Denenberg, Barry 1940- 175
Dengler, Marianna (Herron) 1935- 103
Dengler, Sandy 1939- 54
Brief entry 40

Denim, Sue
    See Pilkey, Dav
Denise, Anika 210
Denise, Christopher 1968- 193
    Earlier sketch in SATA 147
Denman, K.L. 1957- 186
Denmark, Harrison
    See Zelazny, Roger
Dennard, Deborah 1953- 136
    Earlier sketch in SATA 78
Denney, Diana 1910-2000 25
    Obituary 120
Dennis, Morgan 1891(?)-1960 18
Dennis, Wesley 1903-1966 18
Denniston, Elinore 1900-1978
    Obituary 24
Denny, Norman (George) 1901-1982 43
Denos, Julia 202
Denslow, Sharon Phillips 1947- 142
    Earlier sketch in SATA 68
Denslow, W(illiam) W(allace) 1856-1915 16
    See also CLR 15
Dent, Grace 1973- 187
Denton, Kady MacDonald 181
    Earlier sketches in SATA 66, 110
    See also CLR 71
Denton, Terry 1950- 186
Denver, Walt
    See Redding, Robert Hull
    and Sherman, Jory (Tecumseh)
Denzel, Justin F(rancis) 1917-1999 46
    Brief entry 38
Denzer, Ann Wiseman
    See Wiseman, Ann (Sayre)
DePalma, Mary Newell 1961- 185
    Earlier sketch in SATA 139
De Palma, Toni 199
dePaola, Thomas Anthony 1934- 200
    Earlier sketches in SATA 11, 59, 108, 155
    See also CLR 81
    See also SAAS 15
dePaola, Tomie
    See dePaola, Thomas Anthony
deParrie, Paul 1949- 74
DePauw, Linda Grant 1940- 24
De Pretto, Lorenzo 1966- 225
DeRan, David 1946- 76
Derby, Ken 1956- 181
Derby, Kenneth R.
    See Derby, Ken
Derby, Pat 1942- 172
Derby, Sally 1934- 189
    Earlier sketches in SATA 89, 132
de Regniers, Beatrice Schenk (Freedman)
    1914-2000 68
    Obituary 123
    Earlier sketch in SATA 2
    See also SAAS 6
Dereske, Jo 1947- 72
Deriso, Christine Hurley 1961- 210
Derleth, August (William) 1909-1971 5
Derman, Martha (Winn) 74
Derman, Sarah Audrey 1915- 11
DeRoberts, Lyndon
    See Silverstein, Robert Alan
Derom, Dirk 1980- 224
de Roo, Anne Louise 1931-1997 84
    Earlier sketch in SATA 25
    See also CLR 63
deRosa, Dee 70
Derrick, Lionel
    See Cunningham, Chet
Derrickson, Jim 1959- 141
Derry Down Derry
    See Lear, Edward
Derting, Kimberly 1968- 231
Dervaux, Isabelle 1961- 106
Derwent, Lavinia 14
Desai, Anita 1937- 126
    Earlier sketch in SATA 63
DeSaix, Deborah Durland 188

De Saulles, Tony 1958- 119
Desbarats, Peter 1933- 39
de Selincourt, Aubrey 1894-1962 14
de Seve, Peter 1958- 219
de Seve, Randall 198
Deshpande, Chris 1950- 69
Desimini, Lisa 1964- 216
    Earlier sketches in SATA 86, 148
Desjarlais, John 1953- 71
Desjarlais, John J.
    See Desjarlais, John
Desmoinaux, Christel 1967- 149
    Earlier sketch in SATA 103
Desmond, Adrian 1947- 51
Desmond, Adrian J.
    See Desmond, Adrian
Desmond, Adrian John
    See Desmond, Adrian
Desmond, Alice Curtis 1897-1990 8
Desnoettes, Caroline 183
DeSpain, Pleasant 1943- 87
Desputeaux, Helene 1959- 95
Dessen, Sarah 1970- 172
    Earlier sketch in SATA 120
Detine, Padre
    See Olsen, Ib Spang
de Trevino, Elizabeth B.
    See Trevino, Elizabeth B(orton) de
de Trevino, Elizabeth Borton
    See Trevino, Elizabeth B(orton) de
Detwiler, Susan Dill 1956- 58
Deuker, Carl 1950- 196
    Earlier sketches in SATA 82, 150
Deutsch, Babette 1895-1982 1
    Obituary 33
Deutsch, Eva Costabel
    See Costabel, Eva Deutsch
Deutsch, Helen 1906-1992 76
Deutsch, Kurt
    See Singer, Kurt D.
De Valera, Sinead 1879(?)-1975
    Obituary 30
Devaney, John 1926-1994 12
de Varennes, Monique 1947- 168
de Varona, Frank J. 1943- 83
Devereux, Frederick L(eonard), Jr.
    1914-1993 9
Devi, Nila
    See Woody, Regina Jones
DeVillers, Julia 1967- 227
deVinck, Christopher 1951- 85
DeVita, James 195
DeVito, Cara 1956- 80
Devlin, Dorothy Wende
    See Devlin, Wende
Devlin, Harry 1918-2001 136
    Earlier sketches in SATA 11, 74
Devlin, Wende 1918-2002 74
    Earlier sketch in SATA 11
Devon, Paddie 1953- 92
Devons, Sonia 1974- 72
Devorah-Leah 111
de Vos, Gail 1949- 122
de Vries, Anke 1936- 222
DeVries, Douglas 1933- 122
De Waard, E(lliott) John 1935- 7
Dewan, Ted 1961- 226
    Earlier sketches in SATA 108, 157
Dewdney, Anna 232
    Earlier sketch in SATA 184
Dewdney, Selwyn (Hanington) 1909-1979 ... 64
DeWeese, Gene
    See DeWeese, Thomas Eugene
DeWeese, Jean
    See DeWeese, Thomas Eugene
DeWeese, Thomas Eugene 1934- 46
    Brief entry 45
Dewey, Ariane 1937- 178
    Earlier sketches in SATA 7, 109

Dewey, Jennifer (Owings) 1941- 103
    Brief entry 48
    Earlier sketch in SATA 58
Dewey, Kenneth Francis 1940- 39
Dewin, Howie
    See Howie, Betsy
De Wire, Elinor 1953- 180
deWit, Dorothy (May Knowles) 1916-1980 . 39
    Obituary 28
Dexter, Alison 1966- 125
Dexter, John
    See Bradley, Marion Zimmer
Deyneka, Anita 1943- 24
Deyrup, Astrith Johnson 1923- 24
Dezern, Chad 201
de Zubizarreta, Alma
    See Ada, Alma Flor
Dhami, Narinder 1958- 152
Dhondy, Farrukh 1944- 152
    Earlier sketch in SATA 65
    See also CLR 41
Diakite, Baba Wague 1961- 174
Diakite, Penda 1993(?)- 174
Diamand, Emily 1971- 227
Diamond, Arthur 1957- 76
Diamond, Donna 1950- 69
    Brief entry 30
    Earlier sketch in SATA 35
Diamond, Petra
    See Sachs, Judith
Diamond, Rebecca
    See Sachs, Judith
Dias, Earl Joseph 1916- 41
Dias, Ron 1937- 71
Diaz, David 1959(?)- 229
    Earlier sketches in SATA 96, 150, 189
    See also CLR 65
di Bartolo, Jim 225
Dibley, Glin 188
DiCamillo, Kate 1964- 202
    Earlier sketches in SATA 121, 163
    See also CLR 117
Di Certo, J(oseph) J(ohn) 1933- 60
DiCianni, Ron 1952- 107
Dick, Trella Lamson 1889-1974 9
Dickens, Charles 1812-1870 15
    See also CLR 162
Dickens, Charles John Huffam
    See Dickens, Charles
Dickens, Frank
    See Huline-Dickens, Frank William
Dickens, Monica (Enid) 1915-1992 4
    Obituary 74
Dickerson, Roy Ernest 1886-1965
    Obituary 26
Dickinson, Emily 1830-1886 29
Dickinson, Emily Elizabeth
    See Dickinson, Emily
Dickinson, Mary 1949- 48
    Brief entry 41
Dickinson, Mary-Anne
    See Rodda, Emily
Dickinson, Peter 1927- 229
    Earlier sketches in SATA 5, 62, 95, 150
    See also CLR 125
Dickinson, Peter Malcolm de Brissac
    See Dickinson, Peter
Dickinson, Susan 1931- 8
Dickinson, Terence 1943- 102
Dickinson, W(illiam) Croft 1897-1963 13
Dickson, Gordon R. 1923-2001 77
Dickson, Gordon Rupert
    See Dickson, Gordon R.
Dickson, Helen
    See Reynolds, Helen Mary Greenwood Campbell
Dickson, Naida 1916- 8
Diehn, Gwen 1943- 80
Dierssen, Andreas 1962- 190
Diesen, Deborah 1967- 200
Dieterich, Michele M. 1962- 78

Dietz, David H(enry) 1897-1984 10
    Obituary 41
Dietz, Lew 1907-1997 11
    Obituary 95
Diffily, Deborah 159
Di Fiori, Larry
    See Di Fiori, Lawrence
Di Fiori, Lawrence 1934- 130
DiFranco, Anthony (Mario) 1945- 42
Digby, Anne 1935- 72
Digges, Jeremiah
    See Berger, Josef
Digman, Kristina 1959- 176
D'Ignazio, Fred 1949- 39
    Brief entry 35
D'Ignazio, Frederick
    See D'Ignazio, Fred
Di Grazia, Thomas (?)-1983 32
Dijkstra, Lida 1961- 195
Dikty, Julian May
    See May, Julian
Dillard, Annie 1945- 140
    Earlier sketch in SATA 10
Dillard, Kristine 1964- 113
Dillard, Polly Hargis 1916- 24
Dillard, Sarah 1961- 217
Diller, Harriett 1953- 78
Dillon, Anna
    See Scott, Michael
Dillon, Barbara 1927- 44
    Brief entry 39
Dillon, Diane 1933- 194
    Earlier sketches in SATA 15, 51, 106
    See also CLR 44
Dillon, Diane Claire
    See Dillon, Diane
Dillon, Eilis 1920-1994 74
    Autobiography Feature 105
    Obituary 83
    Earlier sketch in SATA 2
    See also CLR 26
Dillon, Jana (a pseudonym) 1952- 117
Dillon, Leo 1933- 194
    Earlier sketches in SATA 15, 51, 106
    See also CLR 44
Dillon, Sharon Saseen
    See Saseen, Sharon (Dillon)
Dils, Tracey E. 1958- 83
Dilson, Jesse 1914-1988 24
Dinan, Carolyn 59
    Brief entry 47
Dines, Carol 1956- 175
Dines, (Harry) Glen 1925-1996 7
Dinesen, Isak
    See Blixen, Karen
Dinessi, Alex
    See Schembri, Jim
Dinneen, Betty 1929- 61
Dinnerstein, Harvey 1928- 42
Dinsdale, Tim(othy Kay) 1924-1987 11
Dion, Nathalie 1964- 213
Dionne, Erin 1975- 217
Diop, Birago (Ismael) 1906-1989
    Obituary 64
Diouf, Sylviane A. 168
Diouf, Sylviane Anna
    See Diouf, Sylviane A.
DiPucchio, Kelly 204
    Earlier sketch in SATA 159
Dirk
    See Gringhuis, Richard H.
Dirks, Wilhelmina 1916- 59
Dirks, Willy
    See Dirks, Wilhelmina
Dirtmeister
    See Tomecek, Steve
DiSalvo, DyAnne 1960- 144
    Earlier sketch in SATA 59
DiSalvo-Ryan, DyAnne
    See DiSalvo, DyAnne

Disch, Thomas M. 1940-2008 92
    Obituary 195
    See also CLR 18
    See also SAAS 15
Disch, Thomas Michael
    See Disch, Thomas M.
Disch, Tom
    See Disch, Thomas M.
Disher, Garry 1949- 125
    Earlier sketch in SATA 81
Disney, Walt(er Elias) 1901-1966 28
    Brief entry 27
Ditchfield, Christin 1973- 226
    Earlier sketch in SATA 189
DiTerlizzi, Tony 1969- 214
    Earlier sketch in SATA 154
DiTerlooney, Tiny
    See DiTerlizzi, Tony
Divakaruni, Chitra Banerjee 1956- 222
    Earlier sketch in SATA 160
Di Valentin, Maria (Amelia) Messuri
    1911-1985 7
Diver, Lucienne 1971- 218
Divine, Arthur Durham 1904-1987
    Obituary 52
Divine, David
    See Divine, Arthur Durham
Divine, L. 229
Dixon, Ann 1954- 212
    Earlier sketches in SATA 77, 127
Dixon, Ann Renee
    See Dixon, Ann
Dixon, Dougal 1947- 190
    Earlier sketches in SATA 45, 127
Dixon, Franklin W.
    See Barrett, Neal, Jr.
    and Goulart, Ron
    and Lantz, Francess L(in)
    and Lerangis, Peter
    and McFarlane, Leslie
    and Stanley, George Edward
    and Stratemeyer, Edward L.
Dixon, Jeanne 1936- 31
Dixon, Paige
    See Corcoran, Barbara (Asenath)
Dixon, Peter L(ee) 1931- 6
Dixon, Rachel 1952- 74
Dizin, Pascal 230
Djoleto, (Solomon Alexander) Amu 1929- ... 80
d'Lacey, Chris 1949- 227
    Earlier sketch in SATA 165
Doak, Annie
    See Dillard, Annie
Doane, Pelagie 1906-1966 7
Dob, Bob 207
Dobell, I(sabel) M(arian) B(arclay)
    1909-1998 11
Dobie, J(ames) Frank 1888-1964 43
Dobkin, Alexander 1908-1975
    Obituary 30
Dobler, Lavinia G. 1910- 6
Dobrin, Arnold 1928- 4
Dobson, Jill 1969- 140
Dobson, Julia 1941- 48
Dobson, Mary 1954- 117
DoCampo, Valeria 1976- 217
Docherty, James
    See Docherty, Jimmy
Docherty, Jimmy 1976- 204
Docherty, Thomas 1955- 218
Dockery, Wallene T. 1941- 27
Dockray, Tracy 1962- 139
Dockrey, Karen 1955- 103
Doctor, Bernard
    See Doctor, Bernard Aquina
Doctor, Bernard Aquina 1950- 81
Doctor X
    See Nourse, Alan E(dward)
Dodd, Ed(ward Benton) 1902-1991 4
    Obituary 68
Dodd, Emma 1969- 203

Dodd, Lynley (Stuart) 1941- 132
    Earlier sketches in SATA 35, 86
    See also CLR 62
Dodd, Marty 1921- 142
Dodd, Quentin 1972- 137
Dodds, Bill 1952- 78
Dodds, Dayle Ann 1952- 201
    Earlier sketches in SATA 75, 150
Doder, Josh 1968- 187
Dodge, Bertha S(anford) 1902-1995 8
Dodge, Fremont
    See Grimes, Lee
Dodge, Gil
    See Hano, Arnold
Dodge, Mary (Elizabeth) Mapes
    1831(?)-1905 100
    Earlier sketch in SATA 21
    See also CLR 62
Dodgson, Charles Lutwidge
    See Carroll, Lewis
Dodson, Kenneth MacKenzie 1907-1999 11
Dodson, Susan 1941- 50
    Brief entry 40
Doerrfeld, Cori 1964- 214
Dogar, Sharon 1962- 211
Dogyear, Drew
    See Gorey, Edward (St. John)
Doherty, Berlie 1943- 111
    Earlier sketch in SATA 72
    See also CLR 21
    See also SAAS 16
Doherty, Charles Hugh 1913- 6
Doherty, Craig A. 1951- 169
    Earlier sketch in SATA 83
Doherty, Katherine M(ann) 1951- 83
Doherty, Kieran 1945- 164
Dokas, Dara 1968- 216
Dokey, Cameron 1956- 97
Dolamore, Jaclyn 1982- 227
Dolan, Edward F(rancis), Jr. 1924- 94
    Brief entry 31
    Earlier sketch in SATA 45
Dolan, Ellen M(eara) 1929-1998 88
Dolan, Sean J. 1958- 74
Dolce, J. Ellen 1948- 75
Dolch, Edward William 1889-1961 50
Dolch, Marguerite Pierce 1891-1978 50
Dollar, Diane (Hills) 1933- 57
Dolson, Hildegarde
    See Lockridge, Hildegarde (Dolson)
Domanska, Janina 1913(?)-1995 68
    Obituary 84
    Earlier sketch in SATA 6
    See also CLR 40
    See also SAAS 18
Dominguez, Angel 1953- 76
Dominguez, Angela N. 1982- 219
Domino, John
    See Averill, Esther (Holden)
Domjan, Joseph (Spiri) 1907-1992 25
Domm, Jeffrey C. 1958- 84
Donahue, Dorothy 178
Donald, Rhonda Lucas 1962- 147
Donalds, Gordon
    See Shirreffs, Gordon D(onald)
Donaldson, Bryna
    See Stevens, Bryna
Donaldson, Gordon 1913-1993 64
    Obituary 76
Donaldson, Joan 1953- 227
    Earlier sketch in SATA 78
Donaldson, Julia 1948- 226
    Earlier sketches in SATA 82, 132, 180
Donaldson, Stephen R. 1947- 121
Donaldson, Stephen Reeder
    See Donaldson, Stephen R.
Doner, Kim 1955- 208
    Earlier sketch in SATA 91
Doney, Todd L. W. 1959- 104
Dong-Sung, Kim 1970- 195

Dong-Sung Kim
  See Dong-Sung, Kim
Donkin, Andrew *219*
Donkin, Nance (Clare) 1915- *95*
Donna, Natalie 1934-1979 .... *9*
Donnelly, Elfie 1950-
  See CLR 104
Donnelly, Jennifer 1963- *154*
Donnelly, Matt 1972- *148*
Donnio, Sylviane *188*
Donofrio, Beverly 1950- *209*
Donoghue, Emma 1969- *101*
Donohue, Moira Rose 1954- *201*
Donoughue, Carol 1935- *139*
Donovan, Frank (Robert) 1906-1975
  Obituary *30*
Donovan, Gail 1962- *217*
Donovan, John 1928-1992 .... *72*
  Brief entry *29*
  See also CLR 3
Donovan, Mary Lee 1961- *86*
Donovan, William
  See Berkebile, Fred D(onovan)
Donze, Mary Terese 1911- *89*
Doob, Leonard W(illiam) 1909-2000 .... *8*
Doodler, Todd H.
  See Goldman, Todd Harris
Dooley, Norah 1953- *74*
Dooling, Michael 1958- *220*
  Earlier sketch in SATA 105
Dor, Ana
  See Ceder, Georgiana Dorcas
Doran, Colleen 1963- *211*
Dore, (Louis Christophe Paul) Gustave
  1832-1883 .... *19*
Doremus, Robert 1913-2010 .... *30*
Doren, Marion (Walker) 1928- *57*
Dorenkamp, Michelle 1957- *89*
Dorflinger, Carolyn 1953- *91*
Dorfman, Joaquin 1979- *180*
Dorfman, Joaquin Emiliano
  See Dorfman, Joaquin
Dorian, Edith M(cEwen) 1900-1983 .... *5*
Dorian, Harry
  See Hamilton, Charles (Harold St. John)
Dorian, Marguerite *7*
Dorin, Patrick C(arberry) 1939- *59*
  Brief entry *52*
Dorman, Brandon *194*
Dorman, Michael 1932- *7*
Dorman, N. B. 1927- *39*
Dormer, Frank W. *200*
Dorris, Michael 1945-1997 .... *75*
  Obituary *94*
  See also CLR 58
Dorris, Michael A.
  See Dorris, Michael
Dorris, Michael Anthony
  See Dorris, Michael
Dorritt, Susan
  See Schlein, Miriam
Dorros, Alex 1991- *194*
Dorros, Arthur 1950- *168*
  Earlier sketches in SATA 78, 122
  See also CLR 42
  See also SAAS 20
Dorros, Arthur M.
  See Dorros, Arthur
Dorson, Richard M(ercer) 1916-1981 .... *30*
Doss, Helen (Grigsby) 1918- *20*
Doss, Margot Patterson *6*
dos Santos, Joyce Audy 1949- *57*
  Brief entry *42*
Dothers, Anne
  See Chess, Victoria (Dickerson)
Dotlich, Rebecca Kai 1951- *182*
Dottig
  See Grider, Dorothy
Dotts, Maryann J. 1933- *35*
Doty, Jean Slaughter 1929- *28*
Doty, Roy 1922- *28*

Doubtfire, Dianne (Abrams) 1918- *29*
Doucet, Sharon Arms 1951- *144*
  Autobiography Feature *144*
  Earlier sketch in SATA 125
Dougherty, Charles 1922- *18*
Dougherty, Terri (L.) 1964- *146*
Doughty, Rebecca 1955- *174*
Douglas, Allen *223*
Douglas, Blaise 1960- *101*
Douglas, Carole Nelson 1944- *73*
Douglas, Garry
  See Kilworth, Garry
Douglas, James McM.
  See Griffin, W. E. B.
Douglas, Kathryn
  See Ewing, Kathryn
Douglas, Leonard
  See Bradbury, Ray
Douglas, Lola
  See Zeises, Lara M.
Douglas, Marjory Stoneman 1890-1998 .... *10*
Douglas, Michael
  See Bright, Robert Sr.)
Douglas, Michael
  See Crichton, Michael
Douglas, Shirley Stewart
  See Tepper, Sheri S.
Douglass, Barbara 1930- *40*
Douglass, Frederick 1817(?)-1895 .... *29*
Douglass, Keith
  See Cunningham, Chet
Douty, Esther M(orris) 1909-1978 .... *8*
  Obituary *23*
Dow, Emily R. 1904-1987 .... *10*
Dow, Vicki
  See McVey, Vicki
Dowd, John David 1945- *78*
Dowd, Siobhan 1960-2007 .... *204*
Dowdell, Dorothy (Florence) Karns 1910- ... *12*
Dowden, Anne Ophelia Todd 1907-2007 .... *7*
  Obituary *180*
  See also SAAS 10
Dowdey, Landon Gerald 1923- *11*
Dowdy, Mrs. Regera
  See Gorey, Edward (St. John)
Dowell, Frances O'Roark 1964- *205*
  Earlier sketch in SATA 157
Dower, Laura 1967- *185*
Dowling, Terry 1947- *101*
Downard, Barry 1956- *202*
Downer, Ann 1960- *155*
Downer, Marion 1892(?)-1971 .... *25*
Downes, Belinda 1962- *180*
Downey, Fairfax D(avis) 1893-1990 .... *3*
  Obituary *66*
Downey, Lisa *214*
Downey, Lynn 1961- *185*
Downham, Jenny 1964- *192*
Downie, John 1931- *87*
Downie, Mary Alice 1934- *171*
  Earlier sketches in SATA 13, 87
Downie, Mary Alice Dawe
  See Downie, Mary Alice
Downing, David A(lmon) 1958- *84*
Downing, Johnette *184*
Downing, Julie 1956- *148*
  Earlier sketch in SATA 81
Downing, Paula E. 1951- *80*
Downing, Warwick
  See Downing, Wick
Downing, Wick 1931- *138*
Dowswell, Paul 1957- *184*
Doyle, A. Conan
  See Doyle, Sir Arthur Conan
Doyle, Sir Arthur Conan 1859-1930 .... *24*
  See also CLR 106
Doyle, Brian 1935- *156*
  Earlier sketches in SATA 67, 104
  See also CLR 22
  See also SAAS 16

Doyle, Charlotte 1937- *178*
  Earlier sketch in SATA 94
Doyle, Charlotte Lackner
  See Doyle, Charlotte
Doyle, Conan
  See Doyle, Sir Arthur Conan
Doyle, Debra 1952- *165*
  Earlier sketch in SATA 105
Doyle, Donovan
  See Boegehold, Betty (Doyle)
Doyle, Eugenie 1952- *225*
Doyle, John
  See Graves, Robert
Doyle, Malachy 1954- *165*
  Earlier sketch in SATA 120
  See also CLR 83
Doyle, Richard 1824-1883 .... *21*
Doyle, Sir A. Conan
  See Doyle, Sir Arthur Conan
Dr. A
  See Asimov, Isaac
  and Silverstein, Alvin
  and Silverstein, Virginia B.
Dr. Alphabet
  See Morice, Dave
Dr. Fred
  See Bortz, Alfred B(enjamin)
Dr. Laura
  See Schlessinger, Laura (Catherine)
Dr. Seuss 1904-1991 .... *100*
  Obituary *67*
  Earlier sketches in SATA 1, 28, 75
  See also CLR 100
Dr. Zed
  See Penrose, Gordon
Drabble, Margaret 1939- *48*
Drackett, Phil(ip Arthur) 1922- *53*
Draco, F.
  See Davis, Julia
Dracup, Angela 1943- *74*
Dragisic, Patricia *116*
Dragonwagon, Crescent 1952- *186*
  Autobiography Feature *186*
  Earlier sketches in SATA 11, 41, 75, 133
  See also SAAS 14
Drake, David 1945- *85*
Drake, David Allen
  See Drake, David
Drake, Frank
  See Hamilton, Charles (Harold St. John)
Drake, Jane 1954- *82*
Drake, Salamanda
  See Barlow, Steve
Drakeford, Dale B 1952- *113*
Drakeford, Dale Benjamin
  See Drakeford, Dale B
Draper, Hastings
  See Jeffries, Roderic
Draper, Sharon
  See Draper, Sharon M.
Draper, Sharon M. 1948- *195*
  Autobiography Feature *146*
  Earlier sketches in SATA 98, 146
  See also CLR 57
Draper, Sharon Mills
  See Draper, Sharon M.
Drapier, M. B.
  See Swift, Jonathan
Drawson, Blair 1943- *126*
  Earlier sketch in SATA 17
Dray, Matt 1967- *177*
Dray, Matthew Frederick
  See Dray, Matt
Dresang, Eliza (Carolyn Timberlake) 1941- . *19*
Drescher, Henrik 1955- *172*
  Earlier sketches in SATA 67, 105
  See also CLR 20
Drescher, Joan E(lizabeth) 1939- *137*
  Earlier sketch in SATA 30
Dressen-McQueen, Stacey *191*

Dreves, Veronica R. 1927-1986
  Obituary *50*
Drew, Patricia 1938- *15*
Drew, Patricia Mary
  See Drew, Patricia
Drewery, Mary 1918- *6*
Drewery, Melanie 1970- *165*
Drewry, Henry N(athaniel) 1924- *138*
Dreyer, Ellen *177*
Drial, J. E.
  See Laird, Jean E(louise)
Drimmer, Frederick 1916-2000 .... *60*
  Obituary *124*
Driskill, J. Lawrence 1920- *90*
Driskill, Larry
  See Driskill, J. Lawrence
Driving Hawk, Virginia
  See Sneve, Virginia Driving Hawk
Dron, Laura
  See Matthews, L. S.
Dronzek, Laura *199*
Drucker, Malka 1945- *214*
  Brief entry *29*
  Earlier sketches in SATA *39, 111*
Drucker, Olga Levy 1927- *79*
Druitt, Tobias
  See Purkiss, Diane
Drummond, Allan 1957- *209*
Drummond, Karona 1965- *220*
Drummond, V(iolet) H(ilda) 1911-2000 .... *6*
Drummond, Walter
  See Silverberg, Robert
Drury, Clare Marie
  See Hoskyns-Abrahall, Clare (Constance Drury)
Drury, Roger W(olcott) 1914-1996 .... *15*
Druse, Eleanor
  See King, Stephen
Dryden, Pamela
  See St. John, Nicole
D.T., Hughes
  See Hughes, Dean
Duane, Diane 1952- *233*
  Brief entry *46*
  Earlier sketches in SATA *58, 95, 145*
Dubanevich, Arlene 1950- *56*
Dubelaar, Thea 1947- *60*
Dubin, Jill *205*
du Blane, Daphne
  See Groom, Arthur William
Duble, Kathleen Benner 1958- *164*
Dubois, Claude K. 1960- *196*
DuBois, Rochelle Holt 1946- *41*
Du Bois, Shirley Graham 1907(?)-1977 .... *24*
  See Graham, Shirley
Du Bois, W. E. B. 1868-1963 .... *42*
Du Bois, William Edward Burghardt
  See Du Bois, W. E. B.
du Bois, William Pene
  See Pene du Bois, William (Sherman)
Duboise, Novella 1911-1999 .... *88*
Dubosarsky, Ursula 1961- *193*
  Earlier sketches in SATA *107, 147*
DuBose, LaRocque (Russ) 1926- *2*
Dubrovin, Vivian 1931- *139*
  Earlier sketch in SATA *65*
DuBurke, Randy *224*
  Earlier sketch in SATA *172*
Ducey, Jean Sparks 1915- *93*
Duchacek, Ivo D(uka) 1913-1988
  Obituary *55*
Du Chaillu, Paul (Belloni) 1835(?)-1903 ..... *26*
Ducharme, Dede Fox
  See Ducharme, Lilian Fox
Ducharme, Lilian Fox 1950- *122*
Ducornet, Erica 1943- *7*
Ducornet, Rikki
  See Ducornet, Erica
Duddle, Jonny 1971(?)- *219*
Duden, Jane 1947- *136*

Duder, Tessa 1940- *117*
  Earlier sketch in SATA *80*
  See also CLR *43*
  See also SAAS *23*
Dudley, Helen
  See Hope Simpson, Jacynth
Dudley, Martha Ward 1909(?)-1985
  Obituary *45*
Dudley, Nancy
  See Cole, Lois Dwight
Dudley, Robert
  See Baldwin, James
Dudley, Ruth H(ubbell) 1905-2001 .... *11*
Dudley-Smith, T.
  See Trevor, Elleston
Due, Linnea A. 1948- *64*
Dueck, Adele 1955- *97*
Dueland, Joy V(ivian) *27*
Duerr, Gisela 1968- *89*
Duey, Kathleen 1950- *199*
  Earlier sketch in SATA *132*
Dufault, Joseph Ernest Nephtali
  See James, Will(iam Roderick)
Duff, Annis (James) 1904(?)-1986
  Obituary *49*
Duff, Maggie
  See Duff, Margaret K(app)
Duff, Margaret K(app) 1916-2003 .... *37*
  Obituary *144*
Duffey, Betsy (Byars) 1953- *131*
  Earlier sketch in SATA *80*
Duffie, Charles 1960- *144*
Duffield, Katy S. 1961- *147*
Duffy, Carol Ann 1955- *165*
  Earlier sketch in SATA *95*
Duffy Stone, Heather *217*
Dugan, Jack
  See Griffin, W. E. B.
Dugan, John Kevin
  See Griffin, W. E. B.
Dugan, Karen *202*
Dugan, Karen M.
  See Dugan, Karen
Dugan, Michael (Gray) 1947- *15*
Duggan, Alfred Leo 1903-1964 .... *25*
Duggan, Maurice 1922-1974 .... *40*
  Obituary *30*
Duggan, Maurice Noel
  See Duggan, Maurice
Dugger, Elizabeth L.
  See Kanell, Beth
Duggleby, John 1952- *94*
Dugin, Andrej 1955- *77*
Dugina, Olga 1964- *77*
du Jardin, Rosamond Neal 1902-1963 .... *2*
Duka, Ivo
  See Duchacek, Ivo D(uka)
Duke, Kate 1956- *192*
  Earlier sketches in SATA *90, 148*
  See also CLR *51*
Duke, Will
  See Gault, William Campbell
Dulac, Edmund 1882-1953 .... *19*
Dumas, Alexandre (pere) 1802-1870 .... *18*
  See also CLR *134*
Dumas, Jacqueline 1946- *55*
Dumas, Philippe 1940- *119*
  Earlier sketch in SATA *52*
du Maurier, Daphne 1907-1989 .... *27*
  Obituary *60*
Dumbleton, Mike 1948- *206*
  Earlier sketches in SATA *73, 124*
Dunbar, Fiona 1961- *167*
Dunbar, Joyce 1944- *213*
  Earlier sketches in SATA *76, 112, 162*
Dunbar, Paul Laurence 1872-1906 .... *34*
Dunbar, Polly 1980(?)- *211*
  Earlier sketch in SATA *181*
Dunbar, Robert E(verett) 1926- *32*
Duncan, Alexandra
  See Moore, Ishbel (Lindsay)

Duncan, Alice Faye 1967- *168*
  Earlier sketch in SATA *95*
Duncan, Gregory
  See McClintock, Marshall
Duncan, Jane
  See Cameron, Elizabeth Jane
Duncan, Julia K.
  See Benson, Mildred
Duncan, Lois 1934- *219*
  Autobiography Feature *141*
  Earlier sketches in SATA *1, 36, 75, 133, 141*
  See also CLR *129*
  See also SAAS *2*
Duncan, Norman 1871-1916
  See YABC *1*
Duncan, Terence
  See Nolan, William F.
Duncombe, Frances (Riker) 1900-1994 .... *25*
  Obituary *82*
Dungy, Anthony
  See Dungy, Tony
Dungy, Tony 1955- *206*
Dunham, Montrew 1919- *162*
Dunham, Montrew Goetz
  See Dunham, Montrew
Dunkle, Clare B. 1964- *223*
  Earlier sketch in SATA *155*
Dunlap, Julie 1958- *84*
Dunleavy, Deborah 1951- *133*
Dunlop, Agnes M. R. (?)-1982 .... *87*
Dunlop, Eileen (Rhona) 1938- *76*
  Earlier sketch in SATA *24*
  See also SAAS *12*
Dunmore, Helen 1952- *201*
Dunn, Anne M. 1940- *107*
Dunn, Carolyn 1965- *208*
Dunn, Harvey T(homas) 1884-1952 .... *34*
Dunn, Herb
  See Gutman, Dan
Dunn, John M. (III) 1949- *93*
Dunn, Judy
  See Spangenberg, Judith Dunn
Dunn, Mary Lois 1930- *6*
Dunnahoo, Terry Janson 1927- *7*
Dunne, Jeanette 1952- *72*
Dunne, Kathleen 1933- *126*
Dunne, Marie
  See Clark, Ann Nolan
Dunne, Mary Collins 1914- *11*
Dunne, Mary Jo
  See Dunne, Mary Collins
Dunnett, Kaitlyn
  See Emerson, Kathy Lynn
Dunnett, Margaret (Rosalind) 1909-1977 ..... *42*
Dunnick, Regan *178*
Dunphy, Madeleine 1962- *219*
Dunrea, Olivier 1953- *233*
  Brief entry *46*
  Earlier sketches in SATA *59, 118, 160*
Dunrea, Olivier Jean-Paul Dominique
  See Dunrea, Olivier
Dunstan Muller, Rachel *221*
Dunton, Dorothy 1912- *92*
Dupasquier, Philippe 1955- *151*
  Earlier sketch in SATA *86*
duPont, Lindsay *207*
duPont, Lindsay Harper
  See duPont, Lindsay
DuPrau, Jeanne 1944- *215*
  Earlier sketch in SATA *144*
Dupuy, T(revor) N(evitt) 1916-1995 .... *4*
  Obituary *86*
DuQuette, Keith 1960- *155*
  Earlier sketch in SATA *90*
Duran, Gloria 1924- *171*
Duran, Gloria Bradley
  See Duran, Gloria
Duranceau, Suzanne 1952- *162*
Durand, Delphine 1971- *200*
Durand, Hallie 1964(?)- *216*

Durango, Julia 1967- 215
  Earlier sketch in SATA *173*
Durant, Alan 1958- 214
  Earlier sketches in SATA *121, 165*
Durant, John 1902- 27
Durbin, William 1951- 174
  Earlier sketch in SATA *143*
Durell, Ann 1930- 66
Durkee, Sarah 173
Durney, Ryan 205
Durrant, Lynda 1954- 212
  Earlier sketches in SATA *96, 148*
Durrant, Sabine 210
Durrell, Gerald (Malcolm) 1925-1995 8
  Obituary 84
Durrell, Julie 1955- 94
Durrett, Deanne 1940- 144
  Earlier sketch in SATA *92*
Durst, Sarah Beth 1974- 203
Dusikova, Maja 1946- 223
Du Soe, Robert C. 1892-1958
  See YABC *2*
Dussling, Jennifer 1970- 143
  Earlier sketch in SATA *96*
DuTemple, Lesley A. 1952- 113
Dutton, Sandra 191
Dutz
  See Davis, Mary Octavia
Duval, Katherine
  See James, Elizabeth
Duval, Kathy 1946- 181
Duvall, Aimee
  See Thurlo, Aimee
  and Thurlo, David
Duvall, Evelyn Millis 1906- 9
Duvall, Jill D. 1932- 102
Duvall, Jill Donovan
  See Duvall, Jill D.
Duvoisin, Roger (Antoine) 1904-1980 30
  Obituary 23
  Earlier sketch in SATA *2*
  See also CLR *23*
Dwiggins, Don(ald J.) 1913-1988 4
  Obituary 60
Dwight, Allan
  See Cole, Lois Dwight
Dwyer, Deanna
  See Koontz, Dean
Dwyer, K.R.
  See Koontz, Dean
Dyck, Peter J. 1914- 75
Dyer, Alan 1953- 218
Dyer, Hadley 1973- 229
Dyer, James (Frederick) 1934- 37
Dyer, Jane 191
  Earlier sketch in SATA *147*
Dyer, Sarah 1978- 212
Dyer, Sarah L.
  See Dyer, Sarah
Dyess, John (Foster) 1939- 76
Dygard, Thomas J. 1931-1996 97
  Obituary 92
  Earlier sketch in SATA *24*
  See also SAAS *15*
Dyke, John 1935- 35

E

E. V. L.
  See Lucas, E(dward) V(errall)
Eagar, Frances (Elisabeth Stuart)
  1940-1978 11
  Obituary 55
Eager, Edward (McMaken) 1911-1964 17
  See also CLR *43*
Eager, George 1921- 56
Eager, George B.
  See Eager, George
Eagle, Ellen 1953- 61

Eagle, Kin
  See Adlerman, Daniel (Ezra)
  and Adlerman, Kimberly M(arie)
Eagle, Mike 1942- 11
Eamer, Claire 1947- 222
Earle, Olive L(ydia) 1888-1982 7
Earle, William
  See Johns, W(illiam) E(arle)
Earls, Nick 1963- 156
  Earlier sketch in SATA *95*
Early, Jack
  See Scoppettone, Sandra
Early, Jon
  See Johns, W(illiam) E(arle)
Early, Margaret 1951- 72
Earnest, Peter 1934- 222
Earnshaw, Brian 1929- 17
Earnshaw, Micky 1939- 88
Earnshaw, Spencer Wright
  See Earnshaw, Micky
Easley, MaryAnn 94
Eason, Alethea 1957- 197
East, Jacqueline 224
Eastman, Charles A(lexander) 1858-1939
  See YABC *1*
Eastman, P(hilip) D(ey) 1909-1986 33
  Obituary 46
Easton, Kelly 1960- 192
  Earlier sketch in SATA *141*
Eastwick, Ivy (Ethel) O(live) 3
Eaton, Anne T(haxter) 1881-1971 32
Eaton, Anthony 1971- 167
Eaton, George L.
  See Verral, Charles Spain
Eaton, Janet
  See Givens, Janet E(aton)
Eaton, Jeanette 1886-1968 24
Eaton, Maxwell III 1981- 199
Eaton, Tom 1940- 22
Ebbeler, Jeff
  See Ebbeler, Jeffrey
Ebbeler, Jeffrey 1974- 206
Ebbitt, Carolyn Q. 1974(?)- 225
Ebel, Alex 1927- 11
Eber, Dorothy (Margaret) Harley 1930- 27
Eberhart, Sheri S.
  See Tepper, Sheri S.
Eberle, Irmengarde 1898-1979 2
  Obituary 23
Eble, Diane 1956- 74
Eboch, Chris 113
Eccles Williams, Ferelith 1920- 22
Echeverria-Bis, Olivia 217
Echeverria Gyorkos, Charmaine 216
Echlin, Kim 1955- 166
Eckblad, Edith Berven 1923- 23
Ecke, Wolfgang 1927-1983
  Obituary 37
Eckert, Allan W. 1931- 91
  Brief entry 27
  Earlier sketch in SATA *29*
  See also SAAS *21*
Eckert, Horst 1931- 72
  Earlier sketch in SATA *8*
  See also CLR *26*
Ecklar, Julia (Marie) 1964- 112
Eddings, David 1931-2009 91
Eddings, David Carroll
  See Eddings, David
Ede, Janina 1937- 33
Edell, Celeste 12
Edelman, Lily (Judith) 1915-1981 22
Edelson, Edward 1932- 51
Edens, Cooper 1945- 166
  Earlier sketches in SATA *49, 112*
Edens, (Bishop) David 1926- 39
Edey, Maitland A(rmstrong) 1910-1992 25
  Obituary 71
Edgerton, Perky 196
Edgeworth, Maria 1768-1849 21
  See also CLR *153*

Edgson, Alison 211
Edgy, Wardore
  See Gorey, Edward (St. John)
Edison, Theodore
  See Stratemeyer, Edward L.
Edler, Tim(othy) 1948- 56
Edmiston, Jim 1948- 80
Edmonds, I(vy) G(ordon) 1917- 8
Edmonds, Walter D(umaux) 1903-1998 27
  Obituary 99
  Earlier sketch in SATA *1*
  See also SAAS *4*
Edmund, Sean
  See Pringle, Laurence
Edsall, Marian (Stickney) 1920- 8
Edwards, Al
  See Nourse, Alan E(dward)
Edwards, Anne 1927- 35
Edwards, Audrey 1947- 52
  Brief entry 31
Edwards, Becky (Jane) 1966- 125
Edwards, Bertram
  See Edwards, Herbert Charles
Edwards, Bronwen Elizabeth
  See Rose, Wendy
Edwards, Cecile Pepin 1916- 25
Edwards, David 1962- 198
Edwards, Dorothy 1914-1982 88
  Obituary 31
  Earlier sketch in SATA *4*
Edwards, F. E.
  See Nolan, William F.
Edwards, Frank B. 1952- 93
Edwards, Gunvor 32
Edwards, Harvey 1929- 5
Edwards, Hazel (Eileen) 1945- 135
Edwards, Herbert Charles 1912- 12
Edwards, Jane Campbell 1932- 10
Edwards, Julia
  See Stratemeyer, Edward L.
Edwards, Julie
  See Andrews, Julie
Edwards, Julie Andrews
  See Andrews, Julie
Edwards, June
  See Bhatia, Jamunadevi
Edwards, Linda Strauss 1948- 49
  Brief entry 42
Edwards, Margaret (Alexander) 1902-1988
  Obituary 56
Edwards, Michelle 1955- 152
  Earlier sketch in SATA *70*
Edwards, Monica le Doux Newton
  1912-1998 12
Edwards, Olwen
  See Gater, Dilys
Edwards, Page (Lawrence, Jr.) 1941-1999 ... 59
Edwards, Pamela Duncan 189
Edwards, R. T.
  See Goulart, Ron
Edwards, Sally (Cary) 1929- 7
Edwards, Samuel
  See Gerson, Noel Bertram
Edwards, Wallace 1957(?)- 170
Edwardson, Debby Dahl 223
Eeckhout, Emmanuelle 1976- 208
Egan, E. W. 1922- 35
Egan, Edward Welstead
  See Egan, E. W.
Egan, Kerry 175
Egan, Lorraine Hopping 1960- 134
  Earlier sketch in SATA *91*
Egan, Tim 1957- 191
  Earlier sketches in SATA *89, 155*
Egermeier, Elsie E(milie) 1890-1986 65
Eggenberger, David 1918- 6
Eggleston, Edward 1837-1902 27
Egielski, Richard 1952- 220
  Earlier sketches in SATA *11, 49, 106, 163*
Egypt, Ophelia Settle 1903-1984 16
  Obituary 38

Ehlert, Lois 1934- *172*
    Earlier sketches in SATA *35, 69, 128*
    See also CLR *28*
Ehlert, Lois Jane
    See Ehlert, Lois
Ehling, Katalin Olah 1941- *93*
Ehrenberg, Pamela 1972- *219*
Ehrenfreund, Norbert 1921- *86*
Ehrenhaft, Daniel 1970- *185*
Ehrenhaft, Daniel Parker
    See Ehrenhaft, Daniel
Ehrhardt, Karen 1963- *184*
Ehrlich, Amy 1942- *217*
    Earlier sketches in SATA *25, 65, 96, 132*
Ehrlich, Bettina Bauer 1903-1985 .... *1*
Ehrlich, Fred *205*
Ehrlich, Fred M.D.
    See Ehrlich, Fred
Ehrlich, H. M.
    See Ziefert, Harriet
Eichenberg, Fritz 1901-1990 .... *50*
    Earlier sketch in SATA *9*
Eichler, Margrit 1942- *35*
Eichner, James A. 1927- *4*
Eidson, Thomas 1944- *112*
Eifert, Virginia (Louise) S(nider) 1911-1966 . *2*
Eige, (Elizabeth) Lillian 1915- *65*
Eiken, J. Melia 1967- *125*
Einhorn, Edward 1970- *204*
Einsel, Naiad *10*
Einsel, Walter 1926- *10*
Einzig, Susan 1922- *43*
Eiseman, Alberta 1925- *15*
Eisenberg, Azriel (Louis) 1903-1985 .... *12*
Eisenberg, Lisa 1949- *155*
    Brief entry *50*
    Earlier sketch in SATA *57*
Eisenberg, Phyllis Rose 1924- *41*
Eisner, Vivienne
    See Margolis, Vivienne
Eisner, Will 1917-2005 .... *165*
    Earlier sketch in SATA *31*
Eisner, William Erwin
    See Eisner, Will
Eitzen, Allan 1928- *9*
Eitzen, Ruth (Carper) 1924- *9*
Ekwensi, C. O. D.
    See Ekwensi, Cyprian
Ekwensi, Cyprian 1921-2007 .... *66*
Ekwensi, Cyprian Odiatu Duaka
    See Ekwensi, Cyprian
Elam, Richard M(ace, Jr.) 1920- *9*
Elborn, Andrew
    See Clements, Andrew
    and Clements, Andrew
Elboz, Stephen 1956- *152*
Eldin, Peter 1939- *154*
Eldon, Kathy 1946- *107*
Eldridge, Marion *199*
Eley, Robin *219*
Elfman, Blossom 1925- *8*
Elgin, Kathleen 1923- *39*
Elia
    See Lamb, Charles
Eliot, A. D.
    See Jewett, Sarah Orne
Eliot, Alice
    See Jewett, Sarah Orne
Eliot, Anne
    See Cole, Lois Dwight
Eliot, Dan
    See Silverberg, Robert
Elish, Dan 1960- *204*
    Earlier sketches in SATA *68, 129*
Elisha, Ron 1951- *104*
Elisofon, Eliot 1911-1973
    Obituary *21*
Elkeles, Simone 1970- *187*
Elkin, Benjamin 1911-1995 .... *3*
Elkins, Dov Peretz 1937- *5*
Ellacott, S(amuel) E(rnest) 1911- *19*

Elleman, Barbara 1934- *147*
Ellen, Jaye
    See Nixon, Joan Lowery
Eller, Scott
    See Holinger, William (Jacques)
    and Shepard, Jim
Ellery, Amanda *216*
Ellestad, Myrvin
    See Ellestad, Myrvin H.
Ellestad, Myrvin H. 1921- *120*
Elliot, Bruce
    See Field, Edward
Elliot, David 1952- *208*
    Earlier sketch in SATA *122*
Elliott, Bruce
    See Field, Edward
Elliott, David 1947- *201*
    Earlier sketch in SATA *163*
Elliott, Don
    See Silverberg, Robert
Elliott, Elizabeth Shippen Green
    See Green, Elizabeth Shippen
Elliott, Janice 1931-1995 .... *119*
Elliott, Joey
    See Houk, Randy
Elliott, Laura Malone 1957- *197*
Elliott, L.M.
    See Elliott, Laura Malone
Elliott, Louise *111*
Elliott, Mark 1949- *210*
Elliott, Odette 1939- *75*
Elliott, Patricia 1946- *176*
Elliott, Sarah M(cCarn) 1930- *14*
Elliott, (Robert) Scott 1970- *153*
Elliott, William
    See Bradbury, Ray
Elliott, Zetta *206*
Ellis, (Mary) Amabel (Nassau Strachey)
    Williams
    See Williams-Ellis, (Mary) Amabel (Nassau
    Strachey)
Ellis, Ann Dee *210*
Ellis, Anyon
    See Rowland-Entwistle, (Arthur) Theodore
    (Henry)
Ellis, Carson 1975- *190*
Ellis, Carson Friedman
    See Ellis, Carson
Ellis, Deborah 1960- *187*
    Earlier sketch in SATA *129*
Ellis, E. S.
    See Ellis, Edward S.
Ellis, Edward S. 1840-1916
    See YABC *1*
Ellis, Edward Sylvester
    See Ellis, Edward S.
Ellis, Ella Thorp 1928- *127*
    Earlier sketch in SATA *7*
    See also SAAS *9*
Ellis, Harry Bearse 1921-2004 .... *9*
Ellis, Helen *232*
Ellis, Herbert
    See Wilson, Lionel
Ellis, Julie 1961- *227*
Ellis, Mel(vin Richard) 1912-1984 .... *7*
    Obituary *39*
Ellis, Richard 1938- *130*
Ellis, Sarah 1952- *179*
    Earlier sketches in SATA *68, 131*
    See also CLR *42*
Ellison, Chris *196*
Ellison, Elizabeth Stow 1970- *209*
Ellison, Emily *114*
Ellison, Lucile Watkins 1907(?)-1979 .... *50*
    Obituary *22*
Ellison, Virginia H(owell) 1910- *4*
Ellsberg, Edward 1891-1983 .... *7*
Ellsworth, Loretta 1954- *199*
Ellsworth, Mary Ellen (Tressel) 1940- *146*
Ellwand, David 1965(?)- *213*

Elmer, Robert 1958- *154*
    Earlier sketch in SATA *99*
Elmore, (Carolyn) Patricia 1933- *38*
    Brief entry *35*
El-Moslimany, Ann P(axton) 1937- *90*
Elschner, Geraldine 1954- *183*
Elspeth
    See Bragdon, Elspeth MacDuffie
Elster, Jean Alicia 1953- *150*
Elting, Mary 1906- *88*
    Earlier sketch in SATA *2*
    See also SAAS *20*
Elvgren, Jennifer Riesmeyer *179*
Elwart, Joan Potter 1927- *2*
Elwell, Peter *220*
Elwood, Ann 1931- *55*
    Brief entry *52*
Elwood, Roger 1943-2007 .... *58*
Ely, Lesley *212*
Elya, Susan Middleton 1955- *202*
    Earlier sketches in SATA *106, 159*
Elzbieta *88*
Ember, Kathi *190*
Emberley, Barbara A. 1932- *146*
    Earlier sketches in SATA *8, 70*
    See also CLR *5*
Emberley, Barbara Anne
    See Emberley, Barbara A.
Emberley, Ed 1931- *146*
    Earlier sketches in SATA *8, 70*
    See also CLR *81*
Emberley, Edward Randolph
    See Emberley, Ed
Emberley, Michael 1960- *232*
    Earlier sketches in SATA *34, 80, 119, 189*
Emberley, Rebecca 1958- *218*
Embry, Margaret Jacob 1919-1975 .... *5*
Emecheta, Buchi 1944- *66*
    See also CLR *158*
Emecheta, Florence Onye Buchi
    See Emecheta, Buchi
Emerson, Alice B.
    See Benson, Mildred
Emerson, Kate
    See Emerson, Kathy Lynn
Emerson, Kathy Lynn 1947- *63*
Emerson, Kevin *209*
Emerson, Ru 1944- *107*
    Earlier sketch in SATA *70*
Emerson, Sally 1952- *111*
Emerson, William K(eith) 1925- *25*
Emert, Phyllis R. 1947- *93*
Emert, Phyllis Raybin
    See Emert, Phyllis R.
Emery, Anne (McGuigan) 1907- *33*
    Earlier sketch in SATA *1*
Emmens, Carol Ann 1944- *39*
Emmett, Jonathan 1965- *188*
    Earlier sketch in SATA *138*
Emmons, Della (Florence) Gould 1890-1983
    Obituary *39*
Emond, Stephen 1979(?)- *231*
Emory, Jerry 1957- *96*
Emrich, Duncan (Black Macdonald)
    1908-1970(?) *11*
Emshwiller, Carol 1921- *174*
    Autobiography Feature *174*
Emshwiller, Carol Fries
    See Emshwiller, Carol
Emslie, M. L.
    See Simpson, Myrtle L(illias)
Ende, Michael (Andreas Helmuth)
    1929-1995 .... *130*
    Brief entry *42*
    Obituary *86*
    Earlier sketch in SATA *61*
    See also CLR *138*
Enderle, Dotti 1954- *203*
    Earlier sketch in SATA *145*

Enderle, Judith (Ann) Ross 1941- 89
  Autobiography Feature *114*
  Earlier sketch in SATA *38*
  See also SAAS *26*
Endle, Kate 207
Enell, Trinka (Gochenour) 1951- 79
Enfield, Carrie
  See Smith, Susan Vernon
Engdahl, Sylvia Louise 1933- 4
  Autobiography Feature *122*
  See also CLR *2*
  See also SAAS *5*
Engel, Christiane 231
Engel, Diana 1947- 70
Engelbreit, Mary 1952- 169
Engelhart, Margaret S. 1924- 59
Engelmann, Kim (V.) 1959- 87
England, George Allan 1877-1936 102
Englart, Mindi Rose 1965- 146
Engle, Eloise
  See Paananen, Eloise (Katherine)
Engle, Margarita 1951- 231
  Earlier sketch in SATA *193*
Englebert, Victor 1933- 8
English, James W(ilson) 1915- 37
English, Karen 202
Engstrom, Elizabeth 1951- 110
Enright, D(ennis) J(oseph) 1920-2002 25
  Obituary *140*
Enright, Dominique 194
Enright, Elizabeth (Wright) 1909-1968 9
  See also CLR *4*
Ensor, Barbara 180
Ensor, Robert (T.) 1922- 93
Enthoven, Sam 1974- 187
Entwistle, (Arthur) Theodore (Henry) Rowland
  See Rowland-Entwistle, (Arthur) Theodore
  (Henry)
Enys, Sarah L.
  See Sloggett, Nellie
Epanya, Christian A(rthur Kingue) 1956- 91
Ephraim, Shelly S(chonebaum) 1952- 97
Ephron, Delia 1944- 197
  Brief entry *50*
  Earlier sketch in SATA *65*
Epler, Doris M. 1928- 73
Epp, Margaret A(gnes) 1913- 20
Eppenstein, Louise (Kohn) 1892-1987
  Obituary *54*
Epple, Anne Orth 1927- 20
Epstein, Anne Merrick 1931- 20
Epstein, Beryl 1910- 31
  Earlier sketch in SATA *1*
  See also CLR *26*
  See also SAAS *17*
Epstein, Beryl M. Williams
  See Epstein, Beryl
Epstein, Perle S(herry) 1938- 27
Epstein, Rachel S. 1941- 102
Epstein, Robin 1972- 230
Epstein, Samuel 1909-2000 31
  Earlier sketch in SATA *1*
  See also CLR *26*
  See also SAAS *17*
Erdman, Loula Grace 1905(?)-1976 .... *1*
Erdoes, Richard 1912- 33
  Brief entry *28*
Erdogan, Buket 187
Erdrich, Karen Louise
  See Erdrich, Louise
Erdrich, Louise 1954- 141
  Earlier sketch in SATA *94*
Erickson, Betty J. 1923- 97
Erickson, Betty Jean
  See Erickson, Betty J.
Erickson, John R. 1943- 136
  Earlier sketch in SATA *70*
Erickson, Jon 1948- 141
Erickson, Phoebe 59
Erickson, Russell E(verett) 1932- 27
Erickson, Sabra Rollins 1912-1995 35

Erickson, Walter
  See Fast, Howard
Ericson, Walter
  See Fast, Howard
Ericsson, Jennifer A. *170*
Erikson, Mel 1937- *31*
Eriksson, Eva 1949- 207
Ering, Timothy Basil *176*
Erlanger, Baba
  See Trahey, Jane
Erlbach, Arlene 1948- *160*
  Earlier sketches in SATA *78, 115*
Erlbruch, Wolf 1948- *181*
Erlich, Lillian (Feldman) 1910-1983 .... *10*
Erlings, Fridrik 1962- *196*
Erlingsson, Friorik
  See Erlings, Fridrik
Ermatinger, James W. 1959- *170*
Ernest, William
  See Berkebile, Fred D(onovan)
Ernst, (Lyman) John 1940- *39*
Ernst, Kathleen
  See Ernst, Kathleen A.
Ernst, Kathleen A. 1959- *162*
Ernst, Kathryn (Fitzgerald) 1942- *25*
Ernst, Lisa Campbell 1957- *212*
  Brief entry *44*
  Earlier sketches in SATA *55, 95, 154*
Erskine, Kathryn *193*
Ervin, Janet Halliday 1923- *4*
Erwin, Will
  See Eisner, Will
Esbaum, Jill *213*
  Earlier sketch in SATA *174*
Esbensen, Barbara J(uster) 1925-1996 .... *97*
  Brief entry *53*
  Earlier sketch in SATA *62*
Eschbacher, Roger *160*
Eschmeyer, R. E. 1898-1989 .... *29*
Escriva, Vivi *182*
Eseki, Bruno
  See Mphahlele, Es'kia
Esekie, Bruno
  See Mphahlele, Es'kia
Eshmeyer, Reinhart Ernst
  See Eschmeyer, R. E.
Eskridge, Ann E. 1949- *84*
Espeland, Pamela (Lee) 1951- *128*
  Brief entry *38*
  Earlier sketch in SATA *52*
Espinosa, Laura 203
Espinosa, Leo 203
Espriella, Don Manuel Alvarez
  See Southey, Robert
Espy, Willard R(ichardson) 1910-1999 .... *38*
  Obituary *113*
Essakalli, Julie Klear 200
Essrig, Harry 1912- *66*
Estep, Irene Compton *5*
Esterl, Arnica 1933- *77*
Estes, Eleanor (Ruth) 1906-1988 .... *91*
  Obituary *56*
  Earlier sketch in SATA *7*
  See also CLR *70*
Estoril, Jean
  See Allan, Mabel Esther
Estrada, Pau 1961- 200
  Earlier sketch in SATA *74*
Etchemendy, Nancy 1952- *166*
  Earlier sketch in SATA *38*
Etchemendy, Nancy Elise Howell
  See Etchemendy, Nancy
Etchison, Birdie L(ee) 1937- *38*
Etchison, Craig 1945- *133*
Etherington, Frank 1945- *58*
Etnier, Jennifer L. 227
Eton, Robert
  See Meynell, Laurence Walter
Ets, Marie Hall 1893-1984 .... *2*
  See also CLR *33*
Ettlinger, Doris 1950- *173*

Eugnia, Maria 222
Eulberg, Elizabeth 1975- 227
Eunson, (John) Dale 1904-2002 5
  Obituary *132*
Evan, Frances Y. 1951- *167*
Evanoff, Vlad 1916- 59
Evans, Cambria 1981- *178*
Evans, Douglas 1953- *144*
  Earlier sketch in SATA *93*
Evans, Eva (Knox) 1905-1998 27
Evans, Freddi Williams 1957- *211*
  Earlier sketch in SATA *134*
Evans, Greg 1947- *143*
  Earlier sketch in SATA *73*
Evans, Hubert Reginald 1892-1986 .... *118*
  Obituary *48*
Evans, Katherine (Floyd) 1901-1964 5
Evans, Larry
  See Evans, Laurence Chubb
Evans, Laurence Chubb 1939- 88
Evans, Lawrence Watt
  See Watt-Evans, Lawrence
Evans, Leslie 1953- *214*
Evans, Lezlie *180*
Evans, Mari 1923- *10*
Evans, Mark *19*
Evans, Nancy 1950- 65
Evans, Nate 201
Evans, Patricia Healy
  See Carpenter, Patricia (Healy Evans)
Evans, (Alice) Pearl 1927- 83
Evans, Shane W. *189*
Evans, Shirlee 1931- 58
Evans, Tabor
  See Cameron, Lou
  and Knott, William C(ecil, Jr.)
  and Wallmann, Jeffrey M(iner)
  and Whittington, Harry (Benjamin)
Evarts, Esther
  See Benson, Sally
Evarts, Hal G., (Jr.) 1915-1989 6
Everett, Gail
  See Hale, Arlene
Evernden, Margery 1916- 5
Eversole, Robyn 1971- 74
Eversole, Robyn H.
  See Eversole, Robyn
Eversole, Robyn Harbert
  See Eversole, Robyn
Evslin, Bernard 1922-1993 83
  Brief entry *28*
  Obituary *77*
  Earlier sketch in SATA *45*
Ewart, Claire 1958- *145*
  Earlier sketch in SATA *76*
Ewart, Franzeska G. 1950- 205
Ewen, David 1907-1985 4
  Obituary *47*
Ewing, Juliana (Horatia Gatty) 1841-1885 ... 16
  See also CLR *78*
Ewing, Kathryn 1921- 20
Eyerly, Jeannette 1908-2008 86
  Obituary *196*
  Earlier sketch in SATA *4*
  See also SAAS *10*
Eyerly, Jeannette Hyde
  See Eyerly, Jeannette
Eyre, Dorothy
  See McGuire, Leslie (Sarah)
Eyre, Frank 1910-1988
  Obituary *62*
Eyre, Katherine Wigmore 1901-1970 26
Ezzell, Marilyn 1937- 42
  Brief entry *38*

F

Fabe, Maxene 1943- 15
Faber, Doris (Greenberg) 1924- 78
 Earlier sketch in SATA 3
Faber, Harold 1919-2010 5
Fabre, Jean Henri (Casimir) 1823-1915 22
Fabry, Glenn 1961- 205
Facklam, Margaret
 See Thomas, Peggy
Facklam, Margery (Metz) 1927- 132
 Earlier sketches in SATA 20, 85
Fadden, David Kanietakeron 196
Fadiman, Clifton (Paul) 1904-1999 11
 Obituary 115
Fagan, Cary 1957- 186
Fagan, Deva 220
Fahs, Sophia Blanche Lyon 1876-1978 102
Failing, Barbara Larmon 182
Fain, Sarah 1971- 204
Fair, David 1952- 96
Fair, Sylvia 1933- 13
Fairfax-Lucy, Brian (Fulke Cameron-Ramsay)
 1898-1974 6
 Obituary 26
Fairfield, Flora
 See Alcott, Louisa May
Fairlie, Gerard 1899-1983
 Obituary 34
Fairman, Joan A(lexandra) 1935- 10
Faithfull, Gail 1936- 8
Falcone, L.M. 1951- 231
 Earlier sketch in SATA 155
Falcone, Lucy M.
 See Falcone, L.M.
Falconer, Ian 1959- 179
 Earlier sketch in SATA 125
 See also CLR 146
Falconer, James
 See Kirkup, James
Falconer, Lee N.
 See May, Julian
Falkner, Brian 1962- 206
Falkner, Leonard 1900-1977 12
Fall, Andrew
 See Arthur, Robert, (Jr.)
Fall, Thomas
 See Snow, Donald Clifford
Faller, Regis 1968- 187
Falls, C(harles) B(uckles) 1874-1960 38
 Brief entry 27
Falls, Kat 232
Falls, Kathleen Moynihan
 See Falls, Kat
Falstein, Louis 1909-1995 37
Falvey, David 1982- 222
Falwell, Cathryn 1952- 196
Fancher, Lou 1960- 228
 Earlier sketch in SATA 177
Fanelli, Sara 1969- 126
 Earlier sketch in SATA 89
Fanning, Leonard M(ulliken) 1888-1967 5
Fantaskey, Beth 1965- 217
Faralla, Dana 1909- 9
Faralla, Dorothy W.
 See Faralla, Dana
Farb, Peter 1929-1980 12
 Obituary 22
Farber, Norma 1909-1984 75
 Obituary 38
 Earlier sketch in SATA 25
Fardell, John 1967- 195
Fardell, John William
 See Fardell, John
Faria, Rosana 213
Farish, Terry 1947- 146
 Earlier sketch in SATA 82
Farjeon, (Eve) Annabel 1919-2004 11
 Obituary 153
Farjeon, Eleanor 1881-1965 2
 See also CLR 34

Farley, Carol (J.) 1936- 137
 Earlier sketch in SATA 4
Farley, Terri 165
Farley, Walter (Lorimer) 1915-1989 132
 Earlier sketches in SATA 2, 43
Farlow, James O(rville, Jr.) 1951- 75
Farmer, Jacqueline 210
Farmer, Nancy 1941- 161
 Earlier sketches in SATA 79, 117
Farmer, Patti 1948- 79
Farmer, Penelope (Jane) 1939- 105
 Brief entry 39
 Earlier sketch in SATA 40
 See also CLR 8
 See also SAAS 22
Farmer, Peter 1950- 38
Farmer, Philip Jose
 See Farmer, Philip Jose
Farmer, Philip Jose 1918-2009 93
 Obituary 201
Farmer, Philipe Jos
 See Farmer, Philip Jose
Farnham, Burt
 See Clifford, Harold B(urton)
Farnsworth, Bill 1958- 186
 Earlier sketches in SATA 84, 135
Farooqi, Musharraf Ali 1968- 207
Farquhar, Margaret C(utting) 1905-1988 13
Farquharson, Alexander 1944- 46
Farquharson, Martha
 See Finley, Martha
Farr, Diana 82
 Earlier sketch in SATA 3
Farr, Finis (King) 1904-1982 10
Farr, Richard 1960- 209
Farrar, Jill
 See Morris, Jill
Farrar, Susan Clement 1917- 33
Farrell, Ben
 See Cebulash, Mel
Farrell, Darren 228
Farrell, John 1951- 204
Farrell, Patrick
 See Odgers, Sally Farrell
Farrell, Sally
 See Odgers, Sally Farrell
Farrer, Vashti 167
Farrington, Benjamin 1891-1974
 Obituary 20
Farrington, S(elwyn) Kip, Jr. 1904-1983 20
Farris, Christine King 1927- 206
Farshtey, Greg(ory T.) 1965- 148
Farthing, Alison 1936- 45
 Brief entry 36
Farthing-Knight, Catherine 1933- 92
Fassler, Joan (Grace) 1931- 11
Fast, Howard 1914-2003 7
 Autobiography Feature 107
Fast, Howard Melvin
 See Fast, Howard
Fasulo, Michael 1963- 83
Fatchen, Max 1920- 84
 Earlier sketch in SATA 20
 See also SAAS 20
Fate, Marilyn
 See Collins, Paul
Father Goose
 See Ghigna, Charles
Fatigati, Evelyn 1948- 24
Fatigati, Frances Evelyn
 See Fatigati, Evelyn
Fatio, Louise 1904-1993 6
Fatus, Sophie 1957- 182
Faulhaber, Martha 1926- 7
Faulkner, Anne Irvin 1906- 23
Faulkner, Frank
 See Ellis, Edward S.
Faulkner, Nancy
 See Faulkner, Anne Irvin
Faulknor, Cliff(ord Vernon) 1913- 86
Faust, Anke 1971- 230

Favole, Robert J(ames) 1950- 125
Fawcett, Katie Pickard 229
Fax, Elton Clay 1909-1993 25
Faxon, Lavinia
 See Russ, Lavinia (Faxon)
Feagles, Anita M.
 See Feagles, Anita MacRae
Feagles, Anita MacRae 1927- 9
Feagles, Elizabeth
 See Day, Beth (Feagles)
Feague, Mildred H. 1915- 14
Fearing, Mark 1968- 224
Fearnley, Jan 1965- 205
 Earlier sketch in SATA 153
Fearrington, Ann (Peyton) 1945- 146
Fecher, Constance
 See Heaven, Constance (Christina)
Feder, Chris Welles 1938- 81
Feder, Harriet K. 1928- 73
Feder, Paula (Kurzband) 1935- 26
Federici, Debbie 1965- 175
Federici, Debbie Tanner
 See Federici, Debbie
Feelings, Muriel 1938- 16
 See also CLR 5
 See also SAAS 8
Feelings, Muriel Lavita Grey
 See Feelings, Muriel
Feelings, Thomas 1933-2003 69
 Obituary 148
 Earlier sketch in SATA 8
 See also CLR 58
 See also SAAS 19
Feelings, Tom
 See Feelings, Thomas
Fehler, Gene 1940- 201
 Earlier sketch in SATA 74
Fehrenbach, T(heodore) R(eed, Jr.) 1925- 33
Feiffer, Jules 1929- 201
 Earlier sketches in SATA 8, 61, 111, 157
Feiffer, Jules Ralph
 See Feiffer, Jules
Feiffer, Kate 1964- 206
 Earlier sketch in SATA 170
Feig, Barbara Krane 1937- 34
Feig, Paul 221
Feikema, Feike
 See Manfred, Frederick (Feikema)
Feil, Hila 1942- 12
Feilen, John
 See May, Julian
Feinberg, Barbara Jane 1938- 123
 Earlier sketch in SATA 58
Feinberg, Barbara Silberdick
 See Feinberg, Barbara Jane
Feinstein, John 1956- 195
 Earlier sketch in SATA 163
Feldman, Anne (Rodgers) 1939- 19
Feldman, Elane 79
Feldman, Eve B. 221
Feldman, Jody 200
Felin, M. Sindy 194
Felix
 See Vincent, Felix
Fell, Derek 1939- 167
Fell, Derek John
 See Fell, Derek
Fellowes, Julian 1950- 198
Fellows, Muriel H. 10
Fellows, Stan 1957- 177
Fellows, Stanley
 See Fellows, Stan
Felsen, Henry Gregor 1916-1995 1
 See also SAAS 2
Felstead, Cathie 1954- 192
Feltenstein, Arlene 1934- 119
Feltenstine, Arlene H.
 See Feltenstein, Arlene
Felton, Harold William 1902-1991 1
Felton, Ronald Oliver 1909- 3
Felts, Shirley 1934- 33

Felts, Susannah 1973- *214*
Fenderson, Lewis H., Jr. 1907-1983 .... *47*
    Obituary *37*
Fenner, Carol (Elizabeth) 1929-2002 .... *89*
    Obituary *132*
    Earlier sketch in SATA *7*
    See also SAAS *24*
Fenner, Phyllis R(eid) 1899-1982 .... *1*
    Obituary *29*
Fensham, Elizabeth *169*
Fenten, Barbara D(oris) 1935- *26*
Fenten, D(onald) X. 1932- *4*
Fenton, Carroll Lane 1900-1969 .... *5*
Fenton, Edward 1917-1995 .... *7*
    Obituary *89*
Fenton, Joe *213*
Fenton, Mildred Adams 1899-1995 .... *21*
Fenwick, Patti
    See Grider, Dorothy
Feravolo, Rocco Vincent 1922- *10*
Ferber, Brenda A. 1967- *184*
Ferber, Edna 1887-1968 .... *7*
Fergus, Charles *114*
Ferguson, Alane 1957- *182*
    Earlier sketch in SATA *85*
Ferguson, Bob
    See Ferguson, Robert Bruce
Ferguson, Cecil 1931- *45*
Ferguson, Peter 1968- *199*
Ferguson, Robert Bruce 1927-2001 .... *13*
Ferguson, Sarah 1959- *180*
    Earlier sketches in SATA *66, 110*
Ferguson, Sarah Margaret
    See Ferguson, Sarah
Ferguson, Walter (W.) 1930- *34*
Fergusson, Erna 1888-1964 .... *5*
Fermi, Laura 1907-1977 .... *6*
    Obituary *28*
Fern, Eugene A. 1919-1987 .... *10*
    Obituary *54*
Fern, Tracey E. *202*
Fernandes, Eugenie 1943- *205*
    Earlier sketches in SATA *77, 139*
Fernandez, Laura 1960- *171*
Ferraiolo, Jack D. *208*
Ferrari, Maria *123*
Ferrari, Michael *223*
Ferrari, Michael J.
    See Ferrari, Michael
Ferreiro, Carmen 1958- *158*
Ferrell, Nancy Warren 1932- *70*
Ferrer, Isabel
    See Riu, Isabel Ferrer
Ferri, Giuliano 1965- *197*
Ferrier, Lucy
    See Penzler, Otto
Ferris, Helen Josephine 1890-1969 .... *21*
Ferris, James Cody
    See McFarlane, Leslie
Ferris, Jean 1939- *202*
    Brief entry *50*
    Earlier sketches in SATA *56, 105, 149*
Ferris, Jeri Chase 1937- *84*
Ferry, Charles 1927- *92*
    Earlier sketch in SATA *43*
    See also CLR *34*
    See also SAAS *20*
Fetz, Ingrid 1915- *30*
Feydy, Anne Lindbergh
    See Sapieyevski, Anne Lindbergh
Fiammenghi, Gioia 1929- *66*
    Earlier sketch in SATA *9*
Fiarotta, Noel
    See Ficarotta, Noel
Fiarotta, Phyllis
    See Ficarotta, Phyllis
Ficarotta, Noel 1944- *15*
Ficarotta, Phyllis 1942- *15*
Fichter, George S. 1922-1993 .... *7*
Ficocelli, Elizabeth *189*

Fidler, Kathleen (Annie) 1899-1980 .... *87*
    Obituary *45*
    Earlier sketch in SATA *3*
Fiedler, Jean(nette Feldman) *4*
Fiedler, Joseph Daniel *159*
Fiedler, Lisa *185*
Field, Dorothy 1944- *97*
Field, Edward 1924- *109*
    Earlier sketch in SATA *8*
Field, Elinor Whitney 1889-1980
    Obituary *28*
Field, Eugene 1850-1895 .... *16*
Field, Gans T.
    See Wellman, Manly Wade
Field, James 1959- *113*
Field, Peter
    See Drago, Harry Sinclair
    and Dresser, Davis
    and Mann, E(dward) B(everly)
Field, Rachel (Lyman) 1894-1942 .... *15*
    See also CLR *21*
Fielding, Kate
    See Oldfield, Jenny
Fields, Bryan W. 1958(?)- *188*
Fields, Lisa 1984(?)- *216*
Fields, Terri 1948- *191*
Fields, T.S.
    See Fields, Terri
Fienberg, Anna 1956- *183*
    Earlier sketch in SATA *112*
Fiery, Ann
    See Barrows, Annie
Fife, Dale (Odile Hollerbach) 1901- *18*
Fighter Pilot, A
    See Johnston, H(ugh) A(nthony) S(tephen)
Figler, Jeanie 1949- *123*
Figley, Marty Rhodes 1948- *158*
    Earlier sketch in SATA *88*
Figueredo, D(anilo) H. 1951- *155*
Figueroa, Pablo 1938- *9*
Fijan, Carol 1918- *12*
Filderman, Diane E(lizabeth) 1959- *87*
Files, Meg 1946- *107*
Fillmore, Parker H(oysted) 1878-1944
    See YABC *1*
Filstrup, Chris
    See Filstrup, E(dward) Christian
Filstrup, E(dward) Christian 1942- *43*
Filstrup, Janie
    See Merrill, Jane
Finbarr, Desmond
    See Zobel Nolan, Allia
Finchler, Judy 1943- *230*
    Earlier sketch in SATA *93*
Finder, Martin
    See Salzmann, Siegmund
Findlay, Jamieson 1958- *169*
Findon, Joanne 1957- *161*
Fine, Anne 1947- *197*
    Earlier sketches in SATA *29, 72, 111, 160*
    See also CLR *25*
    See also SAAS *15*
Fine, Edith Hope *169*
Fine, Howard 1961- *181*
Fine, Jane
    See Ziefert, Harriet
Finger, Charles J(oseph) 1869(?)-1941 .... *42*
Fink, William B(ertrand) 1916- *22*
Finke, Blythe Foote 1922- *26*
Finkel, George (Irvine) 1909-1975 .... *8*
Finkelstein, Norman H. 1941- *220*
    Earlier sketches in SATA *73, 137*
Finkelstein, Norman Henry
    See Finkelstein, Norman H.
Finlay, Alice Sullivan 1946- *82*
Finlay, Winifred Lindsay Crawford
    (McKissack) 1910-1989 .... *23*
Finlayson, Ann 1925- *8*
Finley, Martha 1828-1909 .... *43*
    See also CLR *148*
Finley, Mary Peace 1942- *83*

Finn, Mary *208*
Finney, Jack 1911-1995 .... *109*
Finney, Patricia 1958- *163*
Finney, Shan 1944- *65*
Finney, Walter Braden
    See Finney, Jack
Firer, Ben Zion
    See Firer, Benzion
Firer, Benzion 1914- *64*
Fireside, Bryna J. 1932- *73*
Firmin, Charlotte 1954- *29*
Firmin, Peter 1928- *58*
    Earlier sketch in SATA *15*
Firth, Barbara *179*
Fischbach, Julius 1894-1988 .... *10*
Fischer, John
    See Fluke, Joanne
Fischer, R.J.
    See Fluke, Joanne
Fischer, Scott M. 1971- *195*
Fischer-Nagel, Andreas 1951- *56*
Fischer-Nagel, Heiderose 1956- *56*
Fischler, Shirley (Walton) *66*
Fischler, Stan(ley I.) *66*
    Brief entry *36*
Fischtrom, Harvey 1933-1974 .... *3*
Fishback, Margaret
    See Antolini, Margaret Fishback
Fishbone, Greg R. *195*
Fisher, Aileen (Lucia) 1906-2002 .... *73*
    Obituary *143*
    Earlier sketches in SATA *1, 25*
    See also CLR *49*
Fisher, Barbara 1940- *44*
    Brief entry *34*
Fisher, Carolyn 1968- *154*
Fisher, Catherine 1957- *155*
Fisher, Chris 1958- *80*
Fisher, Clavin C(argill) 1912- *24*
Fisher, Cynthia *195*
Fisher, Dorothy (Frances) Canfield 1879-1958
    See YABC *1*
    See also CLR *71*
Fisher, Gary L. 1949- *86*
Fisher, John 1909-1996 .... *15*
Fisher, John Oswald Hamilton
    See Fisher, John
Fisher, Laura Harrison 1934- *5*
Fisher, Leonard Everett 1924- *176*
    Autobiography Feature *122*
    Earlier sketches in SATA *4, 34, 73, 120*
    See also CLR *18*
    See also SAAS *1*
Fisher, Lois I. 1948- *38*
    Brief entry *35*
Fisher, Margery (Turner) 1913-1992 .... *20*
    Obituary *74*
Fisher, Marshall Jon 1963- *113*
Fisher, Nikki
    See Strachan, Ian
Fisher, Robert (Tempest) 1943- *47*
Fisher, Suzanne
    See Staples, Suzanne Fisher
Fisher, Valorie *214*
    Earlier sketch in SATA *177*
Fishman, Cathy Goldberg 1951- *106*
Fisk, Nicholas
    See Higginbottom, David
Fisk, Pauline 1948- *160*
    Earlier sketch in SATA *66*
Fiske, Tarleton
    See Bloch, Robert (Albert)
Fisscher, Catharina G. M. 1958- *142*
Fisscher, Tiny
    See Fisscher, Catharina G. M.
Fitch, Clarke
    See Sinclair, Upton
Fitch, John IV
    See Cormier, Robert
Fitch, Sheree 1956- *178*
    Earlier sketch in SATA *108*

Fitschen, Dale 1937- 20
Fitzalan, Roger
  See Trevor, Elleston
Fitzgerald, Captain Hugh
  See Baum, L. Frank
FitzGerald, Cathleen 1932-1987
  Obituary 50
Fitzgerald, Dawn *175*
Fitzgerald, Edward Earl 1919-2001 20
Fitzgerald, F(rancis) A(nthony) 1940- 15
Fitzgerald, Joanne 1956- *198*
Fitzgerald, John D(ennis) 1907(?)-1988 20
  Obituary 56
  See also CLR *1*
Fitzgerald, Merni Ingrassia 1955- 53
Fitzgibbon, Terry 1948- *121*
Fitzhardinge, Joan Margaret 1912- 73
  Earlier sketch in SATA *2*
  See also CLR *5*
  See also SAAS *3*
Fitzhugh, Louise (Perkins) 1928-1974 45
  Obituary 24
  Earlier sketch in SATA *1*
  See also CLR *72*
Fitzhugh, Percy Keese 1876-1950 65
Fitzmaurice, Kathryn *217*
Fitzpatrick, Becca 1979- *224*
Fitzpatrick, Marie-Louise 1962- *189*
  Earlier sketch in SATA *125*
FitzRalph, Matthew
  See McInerny, Ralph
Fitz-Randolph, Jane (Currens) 1915- 51
Fitzsimons, Cecilia 1952- 97
Fitzsimons, Cecilia A.L.
  See Fitzsimons, Cecilia
Flack, Marjorie 1897-1958 .... *100*
  See also YABC *2*
  See also CLR *28*
Flack, Naomi John White -1999 40
  Brief entry 35
Flake, Sharon G. *166*
Flanagan, John 1944- *180*
Flanagan, John Anthony
  See Flanagan, John
Flannery, Kate
  See De Goldi, Kate
Flatt, Lizann 1966- 88
Fleagle, Gail S(hatto) 1940- *117*
Fleetwood, Jenni 1947- 80
Fleischer, Jane
  See Oppenheim, Joanne
Fleischhauer-Hardt, Helga 1936- 30
Fleischman, Albert Sidney
  See Fleischman, Sid
Fleischman, John 1948- *145*
Fleischman, Paul 1952- *156*
  Brief entry 32
  Earlier sketches in SATA *39, 72, 110*
  See also CLR *66*
  See also SAAS *20*
Fleischman, Sid 1920-2010 .... *185*
  Earlier sketches in SATA *8, 59, 96, 148*
  See also CLR *15*
Fleischner, Jennifer 1956- *188*
  Earlier sketch in SATA *93*
Fleisher, Paul 1948- *132*
  Earlier sketch in SATA *81*
Fleisher, Robbin 1951-1977 52
  Brief entry 49
Fleishman, Seymour 1918- 66
  Brief entry 32
Fleming, A. A.
  See Arthur, Robert, (Jr.)
Fleming, Alice Mulcahey 1928- 9
Fleming, Candace 1962- *225*
  Earlier sketches in SATA *94, 143, 190*
Fleming, Denise 1950- *173*
  Earlier sketches in SATA *81, 126*
Fleming, Elizabeth P. 1888-1985
  Obituary 48
Fleming, Ian 1908-1964 9

Fleming, Ian Lancaster
  See Fleming, Ian
Fleming, Ronald Lee 1941- 56
Fleming, Sally
  See Walker, Sally M.
Fleming, Stuart
  See Knight, Damon (Francis)
Fleming, Susan 1932- 32
Fleming, Thomas 1927- 8
Fleming, Thomas James
  See Fleming, Thomas
Fleming, Virginia (Edwards) 1923- 84
Flesch, Y.
  See Flesch, Yolande
Flesch, Yolande 1950- 55
Flesch, Yolande Catarina
  See Flesch, Yolande
Fletcher, Charlie *220*
Fletcher, Charlie May Hogue 1897-1977 3
Fletcher, Colin 1922-2007 28
Fletcher, Dirk
  See Cunningham, Chet
Fletcher, George U.
  See Pratt, (Murray) Fletcher
Fletcher, Helen Jill 1910- 13
Fletcher, Ralph 1953- *195*
  Earlier sketches in SATA *105, 149*
  See also CLR *104*
Fletcher, Ralph J.
  See Fletcher, Ralph
Fletcher, Richard E. 1917(?)-1983
  Obituary 34
Fletcher, Rick
  See Fletcher, Richard E.
Fletcher, Susan 1951- *181*
  Earlier sketches in SATA *70, 110*
Fletcher, Susan Clemens
  See Fletcher, Susan
Fleur, Paul
  See Pohl, Frederik
Flexner, James Thomas 1908-2003 9
Flinn, Alex 1966- *198*
  Earlier sketch in SATA *159*
Flint, Helen 1952- *102*
Flint, Russ 1944- 74
Flitner, David, Jr. 1949- 7
Flitner, David Perkins
  See Flitner, David, Jr.
Floca, Brian *190*
  Earlier sketch in SATA *155*
Floethe, Louise Lee 1913-1988 4
Floethe, Richard 1901-1998 4
Floherty, John Joseph 1882-1964 25
Flood, Bo
  See Flood, Nancy Bo
Flood, Nancy Bo 1945- *233*
  Earlier sketch in SATA *130*
Flood, Pansie Hart 1964- *140*
Flood, William 1942- *129*
Flooglebuckle, Al
  See Spiegelman, Art
Flora, James (Royer) 1914-1998 30
  Obituary *103*
  Earlier sketch in SATA *1*
  See also SAAS *6*
Flores-Galbis, Enrique 1952- *186*
Florian, Douglas 1950- *177*
  Earlier sketches in SATA *19, 83, 125*
Flory, Jane Trescott 1917- 22
Flournoy, Valerie 1952- 95
Flournoy, Valerie Rose
  See Flournoy, Valerie
Flowerdew, Phyllis -1994 33
Flowers, Pam 1946- *136*
Flowers, Sarah 1952- 98
Floyd, Gareth 1940- 62
  Brief entry 31
Fluchere, Henri 1914-1991 40
Fluke, Joanne 1943- 88
Flutsztejn-Gruda, Ilona 1930- *170*
Flynn, Barbara 1928- 9

Flynn, Jackson
  See Bensen, Donald R.
  and Shirreffs, Gordon D(onald)
Flynn, Nicholas
  See Odgers, Sally Farrell
Flynn, Pat 1968- *214*
Flynn, Patrick
  See Flynn, Pat
Flynn, Rachel 1953- *171*
  Earlier sketch in SATA *109*
Flynn, Warren (G.) 1950- *154*
Fodor, R. V. 1944- 25
Fodor, Ronald Victor
  See Fodor, R. V.
Fogelin, Adrian 1951- *175*
  Earlier sketch in SATA *129*
Foley, (Anna) Bernice Williams 1902-1987 . 28
Foley, Greg E. 1969- *190*
Foley, June 1944- 44
Foley, (Mary) Louise Munro 1933- *106*
  Brief entry 40
  Earlier sketch in SATA *54*
Foley, Rae
  See Denniston, Elinore
Folke, Will
  See Bloch, Robert (Albert)
Follett, Helen Thomas 1884(?)-1970
  Obituary 27
Folsom, Franklin (Brewster) 1907-1995 5
  Obituary 88
Folsom, Michael (Brewster) 1938-1990 40
  Obituary 88
Fombelle, Timothee de 1973- *218*
Fontenot, Mary Alice 1910-2003 91
  Obituary *209*
  Earlier sketch in SATA *34*
Fontes, Justine *172*
Fontes, Ron 1952- *183*
Foon, Dennis 1951- *119*
Fooner, Michael 22
Foote, Timothy (Gilson) 1926- 52
Forberg, Ati
  See Forberg, Beate Gropius
Forberg, Beate Gropius 1925- 22
Forbes, Anna 1954- *101*
Forbes, Bryan 1926- 37
Forbes, Cabot L.
  See Hoyt, Edwin P(almer), Jr.
Forbes, Esther 1891-1967 .... *100*
  Earlier sketch in SATA *2*
  See also CLR *147*
Forbes, Graham B. 1
Forbes, Kathryn
  See McLean, Kathryn (Anderson)
Forbes, Robert
  See Arthur, Robert, (Jr.)
Ford, A.G. *231*
Ford, Albert Lee
  See Stratemeyer, Edward L.
Ford, Barbara 56
  Brief entry 34
Ford, Bernette *212*
Ford, Bernette G.
  See Ford, Bernette
Ford, B.G.
  See Ford, Bernette
Ford, Brian J(ohn) 1939- 49
Ford, Carolyn 1938- 98
Ford, Carolyn Mott
  See Ford, Carolyn
Ford, Christine 1953- *176*
Ford, David
  See Baldacci, David
  and Baldacci, David
Ford, David B.
  See Baldacci, David
Ford, David Baldacci
  See Baldacci, David
Ford, Elbur
  See Hibbert, Eleanor Alice Burford
Ford, Ellen 1949- 89

Ford, George (Jr.) 31
Ford, Hilary
  See Youd, Samuel
Ford, Hildegarde
  See Morrison, Velma Ford
Ford, Jerome W. 1949- 78
Ford, Jerry
  See Ford, Jerome W.
Ford, John C. 1971- 221
Ford, Juwanda G(ertrude) 1967- 102
Ford, Marcia
  See Radford, Ruby L(orraine)
Ford, Nancy K(effer) 1906-1961
  Obituary 29
Ford, Peter 1936- 59
Ford, S. M.
  See Uhlig, Susan
Forde, Catherine 1961- 170
Foreman, Mark 199
Foreman, Michael 1938- 216
  Earlier sketches in SATA *2, 73, 129, 135, 184*
  See also CLR *32*
  See also SAAS *21*
Foreman, Wilmoth 1939- 153
Forest, Antonia 1915-2003 29
  Obituary 149
Forest, Dial
  See Gault, William Campbell
Forest, Heather 1948- 185
  Earlier sketch in SATA *120*
Forester, C. S. 1899-1966 13
Forester, Cecil Scott
  See Forester, C. S.
Forester, Victoria 214
Forler, Nan 223
Forman, Brenda 1936- 4
Forman, James
  See Forman, James D.
Forman, James D. 1932-2009 70
  Earlier sketch in SATA *8*
Forman, James Douglas
  See Forman, James D.
Forman, Mark L.
  See Forman, M.L.
Forman, M.L. 1964- 215
Forman, Ruth 1970- 186
Formento, Alison 228
Forrest, Elizabeth
  See Salsitz, Rhondi Vilott
Forrest, Mary
  See Pausacker, Jenny
Forrest, Sybil
  See Markun, Patricia Maloney
Forrestal, Elaine 1941- 165
  Earlier sketch in SATA *117*
Forrester, Frank H. 1919(?)-1986
  Obituary 52
Forrester, Helen
  See Bhatia, Jamunadevi
Forrester, Jade
  See Pausacker, Jenny
Forrester, Marian
  See Schachtel, Roger
Forrester, Sandra 1949- 166
  Earlier sketch in SATA *90*
Forrester, Victoria 1940- 40
  Brief entry 35
Forsee, (Frances) Aylesa -1986 1
Forsey, Chris 1950- 59
Forshay-Lunsford, Cin 1965- 60
Forster, E. M. 1879-1970 57
Forster, Edward Morgan
  See Forster, E. M.
Forsyth, Kate 1966- 154
Fort, Paul
  See Stockton, Francis Richard
Forte, Maurizio 1961- 110
Fortey, Richard 1946- 109
Fortey, Richard A.
  See Fortey, Richard

Fortey, Richard Alan
  See Fortey, Richard
Forth, Melissa D(eal) 96
Fortnum, Peggy
  See Nuttall-Smith, Margaret Emily Noel
Fortune, Eric 182
Forward, Robert L(ull) 1932-2002 82
Foster, Alan Dean 1946- 70
Foster, Brad W. 1955- 34
Foster, Doris Van Liew 1899-1993 10
Foster, E(lizabeth) C(onnell) 1902- 9
Foster, Elizabeth 1902- 12
Foster, Elizabeth 1905-1963 10
Foster, F. Blanche 1919- 11
Foster, G(eorge) Allen 1907-1969 26
Foster, Genevieve (Stump) 1893-1979 2
  Obituary 23
  See also CLR *7*
Foster, Gerald L. 198
Foster, Hal
  See Foster, Harold
Foster, Harold 1892-1982 31
Foster, Jeanne
  See Williams, Jeanne
Foster, John
  See Foster, John L(ouis)
  and Furcolo, Foster
Foster, John (Thomas) 1925- 8
Foster, John L(ouis) 1941- 102
Foster, Juliana 196
Foster, Laura Louise (James) 1918- 6
Foster, Leila Merrell 1929- 73
Foster, Lynne 1937- 74
Foster, Margaret Lesser 1899(?)-1979
  Obituary 21
Foster, Marian Curtis 1909-1978 23
Foster, Mark 1961- 197
Foster, Sally 58
Fotheringham, Edwin 201
Foulds, E. V.
  See Foulds, Elfrida Vipont
Foulds, Elfrida Vipont 1902-1992 52
Fountas, Angela Jane 180
Fourie, Corlia 1944- 91
Fourth Brother, The
  See Aung, (Maung) Htin
Fowke, Edith (Margaret) 1913-1996 14
Fowles, John 1926-2005 22
  Obituary 171
Fowles, John Robert
  See Fowles, John
Fowles, Shelley 1956- 205
Fox, Aileen 1907-2005 58
  Obituary 170
Fox, Aileen Mary
  See Fox, Aileen
Fox, Annie 1950- 175
Fox, Charles Philip 1913-2003 12
  Obituary 150
Fox, Christyan 188
Fox, Diane 188
Fox, Eleanor
  See St. John, Wylly Folk
Fox, Fontaine Talbot, Jr. 1884-1964
  Obituary 23
Fox, Fred 1903(?)-1981
  Obituary 27
Fox, Freeman
  See Hamilton, Charles (Harold St. John)
Fox, Geoffrey 1941- 73
Fox, Grace
  See Anderson, Grace Fox
Fox, Helen 1962- 181
Fox, Karen C. 1969- 229
Fox, Larry 30
Fox, Lee 1958- 227
Fox, Lorraine 1922-1976 27
  Earlier sketch in SATA *11*
Fox, Louisa
  See Kroll, Virginia L.

Fox, Mary Virginia 1919- 152
  Brief entry 39
  Earlier sketches in SATA *44, 88*
Fox, Mem 1946- 211
  Earlier sketches in SATA *51, 103, 155*
  See also CLR *80*
Fox, Merrion Frances
  See Fox, Mem
Fox, Michael W(ilson) 1937- 15
Fox, Norma Diane
  See Mazer, Norma Fox
Fox, Paula 1923- 167
  Earlier sketches in SATA *17, 60, 120*
  See also CLR *96*
Fox, Robert J. 1927- 33
Fox, Robert Joseph
  See Fox, Robert J.
Fox-Davies, Sarah 1956- 199
Foyt, Victoria .... 187.
Fradin, Dennis
  See Fradin, Dennis Brindell
Fradin, Dennis Brindell 1945- 185
  Earlier sketches in SATA *29, 90, 135*
Fradin, Judith Bloom 1945- 185
  Earlier sketches in SATA *90, 152*
Frailey, Paige (Menefee) 1965- 82
Frame, Janet 1924-2004 119
Frame, Janet Paterson
  See Frame, Janet
Frame, Paul 1913-1994 60
  Brief entry 33
  Obituary 83
Frances, Miss
  See Horwich, Frances R(appaport)
Franchere, Ruth 18
Francis, Charles
  See Holme, Bryan
Francis, Dee
  See Haas, Dorothy F.
Francis, Dorothy 1926- 127
  Earlier sketch in SATA *10*
Francis, Dorothy B.
  See Francis, Dorothy
Francis, Dorothy Brenner
  See Francis, Dorothy
Francis, Guy 225
Francis, Jaye
  See Pausacker, Jenny
Francis, Pamela (Mary) 1926- 11
Franck, Eddie
  See Cooke, Frank E.
Franco, Betsy 223
  Earlier sketches in SATA *150, 188*
Franco, Eloise (Bauder) 1910- 62
Franco, Johan (Henri Gustave) 1908-1988 ... 62
Franco, Marjorie 38
Franco, Tom 224
Francois, Andre 1915-2005 25
Francoise
  See Seignobosc, Francoise
Frank, Anne 1929-1945 87
  Brief entry 42
  See also CLR *101*
Frank, Annelies Marie
  See Frank, Anne
Frank, Daniel B. 1956- 55
Frank, Emily R.
  See Frank, E.R.
Frank, E.R. 1967- 157
Frank, Helene
  See Vautier, Ghislaine
Frank, Hillary 1976- 148
Frank, John 199
Frank, Josette 1893-1989 10
  Obituary 63
Frank, Lucy 1947- 166
  Earlier sketch in SATA *94*
Frank, Mary 1933- 34
Frank, R., Jr.
  See Ross, Frank (Xavier), Jr.
Frankau, Mary Evelyn Atkinson 1899-1974 .. 4

Frankel, Alona 1937- 66
Frankel, Bernice 9
Frankel, Edward 1910- 44
Frankel, Ellen 1951- 78
Frankel, Julie 1947- 40
Brief entry 34
Frankenberg, Robert 1911- 22
Frankland, David 207
Franklin, Cheryl J. 1955- 70
Franklin, Harold 1926- 13
Franklin, Kristine L. 1958- 124
Earlier sketch in SATA 80
Franklin, Lance
See Lantz, Francess L(in)
Franklin, Madeleine
See L'Engle, Madeleine
Franklin, Madeleine L'Engle
See L'Engle, Madeleine
Franklin, Madeleine L'Engle Camp
See L'Engle, Madeleine
Franklin, Max
See Deming, Richard
Franklin, Steve
See Stevens, Franklin
Franson, Leanne 1963- 223
Earlier sketch in SATA 111
Franson, Scott E. 1966- 192
Franzen, Nils-Olof 1916- 10
Frascino, Edward 48
Brief entry 33
See also SAAS 9
Frasconi, Antonio 1919- 131
Earlier sketches in SATA 6, 53
See also SAAS 11
Fraser, Betty
See Fraser, Elizabeth Marr
Fraser, Elizabeth Marr 1928- 31
Fraser, Eric (George) 1902-1983 38
Fraser, Mary Ann 1959- 214
Earlier sketches in SATA 76, 137
See also SAAS 23
Fraser, Wynnette (McFaddin) 1925- 90
Frasier, Debra 1953- 182
Earlier sketches in SATA 69, 112
Fraustino, Lisa Rowe 1961- 146
Autobiography Feature 146
Earlier sketch in SATA 84
Frazee, Marla 1958- 225
Earlier sketches in SATA 105, 151, 187
Frazer, Megan 1977- 221
Frazetta, Frank 1928-2010 58
Frazier, Craig 1955- 221
Earlier sketch in SATA 177
Frazier, Neta (Osborn) Lohnes 1890-1990 7
Frazier, Sundee T. 1968- 198
Frazier, Sundee Tucker
See Frazier, Sundee T.
Frederic, Mike
See Cox, William R(obert)
Frederick, Heather Vogel 207
Fredericks, Anthony D. 1947- 113
Freed, Alvyn M. 1913-1993 22
Freedman, Benedict 1919- 27
Freedman, Claire 227
Earlier sketch in SATA 185
Freedman, Deborah 1960- 191
Freedman, Jeff 1953- 90
Freedman, Nancy 1920-2010 27
Freedman, Russell 1929- 175
Earlier sketches in SATA 16, 71, 123
See also CLR 71
Freedman, Russell Bruce
See Freedman, Russell
Freeman, Barbara C. 1906-1999 28
Freeman, Barbara Constance
See Freeman, Barbara C.
Freeman, Bill
See Freeman, William Bradford
Freeman, Don 1908-1978 17
See also CLR 90
Freeman, Ira Maximilian 1905-1987 21

Freeman, Kimberley
See Wilkins, Kim
Freeman, Laura 200
Freeman, Lucy (Greenbaum) 1916-2004 24
Freeman, Mae 1907-1985 25
Freeman, Mae Blacker
See Freeman, Mae
Freeman, Marcia S. 1937- 102
Freeman, Marcia Sheehan
See Freeman, Marcia S.
Freeman, Martha 1956- 201
Earlier sketches in SATA 101, 152
Freeman, Nancy 1932- 61
Freeman, Peter J.
See Calvert, Patricia
Freeman, Sarah (Caroline) 1940- 66
Freeman, Tor 1977- 164
Freeman, VicToria
See Freeman, Tor
Freeman, William Bradford 1938- 58
Brief entry 48
Fregosi, Claudia (Anne Marie) 1946- 24
Freitas, Donna 1972- 205
French, Allen 1870-1946
See YABC 1
French, Dorothy Kayser 1926- 5
French, Fiona 1944- 132
Earlier sketches in SATA 6, 75
See also CLR 37
See also SAAS 21
French, Jackie 186
Autobiography Feature 139
Earlier sketches in SATA 108, 139
See French, Jackie Anne
and French, Jacqueline Anne
French, Kathryn
See Mosesson, Gloria R(ubin)
French, Martin 176
French, Michael 1944- 49
Brief entry 38
French, Paul
See Asimov, Isaac
French, S. Terrell 216
French, Simon 1957- 147
Earlier sketch in SATA 86
French, Vivian 209
Earlier sketch in SATA 165
Frenette, Liza 126
Freschet, Gina 1960- 175
Earlier sketch in SATA 139
Frewer, Glyn (M.) 1931- 11
Frey, Darcy 98
Freymann, Saxton 1958(?)- 178
Freymann-Weyr, Garret 1965- 145
Freymann-Weyr, Rhoda Garret Michaela
See Freymann-Weyr, Garret
Frick, C. H.
See Irwin, Constance (H.) Frick
Frick, Constance
See Irwin, Constance (H.) Frick
Fricke, Aaron 1962- 89
Fridell, Ron 1943- 124
Fried, Janice 197
Frieden, Sarajo 232
Friedlander, Joanne K(ohn) 1930- 9
Friedman, Aimee 1979- 189
Friedman, D. Dina 1957- 180
Friedman, Debra 1955- 150
Friedman, Estelle (Ehrenwald) 1920- 7
Friedman, Frieda 1905- 43
Friedman, Hal 230
See Friedman, Harold
Friedman, Ina R(osen) 1926- 136
Brief entry 41
Earlier sketch in SATA 49
Friedman, Jerrold David
See Gerrold, David
Friedman, Judi 1935- 59
Friedman, Laurie 1964- 219
Earlier sketches in SATA 138, 179

Friedman, Marvin 1930- 42
Brief entry 33
Friedman, Robin 1968- 219
Earlier sketch in SATA 162
Friedmann, Stan 1953- 80
Friedrich, Otto (Alva) 1929-1995 33
Friedrich, Priscilla 1927- 39
Friend, Catherine 1957(?)- 194
Friend, David Michael 1975- 195
Friend, Natasha 1972- 184
Friendlich, Dick
See Friendlich, Richard J.
Friendlich, Richard J. 1909- 11
Friermood, Elisabeth Hamilton 1903-1992 5
Friesen, Bernice (Sarah Anne) 1966- 105
Friesen, Gayle 1960- 200
Earlier sketch in SATA 109
Friesen, Jonathan 1967(?)- 206
Friesner, Esther 1951- 207
Earlier sketches in SATA 71, 168
Friesner, Esther M.
See Friesner, Esther
Friis-Baastad, Babbis Ellinor 1921-1970 7
Frimmer, Steven 1928- 31
Frischmuth, Barbara 1941- 114
Friskey, Margaret (Richards) 1901-1995 5
Fritts, Mary Bahr
See Bahr, Mary (Madelyn)
Fritz, Jean (Guttery) 1915- 163
Autobiography Feature 122
Earlier sketches in SATA 1, 29, 72, 119
See also CLR 96
See also SAAS 2
Froehlich, Margaret W(alden) 1930- 56
Frois, Jeanne 1953- 73
Froissart, Jean 1338(?)-1410(?) 28
Froman, Elizabeth Hull 1920-1975 10
Froman, Robert (Winslow) 1917- 8
Fromental, Jean-Luc 1950- 231
Fromm, Lilo 1928- 29
Frommer, Harvey 1937- 41
Frost, A(rthur) B(urdett) 1851-1928 19
Frost, Elizabeth
See Frost-Knappman, Elizabeth
Frost, Erica
See Supraner, Robyn
Frost, Helen 1949- 194
Autobiography Feature 194
Earlier sketches in SATA 157, 183
Frost, Helen Marie
See Frost, Helen
Frost, Lesley 1899-1983 14
Obituary 34
Frost, Robert 1874-1963 14
See also CLR 67
Frost, Robert Lee
See Frost, Robert
Frost, Shelley 1960- 138
Frost-Knappman, Elizabeth 1943- 179
Froud, Brian 1947- 150
Fry, Annette R(iley) 89
Fry, Christopher 1907-2005 66
Fry, Edward Bernard 1925- 35
Fry, Rosalie Kingsmill 1911-1992 3
See also SAAS 11
Fry, Virginia Lynn 1952- 95
Frye, Sally
See Moore, Elaine
Fuchs, Bernie 1932- 162
Earlier sketch in SATA 95
Fuchs, Erich 1916- 6
Fuchshuber, Annegert 1940- 43
Fucile, Tony 221
Fuerst, Jeffrey B. 1956- 143
Fuertes, Gloria 1918-1998 115
Fuge, Charles 1966- 144
Earlier sketch in SATA 74

Fujikawa, Gyo 1908-1998 76
  Brief entry 30
  Obituary 110
  Earlier sketch in SATA 39
  See also CLR 25
  See also SAAS 16
Fujita, Tamao 1905-1999 7
Fujiwara, Kim 1957- 81
Fujiwara, Michiko 1946- 15
Fuka, Vladimir 1926-1977
  Obituary 27
Fulcher, Jennifer
  See Westwood, Jennifer
Fuller, Catherine Leuthold 1916- 9
Fuller, Edmund (Maybank) 1914- 21
Fuller, Iola
  See McCoy, Iola Fuller
Fuller, John G(rant, Jr.) 1913-1990 65
Fuller, Kathleen
  See Gottfried, Theodore Mark
Fuller, Lois Hamilton 1915- 11
Fuller, Margaret 1810-1850 25
Fuller, Maud
  See Petersham, Maud
Fuller, Roy (Broadbent) 1912-1991 87
Fuller, Sarah Margaret
  See Fuller, Margaret
Fults, John Lee 1932- 33
Funk, Thompson 1911- 7
Funk, Tom
  See Funk, Thompson
Funke, Cornelia 1958- 209
  Earlier sketches in SATA 154, 174
  See also CLR 145
Funke, Cornelia Caroline
  See Funke, Cornelia
Funke, Lewis 1912-1992 11
Fuqua, Jonathon Scott 1966- 141
Furbee, Mary R.
  See Furbee, Mary Rodd
Furbee, Mary Rodd 1954- 138
Furchgott, Terry 1948- 29
Furlong, Monica (Mavis) 1930-2003 86
  Obituary 142
Furlonger, Patricia
  See Wrightson, Patricia
Furman, Gertrude Lerner Kerman 1909- 21
Furniss, Tim 1948- 49
Furrow, Robert 1985- 172
Furukawa, Toshi 1924- 24
Fusillo, Archimede 1962- 137
Futcher, Jane P. 1947- 76
Futehali, Zahida
  See Whitaker, Zai
Fyleman, Rose (Amy) 1877-1957 21
Fyson, Jenny Grace
  See Fyson, J.G.
Fyson, J.G. 1904-1998 42

G

Gaan, Margaret 1914- 65
Gaber, Susan 1956- 169
  Earlier sketch in SATA 115
Gaberman, Judie Angell
  See Angell, Judie
Gabhart, Ann
  See Gabhart, Ann H.
Gabhart, Ann H. 1947- 75
Gable, Brian 1949- 195
Gabler, Mirko 1951- 77
Gabriel, Adriana
  See Rojany, Lisa
Gabrys, Ingrid Schubert
  See Schubert-Gabrys, Ingrid
Gackenbach, Dick 1927- 79
  Brief entry 30
  Earlier sketch in SATA 48
Gadd, Jeremy 1949- 116

Gaddis, Vincent H. 1913-1997 35
Gadler, Steve J. 1905-1985 36
Gaeddert, Lou Ann (Bigge) 1931- 103
  Earlier sketch in SATA 20
Gaeddert, Louann
  See Gaeddert, Lou Ann (Bigge)
Gaer, Joseph 1897-1969 118
Gaer, Yossef
  See Gaer, Joseph
Gaetz, Dayle Campbell 1947- 138
Gaffney, Timothy R. 1951- 170
  Earlier sketch in SATA 69
Gaffron, Norma 1931- 97
Gaffron, Norma Bondeson
  See Gaffron, Norma
Gag, Flavia 1907-1979
  Obituary 24
Gag, Wanda (Hazel) 1893-1946 100
  See also YABC 1
  See also CLR 150
Gage, Brian 162
Gage, Wilson
  See Steele, Mary Q(uintard Govan)
Gagliano, Eugene M. 1946- 150
Gagliardo, Ruth Garver 1895(?)-1980
  Obituary 22
Gagnon, Cecile 1936- 58
Gaillard, Jason 1965- 200
Gaiman, Neil 1960- 228
  Earlier sketches in SATA 85, 146, 197
  See also CLR 109
Gaiman, Neil Richard
  See Gaiman, Neil
Gainer, Cindy 1962- 74
Gaines, Ernest J. 1933- 86
  See also CLR 62
Gaines, Ernest James
  See Gaines, Ernest J.
Gaither, Gloria 1942- 127
Gal, Laszlo 1933- 96
  Brief entry 32
  Earlier sketch in SATA 52
  See also CLR 61
Gal, Susan 228
Galbraith, Ben 1980- 200
Galbraith, Kathryn O. 1945- 219
  Earlier sketch in SATA 85
Galbraith, Kathryn Osebold
  See Galbraith, Kathryn O.
Galdone, Paul 1907(?)-1986 66
  Obituary 49
  Earlier sketch in SATA 17
  See also CLR 16
Galindo, Claudia 1979- 203
Galinsky, Ellen 1942- 23
Gall, Chris 1961- 176
Gallagher, Diana G. 1946- 153
Gallagher, Lurlene Nora
  See McDaniel, Lurlene
Gallagher-Cole, Mernie 1958- 206
Gallant, Roy A(rthur) 1924- 110
  Earlier sketches in SATA 4, 68
  See also CLR 30
Gallardo, Evelyn 1948- 78
Gallaz, Christophe 1948- 162
  See also CLR 126
Gallego Garcia, Laura 1977- 173
Gallico, Paul 1897-1976 13
Gallico, Paul William
  See Gallico, Paul
Gallo, Donald R. 1938- 112
  Autobiography Feature 104
Gallo, Donald Robert
  See Gallo, Donald R.
Galloway, Owateka (S.) 1981- 121
Galloway, Priscilla 1930- 227
  Earlier sketches in SATA 66, 112
Gallup, Joan 1957- 128
Galouchko, Annouchka Gravel 1960- 95
Galt, Thomas Franklin, Jr. 1908-1989 5

Galt, Tom
  See Galt, Thomas Franklin, Jr.
Galvin, Matthew R. 1950- 93
Galvin, Matthew Reppert
  See Galvin, Matthew R.
Gamble, Kim 1952- 183
  Earlier sketches in SATA 81, 124
Gambrell, Jamey 82
Gamerman, Martha 1941- 15
Gammell, Stephen 1943- 226
  Earlier sketches in SATA 53, 81, 128
  See also CLR 83
Ganly, Helen (Mary) 1940- 56
Gannett, Ruth Chrisman (Arens)
  1896-1979 33
Gannett, Ruth Stiles 1923- 3
Gannij, Joan 208
Gannij, Joan Levine
  See Gannij, Joan
Gannon, Ned 1974- 205
Gannon, Robert Haines 1931- 8
Gano, Lila 1949- 76
Gans, Roma 1894-1996 45
  Obituary 93
Gant, Matthew
  See Hano, Arnold
Gantner, Susan (Verble) 1939- 63
Gantos, Jack 1951- 169
  Earlier sketches in SATA 20, 81, 119
  See also CLR 85
Gantos, John Bryan, Jr.
  See Gantos, Jack
Ganz, Yaffa 1938- 61
  Brief entry 52
Garafano, Marie 1942- 84
Garant, Andre J. 1968- 123
Garbe, Ruth Moore
  See Moore, Ruth (Ellen)
Garber, Esther
  See Lee, Tanith
Garcia, Cristina 1958- 208
Garcia, Emma 1969- 198
Garcia, Geronimo 1960- 222
Garcia, Kami 1972- 229
Garcia, Yolanda P. 1952- 113
Garcia, Yolanda Pacheco
  See Garcia, Yolanda P.
Gard, Janice
  See Latham, Jean Lee
Gard, Joyce
  See Reeves, Joyce
Gard, Robert Edward 1910-1992 18
  Obituary 74
Gard, (Sanford) Wayne 1899-1986
  Obituary 49
Gardam, Jane 1928- 130
  Brief entry 28
  Earlier sketches in SATA 39, 76
  See also CLR 12
  See also SAAS 9
Gardam, Jane Mary
  See Gardam, Jane
Gardella, Tricia 1944- 96
Garden, Nancy 1938- 147
  Autobiography Feature 147
  Earlier sketches in SATA 12, 77, 114
  See also CLR 51
  See also SAAS 8
Gardiner, John Reynolds 1944-2006 64
  Obituary 174
Gardiner, Lindsey 1971- 144
Gardner, Craig Shaw 1949- 99
Gardner, Dic
  See Gardner, Richard (M.)
Gardner, Graham 159
Gardner, Hugh 1910-1986
  Obituary 49
Gardner, Jane Mylum 1946- 83
Gardner, Jeanne LeMonnier 1925- 5
Gardner, John, Jr. 1933-1982 40
  Obituary 31

Gardner, John Champlin, Jr.
  See Gardner, John, Jr.
Gardner, John E(dward) 1917- *192*
Gardner, Lyn *192*
Gardner, Martin 1914-2010 .... *142*
  Earlier sketch in SATA *16*
Gardner, Miriam
  See Bradley, Marion Zimmer
Gardner, Richard (M.) 1931- *24*
Gardner, Richard A(lan) 1931-2003 .... *13*
  Obituary *144*
Gardner, Sally *229*
  Earlier sketch in SATA *177*
Gardner, Sandra 1940- *70*
Gardner, Scot 1968- *143*
Gardner, Sheldon 1934- *33*
Gardner, Ted
  See Gardner, Theodore Roosevelt II
Gardner, Theodore Roosevelt
  See Gardner, Theodore Roosevelt II
Gardner, Theodore Roosevelt II 1934- *84*
Garelick, May 1910-1989 .... *19*
Garfield, James B. 1881-1984 .... *6*
  Obituary *38*
Garfield, Leon 1921-1996 .... *76*
  Obituary *90*
  Earlier sketches in SATA *1, 32*
  See also CLR *166*
Garfinkle, Debra L.
  See Garfinkle, D.L.
Garfinkle, D.L. *187*
Garis, Howard R. 1873-1962 .... *13*
Garis, Howard Roger
  See Garis, Howard R.
Garland, Mark 1953- *79*
Garland, Mark A.
  See Garland, Mark
Garland, Michael 1952- *208*
  Earlier sketch in SATA *168*
Garland, Sarah 1944- *135*
  Earlier sketch in SATA *62*
Garland, Sherry 1948- *145*
  Autobiography Feature *145*
  Earlier sketches in SATA *73, 114*
Garner, Alan 1934- *69*
  Autobiography Feature *108*
  Earlier sketch in SATA *18*
  See also CLR *130*
Garner, David 1958- *78*
Garner, Eleanor Ramrath 1930- *122*
Garner, James Finn 1960(?)- *92*
Garnet, A. H.
  See Slote, Alfred
Garnett, Eve C. R. 1900-1991 .... *3*
  Obituary *70*
Garofoli, Viviana 1970- *186*
Garou, Louis P.
  See Bowkett, Stephen
Garraty, John A. 1920-2007 .... *23*
  Obituary *189*
Garraty, John Arthur
  See Garraty, John A.
Garren, Devorah-Leah
  See Devorah-Leah
Garret, Maxwell R. 1917- *39*
Garretson, Victoria Diane
  See Cox, Victoria
Garrett, Helen 1895- *21*
Garrett, Randall 1927-1987 .... *180*
Garrett, Richard 1920- *82*
Garrigue, Sheila 1931- *21*
Garrison, Barbara 1931- *163*
  Earlier sketch in SATA *19*
Garrison, Frederick
  See Sinclair, Upton
Garrison, Mary 1952- *146*
Garrison, Peter
  See Gardner, Craig Shaw
Garrison, Webb B(lack) 1919-2000 .... *25*
Garrity, Jennifer Johnson 1961- *124*
Garrity, Linda K. 1947- *128*

Garsee, Jeannine *199*
Garst, Doris Shannon 1894-1981 .... *1*
Garst, Shannon
  See Garst, Doris Shannon
Garth, Will
  See Hamilton, Edmond
  and Kuttner, Henry
Garthwaite, Marion H(ook) 1893-1981 .... *7*
Garton, Malinda D(ean) (?)-1976
  Obituary *26*
Garvie, Maureen 1944- *175*
Garvie, Maureen McCallum
  See Garvie, Maureen
Garza, Carmen Lomas 1948- *182*
Garza, Xavier *184*
Gascoigne, Bamber 1935- *62*
Gaskins, Pearl Fuyo 1957- *134*
Gasperini, Jim 1952- *54*
  Brief entry *49*
Gater, Dilys 1944- *41*
Gates, Doris 1901-1987 .... *34*
  Obituary *54*
  Earlier sketch in SATA *1*
  See also SAAS *1*
Gates, Frieda 1933- *26*
Gates, Susan 1950- *153*
Gates, Viola R. 1931- *101*
Gathorne-Hardy, Jonathan G. 1933- *124*
  Earlier sketch in SATA *26*
Gatti, Anne 1952- *103*
Gatty, Juliana Horatia
  See Ewing, Juliana (Horatia Gatty)
Gauch, Patricia Lee 1934- *228*
  Earlier sketches in SATA *26, 80*
  See also CLR *56*
  See also SAAS *21*
Gauch, Sarah *223*
Gaudasinska, Elzbieta 1943- *190*
Gaul, Randy 1959- *63*
Gault, Clare 1925- *36*
Gault, Frank 1926-1982 .... *36*
  Brief entry *30*
Gault, William Campbell 1910-1995 .... *8*
Gauthier, Gail 1953- *203*
  Earlier sketches in SATA *118, 160*
Gaver, Becky
  See Gaver, Rebecca
Gaver, Rebecca 1952- *20*
Gavin, Jamila 1941- *223*
  Earlier sketches in SATA *96, 125*
Gay, Amelia
  See Hogarth, Grace (Weston Allen)
Gay, Francis
  See Gee, H(erbert) L(eslie)
Gay, Kathlyn 1930- *144*
  Earlier sketch in SATA *9*
Gay, Marie-Louise 1952- *179*
  Earlier sketches in SATA *68, 126*
  See also CLR *27*
  See also SAAS *21*
Gay, Michel 1947- *162*
Gay, Zhenya 1906-1978 .... *19*
Gaze, Gillian
  See Barklem, Jill
Gear, Kathleen M. O'Neal
  See Gear, Kathleen O'Neal
Gear, Kathleen O'Neal 1954- *224*
  Earlier sketches in SATA *71, 166*
Gear, W. Michael 1955- *224*
  Earlier sketches in SATA *71, 166*
Geary, Rick 1946- *142*
Geason, Susan 1946- *122*
Gedalof, Robin
  See McGrath, Robin
Gedge, Pauline (Alice) 1945- *101*
Gee, H(erbert) L(eslie) 1901-1977
  Obituary *26*
Gee, Maurice 1931- *227*
  Earlier sketches in SATA *46, 101*
  See also CLR *56*

Gee, Maurice Gough
  See Gee, Maurice
Geehan, Wayne (E.) 1947- *107*
Geer, Charles 1922- *42*
  Brief entry *32*
Geeslin, Campbell 1925- *163*
  Earlier sketch in SATA *107*
Gehman, Mary W. 1923- *86*
Gehr, Mary 1910(?)-1997 .... *32*
  Obituary *99*
Geipel, Eileen 1932- *30*
Geis, Alissa Imre 1976- *189*
Geis, Darlene Stern 1918(?)-1999 .... *7*
  Obituary *111*
Geisel, Helen 1898-1967 .... *26*
Geisel, Theodor Seuss
  See Dr. Seuss
Geisert, Arthur 1941- *171*
  Brief entry *52*
  Earlier sketches in SATA *56, 92, 133*
  See also CLR *87*
  See also SAAS *23*
Geisert, Arthur Frederick
  See Geisert, Arthur
Geisert, Bonnie 1942- *165*
  Earlier sketch in SATA *92*
Geist, Ken *191*
Gelber, Lisa *210*
Geldart, William 1936- *15*
Gelinas, Paul J. 1904-1996 .... *10*
Gellis, Roberta 1927- *128*
Gellis, Roberta Leah Jacobs
  See Gellis, Roberta
Gellman, Marc *112*
Gelman, Amy 1961- *72*
Gelman, Jan 1963- *58*
Gelman, Rita Golden 1937- *131*
  Brief entry *51*
  Earlier sketch in SATA *84*
Gelman, Steve 1934- *3*
Gemignani, Tony 1973- *220*
Gemming, Elizabeth 1932- *11*
Gendel, Evelyn W. 1916(?)-1977
  Obituary *27*
Gennaro, Joseph F., Jr. 1924- *53*
Gennaro, Joseph Francis, Jr.
  See Gennaro, Joseph F., Jr.
Gentieu, Penny *204*
Gentile, Petrina 1969- *91*
Gentle, Mary 1956- *48*
Gentleman, David (William) 1930- *7*
Gentry, Marita *215*
Geoghegan, Adrienne 1962- *143*
George, Barbara
  See Katz, Bobbi
George, Emily
  See Katz, Bobbi
George, Gail
  See Katz, Bobbi
George, Jean
  See George, Jean Craighead
George, Jean C.
  See George, Jean Craighead
George, Jean Craighead 1919- *226*
  Earlier sketches in SATA *2, 68, 124, 170*
  See also CLR *136*
George, Jessica Day 1976- *210*
George, John L(othar) 1916- *2*
George, Kristine O'Connell 1954- *156*
  Earlier sketch in SATA *110*
George, Lindsay Barrett 1952- *206*
  Earlier sketches in SATA *95, 155*
George, S. C. 1898- *11*
George, Sally
  See Orr, Wendy
George, Sidney Charles
  See George, S. C.
George, Twig C. 1950- *114*
George, W(illiam) Lloyd 1900(?)-1975
  Obituary *30*
Georgiou, Constantine 1927- *7*

Georgiou, Theo
  See Odgers, Sally Farrell
Geraghty, Paul 1959- 130
Gerard, Jean Ignace Isidore 1803-1847 45
Geras, Adele 1944- 180
  Autobiography Feature 180
  Earlier sketches in SATA 23, 87, 129, 173
  See also SAAS 21
Geras, Adele Daphne Weston
  See Geras, Adele
Gerber, Carole 1947- 207
Gerber, Linda 213
Gerber, Merrill Joan 1938- 170
  Autobiography Feature 170
  Earlier sketches in SATA 64, 127
Gerber, Perren 1933- 104
Gerberg, Mort 1931- 64
Gergely, Tibor 1900-1978 54
  Obituary 20
Geringer, Laura 1948- 232
  Earlier sketches in SATA 29, 94, 164
Gerler, William R(obert) 1917-1996 47
Gerrard, Jean 1933- 51
Gerrard, Roy 1935-1997 90
  Brief entry 45
  Obituary 99
  Earlier sketch in SATA 47
  See also CLR 23
Gerritsen, Paula 1956- 177
Gerrold, David 1944- 144
  Earlier sketch in SATA 66
Gershator, David 1937- 180
Gershator, Phillis 1942- 188
  Earlier sketches in SATA 90, 158
Gershon, Dann 1955- 187
Gershon, Gina 1962- 187
Gerson, Corinne 1927- 37
Gerson, Mary-Joan 136
  Earlier sketch in SATA 79
Gerson, Noel Bertram 1914-1988 22
  Obituary 60
Gerstein, Mordicai 1935- 222
  Brief entry 36
  Earlier sketches in SATA 47, 81, 142, 178
  See also CLR 102
Gertridge, Allison 1967- 132
Gervais, Bernadette 1959- 80
Gervay, Susanne 183
Gesner, Clark 1938-2002 40
  Obituary 143
Gessner, Lynne 1919- 16
Geter, Tyrone 150
Getz, David 1957- 91
Getzinger, Donna 1968- 128
Geus, Mireille 1964- 207
Gevirtz, Eliezer 1950- 49
Gevry, Claudine 188
Gewe, Raddory
  See Gorey, Edward (St. John)
Ghan, Linda (R.) 1947- 77
Ghent, Natale 1962- 148
Gherman, Beverly 1934- 123
  Earlier sketch in SATA 68
Ghigna, Charles 1946- 153
  Earlier sketch in SATA 108
Giacobbe, Beppe 1953- 174
Giambastiani, Kurt R. A. 1958- 141
Giannini, Enzo 1946- 68
Gibala-Broxholm, Scott 1959(?)- 205
Gibbons, Alan 1953- 198
  Earlier sketch in SATA 124
Gibbons, Faye 1938- 103
  Earlier sketch in SATA 65
Gibbons, Gail 1944- 201
  Earlier sketches in SATA 23, 72, 104, 160
  See also CLR 8
  See also SAAS 12
Gibbons, Gail Gretchen
  See Gibbons, Gail
Gibbons, Kaye 1960- 117
Gibbs, Adrea 1960- 126

Gibbs, Alonzo (Lawrence) 1915-1992 5
Gibbs, (Cecilia) May 1877-1969
  Obituary 27
Gibbs, Stuart 1969- 230
Gibbs, Tony
  See Gibbs, Wolcott, Jr.
Gibbs, Wolcott, Jr. 1935- 40
Giblin, James Cross 1933- 197
  Earlier sketches in SATA 33, 75, 122
  See also CLR 29
  See also SAAS 12
Gibson, Andrew (William) 1949- 72
Gibson, Barbara L. 205
Gibson, Barbara Leonard
  See Gibson, Barbara L.
Gibson, Betty 1911- 75
Gibson, Jo
  See Fluke, Joanne
Gibson, Josephine
  See Hine, Sesyle Joslin
  and Hine, Al(fred Blakelee)
Gibson, Marley 1966- 225
Gibson, Sarah P. 1962- 211
Gibson, William 1914-2008 66
  Obituary 199
Gibson, William Ford
  See Gibson, William
Gidal, Nachum
  See Gidal, Tim Nachum
Gidal, Sonia (Epstein) 1922- 2
Gidal, Tim Nachum 1909-1996 2
Gidalewitsch, Nachum
  See Gidal, Tim Nachum
Gideon, Melanie 1963- 175
Giegling, John A(llan) 1935- 17
Gifaldi, David 1950- 209
  Earlier sketch in SATA 76
Giff, Patricia Reilly 1935- 203
  Earlier sketches in SATA 33, 70, 121, 160
Giffard, Hannah 1962- 83
Gifford, Carrie 224
Gifford, Clive 1966- 198
Gifford, Griselda 1931- 171
  Earlier sketch in SATA 42
Gifford, Kerri 1961- 91
Gifford, Peggy 1952- 191
Gilani, Fawzia
  See Gilani-Williams, Fawzia
Gilani-Williams, Fawzia 1967- 231
Gilbert, Ann
  See Taylor, Ann
Gilbert, Anne Yvonne 1951- 185
Gilbert, Barbara Snow 1954- 97
Gilbert, Catherine
  See Murdock, Catherine Gilbert
Gilbert, Frances
  See Collings, Gillian
Gilbert, Harriett 1948- 30
Gilbert, (Agnes) Joan (Sewell) 1931- 10
Gilbert, John (Raphael) 1926- 36
Gilbert, Nan
  See Gilbertson, Mildred Geiger
Gilbert, Roby Goodale 1966- 90
Gilbert, Ruth Gallard Ainsworth
  See Ainsworth, Ruth (Gallard)
Gilbert, Sara (Dulaney) 1943- 82
  Earlier sketch in SATA 11
Gilbert, Sheri L. 157
Gilbert, Suzie 1956- 97
Gilbert, W(illiam) S(chwenck) 1836-1911 ... 36
Gilbert, Yvonne
  See Gilbert, Anne Yvonne
Gilbertson, Mildred Geiger 1908-1988 2
Gilbreath, Alice 1921- 12
Gilbreth, Frank B., Jr. 1911-2001 2
Gilbreth, Frank Bunker
  See Gilbreth, Frank B., Jr.
Gilchrist, Jan Spivey 1949- 130
  Earlier sketch in SATA 72
Gilden, Mel 1947- 97

Giles, Gail 196
  Earlier sketch in SATA 152
Gilfond, Henry 2
Gilge, Jeanette 1924- 22
Gili, Phillida 1944- 70
Gill, Derek (Lewis Theodore) 1919-1997 9
Gill, Margery Jean 1925- 22
Gill, Shelley 176
Gill, Stephen 1932- 63
Gillespie, Carol Ann 1951- 158
Gillett, Mary (Bledsoe) 7
Gillette, Henry Sampson 1915- 14
Gillette, J. Lynett 1946- 103
Gillette, Jan Lynett
  See Gillette, J. Lynett
Gilley, Jeremy 1969- 174
Gillham, Bill
  See Gillham, W(illiam) E(dwin) C(harles)
Gillham, W(illiam) E(dwin) C(harles)
  1936- 42
Gilliam, Stan 1946- 39
  Brief entry 35
Gilliland, Alexis A. 1931- 72
Gilliland, Alexis Arnaldus
  See Gilliland, Alexis A.
Gilliland, (Cleburne) Hap 1918- 92
Gilliland, Judith Heide 180
Gillmor, Don 1954- 127
Gilman, Dorothy 1923- 5
Gilman, Esther 1925- 15
Gilman, Laura Anne 178
Gilman, Phoebe 1940-2002 104
  Obituary 141
  Earlier sketch in SATA 58
Gilmore, Iris 1900-1982 22
Gilmore, Kate 1931- 87
Gilmore, Mary (Jean Cameron) 1865-1962 . 49
Gilmore, Rachna 1953- 209
Gilmore, Susan 1954- 59
Gilpin, Stephen 213
  Earlier sketch in SATA 177
Gilroy, Beryl (Agatha) 1924- 80
Gilson, Barbara
  See Gilson, Charles James Louis
Gilson, Charles James Louis 1878-1943
  See YABC 2
Gilson, Jamie 1933- 176
  Brief entry 34
  Earlier sketches in SATA 37, 91
Gimpel, Carolyn
  See Hart, Carolyn
Ginsberg, Blaze 1987- 222
Ginsburg, Mirra 1909-2000 92
  Earlier sketch in SATA 6
  See also CLR 45
Giovanni, Nikki 1943- 208
  Earlier sketches in SATA 24, 107
  See also CLR 73
Giovanni, Yolanda Cornelia
  See Giovanni, Nikki
Giovanni, Yolande Cornelia
  See Giovanni, Nikki
Giovanni, Yolande Cornelia, Jr.
  See Giovanni, Nikki
Giovanopoulos, Paul (Arthur) 1939- 7
Gipson, Billie
  See Letts, Billie
Gipson, Fred(erick Benjamin) 1908-1973 2
  Obituary 24
Girard, Linda (Walvoord) 1942- 41
Giraudon, David 1975- 215
Girion, Barbara 1937- 78
  Earlier sketch in SATA 26
  See also SAAS 14
Girl, Nerdy
  See Castellucci, Cecil
Girouard, Patrick 1957- 155
Girzone, Joseph F. 1930- 76
Girzone, Joseph Francis
  See Girzone, Joseph F.

Gise, Joanne
  See Mattern, Joanne
Gist, E.M. 206
Gittings, Jo (Grenville) Manton 1919- 3
Gittings, Robert (William Victor) 1911-1992 . 6
  Obituary 70
Givens, Janet E(aton) 1932- 60
Givner, Joan 1936- 171
Givner, Joan Mary
  See Givner, Joan
Gladstone, Eve
  See Werner, Herma
Gladstone, Gary 1935- 12
Gladstone, M(yron) J. 1923- 37
Glanville, Brian (Lester) 1931- 42
Glanzman, Louis S. 1922- 36
Glaser, Byron 1954- 154
Glaser, Dianne E(lizabeth) 1937- 50
  Brief entry 31
Glaser, Isabel Joshlin 1929- 94
Glaser, Linda 225
Glaser, Milton 1929- 151
  Earlier sketch in SATA *11*
Glaser, Shirley 151
Glaspell, Susan 1882(?)-1948
  See YABC *2*
Glass, Andrew 1949- 223
  Brief entry 46
  Earlier sketches in SATA *90, 150*
Glass, Linzi 175
Glass, Linzi Alex
  See Glass, Linzi
Glasscock, Amnesia
  See Steinbeck, John
Glassman, Bruce 1961- 76
Glatt, Lisa 1963- 217
Glauber, Uta (Heil) 1936- 17
Glazer, Thomas (Zachariah) 1914-2003 9
Glazer, Tom
  See Glazer, Thomas (Zachariah)
Gleasner, Diana (Cottle) 1936- 29
Gleason, Judith 1929- 24
Gleason, Katherine (A.) 1960- 104
Gleeson, Libby 1950- 142
  Autobiography Feature 142
  Earlier sketches in SATA *82, 118*
Gleiter, Jan 1947- 111
Gleitzman, Morris 1953- 156
  Earlier sketch in SATA *88*
  See also CLR *88*
Glen, Maggie 1944- 88
Glendinning, Richard 1917-1988 24
Glendinning, Sally
  See Glendinning, Sara W(ilson)
Glendinning, Sara W(ilson) 1913-1993 24
Glenn, John W. 195
Glenn, Mel 1943- 93
  Brief entry 45
  Earlier sketch in SATA *51*
  See also CLR *51*
Glenn, Patricia Brown 1953- 86
Glenn, Sharlee 159
Glenn, Sharlee Mullins
  See Glenn, Sharlee
Glennon, Karen M. 1946- 85
Gles, Margaret Breitmaier 1940- 22
Glick, Carl (Cannon) 1890-1971 14
Glick, Ruth 1942- 125
Glick, Ruth Burtnick
  See Glick, Ruth
Glick, Virginia Kirkus 1893-1980
  Obituary 23
Gliewe, Unada (Grace) 1927- 3
Glimmerveen, Ulco 1958- 85
Glines, Carroll V(ane), Jr. 1920- 19
Gliori, Debi 1959- 189
  Earlier sketches in SATA *72, 138*
Globe, Leah Ain 1900- 41
Glori Ann
  See Blakely, Gloria

Glovach, Linda 1947- 105
  Earlier sketch in SATA *7*
Glover, Denis (James Matthews) 1912-1980 . 7
Glubok, Shirley (Astor) 146
  Autobiography Feature 146
  Earlier sketches in SATA *6, 68*
  See also CLR *1*
  See also SAAS *7*
Gluck, Felix 1923-1981
  Obituary 25
Glyman, Caroline A. 1967- 103
Glynne-Jones, William 1907-1977 11
Gobbato, Imero 1923- 39
Gobbletree, Richard
  See Quackenbush, Robert M(ead)
Goble, Dorothy 26
Goble, Paul 1933- 131
  Earlier sketches in SATA *25, 69*
  See also CLR *21*
Goble, Warwick (?)-1943 46
Godden, (Margaret) Rumer 1907-1998 36
  Obituary 109
  Earlier sketch in SATA *3*
  See also CLR *20*
  See also SAAS *12*
Gode, Alexander
  See Gode von Aesch, Alexander (Gottfried
  Friedrich)
Gode von Aesch, Alexander (Gottfried
  Friedrich) 1906-1970 14
Godfrey, Jane
  See Bowden, Joan Chase
Godfrey, Martyn
  See Godfrey, Martyn N.
  and Godfrey, Martyn N.
Godfrey, Martyn N. 1949-2000 95
  See also CLR *57*
Godfrey, William
  See Youd, Samuel
Godkin, Celia 1948- 145
  Earlier sketch in SATA *66*
Godkin, Celia Marilyn
  See Godkin, Celia
Godon, Ingrid 1958- 186
Godown, Jan
  See Annino, Jan Godown
Godwin, Laura 1956- 179
Godwin, Sam
  See Pirotta, Saviour
Godwin, Sarah Massini
  See Massini, Sarah
Goede, Irene 1966- 208
Goedecke, Christopher (John) 1951- 81
Goekler, Susan
  See Wooley, Susan Frelick
Goembel, Ponder 204
Goertzen, Glenda 172
Goettel, Elinor 1930- 12
Goetz, Delia 1898-1996 22
  Obituary 91
Goffe, Toni 1936- 61
Goffstein, Brooke
  See Goffstein, Marilyn Brooke
Goffstein, M. B.
  See Goffstein, Marilyn Brooke
Goffstein, Marilyn Brooke 1940- 70
  Earlier sketch in SATA *8*
  See also CLR *3*
Goforth, Ellen
  See Francis, Dorothy
Gogol, Sara 1948-2004 80
Goh, Chan Hon 1969- 145
Going, Kelly L.
  See Going, K.L.
Going, Kelly Louise
  See Going, K.L.
Going, K.L. 199
  Earlier sketch in SATA *156*
Golann, Cecil Paige 1921-1995 11
Golbin, Andree 1923- 15
Gold, Alison Leslie 1945- 104

Gold, August 1955- 215
Gold, Bernice 150
Gold, Phyllis
  See Goldberg, Phyllis
Gold, Robert S(tanley) 1924- 63
Gold, Sharlya 9
Gold, Susan
  See Gold, Susan Dudley
Gold, Susan Dudley 1949- 147
Goldbach, Veronica 1980- 220
Goldberg, Grace 1956- 78
Goldberg, Herbert S. 1926- 25
Goldberg, Jacob 1943- 94
Goldberg, Jake
  See Goldberg, Jacob
Goldberg, Myla 1972(?)- 210
Goldberg, Phyllis 1941- 21
Goldberg, Stan J. 1939- 26
Goldberg, Susan 1948- 71
Goldberg, Whoopi 1955- 119
Goldberger, Judith M. 1948- 80
Goldblatt, Stacey 1969(?)- 191
Golden, Christie 1963- 167
  Earlier sketch in SATA *116*
Goldentyer, Debra 1960- 84
Goldfeder, Cheryl
  See Pahz, Cheryl Suzanne
Goldfeder, James
  See Pahz, James Alon
Goldfeder, Jim
  See Pahz, James Alon
Goldfinger, Jennifer P. 1963- 185
Goldfrank, Helen Colodny 1912- 6
Goldin, Augusta 1906-1999 13
Goldin, Barbara Diamond 1946- 129
  Autobiography Feature 129
  Earlier sketch in SATA *92*
  See also SAAS *26*
Goldin, David 1963- 101
Golding, Julia 1969- 188
Golding, Theresa Martin 1960- 150
Golding, William 1911-1993
  See CLR *130*
Golding, William Gerald
  See Golding, William
Goldman, Alex J. 1917- 65
Goldman, E. M. 1943- 103
Goldman, Eleanor Maureen
  See Goldman, E. M.
Goldman, Elizabeth 1949- 90
Goldman, Judy 1955- 212
Goldman, Steven 1964- 207
Goldman, Todd Harris 221
Goldring, Ann 1937- 149
Golds, Cassandra 1962- 226
Goldsborough, June 1923- 19
Goldschmidt, Judy 202
Goldsmith, Connie 1945- 147
Goldsmith, Howard 1943- 108
  Earlier sketch in SATA *24*
Goldsmith, John Herman Thorburn 1903-1987
  Obituary 52
Goldsmith, Oliver 1730(?)-1774 26
Goldsmith, Ruth M. 1919- 62
Goldstein, Nathan 1927- 47
Goldstein, Philip 1910-1997 23
Goldston, Robert (Conroy) 1927- 6
Goldstone, Bruce 183
Goldstone, Lawrence A.
  See Treat, Lawrence
Goldszmit, Henryk 1878-1942 65
  See also CLR *152*
Golembe, Carla 1951- 79
Golenbock, Peter 1946- 99
Goll, Reinhold W(eimar) 1897-1993 26
Gollub, Matthew 1960- 134
  Earlier sketch in SATA *83*
Golson, Terry 213
Golson, Terry Blonder
  See Golson, Terry
Gomes, Filomena 1965- 183

Gomez, Elena *191*
Gomez, Elizabeth *133*
Gomez-Freer, Elizabeth
    See Gomez, Elizabeth
Gomi, Taro 1945- *103*
    Earlier sketch in SATA *64*
    See also CLR 57
Gondosch, Linda 1944- *58*
Gonsalves, Rob 1959- *209*
Gonyea, Mark *194*
Gonzales, Chuck *230*
Gonzalez, Catherine Troxell 1917-2000 .... *87*
Gonzalez, Christina
    See Gonzalez, Maya Christina
Gonzalez, Christina Diaz 1969- *231*
Gonzalez, Gloria 1940- *23*
Gonzalez, Julie 1958- *174*
Gonzalez, Julie Sehers
    See Gonzalez, Julie
Gonzalez, Lucia M. 1957- *202*
Gonzalez, Maya
    See Gonzalez, Maya Christina
Gonzalez, Maya Christina 1964- *175*
    Earlier sketch in SATA *115*
Gonzalez, Rigoberto 1970- *147*
Goobie, Beth 1959- *128*
Good, Alice 1950- *73*
Good, Clare
    See Romano, Clare
Good, Karen Hillard *214*
Goodall, Daphne Machin
    See Machin Goodall, Daphne (Edith)
Goodall, Jane 1934- *111*
Goodall, John S(trickland) 1908-1996 .... *66*
    Obituary *91*
    Earlier sketch in SATA *4*
    See also CLR 25
Goodbody, Slim
    See Burstein, John
Goode, Diane 1949- *225*
    Earlier sketches in SATA *15, 84, 114, 170*
Goode, Diane Capuozzo
    See Goode, Diane
Goode, Stephen Ray 1943- *55*
    Brief entry *40*
Goodenow, Earle 1913- *40*
Goodhart, Pippa 1958- *196*
    Earlier sketch in SATA *153*
Goodhue, Thomas W. 1949- *143*
Goodin, Sallie (Brown) 1953- *74*
Goodman, Alison 1966- *111*
Goodman, Deborah Lerme 1956- *50*
    Brief entry *49*
Goodman, Elaine 1930- *9*
Goodman, Emily *217*
Goodman, Joan Elizabeth 1950- *162*
    Earlier sketches in SATA *50, 94*
Goodman, Susan E. 1952- *181*
Goodman, Walter 1927-2002 .... *9*
Goodman Koz, Paula *211*
Goodrich, Carter 1959(?)- *221*
Goodrich, Samuel Griswold 1793-1860 .... *23*
Goodsell, Jane Neuberger 1921(?)-1988
    Obituary *56*
Goodweather, Hartley
    See King, Thomas
GoodWeather, Hartley
    See King, Thomas
Goodwin, Hal
    See Goodwin, Harold L(eland)
Goodwin, Harold L(eland) 1914-1990 .... *51*
    Obituary *65*
    Earlier sketch in SATA *13*
Goodwin, William 1943- *117*
Goor, Nancy (Ruth Miller) 1944- *39*
    Brief entry *34*
Goor, Ron(ald Stephen) 1940- *39*
    Brief entry *34*
Goossen, Agnes
    See Epp, Margaret A(gnes)
Goossens, Philippe 1963- *195*

Gootman, Marilyn E. 1944- *179*
Gopnik, Adam 1956- *171*
Gorbachev, Valeri 1944- *222*
    Autobiography Feature *143*
    Earlier sketches in SATA *98, 143, 184*
Gordion, Mark
    See Turtledove, Harry
Gordon, Ad
    See Hano, Arnold
Gordon, Amy 1949- *197*
    Earlier sketches in SATA *115, 156*
Gordon, Bernard Ludwig 1931-2010 .... *27*
Gordon, Colonel H. R.
    See Ellis, Edward S.
Gordon, David
    See Garrett, Randall
Gordon, Donald
    See Payne, Donald Gordon
Gordon, Dorothy 1893-1970 .... *20*
Gordon, Esther S(aranga) 1935- *10*
Gordon, Frederick *1*
Gordon, Gaelyn 1939-1997
    See CLR 75
Gordon, Garrett
    See Garrett, Randall
Gordon, Gary
    See Edmonds, I(vy) G(ordon)
Gordon, Hal
    See Goodwin, Harold L(eland)
Gordon, Jeffie Ross
    See Enderle, Judith (Ann) Ross
    and Gordon, Stephanie Jacob
Gordon, John
    See Gesner, Clark
Gordon, John (William) 1925- *84*
Gordon, Lew
    See Baldwin, Gordon C(ortis)
Gordon, Margaret (Anna) 1939- *9*
Gordon, Mike 1948- *101*
Gordon, Mildred 1912-1979
    Obituary *24*
Gordon, Selma
    See Lanes, Selma G.
Gordon, Sheila 1927- *88*
    See also CLR 27
Gordon, Shirley 1921- *48*
    Brief entry *41*
Gordon, Sol 1923- *11*
Gordon, Stephanie Jacob 1940- *89*
    Autobiography Feature *114*
    Earlier sketch in SATA *64*
    See also SAAS 26
Gordon, Stewart
    See Shirreffs, Gordon D(onald)
Gordons, The
    See Gordon, Mildred
    and Gordon, Gordon
Gore, Leonid *222*
    Earlier sketch in SATA *185*
Gorelick, Molly C(hernow) 1920-2003 .... *9*
    Obituary *153*
Gorey, Edward (St. John) 1925-2000 .... *70*
    Brief entry *27*
    Obituary *118*
    Earlier sketch in SATA *29*
    See also CLR 36
Gorham, Charles Orson 1868-1936 .... *36*
Gorham, Michael
    See Folsom, Franklin (Brewster)
Gorman, Carol *187*
    Earlier sketch in SATA *150*
Gorman, Jacqueline Laks 1955- *148*
Gorman, Mike *206*
Gormley, Beatrice 1942- *202*
    Brief entry *35*
    Earlier sketches in SATA *39, 127*
Gorog, Judith (Katharine Allen) 1938- *75*
    Earlier sketch in SATA *39*
Gorrell, Gena K. 1946- *170*
Gorsline, Douglas (Warner) 1913-1985 .... *11*
    Obituary *43*

Gorsline, (Sally) Marie 1928- *28*
Gorsline, S. M.
    See Gorsline, (Sally) Marie
Gorton, Julia *218*
Gorton, Kaitlyn
    See Emerson, Kathy Lynn
Gorton, Kathy Lynn
    See Emerson, Kathy Lynn
Goryan, Sirak
    See Saroyan, William
Goschke, Julia 1973- *208*
Goscinny, Rene 1926-1977 .... *47*
    Brief entry *39*
    See also CLR 37
Goss, Clay(ton E.) 1946- *82*
Goss, Gary 1947- *124*
Goss, Mini 1963- *186*
Goto, Scott *203*
Gott, Barry *197*
Gottesman, S. D.
    See Kornbluth, C(yril) M.
    and Lowndes, Robert A(ugustine) W(ard)
    and Pohl, Frederik
Gottfried, Ted
    See Gottfried, Theodore Mark
Gottfried, Theodore Mark 1928- *150*
    Earlier sketch in SATA *85*
Gottlieb, Gerald 1923- *7*
Gottlieb, William P. 1917-2006 .... *24*
Gottlieb, William Paul
    See Gottlieb, William P.
Goudey, Alice E(dwards) 1898-1993 .... *20*
Goudge, Eileen 1950- *88*
Goudge, Elizabeth (de Beauchamp)
    1900-1984 .... *2*
    Obituary *38*
    See also CLR 94
Gough, Catherine
    See Mulgan, Catherine
Gough, Philip 1908-1986 .... *45*
Gough, Sue 1940- *106*
Goulart, Ron 1933- *67*
    Earlier sketch in SATA *1*
Goulart, Ronald Joseph
    See Goulart, Ron
Gould, Alberta 1945- *96*
Gould, Chester 1900-1985 .... *49*
    Obituary *43*
Gould, Jean R(osalind) 1909-1993 .... *11*
    Obituary *77*
Gould, Lilian *6*
Gould, Marilyn 1928- *76*
    Earlier sketch in SATA *15*
Gould, Robert *154*
Gould, Steven 1955- *95*
Gould, Steven Charles
    See Gould, Steven
Gourley, Catherine 1950- *190*
    Earlier sketch in SATA *95*
Gourse, Leslie 1939-2004 .... *89*
Govan, (Mary) Christine Noble 1898-1985 ... *9*
Gove, Doris 1944- *72*
Govenar, Alan 1952- *189*
Govenar, Alan Bruce
    See Govenar, Alan
Govern, Elaine 1939- *26*
Gowen, L. Kris 1968- *156*
Graaf, Peter
    See Youd, Samuel
Grab, Daphne 1971- *233*
Graber, Alexander 1914-1997 .... *98*
    Earlier sketch in SATA *7*
Graber, George Alexander
    See Graber, Alexander
Graber, Janet 1942- *170*
Graber, Richard (Fredrick) 1927- *26*
Grabianski, Janusz 1928-1976 .... *39*
    Obituary *30*
Graboff, Abner 1919-1986 .... *35*
Grace, Fran(ces Jane) *45*

Grace, N.B.
  See Harper, Suzanne
Grace, Theresa
  See Mattern, Joanne
Gracza, Margaret Young 1928- 56
Graduate of Oxford, A
  See Ruskin, John
Grady, Denise 1952- 189
Graeber, Charlotte Towner 106
  Brief entry 44
  Earlier sketch in SATA 56
Graef, Renee 1956- 204
Graeme, Roderic
  See Jeffries, Roderic
Graf, Michael
  See Graf, Mike
Graf, Mike 1960- 164
Grafe, Max 198
Graff, Lisa 1981- 188
Graff, Polly Anne Colver
  See Colver, Anne
Graff, (S.) Stewart 1908-2009 9
Graham, Ada 1931- 11
Graham, Alastair 1945- 74
Graham, Arthur Kennon
  See Harrison, David L.
Graham, Bob 1942- 187
  Earlier sketches in SATA 63, 101, 151
  See also CLR 31
Graham, Brenda Knight 1942- 32
Graham, Charlotte
  See Bowden, Joan Chase
Graham, Christine 1952- 224
Graham, Eleanor 1896-1984 18
  Obituary 38
Graham, Ennis
  See Molesworth, Mary Louisa
Graham, Frank, Jr. 1925- 11
Graham, Georgia 1959- 190
Graham, Ian 1953- 229
  Earlier sketch in SATA 112
Graham, John 1926-2007 11
Graham, Kennon
  See Harrison, David L.
Graham, Larry
  See Graham, Lawrence
Graham, Lawrence 1962- 63
Graham, Lawrence Otis
  See Graham, Lawrence
Graham, Linda
  See Graham-Barber, Lynda
Graham, Lorenz (Bell) 1902-1989 74
  Obituary 63
  Earlier sketch in SATA 2
  See also CLR 10
  See also SAAS 5
Graham, Margaret Bloy 1920- 11
Graham, Robin Lee 1949- 7
Graham, Shirley 1896(?)-1977
  See Du Bois, Shirley Graham
Graham-Barber, Lynda 1944- 159
  Earlier sketch in SATA 42
Graham-Cameron, M.
  See Graham-Cameron, M(alcolm) G(ordon)
Graham-Cameron, M(alcolm) G(ordon)
  1931- 53
  Brief entry 45
Graham-Cameron, Mike
  See Graham-Cameron, M(alcolm) G(ordon)
Grahame, Kenneth 1859-1932 100
  See also YABC 1
  See also CLR 135
Gralley, Jean 166
Gramatky, Hardie 1907-1979 30
  Obituary 23
  Earlier sketch in SATA 1
  See also CLR 22
Grambling, Lois G. 1927- 206
  Earlier sketches in SATA 71, 148
Grambo, Rebecca L(ynn) 1963- 109
Grammer, June Amos 1927- 58

Grand, Samuel 1912-1988 42
Grandits, John 1949- 192
GrandPre, Mary 1954- 229
  Earlier sketch in SATA 184
Grandville, J. J.
  See Gerard, Jean Ignace Isidore
Grandville, Jean Ignace Isidore Gerard
  See Gerard, Jean Ignace Isidore
Granfield, Linda 1950- 160
  Earlier sketch in SATA 96
Grange, Peter
  See Nicole, Christopher
Granger, Margaret Jane 1925(?)-1977
  Obituary 27
Granger, Michele 1949- 88
Granger, Peggy
  See Granger, Margaret Jane
Granowsky, Alvin 1936- 101
Granstaff, Bill 1925- 10
Granstrom, Brita 1969- 224
  Earlier sketches in SATA 111, 167
Grant, Bruce 1893-1977 5
  Obituary 25
Grant, Cynthia D. 1950- 147
  Earlier sketches in SATA 33, 77
Grant, Eva 1907-1996 7
Grant, Evva H. 1913-1977
  Obituary 27
Grant, Gordon 1875-1962 25
Grant, Gwen(doline Ellen) 1940- 47
Grant, Judyann Ackerman 211
Grant, Katie
  See Grant, K.M.
Grant, Katie M.
  See Grant, K.M.
Grant, K.M. 230
  Earlier sketch in SATA 175
Grant, (Alice) Leigh 1947- 10
Grant, Matthew G.
  See May, Julian
Grant, Maxwell
  See Gibson, Walter B(rown)
  and Lynds, Dennis
Grant, Melvyn 183
Grant, Myrna (Lois) 1934- 21
Grant, Neil 1938- 154
  Earlier sketch in SATA 14
Grant, Nicholas
  See Nicole, Christopher
Grant, Richard 1948- 80
Grant, Skeeter
  See Spiegelman, Art
Grater, Michael 1923- 57
Gratz, Alan 1972- 212
Graullera, Fabiola
  See Graullera Ramirez, Fabiola
Graullera Ramirez, Fabiola 225
Gravel, Fern
  See Hall, James Norman
Gravelle, Karen 1942- 166
  Earlier sketch in SATA 78
Graves, Charles Parlin 1911-1972 4
Graves, Keith 191
  Earlier sketch in SATA 156
Graves, Robert 1895-1985 45
Graves, Robert von Ranke
  See Graves, Robert
Graves, Valerie
  See Bradley, Marion Zimmer
Gravett, Emily 1972(?)- 232
  Earlier sketch in SATA 189
Gray, Betsy
  See Poole, Gray Johnson
Gray, Caroline
  See Nicole, Christopher
Gray, Claudia 213
Gray, Dianne E. 183
Gray, Elizabeth Janet
  See Vining, Elizabeth Gray
Gray, Genevieve S(tuck) 1920-1995 4

Gray, Harold (Lincoln) 1894-1968 33
  Brief entry 32
Gray, Jenny
  See Gray, Genevieve S(tuck)
Gray, John Lee
  See Jakes, John
Gray, Judith A. 1949- 93
Gray, Judith Anne
  See Gray, Judith A.
Gray, Keith 1972- 151
Gray, Kes 1960- 153
Gray, Les 1929- 82
Gray, Libba Moore 1937- 83
Gray, Luli 1945- 149
  Earlier sketch in SATA 90
Gray, Marian
  See Pierce, Edith Gray
Gray, Nicholas Stuart 1922-1981 4
  Obituary 27
Gray, Nigel 1941- 104
  Earlier sketch in SATA 33
Gray, (Lucy) Noel (Clervaux) 1898-1983 47
Gray, Patricia (Clark) 7
Gray, Patsey
  See Gray, Patricia (Clark)
Gray, Rita 184
Gray, Steve 1950- 231
Graydon, Shari 1958- 158
Grayland, V. Merle
  See Grayland, Valerie (Merle Spanner)
Grayland, Valerie (Merle Spanner) 7
Grayson, Devin (Kalile) 1970- 119
Grayson, Kristine
  See Rusch, Kristine Kathryn
Grayson, Paul 1946- 79
Graystone, Lynn
  See Brennan, Joseph Lomas
Great Comte, The
  See Hawkesworth, Eric
Greaves, Margaret 1914-1995 87
  Earlier sketch in SATA 7
Greaves, Nick 1955- 77
Greban, Quentin 1977- 223
Gree, Alain 1936- 28
Green, Adam
  See Weisgard, Leonard (Joseph)
Green, Anne Canevari 1943- 62
Green, Brian
  See Card, Orson Scott
Green, Cliff(ord) 1934- 126
Green, Connie Jordan 1938- 80
Green, D.
  See Casewit, Curtis W(erner)
Green, Elizabeth Shippen 1871-1954 139
Green, Hannah
  See Greenberg, Joanne (Goldenberg)
Green, Jane 1937- 9
Green, Jessica 211
Green, John 1977(?)- 170
Green, Mary Moore 1906- 11
Green, Morton 1937- 8
Green, Norma B(erger) 1925- 11
Green, Phyllis 1932- 20
Green, Roger (Gilbert) Lancelyn 1918-1987 . 2
  Obituary 53
Green, (James Le)Roy 1948- 89
Green, Sheila Ellen 1934- 148
  Earlier sketches in SATA 8, 87
Green, Timothy 1953- 91
Greenaway, Kate 1846-1901 100
  See also YABC 2
  See also CLR 111
Greenbank, Anthony Hunt 1933- 39
Greenberg, David 1954- 171
Greenberg, David T.
  See Greenberg, David
Greenberg, Harvey R. 1935- 5
Greenberg, Jan 1942- 211
  Earlier sketches in SATA 61, 125
Greenberg, Joanne (Goldenberg) 1932- 25

Greenberg, Melanie Hope 1954- 214
Earlier sketch in SATA 72
Greenberg, Polly 1932- 52
Brief entry 43
Greenblat, Rodney Alan 1960- 106
Greenburg, Dan 1936- 175
Earlier sketch in SATA 102
Greene, Bette 1934- 161
Earlier sketches in SATA 8, 102
See also CLR 140
See also SAAS 16
Greene, Carla 1916- 67
Earlier sketch in SATA 1
Greene, Carol 102
Brief entry 44
Earlier sketch in SATA 66
Greene, Constance C(larke) 1924- 72
Earlier sketch in SATA 11
See also CLR 62
See also SAAS 11
Greene, Edgar
See Papademetriou, Lisa
Greene, Ellin 1927- 23
Greene, Graham 1904-1991 20
Greene, Graham Henry
See Greene, Graham
Greene, Jacqueline Dembar 1946- 212
Earlier sketches in SATA 76, 131
Greene, Laura Offenhartz 1935- 38
Greene, Meg
See Malvasi, Meg Greene
Greene, Michele 1962- 178
Greene, Michele Dominguez
See Greene, Michele
Greene, Rhonda Gowler 1955- 160
Earlier sketch in SATA 101
Greene, Stephanie 1950- 221
Earlier sketches in SATA 127, 173
Greene, Wade 1933- 11
Greene, Yvonne
See Flesch, Yolande
Greenfeld, Howard (Scheinman) 1928- 140
Earlier sketch in SATA 19
Greenfeld, Josh(ua Joseph) 1928- 62
Greenfield, Eloise 1929- 155
Earlier sketches in SATA 19, 61, 105
See also CLR 38
See also SAAS 16
Greenhaus, Thelma Nurenberg 1903-1984
Obituary 45
Greenhut, Josh
See Mercer, Sienna
Greening, Hamilton
See Hamilton, Charles (Harold St. John)
Greenlaw, M. Jean 1941- 107
Greenleaf, Barbara Kaye 1942- 6
Greenleaf, Peter 1910-1997 33
Greenlee, Sharon 1935- 77
Greeno, Gayle 1949- 81
Greenseid, Diane 1948- 178
Earlier sketch in SATA 93
Greenspun, Adele Aron 1938- 142
Earlier sketch in SATA 76
Greenstein, Elaine 1959- 150
Earlier sketch in SATA 82
Greenwald, Sheila
See Green, Sheila Ellen
Greenwood, Barbara 1940- 129
Earlier sketch in SATA 90
Greenwood, Mark 1958- 202
Greenwood, Pamela D. 1944- 115
Greer, Richard
See Garrett, Randall
and Silverberg, Robert
Gregg, Andrew K. 1929- 81
Gregg, Charles T(hornton) 1927- 65
Gregg, Walter H(arold) 1919- 20
Gregor, Arthur 1923- 36
Gregor, Lee
See Pohl, Frederik
Gregori, Leon 1919- 15

Gregorian, Joyce Ballou 1946-1991 30
Obituary 83
Gregorich, Barbara 1943- 184
Earlier sketch in SATA 66
Gregorowski, Christopher 1940- 30
Gregory, Diana (Jean) 1933- 49
Brief entry 42
Gregory, Harry
See Gottfried, Theodore Mark
Gregory, Jean
See Ure, Jean
Gregory, Kristiana 1951- 212
Earlier sketches in SATA 74, 136
Gregory, Nan 1944- 192
Earlier sketch in SATA 148
Gregory, Philippa 1954- 122
Gregory, Stephen
See Penzler, Otto
Gregory, Valiska 1940- 82
Greif, Jean-Jacques 1944- 195
Greisman, Joan Ruth 1937- 31
Grendon, Stephen
See Derleth, August (William)
Grenville, Pelham
See Wodehouse, P. G.
Gretz, Susanna 1937- 7
Gretzer, John 18
Grewdead, Roy
See Gorey, Edward (St. John)
Grey, Carol
See Lowndes, Robert A(ugustine) W(ard)
Grey, Christopher 191
Grey, Christopher Peter
See Grey, Christopher
Grey, Jerry 1926- 11
Grey, Mini 205
Earlier sketch in SATA 166
Greybeard the Pirate
See Macintosh, Brownie
Grey Owl
See Belaney, Archibald Stansfeld
Gri
See Denney, Diana
Gribbin, John 1946- 159
Gribbin, John R.
See Gribbin, John
Grice, Frederick 1910-1983 6
Grider, Dorothy 1915- 31
Gridley, Marion E(leanor) 1906-1974 35
Obituary 26
Grieco-Tiso, Pina 1954- 108
Grieder, Walter 1924- 9
Griego, Tony A. 1955- 77
Griese, Arnold A(lfred) 1921- 9
Griessman, Annette 1962- 170
Earlier sketch in SATA 116
Grieve, James 1934- 146
Grifalconi, Ann 1929- 210
Earlier sketches in SATA 2, 66, 133
See also CLR 35
See also SAAS 16
Griffin, Adele 1970- 195
Earlier sketches in SATA 105, 153
Griffin, Elizabeth May 1985- 89
Griffin, Gillett Good 1928- 26
Griffin, Judith Berry 34
Griffin, Kitty 1951- 137
Griffin, Peni R. 1961- 193
Earlier sketches in SATA 67, 99
Griffin, Steven A. 1953- 89
Griffin, Steven Arthur
See Griffin, Steven A.
Griffin, W. E. B. 1929- 5
Griffith, Connie 1946- 89
Griffith, Gershom 1960- 85
Griffith, Helen V. 1934- 87
Autobiography Feature 107
Earlier sketch in SATA 39
Griffith, Helen Virginia
See Griffith, Helen V.

Griffith, Jeannette
See Eyerly, Jeannette
Griffith, Saul 1974- 200
Griffiths, Andy 1961- 196
Earlier sketch in SATA 152
Griffiths, G(ordon) D(ouglas) 1910-1973
Obituary 20
Griffiths, Helen 1939- 86
Earlier sketch in SATA 5
See also CLR 75
See also SAAS 5
Grigson, Jane (McIntire) 1928-1990 63
Grimes, Lee 1920- 68
Grimes, Nikki 1950- 218
Earlier sketches in SATA 93, 136, 174
See also CLR 42
Grimly, Gris 186
Grimm, Jacob Ludwig Karl 1785-1863 22
See also CLR 112
Grimm, Wilhelm Karl 1786-1859 22
See also CLR 112
Grimm, William C(arey) 1907-1992 14
Grimm and Grim
See Grimm, Jacob Ludwig Karl
and Grimm, Wilhelm Karl
Grimm Brothers
See Grimm, Jacob Ludwig Karl
and Grimm, Wilhelm Karl
Grimsdell, Jeremy 1942- 83
Grimshaw, Nigel (Gilroy) 1925- 23
Grimsley, Gordon
See Groom, Arthur William
Grindley, Jane Sally
See Grindley, Sally
Grindley, Sally 1953- 148
Gringhuis, Dirk
See Gringhuis, Richard H.
Gringhuis, Richard H. 1918-1974 6
Obituary 25
Grinnell, David
See Wollheim, Donald A(llen)
Grinnell, George Bird 1849-1938 16
Grinspoon, David
See Grinspoon, David H.
Grinspoon, David H. 1959- 156
Grinspoon, David Harry
See Grinspoon, David H.
Gripe, Maria 1923- 74
Earlier sketch in SATA 2
See also CLR 5
Gripe, Maria Kristina
See Gripe, Maria
Gritton, Steve 223
Grobler, Piet 1959- 201
Groch, Judith (Goldstein) 1929- 25
Grode, Redway
See Gorey, Edward (St. John)
Groener, Carl
See Lowndes, Robert A(ugustine) W(ard)
Groening, Matt 1954- 116
Earlier sketch in SATA 81
Grohmann, Susan 1948- 84
Grohskopf, Bernice 7
Grol, Lini R(icharda) 1913- 9
Grollman, Earl A. 1925- 22
Groom, Arthur William 1898-1964 10
Grooms, Duffy 1964- 169
Gross, Alan 1947- 54
Brief entry 43
Gross, Ernie 1913- 67
Gross, Philip 1952- 164
Earlier sketch in SATA 84
Gross, Philip John
See Gross, Philip
Gross, Ruth Belov 1929- 33
Gross, Sarah Chokla 1906-1976 9
Obituary 26
Grosser, Morton 1931- 74
Grosser, Vicky 1958- 83
Grossman, Bill 1948- 126
Earlier sketch in SATA 72

Grossman, Nancy 1940- 29
Grossman, Patricia 1951- 73
Grossman, Robert 1940- 11
Grossmann-Hensel, Katharina 1973- 219
Grote, JoAnn A. 1951- 113
Groten, Dallas 1951- 64
Groth, John (August) 1908-1988 21
    Obituary 56
Groth-Fleming, Candace
    See Fleming, Candace
Grove, Vicki 1948- 151
    Autobiography Feature 151
    Earlier sketch in SATA 122
Grover, Lorie Ann 1964- 168
Grover, Wayne 1934- 69
Groves, Georgina
    See Symons, (Dorothy) Geraldine
Groves, Maketa 1950- 107
Groves, Seli 77
Grubb, Lisa 160
Gruber, Michael 1940- 173
Gruber, Terry (deRoy) 1953- 66
Gruelle, John 1880-1938 35
    Brief entry 32
    See also CLR 34
Gruelle, Johnny
    See Gruelle, John
Gruenberg, Sidonie Matsner 1881-1974 2
    Obituary 27
Gruhzit-Hoyt, Olga (Margaret) 1922- 127
    Earlier sketch in SATA 16
Grummer, Arnold E(dward) 1923- 49
Gruner, Jessica 233
Grunewalt, Pine
    See Kunhardt, Edith
Grunwell, Jeanne Marie 1971- 147
Grupper, Jonathan 137
Gryski, Camilla 1948- 72
Guarino, Dagmar
    See Guarino, Deborah
Guarino, Deborah 1954- 68
Guarnaccia, Steven 233
Guay, Georgette (Marie Jeanne) 1952- 54
Guay, Rebecca 209
Guay-Mitchell, Rebecca
    See Guay, Rebecca
Guback, Georgia 88
Guccione, Leslie Davis 1946- 111
    Earlier sketch in SATA 72
Guck, Dorothy 1913-2002 27
Gudeon, Karla 212
Guerny, Gene
    See Gurney, Gene
Guest, Elissa Haden 1953- 218
    Earlier sketch in SATA 125
Guest, Jacqueline 1952- 135
Guevara, Susan 167
    Earlier sketch in SATA 97
Gugler, Laurel Dee 95
Gugliotta, Bobette 1918-1994 7
Guianan, Eve 1965- 102
Guiberson, Brenda Z. 1946- 211
    Earlier sketches in SATA 71, 124
Guibert, Emmanuel 1964- 181
Guile, Melanie 1949- 152
    Earlier sketch in SATA 104
Guillaume, Jeanette G. Flierl 1899-1990 8
Guillot, Rene 1900-1969 7
    See also CLR 22
Guisewite, Cathy 1950- 57
Guisewite, Cathy Lee
    See Guisewite, Cathy
Gulbis, Stephen 1959- 142
Gulley, Judie 1942- 58
Gump, P. Q.
    See Card, Orson Scott
Gundrey, Elizabeth 1924- 23
Gunn, James E. 1923- 35
Gunn, James Edwin
    See Gunn, James E.
Gunn, Robin Jones 1955- 84

Gunnella 1956- 197
Gunning, Monica Olwen 1930- 161
Gunston, Bill
    See Gunston, William Tudor
Gunston, William Tudor 1927- 9
Gunterman, Bertha Lisette 1886(?)-1975
    Obituary 27
Gunther, John 1901-1970
Guravich, Dan 1918- 74
Gurko, Leo 1914- 9
Gurko, Miriam 1910(?)-1988 9
    Obituary 58
Gurney, Gene 1924- 65
Gurney, James 1958- 120
    Earlier sketch in SATA 76
Gurney, John Steven 1962- 227
    Earlier sketches in SATA 75, 143
Gustafson, Sarah R.
    See Riedman, Sarah R(egal)
Gustafson, Scott 1956- 34
Gustavson, Adam 1974- 214
    Earlier sketch in SATA 176
Guthrie, A(lfred) B(ertram), Jr. 1901-1991 .. 62
    Obituary 67
Guthrie, Anne 1890-1979 28
Guthrie, Donna W. 1946- 105
    Earlier sketch in SATA 63
Gutierrez, Akemi 172
Gutierrez, Rudy 203
Gutman, Bill 128
    Brief entry 43
    Earlier sketch in SATA 67
Gutman, Dan 1955- 221
    Earlier sketches in SATA 77, 139, 188
Gutman, Naham 1899(?)-1981
    Obituary 25
Gutmann, Bessie Pease 1876-1960 73
Guy, Geoffrey 1942- 153
Guy, Ginger Foglesong 1954- 171
Guy, Rosa 1925- 122
    Earlier sketch in SATA 14, 62
    See also CLR 137
Guy, Rosa Cuthbert
    See Guy, Rosa
Guy, Susan 1948- 149
Guymer, (Wilhelmina) Mary 1909- 50
Guzman, Lila 1952- 168
Guzman, Rick 1957- 168
Gwaltney, Doris 1932- 181
Gwynne, Fred(erick Hubbard) 1926-1993 41
    Brief entry 27
    Obituary 75
Gwynne, Oscar A.
    See Ellis, Edward S.
Gwynne, Oswald A.
    See Ellis, Edward S.
Gyorkos, Charmaine Echeverria
    See Echeverria Gyorkos, Charmaine

H

Haab, Sherri 1964- 169
    Earlier sketch in SATA 91
Haar, Jaap ter
    See ter Haar, Jaap
Haarsma, P.J. 183
Haas, Carolyn Buhai 1926- 43
Haas, Dan 1957- 105
Haas, Dorothy F. 46
    Brief entry 43
    See also SAAS 17
Haas, Irene 1929- 96
    Earlier sketch in SATA 17
Haas, James E. 1943- 40
Haas, James Edward
    See Haas, James E.
Haas, Jessie 1959- 215

Haas, (Katherine) Jessie 1959- 135
    Autobiography Feature 135
    Earlier sketch in SATA 98
Haas, Merle S. 1896(?)-1985
    Obituary 41
Habenstreit, Barbara 1937- 5
Haber, Karen 1955- 78
Haber, Louis 1910-1988 12
Hacker, Randi 1951- 185
Hacker, Randi Dawn
    See Hacker, Randi
Hackett, John Winthrop 1910-1997 65
Hacks, Peter 1928-2003
    Obituary 151
Haddix, Margaret Peterson 1964- 224
    Earlier sketches in SATA 94, 125, 187
Haddon, Mark 1962- 223
    Earlier sketch in SATA 155
Hader, Berta (Hoerner) 1891(?)-1976 16
Hader, Elmer (Stanley) 1889-1973 16
Hadithi, Mwenye
    See Hobson, Bruce
Hadley, Franklin
    See Winterbotham, R(ussell) R(obert)
Hadley, Lee 1934-1995 89
    Brief entry 38
    Obituary 86
    Earlier sketch in SATA 47
    See also CLR 40
    See also SAAS 14
Haeffele, Deborah 1954- 76
Haenel, Wolfram 1956- 89
    See also CLR 64
Hafner, Marylin 1925- 179
    Earlier sketches in SATA 7, 121
Haft, Erin
    See Ehrenhaft, Daniel
Hager, Alan 1940- 176
Hager, Alice Rogers 1894-1969
    Obituary 26
Hager, Betty 1923- 89
Hager, Jenna Bush
    See Bush, Jenna
Hager, Sarah 171
Hager, Thomas 1953- 119
Hager, Tom
    See Hager, Thomas
Hagerup, Klaus 1946- 186
Haggard, H(enry) Rider 1856-1925 16
Haggerty, James J(oseph) 1920- 5
Hagon, Priscilla
    See Allan, Mabel Esther
Hague, Kathleen 1949- 49
    Brief entry 45
Hague, Michael 1948- 185
    Brief entry 32
    Earlier sketches in SATA 48, 80, 129
Hague, Michael R.
    See Hague, Michael
Hague, Susan Kathleen
    See Hague, Kathleen
Hahn, Emily 1905-1997 3
    Obituary 96
Hahn, Hannelore 8
Hahn, James (Sage) 1947- 9
Hahn, Lynn 1949- 9
Hahn, Mary Downing 1937- 208
    Autobiography Feature 157
    Brief entry 44
    Earlier sketches in SATA 50, 81, 138, 157
    See also SAAS 12
Hahn, Michael T. 1953- 92
Hahn, Mona Lynn
    See Hahn, Lynn
Haig, Matt 1975- 221
Haig-Brown, Roderick (Langmere)
    1908-1976 12
    See also CLR 31
Haight, Anne Lyon 1895-1977
    Obituary 30

Haight, Rip
See Carpenter, John
Haight, Sandy 1949- 79
Haij, Vera
See Jansson, Tove (Marika)
Hailstone, Ruth 219
Haines, Gail Kay 1943- 11
Haines, Margaret Ann Beck
See Beck, Peggy
Haining, Peter 1940-2007 14
Obituary 188
Haining, Peter Alexander
See Haining, Peter
Hains, Harriet
See Watson, Carol
Hajdusiewicz, Babs Bell 163
Hakim, Joy 1931- 173
Earlier sketch in SATA 83
Halacy, D. S., Jr. 1919-2002 36
See also SAAS 8
Halacy, Dan
See Halacy, D. S., Jr.
Halam, Ann
See Jones, Gwyneth A.
Haldane, Roger John 1945- 13
Hale, Arlene 1924-1982 49
Hale, Bruce 1957- 203
Earlier sketch in SATA 123
Hale, Christy
See Apostolou, Christine Hale
Hale, Dean 1972- 227
Hale, Edward Everett 1822-1909 16
Hale, Glenn
See Walker, Robert W.
Hale, Helen
See Mulcahy, Lucille Burnett
Hale, Irina 1932- 26
Hale, Kathleen 1898-2000 66
Obituary 121
Earlier sketch in SATA 17
Hale, Linda (Howe) 1929- 6
Hale, Lucretia P.
See Hale, Lucretia Peabody
Hale, Lucretia Peabody 1820-1900 26
See also CLR 105
Hale, Marian 194
Hale, Nancy 1908-1988 31
Obituary 57
Hale, Nathan 1976- 210
Hale, Shannon 200
Earlier sketch in SATA 158
Hale, Stephanie 1973- 232
Haley, Amanda 205
Haley, Gail E(inhart) 1939- 161
Autobiography Feature 161
Brief entry 28
Earlier sketches in SATA 43, 78, 136
See also CLR 21
See also SAAS 13
Haley, Neale 52
Halfmann, Janet 1944- 208
Hall, Adam
See Trevor, Elleston
Hall, Adele 1910- 7
Hall, Anna Gertrude 1882-1967 8
Hall, August 207
Hall, Barbara 1961- 68
Hall, Becky 1950- 186
Hall, Beverly B. 1918- 95
Hall, Borden
See Yates, Raymond F(rancis)
Hall, Brian P(atrick) 1935- 31
Hall, Cameron
See del Rey, Lester
Hall, Caryl
See Hansen, Caryl (Hall)
Hall, Donald 1928- 97
Earlier sketch in SATA 23
Hall, Donald Andrew, Jr.
See Hall, Donald
Hall, Douglas 1931- 43

Hall, Elizabeth 1929- 77
Hall, Elvajean 1910-1984 6
Hall, Francie 1940- 166
Hall, James Norman 1887-1951 21
Hall, Jesse
See Boesen, Victor
Hall, Katy
See McMullan, Kate
Hall, Kirsten Marie 1974- 67
Hall, Lynn 1937- 79
Earlier sketches in SATA 2, 47
See also SAAS 4
Hall, Malcolm 1945- 7
Hall, Marcellus 203
Hall, Marjory
See Yeakley, Marjory Hall
Hall, Melanie 1949- 228
Earlier sketches in SATA 78, 116, 169
Hall, Michael 1954- 228
Hall, Patricia 1940- 136
Hall, Rosalys Haskell 1914- 7
Hall, Teri 229
Hall, Willis 1929-2005 66
Hallard, Peter
See Catherall, Arthur
Hallas, Richard
See Knight, Eric
Hall-Clarke, James
See Rowland-Entwistle, (Arthur) Theodore
(Henry)
Hallensleben, Georg 1958- 173
Haller, Dorcas Woodbury 1946- 46
Hallett, Mark 1947- 220
Earlier sketch in SATA 83
Halliburton, Richard 1900-1939(?) 81
Halliburton, Warren J. 1924- 19
Halliday, Brett
See Dresser, Davis
and Johnson, (Walter) Ryerson
and Terrall, Robert
Halliday, William R(oss) 1926- 52
Hallin, Emily Watson 1916-1995 6
Hallinan, P. K. 1944- 39
Brief entry 37
Hallinan, Patrick Kenneth
See Hallinan, P. K.
Hallman, Ruth 1929- 43
Brief entry 28
Hallowell, Tommy
See Hill, Thomas
Hall-Quest, (Edna) Olga W(ilbourne)
1899-1986 11
Obituary 47
Halls, Kelly Milner 1957- 220
Earlier sketch in SATA 131
Hallstead, William F(inn III) 1924- 11
Hallward, Michael 1889-1982 12
Halperin, Michael 156
Halperin, Wendy Anderson 1952- 200
Earlier sketches in SATA 80, 125
Halpern, Julie 1975- 198
Halpin, Brendan 1968- 193
Halpin, Marlene 1927- 88
Halse, Laurie Beth
See Anderson, Laurie Halse
Halsell, Grace (Eleanor) 1923-2000 13
Halsey, Megan 185
Halsted, Anna Roosevelt 1906-1975
Obituary 30
Halter, Jon C(harles) 1941- 22
Halverson, Deborah 202
Halvorson, Adeline 218
Halvorson, Marilyn 1948- 123
Hamalian, Leo 1920- 41
Hamberger, John 1934- 14
Hamblin, Dora Jane 1920- 36
Hambly, Barbara 1951- 108
Hambly, Barbara Joan
See Hambly, Barbara
Hamer, Martyn
See Eldin, Peter

Hamerstrom, Frances 1907-1998 24
Hamil, Thomas Arthur 1928- 14
Hamill, Ethel
See Webb, Jean Francis (III)
Hamilton, (John) Alan 1943- 66
Hamilton, Alice
See Cromie, Alice Hamilton
Hamilton, Anita 1919- 92
Hamilton, Barbara
See Hambly, Barbara
Hamilton, Buzz
See Hemming, Roy G.
Hamilton, Carol (Jean Barber) 1935- 94
Hamilton, Charles (Harold St. John)
1876-1961 13
Hamilton, Charles 1913-1996 65
Obituary 93
Hamilton, Clive
See Lewis, C. S.
Hamilton, Dorothy (Drumm) 1906-1983 12
Obituary 35
Hamilton, Edith 1867-1963 20
Hamilton, Edmond 1904-1977 118
Hamilton, (Muriel) Elizabeth (Mollie)
1906- 23
Hamilton, Emma Walton 1962- 177
Hamilton, Franklin
See Silverberg, Robert
Hamilton, Gail
See Corcoran, Barbara (Asenath)
and Dodge, Mary Abigail
Hamilton, Kersten 1958- 204
Earlier sketch in SATA 134
Hamilton, K.R.
See Hamilton, Kersten
Hamilton, Martha 1953- 183
Earlier sketch in SATA 123
Hamilton, Mary (E.) 1927- 55
Hamilton, Meredith 233
Hamilton, Mollie
See Kaye, M.M.
Hamilton, Morse 1943-1998 101
Earlier sketch in SATA 35
Hamilton, Peter F. 1960- 109
Hamilton, Priscilla
See Gellis, Roberta
Hamilton, Ralph
See Stratemeyer, Edward L.
Hamilton, Virginia 1936-2002 123
Obituary 132
Earlier sketches in SATA 4, 56, 79
See also CLR 127
Hamilton, Virginia Esther
See Hamilton, Virginia
Hamilton-Paterson, James 1941- 82
Hamlet, Ova
See Lupoff, Richard A(llen)
Hamley, D. C.
See Hamley, Dennis
Hamley, Dennis 1935- 69
Earlier sketch in SATA 39
See also CLR 47
See also SAAS 22
Hamley, Dennis C.
See Hamley, Dennis
Hamlin, Peter J. 1970- 84
Hamm, Diane Johnston 1949- 78
Hammer, Charles 1934- 58
Hammer, Richard 1928- 6
Hammerman, Gay M(orenus) 1926- 9
Hammill, Matt 1982- 206
Hammond, Andrew 1970- 181
Hammond, Ralph
See Hammond Innes, Ralph
Hammond, Winifred G(raham) 1899-1992 ... 29
Obituary 107
Hammond Innes, Ralph 1913-1998 116
Hammontree, Marie (Gertrude) 1913- 13
Hample, Zack 1977- 161
Hampshire, Joyce Gregorian
See Gregorian, Joyce Ballou

Hampshire, Susan 1942- 98
Hampson, (Richard) Denman 1929- 15
Hampson, Frank 1918(?)-1985
    Obituary 46
Hampton, Wilborn 1940- 196
    Earlier sketch in SATA 156
Hamre, Leif 1914- 5
Hamsa, Bobbie 1944- 52
    Brief entry 38
Han, Jenny 1981- 175
Han, Lu
    See Stickler, Soma Han
Han, Soma
    See Stickler, Soma Han
Han, Suzanne Crowder 1953- 89
Hancock, Mary A. 1923- 31
Hancock, Sibyl 1940- 9
Hand, Elizabeth 1957- 167
    Earlier sketch in SATA 118
Handford, Martin (John) 1956- 64
    See also CLR 22
Handforth, Thomas (Schofield) 1897-1948 .. 42
Handleman, Philip 1951- 222
Handler, Daniel
    See Snicket, Lemony
Handville, Robert (Tompkins) 1924- 45
Hane, Roger 1940-1974
    Obituary 20
Hanel, Wolfram
    See Haenel, Wolfram
Haney, Lynn 1941- 23
Hanff, Helene 1916-1997 97
    Earlier sketch in SATA 11
Hanft, Josh 1956- 197
Hanft, Joshua E.
    See Hanft, Josh
Hanley, Boniface Francis 1924- 65
Hanlon, Emily 1945- 15
Hann, Jacquie 1951- 19
Hann, Judith 1942- 77
Hanna, Bill
    See Hanna, William (Denby)
Hanna, Cheryl 1951- 84
Hanna, Dan 200
Hanna, Jack (Bushnell) 1947- 74
Hanna, Nell(ie L.) 1908- 55
Hanna, Paul R(obert) 1902-1988 9
Hanna, William (Denby) 1910-2001 51
    Obituary 126
Hannam, Charles 1925- 50
Hannan, Peter 1954- 187
Hannigan, Katherine 170
Hannon, Ezra
    See Hunter, Evan
Hann-Syme, Marguerite 127
Hano, Arnold 1922- 12
Hano, Renee Roth
    See Roth-Hano, Renee
Hanover, Terri
    See Huff, Tanya
Hansen, Amy S. 229
Hansen, Ann Larkin 1958- 96
Hansen, Brooks 1965- 104
Hansen, Caryl (Hall) 1929- 39
Hansen, Ian V. 1929- 113
Hansen, Jennifer 1972- 156
Hansen, Joyce 1942- 172
    Autobiography Feature 172
    Brief entry 39
    Earlier sketches in SATA 46, 101
    See also CLR 21
    See also SAAS 15
Hansen, Joyce Viola
    See Hansen, Joyce
Hansen, Mark Victor 112
Hansen, Ron 1947- 56
Hansen, Ronald Thomas
    See Hansen, Ron
Hansen, Thore 1942- 224
Hanser, Richard (Frederick) 1909-1981 13
Hanson, Joan 1938- 8

Hanson, Joseph E. 1894(?)-1971
    Obituary 27
Hanson, Mary Elizabeth 188
Hanson, Warren 1949- 155
Hansson, Gunilla 1939- 64
Hantman, Clea 200
Hapka, C.A.
    See Hapka, Catherine
Hapka, Catherine 223
Hapka, Cathy
    See Hapka, Catherine
Harald, Eric
    See Boesen, Victor
Harazin, S. A. 210
Harbour, Elizabeth 1968- 221
Harcourt, Ellen Knowles 1890(?)-1984
    Obituary 36
Hard, Charlotte (Ann) 1969- 98
Hardcastle, Michael 1933- 216
    Brief entry 38
    Earlier sketch in SATA 47
Harding, Lee 1937- 32
    Brief entry 31
Hardinge, Frances 1973- 210
Hardt, Helga Fleischhauer
    See Fleischhauer-Hardt, Helga
Hardwick, Richard Holmes, Jr. 1923- 12
Hardy, Alice Dale 67
    Earlier sketch in SATA 1
Hardy, David A(ndrews) 1936- 9
Hardy, Janice 222
Hardy, Jon 1958- 53
Hardy, LeAnne 1951- 154
Hardy, Stuart
    See Schisgall, Oscar
Hare, Norma Q(uarles) 1924- 46
    Brief entry 41
Harel, Nira 1936- 154
Harford, Henry
    See Hudson, W(illiam) H(enry)
Hargis, Wes 219
Hargrave, Leonie
    See Disch, Thomas M.
Hargreaves, (Charles) Roger 1935-1988
    Obituary 56
Hargrove, James 1947- 57
    Brief entry 50
Hargrove, Jim
    See Hargrove, James
Harik, Elsa
    See Marston, Elsa
Harik, Elsa M.
    See Marston, Elsa
Harik, Elsa Marston
    See Marston, Elsa
Hariton, Anca I. 1955- 79
Hark, Mildred
    See McQueen, Mildred Hark
Harkaway, Hal
    See Stratemeyer, Edward L.
Harkins, Philip 1912-1997 6
    Obituary 129
Harlan, Elizabeth 1945- 41
    Brief entry 35
Harlan, Glen
    See Cebulash, Mel
Harlan, Judith 1949- 135
    Earlier sketch in SATA 74
    See also CLR 81
Harland, Richard 1947- 152
Harlee, J. V.
    See Leese, Jennifer L.B.
Harler, Ann
    See Van Steenwyk, Elizabeth (Ann)
Harley, Avis 183
Harley, Bill 1954- 208
    Earlier sketch in SATA 87
Harlow, Joan Hiatt 1932- 226
    Earlier sketch in SATA 157
Harman, Fred 1902(?)-1982
    Obituary 30

Harman, Hugh 1903-1982
    Obituary 33
Harmelink, Barbara (Mary) 9
Harmer, Mabel 1894-1992 45
Harmon, Dan
    See Harmon, Daniel E(lton)
Harmon, Daniel E(lton) 1949- 157
Harmon, Kate
    See Gibson, Marley
Harmon, Margaret 1906- 20
Harmon, Michael 1969- 189
Harmon, Michael B.
    See Harmon, Michael
Harmon, William (Ruth) 1938- 65
Harnan, Terry 1920- 12
Harness, Cheryl 1951- 178
    Earlier sketch in SATA 131
Harnett, Cynthia (Mary) 1893-1981 5
    Obituary 32
Harper, Anita 1943- 41
Harper, Betty 1946- 126
Harper, Charise
    See Harper, Charise Mericle
Harper, Charise Mericle 226
    Earlier sketch in SATA 179
Harper, Elaine
    See Hallin, Emily Watson
Harper, Ellen
    See Noble, Marty
Harper, Jamie 174
Harper, Jessica 1949- 148
Harper, Jo 1932- 169
    Earlier sketch in SATA 97
Harper, Lee 201
Harper, Mary Wood
    See Dixon, Jeanne
Harper, Piers 1966- 161
    Earlier sketch in SATA 105
Harper, Suzanne 194
Harper, Wilhelmina 1884-1973 4
    Obituary 26
Harrah, Madge 1931- 154
Harrah, Michael 1940- 41
Harrah, Monique
    See Harrah, Madge
Harrar, George E. 1949- 124
Harrell, Beatrice Orcutt 1943- 93
Harrell, Janice 1945- 70
Harrell, Sara Gordon 1940- 26
Harrell, Sara Jeanne Gordon
    See Harrell, Sara Gordon
Harries, Joan 1922- 39
Harrill, Ronald 1950- 90
Harrington, Denis J(ames) 1932- 88
Harrington, Evelyn Davis 1911- 5
Harrington, Janice N. 1956- 187
Harrington, Lyn
    See Harrington, Evelyn Davis
Harris, Alan 1944- 71
Harris, Aurand 1915-1996 37
    Obituary 91
Harris, Bob
    See Harris, Robert J.
Harris, Carol Flynn 1933- 135
Harris, Catherine
    See Ainsworth, Catherine Harris
Harris, Christie
    See Harris, Christie (Lucy) Irwin
Harris, Christie (Lucy) Irwin 1907-2002 74
    Autobiography Feature 116
    Earlier sketch in SATA 6
    See also CLR 47
    See also SAAS 10
Harris, Christine 1955- 105
Harris, Colver
    See Colver, Anne
Harris, David 1942- 118
Harris, David William
    See Harris, David
Harris, Dorothy Joan 1931- 153
    Earlier sketch in SATA 13

Harris, Geraldine 1951- 54
Harris, Geraldine Rachel
  See Harris, Geraldine
Harris, Jacqueline L. 1929- 62
Harris, Janet 1932-1979 4
  Obituary 23
Harris, Jesse
  See Standiford, Natalie
Harris, Joan 1946- 146
Harris, Joe 1928- 201
Harris, Joel Chandler 1848-1908 100
  See also YABC *1*
  See also CLR *128*
Harris, John (Wyndham Parkes Lucas) Beynon
  1903-1969 118
Harris, Johnson
  See Harris, John (Wyndham Parkes Lucas)
  Beynon
Harris, Jonathan 1921-1997 52
Harris, Larry Vincent 1939- 59
Harris, Lavinia
  See St. John, Nicole
Harris, Leon A., Jr. 1926-2000 4
Harris, Lois V. 199
Harris, Lorle K(empe) 1912-2001 22
Harris, Maria Guadalupe
  See Harris, M.G.
Harris, Marilyn
  See Springer, Marilyn Harris
Harris, Mark Jonathan 1941- 84
  Earlier sketch in SATA *32*
Harris, Mary K(athleen) 1905-1966 119
Harris, M.G. 231
Harris, Robert J. 1955- 195
Harris, Robie H. 1940- 203
  Brief entry 53
  Earlier sketches in SATA *90, 147*
Harris, Robin
  See Shine, Deborah
Harris, Rosemary (Jeanne) 82
  Earlier sketch in SATA *4*
  See also CLR *30*
  See also SAAS *7*
Harris, Ruth Elwin 1935- 164
Harris, Sherwood 1932-2009 25
Harris, Stephen 1959- 230
Harris, Steven Michael 1957- 55
Harris, Trudy 1949- 191
  Earlier sketch in SATA *128*
Harris-Filderman, Diane
  See Filderman, Diane E(lizabeth)
Harrison, C(hester) William 1913-1994 35
Harrison, Carol
  See Harrison, Carol Thompson
Harrison, Carol Thompson 113
Harrison, David L. 1937- 186
  Earlier sketches in SATA *26, 92, 150*
Harrison, Deloris 1938- 9
Harrison, Edward Hardy 1926- 56
Harrison, Elizabeth (Allen) Cavanna
  1909-2001 30
  Earlier sketch in SATA *1*
  See also SAAS *4*
Harrison, Harry 1925- 4
Harrison, Harry Max
  See Harrison, Harry
Harrison, Mette Ivie 1970- 202
  Earlier sketch in SATA *149*
Harrison, Michael 1939- 106
Harrison, Michelle 1979- 233
Harrison, Molly (Hodgett) 1909-2002 41
Harrison, Sarah 1946- 63
Harrison, Ted
  See Harrison, Edward Hardy
Harsh, Fred (T.) 1925- 72
Harshaw, Ruth H(etzel) 1890-1968 27
Harshman, Marc 1950- 109
  Earlier sketch in SATA *71*
Hart, Alexandra 1939- 14
Hart, Alison
  See Leonhardt, Alice

Hart, Bruce 1938-2006 57
  Brief entry 39
Hart, Carole 1943- 57
  Brief entry 39
Hart, Carolyn 1936- 74
Hart, Carolyn G.
  See Hart, Carolyn
Hart, Carolyn Gimpel
  See Hart, Carolyn
Hart, Jan Siegel 1940- 79
Hart, Joyce 1954- 148
Hart, Karen 185
Hart, Lenore 171
Hart, Philip S. 1944- 180
Hart, Virginia 1949- 83
Harte, Bret 1836(?)-1902 26
Harte, Francis Brett
  See Harte, Bret
Harter, Debbie 1963- 107
Hartfield, Claire 1957- 147
Hartinger, Brent 1964- 217
  Earlier sketches in SATA *145, 174*
Hartland, Jessie 171
Hartley, Ellen (Raphael) 1915-1980 23
Hartley, Fred Allan III 1953- 41
Hartley, William B(rown) 1913-1980 23
Hartling, Peter
  See Hartling, Peter
Hartling, Peter 1933- 66
  See also CLR *29*
Hartman, Bob 1955- 224
Hartman, Carrie 226
Hartman, Cassie 202
Hartman, Dan 1955- 202
Hartman, Evert 1937- 38
  Brief entry 35
Hartman, Jane E. 1928- 47
Hartman, Jane Evangeline
  See Hartman, Jane E.
Hartman, Louis F(rancis) 1901-1970 22
Hartman, Rachel 174
Hartman, Victoria 1942- 91
Hartnett, Sonya 1968- 176
  Earlier sketches in SATA *93, 130*
Hartry, Nancy 219
Hartshorn, Ruth M. 1928- 11
Hartung, Susan Kathleen 192
  Earlier sketch in SATA *150*
Hartwig, Manfred 1950- 81
Harvey, Alyxandra 1974- 227
  Earlier sketch in SATA *189*
Harvey, Brett 1936- 61
Harvey, Edith 1908(?)-1972
  Obituary 27
Harvey, Gill 189
Harvey, Karen D. 1935- 88
Harvey, Roland 1945- 219
  Earlier sketches in SATA *71, 123, 179*
Harvey-Fitzhenry, Alyxandra
  See Harvey, Alyxandra
Harwick, B. L.
  See Keller, Beverly L(ou)
Harwin, Brian
  See Henderson, LeGrand
Harwood, Pearl Augusta (Bragdon)
  1903-1998 9
Haseley, Dennis 1950- 221
  Brief entry 44
  Earlier sketches in SATA *57, 105, 157*
Hashmi, Kerri 1955- 108
Haskell, Arnold L(ionel) 1903-1981(?) 6
Haskins, James
  See Haskins, James S.
Haskins, James S. 1941-2005 132
  Autobiography Feature 132
  Earlier sketches in SATA *9, 69, 105*
  See also CLR *39*
  See also SAAS *4*
Haskins, Jim
  See Haskins, James S.
Hasler, Eveline 1933- 181

Hasler, Joan 1931- 28
Hasnat, Naheed
  See Senzai, N.H.
Hass, Robert 1941- 94
Hassall, Joan 1906-1988 43
  Obituary 56
Hassett, Ann 1958- 162
Hassett, John 162
Hassler, Jon 1933-2008 19
  Obituary 191
Hassler, Jon Francis
  See Hassler, Jon
Hastings, Beverly
  See Barkin, Carol
  and James, Elizabeth
Hastings, Graham
  See Jeffries, Roderic
Hastings, Ian 1912- 62
Hastings, Victor
  See Disch, Thomas M.
Haszard, Patricia Moyes 1923-2000 63
Hatch, Lynda S. 1950- 90
Hathaway, Barbara 164
Hathorn, Elizabeth
  See Hathorn, Libby
Hathorn, Elizabeth Helen
  See Hathorn, Libby
Hathorn, Libby 1943- 232
  Autobiography Feature 232
  Earlier sketches in SATA *74, 120, 156*
Hatkoff, Craig 1954- 192
Hatlo, Jimmy 1898-1963
  Obituary 23
Hatton, Caroline 1957- 205
Hauff, Wilhelm 1802-1827
  See CLR *155*
Haugaard, Erik Christian 1923- 68
  Earlier sketch in SATA *4*
  See also CLR *11*
  See also SAAS *12*
Haugaard, Kay 117
Haugen, Hayley Mitchell 1968- 172
Haugen, Tormod 1945- 66
Hauman, Doris 1898-1984 32
Hauman, George 1890-1961 32
Hauptly, Denis J. 1945- 57
Hauptly, Denis James
  See Hauptly, Denis J.
Hauser, Jill Frankel 1950- 127
Hauser, Margaret L(ouise) 1909- 10
Hausherr, Rosmarie 1943- 86
Hausman, Gerald 1945- 180
  Earlier sketches in SATA *13, 90, 132*
  See also CLR *89*
Hausman, Gerry
  See Hausman, Gerald
Hauth, Katherine B. 1940- 99
Hautman, Pete 1952- 173
  Earlier sketches in SATA *82, 128*
Hautman, Peter Murray
  See Hautman, Pete
Hautzig, Deborah 1956- 106
  Earlier sketch in SATA *31*
Hautzig, Esther Rudomin 1930-2009 148
  Earlier sketches in SATA *4, 68*
  See also CLR *22*
  See also SAAS *15*
Havel, Geoff 1955- 152
Havel, Jennifer
  See Havill, Juanita
Havelin, Kate 1961- 143
Haven, Paul 1971(?)- 213
Haverfield, Mary 225
Havighurst, Walter (Edwin) 1901-1994 1
  Obituary 79
Haviland, Virginia 1911-1988 6
  Obituary 54
Havill, Juanita 1949- 224
  Earlier sketches in SATA *74, 155*
Hawes, Judy 1913- 4

Hawes, Louise 1943- *180*
  Earlier sketch in SATA *60*
Hawk, Fran *222*
Hawke, Rosanne 1953- *165*
  Earlier sketch in SATA *124*
Hawke, Rosanne Joy
  See Hawke, Rosanne
Hawkes, Kevin 1959- *201*
  Earlier sketches in SATA *78, 150*
Hawkes, Nigel 1943- *119*
Hawkesworth, Eric 1921- *13*
Hawking, Lucy 1969- *197*
Hawkins, Arthur 1903-1985 .... *19*
Hawkins, Colin 1945- *162*
  Earlier sketch in SATA *112*
Hawkins, Jacqui *162*
  Earlier sketch in SATA *112*
Hawkins, Jimmy 1941- *188*
Hawkins, Laura 1951- *74*
Hawkins, (Helena Ann) Quail 1905-2002 ...... *6*
  Obituary *141*
Hawkins, Rachel 1979- *228*
Hawkinson, John (Samuel) 1912-1994 ...... *4*
Hawkinson, Lucy (Ozone) 1924-1971 .... *21*
Hawks, Robert 1961- *85*
Hawley, Mabel C. *67*
  Earlier sketch in SATA *1*
Haworth, Danette *207*
Haworth-Attard, Barbara 1953- *215*
Hawthorne, Captain R. M.
  See Ellis, Edward S.
Hawthorne, Nathaniel 1804-1864
  See YABC 2
  See also CLR *163*
Hay, Jeff T. *154*
Hay, John 1915-2011 .... *13*
Hay, Samantha *213*
Hay, Timothy
  See Brown, Margaret Wise
Hayashi, Leslie Ann 1954- *115*
Hayashi, Nancy 1939- *186*
  Earlier sketch in SATA *80*
Haycak, Cara 1961- *180*
Haycock, Kate 1962- *77*
Haycraft, Howard 1905-1991 .... *6*
  Obituary *70*
Haycraft, Molly Costain 1911- *6*
Hayden, Gwendolen Lampshire 1904- *35*
Hayden, Robert
  See Hayden, Robert Earl
Hayden, Robert C(arter), Jr. 1937- *47*
  Brief entry *28*
Hayden, Robert E.
  See Hayden, Robert Earl
Hayden, Robert Earl 1913-1980 .... *19*
  Obituary *26*
Hayden, Torey L. 1951- *163*
  Earlier sketch in SATA *65*
Hayden, Torey Lynn
  See Hayden, Torey L.
Hayes, Carlton J(oseph) H(untley)
  1882-1964 .... *11*
Hayes, Daniel 1952- *109*
  Earlier sketch in SATA *73*
Hayes, Geoffrey 1947- *207*
  Earlier sketches in SATA *26, 91*
Hayes, Joe 1945- *131*
  Earlier sketch in SATA *88*
Hayes, John F. 1904-1980 .... *11*
Hayes, Karel 1949- *207*
Hayes, Rosemary *227*
  Earlier sketch in SATA *158*
Hayes, Sarah 1945- *208*
Hayes, Sheila 1937- *51*
  Brief entry *50*
Hayes, Will *7*
Hayes, William D(imitt) 1913-1976 .... *8*
Haynes, Betsy 1937- *94*
  Brief entry *37*
  Earlier sketch in SATA *48*
  See also CLR *90*

Haynes, David 1955- *97*
Haynes, Linda
  See Swinford, Betty (June Wells)
Haynes, Mary 1938- *65*
Haynes, Max 1956- *72*
Hays, Anna Jane *214*
Hays, H(offmann) R(eynolds) 1904-1980 .... *26*
Hays, Thomas A.
  See Hays, Tony
Hays, Thomas Anthony
  See Hays, Tony
Hays, Tony 1957- *84*
Hays, Wilma Pitchford 1909- *28*
  Earlier sketch in SATA *1*
  See also CLR *59*
  See also SAAS *3*
Hayter, Rhonda *233*
Hayward, Linda 1943- *185*
  Brief entry *39*
  Earlier sketch in SATA *101*
Haywood, Carolyn 1898-1990 .... *75*
  Obituary *64*
  Earlier sketches in SATA *1, 29*
  See also CLR *22*
Hazelaar, Cor *217*
Hazell, Rebecca (Eileen) 1947- *141*
Hazen, Barbara Shook 1930- *178*
  Earlier sketches in SATA *27, 90*
Hazen, Lynn E. *202*
Head, Gay
  See Hauser, Margaret L(ouise)
Head, Tom 1978- *167*
Headley, Elizabeth
  See Harrison, Elizabeth (Allen) Cavanna
Headley, Justina Chen 1968- *176*
Headstrom, (Birger) Richard 1902-1985 ...... *8*
Heady, Eleanor B(utler) 1917-1979 .... *8*
Heagy, William D. 1964- *76*
Heal, Edith 1903-1995 .... *7*
Heal, Gillian 1934- *89*
Heale, Jay (Jeremy Peter Wingfield) 1937- .. *84*
Healey, Brooks
  See Albert, Burton
Healey, Karen 1981- *230*
Healey, Larry 1927- *44*
  Brief entry *42*
Heap, Sue 1954- *187*
  Earlier sketch in SATA *150*
Heaps, Willard A(llison) 1908-1987 .... *26*
Hearn, Diane Dawson 1952- *209*
  Earlier sketch in SATA *79*
Hearn, Emily
  See Valleau, Emily
Hearn, Julie 1958- *212*
  Earlier sketch in SATA *152*
Hearn, Lian
  See Rubinstein, Gillian
Hearn, Sneed
  See Gregg, Andrew K.
Hearne, Betsy 1942- *146*
  Earlier sketches in SATA *38, 95*
Heath, Charles D(ickinson) 1941- *46*
Heath, Veronica
  See Blackett, Veronica Heath
Heaven, Constance (Christina) 1911- *7*
Hebert-Collins, Sheila 1948- *111*
Hecht, George J(oseph) 1895-1980
  Obituary *22*
Hecht, Henri Joseph 1922- *9*
Hechtkopf, Henryk 1910- *17*
Heck, Bessie (Mildred) Holland 1911-1995 . *26*
Heck, Ed 1963- *173*
Heckert, Connie K(aye Delp) 1948- *82*
Hector, Julian *205*
Hedderwick, Mairi 1939- *145*
  Earlier sketches in SATA *30, 77*
Hedges, Sid(ney) G(eorge) 1897-1974 ...... *28*
Hedrick, Irene Hope 1920- *175*
Heelan, Jamee Riggio 1965- *146*
Heerboth, Sharon
  See Leon, Sharon

Heffernan, John 1949- *168*
  Earlier sketch in SATA *121*
Heffron, Dorris 1944- *68*
Hefter, Richard 1942- *31*
Hegamin, Tonya C. 1975- *209*
Hegarty, Reginald Beaton 1906-1973 .... *10*
Hehenberger, Shelly 1968- *126*
Heidbreder, Robert 1947- *196*
  Earlier sketch in SATA *130*
Heidbreder, Robert K.
  See Heidbreder, Robert
Heide, Florence Parry 1919-2011 .... *192*
  Earlier sketches in SATA *32, 69, 118*
  See also CLR *60*
  See also SAAS *6*
Heiderstadt, Dorothy 1907-2001 .... *6*
Heidi Louise
  See Erdrich, Louise
Heidler, David S. 1955- *132*
Heidler, David Stephen
  See Heidler, David S.
Heidler, Jeanne T. 1956- *132*
Heilbroner, Joan Knapp 1922- *63*
Heilbrun, Lois Hussey 1922(?)-1987
  Obituary *54*
Heiligman, Deborah 1958- *193*
  Earlier sketches in SATA *90, 144*
Heilman, Joan Rattner *50*
Heimann, Rolf 1940- *164*
  Earlier sketch in SATA *120*
Heimberg, Justin *232*
Hein, Lucille Eleanor 1915-1994 .... *20*
Heine, Helme 1941- *135*
  Earlier sketch in SATA *67*
  See also CLR *18*
Heinlein, Robert A. 1907-1988 .... *69*
  Obituary *56*
  Earlier sketch in SATA *9*
  See also CLR *75*
Heinlein, Robert Anson
  See Heinlein, Robert A.
Heins, Ethel L(eah) 1918-1997 .... *101*
Heins, Paul 1909- *13*
Heintze, Carl 1922- *26*
Heinz, Bill
  See Heinz, W. C.
Heinz, Brian J. 1946- *181*
  Earlier sketch in SATA *95*
Heinz, Brian James
  See Heinz, Brian J.
Heinz, W. C. 1915-2008 .... *26*
Heinz, Wilfred Charles
  See Heinz, W. C.
Heinzen, Mildred
  See Masters, Mildred
Heisel, Sharon E(laine) 1941- *125*
  Earlier sketch in SATA *84*
Heitzmann, William Ray 1948- *73*
Heitzmann, Wm. Ray
  See Heitzmann, William Ray
Helakoski, Leslie *178*
Helberg, Shirley Adelaide Holden 1919- ... *138*
Heldring, Thatcher *229*
Helfer, Andrew *187*
Helfer, Ralph 1937- *177*
Helfman, Elizabeth S(eaver) 1911-2001 .... *3*
Helfman, Harry Carmozin 1910-1995 .... *3*
Helgerson, Joseph 1950- *181*
Hellard, Susan *232*
  Earlier sketch in SATA *182*
Hellberg, Hans-Eric 1927- *38*
Heller, Linda 1944- *46*
  Brief entry *40*
Heller, Mike
  See Hano, Arnold
Heller, Ruth M. 1924- *112*
  Earlier sketch in SATA *66*
Hellman, Hal
  See Hellman, Harold
Hellman, Harold 1927- *4*

Helman, Andrea (Jean) 1946- *160*
Earlier sketch in SATA *107*
Helmer, Diana Star 1962- *86*
Helmer, Marilyn *160*
Earlier sketch in SATA *112*
Helps, Racey 1913-1971 .... *2*
Obituary *25*
Helquist, Brett *229*
Earlier sketches in SATA *146, 187*
Helweg, Hans H. 1917- *50*
Brief entry *33*
Helyar, Jane Penelope Josephine 1933- *5*
Autobiography Feature *138*
See also SAAS *2*
Hemingway, Edith M. 1950- *223*
Hemingway, Edith Morris
See Hemingway, Edith M.
Hemingway, Edward 1969(?)- *212*
Hemingway, Ernest 1899-1961
See CLR *168*
Hemingway, Ernest Miller
See Hemingway, Ernest
Hemmant, Lynette 1938- *69*
Hemming, Roy G. 1928-1995 .... *11*
Obituary *86*
Hemphill, Helen 1955- *179*
Hemphill, Kris (Harrison) 1963- *118*
Hemphill, Martha Locke 1904-1973 .... *37*
Hemphill, Michael *220*
Hemphill, Stephanie *190*
Hemstock, Gillian 1956- *173*
Henba, Bobbie 1926- *87*
Henbest, Nigel 1951- *55*
Brief entry *52*
Henderley, Brooks *1*
Henderson, Aileen Kilgore 1921- *178*
Henderson, Aileen Mary
See Fox, Aileen
Henderson, Gordon 1950- *53*
Henderson, Kathy 1949- *155*
Brief entry *53*
Earlier sketches in SATA *55, 95*
Henderson, Lauren 1966- *201*
Henderson, LeGrand 1901-1965 .... *9*
Henderson, Nancy Wallace 1916- *22*
Henderson, Zenna (Chlarson) 1917-1983 .... *5*
Hendrickson, Walter Brookfield, Jr. 1936- *9*
Hendrix, John 1976- *208*
Hendry, Diana 1941- *213*
Earlier sketches in SATA *68, 106*
Hendry, Frances Mary 1941- *171*
Earlier sketch in SATA *110*
Hendry, Linda (Gail) 1961- *83*
Heneghan, James 1930- *160*
Earlier sketches in SATA *53, 97*
Henkes, Kevin 1960- *207*
Earlier sketches in SATA *43, 76, 108, 154*
See also CLR *108*
Henn, Astrid *214*
Hennessy, Barbara G.
See Hennessy, B.G.
Hennessy, Barbara Gulbrandsen
See Hennessy, B.G.
Hennessy, B.G. 1951- *175*
Hennesey, Carolyn 1962- *221*
Henney, Carolee Wells 1928- *102*
Henriod, Lorraine 1925- *26*
Henriquez, Emile F. 1937- *170*
Earlier sketch in SATA *89*
Henry, April 1959- *174*
Henry, Ernest 1948- *107*
Henry, Joanne Landers 1927- *6*
Henry, Maeve 1960- *75*
Henry, Marguerite 1902-1997 .... *100*
Obituary *99*
See also CLR *4*
See also SAAS *7*
Henry, Marie H. 1935- *65*
Henry, Marilyn 1939- *117*
Henry, Marion
See del Rey, Lester

Henry, O. 1862-1910
See YABC *2*
Henry, Oliver
See Henry, O.
Henry, Rohan *217*
Henry, T. E.
See Rowland-Entwistle, (Arthur) Theodore
(Henry)
Henschel, Elizabeth Georgie *56*
Henson, Heather *206*
Henson, James Maury
See Henson, Jim
Henson, Jim 1936-1990 .... *43*
Obituary *65*
Henstra, Friso 1928- *73*
Earlier sketch in SATA *8*
See also SAAS *14*
Hentoff, Nat(han Irving) 1925- *133*
Brief entry *27*
Earlier sketches in SATA *42, 69*
See also CLR *52*
Henty, G(eorge) A(lfred) 1832-1902 .... *64*
See also CLR *76*
Heo, Yumi 1964- *206*
Earlier sketches in SATA *94, 146*
Hepler, Heather *177*
Herald, Kathleen
See Peyton, Kathleen Wendy
Herb, Angela M. 1970- *92*
Herbert, Cecil
See Hamilton, Charles (Harold St. John)
Herbert, Don 1917-2007 .... *2*
Obituary *184*
Herbert, Donald Jeffrey
See Herbert, Don
Herbert, Frank 1920-1986 .... *37*
Obituary *47*
Earlier sketch in SATA *9*
Herbert, Frank Patrick
See Herbert, Frank
Herbert, Helen (Jean) 1947- *57*
Herbert, Janis 1956- *139*
Herbert, Wally 1934-2007 .... *23*
Herbert, Walter William
See Herbert, Wally
Herbst, Judith 1947- *74*
Herda, D.J. 1948- *80*
Herge
See Remi, Georges
Heritage, Martin
See Horler, Sydney
Herkimer, L(awrence) R(ussell) 1925(?)- *42*
Herlihy, Dirlie Anne 1935- *73*
Herlong, Madaline
See Herlong, M.H.
Herlong, M.H. *211*
Herman, Charlotte 1937- *203*
Earlier sketches in SATA *20, 99*
Hermanson, Dennis (Everett) 1947- *10*
Hermes, Jules 1962- *92*
Hermes, Patricia 1936- *233*
Earlier sketches in SATA *31, 78, 141, 191*
Hermes, Patricia Mary
See Hermes, Patricia
Hernandez, Natalie Nelson 1929- *123*
Herndon, Ernest *91*
Herold, Ann Bixby 1937- *72*
Herrera, Diego
See Yayo
Herrera, Juan Felipe 1948- *127*
Herrick, Steven 1958- *209*
Earlier sketches in SATA *103, 156*
Herriman, George (Joseph) 1880-1944 .... *140*
Herriot, James 1916-1995 .... *135*
Brief entry *44*
Earlier sketch in SATA *86*
See also CLR *80*
Herrmanns, Ralph 1933- *11*
Herrold, Tracey
See Dils, Tracey E.
Herron, Carolivia 1947- *203*

Herron, Edward A(lbert) 1912- *4*
Herschler, Mildred Barger *130*
Hersey, John 1914-1993 .... *25*
Obituary *76*
Hersey, John Richard
See Hersey, John
Hershberger, Priscilla (Gorman) 1951- *81*
Hershenhorn, Esther 1945- *151*
Hershey, Kathleen M. 1934- *80*
Hershey, Mary *173*
Hershey, Mary L.
See Hershey, Mary
Hersom, Kathleen 1911- *73*
Hertz, Grete Janus 1915- *23*
Herxheimer, Sophie 1963- *220*
Herzig, Alison Cragin 1935- *87*
Herzog, Brad 1968- *131*
Heslewood, Juliet 1951- *82*
Hess, Lilo 1916- *4*
Hess, Paul 1961- *134*
Hesse, Hermann 1877-1962 .... *50*
Hesse, Karen 1952- *215*
Autobiography Feature *113*
Earlier sketches in SATA *74, 103, 158*
See also CLR *141*
See also SAAS *25*
Hest, Amy 1950- *193*
Earlier sketches in SATA *55, 82, 129*
Heuer, Karsten 1968(?)- *202*
Heuer, Kenneth John 1927- *44*
Heuman, William 1912-1971 .... *21*
Heuston, Kimberley 1960- *167*
Heuston, Kimberley Burton
See Heuston, Kimberley
Heuvel, Eric 1960- *224*
Hewes, Agnes Danforth 1874-1963 .... *35*
Hewett, Anita 1918-1989 .... *13*
Hewett, Joan 1930- *140*
Earlier sketch in SATA *81*
Hewett, Richard 1929- *81*
Hewitson, Jennifer 1961- *97*
Hewitt, Margaret 1961- *84*
Hewitt, Sally 1949- *231*
Earlier sketch in SATA *127*
Hext, Harrington
See Phillpotts, Eden
Hey, Nigel 1936- *20*
Hey, Nigel Stewart
See Hey, Nigel
Heyduck-Huth, Hilde 1929- *8*
Heyer, Carol 1950- *130*
Earlier sketch in SATA *74*
Heyer, Marilee 1942- *102*
Earlier sketch in SATA *64*
Heyerdahl, Thor 1914-2002 .... *52*
Earlier sketch in SATA *2*
Heyes, (Nancy) Eileen 1956- *150*
Earlier sketch in SATA *80*
Heyliger, William 1884-1955
See YABC *1*
Heyman, Ken(neth Louis) 1930- *114*
Earlier sketch in SATA *34*
Heyward, (Edwin) DuBose 1885-1940 .... *21*
Heywood, Karen 1946- *48*
Hezlep, William (Earl) 1936- *88*
Hiaasen, Carl 1953- *208*
Hiatt, Shelby *226*
Hibbert, Arthur Raymond
See Hibbert, Christopher
Hibbert, Christopher 1924-2008 .... *4*
Obituary *201*
Hibbert, Eleanor Alice Burford 1906-1993 .... *2*
Obituary *74*
Hickman, Estella (Lee) 1942- *111*
Hickman, Janet 1940- *127*
Earlier sketch in SATA *12*
Hickman, Martha Whitmore 1925- *26*
Hickman, Pamela 1958- *186*
Earlier sketch in SATA *128*
Hickock, Will
See Harrison, C(hester) William

Hickok, Lorena A. 1893-1968 20
Hickox, Rebecca (Ayres) 116
Hicks, Barbara Jean 1953- 165
Hicks, Betty 191
Hicks, Clifford B. 1920- 50
Hicks, Eleanor B.
   See Coerr, Eleanor (Beatrice)
Hicks, Harvey
   See Stratemeyer, Edward L.
Hicks, Peter 1952- 111
Hicyilmaz, Gaye 1947- 157
   Earlier sketch in SATA 77
Hieatt, Constance B(artlett) 1928- 4
Hiebert, Ray Eldon 1932- 13
Hierstein, Judith 212
Hierstein, Judy
   See Hierstein, Judith
Higdon, Hal 1931- 4
Higginbottom, David 1923- 87
   Earlier sketch in SATA 25
Higginbottom, J(effrey) Winslow 1945- 29
Higgins, Dalton 223
Higgins, F.E. 219
Higgins, Fiona
   See Higgins, F.E.
Higgins, Joanna 1945- 125
Higgins, Simon (Richard) 1958- 105
Higginsen, Vy 79
High, Linda Oatman 1958- 188
   Autobiography Feature 188
   Earlier sketches in SATA 94, 145
High, Philip E. 1914- 119
High, Philip Empson
   See High, Philip E.
Higham, David 1949- 50
Higham, David Michael
   See Higham, David
Higham, Jon Atlas
   See Higham, Jonathan Huw
Higham, Jonathan Huw 1960- 59
Highet, Helen
   See MacInnes, Helen (Clark)
Hightman, Jason 1971(?)- 189
Hightman, J.P.
   See Hightman, Jason
Hightower, Florence Cole 1916-1981 4
   Obituary 27
Highwater, Jamake (Mamake)
   1942(?)-2001 69
   Brief entry 30
   Earlier sketch in SATA 32
   See also CLR 17
Hilb, Nora 1953- 178
Hildebrandt, Greg, Jr. 1970- 228
Hildebrandt, Greg 1939- 172
   Brief entry 33
   Earlier sketch in SATA 55
Hildebrandt, Tim 1939-2006 55
   Brief entry 33
Hildebrandt, Timothy
   See Hildebrandt, Tim
Hildebrandts, The
   See Hildebrandt, Greg
   and Hildebrandt, Tim
Hilder, Rowland 1905-1993 36
   Obituary 77
Hildick, E. W.
   See Hildick, Wallace
Hildick, Wallace 1925-2001 68
   Earlier sketch in SATA 2
   See also SAAS 6
Hilgartner, Beth 1957- 58
Hill, Alexis
   See Craig, Mary (Francis) Shura
   and Glick, Ruth
Hill, Anthony R. 1942- 164
   Earlier sketch in SATA 91
Hill, Anthony Robert
   See Hill, Anthony R.
Hill, David 1942- 152
   Earlier sketch in SATA 103

Hill, Donna (Marie) 1921- 124
   Earlier sketch in SATA 24
Hill, Douglas 1935-2007 78
   Earlier sketch in SATA 39
Hill, Douglas Arthur
   See Hill, Douglas
Hill, Elizabeth Starr 1925- 143
   Earlier sketch in SATA 24
Hill, Eric 1927- 133
   Brief entry 53
   Earlier sketch in SATA 66
   See also CLR 13
Hill, Gordon
   See Eldin, Peter
Hill, Grace Brooks 67
   Earlier sketch in SATA 1
Hill, Grace Livingston 1865-1947
   See YABC 2
Hill, Helen M(orey) 1915- 27
Hill, Isabel 225
Hill, Isabel T.
   See Hill, Isabel
Hill, John
   See Koontz, Dean
Hill, Johnson
   See Kunhardt, Edith
Hill, Judy I. R.
   See Roberts, Judy I.
Hill, Kathleen Louise 1917- 4
Hill, Kay
   See Hill, Kathleen Louise
Hill, Kirkpatrick 1938- 188
   Earlier sketches in SATA 72, 126
Hill, Laban
   See Hill, Laban Carrick
Hill, Laban Carrick 170
Hill, Lee Sullivan 1958- 96
Hill, Lorna 1902-1991 12
Hill, Margaret (Ohler) 1915- 36
Hill, Meg
   See Hill, Margaret (Ohler)
Hill, Meredith
   See Craig, Mary (Francis) Shura
Hill, Monica
   See Watson, Jane Werner
Hill, Pamela Smith 1954- 112
Hill, Ralph Nading 1917-1987 65
Hill, Robert W(hite) 1919-1982 12
   Obituary 31
Hill, Ruth A.
   See Viguers, Ruth Hill
Hill, Ruth Livingston
   See Munce, Ruth Hill
Hill, Stuart 1958- 186
Hill, Susan 1942- 183
Hill, Susan Elizabeth
   See Hill, Susan
Hill, Susanna Leonard 1965- 193
Hill, Thomas 1960- 82
Hillcourt, William 1900-1992 27
Hillenbrand, Will 1960- 210
   Earlier sketches in SATA 84, 147
Hiller, Ilo (Ann) 1938- 59
Hillerman, Anthony Grove
   See Hillerman, Tony
Hillerman, Tony 1925-2008 6
   Obituary 198
Hillert, Margaret 1920- 91
   Earlier sketch in SATA 8
Hilliard, Richard 183
Hillman, Ben 1957- 202
Hillman, Elizabeth 1942- 75
Hillman, John 1952- 120
Hillman, Martin
   See Hill, Douglas
Hillman, Priscilla 1940- 48
   Brief entry 39
Hillman, Shane 200
Hills, C.A.R. 1955- 39
Hills, Charles Albert Reis
   See Hills, C.A.R.

Hills, Tad 173
Hilton, Irene Pothus -1979 7
Hilton, James 1900-1954 34
Hilton, Margaret Lynette 1946- 105
   Earlier sketch in SATA 68
   See also CLR 25
   See also SAAS 21
Hilton, Nette
   See Hilton, Margaret Lynette
Hilton, Ralph 1907-1982 8
Hilton, Suzanne 1922- 4
Hilton-Bruce, Anne
   See Hilton, Margaret Lynette
Him, George 1937-1982
   Obituary 30
Himelblau, Linda -2005 179
Himelstein, Shmuel 1940- 83
Himler, Ann 1946- 8
Himler, Ronald 1937- 183
   Earlier sketches in SATA 6, 92, 137
Himler, Ronald Norbert
   See Himler, Ronald
Himmelman, John 1959- 221
   Earlier sketches in SATA 47, 94, 159
Himmelman, John C.
   See Himmelman, John
Hinckley, Helen
   See Jones, Helen Hinckley
Hind, Dolores (Ellen) 1931- 53
   Brief entry 49
Hindin, Nathan
   See Bloch, Robert (Albert)
Hindley, Judy 1940- 179
   Earlier sketch in SATA 120
Hinds, P. Mignon 98
Hinds, Patricia Mignon
   See Hinds, P. Mignon
Hine, Sesyle Joslin 1929- 2
Hines, Anna Grossnickle 1946- 209
   Brief entry 45
   Earlier sketches in SATA 51, 95, 141
   See also SAAS 16
Hines, Gary (Roger) 1944- 136
   Earlier sketch in SATA 74
Hinman, Bonnie 1950- 216
Hinojosa, Maria (de Lourdes) 1961- 88
Hinton, Nigel 1941- 166
Hinton, S. E. 1950- 160
   Earlier sketches in SATA 19, 58, 115
   See also CLR 23
Hinton, Sam 1917-2009 43
Hinton, Susan Eloise
   See Hinton, S. E.
Hintz, Martin 1945- 128
   Brief entry 39
   Earlier sketch in SATA 47
Hintz, Stephen V. 1975- 129
Hippopotamus, Eugene H.
   See Kraus, (Herman) Robert
Hirano, Cathy 1957- 68
Hirao, Amiko 203
Hirsch, Karen 1941- 61
Hirsch, Odo 157
   Earlier sketch in SATA 111
Hirsch, Phil 1926- 35
Hirsch, S. Carl 1913-1990 2
   See also SAAS 7
Hirschfelder, Arlene B. 1943- 227
   Earlier sketches in SATA 80, 138
Hirschi, Ron 1948- 192
   Earlier sketches in SATA 56, 95
Hirschmann, Linda (Ann) 1941- 40
Hirsh, Marilyn 1944-1988 7
   Obituary 58
Hirshberg, Al(bert Simon) 1909-1973 38
Hiscock, Bruce 1940- 204
   Earlier sketches in SATA 57, 137
Hiser, Constance 1950- 71
Hiser, Iona Seibert -1998 4
Hislop, Julia Rose Catherine 1962- 74

Hissey, Jane 1952- *130*
  Autobiography Feature *130*
  Earlier sketches in SATA *58, 103*
Hissey, Jane Elizabeth
  See Hissey, Jane
Hitchcock, Alfred (Joseph) 1899-1980 .... *27*
  Obituary *24*
Hite, Sid 1954- *175*
  Earlier sketches in SATA *75, 136*
Hitte, Kathryn 1919- *16*
Hitz, Demi
  See Demi
Hitzeroth, Deborah L. 1961- *78*
Hnizdovsky, Jacques 1915- *32*
Ho, Jannie *226*
Ho, Louise *185*
Ho, Minfong 1951- *151*
  Earlier sketches in SATA *15, 94*
  See also CLR *28*
Hoagland, Edward (Morley) 1932- *51*
Hoare, Robert J(ohn) 1921-1975 .... *38*
Hoban, Julia *217*
Hoban, Lillian 1925-1998 .... *69*
  Obituary *104*
  Earlier sketch in SATA *22*
  See also CLR *67*
Hoban, Russell 1925- *136*
  Earlier sketches in SATA *1, 40, 78*
  See also CLR *139*
Hoban, Russell Conwell
  See Hoban, Russell
Hoban, Tana 1917(?)-2006 .... *104*
  Obituary *173*
  Earlier sketches in SATA *22, 70*
  See also CLR *76*
  See also SAAS *12*
Hobart, Lois (Elaine) *7*
Hobbie, Holly 1942- *225*
  Earlier sketch in SATA *178*
  See also CLR *88*
Hobbie, Jocelyn *190*
Hobbie, Nathaniel *196*
Hobbs, Leigh 1953- *166*
Hobbs, Valerie 1941- *193*
  Autobiography Feature *145*
  Earlier sketches in SATA *93, 145*
  See also CLR *148*
Hobbs, Will 1947- *177*
  Autobiography Feature *127*
  Earlier sketches in SATA *72, 110*
  See also CLR *59*
Hobbs, William Carl
  See Hobbs, Will
Hoberman, Mary Ann 1930- *228*
  Earlier sketches in SATA *5, 72, 111, 158*
  See also CLR *22*
  See also SAAS *18*
Hobson, Bruce 1950- *62*
Hobson, Burton (Harold) 1933- *28*
Hobson, Laura Z(ametkin) 1900-1986 .... *52*
Hobson, Sally 1967- *172*
  Earlier sketch in SATA *84*
Hoce, Charley E. *174*
Hochman, David *202*
Hochschild, Arlie Russell 1940- *11*
Hockaby, Stephen
  See Mitchell, Gladys (Maude Winifred)
Hockenberry, Hope
  See Newell, Hope Hockenberry
Hodge, Deborah 1954- *163*
  Earlier sketch in SATA *122*
Hodge, P. W.
  See Hodge, Paul W(illiam)
Hodge, Paul W(illiam) 1934- *12*
Hodgell, P(atricia) C(hristine) 1951- *42*
Hodges, C. Walter 1909-2004 .... *2*
  Obituary *158*
Hodges, Carl G. 1902-1964 .... *10*
Hodges, Cyril Walter
  See Hodges, C. Walter
Hodges, Elizabeth Jamison *1*

Hodges, Margaret 1911-2005 .... *167*
  Obituary *172*
  Earlier sketches in SATA *1, 33, 75, 117*
  See also SAAS *9*
Hodges, Margaret Moore
  See Hodges, Margaret
Hodgetts, Blake Christopher 1967- *43*
Hodgkins, Fran 1964- *199*
Hodgkinson, Leigh 1975- *202*
Hodgman, Ann 1956- *198*
Hodgson, Harriet (W.) 1935- *84*
Hoehne, Marcia 1951- *89*
Hoellwarth, Cathryn Clinton
  See Clinton, Cathryn
Hoestlandt, Jo 1948- *221*
  Earlier sketch in SATA *94*
Hoestlandt, Jocelyne
  See Hoestlandt, Jo
Hoexter, Corinne K. 1927- *6*
Hoeye, Michael 1947- *136*
Hof, Marjolijn 1956- *226*
Hoff, Carol 1900-1979 .... *11*
Hoff, Mary (King) 1956- *157*
  Earlier sketch in SATA *74*
Hoff, Syd(ney) 1912-2004 .... *138*
  Obituary *154*
  Earlier sketches in SATA *9, 72*
  See also CLR *83*
  See also SAAS *4*
Hoffman, Edwin D. *49*
Hoffman, Elizabeth P(arkinson) 1921-2003
  Obituary *153*
Hoffman, Mary 1945- *211*
  Earlier sketches in SATA *59, 97, 144*
  See also SAAS *24*
Hoffman, Mat 1972- *150*
Hoffman, Nina Kiriki 1955- *160*
Hoffman, Phyllis M. 1944- *4*
Hoffman, Phyllis Miriam
  See Hoffman, Phyllis M.
Hoffman, Rosekrans 1926- *15*
Hoffmann, E(rnst) T(heodor) A(madeus)
  1776-1822 .... *27*
  See also CLR *133*
Hoffmann, Felix 1911-1975 .... *9*
Hoffmann, Heinrich 1809-1894
  See CLR *122*
Hoffmann, Margaret Jones 1910- *48*
Hoffmann, Peggy
  See Hoffmann, Margaret Jones
Hofher, Catherine Baxley 1954- *130*
Hofher, Cathy
  See Hofher, Catherine Baxley
Hofmeyr, Dianne (Louise) *138*
Hofsepian, Sylvia A. 1932- *74*
Hofsinde, Robert 1902-1973 .... *21*
Hogan, Bernice Harris 1929- *12*
Hogan, Inez 1895-1973 .... *2*
Hogan, James P. 1941-2010 .... *81*
Hogan, James Patrick
  See Hogan, James P.
Hogan, Jamie *192*
Hogan, Linda 1947- *132*
Hogan, Mary 1957- *210*
Hogarth, Burne 1911-1996 .... *89*
  Earlier sketch in SATA *63*
Hogarth, Grace (Weston Allen) 1905-1995 .. *91*
Hogarth, Jr.
  See Kent, Rockwell
Hogarth, (Arthur) Paul 1917-2001 .... *41*
Hogg, Garry 1902-1976 .... *2*
Hogg, Gary 1957- *172*
  Earlier sketch in SATA *105*
Hogner, Dorothy Childs *4*
Hogner, Nils 1893-1970 .... *25*
Hogrogian, Nonny 1932- *74*
  Autobiography Feature *127*
  Earlier sketch in SATA *7*
  See also CLR *95*
  See also SAAS *1*

Hoh, Diane 1937- *102*
  Brief entry *48*
  Earlier sketch in SATA *52*
Hoke, Helen
  See Watts, Helen L. Hoke
Hoke, Helen L.
  See Watts, Helen L. Hoke
Hoke, John 1925-2011 .... *7*
Hoke, John Lindsay
  See Hoke, John
Hokenson, Terry 1948- *193*
Hol, Coby 1943- *126*
Holabird, Katharine 1948- *213*
  Earlier sketches in SATA *62, 135*
Holaday, Bobbie 1922- *153*
Holbeach, Henry
  See Rands, William Brighty
Holberg, Ruth L(angland) 1889-1984 .... *1*
Holbrook, Kathy 1963- *107*
Holbrook, Peter
  See Glick, Carl (Cannon)
Holbrook, Sabra
  See Erickson, Sabra Rollins
Holbrook, Sara *131*
Holbrook, Stewart Hall 1893-1964 .... *2*
Holcomb, Jerry (Leona) Kimble 1927- *113*
Holcomb, Nan
  See McPhee, Norma H.
Holdcroft, Tina *227*
Holden, Elizabeth Rhoda
  See Lawrence, Louise
Holding, James (Clark Carlisle, Jr.)
  1907-1997 .... *3*
Hole, Stian 1969- *204*
Holeman, Linda 1949- *136*
  Autobiography Feature *136*
  Earlier sketch in SATA *102*
Holgate, Doug *225*
Holinger, William (Jacques) 1944- *90*
Holisher, Desider 1901-1972 .... *6*
Holl, Adelaide Hinkle 1910- *8*
Holl, Kristi
  See Holl, Kristi D.
Holl, Kristi D. 1951- *51*
Holl, Kristi Diane
  See Holl, Kristi D.
Holland, Gay W. 1941- *128*
Holland, Isabelle (Christian) 1920-2002 ...... *70*
  Autobiography Feature *103*
  Obituary *132*
  Earlier sketch in SATA *8*
  See also CLR *57*
Holland, Janice 1913-1962 .... *18*
Holland, John L(ewis) 1919- *20*
Holland, Joyce
  See Morice, Dave
Holland, Julia 1954- *106*
Holland, Lynda (H.) 1959- *77*
Holland, Lys
  See Gater, Dilys
Holland, Marion 1908-1989 .... *6*
  Obituary *61*
Holland, Richard 1976- *216*
Holland, Trish *221*
Hollander, John 1929- *13*
Hollander, Nicole 1940(?)- *101*
Hollander, Paul
  See Silverberg, Robert
Hollander, Phyllis 1928- *39*
Hollander, Zander 1923- *63*
Holldobler, Turid 1939- *26*
Holliday, Joe
  See Holliday, Joseph
Holliday, Joseph 1910- *11*
Holling, Holling C(lancy) 1900-1973 .... *15*
  Obituary *26*
  See also CLR *50*
Hollingsworth, Alvin C(arl) 1930- *39*
Hollingsworth, Mary 1947- *166*
  Earlier sketch in SATA *91*
Holloway, Teresa (Bragunier) 1906- *26*

Hollyer, Beatrice 1957- 226
Hollyer, Belinda 204
Holm, (Else) Anne (Lise) 1922-1998 .... *1*
  See also CLR 75
  See also SAAS 7
Holm, Jennifer L. 1968(?)- 183
  Earlier sketches in SATA *120, 163*
Holm, Matthew 1974- 174
Holm, Sharon Lane 1955- 114
  Earlier sketch in SATA *78*
Holman, Felice 1919- 82
  Earlier sketch in SATA *7*
  See also SAAS 17
Holm and Hamel
  See Holm, Jennifer L.
Holmberg, Bo R. 1945- 203
Holme, Bryan 1913-1990 26
  Obituary 66
Holmes, Barbara Ware 1945- 127
  Earlier sketch in SATA *65*
Holmes, Elizabeth 1957- 191
Holmes, Elizabeth Ann
  See Holmes, Elizabeth
Holmes, John
  See Souster, (Holmes) Raymond
Holmes, Liz
  See Holmes, Elizabeth
Holmes, Marjorie (Rose) 1910-2002 .... *43*
Holmes, Martha 1961- 72
Holmes, Mary Tavener 1954- 199
Holmes, Mary Z(astrow) 1943- 80
Holmes, Oliver Wendell 1809-1894 34
Holmes, Peggy 1898- 60
Holmes, Raymond
  See Souster, (Holmes) Raymond
Holmes, Rick
  See Hardwick, Richard Holmes, Jr.
Holmes, Sara Lewis 186
Holmgren, Helen Jean 1930- 45
Holmgren, Sister George Ellen
  See Holmgren, Helen Jean
Holmgren, Virginia C(unningham) 1909- 26
Holmquist, Eve 1921- 11
Holt, K.A.
  See Roy, Kari Anne
Holt, Kimberly Willis 1960- 223
  Earlier sketches in SATA *122, 179*
Holt, Margaret 1937- *4*
Holt, Margaret Van Vechten (Saunders)
  1899-1963 32
Holt, Michael (Paul) 1929- 13
Holt, Rackham
  See Holt, Margaret Van Vechten (Saunders)
Holt, Rochelle L.
  See DuBois, Rochelle Holt
Holt, Stephen
  See Thompson, Harlan
Holt, Victoria
  See Hibbert, Eleanor Alice Burford
Holtei, Christa 1953- 214
Holton, Leonard
  See Wibberley, Leonard
Holtz, Thomas R., Jr. 1965- 203
Holtze, Sally Holmes 1952- 64
Holtzman, Jerome 1926-2008 57
  Obituary 194
Holub, Joan 1956- 229
  Earlier sketches in SATA *99, 149*
Holub, Josef 1926- 175
Holubitsky, Katherine 1955- 165
  Earlier sketch in SATA *121*
Holyer, Erna Maria 1925- 22
Holyer, Ernie
  See Holyer, Erna Maria
Holyfield, John 1969- 227
Holz, Loretta 1943- 17
Holz, Loretta Marie
  See Holz, Loretta
Homel, David 1952- 97
Homze, Alma C. 1932- 17

Honey, Elizabeth 1947- 137
  Autobiography Feature 137
  Earlier sketch in SATA *112*
Honeycutt, Natalie 1945- 97
Hong, Lily Toy 1958- 76
Hong, Maxine Ting Ting
  See Kingston, Maxine Hong
Honig, Donald 1931- 18
Honig, Donald Martin
  See Honig, Donald
Honness, Elizabeth H. 1904- *2*
Hoobler, Dorothy 1941- 161
  Earlier sketches in SATA *28, 109*
Hoobler, Thomas 161
  Earlier sketches in SATA *28, 109*
Hood, Joseph F. 1925- *4*
Hood, Robert E. 1926- 21
Hood, Sarah
  See Killough, (Karen) Lee
Hook, Brendan 1963- 105
Hook, Frances 1912-1983 27
Hook, Geoffrey R(aynor) 1928- 103
Hook, Jeff
  See Hook, Geoffrey R(aynor)
Hook, Martha 1936- 27
Hooker, Richard
  See Heinz, W. C.
Hooker, Ruth 1920-1998 21
hooks, bell 1952(?)- 170
  Earlier sketch in SATA *115*
Hooks, William H(arris) 1921- 94
  Earlier sketch in SATA *16*
Hoon, Patricia Easterly 1954- 90
Hooper, Byrd
  See St. Clair, Byrd Hooper
Hooper, Mary 1948- 205
  Earlier sketch in SATA *160*
Hooper, Maureen Brett 1927- 76
Hooper, Meredith 1939- 159
  Earlier sketches in SATA *28, 101*
Hooper, Meredith Jean
  See Hooper, Meredith
Hooper, Patricia 1941- 95
Hoopes, Lyn Littlefield 1953- 49
  Brief entry 44
Hoopes, Ned E(dward) 1932- 21
Hoopes, Roy 1922-2009 11
Hoose, Phillip 1947- 215
  Earlier sketch in SATA *137*
Hoover, H(elen) M(ary) 1935- 132
  Brief entry 33
  Earlier sketches in SATA *44, 83*
  See also SAAS 8
Hoover, Helen (Drusilla Blackburn)
  1910-1984 12
  Obituary 39
Hope, Christopher 1944- 62
Hope, Christopher David Tully
  See Hope, Christopher
Hope, Laura Lee
  See Goulart, Ron
  and Stanley, George Edward
Hope Simpson, Jacynth 1930- 12
Hopf, Alice (Martha) L(ightner) 1904-1988 ... *5*
  Obituary 55
Hopgood, Tim 1961- 224
Hopkins, A. T.
  See Turngren, Annette
Hopkins, C. M.
  See Hopkins, Cathy
Hopkins, Cathy 1953- 165
Hopkins, Cathy M.
  See Hopkins, Cathy
Hopkins, Clark 1895-1976
  Obituary 34
Hopkins, Ellen 1955- 128
Hopkins, Ellen L.
  See Hopkins, Ellen
Hopkins, Jackie
  See Hopkins, Jackie Mims

Hopkins, Jackie Mims 1952- 178
  Earlier sketch in SATA *92*
Hopkins, Joseph G(erard) E(dward) 1909- ... *11*
Hopkins, (Hector) Kenneth 1914-1988
  Obituary 58
Hopkins, Lee Bennett 1938- 215
  Earlier sketches in SATA *3, 68, 125, 168*
  See also CLR 44
  See also SAAS 4
Hopkins, Lyman
  See Folsom, Franklin (Brewster)
Hopkins, Marjorie 1911-1999 .... *9*
Hopkins, Mary R(ice) 1956- 97
Hopkinson, Amanda 1948- 84
Hopkinson, Deborah 1952- 216
  Autobiography Feature 180
  Earlier sketches in SATA *76, 108, 159, 180*
  See also CLR 118
Hopman, Philip 1961- 177
Hoppe, Joanne 1932- 42
Hoppe, Matthias 1952- 76
Hoppe, Paul 209
Hopper, Nancy J. 1937- 38
  Brief entry 35
Hoppey, Tim 1958- 225
Hopping, Lorraine Jean
  See Egan, Lorraine Hopping
Horacek, Judy 1961- 211
Horaek, Petr 214
  Earlier sketch in SATA *163*
Horenstein, Henry 1947- 108
Horgan, Paul (George Vincent O'Shaughnessy)
  1903-1995 13
  Obituary 84
Horlak, E.E.
  See Tepper, Sheri S.
Horler, Sydney 1888-1954 102
Horley, Alex 1970- 229
Horn, Sandra Ann 1944- 154
Hornblow, Arthur, Jr. 1893-1976 15
Hornblow, Leonora 1920-2005 18
  Obituary 171
Hornblow, Leonora Schinasi
  See Hornblow, Leonora
Horne, Constance 1927- 149
Horne, Richard 1960-2007 169
  Obituary 180
  Earlier sketch in SATA *111*
Horne, Richard Henry Hengist
  1802(?)-1884 29
Horner, Althea (Jane) 1926- 36
Horner, Dave 1934- 12
Horner, Emily 1982- 233
Horner, Jack 1946- 106
Horner, John R.
  See Horner, Jack
Horner, John Robert
  See Horner, Jack
Hornik, Laurie Miller 159
Horniman, Joanne 1951- 167
  Earlier sketch in SATA *98*
Hornos, Axel 1907-1994 20
Hornstein, Reuben Aaron 1912- 64
Horowitz, Anthony 1955- 195
  Earlier sketch in SATA *137*
Horowitz, Dave 1970- 204
  Earlier sketch in SATA *172*
Horowitz, Eli 230
Horowitz, Ruth 1957- 136
Horrocks, Anita 1958- 169
Horse, Harry
  See Horne, Richard
Horsfield, Alan 1939- 153
Horstman, Lisa 1964- 219
Hort, Lenny 179
Horton, James O. 1943- 173
Horton, James Oliver
  See Horton, James O.
Horton, Joan 217
Horton, Madelyn (Stacey) 1962- 77
Horvath, Betty 1927- *4*

Horvath, David 1972(?)- *192*
Horvath, Polly 1957- *194*
  Earlier sketches in SATA *85, 140*
  See also CLR *90*
Horwich, Frances R(appaport) 1908-2001 .... *11*
  Obituary *130*
Horwitz, Elinor Lander *45*
  Brief entry *33*
Horwood, William 1944- *85*
Hosford, Dorothy (Grant) 1900-1952 .... *22*
Hosford, Jessie 1892-1990 .... *5*
Hoshi, Shin'ichi 1926- *101*
Hoshino, Felicia 1968- *189*
Hoskyns-Abrahall, Clare (Constance
  Drury) *13*
Hosler, Danamarie 1978- *184*
Hossack, Sylvia 1939- *83*
Hossack, Sylvie Adams
  See Hossack, Sylvia
Hosseini, Khaled 1965- *156*
Hossell, Karen Price
  See Price, Karen
Hosta, Dar *192*
Hostetler, Marian 1932- *91*
Hostetter, Joyce Moyer 1952- *228*
Houck, Carter 1924- *22*
Hough, Charlotte 1924-2008 .... *9*
  Obituary *202*
Hough, Helen Charlotte
  See Hough, Charlotte
Hough, Judy Taylor 1932- *63*
  Brief entry *51*
  Earlier sketch in SATA *56*
Hough, Richard (Alexander) 1922-1999 ...... *17*
Houghton, Eric 1930- *7*
Houk, Randy 1944- *97*
Houlehen, Robert J. 1918- *18*
Houlton, Peggy Mann 1925(?)-1990 .... *6*
Household, Geoffrey 1900-1988 .... *14*
  Obituary *59*
Housman, Laurence 1865-1959 .... *25*
Houston, Dick 1943- *231*
  Earlier sketch in SATA *74*
Houston, Gloria *138*
  Autobiography Feature *138*
  Earlier sketch in SATA *81*
Houston, James A(rchibald) 1921-2005 .... *74*
  Obituary *163*
  Earlier sketch in SATA *13*
  See also CLR *3*
  See also SAAS *17*
Houston, James D. 1933-2009 .... *78*
  Obituary *203*
Houston, James Dudley
  See Houston, James D.
Houston, James Dudley
  See Houston, James D.
Houston, Jeanne Toyo Wakatsuki
  See Houston, Jeanne Wakatsuki
Houston, Jeanne Wakatsuki 1934- *168*
  Autobiography Feature *168*
  Earlier sketch in SATA *78*
Houston, Juanita C. 1921- *129*
Houtman, Jacqueline 1960- *231*
Houtman, Jacqueline Jaeger
  See Houtman, Jacqueline
Houton, Kathleen
  See Kilgore, Kathleen
Houts, Amy F. *164*
Houts, Michelle *219*
Hovey, Kate *158*
Howard, Alan 1922- *45*
Howard, Alyssa
  See Buckholtz, Eileen (Garber)
  and Glick, Ruth
  and Titchener, Louise
Howard, Arthur 1948- *212*
  Earlier sketch in SATA *165*
Howard, Arthur Charles
  See Howard, Arthur

Howard, Elizabeth Fitzgerald 1927- *119*
  Earlier sketch in SATA *74*
Howard, Ellen 1943- *184*
  Earlier sketches in SATA *67, 99*
Howard, Jane R(uble) 1924- *87*
Howard, Norman Barry 1949- *90*
Howard, P. M.
  See Howard, Pauline Rodriguez
Howard, Paul 1967- *190*
  Earlier sketch in SATA *118*
Howard, Pauline Rodriguez 1951- *124*
Howard, Prosper
  See Hamilton, Charles (Harold St. John)
Howard, Robert West 1908-1988 .... *5*
Howard, Todd 1964- *135*
Howard, Tristan
  See Currie, Stephen
Howard, Vernon (Linwood) 1918-1992 .... *40*
  Obituary *73*
Howard, Warren F.
  See Pohl, Frederik
Howarth, Daniel *222*
  Earlier sketch in SATA *188*
Howarth, David (Armine) 1912-1991 .... *6*
  Obituary *68*
Howarth, Lesley 1952- *94*
Howe, Deborah 1946-1978 .... *29*
Howe, James 1946- *224*
  Earlier sketches in SATA *29, 71, 111, 161*
  See also CLR *9*
Howe, John F. 1957- *79*
Howe, Norma 1930-2011 .... *126*
Howe, Peter 1942- *214*
Howell, Pat 1947- *15*
Howell, S.
  See Styles, (Frank) Showell
Howell, Simmone 1971- *214*
Howell, Virginia
  See Ellison, Virginia H(owell)
Howells, Tania *229*
Howes, Barbara 1914-1996 .... *5*
Howie, Betsy 1962- *215*
Howie, Diana 1945- *122*
Howie, Diana Melson
  See Howie, Diana
Howker, Janni 1957- *72*
  Brief entry *46*
  See also CLR *14*
  See also SAAS *13*
Howland, Ethan 1963- *131*
Howland, Naomi *232*
Hoxter, Holly Nicole 1983- *231*
Hoy, Linda 1946- *65*
Hoy, Nina
  See Roth, Arthur J(oseph)
Hoyle, Geoffrey 1942- *18*
Hoyt, Ard *190*
Hoyt, Edwin P(almer), Jr. 1923- *28*
Hoyt, Erich 1950- *140*
  Earlier sketch in SATA *65*
Hoyt, Olga
  See Gruhzit-Hoyt, Olga (Margaret)
Hrdlitschka, Shelley 1956- *167*
  Earlier sketch in SATA *111*
Hrdlitschka, Shelley Joanne
  See Hrdlitschka, Shelley
Hromic, Alma A.
  See Alexander, Alma
Htin Aung, U.
  See Aung, (Maung) Htin
Hu, Ying-Hwa *173*
Huang, Benrei 1959- *86*
Huang, Nathan 1982(?)- *228*
Hubalek, Linda K. 1954- *111*
Hubbard, Crystal *209*
Hubbard, Jennifer R. *227*
Hubbard, Margaret Ann
  See Priley, Margaret (Ann) Hubbard
Hubbard, Michelle Calabro 1953- *122*
Hubbard, Patricia 1945- *124*

Hubbard, Woodleigh Marx *160*
  Earlier sketch in SATA *98*
Hubbell, Patricia 1928- *186*
  Earlier sketches in SATA *8, 132*
Hubery, Julia *195*
Hubley, Faith Elliot 1924-2001 .... *48*
  Obituary *133*
Hubley, John 1914-1977 .... *48*
  Obituary *24*
Huck, Charlotte S. 1922- *136*
  Earlier sketch in SATA *82*
Hucke, Johannes 1966- *218*
Hudak, Michal 1956- *143*
Hudson, Cheryl Willis 1948- *160*
  Earlier sketch in SATA *81*
Hudson, Jan 1954-1990 .... *77*
  See also CLR *40*
Hudson, Jeffery
  See Crichton, Michael
Hudson, Jeffrey
  See Crichton, Michael
Hudson, (Margaret) Kirsty 1947- *32*
Hudson, Margaret
  See Shuter, Jane (Margaret)
Hudson, W(illiam) H(enry) 1841-1922 .... *35*
Hudson, Wade 1946- *162*
  Earlier sketch in SATA *74*
Huelsmann, Eva 1928- *16*
Huerlimann, Bettina 1909-1983 .... *39*
  Obituary *34*
Huerlimann, Ruth 1939- *32*
  Brief entry *31*
Huff, Barbara A. 1929- *67*
Huff, Tanya 1957- *171*
  Earlier sketch in SATA *85*
Huff, Tanya Sue
  See Huff, Tanya
Huff, T.S.
  See Huff, Tanya
Huff, Vivian 1948- *59*
Huffaker, Sandy 1943- *10*
Huffman, Tom *24*
Huggins, Nathan Irvin 1927-1989 .... *63*
Huggins, Peter 1951- *178*
Hughes, Carol 1955- *217*
  Earlier sketch in SATA *108*
Hughes, Dean 1943- *139*
  Earlier sketches in SATA *33, 77*
  See also CLR *76*
Hughes, Eden
  See Griffin, W. E. B.
Hughes, Edward James
  See Hughes, Ted
Hughes, James Langston
  See Hughes, Langston
Hughes, Langston 1902-1967 .... *33*
  Earlier sketch in SATA *4*
  See also CLR *17*
Hughes, Libby *71*
Hughes, Matilda
  See MacLeod, Charlotte (Matilda)
Hughes, Monica 1925-2003 .... *162*
  Earlier sketches in SATA *15, 70, 119*
  See also CLR *60*
  See also SAAS *11*
Hughes, Monica Ince
  See Hughes, Monica
Hughes, Pat *197*
Hughes, Richard (Arthur Warren)
  1900-1976 .... *8*
  Obituary *25*
Hughes, Sara
  See Saunders, Susan
Hughes, Shirley 1927- *159*
  Earlier sketches in SATA *16, 70, 110*
  See also CLR *15*
Hughes, Susan 1960- *216*
Hughes, Ted 1930-1998 .... *49*
  Brief entry *27*
  Obituary *107*
  See also CLR *131*

Hughes, Thomas 1822-1896 31
  See also CLR 160
Hughes, Virginia
  See Campbell, Hope
Hughes, Walter (Llewellyn) 1910-1993 26
Hughey, Roberta 1942- 61
Hugo, Pierre Brackers de
  See Brackers de Hugo, Pierre
Hugo, Victor 1802-1885 47
Hugo, Victor Marie
  See Hugo, Victor
Huline-Dickens, Frank William 1931- 34
Huling, Jan 172
Huliska-Beith, Laura 232
  Earlier sketch in SATA 175
Hull, Eleanor (Means) 1913- 21
Hull, Eric Traviss
  See Harnan, Terry
Hull, H. Braxton
  See Jacobs, Helen Hull
Hull, Jesse Redding
  See Hull, Jessie Redding
Hull, Jessie Redding 1932- 51
Hull, Katharine 1921-1977 23
Hull, Lise (E.) 1954- 148
Hull, Maureen 1949- 142
Hulme, Joy N. 1922- 161
  Earlier sketches in SATA 74, 112
Hults, Dorothy Niebrugge 1898-2000 6
Humble, Richard 1945- 60
Hume, Lachie 189
Hume, Lotta Carswell 7
Hume, Ruth Fox 1922-1980 26
  Obituary 22
Hume, Stephen Eaton 1947- 136
Hummel, Berta 1909-1946 43
Hummel, Sister Maria Innocentia
  See Hummel, Berta
Hummon, Marcus 1960- 213
Humphrey, Carol Sue 1956- 167
Humphrey, Henry (III) 1930- 16
Humphrey, Kate
  See Forsyth, Kate
Humphrey, Sandra McLeod 1936- 95
Humphreys, Martha 1943- 71
Humphreys, Susan L.
  See Lowell, Susan
Humphries, Tudor 1953- 226
Hundal, Nancy 1957- 128
Huneck, Stephen 1949- 183
  Earlier sketch in SATA 129
Hungerford, Hesba Fay
  See Brinsmead, H(esba) F(ay)
Hungerford, Pixie
  See Brinsmead, H(esba) F(ay)
Hunkin, Tim 1950- 53
Hunkin, Timothy Mark Trelawney
  See Hunkin, Tim
Hunt, Angela Elwell 1957- 159
  Earlier sketch in SATA 75
Hunt, Bernice 1920- 4
Hunt, Charlotte Dumaresq
  See Demi
Hunt, Francesca
  See Holland, Isabelle (Christian)
Hunt, Irene 1907-2001 91
  Earlier sketch in SATA 2
  See also CLR 1
Hunt, Janie Louise 1963- 102
Hunt, Jonathan 1966- 84
Hunt, Joyce 1927- 31
Hunt, Linda 1940- 39
Hunt, Lisa B(ehnke) 1967- 84
Hunt, Mabel Leigh 1892-1971 1
  Obituary 26
Hunt, Morton M(agill) 1920- 22
Hunt, Nigel
  See Greenbank, Anthony Hunt
Hunt, Peter (Leonard) 1945- 76
Hunter, Anne B. 1966- 118

Hunter, Bernice Thurman 1922-2002 85
  Brief entry 45
Hunter, Bobbi Dooley 1945- 89
Hunter, Captain Marcy
  See Ellis, Edward S.
Hunter, Chris
  See Fluke, Joanne
Hunter, Clingham M.D.
  See Adams, William Taylor
Hunter, Edith Fisher 1919- 31
Hunter, Erin
  See Cary, Kate
Hunter, Evan 1926-2005 25
  Obituary 167
Hunter, George E.
  See Ellis, Edward S.
Hunter, Hilda 1921- 7
Hunter, Jana
  See Hunter, Jana Novotny
Hunter, Jana Novotny 190
Hunter, Jim 1939- 65
Hunter, Kristin
  See Lattany, Kristin Hunter
Hunter, Leigh
  See Etchison, Birdie L(ee)
Hunter, Lieutenant Ned
  See Ellis, Edward S.
Hunter, Linzie 1979- 227
Hunter, Mel 1927-2004 39
Hunter, Mollie 1922- 139
  Autobiography Feature 139
  Earlier sketches in SATA 2, 54, 106
  See also CLR 25
  See also SAAS 7
Hunter, Ned
  See Ellis, Edward S.
Hunter, Norman (George Lorimer)
  1899-1995 84
  Earlier sketch in SATA 26
Hunter, Ryan Ann
  See Greenwood, Pamela D.
  and Macalaster, Elizabeth G.
Hunter, Sara Hoagland 1954- 98
Hunter Blair, Pauline
  See Clarke, Pauline
Huntington, Amy 1956- 180
  Earlier sketch in SATA 138
Huntington, Geoffrey 145
Huntington, Harriet E(lizabeth) 1909- 1
Huntley, Amy 225
Huntsberry, William E(mery) 1916- 5
Hurd, Clement (G.) 1908-1988 64
  Obituary 54
  Earlier sketch in SATA 2
  See also CLR 49
Hurd, Edith Thacher 1910-1997 64
  Obituary 95
  Earlier sketch in SATA 2
  See also CLR 49
  See also SAAS 13
Hurd, John Thacher
  See Hurd, Thacher
Hurd, Thacher 1949- 219
  Autobiography Feature 123
  Brief entry 45
  Earlier sketches in SATA 46, 94
Hurley, Jo
  See Dower, Laura
Hurley, Tonya 207
Hurlimann, Bettina
  See Huerlimann, Bettina
Hurlimann, Ruth
  See Huerlimann, Ruth
Hurmence, Belinda 1921- 77
  See also CLR 25
  See also SAAS 20
Hurst, Carol Otis 1933-2007 185
  Earlier sketch in SATA 130
Hurt-Newton, Tania 1968- 84
Hurwin, Davida Wills 1950- 180

Hurwitz, Johanna 1937- 175
  Earlier sketches in SATA 20, 71, 113
  See also SAAS 18
Hurwood, Bernhardt J. 1926-1987 12
  Obituary 50
Husain, Shahrukh 1950- 108
Huser, Glen 1943- 151
Hutchens, Paul 1902-1977 31
Hutchins, Carleen M.
  See Hutchins, Carleen Maley
Hutchins, Carleen Maley 1911-2009 9
  Obituary 206
Hutchins, Hazel J. 1952- 175
  Brief entry 51
  Earlier sketches in SATA 81, 135
  See also SAAS 24
Hutchins, Pat 1942- 178
  Earlier sketches in SATA 15, 70, 111
  See also CLR 20
  See also SAAS 16
Hutchins, Ross Elliott 1906- 4
Hutchison, Linda 1942- 152
Huthmacher, J. Joseph 1929- 5
Hutto, Nelson (Allen) 1904-1985 20
Hutton, Kathryn 1915- 89
Hutton, Sam
  See Jones, Allan Frewin
Hutton, Warwick 1939-1994 20
  Obituary 83
  See also SAAS 17
Huxley, Aldous 1894-1963 63
  See also CLR 151
Huxley, Aldous Leonard
  See Huxley, Aldous
Huxley, Elspeth (Josceline Grant)
  1907-1997 62
  Obituary 95
Hyde, Catherine 232
Hyde, Catherine R.
  See Hyde, Catherine Ryan
Hyde, Catherine Ryan 1955- 224
  Earlier sketch in SATA 141
Hyde, Dayton O(gden) 9
Hyde, Hawk
  See Hyde, Dayton O(gden)
Hyde, Jeannette
  See Eyerly, Jeannette
Hyde, Margaret O. 1917- 139
  Earlier sketches in SATA 1, 42, 76
  See also CLR 23
  See also SAAS 8
Hyde, Margaret Oldroyd
  See Hyde, Margaret O.
Hyde, Shelley
  See Reed, Kit
Hyde, Wayne Frederick 1922- 7
Hylander, Clarence J(ohn) 1897-1964 7
Hyman, Miles 1962- 210
Hyman, Paula Chase
  See Chase, Paula
Hyman, Robin 1931- 12
Hyman, Robin Phiilip
  See Hyman, Robin
Hyman, Trina Schart 1939-2004 95
  Obituary 158
  Earlier sketches in SATA 7, 46
  See also CLR 50
Hymes, Lucia M(anley) 1907-1998 7
Hyndman, Jane Andrews Lee 1912-1978 46
  Obituary 23
  Earlier sketch in SATA 1
Hyndman, Robert Utley 1906-1973 18
Hynes, Pat 98

I

Iannone, Jeanne
  See Balzano, Jeanne (Koppel)
Ibatoulline, Bagram 1965(?)- 225
  Earlier sketch in SATA *174*
Ibbitson, John Perrie 1955- *102*
Ibbotson, Eva 1925-2010 .... *221*
  Earlier sketches in SATA *13, 103, 156*
Ibbotson, M. C(hristine) 1930- 5
Icenoggle, Jodi 1967- *168*
Icenoggle, Jodi O.
  See Icenoggle, Jodi
Ichikawa, Satomi 1949- *208*
  Brief entry 36
  Earlier sketches in SATA *47, 78, 146*
  See also CLR *62*
Idle, Molly Schaar *223*
Iggulden, Hal 1972- *196*
Ignatow, Amy 1977- *233*
Ignoffo, Matthew 1945- 92
Igus, Toyomi 1953- *112*
  Earlier sketch in SATA *76*
Ihimaera, Witi (Tame) 1944- *148*
Ikeda, Daisaku 1928- 77
Ilowite, Sheldon A. 1931- 27
Ilsey, Dent
  See Chapman, John Stanton Higham
Ilsley, Dent
  See Chapman, John Stanton Higham
Ilsley, Velma (Elizabeth) 1918- *12*
Imai, Ayano 1980- *190*
Imai, Miko 1963- *90*
Imershein, Betsy 1953- *62*
Immel, Mary Blair 1930- *28*
Immell, Myra H. 1941- *92*
Impey, Rose 1947- *223*
  Earlier sketches in SATA *69, 152*
Ingalls, Ann *227*
Ingelow, Jean 1820-1897 .... *33*
Ingermanson, Randall 1958- *134*
Ingermanson, Randy
  See Ingermanson, Randall
Ingersoll, Norman 1928- 79
Ingham, Colonel Frederic
  See Hale, Edward Everett
Ingman, Bruce 1963- *182*
  Earlier sketch in SATA *134*
Ingman, Nicholas 1948- 52
Ingold, Jeanette *128*
Ingpen, Robert 1936- *166*
  Earlier sketch in SATA *109*
Ingpen, Robert Roger
  See Ingpen, Robert
Ingraham, Erick 1950- *145*
Ingraham, Leonard W(illiam) 1913-2003 4
Ingram, Scott 1948- *167*
  Earlier sketch in SATA *92*
Ingram, W. Scott
  See Ingram, Scott
Ingrams, Doreen 1906-1997 .... *97*
  Earlier sketch in SATA *20*
Ingrid, Charles
  See Salsitz, Rhondi Vilott
Ingves, Gunilla 1939- *101*
Ingves, Gunilla Anna Maria Folkesdotter
  See Ingves, Gunilla
Inkpen, Mick 1952- *154*
  Earlier sketch in SATA *99*
Innerst, Stacy *232*
Innes, (Ralph) Hammond
  See Hammond Innes, Ralph
Innes, Ralph Hammond
  See Hammond Innes, Ralph
Innes, Stephanie *220*
Innocenti, Roberto 1940- *159*
  Earlier sketch in SATA *96*
  See also CLR *126*
Innocenti and Gallaz
  See Gallaz, Christophe
  and Innocenti, Roberto

Inns, Chris *212*
Inyart, Gene
  See Namovicz, Gene Inyart
Ionesco, Eugene 1909-1994 7
  Obituary 79
Ipcar, Dahlov (Zorach) 1917- *147*
  Autobiography Feature *147*
  Earlier sketches in SATA *1, 49*
  See also SAAS *8*
Ireland, Karin *151*
  Earlier sketch in SATA *101*
Ironside, Jetske 1940- 60
Irvin, Fred 1914- *15*
Irvine, Georgeanne 1955- *72*
Irvine, Joan 1951- *80*
Irving, Alexander
  See Hume, Ruth Fox
Irving, Robert
  See Adler, Irving
Irving, Washington 1783-1859
  See YABC *2*
  See also CLR *97*
Irwin, Ann(abelle Bowen) 1915-1998 89
  Brief entry 38
  Obituary *106*
  Earlier sketch in SATA *44*
  See also CLR *40*
  See also SAAS *14*
Irwin, Constance (H.) Frick 1913-1995 6
Irwin, Hadley
  See Hadley, Lee
  and Irwin, Ann(abelle Bowen)
Irwin, Keith Gordon 1885-1964 .... *11*
Isaac, Joanne 1934- *21*
Isaacs, Anne 1949- *185*
  Earlier sketch in SATA *90*
Isaacs, Jacob
  See Kranzler, George G(ershon)
Isaacson, Philip M(arshal) 1924- 87
Isadora, Rachel 1953(?)- *204*
  Brief entry 32
  Earlier sketches in SATA *54, 79, 121, 165*
  See also CLR *7*
Isbell, Rebecca T(emple) 1942- *125*
Isham, Charlotte H(ickock) 1912- *21*
Ishida, Jui *176*
Ish-Kishor, Judith 1892-1972 .... *11*
Ish-Kishor, Sulamith 1896-1977 .... *17*
Ishmael, Woodi 1914-1995 .... *31*
  Obituary *109*
Isle, Sue 1963- *105*
Isol 1972- *220*
Israel, Elaine 1945- *12*
Israel, Marion Louise 1882-1973
  Obituary 26
Iterson, S(iny) R(ose) Van
  See Van Iterson, S(iny) R(ose)
Ivanko, John D. 1966- *111*
Ivanko, John Duane
  See Ivanko, John D.
Iversen, Jeremy 1980(?)- *174*
Iversen, Jeremy Watt
  See Iversen, Jeremy
Iverson, Carol (L.) 1941- *145*
Iverson, Diane 1950- *122*
Iverson, Eric G.
  See Turtledove, Harry
Ivery, Martha M. 1948- *124*
Ives, David 1951- *173*
Ives, Morgan
  See Bradley, Marion Zimmer
Ives, Penny 1956- *215*
Iwai, Melissa *183*
Iwamatsu, Jun Atsushi 1908-1994 .... *81*
  Earlier sketch in SATA *14*
  See also CLR *4*
Iwamura, Kazuo 1939- *213*
Iwasaki (Matsumoto), Chihiro 1918-1974
  See CLR *18*
Iyengar, Malathi Michelle 1954- *220*

J

Jabar, Cynthia *210*
Jablonski, Carla *184*
Jac, Lee
  See Morton, Lee Jack, Jr.
Jacka, Martin 1943- *72*
Jackson, Alison 1953- *228*
  Earlier sketches in SATA *73, 108, 160*
Jackson, Anne 1896(?)-1984
  Obituary 37
Jackson, Barry
  See Jackson, Barry E.
Jackson, Barry E. *200*
Jackson, C(aary) Paul 1902-1991 6
Jackson, Caary
  See Jackson, C(aary) Paul
Jackson, Charlotte E. (Cobden) 1903(?)-1989
  Obituary 62
Jackson, Dave
  See Jackson, J. David
Jackson, Donna M. 1959- *206*
Jackson, Ellen 1943- *214*
  Earlier sketches in SATA *75, 115, 167*
Jackson, Ellen B.
  See Jackson, Ellen
Jackson, Garnet Nelson 1944- *87*
Jackson, Geoffrey (Holt Seymour) 1915-1987
  Obituary 53
Jackson, Gina
  See Fluke, Joanne
Jackson, Guida M. 1930- *71*
Jackson, J. David 1944- *91*
Jackson, Jacqueline 1928- *65*
Jackson, Jacqueline Dougan
  See Jackson, Jacqueline
Jackson, Jesse 1908-1983 .... *29*
  Obituary 48
  Earlier sketch in SATA *2*
  See also CLR *28*
Jackson, Marjorie 1928- *127*
Jackson, Melanie 1956- *141*
Jackson, Mike 1946- *91*
Jackson, Neta J. 1944- *91*
Jackson, O. B.
  See Jackson, C(aary) Paul
Jackson, Rob 1961- *176*
Jackson, Robert B(lake) 1926- 8
Jackson, Robert Bradley
  See Jackson, Rob
Jackson, Sally
  See Kellogg, Jean (Defrees)
Jackson, Shirley 1919-1965 2
Jackson, Woody 1948- *92*
Jackson Issa, Kai *205*
Jacob, Helen Pierce 1927- *21*
Jacobin
  See Bisson, Terry
Jacobs, Deborah Lynn *187*
Jacobs, Flora Gill 1918-2006 5
  Obituary *178*
Jacobs, Francine 1935- *150*
  Brief entry 42
  Earlier sketch in SATA *43*
Jacobs, Frank 1929- *30*
Jacobs, Helen Hull 1908-1997 .... *12*
Jacobs, Joseph 1854-1916 .... *25*
Jacobs, Judy 1952- *69*
Jacobs, Laurie A. 1956- *89*
Jacobs, Leah
  See Gellis, Roberta
Jacobs, Lee
  See Stone, Tanya Lee
Jacobs, Leland Blair 1907-1992 .... *20*
  Obituary 71
Jacobs, Linda
  See Altman, Linda Jacobs
Jacobs, Lou(is), Jr. 1921- 2
Jacobs, Shannon K. 1947- 77
Jacobs, Susan
  See Quinn, Susan

Jacobs, William Jay 1933- 89
  Earlier sketch in SATA 28
Jacobsen, Laura 177
Jacobson, Daniel 1923- 12
Jacobson, Jennifer
  See Jacobson, Jennifer Richard
Jacobson, Jennifer Richard 1958- 233
  Earlier sketch in SATA 170
Jacobson, Morris K(arl) 1906- 21
Jacobson, Rick 170
Jacopetti, Alexandra
  See Hart, Alexandra
Jacques, Brian 1939-2011 176
  Earlier sketches in SATA 62, 95, 138
  See also CLR 21
Jacques, Robin 1920-1995 32
  Brief entry 30
  Obituary 86
  See also SAAS 5
Jaekel, Susan M. 1948- 89
Jaffe, Michele 179
Jaffe, Michele Sharon
  See Jaffe, Michele
Jaffee, Al(lan) 1921- 66
  Earlier sketch in SATA 37
Jagendorf, Moritz (Adolf) 1888-1981 2
  Obituary 24
Jago 1979- 216
Jahn, Joseph Michael
  See Jahn, Michael
Jahn, Michael 1943- 28
Jahn, Mike
  See Jahn, Michael
Jahn-Clough, Lisa 1967- 193
  Earlier sketches in SATA 88, 152
Jahsmann, Allan Hart 1916- 28
Jakes, John 1932- 62
Jakes, John William
  See Jakes, John
James, Andrew
  See Kirkup, James
James, Ann 1952- 168
  Earlier sketches in SATA 82, 117
James, Betsy 183
James, Bill 1929- 205
James, B.J.
  See James, Brian
James, Brian 1976- 212
  Earlier sketch in SATA 140
James, Bronte
  See Nash, Renea Denise
James, Captain Lew
  See Stratemeyer, Edward L.
James, Charlie 1961- 185
James, Curtis E. 182
James, Dynely
  See Mayne, William
James, Edwin
  See Gunn, James E.
James, Elizabeth 1942- 97
  Earlier sketches in SATA 39, 45, 52
James, Emily
  See Standiford, Natalie
James, Gordon C. 1973- 195
James, Harry Clebourne 1896-1978 11
James, J. Alison 1962- 146
  Earlier sketch in SATA 83
James, Josephine
  See Sterne, Emma Gelders
James, Mary
  See Meaker, Marijane
James, Matt 201
James, Philip
  See del Rey, Lester
  and Moorcock, Michael
James, Robin 1953- 50
James, Robin Irene
  See James, Robin
James, Simon 1961- 202
James, T. F.
  See Fleming, Thomas

James, Tegan
  See Odgers, Sally Farrell
James, Will(iam Roderick) 1892-1942 19
Jameson, W. C. 1942- 93
Jamieson, Ian R.
  See Goulart, Ron
Jamieson, Victoria 218
Jamiolkowski, Raymond M. 1953- 81
Jane, Mary Childs 1909-1991 6
Jane, Pamela 158
Janeczko, Paul B(ryan) 1945- 155
  Earlier sketches in SATA 53, 98
  See also CLR 47
  See also SAAS 18
Janes, Edward C. 1908-1984 25
Janes, Edward Clarence
  See Janes, Edward C.
Janes, J(oseph) Robert 1935- 148
  Brief entry 50
  Earlier sketch in SATA 101
Janeway, Elizabeth (Hall) 1913-2005 19
Janger, Kathleen N. 1940- 66
Jango-Cohen, Judith 1955- 208
Janice
  See Brustlein, Janice Tworkov
Janisch, Heinz 1960- 181
Janni, Rebecca 229
Janosch
  See Eckert, Horst
Janover, Caroline (Davis) 1943- 141
  Earlier sketch in SATA 89
Janovitz, Marilyn 194
Jansen, Jared
  See Cebulash, Mel
Janson, Dora Jane (Heineberg) 1916- 31
Janson, H(orst) W(oldemar) 1913-1982 9
Jansson, Tove (Marika) 1914-2001 41
  Earlier sketch in SATA 3
  See also CLR 125
Janus, Grete
  See Hertz, Grete Janus
Jaques, Faith 1923-1997 97
  Earlier sketches in SATA 21, 69
Jaquith, Priscilla 1908- 51
Jaramillo, Mari-Luci 1928- 139
Jarka, Jeff 221
Jarman, Julia 1946- 198
  Earlier sketch in SATA 133
Jarman, Rosemary Hawley 1935- 7
Jarrell, Mary Von Schrader 1914- 35
Jarrell, Randall 1914-1965 7
  See also CLR 111
Jarrett, Clare 1952- 201
Jarrett, Roxanne
  See Werner, Herma
Jarrie, Martin 1953- 219
Jarrow, Gail 1952- 185
  Earlier sketch in SATA 84
Jarvis, E.K.
  See Ellison, Harlan
  and Silverberg, Robert
Jarvis, Robin 1963- 181
Jarzab, Anna 1984- 227
Jaskol, Julie 1958- 127
Jasner, W. K.
  See Watson, Jane Werner
Jassem, Kate
  See Oppenheim, Joanne
Jauss, Anne Marie 1902(?)-1991 10
  Obituary 69
Javaherbin, Mina 230
Javernick, Ellen 1938- 217
  Earlier sketch in SATA 89
Javins, Marie 1966- 212
Jay, Alison 196
Jay, Stacey 1978(?)- 231
Jayne, Lieutenant R. H.
  See Ellis, Edward S.
Jaynes, Clare
  See Mayer, Jane Rothschild

Jeake, Samuel, Jr.
  See Aiken, Conrad
Jean-Bart, Leslie 1954- 121
Jeapes, Ben 1965- 174
Jecan, Gavriel 1962- 200
Jefferds, Vincent H(arris) 1916- 59
  Brief entry 49
Jefferies, (John) Richard 1848-1887 16
Jeffers, Dawn 189
Jeffers, Oliver 1977- 213
  Earlier sketch in SATA 175
Jeffers, Susan 1942- 202
  Earlier sketches in SATA 17, 70, 129, 137
  See also CLR 30
Jefferson, Sarah
  See Farjeon, (Eve) Annabel
Jeffries, Roderic 1926- 4
Jeffries, Roderic Graeme
  See Jeffries, Roderic
Jenkin-Pearce, Susie 1943- 80
Jenkins, A. M. 1961- 174
Jenkins, Amanda McRaney
  See Jenkins, A. M.
Jenkins, Debra Reid
  See Reid Jenkins, Debra
Jenkins, Emily 1967- 174
  Earlier sketch in SATA 144
Jenkins, Jean 98
Jenkins, Jerry B. 1949- 149
Jenkins, Jerry Bruce
  See Jenkins, Jerry B.
Jenkins, Leonard 189
Jenkins, Marie M(agdalen) 1909- 7
Jenkins, Martin 1959- 216
Jenkins, M.D.
  See Jenkins, Martin
Jenkins, Patrick 1955- 72
Jenkins, Steve 1952- 218
  Earlier sketches in SATA 154, 188
Jenkins, William A(twell) 1922-1998 9
Jenkyns, Chris 1924- 51
Jennewein, James 215
Jennewein, Jim
  See Jennewein, James
Jennings, Christopher S. 1971(?)- 201
Jennings, Coleman A(lonzo) 1933- 64
Jennings, C.S.
  See Jennings, Christopher S.
Jennings, Dana Andrew 1957- 93
Jennings, Elizabeth (Joan) 1926-2001 66
Jennings, Gary 1928-1999 9
  Obituary 117
Jennings, Gary Gayne
  See Jennings, Gary
Jennings, Linda 1937- 211
Jennings, Linda M.
  See Jennings, Linda
Jennings, Patrick 1962- 205
  Earlier sketches in SATA 96, 160
Jennings, Paul 1943- 165
  Earlier sketch in SATA 88
  See also CLR 40
Jennings, Richard W. 1945- 185
  Earlier sketch in SATA 136
Jennings, Robert
  See Hamilton, Charles (Harold St. John)
Jennings, S. M.
  See Meyer, Jerome Sydney
Jennings, Sharon 1954- 231
  Earlier sketch in SATA 95
Jennings, Sharon Elizabeth
  See Jennings, Sharon
Jennison, C. S.
  See Starbird, Kaye
Jennison, Keith Warren 1911-1995 14
Jensen, Kathryn 1949- 81
Jensen, Kristine Mary 1961- 78
Jensen, Niels 1927- 25
Jensen, Vickie (Dee) 1946- 81
Jensen, Virginia Allen 1927- 8
Jenson-Elliott, Cynthia L(ouise) 1962- 143

Jeram, Anita 1965- *219*
   Earlier sketches in SATA *71, 102, 154*
Jerman, Jerry 1949- *89*
Jernigan, E. Wesley 1940- *85*
Jernigan, Gisela (Evelyn) 1948- *85*
Jerome, Elaine *228*
Jeschke, Susan 1942- *42*
   Brief entry *27*
Jessel, Camilla (Ruth) 1937- *143*
   Earlier sketch in SATA *29*
Jessell, Tim *225*
   Earlier sketch in SATA *177*
Jessey, Cornelia
   See Sussman, Cornelia Silver
Jewel
   See Kilcher, Jewel
Jewell, Nancy 1940- *109*
   Brief entry *41*
Jewett, Eleanore Myers 1890-1967 .... *5*
Jewett, Sarah Orne 1849-1909 .... *15*
Jewett, Theodora Sarah Orne
   See Jewett, Sarah Orne
Jezard, Alison 1919- *57*
   Brief entry *34*
Jiang, Cheng An 1943- *109*
Jiang, Ji-li 1954- *101*
Jiang, Zheng An
   See Jiang, Cheng An
Jiler, John 1946- *42*
   Brief entry *35*
Jimenez, Francisco 1943- *219*
   Earlier sketch in SATA *108*
Jinks, Catherine 1963- *207*
   Earlier sketches in SATA *94, 155*
Jobb, Jamie 1945- *29*
Jobling, Curtis *131*
Jocelyn, Ann Henning 1948- *92*
Jocelyn, Marthe 1956- *198*
   Earlier sketches in SATA *118, 163*
Joerns, Consuelo *44*
   Brief entry *33*
Joey D
   See Macaulay, Teresa
Johansen, Krista V.
   See Johansen, K.V.
Johansen, K.V 1968- *186*
Johansen, K.V. 1968- *186*
   Earlier sketch in SATA *129*
Johansson, Philip *163*
John, Antony 1972- *206*
John, Joyce *59*
Johns, Avery
   See Cousins, Margaret
Johns, Elizabeth 1943- *88*
Johns, Janetta
   See Quin-Harkin, Janet
Johns, Linda 1945- *173*
Johns, W(illiam) E(arle) 1893-1968 .... *55*
Johns, Captain W. E.
   See Johns, W(illiam) E(arle)
Johnson, A.
   See Johnson, Annabell
Johnson, A. E.
   See Johnson, Annabell
   and Johnson, Edgar (Raymond)
Johnson, Angela 1961- *188*
   Earlier sketches in SATA *69, 102, 150*
   See also CLR *33*
Johnson, Annabel
   See Johnson, Annabell
Johnson, Annabell 1921- *72*
   Earlier sketch in SATA *2*
Johnson, Art 1946- *123*
Johnson, B. F. 1920- *1*
Johnson, Benjamin F., of Boone
   See Riley, James Whitcomb
Johnson, Bettye 1858-1919
   See Rogers, Bettye
Johnson, Caryn
   See Goldberg, Whoopi

Johnson, Caryn E.
   See Goldberg, Whoopi
Johnson, Caryn Elaine
   See Goldberg, Whoopi
Johnson, Charles R. 1925- *11*
Johnson, Charlotte Buel
   See von Wodtke, Charlotte Buel Johnson
Johnson, Christine 1978- *232*
Johnson, Chuck
   See Johnson, Charles R.
Johnson, Crockett
   See Leisk, David (Johnson)
Johnson, D(ana) William 1945- *23*
Johnson, Daniel Shahid 1954- *73*
Johnson, David
   See Johnson, David A.
Johnson, David A. 1951- *191*
Johnson, D.B. 1944- *183*
   Earlier sketch in SATA *146*
Johnson, Dianne 1960- *130*
   See Johnson, Dinah
Johnson, Dinah *231*
   See Johnson, Dianne
Johnson, Dolores 1949- *69*
Johnson, Donald B.
   See Johnson, D.B.
Johnson, Dorothy M(arie) 1905-1984 .... *6*
   Obituary *40*
Johnson, E(ugene) Harper *44*
Johnson, Edgar (Raymond) 1912-1990 .... *72*
   Earlier sketch in SATA *2*
Johnson, Eleanor Murdock 1892-1987
   Obituary *54*
Johnson, Elizabeth 1911-1984 .... *7*
   Obituary *39*
Johnson, Eric W(arner) 1918-1994 ....
   Obituary *82*
   Earlier sketch in SATA *8*
Johnson, Evelyne 1922- *20*
Johnson, Fred 19(?)-1982 .... *63*
Johnson, Gaylord 1884-1972 .... *7*
Johnson, Gerald White 1890-1980 .... *19*
   Obituary *28*
Johnson, Gillian 1963- *215*
Johnson, Harper
   See Johnson, E(ugene) Harper
Johnson, Harriett 1908-1987
   Obituary *53*
Johnson, James Ralph 1922- *1*
Johnson, James Weldon 1871-1938 .... *31*
   See also CLR *32*
Johnson, Jane 1951- *48*
Johnson, Jen Cullerton 1972- *230*
Johnson, Joan J. 1942- *59*
Johnson, John E(mil) 1929- *34*
Johnson, Johnny 1901-1995
   See Johnson, (Walter) Ryerson
Johnson, Kathleen Jeffrie 1950- *186*
Johnson, Kathryn
   See Jensen, Kathryn
Johnson, La Verne B(ravo) 1925- *13*
Johnson, Layne *222*
   Earlier sketch in SATA *187*
Johnson, Lee Kaiser 1962- *78*
Johnson, Lissa H(alls) 1955- *65*
Johnson, Lois Smith 1894-1993 .... *6*
Johnson, Lois Walfrid 1936- *130*
   Earlier sketches in SATA *22, 91*
Johnson, Margaret S(weet) 1893-1964 .... *35*
Johnson, Marguerite Annie
   See Angelou, Maya
Johnson, Mary Frances K. 1929(?)-1979
   Obituary *27*
Johnson, Maud Battle 1918(?)-1985
   Obituary *46*
Johnson, Maureen 1973- *232*
   Earlier sketch in SATA *200*
Johnson, Meredith Merrell 1952- *104*
Johnson, Milton 1932- *31*
Johnson, Neil 1954- *135*
   Earlier sketch in SATA *73*

Johnson, Pamela 1949- *71*
Johnson, Patricia Polin 1956- *84*
Johnson, Paul Brett 1947- *132*
   Earlier sketch in SATA *83*
Johnson, Rebecca L. 1956- *147*
   Earlier sketch in SATA *67*
Johnson, Rick L. 1954- *79*
Johnson, (Walter) Ryerson 1901-1995 .... *10*
   Obituary *106*
Johnson, Scott 1952- *119*
   Earlier sketch in SATA *76*
Johnson, Sherrie 1948- *87*
Johnson, Shirley K(ing) 1927- *10*
Johnson, Siddie Joe 1905-1977
   Obituary *20*
Johnson, Spencer 1938- *145*
   Brief entry *38*
Johnson, Stacie
   See Myers, Walter Dean
Johnson, Stephen T. 1964- *189*
   Earlier sketches in SATA *84, 141*
Johnson, Steve 1960- *230*
   Earlier sketch in SATA *177*
Johnson, Sue Kaiser 1963- *78*
Johnson, Sylvia A. *166*
   Brief entry *52*
   Earlier sketch in SATA *104*
Johnson, Varian 1977- *229*
Johnson, William R. *38*
Johnson, William Weber 1909-1992 .... *7*
Johnson-Feelings, Dianne
   See Johnson, Dianne
Johnston, Agnes Christine
   See Dazey, Agnes J(ohnston)
Johnston, Annie Fellows 1863-1931 .... *37*
Johnston, Dorothy Grunbock 1915-1979 ...... *54*
Johnston, Ginny 1946- *60*
Johnston, H(ugh) A(nthony) S(tephen)
   1913-1967 .... *14*
Johnston, Janet 1944- *71*
Johnston, Jeffry W. *188*
Johnston, Johanna 1914(?)-1982 .... *12*
   Obituary *33*
Johnston, Julie 1941- *110*
   Autobiography Feature *128*
   Earlier sketch in SATA *78*
   See also CLR *41*
   See also SAAS *24*
Johnston, Lynn 1947- *216*
   Earlier sketch in SATA *118*
Johnston, Lynn Beverley
   See Johnston, Lynn
Johnston, Mark *194*
Johnston, Norma
   See St. John, Nicole
Johnston, Portia
   See Takakjian, Portia
Johnston, Susan Taylor 1942- *180*
   Earlier sketches in SATA *8, 83, 128*
   See Johnston, Tony
Johnston, Tim(othy Patrick) 1962- *146*
Johnston, Tony *226*
   See Johnston, Susan Taylor
Joinson, Carla *160*
Jolin, Paula *186*
Jolivet, Joelle 1965- *221*
Jonas, Ann 1932- *135*
   Brief entry *42*
   Earlier sketch in SATA *50*
   See also CLR *74*
Jonell, Lynne 1956- *196*
   Earlier sketch in SATA *109*
Jones, Adrienne 1915-2000 .... *82*
   Earlier sketch in SATA *7*
   See also SAAS *10*
Jones, Allan Frewin 1954- *204*
Jones, Annabel
   See Lewis, Mary
Jones, Betty Millsaps 1940- *54*
Jones, Carol 1942- *153*
   Earlier sketch in SATA *79*

Jones, Carrie 1971- *229*
　Earlier sketch in SATA *191*
Jones, Charles M.
　See Jones, Chuck
Jones, Charlotte Foltz 1945- *122*
　Earlier sketch in SATA *77*
Jones, Chuck 1912-2002 .... *53*
　Obituary *133*
Jones, Constance *112*
Jones, Constance A.
　See Jones, Constance
Jones, David 1956- *202*
Jones, Diana Wynne 1934-2011 .... *160*
　Earlier sketches in SATA *9, 70, 108*
　See also CLR *120*
　See also SAAS *7*
Jones, Douglas B. *202*
Jones, Douglas C(lyde) 1924-1998 .... *52*
Jones, Elizabeth McDavid *155*
Jones, Elizabeth Orton 1910-2005 .... *18*
　Obituary *164*
Jones, Evan 1915-1996 .... *3*
Jones, Frewin
　See Jones, Allan Frewin
Jones, Geraldine
　See McCaughrean, Geraldine
Jones, Gillingham
　See Hamilton, Charles (Harold St. John)
Jones, Gwyneth A. 1952- *159*
Jones, Gwyneth Ann
　See Jones, Gwyneth A.
Jones, Harold 1904-1992 .... *14*
　Obituary *72*
Jones, Helen Hinckley 1903-1991 .... *26*
Jones, Helen L(ouise) 1903-1973
　Obituary *22*
Jones, Hettie 1934- *42*
　Brief entry *27*
Jones, Hortense P. 1918- *9*
Jones, J. Sydney 1948- *101*
Jones, Jasmine
　See Papademetriou, Lisa
Jones, Jennifer (Berry) 1947- *90*
Jones, Jessie Mae Orton 1887(?)-1983
　Obituary *37*
Jones, John R(obert) 1926- *76*
Jones, Jon Sydney
　See Jones, J. Sydney
Jones, Judith
　See James, Bill
Jones, Kimberly K. 1957- *187*
Jones, Marcia Thornton 1958- *217*
　Earlier sketches in SATA *73, 115*
Jones, Martha T(annery) 1931- *130*
Jones, Mary Alice 1898(?)-1980 .... *6*
Jones, McClure *34*
Jones, Noah Z. *182*
Jones, Patrick 1961- *210*
　Earlier sketch in SATA *136*
Jones, Penelope 1938- *31*
Jones, Rebecca C(astaldi) 1947- *99*
　Earlier sketch in SATA *33*
Jones, Robin D(orothy) 1959- *80*
Jones, Sanford W.
　See Thorn, John
Jones, Sylvie *185*
Jones, Sylvie Michelle
　See Jones, Sylvie
Jones, Terence Graham Parry 1942- *127*
　Brief entry *51*
　Earlier sketch in SATA *67*
Jones, Terry
　See Jones, Terence Graham Parry
Jones, Tim Wynne
　See Wynne-Jones, Tim
Jones, Traci L. *186*
Jones, V. M. 1958- *147*
Jones, Veda Boyd 1948- *119*
Jones, Victoria Mary
　See Jones, V. M.

Jones, Volcano
　See Mitchell, Adrian
Jones, Weyman (B.) 1928- *4*
　See also SAAS *11*
Jones, William Glynne
　See Glynne-Jones, William
Jonk, Clarence 1906-1987 .... *10*
Jonsberg, Barry 1951- *168*
Joos, Francoise 1956- *78*
Joos, Frederic 1953- *78*
Joosse, Barbara 1949- *220*
　Earlier sketches in SATA *52, 96, 164*
Joosse, Barbara M.
　See Joosse, Barbara
Joosse, Barbara Monnot
　See Joosse, Barbara
Jordan, Alexis Hill
　See Glick, Ruth
　and Titchener, Louise
Jordan, Anne Devereaux 1943- *80*
Jordan, Chris
　See Philbrick, Rodman
Jordan, Deloris *191*
Jordan, Devin *221*
Jordan, Don
　See Howard, Vernon (Linwood)
Jordan, Hope Dahle 1905-1995 .... *15*
Jordan, Jael (Michal) 1949- *30*
Jordan, June 1936-2002 .... *136*
　Earlier sketch in SATA *4*
　See also CLR *10*
Jordan, June Meyer
　See Jordan, June
Jordan, Lee
　See Scholefield, Alan
Jordan, Martin George 1944- *84*
Jordan, Robert 1948-2007 .... *95*
Jordan, Robert K.
　See Jordan, Robert
Jordan, Rosa 1939- *191*
Jordan, Roslyn M. *189*
Jordan, Sherryl 1949- *122*
　Earlier sketch in SATA *71*
　See also SAAS *23*
Jordan, Shirley 1930- *154*
Jordan, Tanis 1946- *84*
Jorgensen, Ivar
　See Ellison, Harlan
　and Garrett, Randall
Jorgensen, Mary Venn -1995 .... *36*
Jorgensen, Norman 1954- *157*
Jorgenson, Ivar
　See Silverberg, Robert
Jorisch, Stephane *178*
Joseph, Anne
　See Coates, Anna
Joseph, James (Herz) 1924- *53*
Joseph, Joan 1939- *34*
Joseph, Joseph M(aron) 1903-1979 .... *22*
Joseph, Patrick
　See O'Malley, Kevin
Josephs, Rebecca
　See Talbot, Toby
Josephson, Judith Pinkerton 1943- *198*
Josh
　See Twain, Mark
Joshua, Peter
　See Stone, Peter
Joslin, Mary 1953- *176*
Joslin, Sesyle
　See Hine, Sesyle Joslin
Joubert, Beverly 1957- *204*
Joubert, Dereck *204*
Journet, Mireille
　See Marokvia, Mireille
Joyce, Bill
　See Joyce, William
Joyce, J(ames) Avery 1902-1987 .... *11*
　Obituary *50*
Joyce, Peter 1937- *127*

Joyce, William 1957- *118*
　Brief entry *46*
　Earlier sketch in SATA *72*
　See also CLR *26*
Joyner, Jerry 1938- *34*
Juan, Ana 1961- *179*
Juarez, Fernando *230*
Juarez, Fernando Lopez
　See Juarez, Fernando
Jubb, Sophie *210*
Jubert, Herve *185*
Juby, Susan 1969- *202*
　Earlier sketch in SATA *156*
Jucker, Sita 1921- *5*
Judah, Aaron 1923- *118*
Judd, Cyril
　See Kornbluth, C(yril) M.
　and Merril, Judith
　and Pohl, Frederik
Judd, Denis (O'Nan) 1938- *33*
Judd, Frances K.
　See Benson, Mildred
Jude, Conny *81*
Judge, Lita *192*
Judson, Clara Ingram 1879-1960 .... *38*
　Brief entry *27*
Judy, Stephen
　See Tchudi, Stephen N.
Judy, Stephen N.
　See Tchudi, Stephen N.
Juhasz, Victor 1954- *177*
Jukes, Mavis 1947- *219*
　Brief entry *43*
　Earlier sketches in SATA *72, 111*
　See also SAAS *12*
Jules, Jacqueline 1956- *218*
　Earlier sketches in SATA *148, 183*
Julesberg, Elizabeth Rider Montgomery
　1902-1985 .... *34*
　Obituary *41*
　Earlier sketch in SATA *3*
Julian, Jane
　See Wiseman, David
Jumpp, Hugo
　See MacPeek, Walter G.
Junco, Martha Aviles
　See Aviles, Martha
Jungman, Ann *165*
Jupo, Frank J. 1904-1981 .... *7*
Jurmain, Suzanne 1945- *169*
　Earlier sketch in SATA *72*
Jurmain, Suzanne Tripp
　See Jurmain, Suzanne
Juster, Norton 1929- *220*
　Earlier sketches in SATA *3, 132*
　See also CLR *112*
Justus, May 1898-1989 .... *1*
　Obituary *106*
Jutte, Jan 1953- *231*
Juvenilia
　See Taylor, Ann

K

Kaaberbol, Lene
　See Kaaberbol, Lene
Kaaberbol, Lene 1960- *159*
Kabdebo, Tamas
　See Kabdebo, Thomas
Kabdebo, Thomas 1934- *10*
Kabibble, Osh
　See Jobb, Jamie
Kacer, Kathy 1954- *184*
　Earlier sketch in SATA *142*
Kaczman, James *156*
Kadair, Deborah Ousley *184*
Kadefors, Sara 1965- *218*
Kadesch, Robert R(udstone) 1922- *31*

Kadohata, Cynthia 1956(?)- 228
  Earlier sketches in SATA *155, 180*
  See also CLR *121*
Kadohata, Cynthia L.
  See Kadohata, Cynthia
Kaempfert, Wade
  See del Rey, Lester
Kaestner, Erich 1899-1974 14
  See also CLR *153*
Kagawa, Julie 228
Kahl, Jonathan (D.) 1959- 77
Kahl, M(arvin) P(hilip) 1934- 37
Kahl, Virginia (Caroline) 1919-2004 48
  Brief entry 38
  Obituary 158
Kahn, Joan 1914-1994 48
  Obituary 82
Kahn, Katherine Janus 1942- 220
  Earlier sketches in SATA *90, 167*
Kahn, Peggy
  See Katz, Bobbi
Kahn, Roger 1927- 37
Kahukiwa, Robyn 1940- 134
Kains, Josephine
  See Goulart, Ron
Kaizuki, Kiyonori 1950- 72
Kajikawa, Kimiko 212
Kakimoto, Kozo 1915- 11
Kalashnikoff, Nicholas 1888-1961 16
Kalb, Jonah 1926- 23
Kalbacken, Joan 1925- 96
Kalechofsky, Roberta 1931- 92
Kaler, James Otis 1848-1912 15
Kalis, Jennifer 207
Kalish, Claire M. 1947- 92
Kallen, Stuart A. 1955- 126
  Earlier sketch in SATA *86*
Kallen, Stuart Arnold
  See Kallen, Stuart A.
Kallevig, Christine Petrell 1955- 164
Kalman, Bobbie 1947- 63
Kalman, Maira 1949- 137
  Earlier sketch in SATA *96*
  See also CLR *32*
Kalnay, Francis 1899-1992 7
Kaloustian, Rosanne 1955- 93
Kalow, Gisela 1946- 32
Kalstein, Dave 175
Kamara, Mariatu 214
Kamen, Gloria 1923- 98
  Earlier sketch in SATA *9*
Kamerman, Sylvia E.
  See Burack, Sylvia K.
Kamm, Josephine (Hart) 1905-1989 24
Kammerman, Sylvia K.
  See Burack, Sylvia K.
Kandel, Michael 1941- 93
Kandell, Alice S. 1938- 35
Kane, Bob 1916-1998 120
Kane, Henry Bugbee 1902-1971 14
Kane, Kim 1973(?)- 221
Kane, L. A.
  See Mannetti, Lisa
Kane, Robert W. 1910- 18
Kane, Wilson
  See Bloch, Robert (Albert)
Kanefield, Teri 1960- 135
Kanell, Beth 215
Kaner, Etta 1947- 198
  Earlier sketch in SATA *126*
Kanetzke, Howard W(illiam) 1932- 38
Kangas, Juli 1958- 200
Kann, Elizabeth 180
Kann, Victoria 180
Kanninen, Barbara 196
Kanninen, Barbara J.
  See Kanninen, Barbara
Kanoza, Muriel Canfield
  See Canfield, Muriel
Kantner, Seth 1965- 179

Kanzawa, Toshiko
  See Furukawa, Toshi
Kanzler, John 1963- 188
Kaplan, Andrew 1960- 78
Kaplan, Anne Bernays
  See Bernays, Anne
Kaplan, Bess 1927- 22
Kaplan, Boche 1926- 24
Kaplan, Elizabeth 1956- 83
Kaplan, Elizabeth A.
  See Kaplan, Elizabeth
Kaplan, Irma 1900- 10
Kaplan, Jean Caryl Korn 1926- 10
Kaplow, Robert 1954- 70
Karageorge, Michael
  See Anderson, Poul
Karas, G. Brian 1957- 222
  Earlier sketch in SATA *178*
Karas, George Brian
  See Karas, G. Brian
Karasz, Ilonka 1896-1981
  Obituary 29
Karen, Ruth 1922-1987 9
  Obituary 54
Kark, Nina Mary
  See Bawden, Nina
Karl, Herb 1938- 73
Karl, Jean E(dna) 1927-2000 122
  Earlier sketch in SATA *34*
  See also SAAS *10*
Karlin, Bernie 1927- 68
Karlin, Eugene 1918- 10
Karlin, Nurit 103
  Earlier sketch in SATA *63*
Karlins, Mark 1947- 219
Karnes, Frances A. 1937- 110
Karp, Naomi J. 1926- 16
Karpinski, J. Rick
  See Karpinski, John Eric
Karpinski, John Eric 1952- 81
Karpinski, Rick
  See Karpinski, John Eric
Karr, Kathleen 1946- 212
  Earlier sketches in SATA *82, 127*
Karr, Phyllis Ann 1944- 119
Karwoski, Gail 1949- 127
Karwoski, Gail Langer
  See Karwoski, Gail
Kashiwagi, Isami 1925- 10
Kaslik, Ibi
  See Kaslik, Ibolya Emma
Kaslik, Ibolya Emma 1973- 185
Kassem, Lou 1931- 62
  Brief entry 51
Kastel, Warren
  See Silverberg, Robert
Kastner, Erich
  See Kaestner, Erich
Kastner, Jill (Marie) 1964- 117
  Earlier sketch in SATA *70*
Kasuya, Masahiro 1937- 51
Kasza, Keiko 1951- 191
  Earlier sketch in SATA *124*
Kataphusin
  See Ruskin, John
Katchen, Carole 1944- 9
Katcher, Brian 1975- 203
Kathryn
  See Searle, Kathryn Adrienne
Kato, Aya 1982- 202
Katona, Robert 1949- 21
Katsarakis, Joan Harries
  See Harries, Joan
Katz, Alan 231
  Earlier sketch in SATA *185*
Katz, Avi 1949- 199
Katz, Avner 1939- 103
Katz, Bobbi 1933- 217
  Earlier sketches in SATA *12, 179*
Katz, Fred(eric Phillip) 1938- 6
Katz, Jane B(resler) 1934- 33

Katz, Karen 1947- 232
  Earlier sketches in SATA *158, 195*
Katz, Marjorie P.
  See Weiser, Marjorie P(hillis) K(atz)
Katz, Susan 1945- 156
Katz, Welwyn Wilton 1948- 96
  Autobiography Feature 118
  Earlier sketch in SATA *62*
  See also CLR *45*
Katz, William 1940- 98
Katz, William Loren 1927- 13
Kaufman, Bel 57
Kaufman, Jeff 1955- 84
Kaufman, Joe 1911-2001 33
Kaufman, Joseph
  See Kaufman, Joe
Kaufman, Mervyn D. 1932- 4
Kaufmann, Angelika 1935- 15
Kaufmann, John 1931- 18
Kaula, Edna Mason 1906-1987 13
Kaur Khalsa, Dayal
  See Khalsa, Dayal Kaur
Kavaler, Lucy 1930- 23
Kavanagh, Jack 1920- 85
Kavanagh, P(atrick) J(oseph Gregory)
  1931- 122
Kavanaugh, Ian
  See Webb, Jean Francis (III)
Kay, Alan N. 1965- 144
Kay, Elizabeth 1949- 165
Kay, Guy Gavriel 1954- 167
  Earlier sketch in SATA *121*
Kay, Helen
  See Goldfrank, Helen Colodny
Kay, Jackie 1961- 165
  Earlier sketch in SATA *97*
Kay, Jacqueline Margaret
  See Kay, Jackie
Kay, Julia 205
Kay, Mara 13
Kay, Verla 1946- 210
  Earlier sketch in SATA *120*
Kaye, Danny 1913-1987
  Obituary 50
Kaye, Geraldine (Hughesdon) 1925- 85
  Earlier sketch in SATA *10*
Kaye, Judy
  See Baer, Judy
Kaye, Marilyn 1949- 230
  Earlier sketches in SATA *56, 110*
Kaye, Mary Margaret
  See Kaye, M.M.
Kaye, M.M. 1908-2004 62
  Obituary 152
Kaye, Mollie
  See Kaye, M.M.
Kaye, Peggy 1948- 143
Keach, James P. 1950- 125
Keams, Geri 1951- 117
Keane, Bil 1922- 4
Keane, Dave 1965- 216
Keaney, Brian 1954- 188
  Earlier sketch in SATA *106*
Kearney, Meg 1964- 178
Kearny, Jillian
  See Goulart, Ron
Keat, Nawuth 1964- 222
Keating, Bern
  See Keating, Leo Bernard
Keating, Frank 1944- 143
Keating, Lawrence A. 1903-1966 23
Keating, Leo Bernard 1915- 10
Keats, Emma 1899(?)-1979(?) 68
Keats, Ezra Jack 1916-1983 57
  Obituary 34
  Earlier sketch in SATA *14*
  See also CLR *35*
Keefer, Catherine
  See Ogan, George F.
  and Ogan, Margaret E. (Nettles)

Keefer, Janice Kulyk
　See Kulyk Keefer, Janice
Keegan, Marcia 1943- *104*
　Earlier sketch in SATA *9*
Keehn, Sally M. 1947- *165*
　Earlier sketch in SATA *87*
Keel, Frank
　See Keeler, Ronald F(ranklin)
Keeler, Patricia *183*
Keeler, Patricia A.
　See Keeler, Patricia
Keeler, Ronald F(ranklin) 1913-1983 .... *47*
Keely, Jack 1951- *119*
Keen, Martin L. 1913-1992 .... *4*
Keenan, Sheila 1953- *95*
Keene, Ann T. 1940- *86*
Keene, Ann Todd
　See Keene, Ann T.
Keene, Carolyn
　See Benson, Mildred
　and Goulart, Ron
　and Lerangis, Peter
　and McFarlane, Leslie
　and Stanley, George Edward
　and Stratemeyer, Edward L.
Keens-Douglas, Richardo 1953- *154*
　Earlier sketch in SATA *95*
Keep, Linda Lowery
　See Lowery, Linda
Keep, Richard 1949- *170*
Keep, Richard Cleminson
　See Keep, Richard
Keeping, Charles (William James)
　1924-1988 .... *69*
　Obituary *56*
　Earlier sketch in SATA *9*
　See also CLR *34*
Keeshan, Robert J. 1927-2004 .... *32*
　Obituary *151*
Kehlenbeck, Angela 1959- *186*
Kehoe, Tim 1970- *224*
Kehret, Peg 1936- *212*
　Autobiography Feature *149*
　Earlier sketches in SATA *73, 108, 149*
Keillor, Garrison 1942- *58*
Keillor, Gary Edward
　See Keillor, Garrison
Keir, Christine
　See Pullein-Thompson, Christine
Keiser, Paige *220*
Keister, Douglas 1948- *88*
Keith, Doug 1952- *81*
Keith, Eros 1942- *52*
Keith, Hal 1934- *36*
Keith, Harold (Verne) 1903-1998 .... *74*
　Earlier sketch in SATA *2*
Keith, Robert
　See Applebaum, Stan
Keleinikov, Andrei 1924- *65*
Kelemen, Julie 1959- *78*
Kelen, Emery 1896-1978 .... *13*
　Obituary *26*
Kelleam, Joseph E(veridge) 1913-1975 .... *31*
Kelleher, Anne 1959- *97*
Kelleher, Annette 1950- *122*
Kelleher, Daria Valerian 1955- *79*
Kelleher, Victor (Michael Kitchener)
　1939- *129*
　Brief entry *52*
　Earlier sketch in SATA *75*
　See also CLR *36*
Keller, Beverly L(ou) *91*
　Earlier sketch in SATA *13*
Keller, Charles 1942- *82*
　Earlier sketch in SATA *8*
Keller, Debra 1958- *94*
Keller, Dick 1923- *36*
Keller, Emily *96*
Keller, Gail Faithfull
　See Faithfull, Gail

Keller, Holly 1942- *216*
　Brief entry *42*
　Earlier sketches in SATA *76, 108, 157*
　See also CLR *45*
Keller, Irene (Barron) 1927-2002 .... *36*
　Obituary *139*
Keller, Laurie 1961(?)- *196*
Kelley, Ann 1941- *217*
Kelley, Ellen A. *185*
Kelley, Ellen Chavez
　See Kelley, Ellen A.
Kelley, Gary 1945- *217*
　Earlier sketch in SATA *183*
Kelley, J.A.
　See Kelley, Jane
Kelley, Jane 1954- *231*
Kelley, Leo P(atrick) 1928- *32*
　Brief entry *31*
Kelley, Marty 1971- *211*
Kelley, Patrick (G.) 1963- *129*
Kelley, Patte 1947- *93*
Kelley, True 1946- *179*
Kelley, True (Adelaide) 1946- *130*
　Brief entry *39*
　Earlier sketches in SATA *41, 92*
Kelley, True Adelaide
　See Kelley, True
Kellin, Sally Moffet 1932- *9*
Kelling, Furn L. 1914-2000 .... *37*
Kellogg, Gene
　See Kellogg, Jean (Defrees)
Kellogg, Jean (Defrees) 1916-1978 .... *10*
Kellogg, Steven 1941- *177*
　Earlier sketches in SATA *8, 57, 130*
　See also CLR *6*
Kellogg, Steven Castle
　See Kellogg, Steven
Kellow, Kathleen
　See Hibbert, Eleanor Alice Burford
Kelly, C. M. O.
　See Gibbs, (Cecilia) May
Kelly, Clint 1950- *140*
Kelly, Eric P(hilbrook) 1884-1960
　See YABC *1*
Kelly, Fiona
　See Coleman, Michael
　and Hendry, Frances Mary
　and Jones, Allan Frewin
　and Oldfield, Jenny
　and Welford, Sue
Kelly, Irene 1957- *210*
　Earlier sketch in SATA *147*
Kelly, Jacqueline *216*
Kelly, Jeff
　See Kelly, Jeffrey
Kelly, Jeffrey 1946- *65*
Kelly, Joanne (W.) 1934- *87*
Kelly, Kate 1958- *91*
Kelly, Kathleen M. 1964- *71*
Kelly, Katy 1955- *215*
　Earlier sketch in SATA *169*
Kelly, Lauren
　See Oates, Joyce Carol
Kelly, Laurene 1954- *123*
Kelly, Martha Rose 1914-1983 .... *37*
Kelly, Marty
　See Kelly, Martha Rose
Kelly, Mij *166*
Kelly, Ralph
　See Geis, Darlene Stern
Kelly, Regina Z(immerman) 1898-1986 .... *5*
Kelly, Rosalie (Ruth) *43*
Kelly, Tara *230*
Kelly, Tom 1961- *191*
Kelly, Walt(er Crawford) 1913-1973 .... *18*
Kelsey, Alice Geer 1896-1982 .... *1*
Kelsey, Elin 1961- *159*
Kelsey, Marybeth *216*
Kemly, Kathleen 1958- *197*
Kemnitz, Thomas Milton, Jr. 1984- *152*

Kemnitz, Tom, Jr.
　See Kemnitz, Thomas Milton, Jr.
Kemp, Gene 1926- *75*
　Earlier sketch in SATA *25*
　See also CLR *29*
Kempner, Mary Jean 1913-1969 .... *10*
Kempter, Christa 1945- *187*
Kempton, Jean Welch 1914- *10*
Kenah, Katharine 1949- *182*
Kenda, Margaret 1942- *71*
Kendall, Carol (Seeger) 1917- *74*
　Earlier sketch in SATA *11*
　See also SAAS *7*
Kendall, Gideon 1966- *215*
Kendall, Katherine
　See Applegate, Katherine
Kendall, Lace
　See Stoutenburg, Adrien (Pearl)
Kendall, Martha E. *87*
Kendall, Russ 1957- *83*
Kenealy, James P. 1927- *52*
　Brief entry *29*
Kenealy, Jim
　See Kenealy, James P.
Kennaway, Adrienne 1945- *171*
　Earlier sketch in SATA *60*
Kennedy, Anne 1955- *198*
Kennedy, Anne Vittur
　See Kennedy, Anne
Kennedy, Brendan 1970- *57*
Kennedy, Dana Forrest 1917- *74*
Kennedy, Dorothy M(intzlaff) 1931- *53*
Kennedy, Doug 1963- *189*
　Earlier sketch in SATA *122*
Kennedy, Frances 1937- *192*
Kennedy, James *214*
Kennedy, John F. 1917-1963 .... *11*
Kennedy, John Fitzgerald
　See Kennedy, John F.
Kennedy, Joseph Charles
　See Kennedy, X. J.
Kennedy, Kim *189*
Kennedy, Marlane 1962- *210*
Kennedy, Pamela (J.) 1946- *87*
Kennedy, Paul E(dward) 1929- *113*
　Earlier sketch in SATA *33*
Kennedy, Richard (Pitt) 1910-1989
　Obituary *60*
Kennedy, (Jerome) Richard 1932- *22*
Kennedy, Robert 1938- *63*
Kennedy, T.A. 1953- *42*
　Brief entry *35*
Kennedy, Teresa
　See Kennedy, T.A.
Kennedy, Teresa A.
　See Kennedy, T.A.
Kennedy, William 1928- *57*
Kennedy, William Joseph
　See Kennedy, William
Kennedy, X. J. 1929- *130*
　Autobiography Feature *130*
　Earlier sketches in SATA *14, 86*
　See also CLR *27*
　See also SAAS *22*
Kennell, Ruth Epperson 1893-1977 .... *6*
　Obituary *25*
Kennemore, Tim 1957- *220*
　Earlier sketch in SATA *133*
Kennen, Ally *190*
Kennett, David 1959- *206*
　Earlier sketch in SATA *121*
Kennison, Ruth *202*
Kenny, Ellsworth Newcomb 1909-1971
　Obituary *26*
Kenny, Herbert Andrew 1912-2002 .... *13*
Kenny, Jude
　See Daly, Jude

Kenny, Kathryn
See Bowden, Joan Chase
and Krull, Kathleen
and Sanderlin, Owenita (Harrah)
and Stack, Nicolete Meredith
Kenny, Kevin
See Krull, Kathleen
Kensinger, George
See Fichter, George S.
Kensington, Kathryn Wesley
See Rusch, Kristine Kathryn
Kent, Alexander
See Reeman, Douglas Edward
Kent, David
See Lambert, David
Kent, Deborah Ann 1948- 155
Brief entry 41
Earlier sketches in SATA 47, 104
Kent, Jack
See Kent, John Wellington
Kent, John Wellington 1920-1985 24
Obituary 45
Kent, Lisa 1942- 90
Kent, Mallory
See Lowndes, Robert A(ugustine) W(ard)
Kent, Margaret 1894- 2
Kent, Rockwell 1882-1971 6
Kent, Rose 188
Kent, Sherman 1903-1986 20
Obituary 47
Kenward, Jean 1920- 42
Kenworthy, Leonard S. 1912-1991 6
Kenyon, Karen (Smith) 1938- 145
Kenyon, Kate
See Adorjan, Carol (Madden)
and Ransom, Candice
Kenyon, Ley 1913-1990 6
Keown, Elizabeth 78
Kepes, Juliet A(ppleby) 1919-1999 13
Kephart, Beth 1960- 196
Kerby, Mona 1951- 202
Earlier sketch in SATA 75
Kerigan, Florence 1896-1984 12
Kerley, Barbara 1960- 191
Earlier sketch in SATA 138
Kerman, Gertrude
See Furman, Gertrude Lerner Kerman
Kerns, Thelma 1929- 116
Kerr, Anne Louise
See Mackey, Weezie Kerr
Kerr, Bob 1951- 120
Kerr, Jessica 1901-1991 13
Kerr, (Anne-)Judith 1923-1970 24
Kerr, M. E.
See Meaker, Marijane
Kerr, P.B.
See Kerr, Philip
Kerr, Philip 1956- 168
Kerr, Phyllis Forbes 1942- 72
Kerr, Tom 1950- 77
Kerrin, Jessica Scott 174
Kerry, Frances
See Kerigan, Florence
Kerry, Lois
See Duncan, Lois
Kershen, (L.) Michael 1982- 82
Kerven, Rosalind 1954- 83
Ker Wilson, Barbara 1929- 121
Earlier sketches in SATA 20, 70
See also SAAS 18
Kerz, Anna 1947- 220
Keselman, Gabriela 1953- 128
Kesey, Ken 1935-2001 66
Obituary 131
See also CLR 170
Kesey, Ken Elton
See Kesey, Ken
Kesler, Jay 1935- 65
Kessel, Joyce Karen 1937- 41
Kessler, Cristina 190

Kessler, Ethel 1922- 44
Brief entry 37
Kessler, Leonard P. 1921- 14
Kessler, Liz 1966- 206
Kest, Kristin 1967- 168
Earlier sketch in SATA 118
Kesteven, G. R.
See Crosher, G. R.
Ketcham, Hank
See Ketcham, Henry King
Ketcham, Henry King 1920-2001 28
Brief entry 27
Obituary 128
Ketcham, Sallie 1963- 124
Ketchum, Liza 1946- 132
Earlier sketch in SATA 78
Ketner, Mary Grace 1946- 75
Kettelkamp, Larry (Dale) 1933- 2
See also SAAS 3
Ketteman, Helen 1945- 223
Earlier sketches in SATA 73, 115, 167
Kettle, Peter
See Glover, Denis (James Matthews)
Kevles, Bettyann Holtzmann 1938- 23
Key, Alexander (Hill) 1904-1979 8
Obituary 23
Key, Samuel M.
See de Lint, Charles
Key, Watt 1970- 189
Keyes, Daniel 1927- 37
Keyes, Diane 207
Keyes, Fenton 1915-1999 34
Keyes, Greg 1963- 116
Keyes, J. Gregory
See Keyes, Greg
Keyser, Marcia 1933- 42
Keyser, Sarah
See McGuire, Leslie (Sarah)
Khalid, Mohamed Nor
See Lat
Khalsa, Dayal Kaur 1943-1989 62
See also CLR 30
Khan, Hena 214
Khan, Rukhsana 1962- 231
Earlier sketches in SATA 118, 165
Khanshendel, Chiron
See Rose, Wendy
Kheirabadi, Masoud 1951- 158
Khemir, Sabiha 87
Kherdian, David 1931- 74
Autobiography Feature 125
Earlier sketch in SATA 16
See also CLR 24
Khing, T.T. 1933- 192
Kibbe, Pat (Hosley) 60
Kidd, Diana 1933-2000 150
Kidd, Richard 1952-2008 152
Obituary 194
Kidd, Ronald 1948- 173
Earlier sketches in SATA 42, 92
Kiddell, John 1922- 3
Kiddell-Monroe, Joan 1908-1972 55
Kidwell, Carl 1910- 43
Kiefer, Irene 1926- 21
Kiefer, Kathleen Balmes 1957- 142
Kiepper, Shirley Morgan 1933- 10
Kierstead, Vera M.
See Kierstead-Farber, Vera M.
Kierstead-Farber, Vera M. 1913- 121
Kierstead-Farber, Vera May
See Kierstead-Farber, Vera M.
Kiesel, Stanley 1925- 35
Kiesler, Kate (A.) 1971- 152
Earlier sketch in SATA 90
Kihn, Greg 1952- 110
Kikukawa, Cecily H(arder) 1919- 44
Brief entry 35
Kilaka, John 1966- 223
Kilcher, Jewel 1974- 109
Kile, Joan 1940- 78
Kilgore, Kathleen 1946- 42

Kilian, Crawford 1941- 35
Killdeer, John
See Mayhar, Ardath
Killien, Christi 1956- 73
Killilea, Marie (Lyons) 1913-1991 2
Killingback, Julia 1944- 63
Killough, (Karen) Lee 1942- 64
Kilpatrick, Don 206
Kilreon, Beth
See Walker, Barbara (Jeanne) K(erlin)
Kilworth, Garry 1941- 216
Earlier sketch in SATA 94
Kilworth, Garry D.
See Kilworth, Garry
Kilworth, Garry Douglas
See Kilworth, Garry
Kim, David 1977- 201
Kim, Dong-hwa 1950- 225
Kim, Helen 1899-1970 98
Kim, Joung Un 1970- 205
Kim, Susan 1958- 232
Kimball, Gayle 1943- 90
Kimball, Violet T(ew) 1932- 126
Kimball, Yeffe 1914-1978 37
Kimber, Murray 1964- 171
Kimble, Warren 176
Kimbrough, Emily 1899-1989 2
Obituary 59
Kimeldorf, Martin 1948- 121
Kimeldorf, Martin R.
See Kimeldorf, Martin
Kimenye, Barbara 1940(?)- 121
Kimmel, Elizabeth Cody 209
Earlier sketch in SATA 170
Kimmel, Eric A. 1946- 208
Earlier sketches in SATA 13, 80, 125, 176
Kimmel, Margaret Mary 1938- 43
Brief entry 33
Kimmelman, Burt 1947- 180
Kimmelman, Leslie 1958- 211
Earlier sketches in SATA 85, 156
Kincaid, Jamaica 1949-
See CLR 63
Kincher, Jonni 1949- 79
Kindl, Patrice 1951- 128
Earlier sketch in SATA 82
See also CLR 132
Kindred, Wendy (Good) 1937- 7
Kinerk, Robert 199
Kines, Pat Decker 1937- 12
King, Adam
See Hoare, Robert J(ohn)
King, Alison
See Martini, Teri
King, (Maria) Anna 1964- 72
King, A.S. 1970- 217
King, Billie Jean 1943- 12
King, Christine
See Farris, Christine King
King, Christopher (L.) 1945- 84
King, (David) Clive 1924- 144
Earlier sketch in SATA 28
King, Colin 1943- 76
King, Cynthia 1925- 7
King, Daniel (John) 1963- 130
King, Daren 1972- 197
King, Elizabeth 1953- 83
King, Frank O. 1883-1969
Obituary 22
King, Frank R. 1904-1999 127
King, Jane
See Currie, Stephen
King, Jeanette (Margaret) 1959- 105
King, Larry L. 1929- 66
King, Laurie R. 1952- 88
King, Marian 1900(?)-1986 23
Obituary 47
King, Martin Luther, Jr. 1929-1968 14
King, Mary Ellen 1958- 93
King, Paul
See Drackett, Phil(ip Arthur)

King, Paula
  See Downing, Paula E.
King, Stephen 1947- *161*
  Earlier sketches in SATA *9, 55*
  See also CLR *124*
King, Stephen Edwin
  See King, Stephen
King, Stephen Michael *218*
  Earlier sketch in SATA *157*
King, Steve
  See King, Stephen
King, Thomas 1943- *96*
King, Thomas Hunt
  See King, Thomas
King, Tony 1947- *39*
King, Willie Christine
  See Farris, Christine King
Kingfisher, Rupert *209*
Kingman, Dong (Moy Shu) 1911-2000 .... *44*
Kingman, Lee
  See Natti, Lee
Kingsbury, Evan
  See Walker, Robert W.
Kingsland, Leslie William 1912- *13*
Kingsley, Charles 1819-1875
  See YABC *2*
  See also CLR *167*
Kingsley, Emily Perl 1940- *33*
Kingsley, Kaza *193*
King-Smith, Dick 1922-2011 .... *192*
  Brief entry *38*
  Earlier sketches in SATA *47, 80, 135*
  See also CLR *40*
Kingston, Maxine Hong 1940- *53*
Kingston, Maxine Ting Ting Hong
  See Kingston, Maxine Hong
Kinkade, Sheila 1962- *229*
Kinney, C. Cle(land) 1915- *6*
Kinney, Harrison 1921- *13*
Kinney, Jean Stout 1912- *12*
Kinney, Jeff 1971- *187*
Kinsey, Elizabeth
  See Clymer, Eleanor
Kinsey, Helen 1948- *82*
Kinsey-Warnock, Natalie 1956- *167*
  Earlier sketches in SATA *71, 116*
Kinzel, Dorothy 1950- *57*
Kinzel, Dottie
  See Kinzel, Dorothy
Kipling, Joseph Rudyard
  See Kipling, Rudyard
Kipling, Rudyard 1865-1936 .... *100*
  See also YABC *2*
  See also CLR *65*
Kippax, Frank
  See Needle, Jan
Kirby, David 1944- *78*
Kirby, David K.
  See Kirby, David
Kirby, David Kirk
  See Kirby, David
Kirby, Margaret
  See Bingley, Margaret (Jane Kirby)
Kirby, Pamela F. 1952- *220*
Kirby, Susan E. 1949- *62*
Kirk, Connie Ann 1957- *167*
Kirk, Daniel 1952- *196*
  Earlier sketches in SATA *107, 153*
Kirk, David 1955- *161*
  Earlier sketch in SATA *117*
Kirk, Heather 1949- *166*
Kirk, Ruth (Kratz) 1925- *5*
Kirkham, Dinah
  See Card, Orson Scott
Kirkland, Will
  See Hale, Arlene
Kirkpatrick, Katherine (Anne) 1964- *113*
Kirkup, James 1918-2009 .... *12*
Kirkus, Virginia
  See Glick, Virginia Kirkus

Kirkwood, Kathryn
  See Fluke, Joanne
Kirsch, Vincent X. *211*
Kirshenbaum, Binnie *79*
Kirshner, David S. 1958- *123*
Kirtland, G. B.
  See Hine, Sesyle Joslin
  and Hine, Al(fred Blakelee)
Kirwan, Wednesday *198*
Kish, Eleanor M(ary) 1924- *73*
Kish, Ely
  See Kish, Eleanor M(ary)
Kishida, Eriko 1929- *12*
Kisinger, Grace Gelvin (Maze) 1913-1965 .. *10*
Kissel, Richard *209*
Kissin, Eva H. 1923- *10*
Kissinger, Rosemary K.
  See Updyke, Rosemary K.
Kistler, John M. 1967- *160*
Kitamura, Satoshi 1956- *201*
  Earlier sketches in SATA *62, 98, 143*
  See also CLR *60*
Kitanidis, Phoebe 1977- *230*
Kitchen, Bert
  See Kitchen, Herbert Thomas
Kitchen, Herbert Thomas 1940- *70*
Kite, L. Patricia
  See Kite, Pat
Kite, Pat 1940- *78*
Kitt, Tamara
  See de Regniers, Beatrice Schenk (Freedman)
Kittinger, Jo S(usenbach) 1955- *148*
  Earlier sketch in SATA *96*
Kituomba
  See Odaga, Asenath (Bole)
Kitzinger, Sheila 1929- *57*
Kiwak, Barbara 1966- *103*
Kjelgaard, James Arthur 1910-1959 .... *17*
  See also CLR *81*
Kjelgaard, Jim
  See Kjelgaard, James Arthur
Kjelle, Marylou Morano 1954- *146*
Klages, Ellen 1954- *196*
Klagsbrun, Francine (Lifton) *36*
Klaits, Barrie 1944- *52*
Klam, Cheryl *191*
Klaperman, Gilbert 1921- *33*
Klaperman, Libby Mindlin 1921-1982 .... *33*
  Obituary *31*
Klass, David 1960- *207*
  Earlier sketches in SATA *88, 142*
Klass, Morton 1927-2001 .... *11*
Klass, Sheila Solomon 1927- *219*
  Autobiography Feature *126*
  Earlier sketches in SATA *45, 99*
  See also SAAS *26*
Klause, Annette Curtis 1953- *175*
  Earlier sketch in SATA *79*
  See also CLR *104*
Klaveness, Jan O'Donnell 1939- *86*
Kleberger, Ilse 1921- *5*
Kleeberg, Irene (Flitner) Cumming 1932- *65*
Klein, Aaron E. 1930-1998 .... *45*
  Brief entry *28*
Klein, Bill 1945- *89*
Klein, David 1919-2001 .... *59*
Klein, Frederick C. 1938- *154*
Klein, Gerda Weissmann 1924- *44*
Klein, H(erbert) Arthur *8*
Klein, James 1932- *115*
Klein, Leonore (Glotzer) 1916- *6*
Klein, Lisa 1958- *211*
Klein, Lisa M.
  See Klein, Lisa
Klein, Mina C(ooper) 1906-1979 .... *8*
Klein, Norma 1938-1989 .... *57*
  Earlier sketch in SATA *7*
  See also CLR *162*
  See also SAAS *1*
Klein, Rachel S. 1953- *105*

Klein, Robin 1936- *164*
  Brief entry *45*
  Earlier sketches in SATA *55, 80*
  See also CLR *21*
Klemin, Diana *65*
Klemm, Barry 1945- *104*
Klemm, Edward G., Jr. 1910-2001 .... *30*
Klemm, Roberta K(ohnhorst) 1884-1975 ..... *30*
Kleven, Elisa 1958- *217*
  Earlier sketches in SATA *76, 173*
  See also CLR *85*
Klevin, Jill Ross 1935- *39*
  Brief entry *38*
Kliban, B(ernard) 1935-1990 .... *35*
  Obituary *66*
Klier, Kimberly Wagner *208*
Klimo, Kate *214*
Klimowicz, Barbara 1927- *10*
Kline, Christina Baker 1964- *101*
Kline, James
  See Klein, James
Kline, Jim
  See Kline, Jim
Kline, Lisa Williams 1954- *143*
Kline, Suzy 1943- *193*
  Autobiography Feature *193*
  Brief entry *48*
  Earlier sketches in SATA *67, 99, 152*
Kling, Heidi R. *233*
Klinger, Shula *230*
Kliros, Thea 1935- *106*
Klise, Kate *221*
  Earlier sketch in SATA *181*
Klise, M. Sarah 1961- *180*
  Earlier sketch in SATA *128*
Klots, Alexander Barrett 1903-1989
  Obituary *62*
Klug, Ron(ald) 1939- *31*
Knaak, Richard A. 1961- *166*
  Earlier sketch in SATA *86*
Knaak, Richard Allen
  See Knaak, Richard A.
Knapman, Timothy *200*
Knapp, Edward
  See Kunhardt, Edith
Knapp, Ron 1952- *34*
Knebel, Fletcher 1911-1993 .... *36*
  Obituary *75*
Kneeland, Linda Clarke 1947- *94*
Kneen, Maggie 1957- *221*
Knickerbocker, Diedrich
  See Irving, Washington
Knifesmith
  See Cutler, Ivor
Knigge, Robert (R.) 1921(?)-1987 .... *50*
Knight, Anne (Katherine) 1946- *34*
Knight, Brenda *112*
Knight, Christopher G. 1943- *96*
Knight, Damon (Francis) 1922-2002 .... *9*
  Obituary *139*
Knight, David C(arpenter) 1925-1984 .... *14*
  See also CLR *38*
Knight, Eric 1897-1943 .... *18*
Knight, Eric Mowbray
  See Knight, Eric
Knight, Francis Edgar 1905- *14*
Knight, Frank
  See Knight, Francis Edgar
Knight, Hilary 1926- *132*
  Earlier sketches in SATA *15, 69*
Knight, Joan
  See Knight, Joan (MacPhail)
Knight, Joan (MacPhail) *159*
  Earlier sketch in SATA *82*
Knight, Kathryn Lasky
  See Lasky, Kathryn
Knight, Mallory T.
  See Hurwood, Bernhardt J.
Knight, Ruth Adams 1898-1974
  Obituary *20*
Knight, Theodore O. 1946- *77*

Knobloch, Dorothea 1951- 88
Knoepfle, John (Ignatius) 1923- 66
Knorr, Laura 1971- 200
Knott, Bill
   See Knott, William C(ecil, Jr.)
Knott, William C(ecil, Jr.) 1927- 3
Knotts, Howard (Clayton, Jr.) 1922- 25
Knowles, Anne 1933- 37
Knowles, Jo 1970- 197
Knowles, Johanna Beth
   See Knowles, Jo
Knowles, John 1926-2001 89
   Obituary 134
   Earlier sketch in SATA 8
   See also CLR 98
Knox, Calvin M.
   See Silverberg, Robert
Knox, (Mary) Eleanor Jessie 1909-2000 59
   Earlier sketch in SATA 30
Knox, Elizabeth 1959- 176
Knox, Elizabeth Fiona
   See Knox, Elizabeth
Knox, James
   See Brittain, William
Knox, Jolyne 1937- 76
Knudsen, James 1950- 42
Knudsen, Michelle 1974- 220
   Earlier sketch in SATA 171
Knudson, Mike 1965- 209
Knudson, R. R.
   See Knudson, Rozanne
Knudson, Richard L(ewis) 1930- 34
Knudson, Rozanne 1932-2008 79
   Earlier sketch in SATA 7
   See also SAAS 18
Knutson, Barbara 1959-2005 166
Knutson, Kimberley 115
Knye, Cassandra
   See Disch, Thomas M.
Kobayashi, Masako Matsuno 1935- 6
Kober, Shahar 1979- 213
Koch, Dorothy Clarke 1924- 6
Koch, Kenneth 1925-2002 65
Koch, Kenneth Jay
   See Koch, Kenneth
Koch, Phyllis (Mae) McCallum 1911- 10
Kochalka, James 1967- 196
Kocsis, J. C.
   See Paul, James
Koda-Callan, Elizabeth 1944- 140
   Earlier sketch in SATA 67
Kodera, Craig 1956- 222
Kodman, Stanislawa 201
Koehler, Phoebe 1955- 85
Koehler-Pentacoff, Elizabeth 1957- 160
   Earlier sketch in SATA 96
Koehn, Ilse
   See Van Zwienen, Ilse Charlotte Koehn
Koeller, Carol 192
Koenig, Viviane 1950- 80
Koering, Ursula 1921-1976 64
Koerner, W(illiam) H(enry) D(avid)
   1878-1938 21
Koertge, Ron 1940- 209
   Earlier sketches in SATA 53, 92, 131
Koestler-Grack, Rachel A. 1973- 156
Koff, Richard Myram 1926- 62
Koffinke, Carol 1949- 82
Kogan, Deborah
   See Kogan Ray, Deborah
Kogan Ray, Deborah 1940- 203
   Earlier sketches in SATA 8, 50, 161
Kogawa, Joy 1935- 99
Kogawa, Joy Nozomi
   See Kogawa, Joy
Kogler, Jennie
   See Kogler, Jennifer Anne
Kogler, Jennifer Anne 1982(?)- 174
Kohara, Kazuno 207
Kohl, Herbert 1937- 47

Kohl, Herbert R.
   See Kohl, Herbert
Kohl, MaryAnn F(aubion) 1947- 144
   Earlier sketch in SATA 74
Kohler, Dean Ellis 1947- 226
Kohler, Julilly H(ouse) 1908-1976
   Obituary 20
Kohn, Bernice
   See Hunt, Bernice
Kohn, Rita (T.) 1933- 89
Kohner, Frederick 1905-1986 10
   Obituary 48
Koide, Tan 1938-1986 50
Koike, Kay 1940- 72
Koja, Kathe 1960- 199
   Earlier sketch in SATA 155
Koja, Stephan 198
Kolar, Bob 1960(?)- 206
Kolb, Larry J. 1953- 175
Kolba, St. Tamara 22
Kolibalova, Marketa
   See Kolibalova, Marketa
Kolibalova, Marketa 1953- 126
Koller, Jackie French 1948- 157
   Earlier sketches in SATA 72, 109
   See also CLR 68
Kolodny, Nancy J. 1946- 76
Kolosov, Jacqueline 1967- 199
Komaiko, Leah 1954- 164
   Earlier sketch in SATA 97
Komisar, Lucy 1942- 9
Komoda, Beverly 1939- 25
Komoda, Kiyo 1937- 9
Kompaneyets, Marc 1974- 169
Komroff, Manuel 1890-1974 2
   Obituary 20
Konigsberg, Bill 1970- 207
Konigsburg, E.L. 1930- 194
   Earlier sketches in SATA 4, 48, 94, 126
   See also CLR 81
Konigsburg, Elaine Lobl
   See Konigsburg, E.L.
Koning, Hans 1921-2007 5
   Obituary 182
Koningsberger, Hans
   See Koning, Hans
Konkle, Janet Everest 1917- 12
Kono, Erin Eitter 1973- 177
Konrad, Marla Stewart 218
Konzak, Burt 1946- 151
Koob, Theodora (J. Foth) 1918- 23
Kooiker, Leonie
   See Kooyker-Romijn, Johanna Maria
Koons, James
   See Pernu, Dennis
Koontz, Dean 1945- 165
   Earlier sketch in SATA 92
   See Koontz, Dean R.
Koontz, Dean R. 225
   See Koontz, Dean
Koontz, Dean Ray
   See Koontz, Dean
Koontz, Robin Michal 1954- 136
   Earlier sketch in SATA 70
Kooyker, Leonie
   See Kooyker-Romijn, Johanna Maria
Kooyker-Romijn, Johanna Maria 1927- 48
Kooyker-Romyn, Johanna Maria
   See Kooyker-Romijn, Johanna Maria
Kopelke, Lisa 1963- 154
Kopper, Lisa 1950- 105
   Brief entry 51
Kopper, Lisa Esther
   See Kopper, Lisa
Koppes, Steven N. 1957- 169
Koppes, Steven Nelson
   See Koppes, Steven N.
Korach, Mimi 1922- 9
Koralek, Jenny 1934- 215
   Earlier sketches in SATA 71, 140

Korczak, Janusz
   See Goldszmit, Henryk
Koren, Edward (Benjamin) 1935- 148
   Earlier sketch in SATA 5
Koren, Edward 1935- 206
Korinets, Iurii Iosifovich
   See Korinetz, Yuri (Iosifovich)
Korinetz, Yuri (Iosifovich) 1923- 9
   See also CLR 4
Korman, Bernice 1937- 78
Korman, Gordon 1963- 226
   Brief entry 41
   Earlier sketches in SATA 49, 81, 119, 167
   See also CLR 25
Korman, Gordon Richard
   See Korman, Gordon
Korman, Justine 1958- 70
Kornblatt, Marc 1954- 147
   Earlier sketch in SATA 84
Kornprobst, Jacques 1937- 177
Korte, Gene J. 1950- 74
Korthues, Barbara 1971- 203
Korty, Carol 1937- 15
Koscielniak, Bruce 1947- 153
   Earlier sketches in SATA 67, 99
Koshin, Alexander (A.) 1952- 86
Kositsky, Lynne 1947- 158
Koskenmaki, Rosalie
   See Maggio, Rosalie
Koss, Amy Goldman 1954- 158
   Earlier sketch in SATA 115
Kossin, Sandy (Sanford) 1926- 10
Kossman, Nina 1959- 84
Kostecki-Shaw, Jenny Sue 203
Kostick, Conor 1964- 186
Kotzwinkle, William 1938- 146
   Earlier sketches in SATA 24, 70
   See also CLR 6
Kouhi, Elizabeth 1917- 54
   Brief entry 49
Kouts, Anne 1945- 8
Koutsky, Jan Dale 1955- 146
Kovacs, Deborah 1954- 132
   Earlier sketch in SATA 79
Kovalski, Maryann 1951- 175
   Earlier sketches in SATA 58, 97
   See also CLR 34
   See also SAAS 21
Kowalski, Kathiann M. 1955- 151
   Earlier sketch in SATA 96
Koz, Paula G.
   See Goodman Koz, Paula
Kozjan, Drazen 209
Kraft, Betsy Harvey 1937- 157
Kraft, Erik P. 193
Krahn, Fernando 1935- 49
   Brief entry 31
   See also CLR 3
Krakauer, Hoong Yee Lee 1955- 86
Krakauer, Jon 1954- 108
Krall, Dan 1970- 218
Kramer, George
   See Heuman, William
Kramer, Nora 1896(?)-1984 26
   Obituary 39
Kramer, Remi (Thomas) 1935- 90
Krantz, Hazel (Newman) 12
Kranzler, George G(ershon) 1916- 28
Kranzler, Gershon
   See Kranzler, George G(ershon)
Krasilovsky, Phyllis 1926- 38
   Earlier sketch in SATA 1
   See also CLR 83
   See also SAAS 5
Krasne, Betty
   See Levine, Betty K(rasne)
Krasner, Steven 1953- 154
Krasnesky, Thad 1969(?)- 224
Krasno, Rena 1923- 104
Kratman, Tom 175
Kraus, Joanna Halpert 1937- 87

Kraus, (Herman) Robert 1925-2001 93
    Obituary 130
    Earlier sketches in SATA 4, 65
    See also SAAS 11
Krauss, Ruth 1911-1993 30
    Obituary 75
    Earlier sketch in SATA 1
    See also CLR 42
Krauss, Ruth Ida
    See Krauss, Ruth
Krautter, Elisa (Bialk) 1912(?)-1990 1
    Obituary 65
Krautwurst, Terry 1946- 79
Kray, Robert Clement 1930- 82
Krech, Bob 1956- 185
Krech, Robert
    See Krech, Bob
Kredel, Fritz 1900-1973 17
Kreikemeier, Gregory Scott 1965- 85
Kreloff, Elliot 189
Krementz, Jill 1940- 134
    Earlier sketches in SATA 17, 71
    See also CLR 5
    See also SAAS 8
Kremer, Marcie
    See Sorenson, Margo
Krenina, Katya 1968- 221
    Earlier sketch in SATA 101
Krensky, Stephen 1953- 188
    Brief entry 41
    Earlier sketches in SATA 47, 93, 136
Krensky, Stephen Alan
    See Krensky, Stephen
Kresh, Paul 1919-1997 61
    Obituary 94
Kress, Nancy 1948- 147
    Autobiography Feature 147
    Earlier sketch in SATA 85
Kricher, John C. 1944- 113
Krieger, Melanie 1944- 96
Krinitz, Esther Nisenthal 1927-2001 194
Kripke, Dorothy Karp 30
Krisher, Trudy 1946- 160
    Earlier sketch in SATA 86
Krisher, Trudy B.
    See Krisher, Trudy
Krishnaswami, Uma 1956- 182
    Earlier sketch in SATA 144
Kristiansen, Teddy 1964- 210
Kristiansen, Teddy H.
    See Kristiansen, Teddy
Kristof, Jane 1932- 8
Kroeber, Theodora (Kracaw) 1897-1979 1
Kroeger, Mary Kay 1950- 92
Krohn, Katherine E(lizabeth) 1961- 125
    Earlier sketch in SATA 84
Kroll, Francis Lynde 1904-1973 10
Kroll, Steven 1941-2011 212
    Autobiography Feature 135
    Earlier sketches in SATA 19, 66, 125, 135
    See also SAAS 7
Kroll, Virginia L. 1948- 225
    Earlier sketches in SATA 76, 114, 168
Kroll, Virginia Louisa
    See Kroll, Virginia L.
Kromhout, Rindert 1958- 189
Krommes, Beth 1956- 208
    Earlier sketches in SATA 128, 181
Kronenwetter, Michael 1943- 62
Kroniuk, Lisa
    See Berton, Pierre (Francis de Marigny)
Kropp, Paul 1948- 38
    Brief entry 34
    See also CLR 96
Kropp, Paul Stephan
    See Kropp, Paul
Krosoczka, Jarrett J. 1977- 200
    Earlier sketch in SATA 155
Krovatin, Christopher 1985- 171
Krudop, Walter
    See Krudop, Walter Lyon

Krudop, Walter Lyon 1966- 210
Kruess, James
    See Kruss, James
Kruglik, Gerald 187
Krull, Kathleen 1952- 229
    Autobiography Feature 106
    Brief entry 39
    Earlier sketches in SATA 52, 80, 149, 184
    See also CLR 44
Krumgold, Joseph (Quincy) 1908-1980 48
    Obituary 23
    Earlier sketch in SATA 1
Krupinski, Loretta 1940- 161
    Earlier sketches in SATA 67, 102
Krupnick, Karen 1947- 89
Krupp, E. C. 1944- 123
    Earlier sketch in SATA 53
Krupp, Edwin Charles
    See Krupp, E. C.
Krupp, Robin Rector 1946- 53
Krush, Beth 1918- 18
Krush, Joe 1918-
    See Krush, Joseph P.
Krush, Joseph P. 1918- 18
Kruss, James 1926-1997 8
    See also CLR 9
Kruusval, Catarina 1951- 201
Krykorka, Vladyana 1945- 96
Krystoforski, Andrej 1943- 196
Kubick, Dana 212
Kubie, Eleanor Gottheil
    See Kubie, Nora Gottheil Benjamin
Kubie, Nora Benjamin
    See Kubie, Nora Gottheil Benjamin
Kubie, Nora Gottheil Benjamin 1899-1988 . 39
    Obituary 59
Kubinyi, Laszlo 1937- 94
    Earlier sketch in SATA 17
Kudlinski, Kathleen V. 1950- 213
    Earlier sketch in SATA 150
Kuehnert, Stephanie 1979- 205
Kuenstler, Morton 1927- 10
Kuh, Charlotte 1892(?)-1985
    Obituary 43
Kuharski, Janice 1947- 128
Kuhn, Dwight 199
Kuijer, Guus 1942- 179
Kujoth, Jean Spealman 1935-1975
    Obituary 30
Kuklin, Susan 1941- 163
    Earlier sketches in SATA 63, 95
    See also CLR 51
Kulak, Jeff 1984(?)- 223
Kulikov, Boris 1966- 205
    Earlier sketch in SATA 170
Kulka, Joe 188
Kulling, Monica 1952- 89
Kullman, Harry 1919-1982 35
Kulyk Keefer, Janice 1952- 132
Kumin, Maxine 1925- 12
Kumin, Maxine Winokur
    See Kumin, Maxine
Kunhardt, Dorothy (Meserve) 1901-1979 53
    Obituary 22
Kunhardt, Edith 1937- 67
Kunjufu, Jawanza 1953- 73
Kunstler, Morton
    See Kuenstler, Morton
Kuntz, J(ohn) L. 1947- 91
Kuntz, Jerry 1956- 133
Kupferberg, Herbert 1918-2001 19
Kuratomi, Chizuko 1939- 12
    See also CLR 32
Kurczok, Belinda 1978- 121
Kurelek, William 1927-1977 8
    Obituary 27
    See also CLR 2
Kurian, George 1928- 65
Kurilla, Renee 1981- 231
Kurjian, Judi(th M.) 1944- 127
Kurland, Gerald 1942- 13

Kurland, Michael 1938- 118
    Earlier sketch in SATA 48
Kurland, Michael Joseph
    See Kurland, Michael
Kuroi, Ken 1947- 120
Kurokawa, Mitsuhiro 1954- 88
Kurten, Bjorn (Olof) 1924-1988 64
Kurtz, Jane 1952- 139
    Earlier sketch in SATA 91
    See also CLR 123
Kurtz, Katherine 1944- 182
    Earlier sketches in SATA 76, 126
Kurtz, Katherine Irene
    See Kurtz, Katherine
Kurusa 1942- 226
Kurz, Rudolf 1952- 95
Kushner, Donn (J.) 1927- 52
    See also CLR 55
Kushner, Ellen 1955- 202
    Earlier sketch in SATA 98
Kushner, Ellen Ruth
    See Kushner, Ellen
Kushner, Jill Menkes 1951- 62
Kushner, Lawrence 1943- 169
    Earlier sketch in SATA 83
Kushner, Tony 1956- 160
Kuskin, Karla 1932-2009 164
    Obituary 206
    Earlier sketches in SATA 2, 68, 111
    See also CLR 4
    See also SAAS 3
Kuskin, Karla Seidman
    See Kuskin, Karla
Kusugak, Michael 1948- 143
Kusugak, Michael Arvaarluk
    See Kusugak, Michael
Kutner, Merrily 1948- 196
Kuttner, Paul 1922- 18
Kuyper, Sjoerd 1952- 177
Kuzma, Kay 1941- 39
Kvale, Velma R(uth) 1898-1979 8
Kvasnosky, Laura McGee 1951- 182
    Earlier sketches in SATA 93, 142
Kwasney, Michelle D. 1960- 162
Kyle, Benjamin
    See Gottfried, Theodore Mark
Kyle, Elisabeth
    See Dunlop, Agnes M. R.
Kyte, Kathy S. 1946- 50
    Brief entry 44

L

L., Barry
    See Longyear, Barry B(rookes)
L., Tommy
    See Lorkowski, Thomas V(incent)
Labatt, Mary 1944- 215
Labouisse, Eve Curie
    See Curie, Eve
Labouisse, Eve Denise
    See Curie, Eve
Lace, William W. 1942- 126
Lacey, Joshua
    See Doder, Josh
Lachenmeyer, Nathaniel 1969- 221
Lachner, Dorothea
    See Knobloch, Dorothea
Lachtman, Ofelia Dumas 1919- 179
Lackey, Mercedes
    See Lackey, Mercedes R.
Lackey, Mercedes R. 1950- 127
    Earlier sketch in SATA 81
Lackey, Mercedes Ritchie
    See Lackey, Mercedes R.
Lacoe, Addie 78
Lacombe, Benjamin 1982- 198
Lacome, Julie 1961- 174
    Earlier sketch in SATA 80

LaCour, Nina 1982- 222
Lacy, Leslie Alexander 1937- 6
Lacy, Rick 231
Ladd, Cheryl (Jean) 1951- 113
Ladd, London 1972(?)- 206
Ladd, Louise 1943- 97
Ladd, Veronica
    See Miner, Jane Claypool
Laden, Nina 1962- 148
    Earlier sketch in SATA 85
Lader, Lawrence 1919-2006 6
    Obituary 178
LaDoux, Rita C. 1951- 74
Ladwig, Tim 1952- 223
Ladwig, Timothy
    See Ladwig, Tim
Lady, A
    See Taylor, Ann
Lady Mears
    See Tempest, Margaret Mary
Lady of Quality, A
    See Bagnold, Enid
La Farge, Oliver 1901-1963 19
La Farge, Oliver Hazard Perry
    See La Farge, Oliver
La Farge, Phyllis 14
LaFave, Kim 196
LaFaye, A. 1970- 220
    Earlier sketches in SATA 105, 156
LaFaye, Alexandria R.T.
    See LaFaye, A.
LaFevers, R.L. 191
LaFevers, Robin L.
    See LaFevers, R.L.
Lafferty, Mur 1973- 227
Laffin, John (Alfred Charles) 1922- 31
LaFleur, Suzanne 1983- 221
LaFontaine, Bruce 1948- 176
    Earlier sketch in SATA 114
La Fontaine, Jean de 1621-1695 18
Lafrance, Marie 1955- 197
Lager, Claude
    See Lapp, Christiane (Germain)
Lager, Marilyn 1939- 52
Lagercrantz, Rose (Elsa) 1947- 39
Lagerloef, Selma
    See Lagerlof, Selma
Lagerlof, Selma 1858-1940 15
    See also CLR 7
Lagos, Alexander 232
Lagos, Joseph 231
Laguna, Sofie 1968- 158
LaHaye, Tim 1926- 149
LaHaye, Timothy F.
    See LaHaye, Tim
Laidlaw, Rob 205
Laiken, Deirdre S. 1948- 48
    Brief entry 40
Laiken, Deirdre Susan
    See Laiken, Deirdre S.
Laimgruber, Monika 1946- 11
Lain, Anna
    See Lamb, Nancy
Laing, Alexander (Kinnan) 1903-1976 117
Laing, Martha 1951- 39
Lairamore, Dawn 233
Laird, Christa 1944- 108
    Autobiography Feature 120
    See also SAAS 26
Laird, Elizabeth 1943- 228
    Earlier sketches in SATA 77, 114, 159
    See also CLR 65
Laird, Elizabeth Mary Risk
    See Laird, Elizabeth
Laird, Jean E(louise) 1930- 38
Laite, Gordon 1925- 31
Lake, Harriet
    See Taylor, Paula (Wright)
Lake, Nick 227
Lakeman, Victoria
    See Forester, Victoria

Lakin, Patricia 1944- 190
Laklan, Carli 1907-1988 5
Laliberte, Louise-Andree 1958- 169
Lalicki, Barbara 61
Lalicki, Tom 1949- 186
Lally, Soinbhe 1945- 119
LaMarche, Jim 162
Lamb, Albert 187
Lamb, Beatrice Pitney 1904-1997 21
Lamb, Charles 1775-1834 17
Lamb, Elizabeth Searle 1917- 31
Lamb, G(eoffrey) F(rederick) 10
Lamb, Harold (Albert) 1892-1962 53
Lamb, Lynton (Harold) 1907-1977 10
Lamb, Mary Ann 1764-1847 17
Lamb, Nancy 1939- 80
Lamb, Robert (Boyden) 1941- 13
Lamba, Marie 195
Lambert, David 1932- 84
    Brief entry 49
Lambert, David Compton
    See Lambert, David
Lambert, Janet 1895(?)-1973 25
Lambert, Martha L. 113
Lambert, Saul 1928- 23
Lambert, Stephen 174
Lamburn, Richmal Crompton 1890-1969 5
Lamensdorf, Len 1930- 120
Lamensdorf, Leonard
    See Lamensdorf, Len
Laminack, Lester L. 1956- 163
    Earlier sketch in SATA 120
Lammle, Leslie 1965- 213
Lamont, Priscilla 200
Lamorisse, Albert (Emmanuel) 1922-1970 ... 23
Lampert, Emily 1951- 52
    Brief entry 49
Lamplugh, Lois 1921- 17
Lampman, Evelyn Sibley 1907-1980 87
    Obituary 23
    Earlier sketch in SATA 4
Lamprey, Louise 1869-1951
    See YABC 2
Lampton, Chris
    See Lampton, Christopher F.
Lampton, Christopher
    See Lampton, Christopher F.
Lampton, Christopher F. 67
    Brief entry 47
Lamstein, Sarah 1943- 174
    Earlier sketch in SATA 126
Lamstein, Sarah Marwil
    See Lamstein, Sarah
Lanagan, Margo 1960- 201
    Earlier sketch in SATA 163
Lancaster, Bruce 1896-1963 9
Lancaster, Matthew 1973(?)-1983
    Obituary 45
Lance, Kathryn 1943- 76
Land, Barbara (Neblett) 1923- 16
Land, Jane
    See Borland, Kathryn Kilby
    and Speicher, Helen Ross S(mith)
Land, Myrick (Ebben) 1922-1998 15
Land, Ross
    See Borland, Kathryn Kilby
    and Speicher, Helen Ross S(mith)
Landa, Norbert 1952- 218
Landau, Elaine 1948- 141
    Earlier sketches in SATA 10, 94
Landau, Jacob 1917- 38
Landeck, Beatrice 1904-1978 15
Landin, Les 1923- 2
Landis, J. D. 1942- 60
    Brief entry 52
Landis, James D.
    See Landis, J. D.
Landis, James David
    See Landis, J. D.
Landis, Jill Marie 1948- 101
Landman, Tanya 207

Landmann, Bimba 1968- 176
Landon, Dena 1978(?)- 168
Landon, Lucinda 1950- 56
    Brief entry 51
Landon, Margaret (Dorothea Mortenson)
    1903-1993 50
Landowne, Youme 1970- 211
Landry, Leo 202
Landshoff, Ursula 1908-1989 13
Landstrom, Lena 1943- 206
    Earlier sketch in SATA 146
Landstrom, Olof 1943- 146
Landy, Derek 1974- 210
Lane, Alison Hoffman 215
Lane, Carolyn 1926-1993 10
Lane, Connie
    See Laux, Constance
Lane, Dakota 1959- 166
    Earlier sketch in SATA 105
Lane, Jerry
    See Martin, Patricia Miles
Lane, John (Richard) 1932- 15
Lane, Leena 199
Lane, Margaret 1907-1994 65
    Brief entry 38
    Obituary 79
Lane, Rose Wilder 1887-1968 29
    Brief entry 28
Lanes, Selma G. 1929- 3
Lanes, Selma Gordon
    See Lanes, Selma G.
Lanfredi, Judy 1964- 83
Lang, Andrew 1844-1912 16
    See also CLR 101
Lang, Aubrey 169
Lang, Glenna 1951- 221
Lang, Lang 1982- 208
Lang, Paul 1948- 83
Lang, Susan S. 1950- 68
Lang, T.T.
    See Taylor, Theodore
Langart, Darrell T.
    See Garrett, Randall
Langdo, Bryan 1973- 233
    Earlier sketches in SATA 138, 191
Lange, John
    See Crichton, Michael
Lange, Karen E. 190
Lange, Suzanne 1945- 5
Langley, Andrew 1949- 166
    Earlier sketch in SATA 104
Langley, Charles P(itman) III 1949- 103
Langley, Jonathan 1952- 122
Langley, Noel 1911-1980
    Obituary 25
Langley, Wanda 173
Langner, Nola
    See Malone, Nola Langner
Langone, John (Michael) 1929- 46
    Brief entry 38
Langreuter, Jutta 1944- 122
Langrish, Katherine 177
Langsen, Richard C. 1953- 95
Langstaff, John 1920-2005 68
    Obituary 172
    Earlier sketch in SATA 6
    See also CLR 3
Langstaff, John Meredith
    See Langstaff, John
Langstaff, Launcelot
    See Irving, Washington
Langston, Laura 1958- 186
Langton, Jane 1922- 200
    Autobiography Feature 140
    Earlier sketches in SATA 3, 68, 129, 140
    See also CLR 33
    See also SAAS 5
Lanier, Sidney 1842-1881 18
Lanier, Sterling E. 1927-2007 109
Lanier, Sterling Edmund
    See Lanier, Sterling E.

Lanino, Deborah 1964- *123*
Lankford, Mary D. 1932- *112*
  Earlier sketch in SATA 77
Lannin, Joanne 1951- *121*
Lannin, Joanne A.
  See Lannin, Joanne
Lansdale, Joe R. 1951- *116*
Lansdale, Joe Richard
  See Lansdale, Joe R.
Lansing, Alfred 1921-1975 .... *35*
Lansing, Karen E. 1954- *71*
Lansky, Vicki 1942- *177*
Lanthier, Jennifer 1964- *204*
Lantier-Sampon, Patricia 1952- *92*
Lantz, Fran
  See Lantz, Francess L(in)
Lantz, Francess L(in) 1952-2004 .... *153*
  Autobiography Feature *153*
  Obituary *159*
  Earlier sketches in SATA 63, 109
Lantz, Paul 1908- *45*
Lantz, Walter 1900-1994 .... *37*
  Obituary *79*
Lanza, Barbara 1945- *101*
Lapp, Christiane (Germain) 1948- *74*
Lappin, Peter 1911-1999 .... *32*
Larbalestier, Justine *231*
  Earlier sketch in SATA 178
Lardy, Philippe 1963- *168*
LaReau, Jenna *181*
LaReau, Kara *181*
Larios, Julie 1949- *178*
Larios, Julie Hofstrand
  See Larios, Julie
Larkin, Amy
  See Burns, Olive Ann
Larkin, Maia
  See Wojciechowska, Maia (Teresa)
Larkspur, Penelope
  See Wyatt, Valerie
Laroche, Giles 1956- *221*
  Earlier sketches in SATA 71, 126
LaRochelle, David 1960- *171*
  Earlier sketch in SATA 115
Larom, Henry V. 1903(?)-1975
  Obituary *30*
LaRose, Linda *125*
Larrabee, Lisa 1947- *84*
Larranaga, Ana Martin 1969- *229*
Larrecq, John M(aurice) 1926-1980 .... *44*
  Obituary *25*
Larrick (Crosby), Nancy 1910-2004 .... *4*
Larsen, Anita 1942- *78*
Larsen, Egon 1904- *14*
Larsen, Rebecca 1944- *54*
Larson, Eve
  See St. John, Wylly Folk
Larson, Gary 1950- *57*
Larson, Hope 1982- *205*
Larson, Ingrid D(ana) 1965- *92*
Larson, Jean Russell 1930- *121*
Larson, Kirby 1954- *181*
  Earlier sketch in SATA 96
Larson, Norita D. 1944- *29*
Larson, Norita Dittberner
  See Larson, Norita D.
Larson, William H. 1938- *10*
Larsson, Carl (Olof) 1853-1919 .... *35*
LaSalle, Charles A.
  See Ellis, Edward S.
LaSalle, Charles E.
  See Ellis, Edward S.
Lasell, Elinor H. 1929- *19*
Lasell, Fen H.
  See Lasell, Elinor H.
Lasenby, Jack 1931- *172*
  Earlier sketches in SATA 65, 103
Laser, Michael 1954- *117*
Lash, Joseph P. 1909-1987 .... *43*
Lasher, Faith B. 1921- *12*
Lasker, David 1950- *38*

Lasker, Joe
  See Lasker, Joseph Leon
Lasker, Joseph Leon 1919- *83*
  Earlier sketch in SATA 9
  See also SAAS 17
Laski, Marghanita 1915-1988 .... *55*
Laskin, Pamela L. 1954- *75*
Lasky, Kathryn 1944- *210*
  Earlier sketches in SATA 13, 69, 112, 157
  See also CLR 140
Lasky Knight, Kathryn
  See Lasky, Kathryn
Lass, Bonnie *131*
Lassalle, C. E.
  See Ellis, Edward S.
Lassiter, Mary
  See Hoffman, Mary
Lassiter, Rhiannon 1977- *157*
Lat 1951- *196*
Latham, Barbara 1896- *16*
Latham, Frank B(rown) 1910-2000 .... *6*
Latham, Irene 1971- *228*
Latham, Jean Lee 1902-1995 .... *68*
  Earlier sketch in SATA 2
  See also CLR 50
Latham, Mavis
  See Clark, Mavis Thorpe
Latham, Philip
  See Richardson, Robert S(hirley)
Lathrop, Dorothy P(ulis) 1891-1980 .... *14*
  Obituary *24*
Lathrop, Francis
  See Leiber, Fritz (Reuter, Jr.)
Latimer, Jim 1943- *80*
Latta, Rich
  See Latta, Richard
Latta, Richard 1946- *113*
Latta, Sara L. 1960- *174*
Lattany, Kristin
  See Lattany, Kristin Hunter
Lattany, Kristin (Eggleston) Hunter 1931- . *154*
  Autobiography Feature *154*
  Earlier sketch in SATA 132
Lattany, Kristin Hunter 1931-2008 .... *132*
  Earlier sketch in SATA 12
  See also CLR 3
  See also SAAS 10
Lattimore, Eleanor Frances 1904-1986 .... *7*
  Obituary *48*
Lattin, Ann
  See Cole, Lois Dwight
Lauber, Patricia (Grace) 1924- *138*
  Earlier sketches in SATA 1, 33, 75
  See also CLR 16
Laugesen, Malene *207*
Laugesen, Malene Reynolds
  See Laugesen, Malene
Laugesen, Mary E(akin) 1906-1995 .... *5*
Laughbaum, Steve 1945- *12*
Laughlin, Florence Young 1910-2001 ...... *3*
Laughlin, Rosemary 1941- *123*
Launder, Sally *206*
Laure, Ettagale
  See Blauer, Ettagale
Laure, Jason 1940- *50*
  Brief entry *44*
Laurence, Ester Hauser 1935- *7*
Laurence, Jean Margaret Wemyss
  See Laurence, Margaret
Laurence, Margaret 1926-1987
  Obituary *50*
Laurie, Rona 1916- *55*
Laurie, Victoria *218*
Laurin, Anne
  See McLaurin, Anne
Lauritzen, Jonreed 1902-1979 .... *13*
Lauscher, Hermann
  See Hesse, Hermann
Lauture, Denize 1946- *86*
Laux, Connie
  See Laux, Constance

Laux, Constance 1952- *97*
Laux, Dorothy 1920- *49*
Lavallee, Barbara 1941- *166*
  Earlier sketch in SATA 74
Lavender, David (Sievert) 1910-2003 .... *97*
  Obituary *145*
  Earlier sketch in SATA 64
Lavender, William D. 1921- *143*
Laverne, Christine *175*
Lavert, Gwendolyn Battle 1951-
  See Battle-Lavert, Gwendolyn
Laverty, Donald
  See Blish, James
  and Knight, Damon (Francis)
Lavigne, Louis-Dominique 1949- *107*
Lavine, David 1928- *31*
Lavine, Sigmund Arnold 1908-1986 .... *82*
  Earlier sketch in SATA 3
  See also CLR 35
Lavis, Steve *225*
Lavond, Paul Dennis
  See Kornbluth, C(yril) M.
  and Lowndes, Robert A(ugustine) W(ard)
  and Pohl, Frederik
Law, Stephen *225*
Law, Stephen
  See Law, Stephen
Lawford, Paula Jane 1960- *57*
  Brief entry *53*
Lawhead, Stephen R. 1950- *109*
Lawhead, Steve
  See Lawhead, Stephen R.
Lawler, Janet *222*
Lawlor, Laurie 1953- *137*
  Earlier sketch in SATA 80
Lawlor, William
  See Lawlor, William T.
Lawlor, William T. 1951- *183*
Lawrence, Ann (Margaret) 1942-1987 .... *41*
  Obituary *54*
Lawrence, Caroline 1954- *203*
Lawrence, Iain 1955- *183*
  Earlier sketch in SATA 135
Lawrence, J. T.
  See Rowland-Entwistle, (Arthur) Theodore
  (Henry)
Lawrence, Jerome 1915-2004 .... *65*
Lawrence, John 1933- *30*
Lawrence, Josephine 1890(?)-1978
  Obituary *24*
Lawrence, Louise 1943- *119*
  Earlier sketches in SATA 38, 78
Lawrence, Louise de Kiriline 1894-1992 ..... *13*
Lawrence, Lynn
  See Garland, Sherry
Lawrence, Margery H. 1889-1969 .... *120*
Lawrence, Michael 1943- *132*
Lawrence, Mildred Elwood 1907-1997 .... *3*
Lawrence, R(onald) D(ouglas) 1921- *55*
Lawrinson, Julia 1969- *141*
Lawson, Amy
  See Gordon, Amy
Lawson, Carol (Antell) 1946- *42*
Lawson, Don(ald Elmer) 1917-1990 .... *9*
Lawson, Joan 1906- *55*
Lawson, Julie 1947- *126*
  Earlier sketch in SATA 79
  See also CLR 89
Lawson, Marion Tubbs 1896-1994 .... *22*
Lawson, Robert 1892-1957 .... *100*
  See also YABC 2
  See also CLR 73
Lawton, Clive A. 1951- *145*
Laxdal, Vivienne 1962- *112*
Laybourn, Emma *193*
Layburn, Joe *228*
Laycock, George (Edwin) 1921- *5*
Layne, Laura
  See Knott, William C(ecil, Jr.)
Layne, Steven L. *171*
Layson, Annelex Hofstra 1938(?)- *211*

Layton, Neal 1971- 187
  Earlier sketch in SATA 152
Layton, Neal Andrew
  See Layton, Neal
Lazare, Gerald John 1927- 44
Lazare, Jerry
  See Lazare, Gerald John
Lazarevich, Mila 1942- 17
Lazarus, Keo Felker 1913-1993 21
  Obituary 129
Lea, Alec 1907- 19
Lea, Bob 1952- 203
Lea, Joan
  See Neufeld, John (Arthur)
Leach, Maria 1892-1977 39
  Brief entry 28
Leacock, Elspeth 1946- 131
Leacroft, Helen (Mabel Beal) 1919- 6
Leacroft, Richard (Vallance Becher) 1914- 6
Leaf, Margaret P. 1909(?)-1988
  Obituary 55
Leaf, (Wilbur) Munro 1905-1976 20
  See also CLR 25
Leaf, VaDonna Jean 1929- 26
Leah, Devorah
  See Devorah-Leah
Leakey, Richard E(rskine Frere) 1944- 42
Leal, Ann Haywood 216
Leander, Ed
  See Richelson, Geraldine
Lear, Edward 1812-1888 100
  Earlier sketch in SATA 18
  See also CLR 169
Lears, Laurie 1955- 127
Leasor, James 1923-2007 54
Leasor, Thomas James
  See Leasor, James
Leavitt, Jerome E(dward) 1916- 23
Leavitt, Martine 1953- 170
LeBar, Mary E(velyn) 1910-1982 35
LeBlanc, Annette M. 1965- 68
LeBlanc, L(ee) 1913- 54
LeBox, Annette 1943- 145
Lebrun, Claude 1929- 66
Le Cain, Errol (John) 1941-1989 68
  Obituary 60
  Earlier sketch in SATA 6
Lechner, Jack 201
Lechner, John 1966- 200
Leck, James 1973- 229
Lecourt, Nancy (Hoyt) 1951- 73
Ledbetter, Suzann 1953- 119
Leder, Jane Mersky 1945- 61
  Brief entry 51
Lederer, Muriel 1929- 48
Lederer, William J. 1912-2009 62
Lederer, William Julius
  See Lederer, William J.
Lee, Amanda
  See Baggett, Nancy
  and Buckholtz, Eileen (Garber)
  and Glick, Ruth
Lee, Benjamin 1921- 27
Lee, Betsy 1949- 37
Lee, Carol
  See Fletcher, Helen Jill
Lee, Carol Ann 1969- 185
Lee, Chinlun 182
Lee, Cora 223
  See Anderson, Catherine Corley
Lee, Dennis (Beynon) 1939- 102
  Earlier sketch in SATA 14
  See also CLR 3
Lee, Dom 1959- 146
  Autobiography Feature 121
  Earlier sketch in SATA 83
  See also SAAS 26
Lee, Doris Emrick 1905-1983 44
  Obituary 35
Lee, Edward
  See Lee, J. Edward

Lee, Elizabeth Rogers 1940- 90
Lee, Harper 1926- 11
  See also CLR 169
Lee, Hector Viveros 1962- 115
Lee, Howard N.
  See Goulart, Ron
Lee, Huy Voun 1969- 217
  Earlier sketch in SATA 129
Lee, Insu 213
Lee, J. Edward 1953- 130
Lee, Jared 1943- 215
Lee, Jared D.
  See Lee, Jared
Lee, Jeanne M. 1943- 138
Lee, John R(obert) 1923-1976 27
Lee, Jordan
  See Scholefield, Alan
Lee, Joseph Edward
  See Lee, J. Edward
Lee, Julian
  See Latham, Jean Lee
Lee, Linda
  See Eyerly, Jeannette
Lee, Liz
  See Lee, Elizabeth Rogers
Lee, Lucy
  See Talbot, Charlene Joy
Lee, Lyn 1953- 128
Lee, Manning de Villeneuve 1894-1980 37
  Obituary 22
Lee, Marian
  See Clish, (Lee) Marian
Lee, Marie G. 1964- 178
  Earlier sketches in SATA 81, 130
Lee, Marie Myung-Ok
  See Lee, Marie G.
Lee, Mary Price 1934- 82
  Earlier sketch in SATA 8
Lee, Mildred
  See Scudder, Mildred Lee
Lee, Nelle Harper
  See Lee, Harper
Lee, Richard S. 1927- 82
Lee, Robert C. 1931- 20
Lee, Robert Edwin 1918-1994 65
  Obituary 82
Lee, Robert J. 1921- 10
Lee, Roy
  See Hopkins, Clark
Lee, Sally 1943- 67
Lee, Suzy 193
Lee, Tammie
  See Townsend, Thomas L.
Lee, Tanith 1947- 185
  Earlier sketches in SATA 8, 88, 134
Lee, Virginia 1976- 208
Lee, Y.S. 1974- 232
Leech, Ben
  See Bowkett, Stephen
Leeds, Contance 188
Leedy, Loreen 1959- 175
  Brief entry 50
  Earlier sketches in SATA 54, 84, 128
Leedy, Loreen Janelle
  See Leedy, Loreen
Lee-Hostetler, Jeri 1940- 63
Leekley, Thomas B(riggs) 1910-2001 23
Leeming, Jo Ann
  See Leeming, Joseph
Leeming, Joseph 1897-1968 26
Leemis, Ralph B. 1954- 72
Leese, Jennifer L.B. 1970- 163
Leeson, Muriel 1920- 54
Leeson, R. A.
  See Leeson, Robert (Arthur)
Leeson, Robert (Arthur) 1928- 76
  Earlier sketch in SATA 42
Lee Tae-Jun 1904-1956(?) 194
Lee-Tai, Amy 1964- 189
Leffland, Ella 1931- 65
Leffler, Silke 197

Lefler, Irene (Whitney) 1917- 12
LeFrak, Karen 182
Le Gallienne, Eva 1899-1991 9
  Obituary 68
Legg, Gerald 1947- 143
Legg, Sarah Martha Ross Bruggeman (?)-1982
  Obituary 40
LeGrand
  See Henderson, LeGrand
Le Guin, Ursula K. 1929- 194
  Earlier sketches in SATA 4, 52, 99, 149
  See also CLR 91
Le Guin, Ursula Kroeber
  See Le Guin, Ursula K.
Legum, Colin 1919-2003 10
Lehman, Barbara 1963- 170
  Earlier sketch in SATA 115
Lehman, Bob 91
Lehman, Elaine 91
Lehmann, Debra Lynn
  See Vanasse, Deb
Lehman-Wilzig, Tami 1950- 224
Lehn, Cornelia 1920- 46
Lehne, Judith Logan 1947- 93
Lehr, Delores 1920- 10
Lehr, Norma 1930- 71
Leiber, Fritz (Reuter, Jr.) 1910-1992 45
  Obituary 73
Leibold, Jay 1957- 57
  Brief entry 52
Leichman, Seymour 1933- 5
Leick, Bonnie 205
Leigh, Nila K. 1981- 81
Leigh, Tom 1947- 46
Leigh-Pemberton, John 1911-1997 35
Leighton, Clare (Veronica Hope)
  1899-1989 37
Leighton, Margaret (Carver) 1896-1987 1
  Obituary 52
Leijten, Aileen 216
Leiner, Al(an) 1938- 83
Leiner, Katherine 1949- 93
Leipold, L. Edmond 1902-1983 16
Leisk, David (Johnson) 1906-1975 30
  Obituary 26
  Earlier sketch in SATA 1
  See also CLR 98
Leist, Christina 226
Leister, Mary 1917- 29
Leitch, Patricia 1933- 98
  Earlier sketch in SATA 11
Leitner, Isabella 1924- 86
Lekich, John 202
Leland, Bob 1956- 92
Leland, Robert E.
  See Leland, Bob
Leloup, Genevieve 230
Lematre, Pascal 1967- 225
  Earlier sketch in SATA 176
Lember, Barbara Hirsch 1941- 92
LeMieux, A.C. 1954- 125
  Earlier sketch in SATA 90
LeMieux, Anne
  See LeMieux, A.C.
LeMieux, Anne Connelly
  See LeMieux, A.C.
Lemieux, Michele 1955- 139
Lemke, Horst 1922- 38
Lemna, Don 1936- 216
Lenain, Thierry 1959- 201
Lenanton, Carola Mary Anima Oman
  See Oman, Carola (Mary Anima)
Lenard, Alexander 1910-1972
  Obituary 21
Lendroth, Susan 207
L'Engle, Madeleine 1918-2007 128
  Obituary 186
  Earlier sketches in SATA 1, 27, 75
  See also CLR 57
  See also SAAS 15

L'Engle, Madeleine Camp Franklin
   See L'Engle, Madeleine
Lengyel, Cornel Adam 1915- 27
Lengyel, Emil 1895-1985 3
   Obituary 42
Lennon, John 1940-1980 114
Lennon, John Ono
   See Lennon, John
Leno, Jay 1950- 154
LeNoir, Janice 1941- 89
Lens, Sidney 1912-1986 13
   Obituary 48
Lenski, Lois 1893-1974 100
   Earlier sketches in SATA *1, 26*
   See also CLR *26*
Lent, Blair 1930-2009 133
   Obituary 200
   Earlier sketch in SATA *2*
Lent, Henry Bolles 1901-1973 17
Lent, John 1948- 108
Leodhas, Sorche Nic
   See Alger, Leclaire (Gowans)
Leokum, Arkady 1916(?)- 45
Leon, Carol Boyd 212
Leon, Sharon 1959- 79
Leonard, Alison 1944- 70
Leonard, Anna
   See Gilman, Laura Anne
Leonard, Constance (Brink) 1923- 42
   Brief entry 40
Leonard, Dutch
   See Leonard, Elmore
Leonard, Elmore 1925- 163
Leonard, Elmore John, Jr.
   See Leonard, Elmore
Leonard, Jonathan N(orton) 1903-1975 36
Leonard, Laura 1923- 75
Leonard, Tom 1955- 207
Leonetti, Mike 1958- 202
Leong, Gor Yun
   See Ellison, Virginia H(owell)
Leonhard, Herb 217
Leonhardt, Alice 1950- 152
Lerangis, Peter 1955- 171
   Earlier sketch in SATA *72*
Lerman, Josh 215
Lerner, Aaron 1920-2007 35
   Obituary 179
Lerner, Aaron Bunsen
   See Lerner, Aaron
Lerner, Carol 1927- 86
   Earlier sketch in SATA *33*
   See also CLR *34*
   See also SAAS *12*
Lerner, Gerda 1920- 65
Lerner, Harriet 1944- 101
Lerner, Marguerite Rush 1924-1987 11
   Obituary 51
Lerner, Sharon (Ruth) 1938-1982 11
   Obituary 29
Leroe, Ellen 1949- 99
   Brief entry 51
   Earlier sketch in SATA *61*
Leroe, Ellen W.
   See Leroe, Ellen
Leroe, Ellen Whitney
   See Leroe, Ellen
Leroux, Gaston 1868-1927 65
Leroux-Hugon, Helene 1955- 132
LeRoy, Gen 52
   Brief entry 36
Lerrigo, Marion Olive 1898-1968
   Obituary 29
LeShan, Eda J(oan) 1922-2002 21
   See also CLR *6*
Leshem, Yossi 1947- 222
LeSieg, Theo.
   See Dr. Seuss
Lesinski, Jeanne M. 1960- 120
Leslie, Robert Franklin 1911-1990 7
Leslie, Roger 1961- 168

Leslie, Roger James
   See Leslie, Roger
Leslie, Sarah
   See McGuire, Leslie (Sarah)
LeSourd, Catherine
   See Marshall, (Sarah) Catherine (Wood)
Lessac, Frane
   See Lessac, Frane
Lessac, Frane 1954- 209
   Earlier sketches in SATA *61, 148*
Lessem, Dino Don
   See Lessem, Don
Lessem, Don 1951- 182
   Earlier sketches in SATA *97, 155*
Lesser, Margaret 1899(?)-1979
   Obituary 22
Lesser, Rika 1953- 53
Lester, Alison 1952- 218
   Earlier sketches in SATA *50, 90, 129*
Lester, Helen 1936- 189
   Earlier sketches in SATA *46, 92, 145*
Lester, Julius 1939- 157
   Earlier sketches in SATA *12, 74, 112*
   See also CLR *143*
Lester, Julius Bernard
   See Lester, Julius
Lester, Mike 1955- 206
   Earlier sketch in SATA *131*
Le Sueur, Meridel 1900-1996 6
Leszczynski, Diana 211
Lethcoe, Jason 191
Le Tord, Bijou 1945- 95
   Earlier sketch in SATA *49*
Letts, Billie 1938- 121
Letts, Elizabeth
   See Alalou, Elizabeth
Leuck, Laura 1962- 192
   Earlier sketches in SATA *85, 146*
Leung, Hilary 1975- 225
Leutscher, Alfred (George) 1913- 23
Levai, Blaise 1919- 39
Levchuk, Lisa 215
Leveen, Tom 230
Levenkron, Steven 1941- 86
Leverich, Kathleen 1948- 103
LeVert, John 1946- 55
Levert, Mireille 1956- 211
LeVert, William John
   See LeVert, John
Levete, Sarah 1961- 153
Levin, Betty 1927- 201
   Earlier sketches in SATA *19, 84, 137*
   See also SAAS *11*
Levin, Ira 1929-2007 66
   Obituary 187
Levin, Ira Marvin
   See Levin, Ira
Levin, Marcia Obrasky 1918- 13
Levin, Meyer 1905-1981 21
   Obituary 27
Levin, Miriam (Ramsfelder) 1962- 97
Levine, Abby 1943- 54
   Brief entry 52
Levine, Anna 212
Levine, Betty K(rasne) 1933- 66
Levine, David 1926-2009 43
   Brief entry 35
Levine, Edna S(imon) 35
Levine, Ellen 1939- 190
Levine, Evan 1962- 77
   Earlier sketch in SATA *74*
Levine, Gail Carson 1947- 195
   Earlier sketches in SATA *98, 161*
   See also CLR *85*
Levine, I(srael) E. 1923-2003 12
   Obituary 146
Levine, Joan Goldman 11
Levine, Joseph 1910- 33
Levine, Kristin 1974- 213
Levine, Marge 1934- 81
Levine, Rhoda 14

Levine, Sarah 1970- 57
Levine, Shar 1953- 131
Levine-Freidus, Gail
   See Provost, Gail Levine
Levinson, Nancy Smiler 1938- 211
   Earlier sketches in SATA *33, 80, 140*
Levinson, Riki 99
   Brief entry 49
   Earlier sketch in SATA *52*
Levithan, David 1972- 166
Levitin, Sonia 1934- 192
   Autobiography Feature 131
   Earlier sketches in SATA *4, 68, 119, 131*
   See also CLR *53*
   See also SAAS *2*
Levitt, Sidney (Mark) 1947- 68
Levon, O. U.
   See Kesey, Ken
Levoy, Myron 1930- 49
   Brief entry 37
Levy, Barrie 112
Levy, Constance 1931- 140
   Earlier sketch in SATA *73*
   See also SAAS *22*
Levy, Debbie 1957- 232
Levy, Deborah Marian
   See Levy, Debbie
Levy, Elizabeth 1942- 169
   Earlier sketches in SATA *31, 69, 107*
   See also SAAS *18*
Levy, Janice 172
Levy, Marilyn 1937- 67
Levy, Nathan 1945- 63
Levy, Robert 1945- 82
Lewees, John
   See Stockton, Francis Richard
Lewin, Betsy 1937- 222
   Autobiography Feature 115
   Earlier sketches in SATA *32, 90, 169*
Lewin, Hugh 1939- 72
   Brief entry 40
   See also CLR *9*
Lewin, Ted 1935- 226
   Autobiography Feature 115
   Earlier sketches in SATA *21, 76, 119, 165,
      195*
Lewis, Alice C. 1936- 46
Lewis, Alice Hudson 1895(?)-1971
   Obituary 29
Lewis, Amanda 1955- 80
Lewis, Anthony 1927- 27
Lewis, Anthony 1966- 227
   Earlier sketch in SATA *120*
Lewis, Barbara A. 1943- 73
Lewis, Beverly 1949- 80
Lewis, Brenda Ralph 1932- 72
Lewis, Brian 1963- 128
Lewis, C. S. 1898-1963 100
   Earlier sketch in SATA *13*
   See also CLR *109*
Lewis, Claudia (Louise) 1907-2001 5
Lewis, Clive Staples
   See Lewis, C. S.
Lewis, Cynthia Copeland 1960- 111
Lewis, E. M. 123
   Earlier sketch in SATA *20*
Lewis, Earl Bradley
   See Lewis, E.B.
Lewis, E.B. 1956- 211
   Earlier sketches in SATA *93, 124, 168*
Lewis, Elizabeth Foreman 1892-1958 121
   See also YABC *2*
Lewis, Francine
   See Wells, Helen
Lewis, Harry Sinclair
   See Lewis, Sinclair
Lewis, Hilda (Winifred) 1896-1974
   Obituary 20
Lewis, J. Patrick 1942- 205
   Earlier sketches in SATA *69, 104, 162*
Lewis, Jack P(earl) 1919- 65

Lewis, Jean 1924- 61
Lewis, Jon Samuel
  See Lewis, J.S.
Lewis, Joseph Anthony
  See Lewis, Anthony
Lewis, J.S. 1972- 203
Lewis, Julinda
  See Lewis-Ferguson, Julinda
Lewis, Kevin 173
Lewis, Kim 1951- 217
  Earlier sketches in SATA 84, 136
Lewis, Linda (Joy) 1946- 67
Lewis, Lucia Z.
  See Anderson, Lucia (Lewis)
Lewis, Marjorie 1929- 40
  Brief entry 35
Lewis, Mary 1907(?)-1988 64
  Obituary 56
Lewis, Mervyn
  See Frewer, Glyn (M.)
Lewis, Michael
  See Untermeyer, Louis
Lewis, Naomi 1911-2009 144
  Earlier sketch in SATA 76
Lewis, Paeony 1960- 173
Lewis, Paul
  See Gerson, Noel Bertram
Lewis, Richard 1935- 3
Lewis, Richard 1956- 209
Lewis, Rob 1962- 72
Lewis, Roger
  See Zarchy, Harry
Lewis, Rose 209
Lewis, Rose A.
  See Lewis, Rose
Lewis, Shannon
  See Llywelyn, Morgan
Lewis, Shari 1934-1998 35
  Brief entry 30
  Obituary 104
Lewis, Sylvan R.
  See Aronson, Virginia
Lewis, Thomas P(arker) 1936- 27
Lewis, Wendy A. 1966- 150
Lewis-Ferguson, Julinda 1955- 85
Lewison, Wendy Cheyette 177
Lewiton, Mina 1904-1970 2
Lew-Vriethoff, Joanne 186
Lexau, Joan M. 130
  Earlier sketches in SATA 1, 36
Ley, Willy 1906-1969 2
Leydon, Rita (Floden) 1949- 21
Leyland, Eric (Arthur) 1911- 37
L'Hommedieu, Dorothy Keasley 1885-1961
  Obituary 29
Li, Xiao Jun 1952- 86
Liao, Jimmy 1958- 202
Liatsos, Sandra Olson 1942- 103
Libby, Alisa M. 189
Libby, Barbara M. 153
Libby, Bill
  See Libby, William M.
Libby, William M. 1927-1984 5
  Obituary 39
Liberty, Gene 1924- 3
Lichtenheld, Tom 208
  Earlier sketch in SATA 152
Lichtman, Wendy 1946- 193
Liddell, Kenneth 1912-1975 63
Liddiment, Carol 224
Lidz, Jane 120
Lieb, Josh 1972- 224
Lieberman, E(dwin) James 1934- 62
Liebers, Arthur 1913-1984 12
Lieblich, Irene 1923- 22
Liers, Emil E(rnest) 1890-1975 37
Lies, Brian 1963- 190
  Earlier sketch in SATA 131
Lieshout, Elle van
  See van Lieshout, Elle
Liestman, Vicki 1961- 72

Lietz, Gerald S. 1918- 11
Liew, Sonny 1974- 219
Life, Kay (Guinn) 1930- 83
Lifton, Betty Jean 1926-2010 118
  Earlier sketch in SATA 6
Lifton, Robert Jay 1926- 66
Lightburn, Ron 1954- 91
Lightburn, Sandra 1955- 91
Lightner, A. M.
  See Hopf, Alice (Martha) L(ightner)
Lightner, Alice
  See Hopf, Alice (Martha) L(ightner)
Lignell, Lois 1911- 37
Liles, Maurine Walpole 1935- 81
Lillegard, Dee 184
Lilley, Stephen R. 1950- 97
Lilley, Stephen Ray
  See Lilley, Stephen R.
Lillington, Kenneth (James) 1916-1998 39
Lilly, Nate 182
Lilly, Ray
  See Curtis, Richard
Lim, John 1932- 43
Liman, Ellen (Fogelson) 1936- 22
Limb, Sue 1946- 203
  Earlier sketch in SATA 158
Limburg, Peter R(ichard) 1929- 13
Lin, Grace 1974- 198
  Earlier sketches in SATA 111, 162
Lincoln, C(harles) Eric 1924-2000 5
Lincoln, Christopher 1952- 208
Lincoln, Hazel 187
Lincoln, James
  See Bates, Katharine Lee
Lindbergh, Anne
  See Sapieyevski, Anne Lindbergh
Lindbergh, Anne Morrow 1906-2001 33
  Obituary 125
Lindbergh, Anne Spencer Morrow
  See Lindbergh, Anne Morrow
Lindbergh, Charles A(ugustus, Jr.)
  1902-1974 33
Lindbergh, Reeve 1945- 163
  Earlier sketch in SATA 116
Lindblom, Steven (Winther) 1946- 94
  Brief entry 39
  Earlier sketch in SATA 42
Linde, Gunnel 1924- 5
Lindenbaum, Pija 1955- 183
  Earlier sketches in SATA 77, 144
Lindgren, Astrid (Anna Emilia Ericsson)
  1907-2002 38
  Obituary 128
  Earlier sketch in SATA 2
  See also CLR 119
Lindgren, Barbro 1937- 207
  Brief entry 46
  Earlier sketches in SATA 63, 120
  See also CLR 86
Lindman, Maj (Jan) 1886-1972 43
Lindo, Elvira 1962- 219
Lindop, Edmund 1925- 5
Lindquist, Jennie Dorothea 1899-1977 13
Lindquist, Rowena Cory 1958- 98
Lindquist, Willis 1908-1988 20
Lindsay, Nicholas Vachel
  See Lindsay, Vachel
Lindsay, Norman Alfred William
  1879-1969 67
  See also CLR 8
Lindsay, Vachel 1879-1931 40
Lindsey, Kathleen D(orothy) 1949- 153
Line, David
  See Davidson, Lionel
Line, Les 1935-2010 27
Lines, Kathleen Mary 1902-1988
  Obituary 61
Linfield, Esther 40

Lingard, Joan (Amelia) 1932- 130
  Autobiography Feature 130
  Earlier sketches in SATA 8, 74, 114
  See also CLR 89
  See also SAAS 5
Link, Martin 1934- 28
Linn, Margot
  See Ziefert, Harriet
Linnea, Sharon 1956- 82
Lintern, Tom 228
Lion, Melissa 1976- 176
Lionni, Leo(nard) 1910-1999 72
  Obituary 118
  Earlier sketch in SATA 8
  See also CLR 71
Lipinsky de Orlov, Lino S. 1908- 22
Lipkind, William 1904-1974 15
Lipman, David 1931-2008 21
Lipman, Matthew 1923-2010 14
Lipp, Frederick 204
Lippincott, Bertram 1898(?)-1985
  Obituary 42
Lippincott, Gary A. 1953- 220
  Earlier sketches in SATA 73, 119
Lippincott, Joseph W(harton) 1887-1976 17
Lippincott, Sarah Lee 1920- 22
Lippman, Peter J. 1936- 31
Lipsyte, Robert 1938- 198
  Earlier sketches in SATA 5, 68, 113, 161
  See also CLR 76
Lipsyte, Robert Michael
  See Lipsyte, Robert
Lisandrelli, Elaine Slivinski 1951- 94
Lisker, Sonia O. 1933- 44
Lisle, Holly 1960- 208
  Earlier sketch in SATA 98
Lisle, Janet Taylor 1947- 150
  Brief entry 47
  Earlier sketches in SATA 59, 96
  See also SAAS 14
Lisle, Rebecca 162
Lisle, Seward D.
  See Ellis, Edward S.
Lisowski, Gabriel 1946- 47
  Brief entry 31
Liss, Howard 1922-1995 4
  Obituary 84
Lissiat, Amy
  See Thompson, Colin
Lisson, Deborah 1941- 110
  Earlier sketch in SATA 71
List, Ilka Katherine 1935- 6
Liston, Robert A. 1927- 5
Litchfield, Ada B(assett) 1916-1999 5
Litchfield, Jo 1973- 116
Lithgow, John 1945- 145
Lithgow, John Arthur
  See Lithgow, John
Litowinsky, Olga 1936- 26
Litowinsky, Olga Jean
  See Litowinsky, Olga
Littke, Lael J. 1929- 140
  Earlier sketches in SATA 51, 83
Little, A. Edward
  See Klein, Aaron E.
Little, Douglas 1942- 96
Little, (Flora) Jean 1932- 149
  Earlier sketches in SATA 2, 68, 106
  See also CLR 4
  See also SAAS 17
Little, Lessie Jones 1906-1986 60
  Obituary 50
Little, Mary E. 1912-1999 28
Littlechild, George 1958- 85
Littledale, Freya (Lota) 1929-1992 74
  Earlier sketch in SATA 2
Littlefield, Bill 1948- 83
Littlefield, Holly 1963- 97
Littlesugar, Amy 1953- 176
  Earlier sketch in SATA 122

Littleton, Mark R. 1950- *142*
　Earlier sketch in SATA *89*
Littlewood, Karin *211*
Littman, Sarah Darer *221*
　Earlier sketch in SATA *175*
Litty, Julie 1971- *181*
Litzinger, Rosanne 1948- *196*
Liu, Cynthea *221*
Lively, Penelope 1933- *164*
　Earlier sketches in SATA *7, 60, 101*
　See also CLR *159*
Lively, Penelope Margaret
　See Lively, Penelope
Liverakos, L. A.
　See Gilman, Laura Anne
Liversidge, (Henry) Douglas 1913- *8*
Livesey, Claire (Warner) 1927- *127*
Livingston, Carole 1941- *42*
Livingston, (M.) Irene 1932- *150*
Livingston, Myra Cohn 1926-1996 .... *68*
　Obituary *92*
　Earlier sketch in SATA *5*
　See also CLR *7*
　See also SAAS *1*
Livingston, Richard R(oland) 1922- *8*
Livo, Norma J. 1929- *76*
Liwska, Renata *199*
Ljungkvist, Laura *180*
Llerena Aguirre, Carlos 1952- *19*
Llerena Aguirre, Carlos Antonio
　See Llerena Aguirre, Carlos
Llewellyn, Claire 1954- *196*
　Earlier sketches in SATA *77, 143*
Llewellyn, Grace 1964- *110*
Llewellyn, Richard
　See Llewellyn Lloyd, Richard Dafydd Vivian
Llewellyn, Sam 1948- *185*
　Earlier sketch in SATA *95*
Llewellyn Lloyd, Richard Dafydd Vivian
　1906-1983 .... *11*
　Obituary *37*
Llewelyn, T. Harcourt
　See Hamilton, Charles (Harold St. John)
Lloyd, Alan
　See Lloyd, A.R.
Lloyd, Alan Richard
　See Lloyd, A.R.
Lloyd, Alison 1966- *231*
Lloyd, A.R. 1927- *168*
　Earlier sketch in SATA *97*
Lloyd, David
　See Lloyd, David T.
Lloyd, David T. 1954- *167*
Lloyd, E. James
　See James, Elizabeth
Lloyd, Errol 1943- *22*
Lloyd, Hugh
　See Fitzhugh, Percy Keese
Lloyd, James
　See James, Elizabeth
Lloyd, Megan 1958- *189*
　Earlier sketches in SATA *77, 117*
Lloyd, Norman 1909-1980
　Obituary *23*
Lloyd, (Mary) Norris 1908-1993 .... *10*
　Obituary *75*
Lloyd, Saci 1967- *220*
Lloyd, Sam *183*
Lloyd-Jones, Sally 1960- *179*
Lloyd Webber, Andrew 1948- *56*
Llywelyn, Morgan 1937- *109*
Lo, Ginnie *165*
Lo, Malinda 1974- *222*
Lo, Virginia M.
　See Lo, Ginnie
Lobato, Jose Bento Monteiro 1882-1948 ... *114*
Lobel, Anita (Kempler) 1934- *162*
　Earlier sketches in SATA *6, 55, 96*

Lobel, Arnold (Stark) 1933-1987 .... *55*
　Obituary *54*
　Earlier sketch in SATA *6*
　See also CLR *5*
Lobel, Gillian *181*
Lobsenz, Amelia *12*
Lobsenz, Norman M(itchell) 1919- *6*
Lochak, Michele 1936- *39*
Lochlons, Colin
　See Jackson, C(aary) Paul
Locke, Clinton W. *1*
Locke, Elsie (Violet) 1912-2001 .... *87*
Locke, Gary 1963- *197*
Locke, Lucie 1904-1989 .... *10*
Locke, Robert 1944- *63*
　See also CLR *39*
Locker, Thomas 1937- *109*
　Earlier sketch in SATA *59*
　See also CLR *14*
Lockhart, E.
　See Jenkins, Emily
Lockridge, Hildegarde (Dolson)
　1908-1981 .... *121*
　Earlier sketch in SATA *5*
Lockwood, Mary
　See Spelman, Mary
Lodge, Bernard 1933- *215*
　Earlier sketches in SATA *33, 107*
Lodge, Jo 1966- *173*
　Earlier sketch in SATA *112*
Loeb, Jeffrey 1946- *57*
Loeb, Robert H., Jr. 1917- *21*
Loefgren, Ulf 1931- *3*
Loehfelm, Bill 1969- *153*
Loehr, Mallory *184*
Loehr, Patrick 1968(?)- *194*
Loeper, John J(oseph) 1929- *118*
　Earlier sketch in SATA *10*
Loescher, Ann Dull 1942- *20*
Loescher, Gil 1945- *20*
Loescher, Gilburt Damian
　See Loescher, Gil
Loewer, Jean Jenkins
　See Jenkins, Jean
Loewer, (Henry) Peter 1934- *98*
LoFaro, Jerry 1959- *77*
Lofo
　See Heimann, Rolf
Lofthouse, Liz *199*
Lofting, Hugh (John) 1886-1947 .... *100*
　Earlier sketch in SATA *15*
　See also CLR *143*
Lofts, Norah (Robinson) 1904-1983 .... *8*
　Obituary *36*
Logan, Alysia
　See Divine, L.
Logan, Jake
　See Knott, William C(ecil, Jr.)
　and Krepps, Robert W(ilson)
　and Pearl, Jacques Bain
　and Riefe, Alan
　and Rifkin, Shepard
　and Smith, Martin Cruz
Logan, Mark
　See Nicole, Christopher
Logan, Rochelle 1954- *169*
Logsted, Greg *221*
Logston, Anne 1962- *112*
Logue, Christopher 1926- *23*
Logue, Mary 1952- *161*
　Earlier sketch in SATA *112*
Logue, Mary Louise
　See Logue, Mary
Loh, Morag 1935- *73*
Lohans, Alison 1949- *101*
Loizeaux, William *185*
Loken, Newton Clayton 1919- *26*
Lomas, Steve
　See Brennan, Joseph Lomas
Lomask, Milton (Nachman) 1909-1991 .... *20*
Lombard, Jenny *178*

Lombino, Salvatore
　See Hunter, Evan
LoMonaco, Palmyra 1932- *102*
London, Jack 1876-1916 .... *18*
　See also CLR *108*
London, Jane
　See Geis, Darlene Stern
London, John Griffith
　See London, Jack
London, Jonathan 1947- *221*
　Earlier sketches in SATA *74, 113, 157*
Lonergan, (Pauline) Joy (MacLean) 1909- ... *10*
Lonette, Reisie (Dominee) 1924- *43*
Long, Cathryn J. 1946- *89*
Long, Earlene (Roberta) 1938- *50*
Long, Emmett
　See Leonard, Elmore
Long, Ethan 1968(?)- *223*
　Earlier sketch in SATA *182*
Long, Helen Beecher *1*
Long, Judith Elaine 1953- *20*
Long, Judy
　See Long, Judith Elaine
Long, Kim 1949- *69*
Long, Laura Mooney 1892-1967
　Obituary *29*
Long, Laurel *203*
Long, Loren 1966(?)- *188*
　Earlier sketch in SATA *151*
Long, Melinda 1960- *152*
Long, Sylvia 1948- *179*
　Earlier sketch in SATA *120*
Longbeard, Frederick
　See Longyear, Barry B(rookes)
Longfellow, Henry Wadsworth 1807-1882 ... *19*
　See also CLR *99*
Longfellow, Layne 1937- *102*
Longfellow, Layne A.
　See Longfellow, Layne
Longman, Harold S. 1919- *5*
Longsworth, Polly 1933- *28*
Longtemps, Kenneth 1933- *17*
Longway, A. Hugh
　See Lang, Andrew
Longyear, Barry B(rookes) 1942- *117*
Look, Lenore *180*
Loomans, Diane 1955- *90*
Loomis, Christine *160*
　Earlier sketch in SATA *113*
Loomis, Jennifer A. 1942- *101*
Loomis, Robert D. *5*
Lopez, Angelo (Cayas) 1967- *83*
Lopez, Antonio Castro
　See Castro L., Antonio
Lopez, Barry 1945- *67*
Lopez, Barry Holstun
　See Lopez, Barry
Lopez, Jack 1950- *178*
Lopez, Loretta 1963- *190*
Lopez, Lorraine 1956- *181*
Lopez, Lorraine M.
　See Lopez, Lorraine
Lopez, Mario 1973- *226*
Lopez, Rafael 1961(?)- *198*
Lopshire, Robert 1927-2002 .... *233*
　Earlier sketch in SATA *6*
Loraine, Connie
　See Reece, Colleen L.
Lorbiecki, Marybeth 1959- *172*
　Earlier sketch in SATA *121*
Lord, Athena V. 1932- *39*
Lord, Beman 1924-1991 .... *5*
　Obituary *69*
Lord, Bette Bao 1938- *58*
　See also CLR *151*
Lord, Cynthia *182*
Lord, Doreen Mildred Douglas
　See Lord, Douglas
Lord, Douglas 1904-1992 .... *12*
Lord, Janet *204*
Lord, John Vernon 1939- *21*

Lord, Michele 201
Lord, Nancy J.
  See Titus, Eve
Lord, Patricia C. 1927-1988
  Obituary 58
Lord, Walter 1917-2002 3
Lorde, Diana
  See Reno, Dawn E(laine)
Lorenz, Albert 1941- 115
Lorenzini, Carlo
  See Collodi, Carlo
Lorey, Dean 1967- 193
Lorimer, Janet 1941- 60
Loring, Emilie (Baker) 1864(?)-1951 51
Lorkowski, Thomas V(incent) 1950- 92
Lorkowski, Tom
  See Lorkowski, Thomas V(incent)
Lorraine, Walter (Henry) 1929- 16
Lorrimer, Claire
  See Robins, Patricia
Loss, Joan 1933- 11
Lothrop, Harriet Mulford Stone 1844-1924 . 20
Lottridge, Celia Barker 1936- 157
  Earlier sketch in SATA 112
LoTurco, Laura 1963- 84
Lotz, Wolfgang 1912-1981 65
Loughridge, Stuart 1978- 214
Louie, Ai-Ling 1949- 40
  Brief entry 34
Louis, Catherine 1963- 186
Louis, Pat
  See Francis, Dorothy
Louisburgh, Sheila Burnford
  See Burnford, Sheila (Philip Cochrane Every)
Louise, Anita
  See Riggio, Anita
Louise, Tina 1934- 191
Lourie, Helen
  See Storr, Catherine (Cole)
Lourie, Peter 1952- 183
  Earlier sketches in SATA 82, 142
Lourie, Peter King
  See Lourie, Peter
Love, Ann 1947- 168
  Earlier sketch in SATA 79
Love, D. Anne 1949- 180
  Earlier sketches in SATA 96, 145
Love, Douglas 1967- 92
Love, Judith Dufour
  See Love, Judy
Love, Judy 188
Love, Katherine (Isabel) 1907- 3
Love, Kathleen Ann
  See Love, Ann
Love, Maryann Cusimano 223
Love, Sandra (Weller) 1940- 26
Lovegrove, James 1965- 216
Lovegrove, J.M.H.
  See Lovegrove, James
Lovejoy, Jack 1937- 116
Lovelace, Delos Wheeler 1894-1967 7
Lovelace, Maud Hart 1892-1980 2
  Obituary 23
Lovell, Ingraham
  See Bacon, Josephine Dodge (Daskam)
Lovelock, Brian 1956- 214
Loverseed, Amanda (Jane) 1965- 75
Lovett, Margaret (Rose) 1915- 22
Low, Alice 1926- 156
  Earlier sketches in SATA 11, 76
Low, Elizabeth Hammond 1898-1991 5
Low, Joseph 1911-2007 14
Low, Penelope Margaret
  See Lively, Penelope
Low, William 177
Lowe, Helen 1961- 206
Lowe, Jay, Jr.
  See Loeper, John J(oseph)
Lowell, Pamela 187
Lowell, Susan 1950- 206
  Earlier sketches in SATA 81, 127

Lowenstein, Dyno 1914-1996 6
Lowenstein, Sallie 1949- 116
Lowery, Linda 1949- 151
  Earlier sketch in SATA 74
Lowery, Mike 227
Lowitz, Anson C. 1901(?)-1978 18
Lowitz, Sadyebeth Heath 1901-1969 17
Lowndes, Robert A(ugustine) W(ard)
  1916-1998 117
Lowrey, Janette Sebring 1892-1986 43
Lowry, Lois 1937- 230
  Autobiography Feature 127
  Earlier sketches in SATA 23, 70, 111, 177
  See also CLR 72
  See also SAAS 3
Lowry, Lois Hammersberg
  See Lowry, Lois
Lowry, Peter 1953- 7
Lowther, George F. 1913-1975
  Obituary 30
Loxton, Daniel 1975- 229
Loyie, Larry 1933- 150
Lozansky, Edward D. 1941- 62
Lozier, Herbert 1915- 26
Lubar, David 1954- 190
  Earlier sketch in SATA 133
Lubell, Cecil 1912-2000 6
Lubell, Winifred (A. Milius) 1914- 6
Lubin, Leonard
  See Lubin, Leonard B.
Lubin, Leonard B. 1943-1994 45
  Brief entry 37
Lubka, S. Ruth 1948- 154
Lubner, Susan 185
Luby, Thia 1954- 124
Lucado, Max (Lee) 1955- 104
Lucas, Cedric 1962- 101
Lucas, David 1966- 208
Lucas, E(dward) V(errall) 1868-1938 20
Lucas, Eileen 1956- 113
  Earlier sketch in SATA 76
Lucas, George 1944- 56
Lucas, Jerry 1940- 33
Lucas, Margeaux 186
Lucas, Victoria
  See Plath, Sylvia
Lucashenko, Melissa 1967- 104
Luccarelli, Vincent 1923- 90
Luce, Celia (Geneva Larsen) 1914- 38
Luce, Willard (Ray) 1914-1990 38
Lucht, Irmgard 1937- 82
Lucke, Deb 202
Luckett, Dave 1951- 220
  Earlier sketches in SATA 106, 167
Luckhardt, Mildred Corell 1898-1990 5
Ludden, Allen (Ellsworth) 1918(?)-1981
  Obituary 27
Ludel, Jacqueline 1945- 64
Ludlow, Geoffrey
  See Meynell, Laurence Walter
Ludlum, Mabel Cleland
  See Widdemer, Mabel Cleland
Ludwig, Helen 33
Ludwig, Lyndell 1923- 63
Ludwig, Trudy 1959- 209
  Earlier sketch in SATA 166
Luebs, Robin 1949- 212
Lueders, Edward (George) 1923- 14
Luenn, Nancy 1954- 79
  Earlier sketch in SATA 51
Lufkin, Raymond H. 1897- 38
Lugard, Flora Louisa Shaw 1852-1929 21
Luger, Harriett Mandelay 1914- 23
Luhrmann, Winifred B(ruce) 1934- 11
Luis, Earlene W. 1929- 11
Lujan, Jorge 201
Lukas, Catherine
  See Albee, Sarah
Luke, Pauline 178
Luke, Pauline R.
  See Luke, Pauline

Lum, Bernice 230
Lum, Kate 229
Lum, Peter
  See Crowe, (Bettina) Peter Lum
Lumry, Amanda (R.) 159
Lund, Deb 157
Lund, Doris Herold 1919- 12
Lunde, Darrin 202
Lundebrek, Amy 1975- 213
Lung, Chang
  See Jordan, Robert
Lunge-Larsen, Lise 1955- 184
  Earlier sketch in SATA 138
Lunn, Carolyn (Kowalczyk) 1960- 67
Lunn, Janet (Louise Swoboda) 1928- 110
  Earlier sketches in SATA 4, 68
  See also CLR 18
  See also SAAS 12
Lunsford, Cin Forshay
  See Forshay-Lunsford, Cin
Lupica, Michael
  See Lupica, Mike
Lupica, Michael Thomas
  See Lupica, Mike
Lupica, Mike 1952- 177
Lupoff, Dick
  See Lupoff, Richard A(llen)
Lupoff, Richard A(llen) 1935- 60
Lurie, Alison 1926- 112
  Earlier sketch in SATA 46
Lurie, Morris 1938- 72
Lussert, Anneliese 1929- 101
Lusted, Marcia Amidon 1962- 143
Lustig, Arnost 1926-2011 56
Lustig, Loretta 1944- 46
Lutes, Jason 1967- 210
Luthardt, Kevin 1973- 172
Luther, Frank 1905-1980
  Obituary 25
Luther, Rebekah (Lyn) S(tiles) 1960- 90
Luttmann, Gail
  See Damerow, Gail
Luttrell, Guy L. 1938- 22
Luttrell, Ida (Alleene) 1934- 91
  Brief entry 35
  Earlier sketch in SATA 40
Luttrell, William (J. III) 1954- 149
Lutz, John 1939- 180
Lutz, John Thomas
  See Lutz, John
Lutz, Norma Jean 1943- 122
Lutzeier, Elizabeth 1952- 72
Lutzker, Edythe 1904-1991 5
Luxbacher, Irene 1970- 219
  Earlier sketch in SATA 153
Luzadder, Patrick 1954- 89
Luzzati, Emanuele 1921-2007 7
Luzzatto, Paola Caboara 1938- 38
Ly, Many 1977- 208
Lybbert, Tyler 1970- 88
Lydon, Michael 1942- 11
Lyfick, Warren
  See Reeves, Lawrence F.
Lyle, Katie Letcher 1938- 8
Lynch, Chris 1962- 209
  Earlier sketches in SATA 95, 131, 171
  See also CLR 58
Lynch, Janet Nichols 1952- 221
Lynch, Jay 1945- 204
Lynch, Lorenzo 1932- 7
Lynch, Marietta 1947- 29
Lynch, Patricia (Nora) 1898-1972 9
  See also CLR 167
Lynch, Patrick James
  See Lynch, P.J.
Lynch, P.J. 1962- 213
  Earlier sketches in SATA 79, 122
Lynds, Dennis 1924-2005 47
  Brief entry 37
Lyne, Alison Davis 188

Lyngseth, Joan
  See Davies, Joan
Lynn, Elizabeth A(nne) 1946- 99
Lynn, Mary
  See Brokamp, Marilyn
Lynn, Patricia
  See Watts, Mabel Pizzey
Lynn, Tracy 175
Lyon, Elinor 1921-2008 6
  Obituary 192
Lyon, Elinor Bruce
  See Lyon, Elinor
Lyon, George Ella 1949- 207
  Autobiography Feature 148
  Earlier sketches in SATA 68, 119, 148
Lyon, Lea 1945- 212
Lyon, Lyman R.
  See de Camp, L. Sprague
Lyons, Dorothy M(arawee) 1907-1997 3
Lyons, Grant 1941- 30
Lyons, Jayne 226
Lyons, Marcus
  See Blish, James
Lyons, Mary E. 1947- 195
  Autobiography Feature 195
  Earlier sketches in SATA 93, 142
Lyons, Mary Evelyn
  See Lyons, Mary E.
Lystad, Mary (Hanemann) 1928- 11
Lytle, Elizabeth Stewart 1949- 79
Lytle, Robert A. 1944- 119
Lyttle, Richard B(ard) 1927- 23
Lytton, Deborah 1966- 218
Lytton, Edward G.E.L. Bulwer-Lytton Baron
  See Bulwer-Lytton, Edward
Lytton of Knebworth, Baron
  See Bulwer-Lytton, Edward

                    M

Ma, Wenhai 1954- 84
Maar, Leonard (Frank, Jr.) 1927- 30
Maartens, Maretha 1945- 73
Maas, Selve -1997 14
Maass, Robert 195
Mabie, Grace
  See Mattern, Joanne
Mac
  See MacManus, Seumas
  and Maccari, Ruggero
Macalaster, Elizabeth G. 1951- 115
MacAlister, Katie 159
MacAlister, V. A.
  See McKernan, Victoria
MacAllan, Andrew
  See Leasor, James
MacAodhagain, Eamon
  See Egan, E. W.
MacArthur-Onslow, Annette Rosemary
  1933- 26
Macaulay, David (Alexander) 1946- 137
  Brief entry 27
  Earlier sketches in SATA 46, 72
  See also CLR 14
Macaulay, Teresa 1947- 95
Macauley, Theresa E.
  See Macaulay, Teresa
Macavinta, Courtney 176
MacBeth, George (Mann) 1932-1992 4
  Obituary 70
MacBride, Roger Lea 1929-1995 85
MacCarter, Don 1944- 91
MacClintock, Dorcas 1932- 8
MacCready, Robin Merrow 1959(?)- 190
MacCullough, Carolyn 174
MacDonald, Alan 1958- 192
MacDonald, Amy 1951- 156
  Autobiography Feature 156
  Earlier sketches in SATA 76, 136

MacDonald, Anne Elizabeth Campbell Bard
  -1958
  See MacDonald, Betty
MacDonald, Anne Louise 1955- 217
MacDonald, Anson
  See Heinlein, Robert A.
MacDonald, Betty 1908-1958
  See YABC 1
Macdonald, Blackie
  See Emrich, Duncan (Black Macdonald)
Macdonald, Caroline 1948- 86
  Obituary 111
  See also CLR 60
Macdonald, Dwight 1906-1982 29
  Obituary 33
MacDonald, George 1824-1905 100
  Earlier sketch in SATA 33
  See also CLR 67
MacDonald, Golden
  See Brown, Margaret Wise
Macdonald, Guy 195
Macdonald, James D. 1954- 67
  Earlier sketches in SATA 81, 114, 165, 1
Macdonald, Marcia
  See Hill, Grace Livingston
MacDonald, Margaret Read 1940- 194
  Earlier sketches in SATA 94, 164
Macdonald, Marianne 1934- 113
Macdonald, Mary
  See Gifford, Griselda
Macdonald, Maryann 1947- 189
  Earlier sketch in SATA 72
MacDonald, Ross 1957- 201
Macdonald, Shelagh 1937- 25
MacDonald, Suse 1940- 193
  Brief entry 52
  Earlier sketches in SATA 54, 109
Macdonald, Wendy 217
Macdonald, Wendy M.
  See Macdonald, Wendy
Macdonald, Zillah K(atherine) 1885-1979 ... 11
MacDonnell, Megan
  See Stevens, Serita
MacDougal, John
  See Blish, James
Mace, Elisabeth 1933- 27
Mace, Varian 1938- 49
MacEachern, Stephen 206
MacEwen, Gwendolyn (Margaret)
  1941-1987 50
  Obituary 55
Macfarlan, Allan A. 1892-1982 35
MacFarlane, Iris 1922- 11
MacGill-Callahan, Sheila 1926-2000 78
MacGregor, Carol Lynn 153
MacGregor, Ellen 1906-1954 39
  Brief entry 27
MacGregor-Hastie, Roy (Alasdhair Niall)
  1929- 3
MacGrory, Yvonne 1948- 142
Machado, Ana Maria 1941- 150
MacHale, D.J. 1956- 175
MacHale, Donald James
  See MacHale, D.J.
Machetanz, Frederick 1908- 34
Machin, Sue
  See Williams, Sue
Machin Goodall, Daphne (Edith) 37
Macht, Norm
  See Macht, Norman L.
Macht, Norman L. 1929- 122
Macht, Norman Lee
  See Macht, Norman L.
Macht, Norman Lee
  See Macht, Norman L.
MacInnes, Helen (Clark) 1907-1985 22
  Obituary 44
Macintosh, Brownie 1950- 98
MacIntyre, Elisabeth 1916- 17
MacIntyre, Rod
  See MacIntyre, R.P.

MacIntyre, R.P. 1947- 203
MacIntyre, R.P. 1947- 203
MacIntyre, Wendy 1947- 196
Mack, Jeff 194
Mack, L.V.
  See Kimmelman, Burt
Mack, Stan(ley) 17
Mack, Todd 168
Mack, Tracy 1968- 183
  Earlier sketch in SATA 128
Mackall, Dandi D.
  See Mackall, Dandi Daley
Mackall, Dandi Daley 1949- 218
  Earlier sketches in SATA 118, 177, 182
Mackay, Claire 1930- 97
  Autobiography Feature 124
  Earlier sketch in SATA 40
  See also CLR 43
Mackay, Constance D'Arcy (?)-1966 125
Mackay, Donald 1914-2005 81
  Obituary 173
Mackay, Donald Alexander
  See Mackay, Donald
MacKaye, Percy (Wallace) 1875-1956 32
Mackel, Kathryn 1950- 162
Mackel, Kathy
  See Mackel, Kathryn
MacKellar, William 1914- 4
Macken, JoAnn Early 1953- 201
Macken, Walter 1915-1967 36
Mackenzie, Anna 1963- 212
MacKenzie, Jill (Kelly) 1947- 75
Mackenzie, Robert 1974- 204
Mackey, Ernan
  See McInerny, Ralph
Mackey, Weezie Kerr 188
Mackie, Maron
  See McNeely, Jeannette
Mackin, Edward
  See McInerny, Ralph
MacKinnon, Bernie 1957- 69
MacKinnon Groomer, Vera 1915- 57
MacKinstry, Elizabeth 1879-1956 42
Mackler, Carolyn 1973- 231
  Earlier sketch in SATA 156
MacLachlan, Emily
  See Charest, Emily MacLachlan
MacLachlan, Patricia 1938- 229
  Brief entry 42
  Earlier sketches in SATA 62, 107, 168
  See also CLR 14
MacLane, Jack
  See Crider, Bill
MacLean, Alistair 1922(?)-1987 23
  Obituary 50
MacLean, Alistair Stuart
  See MacLean, Alistair
Maclean, Art
  See Shirreffs, Gordon D(onald)
MacLean, Christine Kole 1962- 177
MacLean, Glynne 1964- 150
MacLean, Jill 1941- 211
MacLeod, Beatrice 1910- 162
  Earlier sketch in SATA 10
MacLeod, Beatrice Beach
  See MacLeod, Beatrice
MacLeod, Charlotte (Matilda) 1922-2005 28
  Obituary 160
MacLeod, Doug 1959- 201
  Earlier sketch in SATA 60
MacLeod, Elizabeth 184
  Earlier sketch in SATA 158
MacLeod, Ellen Jane (Anderson) 1916- 14
MacManus, James
  See MacManus, Seumas
MacManus, Seumas 1869-1960 25
MacMaster, Eve (Ruth) B(owers) 1942- 46
MacMillan, Annabelle
  See Quick, Annabelle
MacMillan, Dianne M(arie) 1943- 125
  Earlier sketch in SATA 84

Macnaughton, Tina 218
  Earlier sketch in SATA *182*
Macneill, Janet
  See McNeely, Jeannette
MacPeek, Walter G. 1902-1973 4
  Obituary 25
MacPhail, Catherine 1946- 197
  Earlier sketch in SATA *130*
MacPherson, Margaret 1908-2001 9
  See also SAAS *4*
MacPherson, Thomas George 1915-1976
  Obituary 30
MacPherson, Winnie 1930- 107
MacRae, Tom 1980- 181
Macrae, Travis
  See Feagles, Anita MacRae
MacRaois, Cormac 1944- 72
Macumber, Mari
  See Sandoz, Mari(e Susette)
Macy, Sue 1954- 227
  Earlier sketches in SATA *88, 134*
Madaras, Lynda 1947- 151
Madden, Colleen 228
Madden, Colleen M.
  See Madden, Colleen
Madden, Don 1927- 3
Madden, Kerry 1961- 168
Madden-Lunsford, Kerry
  See Madden, Kerry
Maddern, Eric 1950- 166
Maddigan, Beth 1967- 174
Maddison, Angela Mary 1923- 10
  See also CLR *24*
Maddock, Reginald (Bertram) 1912-1994 15
Maddox, Jake
  See Trumbauer, Lisa
Madenski, Melissa (Ann) 1949- 77
Madian, Jon 1941- 9
Madigan, Lisa Kay
  See Madigan, L.K.
Madigan, L.K. (?)-2011 224
Madison, Alan 182
Madison, Arnold 1937- 6
Madison, Bennett 220
Madison, Winifred 5
Madonna 1958- 149
Madsen, Gunnar 171
Madsen, Jim 1964- 202
Madsen, Ross Martin 1946- 82
Madsen, Susan A. 1954- 90
Madsen, Susan Arrington
  See Madsen, Susan A.
Maehlqvist, Stefan 1943- 30
Maestro, Betsy (Crippen) 1944- 106
  Brief entry 30
  Earlier sketch in SATA *59*
  See also CLR *45*
Maestro, Giulio 1942- 106
  Earlier sketches in SATA *8, 59*
  See also CLR *45*
Maeterlinck, Maurice 1862-1949 66
Magee, Doug 1947- 78
Magee, Wes 1939- 64
Maggio, Rosalie 1943- 69
Magid, Ken(neth Marshall) 65
Magnus, Erica 1946- 77
Magoon, Kekla 1980- 213
Magoon, Scott 222
  Earlier sketch in SATA *182*
Magorian, James 1942- 92
  Earlier sketch in SATA *32*
Magorian, Michelle 1947- 128
  Earlier sketch in SATA *67*
Magorian, Michelle Jane
  See Magorian, Michelle
Magovern, Peg 103
Magsamen, Sandra 1959- 213
Maguire, Anne
  See Nearing, Penny
Maguire, Eden 232

Maguire, Gregory 1954- 200
  Autobiography Feature 200
  Earlier sketches in SATA *28, 84, 129*
  See also SAAS *22*
Maguire, Gregory Peter
  See Maguire, Gregory
Maguire, Jack 1920-2000 74
Maguire, Jesse
  See Smith, Sherwood
Maguire, Jessie
  See Smith, Sherwood
Maher, Ramona 1934- 13
Mahlqvist, Stefan
  See Maehlqvist, Stefan
Mahon, Julia C(unha) 1916- 11
Mahony, Elizabeth Winthrop
  See Winthrop, Elizabeth
Mahood, Kenneth 1930- 24
Mahy, Margaret 1936- 171
  Earlier sketches in SATA *14, 69, 119*
  See also CLR *155*
Mahy, Margaret May
  See Mahy, Margaret
Maiden, Cecil (Edward) 1902-1981 52
Maidoff, Ilka
  See List, Ilka Katherine
Maifair, Linda Lee 1947- 83
Maik, Henri
  See Hecht, Henri Joseph
Maillu, David G(ian) 1939- 111
Maine, Trevor
  See Catherall, Arthur
Mains, Randolph P. 1946- 80
Maione, Heather 189
Maiorano, Robert 1946- 43
Maisner, Heather 1947- 89
Maison, Della
  See Katz, Bobbi
Maitland, Antony Jasper 1935- 25
Maitland, Barbara 102
Mai-Wyss, Tatjana 1972- 187
Maizels, Jennie 210
Major, Kevin (Gerald) 1949- 134
  Earlier sketches in SATA *32, 82*
  See also CLR *11*
Majure, Janet 1954- 96
Makhijani, Pooja 188
Makie, Pam 1943- 37
Makowski, Silk
  See Sullivan, Silky
Makowski, Silvia Ann
  See Sullivan, Silky
Malam, John 1957- 152
  Earlier sketch in SATA *89*
Maland, Nick 195
Malaspina, Ann 1957- 222
Malcolm, Dan
  See Silverberg, Robert
Malcolm, Jahnna N.
  See Beecham, Jahnna
Malcolmson, Anne
  See von Storch, Anne B.
Malcolmson, David 1899-1978 6
Maletta, Dr. Arlene
  See Feltenstein, Arlene
Maley, Carleen
  See Hutchins, Carleen Maley
Mali, Jane Lawrence 1937-1995 51
  Brief entry 44
  Obituary 86
Malkin, Nina 1959(?)- 179
Mallett, Jerry J. 1939- 76
Malley, Gemma 198
Malley, G.R.
  See Malley, Gemma
Mallory, Kenneth 1945- 185
  Earlier sketch in SATA *128*
Mallowan, Agatha Christie
  See Christie, Agatha
Malmberg, Carl 1904-1979 9
Malmgren, Dallin 1949- 65

Malo, John W. 1911-2000 4
Malone, James Hiram 1930- 84
Malone, Marianne 229
Malone, Nola Langner 1930-2003 8
  Obituary 151
Malone, Patricia 1932- 155
Malone, Peter 1953- 191
Maloney, Pat
  See Markun, Patricia Maloney
Malory, Sir Thomas 1410(?)-1471(?) 59
  Brief entry 33
Maltese, Michael 1909(?)-1981
  Obituary 24
Malvasi, Meg Greene 143
Malvern, Corinne 1905-1956 34
Malvern, Gladys (?)-1962 23
Mama G.
  See Davis, Grania
Mammano, Julie 1962- 202
  Earlier sketch in SATA *107*
Mamonova, Tatyana 1943- 93
Manchel, Frank 1935- 10
Manchess, Gregory 1955- 203
Manchester, William (Raymond)
  1922-2004 65
Mandabach, Brian 1962(?)- 197
Mandel, Brett H. 1969- 108
Mandel, Peter 1957- 87
Mandel, Sally (Elizabeth) 1944- 64
Mandell, Muriel (Hortense Levin) 1921- 63
Manders, John 1957- 219
  Earlier sketch in SATA *175*
Mandine, Selma 1973- 228
Manes, Stephen 1949- 99
  Brief entry 40
  Earlier sketch in SATA *42*
Manfred, Frederick (Feikema) 1912-1994 30
Mangin, Marie France 1940- 59
Mangione, Gerlando 1909-1998 6
  Obituary 104
Mangione, Jerre
  See Mangione, Gerlando
Mango, Karin N. 1936- 52
Mangurian, David 1938- 14
Mania, Cathy 1950- 102
Mania, Robert 1952- 102
Mania, Robert C., Jr.
  See Mania, Robert
Maniatty, Taramesha 1978- 92
Maniscalco, Joseph 1926- 10
Manivong, Laura 1967- 229
Manley, Deborah 1932- 28
Manley, Seon 1921- 15
  See also CLR *3*
  See also SAAS *2*
Mann, Elizabeth 1948- 153
Mann, Josephine
  See Pullein-Thompson, Josephine (Mary
  Wedderburn)
Mann, Kenny 1946- 91
Mann, Pamela 1946- 91
Mann, Patrick
  See Waller, Leslie
Mann, Peggy
  See Houlton, Peggy Mann
Mannetti, Lisa 1953- 57
  Brief entry 51
Mannheim, Grete (Salomon) 1909-1986 10
Manniche, Lise 1943- 31
Manning, Jane 233
  Earlier sketch in SATA *185*
Manning, Jane K.
  See Manning, Jane
Manning, Maurie
  See Manning, Maurie J.
Manning, Maurie J. 211
Manning, Maurie Jo
  See Manning, Maurie J.
Manning, Mick 1959- 176
Manning, Rosemary 1911-1988 10
Manning, Sarra 162

Manning-Sanders, Ruth (Vernon)
  1895(?)-1988 73
  Obituary 57
  Earlier sketch in SATA 15
Mannion, Diane
  See Paterson, Diane
Mannis, Celeste Davidson 173
Mannon, Warwick
  See Hopkins, (Hector) Kenneth
Manos, Helen 199
Mansir, A. Richard 1932- 170
Manson, Ainslie Kertland 1938- 115
Manson, Beverlie 1945- 57
  Brief entry 44
Mantchev, Lisa 221
Mantha, John 1960- 217
Manthorpe, Helen 1958- 122
Mantinband, Gerda (B.) 1917- 74
Manton, Jo
  See Gittings, Jo (Grenville) Manton
Manuel, Lynn 1948- 179
  Earlier sketch in SATA 99
Manushkin, Fran 1942- 205
  Earlier sketches in SATA 7, 54, 93, 166
Manushkin, Frances
  See Manushkin, Fran
Man Without a Spleen, A
  See Chekhov, Anton
Many, Paul 1947- 210
Many, Paul A.
  See Many, Paul
Manzano, Sonia 1950- 167
Mapes, Mary A.
  See Ellison, Virginia H(owell)
Maple, Marilyn 1931- 80
Mappin, Strephyn 1956- 109
Mara, Barney
  See Roth, Arthur J(oseph)
Mara, Jeanette
  See Cebulash, Mel
Mara, Rachna
  See Gilmore, Rachna
Marais, Josef 1905-1978
  Obituary 24
Marasmus, Seymour
  See Rivoli, Mario
Marbach, Ethel
  See Pochocki, Ethel (Frances)
Marcal, Annette B.
  See Callaway, Bernice (Anne)
Marcelino
  See Agnew, Edith J(osephine)
Marcellino, Fred 1939-2001 118
  Obituary 127
  Earlier sketch in SATA 68
March, Carl
  See Fleischman, Sid
Marchant, Bessie 1862-1941
  See YABC 2
Marchant, Catherine
  See Cookson, Catherine (McMullen)
Marcher, Marion Walden 1890-1987 10
Marchesi, Stephen 1951- 114
Marchesi, Steve
  See Marchesi, Stephen
  and Older, Effin
  and Older, Jules
Marchetta, Melina 1965- 170
Marciano, John Bemelmans 1970- 167
  Earlier sketch in SATA 118
  See also CLR 93
Marco, Lou
  See Gottfried, Theodore Mark
Marcus, Leonard S. 1950- 187
  Earlier sketch in SATA 133
Marcus, Paul 1953- 82
Marcus, Rebecca B(rian) 1907- 9
Marcuse, Aida E. 1934- 89
Marek, Margot L. 1934(?)-1987
  Obituary 54
Maren, Julie 1970- 199

Margaret, Karla
  See Andersdatter, Karla M.
Margolin, Harriet
  See Ziefert, Harriet
Margolis, Jeffrey A. 1948- 108
Margolis, Leslie 187
Margolis, Richard J(ules) 1929-1991 86
  Obituary 67
  Earlier sketch in SATA 4
Margolis, Vivienne 1922- 46
Mariana
  See Foster, Marian Curtis
Marie, Geraldine 1949- 61
Mariner, Scott
  See Pohl, Frederik
Marino, Dorothy Bronson 1912- 14
Marino, Gianna 231
Marino, Jan 1936- 114
Marino, Nan 216
Marino, Nick
  See Deming, Richard
Marino, Peter 1960- 179
Marinsky, Jane 227
Mario, Anna
  See Odgers, Sally Farrell
Marion, Henry
  See del Rey, Lester
Maris, Ron 71
  Brief entry 45
Mark, Jan 1943-2006 164
  Obituary 173
  Earlier sketches in SATA 22, 69, 114
  See also CLR 11
Mark, Janet Marjorie
  See Mark, Jan
Mark, Joan T. 1937- 122
Mark, Pauline (Dahlin) 1913-1997 14
Mark, Polly
  See Mark, Pauline (Dahlin)
Mark, Ted
  See Gottfried, Theodore Mark
Markel, Michelle 169
Marker, Sherry 1941- 76
Markert, Jennifer 1965- 83
Markert, Jenny
  See Markert, Jennifer
Markey, Kevin 1965- 215
Markham, Lynne 1947- 102
Markham, Marion M. 1929- 60
Markham, Wendy
  See Staub, Wendy Corsi
Markins, W. S.
  See Jenkins, Marie M(agdalen)
Markle, Sandra 1946- 218
  Brief entry 41
  Earlier sketches in SATA 57, 92, 148, 185
Markle, Sandra L.
  See Markle, Sandra
Marklew, Gilly 211
Marko, Katherine D(olores) 28
Markoosie
  See Patsauq, Markoosie
Marks, Alan 1957- 187
  Earlier sketches in SATA 77, 151
Marks, Burton 1930- 47
  Brief entry 43
Marks, Graham 158
Marks, Hannah K.
  See Trivelpiece, Laurel
Marks, J.
  See Highwater, Jamake (Mamake)
Marks, J(ames) M(acdonald) 1921- 13
Marks, Laurie J. 1957- 68
Marks, Margaret L. 1911(?)-1980
  Obituary 23
Marks, Mickey Klar -1986 12
Marks, Peter
  See Smith, Robert Kimmel
Marks, Rita 1938- 47
Marks, Stan(ley) 14

Marks-Highwater, J.
  See Highwater, Jamake (Mamake)
Markun, Patricia Maloney 1924- 15
Markusen, Bruce (Stanley Rodriguez)
  1965- 141
Marley, Louise 1952- 173
  Earlier sketch in SATA 120
Marlin, Hilda
  See Van Stockum, Hilda
Marlow, Layne 204
Marlow, Max
  See Nicole, Christopher
Marlow, Susan K. 1953- 178
Marlowe, Amy Bell 67
  Earlier sketch in SATA 1
Marlowe, Jack
  See Deary, Terry
Marlowe, Tess
  See Glick, Ruth
Marney, Dean 1952- 90
Marokvia, Artur 1909- 31
Marokvia, Mireille 1908-2008 5
  Obituary 197
Marokvia, Mireille Journet
  See Marokvia, Mireille
Marol, Jean-Claude 1946- 125
Marr, John S(tuart) 1940- 48
Marr, Melissa 1972- 189
Marric, J. J.
  See Butler, William Vivian
  and Creasey, John
Marrin, Albert 1936- 193
  Brief entry 43
  Earlier sketches in SATA 53, 90, 126
  See also CLR 53
Marriott, Alice Lee 1910-1992 31
  Obituary 71
Marriott, Janice 1946- 134
Marriott, Pat(ricia) 1920- 35
Marriott, Zoe 1982- 216
Marriott, Zoe Davina
  See Marriott, Zoe
Marroquin, Patricio
  See Markun, Patricia Maloney
Mars, W. T.
  See Mars, Witold Tadeusz J.
Mars, Witold Tadeusz J. 1912-1985 3
Marsden, Carolyn 1950- 212
  Autobiography Feature 212
  Earlier sketches in SATA 140, 175
Marsden, John 1950- 146
  Earlier sketches in SATA 66, 97
  See also CLR 34
  See also SAAS 22
Marsh, Carole 1946- 127
Marsh, Dave 1950- 66
Marsh, J. E.
  See Marshall, Evelyn
Marsh, James 1946- 73
Marsh, Jean
  See Marshall, Evelyn
Marsh, Joan F. 1923- 83
Marsh, Katherine 1974- 220
Marsh, Paul
  See Hopkins, (Hector) Kenneth
Marsh, Valerie 1954- 89
Marshall, Anthony D(ryden) 1924- 18
Marshall, Bonnie C. 1941- 141
  Earlier sketch in SATA 18
Marshall, Bridget M(ary) 1974- 103
Marshall, (Sarah) Catherine (Wood)
  1914-1983 2
  Obituary 34
Marshall, Douglas
  See McClintock, Marshall
Marshall, Edmund
  See Hopkins, (Hector) Kenneth
Marshall, Edward
  See Marshall, James
Marshall, Evelyn 1897-1991 11
Marshall, Felicity 1950- 116

Marshall, Garry 1934- 60
Marshall, H. H.
　See Jahn, Michael
Marshall, James 1942-1992 75
　Earlier sketches in SATA 6, 51
　See also CLR 21
Marshall, James Edward
　See Marshall, James
Marshall, James Vance
　See Payne, Donald Gordon
Marshall, Janet (Perry) 1938- 97
Marshall, Jeff
　See Laycock, George (Edwin)
Marshall, Kim
　See Marshall, Michael (Kimbrough)
Marshall, Michael (Kimbrough) 1948- 37
Marshall, Percy
　See Young, Percy M(arshall)
Marshall, S(amuel) L(yman) A(twood)
　1900-1977 21
Marsoli, Lisa Ann 1958- 101
　Brief entry 53
Marsten, Richard
　See Hunter, Evan
Marston, Elsa 1933- 156
Marston, Hope Irvin 1935- 127
　Earlier sketch in SATA 31
Marszalek, John F. 1939- 167
Marszalek, John Francis, Jr.
　See Marszalek, John F.
Marszalek, John Francis 1939-
　See Marszalek, John F.
Martchenko, Michael 1942- 154
　Earlier sketches in SATA 50, 95
Martel, Aimee
　See Thurlo, Aimee
　and Thurlo, David
Martel, Suzanne 1924- 99
Martignoni, Margaret E. 1908(?)-1974
　Obituary 27
Martin, Ann M. 1955- 192
　Brief entry 41
　Earlier sketches in SATA 44, 70, 126
　See also CLR 32
Martin, Bill, Jr. 1916-2004 145
　Brief entry 40
　Earlier sketches in SATA 40, 67
　See also CLR 97
Martin, Charles E(lmer)
　See Mastrangelo, Charles E(lmer)
Martin, Christopher
　See Hoyt, Edwin P(almer), Jr.
Martin, C.K. Kelly 207
Martin, Claire 1933- 76
Martin, Courtney Autumn 1984- 205
Martin, David Stone 1913-1992 39
Martin, Donald
　See Honig, Donald
Martin, Dorothy 1921- 47
Martin, Dorothy McKay
　See Martin, Dorothy
Martin, Eugene 1
Martin, Eva M. 1939- 65
Martin, Frances M(cEntee) 1906-1998 36
Martin, Francesca 1947- 101
Martin, Fred 1948- 119
Martin, Fredric
　See Christopher, Matt(hew Frederick)
Martin, George Raymond Richard
　See Martin, George R.R.
Martin, George R.R. 1948- 118
Martin, J(ohn) P(ercival) 1880(?)-1966 15
Martin, Jacqueline Briggs 1945- 188
　Earlier sketches in SATA 98, 149
Martin, Jane Read 1957- 84
Martin, Jeremy
　See Levin, Marcia Obrasky
Martin, Les
　See Schulman, L(ester) M(artin)
Martin, Linda 1961- 82
Martin, Lynne 1923- 21

Martin, Marcia
　See Levin, Marcia Obrasky
Martin, Marvin 1926- 126
Martin, Melanie
　See Pellowski, Michael (Joseph)
Martin, Nancy
　See Salmon, Annie Elizabeth
Martin, Patricia 200
Martin, Patricia A.
　See Martin, Patricia
Martin, Patricia Miles 1899-1986 43
　Obituary 48
　Earlier sketch in SATA 1
Martin, Peter
　See Chaundler, Christine
Martin, Rafe 1946- 175
Martin, Rene 1891-1977 42
　Obituary 20
Martin, Rupert (Claude) 1905- 31
Martin, S. R.
　See Mappin, Strephyn
Martin, Stefan 1936- 32
Martin, Vicky
　See Storey, Victoria Carolyn
Martin, Webber
　See Silverberg, Robert
Martin, Wendy
　See Martini, Teri
Martin, William Ivan, Jr.
　See Martin, Bill, Jr.
Martineau, Diane 1940- 178
Martineau, Harriet 1802-1876
　See YABC 2
Martinet, Jeanne 1958- 80
Martinez, Agnes 167
Martinez, Arturo O. 1933- 192
Martinez, Claudia Guadalupe 1978- 214
Martinez, Ed(ward) 1954- 98
Martinez, Elizabeth Coonrod 1954- 85
Martinez, Rueben 1940- 232
Martinez, Victor 1954-2011 95
Martini, Angela 1972(?)- 223
Martini, Teri 1930- 3
Martini, Therese
　See Martini, Teri
Martino, Alfred C. 1964- 174
Martinson, Janis
　See Herbert, Janis
Martinusen, Cindy
　See Martinusen-Coloma, Cindy
Martinusen, Cindy McCormick
　See Martinusen-Coloma, Cindy
Martinusen-Coloma, Cindy 1970- 218
Marton, Jirina 1946- 230
　Earlier sketches in SATA 95, 144
Marton, Pierre
　See Stone, Peter
Martson, Del
　See Lupoff, Richard A(llen)
Martyr, Paula (Jane)
　See Lawford, Paula Jane
Maruki, Toshi 1912-2000 112
　See also CLR 19
Marvin, Isabel R(idout) 1924- 84
Marx, Patricia Windschill
　See Marx, Trish
Marx, Robert F(rank) 1936- 24
Marx, Trish 1948- 202
　Earlier sketches in SATA 112, 160
Marzani, Carl (Aldo) 1912-1994 12
Marzollo, Jean 1942- 190
　Autobiography Feature 190
　Earlier sketches in SATA 29, 77, 130
　See also SAAS 15
Masefield, John (Edward) 1878-1967 19
　See also CLR 164
Masiello, Ralph 1961- 214
Masoff, Joy 1951- 118
Mason, Adrienne 1962- 163
Mason, Cherie 170

Mason, Edwin A. 1905-1979
　Obituary 32
Mason, Ernst
　See Pohl, Frederik
Mason, F(rancis) van Wyck 1901-1978 3
　Obituary 26
Mason, Frank W.
　See Mason, F(rancis) van Wyck
Mason, George Frederick 1904-2000 14
Mason, Miriam E(vangeline) 1900-1973 2
　Obituary 26
Mason, Prue 195
Mason, Simon 1962- 178
Mason, Tally
　See Derleth, August (William)
Mason, Van Wyck
　See Mason, F(rancis) van Wyck
Mass, Wendy 1967- 196
　Earlier sketch in SATA 158
Mass, William
　See Gibson, William
Masse, Josee 221
Masselman, George 1897-1971 19
Massey, Misty 212
Massie, Dianne Redfield 1938- 125
　Earlier sketch in SATA 16
Massie, Elizabeth 108
Massini, Sarah 213
Masson, Sophie 1959- 179
　Earlier sketch in SATA 133
Masters, Anthony (Richard) 1940-2003 112
　Obituary 145
Masters, Kelly R(ay) 1897-1987 3
Masters, Mildred 1932- 42
Masters, William
　See Cousins, Margaret
Masters, Zeke
　See Bensen, Donald R.
　and Goulart, Ron
Mastrangelo, Charles E(lmer) 1910-1995 70
　Earlier sketch in SATA 69
Masuda, Takeshi 1944- 56
Matas, Carol 1949- 194
　Autobiography Feature 112
　Earlier sketch in SATA 93
　See also CLR 52
Matchette, Katharine E. 1941- 38
Math, Irwin 1940- 42
Mathabane, Mark 1960- 123
Mather, Kirtley F(letcher) 1888-1978 65
Mathers, Petra 1945- 176
　Earlier sketch in SATA 119
　See also CLR 76
Matheson, Richard (Christian) 1953- 119
Matheson, Shirlee Smith 1942- 155
Mathews, Eleanor
　See Mathews, Ellie
Mathews, Ellie 1946(?)- 193
Mathews, Janet 1914-1992 41
Mathews, Judith
　See Goldberger, Judith M.
Mathews, Louise
　See Tooke, Louise Mathews
Mathiesen, Egon 1907-1976
　Obituary 28
Mathieu, Joe 1949- 185
　Brief entry 36
　Earlier sketches in SATA 43, 94
Mathieu, Joseph P.
　See Mathieu, Joe
Mathis, Sharon Bell 1937- 58
　Earlier sketch in SATA 7
　See also CLR 147
　See also SAAS 3
Matlin, Marlee 1965- 181
Matlin, Marlee Beth
　See Matlin, Marlee
Matloff, Gregory 1945- 73
Matott, Justin 1961- 109
Matranga, Frances Carfi 1922- 78
Matray, James I. 1948- 161

Matray, James Irving
See Matray, James I.
Matson, Emerson N(els) 1926- 12
Matson, Morgan 230
Matsui, Tadashi 1926- 8
Matsuno, Masako
See Kobayashi, Masako Matsuno
Matsuoka, Mei 1981- 192
Matte, (Encarnacion) L'Enc 1936- 22
Mattern, Joanne 1963- 122
Mattheson, Jenny 180
Matthew, James
See Barrie, J. M.
Matthews, Aline
See De Wire, Elinor
Matthews, Andrew 1948- 138
Matthews, Caitlin 1952- 122
Matthews, Cecily 1945- 221
Matthews, Downs 1925- 71
Matthews, Elizabeth 1978- 194
Matthews, Ellen
See Bache, Ellyn
Matthews, Ellen 1950- 28
Matthews, Harold Downs
See Matthews, Downs
Matthews, Jacklyn Meek
See Meek, Jacklyn O'Hanlon
Matthews, John (Kentigern) 1948- 116
Matthews, L. S. 183
Matthews, Laura S.
See Matthews, L. S.
Matthews, Liz
See Pellowski, Michael (Joseph)
Matthews, Morgan
See Pellowski, Michael (Joseph)
Matthews, Nicola
See Browne, N.M.
Matthews, Patricia 1927-2006 28
Matthews, Patricia Anne
See Matthews, Patricia
Matthews, Tina 1961- 190
Matthews, Tom L.
See Lalicki, Tom
Matthews, William Henry III 1919- 45
Brief entry 28
Matthiessen, Peter 1927- 27
Mattingley, Christobel (Rosemary) 1931- 85
Earlier sketch in SATA 37
See also CLR 24
See also SAAS 18
Matulay, Laszlo 1912- 43
Matus, Greta 1938- 12
Matzigkeit, Philip 220
Maugham, W. S.
See Maugham, W. Somerset
Maugham, W. Somerset 1874-1965 54
Maugham, William S.
See Maugham, W. Somerset
Maugham, William Somerset
See Maugham, W. Somerset
Maurer, Diane Philippoff
See Maurer-Mathison, Diane V(ogel)
Maurer, Diane Vogel
See Maurer-Mathison, Diane V(ogel)
Maurer-Mathison, Diane V(ogel) 1944- 89
Mauser, Pat Rhoads
See McCord, Patricia
Mauser, Patricia Rhoads
See McCord, Patricia
Maves, Mary Carolyn 1916- 10
Maves, Paul B(enjamin) 1913-1994 10
Mavor, Salley 1955- 125
Mawicke, Tran 1911- 15
Max 1906-1989
See Diop, Birago (Ismael)
Max, Jill
See Bennett, Kelly
Max, Peter 1939- 45
Maxon, Anne
See Best, (Evangel) Allena Champlin
Maxwell, Arthur S. 1896-1970 11

Maxwell, B.E. 1957- 211
Maxwell, Bruce E.
See Maxwell, B.E.
Maxwell, Edith 1923- 7
Maxwell, Gavin 1914-1969 65
Maxwell, Katie
See MacAlister, Katie
Maxwell, William (Keepers, Jr.) 1908-2000
Obituary 128
Maxwell-Hyslop, Miranda 1968- 154
May, Charles Paul 1920- 4
May, Elaine Tyler 1947- 120
May, J. C.
See May, Julian
May, Julian 1931- 11
May, Katie 225
May, Robert Lewis 1905-1976
Obituary 27
May, Robert Stephen 1929-1996 46
May, Robin
See May, Robert Stephen
Mayall, Beth 171
Mayberry, Florence V(irginia) Wilson 10
Maybury, Richard J. 1946- 72
Maybury, Rick
See Maybury, Richard J.
Maydak, Michael S. 1952- 220
Mayer, Agatha
See Maher, Ramona
Mayer, Albert Ignatius, Jr. 1906-1994
Obituary 29
Mayer, Ann M(argaret) 1938- 14
Mayer, Bill 200
Mayer, Danuta 1958- 117
Mayer, Hannelore Valencak 1929- 42
Mayer, Jane Rothschild 1903-2001 38
Mayer, Marianna 1945- 132
Earlier sketches in SATA 32, 83
Mayer, Mercer 1943- 137
Earlier sketches in SATA 16, 32, 73, 129
See also CLR 11
Mayerson, Charlotte Leon 36
Mayerson, Evelyn Wilde 1935- 55
Mayfield, Katherine 1958- 118
Mayfield, Sue 1963- 146
Earlier sketch in SATA 72
Mayhar, Ardath 1930- 38
Mayhew, James 1964- 204
Earlier sketches in SATA 85, 149
Maynard, Olga 1920- 40
Mayne, William 1928-2010 122
Earlier sketches in SATA 6, 68
See also CLR 123
See also SAAS 11
Mayne, William James Carter
See Mayne, William
Maynes, J. O. Rocky, Jr.
See Maynes, J. Oscar, Jr.
Maynes, J. Oscar, Jr. 1929- 38
Mayo, Gretchen Will 1936- 163
Earlier sketch in SATA 84
Mayo, Margaret 1935- 165
Earlier sketches in SATA 38, 96
Mayo, Margaret Mary
See Mayo, Margaret
Mayr, Diane 1949- 197
Mays, Lucinda L(a Bella) 1924- 49
Mays, (Lewis) Victor (Jr.) 1927- 5
Mazellan, Ron 210
Mazer, Anne 1953- 192
Earlier sketches in SATA 67, 105
Mazer, Harry 1925- 167
Earlier sketches in SATA 31, 67, 105
See also CLR 16
See also SAAS 11
Mazer, Norma Fox 1931-2009 198
Earlier sketches in SATA 24, 67, 105, 168
See also CLR 23
See also SAAS 1
Mazille, Capucine 1953- 96
Mazo, Michael 223

Mazza, Adriana 1928- 19
Mazzio, Joann 1926- 74
Mbugua, Kioi Wa 1962- 83
McAfee, Carol 1955- 81
McAllister, Amanda
See Dowdell, Dorothy (Florence) Karns
and Hager, Jean
and Meaker, Eloise
McAllister, Angela 225
Earlier sketch in SATA 182
McAllister, Margaret I. 1956- 169
Earlier sketch in SATA 117
McAllister, M.I.
See McAllister, Margaret I.
McArdle, Paula 1971- 198
McArthur, Nancy 96
McAvoy, Jim 1972- 142
McBain, Ed
See Hunter, Evan
McBain, Georgina 189
McBratney, Sam 1943- 203
Earlier sketches in SATA 89, 164
See also CLR 44
McBrier, Michael
See Older, Effin
and Older, Jules
McCafferty, Jim 1954- 84
McCaffery, Janet 1936- 38
McCaffrey, Anne 1926- 152
Autobiography Feature 152
Earlier sketches in SATA 8, 70, 116
See also CLR 130
See also SAAS 11
McCaffrey, Anne Inez
See McCaffrey, Anne
McCaffrey, Kate 1970- 228
McCaffrey, Mary
See Szudek, Agnes S(usan) P(hilomena)
McCain, Becky Ray 1954- 138
McCain, Murray (David, Jr.) 1926-1981 7
Obituary 29
McCall, Bruce 1935(?)- 209
McCall, Edith (Sansom) 1911- 6
McCall, Virginia Nielsen 1909-2000 13
McCall, Wendell
See Pearson, Ridley
McCall Smith, Alexander
See Smith, Alexander McCall
McCallum, Phyllis
See Koch, Phyllis (Mae) McCallum
McCallum, Stephen 1960- 91
McCampbell, Darlene Z. 1942- 83
McCann, Edson
See del Rey, Lester
and Pohl, Frederik
McCann, Gerald 1916- 41
McCann, Helen 1948- 75
McCannon, Dindga 41
McCants, William D. 1961- 82
McCarter, Neely Dixon 1929- 47
McCarthy, Agnes 1933- 4
McCarthy, Colin (John) 1951- 77
McCarthy, Mary 1951- 203
McCarthy, Meghan 199
Earlier sketch in SATA 168
McCarthy, Ralph F. 1950- 139
McCarthy-Tucker, Sherri N. 1958- 83
McCarty, Peter 1966- 182
McCarty, Rega Kramer 1904-1986 10
McCaslin, Nellie 1914-2005 12
McCaughrean, Geraldine 1951- 173
Earlier sketches in SATA 87, 139
See also CLR 38
McCaughren, Tom 1936- 75
McCauley, Adam 1965- 209
Earlier sketch in SATA 128
McCay, (Zenas) Winsor 1869-1934 134
Earlier sketch in SATA 41
McClafferty, Carla Killough 1958- 137
McClary, Jane Stevenson 1919-1990
Obituary 64

McCleery, Patsy R. 1925- *133*
Earlier sketch in SATA *88*
McClelland, Susan *214*
McClements, George *196*
McClintock, Barbara 1955- *213*
Earlier sketches in SATA *57, 95, 146*
McClintock, Marshall 1906-1967 .... *3*
McClintock, May Garelick
See Garelick, May
McClintock, Mike
See McClintock, Marshall
McClintock, Norah *226*
Earlier sketch in SATA *178*
McClintock, Theodore 1902-1971 .... *14*
McClinton, Leon 1933- *11*
McCloskey, Kevin 1951- *79*
McCloskey, (John) Robert 1914-2003 .... *100*
Obituary *146*
Earlier sketches in SATA *2, 39*
See also CLR *7*
McCloy, James F(loyd) 1941- *59*
McClung, Robert M(arshall) 1916- *135*
Earlier sketches in SATA *2, 68*
See also CLR *11*
See also SAAS *15*
McClure, Gillian Mary 1948- *31*
McClure, Nikki *218*
McColley, Kevin 1961- *80*
See also SAAS *23*
McConduit, Denise Walter 1950- *89*
McConnell, James Douglas Rutherford
1915-1988 .... *40*
Obituary *56*
McCord, Anne 1942- *41*
McCord, David (Thompson Watson)
1897-1997 .... *18*
Obituary *96*
See also CLR *9*
McCord, Jean 1924- *34*
McCord, Pat Mauser
See McCord, Patricia
McCord, Patricia 1943- *159*
Earlier sketch in SATA *37*
McCord, Patricia Sue Rhoads Mauser
See McCord, Patricia
McCormack, Caren McNelly *217*
McCormick, Brooks
See Adams, William Taylor
McCormick, Dell J. 1892-1949 .... *19*
McCormick, (George) Donald (King)
1911-1998 .... *14*
McCormick, Edith (Joan) 1934- *30*
McCormick, Kimberly A. 1960- *153*
McCormick, Patricia 1956- *181*
Earlier sketch in SATA *128*
McCourt, Edward (Alexander) 1907-1972
Obituary *28*
McCourt, Lisa 1964- *214*
Earlier sketches in SATA *117, 159*
McCourt, Malachy 1931- *126*
McCoy, Glenn 1965- *212*
McCoy, Iola Fuller *3*
McCoy, J(oseph) J(erome) 1917- *8*
McCoy, Karen Kawamoto 1953- *82*
McCoy, Lois (Rich) 1941- *38*
McCrady, Lady 1951- *16*
McCrea, James (Craig, Jr.) 1920- *3*
McCrea, Ruth (Pirman) 1921- *3*
McCreigh, James
See Pohl, Frederik
McCrumb, Sharyn 1948- *109*
McCue, Lisa 1959- *212*
Earlier sketches in SATA *65, 177*
McCue, Lisa Emiline
See McCue, Lisa
McCullen, Andrew
See Arthur, Robert, (Jr.)
McCullers, Carson 1917-1967 .... *27*
McCullers, Lula Carson Smith
See McCullers, Carson

McCulloch, Derek (Ivor Breashur) 1897-1967
Obituary *29*
McCulloch, John Tyler
See Burroughs, Edgar Rice
McCulloch, Sarah
See Ure, Jean
McCullough, David 1933- *62*
McCullough, David Gaub
See McCullough, David
McCullough, Frances Monson 1938- *8*
McCullough, Sharon Pierce 1943- *131*
McCully, Emily Arnold
See Arnold, Emily
McCune, Dan
See Haas, Dorothy F.
McCunn, Ruthanne Lum 1946- *63*
McCurdy, Michael (Charles) 1942- *147*
Earlier sketches in SATA *13, 82*
McCusker, Paul 1958- *220*
McCutcheon, Elsie (Mary Jackson) 1937- .. *60*
McCutcheon, John 1952- *97*
McDaniel, Becky Bring 1953- *61*
McDaniel, Lurlene 1944- *218*
Earlier sketches in SATA *71, 146*
McDaniels, Pellom III 1968- *121*
McDaniels, Preston 1952- *192*
McDearmon, Kay *20*
McDermott, Beverly Brodsky 1941- *11*
McDermott, Eleni *156*
McDermott, Gerald (Edward) 1941- *163*
Earlier sketches in SATA *16, 74*
See also CLR *9*
McDermott, Michael 1962- *76*
McDevitt, Jack 1935- *155*
Earlier sketch in SATA *94*
McDevitt, John Charles
See McDevitt, Jack
McDole, Carol
See Farley, Carol (J.)
McDonald, Candice Hartsough 1982- *225*
McDonald, Collin 1943- *79*
McDonald, Gerald D(oan) 1905-1970 .... *3*
McDonald, Jamie
See Heide, Florence Parry
McDonald, Janet 1953-2007 .... *204*
Earlier sketch in SATA *148*
McDonald, Jill (Masefield) 1927-1982 .... *13*
Obituary *29*
McDonald, Joyce 1946- *164*
Earlier sketch in SATA *101*
McDonald, Lucile Saunders 1898-1992 ..... *10*
McDonald, Mary Ann 1956- *84*
McDonald, Megan 1958- *202*
Autobiography Feature *151*
Earlier sketches in SATA *67, 99, 148, 151*
See also CLR *94*
McDonald, Meme 1954- *112*
McDonald, Mercedes 1956- *169*
Earlier sketch in SATA *97*
McDonald, Rae A. 1952- *201*
McDonell, Chris 1960- *138*
McDonnell, Christine 1949- *225*
Earlier sketches in SATA *34, 115*
McDonnell, Flora (Mary) 1963- *146*
Earlier sketch in SATA *90*
McDonnell, Kathleen 1947- *186*
McDonnell, Lois Eddy 1914-2001 .... *10*
McDonnell, Patrick 1956- *221*
Earlier sketch in SATA *179*
McDonough, Yona Zeldis 1957- *73*
McDowell, Marilyn Taylor *217*
McElligott, Matt 1968- *196*
Earlier sketch in SATA *135*
McElligott, Matthew
See McElligott, Matt
McElmeel, Sharron L. 1942- *128*
McElmurry, Jill *198*
Earlier sketch in SATA *159*
McElrath, William N. 1932- *65*
McElrath-Eslick, Lori 1960- *204*
Earlier sketch in SATA *96*

McEntee, Dorothy (Layng) 1902- *37*
McEvoy, Anne *214*
McEwen, Katherine *183*
McEwen, Robert (Lindley) 1926-1980
Obituary *23*
McFadden, Kevin Christopher
See Pike, Christopher
McFall, Christie 1918- *12*
McFall, Gardner 1952- *183*
McFarlan, Donald M(aitland) 1915- *59*
McFarland, Henry "Hammer"
See McFarland, Henry O.
McFarland, Henry O. 1934- *143*
McFarland, Kenton D(ean) 1920- *11*
McFarland, Martha
See Smith-Ankrom, M. E.
McFarlane, Leslie 1902-1977 .... *100*
Earlier sketches in SATA *31, 1, 65, 67*
See also CLR *118*
McFarlane, Leslie Charles
See McFarlane, Leslie
McFarlane, Peter 1940- *95*
McFarlane, Peter William
See McFarlane, Peter
McFarlane, Sheryl P. 1954- *86*
McFarlane, Todd 1961- *117*
McGaw, Jessie Brewer 1913-1997 .... *10*
McGee, Barbara 1943- *6*
McGee, Marni *163*
McGhee, Alison 1960- *231*
Earlier sketch in SATA *196*
McGhee, Alison R.
See McGhee, Alison
McGhee, Holly M.
See Durand, Hallie
McGiffin, (Lewis) Lee (Shaffer) 1908-1978 .. *1*
McGill, Alice *159*
McGill, Marci
See Balterman, Marcia Ridlon
McGill, Marci Ridlon
See Balterman, Marcia Ridlon
McGill, Ormond 1913- *92*
McGinley, Jerry 1948- *116*
McGinley, Phyllis 1905-1978 .... *44*
Obituary *24*
Earlier sketch in SATA *2*
McGinnis, Lila S(prague) 1924- *44*
McGinty, Alice B. 1963- *202*
Earlier sketch in SATA *134*
McGivern, Justin 1985- *129*
McGivern, Maureen Daly
See Daly, Maureen
McGivern, Maureen Patricia Daly
See Daly, Maureen
McGough, Elizabeth (Hemmes) 1934- *33*
McGovern, Ann 1930- *132*
Earlier sketches in SATA *8, 69, 70*
See also CLR *50*
See also SAAS *17*
McGowen, Thomas E. 1927- *109*
Earlier sketch in SATA *2*
McGowen, Tom
See McGowen, Thomas E.
McGrady, Mike 1933- *6*
McGrath, Barbara Barbieri 1953- *230*
Earlier sketches in SATA *108, 169*
McGrath, Robin 1949- *121*
McGrath, Thomas (Matthew) 1916-1990 .... *41*
Obituary *66*
McGraw, Eloise Jarvis 1915-2000 .... *67*
Obituary *123*
Earlier sketch in SATA *1*
See also SAAS *6*
McGraw, William Corbin 1916-1999 .... *3*
McGreal, Elizabeth
See Yates, Elizabeth
McGregor, Barbara 1959- *82*
McGregor, Craig 1933- *8*
McGregor, Iona 1929- *25*
McGrory, Anik *193*
McGuffey, Alexander Hamilton 1816-1896 . *60*

McGuigan, Mary Ann 1949- 228
   Earlier sketch in SATA *106*
McGuire, Edna 1899- *13*
McGuire, Leslie (Sarah) 1945- *94*
   Brief entry 45
   Earlier sketch in SATA *52*
McGuire, Robert *187*
McGuirk, Leslie (A.) 1960- *152*
McGurk, Slater
   See Roth, Arthur J(oseph)
McHargue, Georgess 1941-2011 77
   Earlier sketch in SATA *4*
   See also CLR *2*
   See also SAAS *5*
McHenry, E.B. 1963(?)- *193*
McHugh, (Berit) Elisabet 1941- *55*
   Brief entry 44
McIlvaine, Jane
   See McClary, Jane Stevenson
McIlwraith, Maureen Mollie Hunter
   See Hunter, Mollie
McInerney, Judith W(hitelock) 1945- 49
   Brief entry 46
McInerny, Ralph 1929-2010 93
McInerny, Ralph Matthew
   See McInerny, Ralph
McKaughan, Larry (Scott) 1941- 75
McKay, Donald 1895- 45
McKay, Hilary 1959- 208
   Earlier sketches in SATA *92, 145*
   See also SAAS *23*
McKay, Hilary Jane
   See McKay, Hilary
McKay, Lawrence, Jr. 1948- *114*
McKay, Robert W. 1921- *15*
McKay, Sharon E. 1954- *165*
McKay, Simon
   See Nicole, Christopher
McKean, Dave 1963- *197*
McKean, David Jeff
   See McKean, Dave
McKeating, Eileen 1957- *81*
McKee, David (John) 1935- *158*
   Earlier sketches in SATA *70, 107*
   See also CLR *38*
McKee, Tim 1970- *111*
McKeever, Marcia
   See Laird, Jean E(louise)
McKellar, Danica 1975- *213*
McKelvey, Carole A. 1942- 78
McKelvy, Charles 1950- *124*
McKendrick, Melveena (Christine) 1941- 55
McKendry, Joe 1972- *170*
McKenna, Colleen O'Shaughnessy 1948- .. *136*
   Earlier sketch in SATA *76*
McKenzie, Dorothy Clayton 1910-1981
   Obituary 28
McKenzie, Ellen Kindt 1928- 80
McKernan, Victoria 1957- *171*
McKie, Robin *112*
McKillip, Patricia A. 1948- *174*
   Earlier sketches in SATA *30, 80, 126*
McKillip, Patricia Anne
   See McKillip, Patricia A.
McKim, Audrey Margaret 1909-1999 47
McKimmie, Chris *194*
McKinley, Jennifer Carolyn Robin
   See McKinley, Robin
McKinley, Robin 1952- *229*
   Brief entry 32
   Earlier sketches in SATA *50, 89, 130, 195*
   See also CLR *127*
McKinney, Barbara Shaw 1951- *116*
McKinney, Nadine 1938- 91
McKinty, Adrian *186*
McKissack, Fredrick L. 1939- *162*
   Brief entry 53
   Earlier sketches in SATA *73, 117*
   See also CLR *55*
McKissack, Fredrick Lemuel
   See McKissack, Fredrick L.

McKissack, Patricia C. 1944- *195*
   Earlier sketches in SATA *51, 73, 117, 162*
   See also CLR *129*
McKissack, Patricia L'Ann Carwell
   See McKissack, Patricia C.
McKissack and McKissack
   See McKissack, Fredrick L.
   and McKissack, Patricia C.
McKown, Robin (?)-1976 6
McKy, Katie 1956- *184*
McLaren, Chesley *213*
McLaren, Clemence 1938- *158*
   Earlier sketch in SATA *105*
McLaughlin, Frank 1934- 73
McLaughlin, Julie 1984- *226*
McLaughlin, Lauren *209*
McLaurin, Anne 1953- 27
McLean, Andrew 1946- *172*
   Earlier sketch in SATA *113*
McLean, J. Sloan
   See Gillette, Virginia M(ary)
   and Wunsch, Josephine (McLean)
McLean, Jacqueline
   See Kolosov, Jacqueline
McLean, Janet 1946- *113*
McLean, Kathryn (Anderson) 1909-1966 9
McLean, Virginia Overton 1946- 90
McLean-Carr, Carol 1948- *122*
McLeish, Kenneth 1940-1997 35
McLenighan, Valjean 1947- 46
   Brief entry 40
McLennan, Connie *171*
McLennan, Will
   See Wisler, G(ary) Clifton
McLeod, Bob 1951- *173*
McLeod, Chum 1955- 95
McLeod, Emilie Warren 1926-1982 23
   Obituary 31
McLeod, Kirsty
   See Hudson, (Margaret) Kirsty
McLeod, Margaret Vail
   See Holloway, Teresa (Bragunier)
McLerran, Alice 1933- *137*
   Earlier sketch in SATA *68*
McLimans, David 1949- *182*
McLoughlin, John C. 1949- 47
McMahon, Bob 1956- *208*
McManus, Patrick F. 1933- 46
McManus, Patrick Francis
   See McManus, Patrick F.
McMeekin, Clark
   See McMeekin, Isabel McLennan
McMeekin, Isabel McLennan 1895-1973 3
McMenemy, Sarah 1965- *226*
   Earlier sketch in SATA *156*
McMillan, Bruce 1947- *192*
   Earlier sketches in SATA *22, 70, 129*
   See also CLR *47*
McMillan, Naomi
   See Grimes, Nikki
McMorey, James L.
   See Moyer, Terry J.
McMorrow, Annalisa 1969- *104*
McMullan, Jim 1934- *150*
   Earlier sketch in SATA *87*
McMullan, K. H.
   See McMullan, Kate
McMullan, Kate 1947- *189*
   Brief entry 48
   Earlier sketches in SATA *52, 87, 132*
McMullan, Kate Hall
   See McMullan, Kate
McMullan, Margaret 1960- *203*
McMurtrey, Martin A(loysias) 1921- 21
McNabb, Linda 1963- *147*
McNair, Kate 3
McNair, Sylvia 1924-2002 74
McNamara, Margaret C(raig) 1915-1981
   Obituary 24
McNaught, Harry 32

McNaughton, Colin 1951- *211*
   Earlier sketches in SATA *39, 92, 134*
   See also CLR *54*
McNaughton, Janet 1953- *162*
   Earlier sketch in SATA *110*
McNeal, Laura *194*
McNeal, Tom *194*
McNeely, Jeannette 1918- 25
McNeer, May (Yonge) 1902-1994 81
   Earlier sketch in SATA *1*
McNeese, Tim 1953- *139*
McNeill, Janet
   See Alexander, Janet
McNicholas, Shelagh *191*
McNickle, D'Arcy 1904-1977
   Obituary 22
McNickle, William D'Arcy
   See McNickle, D'Arcy
McNicoll, Sylvia (Marilyn) 1954- *113*
   See also CLR *99*
McNulty, Faith 1918-2005 .... *168*
   Earlier sketches in SATA *12, 84, 139*
McPhail, David 1940- *219*
   Brief entry 32
   Earlier sketches in SATA *47, 81, 140, 183*
McPhail, David M.
   See McPhail, David
McPhail, David Michael
   See McPhail, David
McPhee, Norma H. 1928- 95
McPhee, Peter 1957- *214*
McPhee, Richard B(yron) 1934- 41
McPherson, James M. 1936- *141*
   Earlier sketch in SATA *16*
McPherson, James Munro
   See McPherson, James M.
McQueen, Lucinda 1950- 58
   Brief entry 48
McQueen, Mildred Hark 1908-1978 12
McQuillan, Mary *200*
McRae, Russell (William) 1934- 63
McShean, Gordon 1936- 41
Mc Swigan, Marie 1907-1962 24
McTavish, Sandy
   See Eyerly, Jeannette
McVeity, Jen *148*
McVey, Vicki 1946- 80
McVicker, Charles (Taggart) 1930- 39
McVicker, Chuck
   See McVicker, Charles (Taggart)
McVoy, Terra Elan *220*
McWhirter, A(lan) Ross 1925-1975 37
   Obituary 31
McWhirter, Norris (Dewar) 1925-2004 37
McWilliam, Howard 1977- *219*
McWilliams, Karen 1943- 65
Mdurvwa, Hajara E. 1962- 92
Meacham, Margaret 1952- *203*
   Earlier sketch in SATA *95*
Meachum, Virginia 1918- *133*
   Earlier sketch in SATA *87*
Mead, Alice 1952- *146*
   Earlier sketch in SATA *94*
Mead, Margaret 1901-1978
   Obituary 20
Mead, Russell (M., Jr.) 1935- 10
Mead, Stella (?)-1981
   Obituary 27
Meade, Elizabeth Thomasina 1854(?)-1914(?)
   See CLR *163*
Meade, Ellen
   See Roddick, Ellen
Meade, Holly *207*
Meade, L. T.
   See Meade, Elizabeth Thomasina
Meade, Marion 1934- *127*
   Earlier sketch in SATA *23*
Meader, Stephen W(arren) 1892-1977 .... *1*
Meadmore, Susan
   See Sallis, Susan (Diana)
Meadow, Charles T(roub) 1929- 23

Meadowcroft, Enid LaMonte
See Wright, Enid Meadowcroft (LaMonte)
Meadows, Daisy
See Chapman, Linda
Meadows, Graham (W.) 1934- *161*
Meadows, Michelle *202*
Meaker, M. J.
See Meaker, Marijane
Meaker, Marijane 1927- *160*
Autobiography Feature *111*
Earlier sketches in SATA *20, 61, 99*
See also CLR *29*
See also SAAS *1*
Meaker, Marijane Agnes
See Meaker, Marijane
Means, Florence Crannell 1891-1980 .... *1*
Obituary *25*
See also CLR *56*
Mearian, Judy Frank 1936- *49*
Mebus, Scott 1974- *216*
Mecca, Judy Truesdell 1955- *127*
Mechling, Lauren 1978(?)- *194*
Mechling, Lauren 1978(?)- *194*
Mechner, Jordan 1964- *205*
Medary, Marjorie 1890-1980 .... *14*
Meddaugh, Susan 1944- *176*
Earlier sketches in SATA *29, 84, 125*
Medearis, Angela Shelf 1956- *123*
Earlier sketch in SATA *72*
Medearis, Mary 1915- *5*
Medina, Jane 1953- *167*
Earlier sketch in SATA *122*
Medina, Meg 1963- *212*
Medina, Nico 1982- *193*
Medlicott, Mary 1946- *88*
Mee, Charles L., Jr. 1938- *72*
Earlier sketch in SATA *8*
Meehan, Kierin *218*
Meehl, Brian *204*
Meek, Jacklyn O'Hanlon 1933- *51*
Brief entry *34*
Meek, S(terner St.) P(aul) 1894-1972
Obituary *28*
Meeker, Clare Hodgson 1952- *96*
Meeker, Oden 1919(?)-1976 .... *14*
Meeker, Richard
See Brown, Fornan
Meeks, Esther MacBain *1*
Meggs, Libby Phillips 1943- *130*
Mehdevi, Alexander (Sinclair) 1947- *7*
Mehdevi, Anne (Marie) Sinclair 1947- *8*
Meidell, Sherry 1951- *73*
Meier, Minta 1906- *55*
Meighan, Donald Charles 1929- *30*
Meigs, Cornelia Lynde 1884-1973 .... *6*
See also CLR *55*
Meilach, Dona Z(weigoron) 1926- *34*
Meilman, Philip W(arren) 1951- *79*
Meinstereifel, Ronald L. 1960- *134*
Meisel, Paul *224*
Earlier sketch in SATA *184*
Meister, Cari *204*
Melanson, Luc *198*
Melcher, Daniel 1912-1985
Obituary *43*
Melcher, Frederic Gershom 1879-1963
Obituary *22*
Melcher, Marguerite Fellows 1879-1969 ...... *10*
Meldrum, Christina *206*
Melendez, Francisco 1964- *72*
Melhuish, Eva *199*
Melin, Grace Hathaway 1892-1973 .... *10*
Mellersh, H(arold) E(dward) L(eslie)
1897- *10*
Melling, David *186*
Melmed, Laura Krauss *212*
Melmoth, Sebastian
See Wilde, Oscar
Melnikoff, Pamela (Rita) *97*
Meltzer, Amy 1968- *202*

Meltzer, Milton 1915-2009 .... *201*
Autobiography Feature *124*
Earlier sketches in SATA *1, 50, 80, 128*
See also CLR *13*
See also SAAS *1*
Melville, Anne
See Potter, Margaret
Melville, Herman 1819-1891 .... *59*
Melwood, Mary
See Lewis, E. M.
Melzack, Ronald 1929- *5*
Memling, Carl 1918-1969 .... *6*
Menchin, Scott *188*
Mendel, Jo
See Bond, Gladys Baker
and Gilbertson, Mildred Geiger
Mendelson, Steven T. 1958-1995 .... *86*
Mendelson-Stevens, Serita Deborah
See Stevens, Serita
Mendes, Valerie 1939- *157*
Mendez, Raymond A. 1947- *66*
Mendez, Simon 1975- *215*
Mendonca, Susan
See Smith, Susan Vernon
Mendoza, George 1934- *41*
Brief entry *39*
See also SAAS *7*
Menendez, Shirley (C.) 1937- *146*
Meng, Cece *194*
Meng, Heinz (Karl) 1924- *13*
Mennen, Ingrid 1954- *85*
Menotti, Gian Carlo 1911-2007 .... *29*
Obituary *180*
Menuhin, Sir Yehudi 1916-1999 .... *40*
Obituary *113*
Menville, Douglas 1935- *64*
Menzel, Barbara Jean 1946- *63*
Menzel, Peter 1948- *207*
Mercati, Cynthia *164*
Mercati, Cynthia J.
See Mercati, Cynthia
Mercer, Charles (Edward) 1917-1988 .... *16*
Obituary *61*
Mercer, Jessie *21*
Mercer, Sienna *192*
Meredith, Arnold
See Hopkins, (Hector) Kenneth
Meredith, David William
See Miers, Earl Schenck
Meringoff, Laurene Krasny
See Brown, Laurene Krasny
Meriwether, Louise 1923- *52*
Brief entry *31*
Merlin, Arthur
See Blish, James
Merlin, Christina
See Heaven, Constance (Christina)
Merrell, Billy 1982- *222*
Merriam, Eve 1916-1992 .... *73*
Earlier sketches in SATA *3, 40*
See also CLR *14*
Merrill, Jane 1946- *42*
Merrill, Jane Merrill
See Merrill, Jane
Merrill, Jean (Fairbanks) 1923- *82*
Earlier sketch in SATA *1*
See also CLR *52*
Merrill, Phil
See Merrill, Jane
Merriman, Alex
See Silverberg, Robert
Merriman, Rachel 1971- *149*
Earlier sketch in SATA *98*
Merrit, Elizabeth
See Goudge, Eileen
Merski, Patricia K.
See Merski, P.K.
Merski, P.K. *172*
Mertz, Barbara
See Peters, Elizabeth

Mertz, Barbara Gross
See Peters, Elizabeth
Merveille, David *200*
Merz, Jennifer J. *196*
Meschel, Susan V. 1936- *83*
Meschenmoser, Sebastian 1980- *229*
Meserve, Jessica *211*
Messenger, Charles (Rynd Milles) 1942- *59*
Messer, Stephen 1972- *231*
Messick, Dale 1906-2005 .... *64*
Brief entry *48*
Messier, Claire 1956- *103*
Messieres, Nicole de
See de Messieres, Nicole
Messinger, Carla *198*
Messmer, Otto 1892(?)-1983 .... *37*
Messner, Kate *224*
Mesta, Gabriel
See Moesta, Rebecca
Metaxas, Eric 1963- *211*
Metcalf, Doris H(unter) *91*
Metcalf, Suzanne
See Baum, L. Frank
Metos, Thomas H(arry) 1932- *37*
Metter, Bert(ram Milton) 1927- *56*
Metzenthen, David 1958- *167*
Earlier sketch in SATA *106*
Meunier, Brian 1954- *195*
Meyer, Barbara 1939- *77*
Meyer, Carolyn 1935- *142*
Autobiography Feature *142*
Earlier sketches in SATA *9, 70, 118*
See also SAAS *9*
Meyer, Carolyn Mae
See Meyer, Carolyn
Meyer, Edith Patterson 1895-1993 .... *5*
Meyer, F(ranklyn) E(dward) 1932- *9*
Meyer, Jean Shepherd *11*
Meyer, Jerome Sydney 1895-1975 .... *3*
Obituary *25*
Meyer, June
See Jordan, June
Meyer, Kerstin 1966- *190*
Meyer, L.A. 1942- *221*
Earlier sketches in SATA *12, 144*
Meyer, Louis A.
See Meyer, L.A.
Meyer, Renate 1930- *6*
Meyer, Stephenie 1973- *193*
See also CLR *142*
Meyer, Susan E. 1940- *64*
Meyerhoff, Jenny 1972- *208*
Meyers, Susan 1942- *164*
Earlier sketches in SATA *19, 108*
Meynell, Laurence Walter 1899-1989
Obituary *61*
Meynier, Yvonne (Pollet) 1908- *14*
Mezey, Robert 1935- *33*
Micale, Albert 1913- *22*
Michael, James
See Scagnetti, Jack
Michael, Jan 1947- *216*
Michael, Livi 1960- *172*
Michael, Manfred
See Winterfeld, Henry
Michael, Olivia
See Michael, Livi
Michaelis, Antonia 1979- *215*
Michaels, Barbara
See Peters, Elizabeth
Michaels, Jamie *195*
Michaels, Joanne Louise
See Teitelbaum, Michael
Michaels, Kristin
See Williams, Jeanne
Michaels, Molly
See Untermeyer, Louis
Michaels, Neal
See Teitelbaum, Michael
Michaels, Rune *194*

Michaels, Ski
  See Pellowski, Michael (Joseph)
Michaels, Steve 1955- 71
Michaels, William M. 1917- 77
Michalak, Jamie 1973- 217
Michel, Anna 1943- 49
  Brief entry 40
Michel, Francois 1948- 82
Michelin, Linda 183
Michelson, Richard 198
  Earlier sketch in SATA *173*
Micich, Paul 74
Mickelson, Scott 1963- 213
Micklish, Rita 1931- 12
Micklos, John, Jr. 1956- 173
  Earlier sketch in SATA *129*
Micklos J., John, Jr. 1956-
  See Micklos, John, Jr.
Micucci, Charles (Patrick, Jr.) 1959- 144
  Earlier sketch in SATA *82*
Middleton, Charlotte 230
Middleton, Haydn 1955- 152
  Earlier sketch in SATA *85*
Miers, Earl Schenck 1910-1972 1
  Obituary 26
Migdale, Lawrence 1951- 89
Miglio, Paige 1966- 201
Mikaelsen, Ben 1952- 173
  Earlier sketches in SATA *73, 107*
Mikaelsen, Benjamin John
  See Mikaelsen, Ben
Miklowitz, Gloria D. 1927- 129
  Earlier sketches in SATA *4, 68*
  See also SAAS *17*
Mikolaycak, Charles 1937-1993 78
  Obituary 75
  Earlier sketch in SATA *9*
  See also SAAS *4*
Mild, Warren (Paul) 1922- 41
Milelli, Pascal 1965- 135
Miles, Betty 1928- 78
  Earlier sketch in SATA *8*
  See also SAAS *9*
Miles, Miska
  See Martin, Patricia Miles
Miles, (Mary) Patricia 1930- 29
Miles, Patricia A.
  See Martin, Patricia Miles
Miles, Victoria 1966- 188
Milford, Kate 1976- 233
Milgrim, David 223
  Earlier sketches in SATA *158, 187*
Milgrom, Harry 1912-1978 25
Milhous, Katherine 1894-1977 15
Milich, Zoran 174
Milios, Rita 1949- 79
Militant
  See Sandburg, Carl
Millais, Raoul 1901- 77
Millar, Barbara F. 1924- 12
Millar, Margaret (Ellis Sturm) 1915-1994 61
  Obituary 79
Millard, Glenda 203
Millard, Kerry 204
Millbank, Captain H. R.
  See Ellis, Edward S.
Millen, C(ynthia) M. 1955- 114
Miller, Albert G(riffith) 1905-1982 12
  Obituary 31
Miller, Alice Ann 1958- 150
Miller, Alice P(atricia McCarthy) 22
Miller, Allan 1978- 216
Miller, Christopher 1976- 215
Miller, Debbie 1951- 160
  Earlier sketch in SATA *103*
  See Miller, Debbie S.
Miller, Debbie S. 232
  See Miller, Debbie
Miller, Deborah Uchill 1944- 61
Miller, Don 1923- 15

Miller, Doris R.
  See Mosesson, Gloria R(ubin)
Miller, Eddie
  See Miller, Edward
Miller, Edna Anita 1920- 29
Miller, Edward 1905-1974 8
Miller, Edward 1964- 218
  Earlier sketch in SATA *183*
Miller, Elizabeth 1933- 41
Miller, Ellanita 1957- 87
Miller, Eugene 1925- 33
Miller, Frances A. 1937- 52
  Brief entry 46
Miller, Heather Lynn 1971- 214
Miller, Helen M(arkley) -1984 5
Miller, Helen Topping 1884-1960
  Obituary 29
Miller, Jane (Judith) 1925-1989 15
Miller, Jewel 1956- 73
Miller, John
  See Samachson, Joseph
Miller, Judi 117
Miller, Karen 1949- 210
Miller, Karen Hokanson
  See Miller, Karen
Miller, Kate 1948- 193
Miller, Kirsten 1973- 185
Miller, Louise (Rolfe) 1940- 76
Miller, M. L. 85
Miller, Madge 1918- 63
Miller, Margaret J.
  See Dale, Margaret J(essy) Miller
Miller, Marilyn (Jean) 1925- 33
Miller, Marvin 65
Miller, Mary
  See Northcott, (William) Cecil
Miller, Mary Beth 1942- 9
Miller, Mary Beth 1964- 185
Miller, Maryann 1943- 73
Miller, Natalie 1917-1976 35
Miller, Pat 1951- 214
Miller, Robert H. 1944- 91
Miller, Ron 1947- 185
Miller, Ruth White
  See White, Ruth
Miller, Sandra
  See Miller, Sandy
Miller, Sandra Peden
  See Miller, Sandy
Miller, Sandy 1948- 41
  Brief entry 35
Miller, Sarah 1969- 175
Miller, Virginia
  See Austin, Virginia
Miller, William R. 1959- 116
Miller Brothers
  See Miller, Allan
Milligan, Bryce 1953- 170
Milligan, Spike
  See Milligan, Terence Alan
Milligan, Terence Alan 1918-2002 29
  Obituary 134
  See also CLR *92*
Millington, Ada
  See Deyneka, Anita
Millman, Isaac 1933- 140
Mills, Adam
  See Stanley, George Edward
Mills, Claudia 1954- 191
  Brief entry 41
  Earlier sketches in SATA *44, 89, 145*
Mills, Elaine (Rosemary) 1941- 72
Mills, G. Riley 196
Mills, Joyce C. 1944- 102
Mills, Judith Christine 1956- 130
Mills, Yaroslava Surmach 1925-2008 35
Millspaugh, Ben P. 1936- 77
Millstead, Thomas E. 30
Millward, Gwen 202

Milne, A. A. 1882-1956 100
  See also YABC *1*
  See also CLR *108*
Milne, Alan Alexander
  See Milne, A. A.
Milne, Lorus J. 5
  See also CLR *22*
  See also SAAS *18*
Milne, Margery 5
  See also CLR *22*
  See also SAAS *18*
Milne, Terry
  See Milne, Theresa Ann
Milne, Theresa Ann 1964- 84
Milnes, Irma McDonough 1924- 101
Milonas, Rolf
  See Myller, Rolf
Milone, Karen
  See Dugan, Karen
Milone-Dugan, Karen
  See Dugan, Karen
Milord, Susan 1954- 200
  Earlier sketches in SATA *74, 147*
Milotte, Alfred G(eorge) 1904-1989 11
  Obituary 62
Milstein, Linda 1954- 80
Milton, Ann 134
Milton, Hilary (Herbert) 1920- 23
Milton, John R(onald) 1924- 24
Milton, Joyce 1946- 101
  Brief entry 41
  Earlier sketch in SATA *52*
Milusich, Janice 216
Milverton, Charles A.
  See Penzler, Otto
Milway, Alex 1978- 215
Milway, Katie Smith 1960- 203
Minahan, John A. 1956- 92
Minar, Barbra (Goodyear) 1940- 79
Minard, Rosemary 1939- 63
Minarik, Else Holmelund 1920- 127
  Earlier sketch in SATA *15*
  See also CLR *33*
Miner, Jane Claypool 1933- 103
  Brief entry 37
  Earlier sketch in SATA *38*
Miner, Lewis S. 1909-1971 11
Mines, Jeanette 1948- 61
Mines, Jeanette Marie
  See Mines, Jeanette
Minier, Nelson
  See Stoutenburg, Adrien (Pearl)
Minnitt, Ronda Jacqueline
  See Armitage, David
Minor, Wendell 1944- 199
  Earlier sketches in SATA *78, 109, 164*
Minter, Daniel 1961- 176
Mintonye, Grace 4
Miranda, Anne 1954- 109
  Earlier sketch in SATA *71*
Miranda, Inaki 1983(?)- 207
Mirocha, Paul 192
Mirsky, Jeannette 1903-1987 8
  Obituary 51
Mirsky, Reba Paeff 1902-1966 1
Misako Rocks! 192
Misenta, Marisol
  See Innes, Stephanie
Mishica, Clare 1960- 91
Miskovits, Christine 1939- 10
Miss Frances
  See Horwich, Frances R(appaport)
Miss Read
  See Saint, Dora Jessie
Mister Rogers
  See Rogers, Fred McFeely
Mitchard, Jacquelyn 1956- 219
  Earlier sketches in SATA *98, 168*
Mitchell, Adrian 1932-2008 166
  Obituary 200
  Earlier sketch in SATA *104*

Mitchell, Allison
  See Griffin, W. E. B.
Mitchell, Betty Jo
  See Mitchell, B.J.
Mitchell, B.J. 1931- *120*
Mitchell, Clyde
  See Ellison, Harlan
  and Silverberg, Robert
Mitchell, Cynthia 1922- *29*
Mitchell, (Sibyl) Elyne (Keith) 1913- *10*
Mitchell, Gladys (Maude Winifred)
  1901-1983 .... *46*
  Obituary *35*
Mitchell, Jay
  See Roberson, Jennifer
Mitchell, Joyce Slayton 1933- *142*
  Brief entry *43*
  Earlier sketch in SATA *46*
Mitchell, K. L.
  See Lamb, Elizabeth Searle
Mitchell, Kathy 1948- *59*
Mitchell, Lori 1961- *128*
Mitchell, Margaree King 1953- *84*
Mitchell, Marianne 1947- *145*
Mitchell, Rhonda *89*
Mitchell, Saundra 1974(?)- *217*
Mitchell, Stephen 1943- *199*
Mitchell, Susan
  See Mitchell, Susan K.
Mitchell, Susan K. 1972- *210*
Mitchell, Todd 1974- *191*
Mitchell, Yvonne 1925-1979
  Obituary *24*
Mitchelson, Mitch
  See Mitchelson, Peter Richard
Mitchelson, Peter Richard 1950- *104*
Mitchison, Naomi (Margaret Haldane)
  1897-1999 .... *24*
  Obituary *112*
Mitchnik, Helen 1901-1982 .... *41*
  Brief entry *35*
Mitchum, Hank
  See Knott, William C(ecil, Jr.)
  and Murray, Stuart A. P.
  and Newton, D(wight) B(ennett)
  and Sherman, Jory (Tecumseh)
Mitgutsch, Ali 1935- *76*
Mitsuhashi, Yoko *45*
  Brief entry *33*
Mitton, Jacqueline 1948- *162*
  Earlier sketches in SATA *66, 115*
Mitton, Simon 1946- *66*
Mitton, Tony 1951- *203*
  Earlier sketches in SATA *104, 149*
Miura, Taro 1968- *181*
Mizner, Elizabeth Howard 1907- *27*
Mizumura, Kazue *18*
Mlynowski, Sarah 1977(?)- *180*
Mobin-Uddin, Asma *216*
  Earlier sketch in SATA *172*
Mobley, Joe A. 1945- *91*
Moche, Dinah (Rachel) L(evine) 1936- *44*
  Brief entry *40*
Mochi, Ugo (A.) 1889-1977 .... *38*
Mochizuki, Ken 1954- *146*
  Earlier sketch in SATA *81*
  See also SAAS *22*
Modarressi, Mitra 1967- *200*
  Earlier sketch in SATA *126*
Modell, Frank B. 1917- *39*
  Brief entry *36*
Modesitt, Jeanne 1953- *217*
  Earlier sketches in SATA *92, 143*
Modesitt, L.E., Jr. 1943- *164*
  Earlier sketch in SATA *91*
Modesitt, Leland Exton, Jr.
  See Modesitt, L.E., Jr.
Modrell, Dolores 1933- *72*
Moe, Barbara 1937- *20*
Moe, Jorgen (Ingebretsen) 1813-1882
  See CLR *104*

Moed-Kass, Pnina *169*
Moerbeek, Kees 1955- *98*
Moeri, Louise 1924- *93*
  Earlier sketch in SATA *24*
  See also SAAS *10*
Moesta, Rebecca 1956- *182*
Moffett, Jami 1952- *84*
Moffett, Mark W. 1957(?)- *203*
Moffett, Martha (Leatherwood) 1934- *8*
Mogensen, Suzanne A(ncher) 1946- *129*
Mohammed, Khadra *197*
Mohanty, Raja *223*
Mohn, Peter B(urnet) 1934- *28*
Mohn, Viola Kohl 1914- *8*
Mohr, Nicholasa 1938- *97*
  Autobiography Feature *113*
  Earlier sketch in SATA *8*
  See also CLR *22*
  See also SAAS *8*
Mok, Esther 1953- *93*
Molan, Christine 1943- *84*
Molarsky, Osmond 1909- *16*
Moldon, Peter L(eonard) 1937- *49*
Mole, John 1941- *103*
  Earlier sketch in SATA *36*
  See also CLR *61*
Molesworth, Mary Louisa 1839-1921 .... *98*
  See also CLR *166*
Molin, Charles
  See Mayne, William
Molina, Silvia 1946- *97*
Molk, Laurel 1957- *162*
  Earlier sketch in SATA *92*
Mollel, Tololwa M. 1952- *88*
Molloy, Anne Baker 1907-1999 .... *32*
Molloy, Michael (John) 1940- *162*
Molloy, Paul (George) 1924- *5*
Molnar, Haya Leah 1951(?)- *230*
Moloney, James 1954- *202*
  Autobiography Feature *144*
  Earlier sketches in SATA *94, 144*
Molski, Carol *215*
Momaday, N. Scott 1934- *48*
  Brief entry *30*
Momaday, Navarre Scott
  See Momaday, N. Scott
Monaco, Octavia 1963- *169*
Monagle, Bernie 1957- *121*
Moncure, Jane Belk 1926- *23*
Monjo, F(erdinand) N(icholas III)
  1924-1978 .... *16*
  See also CLR *2*
Monk, Isabell 1952- *136*
Monks, Lydia *189*
Monroe, Chris 1962- *219*
Monroe, Christine
  See Monroe, Chris
Monroe, Lyle
  See Heinlein, Robert A.
Monroe, Marion
  See Cox, Marion Monroe
Monroy, Manuel 1970- *196*
Monsell, Helen Albee 1895-1971 .... *24*
Monson-Burton, Marianne 1975- *139*
Montalbano, Andrea *231*
Montana, Bob 1920-1975
  Obituary *21*
Montanari, Eva 1977- *209*
Montecalvo, Janet *177*
Montenegro, Laura Nyman 1953- *95*
Montero, Gloria 1933- *109*
Montes, Marisa 1951- *144*
Montgomerie, Norah (Mary) 1913- *26*
Montgomery, Constance
  See Cappel, Constance
Montgomery, Elizabeth
  See Julesberg, Elizabeth Rider Montgomery
Montgomery, Elizabeth Rider
  See Julesberg, Elizabeth Rider Montgomery
Montgomery, Hugh (Edward) 1962- *146*

Montgomery, L. M. 1874-1942 .... *100*
  See also YABC *1*
  See also CLR *145*
Montgomery, Lucy Maud
  See Montgomery, L. M.
Montgomery, Michael G. 1952- *208*
Montgomery, Raymond A. (Jr.) 1936- *39*
Montgomery, Rutherford George 1894-1985 . *3*
Montgomery, Sy 1958- *184*
  Autobiography Feature *132*
  Earlier sketches in SATA *114, 132*
Montgomery, Vivian *36*
Monthei, Betty *179*
Montijo, Rhode *179*
Montileaux, Donald F. 1948- *183*
Montpetit, Charles 1958- *101*
Montresor, Beni 1926-2001 .... *38*
  Earlier sketch in SATA *3*
  See also SAAS *4*
Montserrat, Pep *181*
Monty Python
  See Chapman, Graham
  and Cleese, John (Marwood)
  and Gilliam, Terry
  and Idle, Eric
  and Jones, Terence Graham Parry
  and Palin, Michael
Moodie, Craig 1956- *172*
Moodie, Fiona 1952- *133*
Moody, Minerva
  See Alcott, Louisa May
Moody, Ralph Owen 1898-1982 .... *1*
Moon, Carl 1879(?)-1948 .... *25*
Moon, Grace (Purdie) 1877(?)-1947 .... *25*
Moon, Lily
  See Warnes, Tim
Moon, Nicola 1952- *147*
  Earlier sketch in SATA *96*
Moon, Pat 1946- *113*
Moon, Sheila 1910-1991 .... *5*
  Obituary *114*
Moon, Sheila Elizabeth
  See Moon, Sheila
Mooney, Bel 1946- *95*
Mooney, Bill 1936- *122*
Mooney, Elizabeth C(omstock) 1918-1986
  Obituary *48*
Mooney, William
  See Mooney, Bill
Moor, Emily
  See Deming, Richard
Moorcock, Michael 1939- *166*
  Earlier sketch in SATA *93*
Moorcock, Michael John
  See Moorcock, Michael
Moorcock, Michael John
  See Moorcock, Michael
Moore, Anne Carroll 1871-1961 .... *13*
Moore, Cheri
  See Ladd, Cheryl (Jean)
Moore, Clement Clarke 1779-1863 .... *18*
Moore, Cyd 1957- *233*
  Earlier sketches in SATA *83, 133, 186*
Moore, Don W. 1905(?)-1986
  Obituary *48*
Moore, Elaine 1944- *86*
Moore, Eva 1942- *103*
  Earlier sketch in SATA *20*
Moore, Ishbel (Lindsay) 1954- *140*
Moore, Jack (William) 1941- *46*
  Brief entry *32*
Moore, Janet Gaylord 1905-1992 .... *18*
Moore, Jim 1946- *42*
Moore, John Travers 1908- *12*
Moore, Lilian 1909-2004 .... *137*
  Obituary *155*
  Earlier sketch in SATA *52*
  See also CLR *15*
Moore, Liz
  See Moore, M. Elizabeth
Moore, M. Elizabeth 1959- *156*

Moore, Margaret R(umberger) 1903- *12*
Moore, Margie *224*
  Earlier sketch in SATA *176*
Moore, Marianne 1887-1972 .... *20*
Moore, Marianne Craig
  See Moore, Marianne
Moore, Patrick (Alfred Caldwell) 1923- *49*
  Brief entry *39*
  See also SAAS *8*
Moore, Patrick 1959- *184*
Moore, Perry 1971-2011 .... *193*
Moore, Peter 1963- *175*
Moore, Peter G.
  See Moore, Peter
Moore, Raina 1970- *212*
Moore, Ray (S.) 1905(?)-1984
  Obituary *37*
Moore, Regina
  See Dunne, Mary Collins
Moore, Rosalie (Gertrude) 1910-2001 .... *9*
Moore, Ruth (Ellen) 1908-1989 .... *23*
Moore, Ruth Nulton 1923- *38*
Moore, S(arah) E. *23*
Moore, Sarah Margaret
  See Hodges, Margaret
Moore, Stephanie Perry 1969(?)- *214*
Moore, Tara 1950- *61*
Moore, Yvette 1958- *154*
  Earlier sketches in SATA *69, 70*
Moores, Dick
  See Moores, Richard (Arnold)
Moores, Richard (Arnold) 1909-1986
  Obituary *48*
Mooser, Stephen 1941- *75*
  Earlier sketch in SATA *28*
Mora, Francisco X(avier) 1952- *90*
Mora, Pat 1942- *232*
  Earlier sketches in SATA *92, 134, 186*
  See also CLR *58*
Mora, Patricia
  See Mora, Pat
Morais, Flavio *207*
Morales, Magaly *225*
Morales, Yuyi *180*
  Earlier sketch in SATA *154*
Moran, Tom 1943- *60*
Moranville, Sharelle Byars *196*
  Earlier sketch in SATA *152*
Moray Williams, Ursula 1911-2006 .... *3*
  Obituary *177*
  See also SAAS *9*
Mordecai, Martin *220*
Morden, Simon 1966(?)- *211*
Mordhorst, Heidi 1964- *222*
Mordvinoff, Nicolas 1911-1973 .... *17*
More, Caroline
  See Cone, Molly (Lamken)
  and Strachan, Margaret Pitcairn
Moreau, Jean-Pierre
  See Jarrie, Martin
Moreno, Rene King *190*
Moreton, Andrew Esq.
  See Defoe, Daniel
Morey, Charles
  See Fletcher, Helen Jill
Morey, Walt(er Nelson) 1907-1992 .... *51*
  Obituary *70*
  Earlier sketch in SATA *3*
  See also SAAS *9*
Morgan, Alfred P(owell) 1889-1972 .... *33*
Morgan, Alison (Mary) 1930- *85*
  Earlier sketch in SATA *30*
Morgan, Anne 1954- *121*
Morgan, Christopher 1956- *199*
Morgan, Clay 1950- *198*
Morgan, Douglas
  See Macdonald, James D.
Morgan, Ellen
  See Bumstead, Kathleen Mary
Morgan, Geoffrey 1916- *46*

Morgan, Helen (Gertrude Louise)
  1921-1990 .... *29*
Morgan, Jane
  See Cooper, James Fenimore
  and Franklin, Jane (Morgan)
  and Moren, Sally M(oore)
Morgan, Lenore H. 1908-1976 .... *8*
Morgan, Mary 1957- *213*
  Earlier sketches in SATA *81, 114*
Morgan, McKayla
  See Basile, Gloria Vitanza
Morgan, Michaela
  See Basile, Gloria Vitanza
Morgan, Nicola 1961- *161*
Morgan, Nina 1953- *110*
Morgan, Pierr 1952- *122*
  Earlier sketch in SATA *77*
Morgan, Robin (Evonne) 1941- *80*
Morgan, Roxanne
  See Gentle, Mary
Morgan, Sarah (Nicola) 1959- *68*
Morgan, Shirley
  See Kiepper, Shirley Morgan
Morgan, Stacy T(owle) 1959- *104*
Morgan, Stevie
  See Davies, Nicola
Morgan, Tom 1942- *42*
Morgan, Wendy
  See Staub, Wendy Corsi
Morgan-Vanroyen, Mary
  See Morgan, Mary
Morgenstern, Susie Hoch 1945- *133*
Mori, Hana 1909-1990(?) *88*
Mori, Kyoko 1957- *122*
  Autobiography Feature *126*
  See also CLR *64*
  See also SAAS *26*
Moriarty, Jaclyn 1968- *162*
Moriarty, William J. 1930- *127*
Morice, Dave 1946- *93*
Morin, Isobel V. 1928- *110*
Morine, Hoder
  See Conroy, John Wesley
Morley, Ben *228*
Morley, Taia *199*
Morley, Wilfred Owen
  See Lowndes, Robert A(ugustine) W(ard)
Morningstar, Mildred (Whaley) 1912-1997 .. *61*
  Obituary *114*
Morozumi, Atsuko *217*
  Earlier sketch in SATA *110*
Morpurgo, Michael 1943- *225*
  Earlier sketches in SATA *93, 143, 184*
  See also CLR *51*
Morrah, Dave
  See Morrah, David Wardlaw, Jr.
Morrah, David Wardlaw, Jr. 1914-1991 .... *10*
Morreale-de la Garza, Phyllis
  See De la Garza, Phyllis
Morressy, John 1930-2006 .... *23*
Morrill, Leslie H(olt) 1934-2003 .... *48*
  Brief entry *33*
  Obituary *148*
  See also SAAS *22*
Morris, Carla *210*
Morris, Carla D.
  See Morris, Carla
Morris, Chris(topher Crosby) 1946- *66*
Morris, Deborah 1956- *91*
Morris, Desmond 1928- *14*
Morris, Desmond John
  See Morris, Desmond
Morris, Don 1954- *83*
Morris, Gerald 1963- *207*
  Earlier sketches in SATA *107, 150*
Morris, Gerald Paul
  See Morris, Gerald
Morris, Gilbert (Leslie) 1929- *104*
Morris, Jackie *202*
  Earlier sketch in SATA *151*
Morris, Janet (Ellen) 1946- *66*

Morris, Jay
  See Tatham, Julie Campbell
Morris, (Margaret) Jean 1924- *98*
Morris, Jeffrey
  See Morris, Jeffrey Brandon
Morris, Jeffrey B.
  See Morris, Jeffrey Brandon
Morris, Jeffrey Brandon 1941- *92*
Morris, Jennifer E. 1969- *179*
Morris, Jill 1936- *165*
  Earlier sketch in SATA *119*
Morris, Juddi *85*
Morris, Judy K. 1936- *61*
Morris, Oradel Nolen *128*
Morris, Richard 1969- *224*
Morris, Robert A(da) 1933- *7*
Morris, William 1913-1994 .... *29*
Morrison, Angela *218*
Morrison, Bill 1935- *66*
  Brief entry *37*
Morrison, Chloe Anthony Wofford
  See Morrison, Toni
Morrison, Dorothy Nafus *29*
Morrison, Frank 1971- *226*
  Earlier sketch in SATA *185*
Morrison, Gordon 1944- *183*
  Earlier sketches in SATA *87, 128*
Morrison, Joan 1922- *65*
Morrison, Lillian 1917- *108*
  Earlier sketch in SATA *3*
Morrison, Lucile Phillips 1896- *17*
Morrison, Martha A. 1948- *77*
Morrison, Meighan 1966- *90*
Morrison, P.R. *196*
Morrison, Richard
  See Lowndes, Robert A(ugustine) W(ard)
Morrison, Robert
  See Lowndes, Robert A(ugustine) W(ard)
Morrison, Roberta
  See Webb, Jean Francis (III)
Morrison, Slade 1964-2010 .... *228*
Morrison, Susan Dudley
  See Gold, Susan Dudley
Morrison, Taylor 1971- *187*
  Earlier sketches in SATA *95, 159*
Morrison, Toni 1931- *144*
  Earlier sketch in SATA *57*
  See also CLR *99*
Morrison, Velma Ford 1909- *21*
Morrison, Wilbur Howard 1915- *64*
Morrison, William
  See Samachson, Joseph
Morriss, James E(dward) 1932- *8*
Morrissey, Dean *183*
Morrow, Barbara Olenyik 1952- *167*
Morrow, Betty
  See Bacon, Elizabeth
Morrow, Sue Anne 1966- *218*
Morse, C. Scott
  See Morse, Scott
Morse, Carol
  See Yeakley, Marjory Hall
Morse, C.S.
  See Morse, Scott
Morse, Dorothy B(ayley) 1906-1979
  Obituary *24*
Morse, Flo 1921- *30*
Morse, Scott 1973- *200*
Morse, Tony 1953- *129*
Morstad, Julie *232*
Mort, Vivian
  See Cromie, Alice Hamilton
Mortensen, Denise Dowling *179*
Mortensen, Lori 1955- *221*
Mortimer, Anne 1958- *206*
  Earlier sketch in SATA *116*
Mortimer, Mary H.
  See Coury, Louise Andree
Morton, Alexandra (Hubbard) 1957- *144*
Morton, Anthony
  See Arthur, Robert, (Jr.)

Morton, Christine
    See Morton-Shaw, Christine
Morton, Jane 1931- 50
Morton, Joseph C. 1932- 156
Morton, Lee Jack, Jr. 1928- 32
Morton, Miriam 1918(?)-1985 9
    Obituary 46
Morton-Shaw, Christine 1957- 211
Mosatche, Harriet 1949- 122
Mosatche, Harriet S.
    See Mosatche, Harriet
Moscow, Alvin 1925- 3
Mosel, Arlene (Tichy) 1921-1996 7
Moseley, James W(illett) 1931- 139
Moseng, Elisabeth 1967- 90
Moser, Barry 1940- 185
    Earlier sketches in SATA 56, 79, 138
    See also CLR 49
    See also SAAS 15
Moser, Don(ald Bruce) 1932- 31
Moser, Laura 194
Moser, Lisa 192
Moses, Sheila P. 1961- 168
Moses, Will 1956- 178
    Earlier sketch in SATA 120
Mosesson, Gloria R(ubin) 24
Mosher, Richard 1949- 120
Moskin, Marietta D(unston) 1928- 23
Moskof, Martin Stephen 1930- 27
Mosley, Francis 1957- 57
Moss, Don(ald) 1920- 11
Moss, Elaine (Dora) 1924- 57
    Brief entry 31
Moss, Jeff(rey) 1942-1998 73
    Obituary 106
Moss, Marissa 1959- 216
    Earlier sketches in SATA 71, 104, 163
    See also CLR 134
Moss, Miriam 1955- 202
    Earlier sketches in SATA 76, 140
Moss, Thylias 1954- 108
Moss, Thylias Rebecca Brasier
    See Moss, Thylias
Most, Bernard 1937- 134
    Brief entry 40
    Earlier sketches in SATA 48, 91
Mosz, Gosia 1972- 194
Mott, Evelyn Clarke 1962- 133
    Earlier sketch in SATA 75
Motz, Lloyd 1909-2004 20
Mould, Chris 205
Mould, Edwin
    See Whitlock, Ralph
Moulton, Mark Kimball 212
Mouly, Francoise 155
Mountain, Robert
    See Montgomery, Raymond A. (Jr.)
Mountfield, David
    See Grant, Neil
Mourlevat, Jean-Claude 1952- 187
Mourning, Tuesday 206
Moussard, Jacqueline 1924- 24
Mowat, Claire 1933- 123
Mowat, Claire Angel Wheeler
    See Mowat, Claire
Mowat, Farley 1921- 55
    Earlier sketch in SATA 3
    See also CLR 20
Mowat, Farley McGill
    See Mowat, Farley
Mowll, Joshua 1970(?)- 188
Mowry, Jess 1960- 131
    Autobiography Feature 131
    Earlier sketch in SATA 109
    See also CLR 65
Moxley, Sheila 1966- 96
Moyer, Terry J. 1937- 94
Moyes, Patricia
    See Haszard, Patricia Moyes
Moyler, Alan (Frank Powell) 1926- 36
Mozelle, Shirley 179

Mozley, Charles 1915- 43
    Brief entry 32
Mphahlele, Es'kia 1919-2008 119
    Obituary 198
Mphahlele, Ezekiel
    See Mphahlele, Es'kia
Mphahlele, Zeke
    See Mphahlele, Es'kia
Mr. McGillicuddy
    See Abisch, Roslyn Kroop
Mr. Sniff
    See Abisch, Roslyn Kroop
Mr. Tivil
    See Lorkowski, Thomas V(incent)
Mr. Wizard
    See Herbert, Don
Mraz, David 1947- 219
Mrs. Fairstar
    See Horne, Richard Henry Hengist
Muchamore, Robert 1972- 175
Muchmore, Jo Ann 1937- 103
Mude, O.
    See Gorey, Edward (St. John)
Mudgeon, Apeman
    See Mitchell, Adrian
Mueller, Jorg 1942- 67
    See also CLR 43
Mueller, Miranda R. 201
Mueller, Virginia 1924- 28
Muggs
    See Watkins, Lois
Muir, Diana
    See Appelbaum, Diana Muir Karter
Muir, Frank (Herbert) 1920-1998 30
Muir, Helen 1937- 65
Muirhead, Margaret 220
Mukerji, Dhan Gopal 1890-1936 40
    See also CLR 10
Mulcahy, Lucille Burnett 12
Muldrow, Diane 229
Mulford, Philippa G. 1948- 112
    Earlier sketch in SATA 43
Mulford, Philippa Greene
    See Mulford, Philippa G.
Mulgan, Catherine 1931- 24
Mulila, Vigad G.
    See Maillu, David G(ian)
Mull, Brandon 1974- 190
Mullen, Michael 1937- 122
Muller, Billex
    See Ellis, Edward S.
Muller, Birte 1973- 214
Muller, Jorg
    See Mueller, Jorg
Muller, (Lester) Robin 1953- 86
Mullin, Caryl Cude 1969- 130
Mullins, Edward S(wift) 1922- 10
Mullins, Hilary 1962- 84
Mulock, Dinah Maria
    See Craik, Dinah Maria (Mulock)
Mulvihill, William Patrick 1923- 8
Mumford, Ruth
    See Dallas, Ruth
Mumy, Bill 1954- 112
Mun
    See Leaf, (Wilbur) Munro
Munari, Bruno 1907-1998 15
    See also CLR 9
Munce, Ruth Hill 1898- 12
Mundy, Simon 1954- 64
Mundy, Simon Andrew James Hainault
    See Mundy, Simon
Munger, Nancy 170
Munowitz, Ken 1935-1977 14
Munoz, Claudio 208
Munoz, William 1949- 92
    Earlier sketch in SATA 42
Munro, Alice 1931- 29
Munro, Alice Anne
    See Munro, Alice
Munro, Eleanor 1928- 37

Munro, Roxie 1945- 223
    Earlier sketches in SATA 58, 136, 184
Munsch, Bob
    See Munsch, Robert (Norman)
Munsch, Robert (Norman) 1945- 120
    Brief entry 48
    Earlier sketches in SATA 50, 83
    See also CLR 19
Munsinger, Lynn 1951- 221
    Earlier sketches in SATA 33, 94, 177
Munson, Derek 1970- 139
Munson, R. W.
    See Karl, Jean E(dna)
Munson-Benson, Tunie 1946- 15
Munsterberg, Peggy 1921- 102
Muntean, Michaela 182
Munthe, Nelly 1947- 53
Munves, James (Albert) 1922- 30
Munzer, Martha E. 1899-1999 4
Murawski, Darlyne A. 193
Murch, Mel
    See Manes, Stephen
Murdoch, David H(amilton) 1937- 96
Murdoch, Patricia 1957- 192
Murdock, Catherine Gilbert 185
Murhall, J(acqueline) J(ane) 1964- 143
Murphy, Barbara Beasley 1933- 130
    Earlier sketch in SATA 5
Murphy, Claire Rudolf 1951- 137
    Earlier sketch in SATA 76
Murphy, E(mmett) Jefferson 1926- 4
Murphy, Elizabeth Ann Maureen
    See Murphy, Liz
Murphy, Jill 1949- 214
    Earlier sketches in SATA 37, 70, 142
    See also CLR 39
Murphy, Jill Frances
    See Murphy, Jill
Murphy, Jim 1947- 224
    Brief entry 32
    Earlier sketches in SATA 37, 77, 124, 185
    See also CLR 53
Murphy, Joseph E., Jr. 1930- 65
Murphy, Kelly 1977- 190
    Earlier sketch in SATA 143
Murphy, Liz 1964- 210
Murphy, Louise 1943- 155
Murphy, Mary 1961- 196
Murphy, Pat
    See Murphy, E(mmett) Jefferson
Murphy, Patricia J. 1963- 132
Murphy, Rita 180
Murphy, Robert (William) 1902-1971 10
Murphy, Shirley Rousseau 1928- 126
    Earlier sketches in SATA 36, 71
    See also SAAS 18
Murphy, Stuart J. 1942- 157
    Earlier sketch in SATA 115
Murphy, Thomas Basil, Jr. 1935- 191
Murphy, Tim
    See Murphy, Jim
Murphy, Tom
    See Murphy, Thomas Basil, Jr.
Murray, John 1923- 39
Murray, Kirsty 1960- 165
    Earlier sketch in SATA 108
Murray, Marguerite 1917- 63
Murray, Marian 5
Murray, Martine 1965- 125
Murray, (Judith) Michele (Freedman)
    1933-1974 7
Murray, Ossie 1938- 43
Murray, Peter
    See Hautman, Pete
Murrow, Liza Ketchum
    See Ketchum, Liza
Musgrave, Florence 1902-1999 3
Musgrave, Margaret W(ynkoop) 1943- 124
    Earlier sketch in SATA 26
Musgrove, Marianne 207

Mussey, Virginia Howell
   See Ellison, Virginia H(owell)
Mussey, Virginia T.H.
   See Ellison, Virginia H(owell)
Mussi, Sarah 206
Mutel, Cornelia F. 1947- 74
Muth, Jon J. 206
   Earlier sketch in SATA *165*
Mutz
   See Kuenstler, Morton
Mwangi, Meja 1948- 174
My Brother's Brother
   See Chekhov, Anton
Myers, Anna 220
   Earlier sketch in SATA *160*
Myers, Arthur 1917- 91
   Earlier sketch in SATA *35*
Myers, Bernice 81
   Earlier sketch in SATA *9*
Myers, Caroline Elizabeth Clark
   1887-1980 28
Myers, Christopher 1975- 183
   See also CLR *97*
Myers, Edward 1950- 227
   Earlier sketches in SATA *96, 172*
Myers, Elisabeth P(erkins) 1918- 36
Myers, (Mary) Hortense (Powner)
   1913-1987 10
Myers, Jack 1913-2006 83
   Obituary 178
Myers, Jack Edgar
   See Myers, Jack
Myers, Laurie 232
Myers, Lou 1915-2005 81
   Obituary 171
Myers, Louis
   See Myers, Lou
Myers, R.E. 1924- 119
Myers, Robert Eugene
   See Myers, R.E.
Myers, Tim 1953- 176
   Earlier sketch in SATA *147*
Myers, Timothy Joseph
   See Myers, Tim
Myers, Walter Dean 1937- 229
   Brief entry 27
   Earlier sketches in SATA *41, 71, 109, 157,
   193*
   See also CLR *110*
   See also SAAS *2*
Myers, Walter M.
   See Myers, Walter Dean
Myller, Rolf 1926-2006 27
   Obituary 175
Myra, Harold L(awrence) 1939- 46
   Brief entry 42
Myracle, Lauren 1969- 204
   Earlier sketch in SATA *162*
Myrus, Donald (Richard) 1927- 23
Mysterious Traveler, The
   See Arthur, Robert, (Jr.)

N

Na, An *149*
Na, Il Sung *231*
Naaslund, Goorel Kristina 1940- *170*
Nadel, Laurie 1948- *74*
Naden, Corinne J. 1930- *166*
   Earlier sketch in SATA *79*
Nadimi, Suzan *188*
Nadol, Jen *228*
Nagda, Ann Whitehead *199*
Nagel, Andreas Fischer
   See Fischer-Nagel, Andreas
Nagel, Heiderose Fischer
   See Fischer-Nagel, Heiderose
Nagle, Shane *176*

Nahoko, Uehashi
   See Uehashi, Nahoko
Naidoo, Beverley 1943- *180*
   Earlier sketches in SATA *63, 135*
   See also CLR *29*
Nails, Jennifer *213*
Naiyomah, Wilson Kimeli 1977- *226*
Nakae, Noriko 1940- *59*
Nakata, Hiroe *205*
Nakatani, Chiyoko 1930-1981 .... *55*
   Brief entry *40*
   See also CLR *30*
Nally, Susan W. 1947- *90*
Namioka, Lensey 1929- *157*
   Autobiography Feature *116*
   Earlier sketches in SATA *27, 89*
   See also CLR *48*
   See also SAAS *24*
Namovicz, Gene Inyart 1927- *6*
Nance, Andrew *210*
Nanji, Shenaaz 1954- *204*
   Earlier sketch in SATA *131*
Nanogak Agnes 1925- *61*
Napier, Mark
   See Laffin, John (Alfred Charles)
Napoli, Donna Jo 1948- *230*
   Autobiography Feature *230*
   Earlier sketches in SATA *92, 137, 190*
   See also CLR *51*
   See also SAAS *23*
Napp, Daniel 1974- *204*
Narahashi, Keiko 1959- *115*
   Earlier sketch in SATA *79*
Narayan, R. K. 1906-2001 .... *62*
Narayan, Rasipuram Krishnaswami
   See Narayan, R. K.
Nascimbene, Yan 1949- *173*
   Earlier sketch in SATA *133*
Nash, Bruce M(itchell) 1947- *34*
Nash, Frediric Ogden
   See Nash, Ogden
Nash, Linell
   See Smith, Linell Nash
Nash, Mary (Hughes) 1925- *41*
Nash, Ogden 1902-1971 .... *46*
   Earlier sketch in SATA *2*
Nash, Renea Denise 1963- *81*
Nast, Elsa Ruth
   See Watson, Jane Werner
Nast, Thomas 1840-1902 .... *51*
   Brief entry *33*
Nastick, Sharon 1954- *41*
Natale, Vince *196*
Natalini, Sandro 1970- *222*
Natarajan, Srividya *187*
Nathan, Adele (Gutman) 1900(?)-1986
   Obituary *48*
Nathan, Amy *155*
   Earlier sketch in SATA *104*
Nathan, Dorothy (Goldeen) (?)-1966 .... *15*
Nathan, Robert (Gruntal) 1894-1985 .... *6*
   Obituary *43*
Nathanson, Laura Walther 1941- *57*
Nation, Kaleb 1988- *222*
Natti, Lee 1919- *67*
   Earlier sketch in SATA *1*
   See also SAAS *3*
Natti, Susanna 1948- *125*
   Earlier sketch in SATA *32*
Nau, Thomas *186*
Naughtie, Eleanor
   See Updale, Eleanor
Naughton, Bill
   See Naughton, William John (Francis)
Naughton, James Franklin 1957- *85*
Naughton, Jim
   See Naughton, James Franklin
Naughton, William John (Francis)
   1910-1992 .... *86*
Navarra, John Gabriel 1927- *8*
Nayeri, Daniel *232*

Nayeri, Dina *226*
Naylor, Penelope 1941- *10*
Naylor, Phyllis 1933-
   See Naylor, Phyllis Reynolds
Naylor, Phyllis Reynolds 1933- *209*
   Autobiography Feature *152*
   See also CLR *135*
   See also SAAS *10*
Nazarian, Nikki
   See Nichols, Cecilia Fawn
Nazaroff, Alexander I(vanovich) 1898-1981 .. *4*
Nazoa, Aquiles 1920-1976 .... *198*
Neal, Harry Edward 1906-1993 .... *5*
   Obituary *76*
Neal, Michael
   See Teitelbaum, Michael
Nearing, Penny 1916- *47*
   Brief entry *42*
Nebel, Gustave E. *45*
   Brief entry *33*
Nebel, Mimouca
   See Nebel, Gustave E.
Nee, Kay Bonner *10*
Needham, Kate 1962- *95*
Needle, Jan 1943- *98*
   Earlier sketch in SATA *30*
   See also CLR *43*
   See also SAAS *23*
Needleman, Jacob 1934- *6*
Neel, David 1960- *82*
Neel, Preston 1959- *93*
Neff, Henry H. 1973- *221*
Negri, Rocco 1932- *12*
Negrin, Fabian 1963- *189*
Neidigh, Sherry 1956- *204*
Neier, Aryeh 1937- *59*
Neigoff, Anne *13*
Neigoff, Mike 1920- *13*
Neilan, Eujin Kim 1969- *200*
Neilson, Frances Fullerton (Jones)
   1910-2001 .... *14*
Neimark, Anne E. 1935- *145*
   Earlier sketch in SATA *4*
Neimark, Paul G. 1934- *80*
   Brief entry *37*
Neitzel, Shirley 1941- *134*
   Earlier sketch in SATA *77*
Nell
   See Hanna, Nell(ie L.)
Nelscott, Kris
   See Rusch, Kristine Kathryn
Nelson, Blake 1960- *177*
Nelson, Catherine Chadwick 1926- *87*
Nelson, Cordner 1918-2009 .... *54*
   Brief entry *29*
Nelson, Cordner Bruce
   See Nelson, Cordner
Nelson, D.A. 1970- *215*
Nelson, Dawn Ann
   See Nelson, D.A.
Nelson, Drew 1952- *77*
Nelson, Esther L. 1928- *13*
Nelson, Jandy *229*
Nelson, Jim A.
   See Stotter, Mike
Nelson, Julie L. 1970- *117*
Nelson, Kadir *213*
   Earlier sketches in SATA *154, 181*
Nelson, Kris
   See Rusch, Kristine Kathryn
Nelson, Lawrence E(rnest) 1928-1977
   Obituary *28*
Nelson, Marilyn 1946- *60*
   Autobiography Feature *180*
Nelson, Mary Carroll 1929- *23*
Nelson, O. Terry 1941- *62*
Nelson, Peter 1953- *73*
Nelson, Peter N.
   See Nelson, Peter
Nelson, R. A. *197*
Nelson, Richard K(ing) 1941- *65*

Nelson, Robin Laura 1971- *141*
Nelson, Roy Paul 1923- *59*
Nelson, S.D. *181*
Nelson, Sharlene (P.) 1933- *96*
Nelson, Suzanne 1976- *184*
Nelson, Ted (W.) 1931- *96*
Nelson, Theresa 1948- *143*
  Autobiography Feature *143*
  Earlier sketch in SATA *79*
Nelson, Vaunda Micheaux 1953- *220*
Nemeth, Sally *187*
Neri, G. *197*
Neri, Greg
  See Neri, G.
Neri, Gregory
  See Neri, G.
Nerlove, Miriam 1959- *53*
  Brief entry *49*
Nesbit, E. 1858-1924 .... *100*
  See also YABC *1*
  See also CLR *70*
Nesbit, Edith
  See Nesbit, E.
Nesbit, Troy
  See Folsom, Franklin (Brewster)
Nespojohn, Katherine V(eronica) 1912-1975 . *7*
Ness, Evaline (Michelow) 1911-1986 .... *26*
  Obituary *49*
  Earlier sketch in SATA *1*
  See also CLR *6*
  See also SAAS *1*
Ness, Patrick 1971- *207*
Nestor, Larry 1940- *149*
Nestor, William P(rodromos) 1947- *49*
Nethery, Mary *93*
Neubecker, Robert *214*
  Earlier sketch in SATA *170*
Neuberger, Julia (Babette Sarah) 1950- *142*
  Earlier sketch in SATA *78*
Neufeld, John (Arthur) 1938- *131*
  Autobiography Feature *131*
  Earlier sketches in SATA *6, 81*
  See also CLR *52*
  See also SAAS *3*
Neuhaus, David 1958- *83*
Neumeyer, Peter F(lorian) 1929- *13*
Neurath, Marie (Reidemeister) 1898-1986 ..... *1*
Neuschwander, Cindy 1953- *157*
  Earlier sketch in SATA *107*
Neusner, Jacob 1932- *38*
Neville, Charles
  See Bodsworth, (Charles) Fred(erick)
Neville, Emily Cheney 1919- *1*
  See also SAAS *2*
Neville, Mary
  See Woodrich, Mary Neville
Nevins, Albert (Francis) J(erome)
  1915-1997 .... *20*
Nevius, Carol 1955- *186*
Newberger, Devra
  See Speregen, Devra Newberger
Newberry, Clare Turlay 1903-1970 .... *1*
  Obituary *26*
Newbery, John 1713-1767 .... *20*
  See also CLR *147*
Newbery, Linda 1952- *184*
  Earlier sketch in SATA *142*
Newbigging, Martha *198*
Newbold, Greg *199*
Newcomb, Ellsworth
  See Kenny, Ellsworth Newcomb
Newcombe, Eugene A. 1923-1990 .... *45*
  Brief entry *33*
Newcombe, Jack
  See Newcombe, Eugene A.
Newcome, Robert 1955- *91*
Newcome, Zita 1959- *88*
Newell, Crosby
  See Bonsall, Crosby Barbara (Newell)
Newell, Edythe W(eatherford) 1910-1989 .... *11*
Newell, Hope Hockenberry 1896-1965 ...... *24*

Newfeld, Frank 1928- *26*
Newgarden, Mark 1959- *194*
Newhouse, Maxwell 1947- *232*
Newland, Gillian *220*
Newlon, (Frank) Clarke 1905(?)-1982 .... *6*
  Obituary *33*
Newman, Barbara Johansen *191*
Newman, C.J.
  See Newman, Coleman J.
Newman, Coleman J. 1935- *82*
Newman, Daisy 1904-1994 .... *27*
  Obituary *78*
Newman, Gerald 1939- *46*
  Brief entry *42*
Newman, Jeff 1976- *228*
Newman, Jerry
  See Newman, Coleman J.
Newman, Leslea 1955- *134*
  Earlier sketches in SATA *71, 128*
Newman, Margaret
  See Potter, Margaret
Newman, Marjorie *146*
Newman, Matthew (Harrison) 1955- *56*
Newman, Nanette 1934- *162*
Newman, Robert (Howard) 1909-1988 ...... *87*
  Obituary *60*
  Earlier sketch in SATA *4*
Newman, Shirlee P(etkin) *144*
  Earlier sketches in SATA *10, 90*
Newsom, Carol 1948- *92*
  Earlier sketch in SATA *40*
Newsom, Tom 1944- *80*
Newsome, Richard 1964- *233*
Newth, Mette 1942- *140*
Newton, David E(dward) 1933- *67*
Newton, James R(obert) 1935- *23*
Newton, Jill 1964- *200*
Newton, Robert 1965- *191*
Newton, Suzanne 1936- *77*
  Earlier sketch in SATA *5*
Newton, Vanessa
  See Newton, Vanessa Brantley
Newton, Vanessa Brantley 1962(?)- *206*
Ney, John 1923- *43*
  Brief entry *33*
Nez, John *218*
  Earlier sketch in SATA *155*
Nez, John Abbott
  See Nez, John
Ng, Franklin *82*
Ngui, Marc 1972- *229*
Nguyen, Vincent *226*
  Earlier sketch in SATA *187*
Nichol, B(arrie) P(hillip) 1944-1988 .... *66*
Nicholas, Louise D.
  See Watkins, Dawn L.
Nicholls, Judith (Ann) 1941- *61*
Nicholls, Sally 1983- *209*
Nichols, Cecilia Fawn 1906-1987 .... *12*
Nichols, Grace 1950- *164*
  Earlier sketch in SATA *98*
Nichols, Janet (Louise) 1952- *67*
Nichols, Judy 1947- *124*
Nichols, Leigh
  See Koontz, Dean
Nichols, Michael 1952- *215*
Nichols, Nick
  See Nichols, Michael
Nichols, Paul
  See Hawks, Robert
Nichols, Peter
  See Youd, Samuel
Nichols, (Joanna) Ruth 1948- *15*
  See also CLR *149*
Nichols, Travis *206*
Nicholson, C. R.
  See Nicole, Christopher
Nicholson, Christina
  See Nicole, Christopher
Nicholson, Joyce Thorpe 1919-2011 .... *35*
Nicholson, Lois P. 1949- *88*

Nicholson, Robin
  See Nicole, Christopher
Nicholson, William *180*
Nicholson, William 1872-1949
  See CLR *76*
Nickel, Barbara 1966- *188*
Nickell, Joe 1944- *167*
  Earlier sketch in SATA *73*
Nickelsburg, Janet 1893-1983 .... *11*
Nickerson, Betty 1922- *14*
Nickerson, Elizabeth
  See Nickerson, Betty
Nickl, Barbara (Elisabeth) 1939- *56*
Nicklaus, Carol *62*
  Brief entry *33*
Nickle, John *181*
Nickless, Will 1902-1979(?) *66*
Nic Leodhas, Sorche
  See Alger, Leclaire (Gowans)
Nicol, Ann
  See Turnbull, Ann
Nicolas
  See Mordvinoff, Nicolas
Nicolay, Helen 1866-1954
  See YABC *1*
Nicole, Christopher 1930- *5*
Nicole, Christopher Robin
  See Nicole, Christopher
Nicoll, Helen 1937- *87*
Nicolson, Cynthia Pratt 1949- *141*
Ni Dhuibhne, Eilis 1954- *91*
Niehaus, Paddy Bouma
  See Bouma, Paddy
Nields, Nerissa 1967- *166*
Nielsen, Kay (Rasmus) 1886-1957 .... *16*
  See also CLR *16*
Nielsen, Laura F. 1960- *93*
Nielsen, Laura Farnsworth
  See Nielsen, Laura F.
Nielsen, Nancy J. 1951- *77*
Nielsen, Susin 1964- *195*
Nielsen, Virginia
  See McCall, Virginia Nielsen
Nielsen-Fernlund, Susin
  See Nielsen, Susin
Niemann, Christoph 1970- *191*
Nieuwsma, Milton J(ohn) 1941- *142*
Nightingale, Sandy 1953- *76*
Nikolajeva, Maria 1952- *127*
Nikola-Lisa, W. 1951- *180*
  Earlier sketch in SATA *71*
Niland, Deborah 1951- *172*
  Earlier sketch in SATA *27*
Niland, Kilmeny *75*
Nilsen, Anna 1948- *174*
  Earlier sketch in SATA *96*
Nilsson, Eleanor 1939- *117*
  Earlier sketch in SATA *81*
  See also SAAS *23*
Nilsson, Per 1954- *159*
Nimmo, Jenny 1944- *144*
  Earlier sketch in SATA *87*
  See also CLR *44*
Nishimura, Kae *196*
Niven, Larry 1938- *171*
  Earlier sketch in SATA *95*
Niven, Laurence Van Cott
  See Niven, Larry
Niven, Laurence VanCott
  See Niven, Larry
Nivola, Claire A. 1947- *208*
  Earlier sketches in SATA *84, 140*
Nix, Garth 1963- *210*
  Earlier sketches in SATA *97, 143*
  See also CLR *68*
Nixon, Hershell Howard 1923- *42*
Nixon, Joan Lowery 1927-2003 .... *115*
  Obituary *146*
  Earlier sketches in SATA *8, 44, 78*
  See also CLR *24*
  See also SAAS *9*

Nixon, K.
  See Nixon, Kathleen Irene (Blundell)
Nixon, Kathleen Irene (Blundell)
  1894-1988(?) *14*
  Obituary *59*
Nobati, Eugenia 1968- *201*
Nobisso, Josephine 1953- *121*
  Earlier sketch in SATA *78*
Noble, Iris (Davis) 1922-1986 .... *5*
  Obituary *49*
Noble, Marty 1947- *125*
  Earlier sketch in SATA *97*
Noble, Trinka Hakes 1944- *197*
  Brief entry *37*
  Earlier sketch in SATA *123*
Nobleman, Marc Tyler 1972- *203*
Noda, Takayo 1961- *168*
Nodelman, Perry 1942- *101*
Nodset, Joan L.
  See Lexau, Joan M.
Noel Hume, Ivor 1927- *65*
Noestlinger, Christine
  See Nostlinger, Christine
Noguere, Suzanne 1947- *34*
Nolan, Dennis 1945- *166*
  Brief entry *34*
  Earlier sketches in SATA *42, 92*
Nolan, Han 1956- *157*
  Earlier sketch in SATA *109*
Nolan, Janet 1956- *191*
  Earlier sketch in SATA *145*
Nolan, Jeannette Covert 1897-1974 .... *2*
  Obituary *27*
Nolan, Lucy *215*
Nolan, Paul T(homas) 1919- *48*
Nolan, William F. 1928- *88*
  Brief entry *28*
Nolan, William Francis
  See Nolan, William F.
Nolen, Jerdine 1953- *157*
  Earlier sketch in SATA *105*
Noll, Amanda *219*
Noll, Sally 1946- *82*
Nolte, Jack
  See Carter, Scott William
Noonan, Brandon 1979- *184*
Noonan, Diana 1960- *146*
Noonan, Julia 1946- *148*
  Earlier sketches in SATA *4, 95*
Norac, Carl 1960- *166*
Norcross, John
  See Conroy, John Wesley
Nordan, Robert W(arren) 1934-2004 .... *133*
Nordhoff, Charles Bernard 1887-1947 .... *23*
Nordlicht, Lillian *29*
Nordstrom, Ursula 1910-1988 .... *3*
  Obituary *57*
Nordtvedt, Matilda 1926- *67*
Norling, Beth 1969- *149*
Norman, Charles 1904-1996 .... *38*
  Obituary *92*
Norman, Geoffrey *223*
Norman, Howard
  See Norman, Howard A.
Norman, Howard A. 1949- *81*
Norman, James
  See Schmidt, James Norman
Norman, Jay
  See Arthur, Robert, (Jr.)
Norman, Lilith 1927- *120*
  Earlier sketch in SATA *86*
Norman, Mary 1931- *36*
Norman, Steve
  See Pashko, Stanley
Norment, Lisa 1966- *91*
Norris, Gunilla Brodde 1939- *20*
North, Andrew
  See Norton, Andre
North, Anthony
  See Koontz, Dean

North, Captain George
  See Stevenson, Robert Louis
North, Captain George
  See Stevenson, Robert Louis
North, Howard
  See Trevor, Elleston
North, Joan 1920- *16*
North, Milou
  See Erdrich, Louise
North, Robert
  See Withers, Carl A.
North, Sara
  See Bonham, Barbara Thomas
  and Hager, Jean
North, Sherry *201*
North, Sterling 1906-1974 .... *45*
  Obituary *26*
  Earlier sketch in SATA *1*
Northcott, (William) Cecil 1902-1987
  Obituary *55*
Northeast, Brenda V(ictoria) 1948- *106*
Northmore, Elizabeth Florence 1906-1974 . *122*
Norton, Alice Mary
  See Norton, Andre
Norton, Andre 1912-2005 .... *91*
  Earlier sketches in SATA *1, 43*
  See also CLR *50*
Norton, Browning
  See Norton, Frank R. B(rowning)
Norton, Frank R. B(rowning) 1909-1989 ..... *10*
Norton, Mary 1903-1992 .... *60*
  Obituary *72*
  Earlier sketch in SATA *18*
  See also CLR *140*
Nosredna, Trebor
  See Anderson, Bob
Nostlinger, Christine 1936- *162*
  Brief entry *37*
  Earlier sketch in SATA *64*
  See also CLR *12*
Nourse, Alan E(dward) 1928-1992 .... *48*
  See also CLR *33*
Novak, Matt 1962- *204*
  Brief entry *52*
  Earlier sketches in SATA *60, 104, 165*
Novelli, Luca 1947- *61*
Novgorodoff, Danica 1982(?)- *215*
Nowell, Elizabeth Cameron *12*
Noyes, Deborah 1965- *194*
  Earlier sketch in SATA *145*
Nugent, Cynthia 1954- *205*
Nugent, Nicholas 1949- *73*
Numberman, Neil 1981(?)- *220*
Numeroff, Laura 1953- *206*
  Earlier sketches in SATA *28, 90, 142*
  See also CLR *85*
Numeroff Joffe, Laura
  See Numeroff, Laura
Nunes, Lygia Bojunga 1932- *154*
  Earlier sketch in SATA *75*
Nunn, Laura (Donna) Silverstein 1968- *124*
Nurenberg, Thelma
  See Greenhaus, Thelma Nurenberg
Nurnberg, Maxwell 1897-1984 .... *27*
  Obituary *41*
Nussbaumer, Paul (Edmund) 1934- *16*
Nutt, Ken 1951- *163*
  Earlier sketch in SATA *97*
Nuttall-Smith, Margaret Emily Noel 1919- .. *26*
Nuygen, Mathieu 1967- *80*
Nuzum, K. A. *195*
Nuzum, Kathy A.
  See Nuzum, K. A.
Nwapa, Flora (Nwanzuruaha) 1931-1993
  See CLR *162*
Nyberg, (Everett Wayne) Morgan 1944- *87*
Nyce, (Nellie) Helene von Strecker
  1885-1969 .... *19*
Nyce, Vera 1862-1925 .... *19*

Nye, Naomi Shihab 1952- *198*
  Earlier sketches in SATA *86, 147*
  See also CLR *59*
Nye, Robert 1939- *6*
Nyeu, Tao *206*
Nyikos, Stacy A. 1969- *164*
Nystrom, Carolyn 1940- *130*
  Earlier sketch in SATA *67*

O

O. Henry
  See Henry, O.
Oakes, Elizabeth H. 1964- *132*
Oakes, Vanya 1909-1983 .... *6*
  Obituary *37*
Oakley, Don(ald G.) 1927- *8*
Oakley, Graham 1929- *84*
  Earlier sketch in SATA *30*
  See also CLR *7*
Oakley, Helen (McKelvey) 1906- *10*
Oaks, J. Adams *220*
Oana, Katherine 1929- *53*
  Brief entry *37*
Oates, Eddie H. 1943- *88*
Oates, Joyce Carol 1938- *159*
Oates, Stephen B(aery) 1936- *59*
Obed, Ellen Bryan 1944- *74*
Oberdieck, Bernhard 1949- *230*
Oberle, Joseph 1958- *69*
Oberman, Sheldon 1949-2004 .... *85*
  Autobiography Feature *114*
  Obituary *153*
  See also CLR *54*
  See also SAAS *26*
Obligado, Lilian (Isabel) 1931- *61*
  Brief entry *45*
Obrant, Susan 1946- *11*
O'Brian, E.G.
  See Clarke, Arthur C.
O'Brien, Anne Sibley 1952- *213*
  Brief entry *48*
  Earlier sketches in SATA *53, 80*
O'Brien, Caragh M. *232*
O'Brien, E.G.
  See Clarke, Arthur C.
O'Brien, Esse Forrester 1895(?)-1975
  Obituary *30*
O'Brien, Johnny *222*
O'Brien, Patrick 1960- *193*
O'Brien, Robert C. 1918-1973 .... *23*
  See also CLR *2*
O'Brien, Thomas C. 1938-2010 .... *29*
O'Brien, Thomas Clement
  See O'Brien, Thomas C.
O'Callaghan, Julie 1954- *113*
O'Callahan, Jay 1938- *88*
O'Carroll, Ryan
  See Markun, Patricia Maloney
Ochiltree, Dianne 1953- *117*
Ockham, Joan Price
  See Price, Joan
O'Connell, Margaret F(orster) 1935-1977 .... *30*
  Obituary *30*
O'Connell, Peg
  See Ahern, Margaret McCrohan
O'Connell, Rebecca 1968- *212*
  Earlier sketch in SATA *130*
O'Connor, Barbara 1950- *193*
  Earlier sketch in SATA *154*
O'Connor, Francine M(arie) 1930- *90*
O'Connor, Genevieve A. 1914- *75*
O'Connor, George *228*
  Earlier sketch in SATA *183*
O'Connor, Ian 1965- *188*
O'Connor, Jane 1947- *186*
  Brief entry *47*
  Earlier sketches in SATA *59, 103, 150*

O'Connor, Karen 1938- 89
Earlier sketch in SATA 34
O'Connor, Patrick
See Wibberley, Leonard
O'Connor, Richard 1915-1975
Obituary 21
O'Conor, Jane 1958- 78
Odaga, Asenath (Bole) 1937- 130
Earlier sketch in SATA 67
See also SAAS 19
O Danachair, Caoimhin
See Danaher, Kevin
Odanaka, Barbara 159
O'Daniel, Janet 1921- 24
O'Day, Cathy
See Crane, Barbara (Joyce)
O'Dell, Scott 1898-1989 134
Earlier sketches in SATA 12, 60
See also CLR 126
Odenwald, Robert P(aul) 1899-1965 11
Odgers, Sally
See Odgers, Sally Farrell
Odgers, Sally Farrell 1957- 139
Earlier sketch in SATA 72
Odone, Jamison 1980- 209
O'Donnell, Dick
See Lupoff, Richard A(llen)
and Thompson, Don(ald Arthur)
O'Donnell, Liam 1970- 209
Odriozola, Elena 186
Oechsli, Kelly 1918-1999 5
Oertel, Andreas 1966- 230
Oesterle, Virginia Rorby
See Rorby, Ginny
Ofek, Uriel 1926- 36
See also CLR 28
Ofer, Avi 1975- 207
Offenbacher, Ami 1958- 91
Offermann, Andrea 231
Offill, Jenny 1968- 211
Offit, Sidney 1928- 10
Ofosu-Appiah, L(awrence) H(enry) 1920- ... 13
Ogan, George F. 1912-1983 13
Ogan, M. G.
See Ogan, George F.
and Ogan, Margaret E. (Nettles)
Ogan, Margaret E. (Nettles) 1923-1979 13
Ogburn, Charlton (Jr.) 1911-1998 3
Obituary 109
Ogburn, Jacqueline K. 162
Ogilvie, Elisabeth May 1917-2006 40
Brief entry 29
Obituary 176
Ogilvy, Gavin
See Barrie, J. M.
Ogilvy, Ian 1943- 177
Ogilvy, Ian Raymond
See Ogilvy, Ian
Ogle, Lucille Edith 1904-1988
Obituary 59
Ogletree, Charles J. 1952- 175
O'Green, Jennifer
See Roberson, Jennifer
O'Green, Jennifer Roberson
See Roberson, Jennifer
O'Hagan, Caroline 1946- 38
O'Hanlon, Jacklyn
See Meek, Jacklyn O'Hanlon
O'Hara, Elizabeth
See Ni Dhuibhne, Eilis
O'Hara, Kenneth
See Morris, (Margaret) Jean
O'Hara, Mary
See Alsop, Mary O'Hara
O'Hara (Alsop), Mary
See Alsop, Mary O'Hara
O'Hare, Jeff(rey A.) 1958- 105
O'hearn, Kate 225
Ohi, Ruth 1964- 95
Ohiyesa
See Eastman, Charles A(lexander)

Ohlsson, Ib 1935- 7
Ohmi, Ayano 1959- 115
Ohtomo, Yasuo 1946- 37
o huigin, sean 1942- 138
See also CLR 75
Oiseau
See Moseley, James W(illett)
Oke, Janette 1935- 97
O'Keefe, Susan Heyboer 176
Earlier sketch in SATA 133
O'Keeffe, Frank 1938- 99
O'Kelley, Mattie Lou 1908-1997 97
Earlier sketch in SATA 36
Okimoto, Jean Davies 1942- 103
Earlier sketch in SATA 34
Okomfo, Amasewa
See Cousins, Linda
olafsdottir, Gudrun Elin
See Gunnella
Olaleye, Isaac O. 1941- 96
See also SAAS 23
Olander, Johan 1967- 231
Olcott, Frances Jenkins 1872(?)-1963 19
Old, Wendie C(orbin) 1943- 154
Old Boy
See Hughes, Thomas
Oldenburg, E(gbert) William 1936-1974 35
Older, Effin 1942- 114
Older, Jules 1940- 156
Earlier sketch in SATA 114
Oldfield, Jenny 1949- 140
Oldfield, Margaret J(ean) 1932- 56
Oldfield, Pamela 1931- 86
Oldham, June 70
Oldham, Mary 1944- 65
Oldland, Nicholas 1972- 223
Olds, Elizabeth 1896-1991 3
Obituary 66
Olds, Helen Diehl 1895-1981 9
Obituary 25
Oldstyle, Jonathan
See Irving, Washington
O'Leary, Brian (Todd) 1940- 6
O'Leary, Chris 208
O'Leary, Patsy B. 1937- 97
O'Leary, Patsy Baker
See O'Leary, Patsy B.
Oleynikov, Igor 1953- 202
Oliphant, B.J.
See Tepper, Sheri S.
Oliver, Burton
See Burt, Olive Woolley
Oliver, Chad
See Oliver, Symmes C.
Oliver, John Edward 1933- 21
Oliver, Lauren 1982- 228
Oliver, Lin 202
Oliver, Marilyn Tower 1935- 89
Oliver, Mark 1960- 214
Oliver, Narelle 1960- 197
Earlier sketch in SATA 152
Oliver, Shirley (Louise Dawkins) 1958- 74
Oliver, Symmes C. 1928-1993 101
Oliviero, Jamie 1950- 84
Olmsted, Lorena Ann 1890-1989 13
Olney, Ross R. 1929- 13
Olschewski, Alfred (Erich) 1920- 7
Olsen, Barbara 148
Olsen, Carol 1945- 89
Olsen, Ib Spang 1921- 81
Earlier sketch in SATA 6
Olsen, Violet (Mae) 1922-1991 58
Olson, Arielle North 1932- 67
Olson, David J. 1974- 198
Olson, Gene 1922- 32
Olson, Gretchen 187
Olson, Helen Kronberg 48
Olson, Julie 1976- 233
Olson, Kay Melchisedech 1948- 175
Olson, Marianne
See Mitchell, Marianne

Olson-Brown, Ellen 1967- 183
Olten, Manuela 1970- 197
Olugebefola, Ademole 1941- 15
Oluonye, Mary N(kechi) 1955- 111
Om
See Gorey, Edward (St. John)
O'Malley, Donough 208
O'Malley, Kevin 1961- 230
Earlier sketches in SATA 157, 191
Oman, Carola (Mary Anima) 1897-1978 35
O'Mara, Carmel 1965- 166
O'Mara-Horwitz, Carmel
See O'Mara, Carmel
O'Meara, Walter (Andrew) 1897-1989 65
Ommanney, F(rancis) D(ownes) 1903-1980 . 23
Omololu, Cynthia Jaynes 222
O Mude
See Gorey, Edward (St. John)
Oneal, Elizabeth 1934- 82
Earlier sketch in SATA 30
See also CLR 169
O'Neal, Katherine Pebley 1957- 204
O'Neal, Reagan
See Jordan, Robert
O'Neal, Regan
See Jordan, Robert
Oneal, Zibby
See Oneal, Elizabeth
O'neill, Alexis 1949- 220
O'Neill, Amanda 1951- 111
O'Neill, Catharine 203
O'Neill, Gerard K(itchen) 1927-1992 65
O'Neill, Judith (Beatrice) 1930- 34
O'Neill, Mary L(e Duc) 1908(?)-1990 2
Obituary 64
O'Neill, Reagan
See Jordan, Robert
Onslow, Annette Rosemary MacArthur
See MacArthur-Onslow, Annette Rosemary
Onslow, John 1906-1985
Obituary 47
Onyefulu, Ifeoma 1959- 157
Earlier sketches in SATA 81, 115
Opie, Iona (Margaret Balfour) 1923- 118
Earlier sketches in SATA 3, 63
See also SAAS 6
Opie, Peter (Mason) 1918-1982 118
Obituary 28
Earlier sketches in SATA 3, 63
Oppel, Kenneth 1967- 199
Earlier sketches in SATA 99, 153
Oppel, Kenneth Kerry
See Oppel, Kenneth
Oppenheim, Joanne 1934- 174
Earlier sketches in SATA 5, 82, 136
Oppenheim, Shulamith Levey 1928- 177
Oppenheimer, Joan L(etson) 1925- 28
Oppong, Joseph Ransford 1953- 160
Optic, Oliver
See Adams, William Taylor
and Stratemeyer, Edward L.
Oram, Hiawyn 1946- 101
Earlier sketch in SATA 56
Orbach, Ruth Gary 1941- 21
Orback, Craig 197
Orczy, Emma
See Orczy, Baroness Emmuska
Orczy, Emma Magdalena Rosalia Maria Josefa
See Orczy, Baroness Emmuska
Orczy, Emmuska
See Orczy, Baroness Emmuska
Orczy, Baroness Emmuska 1865-1947 40
Orde, A.J.
See Tepper, Sheri S.
O'Reilly, Jackson
See Jordan, Robert
Orenstein, Denise Gosliner 1950- 157
Orgad, Dorit 1936- 199

Orgel, Doris 1929- *148*
  Earlier sketches in SATA *7, 85*
  See also CLR *48*
  See also SAAS *19*
Orgill, Roxane *198*
Oriolo, Joe
  See Oriolo, Joseph D.
Oriolo, Joseph D. 1913-1985
  Obituary *46*
Orlandelli, Alessandro
  See Horley, Alex
Orlean, Susan 1955- *209*
Orleans, Ilo 1897-1962 .... *10*
Orlev, Uri 1931- *135*
  Earlier sketch in SATA *58*
  See also CLR *30*
  See also SAAS *19*
Ormai, Stella *57*
  Brief entry *48*
Ormerod, Jan 1946- *210*
  Brief entry *44*
  Earlier sketches in SATA *55, 70, 132*
  See also CLR *20*
Ormerod, Janette Louise
  See Ormerod, Jan
Ormes, Jackie
  See Ormes, Zelda J.
Ormes, Zelda J. 1914-1986
  Obituary *47*
Ormondroyd, Edward 1925- *14*
Ormsby, Virginia H(aire) 1906-1990 .... *11*
Orona-Ramirez, Kristy 1964- *189*
Orozco, Jose-Luis 1948- *179*
Orr, Katherine S(helley) 1950- *72*
Orr, Wendy 1953- *206*
  Earlier sketches in SATA *90, 141*
Orris
  See Ingelow, Jean
Orth, Richard
  See Gardner, Richard (M.)
Ortiz Cofer, Judith
  See Cofer, Judith Ortiz
Orwell, George 1903-1950 .... *29*
  See also CLR *68*
Orwin, Joanna 1944- *141*
Os, Eric van
  See van Os, Erik
Osborn, Elinor 1939- *145*
Osborn, Jacob 1981(?)- *215*
Osborn, Kathy 1955(?)- *199*
Osborn, Lois D(orothy) 1915- *61*
Osborne, Charles 1927- *59*
Osborne, Chester G(orham) 1915-1987 .... *11*
Osborne, David
  See Silverberg, Robert
Osborne, George
  See Silverberg, Robert
Osborne, Leone Neal 1914-1996 .... *2*
Osborne, Linda Barrett 1949- *215*
Osborne, Mary Pope 1949- *144*
  Earlier sketches in SATA *41, 55, 98*
  See also CLR *88*
Osceola
  See Blixen, Karen
Osgood, William E(dward) 1926- *37*
O'Shaughnessy, Darren
  See Shan, Darren
O'Shaughnessy, Ellen Cassels 1937- *78*
O'shaughnessy, Tam 1951- *221*
O'Shea, Catherine Patricia Shiels
  See O'Shea, Pat
O'Shea, Pat 1931-2007 .... *87*
  See also CLR *18*
Osmond, Edward 1900- *10*
Ossoli, Sarah Margaret
  See Fuller, Margaret
Ostendorf, (Arthur) Lloyd, (Jr.) 1921-2000 .. *65*
  Obituary *125*
Osterweil, Adam 1972- *217*
Ostow, Micol 1976- *223*
  Earlier sketch in SATA *170*

Otfinoski, Steven 1949- *116*
  Earlier sketch in SATA *56*
Otis, James
  See Kaler, James Otis
O'Toole, Thomas 1941- *71*
O'Trigger, Sir Lucius
  See Horne, Richard Henry Hengist
Otten, Charlotte
  See Otten, Charlotte F.
Otten, Charlotte F. 1926- *98*
Otten, Charlotte Fennema
  See Otten, Charlotte F.
Ottley, Matt 1962- *171*
  Earlier sketch in SATA *102*
Ottley, Reginald Leslie 1909-1985 .... *26*
  See also CLR *16*
Otto, Margaret Glover 1909-1976
  Obituary *30*
Otto, Svend
  See Soerensen, Svend Otto
Ouellet, Debbie 1954- *219*
Oughton, Jerrie (Preston) 1937- *131*
  Earlier sketch in SATA *76*
Oughton, (William) Taylor 1925- *104*
Ouida
  See De La Ramee, Marie Louise
Ousley, Odille 1896-1976 .... *10*
Outcalt, Todd 1960- *123*
Overmyer, James E. 1946- *88*
Overton, Jenny (Margaret Mary) 1942- *52*
  Brief entry *36*
Owen, Ann
  See Qualey, Marsha
Owen, Annie 1949- *75*
Owen, Caroline Dale
  See Snedeker, Caroline Dale (Parke)
Owen, Clifford
  See Hamilton, Charles (Harold St. John)
Owen, Dilys
  See Gater, Dilys
Owen, (Benjamin) Evan 1918-1984 .... *38*
Owen, (John) Gareth 1936-2002 .... *162*
  Earlier sketch in SATA *83*
  See also CLR *31*
  See also SAAS *14*
Owen, James A. *185*
Owens, Bryant 1968- *116*
Owens, Dana Elaine
  See Queen Latifah
Owens, Gail 1939- *54*
Owens, Mary Beth *191*
Owens, Thomas S(heldon) 1960- *86*
Owens, Tom
  See Owens, Thomas S(heldon)
Oxenbury, Helen 1938- *149*
  Earlier sketches in SATA *3, 68*
  See also CLR *70*
Oxendine, Bess Holland 1933- *90*
Oz, Frank (Richard) 1944- *60*
Ozer, Jerome S. 1927- *59*

P

Paananen, Eloise (Katherine) 1923-1993 ...... *9*
Pace, Lorenzo 1943- *131*
Pace, Mildred Mastin 1907- *46*
  Brief entry *29*
Pachter, Hedwig (?)-1988 .... *63*
Pack, Janet 1952- *77*
Pack, Robert 1929- *118*
Packard, Edward 1931- *148*
  Earlier sketches in SATA *47, 90*
Packer, Kenneth L. 1946- *116*
Packer, Vin
  See Meaker, Marijane
Pad, Peter
  See Stratemeyer, Edward L.
Page, Eileen
  See Heal, Edith

Page, Eleanor
  See Coerr, Eleanor (Beatrice)
Page, Gail 1950- *205*
Page, Jake 1936- *81*
Page, James Keena, Jr.
  See Page, Jake
Page, Lou Williams 1912-1997 .... *38*
Page, Mary
  See Heal, Edith
Page, Robin 1943- *154*
Pagliarulo, Antonio 1977(?)- *212*
Pagnucci, Susan 1944- *90*
Pahlen, Kurt 1907-2003
  Obituary *147*
Pahz, Cheryl
  See Pahz, Cheryl Suzanne
Pahz, Cheryl Suzanne 1949- *11*
Pahz, James Alon 1943- *11*
Paice, Margaret 1920- *10*
Paige, Harry W(orthington) 1922- *41*
  Brief entry *35*
Paige, Richard
  See Koontz, Dean
Paige, Robin
  See Albert, Susan Wittig
Paillot, Jim *230*
Paine, Penelope Colville 1946- *87*
Paine, Roberta M. 1925- *13*
Paisley, Tom 1932- *11*
  See also CLR *3*
Palatini, Margie *207*
  Earlier sketches in SATA *134, 174*
Palazzo, Anthony D.
  See Palazzo, Tony
Palazzo, Tony 1905-1970 .... *3*
Palder, Edward L. 1922- *5*
Palecek, Josef 1932- *56*
Palecek, Libuse 1937- *89*
Palen, Debbie *195*
Palin, Michael 1943- *67*
Palin, Michael Edward
  See Palin, Michael
Palladini, David (Mario) 1946- *40*
  Brief entry *32*
Pallas, Norvin 1918-1983 .... *23*
Pallister, John C(lare) 1891-1980
  Obituary *26*
Pallotta, Gerard Larry
  See Pallotta, Jerry
Pallotta, Jerry 1953- *186*
Pallotta-Chiarolli, Maria 1960- *117*
Palmer, Bernard (Alvin) 1914-1998 .... *26*
Palmer, C. Everard 1930- *14*
Palmer, (Ruth) Candida 1926- *11*
Palmer, Cyril Everard
  See Palmer, C. Everard
Palmer, Don
  See Benson, Mildred
Palmer, Gary 1968- *231*
Palmer, Hap 1942- *68*
Palmer, Heidi 1948- *15*
Palmer, Helen Marion
  See Geisel, Helen
Palmer, Jessica 1953- *120*
Palmer, Judd 1972- *153*
Palmer, Juliette 1930- *15*
Palmer, Maria
  See Strachan, Ian
Palmer, Maria
  See Brennan, Herbie
Palmer, Robin 1909-2000 .... *43*
Palmer, Robin 1969- *232*
Palmero Caceres, Ana *198*
Palmisciano, Diane *202*
Paltrowitz, Donna 1950- *61*
  Brief entry *50*
Paltrowitz, Donna Milman
  See Paltrowitz, Donna
Paltrowitz, Stuart 1946- *61*
  Brief entry *50*

Pamela, Todd 1950- 124
Pamintuan, Macky 214
  Earlier sketch in SATA 178
Panagopoulos, Janie Lynn 149
Panati, Charles 1943- 65
Panchyk, Richard 1970- 138
Panetta, George 1915-1969 15
Panetta, Joseph N. 1953- 96
Pang, YaWen Ariel 206
Panik, Sharon 1952- 82
Panowski, Eileen Thompson 1920- 49
Pansy
  See Alden, Isabella (Macdonald)
Pantell, Dora (Fuchs) 39
Panter, Carol 1936- 9
Paolini, Christopher 1983- 157
  See also CLR 102
Papademetriou, Lisa 175
Paparone, Pam 185
Paparone, Pamela
  See Paparone, Pam
Papas, Bill
  See Papas, William
Papas, William 1927-2000 50
Papashvily, George 1898-1978 17
Papashvily, Helen (Waite) 1906-1996 17
Pape, D. L.
  See Pape, Donna (Lugg)
Pape, Donna (Lugg) 1930- 82
  Earlier sketch in SATA 2
Paperny, Myra (Green) 1932- 51
  Brief entry 33
Papineau, Lucie 1962- 224
Papp, Robert 1967- 205
Paradis, Adrian A(lexis) 1912- 67
  Earlier sketch in SATA 1
  See also SAAS 8
Paradis, Marjorie Bartholomew
  1886(?)-1970 17
Paradiz, Valerie 1963- 176
Paratore, Coleen
  See Paratore, Coleen Murtagh
Paratore, Coleen Murtagh 1958- 200
Pardo DeLange, Alex 211
Parenteau, Shirley 1935- 199
  Brief entry 40
  Earlier sketch in SATA 47
Parish, Margaret 1927-1988 73
  Obituary 59
  Earlier sketch in SATA 17
  See also CLR 22
Parish, Margaret Holt
  See Holt, Margaret
Parish, Peggy
  See Parish, Margaret
Park, Barbara 1947- 123
  Brief entry 35
  Earlier sketches in SATA 40, 78
  See also CLR 34
Park, Bill
  See Park, W(illiam) B(ryan)
Park, Frances 1955- 171
Park, Ginger 173
Park, Janie Jaehyun 150
Park, Jordan
  See Kornbluth, C(yril) M.
  and Pohl, Frederik
Park, Linda Sue 1960- 200
  Earlier sketches in SATA 127, 173
  See also CLR 84
Park, Nick 1958- 113
Park, Rosina Ruth Lucia
  See Park, Ruth
Park, Ruth 1917(?)-2010 93
  Earlier sketch in SATA 25
  See also CLR 51
Park, W(illiam) B(ryan) 1936- 22
Parke, Marilyn 1928- 82
Parker, Barbara Keevil 1938- 157
Parker, Daniel
  See Ehrenhaft, Daniel

Parker, Elinor Milnor 1906- 3
Parker, Jake 1977- 227
Parker, Julie F. 1961- 92
Parker, Kim 1963- 174
Parker, Kristy 1957- 59
Parker, Lois M(ay) 1912-1996 30
Parker, Margot M. 1937- 52
Parker, Marjorie Blain 1960- 205
  Earlier sketch in SATA 145
Parker, Mary Jessie 1948- 71
Parker, Nancy Winslow 1930- 132
  Earlier sketches in SATA 10, 69
  See also SAAS 20
Parker, Richard 1915-1990 14
Parker, Robert
  See Boyd, Waldo T.
  and Parker, Robert Andrew
Parker, Robert Andrew 1927- 200
Parker, Steve 1954- 213
Parker, Tom S. 215
Parker, Toni Trent 1947-2005 142
  Obituary 169
Parker-Rees, Guy 193
Parker-Rock, Michelle 214
Parkes, Lucas
  See Harris, John (Wyndham Parkes Lucas)
  Beynon
Parkhill, John
  See Cox, William R(obert)
Parkins, David 1955- 218
  Earlier sketch in SATA 176
Parkinson, Curtis 219
Parkinson, Ethelyn M(inerva) 1906-1999 11
Parkinson, Kathryn N. 1954- 71
Parkinson, Kathy
  See Parkinson, Kathryn N.
Parkinson, Siobhan
  See Parkinson, Siobhan
Parkinson, Siobhan 1954- 178
Parks, Deborah A. 1948- 133
  Earlier sketch in SATA 91
Parks, Edd Winfield 1906-1968 10
Parks, Gordon 1912-2006 108
  Obituary 175
  Earlier sketch in SATA 8
Parks, Gordon Roger Alexander
  See Parks, Gordon
Parks, Peggy J. 1951- 143
Parks, PJ
  See Parks, Peggy J.
Parks, Rosa 1913-2005 83
  Obituary 169
Parks, Rosa Louise Lee
  See Parks, Rosa
Parks, Van Dyke 1943- 62
Parlato, Stephen 1954- 222
Parley, Peter
  See Goodrich, Samuel Griswold
Parlin, John
  See Graves, Charles Parlin
Parme, Fabrice 1966- 191
Parnall, Peter 1936- 69
  Earlier sketch in SATA 16
  See also SAAS 11
Paros, Jennifer 210
Parotti, Phillip (Elliott) 1941- 109
Parr, Ann 1943- 144
Parr, Danny
  See Parr, Ann
Parr, Letitia (Evelyn) 1906-1985(?) 37
Parr, Lucy 1924- 10
Parr, Todd 179
  Earlier sketch in SATA 134
Parra, John 1972- 225
Parrish, Anne 1888-1957 27
Parrish, Mary
  See Cousins, Margaret
Parrish, Maxfield
  See Parrish, (Frederick) Maxfield
Parrish, (Frederick) Maxfield 1870-1966 14
Parry, Marian 1924- 13

Parry, Rosanne 212
Parson Lot
  See Kingsley, Charles
Parsons, Alexandra 1947- 92
Parsons, Ellen
  See Dragonwagon, Crescent
Parsons, Garry 197
Parsons, Martin 1951- 116
Parsons, Martin Leslie
  See Parsons, Martin
Parsons, Tom
  See MacPherson, Thomas George
Parsons-Yazzi, Evangeline 172
Partch, Virgil Franklin II 1916-1984 39
  Obituary 39
Parton, Dolly 1946- 94
Parton, Dolly Rebecca
  See Parton, Dolly
Partridge, Benjamin W., Jr. 1915-2005 28
  Obituary 163
Partridge, Benjamin Waring, Jr.
  See Partridge, Benjamin W., Jr.
Partridge, Cora Cheney
  See Cheney, Cora
Partridge, Elizabeth 216
  Earlier sketch in SATA 134
Partridge, Jenny (Lilian) 1947- 52
  Brief entry 37
Pasachoff, Naomi 1947- 147
Pascal, David 1918- 14
Pascal, Francine 1938- 143
  Brief entry 37
  Earlier sketches in SATA 51, 80
  See also CLR 25
Paschal, Nancy
  See Trotter, Grace V(iolet)
Paschkis, Julie 1957- 220
  Earlier sketch in SATA 177
Pascudniak, Pascal
  See Lupoff, Richard A(llen)
Pashko, Stanley 1913-1982 29
Pasqualotto, Chiara 1976- 228
Passailaigue, Thomas E.
  See Paisley, Tom
Pastel, Elyse 201
Pateman, Robert 1954- 84
Patent, Dorothy Hinshaw 1940- 162
  Autobiography Feature 162
  Earlier sketches in SATA 22, 69, 120
  See also CLR 19
  See also SAAS 13
Paterson, A(ndrew) B(arton) 1864-1941 97
Paterson, Banjo
  See Paterson, A(ndrew) B(arton)
Paterson, Diane 1946- 177
  Brief entry 33
  Earlier sketch in SATA 59
Paterson, John (Barstow) 1932- 114
Paterson, Katherine 1932- 204
  Earlier sketches in SATA 13, 53, 92, 133
  See also CLR 127
Paterson, Katherine Womeldorf
  See Paterson, Katherine
Patience, John 1949- 90
Patneaude, David 1944- 233
  Earlier sketches in SATA 85, 159
Paton, Alan 1903-1988 11
  Obituary 56
Paton, Alan Stewart
  See Paton, Alan
Paton, Jane (Elizabeth) 1934- 35
Paton, Priscilla 1952- 98
Paton Walsh, Gillian
  See Paton Walsh, Jill
Paton Walsh, Jill 1937- 190
  Autobiography Feature 190
  Earlier sketches in SATA 4, 72, 109
  See also CLR 128
  See also SAAS 3
Patricelli, Leslie 207

Patrick, Susan
See Robins, Patricia
Patron, Susan 1948- *182*
Earlier sketch in SATA 76
Patsauq, Markoosie 1942-
See CLR 23
Patschke, Steve 1955- *125*
Patt, Beverly *231*
Patten, Brian 1946- *152*
Earlier sketch in SATA 29
Patterson, Charles 1935- *59*
Patterson, Geoffrey 1943- *54*
Brief entry *44*
Patterson, James 1947- *197*
Earlier sketch in SATA 164
Patterson, James B.
See Patterson, James
Patterson, Lillie G. -1999 .... *88*
Earlier sketch in SATA 14
Patterson, Nancy Ruth 1944- *148*
Earlier sketch in SATA 72
Patterson, Valerie O. *223*
Pattison, Darcy (S.) 1954- *126*
Earlier sketch in SATA 72
Pattou, Edith *164*
Patz (Blaustein), Nancy *154*
Paul, Aileen 1917- *12*
Paul, Alison *196*
Paul, Ann Whitford 1941- *209*
Earlier sketches in SATA 76, 110, 168
Paul, Chris 1985- *224*
Paul, David (Tyler) 1934-1988
Obituary *56*
Paul, Dominique 1973- *184*
Paul, Elizabeth
See Crow, Donna Fletcher
Paul, Hamish Vigne Christie 1951- *151*
See also CLR 87
Paul, James 1936- *23*
Paul, Korky
See Paul, Hamish Vigne Christie
Paul, Robert
See Roberts, John G(aither)
Paul, Tessa 1944- *103*
Pauley, Kimberly 1973- *208*
Pauli, Hertha (Ernestine) 1909-1973 .... *3*
Obituary *26*
Paull, Grace A. 1898- *24*
Paulsen, Gary 1939- *231*
Earlier sketches in SATA 22, 50, 54, 79, 111,
158, 189
See also CLR 82
Paulson, Jack
See Jackson, C(aary) Paul
Pauquet, Gina Ruck
See Ruck-Pauquet, Gina
Pausacker, Jenny 1948- *72*
See also SAAS 23
Pausewang, Gudrun 1928- *165*
Earlier sketch in SATA 104
Pavel, Frances 1907- *10*
Paver, Michelle *215*
Earlier sketch in SATA 170
Paxton
See Barr, Nevada
Paxton, Thomas R. 1937- *70*
Paxton, Tom
See Paxton, Thomas R.
Paye, Won-Ldy *185*
Payne, Alan
See Jakes, John
Payne, Bernal C., Jr. 1941- *60*
Payne, C. Douglas
See Payne, C.D.
Payne, C.D. 1949- *133*
Payne, C.F. 1956- *179*
Payne, Chris Fox
See Payne, C.F.
Payne, Donald Gordon 1924- *37*
Payne, Emmy
See West, Emily Govan

Payne, Nina *135*
Payne, Rachel Ann
See Jakes, John
Payson, Dale 1943- *9*
Payzant, Charles *18*
Paz, A.
See Pahz, James Alon
Paz, Natalia Toledo
See Toledo, Natalia
Paz, Zan
See Pahz, Cheryl Suzanne
Peace, Mary
See Finley, Mary Peace
Peacock, Louise *210*
Peacock, Phyllis Hornung 1977- *230*
Peacock, Shane 1957- *192*
Peake, Mervyn 1911-1968 .... *23*
Peale, Norman Vincent 1898-1993 .... *20*
Obituary *78*
Pearce, Ann Philippa
See Pearce, Philippa
Pearce, Carl *229*
Pearce, Emily Smith 1975- *199*
Pearce, Jacqueline 1962- *146*
Pearce, Margaret *104*
Pearce, Philippa 1920-2006 .... *129*
Obituary *179*
Earlier sketches in SATA 1, 67
See also CLR 9
Peare, Catherine Owens 1911- *9*
Pearle, Ida *207*
Pearsall, Shelley 1966- *190*
Pearson, Gayle 1947- *119*
Earlier sketch in SATA 53
Pearson, Jean Mary
See Gardam, Jane
Pearson, Kit 1947- *77*
Autobiography Feature *117*
See also CLR 26
Pearson, Mary E. 1955- *211*
Earlier sketch in SATA 134
Pearson, Michael Parker
See Pearson, Mike Parker
Pearson, Mike Parker 1957- *228*
Pearson, Ridley 1953- *182*
Pearson, Susan 1946- *166*
Brief entry *27*
Earlier sketches in SATA 39, 91
Pearson, Tracey Campbell 1956- *219*
Earlier sketches in SATA 64, 155
Pease, (Clarence) Howard 1894-1974 .... *2*
Obituary *25*
Peavy, Linda 1943- *54*
Peck, Anne Merriman 1884-1976 .... *18*
Peck, Beth 1957- *190*
Earlier sketch in SATA 79
Peck, Jan *159*
Peck, Jeanie J. 1967- *147*
Peck, Marshall III 1951- *92*
Peck, Richard 1934- *228*
Autobiography Feature *110*
Earlier sketches in SATA 18, 55, 97, 110, 158,
190
See also CLR 142
See also SAAS 2
Peck, Richard Wayne
See Peck, Richard
Peck, Robert Newton 1928- *156*
Autobiography Feature *108*
Earlier sketches in SATA 21, 62, 111
See also CLR 163
See also SAAS 1
Peck, Sylvia 1953- *133*
Peck-Whiting, Jeanie J.
See Peck, Jeanie J.
Peddicord, Jane Ann *199*
Pedersen, Janet *193*
Pederson, Sharleen
See Collicott, Sharleen
Pedler, Caroline *197*

Peebles, Anne
See Galloway, Priscilla
Peek, Merle 1938- *39*
Peel, John 1954- *79*
Peel, Norman Lemon
See Hirsch, Phil
Peeples, Edwin A(ugustus, Jr.) 1915-1994 ..... *6*
Peers, Judi 1956- *119*
Peers, Judith May West
See Peers, Judi
Peet, Bill
See Peet, William Bartlett
Peet, Creighton B. 1899-1977 .... *30*
Peet, Mal *227*
Earlier sketch in SATA 171
Peet, Malcolm
See Peet, Mal
Peet, William Bartlett 1915-2002 .... *78*
Obituary *137*
Earlier sketches in SATA 2, 41
See also CLR 12
Peete, Holly Robinson 1964- *229*
Peguero, Leone *116*
Peirce, Lincoln *232*
Pelaez, Jill 1924- *12*
Pelham, David 1938- *70*
Pelikan, Judy 1941- *219*
Pell, Ed(ward) 1950- *157*
Pelletier, Andrew T. *195*
Pelletier, Andrew Thomas
See Pelletier, Andrew T.
Pellowski, Anne 1933- *20*
Pellowski, Michael (Joseph) 1949- *151*
Brief entry *48*
Earlier sketch in SATA 88
Pellowski, Michael Morgan
See Pellowski, Michael (Joseph)
Pelta, Kathy 1928- *18*
Peltier, Leslie C(opus) 1900-1980 .... *13*
Pemberton, Bonnie *191*
Pemberton, John Leigh
See Leigh-Pemberton, John
Pembury, Bill
See Groom, Arthur William
Pemsteen, Hans
See Manes, Stephen
Pendennis, Arthur Esquir
See Thackeray, William Makepeace
Pender, Lydia Podger 1907- *61*
Pendery, Rosemary (Schmitz) *7*
Pendle, Alexy 1943- *29*
Pendle, George 1906-1977
Obituary *28*
Pendleton, Don
See Cunningham, Chet
and Garside, Jack
and Jagninski, Tom
and Krauzer, Steven M(ark)
and Obstfeld, Raymond
Pendleton, Thomas 1965- *206*
Pendziwol, Jean E. 1965- *177*
Pene du Bois, William (Sherman)
1916-1993 .... *68*
Obituary *74*
Earlier sketch in SATA 4
See also CLR 1
Penn, Audrey 1947- *212*
Penn, Audrey 1950- *22*
Penn, Ruth Bonn
See Rosenberg, Eth Clifford
Pennac, Daniel 1944- *155*
Pennage, E. M.
See Finkel, George (Irvine)
Penner, Fred 1946- *169*
Earlier sketch in SATA 67
Penner, Frederick Ralph Cornelius
See Penner, Fred
Penner, Lucille Recht 1942- *226*
Penney, Grace Jackson 1904-2000 .... *35*
Penney, Ian 1960- *76*

Author Index

Penney, Sue 1957- 152
Earlier sketch in SATA 102
Pennington, Eunice 1923- 27
Pennington, Lillian Boyer 1904-2003 45
Pennypacker, Sara 1951- 187
Penrose, Gordon 1925- 66
Penson, Mary E. 1917- 78
Penzler, Otto 1942- 38
Pepe, Phil 1935- 20
Pepe, Philip
See Pepe, Phil
Peppe, Rodney (Darrell) 1934- 74
Earlier sketch in SATA 4
See also SAAS 10
Pepper, Frank S. 1910-1988
Obituary 61
Percy, Charles Henry
See Smith, Dorothy Gladys
Percy, Rachel 1930- 63
Perdomo, Willie 228
Perdrizet, Marie-Pierre 1952- 79
Perenyi, Constance 1954- 93
Perenyi, Constance Marie
See Perenyi, Constance
Perera, Hilda 1926- 105
Perera, Thomas Biddle 1938- 13
Peretti, Frank E. 1951- 141
Earlier sketch in SATA 80
Perez, L. King 1940- 199
Perez, Lana
See Perez, Marlene
Perez, Lucia Angela 1973- 182
Perez, Marlene 170
Pericoli, Matteo 1968- 178
Perkins, Al(bert Rogers) 1904-1975 30
Perkins, Dan
See Tomorrow, Tom
Perkins, Lucy Fitch 1865-1937 72
Perkins, Lynne Rae 1956- 212
Earlier sketches in SATA 131, 172
Perkins, (Richard) Marlin 1905-1986 21
Obituary 48
Perkins, Mitali 1963- 188
Earlier sketch in SATA 88
Perks, Anne-Marie 1955- 122
Perl, Erica S. 222
Earlier sketch in SATA 188
Perl, Lila 72
Earlier sketch in SATA 6
Perl, Susan 1922-1983 22
Obituary 34
Perlman, Janet 1954- 222
Perlman, Rhea 1948- 183
Perlmutter, O(scar) William 1920-1975 8
Pernu, Dennis 1970- 87
Perrault, Charles 1628-1703 25
See also CLR 134
Perret, Delphine 1980- 190
Perret, Gene (Richard) 1937- 76
Perriman, Cole
See Perrin, Pat
Perriman, Cole
See Coleman, Wim
and Perrin, Pat
Perrin, Pat 212
Perrine, Mary 1913-1976 2
Perrins, Lesley 1953- 56
Perrow, Angeli 1954- 121
Perry, Andrea 1956- 190
Earlier sketch in SATA 148
Perry, Barbara Fisher
See Fisher, Barbara
Perry, Elizabeth 1959- 174
Perry, Elizabeth Goodwin
See Perry, Elizabeth
Perry, John 1967- 223
Perry, M. LaVora 232
Perry, Marie Fritz 165
Perry, Patricia 1949- 30
Perry, Phyllis J(ean) 1933- 152
Earlier sketches in SATA 60, 101

Perry, Ritchie (John Allen) 1942- 105
Perry, Roger 1933- 27
Perry, Steve(n Carl) 1947- 76
Pershall, Mary K. 1951- 172
Earlier sketch in SATA 70
Pershing, Marie
See Schultz, Pearle Henriksen
Perske, Robert 1927- 57
Persun, Morgan Reed
See Watkins, Dawn L.
Perversi, Margaret 213
Petach, Heidi 149
Peter
See Stratemeyer, Edward L.
Peters, Alexander
See Hollander, Zander
Peters, Andrew Fusek 1965- 169
Earlier sketch in SATA 107
Peters, Bernadette 1948- 212
Peters, Caroline
See Betz, Eva Kelly
Peters, David
See David, Peter
Peters, Elizabeth 1927- 49
Peters, Emma
See Price, Karen
Peters, Gabriel
See Matott, Justin
Peters, Julie Anne 1952- 197
Earlier sketches in SATA 82, 128
Peters, Linda
See Catherall, Arthur
Peters, Lisa Westberg 1951- 232
Earlier sketches in SATA 74, 115, 161
Peters, Patricia 1953- 84
Peters, Russell M. 1929- 78
Peters, S. H.
See Henry, O.
and Proffitt, Nicholas
Peters, Stephanie True 1965- 224
Petersen, David 1946- 109
Earlier sketch in SATA 62
Petersen, Gwenn Boardman 1924- 12
Petersen, P(eter) J(ames) 1941- 118
Brief entry 43
Earlier sketches in SATA 48, 83
Petersen, Palle 1943- 85
Petersham, Maud 1890-1971 17
See also CLR 24
Petersham, Maud Sylvia Fuller
See Petersham, Maud
Petersham, Miska 1888-1960 17
See also CLR 24
Peterson, Cris 1952- 174
Earlier sketches in SATA 84, 145
Peterson, Dawn 1934- 86
Peterson, Esther (Allen) 1934- 35
Peterson, Hans 1922- 8
Peterson, Harold L(eslie) 1922-1978 8
Peterson, Helen Stone 1910- 8
Peterson, Jean Sunde 1941- 108
Peterson, Jeanne Whitehouse 1939- 159
Earlier sketch in SATA 29
Peterson, John 1924-2002 233
Peterson, Kathleen B. 1951- 119
Peterson, Lorraine 1940- 56
Brief entry 44
Peterson, Mary 215
Peterson, Shelley 1952- 146
Peterson, Will
See Cocks, Peter
Petie, Haris
See Petty, Roberta
Petricic, Dusan 1946- 176
Petrides, Heidrun 1944- 19
Petrie, Catherine 1947- 52
Brief entry 41
Petrone, Valeria 233
Earlier sketch in SATA 186
Petrosino, Tamara 193
Petroski, Catherine (Ann Groom) 1939- 48

Petrovich, Michael B(oro) 1922- 40
Petrovskaya, Kyra
See Wayne, Kyra Petrovskaya
Petruccio, Steven James 1961- 67
Petrucha, Stefan 1959- 213
Petry, Ann 1908-1997 5
Obituary 94
See also CLR 12
Petry, Ann Lane
See Petry, Ann
Pettit, Jayne 1932- 108
Petty, J.T. 1977- 189
Petty, Kate 1951-2007 204
Petty, Roberta 1915- 10
Pevsner, Stella 131
Earlier sketches in SATA 8, 77
See also SAAS 14
Peyo
See Culliford, Pierre
Peyton, K. M.
See Peyton, Kathleen Wendy
Peyton, Kathleen Wendy 1929- 157
Earlier sketches in SATA 15, 62
See also CLR 3
See also SAAS 17
Pfanner, (Anne) Louise 1955- 68
Pfeffer, Susan Beth 1948- 180
Earlier sketches in SATA 4, 83
See also CLR 11
See also SAAS 17
Pfeffer, Wendy 1929- 204
Earlier sketches in SATA 78, 142
Pfeiffer, Janet (B.) 1949- 96
Pfister, Marcus 207
Earlier sketches in SATA 83, 150
See also CLR 42
Pfitsch, Patricia Curtis 1948- 148
Pfitzenmaier, Audrey 1959- 220
Pflieger, Pat 1955- 84
Pham, LeUyen 1973- 201
Earlier sketch in SATA 175
Phelan, Mary Kay 1914- 3
Phelan, Matt 1970- 215
Earlier sketch in SATA 172
Phelan, Terry Wolfe 1941- 56
Phelps, Ethel Johnston 1914-1984 35
Philbrick, Rodman 1951- 163
Philbrick, W. Rodman
See Philbrick, Rodman
Philbrick, W.R.
See Philbrick, Rodman
Philbrook, Clem(ent E.) 1917- 24
Phillipps, J.C. 218
Phillipps, Julie Christine
See Phillipps, J.C.
Phillips, Aileen Paul
See Paul, Aileen
Phillips, Betty Lou
See Phillips, Elizabeth Louise
Phillips, Bob 1940- 95
Phillips, Douglas A. 1949- 161
Phillips, Elizabeth Louise 58
Brief entry 48
Phillips, Gary R. 225
Phillips, Irv(ing W.) 1905-2000 11
Obituary 125
Phillips, Jack
See Sandburg, Carl
Phillips, Leon
See Gerson, Noel Bertram
Phillips, Loretta (Hosey) 1893-1987 10
Phillips, Louis 1942- 102
Earlier sketch in SATA 8
Phillips, Mark
See Garrett, Randall
and Janifer, Laurence M(ark)
Phillips, Mary Geisler 1881-1964 10
Phillips, Michael
See Nolan, William F.
Phillips, (Woodward) Prentice 1894-1981 10
Phillpotts, Eden 1862-1960 24

Phin
See Thayer, Ernest Lawrence
Phipson, Joan
See Fitzhardinge, Joan Margaret
Phiz
See Browne, Hablot Knight
Phleger, Fred B. 1909-1993 34
Phleger, Marjorie Temple 1908(?)-1986 1
Obituary 47
Piaget, Jean 1896-1980
Obituary 23
Piatti, Celestino 1922- 16
Picard, Barbara Leonie 1917- 89
Earlier sketch in SATA 2
See also SAAS 10
Pichon, Liz 174
Pickard, Charles 1932- 36
Pickering, James Sayre 1897-1969 36
Obituary 28
Pickering, Jimmy 195
Pickering, Robert B. 1950- 93
Pielichaty, Helena 1955- 142
Pien, Lark 222
Pienkowski, Jan (Michal) 1936- 131
Earlier sketches in SATA 6, 58
See also CLR 6
Pierce, Edith Gray 1893-1977 45
Pierce, Katherine
See St. John, Wylly Folk
Pierce, Meredith Ann 1958- 127
Brief entry 48
Earlier sketch in SATA 67
See also CLR 20
Pierce, Ruth (Ireland) 1936- 5
Pierce, Sharon
See McCullough, Sharon Pierce
Pierce, Tamora 1954- 187
Brief entry 49
Earlier sketches in SATA 51, 96, 153
Pierce, Terry 178
Pierik, Robert 1921- 13
Piernas-Davenport, Gail 199
Piers, Robert
See Anthony, Piers
Pig, Edward
See Gorey, Edward (St. John)
Pignataro, Anna 1965- 223
Pike, Aprilynne 218
Pike, Bob
See Pike, Robert W.
Pike, Christopher 1954(?)- 156
Earlier sketch in SATA 68
See also CLR 29
Pike, Deborah 1951- 89
Pike, E(dgar) Royston 1896-1980 22
Obituary 56
Pike, R. William 1956- 92
Pike, Robert
See Pike, Robert W.
Pike, Robert W. 1931- 102
Pike, Robert Wilson
See Pike, Robert W.
Pilarski, Laura 1926- 13
Pilgrim, Anne
See Allan, Mabel Esther
Pilkey, Dav 1966- 166
Earlier sketches in SATA 68, 115
See also CLR 160
Pilkey, David Murray, Jr.
See Pilkey, Dav
Pilkington, Francis Meredyth 1907-1993 4
Pilkington, Roger (Windle) 1915-2003 10
Obituary 144
Pilutti, Deb 208
Pin, Isabel 1975- 183
Pinchot, David 1914(?)-1983
Obituary 34
Pincus, Harriet 1938- 27
Pinczes, Elinor J(ane) 1940- 81
Pine, Nicholas 1951- 91
Pine, Tillie S(chloss) 1896-1999 13

Pini, Richard (Alan) 1950- 89
Pini, Wendy 1951- 89
Pinkerton, Kathrene Sutherland (Gedney)
1887-1967
Obituary 26
Pinkett, Jada
See Smith, Jada Pinkett
Pinkney, Andrea Davis 1963- 160
Earlier sketch in SATA 113
Pinkney, Brian 1961- 206
Earlier sketches in SATA 74, 148
See also CLR 54
Pinkney, Gloria Jean 1941- 212
Earlier sketch in SATA 85
Pinkney, J. Brian
See Pinkney, Brian
Pinkney, Jerry 1939- 198
Autobiography Feature 198
Brief entry 32
Earlier sketches in SATA 41, 71, 107, 151
See also CLR 43
See also SAAS 12
Pinkney, John 97
Pinkney, Sandra L. 193
Earlier sketch in SATA 128
Pinkwater, D. Manus
See Pinkwater, Daniel
Pinkwater, Daniel 1941- 210
Earlier sketches in SATA 8, 46, 76, 114, 158
See also CLR 4
See also SAAS 3
Pinkwater, Daniel M.
See Pinkwater, Daniel
Pinkwater, Daniel Manus
See Pinkwater, Daniel
Pinkwater, Jill 188
Pinkwater, Manus
See Pinkwater, Daniel
Pinner, Joma
See Werner, Herma
Pinto, Sara 200
Pioneer
See Yates, Raymond F(rancis)
Piowaty, Kim Kennelly 1957- 49
Piper, Roger
See Fisher, John
Pirner, Connie White 1955- 72
Piro, Richard 1934- 7
Pirot, Alison Lohans
See Lohans, Alison
Pirotta, Saviour 184
Pirsig, Robert M(aynard) 1928- 39
Pita
See Rendon, Maria
Pitcher, C.
See Pitcher, Caroline
Pitcher, Caroline 1948- 214
Earlier sketch in SATA 128
Pitcher, Caroline Nell
See Pitcher, Caroline
Pitman, (Isaac) James 1901-1985
Obituary 46
Pitre, Felix 1949- 84
Pitrone, Jean Maddern 1920- 4
Pittman, Helena Clare 1945- 71
Pitz, Henry C(larence) 1895-1976 4
Obituary 24
Pitzer, Susanna 1958- 181
Piven, Hanoch 1963- 173
Pixley, Marcella 194
Pizer, Vernon 1918- 21
Place, Marian T(empleton) 1910- 3
Place, Robin (Mary) 1926- 71
Plaidy, Jean
See Hibbert, Eleanor Alice Burford
Plain, Belva 1919-2010 62
Plaine, Alfred R. 1898(?)-1981
Obituary 29
Plant, Andrew 214
Plath, Sylvia 1932-1963 96
Platt, Chris 1959- 185

Platt, Kin 1911- 86
Earlier sketch in SATA 21
See also SAAS 17
Platt, Randall 1948- 95
Platt, Randall Beth
See Platt, Randall
Platt, Richard 1953- 218
Earlier sketches in SATA 120, 166
Playfellow, Robin
See Ellis, Edward S.
Playsted, James
See Wood, James Playsted
Plecas, Jennifer 1966- 229
Earlier sketches in SATA 84, 149
Plimpton, George 1927-2003 10
Obituary 150
Plimpton, George Ames
See Plimpton, George
Plomer, William Charles Franklin
1903-1973 24
Plotz, Helen Ratnoff 1913-2000 38
Plourde, Lynn 1955- 218
Earlier sketches in SATA 122, 168
Plowden, David 1932- 52
Plowden, Martha Ward 1948- 98
Plowhead, Ruth Gipson 1877-1967 43
Plowman, Stephanie 1922- 6
Pluckrose, Henry 1931-2011 141
Earlier sketch in SATA 13
Pluckrose, Henry Arthur
See Pluckrose, Henry
Plum, J.
See Wodehouse, P. G.
Plum, Jennifer
See Kurland, Michael
Plumb, Charles P. 1900(?)-1982
Obituary 29
Plume, Ilse 170
Brief entry 43
Plumme, Don E.
See Katz, Bobbi
Plummer, Margaret 1911- 2
Plum-Ucci, Carol 1957- 184
Poblocki, Dan 1981- 224
Pochocki, Ethel (Frances) 1925- 76
Podendorf, Illa (E.) 1903(?)-1983 18
Obituary 35
Podwal, Mark 1945- 224
Earlier sketches in SATA 101, 160
Podwal, Mark H.
See Podwal, Mark
Poe, Edgar Allan 1809-1849 23
Poe, Ty (Christopher) 1975- 94
Pogany, William Andrew 1882-1955 44
Brief entry 30
Pogany, Willy
See Pogany, William Andrew
Pogue, Carolyn 1948- 223
Pogue, David 1963- 231
Pohl, Frederik 1919- 24
Pohlmann, Lillian (Grenfell) 1902-1997 11
Pohrt, Tom 1953- 195
Earlier sketches in SATA 67, 152
Pointon, Robert
See Rooke, Daphne
Points, Larry G. 1945- 177
Earlier sketch in SATA 133
Points, Larry Gene
See Points, Larry G.
Pokeberry, P.J.
See Mitchell, B.J.
POLA
See Watson, Pauline
Polacco, Patricia 1944- 212
Earlier sketches in SATA 74, 123, 180
See also CLR 40
Polacco, Patricia Ann
See Polacco, Patricia
Polak, Monique 1960- 230
Earlier sketch in SATA 178
Polatnick, Florence T. 1923- 5

Polcovar, Jane 1948- 211
Polder, Markus
    See Kruss, James
Polenghi, Evan 1961- 225
Polese, Carolyn 1947- 58
Polese, James 1914- 87
Polette, Nancy (Jane) 1930- 42
Polhamus, Jean Burt 1928- 21
Polhemus, Coleman 210
Policoff, Stephen Phillip 1948- 77
Polikoff, Barbara G. 1929- 162
    Earlier sketch in SATA 77
Polikoff, Barbara Garland
    See Polikoff, Barbara G.
Polisar, Barry Louis 1954- 134
    Earlier sketch in SATA 77
Politi, Leo 1908-1996 47
    Obituary 88
    Earlier sketch in SATA 1
    See also CLR 29
Polking, Kirk 1925- 5
Pollack, Jill S. 1963- 88
Pollack, Merrill S. 1924-1988
    Obituary 55
Polland, Barbara K(ay) 1939- 44
Polland, Madeleine A(ngela Cahill) 1918- ... 68
    Earlier sketch in SATA 6
    See also SAAS 8
Pollema-Cahill, Phyllis 1958- 123
Pollock, Bruce 1945- 46
Pollock, Mary
    See Blyton, Enid
Pollock, Penny 1935- 137
    Brief entry 42
    Earlier sketch in SATA 44
Pollowitz, Melinda Kilborn 1944- 26
Polner, Murray 1928- 64
Polonsky, Arthur 1925- 34
Polseno, Jo 17
Pomaska, Anna 1946- 117
Pomerantz, Charlotte 1930- 177
    Earlier sketches in SATA 20, 80
Pomeroy, Pete
    See Roth, Arthur J(oseph)
Pon, Cindy 1973- 216
Pon, Cynthia 229
Pond, Alonzo W(illiam) 1894-1986 5
Pontiflet, Ted 1932- 32
Poole, Gray Johnson 1906- 1
Poole, Josephine
    See Helyar, Jane Penelope Josephine
Poole, (Jane Penelope) Josephine
    See Helyar, Jane Penelope Josephine
Poole, Lynn 1910-1969 1
Poole, Peggy 1925- 39
Poon, Janice 228
Poortvliet, Rien 1932- 65
    Brief entry 37
Pope, Elizabeth Marie 1917-1992 38
    Brief entry 36
Pope, Kevin 1958- 183
Popescu, Christine
    See Pullein-Thompson, Christine
Poploff, Michelle 1956- 67
Popp, K. Wendy 91
Poppel, Hans 1942- 71
Porfirio, Guy 1958- 197
Portal, Colette 1936- 6
Porte, Barbara Ann 1943- 152
    Brief entry 45
    Earlier sketches in SATA 57, 93
Porter, A(nthony) P(eyton) 1945- 68
Porter, Connie (Rose) 1959(?)- 129
    Earlier sketch in SATA 81
Porter, Donald Clayton
    See Gerson, Noel Bertram
Porter, Eleanor H(odgman) 1868-1920
    See CLR 110
Porter, Gene Stratton
    See Stratton-Porter, Gene

Porter, Janice Lee 1953- 108
    Earlier sketch in SATA 68
Porter, Katherine Anne 1890-1980 39
    Obituary 23
Porter, Kathryn
    See Swinford, Betty (June Wells)
Porter, Pamela 1956- 193
Porter, Sheena 1935- 24
    See also SAAS 10
Porter, Sue
    See Limb, Sue
Porter, Sue 1951- 213
    Earlier sketch in SATA 76
Porter, Tracey 191
Porter, William Sydney
    See Henry, O.
Portis, Antoinette 189
Porto, Tony 1960- 153
Portteus, Eleanora Marie Manthei (?)-1983
    Obituary 36
Posada, Mia 187
Posell, Elsa Z(eigerman) -1995 3
Posesorski, Sherie 216
Posten, Margaret L(ois) 1915- 10
Postgate, Daniel 1964- 216
Posthuma, Sieb 1960- 150
Postier, Jim 1965- 202
Potok, Chaim 1929-2002 106
    Obituary 134
    Earlier sketch in SATA 33
    See also CLR 92
Potok, Herbert Harold
    See Potok, Chaim
Potok, Herman Harold
    See Potok, Chaim
Potter, Alicia 216
Potter, Beatrix 1866-1943 132
    Earlier sketch in SATA 100
    See also YABC 1
    See also CLR 165
Potter, Ellen 1973- 218
Potter, Giselle 187
    Earlier sketch in SATA 150
Potter, Helen Beatrix
    See Potter, Beatrix
Potter, Katherine 217
Potter, Margaret 1926-1998 21
    Obituary 104
Potter, Marian 1915- 9
Potter, Miriam Clark 1886-1965 3
Potter, Ryan 230
Poulin, Stephane 1961- 98
    See also CLR 28
Poulton, Kimberly 1957(?)- 136
Pournelle, Jerry 1933- 161
    Earlier sketches in SATA 26, 91
Pournelle, Jerry Eugene
    See Pournelle, Jerry
Povelite, Kay 1955- 102
Pow, Tom 1950- 163
Powe-Allred, Alexandra
    See Allred, Alexandra Powe
Powell, A. M.
    See Morgan, Alfred P(owell)
Powell, Consie 174
Powell, E. Sandy 1947- 72
Powell, E.S.
    See Powell, E. Sandy
Powell, Pamela 1960- 78
Powell, Patricia Hruby 1951- 136
Powell, Randy 1956- 118
Powell, Richard Stillman
    See Barbour, Ralph Henry
Powell, Robert (Stephenson Smyth) Baden
    See Baden-Powell, Robert (Stephenson Smyth)
Powell, Stephanie 1953- 93
Power, Margaret (M.) 1945- 125
    Earlier sketch in SATA 75
Powers, Anne
    See Schwartz, Anne Powers

Powers, Bill 1931- 52
    Brief entry 31
Powers, Daniel 1959- 164
Powers, J. L. 195
Powers, Jessica
    See Powers, J. L.
Powers, Jessica Lynn
    See Powers, J. L.
Powers, Margaret
    See Heal, Edith
Powers, Tim 1952- 107
Powers, Timothy Thomas
    See Powers, Tim
Powledge, Fred 1935- 37
Poydar, Nancy 190
Poynter, Margaret 1927- 27
Prachaticka, Marketa
    See Kolibalova, Marketa
Prachatika, Marketa
    See Kolibalova, Marketa
Prager, Arthur 44
Prager, Ellen J. 1962- 136
Prange, Beckie 172
Prap, Lila 1955- 177
Praprotnik-Zupancic, Lilijana
    See Prap, Lila
Pratchett, Terence David John
    See Pratchett, Terry
Pratchett, Terry 1948- 185
    Earlier sketches in SATA 82, 139
    See also CLR 64
Prater, John 1947- 149
    Earlier sketches in SATA 72, 103
Prato, Rodica 184
Pratt, Christine Joy 214
Pratt, (Murray) Fletcher 1897-1956 102
Pratt, Kristin Joy 1976- 87
Pratt, Pierre 1962- 208
    Earlier sketches in SATA 95, 166
Preiss, Byron 1953-2005 166
    Brief entry 42
    Earlier sketch in SATA 47
Preiss, Byron Cary
    See Preiss, Byron
Preller, James 1961- 209
    Earlier sketch in SATA 88
Prelutsky, Jack 1940- 171
    Earlier sketches in SATA 22, 66, 118
    See also CLR 115
Prentice, Amy
    See Kaler, James Otis
Prescott, Casey
    See Morris, Chris(topher Crosby)
Presnall, Judith (Ann) Janda 1943- 96
Pressler, Mirjam 1940- 155
Preston, Douglas 1956- 113
Preston, Edna Mitchell 40
Preston, Lillian Elvira 1918- 47
Preus, Margi 209
Preussler, Otfried 1923- 24
Prevert, Jacques 1900-1977
    Obituary 30
Prevert, Jacques Henri Marie
    See Prevert, Jacques
Prevost, Guillaume 1964- 192
Prevost, Mikela 203
Price, Beverley Joan 1931- 98
Price, Charlie 187
Price, Christine (Hilda) 1928-1980 3
    Obituary 23
Price, Garrett 1896-1979
    Obituary 22
Price, Jennifer
    See Hoover, Helen (Drusilla Blackburn)
Price, Joan 1931- 124
Price, Jonathan (Reeve) 1941- 46
Price, Karen 1957- 125
Price, Kathy Z. 1957- 172
Price, Lucie Locke
    See Locke, Lucie
Price, Olive 1903-1991 8

Price, Susan 1955- *128*
  Earlier sketches in SATA *25, 85*
Price, Willard 1887-1983 .... *48*
  Brief entry *38*
Price-Groff, Claire *127*
Priceman, Marjorie 1958- *168*
  Earlier sketches in SATA *81, 120*
Prichard, Katharine Susannah 1883-1969 ..... *66*
Priddy, Roger *227*
Prideaux, Tom 1908-1993 .... *37*
  Obituary *76*
Priestley, Alice 1962- *227*
  Earlier sketch in SATA *95*
Priestley, Chris 1958- *198*
Priestley, Lee (Shore) 1904-1999 .... *27*
Priestly, Doug 1954- *122*
Priestly, Douglas Michael
  See Priestly, Doug
Prieto, Mariana Beeching 1912-1999 .... *8*
Priley, Margaret (Ann) Hubbard 1909-1992
  Obituary *130*
Primavera, Elise 1954- *230*
  Brief entry *48*
  Earlier sketches in SATA *58, 109, 185*
Prime, Derek (James) 1931- *34*
Prince, Alison (Mary) 1931- *86*
  Earlier sketch in SATA *28*
Prince, April Jones 1975- *180*
Prince, J(ack) H(arvey) 1908- *17*
Prince, Joshua *188*
Prince, Maggie *102*
Prineas, Sarah *204*
Pringle, Eric *138*
Pringle, Laurence 1935- *201*
  Autobiography Feature *201*
  Earlier sketches in SATA *4, 68, 104, 154*
  See also CLR *57*
  See also SAAS *6*
Pringle, Laurence Patrick
  See Pringle, Laurence
Prinz, Yvonne 1960- *175*
Prior, Natalie Jane 1963- *106*
Pritchett, Elaine H(illyer) 1920- *36*
Pritchett, Laura 1971- *178*
Pritchett, Laura Rose
  See Pritchett, Laura
Pritts, Kim Derek 1953- *83*
Prochazkova, Iva 1953- *68*
Proctor, Everitt
  See Montgomery, Rutherford George
Proeysen, Alf 1914-1970 .... *67*
  See also CLR *24*
Professor Scribbler
  See Hollingsworth, Mary
Proimos, James 1955- *217*
  Earlier sketch in SATA *173*
Promitzer, Rebecca *229*
Prose, Francine 1947- *198*
  Earlier sketches in SATA *101, 149*
Prosek, James 1975- *216*
Protopopescu, Orel *186*
Protopopescu, Orel Odinov
  See Protopopescu, Orel
Provensen, Alice 1918- *147*
  Earlier sketches in SATA *9, 70*
  See also CLR *11*
Provensen, Martin 1916-1987 .... *70*
  Obituary *51*
  Earlier sketch in SATA *9*
  See also CLR *11*
Provensen, Martin Elias
  See Provensen, Martin
Provenzo, Eugene (F., Jr.) 1949- *142*
  Earlier sketch in SATA *78*
Provist, d'Alain 1906-1989
  See Diop, Birago (Ismael)
Provost, Gail Levine 1944- *65*
Provost, Gary (Richard) 1944-1995 .... *66*
Proysen, Alf
  See Proeysen, Alf
Pruett, Candace (J.) 1968- *157*

Pryor, Bonnie H. 1942- *69*
Pryor, Boori (Monty) 1950- *112*
Pryor, Helen Brenton 1897-1972 .... *4*
Pryor, Michael 1957- *153*
Pucci, Albert John 1920- *44*
Pudney, John (Sleigh) 1909-1977 .... *24*
Pugh, Ellen (Tiffany) 1920- *7*
Pullein-Thompson, Christine 1925-2005 ...... *82*
  Obituary *172*
  Earlier sketch in SATA *3*
Pullein-Thompson, Diana
  See Farr, Diana
Pullein-Thompson, Joanna Maxwell
  1898-1961 .... *82*
Pullein-Thompson, Josephine (Mary
  Wedderburn) *82*
  Earlier sketch in SATA *3*
Pullen, Zachary *189*
Pullman, Philip 1946- *198*
  Earlier sketches in SATA *65, 103, 150*
  See also CLR *84*
  See also SAAS *17*
Pullman, Philip Nicholas
  See Pullman, Philip
Pulver, Harry, Jr. 1960- *129*
Pulver, Robin 1945- *208*
  Earlier sketches in SATA *76, 133*
Puner, Helen W(alker) 1915-1989 .... *37*
  Obituary *63*
Purdy, Carol 1943- *120*
  Earlier sketch in SATA *66*
Purdy, Susan G(old) 1939- *8*
Purkiss, Diane 1961- *194*
Purmell, Ann 1953- *206*
  Earlier sketch in SATA *147*
Purnell, Idella 1901-1982 .... *120*
Purscell, Phyllis 1934- *7*
Purtill, Richard L. 1931- *53*
Purvis, Leland *232*
Pushker, Gloria 1927- *162*
  Earlier sketch in SATA *75*
Pushker, Gloria Teles
  See Pushker, Gloria
Pushkin, Aleksandr Sergeevich
  See Pushkin, Alexander
Pushkin, Alexander 1799-1837 .... *61*
Putnam, Alice 1916- *61*
Putnam, Arthur Lee
  See Alger, Horatio, Jr.
Putnam, Peter B(rock) 1920-1998 .... *30*
  Obituary *106*
Puttapipat, Niroot *199*
Puttock, Simon *178*
Puvilland, Alex *205*
Puvilland, Alexandre
  See Puvilland, Alex
Puybaret, Eric 1976- *299*
  Earlier sketch in SATA *195*
Pyle, Charles S. 1954(?)- *229*
Pyle, Chuck
  See Pyle, Charles S.
Pyle, Howard 1853-1911 .... *100*
  Earlier sketch in SATA *16*
  See also CLR *117*
Pyle, Katharine 1863-1938 .... *66*
Pyne, Mable Mandeville 1903-1969 .... *9*
Pyrnelle, Louise-Clarke 1850-1907 .... *114*

Q

Quackenbush, Robert M(ead) 1929- *133*
  Autobiography Feature *133*
  Earlier sketches in SATA *7, 70*
  See also CLR *122*
  See also SAAS *7*
Qualey, Marsha 1953- *124*
  Earlier sketch in SATA *79*
Qualls, Sean *233*
  Earlier sketch in SATA *177*

Quammen, David 1948- *7*
Quark, Jason
  See Eldin, Peter
Quarles, Benjamin 1904-1996 .... *12*
Quarles, Benjamin Arthur
  See Quarles, Benjamin
Quatermass, Martin
  See Carpenter, John
Quattlebaum, Mary 1958- *185*
  Earlier sketches in SATA *88, 134*
Quay, Emma *173*
  Earlier sketch in SATA *119*
Queen, Ellery
  See Deming, Richard
  and Dannay, Frederic
  and Davidson, Avram (James)
  and Fairman, Paul W.
  and Flora, Fletcher
  and Holding, James (Clark Carlisle, Jr.)
  and Hoch, Edward D.
  and Kane, Henry
  and Lee, Manfred B.
  and Marlowe, Stephen
  and Powell, (Oval) Talmage
  and Sheldon, Walter J(ames)
  and Sturgeon, Theodore (Hamilton)
  and Tracy, Don(ald Fiske)
  and Vance, Jack
Queen Latifah 1970- *185*
Quennell, Marjorie Courtney 1884-1972 ...... *29*
Quentin
  See Sheldon, David
Quentin, Brad
  See Bisson, Terry
Quest, (Edna) Olga W(ilbourne) Hall
  See Hall-Quest, (Edna) Olga W(ilbourne)
Quick, Annabelle 1922-1986 .... *2*
Quigg, Jane (Hulda) (?)-1986
  Obituary *49*
Quigley, Sarah 1976- *220*
Quill, Monica
  See McInerny, Ralph
Quin-Harkin, Janet 1941- *165*
  Earlier sketches in SATA *18, 90, 119*
Quin-Harkin, Janet Elizabeth
  See Quin-Harkin, Janet
Quinlan, Susan E. 1954- *88*
Quinlan, Susan Elizabeth
  See Quinlan, Susan E.
Quinn, Elisabeth 1881-1962 .... *22*
Quinn, Pat 1947- *130*
Quinn, Patrick 1950- *73*
Quinn, Rob 1972- *138*
Quinn, Spencer
  See Abrahams, Peter
Quinn, Susan 1940- *30*
Quinn, Susan Taft
  See Quinn, Susan
Quinn, Theodora K.
  See Kroeber, Theodora (Kracaw)
Quinn, Vernon
  See Quinn, Elisabeth
Quirk, Anne (E.) 1956- *99*
Quixley, Jim 1931- *56*
Quyth, Gabriel
  See Jennings, Gary

R

Ra, Carol F. 1939- *76*
Raab, Evelyn 1951- *129*
Rabb, Margo 1972- *188*
Rabb, M.E.
  See Rabb, Margo
Rabe, Berniece (Louise) 1928- *148*
  Autobiography Feature *148*
  Earlier sketches in SATA *7, 77*
  See also SAAS *10*
Rabe, Olive H(anson) (?)-1968 .... *13*

Rabin, Staton 1958- 162
  Earlier sketch in SATA 84
Rabinowich, Ellen 1946- 29
Rabinowitz, Sandy 1954- 52
  Brief entry 39
Rachlin, Carol K(ing) 1919- 64
Rachlin, Harvey 1951- 47
Rachlin, Harvey Brant
  See Rachlin, Harvey
Rachlin, Nahid 64
Rachlis, Eugene (Jacob) 1920-1986
  Obituary 50
Rackham, Arthur 1867-1939 100
  Earlier sketch in SATA 15
  See also CLR 57
Racoma, Robin Yoko 1953- 207
Raczka, Bob 1963- 228
  Earlier sketches in SATA 163, 191
Radencich, Marguerite C. 1952-1998 79
Rader, Laura 197
Radford, Ruby L(orraine) 1891-1971 6
Radin, Ruth Yaffe 1938- 107
  Brief entry 52
  Earlier sketch in SATA 56
Radlauer, David 1952- 28
Radlauer, Edward 1921- 15
Radlauer, Ruth Shaw 1926- 98
  Earlier sketch in SATA 15
Radley, Gail 1951- 112
  Earlier sketch in SATA 25
Radunsky, Vladimir 177
Radzinski, Kandy 1948- 212
Rae, Gwynedd 1892-1977 37
Raebeck, Lois 1921- 5
Rael, Elsa Okon 1927-
  See CLR 84
Raffi
  See Cavoukian, Raffi
Raftery, Gerald (Bransfield) 1905-1986 11
Ragan-Reid, Gale 1956- 90
Rahaman, Vashanti 1953- 98
Rahn, Joan Elma 1929- 27
Rai, Bali 1971- 152
Raible, Alton (Robert) 1918- 35
Raiff, Stan 1930- 11
Railsback, Lisa 230
Raines, Shirley C(arol) 1945- 128
Rainey, W. B.
  See Blassingame, Wyatt Rainey
Rake, Jody 1961- 157
Rallison, Janette 1966- 183
Ralston, Jan
  See Dunlop, Agnes M. R.
Rama, Sue 190
Ramal, Walter
  See de la Mare, Walter (John)
Ramanujan, A(ttipat) K(rishnaswami)
  1929-1993 86
Rame, David
  See Divine, Arthur Durham
Ramirez, Jose 1967- 198
Ramirez, Orlando L. 1972- 194
Ramos, Jorge 1958- 205
Ramstad, Ralph L. 1919- 115
Ramthun, Bonnie 214
Rana, Indi
  See Rana, Indira Higham
Rana, Indira Higham 1944- 82
Rana, J.
  See Bhatia, Jamunadevi
Ranadive, Gail 1944- 10
Rand, Ann (Binkley) 30
Rand, Gloria 1925- 156
  Earlier sketch in SATA 101
Rand, Paul 1914-1996 6
Randall, Carrie
  See Ransom, Candice
Randall, David 1972- 167
Randall, Florence Engel 1917-1997 5

Randall, Janet
  See Young, Janet Randall
  and Young, Robert W(illiam)
Randall, Robert
  See Garrett, Randall
  and Silverberg, Robert
Randall, Ruth (Elaine) Painter 1892-1971 3
Randell, Beverley
  See Price, Beverley Joan
Randle, Kristen D. 1952- 92
  Autobiography Feature 119
  See also SAAS 24
Randle, Kristen Downey
  See Randle, Kristen D.
Randolph, Boynton M.D.
  See Ellis, Edward S.
Randolph, Ellen
  See Rawn, Melanie
Randolph, Geoffrey
  See Ellis, Edward S.
Randolph, J. H.
  See Ellis, Edward S.
Randolph, Lieutenant J. H.
  See Ellis, Edward S.
Rands, William Brighty 1823-1882 17
Raney, Ken 1953- 74
Rania, Queen of Jordan 1970- 233
Rankin, Joan 1940- 212
  Earlier sketches in SATA 88, 148
Rankin, Laura 1953(?)- 176
Ranney, Agnes V. 1916-1985 6
Ransom, Candice 1952- 222
  Brief entry 49
  Earlier sketches in SATA 52, 89, 135, 183
Ransom, Jeanie Franz 1957- 187
Ransome, Arthur (Michell) 1884-1967 22
Ransome, James E. 1961- 227
  Earlier sketches in SATA 76, 123, 178
  See also CLR 86
Rant, Tol E.
  See Longyear, Barry B(rookes)
Rao, Rohitash 218
Raphael, Elaine
  See Bolognese, Elaine
Raposo, Joseph Guilherme 1938-1989
  Obituary 61
Rapp, Adam 1968- 148
Rappaport, Doreen 211
  Earlier sketch in SATA 151
Rappaport, Eva 1924- 6
Rappoport, Ken 1935- 167
  Earlier sketch in SATA 89
Rarick, Carrie 1911-2002 41
Raschka, Chris 1959- 207
  Earlier sketches in SATA 80, 117, 166
Raschka, Christopher
  See Raschka, Chris
Rascol, Sabina I. 159
Rash, Andy 219
  Earlier sketch in SATA 162
Raskin, Edith Lefkowitz 1908-1987 9
Raskin, Ellen 1928-1984 139
  Earlier sketches in SATA 2, 38
  See also CLR 12
Raskin, Joseph 1897-1982 12
  Obituary 29
Rathjen, Carl Henry 1909-1984 11
Rathmann, Peggy 1953- 157
  Earlier sketch in SATA 94
  See also CLR 77
Ratliff, Thomas M. 1948- 118
Ratner, Sue Lynn
  See Alexander, Sue
Rattigan, Jama Kim 1951- 99
Ratto, Linda Lee 1952- 79
Rattray, Simon
  See Trevor, Elleston
Ratz de Tagyos, Paul 1958- 198
  Earlier sketch in SATA 76

Rau, Dana Meachen 1971- 218
  Earlier sketches in SATA 94, 167
Rau, Margaret 1913- 168
  Earlier sketch in SATA 9
  See also CLR 8
Rauch, Mabel Thompson 1888-1972
  Obituary 26
Raucher, Herman 1928- 8
Raude, Karina 199
Rauh, Sherry
  See North, Sherry
Raum, Elizabeth 1949- 155
Raut, Radhashyam 222
Rave, Friederike 1970- 231
Raven, Margot Theis 184
RavenWolf, Silver 1956- 155
Ravielli, Anthony 1916-1997 3
  Obituary 95
Ravilious, Robin 1944- 77
Ravishankar, Anushka 1961- 200
Rawding, F(rederick) W(illiam) 1930- 55
Rawlings, Marjorie Kinnan 1896-1953 100
  See also YABC 1
  See also CLR 63
Rawlins, Donna 1956- 206
Rawlinson, Julia 212
  Earlier sketch in SATA 175
Rawls, (Woodrow) Wilson 1913-1984 22
  See also CLR 81
Rawlyk, George Alexander 1935- 64
Rawn, Melanie 1954- 98
Rawn, Melanie Robin
  See Rawn, Melanie
Rawson, Katherine 1955- 190
Ray, Carl 1943-1978 63
Ray, Deborah
  See Kogan Ray, Deborah
Ray, Delia 1963- 179
  Earlier sketch in SATA 70
Ray, Irene
  See Sutton, Margaret Beebe
Ray, Jane 1960- 196
  Earlier sketches in SATA 72, 152
Ray, JoAnne 1935- 9
Ray, Mary (Eva Pedder) 1932- 127
  Earlier sketch in SATA 2
Ray, Mary Lyn 1946- 154
  Earlier sketch in SATA 90
Rayban, Chloe 1944- 167
Rayevsky, Robert 1955- 190
  Earlier sketch in SATA 81
Raymond, James Crossley 1917-1981
  Obituary 29
Raymond, Robert
  See Alter, Robert Edmond
Rayner, Catherine 204
Rayner, Hugh 151
Rayner, Mary 1933- 87
  Earlier sketch in SATA 22
  See also CLR 41
Rayner, Shoo
  See Rayner, Hugh
Rayner, William 1929- 55
  Brief entry 36
Raynor, Dorka 28
Raynor, Gemma 1985- 216
Rayson, Steven 1932- 30
Rayyan, Omar 1968- 216
Razzell, Arthur (George) 1925- 11
Razzell, Mary (Catherine) 1930- 102
Razzi, James 1931- 10
Read, Elfreida 1920- 2
Read, Nicholas 1956- 146
Read, Piers Paul 1941- 21
Reade, Deborah 1949- 69
Reader, Dennis 1929- 71
Reading, Richard P(atrick) 1962- 161
Readman, Jo 1958- 89
Ready, Kirk L(ewis) 1943- 39
Reaney, James 1926-2008 43

Reaney, James Crerar
    See Reaney, James
Reardon, Joyce
    See Pearson, Ridley
Reaver, Chap 1935-1993 69
    Obituary 77
Reaver, Herbert R.
    See Reaver, Chap
Reaves, J. Michael
    See Reaves, (James) Michael
Reaves, (James) Michael 1950- 99
Reber, Deborah 189
Recorvits, Helen 191
Redding, Robert Hull 1919- 2
Redekopp, Elsa 61
Redlich, Ben 1977- 181
Redsand, Anna 1948- 184
Redway, Ralph
    See Hamilton, Charles (Harold St. John)
Redway, Ridley
    See Hamilton, Charles (Harold St. John)
Reece, Colleen L. 1935- 116
Reece, Gabrielle 1970- 108
Reed, Amy 1979- 223
Reed, Betty Jane 1921- 4
Reed, Dallas
    See Pendleton, Thomas
Reed, E.
    See Evans, Mari
Reed, Gwendolyn E(lizabeth) 1932- 21
Reed, Kit 1932- 184
    Autobiography Feature 184
    Earlier sketches in SATA *34, 116*
Reed, Lynn Rowe 215
    Earlier sketch in SATA *171*
Reed, Mike 1951- 211
Reed, Neil 1961- 99
Reed, Talbot Baines 1852-1893
    See CLR 76
Reed, Thomas (James) 1947- 34
Reed, William Maxwell 1871-1962 15
Reeder, Carolyn 1937- 97
    Earlier sketch in SATA *66*
    See also CLR 69
Reeder, Colin (Dawson) 1938- 74
Reeder, Colonel Red
    See Reeder, Russell P(otter), Jr.
Reeder, Russell P(otter), Jr. 1902-1998 4
    Obituary 101
Reeder, Stephanie Owen 1951- 102
Reed-Jones, Carol 1955- 112
Reef, Catherine 1951- 223
    Earlier sketches in SATA *73, 128, 189*
Reekie, Jocelyn (Margaret) 1947- 145
Reeman, Douglas Edward 1924- 63
    Brief entry 28
Rees, Celia 1949- 124
Rees, David (Bartlett) 1936-1993 69
    Obituary 76
    Earlier sketch in SATA *36*
    See also SAAS 5
Rees, Douglas 1947- 169
Rees, Ennis (Samuel, Jr.) 1925-2009 3
Rees, (George) Leslie (Clarence)
    1905-2000 105
    Obituary 135
Reese, Bob
    See Reese, Robert A.
Reese, Carolyn Johnson 1938- 64
Reese, Della 1931(?)- 114
Reese, Lyn
    See Reese, Carolyn Johnson
Reese, Robert A. 1938- 60
    Brief entry 53
Reese, (John) Terence 1913-1996 59
Reeve, Joel
    See Cox, William R(obert)
Reeve, Kirk 1934- 117
Reeve, Philip 1966- 201
    Earlier sketch in SATA *170*

Reeve, Rosie 188
    Earlier sketch in SATA *186*
Reeves, Dia 1977- 227
Reeves, Faye Couch 1953- 76
Reeves, James
    See Reeves, John Morris
Reeves, Jeni 1947- 111
Reeves, John Morris 1909-1978 87
    Earlier sketch in SATA *15*
Reeves, Joyce 1911- 17
Reeves, Lawrence F. 1926- 29
Reeves, Ruth Ellen
    See Ranney, Agnes V.
Regan, Dian Curtis 1950- 224
    Autobiography Feature 149
    Earlier sketches in SATA *75, 133, 149*
Regehr, Lydia 1903-1991 37
Reger, James P. 1952- 106
Reger, Rob 1969- 227
Reggiani, Renee 1925- 18
Rehm, Karl M. 1935- 72
Reibstein, Mark 211
Reich, Ali
    See Katz, Bobbi
Reich, Susanna 1954- 214
    Earlier sketch in SATA *113*
Reiche, Dietlof 1941- 159
Reichert, Edwin C(lark) 1909-1988
    Obituary 57
Reichert, Mickey Zucker
    See Reichert, Miriam Zucker
Reichert, Miriam Zucker 1962- 85
Reichert, Renee 172
Reichhold, Jane(t E.) 1937- 147
Reid, Alastair 1926- 46
Reid, Barbara 1922- 21
Reid, Barbara (Jane) 1957- 93
    See also CLR 64
Reid, Desmond
    See Moorcock, Michael
    and McNeilly, Wilfred (Glassford)
Reid, Eugenie Chazal 1924- 12
Reid, John Calvin 21
Reid, (Thomas) Mayne 1818-1883 24
Reid, Meta Mayne 1905-1991 58
    Brief entry 36
Reid, Robin (Nicole) 1969- 145
Reid Banks, Lynne 1929- 165
    Earlier sketches in SATA *22, 75, 111*
    See also CLR 86
Reider, Katja 1960- 126
Reid Jenkins, Debra 1955- 87
Reidy, Jean 228
Reiff, Stephanie Ann 1948- 47
    Brief entry 28
Reig, June 1933- 30
Reigot, Betty Polisar 1924- 55
    Brief entry 41
Reilly, Joan 195
Reim, Melanie (K.) 1956- 104
Reinach, Jacquelyn (Krasne) 1930-2000 28
Reiner, Carl 1922- 151
Reiner, William B(uck) 1910-1976 46
    Obituary 30
Reinfeld, Fred 1910-1964 3
Reinhardt, Dana 1971- 175
Reinhart, Matthew 1971- 197
    Earlier sketch in SATA *161*
Reiniger, Lotte 1899-1981 40
    Obituary 33
Reinsma, Carol 1949- 91
Reinstedt, Randall A. 1935- 101
Reinstedt, Randy
    See Reinstedt, Randall A.
Reisberg, Mira 1955- 82
Reisberg, Veg
    See Reisberg, Mira
Reiser, Lynn 1944- 180
    Earlier sketches in SATA *81, 138*
Reiser, Lynn Whisnant
    See Reiser, Lynn

Reisgies, Teresa (Maria) 1966- 74
Reiss, Johanna 1929(?)- 18
    See also CLR 19
Reiss, Johanna de Leeuw
    See Reiss, Johanna
Reiss, John J. 23
Reiss, Kathryn 1957- 144
    Earlier sketch in SATA *76*
Reit, Seymour Victory 1918-2001 21
    Obituary 133
Reit, Sy
    See Reit, Seymour Victory
Relf, Patricia 1954- 134
    Earlier sketch in SATA *71*
Remark, Erich Paul
    See Remarque, Erich Maria
Remarque, Erich Maria 1898-1970
    See CLR 159
Remi, Georges 1907-1983 13
    Obituary 32
    See also CLR 114
Remington, Frederic S(ackrider)
    1861-1909 41
Remkiewicz, Frank 1939- 217
    Earlier sketches in SATA *77, 152*
Rempt, Fiona 1973- 198
Remy, Georges
    See Remi, Georges
Renaud, Anne 1957- 211
Renaud, Bernadette 1945- 66
Renault, Mary 1905-1983 23
    Obituary 36
Rendell, Joan 28
Rendina, Laura (Jones) Cooper 1902- 10
Rendon, Marcie R. 1952- 97
Rendon, Maria 1965- 116
Renee, Janina 1956- 140
Renfro, Ed 1924- 79
Renick, Marion (Lewis) 1905-1983 1
Renier, Aaron 1977- 202
Renken, Aleda 1907- 27
Renlie, Frank H. 1936- 11
Rennert, Laura Joy 224
Rennert, Richard Scott 1956- 67
Rennison, Louise 1951- 149
Reno, Dawn E(laine) 1953- 130
Rensie, Willis
    See Eisner, Will
Renton, Cam
    See Armstrong, Richard
Renvoize, Jean 5
Resau, Laura 1973- 230
    Earlier sketch in SATA *190*
Resciniti, Angelo G. 1952- 75
Resnick, Michael David
    See Resnick, Mike
Resnick, Mike 1942- 159
    Earlier sketches in SATA *38, 106*
Resnick, Seymour 1920- 23
Retla, Robert
    See Alter, Robert Edmond
Rettig, Liz 199
Rettstatt, Chris
    See Ashland, Monk
Reuter, Bjarne (B.) 1950- 142
    Earlier sketch in SATA *68*
Reuter, Carol (Joan) 1931- 2
Revena
    See Wright, Betty Ren
Revsbech, Vicki
    See Liestman, Vicki
Rex, Adam 1973- 225
    Earlier sketch in SATA *186*
Rex, Michael 191
Rey, H. A. 1898-1977 100
    Earlier sketches in SATA *1, 26, 69*
    See also CLR 93
Rey, Hans Augusto
    See Rey, H. A.
Rey, Luis V. 1955- 201

Rey, Margret 1906-1996 86
  Obituary 93
  Earlier sketch in SATA 26
  See also CLR 93
Rey, Margret Elisabeth
  See Rey, Margret
Reyher, Becky
  See Reyher, Rebecca Hourwich
Reyher, Rebecca Hourwich 1897-1987 18
  Obituary 50
Reynish, Jenny 222
Reynold, Ann
  See Bernardo, Anilu
Reynolds, Aaron 1970- 197
Reynolds, Adrian 1963- 192
Reynolds, C. Buck 1957- 107
Reynolds, Dickson
  See Reynolds, Helen Mary Greenwood Campbell
Reynolds, Helen Mary Greenwood Campbell
    1884-1969
  Obituary 26
Reynolds, Jan 1956- 180
Reynolds, John
  See Whitlock, Ralph
Reynolds, Madge
  See Whitlock, Ralph
Reynolds, Malvina 1900-1978 44
  Obituary 24
Reynolds, Marilyn 1935- 121
  See also SAAS 23
Reynolds, Marilyn M.
  See Reynolds, Marilyn
Reynolds, Marilynn 1940- 141
  Earlier sketch in SATA 80
Reynolds, Pamela 1923- 34
Reynolds, Peter H. 1961- 226
  Earlier sketch in SATA 128
Reynolds, Peter J. 1961- 179
Reynolds, Susan 179
Rhine, Richard
  See Silverstein, Alvin
  and Silverstein, Virginia B.
Rhoades, Diane 1952- 90
Rhodes, Bennie (Loran) 1927- 35
Rhodes, Donna McKee 1962- 87
Rhodes, Frank Harold Trevor 1926- 37
Rhuday-Perkovich, Olugbemisola 227
Rhue, Morton
  See Strasser, Todd
Rhyne, Nancy 1926- 66
Rhynes, Martha E. 1939- 141
Ribbons, Ian 1924- 37
  Brief entry 30
  See also SAAS 3
Ricciuti, Edward R(aphael) 1938- 10
Rice, Alice (Caldwell) Hegan 1870-1942 63
Rice, Bebe Faas 1932- 89
Rice, Charles D(uane) 1910-1971
  Obituary 27
Rice, Dale R. 1948- 42
Rice, Dale Richard
  See Rice, Dale R.
Rice, Dick
  See Rice, R. Hugh
Rice, Earle (Wilmont), Jr. 1928- 151
  Earlier sketch in SATA 92
Rice, Edward 1918-2001 47
  Brief entry 42
Rice, Elizabeth 1913-1976 2
Rice, Eve 1951- 91
  Earlier sketch in SATA 34
Rice, Eve Hart
  See Rice, Eve
Rice, Inez 1907- 13
Rice, James 1934- 93
  Earlier sketch in SATA 22
Rice, John F. 1958- 82
Rice, R. Hugh 1929- 115
Rice, Richard H.
  See Rice, R. Hugh

Rich, Anna 1956- 212
Rich, Barbara
  See Graves, Robert
Rich, Elaine Sommers 1926- 6
Rich, Josephine Bouchard 1912- 10
Rich, Louise Dickinson 1903-1991 54
  Obituary 67
Rich, Naomi 217
Richard, Adrienne 1921- 5
  See also SAAS 9
Richard, James Robert
  See Bowen, Robert Sydney
Richards, Chuck 1957- 170
Richards, Frank
  See Hamilton, Charles (Harold St. John)
Richards, Hilda
  See Hamilton, Charles (Harold St. John)
Richards, Jackie 1925- 102
Richards, Jame 230
Richards, Jean 1940- 135
Richards, Justin 169
Richards, Kay
  See Baker, Susan (Catherine)
Richards, Laura E(lizabeth Howe) 1850-1943
  See YABC 1
  See also CLR 54
Richards, Leigh
  See King, Laurie R.
Richards, Marlee
  See Brill, Marlene Targ
Richards, Norman 1932- 48
Richards, R(onald) C(harles) W(illiam)
    1923- 59
  Brief entry 43
Richards, Walter Alden (Jr.) 1907-1988
  Obituary 56
Richardson, Andrew (William) 1986- 120
Richardson, Carol 1932- 58
Richardson, Frank Howard 1882-1970
  Obituary 27
Richardson, Grace Lee
  See Dickson, Naida
Richardson, Jean (Mary) 59
Richardson, Judith Benet 1941- 77
Richardson, Nigel 1957- 187
Richardson, Robert S(hirley) 1902-1981 8
Richardson, Sandy 1949- 116
Richardson, V.A. 189
Richardson, Willis 1889-1977 60
Richelson, Geraldine 1922- 29
Richemont, Enid 1940- 82
Richler, Mordecai 1931-2001 98
  Brief entry 27
  Earlier sketch in SATA 44
  See also CLR 17
Richman, Sophia 1941- 142
Rich-McCoy, Lois
  See McCoy, Lois (Rich)
Richmond, Robin 1951- 75
Richoux, Pat(ricia) 1927- 7
Richter, Alice 1941- 30
Richter, Conrad (Michael) 1890-1968 3
Richter, Hans Peter 1925-1993 6
  See also CLR 21
  See also SAAS 11
Richter, Jutta 1955- 184
Rickard, Graham 1949- 71
Rico, Don(ato) 1917-1985
  Obituary 43
Riddell, Chris 1962- 219
  Earlier sketches in SATA 114, 166
Riddell, Christopher Barry
  See Riddell, Chris
Riddell, Edwina 1955- 82
Ridden, Brian 1934- 123
  See Ridden, Brian John
Riddle, Tohby 1965- 223
  Earlier sketches in SATA 74, 151
Riddleburger, Sam 202
Riddles, Libby 1956- 140
Ride, Sally 1951- 219

Ride, Sally Kristen
  See Ride, Sally
Rideout, Sandy 194
Rider, D. F.
  See Perrin, Pat
Rider, David F.
  See Perrin, Pat
Ridge, Antonia (Florence) (?)-1981 7
  Obituary 27
Ridge, Martin 1923-2003 43
Ridley, Philip 171
  Earlier sketch in SATA 88
Ridlon, Marci
  See Balterman, Marcia Ridlon
Riedman, Sarah R(egal) 1902-1995 1
Riehecky, Janet 1953- 164
Ries, Lori 185
Riesenberg, Felix, Jr. 1913-1962 23
Rieu, E(mile) V(ictor) 1887-1972 46
  Obituary 26
Riffenburgh, Beau 1955- 175
Rigg, Sharon
  See Creech, Sharon
Riggenbach, Holly
  See Black, Holly
Riggio, Anita 1952- 148
  Earlier sketch in SATA 73
Riggs, Shannon 190
Riggs, Sidney Noyes 1892-1975
  Obituary 28
Riggs, Stephanie 1964- 138
Riglietti, Serena 1969- 189
Rigney, James Oliver, Jr.
  See Jordan, Robert
Rikhoff, Jean 1928- 9
Rikki
  See Ducornet, Erica
Riley, James A. 1939- 97
Riley, James Whitcomb 1849-1916 17
Riley, Jocelyn 1949- 60
  Brief entry 50
Riley, Jocelyn Carol
  See Riley, Jocelyn
Riley, Linda Capus 1950- 85
Riley, Martin 1948- 81
Rim, Sujean 225
Rimbauer, Steven
  See Pearson, Ridley
Rimes, (Margaret) LeAnn 1982- 154
Rinaldi, Ann 1934- 202
  Brief entry 50
  Earlier sketches in SATA 51, 78, 117, 161
  See also CLR 46
Rinard, Judith E(llen) 1947- 140
  Earlier sketch in SATA 44
Rinck, Maranke 1976- 214
Rinder, Lenore 1949- 92
Ring, Elizabeth 1920- 79
Ringdalh, Mark
  See Longyear, Barry B(rookes)
Ringgold, Faith 1930- 187
  Earlier sketches in SATA 71, 114
  See also CLR 30
Ringi, Kjell (Arne Soerensen) 1939- 12
Rinkoff, Barbara Jean (Rich) 1923-1975 4
  Obituary 27
Rinn, Miriam 1946- 127
Riordan, James 1936- 95
Riordan, Rick 208
  Earlier sketch in SATA 174
Rios, Tere
  See Versace, Marie Teresa Rios
Rioux, Jo 226
Rioux, Jo-Anne
  See Rioux, Jo
Ripken, Cal, Jr. 1960- 215
  Earlier sketch in SATA 114
Ripken, Calvin Edward, Jr.
  See Ripken, Cal, Jr.
Ripley, Catherine 1957- 82
Ripley, Elizabeth Blake 1906-1969 5

Ripper, Charles L(ewis) 1929- 3
Ripper, Chuck
  See Ripper, Charles L(ewis)
Rippin, Sally 220
Riq
  See Atwater, Richard
Rish, David 1955- 110
Riskind, Mary 1944- 60
Rissinger, Matt 1956- 93
Rissman, Art
  See Sussman, Susan
Rissman, Susan
  See Sussman, Susan
Ritchie, Barbara Gibbons 14
Ritchie, Scot 1954- 217
Ritter, Felix
  See Kruss, James
Ritter, John H. 1951- 215
  Earlier sketches in SATA *129, 137*
Ritter, Lawrence S(tanley) 1922-2004 58
  Obituary 152
Ritthaler, Shelly 1955- 91
Ritts, Paul 1920(?)-1980
  Obituary 25
Ritz, Karen 1957- 202
  Earlier sketch in SATA *80*
Riu, Isabel Ferrer 1969- 222
Rivera, Geraldo (Miguel) 1943- 54
  Brief entry 28
Rivera, Guadalupe
  See Rivera Marin, Guadalupe
Rivera Marin, Guadalupe 1924- 224
Rivers, Elfrida
  See Bradley, Marion Zimmer
Rivers, Karen 1970- 131
Riverside, John
  See Heinlein, Robert A.
Rivkin, Ann 1920- 41
Rivoli, Mario 1943- 10
Roach, Marilynne K. 1946- 9
Roach, Marilynne Kathleen
  See Roach, Marilynne K.
Roach, Portia
  See Takakjian, Portia
Robb, Don 1937- 194
Robb, Laura 1937- 95
Robberecht, Thierry 1960- 182
Robbins, Frank 1917-1994(?) 42
  Brief entry 32
Robbins, Jacqui 221
Robbins, Ken 1945- 219
  Brief entry 53
  Earlier sketches in SATA *94, 147*
Robbins, Raleigh
  See Hamilton, Charles (Harold St. John)
Robbins, Ruth 1917(?)- 14
Robbins, Tony
  See Pashko, Stanley
Robbins, Wayne
  See Cox, William R(obert)
Robel, S. L.
  See Fraustino, Lisa Rowe
Roberson, Jennifer 1953- 72
Roberson, John R(oyster) 1930- 53
Robert, Adrian
  See St. John, Nicole
Roberton, Fiona 230
Roberts, Bethany 202
  Earlier sketch in SATA *133*
Roberts, Bruce (Stuart) 1930- 47
  Brief entry 39
Roberts, Charles G(eorge) D(ouglas)
  1860-1943 88
  Brief entry 29
  See also CLR *33*
Roberts, David
  See Cox, John Roberts
Roberts, David 1970- 191
Roberts, Diane 1937- 184
Roberts, Elizabeth 1944- 80

Roberts, Elizabeth Madox 1886-1941 33
  Brief entry 27
  See also CLR *100*
Roberts, Jim
  See Bates, Barbara S(nedeker)
Roberts, Jody 218
Roberts, John G(aither) 1913-1993 27
Roberts, Judy I. 1957- 93
Roberts, Katherine 1962- 152
Roberts, Ken 223
  See Lake, Kenneth R(obert)
Roberts, Laura Peyton 232
Roberts, M. L.
  See Mattern, Joanne
Roberts, Marion 1966- 212
Roberts, Nancy Correll 1924- 52
  Brief entry 28
Roberts, Priscilla 1955- 184
Roberts, Terence
  See Sanderson, Ivan T(erence)
Roberts, Willo Davis 1928-2004 150
  Autobiography Feature 150
  Obituary 160
  Earlier sketches in SATA *21, 70, 133*
  See also CLR *95*
  See also SAAS *8*
Robertson, Barbara (Anne) 1931- 12
Robertson, Don 1929-1999 8
  Obituary 113
Robertson, Dorothy Lewis 1912- 12
Robertson, Ellis
  See Ellison, Harlan
  and Silverberg, Robert
Robertson, James I., Jr. 1930- 182
Robertson, James Irvin
  See Robertson, James I., Jr.
Robertson, Janet (E.) 1935- 68
Robertson, Jennifer Sinclair 1942-1998 12
Robertson, Jenny
  See Robertson, Jennifer Sinclair
Robertson, Keith (Carlton) 1914-1991 85
  Obituary 69
  Earlier sketch in SATA *1*
  See also SAAS *15*
Robertson, Mark
  See Robertson, M.P.
Robertson, M.P. 1965- 197
Robertson, Stephen
  See Walker, Robert W.
Robertus, Polly M. 1948- 212
  Earlier sketch in SATA *73*
Robeson, Kenneth
  See Dent, Lester
  and Goulart, Ron
Robeson, Kenneth
  See Johnson, (Walter) Ryerson
Robinet, Harriette Gillem 1931- 104
  Earlier sketch in SATA *27*
  See also CLR *64*
Robins, Deri 1958- 166
  Earlier sketch in SATA *117*
Robins, Patricia 1921- 117
Robins, Rollo, Jr.
  See Ellis, Edward S.
Robins, Seelin
  See Ellis, Edward S.
Robinson, Adjai 1932- 8
Robinson, Aminah Brenda Lynn 1940- 159
  Earlier sketch in SATA *77*
Robinson, Barbara (Webb) 1927- 84
  Earlier sketch in SATA *8*
Robinson, C(harles) A(lexander), Jr.
  1900-1965 36
Robinson, Charles 1870-1937 17
Robinson, Charles 1931- 6
Robinson, Dorothy W. 1929- 54
Robinson, Elizabeth Keeler 1959- 204
Robinson, Eve
  See Tanselle, Eve
Robinson, Fiona 1965- 225
Robinson, Glen 1953- 92

Robinson, Glendal P.
  See Robinson, Glen
Robinson, Jan M. 1933- 6
Robinson, Jean O. 1934- 7
Robinson, Joan (Mary) G(ale Thomas)
  1910-1988 7
Robinson, Kim Stanley 1952- 109
Robinson, Lee 1948- 110
Robinson, Lloyd
  See Silverberg, Robert
Robinson, Lynda S(uzanne) 1951- 107
Robinson, Marileta 1942- 32
Robinson, Maudie Millian Oller 1914- 11
Robinson, Maurice R(ichard) 1895-1982
  Obituary 29
Robinson, Nancy K(onheim) 1942-1994 91
  Brief entry 31
  Obituary 79
  Earlier sketch in SATA *32*
Robinson, Ray 1920- 23
Robinson, Raymond Kenneth
  See Robinson, Ray
Robinson, Shari
  See McGuire, Leslie (Sarah)
Robinson, Sharon 1950- 197
  Earlier sketch in SATA *162*
Robinson, Spider 1948- 118
Robinson, Sue
  See Robinson, Susan Maria
Robinson, Susan Maria 1955- 105
Robinson, Susan Patricia
  See Gates, Susan
Robinson, Suzanne
  See Robinson, Lynda S(uzanne)
Robinson, T(homas) H(eath) 1869-1950 17
Robinson, Tim 1963- 205
Robinson, (Wanda) Veronica 1926- 30
Robinson, W(illiam) Heath 1872-1944 17
Robison, Bonnie 1924- 12
Robison, Nancy L(ouise) 1934- 32
Robles, Harold E. 1948- 87
Robottom, John 1934- 7
Robson, Eric 1939- 82
Roca, Francois 1971- 200
Rocco, John 1967- 188
Roche, A. K.
  See Abisch, Roslyn Kroop
  and Kaplan, Boche
Roche, Denis 1967- 196
  Earlier sketch in SATA *99*
Roche, Denis Mary
  See Roche, Denis
Roche, Luane 1937- 170
Roche, P(atricia) K. 1935- 57
  Brief entry 34
Roche, Terry
  See Poole, Peggy
Rochman, Hazel 1938- 105
Rock, Lois
  See Joslin, Mary
Rock, Maxine 1940- 108
Rocker, Fermin 1907- 40
Rockliff, Mara 224
Rocklin, Joanne 1946- 134
  Earlier sketch in SATA *86*
Rockwell, Anne F. 1934- 194
  Earlier sketches in SATA *33, 71, 114, 162*
  See also SAAS *19*
Rockwell, Anne Foote
  See Rockwell, Anne F.
Rockwell, Bart
  See Pellowski, Michael (Joseph)
Rockwell, Harlow 1910-1988 33
  Obituary 56
Rockwell, Lizzy 1961- 233
  Earlier sketch in SATA *185*
Rockwell, Norman (Percevel) 1894-1978 23
Rockwell, Thomas 1933- 231
  Earlier sketches in SATA *7, 70*
  See also CLR *6*
Rockwood, Joyce 1947- 39

Rockwood, Roy
    See McFarlane, Leslie
    and Stratemeyer, Edward L.
Rodanas, Kristina 1952- *155*
Rodari, Gianni 1920-1980
    See CLR 24
Rodd, Kathleen Tennant
    See Rodd, Kylie Tennant
Rodd, Kylie Tennant 1912-1988 .... *57*
    Obituary *55*
    Earlier sketch in SATA 6
Rodda, Emily 1948- *230*
    Earlier sketches in SATA *97, 146*
    See also CLR 32
Roddenberry, Eugene Wesley 1921-1991 ..... *45*
    Obituary *69*
Roddenberry, Gene
    See Roddenberry, Eugene Wesley
Roddick, Ellen 1936- *5*
Roddie, Shen *153*
Roddy, Lee 1921- *57*
Rodenas, Paula *73*
Rodgers, Frank 1944- *69*
Rodgers, Mary 1931- *130*
    Earlier sketch in SATA 8
    See also CLR 20
Rodman, Emerson
    See Ellis, Edward S.
Rodman, Eric
    See Silverberg, Robert
Rodman, Maia
    See Wojciechowska, Maia (Teresa)
Rodman, Mary Ann *185*
Rodman, (Cary) Selden 1909-2002 .... *9*
Rodowsky, Colby 1932- *164*
    Earlier sketches in SATA *21, 77, 120*
    See also SAAS 22
Rodowsky, Colby F.
    See Rodowsky, Colby
Rodriguez, Alejo 1941- *83*
Rodriguez, Alex 1975- *189*
Rodriguez, Beatrice 1969- *230*
Rodriguez, Christina 1981- *177*
Rodriguez, Edel 1971- *196*
Rodriguez, Luis J. 1954- *125*
Rodriguez, Rachel *180*
Rodriguez, Rachel Victoria
    See Rodriguez, Rachel
Roeder, Virginia Marsh 1926- *98*
Roehrig, Catharine H. 1949- *67*
Roennfeldt, Robert 1953- *78*
Roessel-Waugh, C. C.
    See Waugh, Carol-Lynn Rossel
    and Waugh, Charles G(ordon)
Roets, Lois F. 1937- *91*
Roever, J(oan) M(arilyn) 1935- *26*
Rofes, Eric 1954-2006 .... *52*
Rofes, Eric Edward 1954-2006
    See Rofes, Eric
Roffey, Maureen 1936- *33*
Rogak, Lisa 1962- *80*
Rogak, Lisa Angowski
    See Rogak, Lisa
Rogan, S. Jones *199*
Rogan, Sally Jones
    See Rogan, S. Jones
Rogasky, Barbara 1933- *144*
    Earlier sketch in SATA 86
Roge 1972- *233*
Rogers, (Thomas) Alan (Stinchcombe)
    1937- *81*
    Earlier sketch in SATA 2
Rogers, Bettye 1858-1919 .... *103*
Rogers, Cindy 1950- *89*
Rogers, Emma 1951- *74*
Rogers, Frances 1888-1974 .... *10*
Rogers, Fred McFeely 1928-2003 .... *33*
    Obituary *138*
Rogers, Gregory 1957- *211*
Rogers, Hal
    See Sirimarco, Elizabeth

Rogers, Jacqueline 1958- *213*
Rogers, Jean 1919- *55*
    Brief entry *47*
Rogers, Matilda 1894-1976 .... *5*
    Obituary *34*
Rogers, Pamela 1927- *9*
Rogers, Paul 1950- *98*
    Earlier sketch in SATA *54*
Rogers, Robert
    See Hamilton, Charles (Harold St. John)
Rogers, Sherry *193*
Rogers, W(illiam) G(arland) 1896-1978 .... *23*
Rohan, M. S.
    See Rohan, Michael Scott
Rohan, Michael Scott 1951- *98*
Rohan, Mike Scott
    See Rohan, Michael Scott
Rohmann, Eric 1957- *171*
    See also CLR 100
Rohmer, Harriet 1938- *56*
Rohrer, Doug 1962- *89*
Rojan
    See Rojankovsky, Feodor (Stepanovich)
Rojankovsky, Feodor (Stepanovich)
    1891-1970 .... *21*
Rojany, Lisa *94*
Rokeby-Thomas, Anna E(lma) 1911- *15*
Roland, Albert 1925-2002 .... *11*
Roland, Mary
    See Lewis, Mary
Roleff, Tamara L. 1959- *143*
Rolerson, Darrell A(llen) 1946- *8*
Roll, Winifred 1909-1998 .... *6*
Rollins, Charlemae Hill 1897-1979 .... *3*
    Obituary *26*
Rollins, James 1961- *216*
Rollock, Barbara T(herese) 1924- *64*
Rolston, Steve 1978- *209*
Romack, Janice Reed
    See LeNoir, Janice
Romain, Trevor *134*
Romanenko, Vitaliy 1962- *101*
Romano, Christy
    See Romano, Christy Carlson
Romano, Christy Carlson 1984- *210*
Romano, Clare 1922- *111*
    Earlier sketch in SATA *48*
Romano, Louis G. 1921- *35*
Romano, Melora A. 1966- *118*
Romano, Ray 1957- *170*
Romano, Raymond
    See Romano, Ray
Romijn, Johanna Maria Kooyker
    See Kooyker-Romijn, Johanna Maria
Romyn, Johanna Maria Kooyker
    See Kooyker-Romijn, Johanna Maria
Rong, Yu 1970- *174*
Rongen, Bjoern 1906- *10*
Rongen, Bjorn
    See Rongen, Bjoern
Ronson, Mark
    See Alexander, Marc
Rood, Ronald (N.) 1920- *12*
Rook, Sebastian
    See Jeapes, Ben
Rooke, Daphne 1914-2009 .... *12*
Rooke, Daphne Marie
    See Rooke, Daphne
Rooney, Ronnie 1970- *212*
Roop, Connie 1951- *167*
    Brief entry *49*
    Earlier sketches in SATA *54, 116*
Roop, Constance Betzer
    See Roop, Connie
Roop, Peter 1951- *167*
    Brief entry *49*
    Earlier sketches in SATA *54, 116*
Roop, Peter G.
    See Roop, Peter
Roop, Peter Geiger
    See Roop, Peter

Roos, Maryn *225*
Roos, Stephen 1945- *128*
    Brief entry *41*
    Earlier sketches in SATA *47, 77*
Roosa, Karen 1961- *218*
Roose-Evans, James 1927- *65*
Roosevelt, Eleanor 1884-1962 .... *50*
Root, Barry *232*
    Earlier sketch in SATA *182*
Root, Betty *84*
Root, Kimberly Bulcken *192*
Root, Phyllis 1949- *224*
    Brief entry *48*
    Earlier sketches in SATA *55, 94, 145, 184*
Root, Shelton L., Jr. 1923-1986
    Obituary *51*
Roper, Laura (Newbold) Wood 1911-2003 .. *34*
    Obituary *150*
Roper, Robert 1946- *142*
    Earlier sketch in SATA *78*
Roraback, Robin (Ellan) 1964- *111*
Rorby, Ginny 1944- *94*
Rorer, Abigail 1949- *85*
Rosaler, Maxine *208*
Rosamel, Godeleine de 1968- *151*
Roscoe, D(onald) T(homas) 1934- *42*
Rose, Anne *8*
Rose, Deborah Lee 1955- *185*
    Earlier sketches in SATA *71, 124*
Rose, Elizabeth (Jane Pretty) 1933- *68*
    Brief entry *28*
Rose, Florella
    See Carlson, Vada F.
Rose, Gerald (Hembdon Seymour) 1935- *68*
    Brief entry *30*
Rose, Malcolm 1953- *168*
    Earlier sketch in SATA *107*
Rose, Nancy A.
    See Sweetland, Nancy A(nn)
Rose, Naomi C. *228*
Rose, Ted 1940- *93*
Rose, Wendy 1948- *12*
Rosen, Elizabeth 1961- *205*
Rosen, Lillian (Diamond) 1928- *63*
Rosen, Marvin 1933- *161*
Rosen, Michael 1946- *229*
    Brief entry *40*
    Earlier sketches in SATA *48, 84, 137, 181*
    See also CLR 45
Rosen, Michael J. 1954- *199*
    Earlier sketch in SATA *86*
Rosen, Michael Wayne
    See Rosen, Michael
Rosen, Sidney 1916- *1*
Rosen, Winifred 1943- *8*
Rosenbaum, Maurice 1907-1987 .... *6*
Rosenberg, Amye 1950- *74*
Rosenberg, Dorothy 1906- *40*
Rosenberg, Eth Clifford 1915- *92*
    See also SAAS 22
Rosenberg, Jane 1949- *58*
Rosenberg, Liz 1958- *129*
    Earlier sketch in SATA *75*
Rosenberg, Maxine B(erta) 1939- *93*
    Brief entry *47*
    Earlier sketch in SATA *55*
Rosenberg, Nancy 1931- *4*
Rosenberg, Sharon 1942- *8*
Rosenberry, Vera 1948- *219*
    Earlier sketches in SATA *83, 144*
Rosenblatt, Arthur
    See Rosenblatt, Arthur S.
Rosenblatt, Arthur S. 1938- *68*
    Brief entry *45*
Rosenblatt, Lily 1956- *90*
Rosenbloom, Joseph 1928- *21*
Rosenblum, Richard 1928- *11*
Rosenburg, John M. 1918- *6*
Rosenfeld, Dina 1962- *99*
Rosenstiehl, Agnes 1941- *203*

Rosenthal, Amy Krouse 1965- 222
  Earlier sketch in SATA *177*
Rosenthal, Betsy R. 1957- *178*
Rosenthal, Harold 1914-1999 .... *35*
Rosenthal, M(acha) L(ouis) 1917-1996 .... *59*
Rosenthal, Marc 1949- *193*
Rosenthal, Mark A(lan) 1946- *64*
Rosing, Norbert 1953- *196*
Rosman, Steven M 1956- *81*
Rosman, Steven Michael
  See Rosman, Steven M
Rosoff, Meg 1956- *209*
  Earlier sketch in SATA *160*
Ross, Alan
  See Warwick, Alan R(oss)
Ross, Christine 1950- *172*
  Earlier sketch in SATA *83*
Ross, Clare
  See Romano, Clare
Ross, Dana Fuller
  See Cockrell, Amanda
  and Gerson, Noel Bertram
Ross, Dave
  See Ross, David
Ross, David 1896-1975 .... *49*
  Obituary *20*
Ross, David 1949- *133*
  Earlier sketch in SATA *32*
Ross, Deborah J.
  See Wheeler, Deborah
Ross, Diana
  See Denney, Diana
Ross, Edward S(hearman) 1915- *85*
Ross, Eileen 1950- *115*
Ross, Frank (Xavier), Jr. 1914- *28*
Ross, Jane 1961- *79*
Ross, John 1921- *45*
Ross, Judy 1942- *54*
Ross, Katharine Reynolds
  See Ross, Kathy
Ross, Kathy 1948- *169*
  Earlier sketch in SATA *89*
Ross, Kent 1956- *91*
Ross, Lillian Hammer 1925- *72*
Ross, Michael Elsohn 1952- *170*
  Earlier sketches in SATA *80, 127*
Ross, Pat(ricia Kienzle) 1943- *53*
  Brief entry *48*
Ross, Ramon R(oyal) 1930- *62*
Ross, Stewart 1947- *134*
  Earlier sketch in SATA *92*
  See also SAAS *23*
Ross, Sylvia 1937- *231*
Ross, Tom 1958- *84*
Ross, Tony 1938- *225*
  Earlier sketches in SATA *17, 65, 130, 176*
Ross, Wilda 1915- *51*
  Brief entry *39*
Rossel, Seymour 1945- *28*
Rossell, Judith 1953- *187*
Rossel-Waugh, C. C.
  See Waugh, Carol-Lynn Rossel
Rossetti, Christina 1830-1894 .... *20*
  See also CLR *115*
Rossetti, Christina Georgina
  See Rossetti, Christina
Rossi, Joyce 1943- *116*
Rossotti, Hazel Swaine 1930- *95*
Rostkowski, Margaret I. 1945- *59*
Rostoker-Gruber, Karen *229*
Roth, Arnold 1929- *21*
Roth, Arthur J(oseph) 1925-1993 .... *43*
  Brief entry *28*
  Obituary *75*
  See also SAAS *11*
Roth, Carol *222*
Roth, David 1940- *36*
Roth, Julie Jersild *180*
Roth, Matthue 1978(?)- *174*
Roth, R.G.
  See Roth, Robert

Roth, Rob
  See Roth, Robert
Roth, Robert 1965- *230*
Roth, Roger *190*
Roth, Ruby 1983(?)- *216*
Roth, Stephanie *202*
Roth, Susan L. *181*
  Earlier sketch in SATA *134*
Rothberg, Abraham 1922-2011 .... *59*
Roth-Hano, Renee 1931- *85*
Rothkopf, Carol Z. 1929- *4*
Rothman, Joel 1938- *7*
Rotner, Shelley 1951- *169*
  Earlier sketch in SATA *76*
Rottman, S.L. 1970- *157*
  Earlier sketch in SATA *106*
Rottman, Susan Lynn
  See Rottman, S.L.
Roueche, Berton 1911-1994 .... *28*
Roughsey, Dick 1921(?)-1985 .... *35*
  See also CLR *41*
Roughsey, Goobalathaldin
  See Roughsey, Dick
Rounds, Glen (Harold) 1906-2002 .... *112*
  Obituary *141*
  Earlier sketches in SATA *8, 70*
Rourke, Constance Mayfield 1885-1941
  See YABC *1*
Rouss, Sylvia *211*
Rovetch, Gerda 1925(?)- *202*
Rovetch, L. Bob
  See Rovetch, Lissa
Rovetch, Lissa *201*
Rowan, Deirdre
  See Williams, Jeanne
Rowe, Jennifer
  See Rodda, Emily
Rowe, John A. 1949- *198*
  Earlier sketch in SATA *146*
Rowe, Viola Carson 1903-1969
  Obituary *26*
Rowh, Mark 1952- *90*
Rowland, Florence Wightman 1900-1997 .... *8*
  Obituary *108*
Rowland-Entwistle, (Arthur) Theodore (Henry)
  1925- *94*
  Earlier sketch in SATA *31*
Rowling, J.K. 1965- *174*
  Earlier sketch in SATA *109*
  See also CLR *112*
Rowling, Joanne Kathleen
  See Rowling, J.K.
Rowsome, Frank (Howard), Jr. 1914-1983 .. *36*
Roy, Gabrielle 1909-1983 .... *104*
Roy, Jacqueline 1954- *74*
Roy, James 1968- *218*
Roy, Jennifer
  See Roy, Jennifer Rozines
Roy, Jennifer Rozines 1967- *178*
Roy, Jessie Hailstalk 1895-1986
  Obituary *51*
Roy, Kari Anne 1977(?)- *221*
Roy, Liam
  See Scarry, Patricia (Murphy)
Roy, Ron 1940- *228*
  Brief entry *35*
  Earlier sketches in SATA *40, 110*
Roybal, Laura 1956- *85*
Roybal, Laura Husby
  See Roybal, Laura
Royds, Caroline 1953- *55*
Royston, Angela 1945- *230*
  Earlier sketches in SATA *120, 169*
Rozakis, Laurie E. 1952- *84*
Rozen, Anna 1960- *206*
Rubbino, Salvatore 1970- *220*
Rubel, David 1961- *223*
Rubel, Nicole 1953- *181*
  Earlier sketches in SATA *18, 95, 135*
Rubin, Eva Johanna 1925- *38*

Rubin, Susan Goldman 1939- *182*
  Earlier sketches in SATA *84, 132*
Rubin, Vicky 1964- *193*
Rubinetti, Donald 1947- *92*
Rubinger, Ami 1953- *225*
Rubinstein, Gillian 1942- *158*
  Autobiography Feature *116*
  Earlier sketches in SATA *68, 105*
  See also CLR *35*
  See also SAAS *25*
Rubinstein, Gillian Margaret
  See Rubinstein, Gillian
Rubinstein, Patricia -2003
  See Forest, Antonia
Rubinstein, Patricia Giulia Caulfield Kate
  See Forest, Antonia
Rubinstein, Robert E(dward) 1943- *49*
Rublowsky, John M(artin) 1928- *62*
Rubright, Lynn 1936- *171*
Ruby, Laura *227*
  Earlier sketches in SATA *155, 181*
Ruby, Lois 1942- *184*
  Autobiography Feature *105*
  Brief entry *34*
  Earlier sketches in SATA *35, 95*
Ruby, Lois F.
  See Ruby, Lois
Ruchlis, Hy(man) 1913-1992 .... *3*
  Obituary *72*
Ruckdeschel, Liz *214*
Rucker, Mike 1940- *91*
Ruckman, Ivy 1931- *93*
  Earlier sketch in SATA *37*
Ruck-Pauquet, Gina 1931- *40*
  Brief entry *37*
Ruddell, Deborah 1949- *210*
Ruditis, Paul *190*
Rudley, Stephen 1946- *30*
Rudolph, Marguerita 1908- *21*
Rudomin, Esther
  See Hautzig, Esther Rudomin
Rue, Leonard Lee III 1926- *142*
  Earlier sketch in SATA *37*
Rue, Nancy 1951- *233*
Rue, Nancy N.
  See Rue, Nancy
Rue, Nancy Naylor
  See Rue, Nancy
Rueda, Claudia *183*
Ruedi, Norma Paul
  See Ainsworth, Norma
Ruelle, Karen Gray 1957- *209*
  Earlier sketches in SATA *84, 126*
Ruemmler, John D(avid) 1948- *78*
Ruepp, Krista 1947- *143*
Ruffell, Ann 1941- *30*
Ruffins, Reynold 1930- *125*
  Earlier sketch in SATA *41*
Rugg, Jim *206*
Ruggles, Lucy
  See Williams, Kathryn
Rugoff, Milton 1913- *30*
Ruhen, Olaf 1911-1989 .... *17*
Rui, Paolo 1962- *217*
Rukeyser, Muriel 1913-1980
  Obituary *22*
Rumbaut, Hendle 1949- *84*
Rumford, James 1948- *193*
  Earlier sketch in SATA *116*
Rumsey, Marian (Barritt) 1928- *16*
Rumstuckle, Cornelius
  See Brennan, Herbie
Runholt, Susan *216*
Runnerstroem, Bengt Arne 1944- *75*
Runyan, John
  See Palmer, Bernard (Alvin)
Runyon, Brent *217*
Runyon, Catherine 1947- *62*
Ruoff, A. LaVonne Brown 1930- *76*
Rupp, Rebecca *185*
Rusch, Elizabeth 1966- *198*

Rusch, Kris
    See Rusch, Kristine Kathryn
Rusch, Kristine Kathryn 1960- *113*
Rush, Alison 1951- *41*
Rush, Peter 1937- *32*
Rushdie, Ahmed Salman
    See Rushdie, Salman
Rushdie, Salman 1947-
    See CLR *125*
Rushford, Patricia H(elen) 1943- *134*
Rushmore, Helen 1898-1994 .... *3*
Rushmore, Robert (William) 1926-1986 .... *8*
    Obituary *49*
Ruskin, Ariane
    See Batterberry, Ariane Ruskin
Ruskin, John 1819-1900 .... *24*
Russ, Lavinia (Faxon) 1904-1992 .... *74*
Russell, Charlotte
    See Rathjen, Carl Henry
Russell, Ching Yeung 1946- *107*
Russell, Don(ald Bert) 1899-1986
    Obituary *47*
Russell, Franklin (Alexander) 1926- *11*
Russell, Gertrude Barrer
    See Barrer-Russell, Gertrude
Russell, Helen Ross 1915- *8*
Russell, James 1933- *53*
Russell, Jim
    See Russell, James
Russell, Joan Plummer 1930- *139*
Russell, Natalie 1972- *218*
Russell, P(hilip) Craig 1951- *162*
    Earlier sketch in SATA *80*
Russell, Patrick
    See Sammis, John
Russell, Paul (Gary) 1942- *57*
Russell, Sarah
    See Laski, Marghanita
Russell, Sharman Apt 1954- *123*
Russell, Solveig Paulson 1904-1985 .... *3*
Russo, Marisabina 1950- *188*
    Earlier sketches in SATA *106, 151*
Russo, Monica J. 1950- *83*
Russo, Susan 1947- *30*
Russon, Penni 1974- *179*
Rutgers van der Loeff, An
    See Rutgers van der Loeff-Basenau, An(na)
    Maria Margaretha
Rutgers van der Loeff-Basenau, An(na) Maria
    Margaretha 1910- *22*
Ruth, Rod 1912-1987 .... *9*
Rutherford, Douglas
    See McConnell, James Douglas Rutherford
Rutherford, Meg 1932- *34*
Ruthin, Margaret
    See Catherall, Arthur
Rutkoski, Marie 1977- *219*
Rutland, J. *232*
Rutland, Jarrett
    See Rutland, J.
Rutledge, Jill Zimmerman 1951- *155*
Rutz, Viola Larkin 1932- *12*
Ruurs, Margriet 1952- *215*
    Earlier sketches in SATA *97, 147*
Ruzicka, Rudolph 1883-1978
    Obituary *24*
Ruzzier, Sergio 1966- *210*
    Earlier sketch in SATA *159*
Ryan, Betsy
    See Ryan, Elizabeth (Anne)
Ryan, Cheli Duran *20*
Ryan, Darlene 1958- *176*
Ryan, Elizabeth (Anne) 1943- *30*
Ryan, Jeanette
    See Mines, Jeanette
Ryan, John 1921-2009 .... *22*
Ryan, John Gerald Christopher
    See Ryan, John
Ryan, Margaret 1950- *166*
    Earlier sketch in SATA *78*
Ryan, Mary E. 1953- *61*

Ryan, Mary Elizabeth
    See Ryan, Mary E.
Ryan, Pam Munoz 1951- *197*
    Earlier sketch in SATA *134*
Ryan, Patrick 1957- *138*
Ryan, Peter (Charles) 1939- *15*
Ryan-Lush, Geraldine 1949- *89*
Rybakov, Anatoli (Naumovich) 1911-1998 .. *79*
    Obituary *108*
Rybakov, Anatolii (Naumovich)
    See Rybakov, Anatoli (Naumovich)
Rybolt, Thomas R. 1954- *62*
Rybolt, Thomas Roy
    See Rybolt, Thomas R.
Rybolt, Tom
    See Rybolt, Thomas R.
Rycroft, Nina *228*
Rydberg, Ernest E(mil) 1901-1993 .... *21*
Rydberg, Lou(isa Hampton) 1908- *27*
Rydell, Katy 1942- *91*
Rydell, Wendell
    See Rydell, Wendy
Rydell, Wendy *4*
Ryden, Hope *91*
    Earlier sketch in SATA *8*
Ryder, Joanne 1946- *226*
    Brief entry *34*
    Earlier sketches in SATA *65, 122, 163*
    See also CLR *37*
Ryder, Pamela
    See Lamb, Nancy
Rye, Anthony
    See Youd, Samuel
Rylant, Cynthia 1954- *195*
    Brief entry *44*
    Earlier sketches in SATA *50, 76, 112, 160*
    See also CLR *86*
    See also SAAS *13*
Rymer, Alta May 1925- *34*
Rymond, Lynda Gene *199*

S

S. L. C.
    See Twain, Mark
S., Svend Otto
    See Soerensen, Svend Otto
Saaf, Donald W(illiam) 1961- *124*
Saal, Jocelyn
    See Sachs, Judith
Sabbeth, Carol (Landstrom) 1957- *125*
Saberhagen, Fred 1930-2007 .... *89*
    Obituary *184*
    Earlier sketch in SATA *37*
Saberhagen, Fred T.
    See Saberhagen, Fred
Saberhagen, Fred Thomas
    See Saberhagen, Fred
Saberhagen, Frederick Thomas
    See Saberhagen, Fred
Sabin, Edwin L(egrand) 1870-1952
    See YABC *2*
Sabin, Francene *27*
Sabin, Lou
    See Sabin, Louis
Sabin, Louis 1930- *27*
Sabre, Dirk
    See Laffin, John (Alfred Charles)
Sabuda, Robert (James) 1965- *120*
    Earlier sketch in SATA *81*
Sabuda, Robert 1965- *170*
Sabuda, Robert James
    See Sabuda, Robert
Sachar, Louis 1954- *154*
    Brief entry *50*
    Earlier sketches in SATA *63, 104*
    See also CLR *161*
Sachs, Elizabeth-Ann 1946- *48*

Sachs, Judith 1947- *52*
    Brief entry *51*
Sachs, Marilyn 1927- *164*
    Autobiography Feature *110*
    Earlier sketches in SATA *3, 68*
    See also CLR *2*
    See also SAAS *2*
Sachs, Marilyn Stickle
    See Sachs, Marilyn
Sackett, S(amuel) J(ohn) 1928- *12*
Sackson, Sid 1920- *16*
Sacre, Antonio 1968- *152*
Saddler, Allen
    See Richards, R(onald) C(harles) W(illiam)
Saddler, K. Allen
    See Richards, R(onald) C(harles) W(illiam)
Sadie, Stanley 1930-2005 .... *14*
Sadie, Stanley John
    See Sadie, Stanley
Sadiq, Nazneen
    See Sheikh, Nazneen
Sadler, Catherine Edwards 1952- *60*
    Brief entry *45*
Sadler, Marilyn (June) 1950- *79*
Sadler, Mark
    See Lynds, Dennis
Sadler, Sonia Lynn *230*
Saffer, Barbara *144*
Sagan, Carl 1934-1996 .... *58*
    Obituary *94*
Sagan, Carl Edward
    See Sagan, Carl
Sage, Angie 1952- *197*
Sage, Juniper
    See Brown, Margaret Wise
    and Hurd, Edith Thacher
Sagsoorian, Paul 1923- *12*
Said, S.F. 1967- *174*
Saidman, Anne 1952- *75*
Saint, Dora Jessie 1913- *10*
St. Anthony, Jane *175*
St. Antoine, Sara L. 1966- *84*
St. Clair, Byrd Hooper 1905-1976
    Obituary *28*
St. Crow, Lili
    See Saintcrow, Lilith
Saintcrow, Lilith 1976- *221*
Saint-Exupery, Antoine de 1900-1944 .... *20*
    See also CLR *142*
Saint-Exupery, Antoine Jean Baptiste Marie
    Roger de
    See Saint-Exupery, Antoine de
St. George, Judith 1931- *161*
    Earlier sketches in SATA *13, 99*
    See also CLR *57*
    See also SAAS *12*
St. George, Judith Alexander
    See St. George, Judith
St. James, Blakely
    See Gottfried, Theodore Mark
    and Platt, Charles
St. James, Blakely
    See Griffin, W. E. B.
St. James, Sierra
    See Rallison, Janette
Saint James, Synthia 1949- *152*
    Earlier sketch in SATA *84*
St. John, Lauren 1966- *214*
St. John, Nicole *143*
    Autobiography Feature *143*
    Earlier sketches in SATA *29, 89*
    See also CLR *46*
    See also SAAS *7*
St. John, Patricia Mary 1919-1993
    Obituary *79*
St. John, Philip
    See del Rey, Lester
St. John, Wylly Folk 1908-1985 .... *10*
    Obituary *45*
St. Max, E. S.
    See Ellis, Edward S.

St. Meyer, Ned
  See Stratemeyer, Edward L.
St. Mox, E. A.
  See Ellis, Edward S.
St. Myer, Ned
  See Stratemeyer, Edward L.
St. Tamara
  See Kolba, St. Tamara
Saito, Michiko
  See Fujiwara, Michiko
Sakai, Komako 1966- 213
Sakaki, Ichiro 1969- 192
Sakamoto, Miki 198
Sakers, Don 1958- 72
Sakharnov, S.
  See Sakharnov, Svyatoslav
Sakharnov, Svyatoslav 1923- 65
Sakharnov, Svyatoslav Vladimirovich
  See Sakharnov, Svyatoslav
Saksena, Kate 148
Sakurai, Gail 1952- 153
  Earlier sketch in SATA 87
Salamanca, Lucy
  See del Barco, Lucy Salamanca
Salas, Laura Purdie 1966- 216
Salassi, Otto R(ussell) 1939-1993 38
  Obituary 77
Salat, Cristina 82
Saldana, Rene, Jr. 186
Saldutti, Denise 1953- 39
Sale, Tim 1956- 153
Salem, Kay 1952- 92
Salerni, Dianne K. 231
Salerno, Steven 176
Salinger, J.D. 1919-2010 67
  See also CLR 18
Salinger, Jerome David
  See Salinger, J.D.
Salisbury, Graham 1944- 195
  Earlier sketches in SATA 76, 108, 161
Salisbury, Joyce E(llen) 1944- 138
Salkey, (Felix) Andrew (Alexander)
  1928-1995 118
  Earlier sketch in SATA 35
Salley, Coleen 166
Sallis, Susan (Diana) 1929- 55
Salmieri, Daniel 1983- 208
Salmon, Annie Elizabeth 1899- 13
Salmon, Dena K. 1959(?)- 219
Salonen, Roxane Beauclair 1968- 184
Salsi, Lynn 1947- 130
Salsitz, R. A. V.
  See Salsitz, Rhondi Vilott
Salsitz, Rhondi Vilott 115
Salten, Felix
  See Salzmann, Siegmund
Salter, Cedric
  See Knight, Francis Edgar
Salter, Sydney 220
Saltman, Judith 1947- 64
Saltzberg, Barney 1955- 233
  Earlier sketches in SATA 135, 194
Saltzman, David (Charles Laertes)
  1967-1990 86
Salvadori, Mario (George) 1907-1997 97
  Earlier sketch in SATA 40
Salwood, F.K.
  See Kilworth, Garry
Salzer, L. E.
  See Wilson, Lionel
Salzman, Marian 1959- 77
Salzmann, Siegmund 1869-1945 25
Samachson, Dorothy (Mirkin) 1914-1997 3
Samachson, Joseph 1906-1980 3
  Obituary 52
Sammis, John 1942- 4
Sampson, Emma (Keats) Speed 1868-1947 . 68
Sampson, Fay 1935- 151
  Brief entry 40
  Earlier sketch in SATA 42

Sampson, Fay Elizabeth
  See Sampson, Fay
Sampson, Jeff 1982- 232
Sampson, Michael 1952- 143
  Earlier sketch in SATA 95
Samson, Anne S(tringer) 1933- 2
Samson, Joan 1937-1976 13
Samson, Suzanne M. 1959- 91
Samuels, Barbara 199
Samuels, Charles 1902-1982 12
Samuels, Cynthia K(alish) 1946- 79
Samuels, Gertrude 1910(?)-2003 17
  Obituary 147
Sanborn, Duane 1914-1996 38
Sancha, Sheila 1924- 38
Sanchez, Alex 1957- 151
Sanchez, Anita 1956- 209
Sanchez, Sonia 1934- 136
  Earlier sketch in SATA 22
  See also CLR 18
Sanchez-Silva, Jose Maria 1911- 132
  Earlier sketch in SATA 16
  See also CLR 12
Sand, George X. 45
Sandak, Cass R(obert) 1950-2001 51
  Brief entry 37
Sandberg, (Karin) Inger 1930- 15
Sandberg, Karl C. 1931- 35
Sandberg, Lasse (E. M.) 1924- 15
Sandburg, Carl 1878-1967 8
  See also CLR 67
Sandburg, Carl August
  See Sandburg, Carl
Sandburg, Charles
  See Sandburg, Carl
Sandburg, Charles A.
  See Sandburg, Carl
Sandburg, Helga 1918- 3
  See also SAAS 10
Sandell, Lisa Ann 1977- 175
Sandemose, Iben 1950- 211
Sander, Heather L. 1947- 157
Sanderlin, George 1915- 4
Sanderlin, Owenita (Harrah) 1916- 11
Sanders, Betty Jane
  See Monthei, Betty
Sanders, Nancy I. 1960- 141
  Earlier sketch in SATA 90
Sanders, Scott Russell 1945- 109
  Earlier sketch in SATA 56
Sanders, Winston P.
  See Anderson, Poul
Sanderson, Irma 1912- 66
Sanderson, Ivan T(erence) 1911-1973 6
Sanderson, Margaret Love
  See Keats, Emma
  and Sampson, Emma (Keats) Speed
Sanderson, Ruth 1951- 224
  Earlier sketches in SATA 41, 109, 172
Sanderson, Ruth L.
  See Sanderson, Ruth
Sanders-Wells, Linda 220
Sand-Eveland, Cyndi 211
Sandin, Joan 1942- 197
  Earlier sketches in SATA 12, 94, 153
Sandison, Janet
  See Cameron, Elizabeth Jane
Sandler, Martin W. 216
  Earlier sketch in SATA 160
Sandom, J. Gregory
  See Welsh, T.K.
Sandom, J.G.
  See Welsh, T.K.
Sandoz, Mari(e Susette) 1900-1966 5
Sanford, Agnes (White) 1897-1976 61
Sanford, Doris 1937- 69
Sanford, Rose
  See Simmonds, Posy
Sanger, Amy Wilson 1967- 205
Sanger, Marjory Bartlett 1920- 8
San Jose, Christine 1929- 167

Sankey, Alice (Ann-Susan) 1910- 27
Sansone, Adele 1953- 230
San Souci, Daniel 192
  Earlier sketch in SATA 96
San Souci, Robert D. 1946- 220
  Earlier sketches in SATA 40, 81, 117, 158
  See also CLR 43
Santamaria, Benjamin 1955- 184
Santat, Dan 224
  Earlier sketch in SATA 188
Santesson, Hans Stefan 1914(?)-1975
  Obituary 30
Santiago, Esmeralda 1948- 129
Santopolo, Jill 214
Santore, Charles 1935- 200
Santoro, C.
  See Santoro, Christopher
Santoro, Christopher 218
Santos, Helen
  See Griffiths, Helen
Santrey, Louis
  See Sabin, Louis
Santucci, Barbara 1948- 130
Sapergia, Barbara 1943- 181
Sapet, Kerrily 1972- 214
Sapieyevski, Anne Lindbergh 1940-1993 81
  Brief entry 32
  Earlier sketches in SATA 35, 78
Saport, Linda 1954- 123
Sapp, Allen 1929- 151
Sarac, Roger
  See Caras, Roger A(ndrew)
Sarah, Duchess of York
  See Ferguson, Sarah
Sarasin, Jennifer
  See Sachs, Judith
Sarcone-Roach, Julia 215
Sardinha, Rick 192
Sarg, Anthony Frederick
  See Sarg, Tony
Sarg, Tony 1882-1942
  See YABC 1
Sargent, Pamela 1948- 78
  Earlier sketch in SATA 29
Sargent, Robert 1933- 2
Sargent, Sarah 1937- 44
  Brief entry 41
Sargent, Shirley 1927-2004 11
Sarnoff, Jane 1937- 10
Saroff, Phyllis V. 202
Saroyan, William 1908-1981 23
  Obituary 24
Sartell, Debra 229
Sarton, Eleanor May
  See Sarton, May
Sarton, May 1912-1995 36
  Obituary 86
Sasaki, Chris 182
Sasaki, Ellen Joy 206
Saseen, Sharon (Dillon) 1949- 59
Sasek, Miroslav 1916-1980 16
  Obituary 23
  See also CLR 4
Sasso, Sandy Eisenberg 1947- 162
  Earlier sketches in SATA 86, 116
Sathre, Vivian 1952- 133
  Earlier sketch in SATA 79
Satterfield, Charles
  See del Rey, Lester
  and Pohl, Frederik
Sattgast, L. J.
  See Sattgast, Linda J.
Sattgast, Linda J. 1953- 91
Sattler, Helen Roney 1921-1992 74
  Earlier sketch in SATA 4
  See also CLR 24
Sattler, Jennifer
  See Sattler, Jennifer Gordon
Sattler, Jennifer Gordon 218
Sauer, Julia Lina 1891-1983 32
  Obituary 36

Sauer, Tammi 1972- 223
Sauerwein, Leigh 1944- 155
Saul, Carol P. 1947- 117
  Earlier sketch in SATA 78
Saul, John 1942- 98
Saul, John W.
  See Saul, John
Saul, John Woodruff III
  See Saul, John
Saul, (Ellen) Wendy 1946- 42
Saulnier, Karen Luczak 1940- 80
Saunders, Caleb
  See Heinlein, Robert A.
Saunders, Dave 1939- 85
Saunders, Julie 1939- 85
Saunders, (William) Keith 1910-1994 12
Saunders, Rubie (Agnes) 1929- 21
Saunders, Steven
  See Jones, Allan Frewin
Saunders, Susan 1945- 96
  Brief entry 41
  Earlier sketch in SATA 46
Saunders-Smith, Gail 1952- 169
Sauvain, Philip Arthur 1933- 111
Savadier, Elivia 1950- 228
  Earlier sketches in SATA 79, 164
Savage, Alan
  See Nicole, Christopher
Savage, Blake
  See Goodwin, Harold L(eland)
Savage, Candace 1949- 142
Savage, Deborah 1955- 76
Savage, Jeff 1961- 97
Savage, Katharine James 1905-1989
  Obituary 61
Savage, Stephen 1965- 194
Savage, Thomas 1915-2003
  Obituary 147
Savageau, Cheryl 1950- 96
Savery, Constance (Winifred) 1897-1999 1
Saville, Andrew
  See Taylor, Andrew
Saville, (Leonard) Malcolm 1901-1982 23
  Obituary 31
Saviozzi, Adriana
  See Mazza, Adriana
Savitt, Sam 1917-2000 8
  Obituary 126
Savitz, Harriet May 1933-2008 72
  Earlier sketch in SATA 5
  See also SAAS 26
Sawicki, Mary 1950- 90
Sawyer, (Frederick) Don(ald) 1947- 72
Sawyer, Kem Knapp 1953- 84
Sawyer, Kim Vogel 233
Sawyer, Robert J. 1960- 149
  Earlier sketch in SATA 81
Sawyer, Robert James
  See Sawyer, Robert J.
Sawyer, Ruth 1880-1970 17
  See also CLR 36
Saxby, H.M.
  See Saxby, (Henry) Maurice
Saxby, (Henry) Maurice 1924- 71
Saxon, Andrew
  See Arthur, Robert, (Jr.)
Saxon, Antonia
  See Sachs, Judith
Say, Allen 1937- 161
  Earlier sketches in SATA 28, 69, 110
  See also CLR 135
Sayers, Frances Clarke 1897-1989 3
  Obituary 62
Sayles, Elizabeth 1956- 220
  Earlier sketches in SATA 108, 163
Saylor-Marchant, Linda 1963- 82
Sayre, April Pulley 1966- 233
  Earlier sketches in SATA 88, 131, 191
Sazer, Nina 1949- 13
Scabrini, Janet 1953- 13
Scagell, Robin 1946- 107

Scagnetti, Jack 1924- 7
Scaletta, Kurtis 1968- 215
Scalora, Suza 224
Scamander, Newt
  See Rowling, J.K.
Scamell, Ragnhild 1940- 180
  Earlier sketch in SATA 77
Scandiffio, Laura 227
Scanlon, Elizabeth Garton
  See Scanlon, Liz Garton
Scanlon, Liz Garton 226
Scanlon, Marion Stephany 11
Scannel, John Vernon
  See Scannell, Vernon
Scannell, Vernon 1922-2007 59
  Obituary 188
Scarborough, Elizabeth
  See Scarborough, Elizabeth Ann
Scarborough, Elizabeth Ann 1947- 171
  Earlier sketch in SATA 98
Scarf, Maggi
  See Scarf, Maggie
Scarf, Maggie 1932- 5
Scariano, Margaret M. 1924- 86
Scarlett, Susan
  See Streatfeild, Noel
Scarry, Huck
  See Scarry, Richard McClure, Jr.
Scarry, Patricia (Murphy) 1924- 2
Scarry, Patsy
  See Scarry, Patricia (Murphy)
Scarry, Richard (McClure) 1919-1994 75
  Obituary 90
  Earlier sketches in SATA 2, 35
  See also CLR 41
Scarry, Richard McClure, Jr. 1953- 35
Schachner, Judith Byron 1951- 178
  Earlier sketch in SATA 88
Schachner, Judy
  See Schachner, Judith Byron
Schachtel, Roger 1949- 38
Schachtel, Roger Bernard
  See Schachtel, Roger
Schade, Susan 189
Schaedler, Sally 116
Schaefer, Carole Lexa 173
Schaefer, Jack (Warner) 1907-1991 66
  Obituary 65
  Earlier sketch in SATA 3
Schaefer, Lola M. 1950- 183
  Earlier sketches in SATA 91, 144
Schaeffer, Mead 1898- 21
Schaeffer, Susan Fromberg 1940-2011 22
Schaer, Brigitte 1958- 112
Schallau, Daniel 1966- 222
Schaller, George
  See Schaller, George B.
Schaller, George B. 1933- 30
Schaller, George Beals
  See Schaller, George B.
Schanzer, Rosalyn (Good) 1942- 138
  Earlier sketch in SATA 77
Schatell, Brian 66
  Brief entry 47
Schechter, Betty (Goodstein) 1921- 5
Schechter, Simone
  See Elkeles, Simone
Schecter, Ellen 1944- 85
Scheeder, Louis 1946- 141
Scheer, Julian (Weisel) 1926-2001 8
Scheffer, Victor B(lanchard) 1906- 6
Scheffler, Axel 1957- 230
  Earlier sketch in SATA 180
Scheffler, Ursel 1938- 81
Scheffrin-Falk, Gladys 1928- 76
Scheidl, Gerda Marie 1913- 85
Scheier, Michael 1943- 40
  Brief entry 36
Schell, Mildred 1922- 41
Schell, Orville (Hickok) 1940- 10
Scheller, Melanie 1953- 77

Schellie, Don 1932- 29
Schembri, Jim 1962- 124
Schembri, Pamela 1969- 195
Schemm, Mildred Walker 1905-1998 21
  Obituary 103
Schenker, Dona 1947- 133
  Earlier sketch in SATA 68
Scher, Paula 1948- 47
Scherer, Jeffrey 194
Scherf, Margaret 1908-1979 10
Schermer, Judith (Denise) 1941- 30
Schertle, Alice 1941- 231
  Earlier sketches in SATA 36, 90, 145, 192
Schick, Alice 1946- 27
Schick, Eleanor 1942- 144
  Earlier sketch in SATA 9, 82
Schick, Joel 1945- 31
  Brief entry 30
Schields, Gretchen 1948- 75
Schiff, Ken(neth Roy) 1942- 7
Schiller, Andrew 1919- 21
Schiller, Barbara (Heyman) 1928- 21
Schiller, Pamela (Byrne) 127
Schindel, John 1955- 213
  Earlier sketches in SATA 77, 115
Schindelman, Joseph 1923- 67
  Brief entry 32
Schindler, S.D. 1952- 198
  Brief entry 50
  Earlier sketches in SATA 75, 118, 171
Schindler, Steven D.
  See Schindler, S.D.
Schinto, Jeanne 1951- 93
Schisgall, Oscar 1901-1984 12
  Obituary 38
Schlaepfer, Gloria G. 1931- 154
Schlee, Ann 1934- 44
  Brief entry 36
Schleichert, Elizabeth 1945- 77
Schlein, Miriam 1926-2004 130
  Obituary 159
  Earlier sketches in SATA 2, 87
  See also CLR 41
Schlesinger, Arthur M., Jr. 1917-2007 61
  Obituary 181
  See Schlesinger, Arthur Meier
Schlesinger, Arthur Meier 1888-1965
Schlessinger, Laura (Catherine) 1947- 160
  Earlier sketch in SATA 110
Schlitz, Laura Amy 232
  Earlier sketch in SATA 184
Schloat, G. Warren, Jr. 1914-2000 4
Schlossberg, Elisabeth 221
Schmais, Libby 227
Schmatz, Pat 197
Schmid, Eleonore 1939- 126
  Earlier sketches in SATA 12, 84
Schmid, Paul 231
Schmid, Susan Maupin 208
Schmiderer, Dorothy 1940- 19
Schmidt, Annie M. G. 1911-1995 67
  Obituary 91
  See also CLR 22
Schmidt, C.A. 196
Schmidt, Diane 1953- 70
Schmidt, Elizabeth 1915- 15
Schmidt, Gary D. 1957- 193
  Earlier sketches in SATA 93, 135
Schmidt, James Norman 1912-1983 21
Schmidt, Karen Lee 1953- 185
  Earlier sketch in SATA 94
Schmidt, Lynette 1952- 76
Schmitz, Tamara 207
Schneider, Antonie 1954- 167
  Earlier sketch in SATA 89
Schneider, Christine M. 1972(?)- 171
  Earlier sketch in SATA 120
Schneider, Dick
  See Schneider, Richard H.
Schneider, Elisa
  See Kleven, Elisa

Schneider, Herman 1905-2003 7
  Obituary 148
Schneider, Howie -2007 181
Schneider, Josh 1980- 196
Schneider, Laurie
  See Adams, Laurie
Schneider, Nina 1913-2007 2
  Obituary 186
Schneider, Nina Zimet
  See Schneider, Nina
Schneider, Rex 1937- 44
Schneider, Richard H. 1922- 171
Schneider, Richard Henry
  See Schneider, Richard H.
Schneider, Robyn 1986- 187
Schnirel, James R. 1931- 14
Schnitter, Jane T. 1958- 88
Schnitzlein, Danny 134
Schnur, Steven 1952- 144
  Earlier sketch in SATA 95
Schnurre, Wolfdietrich 1920-1989
  Obituary 63
Schoberle, Cecile 1949- 80
Schock, Pauline 1928- 45
Schoell, William 1951- 160
Schoen, Barbara (Taylor) 1924-1993 13
Schoenherr, Ian 177
Schoenherr, John 1935-2010 66
  Earlier sketch in SATA 37
  See also SAAS 13
Schoenherr, John Carl
  See Schoenherr, John
Schofield, Sandy
  See Rusch, Kristine Kathryn
Scholastica, Sister Mary
  See Jenkins, Marie M(agdalen)
Scholefield, A. T.
  See Scholefield, Alan
Scholefield, Alan 1931- 66
Scholefield, Edmund O.
  See Griffin, W. E. B.
Scholey, Arthur 1932- 28
Scholz, Jackson Volney 1897-1986
  Obituary 49
Schon, Nick 1955- 223
Schone, Virginia 22
Schongut, Emanuel 1936- 184
  Brief entry 36
  Earlier sketch in SATA 52
Schoonover, Frank (Earle) 1877-1972 24
Schoor, Gene 1921- 3
Schories, Pat 1952- 232
  Earlier sketches in SATA 116, 164
Schorr, Melissa 1972- 194
Schorr, Melissa Robin
  See Schorr, Melissa
Schott, Jane A. 1946- 172
Schotter, Roni 190
  Earlier sketches in SATA 105, 149
Schrader, Dave 1967(?)- 225
Schraff, Anne E(laine) 1939- 92
  Earlier sketch in SATA 27
Schram, Penninah 1934- 219
  Earlier sketch in SATA 119
Schrank, Joseph 1900-1984
  Obituary 38
Schrecengost, Maity 1938- 118
Schrecengost, S. Maitland
  See Schrecengost, Maity
Schreck, Karen
  See Schreck, Karen Halvorsen
Schreck, Karen Halvorsen 1962- 185
Schrecker, Judie 1954- 90
Schreiber, Elizabeth Anne (Ferguson)
  1947- 13
Schreiber, Ralph W(alter) 1942- 13
Schreiner, Samuel A(gnew), Jr. 1921- 70
Schroades, John 214
Schroder, Monika 1965- 229
Schroeder, Alan 1961- 98
  Earlier sketch in SATA 66

Schroeder, Binette
  See Nickl, Barbara (Elisabeth)
Schroeder, Russell (K.) 1943- 146
Schroeder, Ted 1931(?)-1973
  Obituary 20
Schubert, Dieter 1947- 217
  Earlier sketches in SATA 62, 101
Schubert, Ingrid 1953- 217
Schubert, Leda 1945(?)- 232
  Earlier sketch in SATA 181
Schubert, Leda Deirdre
  See Schubert, Leda
Schubert-Gabrys, Ingrid 1953- 101
  Earlier sketch in SATA 62
Schuelein-Steel, Danielle
  See Steel, Danielle
Schuelein-Steel, Danielle Fernande
  See Steel, Danielle
Schuerger, Michele R. 110
Schuett, Stacey 1960- 168
  Earlier sketch in SATA 75
Schulke, Flip Phelps Graeme 1930- 57
Schulman, Arlene 1961- 105
Schulman, Janet 1933- 208
  Earlier sketches in SATA 22, 137
Schulman, L(ester) M(artin) 1934- 13
Schulte, Elaine L(ouise) 1934- 36
Schultz, Betty K(epka) 1932- 125
Schultz, Gwendolyn 21
Schultz, James Willard 1859-1947
  See YABC 1
Schultz, Pearle Henriksen 1918- 21
Schulz, Charles M. 1922-2000 10
  Obituary 118
Schulz, Charles Monroe
  See Schulz, Charles M.
Schumacher, Julie 1958- 191
Schumaker, Ward 1943- 96
Schuman, Michael A. 1953- 134
  Earlier sketch in SATA 85
Schur, Maxine
  See Schur, Maxine Rose
Schur, Maxine Rose 1948- 135
  Autobiography Feature 135
  Brief entry 49
  Earlier sketches in SATA 53, 98
Schurfranz, Vivian 1925- 13
Schutzer, A. I. 1922- 13
Schuyler, Pamela R. 1948- 30
Schwabach, Karen 185
Schwager, Tina 1964- 110
Schwandt, Stephen (William) 1947- 61
Schwark, Mary Beth 1954- 51
Schwartz, Alvin 1927-1992 56
  Obituary 71
  Earlier sketch in SATA 4
  See also CLR 89
Schwartz, Amy 1954- 189
  Brief entry 41
  Earlier sketches in SATA 47, 83, 131
  See also CLR 25
  See also SAAS 18
Schwartz, Anne Powers 1913-1987 10
Schwartz, Carol 1954- 77
Schwartz, Charles W(alsh) 1914- 8
Schwartz, David M. 1951- 110
  Earlier sketch in SATA 59
Schwartz, David Martin
  See Schwartz, David M.
Schwartz, Elizabeth Reeder 1912- 8
Schwartz, Ellen 1949- 117
Schwartz, Jerome L.
  See Lawrence, Jerome
Schwartz, Joanne 1960- 220
Schwartz, Joel L. 1940- 54
  Brief entry 51
Schwartz, John 1957- 232
Schwartz, Joyce R. 1950- 93
Schwartz, Julius 1907-2004 45
Schwartz, Perry 1942- 75
Schwartz, Sheila (Ruth) 1929- 27

Schwartz, Stephen (Lawrence) 1948- 19
Schwartz, Virginia Frances 1950- 184
  Earlier sketch in SATA 131
Schwarz, Silvia Tessa Viviane
  See Schwarz, Viviane
Schwarz, Viviane 1977- 204
Schwarz, (Silvia Tessa) Viviane 1977- 141
Schweitzer, Byrd Baylor
  See Baylor, Byrd
Schweitzer, Iris 59
  Brief entry 36
Schweninger, Ann 1951- 168
  Earlier sketches in SATA 29, 98
Schwerin, Doris H(alpern) 1922- 64
Schy, Yael 197
Scieszka, Jon 1954- 199
  Earlier sketches in SATA 68, 105, 160
  See also CLR 107
Scillian, Devin 199
  Earlier sketch in SATA 128
Scioscia, Mary (Hershey) 1926- 63
Sciurba, Katie 1957- 196
Scofield, Penrod 1933- 62
  Obituary 78
Scoggin, Margaret C(lara) 1905-1968 47
  Brief entry 28
Scoltock, Jack 1942- 141
  Earlier sketch in SATA 72
Scoppettone, Sandra 1936- 92
  Earlier sketch in SATA 9
Scot, Michael
  See Rohan, Michael Scott
Scot-Bernard, P.
  See Bernard, Patricia
Scotland, Jay
  See Jakes, John
Scott, Alastair
  See Allen, Kenneth S.
Scott, Ann Herbert 1926- 140
  Autobiography Feature 140
  Brief entry 29
  Earlier sketches in SATA 56, 94
Scott, Bill
  See Scott, William N(eville)
Scott, Bill 1920(?)-1985
  Obituary 46
Scott, Cora Annett (Pipitone) 1931- 11
Scott, Dan
  See Barker, S. Omar
Scott, Elaine 1940- 198
  Earlier sketches in SATA 36, 90, 164
Scott, Elizabeth 1972- 194
Scott, Jack Denton 1915-1995 83
  Earlier sketch in SATA 31
  See also CLR 20
  See also SAAS 14
Scott, Jane (Harrington) 1931- 55
Scott, Jane Wooster 1939- 226
Scott, Jennifer Power 1968- 230
Scott, Jessica
  See De Wire, Elinor
Scott, John 1912-1976 14
Scott, John Anthony 1916- 23
Scott, John M(artin) 1913- 12
Scott, Mary
  See Mattern, Joanne
Scott, Melissa 1960- 109
Scott, Michael 1959- 211
Scott, Michael Peter
  See Scott, Michael
Scott, Mike
  See Scott, Michael
Scott, Richard
  See Rennert, Richard Scott
Scott, Roney
  See Gault, William Campbell
Scott, Sally 1909-1978 43
Scott, Sally 1948- 44
Scott, Sally Elisabeth
  See Scott, Sally

Scott, W. N.
See Scott, William N(eville)
Scott, Sir Walter 1771-1832
See YABC 2
See also CLR 154
Scott, Warwick
See Trevor, Elleston
Scott, William N(eville) 1923- 87
Scotti, Anna
See Coates, Anna
Scotton, Rob 1960- 214
Earlier sketch in SATA 177
Scribner, Charles, Jr. 1921-1995 13
Obituary 87
Scribner, Joanne L. 1949- 33
Scribner, Kimball 1917- 63
Scrimger, Richard 1957- 164
Earlier sketch in SATA 119
Scrimsher, Lila Gravatt 1897-1974
Obituary 28
Scroder, Walter K. 1928- 82
Scroggs, Kirk 187
Scruggs, Sandy 1961- 89
Scudder, Brooke 1959- 154
Scudder, Mildred Lee 1908- 6
See also SAAS 12
Scull, Marie-Louise 1943-1993 77
Scuro, Vincent 1951- 21
Seabrooke, Brenda 1941- 148
Earlier sketches in SATA 30, 88
Seagraves, D.B.
See Seagraves, Donny Bailey
Seagraves, Donny
See Seagraves, Donny Bailey
Seagraves, Donny Bailey 1951- 224
Seaman, Augusta Huiell 1879-1950 31
Seamands, Ruth 1916- 9
Searcy, Margaret Zehmer 1926- 54
Brief entry 39
Searight, Mary W(illiams) 1918- 17
Searle, Kathryn Adrienne 1942- 10
Searle, Ronald (William Fordham) 1920- 70
Earlier sketch in SATA 42
Sears, Stephen W. 1932- 4
Seaskull, Cecil
See Castellucci, Cecil
Sebastian, Lee
See Silverberg, Robert
Sebestyen, Igen
See Sebestyen, Ouida
Sebestyen, Ouida 1924- 140
Earlier sketch in SATA 39
See also CLR 17
See also SAAS 10
Sebrey, Mary Ann 1951- 62
Sechrist, Elizabeth Hough 1903-1991 2
Sederman, Marty 211
Sedges, John
See Buck, Pearl S.
Sedgwick, Marcus 1968- 197
Earlier sketch in SATA 160
Seed, Cecile Eugenie 1930- 86
Earlier sketch in SATA 8
See also CLR 76
Seed, Jenny
See Seed, Cecile Eugenie
Seed, Sheila Turner 1937(?)-1979
Obituary 23
Seeger, Elizabeth 1889-1973
Obituary 20
Seeger, Laura Vaccaro 200
Earlier sketch in SATA 172
Seeger, Pete 1919- 139
Earlier sketch in SATA 13
Seeger, Peter R.
See Seeger, Pete
Seeley, Laura L. 1958- 71
Seever, R.
See Reeves, Lawrence F.
Sefozo, Mary 1925- 82

Sefton, Catherine
See Waddell, Martin
Segal, John 178
Segal, Joyce 1940- 35
Segal, Lore 1928- 228
Autobiography Feature 228
Earlier sketches in SATA 4, 66, 163
See also SAAS 11
Segal, Lore Groszmann
See Segal, Lore
Segar, E(lzie) C(risler) 1894-1938 61
Segovia, Andres 1893(?)-1987
Obituary 52
Seguin, Marilyn W(eymouth) 1951- 91
Seguin-Fontes, Marthe 1924- 109
Seibold, J. Otto 1960- 196
Earlier sketches in SATA 83, 149
See also SAAS 22
Seidel, Ross 95
Seidelman, James Edward 1926- 6
Seiden, Art(hur) 107
Brief entry 42
Seidensticker, John 1944- 200
Seidler, Ann (G.) 1925- 131
Seidler, Tor 1952- 149
Brief entry 46
Earlier sketches in SATA 52, 98
Seidman, Karla
See Kuskin, Karla
Seidman, Laurence Ivan 1925- 15
Seigel, Kalman 1917-1998 12
Obituary 103
Seignobosc, Francoise 1897-1961 21
Seinfeld, Jerry 1954- 146
Seitz, Jacqueline 1931- 50
Seixas, Judith S. 1922- 17
Sejima, Yoshimasa 1913- 8
Selberg, Ingrid (Maria) 1950- 68
Selden, George
See Thompson, George Selden
Selden, Neil R(oy) 1931- 61
Self, Margaret Cabell 1902-1996 24
Selfors, Suzanne 1963- 193
Selick, Henry 1952- 183
Selig, Sylvie 1942- 13
Selkirk, Jane
See Chapman, John Stanton Higham
Sellers, Naomi
See Flack, Naomi John White
Sellier, Marie 1953- 212
Selman, LaRue W. 1927- 55
Selsam, Millicent E(llis) 1912-1996 29
Obituary 92
Earlier sketch in SATA 1
See also CLR 1
Seltzer, Meyer 1932- 17
Seltzer, Richard 1946- 41
Seltzer, Richard Warren, Jr.
See Seltzer, Richard
Selvadurai, Shyam 1965(?)- 171
Selway, Martina 1940- 169
Earlier sketch in SATA 74
Selzer, Adam 1980- 229
Earlier sketch in SATA 192
Selznick, Brian 1966- 210
Earlier sketches in SATA 79, 117, 171
Semel, Nava 1954- 107
Semloh
See Holmes, Peggy
Sendak, Jack 1924(?)-1995 28
Sendak, Maurice 1928- 165
Earlier sketches in SATA 1, 27, 113
See also CLR 131
Sendak, Maurice Bernard
See Sendak, Maurice
Sender, Ruth M(insky) 1926- 62
Sengler, Johanna 1924- 18
Senir, Mirik
See Snir, Mirik
Senisi, Ellen B. 1951- 116

Senisi, Ellen Babinec
See Senisi, Ellen B.
Senn, J(oyce) A(nn) 1941- 115
Senn, Steve 1950- 60
Brief entry 48
Sensel, Joni 1962- 204
Senzai, N.H. 233
Serafini, Frank 201
Serage, Nancy 1924- 10
Seredy, Kate 1899-1975 1
Obituary 24
See also CLR 10
Serfozo, Mary 1925- 194
Seroff, Victor I(ilyitch) 1902-1979 12
Obituary 26
Serra, Sebastia 1966- 202
Serraillier, Ian (Lucien) 1912-1994 73
Obituary 83
Earlier sketch in SATA 1
See also CLR 2
See also SAAS 3
Serros, Michele 175
Serros, Michele M.
See Serros, Michele
Servello, Joe 1932- 10
Service, Pamela F. 1945- 222
Earlier sketch in SATA 64
Service, Robert
See Service, Robert W.
Service, Robert W. 1874(?)-1958 20
Serwadda, W(illiam) Moses 1931- 27
Serwer-Bernstein, Blanche L(uria)
1910-1997 10
Sescoe, Vincent E. 1938- 123
Seskin, Steve 1953- 211
Seth, Mary
See Lexau, Joan M.
Seton, Anya 1904(?)-1990 3
Obituary 66
Seton, Ernest (Evan) Thompson 1860-1946 . 18
See also CLR 59
Seton-Thompson, Ernest
See Seton, Ernest (Evan) Thompson
Seuling, Barbara 1937- 220
Autobiography Feature 220
Earlier sketches in SATA 10, 98, 145, 193
See also SAAS 24
Seuss, Dr.
See Dr. Seuss
Severn, Bill
See Severn, William Irving
Severn, David
See Unwin, David S.
Severn, William Irving 1914- 1
Sewall, Marcia 1935- 119
Earlier sketches in SATA 37, 69
Seward, Prudence 1926- 16
Sewell, Anna 1820-1878 100
Earlier sketch in SATA 24
See also CLR 17
Sewell, Helen (Moore) 1896-1957 38
Sexton, Anne 1928-1974 10
Sexton, Anne Harvey
See Sexton, Anne
Seymour, Alta Halverson 10
Seymour, Jane 1951- 139
Seymour, Tres 1966- 164
Earlier sketch in SATA 82
Sfar, Joann 1971- 182
Shachtman, Tom 1942- 49
Shackleton, C.C.
See Aldiss, Brian W.
Shader, Rachel
See Sofer, Barbara
Shadow, Jak
See Sutherland, Jon
Shadyland, Sal
See Cooper, Louise
Shafer, Audrey 183
Shafer, Robert E(ugene) 1925- 9
Shaffer, Terea 1968- 79

Shahan, Sherry 1949- 216
　Earlier sketches in SATA *92, 134*
Shahn, Ben(jamin) 1898-1969
　Obituary 21
Shahn, Bernarda Bryson
　See Bryson, Bernarda
Shaik, Fatima 114
Shalant, Phyllis 1949- 150
Shan, Darren 1972- 199
　Earlier sketches in SATA *129, 168*
Shan, D.B.
　See Shan, Darren
Shanahan, Lisa 199
Shanberg, Karen
　See Shragg, Karen (I.)
Shane, Harold Gray 1914-1993 36
　Obituary 76
Shange, Ntozake 1948- 157
Shanks, Ann Zane (Kushner) 10
Shannon, David 1959- 228
　Earlier sketches in SATA *107, 152*
　See also CLR *87*
Shannon, George 1952- 202
　Earlier sketches in SATA *35, 94, 143*
Shannon, George William Bones
　See Shannon, George
Shannon, Jacqueline 63
Shannon, Margaret
　See Silverwood, Margaret Shannon
Shannon, Monica 1905(?)-1965 28
Shannon, Terry
　See Mercer, Jessie
Shannon, Terry Miller 1951- 148
Shapiro, Irwin 1911-1981 32
Shapiro, Jody Fickes 1940- 193
Shapiro, Karen Jo 1964- 186
Shapiro, Michelle 1961- 196
Shapiro, Milton J. 1926- 32
Shapiro, Tricia
　See Andryszewski, Tricia
Shapiro, Zachary 1970- 213
Shapp, Charles M(orris) 1906-1989
　Obituary 61
Shapp, Martha Glauber 1910- 3
Sharenow, Robert 193
Sharfman, Amalie 14
Sharkey, Niamh 213
Sharma, Partap 1939- 15
Sharma, Rashmi
　See Singh, Rashmi Sharma
Sharman, Alison
　See Leonard, Alison
Sharmat, Marjorie Weinman 1928- 133
　Earlier sketches in SATA *4, 33, 74*
Sharmat, Mitchell 1927- 127
　Earlier sketch in SATA *33*
Sharp, Anne Wallace 1947- 144
Sharp, Luke
　See Alkiviades, Alkis
Sharp, Margery 1905-1991 29
　Obituary 67
　Earlier sketch in SATA *1*
　See also CLR *27*
Sharp, Zerna A. 1889-1981
　Obituary 27
Sharpe, Jon
　See Duncan, Alice
　and Knott, William C(ecil, Jr.)
　and Messman, Jon
Sharpe, Mitchell R(aymond) 1924- 12
Sharpe, Susan 1946- 71
Sharratt, Nick 1962- 199
　Earlier sketches in SATA *104, 153*
Shasha, Mark 1961- 80
Shattuck, Roger 1923-2005 64
　Obituary 174
Shattuck, Roger Whitney
　See Shattuck, Roger
Shaw, Arnold 1909-1989 4
　Obituary 63
Shaw, Carolyn V. 1934- 91

Shaw, Charles (Green) 1892-1974 13
Shaw, Evelyn S. 1927- 28
Shaw, Flora Louisa
　See Lugard, Flora Louisa Shaw
Shaw, Hannah 1982(?)- 227
Shaw, Janet 1937- 146
　Earlier sketch in SATA *61*
　See also CLR *96*
Shaw, Janet Beeler
　See Shaw, Janet
Shaw, Liane 1959- 222
Shaw, Lisa
　See Rogak, Lisa
Shaw, Margret 1940- 68
Shaw, Mary 1965- 180
Shaw, Nancy 1946- 162
　Earlier sketch in SATA *71*
Shaw, Ray 7
Shaw, Richard 1923- 12
Shawn, Frank S.
　See Goulart, Ron
Shay, Art
　See Shay, Arthur
Shay, Arthur 1922- 4
Shay, Lacey
　See Shebar, Sharon Sigmond
Shea, Bob 231
　Earlier sketch in SATA *188*
Shea, George 1940- 54
　Brief entry 42
Shea, Pegi Deitz 1960- 172
　Earlier sketches in SATA *77, 137*
Shearer, Alex 1949- 204
Shearer, John 1947- 43
　Brief entry 27
　See also CLR *34*
Shearer, Ted 1919- 43
Shearing, Leonie 1972- 184
Sheban, Chris 182
Shebar, Sharon Sigmond 1945- 36
Shecter, Ben 1935- 16
Shedd, Warner 1934- 147
　Earlier sketch in SATA *87*
Sheedy, Alexandra Elizabeth 1962- 39
　Earlier sketch in SATA *19*
Sheehan, Ethna 1908-2000 9
Sheehan, Patty 1945- 77
Sheehan, Sean 1951- 154
　Earlier sketch in SATA *86*
Sheen, Barbara 1949- 143
Shefelman, Janice 1930- 205
　Earlier sketches in SATA *58, 129*
Shefelman, Janice Jordan
　See Shefelman, Janice
Shefelman, Tom 1927- 204
　Earlier sketch in SATA *58*
Sheffer, H. R.
　See Abels, Harriette S(heffer)
Sheffield, Charles 1935-2002 109
Sheffield, Janet N. 1926- 26
Sheikh, Nazneen 1944- 101
Sheinkin, Steve 1968- 204
Sheinmel, Alyssa B. 233
Sheinmel, Courtney 1977- 211
Shekerjian, Regina Tor 16
Shelby, Anne 1948- 85
　Autobiography Feature 121
　See also SAAS *26*
Sheldon, Ann
　See Antle, Nancy
Sheldon, Ann 67
　Earlier sketch in SATA *1*
Sheldon, Aure 1917-1976 12
Sheldon, David 185
Sheldon, Deyan 181
Sheldon, John
　See Bloch, Robert (Albert)
Sheldon, Muriel 1926- 45
　Brief entry 39
Shell, Barry 1951- 176

Shelley, Frances
　See Wees, Frances Shelley
Shelley, John 1959- 202
Shelley, Mary
　See Shelley, Mary Wollstonecraft
Shelley, Mary Wollstonecraft 1797-1851 29
　See also CLR *133*
Shelton, Paula Young 1961- 227
Shelton, William Roy 1919-1995 5
　Obituary 129
Shemie, Bonnie (Jean Brenner) 1949- 96
Shemin, Margaretha (Hoeneveld) 1928- 4
Shen, Michele 1953- 173
Shenker, Michele
　See Shen, Michele
Shenton, Edward 1895-1977 45
Shepard, Aaron 1950- 187
　Earlier sketches in SATA *75, 113*
Shepard, Ernest Howard 1879-1976 100
　Obituary 24
　Earlier sketches in SATA *3, 33*
　See also CLR *27*
Shepard, James R.
　See Shepard, Jim
Shepard, Jim 1956- 164
　Earlier sketch in SATA *90*
Shepard, Mary
　See Knox, (Mary) Eleanor Jessie
Shephard, Esther 1891-1975 5
　Obituary 26
Shepherd, Amanda 201
Shepherd, Donna Walsh
　See Walsh Shepherd, Donna
Shepherd, Elizabeth 4
Shepherd, Irana 173
Shepherd, Roni
　See Shepherd, Irana
Sheppard, Kate 195
Shepperson, Rob 178
Sherburne, Zoa (Lillian Morin) 1912-1995 3
　See also SAAS *18*
Sherk-Savage, Candace
　See Savage, Candace
Sherlock, Patti 71
Sherman, D(enis) R(onald) 1934- 48
　Brief entry 29
Sherman, Diane (Finn) 1928- 12
Sherman, Elizabeth
　See Friskey, Margaret (Richards)
Sherman, Harold (Morrow) 1898-1987 37
　Obituary 137
Sherman, Josepha 163
　Earlier sketch in SATA *75*
Sherman, Michael
　See Lowndes, Robert A(ugustine) W(ard)
Sherman, Nancy
　See Rosenberg, Nancy
Sherman, Pat 174
Sherman, Peter Michael
　See Lowndes, Robert A(ugustine) W(ard)
Sherrard, Valerie 1957- 141
Sherrard, Valerie Anne
　See Sherrard, Valerie
Sherrod, Jane
　See Singer, Jane Sherrod
Sherry, Clifford J. 1943- 84
Sherry, (Dulcie) Sylvia 1932- 122
　Earlier sketch in SATA *8*
Sherwan, Earl 1917- 3
Sherwood, Jonathan
　See London, Jonathan
Sheth, Kashmira 186
Shetterly, Will 1955- 78
　Autobiography Feature 106
Shetterly, William Howard
　See Shetterly, Will
Shiefman, Vicky 1942- 22
Shields, Brenda Desmond (Armstrong)
　1914- 37
Shields, Carol Diggory 174
Shields, Charles 1944- 10

Shields, Gillian 203
Shiels, Barbara
    See Adams, Barbara Johnston
Shiffman, Lena 1957- *101*
Shiga, Jason 1976- 228
Shiina, Makoto 1944- 83
Shimin, Symeon 1902-1984 .... *13*
Shimko, Bonnie 1941- *191*
Shine, Andrea 1955- *104*
Shine, Deborah 1932- 71
Shinn, Everett 1876-1953 .... *21*
Shinn, Sharon 1957- 229
    Earlier sketches in SATA *110, 164*
Shippen, Katherine B(inney) 1892-1980 .... *1*
    Obituary *23*
    See also CLR *36*
Shippey, T. A. 1943- *143*
Shippey, Thomas Alan
    See Shippey, T. A.
Shipton, Eric Earle 1907-1977 .... *10*
Shipton, Jonathan 1948- *215*
Shipton, Paul 1963- *196*
Shiraz, Yasmin *173*
Shirer, William L(awrence) 1904-1993 .... *45*
    Obituary *78*
Shirley, Debra 203
Shirley, Gayle C 1955- 96
Shirley, Gayle Corbett
    See Shirley, Gayle C
Shirley, Jean 1919- 70
Shirreffs, Gordon D(onald) 1914-1996 .... *11*
Shirts, Morris A(lpine) 1922- 63
Shlichta, Joe 1968- 84
Shmurak, Carole B. 1944- *118*
Sholokhov, Mikhail 1905-1984
    Obituary *36*
Sholokhov, Mikhail Aleksandrovich
    See Sholokhov, Mikhail
Shore, Diane Z. 215
    Earlier sketch in SATA *179*
Shore, Diane ZuHone
    See Shore, Diane Z.
Shore, June Lewis 30
Shore, Nancy 1960- *124*
Shore, Robert 1924- 39
Short, Michael 1937- 65
Short, Roger
    See Arkin, Alan
Shortall, Leonard W. *19*
Shortt, Tim(othy Donald) 1961- 96
Shotwell, Louisa Rossiter 1902-1993 .... *3*
Shoulders, Michael 1954- 216
Shoup, Barbara 1947- *156*
    Earlier sketch in SATA *86*
    See also SAAS *24*
Shoveller, Herb *184*
Showalter, Jean B(reckinridge) *12*
Showell, Ellen Harvey 1934- 33
Showers, Paul C. 1910-1999 92
    Obituary *114*
    Earlier sketch in SATA *21*
    See also CLR *6*
    See also SAAS *7*
Shpakow, Tanya 1959(?)- 94
Shpitalnik, Vladimir 1964- 83
Shragg, Karen (I.) 1954- *142*
Shreeve, Elizabeth 1956- *156*
Shreve, Susan
    See Shreve, Susan Richards
Shreve, Susan Richards 1939- *152*
    Brief entry *41*
    Earlier sketches in SATA *46, 95*
Shriver, Jean Adair 1932- 75
Shriver, Maria 1955- *134*
Shriver, Maria Owings
    See Shriver, Maria
Shrode, Mary
    See Hollingsworth, Mary
Shtainmets, Leon 32
Shub, Elizabeth 1915(?)-2004 5
Shuken, Julia 1948- 84

Shulevitz, Uri 1935- *165*
    Earlier sketches in SATA *3, 50, 106*
    See also CLR *61*
Shulman, Alix Kates 1932- 7
Shulman, Dee 1957- *146*
Shulman, Irving 1913-1995 .... *13*
Shulman, Lisa 202
Shulman, Mark 1962- *184*
Shulman, Max 1919-1988
    Obituary 59
Shulman, Milton 1913-2004
    Obituary *154*
Shulman, Neil B(arnett) 1945- 89
Shumsky, Zena
    See Collier, Zena
Shura, Mary Francis
    See Craig, Mary (Francis) Shura
Shusterman, Neal 1962- 201
    Autobiography Feature *140*
    Earlier sketches in SATA *85, 121, 140*
Shuter, Jane (Margaret) 1955- *151*
    Earlier sketch in SATA *90*
Shuttlesworth, Dorothy Edwards *3*
Shwartz, Susan (Martha) 1949- 94
Shyer, Christopher 1961- 98
Shyer, Marlene Fanta *13*
Siberell, Anne 29
Sibley, Don 1922- *12*
Siburt, Ruth 1951- *121*
Siculan, Daniel 1922- *12*
Siddals, Mary McKenna 232
Siddon, Barbara
    See Bradford, Barbara Taylor
Sidgwick, Ethel 1877-1970 .... *116*
Sidjakov, Nicolas 1924- *18*
Sidman, Joyce 1956- *181*
    Earlier sketch in SATA *145*
Sidney, Frank
    See Warwick, Alan R(oss)
Sidney, Margaret
    See Lothrop, Harriet Mulford Stone
Siebert, Diane 1948- *189*
Siegal, Aranka 1930- 88
    Brief entry *37*
Siegel, Beatrice 36
Siegel, Helen
    See Siegl, Helen
Siegel, Robert 1939- 39
Siegel, Robert Harold
    See Siegel, Robert
Siegel, Siena Cherson 1967(?)- *185*
Siegelson, Kim L. 1962- *114*
Sieger, Ted 1958- *189*
Siegl, Helen 1924- 34
Siepmann, Mary Aline
    See Wesley, Mary (Aline)
Sierra, Judy 1945- *195*
    Earlier sketches in SATA *104, 162*
Sieswerda, Paul L. 1942- *147*
Sievert, Terri
    See Dougherty, Terri (L.)
Sigsawa, Keiichi 1972- *211*
Silas
    See McCay, (Zenas) Winsor
Silcock, Sara Lesley 1947- *12*
Silin-Palmer, Pamela *184*
Sill, Cathryn 1953- *221*
    Earlier sketches in SATA *74, 141*
Sill, John 1947- 222
    Earlier sketches in SATA *74, 140*
Sillitoe, Alan 1928-2010 .... *61*
Sills, Leslie (Elka) 1948- *129*
Silly, E. S.
    See Kraus, (Herman) Robert
Silsbe, Brenda 1953- 73
Silva, Joseph
    See Goulart, Ron
Silvano, Wendi 1962- 223
Silver, Jago
    See Jago
Silver, Maggie 216

Silver, Ruth
    See Chew, Ruth
Silverberg, Robert 1935- 91
    Autobiography Feature *104*
    Earlier sketch in SATA *13*
    See also CLR *59*
Silverman, Erica 1955- 222
    Earlier sketches in SATA *78, 112, 165*
Silverman, Janis L. 1946- *127*
Silverman, Mel(vin Frank) 1931-1966 9
Silverman, Robin L. 1954- 96
Silverman, Robin Landew
    See Silverman, Robin L.
Silverstein, Alvin 1933- *124*
    Earlier sketches in SATA *8, 69*
    See also CLR *25*
Silverstein, Herma 1945- *106*
Silverstein, Robert Alan 1959- *124*
    Earlier sketch in SATA *77*
Silverstein, Shel 1932-1999 92
    Brief entry *27*
    Obituary *116*
    Earlier sketch in SATA *33*
    See also CLR *96*
Silverstein, Sheldon Allan
    See Silverstein, Shel
Silverstein, Virginia B. 1937- *124*
    Earlier sketches in SATA *8, 69*
    See also CLR *25*
Silverstein, Virginia Barbara Opshelor
    See Silverstein, Virginia B.
Silverthorne, Elizabeth 1930- 35
Silverwood, Margaret Shannon 1966- *137*
    Earlier sketch in SATA *83*
Silvey, Diane F. 1946- *135*
Sim, David 1953- *162*
Sim, Dorrith M. 1931- 96
Simak, Clifford D(onald) 1904-1988
    Obituary 56
Simard, Remy 1959- *168*
Siminovich, Lorena 1976(?)- *219*
Simmie, Lois (Ann) 1932- *106*
Simmonds, Posy 1945- *130*
    See also CLR *23*
Simmonds, Rosemary Elizabeth
    See Simmonds, Posy
Simmons, Andra 1939- *141*
Simmons, Elly 1955- *134*
Simmons, Michael 1970- *185*
Simms, Laura 1947- *117*
Simner, Janni Lee *113*
Simon, Charlie May
    See Fletcher, Charlie May Hogue
Simon, Francesca 1955- *111*
Simon, Gabriel 1972- *118*
Simon, Hilda Rita 1921- 28
    See also CLR *39*
Simon, Howard 1903-1979 32
    Obituary *21*
Simon, Joe
    See Simon, Joseph H.
Simon, Joseph H. 1913- 7
Simon, Martin P(aul William) 1903-1969 .... *12*
Simon, Mina Lewiton
    See Lewiton, Mina
Simon, Norma (Feldstein) 1927- *129*
    Earlier sketches in SATA *3, 68*
Simon, Seymour 1931- 202
    Earlier sketches in SATA *4, 73, 138*
    See also CLR *63*
Simon, Shirley (Schwartz) 1921- *11*
Simon, Solomon 1895-1970 40
Simonetta, Linda 1948- *14*
Simonetta, Sam 1936- *14*
Simons, Barbara B(rooks) 1934- *41*
Simont, Marc 1915- *126*
    Earlier sketches in SATA *9, 73*
Simpson, Colin 1908-1983 .... *14*
Simpson, Harriette
    See Arnow, Harriette (Louisa) Simpson

Simpson, Jacynth Hope
    See Hope Simpson, Jacynth
Simpson, Lesley 1963- 150
Simpson, Margaret 1943- 128
Simpson, Myrtle L(illias) 1931- 14
Sims, Blanche 168
    Earlier sketch in SATA 75
Sims, Blanche L.
    See Sims, Blanche
Sims, Rudine
    See Bishop, Rudine Sims
Simundsson, Elva 1950- 63
Sinclair, Clover
    See Gater, Dilys
Sinclair, Emil
    See Hesse, Hermann
Sinclair, Jeff 1958- 77
Sinclair, Olga 1923- 121
Sinclair, Rose
    See Smith, Susan Vernon
Sinclair, Upton 1878-1968 9
Sinclair, Upton Beall
    See Sinclair, Upton
Singer, A.L.
    See Lerangis, Peter
Singer, Arthur 1917-1990 64
Singer, Isaac
    See Singer, Isaac Bashevis
Singer, Isaac Bashevis 1904-1991 27
    Obituary 68
    Earlier sketch in SATA 3
    See also CLR 1
Singer, Jane Sherrod 1917-1985 4
    Obituary 42
Singer, Julia 1917- 28
Singer, Kurt D. 1911-2005 38
    Obituary 172
Singer, Marilyn 1948- 201
    Autobiography Feature 158
    Brief entry 38
    Earlier sketches in SATA 48, 80, 125, 158
    See also CLR 48
    See also SAAS 13
Singer, Muff 1942-2005 104
    Obituary 160
Singer, Nicky 1956- 194
Singer, Susan (Mahler) 1941- 9
Singh, Rashmi Sharma 1952- 90
Singleton, Linda Joy 1957- 166
    Earlier sketch in SATA 88
Singleton, L.J.
    See Singleton, Linda Joy
Singleton, Sarah 1966- 214
Sinykin, Sheri
    See Sinykin, Sheri Cooper
Sinykin, Sheri Cooper 1950- 142
    Autobiography Feature 142
    Earlier sketches in SATA 72, 133
Sinykin, Sheril Terri Cooper
    See Sinykin, Sheri Cooper
Siomades, Lorianne 217
Sipiera, Paul P., (Jr.) 1948- 144
    Earlier sketch in SATA 89
Siracusa, Catherine (Jane) 1947- 82
Sirett, Dawn (Karen) 1966- 88
Sirimarco, Elizabeth 1966- 158
Sirof, Harriet 1930- 94
    Earlier sketch in SATA 37
Sirois, Allen L. 1950- 76
Sirvaitis (Chernyaev), Karen (Ann) 1961- ... 79
Sis, Peter 1949- 192
    Earlier sketch in SATA 149
    See also CLR 110
Sisson, Rosemary Anne 1923- 11
Sister Mary Terese
    See Donze, Mary Terese
Sita, Lisa 1962- 87
Sitarski, Anita 200
Sitomer, Alan Lawrence 174
Sitomer, Harry 1903-1985 31
Sitomer, Mindel 1903-1987 31

Sittenfeld, Curtis 1975(?)- 164
Sive, Helen R(obinson) 1951- 30
Sivulich, Sandra (Jeanne) Stroner 1941- 9
Siy, Alexandra 193
Skarmeta, Antonio 1940- 57
Skeers, Linda 1958- 207
Skelly, James R(ichard) 1927- 17
Skelton, Matthew 1971- 185
Skinner, Constance Lindsay 1877-1939
    See YABC 1
Skinner, Cornelia Otis 1901-1979 2
Skipper, G. C. 1939- 46
    Brief entry 38
Sklansky, Amy E(dgar) 1971- 145
Sklansky, Amy E. 1971- 204
Skofield, James 95
    Brief entry 44
Skold, Betty Westrom 1923- 41
Skorpen, Liesel Moak 1935- 3
Skott, Maria
    See Nikolajeva, Maria
Skovron, Jon 1976- 229
Skrypuch, Marsha Forchuk 1954- 134
Skultety, Nancy Laney 1960- 175
Skurzynski, Gloria 1930- 145
    Autobiography Feature 145
    Earlier sketches in SATA 8, 74, 122
    See also SAAS 9
Skurzynski, Gloria Joan
    See Skurzynski, Gloria
Skutch, Robert 1925- 89
Skye, Maggie
    See Werner, Herma
Skye, Obert 200
    Earlier sketch in SATA 170
Slack, Michael 1969- 189
Slackman, Charles B. 1934- 12
Slade, Arthur G. 1967- 221
    Earlier sketches in SATA 106, 149
Slade, Arthur Gregory
    See Slade, Arthur G.
Slade, Christian 1974- 193
Slade, Richard 1910-1971 9
Slade, Suzanne 1964- 226
Slangerup, Erik Jon 1969- 130
Slate, Joseph 1928- 174
    Earlier sketches in SATA 38, 122
Slate, Joseph Frank
    See Slate, Joseph
Slater, Dashka 1963- 179
Slater, David Michael 1970- 212
Slater, Ray
    See Lansdale, Joe R.
Slaughter, Hope 1940- 84
Slaughter, Jean
    See Doty, Jean Slaughter
Slaughter, Tom 1955- 152
Slavicek, Louise Chipley 1956- 144
Slavin, Bill 1959- 199
    Earlier sketches in SATA 76, 148
Slaymaker, Melissa Eskridge 1958- 158
Slayton, Fran Cannon 221
Sleator, William 1945-2011 208
    Earlier sketches in SATA 3, 68, 118, 161
    See also CLR 128
Sleator, William Warner III
    See Sleator, William
Slegers, Liesbet 1975- 154
Sleigh, Barbara 1906-1982 86
    Obituary 30
    Earlier sketch in SATA 3
Slepian, Jan 1921- 85
    Brief entry 45
    Earlier sketch in SATA 51
    See also SAAS 8
Slepian, Janice B.
    See Slepian, Jan
Slicer, Margaret O. 1920- 4
Slier, Debby
    See Shine, Deborah
Sloan, Brian 1966- 172

Sloan, Carolyn 1937- 116
    Earlier sketch in SATA 58
Sloan, Glenna 1930- 120
Sloan, Glenna Davis
    See Sloan, Glenna
Sloane, Eric 1910(?)-1985 52
    Obituary 42
Sloane, Todd 1955- 88
Sloat, Teri 1948- 164
    Earlier sketches in SATA 70, 106
Slobodkin, Florence Gersh 1905-1994 5
    Obituary 107
Slobodkin, Louis 1903-1975 26
    Earlier sketch in SATA 1
Slobodkina, Esphyr 1908-2002 1
    Obituary 135
    See also SAAS 8
Sloggett, Nellie 1851-1923 44
Slonim, David 1966- 207
Sloss, Lesley Lord 1965- 72
Slote, Alfred 1926- 72
    Earlier sketch in SATA 8
    See also CLR 4
    See also SAAS 21
Slote, Elizabeth 1956- 80
Small, Charlie
    See Ward, Nick
Small, David 1945- 216
    Brief entry 46
    Earlier sketches in SATA 50, 95, 126, 183
    See also CLR 53
Small, Ernest
    See Lent, Blair
Small, Mary 1932- 165
Small, Terry 1942- 75
Smallcomb, Pam 1954- 159
Smallman, Steve 227
    Earlier sketch in SATA 197
Smalls, Irene
    See Smalls-Hector, Irene
Smalls-Hector, Irene 1950- 146
    Earlier sketch in SATA 73
    See also CLR 103
Smallwood, Norah (Evelyn) 1910(?)-1984
    Obituary 41
Smaridge, Norah (Antoinette) 1903-1994 6
Smath, Jerry 1933- 198
Smee, Nicola 1948- 167
    Earlier sketch in SATA 76
Smiley, Virginia Kester 1923- 2
Smit, Noelle 1972- 199
Smith, Alexander McCall 1948- 179
    Earlier sketch in SATA 73
Smith, Andrew 1959- 209
Smith, Andrew Anselmo
    See Smith, Andrew
Smith, Andy J. 1975- 207
Smith, Anne Warren 1938- 41
    Brief entry 34
Smith, Barry (Edward Jervis) 1943- 75
Smith, Beatrice S(chillinger) 12
Smith, Betsy Covington 1937- 55
    Earlier sketch in SATA 43
Smith, Betty (Wehner) 1904-1972 6
Smith, Bradford 1909-1964 5
Smith, Brenda 1946- 82
Smith, C. Pritchard
    See Hoyt, Edwin P(almer), Jr.
Smith, Caesar
    See Trevor, Elleston
Smith, Cat Bowman 1939- 201
Smith, Charles R., Jr. 1969- 203
    Earlier sketch in SATA 159
Smith, Craig 1955- 172
    Earlier sketches in SATA 81, 117
Smith, Cynthia Leitich 1967- 215
    Earlier sketch in SATA 152
Smith, D. James 1955- 176
Smith, Danna 216
Smith, Danna Kessimakis
    See Smith, Danna

Smith, Datus C(lifford), Jr. 1907-1999 .... *13*
  Obituary *116*
Smith, Debra 1955- *89*
Smith, Derek 1943- *141*
Smith, Dick King
  See King-Smith, Dick
Smith, D.J.
  See Smith, D. James
Smith, Dodie
  See Smith, Dorothy Gladys
Smith, Doris Buchanan 1934-2002 .... *75*
  Obituary *140*
  Earlier sketch in SATA *28*
  See also SAAS *10*
Smith, Dorothy Gladys 1896-1990 .... *82*
  Obituary *65*
Smith, Dorothy Stafford 1905- *6*
Smith, Duane 1974- *202*
Smith, E(lmer) Boyd 1860-1943
  See YABC *1*
Smith, E(dric) Brooks 1917- *40*
Smith, Elwood H. 1941- *203*
Smith, Emily Wing 1980- *215*
Smith, Emma 1923- *52*
  Brief entry *36*
Smith, (Katherine) Eunice (Young)
  1902-1993 .... *5*
Smith, Frances C(hristine) 1904-1986 .... *3*
Smith, Gary R. 1932- *14*
Smith, Geof 1969- *102*
Smith, George Harmon 1920- *5*
Smith, Gordon 1951- *184*
Smith, Greg Leitich *152*
Smith, H(arry) Allen 1907-1976
  Obituary *20*
Smith, Helene 1937- *142*
Smith, Hope Anita *202*
Smith, Howard E(verett), Jr. 1927- *12*
Smith, Hugh L(etcher) 1921-1968 .... *5*
Smith, Icy 1966- *228*
Smith, Imogene Henderson 1922- *12*
Smith, Jacqueline B. 1937- *39*
Smith, Jada Pinkett 1971- *161*
Smith, James Noel 1950- *193*
Smith, Janet (Buchanan) Adam
  See Adam Smith, Janet (Buchanan)
Smith, Janice Lee 1949- *155*
  Earlier sketch in SATA *54*
Smith, Jean
  See Smith, Frances C(hristine)
Smith, Jean Pajot 1945- *10*
Smith, Jeff 1958- *161*
  Earlier sketch in SATA *93*
Smith, Jeff Allen
  See Smith, Jeff
Smith, Jeffrey Alan
  See Smith, Jeff
Smith, Jenny 1963- *90*
Smith, Jessie
  See Kunhardt, Edith
Smith, Jessie Willcox 1863-1935 .... *21*
  See also CLR *59*
Smith, Jim W.W. *231*
Smith, Joan (Mary) 1933- *54*
  Brief entry *46*
Smith, Johnston
  See Crane, Stephen
Smith, Jos A. 1936- *181*
  Earlier sketches in SATA *73, 120*
Smith, Joseph Arthur
  See Smith, Jos A.
Smith, Judie R. 1936- *80*
Smith, Kirsten 1970- *210*
Smith, Lafayette
  See Higdon, Hal
Smith, Lane 1959- *224*
  Earlier sketches in SATA *76, 131, 179*
  See also CLR *47*
Smith, Lee
  See Albion, Lee Smith
Smith, Lendon H(oward) 1921- *64*

Smith, Lillian H(elena) 1887-1983
  Obituary *32*
Smith, Linda 1949- *177*
Smith, Linell Nash 1932- *2*
Smith, Lucia B. 1943- *30*
Smith, Maggie 1965- *190*
Smith, Margaret Emily Noel Nuttall
  See Nuttall-Smith, Margaret Emily Noel
Smith, Marion Hagens 1913- *12*
Smith, Marion Jaques 1899-1987 .... *13*
Smith, Mary Ellen *10*
Smith, Marya 1945- *78*
Smith, Mike
  See Smith, Mary Ellen
Smith, Nancy Covert 1935- *12*
Smith, Norman F. 1920- *70*
  Earlier sketch in SATA *5*
Smith, Patricia Clark 1943- *96*
Smith, Pauline C.
  See Arthur, Robert, (Jr.)
Smith, Pauline C(oggeshall) 1908-1994 .... *27*
Smith, Philip Warren 1936- *46*
Smith, R. Alexander McCall
  See Smith, Alexander McCall
Smith, Rebecca 1946- *123*
Smith, Robert Kimmel 1930- *77*
  Earlier sketch in SATA *12*
Smith, Robert Paul 1915-1977 .... *52*
  Obituary *30*
Smith, Roland 1951- *193*
  Earlier sketches in SATA *115, 161*
Smith, Rosamond
  See Oates, Joyce Carol
Smith, Ruth Leslie 1902- *2*
Smith, Samantha 1972-1985
  Obituary *45*
Smith, Sandra Lee 1945- *75*
Smith, Sarah Stafford
  See Smith, Dorothy Stafford
Smith, Sharon 1947- *82*
Smith, Sherri L. 1971- *156*
Smith, Sherwood 1951- *206*
  Autobiography Feature *206*
  Earlier sketches in SATA *82, 140*
Smith, Shirley Raines
  See Raines, Shirley C(arol)
Smith, Susan Carlton 1923- *12*
Smith, Susan Mathias 1950- *43*
  Brief entry *35*
Smith, Susan Vernon 1950- *48*
  Brief entry *45*
Smith, Tim(othy R.) 1945- *151*
Smith, Ursula 1934- *54*
Smith, Vian (Crocker) 1920-1969 .... *11*
Smith, Wanda VanHoy 1926- *65*
Smith, Ward
  See Goldsmith, Howard
Smith, William A. 1918- *10*
Smith, William Jay 1918- *154*
  Autobiography Feature *154*
  Earlier sketches in SATA *2, 68*
  See also SAAS *22*
Smith, Winsome 1935- *45*
Smith, Z.Z.
  See Westheimer, David
Smith-Ankrom, M. E. 1942- *130*
Smith-Griswold, Wendy 1955- *88*
Smith Hernandez, Duncan Tonatiuh
  See Tonatiuh, Duncan
Smith-Rex, Susan J. 1950- *94*
Smithsen, Richard
  See Pellowski, Michael (Joseph)
Smithson, Ryan 1985- *216*
Smits, Teo
  See Smits, Theodore R(ichard)
Smits, Theodore R(ichard) 1905-1996 .... *45*
  Brief entry *28*
Smolinski, Dick 1932- *86*
Smothers, Ethel Footman 1944- *149*
  Earlier sketch in SATA *76*
Smucker, Anna Egan 1948- *209*

Smucker, Barbara 1915-2003 .... *130*
  Earlier sketches in SATA *29, 76*
  See also CLR *10*
  See also SAAS *11*
Smucker, Barbara Claassen
  See Smucker, Barbara
Smyth, Iain 1959- *105*
Snedeker, Caroline Dale (Parke) 1871-1956
  See YABC *2*
Sneed, Brad *191*
Sneider, Marian 1932-2005 .... *197*
Snell, Gordon 1933(?)- *228*
Snell, Nigel (Edward Creagh) 1936- *57*
  Brief entry *40*
Snellgrove, L(aurence) E(rnest) 1928- *53*
Snelling, Dennis (Wayne) 1958- *84*
Sneve, Virginia Driving Hawk 1933- *95*
  Earlier sketch in SATA *8*
  See also CLR *2*
Snicket, Lemony 1970- *215*
  Earlier sketches in SATA *126, 187*
  See also CLR *79*
Sniegoski, Thomas E. *195*
Sniegoski, Tom
  See Sniegoski, Thomas E.
Snir, Eleyor *225*
Snir, Mirik 1948- *226*
Snodgrass, Mary Ellen 1944- *75*
Snodgrass, Quentin Curtius
  See Twain, Mark
Snodgrass, Thomas Jefferson
  See Twain, Mark
Snook, Barbara (Lillian) 1913-1976 .... *34*
Snow, Alan 1959- *190*
Snow, Carol 1965- *208*
Snow, Donald Clifford 1917-1979 .... *16*
Snow, Dorothea J(ohnston) 1909- *9*
Snow, Richard F. 1947- *52*
  Brief entry *37*
Snow, Richard Folger
  See Snow, Richard F.
Snow, Sarah *229*
Snyder, Anne 1922-2001 .... *4*
  Obituary *125*
Snyder, Bernadette McCarver 1930- *97*
Snyder, Betsy *230*
Snyder, Carol 1941- *35*
Snyder, Gerald S(eymour) 1933- *48*
  Brief entry *34*
Snyder, Jerome 1916-1976
  Obituary *20*
Snyder, Laurel 1974- *209*
Snyder, Midori 1954- *106*
Snyder, Paul A. 1946- *125*
Snyder, Zilpha Keatley 1927- *226*
  Autobiography Feature *163*
  Earlier sketches in SATA *1, 28, 75, 110, 163*
  See also CLR *121*
  See also SAAS *2*
Snyderman, Reuven K. 1922- *5*
So, Meilo *162*
Sobel, June 1950- *149*
Soble, Jennie
  See Cavin, Ruth
Sobol, Donald J. 1924- *132*
  Earlier sketches in SATA *1, 31, 73*
  See also CLR *4*
Sobol, Harriet Langsam 1936- *47*
  Brief entry *34*
Sobol, Richard *211*
Sobol, Rose 1931- *76*
Sobott-Mogwe, Gaele 1956- *97*
Soderlind, Arthur E(dwin) 1920- *14*
Soentpiet, Chris K. 1970- *159*
  Earlier sketch in SATA *97*
Soerensen, Svend Otto 1916- *67*
Sofer, Barbara 1949- *109*
Sofer, Rachel
  See Sofer, Barbara
Softly, Barbara Frewin 1924- *12*
Sogabe, Aki *207*

Soglow, Otto 1900-1975
  Obituary 30
Sohl, Frederic J(ohn) 1916- 10
Sohr, Daniel 1973- 190
Sokol, Bill
  See Sokol, William
Sokol, William 1923- 37
Sokolov, Kirill 1930- 34
Solbert, Romaine G. 1925- 2
Solbert, Ronni
  See Solbert, Romaine G.
Solheim, James 233
  Earlier sketch in SATA 133
Solomon, Heather M. 188
Solomon, Joan 1930- 51
  Brief entry 40
Solomons, Ikey Esquir
  See Thackeray, William Makepeace
Solonevich, George 1915-2003 15
Solot, Mary Lynn 1939- 12
Solov'ev, Mikhail
  See Soloviov, Michael
Soloviov, Michael 1972- 222
Soman, David 1965- 200
Somerlott, Robert 1928-2001 62
Somers, Kevin 205
Somervill, Barbara A(nn) 1948- 140
Sommer, Angela
  See Sommer-Bodenburg, Angela
Sommer, Carl 1930- 175
  Earlier sketch in SATA 126
Sommer, Elyse 1929- 7
Sommer, Robert 1929- 12
Sommer-Bodenburg, Angela 1948- 113
  Earlier sketch in SATA 63
Sommerdorf, Norma 1926- 131
Sommerdorf, Norma Jean
  See Sommerdorf, Norma
Sommerfelt, Aimee 1892-1975 5
Son, John 160
Sones, Sonya 131
Sonneborn, Ruth (Cantor) 1899-1974 4
  Obituary 27
Sonnenblick, Jordan 1969- 223
  Earlier sketch in SATA 185
  See also CLR 144
Sonnenmark, Laura A. 1958- 73
Soo, Kean 201
Sopko, Eugen 1949- 58
Sorel, Edward 1929- 126
  Brief entry 37
  Earlier sketch in SATA 65
Sorensen, Henri 1950- 115
  Earlier sketch in SATA 77
Sorensen, Svend Otto
  See Soerensen, Svend Otto
Sorensen, Virginia 1912-1991 2
  Obituary 72
  See also SAAS 15
Sorenson, Jane 1926- 63
Sorenson, Margo 1946- 96
Sorley Walker, Kathrine 41
Sorra, Kristin 185
Sorrells, Walter 177
Sorrentino, Joseph N. 1937- 6
Sortor, June Elizabeth 1939- 12
Sortor, Toni
  See Sortor, June Elizabeth
Sosa, Hernan 1977- 203
Soskin, V. H.
  See Ellison, Virginia H(owell)
Soto, Gary 1952- 174
  Earlier sketches in SATA 80, 120
  See also CLR 38
Sotomayor, Antonio 1902-1985 11
Souci, Robert D. San
  See San Souci, Robert D.
Soudley, Henry
  See Wood, James Playsted
Souhami, Jessica 176
Soule, Gardner (Bosworth) 1913-2000 14

Soule, Jean Conder 1919- 10
Soup, Cuthbert
  See Swallow, Gerry
Souster, (Holmes) Raymond 1921- 63
South, Sheri Cobb 1959- 82
Southall, Ivan 1921-2008 134
  Autobiography Feature 134
  Earlier sketches in SATA 3, 68
  See also CLR 165
  See also SAAS 3
Southall, Ivan Francis
  See Southall, Ivan
Southey, Robert 1774-1843 54
Southgate, Vera 54
Souza, Janet
  See Tashjian, Janet
Sovak, Jan 1953- 115
Sowden, Celeste
  See Walters, Celeste
Sowter, Nita 69
Spafford, Suzy 1945- 160
Spagnoli, Cathy 1950- 134
  Earlier sketch in SATA 79
Spain, Sahara Sunday 1991- 133
Spain, Susan Rosson 185
Spalding, Andrea 1944- 150
  Earlier sketch in SATA 101
Spalenka, Greg 1958- 198
Spanfeller, James J. 1930- 19
  See also SAAS 8
Spanfeller, Jim
  See Spanfeller, James J.
Spangenberg, Judith Dunn 1942- 5
Spangler, Brie 212
Spanyol, Jessica 1965- 206
  Earlier sketch in SATA 137
Spar, Jerome 1918- 10
Sparks, Barbara 1942- 78
Sparks, Beatrice (Mathews) 1918- 44
  Brief entry 28
  See also CLR 139
Sparks, Mary W. 1920- 15
Spaulding, Douglas
  See Bradbury, Ray
Spaulding, Leonard
  See Bradbury, Ray
Spaulding, Norma 107
Speare, Elizabeth George 1908-1994 62
  Obituary 83
  Earlier sketch in SATA 5
  See also CLR 8
Spearing, Craig J. 228
Spearing, Judith (Mary Harlow) 1922- 9
Spears, Rick 182
Speck, Katie 196
Speck, Nancy 1959- 104
Specking, Inez 1890-1960(?) 11
Speed, Nell
  See Keats, Emma
  and Sampson, Emma (Keats) Speed
Speed, Nell (Ewing) 1878-1913 68
Speer, Bonnie Stahlman 1929- 113
Speer-Lyon, Tammie L. 1965- 89
Speicher, Helen Ross S(mith) 1915- 8
Speir, Nancy 1958- 210
  Earlier sketch in SATA 81
Spellman, John W(illard) 1934- 14
Spellman, Roger G.
  See Cox, William R(obert)
Spelman, Cornelia Maude 1946- 144
  Earlier sketch in SATA 96
Spelman, Mary 1934- 28
Spelvin, George
  See Lerangis, Peter
  and Phillips, David Atlee
Spence, Cynthia
  See Eble, Diane
Spence, Eleanor (Rachel) 1928- 21
  See also CLR 26
Spence, Geraldine 1931- 47
Spencer, Ann 1918- 10

Spencer, Britt 206
Spencer, Cornelia
  See Yaukey, Grace S(ydenstricker)
Spencer, Donald D(ean) 1931- 41
Spencer, Elizabeth 1921- 14
Spencer, Leonard G.
  See Garrett, Randall
  and Silverberg, Robert
Spencer, William 1922- 9
Spencer, Zane A(nn) 1935- 35
Spengler, Margaret 223
Sper, Emily 1957- 142
Speregen, Devra Newberger 1964- 84
Sperling, Dan(iel Lee) 1949- 65
Sperry, Armstrong W. 1897-1976 1
  Obituary 27
Sperry, Raymond
  See Garis, Howard R.
Sperry, Raymond, Jr. 1
Spetter, Jung-Hee 1969- 134
Spicer, Dorothy Gladys -1975 32
Spiegel, Beth 184
Spiegelman, Art 1948- 158
  Earlier sketch in SATA 109
Spiegelman, Judith M. 5
Spielberg, Steven 1947- 32
Spier, Peter (Edward) 1927- 54
  Earlier sketch in SATA 4
  See also CLR 5
Spilhaus, Athelstan (Frederick) 1911-1998 .. 13
  Obituary 102
Spilka, Arnold 1917- 6
Spillane, Frank Morrison
  See Spillane, Mickey
Spillane, Mickey 1918-2006 66
  Obituary 176
Spillebeen, Geert 1956- 225
Spinelli, Eileen 1942- 225
  Earlier sketches in SATA 38, 101, 150, 186
Spinelli, Jerry 1941- 195
  Earlier sketches in SATA 39, 71, 110, 158
  See also CLR 82
Spink, Reginald (William) 1905-1994 11
Spinka, Penina Keen 1945- 72
Spinner, Stephanie 1943- 132
  Earlier sketches in SATA 38, 91
Spinossimus
  See White, William, Jr.
Spiotta-DiMare, Loren 173
Spires, Ashley 1978- 183
Spires, Elizabeth 1952- 215
  Earlier sketches in SATA 71, 111
Spiridellis, Gregg 1971(?)- 199
Spirin, Gennadii
  See Spirin, Gennady
Spirin, Gennadij
  See Spirin, Gennady
Spirin, Gennady 1948- 204
  Earlier sketches in SATA 95, 134
  See also CLR 88
Spiro, Ruth 208
Spivak, Dawnine 101
Spizman, Robyn Freedman 194
Spohn, David 1948- 72
Spohn, Kate 1962- 147
  Earlier sketch in SATA 87
Spollen, Christopher 1952- 12
Spooner, Michael (Tim) 1954- 92
Spoor, Mike 218
Spowart, Robin 1947- 177
  Earlier sketch in SATA 82
Spradlin, Michael P. 204
Sprague, Gretchen 1926-2003 27
Spranger, Nina 1969- 203
Sprengel, Artie
  See Lerangis, Peter
Sprigge, Elizabeth (Miriam Squire)
  1900-1974 10
Spring, (Robert) Howard 1889-1965 28
Springer, Kristina 226
Springer, Margaret 1941- 78

Springer, Marilyn Harris 1931- 47
Springer, Nancy 1948- 222
  Earlier sketches in SATA 65, 110, 172
Springstubb, Tricia 1950- 78
  Brief entry 40
  Earlier sketch in SATA 46
Spudvilas, Anne 1951- 199
  Earlier sketch in SATA 94
Spurll, Barbara 1952- 78
Spurr, Elizabeth 172
Spykman, E(lizabeth) C(hoate) 1896-1965 .. 10
  See also CLR 35
Spyri, Johanna (Heusser) 1827-1901 100
  Earlier sketch in SATA 19
  See also CLR 115
Squires, Janet 215
Squires, Phil
  See Barker, S. Omar
Srba, Lynne 98
Sreenivasan, Jyotsna 1964- 101
S-Ringi, Kjell
  See Ringi, Kjell (Arne Soerensen)
Staake, Bob 1957- 209
Stacey, Cherylyn 1945- 96
Stacy, Donald
  See Pohl, Frederik
Stadler, John 204
Stadtler, Bea 1921- 17
Stafford, Jean 1915-1979
  Obituary 22
Stafford, Liliana 1950- 141
Stafford, Paul 1966- 116
Stahl, Ben(jamin) 1910-1987 5
  Obituary 54
Stahl, Hilda 1938-1993 48
  Obituary 77
Stahler, David, Jr. 218
  Earlier sketch in SATA 162
Staib, Walter 233
Staines, Bill 1949- 213
Stainton, Sue 187
Stair, Gobin (John) 1912- 35
Stalder, Valerie 27
Stamaty, Mark Alan 1947- 230
  Earlier sketch in SATA 12
Stambler, Irwin 1924- 5
Stamp, Jorgen 1969- 225
Stampler, Ann Redisch 209
Standiford, Natalie 1961- 169
  Earlier sketch in SATA 81
Stanek, Lou Willett 1931- 63
Stang, Judit 1921-1977 29
Stang, Judy
  See Stang, Judit
Stangl, (Mary) Jean 1928- 67
Stanhope, Eric
  See Hamilton, Charles (Harold St. John)
Stankevich, Boris 1928- 2
Stanley, Diane 1943- 213
  Brief entry 32
  Earlier sketches in SATA 37, 80, 115, 164
  See also CLR 46
  See also SAAS 15
Stanley, Elizabeth 1947- 206
Stanley, George Edward 1942-2011 228
  Earlier sketches in SATA 53, 111, 157, 1, 67
Stanley, Jerry 1941- 127
  Earlier sketch in SATA 79
Stanley, Mandy 165
Stanley, Robert
  See Hamilton, Charles (Harold St. John)
Stanley, Sanna 1962- 145
Stanli, Sue
  See Meilach, Dona Z(weigoron)
Stanstead, John
  See Groom, Arthur William
Stanton, Karen 1960- 190
Stanton, Schuyler
  See Baum, L. Frank

Staples, Suzanne Fisher 1945- 207
  Earlier sketches in SATA 70, 105, 151
  See also CLR 137
Stapleton, Marjorie (Winifred) 1932- 28
Stapp, Arthur D(onald) 1906-1972 4
Starbird, Kaye 1916- 6
  See also CLR 60
Stark, Evan 1942- 78
Stark, James
  See Goldston, Robert (Conroy)
Stark, Ken 1943- 199
Stark, Ulf 1944- 124
Starke, Ruth (Elaine) 1946- 129
Starkey, Marion L(ena) 1901-1991 13
Starmer, Aaron 1976- 226
Starr, Ward
  See Manes, Stephen
Starret, William
  See McClintock, Marshall
Starr Taylor, Bridget 1959- 99
Stasiak, Krystyna 49
Staub, Frank 1949- 116
Staub, Frank Jacob
  See Staub, Frank
Staub, Wendy Corsi 1964- 114
Stauffacher, Sue 1961- 199
  Earlier sketch in SATA 155
Stauffer, Don
  See Berkebile, Fred D(onovan)
Staunton, Schuyler
  See Baum, L. Frank
Staunton, Ted 1956- 167
  Earlier sketch in SATA 112
Stead, Erin E. 1982- 232
Stead, Judy 210
Stead, Philip C.
  See Stringer, Helen
Stead, Philip Christian 225
Stead, Rebecca 1968(?)- 228
  Earlier sketch in SATA 188
Steadman, Ralph 1936- 123
  Earlier sketch in SATA 32
Steadman, Ralph Idris
  See Steadman, Ralph
Stearman, Kaye 1951- 118
Stearn, Ted 1961- 218
Stearns, Monroe (Mather) 1913-1987 5
  Obituary 55
Steckler, Arthur 1921-1985 65
Steding, Laurie 1953- 119
Steel, Danielle 1947- 66
Steel, Danielle Fernande
  See Steel, Danielle
Steele, Addison II
  See Lupoff, Richard A(llen)
Steele, Alexander 1958- 116
Steele, Henry Maxwell
  See Steele, Max
Steele, Mary 1930- 94
Steele, Mary Q(uintard Govan) 1922-1992 .. 51
  Obituary 72
  Earlier sketch in SATA 3
Steele, Max 1922-2005 168
  Earlier sketch in SATA 10
Steele, Philip 1948- 140
  Earlier sketch in SATA 81
Steele, William O(wen) 1917-1979 51
  Obituary 27
  Earlier sketch in SATA 1
Steelhammer, Ilona 1952- 98
Steelsmith, Shari 1962- 72
Stefanik, Alfred T. 1939- 55
Steffanson, Con
  See Cassiday, Bruce (Bingham)
  and Goulart, Ron
Steffens, Bradley 1955- 166
  Earlier sketch in SATA 77
Steffensmeier, Alexander 1977- 195
Stegeman, Janet Allais 1923- 49
  Brief entry 49
Steggall, Susan 1967- 182

Steig, William 1907-2003 111
  Obituary 149
  Earlier sketches in SATA 18, 70
  See also CLR 103
Steig, William H.
  See Steig, William
Stein, David Ezra 211
  Earlier sketch in SATA 180
Stein, Janet 1955- 218
Stein, M(eyer) L(ewis) 1920- 6
Stein, Mathilde 1969- 195
Stein, Mini 2
Stein, R(ichard) Conrad 1937- 154
  Earlier sketches in SATA 31, 82
Stein, Wendy 1951- 77
Steinbeck, John 1902-1968 9
Steinbeck, John Ernst
  See Steinbeck, John
Steinberg, Alfred 1917-1995 9
Steinberg, David 1962- 200
Steinberg, D.J.
  See Steinberg, David
Steinberg, Fannie 1899-1990 43
Steinberg, Fred J. 1933- 4
Steinberg, Phillip Orso 1921- 34
Steinberg, Rafael (Mark) 1927- 45
Steinberg, Saul 1914-1999 67
Steincrohn, Maggie
  See Davis, Maggie S.
Steiner, Barbara A(nnette) 1934- 83
  Earlier sketch in SATA 13
  See also SAAS 13
Steiner, Charlotte 1900-1981 45
Steiner, George 1929- 62
Steiner, Joan 199
  Earlier sketch in SATA 110
Steiner, Jorg
  See Steiner, Jorg
Steiner, Jorg 1930- 35
Steiner, K. Leslie
  See Delany, Samuel R., Jr.
Steiner, Stan(ley) 1925-1987 14
  Obituary 50
Steins, Richard 1942- 79
Stem, Jacqueline 1931- 110
Stemple, Heidi E.Y. 1966- 214
Stemple, Jason 179
Steneman, Shep 1945- 132
Stengel, Joyce A. 1938- 158
Stephanie, Gordon
  See Gordon, Stephanie Jacob
Stephens, Alice Barber 1858-1932 66
Stephens, Casey
  See Wagner, Sharon B.
Stephens, Henrietta Henkle 1909-1993 6
Stephens, J.B.
  See Lynn, Tracy
Stephens, Mary Jo 1935- 8
Stephens, Rebecca 1961- 141
Stephens, Reed
  See Donaldson, Stephen R.
Stephens, Suzanne
  See Kirby, Susan E.
Stephens, William M(cLain) 1925- 21
Stephensen, A. M.
  See Manes, Stephen
Stephenson, Kristina 224
Stephenson, Lynda 1941- 179
Stephenson, Lynda A.
  See Stephenson, Lynda
Stepp, Ann 1935- 29
Stepto, Michele 1946- 61
Steptoe, Javaka 1971- 213
  Earlier sketch in SATA 151
Steptoe, John (Lewis) 1950-1989 63
  Earlier sketch in SATA 8
  See also CLR 12
Sterling, Brett
  See Bradbury, Ray
  and Hamilton, Edmond
  and Samachson, Joseph

Sterling, Dorothy 1913-2008 83
  Autobiography Feature 127
  Obituary 200
  Earlier sketch in SATA *1*
  See also CLR *1*
  See also SAAS *2*
Sterling, Helen
  See Watts, Helen L. Hoke
Sterling, Philip 1907-1989 8
  Obituary 63
Sterling, Shirley (Anne) 1948- 101
Stern, Ellen Norman 1927- 26
Stern, Judith M. 1951- 75
Stern, Madeleine
  See Stern, Madeleine B.
Stern, Madeleine B. 1912-2007 14
Stern, Madeleine Bettina
  See Stern, Madeleine B.
Stern, Maggie 1953- 156
Stern, Philip Van Doren 1900-1984 13
  Obituary 39
Stern, Simon 1943- 15
Sterne, Emma Gelders 1894- 6
Steurt, Marjorie Rankin 1888-1978 10
Stevens, April 1963- 208
Stevens, Bryna 1924- 65
Stevens, Carla M(cBride) 1928- 13
Stevens, Chambers 1968- 128
Stevens, Diane 1939- 94
Stevens, Franklin 1933- 6
Stevens, Greg
  See Cook, Glen
Stevens, Gwendolyn 1944- 33
Stevens, Helen 209
Stevens, Jan Romero 1953- 95
Stevens, Janet 1953- 193
  Earlier sketches in SATA *90, 148*
Stevens, Kathleen 1936- 49
Stevens, Leonard A. 1920- 67
Stevens, Lucile Vernon 1899-1994 59
Stevens, Margaret Dean
  See Aldrich, Bess Streeter
Stevens, Patricia Bunning 1931- 27
Stevens, Peter
  See Geis, Darlene Stern
Stevens, Serita 1949- 70
Stevens, Serita Deborah
  See Stevens, Serita
Stevens, Serita Mendelson
  See Stevens, Serita
Stevens, Shira
  See Stevens, Serita
Stevenson, Anna (M.) 1905- 12
Stevenson, Augusta 1869(?)-1976 2
  Obituary 26
Stevenson, Burton Egbert 1872-1962 25
Stevenson, Drew 1947- 60
Stevenson, Emma 207
Stevenson, Harvey 1960- 148
  Earlier sketch in SATA *80*
Stevenson, James 1929- 195
  Brief entry 34
  Earlier sketches in SATA *42, 71, 113, 161*
  See also CLR *17*
Stevenson, Janet 1913- 8
Stevenson, Robert Louis 1850-1894 100
  See also YABC *2*
  See also CLR *107*
Stevenson, Robert Louis Balfour
  See Stevenson, Robert Louis
Stevenson, Sucie
  See Stevenson, Sucie
Stevenson, Sucie 1956- 194
  Earlier sketch in SATA *104*
Stewart, A(gnes) C(harlotte) 15
Stewart, Amber 181
Stewart, Chantal 1945- 173
  Earlier sketch in SATA *121*
Stewart, Charles
  See Zurhorst, Charles (Stewart, Jr.)

Stewart, Eleanor
  See Porter, Eleanor H(odgman)
Stewart, Elisabeth J(ane) 1927- 93
Stewart, Elizabeth Laing 1907- 6
Stewart, Gail B. 1949- 141
Stewart, George Rippey 1895-1980 3
  Obituary 23
Stewart, Jennifer J. 1960- 128
Stewart, Jennifer Jenkins
  See Stewart, Jennifer J.
Stewart, Joel 211
  Earlier sketch in SATA *151*
Stewart, John 1920- 14
Stewart, Mary (Florence Elinor) 1916- 12
Stewart, Mary Rainbow
  See Stewart, Mary (Florence Elinor)
Stewart, Melissa 1968- 209
  Earlier sketches in SATA *111, 167*
Stewart, Paul 1955- 199
  Earlier sketches in SATA *114, 163*
Stewart, Robert Neil 1891-1972 7
Stewart, Sarah 143
Stewart, Scott
  See Zaffo, George J.
Stewart, Trenton Lee 1970- 216
Stewart, W(alter) P. 1924- 53
Stewart, Whitney 1959- 167
  Earlier sketch in SATA *92*
Stewig, John Warren 1937- 162
  Earlier sketches in SATA *26, 110*
Stickler, Soma Han 1942- 128
Stidworthy, John 1943- 63
Stiegemeyer, Julie 180
Stier, Catherine 198
Stiles, Martha Bennett 108
  Earlier sketch in SATA *6*
Still, James 1906-2001 29
  Obituary 127
Stille, Darlene R. 1942- 170
  Earlier sketch in SATA *126*
Stille, Darlene Ruth
  See Stille, Darlene R.
Stillerman, Marci 104
Stillerman, Robbie 1947- 12
Stilley, Frank 1918- 29
Stilton, Geronimo 158
Stimpson, Gerald
  See Mitchell, Adrian
Stimson, James 1964- 213
Stine, Catherine 165
Stine, G(eorge) Harry 1928-1997 136
  Earlier sketch in SATA *10*
Stine, Jovial Bob
  See Stine, R.L.
Stine, R.L. 1943- 194
  Earlier sketches in SATA *31, 76, 129*
  See also CLR *111*
Stine, Robert Lawrence
  See Stine, R.L.
Stinetorf, Louise (Allender) 1900-1992 10
Stinson, Kathy 1952- 98
Stirling, Arthur
  See Sinclair, Upton
Stirling, Ian 1941- 77
Stirling, Nora B(romley) 1900-1997 3
Stirnweis, Shannon 1931- 10
Stobbs, William 1914-2000 17
  Obituary 120
Stock, Carolmarie 1951- 75
Stock, Catherine 1952- 214
  Earlier sketches in SATA *65, 114, 158*
Stockdale, Susan 1954- 206
  Earlier sketch in SATA *98*
Stockham, Peter (Alan) 1928- 57
Stockton, Francis Richard 1834-1902 44
  Brief entry 32
Stockton, Frank R.
  See Stockton, Francis Richard
Stockwell-Moniz, Marc J. 1954- 164
Stoddard, Edward G. 1923- 10
Stoddard, Hope 1900-1987 6

Stoddard, Sandol 1927- 98
  Earlier sketch in SATA *14*
Stoehr, Shelley 1969- 107
Stoeke, Janet Morgan 1957- 202
  Earlier sketches in SATA *90, 136*
Stohl, Margaret 227
Stohner, Anu 1952- 179
Stoiko, Michael 1919- 14
Stojic, Manya 1967- 156
Stoker, Abraham
  See Stoker, Bram
Stoker, Bram 1847-1912 29
Stokes, Cedric
  See Beardmore, George
Stokes, Jack (Tilden) 1923- 13
Stokes, Olivia Pearl 1916- 32
Stolarz, Laurie Faria 1972- 203
Stolz, Mary 1920-2006 133
  Obituary 180
  Earlier sketches in SATA *10, 71*
  See also SAAS *3*
Stolz, Mary Slattery
  See Stolz, Mary
Stone, Alan
  See Svenson, Andrew E(dward)
Stone, David K(arl) 1922- 9
Stone, David Lee 1978- 166
Stone, Eugenia 1879-1971 7
Stone, Gene
  See Stone, Eugenia
Stone, Helen V(irginia) 6
Stone, Idella Purnell
  See Purnell, Idella
Stone, Ikey
  See Purnell, Idella
Stone, Irving 1903-1989 3
  Obituary 64
Stone, Jeff 178
Stone, Jon 1931-1997 39
  Obituary 95
Stone, Josephine Rector
  See Dixon, Jeanne
Stone, Kyle M. 1972- 202
Stone, Lesley
  See Trevor, Elleston
Stone, Mary Hanlon 231
Stone, Peter 1930-2003 65
  Obituary 143
Stone, Phoebe 205
  Earlier sketch in SATA *134*
Stone, Raymond 1
Stone, Rosetta
  See Dr. Seuss
Stone, Tanya Lee 1965- 217
  Earlier sketch in SATA *182*
Stonehouse, Bernard 1926- 140
  Earlier sketches in SATA *13, 80*
Stones, (Cyril) Anthony 1934- 72
Stong, Phil(ip Duffield) 1899-1957 32
Stoops, Erik D(aniel) 1966- 142
  Earlier sketch in SATA *78*
Stoppelmoore, Cheryl Jean
  See Ladd, Cheryl (Jean)
Stops, Sue 1936- 86
Storace, Patricia 193
Storad, Conrad J. 1957- 119
Storey, Margaret 1926- 9
Storey, Victoria Carolyn 1945- 16
Stork, Francisco
  See Stork, Francisco X.
Stork, Francisco X. 1953- 210
Storme, Peter
  See Stern, Philip Van Doren
Storms, Patricia 1963- 217
Storr, Catherine (Cole) 1913-2001 87
  Obituary 122
  Earlier sketch in SATA *9*
Story, Josephine
  See Loring, Emilie (Baker)
Stotko, Mary-Ann 1960- 154
Stott, Ann 219

Stott, Dorothy (M.) 1958- 99
  Earlier sketch in SATA 67
Stott, Dot
  See Stott, Dorothy (M.)
Stotter, Mike 1957- 108
Stotts, Stuart 227
Stout, Shawn K. 226
Stout, William 1949- 132
Stoutenburg, Adrien (Pearl) 1916-1982 3
Stoutland, Allison 1963- 130
Stover, Allan C(arl) 1938- 14
Stover, Jill (Griffin) 1958- 82
Stover, Marjorie Filley 1914- 9
Stowe, Harriet Beecher 1811-1896
  See YABC 1
  See also CLR 131
Stowe, Harriet Elizabeth Beecher
  See Stowe, Harriet Beecher
Stowe, Leland 1899-1994 60
  Obituary 78
Stowe, Rosetta
  See Ogan, George F.
  and Ogan, Margaret E. (Nettles)
Stower, Adam 229
  Earlier sketch in SATA 195
Strachan, Bruce 1959- 205
Strachan, Ian 1938- 85
Strachan, Linda 167
Strachan, Margaret Pitcairn 1908-1998 14
Strahinich, H. C.
  See Strahinich, Helen C.
Strahinich, Helen C. 1949- 78
Strait, Treva Adams 1909-2002 35
Strand, Mark 1934- 41
Strange, Philippa
  See Coury, Louise Andree
Stranger, Joyce
  See Wilson, Joyce M.
Strangis, Joel 1948- 124
Strannigan, Shawn 1956- 93
Strannigan, Shawn Alyne
  See Strannigan, Shawn
Strasnick, Lauren 222
Strasser, Todd 1950- 215
  Earlier sketches in SATA 41, 45, 71, 107, 153
  See also CLR 11
Stratemeyer, Edward L. 1862-1930 100
  Earlier sketches in SATA 1, 67
  See also CLR 166
  See Adams, Harrison
Stratford, Philip 1927- 47
Stratton, Allan 1951- 178
Stratton, J. M.
  See Whitlock, Ralph
Stratton, Thomas
  See Coulson, Robert S(tratton)
  and DeWeese, Thomas Eugene
Stratton-Porter, Gene 1863-1924 15
  See also CLR 87
Strauss, Gwen 1963- 77
Strauss, Joyce 1936- 53
Strauss, Linda Leopold 1942- 127
Strauss, Susan (Elizabeth) 1954- 75
Strayer, E. Ward
  See Stratemeyer, Edward L.
Streano, Vince(nt Catello) 1945- 20
Streatfeild, Mary Noel
  See Streatfeild, Noel
Streatfeild, Noel 1897(?)-1986 20
  Obituary 48
  See also CLR 83
Street, Janet Travell 1959- 84
Street, Julia Montgomery 1898-1993 11
Streissguth, Thomas 1958- 116
Strelkoff, Tatiana 1957- 89
Stren, Patti 1949- 88
  Brief entry 41
  See also CLR 5
Strete, Craig Kee 1950- 96
  Earlier sketch in SATA 44

Stretton, Barbara (Humphrey) 1936- 43
  Brief entry 35
Strickland, Brad 1947- 200
  Earlier sketches in SATA 83, 137, 142
Strickland, Craig (A.) 1956- 102
Strickland, Dorothy S(alley) 1933- 89
Strickland, Michael R. 1965- 144
  Earlier sketch in SATA 83
Strickland, Shadra 209
Strickland, Tessa 173
Strickland, William Bradley
  See Strickland, Brad
Striegel, Jana 1955- 140
Striegel-Wilson, Jana
  See Striegel, Jana
Striker, Lee
  See Clark, Margaret (D.)
Striker, Susan 1942- 63
Stringam, Jean 1945- 233
Stringer, Helen 225
Stringer, Lauren 1957- 183
  Earlier sketch in SATA 129
Stroeyer, Poul 1923- 13
Stromoski, Rick 1958- 111
Strong, Charles
  See Epstein, Beryl
  and Epstein, Samuel
Strong, David
  See McGuire, Leslie (Sarah)
Strong, Jeremy 1949- 175
  Earlier sketches in SATA 36, 105
Strong, J.J.
  See Strong, Jeremy
Strong, Pat
  See Hough, Richard (Alexander)
Strong, Stacie 1965- 74
Stroud, Bettye 1939- 165
  Earlier sketch in SATA 96
Stroud, Jonathan 1970- 213
  Earlier sketches in SATA 102, 159
  See also CLR 134
Stroyer, Poul
  See Stroeyer, Poul
Strug, Kerri 1977- 108
Stryer, Andrea Stenn 1938- 192
Stryker, Daniel
  See Morris, Chris(topher Crosby)
  and Stump, Jane Barr
Stuart, David
  See Hoyt, Edwin P(almer), Jr.
Stuart, Derek
  See Foster, John L(ouis)
Stuart, Forbes 1924- 13
Stuart, Ian
  See MacLean, Alistair
Stuart, Jesse (Hilton) 1906-1984 2
  Obituary 36
Stuart, Ruth McEnery 1849(?)-1917 116
Stuart, Sheila
  See Baker, Mary Gladys Steel
Stuart-Clark, Christopher (Anthony) 1940- .. 32
Stubis, Talivaldis 1926- 5
Stubley, Trevor (Hugh) 1932- 22
Stuchner, Joan Betty 209
Stucky, Naomi R. 1922- 72
Stucley, Elizabeth
  See Northmore, Elizabeth Florence
Stultifer, Morton
  See Curtis, Richard
Sture-Vasa, Mary
  See Alsop, Mary O'Hara
Sturges, Philemon 174
Sturtevant, Katherine 1950- 180
  Earlier sketch in SATA 130
Sturton, Hugh
  See Johnston, H(ugh) A(nthony) S(tephen)
Sturtzel, Howard A(llison) 1894-1985 1
Sturtzel, Jane Levington 1903-1996 1
Stutley, D(oris) J(ean) 1959- 142
Stutson, Caroline 1940- 104

Stuve-Bodeen, Stephanie
  See Bodeen, S. A.
Stux, Erica 1929- 140
Styles, (Frank) Showell 1908- 10
Stynes, Barbara White 133
Suarez, Maribel 1952- 201
Suba, Susanne 4
Suber, Melissa 213
Subond, Valerie
  See Grayland, Valerie (Merle Spanner)
Sudbery, Rodie 1943- 42
Sudyka, Diana 208
Sue, Majella Lue 209
Suen, Anastasia 1956(?)- 157
Sufrin, Mark 1925- 76
Sugarman, Joan G. 1917- 64
Sugarman, Tracy 1921- 37
Sugita, Yutaka 1930- 36
Suhl, Yuri (Menachem) 1908-1986 8
  Obituary 50
  See also CLR 2
  See also SAAS 1
Suhr, Joanne 129
Suid, Murray 1942- 27
Sullivan, Edward T. 206
Sullivan, George (Edward) 1927- 147
  Earlier sketches in SATA 4, 89
Sullivan, Jacqueline Levering 203
Sullivan, Jody
  See Rake, Jody
Sullivan, Kathryn A. 1954- 141
Sullivan, Mary Ann 1954- 63
Sullivan, Mary W(ilson) 1907- 13
Sullivan, Pat
  See Messmer, Otto
Sullivan, Paul 1939- 106
Sullivan, Sarah G. 1953- 179
Sullivan, Silky 1940- 101
Sullivan, Sue
  See Sullivan, Susan E.
Sullivan, Susan E. 1962- 123
Sullivan, Thomas Joseph, Jr. 1947- 16
Sullivan, Tom
  See Sullivan, Thomas Joseph, Jr.
Sully, Tom 1959- 104
Suma, Nova Ren 223
Sumichrast, Jozef 1948- 29
Sumiko
  See Davies, Sumiko
Summerforest, Ivy B.
  See Kirkup, James
Summers, Barbara 1944- 182
Summers, Cassia Joy
  See Cowley, Joy
Summers, James L(evingston) 1910-1973 57
  Brief entry 28
Summertree, Katonah
  See Windsor, Patricia
Summy, Barrie 208
Sumner, William 1971- 229
Sun, Chyng Feng 1959- 90
Sunderlin, Sylvia (S.) 1911-1997 28
  Obituary 99
Sung, Betty Lee 26
Supeene, Shelagh Lynne 1952- 153
Supplee, Suzanne 204
Supraner, Robyn 1930- 101
  Earlier sketch in SATA 20
Supree, Burt(on) 1941-1992 73
Surface, Mary Hall 1958- 126
Surge, Frank 1931- 13
Susac, Andrew 1929- 5
Susi, Geraldine Lee 1942- 98
Sussman, Cornelia Silver 1914-1999 59
Sussman, Irving 1908-1996 59
Sussman, Michael 1953- 217
Sussman, Michael B.
  See Sussman, Michael
Sussman, Susan 1942- 48

Sutcliff, Rosemary 1920-1992 78
    Obituary 73
    Earlier sketches in SATA 6, 44
    See also CLR 138
Sutcliffe, Jane 1957- 138
Sutherland, Colleen 1944- 79
Sutherland, Efua (Theodora Morgue)
    1924-1996 25
Sutherland, Jon 1958- 167
Sutherland, Jonathan D.
    See Sutherland, Jon
Sutherland, Jonathan David
    See Sutherland, Jon
Sutherland, Margaret 1941- 15
Sutherland, Zena Bailey 1915-2002 37
    Obituary 137
Suttles, Shirley (Smith) 1922- 21
Sutton, Ann (Livesay) 1923- 31
Sutton, Eve(lyn Mary) 1906-1992 26
Sutton, Felix 1910(?)-1973 31
Sutton, Jane 1950- 52
    Brief entry 43
Sutton, Larry M(atthew) 1931- 29
Sutton, Margaret Beebe 1903-2001 1
    Obituary 131
Sutton, Myron Daniel 1925- 31
Sutton, Roger 1956- 93
Sutton, Sally 1973- 214
Suzanne, Jamie
    See Hawes, Louise
    and Lantz, Francess L(in)
    and Singleton, Linda Joy
    and Zach, Cheryl (Byrd)
Suzuki, David 1936- 138
Suzuki, David Takayoshi
    See Suzuki, David
Svendsen, Mark 1962- 181
    Earlier sketch in SATA 120
Svendsen, Mark Nestor
    See Svendsen, Mark
Svenson, Andrew E(dward) 1910-1975 2
    Obituary 26
Swaab, Neil 1978- 191
Swaim, Jessica 1950- 202
Swain, Carol 1962- 172
Swain, Gwenyth 1961- 134
    Earlier sketch in SATA 84
Swain, Ruth
    See Swain, Ruth Freeman
Swain, Ruth Freeman 1951- 161
    Earlier sketch in SATA 119
Swain, Su Zan (Noguchi) 1916- 21
Swain, Wilson 1976- 225
Swallow, Gerry 227
Swallow, Pamela Curtis 178
Swamp, Jake 1941- 98
Swan, Susan 1944- 108
    Earlier sketch in SATA 22
Swann, Brian (Stanley Frank) 1940- 116
Swann, E.L.
    See Lasky, Kathryn
Swann, Ruth Rice 1920- 84
Swanson, Diane 1944- 203
Swanson, Helen M(cKendry) 1919- 94
Swanson, June 1931- 76
Swanson, Susan Marie 209
Swanson, Wayne 1942- 167
Swarner, Kristina 1965- 215
Swarthout, Glendon (Fred) 1918-1992 26
Swarthout, Kathryn 1919- 7
Swayne, Sam(uel F.) 1907- 53
Swayne, Zoa (Lourana) 1905- 53
Swearingen, Greg 1976- 225
Sweat, Lynn 1934- 168
    Earlier sketch in SATA 57
Swede, George 1940- 67
Sweeney, James B(artholomew) 1910-1999 . 21
Sweeney, Joyce 1955- 167
    Earlier sketches in SATA 65, 68, 108
Sweeney, Joyce Kay
    See Sweeney, Joyce

Sweeney, Karen O'Connor
    See O'Connor, Karen
Sweeney, Matthew (Gerard) 1952- 156
Sweet, Melissa 1956- 211
    Earlier sketch in SATA 172
Sweet, Sarah C.
    See Jewett, Sarah Orne
Sweetland, Nancy A(nn) 1934- 48
Swenson, Allan A(rmstrong) 1933- 21
Swenson, May 1919-1989 15
Swentzell, Rina 1939- 79
Swiatkowska, Gabi 1971(?)- 180
Swift, Bryan
    See Knott, William C(ecil, Jr.)
Swift, David
    See Kaufmann, John
Swift, Hildegarde Hoyt 1890(?)-1977
    Obituary 20
Swift, Jonathan 1667-1745 19
    See also CLR 161
Swift, Merlin
    See Leeming, Joseph
Swiger, Elinor Porter 1927- 8
Swinburne, Laurence (Joseph) 1924- 9
Swinburne, Stephen R. 1952- 231
    Earlier sketches in SATA 150, 188
Swinburne, Steve
    See Swinburne, Stephen R.
Swindells, Robert (Edward) 1939- 150
    Brief entry 34
    Earlier sketches in SATA 50, 80
    See also SAAS 14
Swinford, Betty (June Wells) 1927- 58
Swinford, Bob
    See Swinford, Betty (June Wells)
Swithen, John
    See King, Stephen
Switzer, Ellen 1923- 48
Swope, Sam 156
Swope, Samuel
    See Swope, Sam
Sybesma, Jetske
    See Ironside, Jetske
Sydney, Frank
    See Warwick, Alan R(oss)
Sydor, Colleen 1960- 207
Sykes, Julie 1963- 202
Sylvada, Peter 1964- 202
Sylver, Adrienne 230
Sylvester, Natalie G(abry) 1922- 22
Syme, (Neville) Ronald 1913-1992 87
    Earlier sketch in SATA 2
Symes, R. F. 77
Symes, Ruth Louise 1962- 179
Symons, (Dorothy) Geraldine 1909- 33
Symons, Stuart
    See Stanley, George Edward
Symynkywicz, Jeffrey B. 1954- 87
Symynkywicz, Jeffrey Bruce
    See Symynkywicz, Jeffrey B.
Synge, (Phyllis) Ursula 1930- 9
Sypher, Lucy Johnston 1907- 7
Szasz, Suzanne (Shorr) 1915-1997 13
    Obituary 99
Szekeres, Cyndy 1933- 157
    Autobiography Feature 157
    Earlier sketches in SATA 5, 60, 131
    See also SAAS 13
Szekessy, Tanja 98
Szpura, Beata 1961- 93
Szuc, Jeff 1975- 220
Szudek, Agnes S(usan) P(hilomena) 57
    Brief entry 49
Szulc, Tad 1926-2001 26
Szydlow, Jarl
    See Szydlowski, Mary Vigliante
Szydlowski, Mary Vigliante 1946- 94
Szymanski, Lois 1957- 91

T

Taback, Simms 1932- 170
    Brief entry 36
    Earlier sketches in SATA 40, 104
    See also CLR 100
Taber, Gladys (Bagg) 1899-1980
    Obituary 22
Tabor, Nancy Maria Grande 1949- 161
    Earlier sketch in SATA 89
Tabrah, Ruth Milander 1921- 14
Tacang, Brian 213
Tackach, James 1953- 123
Tackach, James M.
    See Tackach, James
Tadgell, Nicole 1969- 220
    Earlier sketch in SATA 177
Tafolla, Carmen 1951- 220
Tafolla, Mary Carmen
    See Tafolla, Carmen
Tafuri, Nancy 1946- 192
    Autobiography Feature 192
    Earlier sketches in SATA 39, 75, 130
    See also CLR 74
    See also SAAS 14
Tagg, Christine Elizabeth 1962- 138
Tagliaferro, Linda 173
Taha, Karen T(erry) 1942- 156
    Earlier sketch in SATA 71
Tai, Sharon O. 1963- 153
Tait, Douglas 1944- 12
Takabayashi, Mari 1960- 156
    Earlier sketch in SATA 115
Takahashi, Hideko 209
Takahashi, Rumiko 1957- 163
Takakjian, Portia 1930- 15
Takashima, Misako
    See Misako Rocks!
Takashima, Shizuye 1928- 13
Takayama, Sandi 1962- 106
Takeda, Pete(r M.) 1964- 148
Tal, Eve 1947- 176
Talbert, Marc (Alan) 1953- 154
    Autobiography Feature 154
    Earlier sketches in SATA 68, 99
Talbot, Charlene Joy 1928- 10
Talbot, Toby 1928- 14
Talbott, Hudson 1949- 212
    Earlier sketches in SATA 84, 131
Talifero, Gerald 1950- 75
Talker, T.
    See Rands, William Brighty
Tallarico, Tony 1933- 116
Tallcott, Emogene 10
Tallec, Olivier 1970- 197
Tallis, Robyn
    See Smith, Sherwood
Tallon, Robert 1939- 43
    Brief entry 28
Talmadge, Marian 14
Tamaki, Jillian 1980- 201
Tamar, Erika 1934- 150
    Earlier sketches in SATA 62, 101
Tamarin, Alfred H. 1913-1980 13
Tamburine, Jean 1930- 12
Tames, Richard (Lawrence) 1946- 102
    Earlier sketch in SATA 67
Tamminga, Frederick W(illiam) 1934- 66
Tammuz, Benjamin 1919-1989
    Obituary 63
Tan, Amy 1952- 75
Tan, Amy Ruth
    See Tan, Amy
Tan, Shaun 1974- 198
Tanaka, Beatrice 1932- 76
Tanaka, Shelley 214
    Earlier sketch in SATA 136
Tanaka, Yoko 1947- 215
Tang, Charles 1948- 81
Tang, Greg 172
Tang, You-Shan 1946- 53

Tania B.
  See Blixen, Karen
Tankard, Jeremy 1973- *191*
Tannen, Mary 1943- *37*
Tannenbaum, Beulah Goldstein 1916- *3*
Tannenbaum, D(onald) Leb 1948- *42*
Tanner, Jane 1946- *74*
Tanner, Louise S(tickney) 1922-2000 .... *9*
Tanobe, Miyuki 1937- *23*
Tanselle, Eve 1933- *125*
Tapio, Pat Decker
  See Kines, Pat Decker
Tapp, Kathy Kennedy 1949- *88*
  Brief entry *50*
Tarbescu, Edith 1939- *107*
Tarkington, (Newton) Booth 1869-1946 .... *17*
Tarpley, Natasha A(nastasia) 1971- *147*
Tarr, Judith 1955- *149*
  Earlier sketch in SATA *64*
Tarry, Ellen 1906-2008 .... *16*
  See also CLR *26*
  See also SAAS *16*
Tarshis, Jerome 1936- *9*
Tarshis, Lauren *187*
Tarsky, Sue 1946- *41*
Taschek, Karen 1956- *185*
Tashjian, Janet 1956- *151*
  Earlier sketch in SATA *102*
Tashjian, Virginia A. 1921-2008 .... *3*
Tasker, James 1908- *9*
Tate, Don(ald E.) *159*
Tate, Eleanora E. 1948- *191*
  Earlier sketches in SATA *38, 94*
  See also CLR *37*
Tate, Eleanora Elaine
  See Tate, Eleanora E.
Tate, Ellalice
  See Hibbert, Eleanor Alice Burford
Tate, Joan 1922- *86*
  Earlier sketch in SATA *9*
  See also SAAS *20*
Tate, Mary Anne
  See Hale, Arlene
Tate, Nikki *134*
Tate, Richard
  See Masters, Anthony (Richard)
Tate, Suzanne 1930- *91*
Tatham, Betty *142*
Tatham, Campbell
  See Elting, Mary
Tatham, Julie
  See Tatham, Julie Campbell
Tatham, Julie Campbell 1908-1999 .... *80*
Tavares, Matt *198*
  Earlier sketch in SATA *159*
Tavares, Victor 1971- *176*
Taves, Isabella 1915- *27*
Tayleur, Karen 1961- *213*
Taylor, Alastair 1959- *130*
Taylor, Andrew 1951- *70*
Taylor, Andrew John Robert
  See Taylor, Andrew
Taylor, Ann 1782-1866 .... *41*
  Brief entry *35*
Taylor, Audilee Boyd 1931- *59*
Taylor, Barbara J. 1927- *10*
Taylor, Ben
  See Strachan, Ian
Taylor, Brooke *205*
Taylor, Carl 1937-2010 .... *14*
Taylor, Carrie-Jo
  See Taylor, C.J.
Taylor, Cheryl Munro 1957- *96*
Taylor, C.J. 1952- *224*
Taylor, Cora (Lorraine) 1936- *103*
  Earlier sketch in SATA *64*
  See also CLR *63*
Taylor, Dave 1948- *78*
Taylor, David
  See Taylor, Dave
Taylor, David 1900-1965 .... *10*

Taylor, Debbie A. 1955- *169*
Taylor, Eleanor 1969- *206*
Taylor, Elizabeth 1912-1975 .... *13*
Taylor, Florance Walton *9*
Taylor, Florence M(arian Tompkins)
  1892-1983 .... *9*
Taylor, Gage 1942-2000 .... *87*
Taylor, Geoff 1946- *204*
Taylor, G.P. 1958(?)- *216*
  Earlier sketch in SATA *156*
Taylor, Graham Peter
  See Taylor, G.P.
Taylor, Greg 1951- *221*
Taylor, Herb(ert Norman, Jr.) 1942-1987 ..... *22*
  Obituary *54*
Taylor, J. David
  See Taylor, Dave
Taylor, Jane 1783-1824 .... *41*
  Brief entry *35*
Taylor, Jerry D(uncan) 1938- *47*
Taylor, John Robert
  See Taylor, Andrew
Taylor, Judy
  See Hough, Judy Taylor
Taylor, Kenneth N. 1917-2005 .... *26*
Taylor, Kenneth Nathaniel
  See Taylor, Kenneth N.
Taylor, Kim *180*
Taylor, L(ester) B(arbour), Jr. 1932- *27*
Taylor, Lois Dwight Cole
  See Cole, Lois Dwight
Taylor, Louise Todd 1939- *47*
Taylor, Margaret 1950- *106*
Taylor, Mark 1927- *32*
  Brief entry *28*
Taylor, Mildred D. 1943- *135*
  See also CLR *144*
  See also SAAS *5*
Taylor, Mildred Delois
  See Taylor, Mildred D.
Taylor, Paula (Wright) 1942- *48*
  Brief entry *33*
Taylor, Peter Lane *210*
Taylor, Robert Lewis 1912-1998 .... *10*
Taylor, Sean 1965- *192*
Taylor, Susan Champlin
  See Champlin, Susan
Taylor, Sydney (Brenner) 1904(?)-1978 .... *28*
  Obituary *26*
  Earlier sketch in SATA *1*
Taylor, Theodore 1921-2006 .... *128*
  Obituary *177*
  Earlier sketches in SATA *5, 54, 83*
  See also CLR *30*
  See also SAAS *4*
Taylor, William 1938- *164*
  Earlier sketches in SATA *78, 113*
  See also CLR *63*
Taylor-Butler, Christine 1959- *218*
Tazewell, Charles 1900-1972 .... *74*
Tchana, Katrin
  See Tchana, Katrin Hyman
Tchana, Katrin H.
  See Tchana, Katrin Hyman
Tchana, Katrin Hyman 1963- *177*
  Earlier sketch in SATA *125*
Tchekhov, Anton
  See Chekhov, Anton
Tchen, Richard *120*
Tchudi, Stephen N. 1942- *55*
Teague, Bob
  See Teague, Robert
Teague, Mark 1963- *205*
  Earlier sketches in SATA *68, 99, 170*
Teague, Mark Christopher
  See Teague, Mark
Teague, Robert 1929- *32*
  Brief entry *31*
Teal, Val 1902-1997 .... *10*
  Obituary *114*

Teal, Valentine M.
  See Teal, Val
Teale, Edwin Way 1899-1980 .... *7*
  Obituary *25*
Teasdale, Sara 1884-1933 .... *32*
Tebbel, John (William) 1912-2004 .... *26*
Teckentrup, Britta 1969- *200*
Tedesco, P.R.
  See Naylor, Phyllis Reynolds
Teensma, Lynne Bertrand
  See Bertrand, Lynne
Tee-Van, Helen Damrosch 1893-1976 .... *10*
  Obituary *27*
Teevee, Ningeokuluk 1963- *223*
Tegner, Bruce 1928- *62*
Teitelbaum, Michael 1953- *116*
  Earlier sketch in SATA *59*
Tejima
  See Tejima, Keizaburo
Tejima, Keizaburo 1931- *139*
  See also CLR *20*
Telander, Todd (G.) 1967- *88*
Teleki, Geza 1943- *45*
Telemaque, Eleanor Wong 1934- *43*
Telescope, Tom
  See Newbery, John
Telgemeier, Raina 1977- *228*
Tellegen, Toon 1941- *229*
Teller, Janne 1964- *230*
Tellis, Annabel 1967- *191*
Temkin, Sara Anne Schlossberg 1913-1996 . *26*
Temko, Florence *13*
Tempest, Margaret Mary 1892-1982
  Obituary *33*
Templar, Maurice
  See Groom, Arthur William
Temple, Arthur
  See Northcott, (William) Cecil
Temple, Charles 1947- *79*
Temple, Frances (Nolting) 1945-1995 .... *85*
Temple, Herbert 1919- *45*
Temple, Paul
  See McConnell, James Douglas Rutherford
Temple, William F(rederick) 1914-1989 .... *107*
Tenggren, Gustaf 1896-1970 .... *18*
  Obituary *26*
Tennant, Kylie
  See Rodd, Kylie Tennant
Tennant, Veronica 1947- *36*
Tenneshaw, S.M.
  See Beaumont, Charles
  and Garrett, Randall
  and Silverberg, Robert
Tenniel, John 1820-1914 .... *74*
  Brief entry *27*
  See also CLR *146*
Teplin, Scott *231*
Tepper, Sheri S. 1929- *113*
Tepper, Yona 1941- *228*
Terada, Alice M. 1928- *90*
Terban, Marvin 1940- *54*
  Brief entry *45*
Teresi, Judith M.
  See Goldberger, Judith M.
ter Haar, Jaap 1922- *6*
  See also CLR *15*
Terhune, Albert Payson 1872-1942 .... *15*
Terkel, Susan N(eiburg) 1948- *103*
  Earlier sketch in SATA *59*
Terlouw, Jan (Cornelis) 1931- *30*
Terrazzini, Daniela Jaglenka *218*
Terrell, John Upton 1900-1988
  Obituary *60*
Terrill, Beth *198*
Terrill, Elizabeth
  See Terrill, Beth
Terris, Susan 1937- *77*
  Earlier sketch in SATA *3*
Terry, Luther L(eonidas) 1911-1985 .... *11*
  Obituary *42*

Terry, Margaret
See Dunnahoo, Terry Janson
Terry, Michael 1947- 233
Terry, Walter 1913-1982 14
Terry, Will 1966- 205
Terzian, James P. 1915- 14
Tessendorf, K(enneth) C(harles) 1925-2003 . 75
Obituary 142
Tessler, Manya 200
Tessler, Stephanie Gordon
See Gordon, Stephanie Jacob
Testa, Dom 208
Tester, Sylvia Root 1939- 64
Brief entry 37
Tether, (Cynthia) Graham 1950- 46
Brief entry 36
Tetzner, Lisa 1894-1963 169
Thach, James Otis 1969- 195
Thacher, Mary McGrath 1933- 9
Thackeray, William Makepeace 1811-1863 .. 23
Thaler, Michael C.
See Thaler, Mike
Thaler, Mike 1936- 215
Brief entry 47
Earlier sketches in SATA 56, 93
Thaler, Shmuel 1958- 126
Earlier sketch in SATA 72
Thamer, Katie 1955- 42
Thane, Elswyth 1900-1984(?) 32
Tharp, Louise (Marshall) Hall 1898-1992 3
Obituary 129
Tharp, Tim 1957- 189
Thayer, Ernest Lawrence 1863-1940 60
Thayer, Jane
See Woolley, Catherine
Thayer, Marjorie 1908-1992 74
Brief entry 37
Thayer, Peter
See Wyler, Rose
Thelwell, Norman 1923-2004 14
Themerson, Stefan 1910-1988 65
Thermes, Jennifer 1966- 155
Theroux, Paul 1941- 109
Earlier sketch in SATA 44
Theroux, Paul Edward
See Theroux, Paul
Thesman, Jean 124
Earlier sketch in SATA 74
The Tjong-Khing
See Khing, T.T.
Thieda, Shirley Ann 1943- 13
Thiele, Colin 1920-2006 125
Earlier sketches in SATA 14, 72
See also CLR 27
See also SAAS 2
Thiele, Colin Milton
See Thiele, Colin
Thiesing, Lisa 1958- 159
Earlier sketch in SATA 95
Thimmesh, Catherine 189
Thiry, Joan (Marie) 1926- 45
Thisdale, Francois 1964- 222
Thistlethwaite, Miles 1945- 12
Thollander, Earl 1922- 22
Thomas, Abigail 1941- 112
Thomas, Andrea
See Hill, Margaret (Ohler)
Thomas, Art(hur Lawrence) 1952- 48
Brief entry 38
Thomas, Carroll
See Ratliff, Thomas M.
and Shmurak, Carole B.
Thomas, Dylan 1914-1953 60
Thomas, Dylan Marlais
See Thomas, Dylan
Thomas, Egbert S.
See Ellis, Edward S.
Thomas, Estelle Webb 1899-1982 26
Thomas, Frances 1943- 171
Earlier sketch in SATA 92
Thomas, Garen 213

Thomas, H. C.
See Keating, Lawrence A.
Thomas, Ianthe 1951- 139
Brief entry 42
See also CLR 8
Thomas, J. F.
See Fleming, Thomas
Thomas, Jan 1958- 226
Earlier sketch in SATA 197
Thomas, Jane Resh 1936- 171
Earlier sketches in SATA 38, 90
Thomas, Jerry D. 1959- 91
Thomas, Joan Gale
See Robinson, Joan (Mary) G(ale Thomas)
Thomas, Joyce Carol 1938- 210
Autobiography Feature 137
Earlier sketches in SATA 40, 78, 123, 137
See also CLR 19
See also SAAS 7
Thomas, Lee
See Floren, Lee
and Pendleton, Thomas
Thomas, Lowell Jackson, Jr. 1923- 15
Thomas, Margaret
See Thomas, Peggy
Thomas, Meredith 1963- 119
Thomas, Michael
See Wilks, Michael Thomas
Thomas, Middy 1931- 191
Thomas, Patricia 1934- 199
Earlier sketch in SATA 51
Thomas, Peggy 174
Thomas, Rob 1965- 97
Thomas, Scott 1959- 147
Thomas, Velma Maia 1955- 171
Thomas, Vernon (Arthur) 1934- 56
Thomas, Victoria
See DeWeese, Thomas Eugene
and Kugi, Constance Todd
Thomasma, Kenneth R. 1930- 90
Thomason, Mark 1959- 215
Thomassie, Tynia 1959- 92
Thompson, Alicia 1984- 224
Thompson, Brenda 1935- 34
Thompson, Carol 1951- 189
Earlier sketch in SATA 85
Thompson, China
See Lewis, Mary
Thompson, Colin 1942- 198
Earlier sketches in SATA 95, 163
Thompson, David H(ugh) 1941- 17
Thompson, Eileen
See Panowski, Eileen Thompson
Thompson, George Selden 1929-1989 73
Obituary 63
Earlier sketch in SATA 4
See also CLR 8
Thompson, Harlan 1894-1987 10
Obituary 53
Thompson, Hilary 1943- 56
Brief entry 49
Thompson, Joanna Maxwell Pullein
See Pullein-Thompson, Joanna Maxwell
Thompson, Julian F(rancis) 1927- 155
Brief entry 40
Earlier sketches in SATA 55, 99
See also CLR 24
See also SAAS 13
Thompson, K(athryn Carolyn) Dyble
1952- 82
Thompson, Kate 1956- 204
Thompson, Kay 1912(?)-1998 16
See also CLR 22
Thompson, Lauren 1962- 200
Earlier sketches in SATA 132, 174
Thompson, Lauren Stevens
See Thompson, Lauren
Thompson, Megan Lloyd
See Lloyd, Megan
Thompson, Richard 1951- 184
Thompson, Ruth Plumly 1891-1976 66

Thompson, Sharon 1952- 119
Thompson, Sharon Elaine
See Thompson, Sharon
Thompson, Stith 1885-1976 57
Obituary 20
Thompson, Vivian L(aubach) 1911- 3
Thomson, Bill 1963- 187
Thomson, Celia
See Lynn, Tracy
Thomson, David (Robert Alexander)
1914-1988 40
Obituary 55
Thomson, Melissa 1979- 205
Thomson, Pat 1939- 122
Earlier sketch in SATA 77
Thomson, Peggy 1922- 31
Thomson, Sarah L. 212
Earlier sketch in SATA 178
Thon, Melanie Rae 1957- 132
Thong, Roseanne 174
Thor, Annika 1950- 222
Thorburn, John
See Goldsmith, John Herman Thorburn
Thorn, John 1947- 59
Thorndyke, Helen Louise
See Benson, Mildred
Thorne, Ian
See May, Julian
Thorne, Jean Wright
See May, Julian
Thornhill, Jan 1955- 148
Earlier sketch in SATA 77
Thornton, Hall
See Silverberg, Robert
Thornton, W. B.
See Burgess, Thornton Waldo
Thornton, Yvonne S. 1947- 96
Thornton, Yvonne Shirley
See Thornton, Yvonne S.
Thorpe, E(ustace) G(eorge) 1916- 21
Thorpe, J. K.
See Nathanson, Laura Walther
Thorvall, Kerstin 1925- 13
Thorvall-Falk, Kerstin
See Thorvall, Kerstin
Thrasher, Crystal (Faye) 1921- 27
Threadgall, Colin 1941- 77
Three Little Pigs
See Lantz, Francess L(in)
Thum, Gladys 1920- 26
Thum, Marcella 28
Earlier sketch in SATA 3
Thundercloud, Katherine
See Witt, Shirley Hill
Thurber, James 1894-1961 13
Thurber, James Grover
See Thurber, James
Thurlo, Aimee 161
Thurlo, David 161
Thurman, Judith 1946- 33
Thurman, Mark (Gordon Ian) 1948- 63
Thwaite, Ann (Barbara Harrop) 1932- 14
Tibbetts, Peggy 127
Tibbles, Jean-Paul 1958- 115
Tibo, Gilles 1951- 107
Earlier sketch in SATA 67
Tiburzi, Bonnie 1948- 65
Ticheburn, Cheviot
See Ainsworth, William Harrison
Tichenor, Tom 1923-1992 14
Tichnor, Richard 1959- 90
Tichy, William 1924- 31
Tickle, Jack
See Chapman, Jane
Tidholm, Anna-Clara 1946- 223
Tiegreen, Alan F. 1935- 94
Brief entry 36
Tierney, Fiona 229
Tierney, Frank M. 1930- 54
Tierney, Tom 1928- 113
Tiffault, Benette W. 1955- 77

Tildes, Phyllis Limbacher 1945- *210*
Tiller, Ruth L. 1949- *83*
Tilley, Debbie *190*
Tillman, Nancy *211*
Tillotson, Katherine *224*
Tilly, Nancy 1935- *62*
Tilton, Madonna Elaine 1929- *41*
Tilton, Rafael
   See Tilton, Madonna Elaine
Timberlake, Amy *156*
Timberlake, Carolyn
   See Dresang, Eliza (Carolyn Timberlake)
Timmers, Leo 1970- *190*
Timmins, Jeffrey Stewart 1979- *227*
Timmins, William F(rederick) *10*
Tinbergen, Niko(laas) 1907-1988
   Obituary *60*
Tincknell, Cathy *194*
Tiner, John Hudson 1944- *32*
Tingle, Dolli (?)-
   See Brackett, Dolli Tingle
Tingle, Rebecca *174*
Tingle, Tim *208*
Tingum, Janice 1958- *91*
Tinkelman, Murray 1933- *12*
Tinkham, Kelly A. *188*
Tinkle, (Julien) Lon 1906-1980 .... *36*
Tinling, Marion (Rose) 1904- *140*
Tipene, Tim 1972- *141*
Tippett, James S(terling) 1885-1958 .... *66*
Tirone Smith, Mary-Ann 1944- *143*
Titlebaum, Ellen *195*
Titler, Dale M(ilton) 1926- *35*
   Brief entry *28*
Titmarsh, Michael Angelo
   See Thackeray, William Makepeace
Titus, Eve 1922- *2*
Tjia, Sherwin 1975- *204*
Tjong Khing, The 1933- *76*
Tobias, Katherine
   See Gottfried, Theodore Mark
Tobias, Tobi 1938- *82*
   Earlier sketch in SATA *5*
   See also CLR *4*
Tobin, James *226*
Tocci, C. Lee 1958- *220*
Tocci, Cynthia Lee
   See Tocci, C. Lee
Tocher, Timothy *228*
Todd, Anne Ophelia
   See Dowden, Anne Ophelia Todd
Todd, Barbara 1961- *173*
Todd, Barbara K(eith) 1917- *10*
Todd, Chuck *195*
Todd, H(erbert) E(atton) 1908-1988 .... *84*
   Earlier sketch in SATA *11*
Todd, Loreto 1942- *30*
Todd, Pamela *212*
Todd, Peter
   See Hamilton, Charles (Harold St. John)
Toews, Miriam 1964- *165*
Tofel, Richard J. 1957- *140*
Toft, Di 1958- *233*
Toft, Kim Michelle 1960- *170*
Tokunbo, Dimitrea *187*
Tolan, Stephanie S. 1942- *142*
   Earlier sketches in SATA *38, 78*
Toland, John (Willard) 1912-2004 .... *38*
Tolbert, Steve 1944- *143*
Toledo, Francisco 1940- *198*
Toledo, Natalia 1967- *197*
Tolkien, J. R. R. 1892-1973 .... *100*
   Obituary *24*
   Earlier sketches in SATA *2, 32*
   See also CLR *152*
Tolkien, John Ronald Reuel
   See Tolkien, J. R. R.
Toll, Emily
   See Cannon, Eileen E(mily)
Toll, Nelly S. 1935- *78*

Tolland, W. R.
   See Heitzmann, William Ray
Tolles, Martha 1921- *76*
   Earlier sketch in SATA *8*
Tolliver, Ruby C(hangos) 1922- *110*
   Brief entry *41*
   Earlier sketch in SATA *55*
Tolmie, Kenneth Donald 1941- *15*
Tolstoi, Lev
   See Tolstoy, Leo
Tolstoy, Leo 1828-1910 .... *26*
Tolstoy, Count Leo
   See Tolstoy, Leo
Tolstoy, Leo Nikolaevich
   See Tolstoy, Leo
Tomalin, Ruth *29*
Tomaselli, Rosa
   See Pausacker, Jenny
Tomecek, Steve *172*
Tomes, Margot (Ladd) 1917-1991 .... *70*
   Brief entry *27*
   Obituary *69*
   Earlier sketch in SATA *36*
Tomey, Ingrid 1943- *77*
Tomfool
   See Farjeon, Eleanor
Tomic, Tomislav 1977- *202*
Tomkins, Jasper
   See Batey, Tom
Tomline, F. Latour
   See Gilbert, W(illiam) S(chwenck)
Tomlinson, Heather *192*
Tomlinson, Jill 1931-1976 .... *3*
   Obituary *24*
Tomlinson, Reginald R(obert) 1885-1979(?)
   Obituary *27*
Tomlinson, Theresa 1946- *165*
   Earlier sketch in SATA *103*
   See also CLR *60*
Tommaso, Rich 1970(?)- *200*
Tomorrow, Tom 1961- *223*
Tompert, Ann 1918- *139*
   Earlier sketches in SATA *14, 89*
Tompkins, Troy
   See Cle, Troy
Tonatiuh, Duncan *231*
Toner, Raymond John 1908-1986 .... *10*
Tong, Gary S. 1942- *66*
Tong, Paul *188*
Took, Belladonna
   See Chapman, Vera (Ivy May)
Tooke, Louise Mathews 1950- *38*
Tooke, Susan *173*
Toonder, Martin
   See Groom, Arthur William
Toothaker, Roy Eugene 1928- *18*
Tooze, Ruth (Anderson) 1892-1972 .... *4*
Topaz, Ksenia *212*
Topek, Susan Remick 1955- *78*
Topping, Audrey R(onning) 1928- *14*
Tor, Regina
   See Shekerjian, Regina Tor
Torbert, Floyd James 1922- *22*
Torgersen, Don Arthur 1934- *55*
   Brief entry *41*
Torley, Luke
   See Blish, James
Torrecilla, Pablo 1967- *206*
Torres, Andres Segovia
   See Segovia, Andres
Torres, Daniel 1958- *102*
Torres, J. 1969- *230*
Torres, John A. 1965- *163*
   Earlier sketch in SATA *94*
Torres, John Albert
   See Torres, John A.
Torres, Joseph
   See Torres, J.
Torres, Laura 1967- *146*
   Earlier sketch in SATA *87*
Torres, Leyla 1960- *155*

Torrey, Rich
   See Torrey, Richard
Torrey, Richard *189*
Torrie, Malcolm
   See Mitchell, Gladys (Maude Winifred)
Toten, Teresa 1955- *99*
Totham, Mary
   See Breinburg, Petronella
Touponce, William F. 1948- *114*
Tournier, Michel 1924- *23*
Tournier, Michel Edouard
   See Tournier, Michel
Towle, Ben 1970- *228*
Towle, Wendy 1963- *79*
Towne, Mary
   See Spelman, Mary
Townley, Rod
   See Townley, Roderick
Townley, Roderick 1942- *177*
Townsend, Brad W. 1962- *91*
Townsend, John Rowe 1922- *132*
   Autobiography Feature *132*
   Earlier sketches in SATA *4, 68*
   See also CLR *2*
   See also SAAS *2*
Townsend, Michael 1981- *231*
   Earlier sketch in SATA *194*
Townsend, Sue 1946- *93*
   Brief entry *48*
   Earlier sketch in SATA *55*
Townsend, Susan Lilian
   See Townsend, Sue
Townsend, Thomas L. 1944- *59*
Townsend, Tom
   See Townsend, Thomas L.
Townsend, Wendy 1962- *201*
Townson, Hazel *134*
Toye, William Eldred 1926- *8*
Traherne, Michael
   See Watkins-Pitchford, Denys James
Trahey, Jane 1923-2000 .... *36*
   Obituary *120*
Trapani, Iza 1954- *214*
   Earlier sketches in SATA *80, 116*
Trapp, Maria Augusta von
   See von Trapp, Maria Augusta
Travers, P(amela) L(yndon) 1899-1996 ...... *100*
   Obituary *90*
   Earlier sketches in SATA *4, 54*
   See also CLR *93*
   See also SAAS *2*
Travis, Lucille *133*
   Earlier sketch in SATA *88*
Treadgold, Mary 1910-2005 .... *49*
Trease, (Robert) Geoffrey 1909-1998 .... *60*
   Obituary *101*
   Earlier sketch in SATA *2*
   See also CLR *42*
   See also SAAS *6*
Treat, Lawrence 1903-1998 .... *59*
Tredez, Alain 1926- *17*
Tredez, Denise 1930- *50*
Treece, Henry 1912-1966 .... *2*
   See also CLR *2*
Tregarthen, Enys
   See Sloggett, Nellie
Tregaskis, Richard 1916-1973 .... *3*
   Obituary *26*
Treherne, Katie Thamer 1955- *76*
Trell, Max 1900-1996 .... *14*
   Obituary *108*
Tremain, Ruthven 1922- *17*
Trembath, Don 1963- *168*
   Earlier sketch in SATA *96*
Tremens, Del
   See MacDonald, Amy
Trent, Robbie 1894-1988 .... *26*
Trent, Timothy
   See Malmberg, Carl
Treseder, Terry Walton 1956- *68*
Tresilian, (Cecil) Stuart 1891-(?) *40*

Tresselt, Alvin 1916-2000 7
　See also CLR 30
Trevino, Elizabeth B(orton) de 1904- 29
　Earlier sketch in SATA 1
　See also SAAS 5
Trevor, Elleston 1920-1995 28
Trevor, Frances
　See Teasdale, Sara
Trevor, Glen
　See Hilton, James
Trevor, (Lucy) Meriol 1919-2000 113
　Obituary 122
　Earlier sketch in SATA 10
Trewellard, J.M. 195
Trewellard, Juliet
　See Trewellard, J.M.
Trez, Alain
　See Tredez, Alain
Trez, Denise
　See Tredez, Denise
Trezise, Percy 1923-
　See CLR 41
Trezise, Percy James
　See Trezise, Percy
Triggs, Tony D. 1946- 70
Trimble, Marshall I(ra) 1939- 93
Trimby, Elisa 1948- 47
　Brief entry 40
Tring, A. Stephen
　See Meynell, Laurence Walter
Triplett, Gina 229
Tripp, Eleanor B(aldwin) 1936- 4
Tripp, Janet 1942- 108
Tripp, Jenny 188
Tripp, John
　See Moore, John Travers
Tripp, Nathaniel 1944- 101
Tripp, Paul 1916-2002 8
　Obituary 139
Tripp, Valerie 1951- 168
　Earlier sketch in SATA 78
Tripp, Wallace (Whitney) 1940- 31
Trivelpiece, Laurel 1926- 56
　Brief entry 46
Trivett, Daphne Harwood 1940- 22
Trivizas, Eugene 1946- 84
Trnka, Jiri 1912-1969 43
　Brief entry 32
Trollope, Anthony 1815-1882 22
Trost, Lucille W(ood) 1938- 149
　Earlier sketch in SATA 12
Trott, Betty 1933- 91
Trotter, Deborah W. 184
Trotter, Grace V(iolet) 1900-1991 10
Trottier, Maxine 1950- 175
　Earlier sketch in SATA 131
Troughton, Joanna (Margaret) 1947- 37
Trout, Kilgore
　See Farmer, Philip Jose
Trout, Richard E. 123
Trudeau, Garretson Beekman
　See Trudeau, G.B.
Trudeau, Garry
　See Trudeau, G.B.
Trudeau, Garry B.
　See Trudeau, G.B.
Trudeau, G.B. 1948- 168
　Earlier sketch in SATA 35
Trueit, Trudi
　See Trueit, Trudi Strain
Trueit, Trudi Strain 1963- 179
Trueman, Matthew 183
Trueman, Terry 1947- 178
　Earlier sketch in SATA 132
Truesdell, Judy
　See Mecca, Judy Truesdell
Truesdell, Sue
　See Truesdell, Susan G.
Truesdell, Susan G. 212
　Brief entry 45
　Earlier sketch in SATA 108

Trumbauer, Lisa 1963- 228
　Earlier sketch in SATA 149
Trumbauer, Lisa Trutkoff
　See Trumbauer, Lisa
Truss, Jan 1925- 35
Truss, Lynne 1955(?)- 194
Tryon, Leslie 194
　Earlier sketch in SATA 139
Tubb, Jonathan N. 1951- 78
Tubb, Kristin O'Donnell 1971- 209
Tubby, I. M.
　See Kraus, (Herman) Robert
Tucker, Allan James
　See James, Bill
Tucker, Caroline
　See Nolan, Jeannette Covert
Tucker, James
　See James, Bill
Tudor, Edward
　See Browne, Anthony
Tudor, Tasha 1915-2008 160
　Obituary 205
　Earlier sketches in SATA 20, 69
　See also CLR 13
Tuerk, Hanne 1951- 71
Tugeau, Jeremy 199
Tulloch, Richard 1949- 180
　Earlier sketch in SATA 76
Tulloch, Richard George
　See Tulloch, Richard
Tulloch, Shirley 169
Tully, John (Kimberley) 1923- 14
Tumanov, Vladimir A. 1961- 138
Tung, Angela 1972- 109
Tunis, Edwin (Burdett) 1897-1973 28
　Obituary 24
　Earlier sketch in SATA 1
　See also CLR 2
Tunis, John R(oberts) 1889-1975 37
　Brief entry 30
Tunnell, Michael
　See Tunnell, Michael O.
Tunnell, Michael O. 1950- 157
　Earlier sketch in SATA 103
Tunnell, Michael O'Grady
　See Tunnell, Michael O.
Tunnicliffe, C(harles) F(rederick)
　1901-1979 62
Turck, Mary C. 1950- 144
Turk, Hanne
　See Tuerk, Hanne
Turk, Ruth 1917- 82
Turkle, Brinton 1915- 79
　Earlier sketch in SATA 2
Turlington, Bayly 1919-1977 5
　Obituary 52
Turnbull, Agnes Sligh 1888-1982 14
Turnbull, Ann 1943- 160
　Earlier sketch in SATA 18
Turnbull, Ann Christine
　See Turnbull, Ann
Turnbull, Susan 222
Turner, Alice K. 1940- 10
Turner, Ann 1945- 188
　Autobiography Feature 188
　Earlier sketches in SATA 14, 77, 113, 178
Turner, Ann Warren
　See Turner, Ann
Turner, Bonnie 1932- 75
Turner, Elizabeth 1774-1846
　See YABC 2
Turner, Glennette Tilley 1933- 183
　Earlier sketch in SATA 71
Turner, Josie
　See Crawford, Phyllis
Turner, Megan Whalen 1965- 174
　Earlier sketch in SATA 94
Turner, Pamela S. 1957- 211

Turner, Philip (William) 1925- 83
　Earlier sketch in SATA 11
　See also CLR 89
　See also SAAS 6
Turner, Robyn 1947- 77
Turner, Sheila R.
　See Seed, Sheila Turner
Turngren, Annette 1902(?)-1980
　Obituary 23
Turngren, Ellen (?)-1964 3
Turska, Krystyna (Zofia) 1933- 31
　Brief entry 27
Turteltaub, H. N.
　See Turtledove, Harry
Turtledove, Harry 1949- 166
　Earlier sketch in SATA 116
Turtledove, Harry Norman
　See Turtledove, Harry
Tusa, Tricia 1960- 207
　Earlier sketches in SATA 72, 111
Tusiani, Joseph 1924- 45
Twain, Mark 1835-1910 100
　See also YABC 2
　See also CLR 156
Tweit, Susan J 1956- 94
Tweit, Susan Joan
　See Tweit, Susan J
Tweton, D. Jerome 1933- 48
Twinem, Neecy 1958- 92
Twohill, Maggie
　See Angell, Judie
Tworkov, Jack 1900-1982 47
　Obituary 31
Tyche
　See Papademetriou, Lisa
Tyers, Jenny 1969- 89
Tyers, Kathy 1952- 82
Tyler, Anne 1941- 173
　Earlier sketches in SATA 7, 90
Tyler, Linda
　See Tyler, Linda W(agner)
Tyler, Linda W(agner) 1952- 65
Tyler, Vicki 1952- 64
Tyne, Joel
　See Schembri, Jim
Tyrrell, Frances 1959- 107

U

Ubell, Earl 1926-2007 4
　Obituary 182
Uchida, Yoshiko 1921-1992 53
　Obituary 72
　Earlier sketch in SATA 1
　See also CLR 56
　See also SAAS 1
Udall, Jan Beaney 1938- 10
Uden, (Bernard Gilbert) Grant 1910- 26
Uderzo, Albert 1927-
　See CLR 37
Udovic, David 1950- 189
Udovic, Jane Morris 1947- 224
Udry, Janice May 1928- 152
　Earlier sketch in SATA 4
Uegaki, Chieri 1969- 211
　Earlier sketch in SATA 153
Uehashi, Nahoko 1962- 215
Ueno, Noriko
　See Nakae, Noriko
Ugliano, Natascia 196
Uhlberg, Myron 174
Uhlig, Richard 1970- 195
Uhlig, Susan 1955- 129
Ulam, S(tanislaw) M(arcin) 1909-1984 51
Ullman, Barb Bentler 210
Ullman, James Ramsey 1907-1971 7
Ulm, Robert 1934-1977 17
Ulmer, Louise 1943- 53
Ulmer, Wendy K. 1950- 201

Ulrich, Maureen 1958- 206
Ulriksen, Mark 1957- 210
Ulyatt, Kenneth 1920- 14
Umansky, Kaye 1946- 224
    Earlier sketches in SATA *158, 188*
Unada
    See Gliewe, Unada (Grace)
Uncle Carter
    See Boucher, (Clarence) Carter
Uncle Eric
    See Maybury, Richard J.
Uncle Gus
    See Rey, H. A.
Uncle Mac
    See McCulloch, Derek (Ivor Breashur)
Uncle Ray
    See Coffman, Ramon Peyton
Uncle Shelby
    See Silverstein, Shel
Underhill, Alice Mertie (Waterman)
    1900-1971 10
Underhill, Liz 1948- 53
    Brief entry 49
Underwood, Deborah 1962- 206
Unger, Harlow G. 1931- 75
Unger, Harlow Giles
    See Unger, Harlow G.
Unger, Jim 1937- 67
Ungerer, (Jean) Thomas 1931- 106
    Earlier sketches in SATA *5, 33*
    See also CLR 77
Ungerer, Tomi 1931-
    See Ungerer, (Jean) Thomas
Unkelbach, Kurt 1913-1992 4
Unnerstad, Edith (Totterman) 1900-1982 3
    See also CLR 36
Unobagha, Uzo 139
Unrau, Ruth 1922- 9
Unstead, R(obert) J(ohn) 1915-1988 12
    Obituary 56
Unsworth, Walt(er) 1928- 4
Untermeyer, Bryna Ivens 1909-1985 61
Untermeyer, Louis 1885-1977 37
    Obituary 26
    Earlier sketch in SATA *2*
Unwin, David S. 1918-2010 14
Unwin, David Storr
    See Unwin, David S.
Unwin, Nora S(picer) 1907-1982 3
    Obituary 49
Unzner, Christa 1958- 230
    Earlier sketches in SATA *80, 141*
Unzner-Fischer, Christa
    See Unzner, Christa
Updale, Eleanor 1953- 175
Updyke, Rosemary K. 1924- 103
Upitis, Alvis 109
Urbain, Cat 1956- 211
Urbain, Catherine
    See Urbain, Cat
Urban, Helle (Denise) 1957- 149
Urban, Linda 199
Urbanovic, Jackie 189
Urberuaga, Emilio 1954- 219
Urbigkit, Cat 1965- 196
Urdahl, Catherine 215
Ure, Jean 1943- 192
    Autobiography Feature 192
    Earlier sketches in SATA *48, 78, 129*
    See also CLR 34
    See also SAAS 14
U'Ren, Andrea 1968- 213
    Earlier sketch in SATA *142*
Uris, Leon 1924-2003 49
    Obituary 146
Uris, Leon Marcus
    See Uris, Leon
Ursu, Anne 177
Ury, Allen B. 1954- 98
Uschan, Michael V. 1948- 129

Usher, Margo Scegge
    See McHargue, Georgess
Usher, Mark David
    See Usher, M.D.
Usher, M.D. 1966- 221
Uslan, Michael E. 1951- 169
Uston, Ken(neth Senzo) 1935-1987 65
Uttley, Alice Jane 1884-1976 88
    Obituary 26
    Earlier sketch in SATA *3*
Uttley, Alison
    See Uttley, Alice Jane
Utz, Lois (Marie) 1932-1986 5
    Obituary 50

V

Vaeth, J. Gordon 1921- 17
Vaeth, Joseph Gordon
    See Vaeth, J. Gordon
Vagin, Vladimir (Vasilevich) 1937- 142
Vail, Rachel 1966- 201
    Earlier sketches in SATA *94, 163*
Vainio, Pirkko 1957- 123
    Earlier sketch in SATA *76*
Valen, Nanine 1950- 21
Valencak, Hannelore
    See Mayer, Hannelore Valencak
Valens, Amy 1946- 70
Valens, E(vans) G(ladstone), Jr. 1920-1992 ... 1
Valentine, Johnny 72
Valerio, Geraldo 1970- 180
Valgardson, W. D. 1939- 151
    Earlier sketch in SATA *101*
Valgardson, William Dempsey
    See Valgardson, W. D.
Valleau, Emily 1925- 51
Vamos, Samantha R. 215
Van Abbe, Salaman 1883-1955 18
Van Allsburg, Chris 1949- 156
    Earlier sketches in SATA *37, 53, 105*
    See also CLR 113
Van Anrooy, Francine 1924- 2
Van Anrooy, Frans
    See Van Anrooy, Francine
Vanasse, Deb 1957- 170
Van Buren, David 203
Van Camp, Katie 1981- 222
Vance, Cynthia 207
Vance, Eleanor Graham 1908-1985 11
Vance, Gerald
    See Garrett, Randall
    and Silverberg, Robert
Vance, Marguerite 1889-1965 29
Vance-Abrams, Cynthia
    See Vance, Cynthia
VanCleave, Janice 1942- 116
    Autobiography Feature 123
    Earlier sketch in SATA *75*
Vandenburg, Mary Lou 1943- 17
Vander Boom, Mae M. 14
Vander-Els, Betty 1936- 63
van der Heide, Iris 1970- 183
van der Linde, Laurel 1952- 78
van der Linden, Martijn 1979- 214
van der Meer, Ron 1945- 98
Vanderpool, Clare 1964- 232
van de Ruit, John 1975- 199
Van der Veer, Judy 1912-1982 4
    Obituary 33
Vanderwal, Andrew H. 1956- 219
Vanderwerff, Corrine 1939- 117
Vander Zee, Ruth 199
    Earlier sketch in SATA *159*
Vande Velde, Vivian 1951- 211
    Earlier sketches in SATA *62, 95, 141*
    See also CLR 145
Vandivert, Rita (Andre) 1905-1986 21

Van Draanen, Wendelin 207
    Earlier sketch in SATA *122*
Van Dusen, Chris 228
    Earlier sketch in SATA *173*
Van Duyn, Janet 1910- 18
Van Dyne, Edith
    See Baum, L. Frank
    and Sampson, Emma (Keats) Speed
    and van Zantwijk, Rudolf (Alexander
    Marinus)
Vane, Mitch
    See Vane, Mitchelle
Vane, Mitchelle 176
van Eekhout, Greg 232
van Frankenhuyzen, Gijsbert 1951- 132
Van Genechten, Guido 1957- 165
van Haeringen, Annemarie 193
Van Hook, Beverly 1941- 99
Van Hook, Beverly H.
    See Van Hook, Beverly
Van Hook, Beverly Hennen
    See Van Hook, Beverly
Van Horn, William 1939- 43
van Hout, Mies 1962- 178
Van Iterson, S(iny) R(ose) 26
Van Kampen, Vlasta 1943- 163
    Earlier sketch in SATA *54*
Van Laan, Nancy 1939- 214
    Earlier sketch in SATA *105*
van Lawick-Goodall, Jane
    See Goodall, Jane
Van Leeuwen, Jean 1937- 211
    Autobiography Feature 141
    Earlier sketches in SATA *6, 82, 132, 141*
    See also SAAS 8
van Lhin, Erik
    See del Rey, Lester
van Lieshout, Elle 1963- 217
van Lieshout, Maria 201
Van Loon, Hendrik Willem 1882-1944 18
van Ommen, Sylvia 1978- 186
VanOosting, James 1951- 170
Van Orden, M(erton) D(ick) 1921- 4
van Os, Erik 1963- 217
Van Patter, Bruce 183
Van Reek, Wouter 204
Van Rensselaer, Alexander (Taylor Mason)
    1892-1962 14
Van Riper, Guernsey, Jr. 1909-1995 3
van Rossum, Heleen 1962- 174
Van Rynbach, Iris 1952- 102
Vansant, Rhonda Joy Edwards 1950- 92
Van Steenwyk, Elizabeth (Ann) 1928- 89
    Earlier sketch in SATA *34*
Van Stockum, Hilda 1908-2006 5
    Obituary 179
van Straaten, Harmen 1961- 218
    Earlier sketch in SATA *195*
Van Tuyl, Barbara 1940- 11
van Vogt, A(lfred) E(lton) 1912-2000 14
    Obituary 124
Van Wassenhove, Sue 1951- 202
Van Woerkom, Dorothy (O'Brien)
    1924-1996 21
Van Wormer, Joe
    See Van Wormer, Joseph Edward
Van Wormer, Joseph Edward 1913-1998 35
Van Wright, Cornelius 173
Van Zwienen, Ilse Charlotte Koehn
    1929-1991 34
    Brief entry 28
    Obituary 67
Van Zyle, Jon 1942- 176
    Earlier sketch in SATA *84*
Varela, Barry 180
Varga, Judy
    See Stang, Judit
Varley, Dimitry V. 1906-1984 10
Varley, Susan 1961- 134
    Earlier sketch in SATA *63*
Varon, Sara 195

Vasileva, Tatiana
  See Wassiljewa, Tatjana
Vasiliev, Valery 1949- 80
Vasilieva, Tatiana
  See Wassiljewa, Tatjana
Vasiliu, Mircea 1920- 2
Vass, George 1927- 57
  Brief entry 31
Vaughan, Carter A.
  See Gerson, Noel Bertram
Vaughan, Harold Cecil 1923- 14
Vaughan, Marcia (K.) 1951- 159
  Earlier sketches in SATA 60, 95
Vaughan, Richard 1947- 87
Vaughn, Sam(uel) 1928- 14
Vaughn, Ruth 1935- 14
Vaught, Susan 1965- 195
Vaupel, Robin 198
Vautier, Ghislaine 1932- 53
Vavra, Robert James 1935- 8
Vecsey, George Spencer 1939- 9
Vedral, Joyce L(auretta) 1943- 65
Vega, Denise 216
  Earlier sketch in SATA 174
Vega, Denise B.
  See Vega, Denise
Vega, Diego
  See Adkins, Jan
Veglahn, Nancy (Crary) 1937- 5
Vejjajiva, Jane 1963- 189
Velasquez, Crystal 228
Velasquez, Eric 226
  Earlier sketch in SATA 192
Velasquez, Gloria 1949- 229
  Earlier sketch in SATA 113
Velthuijs, Max 1923-2005 110
  Obituary 160
  Earlier sketch in SATA 53
Venable, Alan (Hudson) 1944- 8
Venable, Colleen A.F. 1980- 233
Venezia, Mike 1945- 150
Venner, Grace Chang
  See Chang, Grace
Ventura, Anthony
  See Pellowski, Michael (Joseph)
Ventura, Piero (Luigi) 1937- 61
  Brief entry 43
  See also CLR 16
Vequin, Capini
  See Quinn, Elisabeth
Verba, Joan Marie 1953- 78
Verboven, Agnes 1951- 103
verDorn, Bethea (Stewart) 1952- 76
Vere, Ed 197
Verissimo, Erico (Lopes) 1905-1975 113
Verne, Jules 1828-1905 21
  See also CLR 88
Verne, Jules Gabriel
  See Verne, Jules
Verner, Gerald 1897(?)-1980
  Obituary 25
Verney, John 1913-1993 14
  Obituary 75
Verniero, Joan C. 1949- 181
Vernon, (Elda) Louise A(nderson) 1914- 14
Vernon, Rosemary
  See Smith, Susan Vernon
Vernon, Ursula 204
Vernor, D.
  See Casewit, Curtis W(erner)
Verr, Harry Coe
  See Kunhardt, Edith
Verral, Charles Spain 1904-1990 11
  Obituary 65
Verrillo, Erica 1953- 199
Verrillo, Erica F.
  See Verrillo, Erica
Verroken, Sarah 1982- 223
Verrone, Robert J. 1935(?)-1984
  Obituary 39
Versace, Marie Teresa Rios 1917- 2

Vertreace, Martha M(odena) 1945- 78
Vesey, A(manda) 1939- 62
Vesey, Mark (David) 1958- 123
Vesey, Paul
  See Allen, Samuel W(ashington)
Vess, Charles 1951- 215
Vestergaard, Hope 178
Vestly, Anne-Cath(arina) 1920-2008 14
  See also CLR 99
Vevers, (Henry) Gwynne 1916-1988 45
  Obituary 57
Viator, Vacuus
  See Hughes, Thomas
Viau, Nancy 208
Vicar, Henry
  See Felsen, Henry Gregor
Vick, Helen Hughes 1950- 88
Vicker, Angus
  See Felsen, Henry Gregor
Vickers, Sheena 1960- 94
Vickery, Kate
  See Kennedy, T.A.
Victor, Edward 1914- 3
Victor, Joan Berg 1942- 30
Vidrine, Beverly Barras 1938- 188
  Earlier sketch in SATA 103
Vieceli, Emma 1979- 210
Viereck, Ellen K. 1928- 14
Viereck, Phillip 1925- 3
Viergutz, Dina Nayeri
  See Nayeri, Dina
Viertel, Janet 1915- 10
Vigliante, Mary
  See Szydlowski, Mary Vigliante
Vigna, Judith 1936- 102
  Earlier sketch in SATA 15
Viguers, Ruth Hill 1903-1971 6
Vila, Laura 207
Vilela, Fernando 1973- 216
Villareal, Ray 187
Villasenor, Edmund
  See Villasenor, Victor E.
Villasenor, Edmundo
  See Villasenor, Victor E.
Villasenor, Victor
  See Villasenor, Victor E.
Villasenor, Victor E. 1940- 171
Villasenor, Victor Edmundo
  See Villasenor, Victor E.
Villeneuve, Anne 230
Villiard, Paul 1910-1974 51
  Obituary 20
Villiers, Alan (John) 1903-1982 10
Vilott, Rhondi
  See Salsitz, Rhondi Vilott
Vincent, Amy
  See Gray, Claudia
Vincent, Eric Douglas 1953- 40
Vincent, Erin 1969- 188
Vincent, Felix 1946- 41
Vincent, Gabrielle 1928-2000 121
  Earlier sketch in SATA 61
  See also CLR 13
Vincent, Mary Keith
  See St. John, Wylly Folk
Vincent, Rachel 1978- 222
Vincent, William R.
  See Heitzmann, William Ray
Vinegar, Tom
  See Gregg, Andrew K.
Vinest, Shaw
  See Longyear, Barry B(rookes)
Vinge, Joan (Carol) D(ennison) 1948- 113
  Earlier sketch in SATA 36
Vining, Elizabeth Gray 1902-1999 6
  Obituary 117
Vinson, Kathryn 1911-1995 21
Vinton, Iris 1906(?)-1988 24
  Obituary 55
Viola, Herman J(oseph) 1938- 126

Viorst, Judith 1931- 172
  Earlier sketches in SATA 7, 70, 123
  See also CLR 90
Vip
  See Partch, Virgil Franklin II
Vipont, Charles
  See Foulds, Elfrida Vipont
Vipont, Elfrida
  See Foulds, Elfrida Vipont
Viramontes, Helena Maria 1954-
  See CLR 285
Viscott, David S(teven) 1938-1996 65
Visser, W(illem) F(rederik) H(endrik)
  1900-1968 10
Vitale, Stefano 1958- 225
  Earlier sketches in SATA 114, 180
Vivas, Julie 1947- 96
Vivelo, Jackie 1943- 63
Vivelo, Jacqueline J.
  See Vivelo, Jackie
Vivelo, Jacqueline Jean
  See Vivelo, Jackie
Vivian, Siobhan 1979(?)- 215
Vizzini, Ned 1981- 179
  Earlier sketch in SATA 125
Vlahos, Olivia 1924- 31
Vlasic, Bob
  See Hirsch, Phil
Voake, Charlotte 180
  Earlier sketch in SATA 114
Voake, Steve 1961- 178
Vo-Dinh, Mai 1933- 16
Vogel, Carole Garbuny 1951- 231
  Earlier sketches in SATA 70, 105
Vogel, Ilse-Margret 1914-2001 14
  See also CLR 170
Vogel, John H., Jr. 1950- 18
Vogt, Esther Loewen 1915-1999 14
Vogt, Gregory L. 94
Vogt, Marie Bollinger 1921- 45
Vohwinkel, Astrid 1969- 207
Voight, Virginia Frances 1909-1989 8
Voigt, Cynthia 1942- 160
  Brief entry 33
  Earlier sketches in SATA 48, 79, 116
  See also CLR 141
Voigt, Erna 1925- 35
Voigt-Rother, Erna
  See Voigt, Erna
Vojtech, Anna 1946- 108
  Earlier sketch in SATA 42
Vollstadt, Elizabeth Weiss 1942- 121
Volponi, Paul 228
  Earlier sketch in SATA 175
Volting, Dr. R.E.
  See Lerangis, Peter
Von Ahnen, Katherine 1922- 93
von Buhler, Cynthia 185
Vondra, J. Gert
  See Vondra, Josef
Vondra, Josef 1941- 121
Vondra, Josef Gert
  See Vondra, Josef
Von Gunden, Kenneth 1946- 113
Von Hagen, Victor Wolfgang 1908-1985 29
von Klopp, Vahrah
  See Malvern, Gladys
von Schmidt, Eric 1931-2007 50
  Brief entry 36
  Obituary 181
von Storch, Anne B. 1910- 1
von Trapp, Maria Augusta 1905-1987 16
von Wodtke, Charlotte Buel Johnson
  1918-1982 46
von Ziegesar, Cecily 1970- 161
Vos, Ida 1931-2006 121
  Earlier sketch in SATA 69
  See also CLR 85
Vosburgh, Leonard (W.) 1912- 15
Votaw, Carol 1961- 201

Voyle, Mary
  See Manning, Rosemary
Vrettos, Adrienne Maria *187*
Vriens, Jacques 1946- *151*
Vugteveen, Verna Aardema
  See Aardema, Verna
Vulture, Elizabeth T.
  See Gilbert, Suzie
Vuong, Lynette Dyer 1938- *110*
  Earlier sketch in SATA *60*
Vyner, Tim 1963- *228*

W

Waas, Uli
  See Waas-Pommer, Ulrike
Waas-Pommer, Ulrike 1949- *85*
Waber, Bernard 1924- *155*
  Brief entry *40*
  Earlier sketches in SATA *47, 95*
  See also CLR *55*
Waber, Paulis *231*
Wachtel, Shirley Russak 1951- *88*
Wachter, Oralee (Roberts) 1935- *61*
  Brief entry *51*
Waddell, Evelyn Margaret 1918- *10*
Waddell, Martin 1941- *232*
  Autobiography Feature *129*
  Earlier sketches in SATA *43, 81, 127, 129*
  See also CLR *31*
  See also SAAS *15*
Waddy, Lawrence 1912-2010 .... *91*
Waddy, Lawrence Heber
  See Waddy, Lawrence
Wade, Mary Dodson 1930- *151*
  Earlier sketch in SATA *79*
Wade, Suzanne
  See Kirby, Susan E.
Wade, Theodore E., Jr. 1936- *37*
Wademan, Peter John 1946- *122*
Wademan, Spike
  See Wademan, Peter John
Wadsworth, Ginger 1945- *223*
  Earlier sketches in SATA *103, 157*
Wagenheim, Kal 1935- *21*
Wagner, Michele R. 1975- *157*
Wagner, Sharon B. 1936- *4*
Wagoner, David (Russell) 1926- *14*
Wahl, Jan (Boyer) 1933- *132*
  Earlier sketches in SATA *2, 34, 73*
  See also SAAS *3*
Wahl, Mats 1945- *186*
Wahman, Wendy *218*
Waide, Jan 1952- *29*
Wainscott, John Milton 1910-1981 .... *53*
Wainwright, Debra *218*
Wainwright, Richard M. 1935- *91*
Wainwright, Ruth
  See Symes, Ruth Louise
Wait, Lea 1946- *137*
Waite, Judy *174*
Waite, Judy Bernard
  See Bernard, Patricia
Waite, Michael
  See Waite, Michael P.
Waite, Michael P. 1960- *101*
Waite, P(eter) B(usby) 1922- *64*
Waites, Joan C. *187*
Waitley, Douglas 1927- *30*
Wakefield, Jean L.
  See Laird, Jean E(louise)
Wakin, Daniel (Joseph) 1961- *84*
Wakin, Edward 1927- *37*
Wakiyama, Hanako 1966- *192*
Walck, Henry Z. 1908(?)-1984
  Obituary *40*
Walden, Amelia Elizabeth *3*
Walden, Mark *188*
Waldherr, Kris 1963- *76*

Waldman, Bruce 1949- *15*
Waldman, Neil 1947- *203*
  Earlier sketches in SATA *51, 94, 142*
Waldrep, Richard *198*
Waldron, Ann Wood 1924-2010 .... *16*
Waldron, Kathleen Cook *176*
Waldron, Kevin 1979- *230*
Wales, Dirk 1931- *205*
Walgren, Judy 1963- *118*
Walker, Addison
  See Walker, Mort
Walker, Addison Mort
  See Walker, Mort
Walker, Alice 1944- *31*
Walker, Alice Malsenior
  See Walker, Alice
Walker, Anna *223*
Walker, Barbara (Jeanne) K(erlin) 1921- *80*
  Earlier sketch in SATA *4*
Walker, Barbara M(uhs) 1928- *57*
Walker, (James) Braz(elton) 1934-1983 .... *45*
Walker, David 1965- *197*
Walker, David G(ordon) 1926- *60*
Walker, David Harry 1911-1992 .... *8*
  Obituary *71*
Walker, Diana 1925- *9*
Walker, Diane Marie Catherine
  See Walker, Kate
Walker, Dick
  See Pellowski, Michael (Joseph)
Walker, Frank 1931-2000 .... *36*
Walker, Holly Beth
  See Bond, Gladys Baker
Walker, Kate 1950- *165*
  Earlier sketch in SATA *82*
Walker, Kathrine Sorley
  See Sorley Walker, Kathrine
Walker, Kristin *228*
Walker, Lou Ann 1952- *66*
  Brief entry *53*
Walker, Louise Jean 1891-1976
  Obituary *35*
Walker, Mary Alexander 1927- *61*
Walker, Mildred
  See Schemm, Mildred Walker
Walker, Mort 1923- *8*
Walker, Pamela 1948- *142*
  Earlier sketch in SATA *24*
Walker, Paul Robert 1953- *154*
Walker, Robert W. 1948- *66*
Walker, Robert Wayne
  See Walker, Robert W.
Walker, Sally M. 1954- *221*
  Earlier sketch in SATA *135*
Walker, Stephen J. 1951- *12*
Walker, Steve *232*
Walker-Blondell, Becky 1951- *89*
Wallace, Barbara Brooks 1922- *136*
  Earlier sketches in SATA *4, 78*
  See also CLR *150*
  See also SAAS *17*
Wallace, Beverly Dobrin 1921- *19*
Wallace, Bill 1947- *169*
  Brief entry *47*
  Earlier sketches in SATA *53, 101*
Wallace, Carol 1948- *218*
Wallace, Chad *229*
Wallace, Daisy
  See Cuyler, Margery
Wallace, Ian 1950- *219*
  Earlier sketches in SATA *53, 56, 141*
  See also CLR *37*
Wallace, John 1966- *155*
  Earlier sketch in SATA *105*
Wallace, John A(dam) 1915-2004 .... *3*
  Obituary *155*
Wallace, Karen 1951- *188*
  Earlier sketches in SATA *83, 139*
Wallace, Nancy Elizabeth 1948- *222*
  Earlier sketches in SATA *141, 186*

Wallace, Nigel
  See Hamilton, Charles (Harold St. John)
Wallace, Paula S. *153*
Wallace, Rich 1957- *233*
  Earlier sketches in SATA *117, 158, 196*
Wallace, Robert 1932-1999 .... *47*
  Brief entry *37*
Wallace, Ruby Ann 1923(?)- *77*
Wallace, William Keith
  See Wallace, Bill
Wallace-Brodeur, Ruth 1941- *169*
  Brief entry *41*
  Earlier sketches in SATA *51, 88*
Wallenfels, Stephen *232*
Wallenta, Adam 1974- *123*
Waller, Leslie 1923-2007 .... *20*
Walley, Byron
  See Card, Orson Scott
Walliams, David 1971- *227*
Wallis, Diz 1949- *77*
Wallis, G. McDonald
  See Campbell, Hope
Wallner, Alexandra 1946- *156*
  Brief entry *41*
  Earlier sketches in SATA *51, 98*
Wallner, John C. 1945- *133*
  Earlier sketches in SATA *10, 51*
Wallower, Lucille *11*
Walrod, Amy 1973(?)- *182*
Walsh, Ann 1942- *176*
  Earlier sketch in SATA *62*
Walsh, Ellen Stoll 1942- *194*
  Earlier sketches in SATA *49, 99, 147*
Walsh, George Johnston 1889-1981 .... *53*
Walsh, Gillian Paton
  See Paton Walsh, Jill
Walsh, Jill Paton
  See Paton Walsh, Jill
Walsh, Joanna 1970- *182*
Walsh, Lawrence 1942- *170*
Walsh, Marissa 1972- *195*
Walsh, Mary Caswell 1949- *118*
Walsh, Mitzy
  See Walsh, Marissa
Walsh, Rebecca *217*
Walsh, Suella *170*
Walsh, V. L.
  See Walsh, Vivian
Walsh, Vivian 1960- *120*
Walsh Shepherd, Donna 1948- *78*
Walter, Frances V. 1923- *71*
Walter, Mildred Pitts 1922- *133*
  Brief entry *45*
  Earlier sketch in SATA *69*
  See also CLR *61*
  See also SAAS *12*
Walter, Villiam Christian
  See Andersen, Hans Christian
Walter, Virginia
  See Walter, Virginia A.
Walter, Virginia A. *134*
Walters, Audrey 1929- *18*
Walters, Celeste 1938- *126*
Walters, Eric 1957- *205*
  Earlier sketches in SATA *99, 155*
Walters, Eric Robert
  See Walters, Eric
Walters, Gregory 1964- *213*
Walters, Helen B. (?)-1987
  Obituary *50*
Walters, Hugh
  See Hughes, Walter (Llewellyn)
Walther, Thomas A. 1950- *31*
Walther, Tom
  See Walther, Thomas A.
Waltner, Elma 1912-1987 .... *40*
Waltner, Willard H. 1909- *40*
Walton, Darwin McBeth 1926- *119*
Walton, Fiona L. M. 1959- *89*
Walton, Richard J. 1928- *4*

Walton, Rick 1957- *204*
  Earlier sketches in SATA *101, 151*
Waltrip, Lela (Kingston) 1904-1995 .... *9*
Waltrip, Mildred 1911- *37*
Waltrip, Rufus (Charles) 1898-1988 .... *9*
Walworth, Nancy Zinsser 1917- *14*
Wang, Gabrielle *212*
Wang, Lin 1973- *221*
Wang, Shaoli *216*
Wangerin, Walter, Jr. 1944- *98*
  Brief entry *37*
  Earlier sketch in SATA *45*
Waniek, Marilyn
  See Nelson, Marilyn
Waniek, Marilyn Nelson 1946-
  See Nelson, Marilyn
Wannamaker, Bruce
  See Moncure, Jane Belk
Warbler, J. M.
  See Cocagnac, Augustin Maurice(-Jean)
Warburg, Sandol Stoddard
  See Stoddard, Sandol
Warburton, Tom 1968(?)- *218*
Ward, David 1967- *213*
Ward, E. D.
  See Gorey, Edward (St. John)
  and Lucas, E(dward) V(errall)
Ward, Ed
  See Stratemeyer, Edward L.
Ward, Helen 1962- *206*
  Earlier sketches in SATA *72, 144*
Ward, Jay 1920-1989
  Obituary *63*
Ward, Jennifer 1963- *226*
  Earlier sketch in SATA *146*
Ward, John (Stanton) 1917- *42*
Ward, Jonas
  See Ard, William
  and Cox, William R(obert)
  and Garfield, Brian (Francis Wynne)
Ward, Lynd (Kendall) 1905-1985 .... *36*
  Obituary *42*
  Earlier sketch in SATA *2*
Ward, Martha (Eads) *5*
Ward, Melanie
  See Curtis, Richard
  and Lynch, Marilyn
Ward, Nicholas John
  See Ward, Nick
Ward, Nick 1955- *190*
Ward, Rachel 1964- *229*
Ward, Tom
  See Stratemeyer, Edward L.
Wardell, Dean
  See Prince, J(ack) H(arvey)
Wardlaw, Lee 1955- *115*
  Earlier sketch in SATA *79*
Ware, Cheryl 1963- *101*
Ware, Chris 1967- *140*
Ware, Leon (Vernon) 1909-1976 .... *4*
Wargin, Kathy-jo 1964- *210*
  Earlier sketch in SATA *145*
Warhola, James 1955- *187*
Warman, Jessica 1981- *225*
Warner, Frank A. *67*
  Earlier sketch in SATA *1*
Warner, Gertrude Chandler 1890-1979 .... *9*
  Obituary *73*
Warner, J(ohn) F. 1929- *75*
Warner, Lucille Schulberg *30*
Warner, Marsha *232*
Warner, Matt
  See Fichter, George S.
Warner, Oliver (Martin Wilson) 1903-1976 . *29*
Warner, Sally 1946- *214*
  Earlier sketch in SATA *131*
Warner, Sunny (B.) 1931- *108*
Warnes, Tim 1971- *216*
  Earlier sketches in SATA *116, 166*
Warnes, Timothy
  See Warnes, Tim

Warnick, Elsa 1942- *113*
Warren, Andrea 1946- *98*
Warren, Betsy
  See Warren, Elizabeth Avery
Warren, Billy
  See Warren, William Stephen
Warren, Cathy 1951- *62*
  Brief entry *46*
Warren, Elizabeth
  See Supraner, Robyn
Warren, Elizabeth Avery 1916- *46*
  Brief entry *38*
Warren, Jackie M. 1953- *135*
Warren, Joshua P(aul) 1976- *107*
Warren, Joyce W(illiams) 1935- *18*
Warren, Mary Phraner 1929- *10*
Warren, Robert Penn 1905-1989 .... *46*
  Obituary *63*
Warren, Scott S. 1957- *79*
Warren, William Stephen 1882-1968 .... *9*
Warrick, Patricia Scott 1925- *35*
Warriner, John 1907(?)-1987
  Obituary *53*
Warsh
  See Warshaw, Jerry
Warshaw, Jerry 1929- *30*
Warshaw, Mary 1931- *89*
Warshofsky, Fred 1931- *24*
Warshofsky, Isaac
  See Singer, Isaac Bashevis
Wartski, Maureen (Ann Crane) 1940- *50*
  Brief entry *37*
Warwick, Alan R(oss) 1900-1973 .... *42*
Wa-sha-quon-asin
  See Belaney, Archibald Stansfeld
Wa-Sha-Quon-Asin
  See Belaney, Archibald Stansfeld
Washburn, Bradford 1910-2007 .... *38*
  Obituary *181*
Washburn, Henry Bradford, Jr.
  See Washburn, Bradford
Washburn, Jan(ice) 1926- *63*
Washburn, Lucia *193*
Washburne, Carolyn Kott 1944- *86*
Washburne, Heluiz Chandler 1892-1970 ...... *10*
  Obituary *26*
Washington, Booker T. 1856-1915 .... *28*
Washington, Donna L. 1967- *159*
  Earlier sketch in SATA *98*
Wasserman, Robin 1978- *207*
Wasserstein, Wendy 1950-2006 .... *94*
  Obituary *174*
Wassiljewa, Tatjana 1928- *106*
Watanabe, Etsuko 1968- *219*
Watanabe, Shigeo 1928- *131*
  Brief entry *32*
  Earlier sketch in SATA *39*
  See also CLR *8*
Waters, John F(rederick) 1930- *4*
Waters, Summer
  See Sykes, Julie
Waters, Tony 1958- *75*
Waterton, Betty 1923- *99*
  Brief entry *34*
  Earlier sketch in SATA *37*
Waterton, Betty Marie
  See Waterton, Betty
Watkins, Dawn L. *126*
Watkins, Gloria Jean
  See hooks, bell
Watkins, Lis
  See Watkins, Liselotte
Watkins, Liselotte 1971- *215*
Watkins, Lois 1930- *88*
Watkins, Peter 1934- *66*
Watkins, Yoko Kawashima 1933- *93*
Watkins-Pitchford, Denys James
  1905-1990 .... *87*
  Obituary *66*
  Earlier sketch in SATA *6*
  See also SAAS *4*

Watling, James 1933- *117*
  Earlier sketch in SATA *67*
Watson, Aldren A(uld) 1917- *42*
  Brief entry *36*
Watson, Amy Zakrzewski 1965- *76*
Watson, B. S.
  See Teitelbaum, Michael
Watson, Carol 1949- *78*
Watson, C.G. *193*
Watson, Clyde 1947- *68*
  Earlier sketch in SATA *5*
  See also CLR *3*
Watson, Helen Orr 1892-1978
  Obituary *24*
Watson, James 1936- *106*
  Earlier sketch in SATA *10*
Watson, Jane Werner 1915- *54*
  Earlier sketch in SATA *3*
Watson, Jesse Joshua *199*
Watson, John H.
  See Farmer, Philip Jose
Watson, Mary 1953- *117*
Watson, N. Cameron 1955- *81*
Watson, Nancy Dingman *32*
Watson, Pauline 1925- *14*
Watson, Renee 1978- *233*
Watson, Richard F.
  See Silverberg, Robert
Watson, Richard Jesse 1951- *211*
  Earlier sketch in SATA *62*
Watson, Sally (Lou) 1924- *3*
Watson, Sasha *211*
Watson, Wendy (McLeod) 1942- *142*
  Earlier sketches in SATA *5, 74*
Watson Taylor, Elizabeth 1915- *41*
Watt, Melanie 1975- *193*
  Earlier sketch in SATA *136*
Watt, Thomas 1935- *4*
Wattenberg, Jane *174*
Watterson, Bill 1958- *66*
Watt-Evans, Lawrence 1954- *121*
Watts, Bernadette 1942- *230*
  Earlier sketches in SATA *4, 103*
Watts, Ephraim
  See Horne, Richard Henry Hengist
Watts, Franklin (Mowry) 1904-1978 .... *46*
  Obituary *21*
Watts, Helen L. Hoke 1903-1990
  Obituary *65*
Watts, Irene N(aemi) 1931- *111*
  Earlier sketch in SATA *56*
Watts, Isaac 1674-1748 .... *52*
Watts, James K(ennedy) M(offitt) 1955- *59*
Watts, Jeri Hanel 1957- *170*
Watts, Julia 1969- *103*
Watts, Leander 1956- *146*
Watts, Leslie Elizabeth 1961- *168*
Watts, Mabel Pizzey 1906-1994 .... *11*
Watts, Nigel 1957-1999 .... *121*
Waugh, C. C. Roessel
  See Waugh, Carol-Lynn Rossel
  and Waugh, Charles G(ordon)
Waugh, Carol-Lynn Rossel 1947- *41*
Waugh, Dorothy -1996 .... *11*
Waugh, Sylvia 1935- *169*
Waugh, Virginia
  See Sorensen, Virginia
Wax, Wendy A. 1963- *219*
  Earlier sketches in SATA *73, 163*
Wayland, April Halprin 1954- *143*
  Earlier sketch in SATA *78*
  See also SAAS *26*
Wayland, Patrick
  See O'Connor, Richard
Wayne, (Anne) Jenifer 1917-1982 .... *32*
Wayne, Kyra Petrovskaya 1918- *8*
Wayne, Richard
  See Decker, Duane
Wayshak, Deborah Noyes
  See Noyes, Deborah

Waystaff, Simon
See Swift, Jonathan
Weales, Gerald (Clifford) 1925- *11*
Weary, Ogdred
See Gorey, Edward (St. John)
Weatherford, Carole Boston 1956- *226*
Earlier sketches in SATA *138, 181*
Weatherill, Cat *203*
Weatherly, Lee 1967- *192*
Weatherly, Myra 1926- *130*
Weatherly, Myra S.
See Weatherly, Myra
Weaver, Brian M.
See Numberman, Neil
Weaver, Harriett E. 1908-1993 .... *65*
Weaver, John L. 1949- *42*
Weaver, Robyn
See Conley, Robyn
Weaver, Robyn M.
See Conley, Robyn
Weaver, Tess *197*
Weaver, Ward
See Mason, F(rancis) van Wyck
Weaver, Will 1950- *217*
Earlier sketches in SATA *88, 109, 161*
Weaver, William Weller
See Weaver, Will
Weaver-Gelzer, Charlotte 1950- *79*
Webb, Christopher
See Wibberley, Leonard
Webb, Jacqueline
See Pearce, Margaret
Webb, Jacquelyn
See Pearce, Margaret
and Pearce, Margaret
Webb, Jean Francis (III) 1910-1991 .... *35*
Webb, Kaye 1914- *60*
Webb, Lois Sinaiko 1922- *82*
Webb, Margot 1934- *67*
Webb, Sharon 1936-2010 .... *41*
Webb, Sophie 1958- *135*
Webber, Andrew Lloyd
See Lloyd Webber, Andrew
Webber, Desiree Morrison 1956- *170*
Webber, Irma E(leanor Schmidt)
1904-1995 .... *14*
Weber, Alfons 1921- *8*
Weber, Bruce 1942- *120*
Earlier sketch in SATA *73*
Weber, Debora 1955- *58*
Weber, EdNah New Rider 1919(?)- *168*
Weber, Elka 1968- *219*
Weber, Jill 1950- *209*
Earlier sketch in SATA *127*
Weber, Judith E(ichler) 1938- *64*
Weber, Ken(neth J.) 1940- *90*
Weber, Lenora Mattingly 1895-1971 .... *2*
Obituary *26*
Weber, Lisa K. *217*
Weber, Lori 1959- *220*
Weber, Michael 1945- *87*
Weber, Sandra 1961- *158*
Weber, William J(ohn) 1927- *14*
Webster, Alice Jane Chandler 1876-1916 ..... *17*
Webster, David 1930- *11*
Webster, Frank V. *67*
Earlier sketch in SATA *1*
Webster, Gary
See Garrison, Webb B(lack)
Webster, James 1925-1981 .... *17*
Obituary *27*
Webster, Jean
See Webster, Alice Jane Chandler
Wechsler, Doug *189*
Wechsler, Herman J. 1904-1976
Obituary *20*
Wechter, Nell (Carolyn) Wise 1913-1989 .. *127*
Earlier sketch in SATA *60*
Weck, Thomas L. 1942- *62*
Wedd, Kate
See Gregory, Philippa

Weddle, Ethel Harshbarger 1897-1996 .... *11*
Wedekind, Annie *204*
Weeks, Sarah *194*
Earlier sketch in SATA *158*
Weems, David B(urnola) 1922- *80*
Wees, Frances Shelley 1902-1982 .... *58*
Weevers, Peter 1944- *59*
Wegen, Ronald 1946-1985 .... *99*
Wegman, William (George) 1943- *135*
Earlier sketches in SATA *78, 129*
Wegner, Fritz 1924- *20*
Wehrman, Vicki *223*
Weidhorn, Manfred 1931- *60*
Weidt, Maryann N. 1944- *85*
Weigel, Jeff 1958- *170*
Weigelt, Udo 1960- *201*
Earlier sketch in SATA *168*
Weihs, Erika 1917-2010 .... *107*
Earlier sketch in SATA *15*
Weik, Mary Hays 1898(?)-1979 .... *3*
Obituary *23*
Weil, Ann Yezner 1908-1969 .... *9*
Weil, Lisl 1910- *7*
Weilerstein, Sadie Rose 1894-1993 .... *3*
Obituary *75*
Weill, Cynthia 1959- *167*
Wein, Elizabeth E. 1964- *151*
Earlier sketch in SATA *82*
Wein, Elizabeth Eve
See Wein, Elizabeth E.
Wein, Hallie
See Zobel Nolan, Allia
Weinberg, Larry
See Weinberg, Lawrence (E.)
Weinberg, Lawrence (E.) *92*
Brief entry *48*
Weinberger, Tanya 1939- *84*
Weiner, Sandra 1922- *14*
Weingarten, Lynn *217*
Weingarten, Violet (Brown) 1915-1976 .... *3*
Obituary *27*
Weingartner, Charles 1922- *5*
Weinheimer, Beckie 1958- *186*
Weinstein, Bruce 1960- *220*
Weinstein, Bruce M.
See Weinstein, Bruce
Weinstein, Ellen Slusky 1959- *200*
Weinstein, Muriel Harris *215*
Weinstein, Nina 1951- *73*
Weinstock, Robert 1967- *204*
Weir, Bob 1947- *76*
Weir, Diana (R.) Loiewski 1958- *111*
Weir, Joan S(herman) 1928- *99*
Weir, LaVada *2*
Weir, Rosemary (Green) 1905-1994 .... *21*
Weir, Wendy 1949- *76*
Weis, Margaret 1948- *164*
Earlier sketches in SATA *38, 92*
Weisberger, Bernard A(llen) 1922- *21*
Weisburd, Stefi 1957- *202*
Weiser, Marjorie P(hillis) K(atz) 1934- *33*
Weisgard, Leonard (Joseph) 1916-2000 .... *85*
Obituary *122*
Earlier sketches in SATA *2, 30*
See also SAAS *19*
Weiss, Adelle 1920- *18*
Weiss, Ann E(dwards) 1943- *69*
Earlier sketch in SATA *30*
See also SAAS *13*
Weiss, Edna
See Barth, Edna
Weiss, Ellen 1953- *44*
Weiss, Harvey 1922- *76*
Earlier sketches in SATA *1, 27*
See also CLR *4*
See also SAAS *19*
Weiss, Jaqueline Shachter 1926- *65*
Weiss, Malcolm E. 1928- *3*
Weiss, Margaret Edith
See Weis, Margaret

Weiss, Miriam
See Schlein, Miriam
Weiss, Mitch 1951- *183*
Earlier sketch in SATA *123*
Weiss, Nicki 1954- *86*
Earlier sketch in SATA *33*
Weiss, Renee Karol 1923- *5*
Weissberger, Ela 1930- *181*
Weissberger, Ela Stein
See Weissberger, Ela
Weissenborn, Hellmuth 1898-1982
Obituary *31*
Weissman, Elissa Brent *217*
Weitzman, David L. 1936- *172*
Earlier sketch in SATA *122*
Wekesser, Carol A. 1963- *76*
Welber, Robert *26*
Welch, Amanda (Jane) 1945- *75*
Welch, D'Alte Aldridge 1907-1970
Obituary *27*
Welch, Holly *206*
Welch, Jean-Louise
See Kempton, Jean Welch
Welch, Pauline
See Bodenham, Hilda Morris
Welch, Ronald
See Felton, Ronald Oliver
Welch, Sheila Kelly 1945- *130*
Welch, Willy 1952- *93*
Weldin, Frauke 1969- *188*
Welford, Sue 1942- *75*
Weller, George 1907-2002 .... *31*
Obituary *140*
Weller, George Anthony
See Weller, George
Welling, Peter J. 1947- *135*
Wellington, Monica 1957- *222*
Earlier sketches in SATA *67, 99, 157*
Wellman, Alice 1900-1984 .... *51*
Brief entry *36*
Wellman, Manly Wade 1903-1986 .... *6*
Obituary *47*
Wellman, Paul I. 1898-1966 .... *3*
Wellman, Paul Iselin
See Wellman, Paul I.
Wellman, Sam 1939- *122*
Wellman, Samuel
See Wellman, Sam
Wells, H. G. 1866-1946 .... *20*
See also CLR *133*
Wells, Helen
See Campbell, Hope
Wells, Helen 1910-1986 .... *49*
Earlier sketch in SATA *2*
Wells, Herbert George
See Wells, H. G.
Wells, J. Wellington
See de Camp, L. Sprague
Wells, June
See Swinford, Betty (June Wells)
Wells, Robert
See Welsch, Roger L(ee)
Wells, Robert E. *184*
Wells, Rosemary 1943- *207*
Earlier sketches in SATA *18, 69, 114, 156*
See also CLR *69*
See also SAAS *1*
Wells, Susan (Mary) 1951- *78*
Wels, Byron G(erald) 1924-1993 .... *9*
Welsbacher, Anne 1955- *89*
Welsch, Roger L(ee) 1936- *82*
Welsh, David
See Hills, C.A.R.
Welsh, Mary Flynn 1910(?)-1984
Obituary *38*
Welsh, T.K. 1956- *184*
Weltevrede, Pieter 1957- *228*
Weltner, Linda R(iverly) 1938- *38*
Welton, Jude 1955- *143*
Earlier sketch in SATA *79*

Welty, S. F.
 See Welty, Susan F.
Welty, Susan F. 1905- 9
Wemmlinger, Raymond 190
Wendelin, Rudolph 1910-2000 23
Weninger, Brigitte 1960- 189
Wensell, Ulises 1945- 229
Wentworth, Robert
 See Hamilton, Edmond
Werlin, Nancy 1961- 161
 Earlier sketches in SATA *87, 119*
Werner, Elsa Jane
 See Watson, Jane Werner
Werner, Herma 1926- 47
 Brief entry 41
Werner, Jane
 See Watson, Jane Werner
Werner, K.
 See Casewit, Curtis W(erner)
Wersba, Barbara 1932- 58
 Autobiography Feature 103
 Earlier sketch in SATA *1*
 See also CLR *78*
 See also SAAS *2*
Werstein, Irving 1914(?)-1971 14
Werth, Kurt 1896-1983 20
Wesley, Alison
 See Barnes, Michael
Wesley, Kathryn
 See Rusch, Kristine Kathryn
Wesley, Mary (Aline) 1912-2002 66
Wesley, Valerie Wilson 1947- 168
 Earlier sketch in SATA *106*
West, Andrew
 See Arthur, Robert, (Jr.)
West, Anna 1938- 40
West, Barbara
 See Price, Olive
West, Betty 1921- 11
West, Bruce 1951- 63
West, C. P.
 See Wodehouse, P. G.
West, Dorothy
 See Benson, Mildred
West, Emily Govan 1919- 38
West, Emmy
 See West, Emily Govan
West, James
 See Withers, Carl A.
West, Jerry
 See Svenson, Andrew E(dward)
West, (Mary) Jessamyn 1902-1984
 Obituary 37
West, John
 See Arthur, Robert, (Jr.)
West, Owen
 See Koontz, Dean
West, Ward
 See Borland, Harold Glen
Westall, Robert (Atkinson) 1929-1993 69
 Obituary 75
 Earlier sketch in SATA *23*
 See also CLR *13*
 See also SAAS *2*
Westaway, Jane 1948- 121
Westcott, Nadine Bernard 1949- 130
Westera, Marleen 1962- 187
Westerberg, Christine 1950- 29
Westerduin, Anne 1945- 105
Westerfeld, Scott 1963- 230
 Earlier sketch in SATA *161*
Westervelt, Virginia Veeder 1914-2005 10
Westheimer, David 1917-2005 14
 Obituary 170
Westheimer, David Kaplan
 See Westheimer, David
Westmacott, Mary
 See Christie, Agatha
Westman, Barbara 70
Westman, Paul (Wendell) 1956- 39
Westmoreland, William C. 1914-2005 63

Westmoreland, William Childs
 See Westmoreland, William C.
Weston, Allen
 See Hogarth, Grace (Weston Allen)
 and Norton, Andre
Weston, Carol 1956- 135
Weston, Carrie 190
Weston, John (Harrison) 1932- 21
Weston, Martha 1947- 119
 Earlier sketch in SATA *53*
Weston, Robert Paul 209
Westphal, Arnold Carl 1897- 57
Westrup, Hugh 102
Westwood, Jennifer 1940-2008 10
 Obituary 192
Wexler, Jerome (LeRoy) 1923- 14
Weyland, Jack 1940- 81
Weyn, Suzanne 1955- 220
 Earlier sketches in SATA *63, 101, 164*
Weyr, Garret
 See Freymann-Weyr, Garret
Wezyk, Joanna 1966- 82
Whaley, Joyce Irene 1923- 61
Whalin, W. Terry 1953- 93
Whamond, Dave 222
Wharf, Michael
 See Weller, George
Wharmby, Margot 63
Wharton, Edith 1862-1937
 See CLR *136*
Wharton, Edith Newbold Jones
 See Wharton, Edith
Wharton, Thomas 1963- 223
Whatley, Bruce 1954- 213
 Earlier sketch in SATA *177*
Wheatley, Arabelle 1921- 16
Wheatley, Nadia 1949- 147
Wheeler, Cindy 1955- 49
 Brief entry 40
Wheeler, Deborah 1947- 83
Wheeler, Janet D. 1
Wheeler, Jill C. 1964- 136
 Earlier sketch in SATA *86*
Wheeler, Jody 1952- 148
 Earlier sketch in SATA *84*
Wheeler, Lisa 1963- 200
 Earlier sketch in SATA *162*
Wheeler, Opal 1898- 23
Whelan, Elizabeth M(urphy) 1943- 14
Whelan, Gloria 1923- 224
 Earlier sketches in SATA *85, 128, 178*
 See also CLR *90*
Whelan, Gloria Ann
 See Whelan, Gloria
Whinnem, Reade Scott 224
Whipple, A(ddison) B(eecher) C(olvin)
 1918- 64
Whipple, Cal
 See Whipple, A(ddison) B(eecher) C(olvin)
Whisp, Kennilworthy
 See Rowling, J.K.
Whistler, Reginald John 1905-1944 30
Whistler, Rex
 See Whistler, Reginald John
Whitaker, Zai 183
Whitcher, Susan (Godsil) 1952- 96
Whitcomb, Jon 1906-1988 10
 Obituary 56
Whitcomb, Laura 1958- 214
 Earlier sketch in SATA *171*
White, Amy Brecount 228
White, Anne Terry 1896-1980 2
White, Bessie (Felstiner) 1892(?)-1986
 Obituary 50
White, Carolyn 1948- 130
White, Dale
 See Place, Marian T(empleton)
White, Dori 1919- 10

White, E. B. 1899-1985 100
 Obituary 44
 Earlier sketches in SATA *2, 29*
 See also CLR *107*
White, Eliza Orne 1856-1947
 See YABC *2*
White, Elwyn Brooks
 See White, E. B.
White, Florence M(eiman) 1910- 14
White, Laurence B(arton), Jr. 1935- 10
White, Lee 223
 Earlier sketch in SATA *176*
White, Martin 1943- 51
White, Nancy 1942- 126
White, Ramy Allison 67
 Earlier sketch in SATA *1*
White, Robb 1909-1990 83
 Earlier sketch in SATA *1*
 See also CLR *3*
 See also SAAS *1*
White, Ruth 1942- 186
 Autobiography Feature 186
 Earlier sketches in SATA *39, 117, 165*
White, Ruth C.
 See White, Ruth
White, T(erence) H(anbury) 1906-1964 12
 See also CLR *139*
White, Tekla N. 1934- 115
White, Timothy (Thomas Anthony)
 1952-2002 60
White, Tom 1923- 148
White, William, Jr. 1934- 16
Whitehead, Don(ald) F. 1908-1981 4
Whitehead, Jenny 1964- 191
Whitehead, Kathy 1957- 176
Whitehouse, Arch
 See Whitehouse, Arthur George Joseph
Whitehouse, Arthur George Joseph
 1895-1979 14
 Obituary 23
Whitehouse, Elizabeth S(cott) 1893-1968 35
Whitehouse, Jeanne
 See Peterson, Jeanne Whitehouse
Whitelaw, Nancy 1933- 166
 Earlier sketch in SATA *76*
Whitesel, Cheryl Aylward 162
Whiting, Sue 1960- 205
Whiting, Susan Allana
 See Whiting, Sue
Whitinger, R. D.
 See Place, Marian T(empleton)
Whitley, David 1984- 225
Whitley, Mary Ann
 See Sebrey, Mary Ann
Whitley, Peggy 1938- 140
Whitlock, Pamela 1921(?)-1982
 Obituary 31
Whitlock, Ralph 1914-1995 35
Whitman, Alice
 See Marker, Sherry
Whitman, Candace 1958- 208
Whitman, Sylvia (Choate) 1961- 135
 Earlier sketch in SATA *85*
Whitman, Walt 1819-1892 20
Whitman, Walter
 See Whitman, Walt
Whitmore, Arvella 1922- 125
Whitmore, Benette 1955- 203
Whitney, Alex(andra) 1922- 14
Whitney, David C(harles) 1921- 48
 Brief entry 29
Whitney, Kim Ablon 162
Whitney, Phyllis A. 1903-2008 30
 Obituary 189
 Earlier sketch in SATA *1*
 See also CLR *59*
Whitney, Phyllis Ayame
 See Whitney, Phyllis A.
Whitney, Sharon 1937- 63
Whitney, Thomas P. 1917-2007 25
 Obituary 189

Whitney, Thomas Porter
  See Whitney, Thomas P.
Whittington, Mary K(athrine) 1941- 75
Whitworth, John 1945- 123
Whybrow, Ian 202
  Earlier sketch in SATA 132
Whyte, Mal(colm Kenneth, Jr.) 1933- 62
Whyte, Mary 1953- 148
  Earlier sketch in SATA 94
Whyte, Ron 1942(?)-1989
  Obituary 63
Whytock, Cherry 177
Wiater, Stanley 1953- 84
Wibbelsman, Charles J(oseph) 1945- 59
Wibberley, Leonard 1915-1983 45
  Obituary 36
  Earlier sketch in SATA 2
  See also CLR 3
Wibberley, Leonard Patrick O'Connor
  See Wibberley, Leonard
Wiberg, Harald (Albin) 1908- 93
  Brief entry 40
Wick, Walter 1953- 148
Wickberg, Susan
  See Rottman, S.L.
Wickens, Elaine 86
Wicker, Ireene 1905(?)-1987
  Obituary 55
Wickstrom, Sylvie 1960- 169
Wickstrom, Thor 1960- 200
Widdemer, Mabel Cleland 1902-1964 5
Widener, Terry 1950- 209
  Earlier sketch in SATA 105
Widerberg, Siv 1931- 10
Wiebe, Rudy 1934- 156
Wiebe, Rudy Henry
  See Wiebe, Rudy
Wieler, Diana (Jean) 1961- 109
Wiener, Lori 1956- 84
Wier, Ester (Alberti) 1910-2000 3
Wiese, Kurt 1887-1974 36
  Obituary 24
  Earlier sketch in SATA 3
  See also CLR 86
Wiesel, Elie 1928- 56
Wiesel, Eliezer
  See Wiesel, Elie
Wiesner, David 1956- 181
  Earlier sketches in SATA 72, 117, 139
  See also CLR 84
Wiesner, Portia
  See Takakjian, Portia
Wiesner, William 1899-1984 5
Wiewandt, Thomas 1945- 231
Wiggers, Raymond 1952- 82
Wiggin, Eric E. 1939- 167
  Earlier sketch in SATA 88
Wiggin, Eric Ellsworth 1939-
  See Wiggin, Eric E.
Wiggin (Riggs), Kate Douglas (Smith)
  1856-1923
  See YABC 1
  See also CLR 52
Wiggins, VeraLee (Chesnut) 1928-1995 89
Wight, Eric 1974- 232
  Earlier sketch in SATA 218
Wight, James Alfred
  See Herriot, James
Wignell, Edel 1936- 69
Wijnberg, Ellen 85
Wijngaard, Juan 1951- 230
Wikland, Ilon 1930- 93
  Brief entry 32
Wikler, Madeline 1943- 114
Wilber, Donald N(ewton) 1907-1997 35
Wilbur, C. Keith 1923- 27
Wilbur, Frances 1921- 107
Wilbur, Helen L. 1948- 204
Wilbur, Richard 1921- 108
  Earlier sketch in SATA 9

Wilbur, Richard Purdy
  See Wilbur, Richard
Wilburn, Kathy 1948- 68
Wilcox, Charlotte 1948- 72
Wilcox, Leah 1975(?)- 207
Wilcox, R(uth) Turner 1888-1970 36
Wilcox, Roger
  See Collins, Paul
Wild, Jocelyn 1941- 46
Wild, Kate 1954- 192
Wild, Margaret 1948- 197
  Earlier sketch in SATA 151
Wild, Robin (Evans) 1936- 46
Wild, Robyn 1947- 117
Wilde, D. Gunther
  See Hurwood, Bernhardt J.
Wilde, Oscar 1854(?)-1900 24
  See also CLR 114
Wilde, Oscar Fingal O'Flahertie Willis
  See Wilde, Oscar
Wilder, Buck
  See Smith, Tim(othy R.)
Wilder, Laura Elizabeth Ingalls
  See Wilder, Laura Ingalls
Wilder, Laura Ingalls 1867-1957 100
  Earlier sketches in SATA 15, 29
  See also CLR 111
Wildish, Lee 231
Wildsmith, Brian 1930- 124
  Earlier sketches in SATA 16, 69
  See also CLR 52
  See also SAAS 5
Wiles, Deborah 171
Wilhelm, Doug 1952- 190
Wilhelm, Hans 1945- 196
  Autobiography Feature 196
  Earlier sketches in SATA 58, 135
  See also CLR 46
  See also SAAS 21
Wilkie, Katharine E(lliott) 1904-1980 31
Wilkin, Eloise 1904-1987 49
  Obituary 54
Wilkins, Frances 1923- 14
Wilkins, Kim 147
Wilkins, Marilyn (Ruth) 1926- 30
Wilkins, Marne
  See Wilkins, Marilyn (Ruth)
Wilkins, Mary Huiskamp 1926- 2
  See also CLR 42
Wilkins, Mary Huiskamp Calhoun
  See Wilkins, Mary Huiskamp
Wilkins, Rose 180
Wilkinson, (Thomas) Barry 1923- 50
  Brief entry 32
Wilkinson, Beth 1925- 80
Wilkinson, Brenda 1946- 91
  Earlier sketch in SATA 14
  See also CLR 20
Wilkinson, (John) Burke 1913-2000 4
Wilkinson, Carole 1950- 210
Wilkinson, Sylvia 1940- 56
  Brief entry 39
Wilkon, Jozef 1930- 133
  Earlier sketches in SATA 31, 71
Wilkowski, Sue 193
Wilks, Michael Thomas 1947- 44
  See Wilks, Mike
Wilks, Mike 224
  See Wilks, Michael Thomas
Will
  See Lipkind, William
Willard, Barbara (Mary) 1909-1994 74
  Earlier sketch in SATA 17
  See also CLR 2
  See also SAAS 5
Willard, Elizabeth Kimmel
  See Kimmel, Elizabeth Cody
Willard, Mildred Wilds 1911-1978 14

Willard, Nancy 1936- 191
  Brief entry 30
  Earlier sketches in SATA 37, 71, 127
  See also CLR 5
Willcox, Isobel 1907-1996 42
Willems, Mo 228
  Earlier sketches in SATA 154, 180
  See also CLR 114
Willett, Edward 1959- 115
Willett, Edward C.
  See Willett, Edward
Willey, Bee 184
Willey, Margaret 1950- 226
  Earlier sketch in SATA 86
Willey, Robert
  See Ley, Willy
Willhoite, Michael A. 1946- 71
William, Kate
  See Armstrong, Jennifer
Williams, Alex 1969- 209
Williams, Arlene 171
Williams, Barbara 1925- 107
  Earlier sketch in SATA 11
  See also CLR 48
  See also SAAS 16
Williams, Barbara 1937- 62
Williams, Beryl
  See Epstein, Beryl
Williams, Brian (Peter) 1943- 54
Williams, Carol Lynch 1959- 212
  Earlier sketch in SATA 110
Williams, Charles
  See Collier, James Lincoln
Williams, Clyde C. 1881-1974 8
  Obituary 27
Williams, Coe
  See Harrison, C(hester) William
Williams, Colleen Madonna Flood 1963- .. 156
Williams, Cynthia G. 1958- 123
Williams, Dar 1967- 168
Williams, Donna Reilly 1945- 83
Williams, Dorothy
  See Williams, Marcia
Williams, Dorothy Snowden
  See Williams, Dar
Williams, Eric (Ernest) 1911-1983 14
  Obituary 38
Williams, Ferelith Eccles
  See Eccles Williams, Ferelith
Williams, Frances B.
  See Browin, Frances Williams
Williams, Garth (Montgomery) 1912-1996 .. 66
  Obituary 90
  Earlier sketch in SATA 18
  See also CLR 57
  See also SAAS 7
Williams, Guy R(ichard) 1920- 11
Williams, Hawley
  See Heyliger, William
Williams, Helen 1948- 77
Williams, J. R.
  See Williams, Jeanne
Williams, J. Walker
  See Wodehouse, P. G.
Williams, Jay 1914-1978 41
  Obituary 24
  Earlier sketch in SATA 3
  See also CLR 8
Williams, Jeanne 1930- 5
Williams, Jenny 1939- 60
Williams, Karen Lynn 1952- 224
  Earlier sketches in SATA 66, 99
Williams, Kathryn 1981- 222
Williams, Kit 1946(?)- 44
  See also CLR 4
Williams, L. E.
  See Williams, Laura E.
Williams, Laura E.
  See Williams, Laura Ellen
Williams, Laura Ellen 180
Williams, Leslie 1941- 42

Williams, Linda 1948- 59
Williams, Louise Bonino 1904(?)-1984
  Obituary 39
Williams, Lynn
  See Hale, Arlene
Williams, Maiya 1962- 230
Williams, Marcia 1945- 159
  Earlier sketches in SATA 71, 97
Williams, Marcia Dorothy
  See Williams, Marcia
Williams, Margery
  See Bianco, Margery Williams
Williams, Mark
  See Arthur, Robert, (Jr.)
Williams, Mark London 1959- 140
Williams, Maureen 1951- 12
Williams, Michael
  See St. John, Wylly Folk
Williams, Patrick J.
  See Griffin, W. E. B.
Williams, Paulette Linda
  See Shange, Ntozake
Williams, Pete
  See Faulknor, Cliff(ord Vernon)
Williams, S. P.
  See Hart, Virginia
Williams, Sam 177
  Earlier sketch in SATA 124
Williams, Selma R(uth) 1925- 14
Williams, Sherley Anne 1944-1999 78
  Obituary 116
Williams, Sheron 1955- 77
Williams, Shirley
  See Williams, Sherley Anne
Williams, Slim
  See Williams, Clyde C.
Williams, Sophy 1965- 135
Williams, Sue 1948-2007 208
Williams, Susan
  See Beckhorn, Susan Williams
Williams, Suzanne
  See Williams, Suzanne Morgan
Williams, Suzanne 1953- 202
  Earlier sketch in SATA 71
Williams, Suzanne M.
  See Williams, Suzanne Morgan
Williams, Suzanne Morgan 1949- 207
Williams, Ursula Moray
  See Moray Williams, Ursula
Williams, Vera B(aker) 1927- 102
  Brief entry 33
  Earlier sketch in SATA 53
  See also CLR 9
Williams-Andriani, Renee 1963- 98
Williams-Ellis, (Mary) Amabel (Nassau
  Strachey) 1894-1984 29
  Obituary 41
Williams-Garcia, Rita 1957- 160
  Earlier sketch in SATA 98
  See also CLR 36
Williamson, Gwyneth 1965- 109
Williamson, Henry (William) 1895-1977 37
  Obituary 30
Williamson, Joanne S(mall) 1926- 122
  Earlier sketch in SATA 3
Williamson, Kate T. 1979- 215
Williamson, Melanie 196
Willis, Charles
  See Clarke, Arthur C.
Willis, Connie 1945- 110
  See also CLR 66
Willis, Cynthia Chapman 215
Willis, Jeanne 1959- 195
  Earlier sketches in SATA 61, 123
Willis, Jeanne Mary
  See Willis, Jeanne
Willis, Meredith Sue 1946- 101
Willis, Nancy Carol 1952- 139
  Earlier sketch in SATA 93
Willis, Paul J. 1955- 113
Willms, Russ 95

Willoughby, Lee Davis
  See Avallone, Michael (Angelo, Jr.)
  and Brandner, Gary (Phil)
  and Deming, Richard
  and DeAndrea, William L(ouis)
  and Laymon, Richard (Carl)
  and Streib, Dan(iel Thomas)
  and Toombs, John
  and Webb, Jean Francis (III)
Willson, Robina Beckles
  See Beckles Willson, Robina
Willson, Sarah
  See Albee, Sarah
Wilma, Dana
  See Faralla, Dana
Wilsdorf, Anne 1954- 191
Wilson, Anne 1974- 224
Wilson, April 80
Wilson, Barbara Ker
  See Ker Wilson, Barbara
Wilson, Beth P(ierre) 8
Wilson, Budge 1927- 55
  Brief entry 51
Wilson, Carletta 1951- 81
Wilson, Carter 1941- 6
Wilson, Charles Morrow 1905-1977 30
Wilson, Christopher B. 1910(?)-1985
  Obituary 46
Wilson, Darryl B(abe) 1939- 90
Wilson, Diane Lee 172
Wilson, Dirk
  See Pohl, Frederik
Wilson, Dorothy Clarke 1904-2003 16
Wilson, Edward A(rthur) 1886-1970 38
Wilson, Ellen (Janet Cameron) (?)-1976 9
  Obituary 26
Wilson, Eric (H.) 1940- 34
  Brief entry 32
Wilson, Erica 51
Wilson, Forrest 1918- 27
Wilson, Gahan 1930- 35
  Brief entry 27
Wilson, Gina 1943- 85
  Brief entry 34
  Earlier sketch in SATA 36
Wilson, (Leslie) Granville 1912- 14
Wilson, Hazel (Hutchins) 1898-1992 3
  Obituary 73
Wilson, J(erry) M. 1964- 121
Wilson, Jacqueline 1945- 199
  Brief entry 52
  Earlier sketches in SATA 61, 102, 153
Wilson, John 1922- 22
Wilson, John 1951- 227
  Earlier sketch in SATA 182
Wilson, John Alexander
  See Wilson, John
Wilson, Johnniece Marshall 1944- 75
Wilson, Jonathan 1950- 181
Wilson, Joyce M. 84
  Earlier sketch in SATA 21
  See also SAAS 24
Wilson, Karma 221
  Earlier sketch in SATA 174
Wilson, Leslie 1952- 166
Wilson, Linda Miller 1936- 116
Wilson, Lionel 1924-2003 33
  Brief entry 31
  Obituary 144
Wilson, Marjorie
  See Wilson, Budge
Wilson, Martin 1973- 205
Wilson, Maurice (Charles John) 1914- 46
Wilson, Nancy Hope 1947- 138
  Earlier sketch in SATA 81
Wilson, Nathan D.
  See Wilson, N.D.
Wilson, N.D. 1978- 194
Wilson, Nick
  See Ellis, Edward S.
Wilson, Phil 1948- 181

Wilson, Ron(ald William) 1941- 38
Wilson, Sarah 1934- 208
  Earlier sketches in SATA 50, 142
Wilson, Tom 1931-2011 33
  Brief entry 30
Wilson, Troy 1970- 169
Wilson, Walt(er N.) 1939- 14
Wilson-Max, Ken 1965- 170
  Earlier sketch in SATA 93
Wilton, Elizabeth 1937- 14
Wilton, Hal
  See Pepper, Frank S.
Wilwerding, Walter Joseph 1891-1966 9
Wimmer, Mike 1961- 194
  Earlier sketch in SATA 70
Winborn, Marsha (Lynn) 1947- 75
Winch, John 1944- 165
  Earlier sketch in SATA 117
Winchester, James H(ugh) 1917-1985 30
  Obituary 45
Winchester, Stanley
  See Youd, Samuel
Windawi, Thura al- 1983(?)- 165
Winders, Gertrude Hecker -1987 3
Windham, Basil
  See Wodehouse, P. G.
Windham, Kathryn T. 1918-2011 14
Windham, Kathryn Tucker
  See Windham, Kathryn T.
Windham, Sophie 184
Windling, Terri 1958- 233
  Earlier sketch in SATA 151
Windrow, Martin
  See Windrow, Martin Clive
Windrow, Martin C.
  See Windrow, Martin Clive
Windrow, Martin Clive 1944- 68
Windsor, Claire
  See Hamerstrom, Frances
Windsor, Linda 1950- 124
Windsor, Patricia 1938- 78
  Earlier sketch in SATA 30
  See also SAAS 19
Wineman-Marcus, Irene 1952- 81
Winer, Yvonne 1934- 120
Winerip, Michael 175
Winfield, Arthur M.
  See Stratemeyer, Edward L.
Winfield, Edna
  See Stratemeyer, Edward L.
Winfield, Julia
  See Armstrong, Jennifer
Wing, Natasha 1960- 200
  Earlier sketch in SATA 82
Wingerter, Linda S. 1973(?)- 207
Winget, Susan 211
Winick, Judd 1970- 124
Winks, Robin William 1930-2003 61
Winn, Alison
  See Wharmby, Margot
Winn, Chris 1952- 42
Winn, Janet Bruce 1928- 43
Winn, Marie 1936(?)- 38
Winnick, Karen B. 1946- 211
Winnick, Karen B(eth) B(inkoff) 1946- 51
Winn-Lederer, Ilene 198
Winslow, Barbara 1947- 91
Winstead, Rosie 180
Winston, Clara 1921-1983 54
  Obituary 39
Winston, Richard 1917-1979 54
Winston, Sherri 1964(?)- 201
Winter, Janet 1926- 126
Winter, Jeanette 1939- 184
  Earlier sketch in SATA 151
Winter, Jonah 1962- 225
  Earlier sketch in SATA 179
Winter, Milo (Kendall) 1888-1956 21
Winter, Paula Cecelia 1929- 48
Winter, R. R.
  See Winterbotham, R(ussell) R(obert)

Winter, Susan 182
Winterbotham, R(ussell) R(obert)
  1904-1971 10
Winterbotham, Russ
  See Winterbotham, R(ussell) R(obert)
Winterfeld, Henry 1901-1990 55
Winters, J. C.
  See Cross, Gilbert B.
Winters, Jon
  See Cross, Gilbert B.
Winters, Katherine
  See Winters, Kay
Winters, Kay 1936- 153
  Earlier sketch in SATA *103*
Winters, Nina 1944- 62
Winters, Paul A. 1965- 106
Winterson, Jeanette 1959- 190
Winterton, Gayle
  See Adams, William Taylor
Winthrop, Elizabeth 1948- 164
  Autobiography Feature 116
  Earlier sketches in SATA *8, 76*
  See also CLR *89*
Winton, Ian (Kenneth) 1960- 76
Winton, Tim 1960- 98
Wintz-Litty, Julie
  See Litty, Julie
Wirt, Ann
  See Benson, Mildred
Wirt, Mildred A.
  See Benson, Mildred
Wirtenberg, Patricia Z. 1932-2007 10
Wirtenberg, Patricia Zarrella
  See Wirtenberg, Patricia Z.
Wirth, Beverly 1938- 63
Wirths, Claudine (Turner) G(ibson)
  1926-2000 104
  Earlier sketch in SATA *64*
Wise, Bill 1958- 191
Wise, Lenny
  See Wise, Leonard
Wise, Leonard 1940- 167
Wise, Leonard A.
  See Wise, Leonard
Wise, Leonard Allan
  See Wise, Leonard
Wise, William 1923- 163
  Earlier sketch in SATA *4*
Wise, Winifred E. 2
Wiseman, Ann (Sayre) 1926- 31
Wiseman, B(ernard) 1922-1995 4
Wiseman, David 1916- 43
  Brief entry 40
Wiseman, Eva 1947- 210
Wishinsky, Frieda 1948- 166
  Earlier sketches in SATA *70, 112*
Wisler, G(ary) Clifton 1950- 103
  Brief entry 46
  Earlier sketch in SATA *58*
Wismer, Donald (Richard) 1946- 59
Wisner, Bill
  See Wisner, William L.
Wisner, William L. 1914(?)-1983 42
Wisnewski, David 1953-2002
  See Wisniewski, David
Wisniewski, David 1953-2002 95
  Obituary 139
  See also CLR *51*
Wister, Owen 1860-1938 62
Witham, (Phillip) Ross 1917- 37
Withers, Carl A. 1900-1970 14
Withers, Pam 1956- 182
Withrow, Sarah 1966- 199
  Earlier sketch in SATA *124*
Witt, Dick 1948- 80
Witt, Shirley Hill 1934- 17
Wittanen, Etolin 1907- 55
Wittels, Harriet Joan 1938- 31
Wittenstein, Vicki Oransky 1954- 228
Wittig, Susan
  See Albert, Susan Wittig

Wittlinger, Ellen 1948- 189
  Autobiography Feature 128
  Earlier sketches in SATA *83, 122*
Wittman, Sally (Anne Christensen) 1941- 30
Witty, Paul 1898-1976 50
  Obituary 30
Wodehouse, P. G. 1881-1975 22
Wodehouse, Pelham Grenville
  See Wodehouse, P. G.
Wodge, Dreary
  See Gorey, Edward (St. John)
Woelfle, Gretchen 1945- 145
Wohlberg, Meg 1905-1990 41
  Obituary 66
Wohlrabe, Raymond A. 1900-1977 4
Wohnoutka, Mike 230
  Earlier sketch in SATA *195*
Wojciechowska, Maia (Teresa) 1927-2002 ... 83
  Autobiography Feature 104
  Obituary 134
  Earlier sketches in SATA *1, 28*
  See also CLR *1*
  See also SAAS *1*
Wojciechowski, Susan 126
  Earlier sketch in SATA *78*
Wojnarowski, Adrian 1970- 190
Wojtusik, Elizabeth 208
Wolcott, Patty 1929- 14
Wold, Allen L. 1943- 64
Wold, Jo Anne 1938- 30
Woldin, Beth Weiner 1955- 34
Wolf, Allan 1963- 192
Wolf, Bernard 1930- 102
  Brief entry 37
Wolf, Erica (Van Varick) 1978- 156
Wolf, Gita 1956- 101
Wolf, J. M.
  See Wolf, Joan M.
Wolf, Janet 1957- 78
Wolf, Joan M. 1966- 193
Wolf, Sallie 1950- 205
  Earlier sketch in SATA *80*
Wolfe, Art 1952- 76
Wolfe, Burton H. 1932- 5
Wolfe, Frances 216
Wolfe, Gene 1931- 165
  Earlier sketch in SATA *118*
Wolfe, Gene Rodman
  See Wolfe, Gene
Wolfe, Gillian 199
Wolfe, Louis 1905-1985 8
  Obituary 133
Wolfe, Rinna (Evelyn) 1925- 38
Wolfenden, George
  See Beardmore, George
Wolfer, Dianne 1961- 167
  Autobiography Feature 117
  Earlier sketch in SATA *104*
Wolff, Alexander (Nikolaus) 1957- 137
  Earlier sketch in SATA *63*
Wolff, Ashley 1956- 203
  Earlier sketches in SATA *50, 81, 155*
Wolff, Diane 1945- 27
Wolff, Ferida 1946- 164
  Earlier sketch in SATA *79*
Wolff, Jason 1972- 213
Wolff, Jennifer Ashley
  See Wolff, Ashley
Wolff, Nancy 202
Wolff, Robert Jay 1905-1977 10
Wolff, Sonia
  See Levitin, Sonia
Wolff, Virginia Euwer 1937- 137
  Earlier sketch in SATA *78*
  See also CLR *62*
Wolfman, Judy 1933- 138
Wolfson, Evelyn 1937- 62
Wolitzer, Hilma 1930- 31
Wolkoff, Judie (Edwards) 93
  Brief entry 37

Wolkstein, Diane 1942- 138
  Earlier sketches in SATA *7, 82*
Wollheim, Donald A(llen) 1914-1990
  Obituary 69
Wolny, P.
  See Janeczko, Paul B(ryan)
Wolters, Richard A. 1920-1993 35
Wondriska, William 1931- 6
Wong, Jade Snow 1922-2006 112
  Obituary 175
Wong, Janet S. 1962- 210
  Earlier sketches in SATA *98, 148*
  See also CLR *94*
Wong, Marissa Lopez 226
Wong, Nicole 214
Woo, Howie 1974- 207
Wood, Addie Robinson
  See Wiggin, Eric E.
Wood, Anne (Savage) 1937- 64
Wood, Audrey 198
  Brief entry 44
  Earlier sketches in SATA *50, 81, 139*
  See also CLR *26*
Wood, Catherine
  See Etchison, Birdie L(ee)
Wood, David 1944- 212
  Earlier sketch in SATA *87*
Wood, Don 1945- 50
  Brief entry 44
  See also CLR *26*
Wood, Douglas 1951- 180
  Earlier sketches in SATA *81, 132*
Wood, Douglas Eric
  See Wood, Douglas
Wood, Edgar A(llardyce) 1907-1998 14
Wood, Esther
  See Brady, Esther Wood
Wood, Frances Elizabeth 34
Wood, Frances M. 1951- 97
Wood, Jacqueline
  See Wood, Jakki
Wood, Jakki 1957- 211
Wood, James Playsted 1905- 1
Wood, Jenny 1955- 88
Wood, John Norris 1930- 85
Wood, June Rae 1946- 120
  Earlier sketch in SATA *79*
  See also CLR *82*
Wood, Kerry
  See Wood, Edgar A(llardyce)
Wood, Kim Marie 134
Wood, Laura N.
  See Roper, Laura (Newbold) Wood
Wood, Linda C(arol) 1945- 59
Wood, Marcia 1956- 80
Wood, Marcia Mae
  See Wood, Marcia
Wood, Nancy
  See Wood, Nancy C.
Wood, Nancy C. 1936- 178
  Earlier sketch in SATA *6*
Wood, Nuria
  See Nobisso, Josephine
Wood, Owen 1929- 64
Wood, Phyllis Anderson 1923- 33
  Brief entry 30
Wood, Richard 1949- 110
Wood, Tim(othy William Russell) 1946- 88
Wood, Wallace 1927-1981
  Obituary 33
Woodard, Carol 1929- 14
Woodburn, John Henry 1914- 11
Woodbury, David Oakes 1896-1981 62
Woodford, Peggy 1937- 25
Woodhouse, Barbara (Blackburn)
  1910-1988 63
Woodhull, Ann Love 194
Wooding, Chris 1977- 166
Wooding, Sharon
  See Wooding, Sharon L(ouise)
Wooding, Sharon L(ouise) 1943- 66

Woodman, Allen 1954- 76
Woodrich, Mary Neville 1915- 2
Woodruff, Elvira 1951- 211
　Earlier sketches in SATA 70, 106, 162
Woodruff, Joan Leslie 1953- 104
Woodruff, Liza 1971(?)- 182
Woodruff, Marian
　See Goudge, Eileen
Woodruff, Noah 1977- 86
Woods, George A(llan) 1926-1988 30
　Obituary 57
Woods, Geraldine 1948- 111
　Brief entry 42
　Earlier sketch in SATA 56
Woods, Harold 1945- 56
　Brief entry 42
Woods, Lawrence
　See Lowndes, Robert A(ugustine) W(ard)
Woods, Margaret 1921- 2
Woods, Nat
　See Stratemeyer, Edward L.
Woods, Titania
　See Weatherly, Lee
Woodson, Jack
　See Woodson, John Waddie Jr.
Woodson, Jacqueline 1964- 189
　Earlier sketches in SATA 94, 139
　See also CLR 49
Woodson, Jacqueline Amanda
　See Woodson, Jacqueline
Woodson, John Waddie Jr. 1913- 10
Woodtor, Dee
　See Woodtor, Delores Parmer
Woodtor, Dee Parmer 1945(?)-2002
　See Woodtor, Delores Parmer
Woodtor, Delores Parmer 1945-2002 93
Wood-Trost, Lucille
　See Trost, Lucille W(ood)
Woodward, (Landon) Cleveland 1900-1986 . 10
　Obituary 48
Woodworth, Chris 1957- 168
Woodworth, Viki 1952- 127
Woody, Regina Jones 1894-1983 3
Woodyadd, Charlotte
　See Hough, Charlotte
Woog, Adam 1953- 125
　Earlier sketch in SATA 84
Wooldridge, Connie Nordhielm 1950- 143
　Earlier sketch in SATA 92
Wooldridge, Frosty 1947- 140
Wooldridge, Rhoda 1906-1988 22
Wooley, Susan Frelick 1945- 113
Woolf, Paula 1950- 104
Woolfe, Angela 1976- 169
Woolley, Catherine 1904-2005 3
　Obituary 166
Woolman, Steven 1969-2004 163
　Earlier sketch in SATA 90
Woolsey, Janette 1904-1989 3
　Obituary 131
Worcester, Donald E(mmet) 1915- 18
Word, Reagan 1944- 103
Work, Virginia 1946- 57
　Brief entry 45
Worline, Bonnie Bess 1914- 14
Wormell, Christopher 1955- 154
　Earlier sketch in SATA 103
Wormell, Mary 1959- 96
Wormser, Richard 1933- 106
　Autobiography Feature 118
　See also SAAS 26
Wormser, Sophie 1897-1979 22
Worth, Richard
　See Wiggin, Eric E.
Worth, Richard 1945- 59
　Brief entry 46
Worth, Valerie 1933-1994 81
　Earlier sketch in SATA 8, 70
　See also CLR 21
Worthington, Leonie 1956- 200

Wortis, Avi
　See Avi
Wortis, Edward Irving
　See Avi
Wosmek, Frances 1917- 29
Woychuk, Denis 1953- 71
Wrede, Patricia C(ollins) 1953- 146
　Earlier sketch in SATA 67
Wriggins, Sally Hovey 1922- 17
Wright, Alexandra 1979- 103
Wright, Betty Ren 1927- 109
　Brief entry 48
　Earlier sketch in SATA 63
Wright, Cliff 1963- 168
　Earlier sketch in SATA 76
Wright, Courtni
　See Wright, Courtni C(rump)
Wright, Courtni C(rump) 1950- 84
Wright, Courtni Crump
　See Wright, Courtni C(rump)
Wright, Dare 1914(?)-2001 21
　Obituary 124
Wright, David K. 1943- 112
　Earlier sketch in SATA 73
Wright, Elinor
　See Lyon, Elinor
Wright, Enid Meadowcroft (LaMonte)
　1898-1966 3
Wright, Esmond 1915-2003 10
Wright, Frances Fitzpatrick 1897-1982 10
Wright, J. B.
　See Barkan, Joanne
Wright, Johanna 220
Wright, Judith 1915-2000 14
　Obituary 121
Wright, Judith Arundell
　See Wright, Judith
Wright, Katrina
　See Gater, Dilys
Wright, Kenneth
　See del Rey, Lester
Wright, Kit 1944- 87
Wright, Leslie B(ailey) 1959- 91
Wright, Maureen 1961- 233
Wright, Michael 1954- 198
Wright, Nancy Means 38
Wright, R(obert) H(amilton) 1906- 6
Wright, Rachel 220
　Earlier sketch in SATA 134
Wright, Simeon 1942- 232
Wright, Susan Kimmel 1950- 97
Wrightfrierson
　See Wright-Frierson, Virginia (Marguerite)
Wright-Frierson, Virginia (Marguerite)
　1949- 110
　Earlier sketch in SATA 58
Wrightson, Alice Patricia
　See Wrightson, Patricia
Wrightson, Patricia 1921-2010 112
　Obituary 215
　Earlier sketches in SATA 8, 66
　See also CLR 154
　See also SAAS 4
Wroble, Lisa A. 1963- 134
Wrongo, I.B.
　See Katz, Alan
Wronker, Lili
　See Wronker, Lili Cassel
Wronker, Lili Cassel 1924- 10
Wryde, Dogear
　See Gorey, Edward (St. John)
Wu, Donald 212
Wu, Elizabeth
　See Wu, Liz
Wu, Liz 184
Wu, Norbert 1961- 155
　Earlier sketch in SATA 101
Wulf, Linda Press 205
Wulffson, Don 1943- 155
　Earlier sketches in SATA 32, 88

Wulffson, Don L.
　See Wulffson, Don
Wummer, Amy 1955- 201
Wunderli, Stephen 1958- 79
Wunsch, Josephine (McLean) 1914- 64
Wunsch, Marjory 1942- 220
　Earlier sketch in SATA 82
Wuorio, Eva-Lis 1918- 34
　Brief entry 28
Wurts, Janny 1953- 98
Wyatt, B. D.
　See Robinson, Spider
Wyatt, David 1968- 185
Wyatt, Jane
　See Bradbury, Bianca (Ryley)
Wyatt, Melissa 1963- 177
Wyatt, Valerie 209
Wyeth, Betsy James 1921- 41
Wyeth, N(ewell) C(onvers) 1882-1945 17
　See also CLR 106
Wyler, Rose 1909-2000 18
　Obituary 121
Wylie, Betty Jane 48
Wylie, Laura
　See Matthews, Patricia
Wylie, Laurie
　See Matthews, Patricia
Wyllie, Stephen 86
Wyman, Andrea 75
Wyman, Carolyn 1956- 83
Wymer, Norman (George) 1911- 25
Wynard, Talbot
　See Hamilton, Charles (Harold St. John)
Wyndham, John
　See Harris, John (Wyndham Parkes Lucas)
　Beynon
Wyndham, Lee
　See Hyndman, Jane Andrews Lee
Wyndham, Robert
　See Hyndman, Robert Utley
Wynne, Patricia J. 210
Wynne-Jones, Tim 1948- 186
　Autobiography Feature 136
　Earlier sketches in SATA 67, 96, 136
　See also CLR 58
Wynne-Jones, Timothy
　See Wynne-Jones, Tim
Wynter, Edward (John) 1914- 14
Wynyard, Talbot
　See Hamilton, Charles (Harold St. John)
Wyshynski, Sue 233
Wyss, Johann David Von 1743-1818 29
　Brief entry 27
　See also CLR 92
Wyss, Thelma Hatch 1934- 202
　Earlier sketches in SATA 10, 140

X

Xavier, Father
　See Hurwood, Bernhardt J.
Xuan, YongSheng 1952- 226
　Autobiography Feature 226
　Earlier sketch in SATA 116

Y

Yaccarino, Dan 192
　Earlier sketch in SATA 141
Yadin, (Rav-Aloof) Yigael 1917-1984 55
Yaffe, Alan
　See Yorinks, Arthur
Yagher, Kevin 1962- 143
Yakovetic, (Joseph Sandy) 1952- 59
Yakovetic, Joe
　See Yakovetic, (Joseph Sandy)
Yamada, Utako 1963- 188
Yamaguchi, Marianne (Illenberger) 1936- 7

Yamaka, Sara 1978- 92
Yamanaka, Lois-Ann 1961- 166
Yamasaki, Katie 206
Yancey, Diane 1951- 138
  Earlier sketch in SATA 81
Yancey, Richard
  See Yancey, Rick
Yancey, Rick 193
Yang, Belle 1960- 170
Yang, James 1960- 190
Yang, Jay 1941- 12
Yang, Mingyi 1943- 72
Yarbrough, Camille 1938- 79
  See also CLR 29
Yarbrough, Ira 1910(?)-1983
  Obituary 35
Yaroslava
  See Mills, Yaroslava Surmach
Yarrow, Peter 1938- 195
Yashima, Taro
  See Iwamatsu, Jun Atsushi
Yates, Elizabeth 1905-2001 68
  Obituary 128
  Earlier sketch in SATA 4
  See also SAAS 6
Yates, Janelle K(aye) 1957- 77
Yates, John 1939- 74
Yates, Kelly 1971- 208
Yates, Louise 1983(?)- 218
Yates, Philip 1956- 212
  Earlier sketches in SATA 92, 149
Yates, Raymond F(rancis) 1895-1966 31
Yaukey, Grace S(ydenstricker) 1899-1994 ... 80
  Earlier sketch in SATA 5
Yayo 1961- 226
Yazzie, Johnson 1946- 205
Ye, Ting-xing 1952- 106
Yeahpau, Thomas M. 1975- 187
Yeakley, Marjory Hall 1908- 21
Yeates, Thomas 1955- 230
Yeatman, Linda 1938- 42
Yeatts, Tabatha 1970- 215
Yee, Brenda Shannon 133
Yee, Lisa 1959- 218
  Earlier sketch in SATA 160
Yee, Paul 1956- 211
  Earlier sketches in SATA 67, 96, 143
  See also CLR 44
Yee, Tammy 206
Yee, Wong Herbert 1953- 172
  Earlier sketches in SATA 78, 115
Yee, Ying S.
  See Lee, Y.S.
Yeh, Chun-Chan 1914- 79
Ye Junjian
  See Yeh, Chun-Chan
Yelchin, Eugene 1956- 232
  Earlier sketch in SATA 196
Yenawine, Philip 1942- 85
Yensid, Retlaw
  See Disney, Walt(er Elias)
Yeo, Wilma (Lethem) 1918-1994 81
  Earlier sketch in SATA 24
Yeoman, John 1934- 80
  Earlier sketch in SATA 28
  See also CLR 46
Yep, Kathleen S. 203
Yep, Laurence 1948- 213
  Earlier sketches in SATA 7, 69, 123, 176
  See also CLR 132
Yep, Laurence Michael
  See Yep, Laurence
Yepsen, Roger B(ennet), Jr. 1947- 59
Yerian, Cameron John 21
Yerian, Margaret A. 21
Yerxa, Leo 1947- 181
Yetska
  See Ironside, Jetske
Yezerski, Thomas F. 1969- 190
Yin 194
Ylvisaker, Anne 1965(?)- 172

Yoder, Carolyn P. 1953- 149
Yoder, Carolyn Patricia
  See Yoder, Carolyn P.
Yoder, Dorothy Meenen 1921- 96
Yoder, Dot
  See Yoder, Dorothy Meenen
Yoder, Walter D. 1933- 88
Yohalem, Eve 219
Yolen, Jane 1939- 230
  Autobiography Feature 111
  Earlier sketches in SATA 4, 40, 75, 112, 158, 194
  See also CLR 149
  See also SAAS 1
Yolen, Jane Hyatt
  See Yolen, Jane
Yonezu, Yusuke 196
Yonge, Charlotte 1823-1901 17
Yonge, Charlotte Mary
  See Yonge, Charlotte
Yoo, Paula 1969(?)- 174
Yoo, Taeeun 191
Yoon, Salina 1972- 204
Yorinks, Adrienne 1956- 171
Yorinks, Arthur 1953- 200
  Earlier sketches in SATA 33, 49, 85, 144
  See also CLR 20
York, Alison
  See Nicole, Christopher
York, Andrew
  See Nicole, Christopher
York, Carol Beach 1928- 77
  Earlier sketch in SATA 6
York, Rebecca
  See Buckholtz, Eileen (Garber)
  and Glick, Ruth
York, Simon
  See Heinlein, Robert A.
Yoshida, Toshi 1911- 77
Yoshikawa, Sachiko 181
Yost, Edna 1889-1971
  Obituary 26
Youd, C. S.
  See Youd, Samuel
Youd, Samuel 1922- 135
  Brief entry 30
  Earlier sketch in SATA 47
  See also CLR 2
  See also SAAS 6
Youme
  See Landowne, Youme
Young, Amy L. 185
Young, Anne Mortimer
  See Mortimer, Anne
Young, Bob
  See Young, Robert W(illiam)
  and Young, James Robert
Young, Carol 1945- 102
Young, Catherine
  See Olds, Helen Diehl
Young, Clarence
  See Garis, Howard R.
  and Stratemeyer, Edward L.
Young, Collier
  See Bloch, Robert (Albert)
Young, Dan 1952- 126
Young, Dianne 1959- 88
Young, Dorothea Bennett 1924- 31
Young, Ed 1931- 211
  Earlier sketches in SATA 10, 74, 122, 173
  See also CLR 27
Young, Ed Tse-chun
  See Young, Ed
Young, Edward
  See Reinfeld, Fred
Young, E.L. 1973- 219
Young, Elaine L.
  See Schulte, Elaine L(ouise)
Young, Emma L.
  See Young, E.L.

Young, James
  See Graham, Ian
Young, Jan
  See Young, Janet Randall
Young, Janet 1957- 188
Young, Janet Randall 1919-1994 3
Young, Janet Ruth
  See Young, Janet
Young, Jeff C. 1948- 132
Young, John
  See Macintosh, Brownie
Young, Judy 1956- 207
  Earlier sketch in SATA 155
Young, Judy (Elaine) Dockrey 1949- 72
Young, Karen Romano 1959- 168
  Earlier sketch in SATA 116
Young, Ken 1956- 86
Young, Lois Horton 1911-1981 26
Young, Louisa 161
Young, Louise B. 1919- 64
Young, Margaret B. 1922-2009 2
Young, Margaret Buckner
  See Young, Margaret B.
Young, Mary 1940- 89
Young, Miriam 1913-1974 7
Young, Ned 233
Young, Noela 1930- 89
Young, (Rodney Lee) Patrick (Jr.) 1937- 22
Young, Percy M(arshall) 1912-2004 31
  Obituary 154
Young, Richard Alan 1946- 72
Young, Robert W(illiam) 1916-1969 3
Young, Ross B. 1955- 150
Young, Ruth 1946- 67
Young, Sara
  See Pennypacker, Sara
Young, Scott A. 1918-2005 5
Young, Scott Alexander
  See Young, Scott A.
Young, Selina 1971-2006 201
Young, Vivien
  See Gater, Dilys
Younger, Barbara 1954- 108
Youngs, Betty 1934-1985 53
  Obituary 42
Younkin, Paula 1942- 77
Yount, Lisa (Ann) 1944- 124
  Earlier sketch in SATA 74
Yourgrau, Barry 179
Yuditskaya, Tatyana 1964- 75
Yue, Stephanie 1984- 231
Yum, Hyewon 211
Yumoto, Kazumi 1959- 153

Z

Zach, Cheryl (Byrd) 1947- 98
  Brief entry 51
  Earlier sketch in SATA 58
  See also SAAS 24
Zacharias, Gary L. 1946- 153
Zadoff, Allen 1967- 224
Zaffo, George J. (?)-1984 42
Zagarenski, Pamela 1969(?)- 183
Zagwyn, Deborah Turney 1953- 138
  Earlier sketch in SATA 78
Zahares, Wade 193
Zahedi, Morteza 1978- 233
Zahidi, Murtiza
  See Zahedi, Morteza
Zahler, Diane 228
Zahn, Timothy 1951- 156
  Earlier sketch in SATA 91
Zaid, Barry 1938- 51
Zaidenberg, Arthur 1908(?)-1990 34
  Obituary 66
Zakanitch, Robert Rahway 1935- 231
Zakanitch, Robert S.
  See Zakanitch, Robert Rahway

Zalben, Jane Breskin 1950- *170*
   Earlier sketches in SATA *7, 79, 120*
   See also CLR *84*
Zallinger, Jean (Day) 1918- *115*
   Earlier sketches in SATA *14, 80*
Zallinger, Peter Franz 1943- *49*
Zambreno, Mary Frances 1954- *140*
   Earlier sketch in SATA *75*
Zanderbergen, George
   See May, Julian
Zappa, Ahmet 1974- *180*
Zappa, Ahmet Emuukha Rodan
   See Zappa, Ahmet
Zappler, Lisbeth 1930- *10*
Zarchy, Harry 1912-1987 .... *34*
Zarin, Cynthia 1959- *192*
   Earlier sketch in SATA *108*
Zaring, Jane (Thomas) 1936- *40*
Zarins, Joyce Audy
   See dos Santos, Joyce Audy
Zaslavsky, Claudia 1917- *36*
Zaugg, Sandra L. 1938- *118*
Zaugg, Sandy
   See Zaugg, Sandra L.
Zaunders, Bo 1939- *137*
Zawadzki, Marek 1958- *97*
Zebra, A.
   See Scoltock, Jack
Zebrowski, George 1945- *67*
Zebrowski, George T.
   See Zebrowski, George
Zecca, Katherine *207*
Zeck, Gerald Anthony 1939- *40*
Zeck, Gerry
   See Zeck, Gerald Anthony
Zed, Dr.
   See Penrose, Gordon
Zei, Alki 1925- *24*
   See also CLR *6*
Zeier, Joan T(heresa) 1931- *81*
Zeinert, Karen 1942-2002 .... *137*
   Earlier sketch in SATA *79*
Zeises, Lara M. 1976- *184*
   Earlier sketch in SATA *145*
Zelazny, Roger 1937-1995 .... *57*
   Brief entry *39*
Zelazny, Roger Joseph
   See Zelazny, Roger
Zeldis, Malcah 1931- *146*
   Earlier sketch in SATA *86*
Zelinsky, Paul O. 1953- *154*
   Brief entry *33*
   Earlier sketches in SATA *49, 102*
   See also CLR *55*
Zellan, Audrey Penn
   See Penn, Audrey
Zemach, Harve
   See Fischtrom, Harvey
Zemach, Kaethe 1958- *149*
   Brief entry *39*
   Earlier sketch in SATA *49*
Zemach, Margot 1931-1989 .... *70*
   Obituary *59*
   Earlier sketch in SATA *21*

Zemach-Bersin, Kaethe
   See Zemach, Kaethe
Zeman, Ludmila 1947- *153*
Zepeda, Gwendolyn 1971- *206*
Zephaniah, Benjamin 1958- *189*
   Earlier sketches in SATA *86, 140*
Zephaniah, Benjamin Obadiah Iqbal
   See Zephaniah, Benjamin
Zephaniah, Benjamin Pbadiah Iqubal
   See Zephaniah, Benjamin
Zerman, Melvyn Bernard 1930-2010 .... *46*
Zettner, Pat 1940- *70*
Zevin, Gabrielle 1977- *176*
Zhang, Christopher Zhong-Yuan 1954- *91*
Zhang, Song Nan 1942- *170*
   Earlier sketch in SATA *85*
Ziefert, Harriet 1941- *205*
   Earlier sketches in SATA *101, 154*
Ziegler, Jack (Denmore) 1942- *60*
Ziemienski, Dennis (Theodore) 1947- *10*
Ziliox, Marc
   See Fichter, George S.
Zillah
   See Macdonald, Zillah K(atherine)
Zim, Herbert S(pencer) 1909-1994 .... *30*
   Obituary *85*
   Earlier sketch in SATA *1*
   See also CLR *2*
   See also SAAS *2*
Zim, Sonia Bleeker 1909-1971 .... *2*
   Obituary *26*
Zima, Gordon 1920- *90*
Zimelman, Nathan 1921- *65*
   Brief entry *37*
Zimmer, Dirk 1943- *147*
   Earlier sketch in SATA *65*
Zimmer, Tracie Vaughn *169*
Zimmerman, Andrea 1950- *192*
   Earlier sketch in SATA *123*
Zimmerman, Andrea Griffing
   See Zimmerman, Andrea
Zimmerman, H. Werner 1951- *101*
Zimmerman, Heinz Werner
   See Zimmerman, H. Werner
Zimmerman, Naoma 1914-2004 .... *10*
Zimmermann, Arnold E. 1909- *58*
Zimmermann, Karl 1943- *211*
Zimmermann, Karl R.
   See Zimmermann, Karl
Zimmett, Debbie
   See Becker, Deborah Zimmett
Zimmy
   See Stratemeyer, Edward L.
Zimnik, Reiner 1930- *36*
   See also CLR *3*
Zindel, Bonnie 1943- *34*
Zindel, Lizabeth *187*
Zindel, Paul 1936-2003 .... *102*
   Obituary *142*
   Earlier sketches in SATA *16, 58*
   See also CLR *85*
Ziner, Feenie
   See Ziner, Florence
Ziner, Florence 1921- *5*

Zingara, Professor
   See Leeming, Joseph
Zinger, Yitskhok
   See Singer, Isaac Bashevis
Zink, Michelle 1969- *220*
Zion, Eugene 1913-1975 .... *18*
Zion, Gene
   See Zion, Eugene
Zobel, Allia
   See Zobel Nolan, Allia
Zobel Nolan, Allia *218*
Zoehfeld, Kathleen Weidner 1954- *193*
Zohorsky, Janet R. 1958- *148*
Zolkower, Edie Stoltz *171*
Zolkowski, Cathy (A.) 1969- *121*
Zollars, Jaime *191*
Zolotow, Charlotte 1915- *138*
   Earlier sketches in SATA *1, 35, 78*
   See also CLR *77*
Zolotow, Charlotte Gertrude Shapiro
   See Zolotow, Charlotte
Zolotow, Ellen
   See Dragonwagon, Crescent
Zonderman, Jon 1957- *92*
Zonia, Dhimitri 1921- *20*
Zonta, Pat 1951- *143*
Zubrowski, Bernard 1939- *90*
   Earlier sketch in SATA *35*
Zubrowski, Bernie
   See Zubrowski, Bernard
Zucker, Jonny *228*
Zucker, Miriam S.
   See Reichert, Miriam Zucker
Zuckerman, Amy *217*
Zuckerman, Andrew 1977- *224*
Zuckerman, Linda *190*
Zudeck, Darryl 1961- *61*
Zug, Mark *204*
Zulkey, Claire 1979- *225*
Zupa, G. Anthony
   See Zeck, Gerald Anthony
Zupancic, Lilijana Praprotnik
   See Prap, Lila
Zurbo, Matt(hew) 1967- *98*
Zurhorst, Charles (Stewart, Jr.) 1913-1989 .. *12*
Zurlo, Tony 1941- *145*
Zuromskis, Diane
   See Stanley, Diane
Zuromskis, Diane Stanley
   See Stanley, Diane
Zusak, Markus 1975- *149*
Zwahlen, Diana 1947- *88*
Zweifel, Frances W. 1931- *14*
Zwerger, Lisbeth 1954- *194*
   Earlier sketches in SATA *66, 130*
   See also CLR *46*
   See also SAAS *13*
Zwinger, Ann (H.) 1925- *46*
Zymet, Cathy Alter 1965- *121*